NATIONAL GALLERY CATALOGUES

D1634460

THE
EARLIER ITALIAN
SCHOOLS

BY
MARTIN DAVIES

A new edition of the *Illustrated General Catalogue* of the National Gallery Collection will be published in 1986 and also at that time the first of a new series of detailed catalogues, with illustrations en suite, dealing with the Dutch School, which will eventually cover the whole Collection. Meanwhile three of the existing schools catalogues have been reprinted, *The Earlier Italian Schools* by Martin Davies (1961), *The Flemish School* by Gregory Martin (1970), and *The Seventeenth and Eighteenth Century Italian Schools* by Michael Levey (1971). Each has been reissued without alteration to the text, but a list of paintings of the relevant school acquired since publication of the catalogue is added as an appendix. For further details about these paintings the reader is referred to the *Illustrated General Catalogue* and to the editions of the *National Gallery Report*, where fuller entries for acquisitions are supplied.

Published by order of the Trustees
National Gallery Publications
The National Gallery
London

© The National Gallery 1951, revised and reprinted 1961
Reprinted 1972, 1986

ISBN 0 901791 29 6

Printed and bound in Great Britain by
William Clowes Limited, Beccles and London

Front Cover
Pisanello, living 1395, died 1455(?), *The Vision of S. Eustace* (detail)

NOTE

THE PRESENT CATALOGUE deals with the pictures of the *Earlier Italian Schools* in the National Gallery. It records also a few miscellaneous items, such as Greco-Roman portraits; but its main subject is the Italian pictures up to the end of the Early Renaissance.

There is no doubt that a broad line of demarcation can be drawn between the Early and the High Renaissance. In some cases, nevertheless, it has been difficult to decide what to put into this catalogue and what to leave out. It appears, for instance, reasonable to class Perugino in the Early Renaissance, and Raphael in the High Renaissance; yet, in point of fact, Perugino died later than Raphael, and one of the Peruginos here catalogued was most probably painted after Raphael's death. Clearly, no division can be made that would in every detail be accepted by everyone as correct. Two lists are given at the end of the present volume, to help the student to find out what is included: a list of the inventory numbers of the pictures, and a list of the attributions that have been changed since the catalogue of 1929 and its supplement of 1939.

Many of the pictures here included were first catalogued at the National Gallery, and most excellently catalogued, by Eastlake and Wornum in the middle of the nineteenth century. Various useful revisions, together with a large number of new entries, have been made for subsequent editions. The most recent was first issued in 1929. Shortly after that date, Mr. E. K. Waterhouse began a complete revision for all the Italian schools, and made entries in typescript for perhaps half the pictures included in the present volume. These entries added much new information, and corrected many errors in the 1929 catalogue, although they are considerably less detailed than what is printed now. Later on, for a few years up to the early part of the last war, Mr. P. M. R. Pouncey made a number of new entries in typescript for the Italian pictures in the National Gallery; he also wrote entries for various acquisitions of Italian pictures after 1929, which were printed in 1939 in a *Supplement to the 1929 Catalogue*. Mr. Pouncey's work contains a large amount of detailed research; unfortunately most of it was for pictures that are not included in the present volume.

I have wished gratefully to acknowledge my indebtedness to previous cataloguers; to Eastlake and Wornum, to the various hands that have made revisions and new entries since their time, to Mr. Waterhouse and Mr. Pouncey. But, lest blame for my errors should wrongly be transferred to other people, I feel bound to add that I am responsible for the accuracy or not of the statements here printed concerning the pictures.

3

Work on this catalogue has extended over several years, and the student, I think, may find some unevenness in the treatment of different pictures. Nevertheless, the principles have remained constant.

The biographical notices of the painters aim at being very brief. If that aim has not always been achieved, it is that it has been necessary in certain cases to define how a picture in the National Gallery, or more often how any pictures, can be associated with a particular name.

Next after the biography come the inventory number and the title of the picture. Descriptions have been for the most part omitted, reference to a reproduction being given instead. Inscriptions on the fronts are indicated, and iconographical identifications are stated; if elucidation of these statements is needed, it is usually made lower down, in the commentary. The measurements have mostly been taken specially for the present catalogue; if not, this is recorded.

The notes on the difficult subject of condition will be the object of some explanation presently.

In the commentary, the subject of the picture is usually treated first, attribution second. No picture in the present catalogue is to my knowledge signed or documented, unless this is explicitly stated. I have attempted to discuss fully any historical evidence concerning the authorship; but the discussion of modern attributions is less full.

The provenance of pictures seems perhaps even more suitable for record in a gallery catalogue than anywhere else; it has therefore been dealt with in some detail.

Besides the already mentioned lists of inventory numbers and changed attributions, there are various indices of the subjects of the pictures.

The statements made in this catalogue are based upon what has been written about the pictures, and upon examination of the pictures themselves. The first of these sources of information includes both printed books and manuscripts.

With regard to printed material, some of the references known to me have been deliberately omitted, in the belief that they would add little or nothing to what is already written; others, no doubt, have been omitted through ignorance. It is, I hope, excusable to point out that the bibliography concerning the pictures in this catalogue is very large; the Italians have been printing learned works for nearly five centuries, and Italian pictures so very often raise problems that are outside the field of art history proper. Further, the resources of the National Gallery Library are limited; indeed, a surprising number of the books cited in this volume seem not to be findable anywhere in England.

With regard to manuscript material, I have tried to make full use of the mss. preserved in the National Gallery; an official catalogue should surely not omit anything of that kind that adds new facts. But the cataloguer of a museum collection is, in my view, under no obligation to consult or cite any manuscripts preserved outside the building. Nevertheless, some mss. that are not in the National Gallery are referred to in the present volume.

It may help other students if I list here the principal manuscripts in London that I have at one time or another consulted.

In the National Gallery itself, apart from various papers mostly concerning individual pictures (the Gallery archives), there are the following collections of mss.:

(1), all that are known to survive of the note-books of Sir Charles Eastlake (Keeper of the National Gallery, 1843–1847; Director, 1855–1865). Most of these notes were made in Italy, usually with reference to possible or probable acquisition for the Gallery; they are of considerable importance.

(2), two volumes of the diary of Otto Mündler (Travelling Agent for the National Gallery, 1855–1858). These also are important. Mündler spent much more of the year abroad than Eastlake did, and he saw more pictures; his notes are usually more detailed than Eastlake's, his judgments perhaps less interesting.

Eastlake's note-books and Mündler's diary form a valuable supplement to Crowe and Cavalcaselle, who were travelling in Italy at about the same time.

(3), some papers of Sir Henry Layard, most of whose pictures passed by bequest to the National Gallery. These are referred to in the present catalogue as the 'Layard MSS. in the National Gallery'; the most valuable item in Layard's own ms. catalogue of his pictures.

(4), some papers of George Salting, most of whose pictures passed by bequest to the National Gallery.

Outside the National Gallery, but in London, I record the following:

(1), the note-books of Sir George Scharf, first Director of the National Portrait Gallery; I have consulted these by kind permission of Sir Henry Hake (Director, 1927–1951). Scharf's notes, often accompanied by useful sketches, are mostly on antiquarian subjects or concern English portraits. But he was responsible for the Old Masters section of the Manchester Exhibition of 1857, and even after 1857 he not infrequently recorded Italian and other foreign pictures he had occasion to see. The references found for the present catalogue are unfortunately not very many.

(2), a vast collection of the papers of Sir Henry Layard is in the Department of MSS. at the British Museum; printed catalogue, *Additions to the Manuscripts, 1911–1915*, 1925, with index of the writers of the letters. Many of these papers are not about pictures. I have looked through the six volumes of letters to and from Morelli, and I have consulted some other volumes. Adolfo Venturi had access to what clearly included these papers for an article on the Layard Collection, which he published in *L'Arte*, 1912, pp. 449 ff. What Venturi says is sometimes not accurate; unfortunately, it has been impossible to control his statements for some of Layard's earliest acquisitions, since the letters Venturi here refers to are not included in the collection now at the British Museum.

(3), a vast amount of ms. by Crowe and Cavalcaselle is at the Victoria and Albert Museum. A glance at some specimens showed that it was unlikely that much beyond what appears in their books could be found in these mss.; so I did not continue the examination.

I will not list here the mss. I have consulted abroad; my studies have been limited by time and are certainly very incomplete, and the references for anything found are given in each case. I imagine that a good deal of new fact concerning the National Gallery pictures could be extracted from mss. in Italy and elsewhere; perhaps the richest sources would be unpublished inventories, and papers connected with the history of certain museums.

To pass on to examination of the pictures: the student will find in this catalogue some indications concerning their preservation. Such notes are inevitably more or less faulty, especially if the picture has not recently been cleaned. I have, as occasion demanded, consulted with the restoring staff, and I am most grateful for their help. It might be thought that the restoring staff should have been made entirely responsible for all the statements on this subject. They could indeed give a better account of the condition of the pictures, if their examination were carried out far more elaborately than mine has been; but such an examination would occupy them for several years, and could not be undertaken. It was considered that, working no more elaborately than I have done, they would not have achieved results substantially more accurate.

The notes here printed are not intended to give a complete statement of the present condition of the pictures; they are addressed to the art-historian, to indicate to him, briefly and as well as may be, whether what he now sees differs notably from the original painter's work. There is, it should be explained, hardly ever any reference to the condition above the paint layer, i.e. to dirt and varnish; although admittedly these may change the appearance of the painter's work as much as over-cleaning or repainting. The word 'undercleaning' is used to indicate uneven cleaning, by which the raised parts of the paint have been made more or less clean, but the hollows have been left dirty.

I think it is essential in a catalogue of important pictures to include some such notes on condition; it is, nevertheless, very difficult to decide in each case how much to say, and the student will probably find that the treatment of different pictures is uneven. I hope that errors in the statements made will not be found disastrously numerous or serious. I should like to add that Mr. F. I. G. Rawlins has most readily taken any scientific photographs for which I asked; but economy demanded that I should ask only when I was sure of the need, so that many pictures included in this volume have not been studied under X-rays or under ultra-violet and infra-red lamps.

I have already made some acknowledgements of the help I have received in the preparation of this catalogue; there is much more on this score that I should like to say. I have had help of various kinds from my colleagues at the National Gallery; particularly, besides those already mentioned, from the Director, the Keeper and the publications staff. I wish also to make particular acknowledgement to Messrs. Christie, Manson and Woods, who have been unfailingly helpful in matters relating to their sales. This would form merely the beginning of a long list, if I were here to thank all the institutions and scholars of whom I have asked help, either in questions relating to the pictures, or in a search for books, or in the consultation of manuscripts. In some cases, the acknowledgement is made in its place in the catalogue. In others, this has not been possible; yet I feel that a list of names here would be inadequate to express my gratitude. A complete list would be, I fear, intolerably long; a selection from among so many kindnesses would seem invidious. Perhaps, therefore, it is best if I say merely that so much help of diverse kinds is not forgotten by me; and that the following catalogue has profited greatly from so many contributions to it.

MARTIN DAVIES

1951

NOTE TO THE SECOND EDITION

THE FIRST EDITION of the present catalogue, published in 1951, went out of print sooner than I could turn to writing revisions. Although it was desirable for the Gallery to have this catalogue on sale, an interval was granted for me to make some changes. The revision is partial; some pictures have not even been looked at again. This does not mean that the changes that have been made have been made hastily, nor that with more time I should have carried out substantial alterations to the character of the catalogue.

New information has come from the cleaning of pictures, and from discussions about these and others with the Conservation Department, which had not long existed in 1951.

There has also been much published in the last decade about the pictures and the painters, partly in direct connection with the catalogue. I have made fairly full references to what I knew of these publications, fuller than for earlier writings; and I am most grateful to all critics who have made useful contributions, whether in correction of what was printed here before or as a supplement to it. Some pages of comment by Professor Roberto Longhi were particularly generous to me; *peraro* is a motto I dare not indeed claim, but should like to claim.

An index of collections has been added in the present edition; this includes present owners who have deposited pictures on loan, if their pictures are given entries in the catalogue. Such an index may indeed reveal interesting facts in itself, but is primarily a signpost to the text of the catalogue, usually the Provenance section. It is in varying degrees uncertain if some of the names indexed ought to be included as owners, but doubtful cases are not so specified in the index. The surname may be all that is given for a collection, maybe covering several generations, or different members of a firm of dealers; on the other hand, a name may be given more fully in the index than in the text, and an attempt has been made to specify collectors who without some definition would be confused with others. Agents are not owners, yet their status is often undefined, and it was thought best to include them; but agents for the National Gallery have been omitted, even though this may impede the curious concerning the activity of some people involved in the art-world and not readily traceable. It seemed improper to include the names of people who contributed money towards purchases; the National Gallery indeed owes much, for instance, to the National Art-Collections Fund, yet a record of this generosity seemed outside the scope of the index. There are entries for the origin of pictures when known, e.g. the church for which a picture was painted, the entry being under the town;

also, in cases considered reasonable, entries for donors of church pictures, whether known from documents or from the ownership of a chapel; also a selection of names of later owners of a chapel. In most cases, a person whose portrait appears in a picture is given an entry. I hope that this attempt at an index will be of use to students working on collections, and that they will be able to help me in correcting mistakes, and in defining more closely the names or activities of some collectors I know too little about.

In the preface to the first edition, I gave up trying to acknowledge all the help I had received. The task would be even more difficult now; and I will confine myself to recording with gratitude use of the Witt Library, the Library of the Warburg Institute and that of the Kunsthistorisches Institut at Florence.

MARTIN DAVIES

EXPLANATIONS

ATTRIBUTION: A picture labelled as *by* a painter or from his *Studio* is presumed to have been produced as his in his shop. If doubt needs emphasis, *Ascribed to* is prefixed. If there seems to be a connection of style but not of hand, *Follower of*, *After*, *Imitator of* or *Style of* is prefixed. *Follower* replaces the word *School*, here reserved for a town or district; *After* indicates a copy of any date; *Imitator of* explains itself; *Style of* indicates a vague relation.

CONDITION: All canvases not mounted on panels have been relined, unless the contrary is stated. Cradling of panels is not noted; damages in the supports, such as cracks in the panels, are usually not noted.

MEASUREMENTS: These are given in inches, followed by metres in brackets. Height precedes width. The size of the painted surface, not of the supporting canvas or panel, is given.

MEDIUM: Most of the pictures here catalogued are painted in tempera or oil or both; no attempt has been made to record which. Frescoes are noted as such.

WOOD: In some cases, the species of wood on which a picture is painted is noted. This matter, nevertheless, has not been pursued. Most early Italian pictures are painted on poplar or lime; the painters themselves seem not always to have minded which (cf. the entry for Crivelli, No. 788).

CANVAS: Sometimes the fabric on which the pictures are painted is not canvas but, for instance, silk. Only in a few cases has the fabric been sent for analysis; for others, the word 'canvas' is used, although it may not be the correct description.

RIGHT AND LEFT: These terms indicate the spectator's right and left, unless the context clearly implies the contrary.

BIBLIOGRAPHY: General works of reference are sometimes cited without full details. This should not cause difficulty; but it may be mentioned here that the page references to the *Acta Sanctorum* by the Bollandists are according to the most recent edition.

ANDREA DI ALOIGI, called L'INGEGNO
active 1484–1516

Andrea di Aloigi, also called L'Ingegno. First recorded, apparently as a painter, in Assisi; again, as an assistant of Perugino's, in 1490. From 1501 he seems to have abandoned painting, living thenceforward in Assisi; it is possible, as Vasari says, that he went blind. Vasari records him with praise as a pupil of Perugino's, but none of his works have been identified; the only one with any claim to consideration is No. 1220 below.

Ascribed to ANDREA DI ALOIGI

1220 THE VIRGIN AND CHILD

Signed (?), A.A.P.

Wood, painted surface, $25\frac{1}{2} \times 17\frac{1}{8}$ (0.65×0.435); including an edging in dark paint all round, which continues to all the edges of the panel.

In general well preserved, but the paint has flaked somewhat. Most of the gold seems to have been renewed; the gold of the signature (?) is apparently old, though somewhat damaged, and a little retouched.

The letters may be a signature, and can be interpreted as *Andreas Assisiensis* (or possibly *Andrea* [di] *Aloigi*) *Pinxit*.[1] If that is true, No. 1220 would be an authenticated work of the painter; the only one. An alternative suggestion of *Aulista d'Angelo Pinxit* seems more improbable;[2] Aulista's obscurity is deeper than Andrea's.

VERSIONS: Very similar pictures in the Abbé Le Monnier Sale, Paris, 15 May, 1909 (lot 53),[3] and with Abels, Cologne (frontispiece to catalogue of October, 1959). A picture rather more varied is at Washington.[4] Another, more varied still, but connected in design, was at Munich and is now in the Rockefeller Collection, New York.[5]

PROVENANCE: In 1821 it belonged to Giovanni Metzger at Florence;[6] later to Volkmann at Florence.[7] Acquired before 1837 by the Rev. J. Sanford;[8] Sanford Catalogues, 1838 (No. 156) and 1847 (No. 26); exhibited at the British Institution, 1848 (No. 104). Sanford's daughter had in 1844 married the 2nd Lord Methuen, and his pictures including No. 1220 were added to the collection at Corsham. Exhibited at the R.A., 1877 (No. 183). Purchased from Lord Methuen, Walker Fund, 1886.

REPRODUCTION: *Illustrations, Italian Schools*, 1937, p. 173. *Plates, Earlier Italian Schools*, 1953, Vol. I, p. 1.

REFERENCES: (1) See Rumohr in *Kunst-Blatt*, 1821, p. 290, and his *Italienische Forschungen*, II, 1827, p. 328. (2) See Milanesi's Toscanelli Sale catalogue, 1883, pp. 114/6. (3) As Umbrian School, reproduced; size 0.72×0.51. (4) Washington, 1941 Catalogue, No. 326 (Perugino); reproduced in the Book of Illustrations;

size, 0·70 × 0·51. A very close version of this by Fadino (Tommaso Aleni of Cremona) is reproduced by Van Marle, *Development of the Italian Schools of Painting*, Vol. XIV, Fig. 326, and appeared at Christie's, 26 February, 1937 (lot 152). (5) Munich, 1904 Katalog, No. 1036, size 0·83 × 0·64; Klassiker der Kunst *Perugino*, 1914, Plate 210; Van Marle, *Development of the Italian Schools of Painting*, Vol. XIV, Fig. 223. (6) *Kunst-Blatt*, 1821, p. 290, and *Italiensche Forschungen*, as in note 1. Rumohr gives enough description to make the identity sure. (7) See Passavant, *Rafael von Urbin*, I, 1839, p. 503, referring back to Rumohr. (8) Sanford, according to his 1838 catalogue, collected his pictures in Italy between 1815 and 1837.

ANDREA DI BONAIUTO DA FIRENZE
active *ca.* 1343, died *ca.* 1377

Recorded in the Physicians' Guild at Florence, *ca.* 1343. On 30 December, 1365, he agreed to terminate the frescoes in the Spanish Chapel, Santa Maria Novella, by the end of 1367. In 1377 Andrea da Firenze (accepted as being the same man) received a final payment for the frescoes of S. Ranieri in the Camposanto at Pisa. He made his will in that year, and seems to have died soon after.

Ascribed to ANDREA DA FIRENZE

5115 THE VIRGIN AND CHILD WITH TEN SAINTS

In separate compartments. From left to right: (1) S. Mark, inscribed S. MARCHUS; (2) S. Peter Martyr, inscribed S. PETRUS. ; (3) S. Thomas Aquinas, inscribed S. THOMAS. ; (4) S. Dominic, inscribed S. DOMINICUS; (5) S. Luke, inscribed S. LUCAS; (6) the Virgin and Child, inscribed . S. MARIA UIRGO . ; (7) S. John the Evangelist, inscribed S. IOHANNES; (8) S. Gregory, inscribed S GREGORIUS; (9) S. Catherine of Alexandria, inscribed S. KATERINA; (10) the Magdalen, inscribed S. MARIA MAD; (11) a bishop with a book, inscribed S. THOMAS (D ?).

Wood. The size of each compartment for the saints is, rounded top, $5\frac{1}{8} \times 3\frac{1}{8}$ (0·13 × 0·08); the size of the Virgin's compartment is, pointed top, $7\frac{1}{8} \times 4\frac{5}{8}$ (0·18 × 0·115). The total size, including the framing, is $11 \times 41\frac{3}{4}$ (0·28 × 1·06).

Very fairly preserved; most of the gold on the framing is new.

The saints are in compartments separated from one another by colonnettes. The 11 pictures are framed together by what is clearly the original frame, although mostly regilt; the inscriptions are under each saint, on the lower part of the frame. At the top, the frame rises to a pediment above the Virgin and Child; the top finial of this has been broken away. The ensemble is clearly complete at the sides, and may also be complete at the bottom.

Meiss[1] claimed that the S. Thomas Bishop is S. Thomas à Becket, and this is accepted by Kaftal.[2] It is a pity that he is not shown as a martyr[3] (S. Peter Martyr and S. Catherine in No. 5115 have palms);

although it cannot be said that Becket is the only possible identification,[4] it does seem the most likely.

The picture, as Meiss points out, is clearly associated with the Dominicans. Both Becket and all the other saints shown on No. 5115 had altars in S. Maria Novella at Florence, and S. Matthew (the missing Evangelist) apparently had not; one of the saints, indeed the one in the principal position, is S. Luke, and it may be that chapels were not often dedicated to S. Luke at the time.

Meiss[5] comments on the peculiar shape (with reflections of an earlier style) and size of No. 5115. His claim that it may be a (reduced) replica of the altarpiece of the chapel of S. Luke in S. Maria Novella seems doubtful, since Vasari appears to say that that picture was signed by Simone Martini.[6]

Meiss's attribution for No. 5115 is to Andrea da Firenze; this appears convincing, with the restriction that the quality seems not high, so it may not be a work of his own hand. As Meiss points out, the composition of the Virgin and Child in No. 5115 corresponds quite closely with those appearing on an attributed picture in the Carmine at Florence,[7] and in one of the documented frescoes at Pisa.[8]

PROVENANCE: From the Collection of Mrs. F. W. H. Myers, who die d in 1937. Presented by her daughter, Mrs. Richard F. P. Blennerhassett, 1940.

REPRODUCTION: *Plates, Earlier Italian Schools*, 1953, Vol. I, p. 212.

REFERENCES: (1) Millard Meiss, *Painting in Florence and Siena after the Black Death*, 1951, p. 175/6. (2) G. Kaftal, *The Iconography of the Saints in Tuscan Painting*, 1952, Col. 989. (3) Becket is best referred to as a martyr; cf. Richa, *Notizie Istoriche delle Chiese Fiorentine*, Vol. IV, 1756, p. 68 and Stefano Orlandi, *Il Necrologio di Santa Maria Novella*, 1955, Vol. II, p. 417 (29 December), also Fra Angelico, No. 663 of the present catalogue, Inner Right Panel, Second Row, No. 9. Kaftal, *loc. cit.*, reproduces a figure from a predella in S. Croce, not shown as a martyr (although other figures in the predella are). This has a damaged inscription that apparently includes the name of Thomas, but in parts seems far from clear; the authenticity of this and the other inscriptions on the predella deserves confirmation. It should be added that on the existing altar dedicated to Becket in S. Maria Novella the inscription (apparently of the XIX Century) does not refer to him as a martyr, although on the altar opposite SS. Cosmas and Damian are so described; Paatz, *Die Kirchen von Florenz*, Vol. III, 1952, p. 703, says the altar is dedicated to S. Thomas Aquinas, but it seems not doubtful that S. Thomas à Becket is right (cf. Fineschi, *Il Forestiero Istruito in Santa Maria Novella*, 1790, p. 13). For details about S. Thomas à Becket in connection with S. Maria Novella, see Orlandi, *op. cit.*, Vol. I, p. 415. (4) There is, for instance, S. Thomas de Cantalupe, whose cult may indeed have been peculiarly English, but who did die in Italy. (5) Meiss, *op. cit.*, pp. 47/8 and 175/6. (6) Vasari, ed. Milanesi, Vol. I, p. 549. (7) Meiss, *op. cit.*, Fig. 64. (8) Just distinguishable in Venturi, *Storia*, Vol. V, Fig. 653.

FRA ANGELICO
active 1417—died 1455

Guido di Pietro, presumed to have been born at Vicchio in the Mugello. According to Vasari he was born *ca.* 1386/8, but there is reason to believe that this is too early. He has long been said to have entered the

Dominican friary of S. Domenico near Fiesole as a novice in 1407, taking his vows in the following year; but P. Stefano Orlandi (*Rivista d'Arte*, 1954, pp. 161ff.) has shown that the date of 1407 is not to be relied on, and proposes *ca.* 1418/20 instead. There is confirmatory evidence that he was not a friar (although already a painter) in 1417 (W. Cohn in the *Rivista d'Arte*, 1955, pp. 207 ff.). A 'Guido di Pietro', reasonably claimed to be him, was paid for an altarpiece on 15 February, 1418; on the other hand, he was already a friar by June 1423 (Cohn in *Memorie Domenicane*, 1956, pp. 218 ff.). On becoming a friar he was known as Fra Giovanni; he is now known by the sobriquet of Angelico, perhaps first used as an epithet in his praise, already so by Fra Domenico di Giovanni da Corella (d. 1483) in the 4th Book of his *Theotocon* (*ca.* 1468). He does not appear to have been formally beatified (although called 'Venerable' on his tombstone); but it is customary in Italian to call him *Il Beato Angelico.*

The Fiesolan friars were dispersed during the years 1409–1418; but it is thought now that this does not concern the biography of Fra Angelico. It is certain that he lived for a considerable time in the friary at Fiesole; indeed there is no evidence that he was ever transferred to another house (cf. the *Archivio Storico Italiano*, 1913, I, p. 14), and he became eventually its prior. Sometime after 1436, he was working extensively for the Dominican friary of S. Marco in Florence (a daughter house of the friary at Fiesole). From 1447 at latest he was a good deal occupied in Rome, and in 1447 also he was painting in Orvieto.

The early records given above are Florentine. It is not known who was Fra Angelico's master; but the picture paid for in 1418 had been allocated in 1413 to Ambrogio di Baldese, and it may be that Fra Angelico was trained by him, or at least by some traditional Florentine painter. His developed style, deeply coloured by his religion, seems to have been formed towards 1430, under the progressive influences then in Florence, particularly (perhaps) Ghiberti.

663 CHRIST GLORIFIED IN THE COURT OF HEAVEN (PREDELLA OF AN ALTARPIECE)

Five panels.

Centre

Christ amid the angelic host. He is shown as it is customary to show Him at the Resurrection, His wounds apparent, blessing, and holding a banner with a red cross on a white ground. Of the figures surrounding Him, S. Michael is identifiable.

Inner Left Panel

At the top on the right is the Virgin. Behind her are three rows of Apostles or Saints of Apostolic character, numbering 21 in all; SS. Peter, Paul and John the Evangelist are clearly identifiable. (See the commentary below.) Behind them, the three rows continue with other saints (Confessors, Hermits and Members of Religious Orders).

Reading from right to left, Top Row: 1, S. Silvester, Pope, his name inscribed S̄. SILVESTER.   2, S. Hilary, his name inscribed ILARI'.   3, S. Martin, inscribed S. MARTINVS.   4, unidentified.   5, S. Dominic, with his lily; his book has an inscription from Psalm xxxvi or xxxvii, 30, DS IVST / MEDI / TABIT' / SAPIE / NTIĀ / & LIN / GVA EI' / LOQᵛET', see below.   6, unidentified.   7, S. Gregory, Pope, inscribed S̄. ḠEGORI'.   8, S. Nicholas with his three balls on a book.   9, S. Francis, with the Stigmata.   10, S. Zenobius (?), see below.

Second Row: 1, S. Jerome as a Cardinal, with pen and a book inscribed SANC/TVS. YE/RONIM' / DOᶜTCTŌ / MASSI/MVS: AD/ EVSTO/CIA'. See below.   2, S. Anthony Abbot, with a crutch.   3, S. Maurus (?).   4, S. Benedict, with rods and a book.   5, S. Augustine with a book; see below.   6, unidentified.   7, S. Thomas Aquinas with a star on his breast; his book bears the remains of an inscription from Psalm ciii or civ, 13, ...SA / ..MO/.... (T)E / IOB' / S DE / FRVTV / OPERV̄ / TVORV̄ / SATIA. See below.   8, S. Anthony of Padua with a Cross.   9, unidentified.   10, S. Bernard (?), with a book; see below.

Third Row: 1, S. Paul the Hermit, in his dress of matted palm leaves. 2, 3, 4, unidentified.   5, S. Giovanni (John) Gualberto, with book and cross; see below.   6, A saint with a book; see below.   7, S. Louis of Toulouse, a Franciscan Bishop with crowns on his cope; the Annunciation is shown on his crozier.   8, S. Onuphrius.   9, unidentified.   10, S. Leonard (?), if (as seems unlikely) the object hanging from his girdle is a fetter.

Inner Right Panel

Reading from left to right, Top Row: The Precursors of Christ.   1, Adam.   2, Eve, in hairy dress, holding three ears of corn (?); see below. 3, Noah, holding the Ark.   4, unidentified.   5, Abraham, with a knife.   6, unidentified.   7, Moses, holding the Tables of the Law. On one is inscribed NON ABE/BIS DEOS A-/LIENOS: N / NON ASS/VMES NO/MEN DEI / TVI IN / VANVz; on the other ET MA/ TVAM / OCIDES / MEECC/ABERIS / NŌ FVR/T FA. See below.   8, unidentified.   9, Aaron, inscribed ARON.   10, Joshua, inscribed *jesue*. 11, S. John the Baptist; see below.   12, Joel, inscribed YOEL.   13, David, with a harp inscribed DAVId.   14, Isaiah, with a scroll inscribed YSAYA.   15, Ezekiel, his cap inscribed EZECIEL.   16, Jeremiah, with a scroll inscribed YEREMIA.   17, Unnamed, his halo left partly unstamped.   18, Daniel, inscribed. *daniel.*   19, Zechariah, with a scroll inscribed SACCARIA.   20, Jonah, with a book inscribed IONA.   21, Habbakkuk, with a scroll inscribed ABACVC.

Second Row: Male Martyrs, all with palms.   1, S. Stephen, Protomartyr, with a stone on his collar.   2, S. Cyprian, inscribed S. CIPRIANVS. 3, S. Clement, inscribed S : CLEMENS.   4, unidentified.   5, S. Vincent, with his millstone; see below.   6, S. Lawrence, with his gridiron.   7, unidentified.   8, S. Barnabas (?), with a book; see below.   9, S. Thomas à Becket, inscribed S : THOMA. See below.   10, S. Peter Martyr, with a book and bloody head.   11, 12, SS. Cosmas and Damian, in medical bonnets, with a box of unguents. 13, S. Sebastian, clothed, holding an arrow; see below. 14, unidentified. 15, S. Ignatius, holding a heart inscribed $\overline{yhs}$ several times; see below. 16, unidentified. 17, S. George(?), in armour; see below. 18, S. Julian (?), or more probably S. Miniato, with a line of blood round his head; see below. 19, unidentified. 20, S. Christopher, without the Christ Child, but with his leafy branch, and with bare legs for wading; see below. 21, S. Sixtus, Pope, inscribed S SISTVS; see below. 22, S. Erasmus, inscribed S: ARASMVS.

Third Row, Female Saints. 1, S. Anne; see below. 2, S. Thecla, the first female martyr; see below. 3, S. Mary Magdalene (?), with prayer beads; see below. 4, S. Martha(?); see below. 5, 6, unidentified. 7, S. Agnes, holding the *Agnus Dei* haloed and wounded in the side; see below. 8, 9, unidentified. 10, S. Cecily, with a crown of red and white roses; see below. 11, unidentified. 12, S. Catherine, crowned, with her wheel. 13, S. Margaret, with a cross; see below. 14, S. Elizabeth of Hungary (?); see below. 15, 16, unidentified. 17, S. Helen, with the True Cross; inscribed on her crown SANCTA. LENA. 18, S. Flavia or S. Felicitas (?); see below. 19, S. Bridget of Sweden, with a book and a lighted candle; see below. 20, S. Clare. 21, S. Reparata (?); see below. 22, unidentified.

Outer Panels

Notes on the identity of these figures are given in the commentary below; here only the inscriptions and emblems are recorded.

Outer Left Panel

Reading from right to left, Top Row: 1, . *b iōdan'*, with book and pen. 2, . *b . reginaldus*. 3, *b . ābrosi'*, with a book and the Holy Ghost at his ear. 4, . *b . nich'laus*. 5, . *b . jachob'*; he is scratching the name $\overline{iyu}$ on his breast. 6, . *b . ERichu'*, with a book; he has a golden cross surmounted by a crown on his habit.

Second and Third Rows together: 1, *.b.iacob'*; he holds a golden pot with a lily, and a dove near his right shoulder seems to belong to him rather than to No. 2. 2, . *b . ērichus*, with a book. 3, . *b . sinuus* (apparently; lettering damaged); he holds a book and a leafy branch. 4, . *b . boninsegĭa*, with a palm and a double-handed saw in his head. 5, . *b . uĭcēti'*, with a book and a flame in his hand. 6, *b . amandu'* with a book. 7, . *b . iōdan'*, with a book and a skull.

Bottom Row: 1, . *b . māgaĭta*, with the Stigmata. 2, . *b . āgnies*. 3, . *b . sibeina* (or *sibrina*). 4 and 5, unnamed.

Outer Right Panel

Reading from left to right, Top Row: 1, Bishop holding a book inscribed BEAT/VS AL/BERTV' / MAN/(N)VS. 2, *b . benedict'*, Pope. 3, *.b . beltad*, (lettering damaged), Martyr Bishop. 4, *. b . latinus*, Cardinal. 5, *.b . gualteri'*, with the Stigmata. 6, . *b . petrus*; $\overline{yhs}$ in his mouth. 7, *.b . unbert'*, with a book and holding a magister's wand.

Second and Third Rows together: 1, . *b . raimūd'*, with a book. 2, . *b .*

iacob'; holding apparently his own heart (inscribed *yh̄u*'), taken from his side. 3, . *b . bona/speme* (lettering damaged); a martyr with a wound in his neck. 4, . *b . johes*; in one hand he holds a church, from the other rays are directed towards the church. 5, . *b . uēturin*', with a book, and the Holy Ghost at his mouth. 6, . *b . māculin*', holding a Cross and three Nails.

Bottom Row: 1, . *b . caterina*, with a book. 2, . *b . māgaita*. 3, . *b . joha. d . floretiᵃ* (lettering damaged). 4, 5 & 6, unnamed.

Wood. The sizes of the painted surfaces are: centre panel, $12\frac{1}{2} \times 28\frac{3}{4}$ (0.32×0.73); inner left panel, $12\frac{1}{2} \times 25\frac{1}{4}$ (0.32×0.64); inner right panel, $12\frac{1}{2} \times 25$ (0.32×0.635); outer left panel, $12\frac{1}{2} \times 8\frac{1}{2}$ (0.32×0.215); outer right panel, $12\frac{1}{2} \times 8\frac{3}{4}$ (0.32×0.22).

In general in excellent condition.

The pictures formed the predella of the high altarpiece in the church of Fra Angelico's own friary of S. Domenico, near Fiesole; some comment on this matter will be made lower down.

Iconographical Commentary

No. 663 is by far the most distinguished hagiological picture in the Gallery. Unfortunately, it has not been possible to identify all the figures. This is partly because it is very difficult to discover what Fra Angelico or his advisers might have known about the Saints, whose lives have been the subject of extensive research since that time; also partly because Fra Angelico has left some figures without identifying marks, and may further have committed some mistakes.

The subject of the central panel is not absolutely clear. It is indeed obvious that Christ is represented glorified in Heaven; it is, nevertheless, slightly odd that the Father and the Holy Ghost should be missing. Christ is depicted as it is customary to depict Him at the Resurrection. It is hard to suppose that some incident is here represented. The picture is clearly not a Last Judgment; possible subjects might be the Ascent from Hell or the Ascension. But the treatment of such subjects would be very peculiar; and this view would not accord very well with the devotional nature of the picture, which is clearly emphasized.

The *Inner Left Panel*, which being on Christ's right hand is the place of honour, poses an odd problem; the group of apostles and saints of apostolic character numbers 21. It is probable that the saints holding a book, who number twelve and certainly include SS. Peter, Paul and John, are Apostles; and the 7th saint in the top row, who holds a scroll, may be S. Matthias, thus completing the number of thirteen. Two of these Apostles, S. John and one other, hold a pen as well as a book, and two others without a book hold a pen; it seems likely that a pen specifies an Evangelist. Of the two Evangelists who were not Apostles, SS. Luke and Mark, a painter may be thought likely to give more prominence to S. Luke; so he may be the first figure of the third row. This makes a total of 15; the remaining six saints, who have no emblems, are presumably representatives of the disciples.[1] Top Row, No. 5; the passage from the Psalms is used in the gradual of the Mass *de communi doctorum*, also

in the introit of the *commune confessoris non Ponteficis*, and therefore in
the service for S. Dominic's own feast. The text is found sometimes in
images of other saints. No. 10; this bishop without attribute has a good
claim to be S. Zenobius. In such a collection of saints on a Florentine
picture, the chief Patrons of Florence are to be expected; cf. Inner Right
Panel, Bottom Row, No. 21 (S. Reparata?). A slight difficulty about S.
Zenobius here is that he is often shown with a short beard; but this is not
invariably the case.[2] Second Row, No. 1: the words on S. Jerome's book
ad Eustochiam refer to his epistles to that saint, who was his pupil. She is
represented on Botticini's altarpiece, No. 227 of this Gallery. The
bungled third word of the inscription seems first to have been written
DOTTO(R); then an attempt was made to turn the first T into a C; when
this failed, a C was added on the line above. No. 5: since the other great
Doctors of the Church are present, S. Augustine can hardly have been
omitted, and this figure seems the only possible one. The Dominicans are
usually said to follow the Rule of S. Augustine, this being mentioned in
the *Golden Legend*; and some significance may be found in his turning as
if to speak to S. Thomas Aquinas, who claimed S. Augustine for his
principal guide. No. 7: the full text of the inscription is *Rigans montes de
superioribus suis*; *de fructu operum tuorum satiabitur terra* (Psalm ciii (civ),
13). These words were quoted by an old man in a vision to S. Thomas,
bidding him accept his doctor's degree, which S. Thomas in his humility
was desirous of refusing; S. Thomas therefore took the degree, using
these words as the text of his *principium*. The same text occurs for S.
Thomas in the main part of the altarpiece at Fiesole, and elsewhere, e.g.
in an altarpiece in S. Marco, Florence (ex-Conservatorio di S. Pietro
Martire).[3] No. 10 seems pretty certainly S. Bernard; No. 9 has the
appearance of being one of his disciples, but it is difficult to suggest who.
Third Row. Although Fra Angelico himself belonged to a Religious
Order, this group of monks and hermits is the worst characterized of the
whole picture. Most of the figures have no adequate distinguishing
marks; and several well-known Orders, such as the Carmelites, Camaldolese, etc., appear to be unrepresented. No. 5: it was customary to represent S. Giovanni Gualberto with a Cross, because of the Crucifix which
bowed Its head at the time of his conversion.[4] No. 6 (with a book): there
seems to be no suitable Founder of an Order, so the writer S. Bonaventure seems just possible, although the saint is not certainly a Franciscan,
and although S. Bonaventure was not canonized until 1482. Some
similar example of S. Bonaventure would be required to make the
identification at all probable.[5]

Inner Right Panel. No. 2: the figure between Adam and Noah is
peculiar. One would naturally take it for a man; the only likely candidate
would then be Abel. But the clothes seem irrelevant to what is recorded
of Abel; and the ears of corn (?) would be a proper attribute for Cain,
who was a farmer, rather than for Abel, who was a shepherd. The figure
would seem therefore to be Eve. Her costume would be the coat of skins
made for her by God, and the ears of corn (?) perhaps a reference to the
present state of mankind, for which indeed Eve is responsible, 'in the

sweat of thy face shalt thou eat bread' (Genesis iii, 19 and 21). Eve wears
a similar dress in Fra Angelico's *Annunciation* at Madrid, which was
formerly in S. Domenico di Fiesole; and there is a figure in some degree
similar in his fresco of the *Descent into Hell* in S. Marco, Florence.
There would be further some significance in putting Eve opposite the
Virgin Mary, but with the Virgin placed forward in front of her group,
and Eve placed behind Adam; many old pictures illustrate the tenet that
it is the Virgin Mary who undid the harm caused to mankind by Eve.
In particular, Fra Angelico was in the habit of illustrating the Fall in the
backgrounds of his *Annunciations*. No. 7: the fragmentary inscription
on the Table of the Law held in Moses' left hand stands for *Honora
patrem tuum et matrem tuam, etc. Non occides. Non moechaberis. Non
furtum facies* (Exodus xx). No. 11: S. John the Baptist has been placed
out of chronological order, perhaps partly to give him prominence as the
Principal Patron of Florence. Second Row, No. 5: it is proper for S.
Vincent to have a millstone as his attribute—according to the Golden
Legend one of the incidents of his passion was to be attached to one and
cast into the sea.[6] No. 8: this prominent figure of apostolic character,
with a book and martyr's palm, was obviously meant to be recognizable.
S. Barnabas seems to be the only candidate. On the main part of the
picture, of which No. 663 formed the predella, the four saints are
Dominic, Thomas Aquinas, Peter Martyr and a figure now identified as
S. Barnabas.[7] This is clearly correct; the picture (see the provenance)
was the high altarpiece of a church dedicated to SS. Dominic and
Barnabas (perhaps even originally to S. Barnabas alone). Barnaba degli
Agli had in fact been the principal benefactor of the friary.[8] In No. 663,
the three Dominican saints reappear, as is natural in the court of heaven;
S. Barnabas is obviously also required, and he may fairly be identified as
the present figure, although with no attribute except a book (referring to
the *Epistle of Barnabas*). Three doubtful points about the identification
may be mentioned. The first is that the figure is separated from the
apostles on the inner left panel; but S. Barnabas' special connection with
the church would justify this. Secondly, the figure here has a martyr's
palm, which is correct for S. Barnabas; but on the main part of the
picture S. Barnabas appears to have no palm. Nothing has been distinguished on the original altarpiece at S. Domenico di Fiesole; but it may
be (subject to confirmation) that Lorenzo di Credi, who played havoc
with the main part of the picture, painted out S. Barnabas' palm. Thirdly,
Kaftal claims that in Florentine painting S. Barnabas is always shown
holding an olive branch. Yet the saint identified as S. Barnabas on the
main part of the altarpiece at Fiesole does not, and the (damaged) S.
Barnabas in the Giovanni da Milano at Prato does not, and clearly
never did; maybe the olive branch was *de rigueur* only at Florence itself.
No. 9: the Dominicans of S. Maria Novella had received a bequest of
land, if they celebrated the Feast of S. Thomas of Canterbury.[9] No. 13:
clearly S. Sebastian. Later in the fifteenth century he was most often
shown naked; but even if Fra Angelico had normally done so, he would
probably have dressed him for the court of heaven. No. 15: undoubtedly

S. Ignatius, Bishop of Antioch. When tortured, he constantly invoked
the name of Jesus Christ; asked why, he replied, That Name is written
in my heart. When he had succumbed, his heart was cut open; within it
in golden letters was the sacred Name.[10] No. 17: S. George is likely. S.
Maurice would be possible, but less likely. No. 18: a similar figure is
seen on a Lorenzo di Credi, formerly at Lockinge, called one of the
many S. Julians, but undoubtedly the wrong one. S. Julian, the husband
of S. Basilissa, would be a possible identification for both figures; he
was scalped. The compiler, nevertheless, inclines to withdraw this suggestion of S. Julian, and proposes S. Miniato instead.[11] No. 20: clearly
S. Christopher. Presumably Fra Angelico was reluctant to show him
carrying the Christ Child in the court of heaven; it is unusual to represent him alone at this date, but some similar cases exist, e.g. a figure
(with the name inscribed) in Jacobello del Fiore's *Paradise* in the
Academy at Venice.[12] No. 21: probably Sixtus II rather than Sixtus I.
Third Row, No. 1: obviously S. Anne, opposite but lower than the
Virgin on the inner left panel. No. 2: from the position, the first female
martyr, i.e. S. Thecla. Her long hair may be a reference to the story that
S. Paul refused to let her cut her hair and put on male attire, in order to
follow him on his missions to remote places. S. Cyprian had a peculiar
devotion to S. Thecla; it is possible that his position immediately above
her may have been chosen for that reason. Nos. 3 and 4: these figures,
not martyrs, and placed before the group of the Virgin Patronesses, are
clearly Biblical. No. 3 with prayer beads may be the penitent Magdalen;
No. 4 might then be S. Martha, who is supposed to have been the first
nun, and is dressed in a way fancifully recalling a nun's habit. No. 7: S.
Agnes' usual attribute of a lamb has been turned into the *Agnus Dei*,
with even a wound in its side. It is not a very great variation, and some
similar examples are known, e.g. by Duccio, No. 47 of the Siena Gallery.
No. 10: it is proper for S. Cecily to wear a crown of red and white roses,
and a similar figure by Fra Angelico exists, where the name is inscribed.
S. Cecily is now chiefly known as Patroness of Music.[13] No. 13: a cross
is the proper attribute of S. Margaret, who escaped from a dragon by
means of a cross or by making the sign of the cross. No. 14: S. Elizabeth
of Hungary seems possible for this figure. One would certainly expect
her in the picture. No. 18: if this martyr is a nun, the décolleté would
suggest a Benedictine nun. S. Flavia is the most obvious martyr nun,
and was a Benedictine. On the other hand, a S. Felicitas with the name
inscribed, and somewhat similar to this, occurs in the altarpiece in the
Academy at Florence by Spinello Aretino, Niccolò di Pietro and
Lorenzo di Niccolò.[14] No. 19: certainly S. Bridget of Sweden. Every
Friday she dropped burning wax from a candle on her arm. Her dress is
not the Bridgittine habit, and should in fact not be so for S. Bridget.[15]
No. 21: apropos of S. Zenobius above, it was remarked that the chief
Patrons of Florence could be expected on this picture; S. Reparata was
a martyr and is correctly represented in civilian costume. It is true that
S. Reparata is often shown wearing a crown.[16]

The two outer panels represent *beati* of Fra Angelico's own Order.

They offer problems of identification even harder than those of the main panels, although in most cases the name is inscribed. It should be stated that these inscriptions are clearly contemporary. S. Vincent Ferrer was canonized in 1455 (publicly in 1458), and S. Catherine of Siena was canonized in 1461; the fact that such popular figures are recorded merely as *beati* is proof that the naming was done very early, presumably being executed by Fra Angelico himself, unless indeed it was at his request by his calligrapher brother Fra Benedetto. There is nothing strange in finding such inscriptions in a Fra Angelico; for instance, the *Coronation of the Virgin* in S. Marco, Florence (ex-S. Maria Nuova) has several saints named on their collars. One may add that the writing corresponds quite well with an autograph of 1436 by Fra Angelico (*Mostra dei Documenti*, Florence, 1955, No. 10; reproduced by Orlandi in *Memorie Domenicane*, January-March 1955, Plate V).

One of the great difficulties in identifying the figures is that several worthies are included, whose cult has even now not been officially approved. Some of these may almost have dropped out of human memory since Fra Angelico's time. The problem is to imagine which members of the Dominican Order a Dominican of the early fifteenth century at Florence would have considered suitable for this picture. It may be added that Christian names only are given, and that several of the figures appear so rarely in pictures that their emblems (if any) are by no means standardized.

Several of these *beati*, as will be seen, were associated with S. Maria Novella, the chief Dominican house at Florence. It is likely that Fra Angelico got most of his names and emblems from traditions current at S. Maria Novella; indeed, several of the more doubtful figures seem to occur painted on the vaulting of the Chiostro Verde there, but so much damaged that they seem useless for identification.

Left Panel

Reading from right to left, Top Row: 1, from his prominent position, certainly Jordanus of Saxony, 2nd Master General, died 1237. 2, Reginald of Orléans, died 1220; his vision of the form of the Dominican habit is the subject of picture No. 3417 below. 3, Ambrogio Sansedonio of Siena, died 1286/7; several pictures of him exist with the Holy Ghost at his ear, as here. This was seen by various persons when he preached (cf. the Bollandists, 20 March, p. 192, §51). 4, presumably Nicholas of Palea (or of Giovinazzo), died 1255. 5, this figure, called James, is writing the name of Jesus on his heart. The act was, however, performed by Henry Amandus Suso, died 1366; there seems to have been a mistake in Angelico's information. Two other James, two Henrys and an Amandus are named on the picture; it is doubtful which name could have been exchanged with which.[17] 6, Henry. Not certainly identified, in spite of his distinctive emblem; see No. 5 above, and the note.

Second and Third Rows together: 1, James. The dove near his right shoulder appears to belong to him rather than to the next figure; in that case, he should be James of Salomonio, died 1314. The pot of lilies

remains obscure; but the Bollandists quote a poem in his honour, in which
a lily is mentioned, and a lily appears to have been accepted in painting
as a suitable emblem for him.[18] See also Top Row, No. 5. 2, Henry; see
Top Row, No. 5. Unidentifiable. 3, Sinuus, apparently; unidentified.[19]
4, Buoninsegna. He was killed in Antioch *ca.* 1268, his family name
being apparently Cicciaporci;[20] he appears also in Fra Angelico's Dominican Tree in S. Marco, Florence.[21] 5, S. Vincent Ferrer, died 1419. 6,
Amandus; unidentifiable, see Top Row, No. 5. 7, no doubt Jordanus of
Pisa (or of Rivalto), died 1311. The skull is unexplained, but one might
guess that he used to take one into the pulpit with him, to point his
sermons. He is said to have been the first important preacher to use the
Italian language.[22]

Bottom Row: Four cloistered Virgins. 1, S. Margaret of Hungary,
died 1271; it is in accordance with tradition to represent her with the
Stigmata.[23] 2, S. Agnes of Montepulciano, died 1317. 3, Sibyllina de
Biscossis, died 1367. 4, Unnamed. The fifth figure is an unnamed *beato*,
a lay brother.

Right Panel

Reading from left to right, Top Row: 1, S. Albert the Great, died 1280.
The spelling of the damaged last word was probably originally *Mang-
nus*.[24] 2, S. Benedict XI, Pope, died 1304. 3, Bertrand; an unidentified
martyr bishop. 4, Cardinal Latino Malabranca, died 1294. He laid the
first stone of the new S. Maria Novella at Florence in 1279.[25] 5, Walter
of Strasbourg, died before 1260; Gerard de Frachet refers to his being
marked with the Stigmata, as here.[26] 6, probably Peter González, died
1246.[27] 7, Humbert of Romans, 5th Master General, died 1277/8.

Second and Third Rows together: 1, presumably S. Raymond of Peña-
fort, 3rd Master General, died 1275. Yet Raymond of Capua, died 1399,
23rd Master General and associated with S. Catherine of Siena, might
have seemed to Fra Angelico a more prominent person. 2, James; see
Left Panel, Top Row, No. 5. The present figure is unidentified, but
James of Bevagna ought to be somewhere in the picture; conceivably the
heart with the name of Jesus is some corruption of the story of the bleed-
ing Crucifix associated with him.[28] 3, Bonaspeme; an unidentified
martyr.[29] 4, John of Salerno, who established the Dominican Order in
Florence, died 1242. The church he holds doubtless stands for S. Maria
Novella in Florence; he was at the head of the group of Dominicans to
whom S. Maria Novella was granted as the first Dominican friary in
Florence.[30] The founder of the friary at Fiesole, John Dominici, might
be thought of as a possible alternative; he died in Hungary in 1419. But
he was a Cardinal, a fact of which Fra Angelico was apparently not un-
aware;[31] so he is to be excluded. 5, Venturino of Bergamo, died 1346.
6, Marcolino Amanni, died 1397; his emblems have not been
explained.

Bottom Row: Four Tertiary Sisters. 1, S. Catherine of Siena, not
represented with the Stigmata. According to the best accounts, her
Stigmata were invisible;[32] it is questionable if Angelico, by her gesture,

is trying to indicate this. 2, Apparently Margaret of Città di Castello, died 1320. Margaret of San Severino, died 1395, is also said to have been a Dominican;[33] the former is, however, the more probable. 3, inscribed Jane of Florence; not Jane of Orvieto, died 1306, but a now almost forgotten Jane of Florence, fl. 1333. Her tomb was a popular object of cult in S. Maria Novella at Florence, until it was discovered that it contained two bodies.[34] 4, unnamed. 5 and 6, two lay tertiaries; since they are without heavenly rays, they were presumably still alive when the picture was painted, and may be the donors, or in some way connected with the production of the picture.

General Commentary

As was stated above, No. 663 was the predella of the high altarpiece of San Domenico near Fiesole. This has been questioned; but the evidence is convincing. Vasari describes in this predella the 'infinite figurine che in una gloria celeste vi si veggiono', which fits No. 663;[35] Rumohr says that the predella was sold from the church in his time and passed into the Valentini Collection,[36] from which Collection it was in fact bought for the National Gallery some 35 years later; and a partial copy of No. 663 by Micheli is now beneath the main part of the altarpiece, which hangs in a chapel of the church.[37] Doubt about the provenance is not possible in the face of such evidence; the argument about the identification of S. Barnabas (Inner Right Panel, Second Row, No. 8) offers some further support. There is yet another iconographical point in confirmation; Brocchi says that the B. Buoninsegna was shown on the Fiesole picture.[38]

The picture was the high altarpiece of the church in Vasari's time, indeed already *ca.* 1501 (see the provenance). It would be most unreasonable to suppose that it had ever been anything else; the church was dedicated to SS. Dominic and Barnabas and, as has been noted above, on the main panel a figure most probably S. Barnabas appears, as well as (certainly) S. Dominic.

The main part of the altarpiece was drastically remodelled by Lorenzo di Credi in or *ca.* 1501.[39] Although it is not apparent that he touched the predella, the possibility of his having done something to it will be referred to presently.

The external evidence for the date of the altarpiece is as follows. It is certainly later than 1419; S. Vincent Ferrer, who died in that year, is shown as dead in the predella. On the other hand, the church was dedicated in 1435;[40] it is reasonable to suppose that the high altarpiece would have been in place for that event, but not necessarily painted much before.[41] The only other piece of evidence is the absence of Giovanni Dominici, the founder of the friary at Fiesole, who died in Hungary in 1419. It has been stated above that he is not shown in the predella; he was obviously a less prominent figure than S. Vincent Ferrer, who died in the same year, so that some delay in the establishing of his cult at Florence may be assumed. His name is indeed inscribed on Fra Angelico's Dominican Tree in S. Marco, Florence;[42] although

the inscription is of dubious authenticity, it seems to have been there
in Vasari's time,[43] and may record Fra Angelico's intention.

One might imagine that the attribution of the high altarpiece of Fra
Angelico's own friary, although it cannot be called documented, would
not present much difficulty. Yet many critics have seen in No. 663 to a
varying extent the work of other hands.[44] Much of this predella is clearly
of exquisite quality. Parts of the inner left panel, nevertheless, seem to be
inferior. Examination suggests that the crude effect is largely due to the
outlining of the features, especially the eyes, in black or brown. These
lines appear to be very old, and may well be by the original painter; but
Lorenzo di Credi, as has been already stated, restored the main part of
the altarpiece, of which No. 663 is the predella, and may have touched
the predella too. In any case, it is possible that some parts of the predella
were executed by an assistant, if indeed Fra Angelico had any studio
assistants at the right time; but it is also possible that what weaknesses
there are are due to haste on Fra Angelico's part, or immaturity.

The main panel, still in the church, and this predella No. 663 are the
principal parts of the altarpiece. Nothing else certainly belonging to
it is known. Crowe and Cavalcaselle say that two small panels of SS.
Matthew and Mark in the Reiset Collection (now at Chantilly) were
originally on the pilasters of the frame.[45] Two panels of SS. Nicholas
and Michael, clearly of the same series, were in the Rev. A. Hawkins
Jones Sale, 26 June, 1957 (lot 151);[46] they have inscriptions on the backs
that they belong to a series of ten that adorned an altar in S. Domenico,
Fiesole. It is rather doubtful if these panels come from the pilasters of the
same altarpiece as No. 663. Fra Angelico's original frame disappeared
long ago. The frame now in the church may well be the one supplied at
the time of Lorenzo di Credi's reconstruction; the painted pilaster
figures now on the frame are recent substitutions.[47] It may be said that,
if the high altarpiece originally had pilasters with saints, early evidence
for identifying them would be desired; and it should be borne in mind
that this was not the only altarpiece by Fra Angelico in the church.
Salmi thinks that two roundels of *The Annunciation* were at the top of
the original frame.[48]

Vasari [49] mentions a ciborium in connection with the high altarpiece.
According to Crowe and Cavalcaselle, this is identical with a tabernacle
once with Bardini, later in the G. Stroganoff Collection at Rome, and
now at Leningrad.[50] It has also been suggested that an Angel in the
Louvre and another in private hands in Paris are fragments of the ciborium,[51] or alternatively two angels at Turin.[52]

COPIES: A partial copy of No. 663 by one Micheli now hangs beneath the main
part of the altarpiece in S. Domenico, Fiesole.[53] A copy of six of the Old Testament figures, beginning with Abraham and going right, is in the Louvre;[54] this
does not appear to be contemporary.

PROVENANCE: No. 663 was the predella of the high altarpiece of San Domenico near Fiesole, which is mentioned *ca.* 1501,[55] and is described by Vasari.[56]
The picture was removed from the high altar, perhaps in 1610, but remained in
the church.[57] No. 663, sold not long before 1827, was acquired by Vincenzo (?)[58]

Valentini, the Prussian Consul at Rome, through the agency apparently of a copyist (Michele?) Micheli, one Morellini and the dealer Metzger.[59] The Valentini property became tied by a *fidecommesso*; but the Angelico was released in favour of Gioacchino Valentini,[60] and sold through Æneas Macbean to the National Gallery in 1860.

REPRODUCTIONS: *Illustrations, Italian Schools*, 1937, pp. 7–9. *Plates, Earlier Italian Schools*, 1953, Vol. I, pp. 2–6.

REFERENCES: (1) The Rev. S. A. van Dijk, O.F.M., kindly gave consideration to this problem of the 21 figures, and made valuable suggestions for the identifications. (2) The clean shaven bishop on Domenico Veneziano's altarpiece in the Uffizi is acceptable as representing S. Zenobius; reproduced by Van Marle, *Development of the Italian Schools of Painting*, Vol. X, Fig. 192. Some further comments on the Patrons of Florence will be found in the entry for Nos. 569/78, Style of Orcagna. It may be remarked that only the obscurer points of iconography are given references here; the others can be found without much difficulty in the books on the saints. (3) Klassiker der Kunst *Fra Angelico*, 1924, Plates 4 and 11. Guérin, *Les Petits Bollandistes*, 7th edition, III, p. 249, gives the story; cf. Kaftal, *Iconography of the Saints in Tuscan Painting*, 1952, col. 980. (4) An (unnamed) example of S. Giovanni Gualberto with a cross by Angelico is reproduced in the Klassiker der Kunst volume on the painter, 2nd edition, 1924, p. 62, where he is wrongly called S. Francis (the S. Francis on that altarpiece is reproduced on p. 66). There is an example, with the name inscribed, by Francesco di Antonio in the Fitzwilliam Museum at Cambridge; reproduced in the *Rivista d'Arte*, 1929, p. 15. (5) A fresco in the Vatican by Fra Angelico (Klassiker der Kunst, 1924, p. 209) is supposed to represent S. Bonaventure, but Dr. Redig de Campos kindly pointed out that this is incorrect. The Vatican fresco therefore offers no confirmation that the saint in No. 663 is S. Bonaventure. (6) The attribute is frequent in Spanish primitives; it is also not particularly rare in Italian pictures, but the saint is often not recognized as S. Vincent. (7) Klassiker der Kunst, 1924, pp. 4, 5. (8) P. Lodovico Ferretti, *La Chiesa e il Convento di San Domenico di Fiesole*, 1901, pp. 13 and 34; cf. also the *Nuovo Osservatore Fiorentino*, 1885, p. 127, A. M. Bandini, *Lettere XII ... della città di Fiesole*, 1786, Col. 31 and Richa, *Notizie Istoriche delle Chiese Fiorentine*, VII, 1758, p. 119. It may be mentioned further that S. Barnabas was particularly associated with Florence from the time of the battle of Campaldino; Richa, *op cit.*, VII, pp. 54/5, and IX, pp. 42 ff. (9) Richa, *Notizie Istoriche delle Chiese Fiorentine*, IV, 1756, p. 68. See further in the entry for Andrea di Bonaiuto (ascribed), No. 5115, especially note 3. (10) One of the relics of S. Maria Novella was part of the head of S. Ignatius (Richa, *op cit.*, III, 1755, p. 47); the reliquary is now in the Bargello (A.S., No. 1). The feast of S. Ignatius was indeed particularly associated with S. Maria Novella; see Vasari, ed. Milanesi, III, p. 197 (under Cecca). Examples of S. Ignatius in Florentine painting occur in Botticelli's S. Barnabas altarpiece in the Uffizi (together with a predella scene of the heart being cut open); in a *Coronation of the Virgin* ascribed to the style of Daddi, No. 3449 of the Academy at Florence, right wing, top left (Offner, *Corpus*, Section III, Vol. V, Plates XXII and XXII⁹); and in a panel ascribed to Raffaellino del Garbo in S. Maria Maddalena dei Pazzi at Florence, No. 69 of the *Mostra di Opere d'Arte trasportate a Firenze durante la Guerra*, 1947. An example of 1486, with the name inscribed, is in the Rijksmuseum at Amsterdam, J. W. Edwin vom Rath Bequest, as Florentine School (a label on the frame, Pier Francesco Fiorentino); see Rijksmuseum, *Verslag van den Hoofddirecteur over het Jaar* 1941, p. 17, No. 21. S. Ignatius is also shown in Lotto's picture of 1508, inv. No. 193, Borghese Gallery at Rome. It may be mentioned that the martyr's palm held by the figure in No. 663 suffices to exclude S. Augustine, who is sometimes shown holding a heart; this emblem for S. Augustine occurs chiefly in Netherlandish and German pictures, but also occasionally in Italian pictures, e.g. in Pintoricchio's polyptych in the Gallery at Perugia (reproduced by Giovanni Cecchini, *La Galleria Nazionale dell'Umbria in Perugia*, 1932, p. 160). (11) For the S. Julian referred to, see the Bollandists, 9 January, p. 586. The Lockinge picture (at one time Lady Wantage's) is reproduced in *Florentine Painting before 1500*, 1919, Burlington Fine Arts Club, Illustrated Catalogue 1920, Plate XXIX; exhibited at Manchester, 1957 (No. 3), lent by Dr. James Hasson. For S. Miniato with a line of blood round his head, see the last scene of Jacopo del Casentino's picture in the church of S. Miniato, Florence (Antal, *Florentine Painting and its Social Background*, 1947, Plate 31). Another example in the same church is a bust, the identification of which seems not doubtful; see Niccoli in the *Rivista d'Arte*, 1933, p. 213 and Fig. 2—he implies that the line of blood is original. What may be another example is in the Robbia-ware lunette on the façade of Ognissanti at Florence; doubtfully identified as S. Ansano in A. Marquand, *Benedetto and Santi Buglioni*, 1921, No. 103, with reproduction. The compiler has not found a literary source for this representation of S. Miniato, which appears to be unusual. (12) Sandra Moschini Marconi, *Gallerie dell'Accademia di Venezia*, Catalogue, XIV and XV Centuries, 1955, Plate 28a. There is another, certain example by Mantegna in the Eremitani at Padua (Klassiker der Kunst *Mantegna*, 1910, Plate 149, as by Pizolo). For other S. Christophers without the Child, name not inscribed, in S. Bartolomeo at Busseto, see the reproduction in the *Inventario degli Oggetti d'Arte d'Italia, Provincia di Parma*, 1934, p. 183; and in the Museo Bandini at Fiesole, the reproduction in the *Catalogo delle Cose d'Arte e di Antichità d'Italia, Fiesole*, 1933, p. 216. (13) For Fra Angelico's picture, see the Klassiker der Kunst *Fra Angelico*, 1924, p. 17; a similar figure with the name inscribed occurs in a Neri di Bicci in the Gallery at Siena, No. 320. It is true that other saints also were shown crowned with roses, for instance S. Dorothy; see what is said about her in the entry for Francesco di Giorgio, No. 1682. Kaftal, *op. cit.*, col. 249 sqq., does not cite any example of the association of S. Cecily with music; his book deals with Tuscan painting up to about 1500. It may be that S. Cecily is not shown with an organ in Italian art earlier than this, though there are XV Century examples from elsewhere (cf. Braun, *Tracht und Attribute der Heiligen in der deutschen Kunst*, 1943, col. 159 sqq.); even, it seems, earlier than the date of No. 663 (see *The Trinity Adored by All Saints* ascribed to the Valencian School *ca.* 1420 in the Metropolitan Museum, New York; name inscribed; reproduced in *Pantheon*, 1928, II. p. 496). (14) Reproduced by Van Marle, *Italian Schools*, Vol. III, Fig. 336. See also the picture by Neri di Bicci in S. Felicita, Florence, where (if it is the same saint) S. Felicitas is shown with her seven children; reproduced in *The Burlington Magazine*, Vol. LXII (1933), p. 223. (15) For the emblem, see Guérin, *Les Petits Bollandistes*, 7th edition, XII, p. 170. A representation with the candle, name inscribed, is on the S. Benedict Retable at Bonson; reproduced on Plate XXIV of *L'Art Religieux Ancien dans le Comté de Nice*, etc. (Musée Masséna), 1932. For another example of S. Bridget, see Van Marle, *op. cit.*, Vol. XVI, Fig. 114 (wrongly called S. Clare (?)). S. Bridget herself did not belong to the Bridgittine Order, see Hélyot, *Histoire des Ordres Monastiques*, IV, 1715, p. 38. There exists a woodcut showing S. Bridget in a dress contrasted with the habit; Campbell Dodgson, *Woodcuts of the XV century in the . . . British Museum*, II, 1935, No. 230a and Plate XCIIIa. In Isak Collijn, *Iconographia Birgittina Typographica*, 1915/8, only a few of the plates show S. Bridget in the Bridgittine habit. (16) S. Reparata does not wear a crown in the principal altarpiece dedicated to her in Florence; reproduced by Ruth Wedgwood Kennedy, *Alesso Baldovinetti*, 1938, Fig. 30. (17) For Suso, cf. for instance, W. L. Schreiber, *Handbuch der Holz- und Metallschnitte des XV. Jahrhunderts*, Vol. III, No. 1698. With regard to the names confused, the V. Rev. W. Gumbley, O.P., and Father Laurent, O.P., who have been good enough to make some valuable suggestions about the Dominicans in this picture, think that the Henry immediately following (No. 6) may be intended for Henry of Cologne, who died on Crusade in 1254; his cult has not been officially recognized. (18) See the Bollandists, 31 May, pp. 458 and 466; the lily is really S. Dominic's lily. The B. James of Salamonio (with the name inscribed) is shown holding a lily and a crucifix, with a rose growing by him, in a fresco in

S. Domenico at Perugia; it is by Anton Maria Fabbrizj or Fabrizi (see Serafino Siepi, *Descrizione Topologico-Istorica della Città di Perugia*, 1822, II, pp. 504, 506). (**19**) Sinibaldus de Alma was Provincial of the Roman Province *ca.* 1264; see Leandro Alberti, *De Viris Illustribus O.P.*, 1517, f. 187v. He seems, however, excessively unlikely, and no explanation of the leafy branch in the picture is forthcoming. A more possible identification, perhaps, is Fino da Barberino, died in 1332, mentioned as one of the *beati* of S. Maria Novella, Florence, by Richa, *Notizie Istoriche delle Chiese Fiorentine*, III, 1755, p. 98. He is included in a series of Dominican worthies painted in the large cloister of S. Maria Novella; V. Fineschi, *Il Forestiero Istruito in S. Maria Novella*, 1790, p. 60. Also mentioned by Giuseppe Maria Brocchi, *Descrizione della Provincia del Mugello*, 1748, pp. 10/11. See further Stefano Orlandi, *Il Necrologio di S. Maria Novella*, 1955, Vol. I, pp. 341/2. (**20**) V. Fineschi, *Memorie Istoriche degli uomini illustri del Convento di S.M.N.*, I, 1790, p. 38. Richa, *Notizie Istoriche delle Chiese Fiorentine*, III, 1755, p. 98 gives his date of death as 1270. This is also the year given by Giuseppe Maria Brocchi, *Vite de' Santi e Beati Fiorentini*, Vol. II, Part I, 1752, pp. 303 ff. Orlandi, *op. cit.*, Vol. I, p. 225, thinks the date of death was 1268. (**21**) Klassiker der Kunst, 1924, p. 112. (**22**) Gaspary, *Storia della Letteratura Italiana*, I, 1887, p. 330. (**23**) The V. Rev. W. Gumbley kindly gave the reference to Laurent Pignon's statement that S. Margaret was always painted with the Stigmata; printed in the *Monumenta Ordinis FF. Prædicatorum Historica*, Vol. XVIII, ed. Meersseman, Rome, 1936, p. 5. There is a picture of the early sixteenth century in the Gallery at Perugia showing S. Margaret of Hungary with the Stigmata and other emblems, between S. Agnes of Montepulciano and the B. Margaret of Città de Castello; the names are inscribed, and although the inscriptions may not be quite as old as the picture, there is not the slightest reason to believe that they are incorrect. See G. Cecchini, *La Galleria Nazionale dell'Umbria in Perugia*, 1932, p. 184, No. 265; photo Soprintendenza, in the Gallery archives (kindly supplied by Prof. Achille Bertini Calosso). S. Margaret's Stigmatization is contrasted with S. Catherine of Siena's in an engraving; A. M. Hind, *Early Italian Engraving*, Vol. I, 1938, F5 and Vol. IV, 1938, Plate 462. (**24**) Cf. Klassiker der Kunst *Fra Angelico*, 1924, p. 150. (**25**) Marchese, *Memorie dei più insigni Pittori, etc. Domenicani*, 2nd edition, 1854, I, p. 43; or the Rev. J. Wood Brown, *The Dominican Church of Santa Maria Novella at Florence*, 1902, p. 64 (name given as Frangipani). According to Moroni's *Dizionario Storico-Ecclesiastico*, he was Latino Frangipani Malabranca, and related to the Orsini family. (**26**) Gerard de Frachet, *Lives of the Brethren*, English translation, 1924, p. 204. (**27**) It cannot be entirely excluded that he is Pietro Strozzi, a preacher and prior of S. Maria Novella (d. 1362). Cf. G. M. Brocchi, *Vite de' Santi e Beati Fiorentini*, I, 1742, p. 581 (traditionally considered a *beatus*); Richa, *op. cit.*, III, 1755, p. 95; Litta, *Famiglie Celebri d'Italia*, Tavola II of the Strozzi family; Orlandi, *op. cit.*, Vol. I, pp. 499 ff. Piero Strozzi is included in a series of Dominican worthies painted in the large cloister of S. Maria Novella; V. Fineschi, *Il Forestiero Istruito in S. Maria Novella*, 1790, p. 70. (**28**) Bollandists, 23 August, p. 720. Kaftal, *op. cit.*, Col. 521, calls this figure James of Salamonio, who, however, seems better identified as Left Panel, Second and Third Rows together, No. 1. (**29**) Michele Piò, *Delle Vite degli Homini Illustri di S. Domenico*, 1620, p. 215, mentions a Bonaspeme as Bishop of Perugia, not as a martyr, died 1251. Laurent Pignon lists a Bonapene of Perugia; see *Monumenta Ordinis FF. Prædicatorum*, Vol. XVIII, 1936, p. 4. If the present figure were not named, he would probably be assumed to be Bernard of Rochefort, died 1242; cf. Klassiker der Kunst *Fra Angelico*, 1924, p. 113. (**30**) Marchese, *op. cit.*, I, pp. 36 ff., or Wood Brown, *op. cit.*, p. 48. (**31**) Compare the figure in Fra Angelico's Dominican Tree at S. Marco (Klassiker der Kunst, 1924, p. 113). The names of some figures on this Tree have been altered and Marchese, *op. cit.*, I, pp. 255 ff., doubts in particular Giovanni Dominici; but the names were noted in Vasari's time (Milanesi's edition, II, p. 508), and may for the most part preserve Fra Angelico's intentions. (**32**) Bollandists, 30 April, p. 910. Cf. the engraving referred to at the end of note 23. (**33**) Michele Piò, *Della...*

Progenie del P. S. Domenico, 1615, pp. 250/1, calls her so. (**34**) Richa, *Notizie Istoriche delle Chiese Fiorentine*, III, 1755, p. 55. She is mentioned by Johannes Meyer, *Liber de Viris Illustribus O.P.*, ed. Loë, 1918, p. 71. Richa's account is followed; Giuseppe Maria Brocchi, *Vite de' Santi e Beati Fiorentini*, Vol. II, Part II, 1761, pp. 31 f. and 95 f., gives an account doubted by Richa, but possibly more accurate. Brocchi claims that S. Maria Novella boasted of two Janes, both blessed and both tertiaries; one called Jane of Orvieto (but distinct from the Jane of Orvieto still well known) who died in 1333, and another properly of Florence, who died a little later, and is referred to in a letter by Franco Sacchetti (*La Battaglia delle Belle Donne*, etc., ed. A. Chiari, Laterza, 1938, p. 101). See further Kaftal, *op. cit.*, Col. 537/8; Sandra Moschini Marconi, *Gallerie dell'Accademia di Venezia*, Catalogue XIV and XV Centuries, 1955, pp. 177/8; Orlandi, *op. cit.*, Vol. I, p. XL and Vol. II, p. 401. (**35**) Vasari, ed. Milanesi, II, p. 510 (not in 1550 edition). (**36**) Rumohr, *Italienische Forschungen*, II, 1827, p. 254. It may be mentioned the Rumohr could probably speak from first-hand knowledge about the Valentini Collection; cf. the Prussian *Jahrbuch*, 1914, *Beiheft*, p. 69 or 1925, *Beiheft*, p. 16. (**37**) Cf. Klassiker der Kunst, 1924, p. 4. (**38**) G. M. Brocchi, *Vite de' Santi e Beati Fiorentini*, Vol. II, Part I, 1752, p. 306. (**39**) Marchese, *op. cit.*, I, p. 229; or better, the *Catalogo delle Cose d'Arte e di Antichità d'Italia*, Fiesole, 1933, pp. 24/5, or the catalogue of the Angelico Exhibition, Rome-Florence, 1955, pp. 12/3. (**40**) Ferretti, *La Chiesa e il Convento di San Domenico di Fiesole*, 1901, p. 34. In the *Nuovo Osservatore Fiorentino*, 1885, p. 127, the date is given as 1438; but 1435 seems surely right (Orlandi in the *Rivista d'Arte*, 1954, p. 170). (**41**) On stylistic grounds a date a few years before is to be preferred; cf. the Catalogue of the Angelico Exhibition, Rome-Florence, 1955, p. 14; Procacci, *Il Beato Angelico*, 1956, p. 12, dates *ca.* 1430/1; Salmi, *Il Beato Angelico*, 1958, p. 98, a little before 1428. (**42**) Klassiker der Kunst, 1924, p. 113. This fresco appears to be datable 1441/2; see the Catalogue of the Angelico Exhibition, Rome-Florence, 1955, p. 132. (**43**) Vasari, ed. Milanesi, II, p. 508. The text is from the edition of 1568; there is no description of these figures in the first edition of 1550. Cf. also what is said about this figure in note 31. (**44**) Van Marle, *Development of the Italian Schools of Painting*, X, pp. 170 ff., even ascribes the whole predella to Zanobi Strozzi, the identification of whose panel paintings is still very uncertain. (**45**) Crowe and Cavalcaselle, *History of Painting in Italy*, I, 1864, p. 584; Gruyer's Chantilly Catalogue, Nos. 4 and 5, sizes given as 0·36 × 0·11 and 0·32 × 0·11. Reproduced by John Pope-Hennessy, *Fra Angelico*, 1952, p. 166. (**46**) Reproduced in the Catalogue of the Angelico Exhibition, Rome-Florence, 1955, Plate VIII; size, 14 × 5½ in. each. Neither these nor the Chantilly pictures would seem the work of Fra Angelico's own hand. (**47**) See especially O. H. Giglioli, *Catalogo delle Cose d'Arte e di Antichità d'Italia*, Fiesole, 1933, pp. 21 ff. (**48**) Salmi, *Il Beato Angelico*, 1958, p. 11; the pictures are reproduced by Van Marle, *Italian Schools*, Vol. X, Figs. 101/2, size not stated. (**49**) Vasari, ed. Milanesi, II, p. 510. (**50**) Crowe and Cavalcaselle, *op. cit.*; not in the 1864 edition; Italian translation, publ. Le Monnier, II, 1883, p. 385; Douglas' edition, IV, 1911, p. 88. See also A. Muñoz, *Pièces de Choix de la Collection du Comte Grégoire Stroganoff*, II, 1911, pp. 19/20; and Klassiker der Kunst, *Fra Angelico*, 1924, pp. 14, 15. Some further details in Bode, *Mein Leben*, 1930, I, p. 123. (**51**) G. Migeon in the *Gazette des Beaux-Arts*, 1909, I, pp. 412/3; Seymour de Ricci, Louvre Catalogue, *Ecoles Etrangères, Italie et Espagne*, 1913, pp. 58/9; *Bulletin de la Société de l'Histoire de l'Art Français*, 1914, p. 158. Salmi, *op. cit.*, p. 115, dates the Louvre angel later. (**52**) Salmi, *op. cit.*, p. 12 and Plate 10 c, d. (**53**) See Klassiker der Kunst, 1924, p. 4. The name of the copyist was supplied to Eastlake; letter in the Gallery archives. He may be identical with the Michele Micheli, stated to have died in September, 1848; for him, see R. C. Fisher in *The Athenaeum*, 26 January, 1907, pp. 109/10. (**54**) Klassiker der Kunst, 1924, p. 9. In the Gatteaux Bequest to the Louvre; 1926 Catalogue, No. 1294D; mentioned by E. Cartier, *Vie de Fra Angelico*, 1857, pp. 442/3, No. CVIII. Probably from the (Giustiniani and d'Acosta) Sale, Paris, 2 *sqq.* December, 1823 (lot 4). (**55**) See the text of the chronicle of the friary, apropos of Lorenzo di Credi's reconstruction, which is well given by O. H. Giglioli, *Catalogo delle Cose d'Arte e di Antichità d'Italia, Fiesole*, 1933, pp. 24/5. Fra Angelico's name is not mentioned; but the reference seems quite precise enough for the identification of the picture. (56) Vasari, ed. Milanesi, II, p. 510 (not in 1550 edition). (57) Giglioli, *op. cit.*, p. 22, says that the picture was removed from the high altar in 1510; but 1610 is probably right (cf. Giglioli, *op. cit.*, pp. 10 and 31/2). (58) F. Stock in the Prussian *Jahrbuch*, 1925, *Beiheft*, note 61, calls him Dominico; but the *fidecommesso* was established by Vincenzo Valentini (document in the Gallery archives). (59) See Rumohr, *Italienische Forschungen*, II, 1827, p. 254; Marchese, *op. cit.*, I, 1854, p. 229; letter of Eastlake to Wornum, 12 December, 1860. According to the *Nuovo Osservatore Fiorentino*, 1885, p. 135, the priest, P. Giacinto Giachi, seems also to have been concerned in the affair. The editor of Vasari (II, p. 510; first in the Le Monnier edition, IV, pp. 29/30) says that the agent was Niccola Tacchinardi. A passage in Crowe and Cavalcaselle, *op. cit.*, I, 1864, p. 576, suggests that this is a confusion with another picture, once apparently in the Valentini Collection; see also Seymour de Ricci's Louvre Catalogue, I, *Italie et Espagne*, 1913, No. 1293, pp. 57/8. (60) The consul's nephew, according to the 1860 N.G. Catalogue.

Ascribed to FRA ANGELICO

2908 ROUNDEL: A MARTYR BISHOP OR ABBOT

On the background to the right, the faint remains of a name,... MEVS (?).

Wood. The picture is a circle, $5\frac{1}{2}$ (0·14) in diameter; it is framed as an octagon, but the piece of wood on which it is painted is rectangular, size $6\frac{3}{8} \times 6\frac{1}{8}$ (0·16 × 0·155).

The left part of the panel is new, consisting of two separate pieces of new wood; the total width of the new part is approximately $1\frac{1}{2}$ (0·035), but the line of junction is not vertical. All the gold in the spandrels (mostly covered by the frame) is modern. The background appears to be modern, and the remains of the inscription are doubtful. The figure itself, although somewhat repainted, is in a very fair state.

No. 2908 is most probably from a frame. It has been confused by Schottmüller and van Marle with another picture.[1] That picture is said to be from an altarpiece at San Domenico at Ficsole, is said to have been in the Samuel Rogers Collection, was bought from Canon Sutton by Langton Douglas, went to America[2] and is perhaps the picture listed by Berenson in 1932 as belonging to Mr. and Mrs. Henry L. Moses, New York. It may be identical with a picture of which a German photograph is in the Gallery archives; that is perhaps the same as one seen by Sir K. Clark at Bottenwieser's in 1929. The photograph shows a picture that seems obviously of the same series as No. 2908, but is not a replica of it.

Berenson in 1936 lists No. 2908 as Fra Angelico in part, and attributes the Moses picture to Fra Angelico. Salmi thinks that No. 2908 is by Zanobi Strozzi on Fra Angelico's design before *ca.* 1438.[3] No. 2908 seems sufficiently near to Fra Angelico to be ascribed to him, or at least to his studio (if he had one).[4]

PROVENANCE: Lent by Lady Lindsay to the New Gallery, 1893/4 (No. 120);[5] Lady Lindsay Bequest, 1912.

REPRODUCTION: *Illustrations, Italian Schools,* 1937, p. 11. *Plates, Earlier Italian Schools,* 1953, Vol. I, p. 7.

REFERENCES: (1) Schottmüller, Klassiker der Kunst *Angelico,* 2nd edition, 1924, p. 203 (as Fra Angelico); Van Marle, *Development of the Italian Schools of Painting,* Vol. X, pp. 118 and 577. (2) Letter from Langton Douglas of 18 December, 1928, in the Gallery archives. (3) Salmi, *Il Beato Angelico,* 1958, p. 87. The remaining part of his remarks may have been misplaced from No. 3417 below. (4) There is reliable evidence concerning Fra Angelico's studio assistants, in his work at Orvieto and the Vatican; otherwise there does not seem to be any. It is nevertheless probable that Fra Angelico took pupils at Florence or Fiesole; cf. the document, which does not mention Fra Angelico's name apparently, referred to by Mario Salmi, *Paolo Uccello Andrea del Castagno Domenico Veneziano,* 1938, p. 139. (5) As S. Nicholas.

Follower of FRA ANGELICO

582   THE ADORATION OF THE KINGS (PREDELLA PANEL FROM AN ALTARPIECE)

The a's and b's embroidered on two of the dresses are merely decoration.

Wood, painted surface, $7\frac{1}{2} \times 18\frac{3}{4}$ (0·19 × 0·475); this includes $\frac{1}{4}$ in. of preparation (?) on the left, which goes up to the edge of the wood.

The condition is good on the whole; although small restorations on some of the heads somewhat affect the character.

Obviously part of a predella. Panels of approximately the same size are the *Marriage of the Virgin* and *Death of the Virgin* in S. Marco, Florence,[1] and the *Nativity* in the collection of Prince Ernst von Sachsen-Meiningen.[2] Some or all of these may perhaps be thought to have come originally from the same altarpiece.

No. 582 cannot pass as Fra Angelico's own work. It might be classed as a studio production, if it were clearer how far Fra Angelico had an organized studio. It seems best to consider it as by a follower. Berenson (1932 Lists) calls it early Domenico di Michelino, Van Marle calls it Zanobi Strozzi;[3] what pictures were painted by these is still very uncertain.

PROVENANCE: From the Collection of Prof. Rosini at Pisa.[4] Purchased with other pictures from the Lombardi-Baldi Collection, Florence, 1857.[5]

REPRODUCTION: *Illustrations, Italian Schools,* 1937, p. 10. *Plates, Earlier Italian Schools,* 1953, Vol. I, p. 8.

REFERENCES: (1) Klassiker der Kunst, 2nd edition, 1924, pp. 24, 25; sizes 0·19×0·50, 0·19×0·51. These panels are very greatly superior in quality to No. 582. They have been claimed to be from the *Coronation* in the Uffizi (ex-S. Maria Nuova); see the catalogue of the Angelico Exhibition, Rome-Florence, 1955 (Nos. 11–12). It should be mentioned, as a point in favour of the association with No. 582, that the S. Marco panels have the remains of a black line surrounding them; outside that, at the sides at least, is a little plain gold. A black line goes round No. 583; and there may be a few traces of original gold on the preparation (?) at the left, though a definite statement could not be made owing to surface accretions. (2) Klassiker der Kunst, 1924, p. 93; size, 0·20 × 0·43. (3) Van Marle, *Development of the Italian Schools of Painting*, Vol. X, p. 182. An article on Zanobi Strozzi as a miniaturist was published by Mirella Levi D'Ancona in *La Bibliofilia*, Vol. LXI, 1959, pp. 1 ff. (4) N. G. 1858 Catalogue, presumably on information supplied to Eastlake. (5) For the history of the Lombardi-Baldi Collection, see Appendix I.

591   THE RAPE OF HELEN BY PARIS

Wood, irregular octagon, painted surface, 20 × 24 (0·51 × 0·61); painted up to the edges all round, so perhaps cut.

The picture is more restored than might seem likely at the first glance; but on the whole it is in very fair state. The damage is especially near the edges.

Presumably part of the decoration of a chest.

There need be no doubt that the subject is the *Rape of Helen*. No less than four women are being carried off to a ship, from a temple. This indeed does not correspond with the classical stories of the Rape of Helen; but according to Dares Phrygius, Helen was taken by Paris from the Temple of Apollo and Artemis (the statue in No. 591 appears to be male) at Helæa in Cythera, and some other women were taken with her.[1] There are numerous later derivations of this form of the story.[2]

The traditional identification of the subject was *The Abduction of the Brides of Venice*.[3] It is an ancient legend that some brides of Venice, perhaps under Doge Pietro Candiano III, were seized by pirates but were recovered at Caorle and brought back to Venice. This gave rise to a popular festival at Venice, the *Festa delle Marie*, on which some girls went to be married in S. Pietro di Castello and thence proceeded to S. Maria Formosa; but this festival ceased in 1379 (though taken up again recently), and in any case the representation of this subject is most unlikely on a Florentine picture.[4]

The dress of the principal woman being carried off in No. 591 (presumably Helen) is ornamented with a cock (?); but it is doubtful if this is meant to be relevant to the subject.

No. 591 was for long catalogued after it entered the Gallery as by Benozzo (Gozzoli). This attribution is usually accepted, although doubts have sometimes been expressed.[5] The figures of the little child in the foreground and the man in armour towards the left (Paris?) do vaguely suggest Benozzo; but there is little or no justification for believing that No. 591 is his. If so, it would necessarily be a very early work; in point of fact, the earliest independent Benozzos known are the frescoes at Montefalco (1450 sqq.).[6] No satisfactory alternative attribution has been made;[7] since the principal influence in No. 591 seems to be that of Fra Angelico, it is here classed in his following.

The costume is somewhat fanciful; but the date of the picture may be deduced as being not far from 1450.

PROVENANCE: From the Collection of the Marchese Albergotti at Arezzo.[8] In the Lombardi-Baldi Collection at Florence; (1845) catalogue, No. 48;[9] purchased with other pictures from Lombardi and Baldi, 1857.[10]

REPRODUCTION: *Illustrations, Italian Schools,* 1937, p. 161. *Plates, Earlier Italian Schools,* 1953, Vol. I, p. 9.

REFERENCES: **(1)** From W. H. Roscher, *Lexikon der Griechischen und Römischen Mythologie,* III, Col. 1596. In the previous column, Roscher cites Dracontius, *De raptu Helenae,* to the effect that Helen (companions not mentioned) was taken by Paris from the Temple of Aphrodite (?) in Cyprus. **(2)** For the story of the Rape of Helen as treated in the Renaissance, see especially Guy de Tervarent *Les Enigmes de l'Art,* III, *L'Héritage Antique,* 1947, pp. 21 ff.; also Edward S. King in the *Journal of the Walters Art Gallery,* 1939, pp. 55 ff. **(3)** So in the Lombardi-Baldi catalogue, referred to under provenance. **(4)** Giustina Renier Michiel, *Origine delle Feste Veneziane,* I, 1829, pp. 91 ff.; Manlio Dazzi, *Feste e Costumi di Venezia,* n.d., p. 4. **(5)** P. Schubring, *Cassoni,* 1923, No. 280, expresses doubt. Berenson, *Drawings of the Florentine Painters,* 1903, I, p. 58, suggested Domenico di Michelino, but later accepted the attribution to Benozzo; see the 1938 edition, I, p. 88 and II, No. 545B. **(6)** According to the evidence conveniently given by Elena Contaldi, *Benozzo Gozzoli,* 1928. **(7)** The 1913 N.G. catalogue suggested Boccati; for him, see No. 558I below, which is not by the same hand as No. 591. Licia Collobi Ragghianti in *Critica d'Arte,* 1950, p. 20 and 1955, p. 44, suggests Zanobi Strozzi. **(8)** N.G. Catalogue, 1858. **(9)** As Gentile da Fabriano. The copy of the catalogue in the Uffizi Library is claimed to be of 1845. **(10)** For the history of the Lombardi-Baldi Collection, see Appendix I.

1406   ALTARPIECE: THE ANNUNCIATION

S. Gabriel advances towards the Virgin, who holds a closed book; above, the Holy Ghost as a Dove. In the background, a garden walled and hedged with roses (the *hortus conclusus*), with a closed gate (the *porta clausa*); in the middle of the garden, a well and a vase with a lily. The capitals of the two columns left and centre carry a coat of arms, two red concentric circles with a central red spot (torteau) on a grey ground.

Wood, $40\frac{3}{4} \times 55\frac{3}{4}$ (1·035 × 1·42). Painted up to the edges all round, and cut considerably all round.[1] There is a vertical join $28\frac{1}{4}$ in. (0·72) from the left; the picture was in fact in two parts in the nineteenth century, and was joined together after its purchase by the Gallery.[2]

Very fair state.

The arms have been called those of the Albizzi family, which is incorrect; they are those of the Lanfredini family.[3]

According to the Woodburn Sale catalogue, and a label of slightly later date on the back, No. 1406 is the picture called Fra Angelico by Vasari,[4] and recorded by him in S. Francesco fuor della Porta a San Miniato, Florence. That picture appears to have remained in the church for a considerable time.[5] It seems unlikely that, when Woodburn acquired No. 1406 in Rome in 1818, a wrong provenance had become attached to it; and since a Lanfredini Chapel is recorded to have existed in the Church,[6] the matter might be considered hardly doubtful, if a rival claimant did not exist.[7]

This church, from which No. 1406 seems very likely to have come, is sometimes known as S. Francesco, but more usually as S. Salvatore al Monte.[8]

An attribution of No. 1406 to Fra Angelico himself, in spite of the apparent support of Vasari, cannot be accepted; the picture is by some not very close follower. Berenson (1932 Lists), Van Marle and L. C. Ragghianti call it Domenico di Michelino.⁹

PROVENANCE: Probably from S. Salvatore al Monte, Florence, as explained above. Imported from Rome in 1818 by Woodburn.¹⁰ No. 10 of an undated Woodburn MS. Inventory;¹¹ Woodburn Sale, 9 June, 1860 (lot 72), bought by F. Nieuwenhuys. Anon. Sale, Christie's, 29 May, 1869 (lot 71).¹² C.-J. Nieuwenhuys Sale, Brussels, 4 May, 1883 (lot 5), bought by Bourgeois. Lent by Stéphane Bourgeois to an exhibition at Paris, *au Profit des Inondés du Midi*, 1887 (No. 1). Purchased, from Bourgeois apparently, through Lawrie and Co., 1894.

REPRODUCTION: *Illustrations, Italian Schools*, 1937, p. 10. *Plates, Earlier Italian Schools*, 1953, Vol. I, p. 10.

REFERENCES: (1) Licia Collobi Ragghianti thinks that a fragment representing *The Expulsion from Paradise* in the Reber Collection at Lausanne may have formed part of No. 1406 at the left; see *Critica d'Arte*, January 1950, p. 365 and Figs. 317 and 319. This may be so; but, to judge from the reproduction, the landscape would fit awkwardly. (2) N.G. MS. Catalogue. (3) J.-B. Rietstap, *Armoiries des Familles contenues dans L'Armorial Général Français*, 1903. The Lanfredini arms appear on a cassone; see the Cook Collection, Large Catalogue, I, 1913, No. 21, reproduced. (4) Vasari, ed. Milanesi, II, p. 513; 1550 edition, p. 370. In Milanesi's Vasari, Vol. IX, p. 256 this picture is wrongly identified with the *Annunciation* in the Prado, which comes from S. Domenico di Fiesole. (5) An *Annunciation* by Fra Angelico is mentioned in the *Ristretto delle Cose più notabili della Città di Firenze*, 2nd edition, 1698, p. 168, 5th edition, 1745, p. 199; in Cambiagi's *L'Antiquario Fiorentino*, 1765, p. 289; and in the *Guida per Osservare con Metodo le Rarità e Bellezze della Città di Firenze*, 1805, p. 293. The picture is no doubt mentioned in other Guides to Florence also; but the matter is not worth pursuing, since these guide-books tend to copy each other, and a mention in a publication of some date is not absolute proof that the picture was still in the church at that date. (6) Domenico Moreni, *Notizie Istoriche dei Contorni di Firenze*, V. 1794, p. 8. (7) This is the *Annunciation* at Montecarlo (Angelico Exhibition, Rome-Florence, 1955, No. 42, with reproduction); there is a local tradition that this picture comes from the church in question (see Poggi in the *Rivista d'Arte*, 1909, pp. 130/2). The provenance is not stated in the first reference known to the compiler to the picture at Montecarlo (F. Gherardi Dragomanni, *Memorie della Terra di San Giovanni nel Val d'Arno Superiore*, 1834, p. 44); the claim is rejected by Salmi, *Il Beato Angelico*, 1958, p. 111. (8) For information concerning it, see W. and E. Paatz, *Die Kirchen von Florenz*, Vol. V, 1953, pp. 49 ff. (9) Van Marle, *Development of the Italian Schools of Painting*, Vol. X, p. 190. L. C. Ragghianti, *loc. cit.* in note 1. (10) Label on the back. (11) In the Gallery archives. (12) Cutting on the back.

3417   THE VISION OF THE DOMINICAN HABIT

Left, the Blessed Reginald of Orléans is ill in bed; to him appear the Virgin and two beautiful damsels. The Virgin holds a specimen of a habit, which she reveals that the Dominicans should henceforth wear; one of her companions holds a box of ointments, wherewith to anoint the Blessed Reginald. Right, the same three celestial figures, with the new Dominican habit, appear to S. Dominic.

Reverse: Remains of a marbled, mostly red, decoration, with a broad white band ornamented with two rows of red triangles, all round except at the top; in the bottom corners, left and right, the ornament is two concentric red circles.

Wood, painted surface, $9\frac{3}{8} \times 11\frac{3}{4}$ (0.24×0.295), excluding white bands of paint, which go all round except at the top. The size of the painted decoration at the back is $9\frac{5}{8} \times 12\frac{1}{8}$ (0.245×0.305); this excludes a chamfer on the right side, which is also covered with paint, different in appearance from the paint at the back, but similar to paint on the left side of the panel. The picture is presumably part of a cupboard (?) door; there is what appears to be the remains of a hinge in the wood on the left side. It has apparently not been cut much at the bottom, but considerably at the top, where the whole white band edging the pattern on the reverse is missing; on the front there may have been at least one other scene above No. 3417.

Very fair condition.

The story of the origin of the Dominican habit is followed fairly exactly in the left part of the picture. It is recorded that the events were revealed to S. Dominic, and this seems to be what the painter is trying to express on the right.[1]

The subject occurs in the predella of Fra Angelico's *Annunciation* at Cortona; the compositions are not similar.[2]

No. 3417 is by some fairly close follower of Fra Angelico. Berenson (1932 Lists) ascribed it to the studio, but this attribution seems improbable.[3]

The picture has been associated with a S. Dominic scene, now in the collection of Sir Thomas Barlow; but this is to be excluded.[4]

PROVENANCE: Before 1885, owned by the Rev. H. E. Richards, Claygate; bought from his widow in 1891 by Sir Charles Archer Cook, by whom presented, 1919.[5]

REPRODUCTION: *Illustrations, Italian Schools*, 1937, p. 11. *Plates, Earlier Italian Schools*, 1953, Vol. I, p. 11.

REFERENCES: (1) The story is given by the Bollandists, 4 August, p. 459. A summary by the donor of the present picture was printed in *The Burlington Magazine*, Vol. XXXV (1919), pp. 175/6. (2) Reproduced by John Pope-Hennessy, *Fra Angelico*, 1952, p. 167. (3) Salmi, *Il Beato Angelico*, 1958, p. 110, also thinks it is a studio work, perhaps from a predella to the *Pietà* (from S. Maria della Croce al Tempio) at Florence. (4) Reproduced by Berenson in *Dedalo*, 1932, p. 528. According to the catalogue of the Italian Exhibition at Birmingham, 1955 (No. 4), the size is $13\frac{1}{2}$ in. $\times$ $18\frac{1}{4}$ in.; this alone would make association unlikely. For the claim, see Licia Collobi Ragghianti in *Critica d'Arte* 1950, p. 18 and 1955, p. 40; see also the catalogue of the Angelico Exhibition, Rome-Florence, 1955, pp. 20/1. (5) The provenance is from a letter from the donor in the Gallery archives.

5581   THE VIRGIN AND CHILD WITH ANGELS

The Virgin and Child are under a *baldacchino* ornamented with shields, on one of which a cross has been scratched.

Wood. The picture has been fixed into a piece of framing; the size of the painted surface is $11\frac{1}{2} \times 8\frac{1}{2}$ (0.29×0.215), the size of the original panel (at the back) is $11\frac{7}{8} \times 8\frac{7}{8}$ (0.30×0.225).

Very good condition.

This picture is by a painter evidently influenced by Fra Angelico, and apparently also by Fra Filippo Lippi in his early, or Masaccesque, phase. A suggestion by Langton Douglas[1] that it is an early work of Giovanni di Piermatteo of Camerino, called Boccati, might seem at first sight attractive; but Boccati appears too provincial to be the painter of No. 5581, and the little that is known about his origins is rather against the suggestion. Boccati came to Perugia in 1445, and an altarpiece in the Gallery at Perugia is from 1446/7; he is generally supposed to have been born ca. 1420, and although it is possible that he was born considerably earlier, and that he was active in Florence in the decade 1430/40, that is usually disbelieved.[2] Berenson[3] doubtfully suggests that No. 5581 is an early work of Domenico Veneziano, which seems unlikely. Longhi[4] thinks that No. 5581 may be a work of ca. 1425/30 by Fra Angelico himself; little is known of Fra Angelico's origins, but it seems most unlikely that he should have painted this picture. Salmi[5] doubtfully suggests that it is an early work by Piero della Francesca. Van Marle[6] thinks that No. 5581 is by the same hand as an *Adoration of the Kings*, wrongly stated to be in the Gallery at Budapest;[7] that picture is derived from a scene by Fra Angelico in S. Marco, Florence,[8] and it is highly doubtful if it has any connection with No. 5581.

PROVENANCE: In the Collection of Miss Sarah Rogers by 1844,[9] and then in the sale of her brother, Samuel Rogers, 2 May, 1856 (lot 614),[10] bought by Charles Sackville Bale; exhibited at the British Institution, 1858 (No. 35),[11] and at the R.A., 1870 (No. 118);[12] Bale Sale, 14 May, 1881 (lot 290),[13] bought by Robinson for the Cook Collection at Richmond.[14] Exhibited at the Burlington Fine Arts Club, 1902 (No. 15), 1920 (No. 16)[15] and 1932/3 (No. 27);[16] at Toledo, U.S.A., 1944/5 (No. 15).[17] Purchased from the Cook Trustees, Champney, Colnaghi and Temple-West Funds, 1945.

REPRODUCTION: *Plates, Earlier Italian Schools*, 1953, Vol. I, p. 12.

REFERENCES: (1) Douglas in *L'Arte*, 1903, p. 108. The attribution is accepted by Pudelko in the *Mitteilungen des Kunsthistorischen Instituts in Florenz*, IV, 1934, p. 199. (2) Douglas' suggestion is rejected by Bombe in Thieme-Becker. For Boccati, see also Luigi Serra, *L'Arte nelle Marche*, 1934, pp. 287 ff. (3) Berenson, Lists of 1932. (4) Longhi in *Critica d'Arte*, Nos. XXV–VI, 1940, pp. 174/5. (5) Mario Salmi in *Arti Figurative*, 1947, pp. 80 ff. (6) R. van Marle, *Development of the Italian Schools of Painting*, Vol. X, pp. 156 and 162, and Vol. XV, p. 12. (7) Photo in the Gallery archives. It is reproduced in the Klassiker der Kunst *Angelico*, 1911, p. 211, or 1924, p. 231. (8) Klassiker der Kunst *Angelico*, 1924, p. 186. (9) Mrs. Jameson, *Companion to the Private Galleries of Art*, 1844, p. 412; cf. also Waagen, *Treasures*, II, 1854, p. 267. The description makes the identification with No. 5581 sure. (10) As Giotto. Miss Rogers bequeathed her pictures (with certain specified exceptions) to her brother; she died in February 1855 and he later on in the same year. (11) As Benozzo (Gozzoli). (12) As Benozzo (Gozzoli). (13) As Angelico. (14) Cook Catalogue, I, 1913, No. 15, as School of Angelico; 1932 Catalogue, as Benozzo (Gozzoli). (15) As probably by an illuminator of the San Marco School, in close contact with Fra Angelico. (16) As Benozzo (Gozzoli). (17) In 1945, also exhibited at Toronto and Ottawa.

ANGELO DI TADDEO GADDI *See* GADDI (AGNOLO)

ANTONELLO DA MESSINA
active 1456, died 1479

Active chiefly at Messina, where he already had a pupil in 1456. According to a reliable source of 1524, his teacher was Colantonio at Naples. Antonello's stay at Naples some years before 1456 is all the more likely in that works by Jan van Eyck and Rogier van der Weyden are recorded to have existed there at about that time; from these he could have adopted his somewhat Netherlandish style. In 1475/6 he visited Venice and painted an altarpiece for the church of San Cassiano there, of which fragments are preserved at Vienna; this picture had a great influence on Venetian painting, partly for reasons of technique, and may have been the original treatment of the Virgin and Child with Saints under architecture of a type followed by Bellini and many other Venetians. Antonello is known chiefly for his portrait heads, many of which are signed and dated.

Former statements that Antonello visited the Netherlands, that he was a pupil of Jan van Eyck, or that he learnt oil painting from Petrus Christus in Milan in 1456 are now discounted as extremely unlikely or impossible.

Literature: J. Lauts in the Vienna *Jahrbuch*, 1933, pp. 15 ff.

673 SALVATOR MUNDI

Signed on a *cartellino: Millesimo quatricentessimo sexstage | simo quinto viij^e Indi antonellus | messaneus me pinxit.*

Wood, painted surface, $15\frac{1}{4} \times 11\frac{3}{4}$ (0·39 × 0·295).

Somewhat worn, e.g. in the shadows. *Pentimenti:* the hand blessing was once more upright, the outlines of the four original fingers being now discernible; the hem of the tunic was also once higher.

The date is contradictory. Indictions give a yearly measure of time during periods of 15 years, and at the end of each period they begin again at 1; 1465 was the 13th indiction, the 8th could be 1460 or 1475. This contradiction is inexplicable. 1465 is the earliest date on a picture by Antonello.

The design seems to be clearly of Netherlandish derivation. Lauts reproduces a slightly later Netherlandish picture, which may be compared;[1] the likeness was greater before the hand on No. 673 was changed to its present form.

VERSION: A variant by a follower of Antonello is stated to exist in the church of Ficarra, Sicily.[2]

PROVENANCE: Said to have come from Naples in the 1840's.[3] Purchased through[4] Cav. Giuseppe Isola and Paolo Orlandi at Genoa, 1861.

REPRODUCTION: *Illustrations, Italian Schools,* 1937, p. 13. *Plates, Earlier Italian Schools,* 1953, Vol. I, p. 13.

REFERENCES: (1) J. Lauts in the Vienna *Jahrbuch*, 1933, p. 31. (2) Cf. E. Brunelli in *L'Arte,* 1908, pp. 223/4. (3) Cf. Crowe and Cavalcaselle, *Painting in North Italy,* II, 1871, p. 84; ed. Borenius, II, 1912, p. 418. The reference is to an anonymous article in the *Journal des Beaux-Arts et de la Littérature*, 1862, p. 13, where it is stated that the picture bears on the back a seal with the arms of the city of Naples; it has now on the back an unidentifiable seal. (4) The name of the proprietor in 1861 is unknown; see Eastlake's note-book.

1141   PORTRAIT OF A MAN

Poplar[1], painted surface, 14 × 10 (0·355 × 0·255). The top and sides may be true edges. The bottom was sawn off to 'reduce the picture to a better shape'; this according to an inscription partly illegible on the back, in Italian and probably of the eighteenth century.[2]

Very good condition. X-rays reveal that the eyes were originally turned the other way.[3]

According to the text on the back, the part sawn off contained a 'description (?)' to the effect that the sitter was Antonello himself. A simple 'Antonellus me pinxit,' misunderstood by ignorant people, might be the origin of this idea; the present position of the eyes is irrelevant to the matter, being normal in Antonello's portraits.[4]

A mature work, dated by Lauts *ca.* 1475.[5]

COPY: A copy was once in the Somzée Collection, Brussels.[6]

PROVENANCE: Possibly the Self-Portrait in the Roberto Canonici Collection at Ferrara, 1632.[7] Said to have been in the Molfino family for generations;[8] there by 1871.[9] Purchased from G. Molfino, Genoa, out of the Lewis Fund, 1883. Cleaned Pictures Exhibition at the National Gallery, 1947/8 (No. 24).

REPRODUCTION: *Illustrations, Italian Schools*, 1937, p. 14. *Plates, Earlier Italian Schools*, 1953, Vol. I, p. 14.

REFERENCES: (1) Letter from B. J. Rendle, of the Forest Products Research Laboratory, in the Gallery archives. (2) Said to have been written by the great grandfather of the Molfino who sold the picture to the Gallery (N.G. MS. Catalogue). (3) Reproduced by Ian Rawlins, *From the National Gallery Laboratory*, 1940, Plate 9. (4) Cf. Martin Davies in *The Burlington Magazine*, Vol. LXXXIX (1947), p. 171. (5) J. Lauts in the Vienna *Jahrbuch*, 1933, p. 67. G. Vigni, *Tutta la Pittura di Antonello da Messina*, 1952, p. 22 and S. Bottari, *Antonello*, 1953, pp. 98/9, put it a little earlier. (6) Exhibited at the New Gallery, 1894/5 (No. 59); cf. Gronau in the *Gazette des Beaux-Arts*, 1895, I, p. 248. No doubt identical with a picture in the Exposition Néerlandaise de Beaux-Arts, Brussels, 1882 (No. 1) (Tableaux Anciens). (7) Giuseppe Campori, *Raccolta di Cataloghi ed Inventarii Inediti*, 1870, p. 112; the brief description corresponds quite well. Campori on p. 105 refers to a fire of 1638, but it does not appear that the whole collection was then destroyed. (8) N.G. MS. Catalogue. Vigni, *op. cit.*, p. 22, says that Molfino is a name occurring in Messina documents in the XV Century. (9) Crowe and Cavalcaselle, *Painting in North Italy*, 1871, II, p. 90.

1166   CHRIST CRUCIFIED

The Virgin and S. John are at the foot of the Cross marked:. I.N.R.I. Three figures in the middle distance, seen to the left of the Cross, are probably the Maries. Signed on a *cartellino:* 1475 / *antonellus messaneus / me pinxit* (retouched).

Wood, painted surface, 16½ × 10 (0·42 × 0·255); not included in these measurements is a strip ¾ in. (2 cm.) wide along the bottom, which is new except for a piece in the middle 1½ in. (4 cm.) long. This old piece, with the *cartellino* and signature, need not have been originally exactly in its present place.[1] The picture is painted up to the edges of the wood at the sides and top, and the top corners are new. Much damaged and restored; of the three principal figures, the Virgin is the best preserved.

The date was read as 1477 until Lauts read 1475;[2] there is no doubt that 1475 is correct, although the last figure, being damaged and re-touched, no longer accurately represents anything.

A *Crucifixion* at Sibiu (Hermannstadt) is of the same general character, but Lauts rightly considers that a very early work.[3] Another at Antwerp is, like No. 1166, dated 1475, and the central figure is again almost identical.[4]

PROVENANCE: Given or bequeathed by the 2nd Marquess of Bute (who died in 1848) to his 3rd cousin Louisa, wife of the 3rd Marquess of Waterford; pur-chased from her, Clarke Fund, 1884.[5]

REPRODUCTION: *Illustrations, Italian Schools*, 1937, p. 13. *Plates, Earlier Italian Schools*, 1953, Vol. I, p. 15.

REFERENCES: (1) The *cartellino* was on the back of the picture when it was acquired. It need not be doubted that it belongs to the present picture. The *Christ* in Palazzo Spinola at Genoa has a *cartellino* with signature on the frame, which does seem there to be the original arrangement; reproduced in the catalogue of the Antonello Exhibition, 2nd edition, Messina, 1953, Plate 13, and by P. Rotondi, *La Galleria Nazionale di Palazzo Spinola a Genova*, 1959, p. 28. (2) J. Lauts in the Vienna *Jahrbuch*, 1933, p. 67. S. Bottari, *Antonello*, 1953, p. 49, pleads for 1477. (3) Reproduced by Lauts, *loc. cit.*, p. 16. (4) Reproduced by Lauts, p. 46. (5) The provenance is recorded in the National Gallery MS. Catalogue, presumably on information supplied by the vendor.

1418   S. JEROME IN HIS STUDY

Lime,[1] painted surface, $18 \times 14\frac{1}{4}$ (0·46×0·365); painted up to the edge at the left, but obviously not cut there.

Excellent state.

The *Anonimo*[2] saw it in 1529, recorded attributions to Antonello, van Eyck and Memlinc, and stated that the style of the figure had suggested to some a repainting of this part by Jacometto; for the last named, see the entries under his name.[3] Lauts[4] convincingly admits No. 1418 as one of Antonello's earliest known works, and claims that it may be derived from a S. Jerome, possibly of similar treatment, that is recorded to have formed one wing of a triptych by van Eyck, in Naples in 1456.

PROVENANCE: In 1529, owned by Antonio Pasqualino at Venice.[5] In Sir Thomas Baring's Collection at Stratton by 1835;[6] exhibited at the British Institution, 1837 (No. 22) and 1845 (No. 66); Sale, 3 June, 1848 (lot 66), bought by Coningham. William Coningham Sale, 9 June, 1849 (lot 29), bought by Smith for Thomas Baring (who bequeathed his pictures to his nephew, Lord Northbrook).[7] Exhibited at the R.A., 1871 (No. 191), at the Guildhall, 1890 (No. 46), at the Burlington Fine Arts Club, 1892 (No. 7a), and at the R.A., 1894 (No. 183). Purchased from the Earl of Northbrook, 1894. Cleaned Pictures Exhibition at the National Gallery, 1947/8 (No. 23).

REPRODUCTION: *Illustrations, Italian Schools*, 1937, p. 15. *Plates, Earlier Italian Schools*, 1953, Vol. I, p. 16.

REFERENCES: (1) Letter from B. J. Rendle, of the Forest Products Research Laboratory, in the Gallery archives. (2) The *Anonimo* (Marcantonio Michiel), ed. Frimmel, 1888, pp. 98/100, with identifying description. (3) Luigi Servolini, *Jacopo de' Barbari*, 1944, pp. 31 ff. dubiously accepts No. 1418 as by Jacometto, whom he wrongly inclines (p. 36) to think identical with Jacopo de' Barbari. (4) J. Lauts in the Vienna *Jahrbuch*, 1933, p. 66. (5) Reference as in note 2. (6) Waagen, *Art and Artists*, 1838, III, p. 42. In the nineteenth century it was at first called Dürer, then for some time van Eyck. (7) J. P. Richter's Northbrook Catalogue, 1889 (No. 150). Mentioned by Waagen, *Treasures*, II, 1854, p. 182.

Follower of ANTONELLO DA MESSINA

2618   THE VIRGIN AND CHILD

Wood, painted surface, $17 \times 13\frac{1}{2}$ (0·43 × 0·345).

Much damaged and restored. The painted framing to the background may be original; it would seem contemporary with the haloes.

On its discovery this picture was called Flemish, Spanish, Portuguese, Russian, and even Oriental;[1] there is, however, no doubt that it is closely connected with Antonello, the head of the Virgin being almost exactly the same as on the picture accepted as by Antonello now at Washington (formerly in the Benson and Mackay Collections).[2] Berenson[3] published a picture doubtless by the same hand in the Walters Art Gallery at Baltimore, called *S. Rosalia of Palermo* or *The Virgin reading*. Bottari[4] ascribed both these pictures to the early period of Antonello, and (without good evidence) then dated the one at Baltimore 1461. The quality of No. 2618 is distinctly inferior to that of No. 1418 above, and it seems most likely to be by a pupil of Antonello's early time; Lauts[5] thinks the painter may be a Spaniard trained in the Netherlandish style.

PROVENANCE: Lent by George Salting to the Burlington Fine Arts Club, 1904 No. 5); Salting Bequest, 1910.

REPRODUCTION: *Illustrations, Italian Schools*, 1937, p. 228. *Plates, Earlier Italian Schools*, 1953, Vol. I, p. 17.

REFERENCES: (1) Cf. H. Cook in *L'Arte*, 1905, p. 130. (2) Reproduced in the Washington Book of Illustrations, and often elsewhere. Cf. R. Longhi in *Unknown Masterpieces*, Vol. I, 1930, No. 15. (3) Berenson, *Venetian Paintings in America*, 1916, pp. 35 ff., where the Walters picture is reproduced. (4) S. Bottari in *Critica d'Arte*, II, 1937, p. 108. Fiocco in *Emporium*, 1950, pp. 56/7, while rejecting Bottari's evidence for the dating, agrees in the attribution to Antonello. (5) J. Lauts in the Vienna *Jahrbuch*, 1933, p. 67 (s.v. Long Island). Lauts wrote further on the subject in *Kunstchronik*, June 1953, pp. 151/2, apropos of a third picture, perhaps by the same hand, which was No. XX (Plate 24) of the Antonello Exhibition at Messina, 1953; Bottari, *Antonello*, 1953, pp. 72 ff., and Plates XXX, XXXII and XXXIII, classes the three connected pictures as by Antonello. Pallucchini in *Arte Veneta*, 1951, p. 195, indicates that No. 2618 is by Antonello; Berenson, in his 1957 lists, p. 7, classes all three pictures as by a close follower.

APOLLONIO DI GIOVANNI
1415 (?)–1465

Florentine School. The dates of birth and death given above are from Colnaghi's *Dictionary of Florentine Painters*. Member of the Physicians' Guild at Florence, 1442. By 1446, he was a partner with Marco del Buono, almost entirely for the production of *cassoni*; for the records of this activity, see Schubring, *Cassoni*, 1923, pp. 443 ff. (also Gualandi, *Memorie*, IV, 1843, p. 140).

See FLORENTINE SCHOOL, No. 4906

ALESSO BALDOVINETTI
ca. 1426-1499

Florentine School; of a well-to-do family. For the dubious evidence of his date of birth, see Colnaghi's *Dictionary of Florentine Painters*, p. 28; E. Londi in the *Rivista d'Arte*, 1906, pp. 191/2; and R. G. Mather in *The Art Bulletin*, March, 1948, p. 26. Mather, p. 28, claims that Baldovinetti was out of Florence *ca.* 1433–46. He joined the Compagnia di S. Luca at Florence in 1448 or 1449. He not only painted, but also worked in mosaic and stained glass. Several authenticated works exist. He seems to have been influenced by Domenico Veneziano, Fra Angelico and Andrea dal Castagno.

Literature: Ruth Wedgwood Kennedy, *Alesso Baldovinetti*, 1938.

758 PORTRAIT OF A LADY IN YELLOW

On her sleeve is a device with three palm leaves tied with two other leaves (?).

Wood, painted surface, $24\frac{3}{4} \times 16$ (0·63 × 0·405). Including the frame, $28\frac{3}{4} \times 20$ (0·73 × 0·505); the frame appears to be original, but is not in one piece with the picture.

Cleaned in 1954. Good condition, although worn in the flesh.

No. 758 was purchased as representing a Contessa Palma of Urbino;[1] the sitter has also been claimed to be Francesca Stati, wife of the poet Angelo Galli of Urbino.[2] She has also been called a sister of Piero Soderini of Florence.[3]

No. 758 was acquired as by Piero della Francesca.[4] The attribution to Baldovinetti was made by Roger Fry,[5] and has been accepted by Mrs. Kennedy and others.[6] Various other suggestions for the authorship have been made;[7] but Baldovinetti seems to be the right man, although admittedly the stylistic comparison has to be made with pictures that are not portraits. Mrs. Kennedy gives some reasons for dating it *ca.* 1465.[8]

PROVENANCE: Stated to have been owned by Conte Pancrazi at Ascoli Piceno;[9] purchased from Egidi, a dealer at Florence, 1866.

REPRODUCTION: *Illustrations, Italian Schools*, 1937, p. 16. *Plates, Earlier Italian Schools*, 1953, Vol. I, p. 18.

REFERENCES: (1) Letter from Egidi, the seller of the picture, in the Gallery archives. A Palazzo Palma exists at Urbino; see *Catalogo delle Cose d'Arte e di Antichità d'Italia, Urbino*, by Luigi Serra, 1932, p. 85, with a reproduction of the courtyard. There was published in *The Sphere*, 6 August, 1927, a statement that a Countess Lavagine delle Palme was a mistress of Federico d'Urbino. (2) E. Giovannetti in the *Illustrazione Italiana*, 26 July, 1925, pp. 75/6, giving the views of Luigi Nardini. The reference is recorded by Mario Salmi, *Paolo Uccello Andrea del Castagno Domenico Veneziano*, 1938, p. 182. (3) Ruth Wedgwood Kennedy, *Alesso Baldovinetti*, 1938, pp. 132/3. The Soderini device to which Mrs. Kennedy refers was, according to Litta, *Famiglie Celebri d'Italia*, Tav. I of the Soderini family, personal to Piero Soderini. The textile referred to in the Bargello is reproduced by F. Rossi, *Il Museo Nazionale di Firenze*, 1932, p. 81; it contains nothing similar to the device on No. 758. (4) So catalogued until 1915. (5) Fry in *The Burlington Magazine*, Vol. XVIII (1911), pp. 311 f. (6) Kennedy, *op. cit.*, pp. 131 ff.; cf. also Berenson's 1932 Lists, and Pudelko in *Pantheon*, 1935, p. 95. (7) E.g. Domenico Veneziano by Schmarsow in *L'Arte*, 1912, pp. 94/5, and by Salmi, *op. cit.*, 1938, Plate 214; A. Pollaiuolo by A. Venturi in *Pantheon*, 1929, p. 14; Uccello by W. Boeck in the *Zeitschrift für Kunstgeschichte*, 1933, pp. 271/2, and by Longhi in *Paragone*, November 1952, p. 33. (8) Kennedy, *op. cit.*, pp. III and 133. (9) Letter from Egidi in the Gallery archives.

JACOPO DE' BARBARI
active 1500, died 1516 (?)

Also *Jacob Walch*. He is referred to as a Venetian, by birth or adoption, but little is known of his activity at Venice. He may have been born about the middle of the fifteenth century, being described as old in 1512. He influenced the young Dürer; this is supposed to have occurred on Dürer's visit to Venice in 1494. In 1500, he was appointed painter to the Emperor at Nuremberg; thereafter he seems to have spent his life at various German courts, and then in the Netherlands in the service of Margaret of Austria, etc. He was dead by 1516 and may have died in that year (cf. J. Duverger's article in the *Mélanges Hulin*, 1931, pp. 142 ff.).

A good many engravings exist, mostly signed with a caduceus; also several pictures signed in one form or another, with dates from 1500. Traces of Venetian influence are perhaps discernible; also that of Dürer and (later on) of Cranach. He painted one of the earliest seduction scenes, and one of the earliest still-lifes.

A *Portrait of Luca Pacioli and another Man* of 1495 at Naples is signed by Jaco. Bar., 'aged twenty' (apparently); it is usually supposed to be by another painter.

3088   A SPARROWHAWK

Oak, painted surface, 7 × 4¼ (0·178 × 0·11); painted up to the edges all round, and possibly cut from a larger picture.

Excellent state.

The subject is most probably a female sparrowhawk.[1]

On the back of the former frame, in a nineteenth-century hand or hands, *Grif d'Anversa* and *Jacopo de Barbaris*; these may be copies from older inscriptions. The first presumably means an *Antwerp Falcon* or *Hawk (grifagno)*. It was the basis in recent editions of the catalogue for an ascription to Adriaen Gryef, a painter active *ca.* 1700. The attribution to Jacopo de' Barbari was made by Mündler.[2] The Gryef theory over-shadowed it for a while; but it has been taken up again recently by Glück,[3] Baldass,[4] Servolini,[5] and Berenson (1957 Lists), and seems quite convincing. Probably rather late work.

PROVENANCE: Obviously the picture sold *ca.* 1859 from the Collection of Count Castellani (previously of Count Bertolazone d'Arache) at Turin.[6] Presented by Sir James Hudson (our minister at Turin, 1851/63) to Sir A. H. Layard;[7] exhibited at South Kensington, 1869 (No. 36); Layard Bequest, 1916.[8]

REPRODUCTION: *Illustrations, Continental Schools*, 1937, p. 147. *Plates, Earlier Italian Schools*, 1953, Vol. I, p. 19.

REFERENCES: (**1**) Letter from E. Banks of the Natural History Museum, in the Gallery archives. (**2**) Layard MSS. in the National Gallery. Cf. also Mündler in the *Zeitschrift für bildende Kunst*, 1869, p. 163. The attribution was accepted by several critics, e.g. by Stiassny in the *Repertorium für Kunstwissenschaft*, 1888, p. 385; by Berenson, *Venetian Painters*, 1894, 1895, 1897; and by Frizzoni in the *Gazette des Beaux-Arts*, 1896, II, p. 462. (**3**) Glück in the Vienna *Jahrbuch*, 1934, p. 192. (**4**) Baldass in *Pantheon*, 1938, p. 322. (**5**) Luigi Servolini, *Jacopo de' Barbari*, 1944, p. 126. (**6**) Mündler, *loc. cit.* In the Le Monnier Vasari, V, 1849, p. 188, a catalogue of the collection of the 'Marchese d'Harache' is referred to; the compiler has not seen this. Dr. Vittorio Viale kindly sent a copy of the un-dated *Inventario di quadri, stampe e statue dell'ill.mo Sig. Conte Bertolazone d'Arache e di Banna, Collaterale nella R.a Camera* (Turin, Biblioteca del Re, MSS., Misc. Patria, Vol. 156), but No. 3088 does not appear to be recorded there. Mündler, in his diary, 11 April, 1856, says that 'Conte Castillane' was nephew and heir to 'Conte Harrach'; to judge from the catalogue of the Arache Sale at Paris, 1859, *Castellani* is the right spelling. (**7**) Layard MSS. in the National Gallery. (**8**) For the history of the Layard Collection, see Appendix IV.

BARNABA DA MODENA
active 1361–1383

From a Milanese family settled in Modena. The records of his activity are, however, not at Modena, but at Genoa, and there is reason to believe that he was already there some time before the earliest record (1361). He paid a visit to Pisa in 1380. Several signed works exist, some dated.

1437 PENTECOST

The Virgin and the twelve Apostles with hands joined in prayer receive the Holy Spirit.

Wood, $21\frac{1}{2} \times 19\frac{3}{4}$ (0·545 × 0·50); painted up to the edges all round. Good state. One of the haloes has been left unstamped by error.

Thought to be one panel of a composite work; C. Ricci suggests that an *Ascension* (size 0·59 × 0·45), in the Capitol (formerly Sterbini Collection) at Rome, belongs to the same series.[1] Longhi further suggested a *Nativity* and a *Flight into Egypt* in the Palazzo del Comune at Bologna.[2]

PROVENANCE: Purchased from Charles Simpson, Linslade House, Leighton Buzzard, 1895.[3]

REPRODUCTION: *Illustrations, Italian Schools*, 1937, p. 17. *Plates, Earlier Italian Schools*, 1953, Vol. I, p. 20.

REFERENCES: (1) C. Ricci in *The Burlington Magazine*, Vol. XXIV (1913/4), p. 65. Size from A. Venturi, *La Galleria Sterbini in Roma*, 1906, No. 13; reproduction in Van Marle, *Development of the Italian Schools of Painting*, IV, Fig. 194. S. Bocconi, *Collezioni Capitoline*, 1950, p. 345, No. 3 (size given as 0·49 × 0·45, apparently by mistake), and Plate 58. (2) Oral communication from R. Longhi. Bologna, *Mostra della Pittura Bolognese del 300*, 1950, Nos. 58, 59; reproduced by P. Rotondi, *Il Polittico di Barnaba da Modena a Lavagnola*, 1955, Fig. 29. The size of these pictures is only 0·39 × 0·28 and 0·38 × 0·28; such subjects in the same ensemble as *Pentecost* and *The Ascension* would seem to imply a series of large extent, most of which would be missing. It is true that the halo patterns correspond well with those of No. 1437. (3) As School of Giotto.

2927   THE CORONATION OF THE VIRGIN: THE TRINITY: THE VIRGIN AND CHILD: THE CRUCIFIXION

Four scenes, and a predella. *Top left*, the Coronation of the Virgin. *Top right*, the Trinity. Christ is shown on a Cross marked .I.N.R.I., supported by God the Father; the Holy Ghost as a Dove. These figures are within a vesica, at the corners of which are the symbols of the four Evangelists; each holds a book inscribed with the opening words of the respective Gospel, except S. Luke who has the opening words of his Chapter II. The Virgin and S. John mourn at the foot of the Cross. *Bottom left*, the Virgin and Child; her halo is inscribed AUE. GRATIA. PLEN, and the Child holds a scroll, now illegible. Two donors are presented by S. Raphael, his halo being inscribed SANCTUS: RAFAELIS. *Bottom right*, the Crucifixion. Christ is on a Cross marked I.N.R.I., and surmounted apparently by a Pelican in her piety. Angels carry off the soul of the good thief (S. Dismas), devils that of the bad thief (Gestas). The Magdalen is at the foot of the Cross. Left foreground, the swooning Virgin attended by the Holy Women and S. John; right foreground, the soldiers casting lots. The *Predella*, divided into two parts, shows the twelve Apostles, for the most part not individually distinguished. Signed on the panel bottom left: *barnabas. de mutina pinxit*. 1374.

Wood. The individual scenes are 13½ × 10¾ (0·34 × 0·275) each; the two parts of the predella each 2½ × 10¾ (0·065 × 0·275). Total, including the strip of framing round the edges, 32¼ × 23¾ (0·82 × 0·605).

The gold backgrounds are new, but the picture is in general in satisfactory state, the scene of the Crucifixion being the most damaged. The original framing has been in parts renewed.

Ricci suggests that the donors may be the Doge and Dogaressa of Genoa, Domenico Fregoso and his wife.[1]

PROVENANCE: Damaged and unidentified seal on the back. Owned by Seroux d'Agincourt, *ca.* 1785.[2] Later in the collection of Sir James Parke, Lord Wensleydale, who lent it to Manchester, 1857 (Provisional Catalogue, No. 300;

Definitive Catalogue, No. 46). Lord Wensleydale died in 1868; his widow died in 1879, and bequeathed the picture to her grandson, Charles Howard, 9th Earl of Carlisle.[3] Presented by his widow, Rosalind, Countess of Carlisle, 1913.

REPRODUCTION: *Illustrations, Italian Schools*, 1937, p. 17. *Plates, Earlier Italian Schools*, 1953, Vol. I, p. 21.

REFERENCES: (1) C. Ricci in *The Burlington Magazine*, Vol. XXIV (1913/4), p. 66. (2) D'Agincourt, *Storia dell'Arte*, IV, 1827, pp. 408/9; VI, 1829, pp. 394/5; and Plate CXXXIII. (3) Label on the back.

BARTOLO DI FREDI
active 1353, died 1410

Sienese School; occasionally active at San Gimignano and Volterra. He occupied some municipal posts at Siena, as well as being a painter. Several authenticated works exist. For the date of the frescoes in the Collegiata at San Gimignano, see Enzo Carli in *Critica d'Arte*, May, 1949, pp. 75 f.

Ascribed to BARTOLO DI FREDI

3896 S. ANTHONY ABBOT (PANEL FROM AN ALTAR-PIECE)

Wood. The size of the picture (cusped and rounded top) is $21\frac{1}{2} \times 12\frac{1}{2}$ ($0\cdot55 \times 0\cdot315$); the size including all the framing is $24\frac{1}{4} \times 14\frac{1}{4}$ ($0\cdot615 \times 0\cdot36$).

Damaged towards the bottom, but in general in very good condition. Part of the frame is old, but for the most part regilt.

Obviously one panel from a triptych or polyptych, of which the other parts have not been identified.

The attribution to Bartolo di Fredi has been accepted by several writers, e.g. by Berenson, 1932 Lists. It is rejected by Enzo Carli (verbal, 1949). Offner (verbal, 1936) ascribed No. 3896 to Giovanni di Nicola da Pisa; van Marle[1] ascribed it to A. Vanni.

PROVENANCE: Henry Willett Collection, Brighton; exhibited at the New Gallery, 1893/4 (No. 12);[2] Sale, 10 April, 1905 (lot 48), bought by Wagner. Presented by Henry Wagner, 1924.

REPRODUCTION: *Illustrations, Italian Schools*, 1937, p. 18. *Plates, Earlier Italian Schools*, 1953, Vol. I, p. 22.

REFERENCES: (1) Van Marle, *Le Scuole della Pittura Italiana*, II, 1934, p. 483. (2) Label on the back. Here, and in the sale, as Florentine School.

MARCO BASAITI
active 1496–1530

Probably of Greek origin, but born at Venice or in Friuli. There are many signed works, some of them dated; the signatures vary in spelling, but are most often *Baxaiti*. An altarpiece in the Frari at Venice, begun by Alvise Vivarini, was finished after Alvise's death in 1503/5 by Basaiti; but there is no good reason for supposing that Basaiti was originally Alvise's pupil, and his beginnings are obscure. Towards 1500–10 he sometimes approached rather closely to Giovanni Bellini, though the nearness of his relationship is disputed.

For the Pseudo-Basaiti, see the commentary to Giovanni Bellini, No. 599.

2498 PORTRAIT OF A YOUNG MAN

Signed, . MARCHVS: BAXAITI.P.

Wood, painted surface, $14\frac{1}{4} \times 10\frac{3}{4}$ (0·365 × 0·27).

Good condition in general. But there are many retouches to reduce the prominence of the wider cracks, and over the half shadows of the flesh and hair; the surface is thus not altogether reliable, but the general character of the modelling is only very slightly affected. *Pentimenti* in his hair to the left and where the cap rests on it.

The craquelure is rather peculiar, but the picture is certainly a genuine Basaiti. The brownish tone is probably characteristic of the earliest Basaitis. The costume indeed would be suitable for a date 1495–1500.

PROVENANCE: Passed by inheritance from the collection of Edward Cheney[1] into that of Col. Alfred Capel Cure of Badger Hall.[2] Exhibited at the R.A. 1886 (No. 161). Francis Capel Cure Sale, 6 May, 1905 (lot 26),[3] bought by Colnaghi. Lent by George Salting to the Burlington Fine Arts Club, Winter, 1907 (No. 6); Salting Bequest, 1910.

REPRODUCTION: *Illustrations, Italian Schools*, 1937, p. 20. *Plates, Earlier Italian Schools*, 1953, Vol. I, p. 23.

REFERENCES: (1) Where seen by Crowe and Cavalcaselle: *Painting in North Italy*, I, 1871, p. 271, or ed. Borenius, 1912, I, p. 275. (2) The property of Edward Cheney (1803–1884), of Badger Hall, passed to his nephew, Col Alfred Capel Cure; see Burke's *Landed Gentry*, 1886. (3) With description.

2499 THE VIRGIN AND CHILD

Signed, .MARCO./ BAXAITI.P. (the second line partly cut away).

Poplar,[1] painted surface, $24\frac{3}{4} \times 18\frac{1}{2}$ (0·63 × 0·47); painted up to the edges all round, and slightly cut at least at the bottom.

Good condition. The most serious damage is on the Child's head, which has been considerably made up. Other obvious damages on the Child's body are of little importance for the style; the flesh parts of the Virgin are well preserved.

An early work.

VERSION: A version without the curtain is in the Liechtenstein Collection;[2] perhaps identical with a picture once in the Tescari Collection, Castelfranco.[3]

PROVENANCE: Probably the picture in the Baron de Beurnonville Sale, Paris, 9–16 May, 1881 (lot 606).[4] Lent by George Salting to the New Gallery, 1894/5 (No. 101); Salting Bequest, 1910.

REPRODUCTION: *Illustrations, Italian Schools*, 1937, p. 22. *Plates, Earlier Italian Schools*, 1953, Vol. I, p. 24.

REFERENCES: (1) Letter from B. J. Rendle, of the Forest Products Research Laboratory, in the Gallery archives. (2) Reproduced by Venturi, *Storia dell'Arte Italiana*, Vol. VII, Part IV, Fig. 396 (wrongly lettered as at Oldenburg); since then, the Child's loin cloth has been removed, and there are some other variations from Venturi's reproduction (a photograph of the picture was taken in 1951 at the National Gallery). Liechtenstein Guide, 1931 (No. 846); size 0·64 × 0·51. (3) Cf. Crowe and Cavalcaselle, *Painting in North Italy*, I, 1871, p. 262, or ed. Borenius, 1912, I, p. 267. Tescari Catalogue, 1875 (No. 329); size, 0·64 × 0·52. (4) With some description; size, 0·62 × 0·45.

See also Follower of GIOVANNI BELLINI, No. 281

LAZZARO BASTIANI
active 1449–died 1512

Lazzaro Bastiani or *Sebastiani*. Venetian School. There are several signed works; the earliest date on a picture is 1484. He seems to have spent much of his time imitating the Vivarini, the Bellini and Carpaccio, but he may also have been the teacher of the last.

1953 THE VIRGIN AND CHILD

Signed, LAZARVS BASTIANVS PINXIT.

Wood, painted surface, $32\frac{3}{4} \times 25\frac{1}{4}$ (0·83 × 0·64); painted up to the edges all round.

The picture is much worn, and considerably repainted.

Seemingly from the painter's middle period.[1]

PROVENANCE: For sale at the Monte di Pietà, Rome, in 1857, and seen there in 1858 by Mündler.[2] Later owned by Father O'Connor, Keighley.[3] Presented by the National Art-Collections Fund, 1905. Exhibited at the National Gallery, N.A.C.F. Exhibition, 1945/6 (No. 1).

REPRODUCTION: *Illustrations, Italian Schools*, 1937, p. 25. *Plates, Earlier Italian Schools*, 1953, Vol. I, p. 25.

REFERENCES: (1) Cf. E. Sandberg-Vavalà's article in *The Burlington Magazine*, Vol. LIX (1931), pp. 124 ff. (2) Monte di Pietà *Catalogo*, December 1857 (No. 252); Mündler's Diary, with identifying description. (3) Reproduction in Bryan's *Dictionary*, 1903/5 edition, s.v. *Sebastiani*.

GENTILE BELLINI
active *ca.* 1460–died 1507

Venetian School: son of Jacopo, and brother of Giovanni Bellini. The evidence, without being sure, is rather in favour of his being older than the latter; if so, he may have been born in 1429. An altarpiece is recorded to have been signed by the three Bellini, and dated (apparently) 1460.

Some organ-shutters in S. Mark's, Venice, are signed by Gentile and dated (by Crowe and Cavalcaselle) 1464; the *Blessed Lorenzo Giustinian* in the Venice Academy is signed and dated 1465. In 1469 he was made *eques* and *comes palatinus* by the Emperor. By 1474 he was working in the *Sala del Gran Consiglio* at Venice, for which later on his principal pictures were painted; everything was destroyed in 1577. In 1479 he went to Constantinople to work for the Sultan Mehmet II, and left again early in 1481; he received (?) from the Sultan titles comparable with what he already had, being called *miles auratus* and *comes palatinus*. Some large subject-pieces in Venice and Milan, in unsatisfactory condition, are authenticated works of his later years.

Gentile was presumably trained by his father Jacopo; but a strong influence of Mantegna is discernible in the organ-shutters supposed to be of 1464. The evidence is insufficient to follow his development at all exactly.

3911   THE VIRGIN AND CHILD ENTHRONED

Signed: .OPVS.GENTILIS.BELLINI.VENETI.EQVITIS.

Wood, rounded top, painted surface, $48 \times 32\frac{1}{2}$ ($1 \cdot 22 \times 0 \cdot 825$); painted up to the edges all round. About $\frac{1}{2}$ in. of the front part of the panel, not included in the above measurements, has been cut away along the upper edge; this cut just eats into the rounded top of the picture, which would have extended to the extreme edge of the panel. Richter[1] thinks the picture had originally a square top; the spandrels are now covered with modern paint, but where this has flaked off there seems to be nothing but gesso.

The flesh, which is much worn, has been very extensively repainted. The gold is new, though there was gold originally; the sky and the blue hills right and left are new. The dress, carpet and throne, although cracked and repaired and certainly not altogether trustworthy, are in very fair state. The signature is in good condition. *Pentimenti*, some visible only under X-rays, in Christ's fingers blessing and His left hip, in the lines of both haloes and in the Virgin's drapery right, at the base of the throne.

The flesh parts in their present state show little of Gentile's style. The picture cannot be from before 1469, when he was knighted.[2] The decorative treatment and some details, such as the tiny trees in the Gothic tradition, would suggest a fairly early date.

PROVENANCE: Richter[3] thinks it is the central panel of a signed altarpiece in six compartments, recorded by various authors in the Mercers' Guild, Venice; there is no specific evidence for this. Probably the signed *Virgin and Child* seen by Mündler in the studio of Paolo Fabris, Venice, in 1857.[4] It was in any case acquired by Sir Charles Eastlake between 1855 and 1865.[5] Lady Eastlake's Sale, 2 June, 1894 (lot 59), bought by Richter for Ludwig Mond. Exhibited at the New Gallery, 1894/5 (No. 47). Mond Bequest, 1924.

REPRODUCTION: *Illustrations, Italian Schools*, 1937, p. 29. *Plates, Earlier Italian Schools*, 1953, Vol. I, p. 26.

REFERENCES: (1) J. P. Richter, *The Mond Collection*, 1910, I, p. 101. (2) It is recorded, though it is confusing, that Gentile received titles described in almost the same terms twice, once from the Emperor Frederick III in 1469 and again from the Sultan in 1479/81. The texts are given by Paoletti, *Documenti Inediti*, 1894, I, p. 18, and Emil Jacobs in the Prussian *Jahrbuch*, 1927, p. 8. But the granting of such titles to Gentile Bellini by the Sultan is disbelieved by Franz Babinger in Österreichische Akademie der Wissenschaften, Philosophisch-Historische Klasse, *Sitzungsberichte*, 237. Band, 3. Abhandlung, 1961, p. 7 of the offprint. (3) Richter, *op. cit.*, pp. 97/8. (4) Mündler's Diary. (5) It was among the pictures acquired by Eastlake during his directorship (1855/65), and in accordance with his wishes offered to the Gallery for sale by Lady Eastlake in 1867.

Ascribed to GENTILE BELLINI

1213   A MAN WITH A PAIR OF DIVIDERS (?)

Canvas, $27\frac{1}{4} \times 23\frac{1}{4}$ ($0 \cdot 69 \times 0 \cdot 59$).

Much rubbed, and restored in the shadows and elsewhere; a new patch in the background at the top. X-rays show that the collar was once higher.

The sitter is unknown. The dividers (?)[1] presumably suggested a mathematician, and then the name of Gerolamo Malatini, a mathematician alive *ca.* 1494, who is said to have taught perspective to Giovanni Bellini and to Carpaccio.[2]

The attribution is more often accepted than not; but Gronau[3] in 1909 doubted it, and so did Berenson (1932 and 1936 Lists; not doubted in the 1957 Lists). The face does suggest Gentile, but the hands seem to be in perhaps too free a style. Venturi proposes a painter akin to Lotto.[4] The date may be from about 1500.

PROVENANCE: Perhaps the 'Portrait of an Architect', size 26 in. $\times$ 22$\frac{1}{2}$ in., Gentil Bellini, from Conte Lechi's Collection at Brescia;[5] then, through Irvine, in the Sir William Forbes Collection, and in his Sale, 2 June, 1842 (lot 12). The Forbes picture was in the W. E. Gladstone Sale, 26 June, 1875 (lot 667), bought by Johnson. No. 1213 is said to have been bought from Agnew's *ca.* 1875 by William Walton of Manchester.[6] Said to have been owned by Martin Colnaghi.[7] Purchased in Milan from J. P. Richter, Walker Fund, 1886.[8]

REPRODUCTION: *Illustrations, Italian Schools*, 1937, p. 27. *Plates, Earlier Italian Schools*, 1953, Vol. I, p. 27.

REFERENCES: (1) A. Barclay of the Science Museum (letter in the Gallery archives) kindly enquired into the nature of the instrument, without reaching any certain identification. He thought that it might be a pair of scribing dividers for measuring and marking out lengths; alternatively, a crushing device or a pair of compasses. (2) This suggestion for the sitter seems to be due to Morelli, who in a letter to Layard, 26 October (1885), wrote, 'Si je ne me trompe pas, ce portrait de Gle Bellini pourrait bien représenter le savant Mulattini qui a donné de leçons de perspective aux frères Bellini' (British Museum, Add. MS., 38965, Layard Papers, Vol. XXXV). For Malatini, see in the *Discorsi letti nella R. Accademia di Belle Arti di Venezia*, 1815, the lecture on the Bellini by Francesco Aglietti, p. 34; the authorities quoted are Luca Pacioli's *Summa de Arithmetica*, 1494 (see the text in Italian in R. Buscaroli, *Melozzo da Forlì*, 1938, p. 134, or in Latin in E. Müntz, *Les Archives des Arts*, 1890, p. 36), and a MS.

Trattato della Perspettiva by Daniele Barbaro, the passage being quoted by Jacopo Morelli, *I Codici MSS. Volgari della Libreria Naniana*, 1776, p. 13. (3) Gronau, *Die Künstlerfamilie Bellini*, 1909, p. 50. (4) A. Venturi, *Storia dell'Arte Italiana*, Vol. VII, Part IV, p. 246. (5) No such picture appears to have existed in the Lechi Collection; information kindly supplied by Conte Fausto Lechi, 6 February, 1950. (6) Information from Mr. Hodgson, 1934. (7) N.G. 1913 (but not 1906) Catalogue. (8) Richter (*The Mond Collection*, 1910, I, p. 48) says that it was without attribution when he acquired it.

3099 THE SULTAN MEHMET II

For the inscriptions see below.

Canvas, perhaps transferred from panel, $27\frac{1}{2} \times 20\frac{1}{2}$ (0·70 × 0·52).

There are now only traces of a very much worn and neglected old picture here, almost entirely repainted, especially in the figure.

In the right-hand bottom corner is an inscription, .MCCCCLXXX./ .DIE.XXV.ME / NSIS NOVEM / BRIS. This is only slightly damaged, and is quite old; but the feeble lettering cannot be ascribed to Gentile Bellini (contrast the signature of No. 3911 above). In the left-hand corner, in similar lettering, are the following remains: ( )IL(?) ISQV( )R / ( )TOR ORBIS, and lower down ( )CVNCT-ARE( ). In the interlining of this old inscription, another, more recent, has been inserted; this new inscription is itself much damaged. It is possible that its author had more remains of the old one to go upon than are visible now, but it is also possible that he trusted to his imagination; thus, at the end of the first line he gives VICTOR, which it appears cannot have been the word of the earlier text. It seems, therefore, pointless to quote the legible parts of the new inscription; but it may be recorded that it includes the names of Mehmet and Gentile Bellini.

There can be no reasonable doubt that the sitter is in fact Mehmet II (1432–1481)[1]; the crowns in the top corners of No. 3099, which appear also in Gentile Bellini's medal of the sitter,[2] have not been added. Some iconographical difficulties, such as the neck's not being extremely thick, may be caused by its condition. A drawing at Constantinople with the head in nearly the same pose[3] confirms the identification.

The attribution, on the other hand, is not proved. Stylistic criticism for No. 3099 is not possible; the inscription seems worthless evidence. Gentile Bellini was, no doubt, the most likely author at the Sultan's court; but Gray has good evidence for ascribing a drawing of the sitter to Costanzo da Ferrara, so Gentile Bellini is not the only possible name[4]. It is here doubtfully kept, although the attribution means very little, because it has long been associated with the picture. There is insufficient evidence for saying if No. 3099 is an original picture or a copy.

VERSIONS: A small portrait, in which the head is very similar, was once in Russia.[5] A drawing that may have some connection is referred to above. Portraits of the sitter by Gentile Bellini are stated to have existed in the Zen Collection at Venice and in Paolo Giovio's Museum at Como. The former is said to be a picture now at Northwick Park;[6] the latter is known from a woodcut, which is probably very inaccurate.[7] A portrait of the Sultan and a younger man, in

Swiss private possession, was published by Franz Babinger in 1961.[8] The Sultan is quite closely similar in pose to No. 3099; this picture has recorded on the back an XVIII (?) century attribution to Gentile Bellini.

PROVENANCE: No. 3099 was bought in 1865 by Layard 'from an old man, the son of an Englishman, who had been a contractor in the service of the Republic (of Venice). This contractor had, according to his son's avowal, secured this portrait, with other property, from the Venturi family in discharge of a debt.'[9] Exhibited at Leeds, 1868 (No. 75), and at South Kensington, 1869 (No. 32). Layard Bequest, 1916.[10]

REPRODUCTIONS: *Illustrations, Italian Schools*, 1937, p. 27. *Plates, Earlier Italian Schools*, 1953, Vol. I, p. 28. An earlier state, in which the fur collar is differently restored, is reproduced by L. Thuasne, *Gentile Bellini et Sultan Mohammed II*, 1888, frontispiece.

REFERENCES: (1) For portraits of Mehmet II, see Basil Gray in *The Burlington Magazine*, Vol. LXI (1932), pp. 4 ff. Cf. also Armenag Sakisian in *The Burlington Magazine*, Vol. LXXIV (1939), pp. 172 ff. (2) G. F. Hill, *Corpus of Italian Medals of the Renaissance*, 1930, No. 432. According to Hill, the three crowns stand for Constantinople, Iconium and Trebizond. On Bertoldo's medal, which seems somehow connected with Gentile's, three crowned figures are labelled Greece (apparently for Magna Grecia), Trebizond and Asia; cf. Emil Jacobs in the Prussian *Jahrbuch*, 1927, pp. 1 ff., and Hill, No. 911. See the comment by Tervarent, *Attributs et Symboles dans l'Art Profane*, 1959, Col. 132. (3) Reproduced by Gray, *loc. cit.*, Plate IIa and by Sakisian, *loc. cit.*, Plate Ic. (4) Gray, *loc. cit.*, frontispiece; Sakisian, *loc. cit.*, Plate IIb. Babinger, *loc. cit.*, in note 8, believes that Costanzo da Ferrara left Constantinople before Gentile Bellini arrived. (5) Reproduced in *Apollo*, February 1935, p. 111, belonging to Arthur L. Erlanger, New York. (6) Tancred Borenius, *Catalogue of Pictures at Northwick Park*, 1921, No. 6. (Not Gentile Bellini and not Mehmet.) (7) Gray, *loc. cit.*, Plate IIb. (8) Prof. Babinger kindly sent the articles in which he discusses this picture, in *SZ am Wochenende*, 7/8 January, 1961, p. 52, and in Österreichische Akademie der Wissenschaften, Philosophisch-Historische Klasse, *Sitzungsberichte*, 237. Band, 3. Abhandlung, 1961. (9) Layard MSS. in the National Gallery, where the date is wrongly given as 1856. For the correct date, see Layard's letter to Morelli, 24 October, 1865 (British Museum, Add. MS. 38966, Layard Papers, Vol. XXXVI). (10) For the history of the Layard Collection, see Appendix IV.

After GENTILE BELLINI (?)

3100   THE DOGE NICCOLÒ MARCELLO (?)

Wood, painted surface, 24½ × 17¾ (0·62 × 0·45); painted up to the edges all round.

The flesh has been a good deal stippled by a restorer, especially in the shadows. The nose has been increased in size, in a *pentimento*.

On the back an inscription, perhaps of the eighteenth century: *Nicolaus. Marcello. Dux* | 1474 | *Bellinus: F.* He was Doge, 1473/4. The identification cannot be considered certain, because the features in No. 3100 correspond only moderately well with the medal of this Doge by the Master G T F;[1] but a picture, perhaps from the same design, by Titian in the Vatican is identified as this Doge on some evidence.[2]

The picture is presumably a copy of a portrait from the life; the postulated original may have been by Gentile Bellini. Berenson (1932 Lists) calls No. 3100 Gentile in great part; he accepts it as by Gentile in the 1957 Lists.

PROVENANCE: Perhaps the 'Doge Niccolò Marcello' called Giovanni Bellini in the collection of John Strange, British Resident at Venice, and offered for sale after his death at the European Museum, May 27 sqq., 1799 (No. 8); later in the E. Coxe Sale, 24 April, 1807 (lot 26), as from Mr. Strange's. In 1844, No. 3100 was owned by the Rev. Charles B. Tayler, Chester.[3] Given by Sir William Boxall in 1876 to Sir A. H. Layard;[4] Layard Bequest, 1916.[5]

REPRODUCTION: *Illustrations, Italian Schools*, 1937, p. 30. *Plates, Earlier Italian Schools*, 1953, Vol. I, p. 29.

REFERENCES: (1) Hill, *Corpus*, 1930, No. 434. (2) For the Vatican Titian cf. Crowe and Cavalcaselle, *Life and Times of Titian*, 1877, I, pp. 112/3 and Hadeln in the *Repertorium für Kunstwissenschaft*, 1910, pp. 101 ff. Reproduced in the Klassiker der Kunst *Titian*, 5th edition, Plate 113. (3) Letter in the Gallery archives. (4) Letter from Layard to Morelli, 9 September, 1876 (British Museum, Add. MS. 38966, Layard Papers, Vol. XXXVI). (5) For the history of the Layard Collection, see Appendix IV.

See also Ascribed to VITTORE CARPACCIO, No. 3098

GIOVANNI BELLINI
active *ca.* 1459–died 1516

Also *Giambellino*; son of Jacopo Bellini, and brother, perhaps younger brother, of Gentile (q.v.). There is no sure evidence for assigning a year to his birth; Gronau (Klassiker der Kunst *Bellini*, 1930) scrupulously avoids doing so. In 1459 he is stated to have acted as a legal witness, being at that time resident apart from his father and brother.* An altarpiece, signed by Jacopo, Gentile and Giovanni, and apparently dated 1460, is recorded to have existed. Giovanni lived and worked in Venice but does not appear to have been employed by the state until 1479; his important works for the *Sala del Gran Consiglio* were destroyed in 1577. (Some idea of his work of this type can be had from the *Martyrdom of S. Mark*, executed mostly by Vittore Belliniano, in the Scuola di S. Marco at Venice; Gronau, Plate 188.)

A definition of Bellini's *oeuvre* is one of the hardest problems in the history of painting. The first difficulty is, despite the destructions, the enormous number of existing pictures, many of them signed, and in one way or another more or less Bellinesque. It is obvious that Bellini had assistants to help him in his studio; indeed, there is documentary proof of that. But the question of what pictures are entirely or for practical purposes Bellini's own is answered largely by personal taste; there is therefore a considerable divergence of view.

It may be remarked in this connection that Morelli's mechanical

* Paoletti *Raccolta di Documenti*, I, *I Bellini*, 1894, p. 11; Archivio di Stato, Venice, deeds of Giuseppe Moisis, Busta 727 (the compiler feels bound to record that he was not fortunate enough to find this document).

theories for distinguishing a genuine Bellini are now exploded; it seems now clear that the signature of an autograph work may be in capitals or in script, with the l's of the same or different lengths. Further, Morelli's disregard of many signatures is seen to be frivolous; if a picture is authentically signed (and many are), it is by Bellini or from his shop, not by an independent painter. Cf. for instance Gronau, *Spätwerke*, 1928, pp. 20 ff. (The Italian translation is in *Pinacotheca*, I, 1928/9, pp. 120 ff.)

Many of the existing Bellinesque pictures are very much damaged, which seriously impedes their classification. It would certainly ease the problem to date them; but that matter offers for the early period almost insuperable difficulties of its own.

The earliest signed and dated works are the *Madonna degli Alberetti* (1487), and the Frari and Murano Altarpieces of 1488. Not only at this time was Bellini by no means young; the style of the two altarpieces differs so much that most of the painting of the one in the Frari has been supposed several years earlier than the date inscribed. This point, which is put very well by Fry, *Giovanni Bellini*, 1900, p. 33, may be true.

Among the existing works, with more or less justification ascribed to Bellini in an earlier time, there is some evidence for dating the four *Carità* altarpieces in the Academy at Venice; these pictures, which are damaged, have recently been cleaned.* It has been thought that a polyptych in SS. Giovanni e Paolo at Venice was being executed *ca.* 1464. This date has been rejected by Giles Robertson in *The Burlington Magazine*, Vol. XCII, 1950, p. 26 (but see his correction in the *Journal of the Warburg and Courtauld Institutes*, 1960, p. 51), and by E. Arslan in the *Bollettino d'Arte*, 1952, pp. 127 ff.; on grounds of costume, a date *ca.* 1475 would be suitable. There is an unreliable tradition that a damaged *Pietà* in the Doge's Palace was once dated 1472.† The other pictures with dates before 1487 in Gronau's 1930 Volume (apart from a portrait of 1474) are a *Resurrection* at Berlin between 1475 and 1478/9, which may be incorrect (see the entry for Andrea Busati, No. 3084); and No. 750 of this Gallery, Venetian School, which can hardly be relevant. The Bagatti-Valsecchi *S. Giustina* may have been finished by 1475 (Bellini Exhibition, 1949, No. 56; see also Pallucchini, *Giovanni Bellini*, 1959, p. 137). There is an apparently reliable statement that the San Giobbe altarpiece (Gronau, Plate 85) is early; this picture is surely Bellini's, but it cannot be very early.

* The four triptychs were Nos. 6–21 of the Bellini Exhibition of 1949; but for their correct arrangement, see Rodolfo Gallo in *Arte Veneta*, 1949, pp. 136 ff. It is disputed if any of these triptychs had or had not been begun by the end of 1462, the phrasing of the document concerning this point being unclear. See Sandra Moschini Marconi, Catalogue of the Accademia at Venice (XIV and XV centuries), 1955, pp. 77 ff., with bibliography. In the *Journal of the Warburg and Courtauld Institutes*, 1960, pp. 49 ff., Giles Robertson suggests that the altarpieces may have been commissioned of Jacopo Bellini and executed in part by Gentile and Giovanni Bellini.

† Bellini Exhibition, 1949 (No. 50), reproduced in the catalogue, with the extensive sixteenth–century alterations removed. Signed by Giovanni Bellini. Hendy ascribes it to Gentile, and this seems correct for much of the picture. Presumably Giovanni Bellini was entrusted with finishing a work left incomplete by Gentile, and did enough to justify his adding his own signature; some parts, indeed, such as the head and hands of Christ and the crown of thorns, differ from what could be expected of Gentile, and may be held to be the work of Giovanni adapting himself to some indications by Gentile.

The evidence for the chronology of Bellini's early works is meagre; and it must be considered in relation to a group of pictures, which (unlike some of those just mentioned) are fully worthy of Bellini and are strongly under Mantegna's influence. One of the principal works of this group is No. 726 below, where the matter receives some further discussion. See further Giles Robertson, *The Earlier Work of Giovanni Bellini* in the *Journal of the Warburg and Courtauld Institutes*, Vol. XXIII, 1960, pp. 45 ff.

Bellini's late style also presents difficult problems, partly because several of the most important works are normally hung in a bad light, or are much damaged, or both. One of the chief pictures of this period is the San Zaccaria altarpiece (dated 1505); others are the *Baptism* in S. Corona at Vicenza (not earlier than 1500; D. Bortolan, *S. Corona ... in Vicenza*, 1889, pp. 263 ff.), and the S. Giovanni Crisostomo altarpiece at Venice (dated 1513).

It may be admitted that to say a picture is by Bellini or not, or to attribute on stylistic grounds a date to it, is to make an ill-defined statement, however true it may appear to be. This point should be remembered in the commentaries below.

It may be added that Bellini was a variable painter. Trained no doubt by his father Jacopo, he was at one time strongly influenced by Mantegna. The visit of Antonello da Messina to Venice in 1475/6 seems certainly to have affected his development, though it is possible that Bellini influenced Antonello as much as Antonello influenced Bellini. Towards the end of his life, Bellini developed a style comparable with the styles of Giorgione and the young Titian; here again, the innovation may be due as much to Bellini himself as to the younger painters' influence on him.

189   THE DOGE LEONARDO LOREDAN, FULL-FACE

Signed on a *cartellino*, IOANNES BELLINVS. (the second L taller than the other letters).

Poplar,[1] painted surface, $24\frac{1}{4} \times 17\frac{3}{4}$ (0·615 × 0·45).

The figure is in excellent state, though the dress suffers somewhat from undercleaning. *Pentimenti* in the outlines of the skull-cap and the chin on the left-hand side.

Leonardo Loredan, born in 1436,[2] was Doge from 1501 to 1521. The age of the sitter and the style of the painting make it likely that the picture is from not long after 1501.

PROVENANCE: Two unidentified seals on the back. Acquired from the Grimani Palace, Venice, by the first Lord Cawdor,[3] who died in 1821. Beckford Collection, Fonthill; sale catalogue of 16[4] October, 1822 (lot 65), but this sale was not held; not in the 1823 sale, but retained by Beckford, from whom purchased in 1844.

REPRODUCTION: *Illustrations, Italian Schools*, 1937, p. 30. *Plates, Earlier Italian Schools*, 1953, Vol. I, p. 30.

REFERENCES: **(1)** Letter from B. J. Rendle, of the Forest Products Research Laboratory, in the Gallery archives. **(2)** Andrea da Mosto, *I Dogi di Venezia*, 1939, p. 149. There are numerous portraits of this doge, which like No. 189 are not authenticated by inscriptions or coats of arms. Yet it appears unnecessary to labour the point that the sitter is correctly identified; cf. for instance Hill, *Corpus of Italian Medals*, 1930, No. 452 and Plate 85, or Alessandro Leopardi's relief, reproduced by Venturi, *Storia dell'Arte Italiana*, Vol. X, Part I, Fig. 308. (**3**) According to the Fonthill catalogue of 1822. Not Lord Cawdor Sale, 5/6 June, 1800. The statement in the 1929 catalogue of the National Gallery that No. 189 was lot 21 of an Anon. Sale, London, 7 February, 1807, is a mistake. It is likely that Beckford had it already by January, 1814; see Boyd Alexander, *Life at Fonthill*, 1957, pp. 142/3. (**4**) So misprinted for 15.

280 THE VIRGIN AND CHILD

Signed on a *cartellino*, IOANNES / BELLINVS.P. (partly effaced; the second L taller than the other letters).

Poplar,[1] $35\frac{3}{4} \times 25\frac{1}{2}$ (0·91 × 0·65); painted up to the edges all round.

Very good condition. The principal damage is a moderate wearing of the shadows of the Child's head and of the landscape right. A few *pentimenti*, the most obvious being in the lower outline of the Virgin's left hand; the Virgin's mantle descended originally at the left where it leaves the jaw, vertically to a point near the Child's left knee.

Often called the *Madonna of the Pomegranate*, which the object held by the Virgin does not seem certainly to be.

The design is related to that of the full-length *Virgin and Child*, No. 286 of the present catalogue, signed by Tacconi and dated 1489. Since the Virgin's raised knee is more clearly understandable in Tacconi's full-length figure, where there is a foot-stool, than in No. 280, it is probable that there existed a design or picture by Bellini at full length; it seems likely that this would have been simply the original of the Tacconi rather than a full-length replica of No. 280. In either case the present picture may be held to be from within a few years of 1489, either earlier or later.[2] Stylistic evidence for its date is somewhat unsure, since there are hardly any fixed points for comparison. Most critics date it at various times during the 1480's; Gronau,[3] however, thinks it of the 1490's, which is possible.

VERSIONS: A picture with some variations is at Worcester, Mass.[4] The Child with the Virgin's supporting hand appears inverted in Mocetto's altarpiece in Santa Maria in Organo, Verona.[5] The design is related to that of Tacconi, No. 286 of this Gallery; partial versions of this in the Scalzi at Venice, at Padua (signed (?) by Filippo Mazzola), in New York (ex-Nemes), with the Virgin's eyes changed and a donor added (signed by Giovanni Bellini), and (a version of the last) at Christie's, 9 June, 1939 (lot 115), also with a signature of Giovanni Bellini.[6]

PROVENANCE: Purchased from Baron Francesco Galvagna, Venice, 1855.[7] Cleaned Pictures Exhibition at the National Gallery, 1947/8 (No. 26).

REPRODUCTION: *Illustrations, Italian Schools*, 1937, p. 32 (without the parapet and signature). *Plates, Earlier Italian Schools*, 1953, Vol. I, p. 31.

REFERENCES: (**1**) Letter from B. J. Rendle, of the Forest Products Research Laboratory, in the Gallery archives. (**2**) Cf. Berenson, *Venetian Painting in America*, 1916, pp. 114/5; he wrongly deduces that No. 280 must be earlier than the Tacconi of 1489. (**3**) Gronau, Klassiker der Kunst *Bellini*, 1930, note to Plate 124. (**4**) Reproduced by Berenson, *loc. cit.* (**5**) Venturi, *Storia dell'Arte*

Italiana, Vol. VII, Part IV, Fig. 407. (6) Cf. Hadeln in the *Zeitschrift für bildende Kunst*, 1912, pp. 289 ff., where the Scalzi and Nemes pictures are reproduced. The latter is Gronau, Klassiker der Kunst *Bellini*, 1930, Plate 117 with note; it was published by the Metropolitan Museum at New York (*The Michael Fried-sam Collection*, 1932, No. 61), but is now in the Friedsam Library of S. Bona-venture's School, St. Bonaventure, New York (letter from Margaretta M. Salinger, 11 February, 1949, in the Gallery archives). The picture at Padua is claimed to be signed *Filipus Maz*(olus) *d*(is.) *Joanis* / (Bel)*li*? (ni p .); see A. Moschetti in the *Bollettino del Museo Civico di Padova*, Vol. X (1907), pp. 151 ff., with a reproduction on p. 152. In the Padua catalogue, 1957, p. 102, the inscription is stated to be illegible. There is a photograph in the Gallery archives of the Christie picture. (7) Mentioned in this collection by Giulio Lecomte, *Venezia*, 1844, p. 276 and by Gianjacopo Fontana, *Manuale ad Uso del Fores-tiere in Venezia*, 1847, p. 238 and *Venezia Monumentale Pittoresca*, 1850 (?), p. 168 of text volume.

599 'THE MADONNA OF THE MEADOW'

Originally on panel (transferred in 1949), painted surface, $26\frac{1}{2} \times 34$ (0·67 × 0·86).

The picture has recently been freed from nineteenth-century restora-tions, and earlier reproductions of it are misleading. The flesh is not well preserved, especially in the shadows; some of these have suffered con-siderably from losses and wearing. The Virgin's dress and the landscape are on the whole in good condition. The recent restorations have been confined to the minimum. *Pentimenti* in the Virgin's headdress.

A detail in the background of a fight between a white bird and a snake has been claimed to be a reminiscence of Virgil, *Georgics*, II, 319/20.[1]

No. 599 has no signature, but it is now generally agreed that it is close in style to Giovanni Bellini's late works. It is particularly near to a Triptych once at Berlin; although not necessarily executed by the same hand, it is certainly near in date. Gronau[2] has given good reasons for dating the Berlin Triptych within a year or two of 1505.

As for the execution of No. 599, it appears practically impossible to fix a standard for Bellini's autograph works of 1500–1510.[3] It would therefore be difficult to claim certainty for the attribution of No. 599 to Bellini himself; yet it would seem capricious to reject as unworthy of the man himself the landscape in No. 599, or the drapery round the Virgin's neck, or her sleeve.[4]

At one time No. 599 was ascribed to the Pseudo-Basaiti, but there seems to be no justification for thinking that there ever was such a painter.[5] Some other attributions for No. 599 have also been made.[6]

DERIVATIONS: The castle in the background reappears with slight variations in pictures at New York (Bache Collection);[7] in the J. G. Johnson Collection, Philadelphia;[8] at Ottawa;[9] and in Lord Wemyss' Collection.[10] The main group in No. 599 recurs, with considerable variations in the Christ, in the Capitol;[11] among other pictures apparently derived, mention may be made of two Catenas at Liverpool[12] and Budapest,[13] and a picture ascribed to Lattanzio da Rimini at Washington.[14] The head and hands of the Virgin in No. 599 are more or less repeated in a female saint in a *Sacra Conversazione* in the Morgan Library, New York,[15] a figure that is copied in yet other pictures.

PROVENANCE: Purchased from Achille Farina, Faenza,[16] 1858.[17]

REPRODUCTION: *Illustrations, Italian Schools*, 1937, p. 21 (before cleaning). *Plates, Earlier Italian Schools*, 1953, Vol. I, p. 32.

REFERENCES: (1) See E. Wind in *The Burlington Magazine*, Vol. XCII (1950), p. 350. (2) See Gronau, Klassiker der Kunst *Bellini*, 1930, Plate 148; Gronau, *Spätwerke des Giovanni Bellini*, 1928, pp. 1 ff. Recorded in *Arte Veneta*, 1949, p. 191, to have been destroyed during the last war. (3) If one may judge from a contemporary mention, one may hold that Bellini's best picture of this period is the San Zaccaria Altarpiece of 1505 (Gronau, Klassiker der Kunst *Bellini*, 1930, p. xv and Plate 160); but this picture is much damaged. (4) No. 599 is called autograph Bellini by Gronau, 1930, Plate 149, and by Berenson, 1932 Lists. Dussler, *Giovanni Bellini*, 1935, p. 147, calls it a studio piece; in his book of the same title, Sammlung Schroll, 1949, pp. 53 and 95, he seems to accept it. (5) No. 599 was for a time called Basaiti: cf. for instance the National Gallery catalogue of 1859; also Crowe and Cavalcaselle, *Painting in North Italy*, I, 1871, p. 267, or ed. Borenius, I, 1912, p. 272, where the authors profess to see the influence of Palma as well as that of Bellini. When Basaiti's name appeared impossible for this and other pictures, a Pseudo-Basaiti was invented; see Gronau, *Spätwerke des Giovanni Bellini*, 1928, pp. 12 ff. (6) J. P. Richter, *Italian Art in the National Gallery*, 1883, p. 80, called it Catena. Frizzoni in the *Archivio Storico Italiano*, 1879, pp. 411/2, called it Bissolo; in the revision of this essay published in his *Arte Italiana del Rinascimento*, 1891, p. 322, Frizzoni accepted it as a Basaiti. (7) Gronau, 1930, Plate 168. (8) J. G. Johnson Collection, No. 183, reproduced in the large catalogue. The picture is without attribution; it is a *Virgin and Child* on a design occurring frequently in Bartolomeo Veneto, Bissolo, etc. (e.g. Bissolo, No. 3083 of the National Gallery). Berenson in the catalogue remarks that the landscape is similar to that of No. 599. (9) *Christ Blessing* at Ottawa; 1957 Catalogue, No. 328, as Giovanni Bellini or his School (reproduced). (10) Lord Wemyss; Unknown Subject, 11 in. × 27⅞ in., as Piero di Cosimo. Photograph in the Gallery archives. (11) Gronau, *Spätwerke des Giovanni Bellini*, 1928, Plate VI. (12) Giles Robertson, *Vincenzo Catena*, 1954, No. 10, with reproduction. (13) Robertson, *op. cit.*, No. 6, with reproduction. (14) Reproduced in the Book of Illustrations. (15) Gronau, 1930, Plate 151. (16) Not Florence, as stated formerly in the National Gallery catalogues; see Eastlake's note-book, and *Journals and Correspondence of Lady Eastlake*, 1895, II, pp. 103/4. He is presumably the man who has an entry in Thieme-Becker. Eastlake notes it under Giovanni Bellini's name at Farina's. (17) 1859 Catalogue as Basaiti. The attribution was changed to Giovanni Bellini in the 1898 Catalogue, on comparison with the Giovanelli picture (Gronau, 1930, Plate 152). No. 599 was given back to Basaiti in the 1913 Catalogue, and remained so ascribed in that of 1929.

726 THE AGONY IN THE GARDEN

A winged *putto* in the sky bears a chalice and wafer; in the distance, Judas and a crowd of soldiers.

Wood, painted surface, 32 × 50 (0·81 × 1·27).

In general in very good state; but Christ's head and hands have lost much of their quality. Elsewhere, the worst damage is in the parts of the pinkish clouds in half-shadow, which are largely new. A few *pentimenti*, e.g. in the rock before which Christ kneels, and in the building on the hill-top right.

The picture has long been held to be one of Bellini's most important early works, but there is no very good evidence for dating it.

A drawing of the same subject in Jacopo Bellini's London sketchbook, which Goloubew dates *ca.* 1440/50, is in a general way of similar design.[1] Mantegna's predella panel of the subject at Tours,[2] from the San Zeno altarpiece, is datable 1457/9; there seem to be reminiscences of Jacopo Bellini or of some other early design, and the resemblances to No. 726 are not particularly close. Another Mantegna of the same subject, No. 1417 of this Gallery, is nearly related to the picture at Tours; but in several of the details where No. 1417 differs from the latter, it approaches No. 726. Thus, Christ's attitude in Nos. 1417 and 726 is almost the same, but inverted;[3] and the winged *putti* are similar in form.

It is certain that Mantegna was precocious, and possible that Bellini was not; if there is no evidence to the contrary, it may be accepted as likely that Bellini's No. 726 was derived from Mantegna's No. 1417.

Mantegna's picture has been identified with an undescribed small work painted in 1459, but this identification is not proved and is not always accepted. Since No. 1417 seems more mature than Mantegna's picture of 1457/9 at Tours, it may be from the earlier 1460's. No. 726 seems therefore unlikely to be much before about 1465.

This dubious date of the middle or late 1460's does not square very well with the dates claimed for some other pictures ascribed to Giovanni Bellini, referred to in the biography above. The evidence is meagre, yet almost contradictory; but in any case No. 726 is accepted as by Giovanni Bellini, and as one of his early works. It is near in style to *The Transfiguration* in the Correr Museum at Venice; No. 1233 below is also near in style.

PROVENANCE: Apparently owned by Consul Joseph Smith (d. 1770) at Venice.[4] Presumably Sir Joshua Reynolds Sale, 13 March, 1795[5] (lot 48), bought by Walton, Beckford Sale, Fonthill, 16 (for 15) October, 1822[6] (lot 77); the same, 10 October, 1823 (lot 77), bought by Bentley. Edward Harman Sale, 28 May, 1847 (lot 412), bought by Bromley.[7] Rev. W. Davenport Bromley Collection, where seen by Waagen;[8] exhibited at Manchester, 1857 (Provisional Catalogue, No. 196; Definitive Catalogue, No. 89); Sale, 12 June, 1863 (lot 62), bought for the National Gallery.

REPRODUCTION: *Illustrations, Italian Schools*, 1937, p. 33. *Plates, Earlier Italian Schools*, 1953, Vol. I, p. 33.

REFERENCES: (1) Goloubew, *Les Dessins de Jacopo Bellini*, Vol. I, 1912, Plate L. (2) Reproduced by Kristeller, *Andrea Mantegna*, London, 1901, Fig. 62. (3) It is, however, an iconographical peculiarity of No. 726 that Christ has no halo. (4) Information kindly supplied by Benedict Nicolson. Among Smith's pictures (according to a list of the English Royal Pictures of 1817/8), No. 326 is as follows: 'Andrea Mantegna. Christ praying on the Mount, & the disciples sleeping, on board. 2 ft. 8½ by 4 ft. 3'. This list, in which is incorporated Smith's lists, is only a copy of an earlier inventory, which, if it exists, has not yet come to light. The entry seems to refer to No. 726. Not found in the catalogue of the Smith Sale of 1776 (Lugt, No. 2550); it has not been established how the picture passed afterwards to Reynolds (?) and Beckford. For information about Consul Smith, see K. T. Parker, *Canaletto Drawings at Windsor Castle*, 1948, Introduction, and Anthony Blunt and Edward Croft-Murray, *Venetian Drawings of the XVII & XVIII Centuries at Windsor Castle*, 1957, Introduction. (5) Many catalogues bear the intended (?) date of 5 March, 1794. (6) With identifying description. This sale did not take place. No. 726 is already mentioned in the Beckford Collection in James Storer's *Description of Fonthill Abbey*, 1812, p. 20;

the passage is quoted by Lewis Melville, *The Life and Letters of William Beckford*, 1910, p. 365. In John Rutter, *A Description of Fonthill Abbey*, 2nd edition, 1822, No. 726 appears to be mentioned twice, on pp. 45 and 52; at least, it would seem unlikely that Beckford owned two such pictures. (7) As from Fonthill. (8) Waagen, *Treasures*, 1854, iii, p. 376, as Bellini; hitherto always as Mantegna.

1233 THE BLOOD OF THE REDEEMER

Christ stands holding the Cross marked . I.N.R.I., on which hangs a crown of thorns; a kneeling angel receives in a chalice the blood from the wound at His side. A parapet behind is ornamented with two classical reliefs, described below; that to the left is a sacrifice at an altar marked DIS MANIB / AVR(EL)IVS. / (   )TI / , the rest of the inscription being hidden.

Wood, painted surface, $18\frac{1}{2} \times 13\frac{1}{2}$ (0·47 × 0·34).

The condition of the two principal figures is very good; some of the shadows on Christ's flesh have been rather rubbed, and in places retouched. There are also various retouches to reduce the effect of cracks. The chalice, which was once of gold, is mostly modern. The pavement is to a large extent new. The bas-reliefs, though somewhat worn, are in most parts well preserved; the feet of the naked man in the one to the right are modern. The landscape and sky have been somewhat damaged, but the buildings right and left are well preserved.

The mystic subject is not uncommon;[1] a picture by Crivelli in the Poldi-Pezzoli Museum may be compared, in which S. Francis takes the place of the angel.[2]

The classical reliefs of No. 1233 do not seem to recur on any other example. On the right, an armed man places his right hand or more probably both hands palm upwards on a tripod; a naked man stands with folded arms behind him; and before him, on a seat of which the arms are winged sphinxes, sits a man in armour but bareheaded (?), holding a wand of Mercury in his left hand and gesticulating with his right. Saxl thinks the subject is Mucius Scaevola before Porsenna, which seems impossible.[3] The other relief is a pagan sacrifice at an altar inscribed as noted above; examination shows that the letters of the word *Aurelius* are complete except for the *e* and the *l*, which are mostly hidden by the angel's wing and are symbolized by three nearly parallel strokes. The man sacrificing holds an ewer in his left hand, and raises his right arm above the altar flame; it may be assumed that he is pouring wine from a patera, but Christ's hand in front conceals his action. Behind the altar is a naked man holding a stick; to the left a satyr playing a double pipe.

It was in the 'Squarcionesque' tradition at Padua to adorn pictures with miscellaneous classical remains; and the principal monument of the kind, the Eremitani frescoes by Mantegna and others, includes some details very like parts of the reliefs on No. 1233. Thus, in the *Judgment of S. James*, there is a throne of sphinxes and a pagan sacrifice at an altar; in *S. James on his Way to Martyrdom*, there is a satyr with a double pipe; and in the *Martyrdom of S. James*, there are similar types of armour. These three frescoes date probably from the middle 1450's.[4]

Saxl is probably right in maintaining that in No. 1233 the reliefs in some way foreshadow or comment upon the main subject;[5] but as their own meaning is not very clear, no precise statement can be made. Yet it is perhaps not without significance that the actual act of pagan sacrifice at the left seems to be cancelled by Christ's outstretched hand.

The picture is by almost every critic accepted as a genuine Bellini, near in date to No. 726 above. The execution of No. 1233, which is not appreciably marred by damage, is weaker than that of No. 726; but it does not follow that No. 1233 must be earlier, and the statements concerning the date of No. 726 above apply fairly exactly to No. 1233 also.[6] The influence of Mantegna is marked in the picture, e.g. in the proportion and pose of the Christ.

PROVENANCE: An unidentified seal on the back. Robert Prioleau Roupell Sale, 25 June, 1887 (lot 63)[7], bought by Murray; purchased from Charles Fairfax Murray, Clarke Fund, 1887.

REPRODUCTION: *Illustrations, Italian Schools*, 1937, p. 34. *Plates, Earlier Italian Schools*, 1953, Vol. I, p.34.

REFERENCES: (1) Cf. E. Panofsky, '*Imago Pietatis*', in the Festschrift Friedländer, 1927, pp. 261 ff., and F. Saxl, *Pagan Sacrifice in the Italian Renaissance*, in *The Warburg Journal*, April 1939, pp. 346 ff. (2) The Crivelli is reproduced by F. Drey, *Carlo Crivelli*, 1927, Plate X. An earlier variant of the subject at Venice is on the back of a polyptych in San Zaccaria (reproduced by Van Marle, *Development of the Italian Schools of Painting*, Vol. XVII, p. 12); according to the inscription on it, this subject there is connected with a relic of the Holy Blood in the Chapel. An example was ordered of Bartolomeo di David in 1510 for a Compagnia del Corpo di Cristo; Milanesi, *Documenti per la Storia dell'Arte Senese*, III, 1856, p. 43. (3) Saxl, *loc. cit.*, p. 351. This had already been suggested by J. P. Richter, *Lectures on the National Gallery*, 1898, p. 36. (4) For the date, cf. the biography of Mantegna in this catalogue; reproductions in Venturi, *Storia dell' Arte Italiana*, Vol. VII, Part III, Figs. 65, 68, 72. Most of these frescoes were terribly damaged during the last war. (5) Saxl, *loc. cit.* (6) In the *Journal of the Warburg and Courtauld Institutes*, 1960, p. 46, Giles Robertson, following a suggestion by J. Wilde, says that the date is unlikely to be after 1464, when the Pope forbade further discussion of the worship of the Holy Blood, about which there had been controversy since 1462. (7) As Vivarini.

1440   S. DOMINIC

In his right hand a lily, and a book labelled *Sanct'. Dominic'*. On the parapet is a *cartellino* with the signature, IOANIS BELLIN OP.; beneath the *cartellino*, a date M.D XV, and on each side of it the words of a half-effaced inscription, IMAGO FRATRIS and THEODORI VRBINATIS.

Canvas, 24¾ × 19½ (0·63 × 0·495); but the edges of the painted area are new, and the original size may have been slightly smaller.

The picture has suffered somewhat from relining, the marks of the supporting canvas being particularly noticeable in the face; but the rubbed effect is exaggerated by undercleaning. Apart from this, the face is in good state, the repairs being of a local character, obvious and not extensive. The hand is less well preserved. The main part of the background is in good condition.

There are many *pentimenti*, which were the subject of an incorrect note by Hadeln.[1] The outlines of the right temple and especially of the skull-cap were at one time considerably lower. But the change to the present form of the skull-cap occurred early on; for the bud of the lily is cut short, not by the first outline, but by the present outline. The lily bud and the lily flower just above it are now partly covered by the halo, which was painted later. But the patterning of the present green background at no point cuts into the lily or the halo; it would seem, therefore, that the patterning was painted last. On the other hand, a green colour for the background was one of the very first things painted; green shows through, not only where the halo is rubbed, but also where the addition to the skull-cap is rubbed.

In the lower part of the picture, the hand was painted later than the lily-stalk or the book, which at one moment met each other with nothing obvious to support them. X-rays prove that the white dress does not continue under the book, but are not clear with regard to the lily-stalk. The book never went below the parapet; its red binding continues beneath the white label on it.

The above facts seem incapable of explanation except as *pentimenti*, which may have dragged on over a period of time, but would not indicate at any moment a change of subject. So far as the compiler can observe, the hand is indistinguishable in style of painting from the face. If it is granted that the hand is by the original painter, the lily (which was painted before the hand) is part of the original picture. If the lily is original, there is no reason to doubt that the subject was always meant to be S. Dominic. Or, to argue the other way round, if one imagines that at one time the lily was not intended, the hand (which was painted later) would have to be sacrificed too; but the book would remain (the white habit does not continue beneath the book), although no hand would be there to support it. It seems indeed clear that S. Dominic was always intended. It is not an argument that the halo is painted over the lily; the picture was clearly painted in stages, the halo being perhaps the last except for the patterning of the curtain, but no change of subject can be deduced.

The *cartellino* with signature has a genuine air, whether it is taken as an autograph signature or a studio mark. But the date, though old, is clearly in a rougher style; and its position outside the *cartellino* is suspicious. Although probably added, it may nevertheless record a good tradition, and there is no need to doubt that the picture was in fact painted in 1515.

Hadeln's theory,[1] on the other hand, is that the picture was originally a portrait of Fra Teodoro da Urbino, and only later turned into a *S. Dominic*. As has been stated, the picture seems clearly always to have been a *S. Dominic*; but the inscription concerning Fra Teodoro remains to be considered. Hadeln thinks that the *cartellino* with signature replaces a word of this inscription, such as *Venerabilis*; this particular word would seem too long for the space, but the thing is theoretically possible. Nevertheless, the inscription is complete as it stands, nor is a word suitable to go between *Fratris* and *Theodori* easily imagined; and on the other hand there is no trace whatsoever of effaced letters in the region of the *cartellino*, and the signature, as has been stated, has a genuine air. It seems therefore reasonable to reverse Hadeln's theory, and say that *Imago Fratris Theodori Urbinatis* was written after the *cartellino*; if the letters have been effaced, it does not mean that they were written earlier than other letters on the picture that have not been effaced, but that at one time or another, perhaps comparatively recently, they were considered uninteresting.

The inscription concerning Fra Teodoro seems, therefore, to be an addition. The letters are too much damaged to be seen very clearly; in the absence of evidence to the contrary, they could be held to be contemporaneous with the insertion of the date of 1515. It cannot be stated definitely why such an addition should have been made; but it is reasonable to suppose that the *model* for the S. Dominic was in fact Fra Teodoro, and that some owner, and preferably the first owner, of the picture knew this and considered it worth recording. It seems that the only mention of Fra Teodoro is of 1514, among the Dominicans of S. Zanipolo.[2]

The attribution of the picture has been disputed. It was long catalogued as by Gentile Bellini; in the years when small weight was allowed to Giambellino's signatures, most critics accepted this, although already in 1909 Gronau[3] saw the stylistic difficulty of associating it with Gentile. Recently, Gronau[4] and Berenson[5] have called it Giovanni. There seems, indeed, little justification for neglecting the signature; and the problem is limited to whether it is by Giovanni himself or from his studio. The technique of a work on canvas cannot easily be compared with that of panel pictures; but the very high quality of No. 1440 makes it reasonable to call it Giovanni himself, although (as is pointed out in the biography) the exact meaning of that phrase is ill-defined. As has been suggested above, the date of 1515 may well be correct; in which case, it would be one of Giovanni's last works.

PROVENANCE: Probably in Palazzo Pesaro, Venice, in 1797.[6] In the collection of Jules Soulages of Toulouse, largely formed *ca.* 1830/40. This collection was bought by a syndicate and brought to England; 1856 Catalogue (No. 582); exhibited at Manchester, 1857 (Provisional Catalogue, No. 1097; Definitive Catalogue, No. 76). Bought by the South Kensington (Victoria and Albert) Museum, 1856; exhibited at Leeds, 1868 (No. 90); lent by the Victoria and Albert Museum, 1895.

REPRODUCTION: *Illustrations, Italian Schools*, 1937, p. 28. *Plates, Earlier Italian Schools*, 1953, Vol. I, p. 35.

REFERENCES: (1) Detlev Freiherr von Hadeln in the *Repertorium für Kunstwissenschaft*, 1907, pp. 536/7. (2) Pietro Paoletti, *La Scuola Grande di San Marco*, 1929, p. 152. (3) Gronau, *Die Künstlerfamilie Bellini*, 1909, p. 50. (4) Gronau, Klassiker der Kunst *Bellini*, 1930, Plate 177 with note. (5) Berenson, 1957 lists. (6) Inventory of Pietro and Giovanni Pesaro, 1797, No. B17, 'Gio.

Bellino, S. Domenico col giglio, in tela,' size 1 ft. 10 in. × 1 ft. 5 in. Venetian measure; see G. Fiocco, *Palazzo Pesaro*, 1925, pp. 28/9 and 36. Not among the 24 lots of the Pesaro Sale in London, 9 July, 1831 (Lugt, No. 12716).

3912 PIETÀ

Inscribed on the background, $\overline{\text{IC}}$ and $\overline{\text{XC}}$.

Wood, painted surface, $37\frac{1}{4} \times 28\frac{1}{4}$ (0·945 × 0·715). Painted up to the edges all round; but traces here and there of incised lines marking the four edges of the paint prove that it has not been cut.

The face of the angel to the right has been much changed by repaint; that of the other angel is in very good condition, and his aureole is largely original. Christ's face has suffered a good deal from a crack, part of the right eye being new; this is not the only damage in this region, but parts, e.g. the mouth, are quite reliable. The rest of the picture is in fair condition, although the above-mentioned crack stretches from top to bottom across the picture; the shadows have cracked a good deal and in some cases been made up.

An early work, but probably later than No. 726 above. By almost every critic accepted as an authentic Bellini.

Richter[1] suggested that it was the top compartment of an altarpiece. It is true that a *Pietà* in the Vatican occupied such a position with regard to the Pesaro altarpiece, but many of Bellini's *Pietàs* are complete pictures, the example in the Brera being a particularly clear case; the perspective of No. 3912 does not support Richter's hypothesis, nor is the absence of a signature decisive.

VARIANT: The Christ reappears inverted in a picture at Berlin, No. 1170A, and reproduced in the Illustrations, reasonably ascribed to Lazzaro Bastiani.[2]

PROVENANCE: Stated to be from the collections of Conte Nuvoloni, Mantua, and the Cav. Cesare Menghini, Mantua.[3] Acquired in 1889 by Richter for Ludwig Mond; exhibited at the New Gallery, 1894/5 (No. 119); Mond Bequest, 1924.

REPRODUCTION: *Illustrations, Italian Schools*, 1937, p. 34. *Plates, Earlier Italian Schools*, 1953, Vol. I, p. 36.

REFERENCES: (1) J. P. Richter, *The Mond Collection*, 1910, I, p. 71. (2) Recorded to have been destroyed during the last war; see *Arte Veneta*, 1949, p. 191. (3) As Mantegna; cf. Richter, *op. cit.*, Table of Contents. There can be little doubt that it is the picture referred to in a letter from Morelli to Layard, 12 November, 1874 (British Museum, Add. MS. 38963, Layard Papers, Vol. XXXIII): 'une "Pietà" de Jean Bellin. Ce tableau appartient à un Monsieur de Mantoue, qui croit d'y posséder un ouvrage de Mantegna'.

3913 THE VIRGIN AND CHILD

Signed on a *cartellino*: IOANNES BELLINVS (the second L taller than the other letters).

Wood, painted surface, 31×23 (0·785 × 0·585); painted up to the edges all round.

In most parts much repainted. Christ's nose and mouth (but not the area between them) are in reliable state. Parts of Christ's body are in very good condition, especially His left shoulder with the shadowed part of the body below and His arm in the upper part; the half shadows here preserve the original finger marks in the paint. The landscape is in good state. There are some *pentimenti* in Christ's limbs, in the line of the Virgin's mantle, and in the rock and castle, which has been extended to the left.

Called by Dussler[1] a studio piece, but the parts noted above as well preserved are by no means unworthy of Bellini himself. From the middle period; this has been symbolized by various datings in the 1480's and 1490's. The castle recurs in a *Virgin and Child* in the Brady Collection, New York (ex-Oldenburg).[2]

PROVENANCE: From the collection of Giacomo Lazzari, Naples (dead by 1843).[3] Bought by Sir Charles Eastlake between 1855 and 1865.[4] Lady Eastlake's Sale, 2 June, 1894 (lot 57), bought by C. Davis for Ludwig Mond. Exhibited at the New Gallery, 1894/5 (No. 79). Mond Bequest, 1924.

REPRODUCTION: *Illustrations, Italian Schools*, 1937, p. 35. *Plates, Earlier Italian Schools*, 1953, Vol. I, p. 37.

REFERENCES: (1) L. Dussler, *Giovanni Bellini*, 1935, p. 147. Cf. also his book of the same title, Sammlung Schroll, 1949, p. 67. (2) Gronau, Klassiker der Kunst *Bellini*, 1930, Plate 128. (3) Catalogue, 1843 (No. 31); the identifying label, with signatures of Dionisio, Paolo and Irene Lazzari and of Aniello d'Aloisio (recorded in Thieme-Becker) is on the back. According to G. Ceci, *Bibliografia per la Storia delle Arti Figurative nell'Italia Meridionale*, 1937, Vol. I, No. 651, the Lazzari Collection was on sale at Naples, 20 April—16 June, 1850. Giacomo Lazzari's Collection was already formed or being formed by 1815, several pictures (though apparently not No. 3913) being recorded by Domenico Romanelli, *Napoli Antica e Moderna*, 1815, Vol. III, p. 117. (4) I.e. during his directorship, and in accordance with his wishes offered to the Gallery for sale by Lady Eastlake in 1867.

Ascribed to GIOVANNI BELLINI

812   THE ASSASSINATION OF S. PETER MARTYR

Left, the Saint is being murdered by Carinus; Brother Dominic attempts to flee from another assassin, centre. Falsely (?) signed (on a genuine *cartellino*), *Ioannes | Bellinus | .p.*; almost effaced, and retouched, the spelling not quite certain.

Wood, painted surface, 39¼×65 (1·00×1·65); painted up to the edges all round. It might seem to have been reduced at the sides, because animals' bodies are cut in two at the edges; but compare the animal half hidden by the Virgin's mantle in Giovanni Bellini, No. 599 above.

Somewhat rubbed; very gravely damaged by cracking and flaking, and extensively repainted.

A small triangle of grass near the saint's ear seems to have been originally the end of the knife, which in almost all representations of S. Peter Martyr traverses his head; X-Rays, without being altogether clear, seem to confirm this. X-Rays also show that, originally, Carinus was apparently bareheaded and was more erect, and held the dagger about a foot above the saint's body, preparing to strike.

S. Peter Martyr is one of the Dominican heroes; yet his murderer Carinus repented so well of his deed that he acquired at least a local reputation as a saint.[1]

The status of No. 812 is a problem. If the signature is genuine, it is either a Bellini or a Bellini studio-piece; but the signature seems rather to be false, in which case No. 812 might be by an independent follower.

The *pentimenti* are sufficient to suggest that No. 812 is the original of the design.

There is no reason to believe that Giovanni Bellini had particular talent for dramatic action; the subject of No. 812, therefore, if he painted it, was unlikely to inspire a wholly successful picture.

The distant landscape in No. 812 is at present greatly inferior to that in No. 599 above, here accepted as by Giovanni Bellini. The main figures in No. 812, although able in some respects, appear not quite like his style. The unsatisfactory condition of the picture, nevertheless, must constantly be borne in mind.

On stylistic grounds, the date of No. 812 is likely to be not long after 1500.

While it appears necessary to stress that the attribution of No. 812 is speculative, it seems reasonable to list it as ascribed to Bellini (but perhaps with intervention from the studio). This is partly out of respect for the recent opinions of Gronau and Berenson.[2] Previously, No. 812 had often not been accepted as Bellini himself; and some alternative names have been suggested. Berenson at one time doubtfully suggested Rocco Marconi.[3] Jacobsen[4] suggested Basaiti, perhaps meaning the Pseudo-Basaiti; but cf. the commentary to No. 599 above. G. M. Richter strangely supposes the execution is partly by Giorgione.[5]

VERSION: A version with a good many differences is in the Courtauld Institute (Lord Lee Collection); it is recorded to have been dated 1509 on the back.[6]

PROVENANCE: Seen by Sir Charles Eastlake in the studio of Natale Schiavone at Venice in 1854[7] and purchased from him in that year.[8] Exhibited at the R.A., 1870 (No. 146); presented by Lady Eastlake, 1870.

REPRODUCTION: *Illustrations, Italian Schools*, 1937, p. 36. *Plates, Earlier Italian Schools*, 1953, Vol. I, p. 38.

REFERENCES: (1) See the *Analecta Bollandiana*, Vol. 26, 1907, pp. 139/40. (2) Gronau, Klassiker der Kunst *Bellini*, 1930, p. 172; Berenson, 1957 Lists. (3) Berenson, *Venetian Painters of the Renaissance*, 1897 (apparently). (4) Jacobsen in the *Repertorium für Kunstwissenschaft*, 1901, p. 341. (5) G. M. Richter, *Giorgio da Castelfranco*, 1937, p. 74 and Catalogue No. 42; he confuses the provenance with that of No. 41 of this Gallery (Cariani). (6) See the catalogue of Lord Lee's Collection, Vol. I, 1923, No. 11, and the Burlington Fine Arts Club *Early Venetian Exhibition*, 1912, No. 30, where stylistic, compositional and icono-graphical differences are noted. See further the Courtauld *Catalogue of the Lee Collection*, 1958 (No. 50). Woodcutters appear in the backgrounds of Lord Lee's picture and of No. 812. They do not seem to have a place in the usual story of the assassination; the Bollandists (29 April, p. 706) merely record that it took place 'in nemore denso'. But there seems to have been a tradition concerning wood-cutters, used for works of art; they appear in the background of the Moretto of this subject in the Ambrosiana (Gombosi, *Moretto*, 1943, No. 143 and Fig. 22), and in a relief on the façade of S. Anastasia at Verona (Venturi, *Storia dell'Arte Italiana*, Vol. VI, Fig. 662). A woodcutter appears also in the background of Lotto's picture in S. Maria della Pace at Alzano Lombardo; *Inventario degli Oggetti d'Arte d'Italia, Provincia di Bergamo*, 1931, p. 145 (reproduced). (7) Eastlake's note-book. (8) It was not among the pictures acquired during his directorship (1855–65) offered for sale by Lady Eastlake in 1867; seen by Waagen, *Supplement*, IV, 1857, p. 114. It is doubtless one of the two Bellinis noted as acquired in Venice by October, 1854, in *Journals and Correspondence of Lady Eastlake*, 1895, II, p. 20.

Studio of GIOVANNI BELLINI

808   A DOMINICAN, WITH THE ATTRIBUTES OF
S. PETER MARTYR ADDED

Signed on a *cartellino: ioannes bellinnus | pinxit* (retouched).

Poplar,[1] painted surface, $23\frac{1}{4} \times 19$ ($0\cdot59 \times 0\cdot48$); painted up to the edge at the bottom.

Covered with a heavily cracked varnish, which makes it difficult to see; but the picture is certainly a good deal damaged. The face in parts, as the nose, seems to be in good condition; but the effect of the left eye has been somewhat altered by restoration, and the mouth to the left is damaged.

The picture has undergone a good many changes.[2] The palm, the sword and the knife have been added; they are fairly old, but are very coarse and not to be connected with the original painter or his studio. The head has been made bare, with hair showing, in replacement of a bonnet; but the bonnet has prominently reappeared. The halo seems to be in the same style as the blood on the head, which is clearly added. It is clear that the original picture was a portrait and not a representation of S. Peter Martyr. Originally, as can be seen in X-Radiographs, the figure was holding a roll of paper vertically, instead of the present palm.[3] The original background seems to have been green, not black as at present.

In contradistinction to the above, there does seem to be a genuine *pentimento* on the picture, revealed by the X-Ray; the mouth was originally partly open, apparently.

The *cartellino* is painted on top of the parapet; but this proves nothing, and it is obviously old. The signature has been written in neither straight nor symmetrically; but there does not seem to be any reason to think that it was added later. The spelling *Bellinnus* is peculiar; it occurs also on the *Virgin and Child* in Santa Maria dell'Orto, Venice, a signature that has apparently not been stated to be false, and seems clearly genuine.[4] In No. 808 the second n seems to have been at first miswritten, but the reading seems sure; there might rather be doubt about some of the retouched letters, yet it is unlikely that any difference would be significant. There is some reason to think that the writing is by a different hand from the signatures of *The Feast of the Gods* at Washington and *The Toilet of Venus* at Vienna.[5]

No. 808 was ascribed by Morelli[6] to Gentile Bellini, because of the form of the ear; it is legitimate to be sceptical about this point of style, especially in a portrait. The ascription, however, had a great success. Eventually Gronau[7] modified it, saying begun by Gentile, finished by Giovanni; and rather strangely added that it shows many connections with No. 1440 (Giovanni Bellini). In Berenson's Lists, 1957, as by Giovanni. The style is not at all clear in the present condition of the picture; unless the signature is proved false, it seems reasonable to call it a production of Giovanni's studio. Some, perhaps considerable, participation by Bellini himself, while not strictly discernible, seems not unlikely.

The date is likely to be towards the end of Bellini's life.

PROVENANCE: Formerly in the collection of the Marchese Sommi-Picenardi at the Torri de' Picenardi, near Cremona, where it is recorded *ca.* 1827.[8] The collection passed by inheritance to the Marchese Araldi Erizzo; his creditors sold this and other pictures in 1869 to Basilini of Milan, from whom purchased, 1870.

REPRODUCTION: *Illustrations, Italian Schools,* 1937, p. 37. *Plates, Earlier Italian Schools,* 1953, Vol. I, p. 39.

REFERENCES: (1) Letter from B. J. Rendle, of the Forest Products Research Laboratory, in the Gallery archives. (2) Cf. Detlev Freiherr von Hadeln in the *Repertorium für Kunstwissenschaft,* 1907, p. 537. (3) X-Radiographs illustrating the comments above are reproduced in *Arte Veneta,* 1950, p. 169. (4) Gronau, Klassiker der Kunst *Bellini,* 1930, Plate 78. (5) This is the tentative view of Alwyn Cole, recorded by John Walker, *Bellini and Titian at Ferrara,* 1956, pp. 95 ff. (6) Morelli, *Munich-Dresden-Berlin,* translated by Mrs. Richter, 1883, p. 10 (note). (7) Gronau, Klassiker der Kunst *Bellini,* 1930, Plate 178 with note. (8) Guido Sommi-Picenardi, *Le Torri de' Picenardi,* 1909, p. 155 (No. 172). There is no further note about No. 808; but the book contains various indications about the history of the Picenardi collection, which are summarized in the entry for Marziale, No. 803.

1455   THE CIRCUMCISION

Signed on a *cartellino:* IOANNES / BELLINVS.

Wood, painted surface, $29\frac{1}{2} \times 40\frac{1}{4}$ (0.75×1.02). Measurements up to the edges of the panel all round; at the sides at least the picture has certainly not been cut.

No. 1455 was cleaned in 1949. The painted surface in general is well preserved; but it is probable that a top layer of grey paint, which remains here and there on the Child, on S. Joseph (?) behind Him, etc., may once have been over all the figures. Several *pentimenti* in the figure of the Child. Some fingermarks are visible in the paint.

The background of No. 1455 is black. In some versions of the design, it is a landscape; e.g. in one at New York, which is dated 1511.[1] Since a landscape is obviously unsuitable for the subject, it is unlikely to be part of Bellini's original conception.

The idea of treating the subject with figures at half-length may well go back to Mantegna; cf. a *Presentation* at Berlin,[2] and a variant of this (unfinished) in the Querini Stampalia Gallery at Venice.[3] Later on, Bellini devised two distinct designs for the *Presentation*[4] and the *Circumcision,* each of which is known in many versions.

The design of *The Circumcision* is sometimes said to be an invention of the 1480's;[5] but there seems to be no example in existence earlier than No. 1455, which Gronau dates soon after 1500.[6] No. 1455 appears to be the best known example of the design, and may be the original version.

Although No. 1455 is perhaps the original, it seems almost impossible to accept much of the execution as being by Bellini's own hand.[7] For instance, the High Priest's white brocade may be contrasted with that of Doge Loredan (No. 189 above). It should, nevertheless, not be forgotten that probably a softening grey layer was once over all the figures.

It is certainly not impossible that Bellini supervised rather than executed an original design. For instance, two altarpieces at Düsseldorf and Baltimore, each representing *The Virgin and Child with Saints*, are usually classed as studio-pieces;[8] and the commissions for these may well have been more important than the commission for *The Circumcision*. The fact that the present design became popular does not prove that the first version of it would have been executed with particular care in Bellini's shop.

The execution of No. 1455 and of other versions has been sometimes ascribed to Catena.[9] It seems likely that the first introduction of Catena's name was due to a misconception: for two versions of the design of the *Presentation*, in the Correr Museum and at Padua, are signed by Vincenzo da Treviso (dalle Destre), whom Crowe and Cavalcaselle thought identical with Vincenzo Catena.[10].

VERSIONS: Numerous versions exist, mostly of poor quality, and not all of them contemporary; Gronau[11] gives indications towards identifying some. A version at New York bears a signature (?) of Giovanni Bellini and a date 1511; this is the same as the Goldschmidt version (1898 sale), often wrongly said to be dated 1508.[12] A copy signed by Marco Bello is at Rovigo.[13] A derivation signed by Bartolomeo Veneto and dated 1506 is in the Louvre.[14] A version at Zagreb, ascribed to Rondinelli in the 1939 Catalogue, is ascribed to Bissolo by Gamulin.[15] In the Leuchtenberg Collection there was a version, and a different picture containing the female figure on the right;[16] this figure also appears in a Previtali at Berlin, No. 39.[17] For Marziale's two pictures of the subject, of 1499 and 1500, which differ considerably, see the entry for Marziale, No. 803.

PROVENANCE: Perhaps the picture in the seventeenth century in the Cristoforo and Francesco Muselli Collection at Verona.[18] By 1727 in the Orleans Collection, from the Duc de Gramont's.[19] It was imported into England in 1798 with the Orleans Collection, though it does not appear in Buchanan's list; exhibited at Bryan's, 26 sqq. Dec. 1798 (No. 122), marked in the National Gallery copy of the catalogue, *Earl of Carlisle*, i.e. reserved by Lord Carlisle for his own collection. Castle Howard Catalogue, 1805 (No. 4). Exhibited at the British Institution, 1851 (No. 46), and at the New Gallery, 1894/5 (No. 84). Presented by the 9th Earl of Carlisle, 1895.

REPRODUCTION: *Illustrations, Italian Schools*, 1937, p. 36 (before cleaning in 1949). *Plates, Earlier Italian Schools*, 1953, Vol. I, p. 40.

REFERENCES: (**1**) Reproduced in the 1941 New York Catalogue, as Catena. (**2**) Reproduced in the Berlin Illustrations. (**3**) Gronau, Klassiker der Kunst *Bellini*, 1930, Plate 42; Bellini Exhibition at Venice, 1949 (No. 46); in both cases as by Giovanni Bellini. (**4**) The *Presentation* is Gronau, *op. cit.*, Plate 189; a variation at Verona is reproduced by Geiger in the Prussian *Jahrbuch*, 1912, p. 13. See further Sandra Moschini Marconi, *Gallerie dell'Accademia di Venezia*,

Catalogue, XIV–XV Centuries, 1955, No. 91, with reproduction. (5) E.g. by
Berenson in *Dedalo*, IV, 1923, p. 116 (1483–90). (6) Gronau, *Spätwerke*, 1928,
pp. 16/7. (7) Gronau, however, calls it Bellini; e.g. in his Klassiker der Kunst
Bellini, 1930, note to Plate 150. Berenson in his 1932 Lists calls it Bellini in
great part. (8) Reproduced by Gronau, 1930, Plates 186/7. (9) No. 1455 was
called Catena in Berenson's *Venetian Painters of the Renaissance*, 1909. See the
comments by Giles Robertson, *Vincenzo Catena*, 1954, p. 80. (10) Cf. Crowe and
Cavalcaselle, *History of Painting in North Italy*, ed. Borenius, I, 1912, pp.
149/50. (11) Gronau, 1930, note to Plate 150. (12) See the New York 1941
Catalogue, s.v. Catena. (13) Crowe and Cavalcaselle, *op. cit.*, p. 291. Reproduced
by Van Marle, *Development of the Italian Schools of Painting*, Vol. XVIII,
Fig. 242. (14) Reproduced by Gronau, *Spätwerke*, 1928, Plate XIII. (15) Grgo
Gamulin in *Zbornik za Umetnostno Zgodovino*, Ljubljana, 1959, pp. 383 ff. (16)
Both reproduced in *L'Arte*, VI, 1903, p. 339. (17) Berlin Illustrations. (18)
Mentioned by Ridolfi, *Le Maraviglie dell'Arte*, 1648, Vol. I, p. 72 of Hadeln's
reprint. Cf. also the Muselli Inventory of 1662, Campori, *Raccolta di Cataloghi*,
1870, pp. 181 and 178. The Muselli pictures were apparently sold into France,
through a dealer 'Aluarese' at some time before 1718; Bartolomeo del Pozzo,
Vite de' Pittori, etc. Veronesi, 1718, p. 94. (19) Orleans Catalogue, 1727,
p. 229.

2901   THE VIRGIN AND CHILD

Wood, painted surface, $32\frac{1}{4} \times 24\frac{1}{2}$ (0·82 × 0·62); painted up to the
edges except at the bottom.

Cleaned in 1959; much damaged. A false signature, IOANNES
BELLINVS / PINXIT, on a false *cartellino*, was removed during the
cleaning.

Berenson, who in his Lists of 1957 ascribes a very large number of
pictures to Bellini, calls No. 2901 Bellini in part; Hetzer,[1] who admits
comparatively few pictures as Bellini's, calls No. 2901 autograph. It
seems to the compiler clearly and well below the level of Bellini's autograph quality.[2] It seems to be a comparatively early work of the studio;
this is sometimes symbolized by putting it at about 1475.

VERSIONS: A version with curtain and landscape is in the Berenson Collection
at Settignano.[3] The design of the Virgin and Child reversed and varied is in the
Fogg Art Museum (Winthrop Bequest);[4] a variant of this is at Padua.[5] A related
composition is at Verona.[6]

PROVENANCE: Lent by Lady Lindsay to the New Gallery, 1894/5 (No. 26);
Lady Lindsay Bequest, 1912.

REPRODUCTION: *Illustrations, Italian Schools*, 1937, p. 32. *Plates, Earlier
Italian Schools*, 1953, Vol. I, p. 41.

REFERENCES: (1) T. Hetzer in the *Zeitschrift für Kunstgeschichte*, 1932, p. 66.
(2) Nevertheless, Pallucchini in *Arte Veneta*, 1951, p. 196, inclined to accept it
as autograph; and Giles Robertson in *The Burlington Magazine*, 1953, p. 28,
had a higher opinion of it than the compiler's. (3) Reproduced by Gamba,
Giovanni Bellini, 1937, Plate 100. (4) Gronau, Klassiker der Kunst *Bellini*, 1930,
Plate 57. (5) The picture and its underdrawing seen from the back during transference are reproduced in *Le Arti*, I, 1938/9, p. 317, figs. 25/6. (6) Gronau, *op.
cit.*, Plate 47. Another version of this was lent by Conte Alessandro Contini
Bonacossi to the Bellini Exhibition, 1949 (No. 53), reproduced in the
catalogue.

3078 THE VIRGIN AND CHILD

Signed on a *cartellino:* ( )OA( )NES BE( )LINVS.

Poplar,[1] $31\frac{1}{2} \times 25\frac{1}{2}$ (0·80 × 0·645). These measurements are up to the edges of the panel all round, and include a painted band of black framing all round, which is not contemporary but covers a continuation of the original picture to the edges.

The upper part of the picture is not in bad state, the lower part has been much damaged. There are original finger-prints in the flesh shadows of the Virgin and (partly overpainted) the Child.

A poor studio piece; from the middle period, and usually dated towards 1490.

VERSIONS: One is in the Museum at Worcester, Mass. (ex-Theodore T. Ellis Collection);[2] another, in the Fogg Art Museum,[3] is perhaps identical with a version once in the Andrea Vendramin Collection.[4] Berenson[5] and Gronau[6] mention other examples on the market.

PROVENANCE: Bought in Paris by Sir A. H. Layard;[7] exhibited at Leeds, 1868 (No. 74) and at South Kensington, 1869 (No. 13); Layard Bequest, 1916.[8]

REPRODUCTION: *Illustrations, Italian Schools*, 1937, p. 35. *Plates, Earlier Italian Schools*, 1953, Vol. I, p. 42.

REFERENCES: (1) Letter from B. J. Rendle, of the Forest Products Research Laboratory, in the Gallery archives. (2) Gronau, Klassiker der Kunst *Bellini*, 1930, Plate 126. Worcester Art Museum, Annual, 1941, pp. 18 and 30/1; acquisition number, 1940, 66. (3) Reproduced by Berenson, *Venetian Painting in America*, 1916, p. 114. (4) See the drawing reproduced by T. Borenius, *The Picture Gallery of Andrea Vendramin*, 1923, Plate 2. (5) Berenson, *op. cit.*, p. 117. (6) Gronau, *op. cit.*, note to Plate 126. (7) Layard MSS. in the National Gallery. It is perhaps the picture (insufficiently described) recommended for purchase by Miner K. Kellogg in a letter from Paris to Layard, 9 March, 1856 (British Museum, Add. MS. 38984, Layard Papers, Vol. LIV). (8) For the history of the Layard Collection, see Appendix IV.

Follower of GIOVANNI BELLINI

281 S. JEROME READING IN A LANDSCAPE

Wood, painted surface, $18\frac{1}{2} \times 13\frac{1}{4}$ (0·47 × 0·34); painted up to the edges all round.

Very good condition. A small piece in the extreme top right corner is new.

Ascribed by Mündler in 1855 to Basaiti;[1] this name was maintained until recently at the Gallery. Execution by Basaiti seems on the whole unlikely, though it should be remarked that there is no adequate study of Basaiti in the light of present views concerning Bellini. It seems in any case certain that the present picture is derived from a design by Giovanni Bellini, perhaps of the 1480's. Gronau[2] (1930) and Berenson (1957 Lists) even ascribe No. 281 to Bellini himself.

VERSIONS, ETC.: An important picture with considerable variations is in the Contini Collection (ex-Papafava).[3] A different design occurs in two versions; one, with a signature of Giovanni Bellini and date 1505, is at Washington (ex-Benson and Mackay),[4] the other is (?) in the Lobkowitz Collection.[5] Yet another variant of the same general scheme is at Oxford.[6] The town and castle in the background of No. 281, which do not recur in the above-mentioned pictures, recur without much variation in Mocetto's engraving of *The Resurrection*.[7]

PROVENANCE: Alleged to have been engraved in the Salvator Rossetti Collection.[8] Purchased from M. Marcovich, Venice, 1855.

REPRODUCTION: *Illustrations, Italian Schools*, 1937, p. 20. *Plates, Earlier Italian Schools*, 1953, Vol. I, p. 43.

REFERENCES: (1) Mündler's Diary. (2) Gronau, Klassiker der Kunst *Bellini*, 1930, Plate 83. Pallucchini in *Arte Veneta*, 1951, p. 196, also thinks it by Giovanni Bellini himself. (3) Gronau, *op. cit.*, Plate 82. It may be identical with a Bellini altarpiece of this subject, once in S. Maria dei Miracoli at Venice, for which Gronau records two old references. (4) Gronau, *op. cit.*, Plate 159. (5) Reproduced by Dvořák and Matějka, *Raudnitzer Schloss*, Prague, 1910, p. 83. (6) Oxford Catalogue, 1951 (No. 55); reproduced in Crowe and Cavalcaselle, *Painting in North Italy*, ed. Borenius, I, 1912, p. 273. A drawing on the same design as this, at Berlin, is reproduced by Hadeln, *Venezianische Zeichnungen des Quattrocento*, 1925, Plate 24, as Carpaccio; Tietze and Tietze-Conrat, *Drawings of the Venetian Painters*, 1944, No. 288. (7) This was pointed out by J. Byam Shaw in *The Connoisseur*, March 1950, p. 60. For the engraving, see A. M. Hind, *Early Italian Engraving*, Vol. V, 1948, p. 163, No. 8 and Vol. VII, 1948, Plate 723. (8) So Mündler was told. A *S. Jerome* by Mansueti was engraved when in the Salvador Orsetti Collection at Venice (Correr Library, Stampe, B11 and C2); this picture is now at Bergamo (Corrado Ricci, *Elenco dei Quadri*, 1930, p. 113, No. 152).

2095 A MAN IN BLACK

Wood, painted surface, $12\frac{1}{4} \times 10$ (0·31 × 0·25).

In unsatisfactory condition. Parts of the nose and right eye are new, nor is the rest of the flesh pure. The original line of the hair to the right was much further out, and the cap has undergone probably more than one change (X-Rays are not altogether clear). Parts of the green curtain above the head are on a black ground; it seems unlikely that the cap extended so high at any time.

Traditionally Antonello,[1] it was ascribed by Berenson (1897 Lists) to Alvise Vivarini, by Suida[2] and Gronau[3] to Giovanni Bellini, by Berenson (1957 Lists) to Andrea da Murano. The style seems derived from Giovanni Bellini more than from anyone else; but the picture is in the unattributable class, and Collins Baker[4] is clearly right in saying that the painter had never really learned to draw. Probably *ca.* 1500.

PROVENANCE: In the John Samuel Collection; lent by his nieces, the Misses Cohen, to the New Gallery, 1893/4 (No. 137), and bequeathed by them with other pictures, as the John Samuel Collection, 1906.

REPRODUCTION: *Illustrations, Italian Schools*, 1937, p. 372. *Plates, Earlier Italian Schools*, 1953, Vol. I, p. 44.

REFERENCES: (1) So in the exhibition of 1893/4. (2) Suida in *The Burlington Magazine*, Vol. LI (1927), p. 187. (3) Gronau, Klassiker der Kunst *Bellini*, 1930, Plate 121. (4) Collins Baker in *The Burlington Magazine*, Vol. L (1927), p. 24.

See also FRANCESCO TACCONI, No. 284

BENOZZO DI LESE (called GOZZOLI)
ca. 1421–1497

Of a Florentine family. Benozzo di Lese (Alesso) is usually known as Gozzoli; this name may be due to some slip in the printing of Vasari's second edition, though there is a little evidence that Benozzo may also have been named Gozzoli. He was studying painting in 1442. In 1444, already trained as a painter, he contracted for three years to work for Ghiberti on the bronze doors of the Baptistery at Florence. In 1447 he was Fra Angelico's principal assistant in Rome and Orvieto; he worked intermittently at the latter place also in 1448 and 1449. 1450/2, Montefalco; 1453, Viterbo. He returned again to Rome before a period of activity at Florence, 1459 till 1462 or 3. Then he worked at San Gimignano. From 1468 until 1494 or 5, almost continually in Pisa. He died at Pistoia. Much of his work was in fresco. For various documents concerning his life, see R. G. Mather in *The Art Bulletin*, March, 1948, pp. 40 ff.

283 ALTARPIECE: THE VIRGIN AND CHILD ENTHRONED AMONG ANGELS AND SAINTS

The Virgin's halo is inscribed, .AVE MARIA GRATIA PLENA DOMINV'; on the hem of her robe is AVE REGINA CELORVM MATER ANGELORVM SANCTA ES QVA MVNDO LVX EST ORT(A). Christ's halo is inscribed HIESVS CRISTVS.

On the left, SS. John the Baptist and Zenobius stand, and S. Jerome kneels. The Baptist's halo is inscribed, .SANCT' IOHANNES BAT(T)ISTA. S. Zenobius' halo is inscribed, .SANTV' ZENOBIVS. The orphrey of his cope is ornamented with the following scenes, ascending on the right and then descending on the left: (1) the Angel appearing to S. Joachim; (2) The Birth of the Virgin; (3) The Presentation of the Virgin; (4) The Marriage of the Virgin; (5) The Annunciation; (6) The Nativity; (7) Christ Disputing with the Doctors; (8) The Calling of SS. Peter and Andrew. S. Jerome's halo is inscribed, .SANCTVS HIERONIMV'.

On the right, SS. Peter and Dominic stand, and S. Francis kneels. S. Peter's halo is inscribed, .SANCTVS PETRVS APOSTOLVS. On the collar of his garment is inscribed, TV ES PETRVS & SVPER ANC; the book he holds is inscribed, TV ES CRISTVS FILIVS DEI VIVI. S. Dominic's halo is inscribed, .SANCTVS DOMINICVS. S. Francis' halo is inscribed, .SANCTVS FRANCISCVS.

Wood, painted surface, $63\frac{3}{4} \times 67$ ($1\cdot62 \times 1\cdot70$).[1]

In general the picture is very well preserved; but the trees in the background are partly modern, and the sky is rather damaged.

On the Virgin's robe in one of Benozzo's altarpieces of 1466 at San Gimignano is an inscription comparable with the one here, AVE REGINA COELORVM MATER ANGELORVM SALVE RADIX QVA MVNDO LVX SURREXIT.[2] The scene of the Calling of S.

Peter on S. Zenobius' cope here is according to Luke v, 1 sqq. The two inscriptions on the figure of S. Peter here are from Matthew xvi, 16–18.

Although there is a break in the provenance, there can be no doubt that No. 283 is the picture that on 23 October, 1461, Benozzo contracted to paint for the Compagnia di Santa Maria della Purificazione e di San Zanobi, known as the Compagnia di San Marco, at Florence.[3] In the contract, the six saints are specified in their identity and their relative positions exactly as they occur on No. 283.

The Confraternity had been attached to San Marco long before the Dominicans took over the church in 1435/6. Medicean patronage of the Dominicans in San Marco resulted in a great extension of the buildings, with much new construction. At the time of the contract with Benozzo, the Confraternity appear to have been in the process of building a new Oratory for themselves in the precincts of San Marco.[4] Whatever the state of the Confraternity's building, they certainly paid attention to having a new altarpiece. On 30 August, 1461, they refer to this as having previously been begun.[5] The reference may mean merely that the panel had been provided, and the frame carved; in the contract of 23 October, 1461, Benozzo was made responsible for getting all the necessary gilding done, and for painting with his own hand the picture, its predella and all necessary ornamentation.[6] The whole was to be finished by 1 November, 1462.

The saints, as already remarked, are specified exactly as they appear on No. 283. The Madonna Enthroned, on the other hand, was to be a copy of the figure on the high altarpiece of San Marco.[7] That picture is by Fra Angelico; either the clause in the contract was modified, or Benozzo interpreted it with peculiar licence.[8]

According to the contract, the predella was to contain stories of the saints shown on the altarpiece; no story of the Virgin Mary is specified. On such altarpieces, the contract goes on, it was customary to place the donor's arms on a shield; here Benozzo was to paint two *putti* dressed in white, with garlands of olive on their heads, holding the shield marked with the letters $\bar{P}$ $\bar{S}$ $\bar{M}$.

Five predella panels are now known, which it is reasonable to assume are part(?) of the predella of No. 283. (1) The Death of Simon Magus, in the Royal Collection;[9] (2) A Miracle of S. Dominic, in the Brera at Milan;[10] (3) A Miracle of S. Zenobius, at Berlin;[11] (4) The Dance of Salome and Beheading of S. John the Baptist, in the Kress Collection;[12] (5) The Purification of the Virgin (or Presentation in the Temple), in the J. G. Johnson Collection at Philadelphia.[13] The last might seem doubtful, since the contract seems rather to imply no scene of the Virgin Mary in the predella. But the subject is suitable for the Confraternity of the Purification; it is rather pointedly omitted from the scenes on S. Zenobius' cope in No. 283; and the size, the halo-pattern and the style of the Johnson picture correspond with those of the other predella panels. The predella panels still missing (if these were in fact painted) are the scenes from the lives of SS. Francis and Jerome; the picture of the two *putti* with the shield is also missing.

PROVENANCE: As already explained, painted for the Compagnia di Santa Maria della Purificazione e di San Zanobi, known as the Compagnia di San Marco, at Florence.[14] Their new Oratory, still attached to San Marco, was still unfinished *ca.* 1465/6. They did not in any case enjoy it long; the Dominicans of San Marco needed the site, and offered the Confraternity ground in the Via San Gallo at Florence, where yet another Oratory was built. The move took place in 1506. The picture is mentioned in the new Oratory in an inventory of 1518.[15] By an arrangement of 1685, confirmed by his will of 1690, Domenico di Santi Melani effected a considerable change in the status of the Confraternity; he built on adjoining ground a *hospice*, which he put under the Confraternity's control.This foundation was known as the Ospedale del Melani or dei Pellegrini; the picture is recorded in the Refectory there by Richa in 1757. The Ospedale was later suppressed, in 1775; the buildings were acquired by the Marchese Orazio Zanobi Pucci, but the Society was still existing in 1802.[16] Exactly what happened to the picture has not been discovered. No. 283 is recorded in the Rinuccini Collection at Florence, 1842,[17] and in the Sale Catalogue (after the death of the last Rinuccini, Marchese Pietro Francesco), 1852 (No. 131). Not sold at the sale, and purchased from the Rinuccini Estate, 1855. On loan at Westminster Abbey, 1945/8.

VERSION: See No. 2863 below.

REPRODUCTION: *Illustrations, Italian Schools*, 1937, p. 162. *Plates, Earlier Italian Schools*, 1953, Vol. I, p. 45.

REFERENCES: (1) These measurements exclude modern paint up to the edges of the panel at the top and sides. The painted surface has perhaps been somewhat reduced at the bottom. (2) Van Marle, *Development of the Italian Schools of Painting*, Vol. XI, Fig. 118. The inscription is quoted by Cavalcaselle e Crowe, *Storia della Pittura in Italia*, Vol. VIII, p. 79. These inscriptions are variants from the beginning of one of the Antiphons used after Compline in the Catholic Church: *Ave, Regina caelorum | Ave, Domina Angelorum: | Salve, radix, salve, porta, | Ex qua mundo lux est orta.* (3) The contract was published by Zanobi Bicchierai in his pamphlet, *Alcuni Documenti Artistici non mai stampati*, Nozze Farinola-Vai, 1855; also, more accessibly, by L. Tanfani Centofanti, *Notizie di Artisti tratte dai Documenti Pisani*, 1897, pp. 83/6, and by Corrado Ricci in his article in the *Rivista d'Arte*, 1904, pp. 1 ff. The document in question is not signed by the contracting parties; but it is presumably an accurate copy of what was signed, since there is another record that the date given (23 October, 1461) is that of the contract for the picture (Horne in *The Burlington Magazine*, Vol. VII (1905), p. 382, Doc. II). (4) Richa, *Notizie Istoriche delle Chiese Fiorentine*, Vol. V (1757), pp. 329 ff., esp. p. 331. Some more about the Confraternity can be found in the part of the Chronicle of San Marco published in the *Archivio Storico Italiano*, 1913, I, p. 15. (5) Horne, *loc cit.*, Doc. I. (6) See the texts in the references given in note 3. (7) *La fighura di nostra Donna chon la sedia nel modo et forma et chon ornamenti chome et in similitudine della tavola dello altare maggiore di sancto Marcho di Firenze.* (8) See the reproduction of the picture in the Klassiker der Kunst *Angelico*, 1924, p. 144. (9) Exhibition of the King's Pictures at the Royal Academy, 1946/7, No. 180, size 9½ in. × 14 in.; reproduced in the Souvenir of the Exhibition. (10) Catalogue, *ca.* 1931, No. 475, size 0·25 × 0·35; reproduced by Van Marle, *op. cit.*, Vol. XI, Fig. 112. (11) 1931 Catalogue, No. 60C, size 0·24 × 0·34; reproduced in the Berlin Illustrations. (12) *Paintings and Sculpture from the Kress Collection, Acquired by the Samuel H. Kress Foundation* 1945–1951, Washington, 1951 (No. 13), reproduced; size, 9¼ in. × 13½ in. See the article on this, and the rest of the altarpiece, by Fern Rusk Shapley in the *Gazette des Beaux-Arts*, February 1952, pp. 77 ff.; all five predella panels are there reproduced, and it is suggested that there are no missing ones. (13) Catalogue, 1913, I, No. 38, reproduced; size 8⅝ in. × 13½ in. Four small panels by Benozzo, some of which show some compositional connections with some of the above mentioned predella, formerly in the Alessandri Collection, are now at New

York; see the Catalogue of Italian, etc., Paintings, 1940, pp. 31 ff., Nos. 15.106. 1–4, with reproductions. The connection with the predella panels here mentioned is not very close, and the New York series is of no relevance for any panels missing from the predella of No. 283. (14) The earlier provenance, unless otherwise stated, is from Richa, *Notizie Istoriche delle Chiese Fiorentine*, Vol. V, 1757, pp. 329 ff. (15) Horne in *The Burlington Magazine*, Vol. VII, 1905, p. 383, Doc. III. (16) (Follini and Rastrelli), *Firenze Antica e Moderna*, VIII, 1802, p. 328; in Vol. IV, 1792, p. 309, the authors speak of Benozzo's picture as having been in the hospital, but it seems no longer to have been available to be seen. Cf. also Vasari, ed. Milanesi, Vol. III, p. 46. It would appear that, at the time of the suppression, the hospital and the Confraternity were considered distinct. This seems established by Insertion No. 28, between pp. 228 and 229 of Vol. I of MS. 226 in the Moreniana Library at Florence (attached to the Riccardiana), entitled *Compendio di Notizie Istoriche delle chiese di Firenze e di alcune suburbane divise nei suoi quartieri*. It is there stated, and the information is clearly contemporary, that the hospital was suppressed on 20 September, 1775, that the effects had already been sold in January, 1774, and that Marchese Zanobi Pucci adapted the buildings to his use in 1776; but that what was esteemed to be the property of the Confraternity was considered quite distinct, and was not included in the sales. Orazio Zanobi Pucci's son married the widow of Marchese Bossi, and the buildings passed to the Bossi family; cf. Luigi Passerini, *Storia degli Stabilimenti di Beneficenza ... della Città di Firenze*, 1853, p. 125, in conjunction with Litta's *Famiglie Celebri d'Italia*, Tav. VIII of the Pucci family. (17) Murray's *Hand-Book for Travellers in Northern Italy*, 1842, p. 550 ('a Madonna and Saints'). *Catalogo dei Quadri ed altri Oggetti della Galleria Rinuccini*, 1845, Quinta Stanza, p. 15, No. 28 (no provenance given).

After BENOZZO di Lese (called Gozzoli)

2863 THE VIRGIN AND CHILD ENTHRONED WITH ANGELS

The Virgin's halo is inscribed AVE.MARIS.STELLA.DEI.MATE(R). Christ's halo is inscribed PAX.VOBIS. The angels' haloes are inscribed,.AVE.GRAZIA.PLENA.

Wood, painted surface, 54×35 ($1 \cdot 37 \times 0 \cdot 89$). Including a piece of framing, which appears to be original, $57\frac{1}{2} \times 38\frac{1}{2}$ ($1 \cdot 46 \times 0 \cdot 975$).

Much damaged and restored. Most of the architecture and the flowers appear to be new in surface, but apparently correspond with original remains beneath. The gold background appears to be substantially old.

A variant of Benozzo's altarpiece, No. 283 above, with the attendant saints omitted; two extra angels added, apparently from a design of Donatello's;[1] and some other variations. Benozzo's altarpiece, as explained in the entry for it, was commissioned in 1461 at Florence. No. 2863 seems clearly to be a copy from that, and therefore done after; not necessarily very long after. It is probably by some Florentine hand, and it is not entirely to be excluded that it was painted in Benozzo's studio. Berenson, in various editions of his lists, has suggested attributions to Bonfigli and Caporali; but both these men were independent masters at Perugia long before the presumed date of No. 2863, and it is awkward to conceive of their copying a picture by Benozzo that was in Florence. In any case, the condition of No. 2863 renders it hardly fit for receiving an attribution.

PROVENANCE: Rev. Walter Davenport Bromley Sale, 13 June, 1863 (lot 149), bought by Wilson.[2] Lent by William Graham to the R.A., 1885 (No. 231); Graham Sale, 9 April, 1886 (lot 343), bought by Wagner. Lent by Henry Wagner to the New Gallery, 1893/4 (No. 43) and to the Grafton Galleries, 1911 (No. 15). Presented by Henry Wagner, 1912.

REPRODUCTION: *Illustrations, Italian Schools*, 1937, p. 162. *Plates, Earlier Italian Schools*, 1953, Vol. I, p. 46.

REFERENCES: (1) This was pointed out by Hans Kauffmann, *Donatello*, 1935, p. 218, note 210. See also *The Art Bulletin*, March 1948, pp. 11 ff. and June 1948, pp. 143 ff. (esp. p. 144, note 7), where the Donatellian reliefs with angels corresponding fairly closely with the two here are discussed and reproduced. (2) The description in the sale catalogue makes the identity sure.

BENVENUTO DI GIOVANNI
1436, not earlier than 1509

Sienese School; first recorded as active in 1453. Last recorded in 1509, he is supposed to have died *ca* 1518. Several authenticated works exist. His son Gerolamo followed his style closely.

909 TRIPTYCH: THE VIRGIN AND CHILD, WITH SS. PETER AND NICHOLAS

On the lower part of the central panel are the inscriptions: AVE and GRA many times (all new?); REGINA CELI LETTARE ALLE-LVIA; and the signature, OPVS BENVENVTI IOANES DE SENIS MCCCCLXXVIIII. Beneath S. Peter is inscribed, SANTVS PETRVS APOSTOLVS. S. Nicholas is shown with the Pietà on his morse, and unidentified single figures on the orphrey of his cope; inscription, SANTVS NICHOLAVS DEBARI.

Wood. Central panel, painted surface, $67\frac{1}{4} \times 26$ ($1 \cdot 71 \times 0 \cdot 66$), painted up to the edges all round; side panels, each, painted surface, $67 \times 19\frac{3}{4}$ ($1 \cdot 70 \times 0 \cdot 50$), painted up to the edges all round.

Almost entirely regilt. Also considerably repainted, of the principal faces that of S. Nicholas being the worst; but in general the repairs do not much harm the original style, which is clearly recognizable in many places on the flesh.

The words in praise of the Virgin form an Easter antiphon in the Roman Catholic Church.[1]

PROVENANCE: In the collection of A. Grazioli, Rome, 1839;[2] still in Rome in 1856,[3] and apparently sold from the Grazioli Collection in 1858.[4] Lent by Alexander Barker to Leeds, 1868 (No. 3). The central panel was acquired at the Barker Sale, 6 June, 1874 (lot 57). The side panels were not included in this sale; they were purchased at the sale of pictures belonging to representatives of the late Mrs. Roe and the late J. E. Roe, from the Barker Collection, 21 June 1879 (lot 449).[5]

REPRODUCTION: *Illustrations, Italian Schools,* 1937, p. 38. *Plates, Earlier Italian Schools,* 1953, Vol. I, p. 47.

REFERENCES: (1) J. J. M. Timmers, *Symboliek en Iconographie der Christelijke Kunst,* 1947, p. 459. (2) Rosini, *Storia della Pittura Italiana,* 1st volume of the plates, 1839, Plate lvii. (3) Mündler's diary, 8 September, 1856. (4) This is the date given by Mündler in the *Zeitschrift für bildende Kunst,* 1867, p. 299. (5) As C. Crivelli.

2482   THE VIRGIN AND CHILD

The Virgin's halo is inscribed, AVE GRASIA PLENA DOMINVS TECVz.

Wood, painted surface, $20\frac{1}{2} \times 13\frac{1}{2}$ ($0\cdot52 \times 0\cdot345$).

In general in very good condition except for the Virgin's mantle; suffers a little from past flaking.

The attribution of this picture is generally accepted.

PROVENANCE: In the Collection of George Salting by 1883;[1] exhibited at the Burlington Fine Arts Club, 1904 (No. 47); Salting Bequest, 1910.

REPRODUCTION: *Illustrations, Italian Schools,* 1937, p. 38. *Plates, Earlier Italian Schools,* 1953, Vol. I, p. 48.

REFERENCE: (1) Salting MSS. The name originally written was that of Fra Carnevale, but this has been changed by Salting to Benvenuto's.

AMBROGIO BERGOGNONE
active 1481, died 1523 (?)

Ambrogio (di Stefano) da Fossano, called *Bergognone* or *Borgognone.* Active at Milan, where in the guild, 1481; from 1488 until 1494/5, and occasionally later, he was working at the Certosa di Pavia. There are a number of documented and dated works. His style derives chiefly from Foppa, and remained almost entirely uninfluenced by Leonardesque taste. A distinction between early and late Bergognones can be made, although his manner did not evolve much.

The part of his *œuvre* attributable to his brother Bernardino cannot be accurately decided. Bernardino, active 1492–1523, is known to have assisted Ambrogio at the Certosa di Pavia and at Lodi; a picture by him, signed and dated 1523, is in the Brera (reproduced in the *Bollettino d'Arte,* April, 1931, p. 457). A picture at Bonn, initialled and dated 1506, is claimed to be his by Suida in the *Rivista d'Arte,* 1957, pp. 172/3.

There was another Ambrogio (di Giorgio) Borgognone, a Pavian painter, apprenticed 1481–died 1513/8.

298   ALTARPIECE: THE VIRGIN AND CHILD WITH SS. CATHERINE OF ALEXANDRIA AND SIENA

A piece of coral hangs from the Child's neck; the Virgin's halo is inscribed, AVE MARIS STELLA DEI MA(ter). The edges of the Virgin's veil and mantle are ornamented with letters, which occasionally form words; the following may be recorded, MARIA MATER GRATIE / . . . /(t)IBI DOM(inu) / S EST DEV(s) / PIETATE TVA NOS.... On the left, S. Catherine of Alexandria, her halo inscribed (San)CTA KATERINA MARTIR; on the right, S. Catherine of Siena, her halo inscribed SANCTA KATERINA DE SE(nis).

Poplar,[1] rounded top, painted surface, $73\frac{3}{4} \times 51$ ($1 \cdot 875 \times 1 \cdot 295$). The measurements are taken from the incised lines marking the limit of the picture; here and there some unfinished painting continues raggedly beyond. The painted surface continues to the extreme bottom edge, which however does not seem likely to have been cut.

The paint in the principal parts is well preserved.

There was formerly a lunette to the picture, a *pietà* with the dead Christ on the lap of the seated Madonna. Right (?), S. John kneeling; beyond him, a portion of a column (?), with a crown of thorns on it; on the other side, the Magdalen kneeling with clasped hands. All under a coffered arch; a hanging behind the two central figures, sky on each side.[2] This lunette was purchased for the National Gallery at the same time as No. 298, but was not despatched to England until 1860 and perished *en route* at sea.

The altarpiece is obviously the one described by P. Matteo Valerio in the Certosa di Pavia.[3] It was presumably painted during Bergognone's first and chief period of activity there; two altarpieces still in the Certosa are dated 1490 and 1491.

COPY: A copy of No. 298 (without the lunette) takes the place of the original at Rebecchino (see the Provenance); it is apparently by the daughter of Carlo Tadeo, through whom No. 298 was purchased.[4]

PROVENANCE: Obviously the picture mentioned in the Certosa di Pavia by Prior Matteo Valerio, who was living there from 1604 until 1645.[5] Presumably it hung in the fifth chapel off the left aisle of the nave, which is dedicated to the two SS. Catherine; a *Virgin and Child with the two SS. Catherine* by Francesco del Cairo (1607–1665) is now there, and was already there in 1771.[6] No. 298 with its lunette was discovered in 1857 in the Chapel of Rebecchino near Pavia, which had been once a dependency of the Certosa; purchased thence through Carlo Tadeo, 1857.

REPRODUCTION: *Illustrations, Italian Schools*, 1937, p. 52. *Plates, Earlier Italian Schools*, 1953, Vol. I, p. 49.

REFERENCES: (1) Letter from B. J. Rendle of the Forest Products Research Laboratory, in the Gallery archives. (2) The description is based on Eastlake's notes taken in front of the picture. G. L. Calvi, *Notizie sulla vita...dei... pittori...in Milano*, II, 1865, pp. 246/7, who also had seen the lunette, describes it as representing 'Cristo deposto dalla croce sulle ginocchia della madre, con la Maddalena ed uno dei suoi discepoli'. (3) *Lancona di santa Caterina da Siena, e santa Catarina martire*. See Luca Beltrami's *Ambrogio Fossano*, 1895, Nos. 84 and 138. (Beltrami's No. 139 is the lunette.) P. Matteo Valerio's complete text is printed in the *Archivio Storico Lombardo*, 1879, pp. 134 ff.; on p. 136 he seems to imply that No. 298 is of 1490. (4) Letter from Prof. Panazza of Pavia, 1947, in the Gallery archives. For the authorship of the copy, see Carlo Magenta, *La Certosa di Pavia*, 1897, p. 298. (5) See note 3. Valerio also records (pp. 135/6) that Bergognone 'fecit imaginem B. Caterinae de Senis in claustro magno pretio de anno 1489 L.74', and 'fece una Beata Catarina da Siena nel Claustro, hora chiusa ov'è il sposalizio di detta santa, L.74' (implied of 1488 or 1489). It is not clear if this is a fresco or a picture. If the latter, it presumably (rather than No. 298) is the 'tavola di Santa Caterina da Senia esistente in detta Certosa nella sala del Capitolo', of 1489, noted as Bergognone's by Albuzzi (1776?); see *L'Arte*, July 1951–June 1952, p. 30 of the supplement and (for Albuzzi's date), *L'Arte*, July 1948–July 1951, pp. iv ff. of the supplement. (6) See J. J. Volkmann, *Historisch-Kritische Nachrichten*, 1771, III, p. 758. For Francesco del Cairo's dates, see Stella Matalon in the *Rivista d'Arte*, 1930, pp. 498 and 506; on p. 515 the Certosa altarpiece is reproduced.

1077 THE VIRGIN AND CHILD WITH TWO ANGELS

The hem of the Virgin's mantle is ornamented with letters, which in one place form the word B'NARDINO.

Wood, painted surface, $36\frac{1}{2} \times 22\frac{3}{4}$ (0·93 × 0·575). Painted up to the edges all round.

Good state.

At one time wrongly associated with Nos. 1077A and B below as the central panel of a triptych.

A very early work, still strongly under the influence of Foppa, and perhaps dating from *ca.* 1480/5.

The presence of the word Bernardino on the Virgin's mantle would not appear to be a good reason for ascribing the picture to Ambrogio's brother of that name. The ornaments on the seat may be compared with Leonardo's more elaborate designs of knots, which are probably of later date.[1]

PROVENANCE: Doubtless No. 26 of a catalogue of the Melzi Collection, Milan, early nineteenth century. Stated later to have been in the Scotti Collection.[2] Purchased from Giuseppe Baslini, Milan, 1879. Exhibited at Milan, *Arte Lombarda*, 1958 (No. 375).

REPRODUCTION: *Illustrations, Italian Schools*, 1937, p. 53. *Plates, Earlier Italian Schools*, 1953, Vol. I, p. 50.

REFERENCES: (1) A. M. Hind, *Early Italian Engraving*, Vol. V, 1948, pp. 93 ff. and Vol. VI, 1948, Plates 626/8; reproduced also in the *Bollettino d'Arte*, November 1924, pp. 220/4. (2) National Gallery MS. Catalogue. The Melzi d'Eril Collection was formed for the most part by Conte Giacomo, who died in 1802. In 1835, the pictures were divided between three heirs, one of whom, Donna Barbara, did marry Duca Tommaso Gallarati Scotti. See Giulio Carotti, *Capi d'Arte appartenenti a S.E. la Duchessa Joséphine Melzi d'Eril-Barbò*, 1901, pp. 9 ff., 140 ff.; the undated Melzi catalogue is reprinted in this volume.

1077A THE AGONY IN THE GARDEN (ONE PANEL FROM AN ALTARPIECE)

On Christ's halo, IESVS CRISTVS; letters on His robe in one place form the word MERITIS. The angel holds a cup, in which are the symbols of the Passion, Cross, Crown of Thorns, Spear and Sponge. In the middle distance, the three disciples; Judas enters furtively at the gate.

Wood, rounded top, original painted surface, $39\frac{1}{4} \times 17\frac{3}{4}$ (0·995 × 0·45). These measurements are taken according to the incised lines marking the limits of the picture; unfinished paint continues raggedly a little beyond, especially in the spandrels at the top. Another set of incised lines shows that at one time the original shape of the painted surface was to have been $39\frac{1}{2} \times 15\frac{3}{4}$ ($1\cdot00 \times 0\cdot40$), rounded top; parts of the painting at the sides, outside the smaller measurement, but within the painted area first given, have been left slightly unfinished.

Excellent state.

For the commentary, etc., see under No. 1077B.

1077B CHRIST CARRYING THE CROSS (ONE PANEL FROM AN ALTARPIECE)

His halo is inscribed, IESVS AVE NAZARENVS: the letters on His robe are merely decoration. In the left-hand bottom corner, 1501 / FF. Q.O (the lower line hidden by the frame; contemporary?).

Wood, rounded top, painted surface, $39\frac{1}{2} \times 17\frac{3}{4}$ ($1\cdot00 \times 0\cdot45$). The measurements are taken as for No. 1077A; here also the picture was originally to have been narrower ($15\frac{3}{4}$ in.), but the incised lines are less obvious.

Condition very good, but a little less so than No. 1077A. The arm of the Cross was apparently once placed higher.

Nos. 1077A and B obviously once formed part of a polyptych or triptych; No. 1077 above has been wrongly supposed to be the central panel. Nos. 1077A and B are late works; 1501 may be their date. The inscription on No. 1077B is, nevertheless, not wholly convincing, and the second line is obscure.

PROVENANCE: Doubtless Nos. 41, 42 of a catalogue of the Melzi Collection, Milan, early nineteenth century. Stated later to have been in the Scotti Collection.[1] Purchased from Giuseppe Baslini, Milan, 1879.

REPRODUCTIONS: *Illustrations, Italian Schools*, 1937, p. 53. *Plates, Earlier Italian Schools*, 1953, Vol. I, pp. 51, 52.

REFERENCE: (1) N.G. MS. Catalogue. Cf. note 2 for the entry to No. 1077 above.

1410 THE VIRGIN AND CHILD

The Child is playing with a rosary; the Virgin's halo is inscribed, AVE MARIA GRATIA PLENA DOMIN. The book on the parapet is inscribed: *Domine labra | m aperies & | os meum | anuntiabit laudez | tuam Deus m | adiutoriu meū | intende mē ad | adiuvandum me | festina Grīā prī | et filio et sp*(iri)*to | sancto Sicut | erat in p̄ripī | n..c & semp.* The background to the right shows the unfinished façade of the Certosa di Pavia, with the transept behind.

Poplar,[1] painted surface, $21\frac{3}{4} \times 14$ ($0\cdot55 \times 0\cdot355$).

Very good condition; two obvious damages by Christ's left eye.

The first parts of the inscription on the book are from Psalms l, 17 (li, 15) and lxix, 2 (lxx, 1). The whole passage is said at matins, according to the Roman Catholic Breviary.

The unfinished state of the Certosa buildings in the background of No. 1410 most probably indicates a date of about 1488 or very soon after.[2]

PROVENANCE: Said to have been given by one of Napoleon's generals or by
Napoleon himself to Contessa Elisabetta Ottolini Visconti, Milan;[3] seen in her
house by Sir Charles Eastlake shortly before his death (1865).[4] She did not know
of his death, and the picture was offered for sale by her to him on 12 October,
1866.[5] After some negotiations, it was acquired by Lady Eastlake through Paolo
Orlandi in Milan on 16 October, 1867.[6] Lady Eastlake's Sale, 2 June, 1894 (lot
64), bought by Murray for the National Gallery.

REPRODUCTION: *Illustrations, Italian Schools*, 1937, p. 54. *Plates, Earlier
Italian Schools*, 1953, Vol. I, p. 53.

REFERENCES: (1) Letter from B. J. Rendle of the Forest Products Research
Laboratory, in the Gallery archives. (2) Cf. Cagnola in the *Rassegna d'Arte*,
1914, p. 219. (3) Victoria and Albert Museum Library, 86 M 39. Letter (No.
48) from Paolo Orlandi, Turin, to Lady Eastlake, 25 December, 1866: 'seppi
colà da persona confidente della Contessa che quel prezioso quadretto fu dono
di un Generale di N.° 1.° o del Console stesso della republica francese; se ciò è,
non dubito, che fece parte della spoliazione fatta da quei Signori alla Certosa di
Pavia'. Letter (No. 50) from Paolo Orlandi, Milan, to Lady Eastlake, 12 November, 1867, reporting that the Countess had said that 'senza il caso datosi d'essere
l'ultimo quadro gustato' (by Sir Charles Eastlake), 'non avrei mai venduto per
qualunque somma questo quadretto che era dono di persona a me carissima'.
(4) See the second letter quoted in the previous note; also, in the same collection, letter No. 39, from Elisabetta Ottolini Visconti, Milan, to Sir Charles
Eastlake, 12 October, 1866. (5) See letter No. 39, referred to in the previous
note. (6) Same collection, letter No. 51, Paolo Orlandi, Milan, to Lady Eastlake,
16 October, 1867. In the same collection, letters No. 49 (Paolo Orlandi to Lady
Eastlake, 1 September, 1867) and 52 (the same to the same, 25 December, 1867)
also refer to the acquisition of this picture. The Ottolini provenance is recorded
in the Eastlake Sale of 1894, and there is no doubt at all concerning the identity
of the picture.

Ascribed to AMBROGIO BERGOGNONE

779–780 MEMBERS   OF   A   CONFRATERNITY   (?)
          (FRAGMENTS)

(779) The heads or busts of nine kneeling men, and part of a male (?)
Patron Saint.

Silk or canvas, mounted on wood, painted surface, $25\frac{3}{8} \times 16\frac{1}{2}$ (0·645 ×
0·42), each.

The paint is very thin, and has been much damaged by flaking and
extensively repaired; the style of the original, however, is very fairly
preserved in some of the heads.

(780) The heads or busts of fourteen kneeling women, and part of a
Patron Saint.

Silk or canvas, mounted on wood, painted surface, $25\frac{3}{8} \times 16\frac{1}{2}$ (0·645 ×
0·42).

Condition as for No. 779, but perhaps rather worse; the style of the
original, however, is very fairly preserved in the three principal faces in
the front row.

Said to be parts of a Standard, said to have been once in the Certosa
di Pavia.[1] What is left of the style is reminiscent of Ambrogio

Bergognone, but the attribution is not certain. They are admitted by Berenson (1932 Lists). At one time catalogued as of the Milanese School, with the suggestion that they might be by Butinone or Zenale;[2] Carotti thinks them early works of Boltraffio.[3] Formerly called 'Family Portraits,' which is very unlikely.

PROVENANCE: According to a record of Molteni's statements, acquired at an auction in Milan by a dealer, from whom acquired by Molteni; Molteni bought the whole Standard, but divided it up and kept only the less ruined portions.[4] Bought from Giuseppe Baslini, Milan, 1867.

REPRODUCTIONS: *Illustrations, Italian Schools*, 1937, p. 232. *Plates, Earlier Italian Schools* 1953, Vol. I, p. 54.

REFERENCES: (1) According to a letter in the Gallery archives from Cav. Bertini, 11 February, 1868, Molteni had given to Bertini another fragment (*God the Father*). Cf. also Crowe and Cavalcaselle, *Painting in North Italy*, II, 1871, pp. 47/8, or ed. Borenius, II, 1912, p. 368. (2) Cf. H. Cook in *The Burlington Magazine*, Vol. V (1904), p. 199. (3) G. Carotti in *Le Gallerie Nazionali Italiane*, 1899, p. 304. (4) References as in note 1.

Style of AMBROGIO BERGOGNONE

3080 S. PAUL (PANEL FROM AN ALTARPIECE)
See No. 3081 below.

3081 S. AMBROSE (?) (PANEL FROM AN ALTARPIECE)

Each, poplar,[1] painted surface, $43\frac{1}{2} \times 16\frac{1}{2}$ ($1 \cdot 10 \times 0 \cdot 42$), approx. The edges at the sides are ragged; at the top and the bottom the panels, which are warped, have been cut into at the front to fit them into the frames, and it is possible that the original heights were slightly greater. As is quite common, the support is not plain wood, but wood covered with a fabric; in the case of No. 3081, the fabric is silk.[2]
Gravely damaged.

The subject of No. 3081 is a Bishop; and since it is a Milanese picture, he is likely to be S. Ambrose.

To judge by the perspective, perhaps from the upper tier of an altarpiece in compartments.

Acquired by Layard as by Bergognone. They cannot be by him, but it seems justifiable to associate them with his manner; their condition forbids a more precise attribution.

PROVENANCE: Brought by Sir Austen Henry Layard from Bruschetti, Milan;[3] exhibited at South Kensington, 1869 (Nos. 22, 23); Layard Bequest, 1916.[4]

REPRODUCTIONS: *Illustrations, Italian Schools*, 1937, pp. 234, 235. *Plates, Earlier Italian Schools*, 1953, Vol. I, p. 55.

REFERENCES: (1) Letter from B. J. Rendle, of the Forest Products Research Laboratory, in the Gallery archives. The specimen of No. 3081 sent to him was

too much decayed for certainty, but was probably of poplar, like that from
No. 3080. (2) The fabric was exposed by an old damage at the bottom of the
picture, and a piece could be removed for analysis, which was kindly carried out
by Dr. W. T. Astbury of Leeds University (letter in the Gallery archives).
(3) Layard MSS. in the National Gallery. It seems probable that they are the
'due figure, opere di Bergognone . . . bellissime, e con la cifra dell'autore' (sic),
acquired from Bruschetti by Layard through Saverio Cavallari ca. 1856; see
A. Venturi in L'Arte, 1912, p. 450. See also Sir A. Henry Layard, Autobiography and Letters, ed. W. N. Bruce, 1903, II, p. 210, letter of 7 September,
1856, apropos of Bergognone: 'I think I have succeeded in picking up a couple
of specimens of his. They are not in his best manner, etc.' (4) For the history of
the Layard Collection, see Appendix IV.

BERTUCCI See GIOVANNI Battista of Faenza

Francesco BISSOLO
active 1492, died 1554

First mentioned as working in the Doge's Palace, Venice, at a modest
wage. There are a good many signed works, some dated; he died in
1554, but the latest date on a picture is 1530. His style is derived from
that of Giovanni Bellini towards 1500.

3083 THE VIRGIN AND CHILD WITH SS. MICHAEL AND VERONICA AND TWO DONORS

.MICHA EL. is inscribed on S. Michael's dress; S. Veronica holds
a kerchief with the image of Christ.

Wood, painted surface, $24\frac{1}{2} \times 33\frac{1}{8}$ (0·62 × 0·84); painted up to the
edges all round.

Very fair state. Pentimenti in S. Michael's left wing and the forehead
of the female donor.

The design of the Virgin and Child occurs very frequently, sometimes
alone, sometimes with saints as here. It was probably invented by
Giovanni Bellini about 1500; there exist examples by Bissolo[1] and
Bartolomeo Veneto.[2]

PROVENANCE: Perhaps from the Pesaro Collection, Venice.[3] Owned by Pope
Gregory XVI (Capellari, died 1846); purchased from his heirs by Sir A. H.
Layard.[4] Exhibited at South Kensington, 1869 (No. 9); Layard Bequest, 1916.[5]

REPRODUCTION: Illustrations, Italian Schools, 1937, p. 41. Plates, Earlier
Italian Schools, 1953, Vol. I, p. 56.

REFERENCES: (1) E.g. at Venice, Gronau's Klassiker der Kunst Bellini, 1930,
Plate 191, and note. It is reproduced as Bartolomeo Veneto by Venturi with
other examples of the design in L'Arte, 1899, pp. 432 ff. (2) E.g. Venturi, Storia
dell'Arte Italiana, Vol. VII, Part IV, Fig. 440 (signed and dated 1505). (3) In
the 1797 Inventory of the Collection of Pietro and Giovanni Pesaro, No. C 131 is
described as 'Madonna; Bambino, S. Michele, S. Veronica e due ritratti,
in tavola', size 1 ft. 9 in. × 2 ft. 5 in. Venetian measure, with an attribution to
Gio. dal Buon C° (presumably Buonconsiglio); see G. Fiocco, Palazzo Pesaro,

1925, p. 43. Not among the 24 lots of the Pesaro Sale, London, 9 July, 1831 (Lugt, No. 12716). (4) Layard MSS. in the National Gallery. (5) For the history of the Layard Collection, see Appendix IV.

3915 THE VIRGIN AND CHILD WITH S. PAUL AND A FEMALE MARTYR

Wood, painted surface, $30\frac{3}{4} \times 46\frac{1}{4}$ (0.78×1.175).

Considerably repainted.

The group of the Virgin and Child is taken from Bellini's San Zaccaria altarpiece of 1505;[1] it occurs in other pictures by Bissolo also.[2]

VERSION: Gronau notes a variant once in the Raffauf Collection, Constantinople.[3]

PROVENANCE: Bought from the collection of Conte F. Balladoro, Verona, by J. P. Richter in 1887. Acquired by Ludwig Mond, 1888;[4] exhibited at the R.A., 1891 (No. 104), and at the New Gallery, 1894/5 (No. 155); Mond Bequest, 1924.

REPRODUCTION: *Illustrations, Italian Schools*, 1937, p. 41. *Plates, Earlier Italian Schools*, 1953, Vol. I, p. 57.

REFERENCES: (1) Gronau, Klassiker der Kunst *Bellini*, 1930, Plate 160. (2) E.g. in the Academy and in the Church of the Redentore at Venice; reproduced in Venturi, *Storia dell'Arte Italiana*, Vol. VII, Part IV, Figs. 363 and 365. (3) Gronau in Thieme-Becker, Vol. IV, p. 68. Raffauf-Horchheim Sale, Berlin, 3 February, 1914 (lot 52), Plate 12; it corresponds quite closely with No. 3915, except that the female saint in the Raffauf picture is characterized as S. Catherine of Alexandria. (4) Richter, *The Mond Collection*, 1910, I, Table of Contents.

Boccaccio BOCCACCINO
active 1493, died 1524/5

Cremonese School. He worked in Genoa in 1493, in Ferrara 1497–1500, and in Venice; but his chief activity was at Cremona, especially from 1506. Vasari says that he was 58 years old at death, but Puerari, *Boccaccino*, 1957, p. 201, claims that he was born not later than 1465. A good many authenticated pictures and frescoes exist. His style reflects Ferrarese and Venetian influences.

His grandson of the same names was also a painter (see Thieme-Becker).

Ascribed to Boccaccio BOCCACCINO

806 ALTARPIECE: THE WAY TO CALVARY

Christ, the Virgin, the Holy Women and S. John are present. The procession continues in the background on the right; there are seen the two thieves, and two horsemen with banners inscribed (S) P Q R. Golgotha further back still.

Wood, painted surface, $52 \times 51\frac{1}{2}$ (1.32×1.31).

On the whole in good condition; Christ's face is somewhat repainted.

There are a good many *pentimenti*. Thus, the outline of the horse continues through the head of the furthermost Holy Woman and (in part at least) through that of the turbaned Holy Woman further right; the latter figure has several changes in the outlines. The figure behind S. John has had the position of his head changed. In the landscape at the extreme left, the mound-like hill is a *pentimento*, and so in part at least are the similar hills right centre.

The attribution of No. 806 has sometimes seemed to be settled by its provenance; indeed, if it is the picture recorded as by Boccaccino in S. Domenico at Cremona by the Anonimo Morelliano,[1] the attribution could hardly be questioned.[2] The identification of No. 806 with the Anonimo's picture at Cremona may be correct;[3] but it is not proved,[4] and in the present state of knowledge the attribution of No. 806 must depend upon stylistic criticism.

Critics may have been influenced in their judgments by the supposed provenance, but in any case, they have tended on the whole to accept No. 806 as an early Boccaccino. It was acquired by the Gallery under this name. Crowe and Cavalcaselle[5] do not accept it, but say that it is reminiscent of Boccaccino. Frizzoni at one time accepted it, but later took the view that it is by a contemporary of Boccaccino, probably Cremonese.[6] Schweitzer[7] accepts it as a late work (which seems impossible). Berenson in his Lists of 1907 did not accept it as a Boccaccino, but in his 1932 Lists admits it with a question mark. Venturi[8] accepts it as early. Gronau[9] accepts it as early, and near in date to a picture which he reproduces, signed and dated 1491 or 1497. Accepted by Longhi and Puerari.[10] A date of *ca.* 1500 suits the costume (note by Miss Stella M. Pearce).

Sacchi[11] claims that certain figures in No. 806 are exactly repeated in a signed Boccaccino at Venice, and in Boccaccino's fresco of *The Marriage of the Virgin* in Cremona Cathedral;[12] but this is incorrect.

The man at the extreme left of the picture, in the foreground, might be the portrait of the painter.

PROVENANCE: For the possibility that No. 806 comes from S. Domenico at Cremona, see above. No. 806 is first certainly recorded *ca.* 1827 in the Collection of the Marchese Sommi-Picenardi at the Torri de' Picenardi near Cremona.[13] The collection passed by inheritance to the Marchese Araldi Erizzo, whose creditors sold this and other pictures to Baslini in 1869.[14] Purchased from Baslini, Milan, 1870.

REPRODUCTION: *Illustrations, Italian Schools*, 1937, p. 40. *Plates, Earlier Italian Schools*, 1953, Vol. I, p. 58.

REFERENCES: (1) See the *Anonimo Morelliano (Michiel)*, ed. Frizzoni, 1884, p. 86: 'La palletta della nostra Donna a man sinistra della porta del coro fu de mano del Boccacino. L'altra palletta del Cristo tirato alla Croce, dall'altro lato fu de mano del detto.' Frimmel, in his edition of the *Anonimo Morelliano*, 1888, pp. 40, 42, gives a text no doubt more correct, but with merely verbal differences. The Anonimo's notes on Cremona seem to be no earlier than 1522, and perhaps not much later; cf. Frizzoni, pp. 84/5 (his dates are not quite accurate). F. Nicolini, *L'Arte Napoletana del Rinascimento e la Lettera di Pietro Summonte*, 1925, p. 79, suggests that Michiel's visit to Cremona was probably of 1517/8;

but this seems unlikely. Some National Gallery catalogues date the passage *ca.* 1537, but there seems to be no evidence for that. (2) The Anonimo does not specify Boccaccio Boccaccino; but, to judge of what he mentions at Cremona, he probably did mean Boccaccio Boccaccino when he referred to Boccaccino. In point of fact, an altar next a side-door of S. Domenico (leading into the street) did have an altarpiece by Camillo Boccaccino, *The Virgin and Child with S. Michael and the B. Ambrogio Sansedoni*; cf. A. M. Panni, *Distinto Rapporto delle Dipinture . . . di Cremona*, 1762, p. 69. G. B. Zaist, *Notizie Istoriche de' Pittori etc. Cremonesi*, 1774, I, p. 133, states that it is signed and an early work, i.e. perhaps early enough for the Anonimo to have seen; F. Sacchi, *Notizie Pittoriche Cremonesi*, 1872, p. 51, as in the Palazzo di Giustizia; reproduced by E. Signori, *Cremona*, 1928, p. 117 (in the Museo Civico); also reproduced by A. Venturi, *Storia dell'Arte Italiana*, Vol. IX, Part VI, Fig. 488; Puerari, *La Pinacoteca di Cremona*, 1951, Fig. 94 and p. 78 (as soon after 1532). (3) As has been seen in note 1, the Anonimo mentions a picture of the same subject as No. 806, which further he says was a small altarpiece. This may be considered fair evidence for the identity with No. 806. (4) There seems to be no mention except the Anonimo's of any picture in S. Domenico at Cremona that could be No. 806. The church is now destroyed; Sacchi, *op. cit.*, p. 42, identifies the Anonimo's 'porta del coro' as the door leading into the sacristy. If that is correct, Boccaccino's *Way to Calvary* was probably removed from its place not later than *ca.* 1572. On the right-hand side of the sacristy door (confirmed by G. Aglio, *Le Pitture e le Sculture della Città di Cremona*, 1794, p. 55; Zaist, *op. cit.*, pp. 121 and 204 is confused about this), an altar was erected in accordance with the will of Giovanni Battista Picenardi, who died in 1572 (1573 n.s. ?). The altarpiece of this new altar, representing *The Nativity*, was commissioned of Bernardino Campi in 1574; he finished his picture in the same year, and it was signed and dated 1574. See Sacchi, *op. cit.*, pp. 247/9 and 78; also A. Lamo, *Discorso intorno alla scoltura, et pittura*, 1584, pp. 95/6. (The present whereabouts of Campi's altarpiece appears to be unknown; it was sold in 1890 to Cav. Alfonso Reichman or Reichmann—see G. Sommi-Picenardi, *Le Torri de' Picenardi*, 1909, pp. 139 and 143; see also *Cremona, Mostra di Antiche Pitture*, 1948, No. 35. According to Grasselli, *Guida . . . di Cremona*, 1818, pp. 56 and 191, a copy of it—by some Boccaccino—replaced the original at some time in S. Domenico. G. Sommi-Picenardi, *op. cit.*, p. 143, says that the copy was put in the church in 1796, that it is by Fr. Boccaccino, and that at the time he wrote it was at the Torri de' Picenardi.) It is to be noted that the altar of *ca.* 1572 belonged to the Picenardi family, and that No. 806 was in the Picenardi Collection in the nineteenth century; this has been perhaps rashly held to confirm the provenance of No. 806 from S. Domenico at Cremona. The student might imagine that the history of Boccaccino's *Virgin and Child*, on the other side of the Anonimo's 'porta del coro' in S. Domenico, might be of interest for the history of No. 806; but that can hardly be claimed to be so. (a) the Anonimo does not say that the two pictures were connected in any way, except in location and authorship. (b) what was presumably the Anonimo's *Virgin and Child* is recorded in the choir of S. Domenico (signed, not dated), by Zaist, *op. cit.*, I, p. 68; but no evidence is known that any picture that could be No. 806 was then still in the church. (c) Zaist's *Virgin and Child* had apparently gone from the church by 1794; see Aglio, *op. cit.*, p. 44 ff. Sacchi, *op. cit.*, pp. 42/3, claims that it is identical with a *Virgin and Child* (size 1·15 × 0·52) in the nineteenth century in the Picenardi Collection (G. Sommi-Picenardi, *op. cit.*, p. 157, No. 203 of a catalogue of *ca.* 1827); and No. 806 was in the Picenardi Collection at the same time. Yet all this, which might seem to be confirmatory evidence, turns out to be rather the contrary. For one thing, almost all the Picenardi pictures (not indeed the already mentioned Bernardino Campi) were not of Picenardi provenance, but came in from the Biffi-Sommi Collection. Further, if Sacchi is right, No. 806 had been in S. Domenico in a place where by *ca.* 1572 the Picenardi had an altar; and in that case, the location of Boccaccino's *Virgin and Child* is also known, and that altar is not recorded to have belonged to the Picenardi. (The altarpiece painted for it later, by Giulio Campi, seems actually to be missing.) It may be said that, even if the Anonimo's two Boccaccinos were both later in the Picenardi Collection, their history appears to have been largely independent. It should be added that, in any case, Boccaccino's *Virgin and Child* in the Picenardi Collection may have disappeared; Gronau in *Belvedere*, 1929, p. 254, suggests that it may be the picture now in the Liechtenstein Collection, but the size does not correspond very well with the size given by Sacchi. Further, Gronau says that the Liechtenstein picture has the remains of a date as well as a signature; but in that case, it can hardly be the same as the picture Zaist records in S. Domenico, which he positively says was without date. See further the comments by Puerari, *Boccaccino*, 1957, p. 203, note 110. (5) Crowe and Cavalcaselle, *History of Painting in North Italy*, II, 1871, p. 446. (6) Frizzoni in the *Archivio Storico Italiano*, 1879, II, pp. 413/4, and his *Arte Italiana del Rinascimento*, 1891, pp. 326/7. (7) E. Schweitzer in *L'Arte*, 1900, pp. 45/6. (8) A. Venturi, *Storia dell'Arte Italiana*, Vol. VII, Part III, p. 728, and Vol. VII, Part IV, p. 671. (9) Gronau in *Belvedere*, 1929, p. 252. The picture of 149(.) reproduced by Gronau seems to be the same as the one (with many differences) reproduced by Puerari, *Boccaccino*, 1957, Fig. 26. (10) R. Longhi, *Officina Ferrarese*, 1934, p. 119; Puerari, *Boccaccino*, 1957, pp. 79 ff. and 225 (as of 1499-1500). Both writers make comments on stylistic influences from other painters. (11) F. Sacchi, *Notizie Pittoriche Cremonesi*, 1872, p. 41. (12) Puerari, *Boccaccino*, 1957, Figs. 102 and 132. (13) See Guido Sommi–Picenardi, *Le Torri de' Picenardi*, 1909. pp. 138/9 and p. 141 (No. 8); as A. Mantegna. (The catalogue here printed was written by the Marchese Giuseppe Picenardi *ca.* 1827.) G. Sommi–Picenardi, *loc. cit.*, notes that it had been ascribed to Carpaccio and Cosimo Tura as well as to Mantegna, but was at the time of sale held to be by Boccaccino. (14) The collection had been formed for the most part by Conte Giovanni Battista Biffi; it was moved from Cremona to the Torri de' Picenardi *ca.* 1827. See further in the entry for Marziale, No. 803.

See also Ascribed to ANDREA PREVITALI, No. 3111

GIOVANNI ANTONIO BOLTRAFFIO
ca. 1466/7(?)—1516

Another, perhaps better, spelling is *Beltraffio*. The date of birth is from his tomb; according to the Milanese necrology, he was only 45 years old at death (see E. Motta in the *Archivio Storico Lombardo*, 1891, p. 259). Active at Milan. He appears to have been Leonardo's principal pupil; mentioned in Leonardo's studio in 1491, he seems to have been working independently by 1498. The *S. Barbara* at Berlin is a documented work, ordered in 1502; the *Casio Madonna* in the Louvre is said by Vasari to have been signed and dated 1500; an altarpiece from Lodi at Budapest is datable *ca.* 1508. These dates are not adequate for establishing any exact chronological order for the pictures grouped as Boltraffio's.

728 THE VIRGIN AND CHILD (FRAGMENT?)

The curtain is inscribed AVE / AVE / .MA., partly new. Two inventory numbers, 1114 and +.103.+.

Wood, painted surface, $36\frac{1}{2} \times 26\frac{1}{2}$ (0·925 × 0·67); painted up to the edges all round.

The condition is quite good on the whole, but there are numerous retouches, including many on important outlines. There are several *pentimenti* in Christ's limbs, some visible only under X-Rays; X-Rays also show changes in the Virgin's eyes, the line of her right shoulder, and the line of her collar, which to the right seems to have been left somewhat ragged at the first painting.

It is possible that this is the central fragment of a large altarpiece.

Suida[1] dates it *ca.* 1498. There is little justification for attaching a particular year to the work, but Suida may well be right in thinking it early; the Child's hair is very Leonardesque.

The design of the Child, somewhat varied, reappears in No. 1300 of the present catalogue, Follower of Leonardo.

PROVENANCE: Coll. Lord Northwick, where seen by Waagen;[2] Sale, 3 August, 1859 (lot 576),[3] bought by Finney for the Rev. W. Davenport Bromley. Davenport Bromley Sale, 12 June, 1863 (lot 159), purchased for the National Gallery.

REPRODUCTION: *Illustrations, Italian Schools*, 1937, p. 42. *Plates, Earlier Italian Schools*, 1953, Vol. I, p. 59.

REFERENCES: (1) Suida, *Leonardo und sein Kreis*, 1929, p. 189. (2) Waagen, *Treasures*, 1854, iii, p. 201 (ascribing it to Boltraffio). There is no description, but it seems unreasonable to doubt the identity. (3) As Verrocchio, with some description. It may well be the *Virgin and Child* by A. Verocchio, lent by Lord Northwick to the British Institution, 1847 (No. 58). This may be the "Andrea Veronica. 'The Adoration'; antique" recorded among the pictures at Northwick Park in *The Art-Union*, 1846, p. 274.

3916   A MAN IN PROFILE

Wood, painted surface, $22\frac{1}{4} \times 16\frac{3}{4}$ (0·565 × 0·425).

Fair state. Two previous attempts at the collar are visible on the surface; another still higher up is revealed by X-Rays.

A portrait, traditionally supposed to be of the same man full-face, size 0·54 × 0·40, was exhibited at the R.A., 1930 (No. 306; Memorial Catalogue, No. 309).[1] The two pictures were formerly in two Frizzoni Collections at Bergamo; one of these was removed to Milan in 1856,[2] the other (containing No. 3916) to Bellagio.

PROVENANCE: Seen in a Frizzoni Collection at Bergamo in 1855; then, in 1862 and 1864, in the Villa Frizzoni at Bellagio (i.e. Federico Frizzoni de Salis).[3] Acquired by Sir William Boxall, who died in 1879, bequeathing it to Lady Eastlake;[4] her Sale, 2 June, 1894 (lot 60), bought by C. Davis for Ludwig Mond. Exhibited at the New Gallery, 1897/8 (No. 135), and at the Burlington Fine Arts Club, 1898 (No. 48). Mond Bequest, 1924.

REPRODUCTION: *Illustrations, Italian Schools*, 1937, p 43. *Plates, Earlier Italian Schools*, 1953 Vol. I. p. 60.

REFERENCES: (1) Contini Collection. Reproduced by Malaguzzi Valeri, *La Corte di Lodovico il Moro*, Vol. III, 1917, p. 86 (then in the Gustavo Frizzoni Collection). G. Frizzoni in the *Gazette des Beaux-Arts*, 1898, II, p. 302 and in the *Rassegna d'Arte*, 1911, p. 44, says that the two portraits represent the same man. The claim seems very unlikely, since the Contini portrait is described as having 'occhi castani' and 'cappelli castano-rossiccio'. In No. 3916, the hair is indeed extensively repainted; but two cleaning tests have showed that, while there is a warm brown ground in the area, there is nothing in the original paint remaining that could be called brown or auburn, the paint is all black or shades of grey. It seems therefore excessively unlikely that the hair in its original, complete state could have been brown. The eye of No. 3916 should now be called black, and is unlikely ever to have been of a different colour. One may add that it is unlikely that the man's sallow complexion was ever much warmer than now. These matters affect any attempt to identify the sitter of No. 3916 as the poet Gerolamo Casio. The portraits claimed to be of him cannot be fully discussed in this place, and it must suffice to record that the two that should be the basis for discussion (each in a condition that must be allowed for by students) are the portrait in the Brera at Milan (Malaguzzi Valeri, *op. cit.*, Fig. 76 on p. 85) and the portrait in Boltraffio's altarpiece in the Louvre (Suida, *Leonardo und sein Kreis*, 1929, Fig. 214). Maria Reggiani Rajna (*Un po' d'ordine fra tanti Casii* in *Rinascimento*, 1951, pp. 337 ff.), whose note on the eyes and hair of the Contini portrait (p. 379) has been quoted, there says that the colour of the hair in the Contini and Brera pictures corresponds. On p. 381 she says that the eyes in the Brera portrait are really brown with a very few small greenish touches. D.ssa Mecheri and D.ssa Ottino of the Brera kindly confirmed that the hair in that picture is 'rossiccio-castano', but said that the colour of the eyes should be called grey, or (more elaborately,) 'di un grigio aurato con venature di verde'. In the Louvre altarpiece, the hair of the portrait (as seen at present) is brown and the eye seems to be dark brown (information from Mme. Béguin of the Louvre). In view of this, Rajna (p. 381) is clearly justified in her reluctance to identify Casio for No. 3916; she continues prudent about the identification in *Bologna, Rivista del Comune*, 15 April, 1952, p. 31. Nevertheless, C. Pedretti (*Documenti e Memorie riguardanti Leonardo da Vinci a Bologna e in Emilia*, 1953, p. 25) considers the identification probable. The compiler thinks it excluded, whatever may be believed about various further pictures claimed to represent Casio. (2) Mündler's Diary, 18 March, 1856. The two Frizzoni were the brothers Giovanni (1806–1849) and Federico (1807–1893); see the *Rassegna d'Arte*, 1911, p. 44, and the Prussian *Jahrbuch*, 1925, *Beiheft*, note 166 or 1943, *Beiheft*, note 207. (3) Eastlake's note-books, with identifying descriptions. (4) J. P. Richter, *The Mond Collection*, 1910, Vol. II, p. 380.

Follower of GIOVANNI ANTONIO BOLTRAFFIO

2496   THE VIRGIN AND CHILD

There are traces of an inscription along the parapet; it was apparently devotional, (A?)E......(M)ARIA PRO ME FILIVM ORA being detectable.

Wood, painted surface, 20 × 14¾ (0·51 × 0·375). Painted up to the edges all round.

Good condition, except for some obvious local damages; the Child's hair rather rubbed. The haloes are new. There are a few small corrections in the outlines.

This picture and No. 2673 below are members of a group, classed by Suida[1] as by a Pseudo-Boltraffio whose activity he puts at about 1510–1530. They are sometimes ascribed to Boltraffio himself;[2] they might be acceptable as late works, but it seems unlikely that he descended to this dry, meagre style. To call them *Studio* would imply that Boltraffio had assistants in his studio, which is uncertain; such a classification might be more justifiable if an undoubted original of one of the designs in the group were known. It seems most likely that they are by one or more followers.

DRAWING: A *Head of the Virgin* at Windsor[3] is nearly but not quite in the same pose, and differs in the headdress.

VERSIONS: A version with slight variations, on the same scale but with a slightly larger field (size 21 in. × 15½ in.), was in the Crespi Sale, 1914, etc.[4] A version with the Virgin considerably changed is in the magazine of the Berlin Museum.[5] A variant with a rock in the place of the curtain (size 0·345 × 0·26) was formerly with Trotti.[6] The Child appears inverted in a picture at Washington.[7] The design of the Child is, further, nearly related to that on a lunette in S. Onofrio, Rome, variously ascribed but probably datable *ca.* 1503/6;[8] it also appears in two pictures by Marco d'Oggiono, one of which is datable 1524.[9] Suida also mentions a headless drawing at Bayonne,[10] which varies somewhat.

PROVENANCE: Possibly, but not probably, in Lord Shrewsbury's Sale, 8 July, 1857 (lot 264),[11] bought by Nieuwenhuys. Bought by Charles Loeser at an antique shop in Paris, 1893.[12] In the collection of George Salting by 1900;[13] exhibited at the R.A., 1902 (No. 27); on loan to the Gallery from 1902; Salting Bequest, 1910. Exhibited at the R.A., *Leonardo da Vinci*, 1952 (No. 249).

REPRODUCTION: *Illustrations, Italian Schools*, 1937, p. 42. *Plates, Early Italian Schools*, 1953, Vol. I, p. 61.

REFERENCES: (1) Suida, *Leonardo und sein Kreis*, 1929, pp. 194 ff. (2) E.g. by Berenson, 1932 Lists. (3) Sir K. Clark, *Leonardo: Drawings at Windsor Castle*, 1935, No. 12509, with reproduction. The drawing, as Clark states, is not by Leonardo. (4) Reproduced by Venturi, *Storia dell'Arte Italiana*, Vol. VII, Part IV, Fig. 701. Lent by Comm. Luigi Bellini to the Mostra Antiquaria at Florence, 1953, No. 714 (the reproduction there shows some variations). (5) Reproduced in the *Monatshefte für Kunstwissenschaft*, 1920, Tafel 8. (6) A reproduction of the Trotti picture is in the Witt Library. (7) Washington, No. 524 (Kress Loan); reproduced in the *Book of Illustrations*, 1941, as Boltraffio. (8) Suida, *op. cit.*, Fig. 220. (9) Reproduced in *L'Arte*, 1905, pp. 416 and 419. (10) Suida, *op. cit.*, p. 215; reproduced by E. Müntz, *Leonardo da Vinci*, London, 1898, Plate 25 (Léon Bonnat, Paris). (11) As Cesare da Sesto. (12) Cf. *L'Arte*, 1895, p. 210 (reproduced, p. 207). (13) Salting MSS.

2673 NARCISSUS

Wood, painted surface, 9⅛ × 10⅜ (0·23 × 0·265). Painted up to the edges all round except at the top; the paint at the right-hand edge is, however, entirely new.

Considerably damaged and restored; the face is not the worst preserved part, but is in untrustworthy state. The landscape and the part of the rock between the landscape and the profile is in good condition.

For the attribution, see No. 2496 above. The profile reappears very similar, not only in the other version to be noted, but also in a *S. Sebastian* in a Frizzoni Collection,[1] and in a drawing in the Louvre.[2] It is related in type to a fancy profile of Leonardo's, found in some drawings; Möller,[3] with little justification, thinks that they are all portraits of Salai, a boy in Leonardo's workshop.

VERSION: A version is in the Uffizi; it has a larger field to the right with an opening in the rocks, and some other slight variations.

PROVENANCE: Possibly in the Anon. (M. Littlehales) Sale of Italian Pictures lately consigned from Rome, 2 March, 1804 (lot 5), as Raphael, *The Story of Narcissus*, from the Borghese Gallery.[4] Possibly Walsh Porter Sale, 14 April, 1810 (lot 1), as Bellini, from the Villa Aldobrandini, bought by Barnet.[5] It was certainly exhibited at the R.A., 1870 (No. 113), lent by Lady Taunton.[6] It had passed to Lord Taunton's son-in-law, Sir Arthur Ellis, by 1895;[7] by him lent to the Burlington Fine Arts Club, 1898 (No. 47a).[8] Acquired by George Salting; exhibited at the Burlington Fine Arts Club, Winter, 1908 (No. 17); Salting Bequest, 1910.

REPRODUCTION: *Illustrations, Italian Schools*, 1937, p. 43. *Plates, Earlier Italian Schools*, 1953, Vol. I, p. 62.

REFERENCES: (1) Suida, *Leonardo und sein Kreis*, 1929, Fig. 234. (2) Suida, *op. cit.*, Fig. 231. (3) E. Möller in the Vienna *Jahrbuch*, 1928, pp. 139 ff. (4) This would be the *Narciso, Raffaele* in the Borghese Inventory (actually of *ca.* 1790) published in *Archivi*, 1937, p. 222, 3rd Room, No. 16. (5) It was settled in 1769 that the Aldobrandini fortune and title should be held by the second son of the head of the Borghese family (cf. the *Enciclopedia Italiana*); the provenance in these two sales may therefore perhaps be held to be the same. For further details of the Aldobrandini fortune, see the entry for Luini, No. 18. The compiler did not identify any picture corresponding with No. 2673 in an inventory of Giovanni Battista Pamphilj Aldobrandini, referred to in the entry for Mantegna, No. 1417, note 17; the record may be there, but cf. Luini, No. 18, note 13. (6) As Luini; not in Waagen's account of the Labouchere (i.e. Taunton) Collection. (7) Label on the back. Lord Taunton died in 1869, Lady Taunton in 1892. (8) As Boltraffio.

Benedetto BONFIGLI
active 1445, died 1496

Of Perugia, where active for the most part; but in 1450 he was at work in the Vatican. In 1454 he contracted to paint a series of frescoes for the Priors' Chapel in the Town Hall at Perugia, which were not quite complete at his death. These are the basis for identifying his style. He also painted a picture for S. Domenico at Perugia in collaboration with Bartolomeo Caporali, *ca.* 1467/8; this picture is generally accepted as being identical with a polyptych now in the Gallery at Perugia. Bonfigli appears to have been much influenced by Benozzo di Lese (Gozzoli), and to have adapted himself hardly at all to the developments of painting at Perugia towards the end of the fifteenth century.

Ascribed to BENEDETTO BONFIGLI

1843   THE ADORATION OF THE KINGS, AND CHRIST ON THE CROSS

S. Joseph is present at the Adoration.

Wood, painted surface, $14\frac{3}{4} \times 19\frac{1}{2}$ (0·375 × 0·495).
Excellent state.

Possibly a fragment of a predella; or perhaps rather a complete small picture.

Berenson, in his Lists of 1932, ascribes this picture to Bartolomeo Caporali. The styles of Caporali and of Bonfigli appear in some cases to be barely distinguishable; but No. 1843 seems to be rather by Bonfigli, to whom it is often ascribed.[1]

PROVENANCE: *Gentile da Fabriano* is written on the back. Conte Fabiani Sale, Gubbio, April–May, 1882 (lot 128).[2] Purchased from Elia Volpi, Florence, 1901.

REPRODUCTION: *Illustrations, Italian Schools*, 1937, p. 44. *Plates, Earlier Italian Schools*, 1953, Vol. I, p. 63.

REFERENCES: (1) E.g. by U. Gnoli, *Pittori e Miniatori nell'Umbria*, 1923, p. 62. (2) Perhaps bought in, since it is mentioned in the Palazzo Fabiani by O. Lucarelli, *Guida Storica di Gubbio*, 1886, p. 50 (No. 50). For the identity with No. 1843, cf. W. Bombe, *Geschichte der Peruginer Malerei*, 1912, p. 102.

BONO DA FERRARA
active 1442 (?)–1461 (?)

A painter of this name was working for the Cathedral of Siena in 1442 and 1461 (cf. L. N. Cittadella, *Documenti ed Illustrazioni Risguardanti la Storia Artistica Ferrarese*, 1868, p. 364). The same or another was active at the Ferrarese court in 1450, and probably the beginning of 1451; mentioned (but probably absent) in 1452 (see Campori in the *Atti della Deputazione di Storia Patria*, Modena, 1885, p. 544).

These notices are supposed to refer to the man who describes himself as a pupil of Pisanello on No. 771 below. A signature or inscription OPVS BONII occurs on a fresco (bombed during the last war) of *S. Christopher carrying the Infant Christ*, in the chapel of the Eremitani at Padua painted by Mantegna and others. The date of this is probably 1451 (the same Bono seems to have been in Padua in 1449, and to have left Padua in 1451; see E. Rigoni in *Arte Veneta*, 1948, pp. 142/3, where the dates given for Bono's presence in Padua do not exclude his identity with the Bono active at Ferrara, according to the dates given by Campori).

The style of the fresco at Padua seems to reflect that of Piero della Francesca, who was probably working in Ferrara about 1450, and to have been adapted, perhaps considerably, to the 'squarcionesque' exigencies of the chapel. Although it is superficially very different from No. 771, it is not impossible that they are by the same hand, and two deer in the background of the fresco (there is one in No. 771) may be considered a reminiscence of Pisanello.

771 S. JEROME IN A LANDSCAPE

Signed on a *cartellino*: .BONVS. FERARIENSIS. / .PISANJ. DISIPVLVS. See the comment below.

Poplar,[1] painted surface, 20½ × 15 (0·52 × 0·38); painted up to the edges top and bottom.

Good condition. Most of the gold on the high-lights of the hills seems to be new, but part of that on the hill to the right seems to be genuine; there can be little doubt that old indications would have been followed for any new gold, gold having been used on the picture in even stranger places (as the lion's eyes). Technically, no reason has been found to doubt the genuineness of the signature.[2] There is a *pentimento* in the line of the saint's head.

The style is near to that of Pisanello; some writers have even attributed the picture to him, and have called the signature a forgery.[3] On comparison with the two pictures in the National Gallery accepted as Pisanello's, the compiler does not think that the execution of No. 771 is by Pisanello; the picture seems to be, as stated in the inscription, by a pupil.[4] According to the inscription, the pupil is Bono da Ferrara. The picture may be derived from a lost Pisanello of this subject; a fragmentary drawing in the Lugt Collection, showing some general connections with No. 771, may be connected with Pisanello in this way too.[5] Some heads of old men in paintings or drawings ascribed to Pisanello and his following are rather similar, and may be compared in Richter's reproductions.[6]

If the painter is the same as the man who painted the Padua fresco, the present picture would seem considerably earlier than the fresco; but exact dating does not seem possible at present.

PROVENANCE: In the Costabili Collection at Ferrara; 1838 Catalogue, I, No. 34; still there in 1858.[7] Acquired by Sir Charles Eastlake, who died in 1865; purchased from Lady Eastlake, at the price Sir Charles Eastlake had paid for it, 1867. Exhibited at Verona, 1958 (No. 115).

REPRODUCTION: *Illustrations, Italian Schools*, 1937, p. 48. *Plates, Earlier Italian Schools*, 1953, Vol. I, p. 64.

REFERENCES: (1) Letter from B. J. Rendle, of the Forest Products Research Laboratory, in the Gallery archives. (2) There was some comment on this matter in the first edition of the present catalogue; because the form of the letters is clearly poor, and after the genuineness had been denied or questioned at the Verona Exhibition of 1958, Mr. N. S. Brommelle, then of the National Gallery Conservation Department, made a technical enquiry by visual examination and with cleaning tests. The visual examination showed nothing definite against the genuineness; the cleaning tests were with a solvent of a strength which would have been used to clean the picture, and the black paint was found completely insoluble in this solvent, also in water. It would be wrong to say that this enquiry proves that the signature is genuine, but it provides evidence in that sense that should not be dismissed without strong reasons. (3) E.g. A. Venturi in *L'Arte*, 1922, pp. 105 ff. Degenhart, *Pisanello* (Chiantore, Turin, 1945), p. 73, says it is either a Pisanello or a studio copy of a Pisanello; but there seems no good reason for modifying what is written on the picture itself. (4) The attribution to Pisanello was brought up again more or less definitely by several critics on the occasion of the picture's exhibition at Verona in 1958, e.g. by Longhi in *Paragone*, November 1958, p. 76. (5) Reproduced in the Verona Exhibition Catalogue, *Da Altichiero a Pisanello*, 1958, Plate CXX; cf. the next note. (6) G. M. Richter in *The Burlington Magazine*, Vol. LV (1929), pp. 59 ff., Plates II and III; Plate II seems to be connected with the Lugt drawing, referred to in the previous note. (7) Mündler's Diary, March 1858.

Francesco BONSIGNORI

Formerly, and less well, *Monsignori*. The dates of birth and death are from Vasari (edition of 1568), who further says he was born at Verona; the date of death is much more sure than the date of birth. From about 1490 (according to Vasari, by 1487) he was active at the Gonzaga court in Mantua. There are several authenticated pictures in Verona, dated from 1483 onwards; others are reasonably ascribed, in provenance from Mantuan churches. An authenticated late work is in SS. Nazaro e Celso, Verona (see Gerola in *Madonna Verona*, 1914, p. 202). Bonsignori may have been influenced by the Venetians, but from 1488 a marked dependence on Mantegna is noticeable.

736 PORTRAIT OF AN ELDERLY MAN

Signed on a *cartellino*, *Franciscus . Bonsignorius . Veronensis . p | . 1487* .

Wood, painted surface, $16\frac{1}{2} \times 11\frac{3}{4}$ (0·42 × 0·295).

Good condition. Of the comparatively small amount of repaint, that under his left eye is in a part important for the modelling; there is also some damage to his right eyeball, and elsewhere.

In the Bernasconi catalogue (1851) and thenceforward, called *A Venetian Senator*; Borenius[1] says the costume is in favour of this. Solari's portrait, No. 923 of this Gallery (q.v.), was also formerly called a Venetian senator; the dress differs somewhat.

DRAWING: A study in chalk for No. 736 (size 0·36 × 0·262) is in the Albertina at Vienna.[2]

PROVENANCE: A portrait with the same signature was in the eighteenth century in the Museo Cappello, Venice.[3] Bought by Cesare Bernasconi, Verona, from a painter of Venice, *ca.* 1848.[4] Purchased from Cesare Bernasconi, 1864.

REPRODUCTION: *Illustrations, Italian Schools*, 1937, p. 49. *Plates, Earlier Italian Schools*, 1953, Vol. I, p. 65.

REFERENCES: (1) Crowe and Cavalcaselle, *Painting in North Italy*, ed. Borenius, 1912, II, p. 184. This may be true, but receives little support from Cesare Vecellio's *Habiti Antichi et Moderni*, ed. 1598, pp. 62 and 80. See also the entry for Andrea Solari, No. 923. (2) *Italian Drawings Exhibited at the Royal Academy*, 1930, No. 176 and Plate CL; Albertina Exhibition (Arts Council), 1948, No. 8. (3) Maffei, *Verona Illustrata*, 1732, Part III, Col. 156. There is a not very clear statement by Bernasconi in the Gallery archives that No. 736 does come from the Capello (*sic*) Collection. (4) Statement by Bernasconi, 28 December, 1863, in the Gallery archives. No. 736 is recorded in the Bernasconi Catalogue, 1851 (No. 16).

3091 THE VIRGIN AND CHILD WITH FOUR SAINTS

Canvas, 19 × 42 (0·48 × 1·07).

Has suffered a great deal from flaking; some prominent parts, such as the Virgin's left eye, are a good deal repainted.

The Saints are not identifiable. The figure on the left with a book is probably a Franciscan; the one of dubious sex on the right is a martyr.

The group of the Virgin and Child is derived, in reverse except for the hands, from an engraving by Mantegna;[1] Mantegna's group inverted occurs in an engraving by Giovanni Maria da Brescia.[2] The frieze-like composition is also probably a reminiscence of Mantegna.[3] The picture is acceptable as a comparatively late work of Bonsignori's.[4]

VERSIONS: The engravings no doubt account for the existence of several related pictures. Kristeller[5] lists No. 143 of the Verona Museum (Francesco Morone ?),[6] a picture at Frankfort,[7] and another belonging to the Marquis Marcello Durazzo-Adorno at Genoa; in another place, Kristeller[8] compares a Virgin and Child Enthroned, at Lord Wemyss'. A copy of No. 3091 was in the Otto Beit Collection at Tewin Water.[9] Crowe and Cavalcaselle[10] mention a version with different saints, once in the Gonzaga Collection, later owned by Count Colloredo at Goritz (presumably Görz, Gorizia).

PROVENANCE: Bought by Sir A. H. Layard from Baslini, Milan, ca. 1863;[11] exhibited at South Kensington, 1869 (No. 40); Layard Bequest, 1916.[12]

REPRODUCTION: Illustrations, Italian Schools, 1937, p. 49. Plates, Earlier Italian Schools, 1953, Vol. I, p. 66.

REFERENCES: (1) Reproduced by Kristeller, Mantegna, London, 1901, p. 392. A. M. Hind, Early Italian Engraving, Vol. V, 1948, p. 10 and Vol. VI, 1948, Plate 486. (2) Hind, op. cit., Vol. V, 1948, p. 58, No. 3 and Vol. VI, 1948, Plate 569. (3) Cf. Venturi, Storia dell'Arte Italiana, Vol. VII, Part III, Fig. 375. (4) The attribution seems to be due to Morelli; letters from Morelli to Layard, 3 January, 1865, and Layard to Morelli, 30 December, 1864 (cf. note 11). (5) Kristeller, op. cit., p. 445. (6) This picture is now catalogued as Gerolamo dai Libri; Venturi, Storia dell'Arte Italiana, Vol. VII, Part IV, Fig. 509. (7) Catalogues of 1900, No. 6, and of 1924, No. 1105 (Veronese School); photograph in the Gallery archives. (8) Kristeller, op. cit., p. 455. (9) Catalogue, 1913, No. 131; noted by E. K. Waterhouse. It was in the Mrs. Arthur Bull Sale, 25 October, 1946 (lot 24); photograph in the Gallery archives. (10) Crowe and Cavalcaselle, Painting in North Italy, I, 1871, p. 478, or ed. Borenius, 1912, II, p. 186. (11) Letter from Morelli to Layard, 3 January, 1865; also mentioned on 26 October, 1864, and in letters from Layard to Morelli, 5 and 30 December, 1864 (British Museum, Add. MSS. 38963 and 38966, Layard Papers, Vols. XXXIII and XXXVI). A. Venturi in L'Arte, 1912, p. 451, gives the date of acquisition as 1864, but it seems to have been the previous year. See also the Layard MSS. in the National Gallery. (12) For the history of the Layard Collection, see Appendix IV.

BORGOGNONE, AMBROGIO See BERGOGNONE

SANDRO BOTTICELLI
ca. 1445–1510

Alessandro, son of Mariano (Filipepi) of Florence, called Botticelli. Possibly trained as a goldsmith by one of his brothers, Antonio (but cf. the comments by R. Salvini, Tutta la Pittura del Botticelli, 1958, Vol. I, p. 31). According to a pre-Vasarian tradition, trained in painting by Fra Filippo Lippi. In 1470 he painted a figure of Fortitude, now in the Uffizi. He was a member of the Compagnia di San Luca in 1472. He was active almost entirely at Florence and in its neighbourhood, but in 1481/2 he was in Rome, painting in the Sistine Chapel. Towards the end of his life his religious views were apparently influenced, though it is difficult to define exactly in what way, by the teachings and death of Savonarola; previously, although extremely active as a painter of religious subjects, he had also painted a good many pagan pictures. He ran an active studio.

592   THE ADORATION OF THE KINGS

The Virgin and Child with S. Joseph are towards the right; the Kings and their immense train stretch across the picture. On the extreme right are two shepherds.

Reverse: A drawing on the unprimed wood of a female figure with a shield; also part of a face, and other, incomprehensible scribbles.

Wood, painted surface, $19\frac{3}{4} \times 53\frac{1}{2}$ (0·50 × 1·36); these measurements exclude about 1 in. of new paint both left and right. The picture is fixed in a strip of modern framing.

Considerably worn. The picture was cleaned in 1940, when it was retouched no more than was necessary to make it fit for exhibition; notably on the dresses of the Virgin and S. Joseph, and of the kneeling man left centre. There are *pentimenti* in the dresses of the Virgin and S. Joseph, in S. Joseph's head, etc. There appear once to have been several extra heads in front of the wall, slightly to the left of the centre; the turban of the standing man still further to the left was once designed to be higher.

This picture seems to the compiler to be acceptable on stylistic grounds as (at least substantially) one of Botticelli's earliest works.[1] The Virgin is still somewhat in the manner of Fra Filippo Lippi. Some smoothly painted figures, especially in the left centre, second row, are near in style to the early work of Filippino Lippi, as exemplified in No. 1124 of this Gallery. A collaboration between the two painters has been claimed;[2] yet these Filippinesque figures may be thought more vigorous than any that Filippino himself would have painted, and the variations in style in the picture could be due to the unfixed style of a single painter, perhaps working over several years. In the rocks and landscape in the centre, it is possible to imagine some influence of the van Eyck school.

The drawings or scribbles on the back of the picture could be by the painter of the front.[3]

PROVENANCE: In the collection of the Marchese Ippolito Orlandini at Florence.[4] In the Lombardi-Baldi Collection at Florence by 1845.[5] Purchased with other pictures from Lombardi and Baldi, Florence, 1857.[6] Cleaned Pictures Exhibition at the National Gallery, 1947/8 (No. 27).

REPRODUCTIONS: The front (before cleaning) is reproduced in the *Illustrations, Italian Schools*, 1937, p. 56. *Plates, Earlier Italian Schools*, 1953, Vol. I, p. 67. The principal drawing on the back is reproduced in *Paintings and Drawings on the Backs of National Gallery Pictures*, 1946, Plate 8; the other scribbles have been photographed.

REFERENCES: (1) Cf. for instance Horne, *Sandro Botticelli*, 1908, pp. 13/4. The attribution was perhaps first made by J. P. Richter, *Italian Art in the*

National Gallery, 1883, p. 24. Crowe and Cavalcaselle, *History of Painting in Italy,* II, 1864, p. 451, accept the earlier attribution to Filippino Lippi. (2) In the first edition of this catalogue, it was considered probable that Botticelli was simply adapting himself to Filippino's manner. This suggestion raises some difficulty about the date, as was pointed out by Robertson in *The Burlington Magazine,* January 1953, p. 28. Salvini in *Saggi su Filippino Lippi,* 1957, pp. 58/9, claims collaboration in No. 592 between Botticelli and Filippino; he suggests that either the composition is Filippino's and that Botticelli worked on the execution in parts, or that the picture was designed by Botticelli *ca.* 1465 but not completed until *ca.* 1471/2, in part by Filippino. The former view is developed in Salvini's *Tutta la Pittura del Botticelli,* 1958, Vol. I, pp. 42/3. A student's opinion on these comments would be affected by his personal opinion on what early pictures by Botticelli exist; the compiler inclines to believe that, without unexpected increases in present knowledge, the problem of No. 592 is unlikely to be convincingly settled. This view is reflected in the opening sentence on the style in the text above; several restrictions have been added in the paragraph on the style to what appeared in the first edition of this catalogue. It may be added that some details of costume, on which there are notes in the Gallery archives by Stella M. Pearce, suggest a date in the later 1470's; if work was done on the picture so late, it would seem (on stylistic grounds) that it was not very extensive. An article by H. Ruhemann on the technique of the picture, with some special photographs reproduced, appeared in *Studies in Conservation,* Vol. II, March 1955, pp. 17 ff. (3) Cf. Berenson, *Drawings of the Florentine Painters,* 1938, II, No. 567B. (4) As Filippo Lippi; see Federigo Fantozzi, *Nuova Guida . . . della Città e Contorni di Firenze,* 1849, p. 488 (presumably merely a reprint from an earlier edition, not proving that the picture was still there in 1849). (5) As Filippino Lippi, in a Lombardi-Baldi Catalogue, No. 50; the catalogue is not dated, but the copy in the Uffizi Library is claimed to be of 1845. (6) For the history of the Lombardi-Baldi Collection, see Appendix I.

626 PORTRAIT OF A YOUNG MAN

Wood, painted surface, $14\frac{3}{4} \times 11\frac{1}{8}$ (0·375 × 0·282); painted up to the edges all round. At the top at least it seems clearly not to have been cut.

Very good condition, except for black spots on the flesh.

Formerly catalogued as by Masaccio; this attribution, with doubt expressed in the more recent editions, was retained until 1881. Ulmann and Bode do not accept the attribution to Botticelli.[1] The picture appears to be of Botticelli's middle period.[2]

PROVENANCE: On the back is written *May* 12 1804; i.e. the (Col. Matthew Smith) Sale, where lot 82, clearly identifiable with No. 626, was bought Northwick.[3] On the back is also the seal of an owner, not at present identified; a crescent (?) on a fess dancetty between three roses, the crest a lion passant on a helmet. Recorded in Lord Northwick's Collection in 1837[4]. Exhibited at Manchester, 1857 (Provisional Catalogue, No. 38; Definitive Catalogue, No. 51).[5] Northwick Catalogue, 1858 (No. 74). Purchased, Northwick Sale, 11 August, 1859 (lot 1127).

REPRODUCTION: *Illustrations, Italian Schools,* 1937, p. 55. *Plates, Earlier Italian Schools,* 1953, Vol. I, p. 68.

REFERENCES: (1) Hermann Ulmann, *Sandro Botticelli,* 1893, pp. 52/3 and 152. Bode, *Sandro Botticelli,* Klassiker der Kunst, 1926, Plate 130 and note. The attribution to Botticelli seems quite sure; it was perhaps first made, in a rather tentative way, by Crowe and Cavalcaselle, *History of Painting in Italy,* I, 1864, pp. 548/9. (2) Horne, *Sandro Botticelli,* 1908, p. 126, ascribes it to the time immediately after Botticelli's return from Rome, i.e. soon after 1482. Salvini, *Tutta la Pittura del Botticelli*, 1958, Vol. II, p. 40 and Plate 7, agrees. (3) Masaccio, Self-Portrait. The date of the sale was, for the first edition of the present catalogue, read as May 18, 1804; although the writing is not very clear, 12 is to be accepted as definitely correct. (4) Waagen, *Kunstwerke*, 1837, II, pp. 203/4, suggesting Filippino; Waagen, *Treasures*, 1854, III, p. 196, as Masaccio. Recorded in the Northwick Collection in the *Cheltenham Looker-On*, 17 December, 1842, p. 806; Northwick Catalogues, 1843 (No. XCV) and 1846 (No. CCXLIX); *The Art-Union*, 1846, p. 254. (5) The label of the Manchester Exhibition is on the back; here and in some other places called a self-portrait by Masaccio.

915 VENUS AND MARS

Wood, painted surface (sight), $27\frac{1}{4} \times 68\frac{1}{4}$ (0.69×1.735).

Good condition. The gold on Venus' hair and dress is mostly new. The shadows on the body of Mars are partly worn. The pink drapery on which he lies is much damaged; it had been entirely overpainted until the picture was cleaned in 1943. The face of the satyr in Mars' cuirass is rather damaged, and there are various blemishes of lesser importance elsewhere on the picture.

Pentimenti in the lines of the right cheek and the neck of Mars, and elsewhere on his body. On the left arm of Venus, the drapery was once more bunched at the shoulder; it was apparently intended once to lie flatly over her wrist.

The subject of No. 915 is not altogether clear,[1] but it need not be doubted that the picture in fact represents *Venus and Mars*. There are some clues on the picture itself; for instance, the armour, suitable for Mars, and the sea in the distance, recalling the story that Venus rose from the sea. But the most convincing argument is from a picture by Piero di Cosimo at Berlin.[2] That picture does indeed differ somewhat in the iconography from No. 915, but many details correspond precisely; and the subject of that picture was admitted as *Venus and Mars* by Vasari.[3]

It can therefore be granted that No. 915 represents *Venus and Mars*; what the picture actually shows is as follows. Mars is asleep, and it appears that a little satyr is trying to wake him, by blowing at a shell near his ear. Perhaps this is being done at the bidding of Venus, who is not asleep. Two other little satyrs appear to be carrying away the helmet and lance of Mars; and a fourth, holding a gourd, is occupying his cuirass. Mars as he lies is likely to be stung about the head by some wasps issuing from a tree. A possible significance of these wasps will be referred to presently, but the principal meaning may be expected to be concerned with the subject of the picture.[4] There seems no doubt that the intention is erotic, and that in a general way it signifies that Love is better than War; it is noteworthy that Mars should be asleep, and that Venus should need to call his attention to herself, if indeed that is what she is doing.[5]

Presumably some humanist indicated to Botticelli what should be put into the picture; but the literary source is not known.[6] Gombrich, however, insists that the literary source for the satyrs carrying the lance and the satyr in the cuirass is a passage in Lucian.[7] Botticelli's figures indeed correspond too closely with Lucian's words for it to be purely a chance; but Lucian is describing the Marriage of Alexander and Roxana, which is certainly not the subject here.[8] The insertion into this picture of *Venus and Mars* of motives associated with another antique subject adds to the difficulty of understanding the main subject.

Gombrich[9] suggests that the wasps in the right-hand corner may be a punning reference to the Vespucci family, for whom the picture may have been painted. This seems possible.[10] Gombrich makes or records some further suggestions about the meaning of the picture.[11]

No. 915 is clearly acceptable as Botticelli's work, apparently of his middle period.[12] The painting of the satyrs is on the whole inferior to that of the main figures; but all may be by Botticelli himself.

DERIVATIONS: No. 916 below, Follower of Botticelli, is perhaps in part derived from No. 915, though the compositions are not closely connected; there is a variant version of No. 916 in the Louvre, referred to in the entry. Piero di Cosimo's picture at Berlin has been referred to in the text above. A mirror-frame in the Victoria and Albert Museum seems to be connected with No. 915, not very closely, and perhaps rather for the subject than the figures.[13]

PROVENANCE: Bought not later than 1869 by Alexander Barker in Florence.[14] Exhibited at the Burlington Fine Arts Club, 1871 (No. 60). Purchased at the Barker Sale, 6 June, 1874 (lot 88). Cleaned Pictures Exhibition at the National Gallery, 1947/8 (No. 28).

REPRODUCTION: *Illustrations, Italian Schools*, 1937, p. 57 (before cleaning). *Plates, Earlier Italian Schools*, 1953, Vol. I, p. 69.

REFERENCES: (1) Recent accounts of it are by E. H. Gombrich in the *Journal of the Warburg and Courtauld Institutes*, Vol. VIII (1945), pp. 46 ff. (referred to in the following notes as Gombrich, *loc. cit.*), and by E. Wind, *Pagan Mysteries of the Renaissance*, 1958, pp.84/5. They are not fully in agreement with each other, and say more than is recorded here. (2) Berlin, 1931 Catalogue, No. 107; reproduced in the Illustrations. (3) Vasari, ed. Milanesi, IV, p. 140; not in the 1550 edition. The iconographical differences would be rather long to describe, and can be seen in the reproductions of the picture. (4) Wind, *op. cit.*, pp. 84/5, associates the wasps with *pugnacitas*, and it seems likely that one meaning for them, maybe the principal one, is to recall what Mars normally is. Guy de Tervarent, *Attributs et Symboles dans l'Art Profane*, 1959, col. 208, tentatively associates the phrase 'to bring a hornet's nest about one's ears' (in reference to the catastrophe of the story of Mars and Venus). This phrase seems connected with words used by Plautus, cited in the form 'irritari crabrones' in the *Adagia* of Erasmus; but it does not seem that this saying quite fits the subject of No. 915. (5) J. Mesnil, *Botticelli*, 1938, p. 55, thinks that the picture shows the different effects of love in male and female. (6) Wickhoff in the Prussian *Jahrbuch*, 1906, p. 206, claims that the scene of No. 915 and the Berlin Piero di Cosimo is from Reposianus, *De Concubitu Martis et Veneris* (published in the Loeb series, 1934, *Minor Latin Poets*, ed. J. W. and A. M. Duff); there are some points of similarity, but they seem insufficient to justify the claim. (7) Gombrich, *loc. cit.*, p. 48. Comparable conceptions are found in some classical monuments; e.g. in two Pompeian paintings of Hercules and Omphale, reproduced by Reinach, *Répertoire des Peintures Grecques et Romaines*, pp. 191/2. (8) Lucian's complete description was used, not many decades later, for the subject of *Alexander and Roxana* by Sodoma and others. See R. H. H. Cust, *Giovanni Antonio Bazzi*, 1906, pp. 138 ff., and R. Förster in the Prussian *Jahrbuch*, 1894, pp. 182 ff. and 1922, pp. 133/4. (9) Gombrich, *loc. cit.*, p. 49. (10) Vasari indeed records that Giovanni Vespucci in his Palace in Florence had a room decorated by Botticelli; there were many pictures with many figures let into the wall. This particular Palace apparently did not belong to the Vespucci until 1499, and on stylistic grounds No. 915 must be considerably earlier. If therefore No. 915 formed part of this decoration, the decoration itself would have been moved to the new Palace from an earlier one. Actually, there is no need to suppose that No. 915 belonged to this particular member of the Vespucci family or, if so, that it formed part of the decoration of this particular room. For the decorations of the Vespucci Palace, see Vasari, 1550 edition, p. 492; ed. Milanesi, III, p. 312; and Horne, *Sandro Botticelli*, 1908, p. 282. The use of panels such as No. 915 with large figures is not quite certain; they may have been for insertion in the wainscoting, or sometimes for large pieces of furniture, such as a bed-head. For the painted bed of 1337 at Pistoia, see Schubring, *Cassoni*, 9123, Plate VII; cf. also R. W. Kennedy, *Alesso Baldovinetti*, 1938, p. 236 (record of 1463, no colours mentioned). There is no need to suppose that No. 915 was used for a cassone. (11) Gombrich, *loc. cit.*, pp. 46 ff. The compiler is disinclined to exclude that Botticelli himself may have made mistakes in painting what he was asked. (12) Horne, *Sandro Botticelli*, 1908, pp. 140/1, dates it *ca.* 1485. Salvini, *Tutta la Pittura del Botticelli*, 1958, Vol. II, p. 41, dates it *ca.* 1483. (13) Victoria and Albert Museum, *Catalogue of Italian Sculpture* by Sir Eric Maclagan and Margaret H. Longhurst, 1932, Vol. I, p. 49, No. 5887-1859, as Antonio Pollaiuolo (?), and Vol. II, Plate 62a. (14) According to the Barker Sale Catalogue, acquired in Florence; on loan from Barker at the Victoria and Albert Museum in 1869 (see *The Athenaeum*, 30 October, 1869, p. 568). Not mentioned among the Botticellis of the Barker Collection in Crowe and Cavalcaselle, *History of Painting in Italy*, 1864, p. 427.

1033   TONDO: THE ADORATION OF THE KINGS

The Virgin and Child and S. Joseph are in the centre; the Kings and their numerous followers are disposed around. A few shepherds are also present.

Wood, tondo, painted surface (sight) $51\frac{1}{2}$ in. (1·315) in diameter.

Cleaning and restoration of this picture completed in 1956. It has suffered from flaking and cracking; also from wearing, but not very seriously. On the whole, the condition is good. *Pentimenti* in the architecture. Arches once continued over the sky on the right, at the height of those on the left; the pilaster on which is the peacock was intended at one time to reach the top of the picture. Near the left edge, there is the beginning of a capital and arch, the capital being at the height of the two capitals in the centre in front of the roofing. Besides these, and some other alterations that may be minor, there are incised lines, some of them probably made only for guidance. In the figures there are also some changes, e.g. in the dress of the man in the foreground slightly right of centre and turned away, and in the horse immediately to the right of him.

An early work, but in the compiler's view clearly rather later than No. 592 above.[1]

Waagen[2] suggested a compositional connection with Ghiberti's relief of the Queen of Sheba and Solomon, on the Door of Paradise of the Florentine Baptistery; this seems quite possible.

Konody thinks that the young man turning to face the spectator is a portrait of the painter.[3]

DERIVATION: A tondo of the same subject in the Ryerson Collection at Chicago, ascribed to Botticini, seems to be derived.[4]

PROVENANCE: Possibly the tondo of the *Epiphany* mentioned by Vasari in Casa Pucci at Florence.[5] No. 1033 was in the Guicciardini Palace at Florence in 1807, and was sold in 1810, apparently to Dubois;[6] it appeared in the William Coningham Sale, 9 June, 1849 (lot 38), bought by Coningham.[7] In the Collection of W. Fuller Maitland at Stansted Hall, where seen by Waagen.[8] Exhibited at the R.A., 1872 (No. 217). Stansted Hall Catalogue, 1872, p. 13.[9] Purchased from W. Fuller Maitland, 1878.[10]

REPRODUCTION: *Illustrations, Italian Schools*, 1937, p. 58. *Plates, Earlier Italian Schools*, 1953, Vol. I, p. 70.

REFERENCES: (1) Horne, *Sandro Botticelli*, 1908, p. 38, dates it *ca.* 1476; other critics have suggested other dates early in Botticelli's career. Salvini, *Tutta la Pittura del Botticelli*, 1958, Vol. I, pp. 44/5 and Plate 38, dates it soon after 1472. He suggests that some details, e.g. heads of the remoter followers of the Magi in the left centre, may be by Filippino Lippi; some types are suggestive of what is presumed to be the early style of Filippino, but his intervention in No. 1033 seems to the compiler unlikely. (2) Waagen, *Treasures*, III, 1854, p. 3. Cf. J. von Schlosser, *Leben und Meinungen des Florentinischen Bildners Lorenzo Ghiberti*, 1941, Plate 59. (3) Konody in *The Connoisseur*, January, 1908, p. 45. (4) Van Marle, *Development of the Italian Schools of Painting*, Vol. XIII, Fig. 271. (5) Vasari, ed. Milanesi, III, p. 313 (text of 1568); not in the 1550 edition. Conte Paolo Guicciardini (letter of 3 August, 1948) has kindly searched in his archives, and has suggested a possible way in which the picture could have passed from the Pucci family to his own. By a document of 1698, various pictures were divided among the sons of Roberto Pucci, and 'due quadri di braccia 3, in una cornice dorata, raffiguranti uno la resurrezione del Signore l'altro i tre Magi' passed to Cosimo Pucci. Cosimo died without heirs in 1707, and the pictures may then have gone to his eldest brother, Giulio. Giulio's daughter Luisa Ninfa Pucci married in 1720 Francesco di Lorenzo Guicciardini. It is not proved that No. 1033 is here referred to, but it seems possible. (6) No. 1033 and the Fra Filippo Lippi tondo of the same subject (ex-Cook; 1951, Kress Loan to Washington) were in the Coningham Sale of 1949, both stated to be from the Guicciardini Palace at Florence. In view of this, the two pictures can be identified with certainty in an old inventory of Guicciardini possessions at Florence. This inventory, here recorded by permission of Conte Paolo Guicciardini, is entitled *Nota dei Quadri esistenti nella Galleria dell'Ill͞mi: SS. Conte Francesco, e Colonnello Ferdinando Fratelli Guicciardini situata nel Quartiere dell'Illma: Sig.ʳᵃ Contessa Caterina Loro Madre*, and headed *A di primo Settembre 1807*. On p. 2 is: Un tondo in tavola antico esprimente l'adorazione dei Magi del Botticello Raro; and on p. 3: Altro tondo Antico esprimente pure l'adorazione de' Magi del Botticelli. This inventory has been altered in parts to accord with a sale in July, 1810, to M. Dubois; the entries for the two tondi were made in 1807, and the prices added in different writing show that the pictures were included in the sale of 1810. The reference for the inventory is Archivio Guicciardini, filza XXXV seconda, n. 5. It seems possible that these pictures are listed in H. Delaroche, *Catalogue d'une collection de tableaux*, belonging to M. Dubois, Commissaire de la Police à Florence, 1813; but the British Museum copy of this catalogue has been destroyed, and the compiler has been unable to consult another. (7) To judge from the descriptions in the sale catalogue, lot 34 is clearly the Cook picture, and lot 38 (as Filippino Lippi) is No. 1033. The provenance of these two pictures has often been confused, e.g. by Crowe and Cavalcaselle, *History of Painting in Italy*, II, 1864, p. 350, and in the large Cook catalogue. (8) Waagen, *Treasures*, III, 1854, p. 3, as Fra Filippo Lippi, as from Coningham. (9) In both cases as by Filippino Lippi. (10) As by Filippino Lippi or Sandro Botticelli.

1034 MYSTIC NATIVITY

The Virgin, the Child, S. Joseph, the ox and the ass are in the centre, under a penthouse attached to a cave. On the right, an angel holding an olive branch introduces two men crowned with olive (the Shepherds); on the left another angel with an olive branch introduces three men also crowned with olive (presumably the Magi). A scroll held by the second angel is inscribed. . . . NIVS DEI . . .; the inscription on the scroll held by the first angel is illegible (presumably together for *Ecce Agnus Dei, ecce qui tollit peccatum mundi*).

On the penthouse roof are three angels in red, white and green, crowned with olive and holding two olive branches and a book. In the sky, the heavens are opened and 12 angels dance, holding branches of olive to which are attached golden crowns and scrolls. Some of the scrolls are inscribed (damaged): SACRARIVM.I(N BETHL?); MATER̄ DE(I); VIRGO.VIRGINVM; SPŌSA.DEI.PATRIS. ADMIRĀDA; VE(   ) FECHVNDA; SPERAN(   ); RE-GINA . SOPRA . TVT(?); REGINA . SOLA . MV̄DI; and a few others, even more illegible. Several other scrolls are inscribed GLORIA. IN.EXCELSIS.DEO (more or less damaged).

In the foreground, three angels holding olive branches embrace three men crowned with olive. The scroll of the left-hand angel is inscribed: .OMINIBVS.BO. . .; the scroll of the central angel:.ET.INTERA. . .; the scroll of the right hand angel: OMINIBVS.BONE.VOLVN-TATIS. (In conjunction with the scrolls of the angels in the sky, this is from Luke ii, 14, *Gloria in altissimis Deo, et in terra pax hominibus bonae voluntatis.*)

Near this foreground, devils scuttle underground.

At the top is an inscription, which is also a signature: ΤΑΥΤΗΝ. ΓΡΑΦΗΝ.ΕΝ.ΤѠi.ΤΕΛΕΙ.ΤΟΥ.Χ.ΣΣΣΣΣ.ΕΤΟΥΣ.ΕΝ.ΤΑΙΣ. ΤΑΡΑ(Χ)ΑΙΣ.ΤΗΣ.ΙΤΑΛΙΑΣ.ΑΛΕΖΑΝΔΡΟΣ.ΕΓѠ.ΕΝ.ΤѠi. ΜΕΤΑ.ΧΡΟΝΟΝ.ΗΜΙΧΡΟΝѠi.ΕΓΡΑΦΟΝ.ΠΑΡΑ.ΤΟ. ΕΝΔΕΚ / ΑΤΟΝ.ΤΟΥ.ΑΓΙΟΥ.ΙѠΑΝΝΟΥ.ΕΝ.ΤѠi. ΑΠΟΚΑΛΥΨΕѠΣ.Β$^{\Omega i}$ΟΥΑΙ.ΕΝ.ΤΗi.ΛΥΣΕΙ.ΤѠΝ.Γ.(Κ)ΑΙ. ΗΜΙΣΥ.ΕΤѠΝ.ΤΟΥ.ΔΙΑΒΟΛΟΥ.ΕΠΕΙΤΑ.ΔΕΣΜΟΘΗΣΕΤΑΙ. ΕΝ ΤѠi.ΙΒ$^{\Omega i}$.ΚΑΙ./ΒΛΕΨΟΜΕΝ.(ΣΑΦ?...)ΝΟΝ.ΟΜΟΙΟΝ. ΤΗi ΓΡΑΦΗi.ΤΑΥΤΗi.

(I Sandro painted this picture at the end of the year 1500 (?) in the troubles of Italy in the half time after the time according to the 11th chapter of S. John in the second woe of the Apocalypse in the loosing of the devil for three and a half years then he will be chained in the 12th chapter and we shall see clearly (?). . . as in this picture.)

Canvas,[1] 42¾×29½ (1·085×0·75).

Cleaned in 1958. Somewhat affected by previous flaking and rubbing. The inscription at the top is painted over blue, but there has been found no technical reason to doubt its authenticity.

No. 1034 is signed in the Greek inscription, and is the only signed picture by Botticelli. J. Mesnil brings it into relation with Botticelli's only signed drawing (for Dante, *Paradiso*, Canto XXVIII), and reasonably claims that in both cases the introduction of Botticelli's name has primarily a devotional significance.[2] The problem of the rest of the Greek inscription will be discussed presently.

As for the other inscriptions, *Ecce Agnus Dei, ecce qui tollit peccatum mundi* (if that is what was written on the picture) is what S. John the Baptist says in reference to Christ in John i, 29.[3] *Gloria in altissimis Deo, et in terra pax hominibus bonae voluntatis* is, as has been already indicated, the Christmas message according to Luke ii, 14.[4] The remaining, fragmentary inscriptions seem to be from some litany in praise of the Virgin at the Nativity; the source has not been identified,[5] but there is no reason at all to suppose that the words have any esoteric meaning. These inscriptions on the picture are much damaged. The texts have been given above as accurately as possible; they are obviously in Latin, and if in one or two cases the fragments appear to be in Italian, it may be that the reading is wrong.

No. 1034 represents the Nativity, mostly according to S. Luke; it is treated with mystic enthusiasm, and with the incidents squeezed together, but with an exactness that is unusual in pictures and therefore appears strange. The three angels embracing the three men crowned with olive in the foreground are, apparently, not repeated in any other picture; but it might be difficult to illustrate very differently the latter part of S. Luke's Christmas message. As for the Shepherds and the figures fairly obviously the Magi, it is peculiar that they should be associated apparently with the words of S. John the Baptist; but these words are suitable to the Shepherds and the Magi. The other incidents in the picture either follow the Gospels exactly, or can be deduced from the Gospels without much strain.

Botticelli's mystic enthusiasm is symbolized in this picture by his return to a mediæval manner, with the Virgin larger than any other figure and tiny trees unlike the style of the Florentine Renaissance.[6]

Here, but for the inscription at the top, the commentary would come to an end. But some critics have concentrated their attention on this inscription, and made many deductions from it about the picture underneath.[7]

The inscription is written in Greek, perhaps to conceal its meaning from prying eyes. Its obscurity is due partly to chance; the word indicating what, according to the inscription, we do see clearly (?) on the picture has been rendered illegible by damage.[8] Its obscurity is due even more to the character of apocalyptic utterances, which are rarely clear and sometimes inexact. Thus, according to the inscription, the devil is chained in the 12th chapter of Revelation; but it is in the 20th chapter of that work that he is chained, and he is not chained at all in No. 1034.

Although one may feel inclined to leave Botticelli to hide his hidden meanings undisturbed, it is desirable to attempt some comment on the inscription. The date is almost certainly the end of the year 1500;[9]

more precisely, according to our calendar, the end of 1500 or the beginning of 1501. Botticelli's reference to 'the troubles of Italy' indicates that contemporary history was in his mind. It is implied that these troubles had begun a time and a half before the picture was painted. If a time and a half means a year and a half,[10] the date would be most probably towards the middle of 1499; at about that time, Cesare Borgia invaded Romagna and Louis XII invaded North Italy, and Botticelli may have been thinking of these troubles, or perhaps of something different. The inscription implies that within a period, perhaps of two years (or perhaps not),[11] something like the Reign of Peace at the Nativity was to occur. There are references in it to Revelation xi and (wrongly) xii; it is uncertain what words or sentences in these references Botticelli considered applicable to his prophecy of 1500/1 (?). Since he was a Florentine, one would expect him to refer his dark utterances chiefly to Florence; it is uncertain whether this is so for No. 1034, but the probability is increased by the analogy of another mystic picture ascribed to Botticelli, in the Fogg Art Museum, where the fate of Florence is the subject.[12]

It is at this point that Botticelli's relationship to Savonarola must be discussed.[13] It is often asserted that he was a follower of Savonarola, and that No 1034 was painted under Savonarola's influence; but it is doubtful if either of these assertions is strictly true.

Vasari says that Botticelli towards the end of his life became a follower of Savonarola, or *piagnone*.[14] Such a statement by Vasari, recorded only 40 years after Botticelli's death, is clearly based on something; but in this case it may be that Vasari confused Sandro Botticelli with his brother, the *piagnone* Simone.[15] Indeed, the most precise reason for supposing that Sandro Botticelli was a follower of Savonarola is that he was living in the same house in Florence with Simone from ca. 1493/5.[16] There is admittedly a record that Sandro was curious to know how Savonarola's death came about;[17] but that proves little, and other documentary evidence concerning Sandro does not favour the view that he was a *piagnone*.[18] Nor can much confirmation of this be found in Botticelli's pictures.[19]

The evidence concerning Botticelli's relationship in general to Savonarola seems therefore indecisive; nor does it seem possible to establish a precise relationship for No. 1034.

The argument for associating it with Savonarola runs as follows. The Greek inscription refers to the 11th chapter of Revelation. The 11th chapter of Revelation gives an account of two witnesses, due to be killed by the beast from the bottomless pit. In May, 1498, Savonarola, Domenico da Pescia and Silvestro Maruffi were martyred. Silvestro Maruffi was a minor figure. Therefore the two witnesses of the 11th chapter of Revelation were identified with Savonarola and Domenico da Pescia. Therefore picture No. 1034 is connected with Savonarola.

No one could deny that an apocalyptic argument might run like that. But the argument would seem to lack cogency, unless it is proved that some people ca. 1500 did identify Savonarola and Domenico da Pescia with the two witnesses of Revelation. This, in spite of some search, the compiler has been unable to prove. For instance, Fra Benedetto compares Savonarola to Jesus Christ, to Amos, to Zacharias, to Jeremiah and to Isaiah, and quotes Psalm lxv (lxvi) about him.[20] 'Burlamacchi' compares Savonarola to Elisha.[21] But there appears to be no reference in either writer to the two witnesses of the 11th chapter of Revelation.

In point of fact, the inscription on No. 1034 does not mention the two witnesses either. Nor is it easy to understand what precise relation the picture could have to Savonarola. It has already been stated that the Greek inscription may indicate that 'the troubles of Italy' began towards the middle of 1499; but Savonarola was martyred in May, 1498. The character of the prophecy in the Greek inscription does not seem particularly Savonarolan. Savonarola was happiest prophesying calamities, reaching (it is said) up to the siege of Florence in 1529; and when Savonarola did prophesy good fortune, he was in the habit of demanding a period of penitence first. The Greek inscription in No. 1034, on the other hand, seems to prophesy a Reign of Peace comparatively soon, and says nothing about penitence.

It appears therefore that No. 1034 has no precise connection with Savonarola. The meaning of the Greek inscription, whatever it may have been, may well not have been at all what his followers would have approved. This is not to say that there are not some parallels between the picture and Savonarola's works. It would indeed be most surprising if there were none; No. 1034, as has been noted, is a work of religious enthusiasm, and Savonarola was a celebrated and almost contemporary religious enthusiast. The closest parallel with No. 1034 in Savonarola's works appears to be in one of his sermons on the Nativity.[22]

It has been assumed in this discussion that the Greek inscription expresses (or conceals) Botticelli's own feelings. It does sound personal; probably No. 1034 was painted by Botticelli for his own devotion,[23] or at least for someone whose views he well understood.

PROVENANCE: From the Villa Aldobrandini at Rome.[24] W. Young Ottley Sale, London, 25 May, 1811 (lot 32), bought in;[25] W. Young Ottley Sale, 4 March, 1837 (lot 75), bought by Brown. Purchased from Smith in 1847 by W. Fuller Maitland of Stansted Hall.[26] Exhibited at Manchester, 1857 (Provisional Catalogue, No. 51; Definitive Catalogue, No. 78); at Leeds, 1868 (No. 32); at the R.A., 1871 (No. 278); and at the Burlington Fine Arts Club, 1871 (No. 21). Stansted Hall Catalogue, 1872, p. 8. Exhibited with other Fuller Maitland pictures at the South Kensington Museum in the 1870's.[27] Purchased from W. Fuller Maitland, 1878.

REPRODUCTION: *Illustrations, Italian Schools*, 1937, p. 59. *Plates, Earlier Italian Schools*, 1953, Vol. I, p. 71. Photographed since cleaning in 1958.

REFERENCES: (1) The picture was already noted to be on canvas in the Ottley Sale Catalogue of 1811; it is not, however, excluded that it has been transferred from panel. (2) J. Mesnil, *Botticelli*, 1938, pp. 174/5. (3) *Behold, the Lamb of God, which taketh away the sin of the world.* (4) Translated, in our Revised Version, *Glory to God in the highest, And on earth peace among men in whom he is well pleased.* Our Authorized Version gives the passage differently. (5) Horne, *Sandro Botticelli*, 1908, p. 300, says that he searched in vain for the source. (6) Cf. J. Mesnil, *Botticelli*, 1938, pp. 176/7, and John Pope–Hennessy, *Botticelli*,

The Nativity, Gallery Books, No. 15, p. 12. (**7**) The first to comment competently on the inscription was Sidney Colvin in *The Academy*, 15 February, 1871, pp. 130/2. Horne, *Sandro Botticelli*, 1908, pp. 294 ff., has also written at length about the inscription. See also Salvini, *Tutta la Pittura del Botticelli*, 1958, Vol. II, pp. 65/6. (**8**) Horne, *op. cit.*, pp. 294/5, and others have reconstructed the word as πατούμενον, 'him trodden down'; this does not seem possible, the third letter being fairly certainly a Φ. The first does not correspond exactly with π appearing elsewhere in the inscription; it may be considered a σ, but it is of a form different from any other σ there. The second letter seems to be α, but does not correspond exactly with other α's. (**9**) Cf. for instance Horne, *op. cit.*, p. 295, for a discussion of the year intended by the symbols ΧΣΣΣΣ. (**10**) Horne, *op. cit.*, p. 295, quotes Savonarola's note to Revelation xi that a time means a year; whether picture No. 1034 is precisely Savonarolan or not, this is contemporary evidence that the word 'time' in this connection could be interpreted to mean 'year'. (**11**) If a 'time' means a 'year' and a 'year' means a 'year', the prophecy seems to be for two years after the date of the picture; but this interpretation is of dubious validity. (**12**) See. J. Mesnil, *Botticelli*, 1938, pp. 169 f. and Plate XCVIII. The attribution of the Fogg picture to Botticelli's own hand is not always accepted. (**13**) The best account of Savonarola in connection with Botticelli is by J. Mesnil, *Botticelli*, 1938, Chapter XI. (**14**) Vasari; 1550 edition, pp. 494/5; ed. Milanesi, Vol. III, pp. 317/8 (text of 1568). (**15**) Simone was a strong believer in Savonarola. See for instance P. Villari and E. Casanova, *Scelta di Prediche e Scritti di Fra Girolamo Savonarola*, 1898, pp. 453 ff., where Simone's chronicle (according to a partial copy in the Vatican) is printed. (**16**) Horne, *Sandro Botticelli*, 1908, pp. 266 ff. (**17**) Horne, *op. cit.*, pp. 291/2, and Docs. XLVI, LV. (**18**) Cf. for instance Horne, *op. cit.*, pp. 276/7. (**19**) Apart from the present picture, which in this aspect is about to be discussed, there are only two works that can be connected with Savonarola. (*a*) Vasari, 1550, pp. 494/5, says that Botticelli produced a print of Savonarola's *Trionfo della Fede* (meaning presumably the *Trionfo della Croce di Cristo*). But no such print is now identifiable; see Horne, *op. cit.*, pp. 274, 288, and A. M. Hind, *Early Italian Engraving, A Critical Catalogue*, Part I, Vol. I, 1938, pp. 139/40. (*b*) the already mentioned picture in the Fogg Art Museum has a possible Savonarolan connection. J. Mesnil, *Botticelli*, 1938, pp. 169/70, is clearly right in claiming that in this picture Florence is being protected. In particular, Florence is being protected by shields showing a red cross on a white ground, which as Mesnil rightly points out is the arms of the Florentine people. But the red cross was also a Savonarolan emblem; cf. for instance *Diario Fiorentino di Luca Landucci*, ed. Iodoco del Badia, 1883, p. 128, and P. Villari and E. Casanova, *Scelta di Prediche e Scritti di Fra Girolamo Savonarola*, 1898, pp. 490/1. It appears therefore not impossible that there is some Savonarolan reference in the picture. For the origin of Savonarola's red crosses, see 'Fra Pacifico Burlamacchi,' *La Vita del Beato Ieronimo Savonarola*, ed. Piero Ginori Conti, 1937, p. 127, referring to a vision which is doubtless that printed by P. Villari and E. Casanova, *op. cit.*, p. 358. (**20**) Fra Benedetto, *Cedrus Libani*, in the *Archivio Storico Italiano*, Appendice, Vol. VII, 1849, pp. 59 ff., esp. pp. 79 and 94. (**21**) 'Fra Pacifico Burlamacchi,' *La Vita del Beato Ieronimo Savonarola*, ed. Piero Ginori Conti, 1937, Prologue (p. 3). The reference is to IV Kings viii, 4; in the English Bible, II Kings, viii, 4. (**22**) See *Sermoni e Prediche di F. Girolamo Savonarola*, Prato, 1846, for Advent 1493 apparently, XIX, *Della Natività di Cristo*, pp. 477 ff. Savonarola's text is from Psalm lxxxiv, 11/2 (lxxxv, 10/1), 'Misericordia et veritas obviaverunt sibi; justitia et pax osculatae sunt. Veritas de terra orta est, et justitia de caelo prospexit.' See especially pp. 485/6, where at the Nativity Savonarola says: 'e subito veggo discendere dal seno del Padre Eterno una veneranda donna con un ramo d'ulivo in mano, e veniva cantando, *Misericordia Domini plena est terra*. Cioè la terra della Vergine Santa fu ripiena della misericordia del Signore, la quale sollecitava e pregava il Fanciullo che uscisse fuora; e così, *Veritas de terra orta est* . . . . Or subito che questa verità fu uscita fuora, la misericordia si scontrò con lei, e tutte a due s'abbracciorno e dissono: *Universae viae Domini misericordia et veritas.* . . . La giustizia risguardò dal cielo . . . e discese subito in terra, clamando e cantando: *Gloria in excelsis Deo.* Ed ecco dall'altra parte del cielo venne una donna in abito semplice, bianco e puro, bellissima e graziosa, e con impeto grande corse inverso la giustizia e insieme si baciorno, e così: *Iustitia et pax obsculatae sunt.* E subito una di loro, che era Madonna Pace, disse: *Et in terra pax hominibus bonae voluntatis.'* This is a good deal farther from S. Luke than picture No. 1034 is, and a good deal nearer to the traditional 'Parliament of Heaven,' for which see Samuel C. Chew, *The Virtues Reconciled*, 1947, pp. 35 ff. On 5 December, 1494, apparently, Savonarola refers again to this text, with the interpretation of *veritas* as a scourge for Florence, which is quite different from picture No. 1034; see P. Villari and E. Casanova, *Scelta di Prediche e Scritti di Fra Girolamo Savonarola*, 1898, p. 71. Some doubt about the date of these sermons is expressed by Villari and Casanova, *op. cit.*, p. 31. **(23)** J. Mesnil, *Botticelli*, 1938, p. 175. **(24)** According to the Ottley Sale Catalogue of 1811. Ottley was in Italy *ca.* 1791/9. Ramdohr, *Ueber Mahlerei und Bildhauerarbeit in Rom*, II, 1787, p. 182, mentions without any details in the Villa Aldobrandini ' eine Sammlung von Gemählden der ersten Meister nach Wiederherstellung der Mahlerei.' The Villa Aldobrandini was sold in 1800; see L. Càllari, *Le Ville di Roma*, 1934, p. 178. The owner at the time of the sale appears to have been Francesco Borghese (1776–1839), who bore the title of Prince Aldobrandini, and later became Prince Borghese and Duca Salviati. For further details of the Aldobrandini inheritance, see the entry for Luini, No. 18. The compiler did not identify any picture corresponding with No. 1034 in an inventory of Giovanni Battista Pamphilj Aldobrandini, referred to in the entry for Mantegna, No. 1417, note 17; the record may be there, but cf. Luini, No. 18, note 13. **(25)** Mentioned in the Ottley Collection by Waagen, *Kunstwerke*, 1837, I, p. 397. **(26)** The date of acquisition was given as 1851 in the 1st edition of this catalogue, but that was a different picture; the matter is put beyond doubt in Smith's *Day-Books* in the Victoria and Albert Museum, III (1837–1848), p. 691 and IV (1848–1867), p. 160. The picture is mentioned in the Maitland Collection by Waagen, *Treasures*, III, 1854, p. 3. **(27)** Horne, *Sandro Botticelli*, 1908, p. 294.

3918 FOUR SCENES FROM THE EARLY LIFE OF S. ZENOBIUS (FROM A SERIES)

From left to right: (1) S. Zenobius renounces the bride chosen for him by his parents, and walks off; (2) S. Zenobius is baptized by S. (?) Theodorus or Theodosius, Bishop of Florence; (3) S. Zenobius' mother Sophia is baptized in the presence of her husband Lucianus and her son; (4) S. Zenobius is consecrated as Bishop of Florence by the Pope, S. Damasus.

Wood, painted surface, $26\frac{1}{4} \times 58\frac{3}{4}$ (0·665 × 1·495).
Excellent condition.
For the commentary, etc., see No. 3919 below.

3919 THREE MIRACLES OF S. ZENOBIUS (FROM A SERIES)

From left to right: (1) Two young men, having ill-treated their mother, were cursed by her into gnawing their own flesh; S. Zenobius exorcizes them; (2) S. Zenobius restores to life the son of a noble lady of Gaul. She had left him in the saint's charge during her pilgrimage to Rome, but the child had died; (3) S. Zenobius outside the Cathedral of Florence restores the sight of a blind beggar, who had promised to become a Christian if he could see.

Wood, painted surface, $25\frac{1}{2} \times 55$ (0.65×1.395).
Excellent condition.

Two pictures by Botticelli besides Nos. 3918/9 exist, showing incidents from the life of S. Zenobius. One in the Metropolitan Museum, New York, shows three other miracles; size, $26\frac{1}{2} \times 59\frac{1}{4}$.[1] The other at Dresden shows three episodes of one miracle, and the death of the saint; size, 0.66×1.82.[2] The sizes vary somewhat, especially in the lengths, and Nos. 3918/9 have not been cut, except just possibly No. 3919 at the top; but all four are clearly from the same series. The stories illustrated in Nos. 3918/9 can be found in Horne and Richter;[3] S. Zenobius (died 407 or 424) was Bishop of Florence, and is one of the Patrons of the City. The well-known miracle of the withered elm bursting into leaf on being touched by S. Zenobius' bier is not included on the existing panels; possibly the series is not complete.

The original provenance of the pictures is not known; presumably they decorated some panelling, perhaps in a room belonging to a church or religious community, presumably at Florence. The Dresden picture is said by Rumohr[4] to have come from the Compagnia di San Zenobio at Florence. It is equally uncertain whether he had good authority for his statement, and what he meant. It seems fairly sure that the Compagnia di San Zanobi or dei Laudesi attached to the Cathedral of Florence never owned any such pictures.[5] Conceivably Rumohr may have meant some other society, such as that of the Purificazione della Madonna e di San Zanobi, known as the Compagnia di San Marco; there is no confirmation that these Botticellis were there.[6]

Although Richter[7] maintained that the pictures are early works of Botticelli, there is no justification for this view. Horne[8] puts them as late as *ca.* 1505, and other critics have suggested various late dates.

PROVENANCE: Like the pictures at New York and Dresden, Nos. 3918/9 come from the Rondinelli Collection at Florence.[9] Bought in 1891 by J. P. Richter for Dr. Ludwig Mond.[10] Exhibited at the R.A., 1894 (Nos. 158 and 164). Mond Bequest, 1924.

REPRODUCTIONS: *Illustrations, Italian Schools*, 1937, pp. 60/1. *Plates, Earlier Italian Schools*, 1953, Vol. I, p. 72.

REFERENCES: (1) New York, Italian and Spanish Catalogue, 1940, No. 11.98, pp. 48/9. Some change due to the removal of repaint by cleaning is illustrated in *The Art News*, November, 1946, p. 34. (2) Dresden, *Die Romanischen Länder*, 1929, No. 9. (3) H. P. Horne, *Sandro Botticelli*, 1908, pp. 308 ff.; J. P. Richter, *The Mond Collection*, II, 1910, pp. 401 ff. For S. (?) Theodorus, see further in Richa, *Notizie Istoriche delle Chiese Fiorentine*, VI, 1757, pp. 280 f. For an inscription at Florence, commemorating the second miracle in No. 3919, see (Follini and Rastrelli), *Firenze Antica e Moderna*, V, 1794, pp. 79 ff., or F. Bigazzi, *Iscrizioni e Memorie della Città di Firenze*, 1886, p. 4. (4) Rumohr, *Italienische Forschungen*, II, 1827, p. 273. It had previously been mentioned without provenance in *Kunst-Blatt*, 1823, pp. 207/8 and 1824, p. 199.

(5) Nevertheless, this provenance is accepted by W. and E. Paatz, *Die Kirchen von Florenz*, Vol. III, 1952, p. 612, note 746. (6) See Poggi in the *Rivista d'Arte*, 1916, pp. 62 ff. For the history of the Compagnia di San Marco, see the chapter headed Spedale del Melani in Richa, *Notizie Istoriche delle Chiese Fiorentine*, V, 1757, pp. 329 ff.; also the entry for Benozzo, No. 283 of the present catalogue. (7) Richter, *loc. cit.* in note 3, and elsewhere. (8) Horne, *loc. cit.* in note 3. Salvini, *Tutta la Pittura del Botticelli*, 1958, Vol. II, pp. 67/8, thinks probably 1500/5. (9) Cf. Horne, *op. cit.*, p. 308. A letter of 1931 from J. P. Richter in the Gallery archives offers confirmation, and corrects some details; but Richter asked that these should not be published. (10) Richter, *op. cit.*, list at the beginning of Vol. II.

Studio of SANDRO BOTTICELLI

226 TONDO: THE VIRGIN AND CHILD WITH S. JOHN AND TWO ANGELS

Wood, *tondo* or, more exactly, slightly oval, painted surface, $45 \times 44\frac{1}{2}$ ($1 \cdot 145 \times 1 \cdot 13$).

Good condition. There is a *pentimento* at the shoulder of the angel on the left, and there are painted out leaves in front of the farther wings of both angels.

The quality of various parts of this *tondo* seems to vary slightly, but it seems impossible to believe that any of the executants was Botticelli himself.

VERSION: A very similar picture, in the Palazzo Rospigliosi-Pallavicini, Rome, has sometimes been confused with No. 226.[1]

PROVENANCE: Formerly owned by the Polli family, Florence.[2] Purchased from J. H. Brown, Florence, 1855.

REPRODUCTION: *Illustrations, Italian Schools*, 1937, p. 61. *Plates, Earlier Italian Schools*, 1953, Vol. I, p. 73.

REFERENCES: (1) E.g. in the Klassiker der Kunst *Botticelli*, 1926, p. 126. See F. Zeri, *La Galleria Pallavicini in Roma*, 1959, No. 68, reproduced. (2) N.G. Report, 1855.

275 TONDO: THE VIRGIN AND CHILD WITH S. JOHN AND AN ANGEL

Wood, painted surface, diameter $33\frac{1}{4}$ ($0 \cdot 845$). In parts painted up to the edges; this is clearly not due to cutting, but to efforts to squeeze the composition into a tondo shape.

Very good condition.

An inscription on the back, in writing apparently contemporary with the painting, reads *M (?) Giuljano da san Ghallo*. This led Richter[1] to attribute the picture to the well-known architect of that name. A signature in pigment on the unprimed back of a picture would in itself be very unlikely; in this particular case, the writing is at a considerable angle to what is the horizontal for the picture, and it seems incredible that Giuliano da Sangallo should have been so careless about a signature. It is often thought that he may have commissioned the picture, which is possible. It is also possible that the picture was put aside in Botticelli's studio with Sangallo's name on the back, to indicate that it was to be sent to him to fit up the frame.[2]

The picture was formerly ascribed to Botticelli himself. It seems probable that the execution is due entirely to an assistant, although the picture was doubtless sold from the shop as a Botticelli, and although it is better in quality than most Botticelli studio-pieces.[3] Salvini accepts a date *ca.* 1490.[4]

VERSIONS: An apparently inferior version was in the Yerkes Sale, New York, 1910.[5] Another inferior version, larger than No. 275, was seen by Eastlake at the Monte di Pietà, Rome, in 1856;[6] perhaps the same as the version in Lord Crawford's Sale, 11 October, 1946 (lot 30).[7] Another version of the same size as No. 275 was offered by Engineer Pécarrère, Pau, in 1900.[8]

PROVENANCE: From the Collection of the Abate Carlo Bianconi of Bologna and Milan, who died in 1802,[9] it passed to Giovanni Giuseppe Bianconi of Bologna,[10] from whom purchased, 1855.

REPRODUCTION: *Illustrations, Italian Schools*, 1937, p. 54. *Plates, Earlier Italian Schools*, 1953, Vol. I, p. 74.

REFERENCES: (1) J. P. Richter, *Lectures on the National Gallery*, 1898, pp. 63/4. Degenhart in the *Römisches Jahrbuch für Kunstgeschichte*, 1955, pp. 233/4, reproduces the inscription and accepts the picture as by Giuliano da Sangallo. (2) Giuliano da Sangallo did make the frame of Botticelli's altarpiece of *ca.* 1485, No. 106 at Berlin; see H. P. Horne, *Sandro Botticelli*, 1908, p. 136 and Doc. No. XXV, which is reprinted from I. B. Supino, *Sandro Botticelli*, 1900, p. 83. A further reference to his activity in this field, *ca.* 1485/8, can be found in P. E. Küppers, *Die Tafelbilder des Domenico Ghirlandaio*, 1916, p. 89. (3) Cf. Hermann Ulmann, *Sandro Botticelli*, 1893, p. 123. (4) Salvini, *Tutta la Pittura del Botticelli*, 1958, Vol. II, p. 75. (5) Yerkes Catalogue, 1904, I, No. 4, with reproduction; diameter 29 in.; from the Galleria del Nero, Rome. (6) Eastlake's note-book. No doubt identical with No. 2770 of the *Catalogo de' Quadri etc. esistenti nella Galleria del Sagro Monte di Pietà di Roma*, December 1857, *La Madonna il Bambino e due Angeli*, tondo, diameter 1·05. (7) Diameter, 41 or 42 in.; stated to be from the Campana Collection, Rome, and to have been bought by Lord Crawford from Pinti in 1874. Reproduced in the Catalogue of the Summer Exhibition at Frank T. Sabin's, 1953 (No. 21). (8) Letter in the Gallery archives. (9) See Thieme-Becker, and the *Guida del Forestiere per la Città di Bologna* by Girolamo Bianconi, 1820, p. 463. (10) The provenance is from the N.G. Report for 1856, where it is stated that this is the picture mentioned as a Ghirlandaio in the house of the late Prof. Bianconi by Petronio Bassani, *Guida agli amatori delle Belle Arti…per la città di Bologna*, I, i, 1816, p. 104, *Q. della B.V. con il Bambino, ec.* The picture is No. 3 (as Botticelli) of the *Catalogo delle Pitture e Sculture possedute dalla Famiglia Bianconi in Bologna, le quali appartenero per la maggior parte alla collezione dell'abate Carlo Bianconi*, 1854.

782 THE VIRGIN AND CHILD

Wood, painted surface, $32\frac{3}{4} \times 25\frac{1}{2}$ (0·83 × 0·65); painted up to the edges all round.

Good condition; some of the gold is new. Some *pentimenti* in the outlines.

VERSIONS: Versions of this design, more or less varied, occur very frequently; it is possible that all such pictures derive ultimately from a Botticelli in the Louvre.[1] Pictures closely corresponding with No. 782 are (1) in the Crespi Collection, Milan (ex-Liechtenstein Gallery at Vienna);[2] (2) at Lille;[3] (3) in the former Aynard Collection at Lyons.[4] A variant as a tondo with S. John added was in the R. von Kaufmann Collection at Berlin.[5] Another group of pictures that shows some similarity of design to No. 782 includes (1) at Dresden;[6] (2) Frankfort;[7] (3) the Palazzo Vecchio at Florence;[8] (4) the Vernon Watney Collection;[9] (5) Oxford.[10] Yet another connected group is in (1) the Max Epstein Collection, Chicago;[11] (2) the former Austen Collection.[12]

PROVENANCE: Formerly owned by Conte Angiolo Galli Tassi at Florence; he bequeathed it in 1863 with other property to the Arcispedale di S. Maria Nuova and other hospitals in Tuscany, for whose benefit it was sold.[13] Purchased at Milan from G. Baslini, 1867.

REPRODUCTION: *Illustrations, Italian Schools*, 1937, p. 62. *Plates, Earlier Italian Schools*, 1953, Vol. I, p. 75.

REFERENCES: (1) Klassiker der Kunst *Botticelli*, 1926, p. 11. (2) Liechtenstein *Führer*, 1931, No. 852, reproduced, ex-coll. Ginori at Florence; also reproduced by Van Marle, *Development of the Italian Schools of Painting*, Vol. XII, Fig. 141. Salvini, *Tutta la Pittura del Botticelli*, 1958, Vol. II, p. 76, states that it passed to the Crespi Collection, Milan. (3) 1893 Catalogue, No. 305; photograph Archives Photographiques, No. P 7311. (4) Aynard Sale, Paris, 1 December, 1913 (lot 40), reproduced; apparently identical with lot 31 of the Mrs. Leverton Harris Sale, 8 June, 1928. (5) Sale, 4 sqq. December, 1917 (lot 20), reproduced; from a Pallavicini Collection in Hungary. (6) Large Catalogue, *Die Romanischen Länder*, 1929 (No. 8), reproduced. (7) Van Marle, *op. cit.*, Vol. XII, Fig. 145. (8) A. Lensi, *Palazzo Vecchio*, 1929, reproduced on p. 357. (9) Catalogue, 1915 (No. 22), ex-Bammeville, Barker, Osmaston and Leyland Collections. (10) Ruskin Sale, 20 May, 1931 (lot 122), reproduced. Oxford, 1951 Catalogue, No. 71. (11) Ex-Jules Féral. Klassiker der Kunst *Botticelli*, 1926, p. 4. (12) Sale, 18 March, 1921 (lot 85), reproduced. This and the preceding are both reproduced in the *Gazette des Beaux-Arts*, 1907, ii, p. 10. (13) The Director's MS. Report of Proceedings on the Continent, January 1868, gives an indication of the provenance. C. Morelli, *Gli Spedali di Parigi e di Londra—L'Arcispedale di Santa Maria Nuova*, etc., 1863, p. 3, and O. Andreucci, *Della Biblioteca e Pinacoteca dell'Arcispedale di S. Maria Nuova*, 1871, p. 21, say that the Galli Tassi bequest was for the benefit of S. Maria Nuova and the other hospitals in Tuscany, and that the testator directed that the pictures, etc., included in the bequest should be sold. For the date of the bequest and spelling of the name, see (Isidoro del Lungo), *Il R. Arcispedale di S. Maria Nuova: I Suoi Benefattori: Sue Antiche Memorie*, 1888, p. 36.

2497   TONDO: THE VIRGIN AND CHILD WITH S. JOHN THE BAPTIST

An inscription on S. John's scroll reads .ECCE.AGNVS./.DEI.

Wood, *tondo* or, more exactly, slightly oval, painted surface, $37\frac{1}{2} \times 37$ (0·955 × 0·94); painted up to the edges all round.

Good condition in general; some of the gold is new. *Pentimenti* in some of the outlines.

VERSIONS: Two versions with some differences are known. (1) At Cardiff, formerly in the Fuller Maitland Collection, diameter 34 in.[1] (2) Formerly in the Lord Grimthorpe and Fairfax Murray Collections, diameter $45\frac{1}{2}$ in.[2]

PROVENANCE: Stated to come from the collection of the Marchese Patrizi at

Rome.[3] Acquired by George Salting before 1889, probably before 1885 and perhaps before 1883.[4] Salting Bequest, 1910.

REPRODUCTION: *Illustrations, Italian Schools*, 1937, p. 63. *Plates, Earlier Italian Schools*, 1953, Vol. I, p. 76.

REFERENCES: (1) Acquired in Rome in 1842, according to the Stansted Hall Catalogue, 1872, p. 7; Fuller Maitland Sale, 14 July, 1922 (lot 53), reproduced. Cardiff, *Catalogue of Oil-Paintings*, 1955, p. 135, No. 747. (2) From a Collection at Arezzo; Lord Grimthorpe Sale, 12 May, 1906 (lot 20), reproduced; Fairfax Murray Sale, Paris, 15 June, 1914 (lot 4), reproduced; Fairfax Murray Sale, 14 December, 1917 (lot 34), reproduced. (3) Salting MSS. (4) This is deducible from the Salting MSS. In the 1929 Catalogue No. 2497 was wrongly said to have been acquired by Salting *ca.* 1875. That note of Salting's refers to a different picture, which he sold in 1885 to R. H. Benson; Benson Catalogue, 1914 (No. 26); later in the E. W. Edwards Collection, Cincinnati, and reproduced in *The Burlington Magazine*, Vol. LVII (1930), p. 153.

2906 THE VIRGIN AND CHILD WITH A POMEGRANATE

Wood, painted surface, $26\frac{3}{4} \times 20\frac{3}{4}$ (0.68×0.53). The partly cut off book in the right-hand bottom corner suggests that the picture may have been cut somewhat, at any rate at the bottom and right-hand sides.

A good deal of retouching somewhat alters the character of the picture.

VERSION: A rather similar design (inverted) occurs in a picture at Washington, formerly Corsini, Florence.[1]

PROVENANCE: A stencil mark 548 X is apparently that of the Prince Jerome Napoleon Sale, London, 9 May, 1872; so presumably lot 301, bought by Johnson.[2] Lent by Lady Lindsay to the New Gallery, 1893/4 (No. 121); Lady Lindsay Bequest, 1912.

REPRODUCTION: *Illustrations, Italian Schools*, 1937, p. 65. *Plates, Earlier Italian Schools*, 1953, Vol. I, p. 77.

REFERENCES: (1) Washington, 1941 Catalogue, No. 21; reproduced in the Book of Illustrations. (2) 'The Virgin in red and blue dress holding the Infant Saviour, seated on a table, a landscape is seen through an open window—*on panel* (0.65 by 0.52).' No. 2906 does not show the Child seated; but otherwise the description corresponds, and there does not appear to be any other claimant for identity with the Napoleon picture.

Follower of SANDRO BOTTICELLI

589 THE VIRGIN AND CHILD WITH AN ANGEL

Wood, painted surface, $27\frac{1}{2} \times 19$ (0.70×0.48).

By no means in bad condition; but the surface is disturbed by past flaking and uneven cleaning. Obvious vertical cracks. *Pentimenti* in the angel's head. In the architecture are several lines, some perhaps indicating proposed differences, but mostly guides for the painter in his perspective.

No. 589 was catalogued in 1929 as from the School of Fra Filippo Lippi. The composition is derived from a picture by Fra Filippo Lippi in the Uffizi.[1] The decoration of the Virgin's dress is also apparently a

Filippesque derivation.[2] The colour is somewhat reminiscent of Fra Filippo Lippi, and so are some details of the handling, e.g. the hair of the Child. No. 589 seems, nevertheless, more advanced in style than anything carried out by Fra Filippo; and there is good reason for associating it with the young Botticelli.[3] Among the numerous derivations from Fra Filippo's already mentioned picture in the Uffizi,[4] much the nearest in style to No. 589 is a picture at Naples;[5] and that picture is probably an early work by Botticelli.

Although the style of No. 589 corresponds fairly closely with that of the picture at Naples, it is so very much weaker that one should postulate a difference of hand.[6] No. 589 might be supposed to be merely a Botticelli studio-piece.[7] But the Naples picture, if by Botticelli, is a very early work indeed, and it is doubtful if Botticelli's studio at such a time would have been competent to produce No. 589. It is probably better to think of No. 589 as a nearly contemporary imitation, not necessarily done under Botticelli's supervision.[8]

The architecture in No. 589 apparently does not recur in any picture of the School. It is sufficiently coherent to suggest that the painter of No. 589 may have been practically interested in architecture, or may have had the use of a drawing by some such person.

VARIANTS: See above.

PROVENANCE: On the back is a seal of export from Italy, and another seal with the words *Roma Terra* and *Lettere* round an umbrella. From Sig. Zambrini of Imola.[9] Purchased with other pictures from Lombardi and Baldi, Florence, 1857.[10]

REPRODUCTION: *Illustrations, Italian Schools*, 1937, p. 190. *Plates, Earlier Italian Schools*, 1953, Vol. I, p. 78.

REFERENCES: (1) Reproduced by J. Mesnil, *Botticelli*, 1938, Plate II, and frequently elsewhere. (2) Compare the tondo in the Pitti, reproduced by Van Marle, *Development of the Italian Schools of Painting*, Vol. X, Figs. 259, 260. Compare also a derivation from the central figure of this tondo, ascribed to Fra Filippo Lippi, at Washington: 1941 Catalogue, No. 407, reproduced in the *Illustrations*, also catalogued at Knoedler's, New York, *Italian Renaissance Portraits*, 1940 (No. 3). (3) J. Mesnil, *Botticelli*, 1938, p. 16, inclines to accept it as a Botticelli. Crowe and Cavalcaselle, *History of Painting in Italy*, II, 1864, pp. 332 and 349/50, considered it between Botticelli and Filippino. (4) The picture referred to in the 1929 Catalogue as a replica of No. 589, in the Davenport Bromley Sale, 1863 (lot 75), is actually No. 2508 of this Gallery, Florentine School. (5) Naples, Catalogo by Aldo de Rinaldis, 1928 (No. 46), reproduced on Plate 14; J. Mesnil, *Botticelli*, 1938, Plate III. The size of the Naples picture is 1·00 × 0·71, so the figures are on a considerably larger scale than those of No. 589. There are many differences from No. 589, including an extra angel; the position of the Child's left arm and leg; and the absence of the book in the foreground, right. Further, the background of the Naples picture is different, the scene there being the *Hortus Conclusus*. (6) Nevertheless, Salvini, *Tutta la Pittura del Botticelli*, 1958, Vol. I, p. 36, accepts both as by Botticelli; he dates No. 589 a little earlier than the Naples picture, which he dates *ca.* 1468/9. For Mesnil's opinion, see note 3. (7) Berenson, in his Lists of 1932, calls it so. (8) A cartoon by a good man could sometimes be got hold of by inferior painters outside the studio; see *Der Literarische Nachlass Giorgio Vasaris*, ed. K. Frey, I, 1923, p. 189. The date of Vasari's letter is indeed 1547, but the practice had presumably been going on for a long time. The pictures classed in the present catalogue as from Botticelli's studio were probably or at least possibly sold as Botticelli's from his shop; this appears unlikely for No. 589, which is why another classification is given. (9) N. G. Catalogue, 1859; presumably Eastlake had the information from Lombardi or Baldi. (10) As Fra Filippo Lippi. For the history of the Lombardi-Baldi Collection, see Appendix I.

598   S. FRANCIS

The Saint stands contemplating a Crucifix; ten angels.

Wood, painted surface, $19\frac{1}{2} \times 12\frac{1}{2}$ (0.495×0.32); painted up to the edges except at the bottom.

On the whole in good condition; but there are a number of damages, e.g. round the Saint's right foot (where there is a *pentimento*), on his left hand and in the top right corner.

Presumably a single panel for private devotion, and not part of a larger ensemble.

No. 598 was cleaned in 1940, at which time a false inscription along the bottom was removed. It read: HVNC SEQVANTVR . HVIC. IVNGANTVR . QVI EX EGIPTO EXEVNT . IN QVO NOBIS CLARA . LVCE . / VEXILLA . REGIS . PRODEVNT . (space) AD MCCCCXCII.[1]

It is unnecessary to retain any shred of belief that No. 598 was painted in 1492. It was in the 1929 Catalogue called Filippino Lippi.[2] It may well be by the same hand as No. 1345 of the Louvre,[3] which is often ascribed to the young Botticelli;[4] indeed, both it and No. 598 have some similarities to his early work.[5] But No. 598 is not acceptable as by the same hand as No. 592 of the National Gallery, which has at least been claimed to be one of the earliest Botticellis;[6] it seems clearly by an inferior man, painting under the influence of Botticelli's early style.[7]

PROVENANCE: In the Collection of Conte Giovanni Battista Costabili at Ferrara by 1841;[8] purchased from that collection in 1858.

REPRODUCTION: *Illustrations, Italian Schools*, 1937, p. 185 (before cleaning, and with a piece missing from the bottom). *Plates, Earlier Italian Schools*, 1953, Vol. I, p. 79.

REFERENCES: (1) The words form with some variations the fifth verse of a Hymn to S. Francis, beginning *Decus morum*, printed in the *Breviarium secundum ritum Romanum Venetiis impressum arte et impensis Andree de Torresanis de Asula*, 1495, and reprinted by H. A. Daniel, *Thesaurus Hymnologicus*, I, 1841, pp. 319/20. (2) The attribution to Filippino was accepted by Mündler (*Diary*, March, 1858), by Eastlake (*Note-book*, August, 1858) and by Crowe and Cavalcaselle, *History of Painting in Italy*, II, 1864, p. 452. Perhaps first rejected by J. P. Richter, *Italian Art in the National Gallery*, 1883, p. 29. (3) Reproduced by Van Marle, *Development of the Italian Schools of Painting*, Vol. XII, Fig. 3. The picture appears as School of Fra Filippo Lippi in Seymour de Ricci's Catalogue of the Louvre, *Ecoles Etrangères, Italie et Espagne*, 1913; in Hautecœur's Catalogue, *Ecole Italienne et Ecole Espagnole*, 1926, it appears on p. 148 as by the Master of the Oriental Sash. (The Master of the Oriental Sash is an agglomeration put together by O. Sirèn in the Blakeslee Galleries Sale Catalogue, New York, 21/3 April, 1915, Introduction; Sirèn does not ascribe No. 598 to him, but No. 589 of this catalogue, Follower of Botticelli.) (4) E.g. by Carlo Gamba, *Botticelli*, 1936, pp. 98/9, and by J. Mesnil, *Botticelli*, 1938, p. 227. (5) Berenson, in his Lists of 1932, does not dispute the date of 1492 then on the picture, and calls it a copy made in 1492 of an early Botticelli. (6) See the entry. (7) Jacobsen in the *Repertorium für Kunstwissenschaft*, 1901, p. 354, calls No. 598 perhaps Raffaellino del Garbo; A. Scharf, *Filippino Lippi*, 1935, No. 162, calls it Botticini. (8) Catalogo, Part IV, 1841, No. 424, as Matteo di Giovanni.

916   AN ALLEGORY

A gravid woman in a white gown is lying on the ground; three putti with fruit and flowers.

Wood, painted surface (sight), $36\frac{1}{4} \times 68$ (0·92 × 1·73).

The paint is well preserved, except where numerous cracks in the panel have caused trouble.

The picture was, in 1929, entitled *Venus reclining with Cupids*, and this may correctly indicate the subject. But it seems more likely that some allegory of Fertility is intended.[1]

This picture was ascribed to Jacopo del Sellaio by M. Logan;[2] it was catalogued as by him in 1929, and the attribution was accepted by Berenson in his Lists of 1932. The œuvre of Sellaio is somewhat ill-defined, as is explained in his biography in this catalogue; in any case, No. 916 does not appear to belong to the group most reasonably classed as by Sellaio.[3] It is by some feeble imitator of Botticelli, and seems to be partly derived from Botticelli's *Venus and Mars*, No. 915 above.

For the use made of panels such as this, see the entry for Botticelli, No. 915 above, note 10.

VERSION: A variant, not necessarily by the same hand, is in the Louvre.[4]

PROVENANCE: Probably identical with a picture in the collection of Cardinal Fesch at Rome (not among the pictures brought by him from France in 1815);[5] 1841 Catalogue, No. 2320; Sale, 1845 (lot 1791), bought by Aducci. In the collection of Alexander Barker, London, where seen by Waagen;[6] purchased at the Barker Sale, 6 June, 1874 (lot 89).[7]

REPRODUCTION: *Illustrations, Italian Schools*, 1937, p. 329. *Plates, Earlier Italian Schools*, 1953, Vol. I, p. 80.

REFERENCES: (1) This was already indicated in the Fesch Catalogue of 1841, for a picture probably identical with No. 916 (see the provenance); A. L. Mayer in *Pantheon*, 1933, p. 14, also inclines to this view. Eugénie Strong, *Terra Mater or Italia?*, in the *Journal of Roman Studies*, Vol. XXVII (1937), pp. 114 ff., pointed out the similarity of No. 916 to the classical group of *Terra Mater*, of which she reproduces several examples. (2) M. Logan in the *Revue Archéologique*, 1899, II, p. 480. (3) Compare Horne, *Sandro Botticelli*, 1908, pp. 141/2. Schubring, *Cassoni*, 1923, Nos. 314/5, gives entries for No. 916 and the variant of it in the Louvre, with a reference to Ulmann's views on the attribution. A. L. Mayer in *Pantheon*, 1933, p. 14, doubtfully ascribes No. 916 to Bartolomeo di Giovanni (Alunno di Domenico). (4) Paris, Louvre, No. 1299; in the Italian Catalogues by Seymour de Ricci, 1913, and Hautecoeur, 1926, as School of Botticelli; reproduced by Van Marle, *Development of the Italian Schools of Painting*, Vol. XII, Fig. 271. Height, 0·845 or (with addition) 0·865; width, 2·18 (information kindly sent by Mme. Béguin). (5) The Louvre claims that the version there is the one from the Fesch Sale. But the size of the Fesch picture was 3 ft. × 5 ft. 3 in., pied du roi; and this fits much better with the size of No. 916 than with that of the Louvre picture (0·845 × 2·18). There are no Fesch labels on the back of either picture. (6) Waagen, *Treasures*, IV, 1857, p. 72, as Botticelli. (7) As Botticelli. Crowe and Cavalcaselle, *History of Painting in Italy*, II, 1864, p. 427, had accepted No. 916 as a Botticelli.

2082   A LADY IN PROFILE

Reverse: a winged figure, presumably an angel, stands on a rock before a wood. In one hand is an armillary sphere, with a scroll apparently inscribed CHI B / I / N; in the other hand, perhaps moss.

Wood, painted surface (sight), $23\frac{1}{4} \times 15\frac{3}{4}$ (0·59 × 0·40); the reverse is of the same size.

The front is considerably damaged; the reverse is in very fair state.

The reverse is obviously an allegory of something, but it has not been discovered of what.[1]

The front is an inferior version of a picture attributed to Botticelli, formerly owned by Dr. Noak at Berlin.[2] Other rather similar profiles exist from the entourage of Botticelli; it is uncertain if they are portraits, or merely illustrations of some feminine ideal.

No. 2082 is by some pedestrian follower of Botticelli.

VERSION: See above.

PROVENANCE: Lent by Alexander Barker to Leeds, 1868 (No. 9a);[3] Barker Sale, 6 June, 1874 (lot 90), bought by John Samuel. Exhibited at the New Gallery, 1893/4 (No. 164), lent by the Misses Cohen, nieces of John Samuel. Bequeathed with other pictures by the Misses Cohen, as the John Samuel Collection, 1906.

REPRODUCTIONS: *Illustrations, Italian Schools*, 1937, p. 64 (both front and reverse). *Plates, Earlier Italian Schools*, 1953, Vol. I, p. 81 (front only).

REFERENCES: (1) Berenson, *Drawings of the Florentine Painters*, 1938, No. 573, mentions a drawing in the Cod. 1711 (*Fior di Virtù*) of the Riccardiana Library at Florence. He notes a 'correspondence in action' between that and the reverse of No. 2082; but the emblems differ, and the correspondence is very slight. (2) Klassiker der Kunst *Botticelli*, 1926, Plate 24. Recorded as a Cimabue in the *Recueil de Gravures au Trait*, etc., Lebrun Collection, Paris, I, 1809, Plate I. (3) As *The Painter's Wife*.

3082   THE VIRGIN AND CHILD

Wood, painted surface, $11\frac{5}{8} \times 7\frac{3}{4}$ (0·295 × 0·195); painted up to the edges all round.

Fairly good condition.

Derived from the central part of Botticelli's S. Barnaba altarpiece in the Uffizi.[1] The picture is by some feeble hand, more or less contemporary with Botticelli, but not certainly or even probably done in Botticelli's studio. On the back is the obscure inscription: .*S.Bartholomeo* / L'.ANNO M.CCCCXII(I?).

VERSIONS: As already stated, derived from the S. Barnaba Altarpiece, of which several other derivations are known.

PROVENANCE: Given to Sir Austen Henry Layard by 'J. Miner Kellogg.'[2] Exhibited at South Kensington, 1869 (No. 50). Layard Bequest, 1916.[3]

REPRODUCTION: *Illustrations, Italian Schools*, 1937, p. 65. *Plates, Earlier Italian Schools*, 1953, Vol I, p. 82.

REFERENCES: (1) Klassiker der Kunst *Botticelli*, 1926, p. 61. (2) Layard MS. Catalogue, No. 11. The donor appears to have been a painter, since 'J. M. Kellogg' gave one of his own pictures to Layard (MS. Catalogue, No. 65). Possibly he is identical with Miner K. Kellogg (see Thieme-Becker), who was in correspondence with Layard (letters in the Layard Papers at the British Museum); further information about Miner K. Kellogg by E. P. Richardson in *The Art Quarterly*, Autumn 1960, pp. 271 ff. (3) For the history of the Layard Collection, see Appendix IV.

Francesco BOTTICINI
ca. 1446–1497

A Florentine painter and craftsman. The date of birth and the surname are from Milanesi's Vasari, IV, p. 245. The documents refer to him as Francesco di Giovanni; but there is some confirmation that he was called Botticini also (Milanesi, *Nuovi Documenti*, 1901, No. 193). He is assumed to be the man who was apprenticed to Neri di Bicci in 1459, and ran away 9 (?) months later (Milanesi's Vasari, II, p. 87).

The only work documented as by the painter we call Botticini is a tabernacle at Empoli, commissioned in 1484; Francesco seems to have more or less completed this tabernacle in 1491, but some work was done on it after his death by his son Raffaello in 1504. E. Kühnel, *Francesco Botticini*, 1906, Plates I and II, reproduces the pictures included in this tabernacle, which were Nos. 28, 30 and 31 of the *Mostra di Opere d'Arte Restaurate* at the Academy of Florence, 1946/7.

A number of works classed as by the Master of the Rossi altarpiece from a picture at Berlin) were assembled as members of a stylistic group by Bode (Prussian *Jahrbuch*, 1886, pp. 231 ff.; some rather confused indications already in Crowe and Cavalcaselle, *History of Painting in Italy*, II, 1864, pp. 452 ff.). These pictures were then associated with the tabernacle at Empoli, and therefore ascribed to Botticini. This was first done by Schmarsow (?); see the *Festschrift zu Ehren des Kunsthistorischen Instituts in Florenz*, 1897, pp. 125/6—an essay stated to have been first published in 1887.

The pictures ascribed to Botticini have various points in common; but the attribution to a single hand of works in general so humdrum is somewhat subjective. According to the commonly accepted view, he spent his time imitating in turn the prominent painters of his day. One may feel that there is some reason for doubting the homogeneity of the group; there has indeed been difference among critics as to the acceptance or rejection of individual items.

An altarpiece in the Musée André at Paris is dated 1471; the Rossi altarpiece at Berlin is dated 1475. If No. 1126 below is by Botticini, he would seem to have been influenced by Fra Filippo Lippi, and possibly by Botticelli.

The most accurate account of him is given by Pèleo Bacci in the *Bollettino d'Arte*, 1924/5, pp. 337 ff.

227 ALTARPIECE: S. JEROME IN PENITENCE, WITH
SAINTS AND DONORS

An altarpiece, complete in its original frame. Centre, in an inner
framing, S. Jerome kneels before a crucifix marked INRI; his name is
inscribed below, .S.IERONIMVS. Left, S. Damasus, Pope, his name
S.DAMMASVS.inscribed, with figures of the Annunciation, S. John
the Baptist, and another saint embroidered on his cope; also, S. Eusebius, with a book, his name inscribed S.EVSHBIVS. Right, S. Paula
with a book, her name inscribed .S.PAVLA.; and S. Eustochium with
a lily, her name inscribed .S.EVSTOCIVz. In front kneel two donors,
the boy being presumably the son of the other, who may be Gerolamo
Rucellai. The predella has the Rucellai arms at each end. Its four scenes
are, from left to right: (1) S. Jerome taking the thorn out of the lion's
paw; (2) S. Jerome's vision when a young man and very ill, that he was
beaten at God's command for being a Ciceronian rather than a Christian;
(3) the death of S. Jerome, with a haloed priest present; (4) S. Jerome,
and S. John the Baptist with a scroll inscribed ECCE A, appear to S.
Augustine. The ends of the predella at the sides contain a simple painted
pattern, the same at each end.

The pilasters of the frame include a device of two (?) feathers in a
diamond ring; on the cornice at the sides the device is three feathers in
a diamond ring.

Wood. The size of the painted surface of the main panel is 60×68
($1 \cdot 525 \times 1 \cdot 73$). The framing surrounding the figure of S. Jerome himself
is fixed on to the front of the picture; the size of S. Jerome's compart-
ment is $47\frac{1}{2} \times 20$ ($1 \cdot 21 \times 0 \cdot 51$), rounded top. The size of the predella,
painted surface, is $6\frac{1}{2} \times 87\frac{3}{4}$ ($0 \cdot 165 \times 2 \cdot 23$); the four predella scenes are
each about 16 in. ($0 \cdot 40$) wide, but vary somewhat. The size of the painted
pattern at each end of the predella, at the sides, is $6\frac{1}{2} \times 8$ ($0 \cdot 165 \times 0 \cdot 20$).
The total size of the altarpiece, including the frame, is $92\frac{1}{2} \times 101\frac{1}{2}$
($2 \cdot 35 \times 2 \cdot 58$), approx.

Good condition.

This picture comes from the church of the Hermits of S. Jerome of
Fiesole, at Fiesole. The donors are, from the arms, members of the
Rucellai family; the man seems likely to be Gerolamo di Piero di Cardinale Rucellai, who died in 1497(?), and whose tomb is near where the
picture hung.[1] The devices on the frame are rather puzzling. They were
much used by the Medici; but two feathers in a diamond ring do occur
prominently on the Palazzo Rucellai at Florence, and in the Cappella
Rucellai in S. Pancrazio there.[2]

The Religious Order was founded by the Blessed(?) Charles of Monte-
granelli, apparently of the family of the Conti Guidi, who died in 1417 or
1419. He took up a penitential retreat on the hill of Fiesole, being a
member of the Third Order of S. Francis, between 1360 and 1386; it
was ca. 1404/6 that his own Order received official recognition. It was
known as the Order of S. Jerome of Fiesole, to distinguish it from other
Hieronymite communities. It had a considerable extension at one time,
the house at Fiesole remaining the head, and was suppressed in 1668.[3]

The four saints surrounding S. Jerome (died 420) on No. 227 were all connected with him in life. S. Damasus, Pope, who died in 384, instructed S. Jerome to make the translation of the Bible known as the Vulgate. S. Eusebius of Cremona, a monk who died in 423, was a friend of S. Jerome, and his supporter against the errors started by Origen. S. Paula, who died in 404, followed S. Jerome to Palestine, and became the abbess of a nunnery founded by him at Bethlehem. Her daughter, S. Eustochium (Julia), who died in 419, was a pupil of S. Jerome, and succeeded her mother as abbess at Bethlehem.

Of the scenes in the predella, No. 1 needs no comment, and No. 2 is from a story told by S. Jerome himself.[4] In No. 3, the haloed priest has not been identified. No. 4 seems to be a mixture of two closely connected incidents; (a) S. Augustine is interrupted in an epistle he was preparing to write to S. Jerome, by a light and a voice which explained that it was the soul of Jerome, who had just died;[5] (b) on the same evening, S. Augustine was inditing an epistle in honour of S. Jerome, but fell asleep; S. Jerome with two crowns and S. John the Baptist with three, amid a host of angels, appeared to him, and the full glory of S. Jerome was revealed.[6] It is clearly mostly (b) that is illustrated here. A possible subsidiary reason for S. Augustine's presence on this particular picture is that in 1441 the Hieronymites of Fiesole began to follow S. Augustine's Rule.[7]

The grey dresses of the principal figures undoubtedly echo the habit of the Hieronymites of Fiesole. They had been at first dressed as members of the Third Order of S. Francis, to which their founder had belonged; but in 1460 most of them, including the mother-house at Fiesole, changed to a grey dress with leather belt. S. Eusebius is presumably dressed correctly, but with the belt not showing; S. Jerome himself has rather vague indications of a belt.[8]

On its acquisition by the National Gallery, the picture was ascribed by Eastlake to Cosimo Rosselli.[9] Then for a time it was anonymous. It belongs to the group called now Botticini. As it is more likely to be by Botticini than No. 1126 below, a distinction in the form of attribution is made, but see the biography above for the dubious œuvre of this painter. As has been indicated already, the picture is unlikely to be earlier than 1460.

DRAWING: A drawing said to be for the S. Jerome is at Budapest.[10]

PROVENANCE: As explained above, from the Hieronymite church of S. Gerolamo, Fiesole. The Order was suppressed in 1668, and the church and the surrounding property passed to the Bardi di Vernio family, apparently partly secularized and partly as an abbacy in commendam.[11] The picture is twice recorded at the end of the eighteenth century, hanging at the first altar on the left in the church;[12] these are the first known records of the picture's existence, but there is no reason to suppose that it had ever been moved since it was first set up. The last representative of the Bardi family was Conte Piero de' Bardi, and in 1798 the property was acquired by Cav. Priore dell'Ordine di Santo Stefano Pietro Leopoldo Ricasoli.[13] He died in 1850, and the property passed to a grandson, Cav. Ugo de' Ricasoli (b. 1837).[14] The picture was after 1852 removed by the Ricasoli family to Florence; purchased from the guardian of Count Ricasoli, a minor, in 1855.[15]

REPRODUCTIONS: *Illustrations, Italian Schools*, 1937, p. 66 (main panel). *Plates, Earlier Italian Schools*, 1953, Vol. I, pp. 83, 84 (including predella). Specimens of the device on the frame, one with two feathers, one with three feathers, in a ring have been photographed. The designs at the ends of the predella at the sides have not been photographed.

REFERENCES: (1) 1497 appears to be correct for Gerolamo's death, and 1436 is given for his birth; he was twice married, but children are not recorded. See Luigi Passerini, *Genealogia e Storia della Famiglia Rucellai*, 1861, Tavola XIII and p. 95. The stone marking his tomb is still on the pavement of the church, near where No. 227 hung; it is inscribed DI.GIROLAMO.DI.PIERO.DI. CHARDINALE.RVCIELAI.MCCCCLXXVIIII., is illustrated by Dionisio Brunori, *L'Eremo di S. Girolamo di Fiesole*, 1920, p. 32, and recorded by Domenico Moreni, *Notizie Istoriche dei Contorni di Firenze*, III, 1792, p. 153. Gerolamo may have acquired the tomb for his family before dying himself. (2) The 'Medicean' device is the subject of comment in the entry for Filippo Lippi, Nos. 666/7. If it is true that the use of this device by the Rucellai is due to the marriage of Bernardo Rucellai with a sister of Lorenzo the Magnificent, then it would be unlikely that Gerolamo could be the right Rucellai here; for Bernardo and Gerolamo were only fourth cousins. The evidence in favour of Gerolamo is, however, very fair; and it seems probable that the Rucellai used this device, not because of a marriage with a Medici, but for some other reason. (3) See Hélyot, *Histoire des Ordres Monastiques*, etc., IV, 1715, pp. 18 ff., and the Bollandists, 7 September, p. 3 (*Praetermissi*); cf. also Moreni, *op. cit.*, III, 1792, pp. 146 ff., Giuseppe Maria Brocchi, *Vite de' Santi e Beati Fiorentini*, Vol. II, Part II, 1761, pp. 195 ff., Litta, *Famiglie Celebri d'Italia*, Guidi di Romagna, Tav. XIII, and Brunori, *op. cit.*, pp. 5, 10, 13. (4) The story occurs in the Golden Legend. A convenient summary of it is given by Louise Pillion in the *Gazette des Beaux-Arts*, 1908, i, pp. 307/8. The picture she there describes and reproduces, a predella panel from an altarpiece No. 1320 in the Louvre (now on deposit at Chartres), comes from the same church as No. 227. The two scenes are so closely connected that it is probable that the treatment of one is derived from the other; the picture belonging to the Louvre is apparently rather earlier than No. 227, but see further in note 8. Another, differing treatment of the same story is illustrated, together with the predella in the Louvre, in *Dedalo*, July, 1932, pp. 520/1. (5) Pillion, *loc. cit.*, p. 310; this is undoubtedly the scene in the predella of the already mentioned picture belonging to the Louvre (see Pillion's reproduction). (6) Pillion, *loc. cit.*, p. 311; or better, J. P. Richter, *The Mond Collection*, II, 1910, pp. 503 ff., referring to Signorelli, No. 3946 of the National Gallery, where the subject is represented fairly accurately. See also the more elaborate comments by Helen I. Roberts in *The Art Bulletin*, 1959, pp. 283 ff. (7) Hélyot, *op. cit.*, p. 22. (8) Hélyot, *op. cit.*, pp. 23/4. In the already mentioned picture belonging to the Louvre (reproduced by Pillion, *loc. cit.*, p. 305), the belt is clear on S. Jerome. One may therefore say that that picture, although in the style of Fra Angelico, is not earlier than 1460; unless indeed the belt is an alteration, concealing an original Franciscan cord. It may be mentioned that the church from which that picture and No. 227 come was under construction apparently in 1450, 1451 and 1462; see Brunori, *op. cit.*, p. 17, quoting Moreni, *op, cit.*, p. 150, and Gaye, *Carteggio*, I, 1839, pp. 559 and 565. (9) N.G. Report, 1856. (10) Degenhart in *Old Master Drawings*, V, 1930/1, pp. 49 ff. and Fig. 31; Berenson, *Drawings of the Florentine Painters*, 1938, II, No. 587A. (11) See Brocchi, as in note 3, pp. 211/2, and Giunio Carbone, *L'Eremo di San Girolamo ora Villa Ricasoli sulla Collina di Fiesole*, (1852), p. 5. Brunori, *op. cit.*, pp. 38/9, remains doubtful about what happened after the suppression of the Hieronymite Order in 1668. It can, nevertheless, not be doubted that some part at least of the property was occupied as a villa by the Bardi di Vernio. Bardi ownership is recorded in the *Ristretto delle Cose più notabili della Città di Firenze*, 2nd edition, 1698, p. 159 and in (an addition to ?) Baldinucci, *Notizie de' Professori del Disegno, Opere*, V, 1811, p. 171 or I, 1845, p. 423. In MS. 226 of the Moreniana

Library (attached to the Riccardiana) at Florence, Vol. III, p. 236, the place is referred to as 'Villa de' Conti Bardi di Vernio.' The manuscript is entitled *Compendio di Notizie Istoriche delle chiese di Firenze e di alcune suburbane divise nei suoi quartieri*. See also Moreni, *op. cit.*, III, p. 157; A. M. Bandini, *Lettere XII...della Città di Fiesole*, 1800, p. 133. (12) A. M. Bandini, *Lettere XII...della Città di Fiesole*, 1776, Col. 88 (edition of 1800, pp. 139/40); Moreni, *loc. cit.* in note 1. (13) Bandini, *op. cit.*, edition of 1800, p. 133; Carbone, *loc. cit.*; Luigi Passerini, *Genealogia e Storia della Famiglia Ricasoli*, 1861, Tav. VIII; cf. also Guido Carocci, *I Dintorni di Firenze*, 1907, I, p. 120. (14) Carbone, *loc. cit.* (15) N.G. Report, 1856; cf. Carbone, *loc. cit.*

Ascribed to FRANCESCO BOTTICINI

1126 ALTARPIECE: THE ASSUMPTION OF THE VIRGIN

The heavens are opened to show the nine Orders of Angels, and the Virgin kneeling before Christ, who holds a book inscribed $A\Omega$. All the angelic hierarchies except the 7th and 9th contain saints as well. In the 8th are four figures, SS. Peter and John the Baptist, an Evangelist (?; S. Matthew ?) and S. Mary Magdalene. In the other rows, identifications are in many cases doubtful or impossible; some are Abraham, SS. Andrew, Augustine, Bartholomew and Catherine of Alexandria, David, SS. Dominic, James the Greater, Jerome and Lawrence, Moses, SS. Paul and Stephen. S. Benedict is also doubtless present. Below, the twelve Apostles, with S. Peter prominent, stand on either side of the Virgin's tomb, which is filled with lilies. On the left kneels the donor, Matteo Palmieri, before a view of Florence, the Mugnone river, the Badia di Fiesole, etc. (described more fully below). On the right, the donatrix is presumably his wife.

Wood, $90 \times 148\frac{1}{2}$ ($2 \cdot 285 \times 3 \cdot 77$).[1]

Cleaned in 1959. The picture has been somewhat overcleaned in the past, especially in the lower part (main figures and landscape).[2] The faces of the donors have been scratched; the commentary below suggests that this may have been deliberate.

The picture was the altarpiece in a chapel in S. Pier Maggiore, a church belonging to Benedictine nuns, at Florence. The donor is Matteo Palmieri, b. 1406, d. 1475, a Florentine of rather humble origin, who occupied a number of Government posts, and was also fairly well known in his time as a writer. He married in 1433 Niccolosa, daughter of Niccolò Serragli, who was still alive in 1458 and probably survived her husband.[3]

The view behind Matteo Palmieri was identified by Margaret Stokes, who published a drawing taken in 1889 from nearly the same spot.[4] The walled city in the distance is Florence, with the Cathedral and Palazzo Vecchio identifiable; possibly S. Pier Maggiore just in front of Palmieri's face. The stream in the middleground is the Mugnone; the bridge is at the spot occupied by the Ponte alla Badia, but is shown with three arches, whereas the Ponte alla Badia has only one, apparently the original arrangement.[5] The group of buildings above, at the left of the picture, is the Badia di Fiesole; they are roughly indicated, but the Chapel of S. Romolo (now destroyed) is shown attached to the side of the church.[6] The house on the skyline higher up is presumably the Villa Luna.[7] The two buildings further to the right and lower down on the same hill are those of a farm (Schifanoia) owned by Matteo Palmieri.[8]

The view on the other side of the picture has not been identified. The possibility that the town there shown is meant to be Prato was noted in the first edition of this catalogue, because the Virgin's girdle which she left with S. Thomas at her Assumption is preserved at Prato; but the town is so slightly shown that it seems more likely to be fanciful.

The date of No. 1126 is relevant to its attribution; it has not been established with certainty, but probabilities can be recorded.

Vasari[9] says that Matteo Palmieri's wife is shown on the picture, and that Matteo himself dictated the design; there is reason to believe that both these statements are true. First, for the identity of the donatrix, Matteo's wife is the obvious person, and it is possible that her name was once inscribed on the picture or its frame.[10] Although in the published records she does not appear to be mentioned after 1458, it is probable that she survived her husband.[11] The chief difficulty is that she appears to be dressed, not as the wife of a Florentine citizen, but as a widow or a nun;[12] possibly the picture, ordered by Matteo towards the end of his life, was not finished until after his death in 1475. A possible date, therefore, would be *ca.* 1474/6.

The buildings shown in the picture seem not to be of great help for the dating. It was recorded in the first edition of this catalogue that the dome of the Cathedral of Florence was shown apparently with the ball above the lantern; but what was thought to be the ball was a touch of repaint now removed, and it is impossible to say if the ball was there originally.[13] The Badia at Fiesole, shown in the picture, was not finished until 1466 or 1467,[14] but this should not be claimed as proof that the picture is later.

Vasari's second point is that Matteo planned the scheme of the picture; there is internal evidence on the picture that this is true.

Palmieri wrote a poem entitled *Città di Vita*,[15] in imitation of the *Divina Commedia*. It owes its origin to two appearances to the author of his dead friend, Cipriano Rucellai, in 1451 and 1455;[16] it was on the first occasion that an essential –and heretical—tenet of the poem was revealed, that human souls are the angels who remained neutral when Lucifer fell.[17] It should not be doubted that this point is illustrated in the picture, where various saints are shown in the hierarchy of angels; these saints are clearly some of the neutral angels, who have passed through their period of life upon earth, and having merited salvation take up again their original angelic positions.[18]

This confirms Vasari's statement that Palmieri himself planned the picture.[19] Clearly the design would have been made before Palmieri's death in 1475; but there is no proof that the picture was actually completed by then.[20] On the other hand, the execution can hardly have been much delayed; the picture so clearly illustrates the poem, that it could hardly have been set up in Palmieri's chapel after the poem itself had become suspect of heresy. Palmieri kept his poem very secret during his life;[21] but as soon as he was dead it was read and suspicion gathered round it.[22] It is doubtful if it was ever formally condemned;[23] but one may suppose that it would have been if it had been published. There is even some evidence that the author's bones were dug up and reburied in unconsecrated ground.[24] It is therefore unlikely that the picture could have been set up in its place much after 1475; it was most probably already there when Palmieri and his works became suspect, and although it was not actually removed as being unsuitable, it was then or later covered with a veil.[25]

The picture, therefore, is very unlikely to date from long after 1475, and there is some reason for accepting *ca.* 1474/6 as a probable date.

The picture is ascribed by Vasari to Botticelli,[26] and this view has had defenders.[27] Botticelli's style in 1470 is known.[28] Even if an attribution to Botticelli a few years before 1470 might be defended on stylistic grounds, No. 1126 is, in quality, unworthy of Botticelli. It is even unnecessary to believe that the design may be his, since it is probably due to Palmieri himself. Botticelli's name is therefore best excluded.

The style has some affinity with the works now classed as Botticini's;[29] although the picture is not in every respect characteristic of Botticini, it seems possible that it is his. It is, however, a difficulty that, dated 1471 and 1475, in the Musée André at Paris and at Berlin, there exist pictures more reasonably attributable to Botticini than No. 1126 is.

DRAWINGS: Two related drawings are at Stockholm.[30] A connected drawing is in the Janos Scholz Collection.[31] A drawing at Christ Church, Oxford, is said by Degenhart to be connected.[32]

PROVENANCE: First recorded in 1550 in Matteo Palmieri's chapel in S. Pier Maggiore, Florence.[33] Suspected of heresy, the picture was at one time or another covered with a veil;[34] but it does not appear to have been moved from its place until the church was destroyed following an accident in 1783.[35] It remained in the possession of the Palmieri family,[36] and is stated to have been stored for a long time at the Uffizi or the Accademia there; eventually it was sold by the last of the Palmieri descendants, a lady apparently, possibly with surname Brocchi, to Luigi Riccieri. It passed through various hands, being with Metzger in Florence in 1828; it was sold, in Paris apparently, to Woodburn, who brought it to England in 1846 and sold it to the Duke of Hamilton.[37] Seen at Hamilton Palace by Waagen.[38] Exhibited at the R.A., 1873 (No. 191). Purchased at the Hamilton Sale, 24 June, 1882 (lot 417).[39]

REPRODUCTION: *Illustrations, Italian Schools*, 1937, p. 66. *Plates, Earlier Italian Schools*, 1953, Vol. I, pp. 85/6.

REFERENCES: (1) Measurements by P. Pouncey. (2) Baldinucci, *Notizie dei Professori del Disegno*, I, 1845, p. 568, says that it was badly overcleaned some years before he wrote; Baldinucci died in 1696, this part of his book not being published till some time after his death. (3) To be strictly accurate, the identity of the donor does not depend upon contemporary evidence, and is first recorded by Vasari in 1550; but it does not seem worth while labouring the point that the identification is correct. For Matteo Palmieri's life, see Antonio Messeri's article in the *Archivio Storico Italiano*, 1894, i, pp. 257 ff. There is a considerable literature about him, some of which is not very accurate. Two other portraits of Palmieri exist; a bust of 1468 by Antonio Rossellino (Venturi, *Storia dell'Arte*

Italiana, Vol. VI, Fig. 409), and a miniature of *ca.* 1473 (reproduced by Margaret Rooke, Smith College Studies in Modern Languages, Vol. VIII, 1926/7, p. 167; ascribed by Berenson to Botticini in his *Florentine Drawings*, 1938, Vol. II, No. 588). (4) Margaret Stokes, *Six Months in the Apennines*, 1892, Fig. 88 (p. 263). The compiler found what appeared to be more exactly the spot, not very far away. (5) Guido Carocci, *I Dintorni di Firenze*, 1907, I, p. 171. In G. Lami, *Lezioni di Antichità Toscane*, 1766, Vol. I, pp. xxvii ff., followed by A. M. Bandini, *Lettere XII...della Città di Fiesole*, 1776, Col. 58 or 1800, pp. 80/1, there are comments upon this point, and the suggestion as a possible alternative that the bridge is one higher up the Mugnone; but this would not, it seems, suit the view-point. (6) Carocci, *op. cit.*, I, pp. 102 ff. Margaret Stokes, *loc. cit.* in note 4, says the tower really belongs to San Domenico di Fiesole, which is situated some way behind; but this does not seem possible. For what is doubtless a more accurate view of this region, see the woodcut view of Florence (with a chain) and the connected engraving; reproduced in the Prussian *Jahrbuch*, 1914, pp. 93 and 95, and by A. M. Hind, *Early Italian Engraving*, Vol. I, 1938, B III 18 and Vol. III, 1938, Plate 215. (7) Carocci, *op. cit.*, I, p. 93. (8) The Villa Palmieri now occupies this site. It may be that it was not Matteo Palmieri himself but one of his successors who built the villa, since Matteo in his cadastral declarations speaks only of a farm; see Messeri, *op. cit.* in note 3, pp. 322 and 324. (9) Vasari, ed. Milanesi, III, pp. 314/5; 1550 edition, pp. 492/3. (10) Richa, *Notizie Istoriche delle Chiese Fiorentine*, I, 1754, p. 158, seems to say this; he does indeed make a minor error in her name, so the point cannot be pressed. (11) This is an *argumentum ex silentio* from Messeri's article, which is so detailed for the whole of Matteo Palmieri's life that his not recording her death affords a presumption that she died later. It should nevertheless be added that the Catasto of 1480 (Quartiere S. Giovanni, Gonfalone Chiavi) seems not to mention her. (12) Among possible alternatives to Niccolosa Palmieri, Matteo's sister Maddelena married in 1435, after which no records of her appear to be published; she seems so unlikely that she may be left out of account (though it may be recalled that the Magdalen has a very high position in the picture). His mother Tommasa might appear more suitable, since she was widowed in 1428. She did not die until 1462; but a date before 1462 is on various grounds unlikely for the picture. Some nun in S. Pier Maggiore would presumably be possible. (13) The ball was placed in position in 1471; see C. von Fabriczy, *Filippo Brunelleschi*, 1892, p.554. Cf. also Busse in the Prussian *Jahrbuch*, 1930, p. 118. (14) Fabriczy, *op. cit.*, p. 608. (15) Published by Margaret Rooke in Smith College Studies in Modern Languages, 1926/7 and 1927/8. (16) This is the evidence in the commentary on the poem by Palmieri's friend, Leonardo Dati; the relevant text is printed in A. M. Bandini, *Catalogus Codicum MSS. Bibliothecæ Mediceæ-Laurentianæ*, V. 1778, Col. 81 sqq., and summaries of it are given by J. A. Symonds, *Renaissance in Italy*, V, 1898, pp. 480 ff., and by Diego Angeli in *L'Arte*, 1896, pp. 63 f. (17) Palmieri in his poem (Cantica I, Capitolo X, tercets 18 sqq.) even offers a proof of this tenet. In Revelation, xii, 4, it is indicated that a third part of heaven rebelled. S. Augustine says that the angels that fell are equal in number to the souls that will be saved; in what Palmieri calls the *sacre carte* (the Bible, presumably), it is stated that the souls saved will be equal in number to the angels who remained loyal to God. Therefore the loyal angels formed one third of heaven; since another third fell, the remaining third must have been the neutral angels, who are thus equal in number to the souls saved. Further, these neutral angels must be somewhere; and it would be hard if they faced the Last Judgment without having had some further opportunity of expressing their character in a positive way. It seemed for these reasons obvious to Palmieri that the neutral angels and human souls are identical. The difficulty that at the Last Day heaven will be only two-thirds full is perhaps not peculiar to Palmieri's theory. The further difficulty that all men will have to be saved in order to make up the right number in heaven did strike the author. Since part of his poem deals with the torments of the damned, it could hardly fail to; his answer that the ways of God are inscrutable satisfied him. For the connection between this tenet and a revival of interest in Origen in the XV Century in Italy, see the essay by E. Wind in *Studies in Art and Literature for Belle da Costa Greene*, 1954, pp. 412 ff. **(18)** According to the best authorities, some angels from all the nine Orders fell with Lucifer; see A. Vacant and E. Mangenot, *Dictionnaire de Théologie Catholique*, IV, s.v. *Démon*, esp. Col. 401. By analogy, it would appear likely that some angels from all the nine Orders remained neutral; yet in the picture no saints are shown in the 7th and 9th circles. Possibly this is due to pictorial convenience rather than to some esoteric dogma. **(19)** In the last cantos of his poem, Palmieri mentions a number of Saints and Old Testament worthies. There is some correspondence with what is seen in No. 1126; some further identifications might be proposed therefrom for figures in the picture, but it is doubtful if the two match exactly. This may be thought a point against the view that Palmieri planned the picture himself; but it is not very strong, if only because the subject of the picture is distinct from what is described in the poem. **(20)** In the funeral oration for Palmieri, his pious donations are briefly referred to; and the phrase 'rerum immortalis Dei cultui dicatarum amplitudo' might, it is true, be stretched to imply that this immense picture already existed. The text of the oration is printed by F. Fossi, *Monumenta ad Alamanni Rinuccini vitam contexendam*, 1791, pp. 122 ff. **(21)** The church authorities would not have permitted a public funeral, with a copy of the wicked poem on the coffin, if they had known about it: unless indeed they had found nothing objectionable (but cf. the comments by Vespasiano di Bisticci, *Vite di Uomini Illustri*, ed. A. Bartoli, 1859, p. 501, or ed. L. Frati, II, 1893, p. 219, partly quoted in the next note). Palmieri indeed showed his poem to Leonardo Dati for advice. He may have shown it to others too, e.g. to Marsilio Ficino; in correction of the compiler's doubt previously expressed, Ficino did refer to Palmieri as *poeta theologicus* (information kindly sent by E. Wind). Symonds, *loc. cit.* in note 16, says that Palmieri himself claims to have published the poem; but in the text in question (printed by M. Rooke, *op. cit.*, 1st Vol., p. xxii) the word used, *edidi*, seems to mean 'begot', i.e. wrote, rather than 'published'. **(22)** See Bisticci, as in the previous note; *morto che fu, subito apersono questo libro, e lo mostrorono a più uomini dotti in teologia, a fine che se vi fussino cose contro alla fede, il libro non si pubblicasse.* There is confirmatory evidence from other sources, e.g. the reference to Palmieri by Luigi Pulci in his *Morgante Maggiore*, quoted by D. Angeli in *L'Arte*, 1896, p. 68, and by M. Rooke, *op. cit.*, 1st Vol., p. ix. **(23)** The tone of some references to the poem would presumably have been different, if it had been condemned; e.g. the following by Cristoforo l'Altissimo, published in 1533, and quoted by Messeri, *op. cit.* in note 3, p. 265, *compose poemi alti et pregiati / che ingiustamente d'alcuni son dannati.* Further, Albertini in his *De Mirabilibus Novae et Veteris Romae*, Bâle edition, 1519, f. 95r, mentions Palmieri with approval; the book is dedicated to the Pope. **(24)** G. B. Gelli, *I Capricci del Bottaio*, 5th edition, 1551, pp. 118/9 says so. **(25)** See Richa, *op. cit.*, I, 1754, pp. 160 f. The period of the veiling is somewhat doubtful; it seems, for instance, certain that Vasari actually saw the picture. Presumably it was veiled later, when Palmieri had usurped a reputation as a heretic. It was uncovered not long before 1657, according to Rosselli's *Sepoltuario*, I, p. 504 (as quoted by Margaret Rooke in the second volume of her publication of the *Città di Vita*, p. 265). It was visible in 1732 (Bottari and Ticozzi, *Raccolta di Lettere*, II, 182, p. 336). **(26)** Vasari, ed Milanesi, III, pp. 314/5. **(27)** E.g. Anna Maria Brizio in *L'Arte*, 1933, pp. 108 ff. **(28)** The *Fortezza* in the Uffizi; reproduced by Van Marle, *Development of the Italian Schools of Painting*, XII, Fig. 5. **(29)** See E. Kühnel, *Francesco Botticini*, 1906, p. 10, and the biography above. The picture was first grouped with Botticini by Bode (letter in the Gallery archives); the name was then not established, and Bode referred to the painter as the Master of the Rossi Altarpiece (a picture at Berlin). See Bode's publication in the Prussian *Jahrbuch*, 1886, pp. 233 f.; his argument that No. 1126 is earlier than 1468 because the donor here appears younger than in Rossellino's bust of that year is unconvincing. **(30)** Berenson, *Florentine Drawings*, 1938, Vol. II, No. 591B, Four Figures, and No. 591C, Christ Blessing. No. 591B is reproduced in Schönbrunner and

Meder's series, No. 1067. In one corner is Christ blessing the Virgin, roughly corresponding with the picture. The main part of the drawing is two angels, one of which corresponds pretty well with the one on the picture in the 6th row, on the right of the saint with a cross (S. Andrew). No. 591C is reproduced by Berenson in his book, Vol. III, Fig. 134, and in the *Gazette des Beaux-Arts*, 1932, II, p. 275; this corresponds well with the figure in the picture. (31) This shows on the left the three Apostles on the right in the picture, and on the right the three on the left. W. Suida, *Bramante Pittore e il Bramantino*, 1953, Fig. 102, as Bramantino: Exhibition of *Drawings from Tuscany and Umbria* (Janos Scholz Collection) at Oakland and Berkeley, 1961, No. 42 (reproduced) as circle of Domenico Ghirlandaio. (32) Christ Church drawings catalogue, by C. F. Bell, 1914, p. 40, No. B 8, as by Lorenzo di Credi; Degenhart in *Old Master Drawings*, V, 1930, p. 51; Berenson, *Florentine Drawings*, 1938, II, No. 706; reproduced in the *Rivista d'Arte*, 1932, p. 297, photograph in the Gallery archives. The drawing is a drapery study, apparently not closely connected either in detail or in style with the figures on the picture. (33) Vasari, 1550 edition, pp. 492/3. (34) See note 25. (35) See the account of the destruction of S. Pier Maggiore given by D. Angeli in *L'Arte*, 1896, p. 70 (with date 1785); or better (Follini and Rastrelli), *Firenze Antica e Moderna*, III, 1791, p. 375, and VIII, 1802, p. 335. The authors describe the picture in their Vol. V, 1794, pp. 87/90. (36) A. M. Bandini, *Lettere XII . . . della Città di Fiesole*, 1800, p. 80, says that, after the destruction of the church, the picture was transferred to Casa Palmieri. (37) For Metzger, see the Prussian *Jahrbuch*, 1914, Beiheft, pp. 63 and 65, and 1925, Beiheft, pp. 4, 5, 9. For Woodburn, the date at which he imported the picture and its storage at the Accademia, Florence, see J. Dennistoun, *Memoirs of the Dukes of Urbino*, 1851, Vol. II, p. 150. For Woodburn, see also *The Times*, 26 June, 1882 (quoted in Redford's *Art Sales*, I, p. 330). Most of the rest of the statement is from Kirkup, who saw the picture in Riccieri's hands, and told the story to Browning, who told it to the Director of the National Gallery in 1884; document in the Gallery archives. See also Milanesi's Vasari, III, p. 315. The editor of Baldinucci, I, 1845, p. 568, says that it was sold by the Brocchi family to the Florentine Accademia; this appears to be a confused record. (38) Waagen, *Treasures*, 1854, III, p. 296. (39) As by Botticelli.

BRAMANTINO
living 1490, died 1530

Bartolomeo Suardi, called *Bramantino*. There is some reason to believe that he was born not later than 1465. He lived at Milan, but visited Rome, where he is recorded in 1508. In 1525 he was appointed painter and architect to Francesco Sforza II. He was dead in 1530, and it seems clear that it was in that year that he died.

It is somewhat difficult to attach paintings to the historical Bramantino. Vasari and the Milanese sources tend to confuse him with Bramante, and several rather famous pictures, from early times ascribed to one or the other, are recognizably by Foppa, etc.; the value of any tradition respecting Bramantino is, therefore, a point to be considered. In spite of these difficulties, the core of the group called Bramantino by modern scholars is not only coherent, but is likely to be rightly named.

The point of departure for ascription is, it seems, a fragmentary ruined fresco, a *Pietà* in the Ambrosiana (from Santo Sepolcro), Milan; a triptych in the Ambrosiana (formerly Melzi) and (it seems) a *Virgin and Child* in the Brera, No. 279, have less good, but respectable, traditions attached to them. A *Flight into Egypt* at Locarno carries a signature suspected by Crowe and Cavalcaselle, and in the catalogue of the Luini Exhibition, 1953, pp. 24/5; there is some reason for supposing that it was painted *ca.* 1522.

The dating of Bramantino's pictures depends almost entirely on internal evidence, and is very uncertain. It is probable that he was influenced by the old Lombard tradition of Butinone and Foppa. His nickname implies that he was a close imitator of Bramante, but whether as painter or architect is uncertain. It is, however, fairly clear that he exercised a powerful influence on younger painters, in particular Luini and Gaudenzio Ferrari.

3073   THE ADORATION OF THE KINGS

The Virgin and Child in the centre, S. Joseph (?) and the Moorish King on either side; the other two Kings with gifts are in the foreground, right and left. The Virgin's footstool has pseudo-Eastern lettering.

Poplar,[1] painted surface, $22\frac{3}{8} \times 21\frac{5}{8}$ (0.57×0.55).

Much damaged and restored. None of the heads are in good condition, though one or two can pass as fair; the legs and feet to the right are well preserved. The green drapery of the young King to the right is also in good condition. *Pentimenti* in some of the feet, etc. X-Rays reveal alterations in the landscape to the right. The rocks had two oblique lines of division instead of one, and seem to have been crowned with an enormous castle, the towers of which have been extended to make the present peaks. Behind the foreground figures on the right were some further fragments of the present ruined building.[2]

The name of Bramantino for No. 3073 was first suggested by Mündler;[3] it has remained as clearly correct, according to the definition of Bramantino given in the biography above. The picture is likely to be an early work; Suida[4] dates it apparently at the end of the 1490's.

PROVENANCE: In the Manfrin Collection, Venice;[5] bought therefrom by Sir A. H. Layard, *ca.* 1863.[6] Exhibited at South Kensington, 1869 (No. 37), and at the R.A., 1870 (No. 54). Layard Bequest, 1916.[7]

REPRODUCTION: *Illustrations, Italian Schools*, 1937, p. 67. *Plates, Earlier Italian Schools*, 1953, Vol. I, p. 87.

REFERENCES: (1) Letter from B. J. Rendle, of the Forest Products Research Laboratory, in the Gallery archives. (2) Reproduced by W. Suida, *Bramante Pittore e il Bramantino*, 1953, Plate LXVIII. (3) Letter from Eastlake to Wornum, 8 October, 1863. The altarpiece by Foppa, No. 729 of this Gallery, had just been purchased as by Bramantino; Eastlake (summer, 1863) compared it to his own satisfaction with the Santo Sepolcro *Pietà* and the Ambrosiana (Melzi) Triptych. It is therefore possible that Mündler's attribution for No. 3073 did not mean exactly what one would nowadays assume. (4) Suida, *op. cit.*, pp. 67 ff. He says that the two standing figures on each side of the Virgin and Child are prophets, probably Isaiah and Daniel; the compiler does not accept this. (5) Presumably Manfrin MS. Catalogue, 1851, Stanza H., No. 7, as Mantegna; *Catalogo dei quadri esistenti nella Galleria Manfrin in Venezia*, 1856 (No. 341), *Adorazione de' Magi*, Andrea Mantegna, Tavola, 0.61×0.59. The Manfrin Collection was formed, at least in part, by Conte Girolamo Manfrin, who died in 1801 according to *Il Forestiere Istruito . . . della Città di Venezia*, 1822, p. 295. According to the catalogue of the A. M. Plattis Sale, Paris, 13/4 May, 1870, the collection was formed *ca.* 1748 (perhaps meaning from that date onwards), and in 1848 was divided between the Marquise Bortolina Plattis veuve du Baron Sardagna and the Marquis Antonio Maria Plattis. According to the Manfrin sale catalogue of 1897, the collection was divided in 1849 between the Marchese Antonio Plattis and the Marchesa Bortolina Plattis nei Sardagna; her part or some of it remained in the Palazzo Manfrin until 1897. (6) Cf. the letter referred to in note 3. (7) For the history of the Layard Collection, see Appendix IV.

Giovanni BUONCONSIGLIO
active 1495, died 1535/7

Called *Il Marescalco*. School of Vicenza; from 1495 he seems to have lived fairly continuously at Venice, but he kept up an association with Vicenza. He was influenced by Montagna and Bellini, and there are dated works from 1497.

3076   S. JOHN THE BAPTIST

On the scroll, ECCE.AGNS / DEI.

Wood, painted surface, $18\frac{3}{4} \times 16\frac{1}{2}$ (0·475 × 0·42); painted up to the edges all round.

Good condition, except that there is some overcleaning, and the panel is cracked.

Formerly ascribed to Montagna,[1] it was recognized by Morelli as a Buonconsiglio;[2] Borenius[3] considers it a rather late work.

PROVENANCE: Bought from Conte di Thiene, Vicenza, by Sir A. H. Layard;[4] exhibited at South Kensington, 1869 (No. 21); Layard Bequest, 1916.[5]

REPRODUCTION: *Illustrations, Italian Schools*, 1937, p. 70. *Plates, Earlier Italian Schools*, 1953, Vol. I, p. 88.

REFERENCES: (1) Still as such in Crowe and Cavalcaselle, *Painting in North Italy*, I, 1871, p. 433; Borenius' edition, 1912, II. p. 134. (2) Layard MSS. in the National Gallery; cf. also Morelli, *Della Pittura Italiana* (Borghese and Doria), 1897, p. 276. (3) Borenius, *The Painters of Vicenza*, 1909, p. 189. (4) Layard MSS. in the National Gallery (as from Count Tieni). It seems to have been bought at the same time as Gerard David, No. 3067, which was lent by Layard to the British Institution in 1862, and may have been bought by him in 1860 (*Sir A. Henry Layard, Autobiography and Letters*, ed. W. N. Bruce, 1903, II, p. 228). (5) For the history of the Layard Collection, see Appendix IV.

Andrea BUSATI
active 1503–1528

Active at Venice. He seems to have been born not earlier than *ca.* 1470, and is first mentioned in 1503. He made his will in 1528.

A signed picture at Venice is sometimes held to be later than 1529, but the date does not appear to have been satisfactorily established (cf.

the catalogue of the Accademia at Venice, 1955, No. 93). Another signed picture is at Vicenza; both are reproduced by Van Marle, *Development of the Italian Schools of Painting*, Vol. XVII, Figs. 282/3. The picture at Venice is compositionally connected with one of 1516 (?), ascribed to Cima, once in the Academy at Vienna (Van Marle, *op. cit.*, Vol. XVII, Fig. 232), and now with two other figures restored to it in the Ca d'Oro at Venice (Borenius in *The Burlington Magazine*, Vol. LXXIV (1939), p. 13).

No. 3084 below is also signed, and is derived from a Cima at Leningrad.

A fourth picture appeared at Christie's in the Marquess of Exeter Sale, 25 February, 1949 (lot 81), as Bonifazio. This damaged and altered work is stylistically unlike the other three. On a *cartellino* is the inscription M.D.XXI / ANDRE/AS.BV/SSATVS / FACIE/BAT; this is on top of another inscription (presumably a signature), in which the name BVSS*/TI is legible. (Photograph in the Gallery files.)

Two of Andrea Busati's brothers appear to have been painters, Luca Antonio, and Francesco. The former is presumably the Luca Antonio Buscatti, whose signed picture in the Ringling Museum at Sarasota is reproduced by Suida in *Art in America*, January, 1944, pp. 5 ff.

3084 THE ENTOMBMENT

The dead Christ is supported by the Virgin; on the right, the Magdalen and a Holy Woman; on the left, SS. John, Nicodemus and Joseph of Arimathea. Golgotha with the three crosses in the background. Signed on a *cartellino* (only the first two words are certain): *Andreas busatti f(   )t do | (s ?)i(p ?)ulus Joanne(s ?) belinu(s ?)*.

Poplar,[1] painted surface, $43\frac{3}{4} \times 36$ ($1 \cdot 115 \times 0 \cdot 915$); painted up to the edges all round.

A good deal damaged and restored. According to the Layard MSS. in the National Gallery, two *putti* were once seated on the parapet, but were additions that could be removed.

The signature has suffered a great deal, and has been irresponsibly repaired. The first upright of the *u* of *busatti* has had an extra stroke added newly to it. The name seems clearly to end in *tti*, rather than *ti*; in either case, the signature may be accepted as certainly that of Andrea Busati. The rest of the inscription, especially the second line, is suspect, and it is by no means certain that Busati meant to call himself a disciple of Giovanni Bellini.

Morelli[2] claims to have been the first to read the signature, in Molteni's studio in 1858 (?); his version is, *Ops B..t.ani Lu.iani disc.pulus Ioannis Bellinus*, but it is not credible that this was ever so. The new addition of a stroke to the *u* of the surname made it possible on careless examination to read *luciani*, and Morelli rashly accepted the picture as Sebastiano del Piombo's. Crowe and Cavalcaselle[3] very properly raised doubts, but the picture had a great success as Sebastiano's earliest work. The first to read the signature at all correctly was Georg Gronau.[4]

The group of figures in No. 3084 is derived fairly exactly from a Cima in the Stroganoff Bequest to the Hermitage, Leningrad, and now at Moscow,[5] which Burckhardt[6] dates *ca.* 1510. The bridge and buildings in the landscape, however, seem taken from a *Resurrection* at Berlin ascribed to Giovanni Bellini;[7] this motive was popular, occurring also in pictures by Bartolomeo Veneto,[8] in No. 3086 of this Gallery,[9] and in a Cimesque *Pietà* stated to be signed *Antonellus R(oartis?)* in the church of S. Pietro at San Giovanni Bianco (Frazione di San Pietro d'Orzio) near Bergamo.[10] There is a variant of it in the Busati at Venice, which does not occur in the Cimesque version of that picture in the Ca d'Oro (formerly the Academy at Vienna).[11]

The style of the Busati at Venice corresponds quite well with that of No. 3084. The date of No. 3084 is on stylistic grounds after 1500, perhaps *ca.* 1510.

PROVENANCE: From the Manfrin Collection, Venice;[12] bought by Sir A. H. Layard, 1862(?)[13]. Exhibited at South Kensington, 1869 (No. 1). Layard Bequest, 1916.[14]

REPRODUCTION: *Illustrations, Italian Schools*, 1937, p. 373. *Plates, Earlier Italian Schools*, 1953, Vol. I, p. 89.

REFERENCES: (1) Letter from B. J. Rendle, of the Forest Products Research Laboratory, in the Gallery archives. (2) Cf. J. P. R(ichter)'s publication of Lermolieff (Morelli's) views in the *Zeitschrift für bildende Kunst, Beiblatt (Kunst-Chronik)*, 1878, Cols. 554/5. (3) Crowe and Cavalcaselle, *Painting in North Italy*, 1871, p. 311, or ed. Borenius, 1912, Vol. III, p. 204. The attribution to Sebastiano del Piombo was also rejected (among others) by Ludwig and Bode in the Prussian *Jahrbuch*, 1903, p. 140, and by Berenson, *Venetian Painting in America*, 1916, p. 209. R. Pallucchini, *Sebastian Viniziano*, 1944, pp. 22/3, gives a substantial account of the attributions for No. 3084. (4) Gronau; a proof of an (unpublished?) article on the subject for *The Burlington Magazine* exists in the Gallery archives. (5) Reproduced in *Arte Veneta*, 1957, p. 49, and L. Coletti, *Cima da Conegliano*, 1959, Plate 27, Cf. Botteon-Aliprandi, *Ricerche*, 1893, pp. 167/8. There is also a picture at Gubbio, with the composition partly similar; reproduced by E. Giovagnoli, *Gubbio nella Storia e nell'Arte*, 1932, Fig. 111. (6) Rudolf Burckhardt, *Cima da Conegliano*, 1905, p. 122. Coletti, *loc. cit.* and p. 100, puts the Moscow picture much earlier. (7) Gronau, Klassiker der Kunst *Bellini*, 1930, Plate 67. The Berlin picture is fully discussed in Ludwig and Bode's article in the Prussian *Jahrbuch*, 1903, pp. 131 ff. It is identified with a work which had been called 1475/9, but as derivations from it are all considerably later, this date seems rather unlikely. The picture is often accepted as Bellini's; but for doubts about the style, see L. Dussler, *Giovanni Bellini*, 1935, pp. 154/5. There is a drawing connected with the landscape here under discussion in the Ambrosiana at Milan; Fig. 8, p. 439, of Venturi's article on Bartolomeo Veneto in *L'Arte*, 1899; Tietze and Tietze-Conrat, *Drawings of the Venetian Painters*, 1944, No. 347 (with note). (8) E.g. the *Virgin and Child* at Bergamo, signed and dated 1505, reproduced by Venturi, *Storia*, Vol. VII, Part IV, Fig. 440. (9) *Illustrations, Italian Schools*, 1937, p. 100; in the present catalogue under Venetian School. (10) Reproduced in the *Inventario degli Oggetti d'Arte e di Antichità d'Italia, Provincia di Bergamo*, 1931, p. 393; also in Berenson's 1959 Lists, Plate 481. (11) Reproduced by Van Marle, *Development of the Italian Schools of Painting*, Vol. XVII, Figs. 282 and 232. (12) As Cima. Mentioned as Cima in the Manfrin Collection in Eastlake's note-book, 1855, with the size given, and the comment 'ruined—& not good specimen of him—old copy?' Mentioned in Eastlake's note-book of 1857, No. 368, 'Copy from large Cima at Fabris.' Manfrin Catalogue, 1856 (No. 368), as Cima. The Manfrin

Collection was formed, at least in part, by Conte Girolamo Manfrin, who died in 1801 according to *Il Forestiere Istruito . . . della Città di Venezia*, 1822, p. 295. According to the catalogue of the A. M. Plattis Sale, Paris, 13/4 May, 1870, the collection was formed *ca.* 1748 (perhaps meaning from that date onwards) and in 1848 was divided between the Marquise Bortolina Plattis veuve du Baron Sardagna and the Marquis Antonio Maria Plattis. According to the Manfrin Sale Catalogue of 1897, the collection was divided in 1849 between the Marchese Antonio Plattis and the Marchesa Bortolina Plattis nei Sardagna; her part or some of it remained in the Palazzo Manfrin until 1897. (13) Cf.*L'Arte*, 1912, p. 450. (14) For the history of the Layard Collection, see Appendix IV.

Bernardino BUTINONE
active 1484–1507

From Treviglio. The two most important works associated with him, an altarpiece at Treviglio and frescoes in S. Pietro in Gessate at Milan, were executed in conjunction with Bernardo Zenale. The frescoes (much damaged) are probably datable 1489/93; the altarpiece was commissioned in 1485, but the painters were still in dispute about it in 1507. There exist also two works signed by Butinone alone; a triptych in the Brera of 1484 (once wrongly read as 1454) and a small picture in the Borromeo Collection (wrongly doubted by Morelli).* Butinone studies owe much to Malaguzzi Valeri, and were pursued further by Salmi in *Dedalo*, November–December, 1929, pp. 336 ff. and 395 ff. According to Salmi, apart from reminiscences of Lombard Gothic tradition, the first and strongest influence on Butinone was that of Mantegna, later that of Foppa and others.

Ascribed to Bernardino BUTINONE

3336 THE ADORATION OF THE SHEPHERDS (PANEL FROM A SERIES)

Poplar,[1] painted surface, $9\frac{3}{4} \times 8\frac{1}{2}$ (0·248×0·215); painted up to the edges all round.

Good state.

The following panels in a comparable style are recorded: (1) *The Adoration of the Kings* (whereabouts unknown).[2] (2) *The Circumcision*, at Bergamo (0·25×0·20).[3] (3) *The Flight into Egypt*, at Chicago ($9\frac{7}{8} \times 8\frac{1}{4}$).[4] (4) *Christ among the Doctors*, at Edinburgh ($9\frac{7}{8} \times 8\frac{3}{8}$).[5] (5) *The Baptism*, at Keir ($10\frac{1}{4} \times 8\frac{1}{4}$).[6] (6) *The Marriage at Cana*, in the Borromeo Collection (0·26×0·21).[7] (7) *Christ in the House of Martha*, in the Suida Collection (0·25×0·20).[8] (8) *Christ before Pilate* (?), (0·235×0·205), at Burg Liechtenstein; see note 9. (9) *The Descent from the Cross*, at Chicago ($9\frac{7}{8} \times 7\frac{3}{4}$).[10] (10) *The Lamentation over the Dead Christ*, in the Crespi Morbio (now Aldo Crespi) Collection (0·25×0·22).[11] (11) *The Resurrection* in the Crespi Morbio (now Aldo Crespi) Collection (0·25×

* For a picture where the signature of Zenale (with date 1503) seems to have been wrongly doubted, see Suida in the *Rivista d'Arte*, 1957, pp. 161 f.

0·22).[12] (12) *The Incredulity of S. Thomas*, at Pavia (0·24×0·22).[13] (13) *The Last Judgment*, with Knoedler's, New York (0·235×0·24).[14]

These pictures have only slight variations of size and considerable similarities of style, and have been supposed to come from a single ensemble. Some scenes would clearly be missing. A triptych on a rather smaller scale in the Castello Sforzesco, ascribed to Butinone, may give an indication of what the original form would have been like.[15] A suggestion that the panels come from more than one series has been made.[16]

Most of the pictures listed above, including No. 3336, were published by Salmi as early works of Butinone, perhaps *ca.* 1480.[17] This seems likely enough;[18] an alternative would be to ascribe them to an imitator, and date them a little later.[19]

The cap worn by the Child in No. 3336 appears also in other pictures;[20] its use seems to be in a Paduan and Venetian tradition.

PROVENANCE: Purchased *ca.* 1905 in Paris by Roger Fry,[21] from whom purchased, Florence Fund, 1918.[22] Exhibited at Milan, *Arte Lombarda*, 1958 (No. 464).

REPRODUCTION: *Illustrations, Italian Schools*, 1937, p. 268. *Plates, Earlier Italian Schools*, 1953, Vol. I, p. 90.

REFERENCES: (1) Letter from B. J. Rendle, of the Forest Products Research Laboratory, in the Gallery archives. (2) Reproduced in *Dedalo*, November 1929, p. 344. (3) Reproduced in *Dedalo, loc. cit.*, p. 346. (4) Reproduced in *The Burlington Magazine*, Vol. LI (1927), p. 241, and in *Dedalo, loc. cit.*, p. 347. (5) Reproduced in the *Illustrations*, National Gallery of Scotland, 1937, p. 19 .(6) Reproduced in the catalogue of the Lombard Exhibition at Milan, 1958, Plate CLXXXVIII. (7) Reproduced in *Dedalo, loc. cit.*, p. 349. (8) Reproduced in *Dedalo, loc. cit.*, p. 348. (9) Reproduced by Suida in *Œsterreichische Kunstschätze*, Vol. I, 1911, Plate LX. This item should probably be omitted, since the subject is very doubtfully identified, and Salmi (*Dedalo*, December, 1929, p. 426) rejects the attribution. (10) Reproduced in *The Burlington Magazine*, Vol. LI (1927), p. 241. (11) Reproduced in *Dedalo, loc. cit.*, p. 342. (12) Reproduced in *Dedalo, loc. cit.*, p. 342. (13) Reproduced in *Dedalo, loc. cit.*, p. 350. (14) Published by Zeri in *The Burlington Magazine*, 1955, p. 77; also reproduced in the catalogue of the Lombard Exhibition at Milan, 1958, Plate CXC. (15) Reproduced in the *Rassegna d'Arte*, 1904, p. 39. Zeri in *The Burlington Magazine*, 1955, p. 77, rightly points out that too many scenes are lacking for a definite hypothesis to be advanced, and considers some further possibilities. (16) Considered probable in the catalogue of the Lombard Exhibition at Milan, 1958, p. 149. (17) Salmi in *Dedalo, loc. cit.*, p. 352. No. 3336 had already been associated with Butinone by Longhi in *L'Arte*, 1919, p. 79. (18) No. 3336 is accepted as Butinone's by Berenson, 1932 Lists. (19) In the catalogue of the Lombard Exhibition at Milan, 1958, p. 149, it is claimed that there are variations of style between the panels, in part probably attributable to execution by assistants. (20) Examples by Antonio da Negroponte and Crivelli are reproduced by Venturi, *Storia*, Vol. VII, Part III, Figs. 237 and 272. (21) N.G. Report, 1918. (22) As Bernardo da Parenzo.

VITTORE CARPACCIO
active 1490, died 1523/6

The name is correctly *Scarpazza*, latinized into *Carpathius*; many different spellings are recorded, though the one now always used does not seem to occur before the seventeenth century. He was probably from a family established in the Venetian islands, in which case he may be identical with a Vittore said to have been born not later than 1457; but Pignatti in *Venezia e l'Europa*, 1956, pp. 224 f., points out that this date for his birth does not follow from the evidence. An alternative theory, with hardly any evidence in its favour, is that he was an Istrian. An altarpiece at Zara is sometimes (on very doubtful evidence) dated 1480. Dates running from 1490 to 1495 are on pictures of his S. Ursula series at Venice; other cycles and altarpieces exist, many of them signed and dated. He may have been trained by Lazzaro Bastiani, but was obviously influenced by Gentile Bellini, and imitated also other painters (e.g. Giovanni Bellini). He is likely to have been a rapid executant; but the amount of his work surviving seems to imply a well-organized studio, in which his two painter sons may have helped. His style evolved very little.

3085 S. URSULA TAKING LEAVE OF HER FATHER (?)

The principal figures may be S. Ursula, her father King Maurus, and a few of the 11,000 Virgins. Two letters lying on the parapet in front are now illegible; it is doubtful if they ever contained words.

Spruce,[1] painted surface, $29\frac{1}{2} \times 35$ (0·75 × 0·885); painted up to the edge at the bottom.

Fair state on the whole; but parts, especially the landscape to the left in the middle and far distance, have been extensively rubbed and repaired.

The action is obscure. It was at one time called *The Landing of Caterina Cornaro at Cyprus*, or *The Meeting of S. Ursula and her Bridegroom*, which are both unsatisfactory. The identification given is, it seems, always accepted now; it is perhaps just possible, but unlikely. The crowned figure seems too young for S. Ursula's father; the iconography differs very greatly from the treatment by Carpaccio at Venice;[2] and the subject is not likely to occur at all except as part of a cycle, which would be assumed to be all destroyed except for this picture. It is doubtful if anyone would have thought of S. Ursula for No. 3085 if Carpaccio had not painted her legend at Venice. His iconography is so fanciful that a convincing identification of the subject is unlikely.

Fiocco[3] thinks that No. 3085 shows evidence of studio help; this is very possible, but it is most often accepted as by Carpaccio. There is no good evidence for attaching a date to it.

DRAWING: A drawing in the Hermitage of two figures, of which one corresponds closely with the principal standing woman, was published by M. Dobroklonsky.[4]

PROVENANCE: Bought from the Manfrin Collection, Venice, *ca.* 1862[5] by Sir A. H. Layard; exhibited at Leeds, 1868 (No. 72), and at South Kensington, 1869 (No. 14); Layard Bequest, 1916.[6]

REPRODUCTION: *Illustrations, Italian Schools*, 1937, p. 84. *Plates, Earlier Italian Schools*, 1953, Vol. I, p. 91.

REFERENCES: (1) Letter from B. J. Rendle, of the Forest Products Research Laboratory, in the Gallery archives. (2) Reproduced by Ludwig and Molmenti, *V. Carpaccio*, 1906, p. 128. (3) Giuseppe Fiocco, *Carpaccio*, 1931, p. 76. (4) *Belvedere*, 1931, I, reproduction opp. p. 202; Tietze and Tietze-Conrat, *Drawings of the Venetian Painters*, 1944, No. 610, without reproduction. (5) Cf. *L'Arte*, 1912, p. 450. It was certainly Layard's by 1864; letter from Morelli to Layard, 20 February, 1864 (British Museum, Add. MS. 38963, Layard Papers, Vol. XXXIII). It is clearly the Carpaccio in the Manfrin Collection, marked in Eastlake's note-book, 1855, as 'very poor—without inscription'; also recorded there by F. Zanotto, *Nuovissima Guida di Venezia*, 1856, p. 345; *Catalogo dei quadri esistenti nella Galleria Manfrin in Venezia*, 1856 (No. 345), *Stersola in atto di congedarsi dal padre*, Tavola, 0·76×0·91. P. Selvatico e V. Lazari, *Guida di Venezia*, 1852, p. 299. The Manfrin Collection was formed, at least in part, by Conte Girolamo Manfrin, who died in 1801 according to *Il Forestiere Istruito . . . della Città di Venezia*, 1822, p. 295. According to the catalogue of the A. M. Plattis Sale, Paris, 13/4 May, 1870, the collection was formed *ca.* 1748 (perhaps meaning from that date onwards) and in 1848 was divided between the Marquise Bortolina Plattis veuve du Baron Sardagna and the Marquis Antonio Maria Plattis. According to the Manfrin sale catalogue of 1897, the collection was divided in 1849 between the Marchese Antonio Plattis and the Marchesa Bortolina Plattis nei Sardagna; her part or some of it remained in the Palazzo Manfrin until 1897. (6) For the history of the Layard Collection, see Appendix IV.

Ascribed to VITTORE CARPACCIO

3098 THE ADORATION OF THE KINGS

Canvas, $43\frac{1}{4} \times 82\frac{1}{4}$ (1·10 × 2·09).

The picture is severely damaged, being much worn and sunk. There is also a good deal of repaint, though it would be untrue to say that the surface has been entirely gone over. The figures have no doubt lost considerably in quality, but for the most part the original style is still detectable; the head of the foremost king is one of the best preserved. The rocks are fairly free from repaint.

The figure to the left, perhaps in penitential garb, might be the donor. Fiocco claims that the landscape represents the Lake of Garda, which seems unlikely.[1]

No. 3098 was formerly catalogued as by Gentile Bellini.[2] This attribution has usually been accepted, although from time to time doubt has been expressed.[3] In the compiler's view, the doubt is justified. Several of the principal figures and the cave in No. 3098 are markedly Mantegnesque;[4] it is true that to begin with Gentile Bellini was Mantegnesque, but the authenticated works of his early time are not similar to No. 3098. Gentile's *Procession in S. Mark's Square*, an authenticated work of 1496, is not similar to No. 3098 either. Berenson[5] says that there are reasons for putting No. 3098 at about 1485.

Crowe and Cavalcaselle,[6] without disputing the attribution to Gentile for No. 3098, said that it reminded them much of Carpaccio. Gamba[7] went further, and thought that the execution may have been partly by the young Carpaccio. Nothing is known for sure of Carpaccio's works before 1490; it is perhaps rash to guess at what his earlier pictures may have been, especially for the case of No. 3098, which is much damaged.

The attribution to Carpaccio, nevertheless, receives some confirmation from the researches of Tietze and Tietze-Conrat. They pointed out that several of the figures in No. 3098 recur in a drawing of *The Adoration of the Kings* in the Uffizi, acceptable as Carpaccio's; also in pictures of varying subject by Carpaccio.[8] It is true that Tietze and Tietze-Conrat do not deduce that No. 3098 is by Carpaccio. Their explanation of the circumstances might seem justified,[9] if there were strong reasons for ascribing No. 3098 to Gentile Bellini. But the reasons appear not to be strong; and it would seem better to believe the case similar to other cases, apparently typical of Carpaccio,[10] and ascribe No. 3098 to the same hand as the drawing and the other pictures in which these figures occur.[11]

If No. 3098 is an early work by Carpaccio, one could deduce that Carpaccio was influenced by Mantegna; presumably also by Gentile Bellini, and perhaps by Giovanni Bellini.[12]

An *Adoration of the Kings* at Padua[13] is conceivably in a general way reminiscent of No. 3098. It cannot be entirely excluded that the two pictures may be (very free) derivations from some lost work, perhaps by Gentile Bellini. This, however, would seem not to affect the proposed attribution of No. 3098 to Carpaccio.

PROVENANCE: Bought by Sir Austen Henry Layard from Favenza of Venice in 1865; Favenza had 'bought it from Count Thieni of Vicenza. It was formerly in the family chapel of the Thieni family in S. Bortolo at Vicenza, and was removed some twenty years ago' (i.e. *ca.* 1845) 'by the present Count when the Church was pulled down.'[14] No. 3098, nevertheless, seems not to be mentioned in any of the guide-books as in S. Bartolomeo, Vicenza; though there was in that Church a rather well-known *Adoration of the Kings* by Fogolino, now in the Gallery of the town.[15] Exhibited at South Kensington, 1869 (No. 7). Layard Bequest, 1916.[16]

REPRODUCTION: *Illustrations, Italian Schools*, 1937, p. 26. *Plates, Earlier Italian Schools*, 1953, Vol. I, p. 92.

REFERENCES: (1) Fiocco in *Madonna Verona*, 1913, p. 127. He mentions particularly the castle of Malcesine; but the castle of Malcesine as reproduced in G. Solitro, *Il Lago di Garda*, 1904, pp. 125/6, is quite different from anything seen in No. 3098. (2) Layard, announcing the acquisition of No. 3098 in a letter of 13 October, 1865, to Morelli, stated that the picture is by Gentile Bellini (British Museum, Add. MS. 38966, Layard Papers, Vol. XXXVI.) (3) Gronau, *Die Künstlerfamilie Bellini*, 1909, p. 50, seems to be not quite satisfied with the attribution to Gentile. A. Venturi, *Storia dell'Arte Italiana*, Vol. VII, Part IV, 1915, pp. 248 and 556, ascribes the picture to a follower of Gentile and Giovanni Bellini. Berenson, *Three Essays in Method*, 1927, pp. 63/7 (essay dated 1924), says that previously he had doubted the attribution to Gentile, but had overcome these doubts. G. Fiocco in *Madonna Verona*, 1913, pp. 126/7, claims that the colour of No. 3098 is impossible for Gentile Bellini, and ascribes the picture to Domenico Morone, which seems unlikely. (Berenson, *loc. cit.*, says that he too had thought of Domenico Morone at one time.) Among recent supporters of the attribution to Gentile Bellini may be cited Pallucchini in *Arte Veneta*, 1951, p. 196 (apparently) and Berenson, 1957 Lists. (4) Cf. the *Adoration of the Kings* in the Uffizi; Klassiker der Kunst *Mantegna*, 1910, p. 94. (5) Berenson, *op. cit.*, p. 65. The date claimed is given as 1495 in the Italian version (*Dedalo*, Vol. V, 1924/5, p. 768); but this seems to make the attribution to Gentile Bellini no easier. (6) Crowe and Cavalcaselle, *Painting in North Italy*, 1871, I, p. 129 or ed. Borenius, I, 1912, p. 130. (7) Carlo Gamba, *Giovanni Bellini*, 1937, pp. 91/2. (8) The drawing is H. Tietze and E. Tietze-Conrat, *The Drawings of the Venetian Painters*, 1944, No. 606 and Plate XX (Fiocco, *Carpaccio*, n.d., Plate LXXXVI). As Tietze and Tietze-Conrat point out, S. Joseph and the men standing by him in No. 3098 recur (but separated) in the drawing. It should be added that the first kneeling king in No. 3098 corresponds closely with the second kneeling king in the drawing. Tietze and Tietze-Conrat go on to say that the group of men standing recurs in a picture by Carpaccio (Fiocco, *op. cit.*, Plate CVII), and S. Joseph (fairly closely) in another (Fiocco, *op. cit.*, Plate CXLV). They add that the Turk standing in No. 3098 between the two foremost kings recurs in pictures by Carpaccio (Fiocco, *op. cit.*, Plate CXXXI and to a less extent Plate CLX). Jan Lauts pointed out that the horseman leaning backwards right centre recurs fairly exactly, but in armour, in the *Martyrs of Ararat* (Fiocco, *op. cit.*, Plate CLXIX, top), and with other variations in the background of the *Death of S. Jerome* (Fiocco, *op. cit.*, Plate XCVI). For connections between the Uffizi drawing (where it does not correspond with No. 3098) and other works by Carpaccio, see Tietze and Tietze-Conrat, No. 606. (9) Tietze and Tietze-Conrat, *op. cit.*, pp. 139 ff., give their views on this problem, which they link up with other suggestions for believing in Carpaccio's dependence on Gentile Bellini. (10) See Tietze and Tietze-Conrat's catalogue for the recurrence of figures in different drawings and paintings by Carpaccio. (11) Giles Robertson in *The Burlington Magazine*, 1953, p. 28, approves of the association with Carpaccio. (12) No. 3098, especially in the landscape, has reminded several critics of Giovanni Bellini; cf. the references given above to Gronau and Gamba. R. Longhi in *Vita Artistica*, 1927, p. 134, ascribes it to Giovanni Bellini. (13) It has been variously ascribed; reproduced as by Mansueti in Crowe and Cavalcaselle, *Painting in North Italy*, ed. Borenius, I. 1912, p. 223; suggested as Gentile Bellini and Mansueti in the Padua Catalogue, 1957, pp. 99–101 (reproduced). Another picture at Padua, in the Cathedral, is in design about as like or unlike No. 3098; reproduced in the *Inventario delle Cose d'Arte d'Italia, Provincia di Padova*, 1936, p. 75. (14) Layard MSS. in the National Gallery. For the date of acquisition, see also Layard's letter to Morelli, 13 October, 1865 (British Museum, Add. MS. 38966, Layard Papers, Vol. XXXVI), or *L'Arte*, 1912, p. 452. The proper name of the former owner is Conte di Thiene. Many pictures from S. Bartolomeo at Vicenza were acquired for the Gallery of the town in 1833 (G. Fasolo, *Guida del Museo Civico di Vicenza*, 1940, p. 51); Barbieri, Cevese and Magagnato, *Guida di Vicenza*, 1953, p. 310, say that the church was destroyed in 1838. (15) Some additional doubt about the provenance might be deduced from the remark of Berenson, *loc. cit.*, that No. 3098 had some influence on painting at Verona; so that a provenance from Verona would be convenient. But the provenance from the Thiene family would seem quite reliable. (16) For the history of the Layard Collection, see Appendix IV.

Andrea dal CASTAGNO
ca. 1421 (?)–1457

Andrea di Bartolo di Simone. Known as Andrea dal Castagno from his place of birth (now called Castagno d'Andrea). Often in the fifteenth century called *Andreino degli Impiccati*, from some lost frescoes of political victims at Florence.

He was active at Florence, but his earliest surviving dated works are frescoes of 1442, apparently done in collaboration with Francesco da Faenza, and perhaps with others, in S. Zaccaria at Venice (see Muraro in *The Art Bulletin*, June 1959, pp. 151 ff.; Fiocco, *L'Arte di Andrea Mantegna*, 1959, p. 47). In 1444 he joined the Guild of Physicians at Florence. There are works either documented, or with very good traditions as to authorship attached to them, in the Castagno Museum at Florence, the Cathedral of Florence, the Berlin Gallery, etc.

Literature: Alberto M. Fortuna, *Andrea dal Castagno*, 1957.

Ascribed to ANDREA DAL CASTAGNO

1138   THE   CRUCIFIXION   (PREDELLA   PANEL   FROM   AN
        ALTARPIECE)

Christ hangs on the Cross, marked $\overline{\text{INRI}}$, between the two Thieves; the Virgin and S. John stand below.

Wood, painted surface, $11\frac{1}{4} \times 13\frac{3}{4}$ (0.285×0.35). Including the gold band that surrounds the picture except at the top, the measurements are $11\frac{1}{2} \times 14\frac{1}{4}$ (0.29×0.36).

So far as the dirty condition of the picture allows one to see, No. 1138 is well preserved except for the gold, which has mostly disappeared. The peculiar effect around S. John's head is due to a mixture of under-cleaning and overcleaning or flaking. The landscape continues under the Virgin's dress a little, especially at her right, and in parts under the Crosses.

No. 1138 is clearly one panel from a predella. Another panel certainly from the same series is *The Resurrection* in the Frick Collection at New York.[1] A picture of *The Capture of Christ* has been claimed to be a pendant to *The Resurrection*.[2] A *Last Supper* at Edinburgh is probably from the same series.[3] A *Flagellation*, formerly in the Berenson Collection, but now destroyed or stolen, has also been claimed to be from the same predella.[4]

The altarpiece, from which No. 1138 and some or all of the pictures just mentioned come, is unknown.[5]

The attribution of No. 1138 to Castagno is usually accepted.[6] An association with Castagno is perhaps not absolutely convincing; and in any case, the weakness of some parts, e.g. the figures of the thieves, suggests that the execution is not by Castagno himself. It may neverthe-less be mentioned that the most characteristic works of Castagno are large and on the whole coarsely executed figures; it is not known what his style was for small figures, nor how far his quality may have des-cended for the execution of a predella.[7]

PROVENANCE: Alleged to have belonged to an engineer at Perugia in the 1870's.[8] Purchased from Charles Fairfax Murray, Florence, 1883.

REPRODUCTION: *Illustrations, Italian Schools*, 1937, p. 91. *Plates, Earlier Italian Schools*, 1953, Vol. I, p. 93.

REFERENCES: (1) Reproduced by Mario Salmi, *Paolo Uccello Andrea del Castagno Domenico Veneziano*, 1938, Plate 175; size, $11\frac{1}{4} \times 13\frac{1}{4}$. F. M. Biebel of the Frick Collection has kindly confirmed (letter of 19 March, 1947) that the material condition of the edges of this picture and of N.G. No. 1138 corresponds except on the right where the Frick picture has been cut. *The Resurrection*, so far as the compiler is aware, is first recorded (as by Piero della Francesca) in the collection of the engineer Cav. Vincenzo Funghini at Arezzo in 1891; see G. F. Pichi, *La Vita e le Opere di Piero della Francesca*, 1892, p. 63. The passage is quoted by Cavalcaselle e Crowe, *Storia della Pittura in Italia*, Vol. VIII, 1898, pp. 253/4, where it is added that Funghini was then dead. The compiler considers that this is identical with the Frick picture, although the provenance usually stated for that is varied. The picture is presumably identical with one lent by Werner Weisbach to the Renaissance Exhibition at Munich, 1901 (No. 5); some confirmation in a descriptive note in the *Repertorium für Kunstwissenschaft*, 1901, p. 321. (2) Pichi, *op. cit.*, p. 63, or Cavalcaselle e Crowe, *op. cit.*, pp. 253/4; the picture, also in the Funghini Collection as Piero della Francesca, is described in some detail. Massimiliano Falciai, *Arezzo*, 1910, pp. 156 ff., describes the collection of Sa. Felice Laschi vedova Funghini, and records what must be this picture on p. 158; recorded as still there in the 2nd edition, 1926, pp. 152/3. There seems to be no good evidence that Funghini owned, or even knew of any further pictures of the same series as his *Resurrection* and *Capture*. (3) Size, $10\frac{1}{2} \times 13\frac{3}{8}$; Edinburgh Catalogue, 1957, No. 1210; reproduced in the *Illustrations*, 1952, p. 23. The panel appears to have been cut down slightly, but on two of the sides gilt bands similar to those of No. 1138 still exist; information kindly supplied by Stanley Cursiter. The style of the Edinburgh picture does not correspond very well with that of No. 1138 and the Frick *Resurrection*. (4) Reproduced by Salmi, *op. cit.*, Plate 177, as Studio; size, 0·292×0·35. (5) R. Langton Douglas in *The Art Quarterly*, Autumn, 1945, p. 288, claims that the pictures formed the predella of the 'Poggibonsi Altarpiece,' for which see the entry for No. 584, Tuscan School. (6) E.g. by Salmi, *op. cit.*, p. 167. It was called too weak for Castagno by Jacobsen in the *Repertorium für Kunstwissenschaft*, 1901, p. 346. (7) Mirella Levi D'Ancona (in the large Frick Catalogue, Vol. XII, 1955, pp. 75 ff., or better in the *Rivista d'Arte*, 1956, pp. 73 ff.) ascribed No. 1138 and the Frick *Resurrection* to the young Antonio del Pollaiuolo; there are some stylistic points of contact with Pollaiuolo, and with other painters she mentions, but the pictures seem to the compiler less far from Castagno. She points out that the Christ in No. 1138 corresponds quite closely with the Christ in *S. Antonino at the Foot of the Cross* in S. Marco, Florence, sometimes ascribed to Pollaiuolo or to Baldovinetti (S. Antonino died in 1459). She further points out that it is unusual for the scene of the Crucifixion to show only Christ, the two thieves, the Virgin and S. John. (8) This is Weisbach's statement as given by Pudelko in *The Burlington Magazine*, Vol. LXVIII (1936), p. 239; it seems true that Weisbach's own picture (the Frick *Resurrection*) belonged to an engineer at Arezzo in the 1890's. R. Langton Douglas in *The Art Quarterly*, Autumn, 1945, p. 288, says that No. 1138 and others of the series belonged to 'Fungini' before 1880, and were sold at auction at Perugia in 1880; but these statements may involve some confusion.

CAVAZZOLA *See* PAOLO MORANDO

CESARE DA SESTO
ca. 1477–1523

Born apparently at Sesto Calende; active mostly in Milan. His date of birth is from his age stated at death. In 1523 he contracted for an altarpiece, of which the chief parts are now in the Castello Sforzesco at Milan. Other pictures, of which the principal is a *Baptism* in the Scotti

Collection at Milan, are mentioned in early sources such as Vasari and Lomazzo, and are to be considered certain. Further, a good many drawings can be established as by him, which in turn confirm the attribution of other pictures.

A body of works is thus identifiable; but lack of dates makes his development a somewhat obscure problem. Vasari (but not in his first edition) speaks of a *Cesare da Milano*, collaborator of Baldassare Peruzzi at Ostia, date not given; it is uncertain if Cesare da Sesto is referred to, or (if so) what stylistic effect may be deduced. Some of Cesare's paintings show a considerable influence of Leonardo; these are supposed to be comparatively early works, but it is not clear what previous training he may have had. His late altarpiece in the Castello Sforzesco, on the other hand, is markedly in Raphael's later style; the chief period of influence by Raphael or his followers may well coincide with a stay in Southern Italy (*ca.* 1515–20 ?), which is deducible from the record of works by Cesare or under his influence at Naples, Salerno and Messina.

Lomazzo (*Trattato*, 1584, p. 188) says that the landscape of the Scotti *Baptism* is by Barnazano (or Bernazzano,) a name mentioned also by Vasari, but not at present known from contemporary documents; this landscape shows affinities with the Netherlandish manner associated with Patenier.

Cesare da Sesto's style was continued by Cesare Magni, of whom several signed works are known.

Studio of CESARE da Sesto

2485   SALOME

On the reverse, some drawings in pigment on the unprimed wood; the two principal figures might represent *Christ Appearing to the Magdalen*, but there seems to be a third smaller figure lower down.

Poplar,[1] painted surface, $53\frac{1}{4} \times 31\frac{1}{2}$ ($1\cdot35 \times 0\cdot80$); painted up to the edges all round.

In very fair condition; but the repaints are not confined to various obvious places on the heads.

The attribution of the design to Cesare da Sesto is not disputed. Three variants are known: (*a*) the present one, of which the original is usually admitted to be a picture at Vienna; (*b*) the same figures, with a third figure added between them, of which there is no trace in No. 2485, either by ordinary light or under X-Rays; (*c*) a seven-figure composition, known only in a drawing at Detroit. The subject was popular in the Milanese School; there exist several well-known pictures by Luini and Andrea Solari.

Suida's latest view[2] is that No. 2485 is a studio replica of the picture at Vienna. Except for the colours, the two pictures are very similar. The principal difference is that here Salome wears a sash, the ends of which reach nearly to the ground; this is of dubious antiquity, and has been painted on top of the dress and various ornaments, which correspond closely with the Vienna version. Salome's brooch and collar differ much less than might appear from the brooch and collar at Vienna; the design is closely similar, but has here been painted in a very unfinished manner.

Suida's latest attribution has been accepted; it is a middle view between the two other possible classifications, Cesare himself or a copy. The picture is at least likely to be later than the one at Vienna; for the top part of Salome's left sandal, present at Vienna, has here been removed in what seems to be an original *pentimento*. Further, all the details of drawing, especially those that are not prominent, are here inferior. An example is the executioner's loin-cloth or knotted shirt, of which there is a sketch at Windsor; in the drawing there is a coherent knot, at Vienna something of a knot, here no knot. Finally, the style of the drawings on the back of No. 2485 seems rather too mannered for Cesare; but they need not be by the painter of the front. These considerations make it likely that the picture is a studio piece or a copy rather than an original repetition.

DRAWINGS: (a) a sheet at Windsor with the executioner's hand and (at right angles) his knotted shirt, etc.;[3] (b) Salome's arm at Venice, according to Suida;[4] this is presumably distinct from a similar arm also at Venice, rightly published by Suida[5] as for the Scotti *Baptism*, and wrongly by Malaguzzi Valeri[6] as for a *S. Jerome*; (c) a seven-figure composition at Detroit;[7] Salome is very similar; (d) the three heads of Salome, S. John and the Executioner in the Arcivescovado at Milan (Monti Bequest, 1650); these are mentioned by Latuada[8] as by Cesare da Sesto, but according to Suida[9] are only copies.

VERSIONS: Frequent. The following may be cited: (a) once in the Zecca at Milan according to Vasari.[10] (a different design?); (b) with Cesare Negruolo, Milan;[11] maybe the same as the next; (c) passed from Lomazzo's possession into that of the Emperoi Rodolph II;[12] this is presumably the picture now at Vienna;[13] (d) the Orleans version;[14] Suida[15] quotes Baldinucci, and claims that this version had been in San Giovanni Decollato at Milan, and was given by Conte Archinto to Mazarin in 1630; what is claimed to be this version has since appeared several times in the sale room, e.g. in the Moret Sale, Paris, 12 February, 1857 (lot 42),[16] and is reproduced in the catalogue of the Henri de la Broise Sale, Paris, 10 June, 1931 (lot 15); this version has a third figure; (e) a copy of the San Giovanni Decollato picture, by A. Figino, 1548–1608, replaced the original in the church at Milan;[17] (f) Cornwall Legh Collection,[18] with a third figure; (g) Hampton Court, with a third figure;[19] (h) fragments in the Borromeo Collection, Milan.[20]

PROVENANCE: Perhaps the picture which belonged to a Galeazzo Sforza (Galeazzo of the Pesaro Branch, who died in 1519?),[21] and later to Caterina Nobili Sforza, Contessa di Santafiora, in whose possession at Rome it was recorded without attribution in 1597.[22] Caterina Sforza died in 1605. Her Palace in Rome, and probably her version of Raphael's *Fornarina*, passed into the possession of the Barberini; No. 2485 is claimed to be from Palazzo Barberini, and its identity with the Sforza picture may therefore also be claimed. On the back of No. 2485, C F B (Cardinale Francesco Barberini?). The Barberini picture is not in the 1631 Barberini Inventory, but probably in that of Cardinale Carlo Barberini, 1704.[23] Seen in Palazzo Barberini by Ramdohr.[24] Presumably the picture in a sale of Barberini pictures at Christie's, 30 March, 1805 (lot 38), bought by Tucker.[25] But the Barberini picture is also claimed to have been bought from Palazzo Barberini in 1799 by Collot; then to have been in the Collot Sale, Paris, 29 March, 1855, bought by Thibaudeau; Adolphe Thibaudeau Sale,

Paris, 13/4 March, 1857.[26] Perhaps Charles Scarisbrick Sale, London, 13 May, 1861 (lot 243), bought by the Rev. Walter Davenport Bromley.[27] George Salting bought No. 2485 from the Rev. —. Hawkins in 1875;[28] exhibited at the Burlington Fine Arts Club, 1896 (No. 16); Salting Bequest, 1910.

REPRODUCTIONS: *Illustrations, Italian Schools*, 1937, p. 95. *Plates, Earlier Italian Schools*, 1953, Vol. I, p. 94. The drawings on the reverse are reproduced in *Paintings and Drawings on the Backs of National Gallery Pictures*, 1946, Plate 30.

REFERENCES: (1) Letter from B. J. Rendle, of the Forest Products Research Laboratory, in the Gallery archives. (2) Suida in Thieme-Becker, s.v. Sesto. (3) Clark's *Catalogue of the Drawings of Leonardo da Vinci at Windsor*, No. 12559, with reproduction. (4) Suida, *Leonardo und sein Kreis*, 1929, p. 220. (5) Suida in *Monatshefte für Kunstwissenschaft*, 1920, Tafel 54. (6) Malaguzzi Valeri in the *Rassegna d'Arte*, 1908, p. 25. (7) A reproduction is in the Gallery archives. (8) S. Latuada, *Descrizione di Milano*, 1737/8, II, p. 85. (9) Suida in *Monatshefte*, 1920, p. 257. (10) Vasari, ed. Milanesi, VI, p. 518. (11) Lomazzo, *Trattato*, 1584, p. 339. (12) Lomazzo, *Idea*, 1591, p. 158. (13) Vienna, 1928 and 1938 Catalogues, under Sesto, with a wrong Orleans provenance. (14) Orleans Catalogue, 1727, p. 28, as A. Solario; engraved in the *Galerie du Palais Royal*, 1786, Vol. I, Plate III, as Leonardo. (15) Suida in Thieme-Becker, s.v. Sesto; Baldinucci, *Vite*, ed. 1845 sqq., II, p. 292. See also Carlo Torre, *Il Ritratto di Milano*, 1674, p. 304. (16) Blanc, *Trésor de la Curiosité*, II, p. 555, as Luini. Cf. also the *Revue Universelle des Arts*, Vol. IV, p. 556. (17) As note 15; also Latuada, *Descrizione di Milano*, 1737/8, V, p. 429. (18) Leeds Exhibition, 1868 (No. 130), and Burlington Fine Arts Club, 1898 (No. 15). Reproduced in the undated High Legh Catalogue, by J. H. Carter, No. 72. (19) Hampton Court, 1929 Catalogue, among the stored pictures. Described in E. Law's *Historical Catalogue*, etc., 1881 (No. 241); it has Charles I's brand on the back. (20) Suida in *Monatshefte*, 1920, p. 257. (21) This is Gronau's suggestion in an (unpublished?) proof for the Burlington Magazine in the Gallery archives. (22) See Lisa Corsini Sforza in *L'Arte*, 1898, pp. 273 ff. (23) L. C. Sforza, *loc. cit.*, p. 277. (24) Ramdohr, *Ueber Mahlerei, etc.*, 1787, II, p. 314, as School of Leonardo. (25) As L. da Vinci. Cf. Redford, *Art Sales*, I, p. 93. (26) Blanc, *Trésor de la Curiosité*, II, pp. 507 and 539, as Leonardo. (27) As L. da Vinci, as from the Barberini Palace; no Collot or Thibaudeau provenance. (28) Salting MSS., as Luini; but see the Burlington Fine Arts Club Catalogue, 1898, for the name of the vendor.

GIOVANNI BATTISTA CIMA DA CONEGLIANO
1459/60(?)–1517/8

It is not to be doubted that Cima was his surname, although he does not appear to have used it for his signatures. He was from Conegliano, where he is claimed to have lived until 1489; he is known to have been active at Venice from 1492 to 1516. An altarpiece at Vicenza is signed and dated 1489. There are many authenticated works, some of them datable; but his style evolved little. He is sometimes said to have been trained by Giovanni Bellini, in which case he did not spend his whole youth at Conegliano. Some of his designs occur in several versions; sometimes these are merely copies by assistants or followers, in other cases it need not be doubted that Cima himself repeated his compositions.

300   THE VIRGIN AND CHILD

Signed: .IOANNES BAPTISTA.P., above which are the remains of an inventory number 29.

Wood, painted surface, $27\frac{1}{4} \times 22\frac{1}{2}$ (0·695 × 0·57); painted up to the edges all round.

Good condition, but not free from repairs, especially in the flesh shadows.

Hadeln in Thieme-Becker and Berenson (1957 Lists) call this a late work. Botteon and Aliprandi[1] say that the town and castle in the background are those of Conegliano; they also say that an obviously different group of buildings in the background of an altarpiece at Parma is the same castle from much the same point of view.[2]

VERSIONS: (1) Venice, No. 597;[3] (2) the Louvre, Schlichting Bequest;[4] (3) once in the Liechtenstein Collection, Vienna;[5] (4) Hermitage, ex-Kotchoubey;[6] (5) Soviet Sale, Berlin, November 1928 (lot 364), now at Raleigh;[7] (6) Palazzo Doria, Rome.[8] The compiler is not claiming that all of these are by Cima himself.

PROVENANCE: Maybe a picture in an auction at Paris, 1857.[9] Purchased from M. Roussel, Paris, 1858.

REPRODUCTION: Illustrations, Italian Schools, 1937, p. 96. Plates, Earlier Italian Schools, 1953, Vol. I, p. 95.

REFERENCES: (1) Botteon and Aliprandi, Ricerche, etc., 1893, pp. 114/5. (2) Botteon-Aliprandi, op. cit., p. 152; reproduced by Venturi, Storia dell'Arte Italiana, Vol. VII, Part IV, Fig. 326. (3) Venice Accademia, Catalogue, XIV and XV Centuries, 1955, No. 123, reproduced; on deposit at Treviso (Fig. 22 of the 1959 Treviso Guida). Most of the details of the background as well as the main figures here correspond with No. 300. (4) Reproduced by L. Coletti, Cima da Conegliano, 1959, Plate 99c; Coletti also reproduces four of the other versions. (5) Photograph in the Gallery archives. Perhaps the picture lent by O. Schuster to Amsterdam, Italian Exhibition, 1934 (No. 79); reproduced in the Rivista del R. Istituto d'Archeologia e Storia dell'Arte, 1935, Plate II between pp. 222 and 223. Perhaps the picture that appeared at Sotheby's, 18 May, 1949 (lot 74) and/or in the Hon. Mrs. Sandeman Sale, 1 July, 1953 (lot 44); photographs in the Gallery archives. (6) Reproduced in Les Anciennes Ecoles de Peinture dans les Palais et les Collections Privées Russes, 1910, p. 35, and in Arte Veneta, 1957, p. 50. According to a note in Crowe and Cavalcaselle, Painting in North Italy, ed. Borenius, 1912, Vol. I, p. 247, this had been in the Leuchtenberg Collection. (7) Reproduced in the 1928 Sale Catalogue, and in the Raleigh Catalogue, 1956, No. 182 (wrongly as ex-Kotchoubey). (8) Photo, Anderson 5459. (9) Mireur, Dictionnaire des Ventes d'Art, Vol. II, p. 192.

634 THE VIRGIN AND CHILD WITH A GOLDFINCH

Signed: .IOANES.BAPTISTA.CONEGLA^S.P.

Poplar,[1] painted surface, $21 \times 17\frac{1}{4}$ (0·535 × 0·435); painted up to the edges all round.

Good condition; some local damages.

Hadeln in Thieme-Becker and Berenson (1957 Lists) call this a late work.

VERSIONS: At Berlin, reproduced in the Book of Illustrations. The same design in a Cinquecento style in the J. G. Johnson Collection, Philadelphia, No. 192.[2]

PROVENANCE: Three unidentified seals on the back. Lord Powerscourt Sale, 19 April, 1845 (lot 60), bought by Coningham. W. Coningham Sale, 9 June,

1849 (lot 41), bought by Nieuwenhuys.[3] Purchased with the rest of the Edmond Beaucousin Collection, Paris, 1860.[4]

REPRODUCTION: *Illustrations, Italian Schools*, 1937, p. 96. *Plates, Earlier Italian Schools*, 1953, Vol. I, p. 96.

REFERENCES: (1) Letter from B. J. Rendle, of the Forest Products Research Laboratory, in the Gallery archives. (2) Catalogue of the J. G. Johnson Collection, I, *Italian Paintings* by B. Berenson, 1913, No. 192, with reproduction, as Sebastiano del Piombo; Venturi, *Storia dell'Arte Italiana*, Vol. VII, Part IV, Fig. 495. (3) With identifying description. (4) Presumably it is the Cima noted as already in the Beaucousin Collection by Claudius Tarral, *Observations sur le Classement Actuel des Tableaux du Louvre*, 1850, p. 8.

816   ALTARPIECE: THE INCREDULITY OF S. THOMAS

Inscribed on a *cartellino* in the centre (partly effaced and retouched): 15(0)4........ ....(norio?) / (i)n tepo d( ) m⁰ Boneto tentor f(u?) (a?)gnolo (d?) radjo( ) Cop(ag?)n(o?) e / ....panjgaja e p̄ pant(i?)nian (bauiero?) p̄ an / dres( ).....nusa Consi( ) fo fata qusta opera. Signed on another *cartellino* to the right (retouched), *Joanes Baptiste Coneglanēsis / opus*; to this has been added the date 1504.

Wood, irregular top, painted surface, $115\frac{3}{4} \times 78\frac{1}{2}$ (2.94×1.995); painted up to the edges all round. An inch or so is missing from the top.

The picture was suffering from neglect until it was sent about 1820 for restoration to Venice; during negotiations for paying the restorer's bill, it (accidentally) passed 'many hours' under the waters of the Grand Canal.[1] Further restorations are recorded, and it is not surprising that it appears as extensively damaged and repaired; but some of Cima's quality remains. The signature in brown has been fairly carefully gone over in brown; subsequently a few careless retouches in black were added, and the date (in black) was taken over from the other *cartellino*.

In 1497 the Scuola di S. Tommaso or dei Battuti decided to commission a picture for their altar of S. Thomas in S. Francesco, Portogruaro. No. 816 was being painted by 1502, and was brought to Portogruaro from Venice in 1504; a dispute with Cima about the price lasted until 1509.[2] The *cartellino* in the centre on the picture gave the names of Officers of the Confraternity. Although the text is so much damaged and retouched, three names are identifiable; Boneto Tentor was (it seems) Treasurer in 1504, Angelo de Radino was *gastaldo* in 1502, and Andrea de la Nussa was a witness in the dispute in 1507.[3]

VERSIONS: In an altarpiece at Venice containing the figures of Christ, the doubting Thomas and S. Magnus by Cima there are some similarities.[4] No. 816 was copied with variations in an altarpiece of 1505/6 in S. Niccolò at Treviso, sometimes attributed to Sebastiano del Piombo.[5] A copy by Eugenio Bonò, probably *ca.* 1870, is stated to be in S. Andrea at Portogruaro.[6]

PROVENANCE: The altarpiece remained until the nineteenth century in S. Francesco, Portogruaro; the church was demolished in 1828, and after its return from restoration in Venice, the picture was transferred in 1833 to S. Andrea, whence it was removed to the Town Hall in 1861. The joint owners were the Commune and the Hospital,[7] from whom it was purchased in 1870.

REPRODUCTION: *Illustrations, Italian Schools*, 1937, p. 97. *Plates, Earlier Italian Schools*, 1953, Vol. I, p. 97.

REFERENCES: (1) See Botteon and Aliprandi, *Ricerche*, etc., 1893, p. 99. Much of what they wrote is from information by Dario Bertolini, whose article on the picture appeared in *Arte e Storia*, Vol. XIII, 1894, pp. 137 ff. (2) Botteon-Aliprandi, *op. cit.*, pp. 216 ff. (3) Botteon-Aliprandi, *op. cit.*, pp. 218, 217, 222. (4) Reproduced by Crowe and Cavalcaselle, *Painting in North Italy*, ed. Borenius, 1912, Vol. I, p. 246. (5) Cf. Fiocco in *L'Arte*, 1912, pp. 293 ff., with a reproduction; but the attribution to Sebastiano del Piombo is now often rejected, and the date disputed (cf. *Catalogo delle Cose d'Arte e di Antichità d'Italia, Treviso*, by Luigi Coletti, 1935, pp. 403/4; R. Pallucchini, *Sebastian Viniziano*, 1944, pp. 23/4). (6) See Bertolini's article (reference in note 1). (7) Botteon-Aliprandi, *op. cit.*, pp. 98/100.

1120   S. JEROME IN A LANDSCAPE

Wood, painted surface, $12\frac{5}{8} \times 10$ ($0 \cdot 32 \times 0 \cdot 255$).

Very good condition. Small *pentimenti* top right, in the leaves and rock.

It is usual for S. Jerome to kneel before a Crucifix; here it is a rude Cross, from beneath which a serpent crawls.

Dated by Burckhardt 1504/10.[1] Berenson (1957 Lists) calls it Early.

PROVENANCE: According to a label on the back, bought in Venice, 1770, from the Collection of the Nuncio of Verona; according to the Hamilton Sale Catalogue, the purchaser was Mr. Strange. Possibly John Strange Collection, exhibited for sale at the European Museum, 17 sqq. May, 1799 (No. 146).[2] In the Collection of William Beckford at Fonthill; Sale, 15 October, 1822 (lot 35),[3] but this sale was not held; not in the 1823 Sale. Seen by Waagen in Beckford's tower at Bath;[4] in 1844 it passed by inheritance to the Duke of Hamilton.[5] Bought at the Hamilton Palace Sale, 17 June, 1882 (lot 26).

REPRODUCTION: *Illustrations, Italian Schools*, 1937, p. 98. *Plates, Earlier Italian Schools*, 1953, Vol. I, p. 98.

REFERENCES: (1) R. Burckhardt, *Cima*, 1905, p. 116. (2) S. Jerome in a small landscape, Civetta. Not identified in the John Strange auction sales, 27/9 January, 1774, 14/5 June, 1775, 15 sqq. 19 sqq. and 28/9 March, 1800, nor in the sale by private contract, 10 sqq. December, 1789. (3) Here and in the Hamilton Sale as Herri met de Bles (Civetta). (4) Waagen, *Art and Artists*, 1838, Vol. III, p. 118. (5) The 10th Duke of Hamilton married a daughter of William Beckford.

1310   CHRIST CROWNED WITH THORNS

Wood, painted surface, $14\frac{1}{2} \times 11\frac{1}{2}$ ($0 \cdot 37 \times 0 \cdot 29$).

Considerably repainted.

When acquired, it was attributed to Giovanni Bellini, and Longhi[1] calls it of Bellini's school; but the usual attribution to Cima seems reasonable.[2] Burckhardt[3] calls it late work, 1510/6. Berenson (1957 Lists) also calls it Late.

VERSION: Coletti[4] reproduces one in the Collection of Professor Nigro, Genoa.

PROVENANCE: In the Perkins Collection at Chipstead; there by 1856.[5] Purchased at the sale of George Perkins (who died in 1879), 14 June, 1890 (lot 37).[6]

REPRODUCTION: *Illustrations, Italian Schools*, 1937, p. 98. *Plates, Earlier Italian Schools*, 1953, Vol. I, p. 99.

REFERENCES: (1) R. Longhi in *Pinacotheca*, 1928/9, p. 159. L. Coletti, *Cima da Conegliano*, 1959, Plate 151a, thinks it is by Giovanni Bellini. (2) Perhaps first as Cima (with a query) in Berenson's *Venetian Painters*, 1897. (3) R. Burckhardt, *Cima*, 1905, p. 116. (4) Coletti, *op. cit.*, Plate 151b. (5) As Carlo Dolci; Scharf, General Notes, No. II, p. 53, in the National Portrait Gallery. (6) As Carlo Dolci.

2505 DAVID AND JONATHAN

David is carrying the head of Goliath.

Wood, painted surface, $16 \times 15\frac{1}{2}$ (0·405 × 0·395); painted up to the edges all round.

Very fair state.

Burckhardt[1] and Hadeln[2] say it is from about 1500. Berenson (1957 Lists) calls it Early. Coletti[3] calls it late.

PROVENANCE: 'O.M.' on the back; said to come from the Modici Collection, Naples.[4] Bought in 1898 by George Salting;[5] exhibited at the Burlington Fine Arts Club, 1902 (No. 23); Salting Bequest, 1910.

REPRODUCTION: *Illustrations, Italian Schools*, 1937, p. 100. *Plates, Earlier Italian Schools*, 1953, Vol. I, p. 100.

REFERENCES: (1) R. Burckhardt, *Cima*, 1905, p. 117. (2) Hadeln in Thieme-Becker. (3) L. Coletti, *Cima da Conegliano*, 1959, Plate 138. (4) N.G. Report for 1910. (5) Salting MSS.

2506 THE VIRGIN AND CHILD

Signed: IOANNES BAPTISTA.P.

Wood, painted surface, $25\frac{1}{2} \times 20\frac{1}{2}$ (0·65 × 0·52); painted up to the edges all round.

Good condition in general. *Pentimenti* in the Child's ear, and in the Virgin's hood at each side.

Burckhardt[1] and Berenson[2] have called this a studio-piece, but it seems to be an autograph Cima.

VERSIONS: There is a version in the Cini Collection, Venice.[3] The design also occurs inverted, e.g. in the Lockinge Collection,[4] and in the Gardner Museum at Boston.[5] Other examples,[6] and other related designs exist.

PROVENANCE: Perhaps from the Patrizi Collection, Rome.[7] Bought by George Salting in 1898;[8] Salting Bequest, 1910.

REPRODUCTION: *Illustrations, Italian Schools*, 1937, p. 97. *Plates, Earlier Italian Schools*, 1953, Vol. I, p. 101.

REFERENCES: (1) R. Burckhardt, *Cima*, 1905, p. 117. (2) Berenson, *Venetian Painting in America*, 1916, p. 201; it appears in his list of 1957 as by Cima only 'in great part.' (3) L. Coletti, *Cima da Congeliano*, 1959, Plate 95 (wrongly lettered as in the National Gallery). This seems clearly the same as the picture once in the Palazzo Caregiani, Venice, reproduced in *L'Arte*, 1904, p. 75. (4) Reproduced by Berenson, 1957 Lists, Plate 460, and by Coletti, *op. cit.*, Plate 94. (5) Reproduced in P. Hendy's Gardner Catalogue, 1931 and by Coletti *op.*

cit., Plate 118. (6) Coletti, *op. cit.*, Plate 97, reproduces one (apparently poor) at Bergamo. (7) According to the National Gallery Report for 1910. (8) Salting MSS.

4945   A MALE SAINT (PANEL FROM AN ALTARPIECE)

4946   S. SEBASTIAN (PANEL FROM AN ALTARPIECE)

Wood, each, painted surface, $40\frac{5}{8} \times 16$ ($1 \cdot 03 \times 0 \cdot 41$); painted up to the edges all round.

The S. Sebastian is in fair state, though it has suffered from flaking, and some of the face is marred. A triangle in the left bottom corner, about 1 in. high and 2 in. wide, is a replacement; further, the painted surface of all the lower part including both feet is uniformly new, with a painted craquelure. The new surface extends upwards over most of the pilasters and the spandrels of the niche, but the niche itself is largely old. The other panel is in comparable state, but rather better; thus, the painting of the feet is only mostly new, etc.

No. 4945 has been identified as S. Mark, S. Luke or S. James; the first is quite likely.

An *Annunciation* in the Hermitage, 1·43 m. high and dated 1495, is said on rather shaky evidence to be identical with a picture removed between 1664 and 1674 from the altar of a chapel belonging to the Zeno family in S. Maria de' Crocicchieri (Padri Crociferi, now Gesuiti), Venice.[1] Ridolfi[2] and Martinioni[3] in their account of the Zeno picture say that it was flanked by figures of SS. Mark and Sebastian, which Crowe and Cavalcaselle,[4] Botteon[5] and Burckhardt[6] propose to identify with Nos. 4945/6. One or the other of these identifications may be correct, but apparently not both. Considerations of altarpiece-structure would seem to forbid the association of the Hermitage picture with Nos. 4945/6; Richter[7] made this point, which was accepted by Hadeln.[8]

Cima in these figures appears to have been influenced by the sculpture of Pietro Lombardi.

Berenson (1932 Lists) called the pictures Early, but in his 1936 and 1957 Lists changed this to Late.

PROVENANCE: Bought in 1854 from Schiavone, Venice, by Sir Charles Eastlake.[9] Exhibited at the R.A., 1871 (Nos. 93, 91), and at the Burlington Fine Arts Club, 1871 (Nos. 3 and 7), lent by Lady Eastlake; Sale, 2 June, 1894 (lot 68), bought by Richter for Ludwig Mond. Mond Bequest, 1924; but Sir Robert Mond had a life-interest in the pictures, which did not enter the Gallery until 1938.

REPRODUCTIONS: *Plates, Earlier Italian Schools*, 1953, Vol. I, p. 102.

REFERENCES: (1) Boschini, *Le Minere*, 1664, p. 421, mentions it, but in the 1674 edition, entitled *Le Ricche Minere*, Sestier di Canareggio, pp. 10/11, he says that it had been removed. Cf. also R. Burckhardt, *Cima*, 1905, p. 30, where the picture is reproduced. (2) Ridolfi, *Le Maraviglie dell'Arte* of 1648, Hadeln's reprint, 1914, I, p. 76. (3) Sansovino, *Venetia Città Nobilissima*, con aggiunta da D. Giustiniano Martinioni, 1663, p. 169. No mention in Sansovino's first edition of 1581. Mentioned without detail in Stringa's Sansovino, 1604, f.

147r. (4) Crowe and Cavalcaselle, *Painting in North Italy*, I, 1871, p. 243. (5) Botteon/Aliprandi, *Ricerche*, 1893, p. 117. (6) R. Burckhardt, *Cima*, 1905, pp. 30 ff. (7) J. P. Richter, *The Mond Collection*, 1910, I, pp. 107 ff. (8) Hadeln in Thieme-Becker. This matter is discussed by Lasareff in *Arte Veneta*, 1957, p. 42. (9) Seen at Schiavone's in 1854 (Eastlake's note-book). They were not included in the list of pictures acquired by him during his directorship (1855–65), which were all (?) offered for sale by Lady Eastlake to the Gallery in 1867; doubtless the two single figures by Cima noted as acquired in Venice by October, 1854, in *Journals and Correspondence of Lady Eastlake*, 1895, II, p. 20. They were seen in Eastlake's Collection by Waagen, *Treasures*, IV, 1857, pp. 114/5.

Ascribed to GIOVANNI BATTISTA CIMA DA CONEGLIANO

3113 THE VIRGIN AND CHILD WITH SS. JOHN THE EVANGELIST (?) AND NICHOLAS

Canvas, $20 \times 27\frac{3}{4}$ (0·51 × 0·705).
Much damaged and retouched.

The condition makes it impossible to say if the picture was by Cima, from the studio or by a follower. Burckhardt[1] calls it a studio-piece; Berenson (1957 Lists) admits it as a late work. Coletti admits it as late.[2]

PROVENANCE: Bought from Favenza, Venice, *ca.* 1866, by Sir A. H. Layard;[3] Layard Bequest, 1916.[4]

REPRODUCTION: *Illustrations, Italian Schools*, 1937, p. 99. *Plates, Earlier Italian Schools*, 1953, Vol. I, p. 103.

REFERENCES: (1) R. Burckhardt, *Cima*, 1905, p. 120. (2) L. Coletti, *Cima da Conegliano*, 1959, Plate 132. (3) The Layard MSS. in the National Gallery record that No. 3113 was acquired with No. 3112 below; see the entry for that picture. (4) For the history of the Layard Collection, see Appendix IV.

After GIOVANNI BATTISTA CIMA DA CONEGLIANO

3112 THE VIRGIN AND CHILD WITH SS. PAUL AND FRANCIS (?)

Poplar[1], painted surface, $19\frac{1}{2} \times 34\frac{1}{4}$ (0·495 × 0·87). Painted up to the edges all round; the above measurements include new additions to the panel of $\frac{7}{8}$ in. (2·2 cm.) along the top and $1\frac{3}{4}$ in. (4·5 cm.) along the bottom.

Somewhat damaged, but much of the flesh is apparently in good condition. The impastoed technique is unlike Cima's work, and the picture seems to be a copy; but the possibility that it was once an unfinished lay-in by Cima cannot be ignored, especially as no other version of this design is recorded.

No. 3112 is called a studio-piece by Burckhardt;[2] Berenson (1957 Lists) admits it as a late work; so does Coletti.[3]

PROVENANCE: Bought from Favenza, Venice, *ca.* 1866 by Sir A. H. Layard;[4] exhibited at Leeds, 1868 (No. 76), and at South Kensington, 1869 (No. 16); Layard Bequest, 1916.[5]

REPRODUCTION: *Illustrations, Italian Schools,* 1937, p. 99. *Plates, Earlier Italian Schools,* 1953, Vol. I, p. 103.

REFERENCES: (1) Letter from B. J. Rendle, of the Forest Products Research Laboratory, in the Gallery archives. The two planks making up the original support are both of poplar; the upper addition is also of poplar; the lower addition is of spruce. (2) R. Burckhardt, *Cima,* 1905, p. 120. (3) L. Coletti, *Cima da Conegliano,* 1959, Plate 137. (4) The purchase from Favenza is recorded in the Layard MSS. in the National Gallery. 1866 seems to be the date of acquisition; see letters from Morelli to Layard, 3 November, 1866, and Layard to Morelli, 6 November, 1866 (British Museum, Add. MSS. 38963 and 38966, Layard Papers, Vols. XXXIII and XXXVI). (5) For the history of the Layard Collection, see Appendix IV.

FRANCESCO DEL COSSA
ca. 1435–*ca.* 1477

Ferrarese School. His date of birth is from an epigram, giving his age at death with extreme precision; unfortunately the exact year of his death is not quite certain. Luciano Chiappini in the *Deputazione Ferrarese di Storia Patria, Atti e Memorie,* N.S. Vol. XIV, 1955, p. 111, gives his dates as *ca.* 1436–*ca.* 1478. First recorded at Ferrara in 1456. Also recorded in 1470 at Ferrara; he had just painted some of the frescoes in the Palazzo di Schifanoia there. Soon after, he removed to Bologna, where he appears to have settled. His adaptations to a fresco in the Madonna del Baraccano there are signed, and are of 1472. An altarpiece in the Bologna Gallery is signed and dated 1474. He was apparently influenced by Mantegna and the Squarcionesques, and by Piero della Francesca.

597 S. VINCENT FERRER (?) (CENTRAL PANEL FROM AN ALTARPIECE)

The book he holds is inscribed with odd letters. Above, Christ in a mandorla, and angels, some of them holding some of the Instruments of the Passion (Cross, Column, Spear, Sponge, Scourge, Nails).

Wood, rounded top, painted surface, $60\frac{1}{2} \times 23\frac{1}{2}$ (1·535 × 0·60). Painted up to the edges at the sides and bottom, but obviously not cut to any relevant extent.

Very good condition; some damage in the small figures at the top. *Pentimenti* in the uplifted finger of the Saint's right hand, and probably in the line of his head.

No. 597 is first surely recorded in 1841, as *S. Hyacinth* by Marco Zoppo.[1] The present attribution to Cossa is so clearly right that it needs no justification.

There is not much reason to suppose that the subject was correctly identified in 1841. S. Hyacinth, a Dominican active in Poland, was not canonized until long after No. 597 was painted; and it is difficult to believe that he enjoyed an unofficial cult in Italy to any notable extent.[2]

It can indeed hardly be doubted that the saint in No. 597 is S. Vincent Ferrer. It is true that the inscription often associated with that saint in pictures is missing;[3] but the figures of Christ and angels may be thought to be equivalent to the figure of Christ in Judgment, often shown in the sky in association with S. Vincent Ferrer.[4]

The probability that this identification is correct is increased by the following circumstances. There was in S. Petronio at Bologna a chapel belonging to the Griffoni family. It was dedicated to S. Vincent Ferrer,[5] and the altarpiece represented S. Vincent Ferrer and other, undescribed saints.[6] Vasari, who mentions this altarpiece, attributed it to Lorenzo Costa;[7] but it is for practical purposes sure that Vasari should have written Cossa, since payment for the frame was claimed in 1473,[8] and this date suits the activity of Cossa but seems impossible for Costa. It is a reasonable and widely accepted hypothesis that No. 597 is the central panel of the S. Petronio altarpiece, and therefore that the saint represented is S. Vincent Ferrer.

The member of the Griffoni family associated with the altarpiece in S. Petronio was named Floriano.[9]

Flanking figures of S. Peter and S. John the Baptist in the Brera at Milan are, on pictorial grounds, certainly side panels to No. 597.[10]

The identification of other parts of the altarpiece presents peculiar difficulties. The part most seriously deserving consideration is a predella in the Vatican.[11] Details of the style correspond very well with No. 597 and the two saints in the Brera. Further, Vasari and others[12] speak of the predella of the altarpiece in S. Petronio with praise; and the quality of the predella in the Vatican is high. There are, nevertheless, two difficulties in this identification. One is the perspective; whereas in the triptych formed by No. 597 and the two Brera pictures the perspective is rigidly centralized, in the Vatican predella the centre of perspective is displaced towards the left.[13] The other difficulty is in the subject of the Vatican predella; it is indeed claimed to show various miracles of S. Vincent Ferrer, but this may not have been satisfactorily demonstrated.[14]

Longhi[15] believes that various further panels belonged to this altarpiece. No old records in support of his views have yet been found. Two pictures of a male saint and S. Lucy at Washington were, Longhi thinks, placed above the side panels of SS. Peter and John the Baptist. The two saints at Washington appear rather heavy for the position suggested, and their haloes stamped flat against the gold background differ in style from the haloes in No. 597 and the Brera pictures. Longhi's chief argument is that the male saint at Washington holds a flower, which he thinks may indicate that the saint is S. Florian; and the name saint of the donor, Floriano Griffoni, could properly have been shown on the altarpiece.[16]

Longhi further believes that a *Crucifixion*, also at Washington, was fitted into the altarpiece above No. 597; but it appears all too slight for this space. He also thinks that the pilasters of the altarpiece were ornamented with figures of saints, and lists 7 out of the 8 he postulates. The attribution of these little pictures has hovered between Cossa and Ercole de' Roberti; the latter name seems correct. More facts would be needed to make these identifications quite convincing. [17]

Longhi also thinks that two *tondi* representing *The Annunciation*, in the Cagnola Collection, were part of the altarpiece. Their style seems to accord quite well with that of the small figures in No. 597; but the position Longhi suggests at the summit of the pilasters seems unhappy.

Longhi's suggestions may be, in part at least, correct; but it is desirable to state that they are not proved.[18]

It was stated at the beginning that the attribution of No. 597 to Cossa needs no justification; also that some of the pictures claimed to be associated are usually ascribed to Cossa, others rather to Ercole de' Roberti. The relations between Cossa and Roberti are not certainly defined; but it is quite admissible that they may both have worked on one altarpiece.

PROVENANCE: Most probably (as explained above) the central panel of the altarpiece in the Griffoni Chapel (dedicated to S. Vincent Ferrer) in S. Petronio at Bologna.[19] The Griffoni Chapel passed, under unknown circumstances, to the Aldrovandi family in the eighteenth century;[20] soon after, the Aldrovandi and Cospi families exchanged chapels in S. Petronio.[21] It seems to have been on this occasion that the altarpiece may have been removed to the Casa Aldrovandi, perhaps by Cardinal Pompeo Aldrovandi.[22] No. 597 is first certainly recorded in 1841 in the Costabili Collection at Ferrara.[23] Purchased thence in 1858.

REPRODUCTION: *Illustrations, Italian Schools*, 1937, p. 110. *Plates, Earlier Italian Schools*, 1953, Vol. I, p. 104.

REFERENCES: (1) C. Laderchi, *Catalogo della Quadreria Costabili*, IV, 1841, No. 415. (2) It may nevertheless be mentioned that a life of S. Hyacinth is included in a collection of lives by the Fifteenth Century Bolognese Dominican Gerolamo Borselli, MS. at Bologna, No. 1999; see the *Analecta Bollandiana*, Vol. 42, pp. 353 and 461. (3) *Timete Dominum, et date illi honorem, quia venit hora judicii ejus* (Revelation xiv, 7). (4) Cf. for instance the picture in the Academy at Florence, ascribed to Giovanni Francesco da Rimini: Melozzo Exhibition at Forlì, 1938, Catalogo, p. 71, No. 6, Plate 41B. See further Kaftal, *Iconography of the Saints in Tuscan Painting*, 1952, Cols. 1021 sqq. His first explanation is that S. Vincent's claim to be the angel of the Apocalypse, speaking the words quoted in the previous note, was miraculously proved at Salamanca. It may be noted that S. Vincent is sometimes shown in the sky, e.g. in the S. Zanipolo triptych ascribed to Giovanni Bellini (without the text), in a Lotto at Recanati (reproduced by P. Bianconi, *Tutta la Pittura di Lorenzo Lotto*, 1955, Plate 27) and in a print wrongly called S. Dominic (Hind, *Early Italian Engraving*, Vol. IV, 1938, Plate 445). S. Vincent is even shown winged sometimes, though the compiler does not know of any case of the XV century; example, a winged S. Vincent in the pulpit by Domenico Tiepolo (the picture reproduced in *Arte Veneta*, 1959/60, p. 303; the corresponding print reproduced by M.-M. Gorce, *Saint Vincent Ferrier*, 1924, Frontispiece, and by P. Molmenti, *Acque-Forti dei Tiepolo*, 1896, p. 121). (5) I. B. Supino, *L'Arte nelle Chiese di Bologna*, II, 1938, p. 196. (6) Malvasia, *Pitture di Bologna*, 1706, p. 259. (7) Vasari; not in 1550 edition; Milanesi's edition, Vol. III, pp. 133/4 and 142/3. (8) On 19 July, 1473, Agostino de' Marchi of Crema demanded payment for the frame of the altarpiece of Floriano Griffoni; I. B. Supino, *L'Arte nelle Chiese di Bologna*, II, 1938, p. 196. (9) See the previous note; he is clearly the man mentioned by Supino as having made his will in 1483. Considerable research concerning the Griffoni family has been carried out for the new edition of Muratori's *Rerum Italicarum Scriptores*, Vol. XVIII, Part II, 1902, Matthae de Griffonibus, *Memoriale Historicum de Rebus Bononiensium*, ed. Frati and Sorbelli, pp. xiv, xviii and 122/3. It would appear that the man associated with the altarpiece in S. Petronio was Floriano, son of another Floriano who had married in 1421 and died in 1434. This younger Floriano married Lodovica Lambertini in 1450; he was certainly still alive in 1465 (same edition of Muratori, Vol. XXXIII, Part I, Cherubino Ghirardacci, *Della Historia di Bologna*, Vol. III, ed. Sorbelli, p. 188). (10) Brera, *Catalogo*, *ca.* 1935, p. 108, Nos. 449, 449 *bis*; Venturi, *Storia dell'Arte Italiana*, Vol. VII, Part III, Figs. 469, 470. The association with No. 597 was pointed out by Crowe and Cavalcaselle, *History of Painting in North Italy*, 1871, I, p. 528. (11) Vatican, *Guida*, 1933, pp. 104/5, No. 286, as Cossa; size, 0·272 × 2·127 (letter from Dr. Redig de Campos, 28 October, 1948). The execution is often ascribed to Ercole de' Roberti. Cf. G. Frizzoni in the *Zeitschrift für bildende Kunst*, 1888, pp. 299 ff. All that is proved concerning its provenance is that in June, 1830, it was offered for sale to the Papal Government, and refused, by a dealer, Feliciano Brizi, di Città di Castello, domiciliato in Lugo (doubtfully as Mantegna or Melozzo); and that in April, 1839, it was again offered by the same Feliciano Brizi, then living in Viterbo, and was purchased in that year (no attribution). See Rome, Archivio di Stato, Camerlengato, II, sez. IV, Nos. 1446 and 2941; the references kindly supplied by Monseigneur Le Grelle. An attribution to Benozzo, due to Baron Camuccini and Luigi Grifi, was put forward in a pamphlet of 1841, *Sopra un dipinto attribuito a Benozzo Gozzoli*, and in the *Galleria di Quadri al Vaticano*, *Indicazione Antiquaria*, Parte Seconda, 1843, p. 83, No. XXXV (not catalogued in the 1840 edition). A modern copy of this picture was presented to the National Gallery by His Holiness Pope Pius XI in 1930; inventory number, 597A. (12) Vasari; not in the 1550 edition; Milanesi's edition, Vol. III, pp. 133/4 and 142/3, as Ercole Ferrarese. Pietro Lamo, *Graticola di Bologna*, 1844, p. 39. Antonio di Paolo Masini, *Bologna Perlustrata*, 3rd edition, 1666, I, p. 111. (13) This is pointed out by R. Longhi, *Officina Ferrarese*, 1934, p. 169. Longhi wonders if the right-hand end of the predella may be a later addition by the painter; equally well or better, the left-hand end might have been cut away. In point of fact, the original edges of the picture have all been cut, but there is no proof that as much as a whole scene has been either added or cut away (kindly communicated by Dr. Redig de Campos). On pictorial grounds, nevertheless, a substantial cut does seem likely. (14) So far as the compiler is aware, the interpretation of the various scenes as miracles of S. Vincent Ferrer is due to Frizzoni (*Zeitschrift für bildende Kunst*, 1888, p. 300). See also the better comments by A. Neppi, *Francesco del Cossa*, 1958, pp. 29 ff. In 1830 (cf. note 11), the subject was supposed to be miracles of S. Antonino. In 1839 the owner thought the subject was miracles of S. Vincent Ferrer; the Vatican authorities rejected this when they acquired the picture, and were at some pains to show that the subject was miracles of S. Hyacinth (cf. the pamphlet of 1841 and the catalogue of 1843, referred to in note 11). Their explanations seem more precise than Frizzoni's; and while it may be admitted that S. Hyacinth is most probably wrong, it would seem that further study of this problem is needed. (15) Roberto Longhi, *Officina Ferrarese*, 1934, pp. 48 ff., Plates 63/5, 91/3; and *Ampliamenti nell'Officina Ferrarese*, 1940, pp. 5 ff., Plates III–VI. (16) This saint was called S. Martin, and the pictures were called Zoppo, when owned by Conte Beni at Gubbio. Mündler's Diary, 3 June, 1858; M. Guardabassi, *Indice-Guida*, *Provincia dell'Umbria*, 1872, p. 104; Comte U. Beni Sale, Gubbio, April/May, 1882 (lots 4, 5). S. Florian (name inscribed) does hold a flower in a Vecchietta altarpiece at Pienza; Kaftal, *op. cit.*, Fig. 433. It would be useful to cite a case at Bologna, since among various S. Florians one is a Patron of that City; by the time of No. 597 *his* emblem may have been becoming standardized as an axe, two representations (name not inscribed) being in the windows of S. Petronio (G. Marchini, *Le Vetrate Italiane*, 1955, Fig. xxiii on p. 33 and Plate 70a). (17) One of the pictures represents S. Petronius, which certainly indicates a Bolognese provenance. E. K. Waterhouse in *The Burlington Magazine*, Vol. LXVIII (1936), p. 151, pointed out that two of the pictures were claimed to come from a shrine at Padua (Mrs. Jameson, *Private Galleries*, 1844, p. 412, and the Rogers Sale Catalogue). Longhi's reasons for rejecting this may appear somewhat subjective. In point of fact, what were obviously these pictures had previously appeared without provenance in the Simon M'Gillivray Sale, 7 May, 1825 (lots 65, 66). There is further a note in the National Gallery in Wornum's writing that the S. Michael had written on the back 'Andrea Mantegna—esiste in Grande in Padova agli Eremitani' (not there now), which might be the origin of the claim 'from a shrine at Padua.' (18) See further the comments on various pictures claimed to be parts of the Griffoni altarpiece, made by E. Ruhmer, *Francesco del Cossa*, 1959, pp. 77 ff. and 85. (19) Bernath's suggestion in Thieme-Becker that it perhaps came from some chapel of S. Hyacinth in S. Domenico at Ferrara seems to be based on nothing. Jacobsen (*Zeitschrift für bildende Kunst*, 1896, pp. 183/5) says that it can't be from S. Petronio at Bologna, because on stylistic grounds it dates from Cossa's Ferrarese period; there is no evidence for saying this. (20) In Malvasia's *Pitture di Bologna*, 1706, p. 259, the chapel is recorded as still belonging to the Griffoni, with the picture in it. (21) Supino, *loc. cit.* (22) According to Malvasia's *Pitture di Bologna*, 1732, p. 263, the chapel had by then passed to the Cospi, and the picture had already gone. Its alleged fate is recorded in the *Guida di Bologna*, 1776, p. 215 (according to Baruffaldi, *Vite de' Pittori e Scultori Ferraresi*, I, 1844, p. 111, note), and in a reprint, *Pitture Scolture ed Architetture delle Chiese*, etc., *di Bologna*, publ. Longhi, 1782, p. 243. In point of fact, Pompeo Aldrovandi became a cardinal only in 1734 (Migne's *Dictionnaire des Cardinaux*); further, in the Oretti MSS. in the Biblioteca dell'Archiginnasio at Bologna (B 104), there is a list of pictures in the Aldrovandi Collection, but this altarpiece is not recorded there. (23) C. Laderchi, *Catalogo della Quadreria Costabili*, IV, 1841, No. 415.

CREDI *See* LORENZO DI CREDI

CARLO CRIVELLI
active 1457–1493

He had a second Christian name, *Giovanni*. He was a native of Venice, where he is recorded in 1457; but he may have left soon after. In 1465 he is recorded as a citizen and inhabitant of Zara (see P. Zampetti in *Arte Veneta*, 1959/60, pp. 227/8). Thereafter he seems to have spent most of his life in the Marches. 1468, Altarpiece at Massa Fermana; thereafter he lived much at Ascoli Piceno. He was knighted by Ferdinand II of Naples in 1490. His *Coronation of the Virgin* in the Brera is dated 1493. He was dead by 1500, probably not long before. His style derives from the Muranese and Paduans; there are many signed works, some of them dated. His pictures usually contain some fruits, often arranged as swags.

602 PIETÀ (PANEL FROM A POLYPTYCH)

The Dead Christ is supported by two angels. Signed (?): CAROLVS. CRIVELLVS.VENETVS.PINSIT. (This signature may well be false.)

Poplar,[1] rounded top, painted surface, $28\frac{1}{2} \times 21\frac{3}{4}$ (0·725 × 0·555). The width is taken between the incised lines marking the edges of the gold;

in the lower part, which is painted, not gilt, the width was probably about $\frac{1}{2}$ in. more, but the true edge is identifiable only on the left. The original framing had a capital on each side at the spring of the arch; the space on the picture surface covered by these was originally left blank, but has been filled up with new paint (including a part of each angel's wing).

The condition is in parts pure, but there are extensive repairs. The most important is an area entirely new at the top, right centre; this is mostly in the gold, but includes the right-hand part of Christ's head, most of His hanging hair, and most of the profile and the right shoulder of the angel to the right. The shadows on Christ's body and arm are not entirely new like the above, but have been much gone over.

The signature has often been commented on as an oddity; it was normal for a *Pietà* such as No. 602 to occupy the centre of the upper tier in a Crivellesque polyptych, where a signature would be hard to see. It could be objected that Crivelli's *Pietàs* at Boston and in the Vatican are signed; but the case of No. 602 is peculiar. As will be explained below, a *Virgin and Child* at Brussels was almost certainly the central panel of the main tier of the altarpiece from which No. 602 comes; this *Virgin and Child* has, as it should, a signature, which further is exactly similar in its text and closely similar in its lettering to the one here.[2] It is *a priori* likely that the one here is false; but examination through a lens and various tests have failed to settle one way or the other the problem of its authenticity. There would indeed be no oddity if No. 602 was originally a picture by itself, and not part of an altarpiece; but the evidence about to be given seems to the compiler unfavourable to this view.

No. 602 is stated to be part of an altarpiece from the Church of the Franciscans (Frati Conventuali Riformati) at Montefiore dell'Aso, near Fermo.

Other panels with a claim to be from the same altarpiece are a *Virgin and Child* and a *S. Francis* at full length at Brussels, and predella figures of *Christ and Seven Apostles*, no doubt those formerly in the Cornwall Legh Collection. All these pictures were seen at Vallati's in Rome in 1858 by Mündler;[3] Vallati had 'lately purchased' them, though Mündler does not record from whom. Eastlake, also in 1858, also at Vallati's, saw No. 602 and other panels which he does not describe; Eastlake records the provenance from Montefiore, presumably on Vallati's authority.[4]

The above-mentioned fragments do not form a complete whole. Other Crivellesque panels were in the same church at Montefiore, now in S. Lucia there. The S. Lucia panels have often not been accepted as by Crivelli himself; but it seems highly probable that they formed part of the same altarpiece as the pictures in Brussels.[5]

The connection of the predella panels is more doubtful; the halo patterns are different, and stylistic criticism is difficult. It may, however, have been in Crivelli's tradition to carry out material variations between altarpiece and predella. It might be thought a further difficulty that S. Peter occurs in the Cornwall Legh series, and also in one of the main panels at Montefiore; but this peculiarity is found in Crivelli's poly-ptych in Ascoli Cathedral, also in a polyptych assigned to Vittorio Crivelli at Torre di Palme.[6]

Whether or not the Cornwall Legh panels are from the predella, its original extent is uncertain. While it is unlikely that a predella would have been complete with Christ and only seven Saints (who must be Apostles), there need not have been twelve; thus, Crivelli's already mentioned altarpiece in Ascoli cathedral shows ten Apostles in the predella.[7]

The date of No. 602 has been claimed to be within a year or two of 1472, but Pallucchini and Zampetti put the Montefiore pictures a little later.[8] The subject of the *Dead Christ supported by Putti* is obviously of Donatellesque derivation;[9] this is an early example on a picture, but Giorgio Schiavone, No. 630 of this catalogue, is almost certainly earlier, and other pictures are likely to be.[10]

VARIANT: A free derivation, part of an altarpiece by Pietro Alamanno (not signed), is at Ascoli.[11]

PROVENANCE: As explained above, most probably from Montefiore dell'Aso. The altarpiece is said to have been broken up in Napoleonic times;[12] but the first certain knowledge of No. 602 is that it was seen by Mündler and Eastlake at Vallati's, Rome, in 1858.[13] Purchased from Cav. P. Vallati, 1859.

REPRODUCTION: *Illustrations, Italian Schools*, 1937, p. 114. *Plates, Earlier Italian Schools*, 1953, Vol. I, p. 105.

REFERENCES: *General*: L. Testi, *Storia della Pittura Veneziana*, Vol. II, 1915, p. 672; F. Drey, *Carlo Crivelli*, 1927, pp. 125/7.

In text: (1) Letter from B. J. Rendle, of the Forest Products Research Laboratory, in the Gallery archives. (2) This was already noted by Mündler in his diary for 1858; he saw the two pictures in the same room. Dr. P. Coremans (letter of 15 March, 1948, in the Gallery archives) examined the signature at Brussels, and believes that it is authentic. (3) Mündler's Diary. The Cornwall Legh series is recorded in photographs, of which prints are in the National Gallery. The *Christ* is now at Williamstown (Sterling and Francine Clark Art Institute), Exhibit 15, 1961, No. 402, reproduced. Two of the Apostles are at Detroit (1930 Catalogue, Nos. 45, 46, reproduced); two in the Kress Collection, now at Honolulu (Drey, *op. cit.*, Plate XVIII); two in the Bearsted Collection at Upton (reproduced in *Kunstchronik*, May 1931, p. 14); the seventh is the picture in the Lehman Collection (reproduced in the catalogue of the exhibition of the Collection at Cincinnati, 1959, No. 97). It is not absolutely proved that these are the pictures from Vallati's, but it would be unreasonable to feel much doubt about it; G. McN. Rushforth, *Carlo Crivelli*, 1900, p. 96, does, in fact, state that they were bought by the late Mr. G. Cornwall Legh from Cav. Vallati at Rome about the same date as the others. (4) Eastlake's note-books. (5) Reproduced in the *Inventario degli Oggetti d'Arte d'Italia, Provincie di Ancona e Ascoli Piceno*, 1936, p. 293; better in the catalogue of the *Mostra della Pittura Veneta nelle Marche*, Ancona, 1950, Plates 21–25. Provenance referred to in Testi, *Storia della Pittura Veneziana*, Vol. II, 1915, pp. 687/8; see also P. Zampetti, *Carlo Crivelli nelle Marche*, 1952, pp. 26 ff. The compiler saw the Montefiore and Brussels pictures together at Amsterdam in 1953, and feels satisfied that they belong to the same altarpiece; the halo patterns of the main S. Lucia panels correspond quite closely with the halo of the S. Francis at Brussels, and the arrangement of the flooring is also quite closely comparable. In the Brussels Catalogue of 1949, the width of the *S. Francis* is given as 0·595; but the width of the original panel, excluding modern additions, is 0·52, and the width of the original painted surface, marked by incised lines, is 0·475. The arch of the *S. Francis* began where the marks of capitals in the original frame are still discernible, which is at about the height of his eyes. Measured from the bottom (which may have been cut), the height of the S. Francis panel to the top of the decoration of the step is 0·13, to the edge of the floor 0·165, to the back of the floor 0·345, to the top of the decoration of the parapet 0·57, to the top of the parapet 0·62. Similar measurements for the three main S. Lucia panels are: (S. Peter) 0·053, 0·086, 0·268, 0·517, 0·54; (S. Catherine) 0·053, 0·085, —, —, 0·538; (S. Lucy) 0·067, 0·10, 0·295, 0·529, 0·555. These three panels have all been cut at the bottom, but the measurements of the internal divisions can be seen to correspond closely with those of the *S. Francis*. As a matter of curiosity, it may be added that the *S. Francis* panel has on the unprimed wood of the back a large drawing of a nude, apparently a bearded old man holding an open book in his right hand, not unlike the S. Peter in the Ascoli polyptych, but inverted (Drey, *op. cit.*, Plate XXX; photograph of the drawing kindly sent by Mlle. Janson). (6) Reproduced by Testi, *Storia della Pittura Veneziana*, Vol. II, 1915, p. 704. (7) The following pictures, not recorded to be from Vallati's shop, have been associated. A *S. Peter Martyr* is said to have balanced the *S. Francis* now at Brussels, but this picture is lost; the authority for its existence appears to be E. Fétis, *Catalogue...du Musée Royal de Belgique*, 2nd edition, 1865, p. 121. A *S. Bernardino* (same size as the *S. Francis*) seems irrelevant; see Fiocco in *Pantheon*, June, 1931, p. 248. Two small *Apostles* are in the Castello Sforzesco at Milan (Drey, *op. cit.*, Plate XVII). Their halo pattern differs a good deal from those of the Cornwall Legh series, which vary only slightly among themselves; the hems of the dresses also differ; and they seem clearly to be from a different series. A small figure in the Prœhl Collection, Amsterdam, has also been wrongly associated; it is said to represent *S. Philip*, but is more probably *S. Andrew*, who already occurs in the Cornwall Legh series; exhibited at Amsterdam, Italian Exhibition, 1934 (No. 100), and reproduced in the catalogue of the Carl Moll Sale, Berlin, 15/9 March, 1917 (lot 9). Zampetti, *op. cit.*, pp. 30/1, adds a half-length figure in the former O. Lanz Collection at Amsterdam (Drey, *op. cit.*, Plate XLI); the compiler does not accept this association, nor can he accept Zampetti's reconstruction of the predella. (8) R. Pallucchini in *Arte Veneta*, 1950, p. 22; Zampetti, *op. cit.*, p. 33. (9) Donatello's relief in the Santo at Padua is reproduced by Venturi, *Storia dell'Arte Italiana*, Vol. VI, Fig. 201. (10) Two examples that may be earlier are a Mantegnesque fresco in the Ovetari Chapel in the Eremitani at Padua (reproduced in the *Bollettino d'Arte*, April, 1926, p. 476), and Giovanni Bellini's picture in the Correr Museum at Venice (reproduced in the catalogue of the Bellini Exhibition at Venice, 1949, No. 26). (11) Reproduced by Testi, *op. cit.*, p. 712. (12) Brussels Catalogue, 1865, as in note 7. (13) Mündler's Diary and Eastlake's Note-book. No. 602 has been said to be identical with a picture once owned by Prof. Minardi at Rome (cf. A. Ricci, *Memorie*, 1834, i, p. 209); but this seems unlikely, and the Minardi picture may be the picture in the J. G. Johnson Collection at Philadelphia (Drey, *op. cit.*, Plate XIV).

668   THE VISION OF THE BLESSED GABRIELE

The Blessed Gabriele, a Franciscan, kneels barefoot in a landscape; his prayer book and his shoes are on the ground by him. A few trees symbolize a wood, above which in a mandorla the Virgin and Child appear to him in the sky. In the middle distance, the head of another Franciscan is visible, and a chapel (for S. Francesco ad Alto, Ancona). Signed: OPVS. KAROLI. CRIVELLI. /. VENETI.

Poplar,[1] original painted surface, $55\frac{1}{2} \times 34\frac{1}{4}$ (1·41 × 0·87). A simple band of painted framing goes all round, with a capital on each side at the top; this is not contemporary. Apart from this, in excellent state.

When No. 668 was acquired, the identity of the subject was preserved by tradition; the provenance proves that this tradition is correct. Gabriele,[2] Superior of the Convent of S. Francesco ad Alto, Ancona, died in 1456; the Virgin appeared to him at night in a wood near the friary, where he was praying. Although not beatified until 1753, he enjoyed a reputation for sanctity, and Crivelli has painted him with an aureole. Following a brief of Pope Innocent VIII in 1489, his body was transferred from its grave to a sculptured tomb in S. Francesco ad Alto, erected by the Ferretti family.[3]

The subject of the Blessed Gabriele's Vision appears also on a marble lunette still preserved at Ancona.[4] The elements of the scene there are much the same as in No. 668, the aureole and shoes recurring; but the Virgin and Child there appear more properly in a tree, there is no second Franciscan and no chapel. It would seem that in Crivelli's picture the iconography has been made to conform with the *Stigmatization of S. Francis*. Another picture of the Blessed Gabriele's Vision is noted in the Bishop's Palace at Ancona, said to be a seventeenth-century copy of a fifteenth-century original;[5] another (?) picture is recorded to have been in S. Francesco ad Alto, by Niccolò Bertuzzi or Bertucci (active 1737, died 1777).[6]

No. 668, to judge from its provenance as given below, seems to have been ordered by the Ferretti family. It is first surely recorded (in 1753), hanging over the Blessed Gabriele's tomb, which the Ferretti had had made at the time of the Pope's brief of 1489. Crivelli, on the other hand, was knighted in 1490, and seems always to have included this distinction in his subsequent signatures. No. 668 may therefore with some probability be dated 1489/90, though a rather earlier date cannot be excluded. Leoni,[7] referring to what must be this picture, states that it was painted in 1466; this may be a misprint for 1456, the year of the Blessed Gabriele's death, but the style of No. 668 excludes either date.

PROVENANCE: No. 668 is perhaps referred to in S. Francesco ad Alto, Ancona, by Francesco Ferretti in 1685; it is certainly recorded there, hanging above the Blessed Gabriele's tomb, by P. Vincenzo Maria Ferretti, in 1753.[8] Still there in 1777.[9] Not recorded there in Maggiori's Guide to Ancona, 1821. It seems to have belonged to the Ferretti family, not to the Church, for what must be No. 668 is recorded by Leoni in 1832 as in an oratory in the house of Raimondo Ferretti at Ancona.[10] Engraved in 1856.[11] It passed into the collection of Alexander Barker, London; exhibited at the British Institution, 1858 (No. 26); purchased from Alexander Barker, 1861.

REPRODUCTION: *Illustrations, Italian Schools*, 1937, p. 114. *Plates, Earlier Italian Schools*, 1953, Vol. I, p. 106.

REFERENCES: General: Iole Bovio Marconi in the *Bollettino d'Arte*, March, 1929, pp. 398 ff.

In text: (1) Letter from B. J. Rendle, of the Forest Products Research Laboratory, in the Gallery archives. (2) He is usually called the B. Gabriele Ferretti. According to Antonio Leoni, *Ancona Illustrata*, 1832, p. 208, his father was a Menmo, and it was his mother who was a Ferretti; but this view is rejected, apparently with good reason, by Stanislao Melchiorri, *Leggenda del Beato Gabriele de' Ferretti di Ancona*, 1844, pp. 21/3. (3) The Church was secularized in 1860, and the tomb was removed to the crypt of the Cathedral; reproduced by I. B. Marconi, *loc. cit.*, also by L. Serra, *L'Arte nelle Marche*, II, 1934, p. 148. **(4)** Cf. I. B. Marconi, *loc. cit.*, where the relief is reproduced; also by Serra, *op. cit.*, p. 148. This lunette, like No. 668, has no inscription identifying the subject; but like No. 668 it comes from S. Francesco ad Alto in Ancona, so that the identification is sure. **(5)** *Inventario degli Oggetti d'Arte d'Italia, Provincie di Ancona e Ascoli Piceno*, 1936, p. 27. **(6)** (A. Maggiori), *Le Pitture*, etc. *d'Ancona*, 1821, p. 16. **(7)** Leoni, *op. cit.*, p. 209; quoted by I. B. Marconi, *loc. cit.*, p. 407. **(8)** See the references, as given and in part quoted, by I. B. Marconi, *loc. cit.*, pp. 400, 406/7. **(9)** Bologna, Biblioteca dell'Archiginnasio, Oretti MSS., B 165 II. **(10)** Leoni, *op. cit.*, p. 209. **(11)** I. B. Marconi, *loc. cit.*

724 ALTARPIECE: THE VIRGIN AND CHILD WITH SS. JEROME AND SEBASTIAN (THE 'MADONNA DELLA RONDINE')

An altarpiece complete in its original frame. In the main panel, the Virgin is seated on a throne, on which is perched a swallow ('rondine'); the Child wears a piece of coral and holds an apple. Left, S. Jerome; right, S. Sebastian (clothed). On the step at the bottom are the arms of the Ottoni family, and the signature: .CAROLVS.CRIVELLVS. VENETVS.MILES.PINXIT.

In the *predella*, from left to right: (*a*) *S. Catherine of Alexandria*; (*b*) *S. Jerome* doing penance before a Crucifix (a dragon and many animals in the landscape, as well as his lion); (*c*) *The Nativity*, at Night (not treated naturalistically); to the right, the Annunciation to the Shepherds; (*d*) *The Martyrdom of S. Sebastian*; (*e*) *S. George and the Dragon*, with the Princess kneeling behind.

Wood. The painted surface of the main panel (poplar[1]) is $59\frac{1}{4} \times 42\frac{1}{4}$ ($1 \cdot 505 \times 1 \cdot 07$). The painted surfaces of the predella scenes are: (*a*) $11\frac{1}{2} \times 8\frac{3}{8}$ ($0 \cdot 29 \times 0 \cdot 215$); (*b*) $11\frac{1}{2} \times 13$ ($0 \cdot 29 \times 0 \cdot 33$); (*c*) $11\frac{1}{2} \times 14\frac{1}{2}$ ($0 \cdot 29 \times 0 \cdot 37$); (*d*) $11\frac{1}{2} \times 12\frac{3}{4}$ ($0 \cdot 29 \times 0 \cdot 325$); (*e*) $11\frac{3}{8} \times 8\frac{3}{8}$ ($0 \cdot 285 \times 0 \cdot 215$). The parts (*b*), (*c*) and (*d*) are on one board, which stretches right and left to the edges of the frame; (*a*) and (*e*) are fixed in front of this board at each end.

Excellent state, except for an obvious crack in the predella. The frame has mostly been regilt, and cut about somewhat.

Not earlier than 1490, because the signature includes Crivelli's title of 'miles.' The arms on the picture are those of the Ottoni, the ruling family at Matelica, whence this picture comes.[2]

It was usual in Italian Quattrocento painting for S. Sebastian to be represented naked (as indeed he is in the predella); clothed S. Sebastians do, however, occur not infrequently, and seem in particular to be in a Vivarinesque tradition.[3] In the predella, the comparatively large-scale figure of S. Catherine on the left corresponds with the much smaller figure of S. George on the right. The predella scenes of S. Jerome, the Nativity and S. George may be compared with the designs in Jacopo Bellini's sketchbooks in London and Paris; there may well be a loose connection—thus, Jacopo Bellini also gives his S. Jeromes dragons and other animals as well as a lion. The *Nativity* in No. 724 has some compositional similarity with a small picture at Strasbourg, often ascribed to Crivelli, but used by Drey as the name-piece for his 'Master of the Strasbourg Adoration.'[4]

PROVENANCE: By 1795/6 in San Francesco, Matelica;[5] presumably it had been painted for an Ottoni chapel there. In 1862 it was somewhat forcibly[6] removed from the Church by Conte Luigi de Sanctis, from whom purchased, 1862.

REPRODUCTION: *Illustrations, Italian Schools*, 1937, p. 115. *Plates, Earlier Italian Schools*, 1953, Vol. I, pp. 107–112.

REFERENCES: (1) Letter from B. J. Rendle, of the Forest Products Research Laboratory, in the Gallery archives. (2) Cf. Litta, *Famiglie Celebri d'Italia*, for the Ottoni family. (3) E.g. in an Antonio Vivarini of 1464 in the Vatican (Testi, *Storia della Pittura Veneziana*, II, 1915, p. 396). (4) F. Drey, *Carlo Crivelli*, 1927, Plate XCIII. (5) The earliest mention seems to be by Lanzi, *Storia Pittorica della Italia*, Vol. II, Part I, 1795/6, p. 15; also mentioned by A. Ricci, *Memorie*, 1834, i, p. 214. (6) See *Le Gallerie Nazionali Italiane*, II, 1896, pp. 325/6, and *Il Raffaello*, Urbino, 1879, pp. 38/9.

739 ALTARPIECE: THE ANNUNCIATION, WITH S. EMIDIUS

A sumptuous scene. The Virgin kneels at a prie-dieu in her bedroom; the Holy Ghost descends towards her head along a ray, which has its origin with God in the heavens, and pierces the wall of the building. In the street outside, S. Gabriel with a lily kneels, accompanied by S. Emidius (Emygdius) holding a model of the town of Ascoli, whose Patron he is. At the bottom is the inscription,.LIBERTAS. / ECCLESIASTICA, and the arms (from left to right) of Prospero Caffarelli (Bishop of Ascoli), Pope Innocent VIII, and the City of Ascoli. Signed: OPVS.CARO / LI.CRIVELLI. / VENETI, and dated,.1486.

Panel transferred to canvas, painted surface, $81\frac{1}{2} \times 57\frac{3}{4}$ ($2 \cdot 07 \times 1 \cdot 465$).

The condition is remarkably good for a transferred picture. What damage there is is particularly apparent in certain important parts; the face of S. Emidius, S. Gabriel's left hand and (to a less extent) the Virgin's face. Various parts of the picture have suffered a slight loss of crispness, but the condition in general is very good.

In 1482, Pope Sixtus IV granted the citizens of Ascoli Piceno certain rights of self-government under the general control of the Church. News of this privilege reached the town on 25 March, the Feast of the Annunciation;[1] a procession went each year thereafter on that date, to celebrate the event, to the Church of the Santissima Annunziata (PP. Minori Osservanti).[2] An *Annunciation*, signed and dated by Pietro Alamanno, 1484, with the commemorative words *Libertas Ecclesiastica*, is now in the Gallery of the town.[3] No. 739 is a second commemorative picture of the same event; it hung in the Church to which the procession used to make its way. Sixtus IV was succeeded as Pope by Innocent VIII in 1484; hence it is that the arms of the latter appear on the picture. Prospero Caffarelli was Bishop of Ascoli from 1464 to 1500. The presence of S. Emidius in No. 739 is explained by the circumstances; it is rather rare for extraneous saints to be involved in an *Annunciation*, but some other examples (not altogether similar) do occur.[4] The motive of a ray piercing the wall of a building is perhaps unique; thus, in an *Annunciation* by

Jacopo Bellini rather similarly arranged, the architecture has been constructed to avoid this.[5]

Some parts of the architectural setting in No. 739 are elaborated from Crivelli's *Annunciation* of 1482 at Frankfort;[6] in particular, the bush growing in a majolica jar at the grated window. The details of No. 739, although impossibly rich, are not merely invented; thus, carpets hanging from parapets occur also in Antonello's *S. Sebastian* at Dresden,[7] and in Mantegna's *Arrow missing S. Christopher* at Padua.[8] The bar in front of the first floor windows is not an invention of Crivelli's: compare, for instance, one of the *Miracles of S. Bernardino* at Perugia.[9] Perhaps it was used for supporting a sun-blind; cf. Niccolò di Buonaccorso, No. 1109 of this Gallery.

PROVENANCE: Recorded *ca.* 1724 in the SS. Annunziata, Ascoli; the altar over which it had hung was at that time dedicated to the Immaculate Conception, and the picture had been transferred to the Capella domestica.[10] Orsini (1790) mentions it in the Friary;[11] it was removed to the Brera, Milan, in 1811.[12] Exchanged with Count Auguste-Louis de Sivry, 1820.[13] Edward Solly Sale, London, 8 May, 1847 (lot 35), bought by Graves. In the collection of the Rt. Hon. H. Labouchere (later Lord Taunton); exhibited at the British Institution, 1847 (No. 56); presented by Lord Taunton, 1864.

REPRODUCTIONS: *Illustrations, Italian Schools,* 1937, p. 116. *Plates, Earlier Italian Schools,* 1953, Vol. I, p. 113. A pamphlet reproducing many details of this picture was issued by the National Gallery in 1947.

REFERENCES: (1) The confirmatory Bull was sent on 19 July. The citizens of Ascoli voluntarily surrendered this privilege in 1502. See Francesco Antonio Marcucci, *Saggio delle Cose Ascolane,* 1766, pp. 350 and 359. (2) Tullio Lazzari, *Ascoli in Prospettiva,* 1724 (?), pp. 87/8. G. Fabiani, *Ascoli nel Quattrocento,* Vol. I, 1950, p. 124, records the proposal to have an annual procession from the time of the first anniversary. (3) Drey, *Carlo Crivelli,* 1927, Plate LXXXIV. An inscription at the bottom makes it clear that this is a civic picture; there are, in fact, various records of its hanging in the Chapel of the Town Hall. The inscription is given by Orsini, *Descrizione,* etc., *della Città di Ascoli,* 1790, pp. 60/1. Orsini wrongly ascribes the picture to Crivelli; the signature of Alamanno is indeed not in an obvious place. (4) Compare, for instance, Serra, *L'Arte nelle Marche,* 1934, Fig. 417; a Fra Angelico in S. Marco at Florence (Klassiker der Kunst *Angelico,* 1924, Plate 123); a Bonfigli at Perugia (Van Marle, *Development of the Italian Schools of Painting,* Vol. XIV, reproduced opposite p. 120). (5) British Museum Sketchbook; Goloubew, *Les Dessins de Jacopo Bellini,* I, 1912, Plate XCIV. (6) Drey, *op. cit.,* Plate LI. (7) Reproduced by Drey, *op .cit.,* p. 77. (8) Venturi, *Storia dell'Arte Italiana,* Vol. VII, Part III, Fig. 77. (9) Venturi, *Storia dell'Arte Italiana,* Vol. VII, Part II, Fig. 360. (10) Lazzari, *loc. cit.,* in note 2. The date of the book appears to be 1724, but in the National Gallery copy has been altered in manuscript to 1734. G. Fabiani, *Ascoli nel Quattrocento,* Vol. II, 1951, p. 145, cites from a will of 1571 that Pietro Falconieri wished to be buried 'ante altare Annuntiate picte manu quondam Caroli Crivelli Veneti'; it is implied that the church is the SS. Annunziata, and it seems clear that No. 739 is referred to. (11) Orsini, *op. cit.,* p. 183. (12) Cantalamessa Carboni, *Memorie,* etc., 1830, pp. 116/7; A. Ricci, *Memorie,* 1834, i, p. 213; Testi, *Storia della Pittura Veneziana,* II, 1915, pp. 559/60, 644, 679. (13) See Corrado Ricci, *La Pinacoteca di Brera,* 1907, pp. 92, 128, 134/5, 137; Testi, as above. Testi ties himself in knots about the provenance. He postulates another Crivelli of the same subject, also removed to the Brera from the same church at Ascoli (!), on the ground that the picture ceded to Sivry was in bad condition, and cannot therefore be the same as No. 739. The fact that No. 739 had to be transferred (in 1881) is sufficient justification for admitting that it may have seemed in bad condition in 1820. It is true that there is a break in the provenance between 1820 and 1847; but descriptions of the Ascoli picture before 1820 make its identity with No. 739 sure.

788 'THE DEMIDOFF ALTARPIECE'

Thirteen panels in three tiers; the figures in the middle tier are at half length, the others at full length.

LOWEST TIER (from left to right):

S. John the Baptist. He holds a scroll inscribed, ECCE.AGNVS. DEI.QVI / MO.

Poplar,[1] arched top, painted surface, $54\frac{1}{2} \times 15\frac{3}{4}$ (1·385 × 0·40).

S. Peter. A Crucifix surmounts his staff; on his cope are identifiable SS. Paul, Andrew and Bartholomew. This figure more than any of the others is distinguished by raised ornament, partly in gesso, partly (as the keys) in wood.

Lime,[1] arched top, painted surface, $54\frac{3}{4} \times 16$ (1·39 × 0·405).

The Virgin and Child. Signed: OPVS.KAROLI.CRIVELLI. VENETI.1476.

Lime,[1] arched top, painted surface, $58\frac{1}{2} \times 25$ (1·485 × 0·635). Painted up to the edge at the bottom; the lowest band of paint is quite plain, and although a cut along the bottom is possible, it seems unlikely that this band of plain paint was ever much larger than now.

S. Catherine of Alexandria.

Poplar,[1] arched top, painted surface, $54 \times 15\frac{3}{4}$ (1·375 × 0·40). Cut about $\frac{1}{2}$ in. (1 cm.) at the bottom.

S. Dominic.

Poplar,[1] arched top, painted surface, $54\frac{1}{4} \times 15\frac{3}{4}$ (1·375 × 0·40). Cut about $\frac{1}{4}$ in. ($\frac{1}{2}$ cm.) at the top.

MIDDLE TIER (from left to right):

S. Francis.

Poplar,[1] arched top, painted surface, $24 \times 15\frac{1}{2}$ (0·61 × 0·395). Painted up to the edge at the bottom and possibly cut there.

S. Andrew.

Poplar,[1] arched top, painted surface, $24 \times 15\frac{3}{4}$ (0·61 × 0·40). Painted up to the edge at the bottom and possibly cut there.

S. Stephen.

Poplar,[1] arched top, painted surface, $24 \times 15\frac{3}{4}$ (0·61 × 0·40). Painted up to the edge at the bottom and possibly cut there.

S. Thomas Aquinas. A monk or friar is conversing with another figure inside the church he holds.

Poplar,[1] arched top, painted surface, $23\frac{3}{4} \times 15\frac{1}{2}$ ($0\cdot605 \times 0\cdot395$). Painted up to the edge at the bottom and possibly cut there.

TOPMOST TIER (from left to right; at present exhibited separately and in a different order):

S. Jerome.

Poplar,[1] arched top, painted surface, $35\frac{3}{4} \times 10\frac{1}{4}$ ($0\cdot91 \times 0\cdot26$). Cut about $\frac{1}{2}$ in. ($1\frac{1}{2}$ cm.) at the bottom.

S. Michael. A man and a woman in his scales.

Poplar,[1] arched top, painted surface, $35\frac{1}{2} \times 10\frac{1}{2}$ ($0\cdot905 \times 0\cdot265$). Cut about $\frac{3}{4}$ in. (2 cm.) at the top.

S. Lucy.

Lime,[1] arched top, painted surface, $35\frac{3}{4} \times 10\frac{1}{2}$ ($0\cdot91 \times 0\cdot265$). Cut about $\frac{1}{2}$ in. ($1\frac{1}{2}$ cm.) at the bottom. Her hair and veil once extended somewhat, left and right; incised lines mark the principal outlines, and the gold has been left unpatterned in these areas.

S. Peter Martyr.

Poplar,[1] arched top, painted surface, $35\frac{1}{2} \times 10\frac{1}{2}$ ($0\cdot905 \times 0\cdot265$). Cut about $\frac{1}{2}$ in. ($1\frac{1}{2}$ cm.) at the bottom.

The measurements given above are all taken, so far as the bottom is concerned, from the edge of the paint; for the sides and top, from the incised line marking the limit of the goldwork and paint. The gold, however, continues in places a little beyond this line, but unpatterned; the paint also continues here and there a little, sometimes in a finished condition. The line in the gold marking the arched top is scalloped in the lowest tier, plain in the others. The measurements of the cuts noted above are those of the paint or gold, not of the panels;[2] there is no evidence to settle if any cuts at the bottoms of the four middle pictures are slight or not.

The condition is in general excellent. The gold backgrounds of the middle tier are slightly less well preserved than those of the others.

The thirteen panels making up the Demidoff altarpiece have been the subject of diverse views. It is often stated that they are parts of at least two different altarpieces, not necessarily of the same date but probably from the same church;[3] what evidence there is is against this, although the arrangement of the panels in their frame is probably wrong.

Tullio Lazzari (1724?)[4] records a polyptych on the high altar of S. Domenico, Ascoli Piceno. He notes all the figures except the Baptist in the lower tier of No. 788, in sufficient detail to make certain the identity with this part at least; but it is not certain or even probable that the polyptych in S. Domenico consisted of only this one row of figures.

Lazzari's mention is the authentic record of the altarpiece in its (presumably) original form and position; the present confusion about it seems to some extent due to A. Ricci (1834).[5] Ricci, partly in quotation

of a lost MS. by F. Bartoli of the end of the eighteenth century, refers
(1) to a *Virgin and Child with SS. Peter, Paul, Dominic and Catherine*, of
1476, once in S. Domenico, Ascoli; (2) to a *Virgin and Child*, also of
1476, also once in the church; (3) to an engraving of the middle panel of
No. 788. Ricci seems to think that these are three different pictures,
whence perhaps comes the view commonly held that No. 788 is a composite affair; but Ricci is untrustworthy, and his three pictures are
probably no more than one.

It is indeed uncertain if there was any polyptych by Crivelli in S.
Domenico at Ascoli except the high altarpiece described by Lazzari.[6]
And it would have been difficult, especially if the panels did come from
various churches, to assemble works by Crivelli that would go so well
together as the parts of No. 788. The twelve saints are all different, as
they must be in the main compartments of a single altarpiece. The style
of the haloes and of the stamped damask pattern is consistent throughout. And all the panels (in spite of what is sometimes said about the top
row[7]) are recognizably in an early Crivellesque manner; this is true even
of the *S. Peter Martyr*, where the execution appears to be perhaps from
the studio.

It is difficult to believe that anyone making one altarpiece from several
would have got all these points right; but while it seems on the whole
likely that the 13 parts of No. 788 are from a single original, it is not
certain that the original has been preserved complete, and it is very
improbable that the XIX Century arrangement is correct.

An altarpiece of three principal tiers is in itself unusual. It is hardly
credible that a construction elaborate enough to be so arranged should
have no predella. The Baptist may well have occupied the place now
given to S. Peter;[8] then his gesture would more properly indicate the
Child. S. Dominic and S. Catherine are also perhaps inverted; S.
Dominic in a Dominican altarpiece might most naturally be next to the
Virgin and Child, at Whom, indeed, his glance seems to be directed.
The absence of a central picture for the middle tier is most peculiar; all
the figures of this tier may have been cut down. The top panels seem
clearly inadequate, and their perspective is unlikely at such a height.

VARIANTS: The Virgin is partially repeated in a picture at Budapest.[9] Some
of the other figures, as S. Peter and S. Catherine, are stock types of Crivelli,
and recur with modifications elsewhere.

PROVENANCE: As explained above, part of the Demidoff altarpiece, and very
possibly the whole (in a different arrangement?), was the high altarpiece in San
Domenico, Ascoli Piceno; seen there ca. 1724 by Lazzari, but not mentioned in
subsequent guides, and perhaps removed from the church when the whole was
reconstructed in 1766 (or 1776?) by L. Giosafatti.[10] The next certain thing
known is that all the present assemblage was in the collection at Rome of Cardinal Francesco Saverio Zelada (died 1801), part at least by 1795/6;[11] it is possible that Cardinal Zelada acquired them through Grossi,[12] who appears to have
been a dealer in Rome. They passed later into the Rinuccini Collection, Florence;[13] Catalogo, 1845, Quinta Stanza, pp. 14/5;[14] Sale, after the death of the
last Rinuccini, Marchese Pietro Francesco, at Palazzo Rinuccini, 1 sqq. May,
1852 (lots 462–470).[15] They were bought by Prince Anatole Demidoff, who had
them put together as the principal altarpiece of the Catholic Chapel of his Villa

of San Donato, near Florence.[16] Still in the Demidoff Collection in 1866.[17] Purchased from G. H. Phillips, Paris, 1868.

REPRODUCTIONS: *Illustrations, Italian Schools*, 1937, p. 117. *Plates, Earlier Italian Schools*, 1953, Vol. I, pp. 114–122.

REFERENCES: (1) Letter from B. J. Rendle, of the Forest Products Research Laboratory, in the Gallery archives. (2) Some of the existing reproductions are unclear in effect. (3) See what is said by Rushforth, *Carlo Crivelli*, 1900, p. 90; Drey, *Carlo Crivelli*, 1927, p. 62; Berenson, *Venetian Painting in America*, 1916, p. 20. (4) Lazzari, *Ascoli in Prospettiva*, p. 76. The date appears to be 1724, but in the National Gallery copy has been altered in manuscript to 1734. The text is quoted by L. Testi, *Storia della Pittura Veneziana*, II, 1915, pp. 647/5; Testi's comments are careful, but pedantic. (5) Amico Ricci, *Memorie ...della Marca d'Ancona*, 1834, i, pp. 211/2. (6) It is true that Lazzari (p. 74, Testi, p. 674) mentions another (?); he does not describe its subject, but his text suggests that it was not of the first quality. This may have been a second polyptych by Crivelli. But, if it remained in the church after the reconstruction by L. Giosafatti in 1766 (or 1776?), it might (it seems) be identical with an altarpiece described in the sacristy by Orsini (*Descrizione...della città di Ascoli*, 1790, pp. 44/5). Orsini's picture represented *la Madonna col Bambino, che sposa S. Catarina, e ci si vede dipinto S. Domenico, S. Giacomo Minore, e S. Stefano. Nel timpano ci sono tre mezze figure, che rappresentano la Pietà, con due Santi Domenicani*; attributed to, but obviously not signed by, Crivelli. Orsini's picture seems to be identical with a picture still in the church in 1853 (Carducci, *Monumenti di Ascoli*, p. 214; perhaps an early Cola), but now in the Gallery at Ascoli; reproduced by L. Serra, *L'Arte nelle Marche*, 1934, Fig. 398. (7) E.g. by Berenson, *Venetian Painting in America*, 1916, p. 20. In his Lists of 1957, Berenson says that all the figures except the Virgin and Child are later than 1476. (8) Cf. Crivelli's polyptych in the Cathedral of Ascoli (Drey, *Carlo Crivelli*, 1927, Plate XXVIII). The analogy seems quite good, but cannot be pressed unless it were proved that the Ascoli polyptych can never have been rearranged. (9) Drey, *Carlo Crivelli*, 1927, Plate XLIV. (10) B. Orsini, *Descrizione delle Pitture...della insigne Città di Ascoli*, 1790, p. 43, says that the reconstruction was in 1776. Giuseppe Ignazio Ciannavei, *Compendio di Memorie Istoriche spettanti alle Chiese Parrocchiali della Città di Ascoli nel Piceno*, etc., 1797, p. 249, says that it was in 1766. G. Fabiani, *Ascoli nel Quattrocento*, Vol. II, 1951, p. 85, says 1764/6. (11) L. Lanzi, *Storia Pittorica della Italia*, Vol. II, Part I, 1795/6, pp. 15/6, with wrong date (corrected in subsequent editions). The identity of the picture is made certain by the engraving in D'Agincourt, *Storia dell'Arte, Tavole*, 1829, Plate CXXXVIII. Eventually, even if not to begin with, Cardinal Zelada had all the thirteen panels; see the explicit statement in the Rinuccini Sale Catalogue, 1852 (Carlo Pini and Carlo Milanesi, *Quelques Tableaux de la Galerie Rinuccini*, p. 19). (12) Cf. A. Ricci, *op. cit.*, I, p. 211. (13) In the will of Cardinal Francesco Saverio Zelada, which was opened on 19 December, 1801, it is stated that he had previously given much property, including pictures, to Marchese Alessandro Rinuccini (1745–1805); the Cardinal confirmed this gift in his will. It is possible that the Demidoff altarpiece was included in this gift. It is recorded that the brother of Alessandro Rinuccini, Cardinal Giovanni (1743–1801), was a friend of Cardinal Zelada's, with whom he shared an interest in works of art; see G. Aiazzi, *Ricordi Storici di Filippo di Cino Rinuccini*, 1840, pp. 211 ff. The passage in Cardinal Zelada's will is from Rome, Archivio di Stato, Notari del Tribunale dell'A.C., Vol. 5509, Notaro Apollonio Passari, f. 1369r; copy in Rome, Archivio Storico Capitolino, Testamenti A. Passari, 1801/3, No. 149. (14) P. 14: No. 8, S. Girolamo e S. Pier martire; No. 9, Madonna' in trono col Bambino; No. 10, San Michele e S. Lucia; No. 17, S. Tommaso e S. Stefano; No. 19, S. Caterina delle Ruote; No. 20, S. Pietro; No. 21, S. Domenico; No. 22, S. Gio. Battista. P. 15: No. 23, S. Andrea e S. Francesco. (15) All the thirteen panels are described in the Rinuccini Sale Catalogue. Crowe and Cavalcaselle subsequently saw the altarpiece in the Villa Demidoff, and gave a hurried and inaccurate description of it; Testi, *op. cit.*, p. 674, wrongly deduces from their account that the 13 panels of No. 788 were not together then. (**16**) Cesare da Prato, *Firenze ai Demidoff*, 1886, p. 425. Prince Demidoff's acquisition seems to have been made only in 1854; see *Deutsches Kunstblatt*, 30 March, 1854, p. 116. (**17**) Boxall's report, 25 May, 1866, in the Gallery archives.

807 ALTARPIECE: THE VIRGIN AND CHILD WITH
        SS. FRANCIS AND SEBASTIAN

The donatrix kneels by S. Francis. An inscription runs along the bottom: ALMAE CONSOLATIONIS MATRI. MARIAE: PRIO-RES.POSTEROSQ' MISERATA SVOS: ORADEA.IOAMNIS: AERE PROPRIO / NON MODICO DICAVIT. Signed: OPVS. CAROLI.CRIVELLI.VENETI.MILES.1491.

Poplar,[1] painted surface, $69 \times 59\frac{1}{2}$ ($1 \cdot 75 \times 1 \cdot 51$). Very slightly cut at each side. The vertical measurements are taken from what seem intended as the edges of the paint (the height of the panel is $70\frac{3}{4}$ in., $1 \cdot 795$ m.).
Excellent state except for splits in the constituent panels.

The donatrix is Oradea, widow of Giovanni Becchetti, who in compliance with the desire expressed in her husband's will founded in 1490 an altar dedicated to S. Maria della Consolazione in S. Francesco at Fabriano.[2]

PROVENANCE: As noted above, from a chapel dedicated to S. Maria della Consolazione in S. Francesco at Fabriano. Recorded (without details) as still there by Venanzo Benigni (1677–1747).[3] Purchased in 1841, in Rome,[4] by Richard, 2nd Marquess of Westminster; exhibited at the British Institution, 1848 (No. 109). Bequeathed by him to his wife in 1869. Presented by Elizabeth Mary, widow of the 2nd Marquess of Westminster, 1870.

REPRODUCTION: *Illustrations, Italian Schools*, 1937, p. 118. *Plates, Earlier Italian Schools*, 1953, Vol. I, p. 123.

REFERENCES: (**1**) Letter from B. J. Rendle, of the Forest Products Research Laboratory, in the Gallery archives. (**2**) These facts were kindly pointed out to the compiler by Bruno Molajoli, who records the provenance in his *Guida Artistica di Fabriano*, 1936, p. 25. They are derived from an article by Romualdo Sassi, *Arte e Storia fra le rovine d'un antico tempio francescano*, in the *Rassegna Marchigiana*, May/June, 1927, p. 348. Sassi gives a reference from the local archives to indulgences attached to the altar in 1490, which (it cannot be doubted) give sufficient details for certainty of identification; in view of this, a clearly wrong provenance from the Dominicans at Fermo, derived from A. Ricci, *Memorie*, 1834, i, p. 214, need not be discussed. (**3**) Venanzo Benigni, *Compendioso Ragguaglio delle Cose più notabili di Fabriano*, 1924, p. 99. The date of the removal of the picture is not known; for some facts about the later history of the church, which no longer exists, see Oreste Marcoaldi, *Guida e Statistica ...di Fabriano*, 1873, pp. 160/1, and Molajoli, *op. cit.*, p. 40. (**4**) N.G. Catalogue, 1870; and letter from Lady Westminster, 26 January, 1872, in the Gallery archives.

906 THE IMMACULATE CONCEPTION

The Virgin is standing with joined hands. Left and right, a glass vase with a lily, and a majolica jug with roses; the Sun and the Moon are incised in the gold background by her head. Two angels hold over her a crown, and a scroll inscribed: VT.INMENTE. DEI.ABINITIO. CONCEPTA.FVI.ITA.ET.FACTA.SVM. At the top, God the Father in a glory of cherubim, and the Dove. Signed on a *cartellino:* KAROLI . CHRIVELLI . / VENETI . MILITIS . PINSIT. / 1492 (the left hand side of this inscription is much restored).

Wood, painted surface, $76\frac{1}{2} \times 36\frac{3}{4}$ (1·945 × 0·935). The measurements are taken from the edges of the paint, which though ragged for Crivelli may well be the original.

Good condition on the whole. Fairly numerous and large local damages, due especially to cracks, are to be found chiefly on the gold background. The most important part seriously affected is the face of the angel to the right, which is new; but the picture preserves fairly well Crivelli's intention.

Perhaps the earliest dated picture of *The Immaculate Conception.*[1] In Ecclesiasticus xxiv, 14 (9 in the English version), is the text *Ab initio et ante saecula creata sum*; see also Proverbs viii, 23/4.

PROVENANCE: Clearly identical with a picture sold a few years before 1834 from S. Francesco, Pergola.[2] Alexander Barker Collection, London, by 1871;[3] Sale, 6 June, 1874 (lot 64), purchased for the National Gallery.

REPRODUCTION: *Illustrations, Italian Schools*, 1937, p. 118. *Plates, Earlier Italian Schools*, 1953, Vol. I, p. 124.

REFERENCES: (1) For the *Immaculate Conception*, cf. Montgomery Carmichael, *Francia's Masterpiece*, 1909; R. Ligtenberg in the *Mededeelingen van het Nederlandsch Historisch Instituut te Rome*, 1931, pp. 65 ff.; and Karl Künstle, *Ikonographie der christlichen Kunst*, Vol. I, 1928, pp. 646 ff. See also the entry for Venetian School, No. 4250. (2) Amico Ricci, *Memorie*, 1834, i, pp. 215 and 228; his note on the subject of the picture and its signature (though he commits some verbal errors) makes the identification certain. The National Gallery Catalogues, however, have followed the Barker Sale Catalogue in saying that the picture is from 'the Malatesta chapel in the Church of San Francesco at Rimini.' It would be curious to discover the origin of this statement; for the whole of San Francesco is known as the *Tempio Malatestiano*. In any case, no Crivelli seems recorded ever to have been at Rimini. There is, however, in San Francesco a Chapel of the Conception, the picture being a copy of a Maratta by the Padre Giuseppe Alemanni, 1675–1739; the absurd sequence P. Alemanni —Pietro Alamanno—Carlo Crivelli suggests itself. It is true that some earlier picture of the *Immaculate Conception* was in existence in 1574/8. See Corrado Ricci, *Il Tempio Malatestiano*, p. 236 and note 156 on pp. 248/9; fig. 280. (3) Crowe and Cavalcaselle, *Painting in North Italy*, I, 1871, p. 95.

907　(A) S. CATHERINE OF ALEXANDRIA

Lime,[1] painted surface, $14\frac{7}{8} \times 7\frac{1}{2}$ (0·38 × 0·19).

(B) S. MARY MAGDALENE

Lime,[1] painted surface, $14\frac{3}{4} \times 7\frac{1}{4}$ (0·375 × 0·185).

Both panels, especially the S. Catherine, in very good condition.

Presumably from the pilasters of a frame, or a predella. Two male figures, once in the same collection (Barker) as No. 907,[2] are identical with the *SS. Anthony of Padua and Dominic* in the Lanz Collection, Amsterdam.[3] These Lanz pictures are not connected with No. 907; it is claimed[4] that they are from the same series as *SS. Bonaventure* (called Jerome) *and Bernard* at Berlin,[5] which seems very likely, though there is some doubt about the sizes.

No. 907 is often classed as the work of Crivelli himself,[6] but may be only of studio execution. It is here given the benefit of the doubt, although the predella of No. 724 above, for instance, must be admitted to be greatly superior in quality. Drey[7] ascribes No. 907 to a pupil he calls the *Master of the Strasbourg Adoration*. The *S. Mary Magdalene* is partly similar to a large figure of the same subject.[8]

PROVENANCE: In the Alexander Barker Collection, London, by 1865;[9] exhibited at the British Institution, 1858 (Nos. 22, 24); at Leeds, 1868 (Nos. 13, 15).[10] Purchased at the Barker Sale, 6 June, 1874 (lot 63).

REPRODUCTIONS: *Illustrations, Italian Schools*, 1937, p. 119. *Plates, Earlier Italian Schools*, 1953, Vol. I, p. 125.

REFERENCES: (1) Letter from B. J. Rendle, of the Forest Products Research Laboratory, in the Gallery archives. (2) Crowe and Cavalcaselle, *Painting in North Italy*, I, 1871, p. 95, say that they are from the same series. (3) Drey, *Carlo Crivelli*, 1927, p. 129, and Plate XXVII (provenance confirmed by A. van Schendel, 18 January, 1949). (4) Catalogue of the Italian Exhibition at Amsterdam, 1934, No. 99. (5) Drey, *op. cit.*, Plate XXVI. (6) E.g. by Berenson, 1957 Lists. (7) Drey, *op. cit.*, p. 107. (8) Drey, *op. cit.*, Plate LV. (9) Waagen, *Treasures*, 1854, ii, p. 127. (10) As *SS. Catherine* and *Lucy*; but the labels are on the backs.

Ascribed to CARLO CRIVELLI

3923   SS. PETER AND PAUL (PANEL FROM AN ALTARPIECE)

Poplar,[1] painted surface, $36\frac{3}{4} \times 18\frac{1}{2}$ ($0 \cdot 93 \times 0 \cdot 47$). Cut at the top, the incised line marking the edges of the gold being visible only at the sides; the condition at the bottom is too ragged and damaged for a definite opinion, but the cut if any is not much.

The condition in general is not bad; although there are a good many washes and retouches, the figures on the whole are reliable.

Obviously one panel from a polyptych, presumably from the left side of the main tier. According to the evidence given in note 4, it was once surmounted by a semi-circular lunette.

The style of No. 3923 seems to the compiler to be inferior to that of Crivelli's authentic works. Drey[2] gives it to a pupil he calls the Master of the Brera Predelle. Many critics, and recently Longhi and Zeri, call it Crivelli.[3] The date may be from the 1470's.

PROVENANCE: Probably from Porto S. Giorgio (Porto di Fermo).[4] First surely recorded in the collection of F. R. Leyland, of Liverpool and London; exhibited at the R.A., 1882 (No. 197); Leyland Sale, 28 May, 1892 (lot 100), bought by Frickenhaus (for Mond). Mond Bequest, 1924.

REPRODUCTION: *Illustrations, Italian Schools*, 1937, p. 119. *Plates, Earlier Italian Schools*, 1953, Vol. I, p. 126.

REFERENCES: (1) Letter from B. J. Rendle, of the Forest Products Research Laboratory, in the Gallery archives. (2) F. Drey, *Carlo Crivelli*, 1927, p. 105. (3) R. Longhi, *Viatico per Cinque Secoli di Pittura Veneziana*, 1946, p. 57; Federico Zeri in *The Burlington Magazine*, Vol. XCII (1950), pp. 197 f. The attribution is accepted also by Pallucchini in *Arte Veneta*, 1951, p. 195, and by Berenson in his 1957 Lists. (4) The provenance for No. 3923 is complicated, and the evidence for it unsatisfactory, so it seems best to discuss the whole matter, not in the text of the entry, but here in a note. Amico Ricci, *Memorie*, 1834, I, pp. 209 and 227, describes Crivelli's works in the Church of S. Giorgio at Porto di Fermo or Porto S. Giorgio; this is the only record, and Ricci is not altogether reliable. He says that there was in the Church an altarpiece acceptable as by Crivelli; in the centre, the Virgin and Child, the Virgin seated on a marble throne, with ornaments of intertwined fruits, flowers and leaves; at the sides, SS. Peter and Paul, and S. George on horseback; the Entombment above. Ricci further notes two other pictures in the same Church, each with saints at full length (mostly bishops), arranged in two tiers, and perhaps part of the picture with the Virgin and Child, etc. Further, perhaps also fragments of the same, several half-length saints in the Salvatori Collection in the town. It cannot be claimed that these descriptions are as clear as possible; but Ricci certainly did not deny that the altarpiece may even in his time have been partly broken up; there may have been enough pictures to come from more than one altarpiece; and, if Ricci's description of the main part is complete, the picture with S. George must have been large enough to balance the two figures of S. Peter and S. Paul. In any case, nothing more is known of the pictures at Porto di Fermo, and the next record to be mentioned is a description in *The Athenaeum*, 1851, p. 723 (among pictures in Lord Ward's, later the Dudley Collection, exhibited at the Egyptian Hall): "three pictures, in compartments of the same frame. In the central one is 'The Virgin and Child' surrounded by Saints:—in the side compartments are, St. George conquering the Dragon,—Saints Peter and Paul, with their emblems,—St. Catherine,—and many other like goodly personages." Next, Waagen, *Treasures*, II, 1854, p. 235, noted this picture (for which he gives no provenance): 'The Virgin and Child. On the right wing, in two rows, St. Peter and St. Paul, St. Catherine and St. Jerome; on the left, St. George, St. Anthony the Hermit, St. Lucy and another Saint.' It will be indicated presently that 'and another Saint' may be an invention of Waagen's. Invention or not, Waagen's description corresponds very closely with the description of the Ward-Dudley picture by Crowe and Cavalcaselle, *Painting in North Italy*, I, 1871, p. 91, or ed. Borenius, I, 1912, p. 90. Crowe and Cavalcaselle add to Waagen that S. George was on horseback, and that the saints above, 'Sts. Catherine, Jerom, Lucy, and another,' were in lunettes; they also add that the Dudley picture had been long exhibited at the Egyptian Hall, and that it came from 'the Church del Porto at Fermo.' As for Ricci's *Entombment*, nothing in connection with the main parts of the altarpiece is said by Waagen or by Crowe and Cavalcaselle. Nevertheless, Ricci's picture may be identical with a representation of this subject that certainly was in the Dudley Collection, possibly not mentioned by Waagen, but recorded by Crowe and Cavalcaselle, *op. cit.*, I, 1871, p. 91. The main Dudley picture appeared in an Anon. (Dudley) Sale, 7 April, 1876 (lot 135), bought by Martin Colnaghi. The entry in the sale catalogue is as follows: 'An altarpiece with the Madonna and Child enthroned in the centre, SS. Peter and Paul on the right side, and St. George and the Dragon on the left, half-length figures of four saints above.' In the *Chronique des Arts*, 1876, p. 158, the description is of a Virgin and Child, the Child holding an apple; 'à leurs côtés, dans des niches, saint Pierre et saint Paul, saint Georges tuant le Dragon," and above, SS. Ottilia, Anthony, Jerome and Catherine of Alexandria. This description is, at least in part, independent of the description in the sale catalogue; the two would seem to prove that Waagen, and Crowe and Cavalcaselle, were wrong in bringing S. Anthony down on to the main tier and mentioning an extra, unnamed saint in the upper tier. This prolonged account of not very satisfactory evidence leads us to consider what the pictures actually may be. The *Virgin and Child* from the Dudley Collection, and presumably from Porto di Fermo, may be identical with a picture till recently in the Cook Collection, and now at Washington. In the large Cook Catalogue, Vol. I, 1913, No. 131, this picture is stated to have been formerly in the collection of the Earl of Dudley (sold privately); this may be considered equivalent to a provenance from the Anon. (Dudley) Sale of 1876. Since the Cook picture contains fruits and leaves, but no flowers, it is not proved to be identical with Ricci's picture. John Walker (letter of 5 January, 1951) kindly gave the information that there is no Christie stencil mark on the back. The *SS. Peter and Paul* is supposed to be No. 3923; the *S. George* is supposed to be the picture in the Gardner Museum at Boston (Catalogue by Philip Hendy, 1931, pp. 113 ff.). There seems to be no proof of this; arguments in favour are that No. 3923 and the Gardner picture were from 1882 both in the Leyland Collection, that the sizes correspond very well, and so do the halo-patterns. Yet No. 3923 would form a somewhat curious pendant to the Gardner *S. George;* the style and quality of the Gardner picture, which seem to correspond quite well with those of the Cook picture, seem not to correspond with those of No. 3923; and the flooring of the Cook *Virgin and Child* and of No. 3923 are somewhat discordant (the Gardner *S. George*, being in a landscape, is not comparable in this respect). Federico Zeri in *The Burlington Magazine*, Vol. XCII (1950), pp. 197 f., discusses this problem and adds a lunette representing *SS. Catherine and* (apparently) *Jerome*; this is now at Kansas City (Kress Collection; Catalogue, 1952, No. 14). Another lunette, at Cracow, was published by Jan Bialostocki in *The Burlington Magazine*, 1956, p. 370. These two lunettes seem convincingly the Dudley ones. Zeri further follows Longhi in claiming the identity of Ricci's *Pietà* with the *Pietà* at Detroit (ex-Dudley). It may be said, in the present state of knowledge, that the pictures mentioned are quite likely all to have come from Porto di Fermo; but this would not prove that they are all by Crivelli's own hand.

Benedetto DIANA
active 1482, died 1525

His surname was really *Rusconi*, but he used *Diana* in the signatures of his pictures. He seems to have been trained in the tradition of Gentile Bellini.

2725 SALVATOR MUNDI

Signed, *Benedictus.diana.pinxit* (retouched).

Wood, painted surface, $30 \times 23\frac{1}{4}$ (0·76 × 0·59); painted up to the edges all round.

The flesh parts are much worn and repaired. Most of the surname of the signature is false, but there is enough of the original to make sure that it has been correctly reconstructed.

PROVENANCE: From the Collection of Conte Contin di Castel-Seprio, Venice.[1] Lawrie and Co. Sale, Christie's, 28 January, 1905 (lot 52),[2] bought by Carfax. Presented by Sir Claude Phillips in memory of his sister Eugénie, 1910.

REPRODUCTION: *Illustrations, Italian Schools*, 1937, p. 120. *Plates, Earlier Italian Schools*, 1953, Vol. I, p. 127.

REFERENCES: (1) Cf. Ludwig in the Prussian *Jahrbuch*, 1905, Beiheft, p. 57, with identifying description. (2) The marks of this sale are on the back of the picture.

DOMENICO Veneziano
active 1438, died 1461

Of Venetian origin, but classed in the Florentine School. In 1438 he was in Perugia. 1439–45 (with interruptions, it seems), he was painting frescoes in S. Egidio (S. Maria Nuova), Florence; the work is mostly lost. For this series, see Mario Salmi in *Atti e Memorie dell'Accademia* ... '*La Colombaria*,' 1947, pp. 421 ff, and, for the documents, Ottavio Andreucci, *Della Biblioteca e Pinacoteca dell'Arcispedale di Santa Maria Nuova*, 1871, pp. 79–80. Domenico's principal surviving work is a signed altarpiece in the Uffizi.

766   FRESCO: HEAD OF A BEARDLESS SAINT (FRAGMENT)

Fresco, transferred to tile, 17 × 14 (0·43 × 0·355).
Much repainted.
For the commentary, etc., see No. 1215 below.

767   FRESCO: HEAD OF A BEARDED SAINT (FRAGMENT)

Fresco, transferred to tile, 17¾ × 14 (0·45 × 0·355).
Even more repainted than No. 766 above, so that the style of the original painter is almost entirely concealed.
For the commentary, etc., see No. 1215 below.

1215   FRESCO: THE VIRGIN AND CHILD ENTHRONED (FRAGMENT)

God the Father and the Holy Ghost appear above. Signed: DOMICVS / D. VENECIIS. P.

Fresco, transferred to canvas, 95 × 47½ (2·41 × 1·205).[1]
Very seriously damaged.

Nos. 766, 767 and 1215 are the surviving fragments of a street tabernacle, painted at the Canto de' Carnesecchi, not far from the Piazza Santa Maria Novella, Florence. The two heads were 'nelle due grossezze del muro, o ali del tabernacolo'; the remaining part of the figures, being 'quasi distrutto dal tempo,' was not removed from the wall in 1851, when Nos. 766, 767 and 1215 were detached.[2]

Vasari[3] says that the tabernacle was one of Domenico's first works in Florence, but there is no necessity to believe that he is right.[4]

PROVENANCE: Painted, as explained above, as a tabernacle at the Canto de' Carnesecchi, Florence. Some property that included this fresco was sold in 1851 by the Marchesa Marianna Venturi vedova Ginori Lisci to Don Ercole dei Principi Pio di Savoia; in the same year he had the pieces removed from the wall by Giovanni Rizzoli. The three fragments were seen in his house in 1858 by Eastlake.[5] In 1859, Prince Pio sold No. 1215, and possibly the other two fragments also, to L. Hombert. Nos. 766, 767 were acquired by Sir Charles Eastlake in 1862,[6] and purchased after his death from his collection, at the price he had paid for them, in 1867. No. 1215 was sold in 1865 by Hombert to

Lord Lindsay, later 25th Earl of Crawford. Exhibited at the R.A., 1871 (No. 269). He died in 1880 and was succeeded by his son, who presented the fresco in 1886.

REPRODUCTIONS: *Illustrations, Italian Schools*, 1937, pp. 123/4. *Plates, Earlier Italian Schools*, 1953, Vol. I, pp. 128–130.

REFERENCES: (1) Measurements from the 1929 Catalogue. (2) This, and a good deal of the documentation concerning the provenance, from a file of papers in the Gallery archives, presented by Lord Crawford with No. 1215. The type of tabernacle may have corresponded with one at the Villa Orsini at Brozzi, reproduced in *Emporium*, April, 1942, p. 163. (3) Vasari, 1550, p. 413; ed. Milanesi, II, p. 675. (4) Pudelko in *Mitteilungen des Kunsthistorischen Instituts in Florenz*, IV, 1934, pp. 179 f., thinks it is of 1454/5; Salmi, *Paolo Uccello, Andrea del Castagno, Domenico Veneziano*, 1938, p. 79, thinks it is of 1430/40. Muraro and Hartt in *The Art Bulletin*, 1959, pp. 158 and 178, date it *ca.* 1442. (5) Eastlake's note-book. See also Crowe and Cavalcaselle, *History of Painting in Italy*, II, 1864, p. 317. (6) Eastlake's letter to Wornum, 5 November, 1863.

DUCCIO
active 1278, died 1319

Duccio di Buoninsegna, a painter active chiefly at Siena. In 1285 he contracted to paint a large picture for Santa Maria Novella, Florence; this is probably the 'Rucellai Madonna' (cf. Giulia Sinibaldi and Giulia Brunetti, *Pittura Italiana del '200 e '300, Catalogo della Mostra Giottesca di Firenze del* 1937, 1943, pp. 107 ff.; Luisa Marcucci, *Gallerie Nazionali di Firenze, I Dipinti Toscani del Secolo XIII*, 1958, pp. 64 ff.) Duccio's principal work is the *Maestà*, or former high-altarpiece of the Cathedral of Siena; he contracted to paint this with his own hand on 9 October, 1308, and it was placed in the cathedral on 9 June, 1311.

Duccio was the first eminent painter of the Sienese School.

566 TRIPTYCH: THE VIRGIN AND CHILD WITH SAINTS

In the tympanum above the central panel are seven figures. Reading from left to right, they are: (1) Daniel; scroll inscribed with a text from Daniel ii, 45 (cf. also v. 34), (d)*e mō/*(t)*e ab/cisus | est la/pis si/ne m*(a)*/nib'*. (2) Moses; scroll inscribed with a text adapted from Exodus iii, 2, *Vidb*( )*/ q' *(ru)*b' | ardebat | *(e)*t non/ combu/reba/tur.* (3) Isaiah; the scroll is much damaged, but the text (the letters of which not even a fragment remains being printed in brackets), must be that of Isaiah vii, 14, *Ecc*(e) *| uir*(go) *| *(cō)*c*(i)*p*(i)/(et). et | *(pa)*ri/*(et) *fi/lium.* (4) The central figure, David; the remains of his name, *uid*, is inscribed on the background. (5) Abraham; scroll inscribed with a text adapted from Genesis xxii, 18, or xxvi, 4, *In seīe | tuo be/nedicen/tur om/nes gē/tes.* (6) Jacob; scroll inscribed with a text from Genesis xxviii, 17, . .(do)*m'/dei et | porta/ celi.* (7) Jeremiah; scroll inscribed with a text adapted from Jeremiah xxxi, 22, *Nou*(um) (?) *| faciet | *(d?)*o' s t/eram | mlier | circū/dabit | *(ui/ rum).

Left wing, S. Dominic; with the name inscribed, S̄ DO/MINIC'.

Right wing, S. Aurea (?); with the remains of the name inscribed, SCA AU.

Reverse: the reverse retains most of its covering of original paint, which is nearly plain for the central panel, but patterned for the wings.[1]

Wood. The size of the central panel of the Virgin and Child, without the framing, is $16\frac{3}{4} \times 13\frac{1}{2}$ (0·425 × 0·345), rounded top; the total size of the central panel, including the framing, the tympanum and the base, is $24\frac{1}{8} \times 15\frac{3}{8}$ (0·615 × 0·39), pointed top. For the wings, the size of S. Aurea's(?) panel, excluding the framing, is $16\frac{1}{2} \times 6\frac{1}{2}$ (0·42 × 0·165); the painted area on the reverse of this wing is $17\frac{3}{4} \times 8\frac{1}{8}$ (0·45 × 0·205). The size of S. Dominic's panel, excluding the framing, is $16\frac{1}{2} \times 6\frac{1}{4}$ (0·42 × 0·16); the painted area on the reverse of this wing is $17\frac{3}{4} \times 7$ (0·45 × 0·18). For the central panel, and the wings (which have irregular tops), it is the greatest height that is given.

Cleaned in 1959; very well preserved.

The saint on the right wing is probably S. Aurea of Ostia,[2] although the inscription is not preserved for the latter part of the name. It is true that she does not carry a martyr's palm, as S. Aurea should, but martyrs in early Sienese painting often do not. It is also true that her only emblem, a cross, does not appear to be normally associated with S. Aurea. Some confirmation that S. Aurea is here intended is given by two other Sienese pictures, where the name is inscribed.[3] Both of these are pictures with a Dominican association, just as No. 566 is; but the link between Sienese painting, the Dominican Order and S. Aurea has not been clearly established.[4]

The patriarchs and prophets in the tympanum seem to be mingled in no logical order; the readings of the scrolls are given in a reliable form, although the student by his naked eye is unlikely to be able to check much of them. All these figures appear with similar types, and (except for Jeremiah) with the same texts as here, in a polyptych at Siena, ascribed to Duccio.[5] Most of these texts are applicable in a mystic way to the Virgin Mary.

The Virgin and Child in No. 566 is rather similar to the Duccio in the Stoclet Collection at Brussels.[6] No. 566 appears to be rather earlier in style than Duccio's *Maestà* of 1308/11.

PROVENANCE: Stated to be from a private collection at Pisa.[7] Purchased with the Lombardi-Baldi Collection, Florence, 1857.[8]

REPRODUCTIONS: *Illustrations, Italian Schools*, 1937, p. 128. *Plates, Earlier Italian Schools*, 1953, Vol. I, pp. 131–134.

REFERENCES: (1) See *Paintings and Drawings on the Backs of National Gallery Pictures*, published by the Gallery, 1946, Plate 6, with note. A very similar patterning is on the back of the wings of a triptych at Boston, ascribed to Duccio; reproduced in the Boston *Bulletin*, June, 1946, p. 38. (2) She is, it may be mentioned, most unlikely to be the B. Alda or Auda, a Sienese widow who died in 1309. (3) A Lippo Vanni in SS. Domenico e Sisto, Rome, reproduced by Weigelt, *Sienese Painting of the Trecento*, n.d., Plate 114. A triptych ascribed to Lippo Vanni in the Walters Art Gallery, Baltimore, reproduced by Berenson, *Essays in the Study of Sienese Painting*, 1918, Fig. 16. (4) P. Pecchiai, *La Chiesa dello Spirito Santo dei Napoletani*, etc., 1953, p. 10, says that the Dominican convent of S. Aurea, Rome, was in existence not very long after 1320. On pp. 37/8 he states that the Lippo Vanni in SS. Domenico e Sisto comes from S. Aurea; cf. Armellini, *Le Chiese di Roma*, 1942, Vol. II, p. 1259. (5) Siena, *Catalogo*, 1933, No. 47; reproduced by Enzo Carli, *Capolavori dell'Arte Senese*, 1946, Plate XXIX. (6) Ex-Stroganoff; Weigelt, *op. cit.*, Plate 11; Van Marle, *Development of the Italian Schools of Painting*, II, Fig. 4. (7) N.G. MS. Catalogue. (8) For the history of the Lombardi-Baldi Collection, see Appendix I.

1139   THE ANNUNCIATION (PREDELLA PANEL FROM AN ALTARPIECE)

S. Gabriel approaches from the left, and the Virgin looks up from her book, which is inscribed with the prophecy of Isaiah vii, 14: *Ecce | uirgo | concipi|et & pa|( )et | filiū | & uoc|abitur*. Above, the Holy Spirit descends from God in the form of a dove.

Wood, painted surface, $17 \times 17\frac{1}{4}$ ($0\cdot43 \times 0\cdot44$). The picture continues to the edge of the panel at the bottom; the paint has here been renewed, but the canvas covering the wood, which appears to be the original canvas, shows here and there along the bottom edge, so it is probable that the original picture continued at least as far as the present bottom of the panel. The corners of the picture were once covered by cross-pieces of the original frame; the evidence for this can be seen at the top left corner.

The condition is good for a picture of such antiquity; but the Virgin's face is damaged, and about 1 in. of the paint along the bottom is new.

The present picture, like Nos. 1140 and 1330 below, is from the predella of Duccio's *Maestà*; in point of fact, this does not seem to be strictly capable of proof, but it would be most unreasonable to doubt it. Duccio's *Maestà* was a double-sided altarpiece, painted in 1308/11 for the high altar of Siena Cathedral. The details concerning this altarpiece would be too long for the present catalogue.[1] It is sufficient to state that the front, representing the Virgin and Child with Saints and Angels, and the back, representing scenes from the Passion, are in the Cathedral Museum at Siena. Above and below these main portions, pinnacles and a predella ornamented the altarpiece on both sides; some parts of these are also in the Cathedral Museum, others must have been removed from the Cathedral at an undefined date and in an unexplained way.[2] The predella is reasonably supposed on the front part to have shown scenes from the early life of Christ, and at the back scenes from His ministry.

To judge from the existing panels assumed to have formed the predella at the front, it is clear that these scenes were separated from each other by figures of prophets. No. 1139 may well have been the panel at the extreme left; in any case, it would appear to have been on the left of, and next to, the Nativity formerly at Berlin and now at Washington. The prophet separating the two scenes, who is attached to the Washington picture, is Isaiah; he holds a scroll with the same text from Isaiah vii, 14, that the Virgin is reading in No. 1139. Indeed, the Isaiah at Washington is pointing to the left, i.e. towards the scene enacted in No. 1139, and away from the Nativity.

The contract specifies that Duccio was to paint his altarpiece with his own hand.[3]

An early retable dedicated to S. Peter at Siena, which seems partly to foreshadow Duccio's style, includes a scene of the Annunciation in which the figures to some extent correspond with those of No. 1139.[4]

DERIVATION: An adaptation of the design appears in a triptych formerly in the Blumenthal Collection, New York;[5] now in the Metropolitan Museum there.

PROVENANCE: Duccio's double-sided *Maestà* was set up in Siena Cathedral on 9 June, 1311; in 1506, its place on the high altar was taken by a bronze tabernacle by Vecchietta.[6] The major part of it remained in the Cathedral or the Cathedral precincts, except apparently for a brief period in 1777, when it was removed to S. Ansano in Castelvecchio to be cut in two.[7] It is possible that Della Valle saw No. 1139 in the Cathedral in the eighteenth century;[8] but the picture he noted as an *Annunciation* may have been really the *Annunciation of the Virgin's Death*, which is now in the Cathedral Museum at Siena. In a Cathedral inventory in 1795, twelve little pictures as well as the two main portions are recorded; it is not certain if these twelve are all included among the small pictures now in the Cathedral Museum.[9] No. 1139, which is reasonably assumed once to have formed part of the Maestà, the date of separation being unknown, was purchased out of the Clarke Fund from C. Fairfax Murray of Florence in 1883.

REPRODUCTION: *Illustrations, Italian Schools*, 1937, p. 127. *Plates, Early Italian Schools*, 1953, Vol. I, p. 135.

REFERENCES: (1) The best account of Duccio's *Maestà* is by Weigelt in the *Bullettino Senese di Storia Patria*, 1909, pp. 191 ff. Weigelt examined the material condition of a number of the panels, and was able to make some precise statements about their original form and position. Cf. also Milanesi, *Documenti per la Storia dell'Arte Senese*, I, 1854, pp. 166 ff.; A. Lisini in the *Bullettino Senese di Storia Patria*, 1898, fasc. 1; V. Lusini in the *Rassegna d'Arte Senese*, 1912, pp. 67 ff.; Pèleo Bacci, *Francesco di Valdambrino*, 1936, Chapter VII; Enzo Carli, *Il Museo dell'Opera*, etc., 1946, pp. 35 ff. (2) The four panels formerly in the Benson Collection are stated to be 'from Colle Alto in the Val d'Elsa' (*Catalogue of Italian Pictures . . . collected by Robert and Evelyn Benson*, 1914, p. 4). There can be little doubt that they are identical with the four pictures, each called *Storia di Gesù Cristo, di Duccio della Boninsegna*, owned by the Sigg. Dini FF. Giuseppe e Marziale; see the *Catalogo degli oggetti d'arte antica presentati alla mostra comunale di Colle di Val d'Elsa*, 6–8 September, 1879, Nos. 80–83. (3) Milanesi, *op. cit.*, I, p. 167. (4) Siena Catalogue by Cesare Brandi, 1933, p. 110; Giulia Sinibaldi and Giulia Brunetti, *Pittura Italiana del '200 e '300, Catalogo della Mostra Giottesca di Firenze del 1937*, 1943, No. 28. *The Calling of Peter and Andrew* on the same retable also has some, rather remote, compositional connection with Duccio's version of the same scene, formerly in the Benson Collection, and now at Washington. (5) George and Florence Blumenthal Catalogue, I, 1926, Plate XVI; Van Marle, *Development of the Italian Schools of Painting*, II, Fig. 55. (6) References as in note 1, where some details about the movements of the picture within the cathedral can be found. (7) Pèleo Bacci, *Francesco di Valdambrino*, 1936, p. 186. (8) Della Valle, *Lettere Sanesi*, II, 1785, p. 72. (9) Bacci, *op. cit.*, p. 187. It is only incidentally that Bacci refers to Duccio's picture; there may remain unpublished records that would throw further light on when the various mutilations occurred.

1140   JESUS OPENS THE EYES OF A MAN BORN BLIND
         (PREDELLA PANEL FROM AN ALTARPIECE)

Christ, followed by the twelve apostles, touches the eye of a beggar; on the right, the same beggar, having washed in the pool of Siloam, recovers his sight.

Wood, painted surface, $17 \times 17\frac{3}{4}$ (0.435×0.45), not quite rectangular; painted up to the edges all round.

The condition is fair, but less good than would appear superficially. In particular, the face and left hand of the beggar on the right are wholly new.

Several miracles of healing the blind are recorded in the Gospels, but the subject here is undoubtedly the one described in John ix, 1 sqq.[1]

This and No. 1330 below are reasonably supposed to be from the back part of the predella of Duccio's *Maestà*; the whole of the predella on this side appears to have been occupied with scenes of Christ's ministry. See further in the commentary to No. 1139 above.

PROVENANCE: Purchased, Clarke Fund, from C. Fairfax Murray of Florence, 1883.

REPRODUCTION: *Illustrations, Italian Schools*, 1937, p. 129. *Plates, Earlier Italian Schools*, 1953, Vol. I, p. 136.

REFERENCE: (1) The subject is treated in a very similar way in a drawing in the British Museum; see British Museum, *Italian Drawings, The Fourteenth and Fifteenth Centuries*, catalogue by A. E. Popham and Philip Pouncey, 1950, I, No. 269, and II, Plate CCXXXIII. For this subject, see Pieter Singelenberg in *The Art Bulletin*, 1958, pp. 105 ff.

1330 THE TRANSFIGURATION (PREDELLA PANEL FROM AN ALTARPIECE)

Centre, Christ; on the left, Moses; on the right, Elijah. Below, the three apostles, Peter, John and James.

Wood, painted surface, $17\frac{3}{8} \times 18\frac{1}{8}$ (0.44×0.46). The size of the panel, which is the same as that of the picture together with its frame, is $19\frac{1}{4} \times 20$ (0.49×0.51), not quite rectangular. The frame is not in one piece with the panel, but is pretty clearly the original; the piece along the bottom, at least, seems to have been removed and refixed at some time. There is no evidence that the corners of this picture were ever hidden by cross-pieces of the frame; contrast No. 1139 above.[1]

Cleaned in 1951/2. No original paint is left on a substantial part of the central Apostle, and in general the whole lower part of the picture is damaged. The upper part is by no means badly preserved for a picture of the period; indeed, the figure of Christ, and the gold background are in good condition.

Like No. 1140 above, this picture is reasonably assumed to be from the back part of the predella of Duccio's *Maestà*.

PROVENANCE: Acquired in Siena by R. H. Wilson, a few years before he presented it to the Gallery in 1891.[2]

REPRODUCTION: *Illustrations, Italian Schools*, 1937, p. 129. *Plates, Earlier Italian Schools*, 1953, Vol. I, p. 137 (both before cleaning). Reproduced after cleaning in the Report, *The National Gallery, 1938–1954*, 1955, Fig. 7.

REFERENCES: (1) No 1330 is reasonably assumed to be from the predella of the back of Duccio's altarpiece. It is very unlikely that any of the predella panels from this part had cross-pieces at the corners of the frames; *The Marriage at Cana* at Siena, which appears to be from this series, has indeed such cross-pieces, but the frame is apparently not original. (**2**) Letter in the Gallery archives.

Follower of DUCCIO

565 THE VIRGIN AND CHILD WITH SIX ANGELS (FRAGMENT)

Transferred from wood, pointed top, 74×65 (1·88×1·65).

The picture would seem to have been cut, especially along the bottom; in that case the Virgin could have been shown originally at full length, as in the *Mastà* ascribed to Duccio from S. Maria Novella at Florence.[1] It must be added that, unlikely as it seems, the picture may not have been cut, at any rate not substantially. Incised lines are visible at the edges of the top part and, less well, here and there at the sides and bottom; these might have been made by the original painter to mark the limits of his picture, though there does not appear to be any technical proof that the incisions were not done later.

The preservation is not very satisfactory, and in particular some parts are modern reconstructions, the chief areas being on the angels. Chief new parts of the angels on the left: for the topmost one, part of the hair, the wing and most of the dress; for the middle one, his right hand; for the lowest one, his left wing and hand and the pink dress round about. On the right-hand side, the face and hair of the topmost angel are new. There are on the picture some other smaller reconstructions of important parts. When the wood support had been removed from the picture during the transference, some very slight drawings and a short inscription (apparently illegible) were found on the back of the original canvas that had covered the wood; these have been photographed.

This picture is stated to come from Santa Croce at Florence,[2] and is apparently identical with a Virgin and Child ascribed to Cimabue, which Vasari recorded as hanging on a pilaster in the choir of the church.[3] It was therefore ascribed to Cimabue from the time of its acquisition by the Gallery in 1857, until in 1898 J. P. Richter recognized that it is Sienese.[4] An ascription to the following of Duccio is justifiable in the present state of knowledge, although the similarity to Duccio's own works is not very close. Pictures that have been associated in style are a Virgin and Child Enthroned, No. 18 of the Siena Gallery, traditionally (and wrongly) ascribed to Gilio;[5] a Virgin and Child, No. 592 of the Siena Gallery, ascribed in the 1933 catalogue to the Master of the London Maestà;[6] and a damaged fresco at Casole.[7] The compiler accepts No. 18 of the Siena Gallery as by the same hand as No. 565, but considerable doubt about the attribution has been expressed.[8] It has been suggested at various times that one or other of these pictures might be early works of Pietro Lorenzetti, and Weigelt makes some such suggestion in a very tentative way for No. 565;[9] an attribution to the young Pietro Lorenzetti could possibly be right, but must be considered at present as extremely uncertain.

A picture apparently unpublished, of which the compiler has seen no reproduction, is stated to have compositional, iconographic, and stylistic connections with No. 565.[10]

PROVENANCE: Apparently the *Virgin and Child* recorded by Vasari on a pilaster in the choir of Santa Croce, Florence;[11] Vasari's picture is apparently the same as an undescribed work recorded in a different place in the church by Bocchi in 1591.[12] Bocchi's picture is recorded to have been removed to the Tosinghi-Spinelli chapel in 1595, where it is recorded (as a *Madonna*) in Rosselli's *Sepoltuario*, MS. of 1657.[13] No. 565 was purchased by Lombardi and Baldi from the Convent of S. Croce;[14] acquired with other pictures from the Lombardi-Baldi Collection, Florence, 1857.[15]

REPRODUCTION: *Illustrations, Italian Schools*, 1937, p. 130 (from a photograph taken before the cleaning of the picture in 1934/5). *Plates, Earlier Italian Schools*, 1953, Vol. I, p. 138.

REFERENCES: (1) Van Marle, *Development of the Italian Schools of Painting*, Vol. II, Fig. 1. (2) N. G. MS. Catalogue, and printed catalogue and Report of 1858; no doubt the statement had been supplied by Messrs. Lombardi and Baldi. (3) Vasari, 1550 edition, p. 127; 1568 edition, I, p. 83; Milanesi's edition, I, p. 249; Frey's edition, 1911, I, pp. 392 and 429/30. The picture is also mentioned by Antonio Petrei; see *Il Libro di Antonio Billi*, ed. Frey, 1892, p. 57. (4) J. P. Richter, *Lectures on the National Gallery*, 1898, p. 8. (5) Van Marle, *op. cit.*, Vol. II, Fig. 54; Siena Catalogue, 1933, by Cesare Brandi, p. 19, as Anonimo Duccesco. (6) Siena Catalogue, 1933, p. 175, with reproduction. (7) This fresco, which is somewhat separate from the other works mentioned, is ascribed to Segna by P. Bacci, *Fonti e Commenti per la Storia dell'Arte Senese*, 1944, pp. 25 ff., and Plates 8–11. Also reproduced in the *Rassegna d'Arte*, 1919, p. 96, and by E. Cecchi, *Pietro Lorenzetti*, 1930, Plates I, II. (8) Some bibliographical references will be found in the Siena Catalogue, 1933; cf. notes 5 and 6 above. F. M. Perkins in *La Balzana*, 1928, pp. 100 and 112, admits some similarity of style for the two pictures at Siena and No. 565, but does not admit that No. 565 is by the same hand as either. On the other hand, Toesca (*Il Trecento*, 1951, p. 517) associates No. 565 with Siena No. 18, as by a painter between Duccio and Pietro Lorenzetti. (9) Weigelt, *Sienese Painting of the Trecento*, n.d., p. 71. (10) See Gertrude Coor-Achenbach in *The Art Bulletin*, June 1960, p. 143. (11) See note 3. (12) Francesco Bocchi, *Le Bellezze della Città di Fiorenza*, 1591, p. 153. (13) From Walter and Elisabeth Paatz, *Die Kirchen von Florenz*, I, 1940, pp. 595 and 687/8, partly on information from P. Saturnino Mencherini, *Santa Croce*, 1929, p. 31. Cinelli's revision of Bocchi's Guide to Florence, 1677, p. 316, merely records that the picture mentioned by Bocchi had been removed. Presumably Bocchi's picture is the same as the *madone* seen in 1739 in Santa Croce by Charles de Brosses, *Lettres Familières sur l'Italie*, ed. Yvonne Bezard, 1931, I, pp. 357/8 (the passage is reprinted in *Emporium*, July, 1942, p. 299). (14) N.G. Report, 1858. (15) For the history of the Lombardi-Baldi Collection, see Appendix I.

FERRARESE(?) SCHOOL

3069 MYSTIC FIGURE OF CHRIST

Christ is shown seated, apparently on a tree-trunk. He wears the Crown of Thorns; His hands and feet are bare, and without Wounds. A broken rope is tied loosely round His neck. He is seated under a porch, in the open air. Top right, apparently the moon.

Reverse: marbled painting.

Wood, painted surface, 20 × 13⅛ (0·51 × 0·335).

Most of Christ's figure is fairly well preserved, but there is much repaint on His head. The perspective lines of the flooring show strongly through His feet and the lower part of His robe. He once had, or was intended to have a halo.

The subject has not been precisely identified. The scene might be claimed to be at Golgotha, while the Cross is being made ready; but if so, it would be treated in a mystic way, and it seems possible that No. 3069 represents some at present unidentified Vision.[1]

No. 3069 was classed in the Ferrarese School in the 1929 Catalogue; this may be true, although the closest stylistic relationship appears to be with Marco Zoppo rather than with any painter strictly Ferrarese.[2] Berenson, in his 1932 Lists, ascribes it to Leonardo Scaletti, which is not satisfactory.

VERSIONS: A version, closely corresponding except in colour, apparently by the same hand as No. 3069, is in the Liechtenstein Collection;[3] in that picture, the fingers of Christ's hands are not spread out,[4] there is no moon in the sky, and there are differences in the architectural decoration and in the landscape. Another variant, not by the same hand as No. 3069, shows Christ in white, seated upon a stone (?), no porch, and with the Magdalen kneeling before Him; it belonged to Baron Tucher at Vienna.[5]

PROVENANCE: From the Costabili Collection at Ferrara; Catalogue, I, 1838 (No. 36).[6] Bought by Sir Austen Henry Layard probably in 1866.[7] Exhibited at South Kensington, 1869 (No. 47).[8] Layard Bequest, 1916.[9]

REPRODUCTION: *Illustrations, Italian Schools*, 1937, p. 131. *Plates, Earlier Italian Schools*, 1953, Vol. I, p. 139.

REFERENCES: (1) Some rather, but not exactly, similar subjects are referred to by E. Mâle, *L'Art Religieux de la Fin du Moyen Age en France*, 2nd edition, 1922, pp. 94 ff., Figs. 44, 48, and by Karl Künstle, *Ikonographie der Christlichen Kunst*, I, 1928, p. 486. (2) R. Longhi, *Officina Ferrarese*, 1934, p. 167, calls No. 3069, and the variant about to be mentioned in the Liechtenstein Collection, near to Zoppo; he doubtfully ascribes some other pictures to the same hand. (3) Liechtenstein Gallery, as Zoppo; *Führer* by A. Kronfeld, 1927 (No. 860), size 0·54 × 0·35; Catalogue of the Liechtenstein Exhibition at Lucerne, 1948 (No. 37), and Plate IV, as bought in Venice in 1883. Also reproduced by Venturi, *Storia dell'Arte Italiana*, Vol. VII, Part III, Fig. 57, as Pizzolo. The Liechtenstein picture may be identical, (*a*) with a version recorded by Crowe and Cavalcaselle, *History of Painting in North Italy*, I, 1871, p. 375, as belonging to Count Massa at Ferrara; (*b*) with a version recorded at Guggenheim's by Layard in his MS. Catalogue, No. 61. (4) The X-Ray shows no alteration in the hands in No. 3069. (5) Reproduced in the *Münchner Jahrbuch der bildenden Kunst*, 1908, I, p. 27, as Parentino. No doubt identical with a picture recorded by Crowe and Cavalcaselle, *loc. cit.* in note 3, as then in the Canonici Collection at Ferrara. (6) As Bono. The Costabili brand is on the back of No. 3069. (7) A letter from Layard to Morelli, 20 October, 1866 (British Museum, Add. MS. 38966, Layard Papers, Vol. XXXVI), records acquisitions just made from the Costabili Collection, but without listing the pictures. (8) As Bono. (9) For the history of the Layard Collection, see Appendix IV.

DEFENDENTE FERRARI
active 1511–1535 (?)

Of Chivasso in Piedmont; the dates are those of his authenticated works. These authenticated and dated works bear a signature in monogram, and for one (the Ranverso altarpiece) there is also a contractual document giving the full name. Other monogrammed pictures are without date. There are also a good many pictures bearing dates but not signed; the earliest, among those usually accepted as Defendente Ferrari's, are a *Nativity at Night* in the Civic Museum, Turin (1510 on the back), and a picture once in the Kaiser Friedrich Museum, Berlin (1511). According to Anna Maria Brizio, there are pictures acceptable as Defendente Ferrari's from 1500 onwards.

Documents exist concerning three Defendente Ferraris at Chivasso: (1) the son of Francesco, referred to as 'magister' in 1528 and still alive in 1542 and perhaps in 1547; (2) his first cousin, b. 1509, probably died young; (3) the brother of the latter, b. 1512. It is possible that (1) is the author of the pictures, although he is never referred to in the documents as being a painter, and although he seems to be of a younger generation. Cf. A. Baudi di Vesme in the *Bollettino della Società Piemontese di Archeologia e Belle Arti*, 1922, pp. 1 ff.

The style of Defendente Ferrari's authenticated works seems hardly to evolve at all; attributions of pictures differing somewhat from these are doubtful, especially as there is some evidence for believing some of these doubtful works to be by Spanzotti. Cf. A. M. Brizio in *L'Arte*, 1924, pp. 211 ff.; Vittorio Viale, *Gotico e Rinascimento in Piemonte*, 1939, pp. 78 ff.; Anna Maria Brizio, *La Pittura in Piemonte*, 1942, pp. 45 ff.; L. Mallé in the *Bollettino della Società Piemontese di Archeologia e di Belle Arti*, 1952/3, pp. 76 ff.

Style of DEFENDENTE FERRARI

1200 S. PETER MARTYR AND A BISHOP SAINT (PANEL FROM AN ALTARPIECE)

On the back is a drawing of concentric squares, in pigment on the unprimed wood.

Poplar,[1] painted surface, $30 \times 20\frac{1}{2}$ (0·765 × 0·52).
For the commentary, etc., see No. 1201 below.

1201 SS. NICHOLAS OF TOLENTINO AND JOHN THE BAPTIST (PANEL FROM AN ALTARPIECE)

S. Nicholas holds a book inscribed, PRE / CEP / TA / PAT / RIS / MEI / SER / VAVI.; his Crucifix is inscribed, I.N.R.I. The Baptist holds a scroll inscribed, ECCE AGN / DEI QVI TOLLIT.

Poplar,[1] painted surface, $30 \times 20\frac{1}{2}$ (0·765 × 0·52).

Both panels are in very good condition, but suffer somewhat from undercleaning.

S. Nicholas of Tolentino was in the 1929 Catalogue wrongly called a Franciscan (?). S. Nicholas of Tolentino appears frequently in Piedmontese painting with the same attributes as here;[2] his identity is certified in a Benozzo in S. Agostino at San Gimignano, where his name is on his halo, and the inscription is given more fully as *Ego patris mei Augustini precepta servavi et maneo in eius dilectione*. The words (except for *Augustini*) are a quotation from John xv, 10.[3]

Nos. 1200 and 1201 are clearly from the upper tier of an altarpiece in compartments. Weber[4] suggested that a *SS. Francis and Agatha with Kneeling Donor* (1·30 × 0·58) in the Academy at Turin was the left-hand panel of the main tier. There is much to be said for this view; the Turin picture contains halo patterns and a rosetted ceiling very similar to those on Nos. 1200/1, and the style seems to correspond closely. Two pictures in the Brera at Milan seem clearly to have been the other two panels of the main tier of the altarpiece; they represent *S. Andrew* (central) and *SS. Catherine and Sebastian* (right).[5] The size of each is 1·28 × 0·59. The halo and floor patterns at Milan correspond very closely with those at Turin. Strips of rosetted ceilings, most of which have been cut away, are visible on the original pictures at Milan; the proportions of the patterning are somewhat different, but seem to correspond sufficiently. The style again corresponds closely. A possible objection to this reconstruction is that the Turin and Milan panels are rather wider than Nos. 1200/1, which have not been cut.

If this reconstruction is correct, the altarpiece was dedicated to S. Andrew.

The attribution of Nos. 1200/1 is doubtful. Like the panels at Turin and Milan, they are similar in style to Defendente Ferrari, without appearing convincingly his.[6] An alternative name would be Spanzotti; it is explained in his biography that attributions to him of pictures near in style to Defendente Ferrari are uncertain.[7] Maybe the pictures are by some different, hitherto unidentified painter.

PROVENANCE: From Piedmont.[8] Bought from Baslini, Milan, Walker Fund, 1885.[9]

REPRODUCTIONS: *Illustrations, Italian Schools*, 1937, pp. 206/7. *Plates, Earlier Italian Schools*, 1953, Vol. I, p. 140.

REFERENCES: (1) Letter from B. J. Rendle, of the Forest Products Research Laboratory, in the Gallery archives. (2) Vittorio Viale, *Gotico e Rinascimento in Piemonte*, 1939, Plates 52 (wrongly as S. Bernardino), 60, 109. (3) The Benozzo is reproduced by E. Ricci, *Mille Santi nell'Arte*, 1931. G. Magherini and E. Giovagnoli, *La Prima Giovinezza di Raffaello*, 1927, p. 52, quote Comin Ventura, *Vita del B. S. Nicola da Tolentino*, 1597, p. 84, to the effect that this text for pictures of S. Nicholas was chosen by Pope Eugenius; the reference must be to Pope Eugenius IV, who did canonize him. (4) Weber in Thieme-Becker, s.v. Macrino d'Alba; see also Viale, *op. cit.*, p. 81 and Plate 71. (5) Viale, *op. cit.*, pp. 84/5 and Plate 55. A strip down the right side of the Two Saints is new paint, and was originally not painted but covered by the frame (information from Mauro Pellicioli). Anna Maria Brizio, *La Pittura in Piemonte*, 1942, pp. 51/2 and 199, accepts that the Turin and Brera pictures are from the same altarpiece, but says nothing about the possible connection of Nos. 1200/1. (6) Berenson, *North Italian Painters*, 1907, and 1932 Lists, calls the London, Turin and Milan pictures Defendente Ferrari. So does Anna Maria Brizio, *op. cit.*, pp. 198/9; her views on Defendente Ferrari's development are given on pp. 45 ff. (7) Viale, *op. cit.*, pp. 81 and 84/5, inclines to an attribution to Spanzotti for the Turin and Milan panels. In a letter of 14 January, 1948 (in the Gallery archives), he maintained his view that these pictures, and hence Nos. 1200/1, are not by Defendente; claimed that it was impossible to classify all the Piedmontese pictures of this style under only two names, Defendente and Spanzotti; and added that for the moment Nos. 1200/1 should be associated with Defendente Ferrari rather than with Spanzotti. (8) National Gallery MS. Catalogue. (9) As Macrino d'Alba, an attribution hitherto maintained at the National Gallery. It is certainly wrong; by a slip, Anna Maria Brizio, *op. cit.*, p. 240, lists Nos. 1200/1 as Macrino, as well as on p. 198 as Defendente.

FIORENZO DI LORENZO
ca. 1440 (?)–1522/5

A Perugian painter, born certainly before 1447, and probably *ca.* 1440 or earlier. His activity is perhaps recorded in 1455/6 at Perugia (U. Gnoli, *Pittori e Miniatori nell'Umbria*, 1923, p. 112); he appears to have matriculated at Perugia between 1463 and 1469. One picture signed and dated 1487 is at Perugia; very few other authenticated works are known. He seems to have confined himself to a local activity at Perugia; some Florentine influences in his work do not necessarily imply a training at Florence.

1103 PART OF AN ALTARPIECE

Central panel, the Virgin and Child with angels, S. Francis introducing a donor, and S. Bernardino; right panel, S. Bartholomew; left panel, S. John the Baptist, with a scroll inscribed . ECCIE AGNVS DEI.

Wood. The sizes of the painted surfaces are: central panel, $48\frac{1}{4} \times 32\frac{3}{4}$ ($1 \cdot 22 \times 0 \cdot 83$); side panels, each, $48\frac{3}{8} \times 19\frac{1}{4}$ ($1 \cdot 225 \times 0 \cdot 49$). The sizes of the side panels include additions on new wood of 1 in. on the right of S. John the Baptist, and of $\frac{1}{2}$ in. on the left of S. Bartholomew. All the painted surfaces continue to the edges of the panels all round, except in the top corners; all three pictures were originally arched at the tops, and parts of these arches together with marks at their springs, where there were capitals in the original frame, are distinguishable.

The line of the ground in the three pictures, and the marks of the capitals so far as they can be seen, indicate that the central panel has been cut at the bottom about $8\frac{1}{4}$ in., if the side panels have not been cut at the bottom at all. To judge from the slight evidence of the remains of the arches, the central panel has been cut at the top about 6 in., and the side panels about 14 in.[1]

Good condition in general. Many of the important outlines are damaged; this appears due originally to the contours not being in the places allowed for when the pictures were laid in. This damage is worst in the central panel, but occurs also on the wings, e.g. on the tops of the saints' heads, and in the Baptist's right arm. The three pictures have also suffered from cracking.

It has been stated[2] that the Baptist and S. Bartholomew were originally on the same side of the central panel (which does not appear credible), and that two other saints on the other side (now lost) completed a pentaptych.

The attribution of No. 1103 to Fiorenzo di Lorenzo is reasonable.[3]

The composition of the central panel corresponds with that of a panel of 1457 or 1458 by Niccolò di Liberatore da Foligno (Alunno) in the Deruta Museum (formerly S. Francesco there), and rather less closely with that of a Benozzo, perhaps rather earlier, at Vienna.[4]

If it is desired to explain, without a visit by Fiorenzo to Florence, the Verrocchiesque character of some parts of No. 1103, one may perhaps suggest an influence from a tabernacle at S. Maria di Monteluce, Perugia, usually admitted as by the Verrocchiesque Francesco di Simone Ferrucci.[5] This tabernacle is of 1483; No. 1103 appears from the style a rather early work of Fiorenzo di Lorenzo, but the evidence is insufficient to show that it is necessarily earlier than 1483.[6]

PROVENANCE: In the Monaldi Collection, Perugia, by 1872.[7] Purchased from the Marchese Perolo Monaldi, Perugia, 1881.

REPRODUCTION: *Illustrations, Italian Schools*, 1937, p. 134. *Plates, Earlier Italian Schools*, 1953, Vol. I, p. 141.

REFERENCES: (1) It may be noted that the three panels obviously belong together, although there is some variation in the halo patterns, and although the gold background of the wings is patterned, while that of the central panel is not patterned. The floor in all three corresponds exactly, and so does the style. (2) Apparently first in the *Descriptive and Historical Catalogue of the National Gallery*, 1889. (3) Borenius, in a note to Crowe and Cavalcaselle, *History of Painting in Italy*, V, 1914, p. 270, calls it a studio work; Jacobsen in the *Repertorium für Kunstwissenschaft*, 1901, p. 350, inclines to the same view. (4) Reproduced by W. Bombe, *Geschichte der Peruginer Malerei*, 1912, Figs. 63, 64 (No. 1103 is Fig. 62). There is some evidence that Giannicola di Paolo copied the Deruta picture in 1494; see U. Gnoli, *Pittori e Miniatori nell' Umbria*, 1923, p. 136. A fairly exact copy of the Benozzo, ascribed to Ugolino di Gisberto, is reproduced by Gnoli, *op. cit.*, p. 338. The date of the Deruta picture is uncertain: A. Rossi, *I Pittori di Foligno*, 1872, p. 31, gives the signature with the date 1457; S. Frenfanelli Cibo, *Niccolò Alunno*, 1872, p. 115, gives the signature with the date 1458; the catalogue of the Perugia Exhibition, 1907, p. 36, No. 18, gives the signature with the date 1458 (?). (5) Venturi, *Storia dell'Arte Italiana*, Vol. VI, Fig. 492. (6) Bombe, *op. cit.*, p. 129, calls it early; Gnoli, *op. cit.*, p. 114, calls it *ca.* 1478. (7) Mariano Guardabassi, *Indice-Guida dei Monumenti Pagani e Cristiani . . . nella Provincia dell'Umbria*, 1872, p. 201, Nos. 32–4, as Fiorenzo di Lorenzo. Nos. 101 and 102 of the *Elenco dei Quadri della Galleria del fu Marchese Giovanni Battista Monaldi di Perugia*, 1878.

Ascribed to FIORENZO DI LORENZO

2483   THE VIRGIN AND CHILD

Wood, painted surface, $19 \times 14\frac{1}{2}$ (0·48 × 0·37).

Good condition, the Child's face rather rubbed; much new gold.

The framing is fixed to the panel, but seems not to be original.

Gnoli[1] thinks that this is Fiorenzo's latest known work; this is possible, although there is little evidence of what Fiorenzo's late style may have been. Fry,[2] while agreeing with the attribution to Fiorenzo, remarked on some similarity to the work of Pintoricchio. Berenson, in his 1932 Lists, ascribed the picture to Pintoricchio himself; this appears difficult to accept, but Zeri agrees with Berenson's attribution.[3]

The composition is of a type associated with Verrocchio;[4] but it is doubtful if a direct Florentine influence need be assumed for this picture.

VERSION: In a *Virgin and Child with S. Jerome* at Boston, the Virgin is very similar.[5]

PROVENANCE: Bought by George Salting in 1898;[6] lent by him to the Burlington Fine Arts Club, Umbrian Exhibition, 1909 (No. 1); Salting Bequest, 1910.

REPRODUCTION: *Illustrations, Italian Schools*, 1937, p. 135. *Plates, Earlier Italian Schools*, 1953, Vol. I, p. 142.

REFERENCES: (1) U. Gnoli, *Pittori e Miniatori nell'Umbria*, 1923, p. 115. (2) Roger Fry in *The Burlington Magazine*, Vol. XVI (1910), p. 267. (3) Zeri in the *Bollettino d'Arte*, 1953, p. 136. (4) Cf. for instance the picture at Berlin, reproduced by Van Marle, *Development of the Italian Schools of Painting*, Vol. XI, Fig. 323. (5) Reproduced by Van Marle, *op. cit.*, Vol. XIV, Fig. 118. (6) Salting MSS.

FLORENTINE SCHOOL

585 PORTRAIT OF A LADY IN RED

Wood, painted surface, $16\frac{1}{2} \times 11\frac{1}{2}$ (0·42 × 0·29); excluding a narrow band painted black all round.

Very good condition. There is a little repaint on the flesh, e.g. at the tip of the nose; and there is some damage in the background. *Pentimento* in the back of the neck.

No. 585 was acquired as the portrait of Isotta da Rimini; this identification was perhaps made from some vague similarity to one of Matteo de' Pasti's medals.[1] One of these medals, in which the costume is rather similar to that in No. 585, is dated 1446; but No. 585 may be rather later.[2]

The picture was purchased as by Piero della Francesca, and was later catalogued as Umbrian School, School of the Pollaiuolo, Ascribed to Uccello. Crowe and Cavalcaselle thought it by a follower of Uccello.[3] Ascribed by Schmarsow[4] to Antonio del Pollaiuolo, and by Salmi[5] to a follower of Antonio del Pollaiuolo. In Berenson's Lists of 1932 as by Domenico Veneziano.

A portrait of similar type, but in reverse, is recorded in the F. J. Fisher Collection at Detroit.[6]

COPY: Van Marle says that a copy on canvas was shortly before 1929 on the Paris market.[7]

PROVENANCE: From the collection of Conte Ferdinando, and then his son, Conte Carlo Guicciardini at Florence.[8] Purchased with other pictures from Lombardi and Baldi, Florence, 1857.[9]

REPRODUCTION: *Illustrations, Italian Schools*, 1937, p. 363. *Plates, Earlier Italian Schools*, 1953, Vol. I, p. 143.

REFERENCES: (1) G. F. Hill, *Corpus of Italian Medals*, 1930, Nos. 167 sqq. and 187 sqq., and Plates 32 and 35. Conte Paolo Guicciardini (letter of 3 August, 1948) has kindly pointed out that Luigi di Piero di Luigi Guicciardini was ambassador to Sigismondo Malatesta in 1453; a portrait of Isotta might thus have entered the Guicciardini Collection, whence No. 585 certainly comes, and this may perhaps be taken as some confirmation of the identification for the sitter. (2) Jean Lipman in *The Art Bulletin*, 1936, p. 101, puts it in the period 1450–75. (3) Crowe and Cavalcaselle, *History of Painting in Italy*, Vol. II, 1864, p. 543. (4) A Schmarsow in *L'Arte*, 1912, p. 95. (5) Mario Salmi, *Paolo Uccello Andrea del Castagno Domenico Veneziano*, 1938, p. 113. (6) Reproduced as by Antonio del Pollaiuolo in *Pantheon*, 1929, p. 12, and by W. R. Valentiner, *Unknown Masterpieces*, I, 1930, No. 13. (7) Van Marle, *Development of the Italian Schools of Painting*, Vol. XI, p. 337. (8) 'Conte Carlo Guicciardini' is apparently on information supplied to Eastlake. The Guicciardini arms are in fact on a label and on a seal on the back; and they are of a form used by the father of Conte Carlo, Ferdinando di Lorenzo, b. 1782, d. 1833 (letter of 2 July, 1948, from Conte Paolo Guicciardini, in the Gallery archives). The picture is not identifiable in the Guicciardini inventory of 1807, referred to in the entry for Botticelli, No. 1033. (9) For details concerning the Lombardi-Baldi Collection, see Appendix I.

1196 THE COMBAT OF LOVE AND CHASTITY

Love is shooting arrows against Chastity (embodied as Petrarch's Laura). Chastity protects herself by a shield, which breaks Love's golden arrows; she holds a chain, by which Love is destined to be bound.

Wood, painted surface, $16\frac{3}{4} \times 13\frac{3}{4}$ (0.425×0.35); painted up to the edges all round.

Very good condition; some damage on Love's face.

The subject is from Petrarch's *Triumphs*, and represents an early moment in the victory of Chastity over Love.[1] A picture at Turin continues the story, showing *Love Bound on the Car of Chastity*.[2] Four pictures in private possession at Genoa are said to be from the same series.[3] These pictures may have decorated a *cassone* or other piece of furniture.

The picture at Turin shows a view of Florence in the background; this confirms what is indeed fairly clear from the style, that the pictures are Florentine. The precise attribution has not been settled. Morelli thought that they were by a painter related to Filippino Lippi and Botticelli.[4] Jacobsen and Schubring ascribed them to a follower of Botticelli.[5] Toesca[6] ascribed them to a follower of Domenico Ghirlandaio; G. L. (G. Lorenzetti)[7] to a miniaturist follower of Domenico Ghirlandaio. Berenson[8] calls them Cosimo Rosselli. A Venturi[9] ascribed them to Benedetto Ghirlandaio. Gronau [10] rejected the attribution to Cosimo Rosselli. R. Carità calls them Bartolomeo di Giovanni.[11]

PROVENANCE: From the collection of the Marchese Crosa di Vergagni, Genoa.[12] Purchased from F. A. Y. Brown, Genoa, Lewis Fund, 1885.[13]

REPRODUCTION: *Illustrations, Italian Schools*, 1937, p. 315. *Plates, Earlier Italian Schools*, 1953, Vol. I, p. 144.

REFERENCES: (1) Relevant passages in Petrarch are lines 22/3, 34/6, 67, 118/9 and 122 in the *Triumph of Chastity*; see *Die Triumphe Francesco Petrarcas*, ed. Carl Appel, 1901, pp. 226 ff., or Petrarch, *Le Rime Sparse e i Trionfi*, ed. Ezio Chiòrboli, 1930, *Trionfo della Pudicizia*, pp. 326 ff. (2) Turin, 1899 Catalogo, No. 106; size, 0·42 × 0·65; reproduced by P. Schubring, *Cassoni*, 1923, Plate LXXVIII. They are clearly from the same series; apart from anything else, the shields shown in the two pictures are closely similar. (3) These pictures appear never to have been reproduced; so it is difficult to certify the usual claim that they are from the same series as No. 1196 and the picture at Turin. They are mentioned in Palazzo of the Marchese Agostino Adorno at Genoa as by Mantegna in the *Guida di Genova* by F. Alizeri, II, 1847, p. 435, who on p. 426 says apparently that the collection was formed by this man; they were seen in Palazzo Adorno by Eastlake in 1861 and 1862 (Eastlake's note-books). In the National Gallery MS. Catalogue, entry for No. 1196 in 1885, it is reported that they had passed by inheritance from Marchese Adorno to his daughter Contessa Durazzo; Camilla, a cousin of Agostino Adorno, married in 1843 Marchese Bandinello di Marcello Francesco Durazzo (Litta, *Famiglie Celebri d'Italia*, Tav. III of the Adorno family). They are recorded as at the Palazzo Adorno, Genoa, in Berenson's *Florentine Painters*, 1909. What appears to be the best description of these pictures occurs as follows in Prince d'Essling (Duc de Rivoli) and E. Müntz, *Pétrarque, ses études d'art*, etc., 1902, p. 142: 'Nous y voyons, dans le premier tableau, l'Amour étendu, les bras liés derrière le corps, et maintenu par deux femmes, tandis que d'autres femmes, debout, saisissent ses ailes, son carquois, et brisent ses flèches. Dans un admirable paysage, peuplé de petites figures, on aperçoit un char qui porte un trône orné de pierreries, des colonnes de marbre avec des chapiteaux d'or, et deux licornes couchées.—Le second panneau représente l'Amour, nu, enchaîné, devant son char, qui est conduit par des femmes et qui entre dans un temple à portique et à colonnes cannelées. Plus loin, se tient, attaché à une colonne de marbre surmontée d'une statue, un autre groupe de femmes. Au premier plan, sont assis deux jeunes gens. Près du char on aperçoit des licornes.—Il n'est pas impossible que l'*Histoire de Judith* et celle *de Jugurtha*, qui fait suite à ces deux scènes, soient là pour symboliser le Triomphe de la Renommée.' (4) G. Morelli, *Borghese and Doria-Pamfili Galleries*, translated by C. J. Ffoulkes, 1892, pp. 86/7. (5) E. Jacobsen in *L'Arte*, 1897, p. 126; P. Schubring, *Cassoni*, 1923, Nos. 325 sqq. (6) P. Toesca in *L'Arte*, 1903, pp. 245/6. (7) G. L. in *L'Arte*, 1910, p. 320. (8) Berenson, Lists of 1932; see also Lists of 1901 and 1909 (Florentine Painters). (9) Venturi, *Storia dell'Arte Italiana*, Vol. VII, Part I, p. 768. (10) Gronau in Thieme-Becker, Vol. XXIX, p. 36, where a few other pictures are listed as being by the same hand. (11) R. Carità in the *Bollettino d'Arte*, 1949, pp. 270 ff., with several references to the literature. (12) This is stated in the National Gallery MS. and printed catalogues; there is no reason to doubt it. Confirmation may be found in the fact that the picture at Turin, obviously of the same series, was presented by the Marchese Crosa di Vergagni in 1847 (?) (the Turin catalogue of 1899 gives the date as 1847, R. Carità in the *Bollettino d'Arte*, 1949, p. 271, gives 1857); and F. Alizeri in his *Guida di Genova*, II, 1847, p. 1349, records in the Nicolò Crosa di Vergagni Collection at Genoa 'Due trionfi del Petrarca di Sandro Botticelli.' Carità, *loc. cit.*, claims that an earlier provenance from Palazzo Adorno, Genoa, was suggested for the Turin picture by Cavalcaselle e Crowe, *Storia della Pittura in Italia*, Vol. VI, 1894, pp. 280/2. But Cavalcaselle and Crowe do not say this; nor do Crowe and Cavalcaselle, *History of Painting in Italy*, ed. Douglas and De Nicola, IV, 1911, p. 263; nor does their source, Mündler, in the *Zeitschrift für bildende Kunst*, Vol. II, 1867, p. 279. (13) As Botticelli.

1199 TONDO: THE VIRGIN AND CHILD, S. JOHN AND AN ANGEL

Wood, circular, painted surface, diameter, $27\frac{1}{2}$ (0·695). Including the frame, slightly oval, $41 \times 40\frac{1}{2}$ (1·04 × 1·03).

Excellent state; original frame.

The design of the Virgin and Child appearing on No. 1199 was one of the most popular in fifteenth-century Florence; possibly the best existing example appeared in the Aynard Sale, Paris, 1/4 December, 1913 (lot 43).[1] The Aynard picture is sometimes held to be the original, and to be by Pesellino. The type of the Virgin is not far from Fra Filippo Lippi, although no exact original by Fra Filippo appears to be known. The angel in No. 1199 is copied, without the wings but otherwise very closely, from the Angel of Fra Filippo's *Annunciation* at Munich (from the Murate at Florence).[2] The S. John in No. 1199 recurs in several works.[3]

The production of pictures such as No. 1199 appears to have been the *raison d'être* of one or more Florentine studios in the fifteenth century. The existing works were ascribed to Pier Francesco Fiorentino, then to a pseudo-Pier Francesco Fiorentino; in the biography of the former it is explained that these classifications are not justified.

VERSIONS: A tondo, diameter $27\frac{1}{2}$ in., lent by T. Lowinsky to the Burlington Fine Arts Club, 1923/4 (No. 105), is stated to be of the same composition as No. 1199.[4] Some of the numerous variants are referred to in note 1.

PROVENANCE: Purchased from Baslini at Milan, Walker Fund, 1885.[5]

REPRODUCTION: *Illustrations, Italian Schools*, 1937, p. 227 (without the frame). *Plates, Earlier Italian Schools*, 1953, Vol. I, p. 145 (with the frame).

REFERENCES: (1) The Aynard picture is reproduced in the Sale catalogue; also in *Dedalo*, 1932, p. 667, and in the *Rivista d'Arte*, 1938, p. 137. Some variants of the design, conveniently reproduced, are as follows. The Virgin and Child alone: Berlin, 1931 Katalog, No. 71A, s.v. Fiorentino, reproduced in the Berlin Illustrations, and by Van Marle, *Development of the Italian Schools of Painting*, Vol. XIII, Fig. 297; Victoria and Albert Museum, Ionides Collection, Catalogue, 1925, Plate 27; Nancy, reproduced in *Dedalo*, July 1926, p. 100; Philadelphia, J. G. Johnson Collection, Catalogue, Vol. I, 1913, No. 41, reproduced in the *Rassegna d'Arte*, 1905, p. 116; Washington, No. 646, reproduced in *Paintings and Sculpture from the Widener Collection*, 1948, Plate 6. The Virgin and Child, with a S. John as in No. 1199 but inverted; Havemeyer Sale, New York, 10 April, 1930 (lot 112), with reproduction; and, with another figure added, in the Hermitage at Leningrad, reproduced in *Art in America*, June, 1935, p. 104, Fig. 1. The Virgin and Child with a different S. John occurs at Kiev; reproduced in *Art in America*, June, 1935, p. 104, Fig. 3. (2) R. Œrtel, *Fra Filippo Lippi*, 1942, Figs. 64, 65. This angel recurs also in a tondo at Narbonne (Reinach, *Répertoire*, V. p. 129, and Plate xxi of the 1923 Narbonne Catalogue), where a second angel is from the Doria *Annunciation* (Œrtel, *op. cit.*, Fig. 62) and the other figures—the Virgin, the Child, S. John the Baptist, God the Father and the Holy Ghost—are from the Berlin *Nativity* (Œrtel, *op. cit.*, Fig. 94). (3) Two have been mentioned in note 1. Another, with a differing Virgin and Child, is in the Fogg Art Museum at Cambridge, Mass. (Catalogue, 1919, No. 10, with reproduction); similar to this, but with God the Father added, at Zagreb (Catalogue, Italian Schools, 1939, No. 23 (51), with reproduction). See also the picture at Poppi, reproduced in the *Bollettino d'Arte*, 1952, p. 257. (4) Van Marle, *Development of the Italian Schools of Painting*, Vol. XIII, p. 450. (5) As Florentine School. Catalogued, 1889–1906, as Tuscan School; then as Pier Francesco Fiorentino.

2492 TONDO: THE HOLY FAMILY WITH ANGELS

GI / N / A is legible on the Virgin's collar; perhaps once preceded by RE. Rays are shown descending from a cloud towards the Child.

Wood, circular, diameter $49\frac{1}{2}$ (1·26) approx. The measurements are within an incised line, which continues all the way round. The paint extends to the edges of the panel (diameter $52\frac{1}{2}$ (1·33)); but outside the incised line, the paint is entirely or almost entirely new.

Good condition.

Formerly ascribed to Jacopo del Sellaio.[1] It seems to be[2] from the same milieu, or even by the same hand, as various pictures, the chief of which are two altarpieces in S. Spirito at Florence[3] and another at Volterra.[4] Berenson[5] calls these three altarpieces Raffaelle Carli; but this is doubtful.[6] The works, including No. 2492, are somewhat eclectic, but seem to show the influence of Ghirlandaio as much as anybody's.

PROVENANCE: Bought by George Salting apparently in 1889.[7] On loan at the National Gallery in 1899[8] and 1900.[9] Salting Bequest, 1910.

REPRODUCTION: *Illustrations, Italian Schools*, 1937, p. 329. *Plates, Earlier Italian Schools*, 1953, Vol. I, p. 146.

REFERENCES: (1) See M. Logan in the *Revue Archéologique*, 1899, II, p. 480. (2) This was suggested by P. Pouncey. (3) One is reproduced by Van Marle, *Development of the Italian Schools of Painting*, Vol. XIII, Fig. 80. The other has been photographed by Alinari, No. 4731. (4) Reproduced by Katharine B. Neilson, *Filippino Lippi*, 1938, Fig. 97. (5) Berenson, *Drawings of the Florentine Painters*, 1938, pp. 111 ff. He considers Raffaelle Carli distinct from Raffaellino del Garbo. (6) For Raffaellino del Garbo, etc., see the biography in this catalogue. The whole problem is doubtful; this particular group is particularly doubtful. (7) Salting MSS., as Credi or Garbo. (8) See note 1. (9) Salting MSS., as School of Ghirlandaio.

2508 THE VIRGIN AND CHILD WITH TWO ANGELS

In the *Hortus Conclusus*. The Virgin's collar is inscribed *ave.regi(na). celi*.

Wood, painted surface, $27\frac{1}{4} \times 19\frac{5}{8}$ (0·695 × 0·50).

Good condition in general. The Virgin's halo and the top of her head were once higher up; the same is apparently true of the Child's halo also.

The composition of this picture is related to that of No. 589, Follower of Botticelli; both pictures, and others more or less similar, are derived ultimately from Fra Filippo Lippi's *Virgin and Child with Two Angels* in the Uffizi.[1] The types of No. 2508 differ a good deal from Lippi's.

No. 2508, like several others related in composition, has been ascribed to the young Botticelli.[2] So far as No. 2508 is concerned, the compiler does not accept that view.[3] Its execution is obviously nearer to the style we attribute to Verrocchio; but its quality is not very high.

VARIANTS: See above.

PROVENANCE: From Sir Augustus Callcott's Collection.[4] (Lord Orford) Sale, 28 June, 1856 (lot 258), bought by D. Bromley.[5] In the collection of the Rev. Walter Davenport Bromley, where seen by Waagen;[6] Sale, 12 June, 1863 (lot

75), bought by Bale. Charles Sackville Bale Sale, 14 May, 1881 (lot 296), bought by (Sampson S.) Lloyd. (Sampson S. Lloyd) Sale, 13 July, 1895 (lot 104), bought by Fairfax Murray. In the collection of George Salting, 1904;[7] Salting Bequest, 1910.

REPRODUCTION: *Illustrations, Italian Schools*, 1937, p. 135. *Plates, Earlier Italian Schools*, 1953, Vol. I, p. 147.

REFERENCES: (1) Reproduced by J. Mesnil, *Botticelli*, 1938, Plate II, and frequently elsewhere. (2) E.g. by Berenson in his Lists of 1932; and by Carlo Gamba, *Botticelli*, 1936, pp. 90/1. Salvini, *Tutta la Pittura del Botticelli*, 1958, Vol. I, p. 37, and Plate 13B, says that it is by Botticelli, perhaps in Verrocchio's studio, perhaps with some intervention by Verrocchio. (3) Cf. J. Mesnil, *Botticelli*, 1938, p. 194 (note 11), and E. K. Waterhouse in *The Burlington Magazine*, Vol. LXXIV (1939), p. 99. (4) Not in the Sale of 10 May, 1845. (5) As ex-Callcott; in this and the following sales as by Filippo Lippi. (6) Waagen, *Treasures*, IV, 1857, p. 167, as Pesellino. (7) Salting MSS.

3120 FRESCO: HEAD OF MALE SAINT (FRAGMENT)

Fresco, irregular shape, $16\frac{1}{2} \times 13$ (0.42×0.33).

Much damaged; the corners at the bottom right and left are new.

This fragment is from the church of the Carmine at Florence;[1] there is good evidence that it is from the chapel dedicated to S. Andrew, founded by Ugolino di Bonsi after 1365.[2] Some fragments from the same series, in very poor condition, are stated to be still in the chapel, behind more modern decoration.[3] The concave surface of No. 3120 rather suggests that it was from a vault; but it is impossible to say of what scene this head formed a part. No. 3120 is too much damaged to make an attribution worth while.

PROVENANCE: As explained above, from the Chapel of S. Andrea in the Carmine at Florence, founded by Ugolino di Bonsi after 1365. The Carmine was largely destroyed by fire in 1771 and thereafter reconstructed, with an altered arrangement of the chapels. No. 3120 is presumably one of the fragments discovered in the Carmine in September, 1859;[4] in the collection of Sir Austen Henry Layard by 1864.[5] Exhibited at South Kensington, 1869 (No. 53); Layard Bequest, 1916.[6]

REPRODUCTION: *Plates, Earlier Italian Schools*, 1953, Vol. I, p. 148.

REFERENCES: (1) Layard MSS. in the National Gallery. (2) Crowe and Cavalcaselle, *History of Painting in Italy*, I, 1864, p. 365, mention No. 3120 as being from the Velluti Chapel. Velluti is, however, a mistake and the correction to Bonsi was made in the Italian edition, Vol. II, 1883, p. 35. The correction was doubtless due to Santi Mattei, *Ragionamento intorno all'antica chiesa del Carmine di Firenze*, 1869, p. 13. Mattei does not mention No. 3120 explicitly, but does refer to the passage in Crowe and Cavalcaselle, claiming that the chapel in question is the Bonsi Chapel, that he Mattei discovered the remains of frescoes in it in September, 1859, and that it was he who showed these remains to Cavalcaselle and to Ugo Baldi. For the history of the chapel, see Ugo Procacci in the *Rivista d'Arte*, 1932, pp. 156/7 and 192. It may be mentioned that this chapel is distinct from the Manetti Chapel in the Carmine at Florence, from which comes No. 276 of this catalogue, Spinello Aretino. (3) Procacci, *loc. cit.*; but Procacci in the *Bollettino d'Arte*, Vol. XXVII, 1933/4, p. 332, states that attempts to find further remains in the chapel revealed nothing. (4) Santi Mattei, as in note 2. (5) Crowe and Cavalcaselle, as in note 2. (6) For the history of the Layard Collection, see Appendix IV.

3627 ROUNDEL: GOD THE FATHER

Wood, painted surface, roundel, diameter $4\frac{1}{8}$ (0·105). Including the frame, the diameter is $5\frac{1}{8}$ (0·13).

So far as can be seen, this appears to be well preserved, including the gold.

Apparently a fragment from a frame.

Formerly catalogued as by Masaccio, and said to be probably from the frame of Masaccio's Pisan altarpiece. This view has had supporters,[1] but doubt has also been expressed.[2] Longhi[3] calls it Venetian ca. 1450/65, near early Giovanni Bellini under the influence of Antonio Vivarini, and perhaps from the frame of one of the Carità altarpieces.[4] It would seem, nevertheless, to be Florentine.

PROVENANCE: Acquired in London ca. 1908 by Charles Ricketts and Charles Shannon[5] and lent by them to the Burlington Fine Arts Club, *Florentine Painting before 1500*, 1919 (No. 5). Presented by Charles Ricketts and Charles Shannon, through the N.A.C.F., 1922. Exhibited at the National Gallery, N.A.C.F. Exhibition, 1945/6 (No. 29).

REPRODUCTION: *Illustrations, Italian Schools*, 1937, p. 223. *Plates, Earlier Italian Schools*, 1953, Vol. I, p. 149.

REFERENCES: (1) E.g. Sir Claude Phillips in *The Burlington Magazine*, Vol. XXXIV (1919), p. 210, and Berenson, 1932 Lists. See the entry for Masaccio, No. 3046 in this catalogue. (2) The attribution to Masaccio is rejected by Toesca in the *Enciclopedia Italiana*, Vol. XXII, p. 475. Mario Salmi, *Masaccio*, 1948, pp. 118 and 225 f., and Plate 216, calls it imitator of Masaccio. (3) R. Longhi in *Critica d'Arte*, Nos. XXV/VI, 1940, p. 181. (4) The Carità altarpieces are reproduced in the Catalogue of the Giovanni Bellini Exhibition at Venice, 1949 (Nos. 6–21); the panels correctly arranged in *Arte Veneta*, 1949, pp. 136 ff., Plates 155–158. (5) See *Self-Portrait taken from the Letters and Journals of Charles Ricketts, R.A.*, 1939, p. 149, letter from Ricketts to Sydney Cockerell, 16 October, 1908; acquired as a Russian icon, near Whiteley's in Bayswater.

3826 CASSONE, WITH THE STORY OF THE SCHOOLMASTER OF FALERII

A chest of carved and gilded wood. The picture on the front illustrates the following story. When the Roman leader Camillus laid siege to Falerii, the citizens were able to continue their usual pursuits; in particular, the boys were taken by their schoolmaster to play and exercise, not only within the town (probably shown, centre background), but also outside the walls (right centre, background). Eventually the schoolmaster led his pupils outside the walls (centre middle distance), but this time with the intention of betraying the city. In the right foreground, he is shown with his pupils kneeling before Camillus. Camillus refused to profit by this treachery, and gave the boys rods and scourges to punish the schoolmaster and drive him back into the city (not shown). The Falerians, moved by the justice of Camillus, sent ambassadors to him (left middle ground). The ambassadors, and Camillus holding the key of the city he has received from them, are shown again in the left foreground; SPQR is on one of the banners.

At the ends of the cassone are painted panels, each with two naked children. Above and below, are strips of painted patterning, both at the front and at the sides. Inside the lid is a decorative design (mostly stencilled).

Wood. The size of the main picture is $15\frac{1}{8} \times 50\frac{1}{4}$ ($0\cdot385 \times 1\cdot28$); the picture at the left end, $15\frac{1}{4} \times 19$ ($0\cdot39 \times 0\cdot485$); the picture at the right end, $15\frac{1}{2} \times 19$ ($0\cdot395 \times 0\cdot485$). The size of the painted decoration inside the lid is $13\frac{1}{2} \times 60$ ($0\cdot34 \times 1\cdot52$), approx. The total size of the cassone is $38 \times 78\frac{1}{2} \times 29\frac{1}{2}$ ($0\cdot97 \times 2\cdot00 \times 0\cdot75$), approx.

The three main paintings are very much damaged. It is doubtful if any of the gilding is old. The painting inside the lid, on the other hand, is in general in good condition, though damaged in part by cracking.

A *cassone* is a chest, which was often much decorated; the usual occasion for its commission was a marriage.[1]

The story of M. Furius Camillus and the Schoolmaster of Falerii (394 B.C.) is told by Plutarch and others.[2]

Schubring calls the paintings on No. 3826 Florentine *ca.* 1440, from the circle of the Anghiari Master.[3] The pattern inside the lid recurs inside the lid of a cassone which Schubring dates from 1461,[4] and inside the lids of the Morelli-Nerli cassoni, which have been identified from the arms as being for a marriage of 1472.[5]

PROVENANCE: From the Collection of Lady Lindsay;[6] presented by her daughters, the Misses Lindsay, 1912.

REPRODUCTIONS: *Illustrations, Italian Schools*, 1937, p. 136 (main picture). *Plates, Earlier Italian Schools*, 1953, Vol. I, pp. 149–150.

REFERENCES: (1) See P. Schubring, *Cassoni*, 1923. (2) Plutarch's *Life of Camillus* (Everyman edition, Vol. I, pp. 198/9); the story is also told by Livy. Schubring (*Belvedere*, 1930, ii, p. 1) claims that Plutarch is here the source, though this seems uncertain. (3) Schubring in *Belvedere*, 1930, ii, p. 1. For the Anghiari Master, see Schubring in *The Burlington Magazine*, Vol. XXII (1912/3), pp. 158 ff., and his *Cassoni*, 1923, p. 243. Attributions of works to this name are very doubtful; several of Schubring's are attacked by Longhi in *Critica d'Arte*, 1940, p. 187. (4) Florence, Bardini; Schubring, *Cassoni*, 1923, Nos. 283/5 and Plate LXVI. (5) *Catalogue of the Lee Collection* (Courtauld Institute of Art), 1958 (No. 58); see also *The Illustrated London News*, 28 February, 1948, p. 248, and (for the second lid) letter of Tomas Harris, 19 March, 1949, in the Gallery archives. The front of one cassone represents the Schoolmaster of Falerii, similar in arrangement to the treatment of the story in No. 3826. Apart from this, and the pattern inside the lids, the forms of the Bardini and Morelli-Nerli cassoni differ from No. 3826. The paintings on the Morelli-Nerli cassoni also differ in style; Schubring's reproduction of the Bardini cassone is not clear on this point. (6) Letter in the Gallery archives.

3895 WING OF A DIPTYCH: THE DEAD CHRIST AND THE VIRGIN

Reverse: a painted Cross, with some of the Instruments of the Passion (spear, sponge, hammer, three nails, and vessel for vinegar(?)).

Wood, painted surface, $23 \times 15\frac{1}{4}$ ($0\cdot585 \times 0\cdot385$), excluding about $\frac{3}{4}$ in. of brown paint at the sides and the bottom. The size of the painting on the reverse is $23\frac{1}{8} \times 15\frac{1}{2}$ ($0\cdot59 \times 0\cdot395$). The condition of the gold patterning on the front shows that the picture has been cut about $1\frac{1}{2}$ in. at the top, not counting a possible further $\frac{3}{4}$ in. of edging.

Cleaned in 1951/2. Very considerably damaged, the worst losses being in the lining of the Virgin's mantle; but the extensive overpainting removed during the cleaning covered much original paint not badly preserved. The reverse has many lacunae.

The other wing of this diptych is in the Lehman Collection at New York, representing S. John the Evangelist and presumably the Magdalen; it is cradled, and apparently retains no painting on the back.[1]

The subject here is divided as a diptych.[2] The pseudo-cufic ornamentation of the gold background occurs with variations in other pictures.[3] The pot on the reverse, although the nails are actually placed in it, would seem to be the 'vessel full of vinegar' of John xix, 29. A triptych with Instruments of the Passion on the outsides of the wings is in the Accademia at Venice.[4]

No. 3895 entered the Gallery as by Ambrogio Lorenzetti,[5] but it appears rather to be Florentine. H. D. Gronau calls it style of Daddi;[6] Berenson in his 1936 Lists doubtfully suggests a Neapolitan follower of Giotto; Coletti puts it into relation with 'Giottino'.[7] Some critics find it not quite Florentine in style;[8] but in any case No. 3895 is near to a somewhat damaged *Crucifixion* in the Louvre,[9] which is sometimes admitted as being by the same hand.[10]

PROVENANCE: Thomas Watson Jackson Sale, 14 May, 1915 (lot 49),[11] bought by Wagner. Presented by Henry Wagner, 1924.

REPRODUCTIONS: *Illustrations, Italian Schools*, 1937, p. 195 (front). *Plates, Earlier Italian Schools*, 1953, Vol. I. p. 151 (front). Both before cleaning. The reverse is reproduced in *Paintings and Drawings on the Backs of National Gallery Pictures*, 1946, Plate 37.

REFERENCES: (1) Published by H. D. Gronau in *The Burlington Magazine*, Vol. LIII (1928), pp. 78 ff., with reproduction. Lehman Catalogue, 1928, No. XXVII, as ex-Duchess of Norfolk; size, $23 \times 15\frac{5}{8}$ (0.575 *sic* $\times 0.39$). Information about the back kindly given by Mrs. E. E. Gardner, 1955. (2) Compare a diptych painted on ivory in the Ambrosiana at Milan, reproduced by Toesca, *Il Trecento*, 1951, Fig. 672. The subject is studied by E. Panofsky, *Imago Pietatis*, in the *Festschrift Friedländer*, 1927, pp. 261 ff. (3) E.g. in a picture ascribed to the Biadaiolo Illuminator: Offner, *Corpus*, Section III, Vol. II, Part I, 1930, Plate XIX. (4) 1955 Catalogue, XIV and XV Centuries, No. 16, reproduced. (5) Borenius in *The Burlington Magazine*, Vol. XXVII (1915), p. 27, calls it style of the Lorenzetti. The Lehman wing has also been associated with the Sienese School; Lehman Catalogue, *cit.*, as Sienese, perhaps under the influence of Simone Martini at Avignon; S. Ameisonowa in the *Rivista d'Arte*, 1939, pp. 118/9, as Master of the S. George Codex. (6) H. D. Gronau, *loc. cit.* in note 1. (7) L. Coletti in *Emporium*, 1942, pp. 470/2. L. Venturi, *Pitture Italiane in America*, 1931, Plate XLII, calls the Lehman picture Florentine. See further the exhibition catalogue of the Lehman Collection, Paris, 2nd edition, 1957 (No. 32). (8) G. M. Richter in *The Burlington Magazine*, Vol. LIX (1931), p. 251, is reminded of the Maestro delle Vele in the types of the Lehman picture, but sees a Sienese character in the goldwork. See also note 5 for various Sienese attributions. (9) Seymour de Ricci's Catalogue, *Ecoles Etrangères, Italie et Espagne*, 1913, p. 190, No. 1665A, as Sienese; reproduced by Coletti in *Emporium*, 1942, p. 474, Fig. 14. (10) Berenson in his 1936 Lists calls the Louvre picture 'Maso.' Coletti, *loc. cit.*, admits the identity of hand. Sergio Bettini, *Giusto de' Menabuoi*, 1944, p. 57, does not. (11) As Sienese.

4208   THE BAPTISM OF CHRIST (PART OF AN ALTAR-PIECE?)

S. John baptizes Christ; the Holy Ghost descends as a Dove.

Wood, painted surface, irregular octagon, $12\frac{1}{4} \times 8\frac{1}{4}$ (0·31 × 0·21). Including the framing, $15\frac{1}{4} \times 11\frac{1}{4}$ (0·385 × 0·285).

Very good condition. The framing is newly gilt, but may be, in parts at least, the original.

Perhaps an end panel from a predella.

Sirèn[1] ascribes it to Agnolo Gaddi. Berenson, in his 1932 Lists, says that it is by a Giottesque after 1350, tending towards Lorenzo Monaco. Salvini[2] calls it a late Gerinesque.

PROVENANCE: No doubt Warner Ottley Sale, 30 June, 1847 (lot 77), bought by Anthony.[3] Rev. J. Fuller Russell Sale, 18 April, 1885 (lot 96),[4] bought by Wagner. Henry Wagner Sale, 16 January, 1925 (lot 50),[5] bought by Martin. Presented by Viscount Rothermere, 1926.[6]

REPRODUCTION: *Illustrations, Italian Schools*, 1937, p. 137. *Plates, Earlier Italian Schools*, 1953, Vol. I, p. 152.

REFERENCES: (1) Sirèn, *Giottino*, 1908, p. 93. (2) R. Salvini, *L'Arte di Agnolo Gaddi*, 1936, p. 185. (3) As Cavallini. An Ottley provenance is stated for the picture in the Fuller Russell Sale, and lot 77 of the 1847 Ottley Sale fits; further, Anthony appears to have been acting for Fuller Russell at this sale—see the entry for Ugolino di Nerio, No. 1188, note 13. (4) As Cavallini. Presumably the picture, recorded briefly but with an Ottley provenance, in the Fuller Russell Collection *ca.* 1863 (Scharf's sketch-books, No. 66, p. 107, in the National Portrait Gallery). (5) As Cavallini. The marks of the Wagner sale are still on the back of No. 4208. (6) As School of Bernardo Daddi.

4906   CASSONE, WITH A TOURNAMENT SCENE

A chest of carved and gilded wood. A painting on the front represents a tournament in a square before a church (perhaps for the Piazza S. Croce at Florence). One of the onlookers is a winged, mounted figure. The church has over the doorway coats of arms, a red cross on a white ground (the Florentine people), and an eagle probably meant for the *Parte Guelfa*. On stands for spectators to the right are more coats of arms; the Florentine people repeatedly; several times a coat probably meant for Spinelli (see below), with the inscription LIBERTAS; and several times a coat or device (see below), a white object, with the inscriptions LIBERTAS and P NON FALIRE (the spelling varies). This last coat or device occurs also on the dresses of several of the men shown in the painting; also centre bottom, below the painting; also, somewhat varied and carved, on the wood left and right of the painting. The coat probably meant for Spinelli also occurs left and right of the painting, not carved.

At the sides of the cassone are painted panels, each with an armoured figure on a horse and two footmen; one of the riders has wings, the other arms or a device perhaps meant to be two spools.

Wood. The size of the main picture is $15 \times 51\frac{1}{4}$ (0.38×1.30); each side picture, $14\frac{3}{4} \times 17\frac{3}{4}$ (0.37×0.45). The total size of the cassone is $40\frac{1}{2} \times 80 \times 26$ ($1.03 \times 2.03 \times 0.66$), approx.

The chest itself is not in very good condition, the feet and some other parts of the woodwork being new. The pictures, on the other hand, are in fair state. It is doubtful if any of the gilding is old.

A *cassone*, like No. 3826 above, which see.

Little can be stated for sure concerning this piece of furniture. The tournament scene appears rather fantastic, and may well not record any historical occasion; nor is a precise location necessarily intended. Some of the coats of arms are pretty clearly intended for Spinelli, although the colours are wrong; it is doubtful if any part of these arms is old. It was doubtfully accepted in the 1939 Supplement to the Catalogue that the other principal coat of arms, or perhaps rather device, may have been connected with the Tanagli family; the Tanagli did at least once use a comparable device with the same motto (*Pour non failir*), though their arms themselves are different.[1] In the painted examples of this coat or device on No. 4906, the object represented does look like a pair of pincers (*tanaglia*); but the carved examples seem to consist of two separate things like nails or pins, connected by a ribbon. The frequent repetition of the word *Libertas* may refer to the arms of the Priori of Florence, where this word is included.

Berenson (1932 Lists) gives No. 4906 to the Master of the Jarves Cassoni,[2] who he says was also responsible for drawings for certain miniatures in a codex of Virgil in the Biblioteca Riccardiana, Florence.[3] Salmi,[4] while disagreeing with much of what Berenson claims for the Master of the Jarves Cassoni, seems to agree in associating No. 4906 with some miniatures in this Virgil codex.

Some of the items listed by Berenson as Master of the Jarves Cassoni are claimed by Stechow[5] to be from the shop of Marco del Buono and Apollonio di Giovanni; this is deduced from a cassone front at Oberlin College and its pendant (destroyed during the war),[6] where the coats of arms (Rucellai and Vettori) correspond with an entry in Marco del Buono and Apollonio di Giovanni's bottega book.[7] If critical opinion decides that No. 4906 is from the same shop as the Oberlin panel, it would be possible to label it Marco del Buono or Apollonio di Giovanni; the Spinelli family, whose arms are probably intended on No. 4906, is not mentioned in the bottega book, so No. 4906 might have to be dated outside the period of the book, which runs from 1446 to 1463 (or 1465 ?). If the date of No. 4906 is after the bottega book,[8] there would be some reason for labelling it Marco del Buono; Apollonio di Giovanni is known to have died in 1465.

PROVENANCE: Bequeathed by Sir Henry Bernhard Samuelson, Bart., in memory of his father, 1937.

REPRODUCTIONS: *Plates, Earlier Italian Schools*, 1953, Vol. I, pp. 153–154.

REFERENCES: (1) For the Tanagli arms with the device and motto added, see Memlinc's altarpiece at Danzig (reproduced by Friedländer, *Altniederländische Malerei*, Vol. VI, Plates VII–X). A. Warburg, in the Prussian *Jahrbuch*, 1902, pp. 250 ff., esp. p. 255, says that the motto was not a permanent adjunct to the Tanagli arms; reprint in Warburg's *Gesammelte Schriften, Die Erneuerung der heidnischen Antike*, 1932, I, pp. 192 ff., with addition concerning No. 4906 on pp. 374 f. (2) The four Jarves *cassoni* listed by Berenson are reproduced in Sirèn, *Catalogue of the Jarves Collection*, 1916, Nos. 33–36. (3) See also Berenson, *Drawings of the Florentine Painters*, 1938, No. 1842; one of the drawings is reproduced by Sidney Colvin, *A Florentine Picture-Chronicle*, 1898, Fig. 69. 20 of the finished miniatures are reproduced by Schubring, *Cassoni*, Plates L–LIII; in his text volume, Schubring numbers these 225–244, under the name of the Dido-Master. (4) Mario Salmi, *Paolo Uccello Andrea del Castagno Domenico Veneziano* (1936), p. 114; 2nd edition, 1938, p. 156. (5) W. Stechow in the *Bulletin of the Allen Memorial Art Museum*, Oberlin College, June, 1944, pp. 5 ff. See further the article *Apollonio di Giovanni* by E. H. Gombrich in *The Journal of the Warburg* and *Courtauld Institutes*, 1955, pp. 16 ff. (6) Both reproduced, but not very clearly, by Stechow, *loc. cit.* (7) The bottega book is printed by Schubring, *Cassoni*, 1923, pp. 443 ff.; the Rucellai-Vettori entry is on p. 450. (8) In the Supplement to the Catalogue, 1939, the date is claimed to be *ca.* 1460/70.

5930 SS. CATHERINE AND BARTHOLOMEW (RIGHT WING OF A TRIPTYCH)

The names are inscribed: [S] / .CHATERINA., and .S./.BAR-TOLOMEV.

Wood, painted surface, $32\frac{1}{2} \times 20$ (0.83×0.51). The picture has an uncusped pointed-arched top, of which the upper 2–3 in. have been cut away; the edging of the gold in this arched part is almost entirely new, but follows the original shape. Probably cut slightly at the bottom.

Fair state.

The names of the saints are on a sort of cartellino on the gold background, which is somewhat unusual.[1]

Apparently of the Florentine School, late fourteenth or even early fifteenth century.

PROVENANCE: Purchased in 1920 from or through Alphonse Kann, Paris, by Herbert Charles Coleman,[2] by whom bequeathed, 1949.[3]

REPRODUCTION: *Plates, Earlier Italian Schools*, 1953, Vol. I, p. 155.

REFERENCES: (1) Comparable forms occur on a *S. Catherine* (Offner, *Corpus*, Section III, Vol. IV, Plate XIII) and a *S. Benedict* (Mostra Giottesca, Florence, 1937, large catalogue by G. Sinibaldi and G. Brunetti, 1943, No. 154, with reproduction), both of which have been associated with Bernardo Daddi; also sometimes in earlier works. (2) Letter in the Gallery archives. (3) With an attribution to Spinello Aretino.

6266 THE VIRGIN AND CHILD

Wood, painted surface, $19\frac{1}{2} \times 13\frac{1}{4}$ (0.495×0.335).

Good condition.

The design of the Virgin and Child with slight variations (and diverse backgrounds) occurs in many versions; it may be considered one of the stand-bys of Florentine shops of the time. Two versions that have been assigned to Pesellino are in the Isabella Stewart Gardner Museum at Boston[1] and at Esztergom;[2] it may well be that the design was invented by him.[3] The execution of No. 6266, clearly one of the better examples, has been ascribed to Piero di Lorenzo[4] and to Don Diamante.[5] Some of the versions have extra figures; a good many of them are associated with the pseudo-Pier Francesco Fiorentino.[6]

VERSIONS: See above.

PROVENANCE: Said to have been in a house in Florence belonging to a family hailing from Prato;[7] stated to have belonged to Bardini at Florence.[8] Coll. Sir Thomas Gibson Carmichael (Lord Carmichael); Sale, 13 May, 1902 (lot 271), presumably bought in. Bequeathed by Lord Carmichael (d. 1926), with a life-interest to his widow; entered the Gallery collection in 1956. Lent to Edinburgh, 1958.

REPRODUCTION: In *Apollo*, 1925, I, p. 65.

REFERENCES: (1) Catalogue, 1931, pp. 257 ff., reproduced. (2) Catalogue, 1948, pp. 74/6, Fig. 84, as Lippi (?). The attribution to Pesellino of this and the Gardner version is accepted by Berenson, Lists of 1932 and 1936. (3) See Hendy in *The Burlington Magazine*, Vol. LIII, 1928, pp. 67 ff. (4) By Borenius in *Apollo*, 1925, I, p. 65. He associates it stylistically with a *Nativity* in the Louvre (Van Marle, *Italian Schools*, Vol. X, Fig. 305). (5) Berenson, Lists of 1932 and 1936. (6) It seems of little use to make a list of examples recorded in literature; references to reproductions of some of them are as follows. Budapest, Catalogue, *Byzantische* etc., 1916, p. 44, No. 55; Cambridge (Fogg), 1919 Catalogue, No. 10; Liverpool, *Twenty Old Masters*, 1948, p. 7; Paris, Musée André, Van Marle, *op. cit.*, Vol. XIII, Fig. 296; Washington, 1941 Illustrations, p. 164; Zagreb, 1939 Catalogue, No. 23. Among further references may be cited the catalogue of Sir Thomas Merton's Collection, 1950, No. XIII; Van Marle, *op. cit.*, Vol. XIII, Fig. 295; *The Burlington Magazine*, 1930, II, p. 219; *Pantheon*, 1930, p. 265 (and *The Burlington Magazine*, 1930, II, p. 219); *Dedalo*, 1932, pp. 686/7; the *Rassegna d'Arte*, 1922, p. 189. (7) Borenius in *Apollo*, 1925, I, p. 67. (8) Borenius in *Lord Carmichael of Skirling*, a memoir prepared by his wife, 1929, p. 254; this may be thought to be confirmed by W. Weisbach, *Francesco Pesellino*, 1901, p. 114.

FLORENTINE(?) SCHOOL

1299   PORTRAIT OF A YOUNG MAN

Wood, painted surface, $22 \times 14\frac{1}{2}$ ($0 \cdot 56 \times 0 \cdot 37$).

Somewhat repainted; but it may be doubted if the general character has been greatly changed.

Ascribed by Küppers[1] to Domenico Ghirlandaio, and by Berenson (1932 Lists) to Ghirlandaio in part. It was indeed in the 1929 catalogue classed as School of Ghirlandaio; but its connection with that painter appears rather remote, and it may even not be Florentine. Its low quality makes any attempt at precise attribution both unnecessary and unreliable.

PROVENANCE: Purchased from Stefano Bardini, Florence, 1889.[2]

REPRODUCTION: *Illustrations, Italian Schools*, 1937, p. 153. *Plates, Earlier Italian Schools*, 1953, Vol. I, p. 155.

REFERENCES:(1) P. E. Küppers, *Die Tafelbilder des Domenico Ghirlandaio*, 1916, pp. 43/4. (2) J. P. Richter (letter to Layard, 5 March, 1890) says that Bardini had had it for some years; British Museum, Add. MS. 39045, Layard Papers, Vol. CXV.

VINCENZO FOPPA
active 1456, died 1515/6

A Brescian, he was domiciled from about 1456 until 1490 at Pavia, thereafter at Brescia; but he made frequent journeys. There are several documented and dated works.

729   ALTARPIECE: THE ADORATION OF THE KINGS

The Virgin and Child and S. Joseph left, the Kings and their followers centre and right, the Star above.

Poplar,[1] painted surface, 94×83 ($2 \cdot 39 \times 2 \cdot 105$).

The condition is good for a picture of its size and date, and exceptionally good for a Foppa, although it is by no means free from damage. The most serious damage is to the figure of the Virgin; Foppa made several attempts at her hood, and now in some parts of the overlaps there is no original paint left. The Virgin's blue robe in general is down to the preparatory layer, most of the folds on it now not being original. S. Joseph's right thumb is new. Some (but not all) of the shadows on the faces have been worn; much the worst cases are the heads of the Virgin and of the negro right centre in the second row. There has been a good deal of flaking down the right-hand side. Parts of the paint surface are somewhat ragged in effect, as indeed is usual with Foppa. It may be remarked that much irresponsible repainting was removed in 1935/6.

There are several *pentimenti* besides those already noticed round the Virgin's head. There are two other outlines to the ox's back; S. Joseph's turban was once more upright; and both front legs of the horse on the right have been changed.

A late work.[2] There are some, not very close, similarities to a drawing at Berlin, assigned to Foppa, subject *The Justice of Trajan*; this drawing in its turn has some connection with an engraving of the same subject by Giovanni Maria da Brescia, 1502.[3]

The detail of the page stooping to remove one of the Kings' spurs is not particularly recondite; but it is perhaps worth recording that this motive appears in one of Jacopo Bellini's drawings,[4] also in Gentile da Fabriano's *Adoration of the Kings* in the Uffizi.

COPY: A small derivative with variations is stated to be in the sacristy of S. Maria Novella, Florence.[5]

PROVENANCE: In the collection of Cardinal Fesch in France, then (from 1815) at Rome; 1841 Catalogue, No. 1295;[6] Sale, 1845, lot 875,[7] bought by Bromley. Purchased at the Rev. Walter Davenport Bromley Sale, London, 13 June, 1863 (lot 155).

REPRODUCTION: *Illustrations, Italian Schools*, 1937, p. 139. *Plates, Earlier Italian Schools*, 1953, Vol., I p. 156.

REFERENCES: (1) Letter from B. J. Rendle, of the Forest Products Research Laboratory, in the Gallery archives. (2) Ffoulkes and Maiocchi, *Vincenzo Foppa*, 1909, pp. 207/10, date it at the end of the fifteenth or even beginning of the sixteenth century, and suggest that it may have come from Brescia. F. Wittgens, *Vincenza Foppa*, 1949, p. 107, dates it at the beginning of the sixteenth century. The attribution to Foppa is due to Crowe and Cavalcaselle, *Painting in North Italy*, 1871, II, pp. 7/8. (3) Ffoulkes and Maiocchi, *op. cit.*, pp. 47 ff., with reproductions. For a further discussion of this, and other drawings, see K. T. Parker in *Old Master Drawings*, Vol. XIII, 1938, pp. 6 ff.; F. Wittgens, *op. cit.*, p. 94; A. M. Hind, *Early Italian Engraving*, Vol. V, 1948, p. 57, and Vol. VI, 1948, Plate 568. (4) V. Goloubew, *Les Dessins de Jacopo Bellini*, 1908/12, II, Plate XXIX. (5) Ffoulkes and Maiocchi, *op. cit.*, p. 210. (6) As Manner of the fourteenth century. (7) As Bramantino.

FRANCESCA (PIERO DELLA)
See PIERO DELLA FRANCESCA

FRANCESCO DI ANTONIO
ca. 1394–1433 or later

Florentine School. In an income tax return of 1427, he gave his age as 33, and he joined the Physicians' Guild at Florence in 1429 (see G. Gronau in the *Rivista d'Arte*, 1932, pp. 383/4; also Frey, *Die Loggia dei Lanzi*, 1885, pp. 318 and 366, who in the second reference wrongly attributes to him the surname of *Banchi*). There is a triptych signed and dated 1415 (?) in the Fitzwilliam Museum at Cambridge (*Catalogue of Pictures in the Marlay Bequest*, 1927, No. 33). A fresco of *The Coronation* in S. Francesco at Figline is signed (cf. M. Salmi, *Masaccio*, 1948, p. 218). He was in 1429 paid for painting two organ shutters for Orsanmichele at Florence, which are identified as two pictures formerly in the Toscanelli Collection, and now in the Academy at Florence. He is presumably the same man as the Francesco Fiorentino, a follower of Lorenzo Monaco's according to Vasari; Vasari says that he painted a tabernacle in the Piazza S. Maria Novella at Florence (Vasari, 1550 edition, p. 216; ed. Milanesi, II, p. 25). All these pictures are reproduced by M. Salmi in the *Rivista d'Arte*, 1929, pp. 1 ff.

Ascribed to FRANCESCO DI ANTONIO

1456 THE VIRGIN AND CHILD WITH SIX ANGELS AND TWO CHERUBIM

On sleeves of the angels are inscribed *aue $\overline{yhs}$*, *a yh*, and perhaps *oša* (*u*?) (somewhat damaged). A strip of gilt scroll-work in relief has been fixed into the (modern) frame, in the position of a predella; it includes three painted quatrefoils of the Virgin, the dead Christ and S. John.

Wood. The size of the main picture is, pointed top, $33\frac{1}{2} \times 21\frac{1}{4}$ (0·85 ×

0·54), approx.; the edges of the picture have been somewhat damaged for the new frame. The size of the 'predella' is $2\frac{3}{4} \times 18$ (0·07 × 0·455); the diameter of the painted quatrefoils is, each, $2\frac{1}{2}$ (0·065).

Good condition.

It is not quite certain that the 'predella' originally belonged to the main picture.

In the 1929 Catalogue as Italian School. It was ascribed by Berenson to the school of Sassetta, and not improbably Priamo della Quercia,[1] a view later rejected by Berenson himself and by other critics.[2] Ascribed by Longhi to Andrea di Giusto.[3] Recently ascribed by Berenson to Francesco di Antonio.[4] Pudelko called it rather the Master of the Adimari Cassone,[5] whom Berenson thinks to be the same man as Francesco di Antonio. Longhi, who does not, has recently withdrawn his Andrea di Giusto attribution, accepts No. 1456 as being by Francesco di Antonio, and rejects Pudelko's view that it is by the Adimari Master.[6] No. 1456 appears to differ somewhat from Francesco di Antonio's triptych at Cambridge.

PROVENANCE: Presented by J. P. Heseltine, 1895.[7]

REPRODUCTION: *Illustrations, Italian Schools*, 1937, p. 175 (without the 'predella'). *Plates, Earlier Italian Schools*, 1953, Vol. I, p. 157.

REFERENCES: (1) Berenson in *The Burlington Magazine*, Vol. III (1903), p. 184. (2) E.g. by G. de Nicola in the *Rassegna d'Arte*, 1918, p. 74. (3) R. Longhi in *Pinacotheca*, 1928, p. 38. (4) Berenson, Lists of 1932 and 1936, s.v. Banchi. (5) Pudelko in *Florenz, Kunsthistorisches Institut, Mitteilungen*, Vol. IV (1932/4), p. 163. (6) R. Longhi in *Critica d'Arte*, 1940, pp. 186/7. He suggests a date of 1425/6. (7) As Italian; the N.G. 1895 Report suggested the school of Gentile da Fabriano.

FRANCESCO di Giorgio
1439–1510/2

Sienese School. Painter, sculptor, architect and engineer. First recorded as active, both as sculptor and painter, in 1464. In partnership with Neroccio for a time until *ca.* 1475. From 1477 at latest, in the service of the Duke of Urbino for some years. Apart from this, active chiefly at Siena, but also at Naples and elsewhere in Italy. Painting was not his most important activity. There is an authenticated picture at Siena; a second one there is probably authenticated also. See Allen Stuart Weller, *Francesco di Giorgio*, 1943.

1682   S. DOROTHY AND THE INFANT CHRIST

Wood, painted surface, $13\frac{1}{8} \times 8\frac{1}{8}$ (0·33 × 0·205). Size of the panel, $15\frac{1}{4} \times 10\frac{1}{4}$ (0·385 × 0·26); the framing covering the difference in these dimensions at the front is not the original.

Good condition; much of the gold is original.

When S. Dorothy was tortured on account of her faith, she suffered everything patiently for the love of Jesus Christ, in whose garden (she said) she had gathered delightful roses and apples. As she was being led off to be beheaded, one Theophilus asked her scornfully to let him have some of those roses. The season was winter; but when S. Dorothy knelt down on the block, a Child appeared brilliantly clad, carrying a basket with three roses and three apples. Take them, the Virgin Martyr begged, to Theophilus; the Child, who was Christ Himself, did so, and Theophilus was converted and received forthwith the crown of martyrdom.[1]

The apples have been omitted from the picture here. Weller[2] says that the subject of S. Dorothy is frequent in German art; he suggests that No. 1682 may be taken from some German print, and reproduces a possible prototype.[3] There are, nevertheless, some more or less similar representations in Early Italian, and perhaps in central Italian painting.[4] It should be added that the story was quite a well-known one; Francesco di Giorgio could have painted the subject as in No. 1682 from some literary source alone, without having seen any painted or engraved version.

Two panels, each showing *Two Flagellants*, have been associated with No. 1682,[5] but Weller is clearly right in saying that they do not come from the same ensemble.[6]

No. 1682 is generally accepted as a work of Francesco di Giorgio;[7] Weller dates it very early (before 1466).[8]

PROVENANCE: Exhibited at the New Gallery (Bardini Collection), Autumn 1898 (No. 116). Stefano Bardini of Florence Sale, London, 7 June, 1899 (lot 486),[9] bought by Agnew. Purchased from Agnew at cost price, 1899.

REPRODUCTION: *Illustrations, Italian Schools*, 1937, p. 142. *Plates, Earlier Italian Schools*, 1953, Vol. I, p. 158.

REFERENCES: (1) Cf. the Garnier edition of the *Golden Legend*; the story of S. Dorothy is not in Jacobus de Varagine's original compilation, but is one of the additions. (2) A. S. Weller, *Francesco di Giorgio*, 1943, pp. 55/6. (3) Weller, *op. cit.*, Fig. 5. (4) An angel takes the place of the Child in a fresco (inscribed S. Dorotea) in S. Zeno at Verona; E. Sandberg Vavalà, *La Pittura Veronese*, 1926, Fig. 24. A figure with the name inscribed, holding a basket of roses, is on a polyptych by Andrea Belunello at Forni di Sopra; reproduced in the Catalogue of the Pordenone Exhibition at Udine, 1939, No. 4. A figure holding a basket of roses, identified as S. Dorothy, is seen in a picture in S. Maria Calchera at Brescia, assigned to Moretto; reproduced by A. Morassi, *Brescia (Catalogo delle Cose d'Arte e di Antichità d'Italia)*, 1939, p. 381. In a Gentile da Fabriano at Urbino, the Virgin holds the Child, Who offers (?) a basket of roses to a female saint, called S. Rosa; reproduced by Van Marle, *Italian Schools*, Vol. VIII, Fig. 13, as *The Mystical Marriage of S. Catherine*. The compiler does not know that the saint there cannot be S. Dorothy (for what may be thought a rather similar treatment, outside Italy, see J. Braun, *Tracht und Attribute der Heiligen in der deutschen Kunst*, 1943, Fig. 272). A picture called *The Virgin and Child*, but possibly representing *S. Dorothy and the Infant Christ*, as in No. 1682, ascribed to Ambrogio Bergognone, is in the church of S. Carlo, Palazzago (Frazione di Burligo); see the *Rassegna d'Arte*, 1907, p. 76 (reproduction), and the *Inventario degli Oggetti d'Arte d'Italia*, I, *Provincia di Bergamo*, 1931, pp. 352, 354 (reproduction). One may further perhaps wonder if a fresco ascribed to Barna in S. Pietro at San Gimignano really includes the Virgin and Child, as claimed, rather than S. Dorothy and the Infant Christ; see Van Marle, *Italian Schools*, Vol II, Fig. 195. In any case, S. Dorothy among groups of saints is not particularly uncommon in Italian painting; see, for instance, on *The Annunciation* in the

Academy at Florence (No. 8606) ascribed to Giovanni del Biondo, the figure
with the name inscribed, wearing a wreath of red and white roses—which
implies knowledge of the story of Theophilus. (5) Chantilly, 1899 Catalogue,
No. 8, Ecole Italienne, *Deux Flagellants*, 0·29 × 0·19. Bayonne, Musée Bonnat,
Catalogue Sommaire, 1930, No. 877, Bonfigli, *Fragment de prédelle*, 0·29 × 0·19
or 'avec la base,' 0·36 × 0·24. Both are reproduced by Weller, *op. cit.*, Figs. 6, 7.
Both under Bonfigli in Berenson's 1932 Lists. Two pictures, each 0·28 × 0·18,
each with Franciscan scenes, at Munich, are claimed to be from the same series;
Quattro Maestri del Primo Rinascimento Exhibition, Florence, 1954 (No. 38),
reproduced, as ascribed to Domenico Veneziano (the subject of one wrongly
identified). All four pictures are discussed in British Museum, *Italian Drawings,
The Fourteenth and Fifteenth Centuries*, catalogue by A. E. Popham and Philip
Pouncey, 1950, I, pp. 159/60. See further *The British Museum Quarterly*, fasc. 3
for 1952, pp. 62/3 (drawing from Pepper Arden). (6) Weller, *op. cit.*, p. 57. (7)
Jacobsen, however, in the *Repertorium für Kunstwissenschaft*, 1901, p. 351,
doubtfully suggested Neroccio. (8) Weller, *op. cit.*, pp. 54/5. (9) No. 363 of the
Portfolio; as Francesco di Giorgio, *The Virgin and Infant Saviour*.

Francesco FRANCIA
ca. 1450–1517/8

Francesco Raibolini, of Bologna; the name *Francia* may be merely a
variant of Francesco, or may be from the name of a goldsmith, to whom
he is said to have been apprenticed. 1450 is the date of birth given by
Vasari (somewhat doubtfully in his first edition). It does not appear to
have been settled if the date of death was 1517 or 1518. He matriculated
in the goldsmiths' guild at Bologna in 1482. First mentioned as a painter
in 1486. His pictorial style appears to have been influenced by the
Ferrarese and Lorenzo Costa. He had a number of pupils and imitators.

179 ALTARPIECE: THE VIRGIN AND CHILD WITH S. ANNE AND OTHER SAINTS

On the left, SS. Sebastian and Paul; on the right, SS. Lawrence and
Benedict (?; in a white habit). In the foreground, the infant S. John holds
a scroll inscribed ECCE AGNVS DEI. On a capital in the centre is
sculptured Abraham sacrificing Isaac. Signed: FRĀNCIA.AVRIFEX.
BONONIĒSIS.P.(much restored).

Canvas, transferred from wood, $76\frac{3}{4} \times 71$ (1·95 × 1·805).
Not badly preserved for a transferred picture; the general effect has
been somewhat weakened, but the quality is not greatly disturbed.
For the commentary, etc., see No. 180 below.

180 LUNETTE TO NO. 179: PIETÀ

The dead Christ, the Virgin and two angels.

Wood, painted surface, flattened semicircle, $37 \times 72\frac{1}{2}$ (0·94 × 1·845).
The picture has been made up with spandrels to form a rectangle with
the two top corners slightly cut; the spandrels are painted with a decorative design, perhaps of the eighteenth or early nineteenth century, and

the total size of the rectangle is $38\frac{3}{4} \times 75$ (0.985×1.91). The original paint reaches the edge of the picture as it is now along the bottom; but this bottom edge would seem not to have been cut, or only very slightly.

The figures are on the whole reasonably well preserved, although many of the shadows are damaged. It is not certain if the present black background is original.

Nos. 179/180 formed the altarpiece in the Chapel of S. Anne in S. Frediano at Lucca.[1] Lodovico di Lorenzo Buonvisi expressed a wish before his death that masses should be celebrated in S. Frediano; in extension of this wish, his brother Benedetto, in conjunction with another brother Paolo, founded the Chapel of S. Anne in S. Frediano. The building was completed by 11 June, 1511, on which day a chaplain was appointed; at that date, the altarpiece and other ornaments were in the hands of the various masters commissioned to carry them out, and Benedetto promised that they would be put in their places in the chapel as soon as they were delivered.[2] It is clear from the signature on No. 179 that the altarpiece was completed, or at worst almost completed, before Francia's death in 1517/8.

It is to be noted that the donors' father (referred to as already dead in 1511) was named Lorenzo, and that one of the donors was named Paolo; this would account for the presence of SS. Lawrence and Paul on No. 179. By analogy, the saint on the extreme right should be S. Benedict, in memory of the principal donor, Benedetto Buonvisi; S. Benedict is indeed sometimes shown in a white habit, but the reason in this case has not been discovered.[3] This saint is traditionally called S. Romuald;[4] but no reason for S. Romuald's presence on the picture has been found, and S. Romuald is normally shown with a longer beard than here, and with a crutch. The fourth saint, S. Sebastian, was probably chosen as the chief protector against the Plague, from which Lucca is stated to have suffered in 1510.[5]

The reason why Francia was chosen to paint this altarpiece for a church at Lucca has not been discovered.

VARIANT: Among the various *Pietàs* by Francia or his following, a picture at Berlin seems to be the closest to No. 180; the designs may fairly be called connected, although the variations are considerable.[6]

PROVENANCE: As explained above, Nos. 179/180 formed the altarpiece in the chapel of S. Anne in S. Frediano at Lucca.[7] The chapel was founded by Benedetto Buonvisi in conjunction with his brother Paolo, the patronage to pass to their heirs. Still in the chapel in 1721.[8] At some time the picture was removed to the Buonvisi Palace at Lucca.[9] The last of the Buonvisi was Francesco di Girolamo, who died in 1800.[10] The Buonvisi property passed to Francesco Montecatini, son of Nicolao Montecatini who had married Maria Caterina Buonvisi. After prolonged negotiations, Nos. 179/180 were sold into the Ducal Collection at Lucca, *ca.* 1823 or soon after.[11] The acquisition was made either by Maria Louisa Josephine, Duchess of Lucca (Queen of Etruria), or by her son and successor, Carlo Lodovico di Borbone, Duke of Lucca.[12] Nos. 179/180 were brought to London for sale, with other pictures from the Lucca Collection (agent, Carlo Galvani);[13] on view at the Society of Painters in Water-Colours, London, July, 1840 (Nos. 8, 9). Bought by E. G. Flight in 1840, from whom purchased through W. Buchanan,[14] 1841.

REPRODUCTION: *Illustrations, Italian Schools*, 1937, p. 143. *Plates, Earlier Italian Schools*, 1953, Vol. I, pp. 159–160.

REFERENCES: (1) The picture is first specifically mentioned by Vasari, 1550, p. 535 (Milanesi's edition, Vol. III, p. 543). (2) The document indicating the date of Francia's working on the altarpiece (Francia's name is not mentioned, but there is no reason to suppose that Benedetto Buonvisi tried some other painter first and later transferred the commission to Francia) is the one concerning the appointment of a chaplain for the chapel, 11 June, 1511. See Archivio di Stato at Lucca, Archivio Buonvisi, Parte I, No. 36, ff.16–21, a later copy of the same document being in the same collection, Parte I, No. 43, ff. 20–24; *Inventario del R. Archivio di Stato in Lucca*, V, Archivi Gentilizi, 1946, pp. 112 and 115. The relevant part of the original text is as follows: (f. 16v) (Benedetto Buonvisi) 'Exposuit et dixit quod ipsi' (Benedetto and Paolo) 'post mortem quondam Bone memorie Lodouici eorum fratris germanj, Et in executionem pie voluntatis dicti quondam Lodouici Celebrare fecit, et in futurum Celebrari intendunt quotidie unam missam in prefata ecclesia santi Fridianj Quam etiam in futurum celebrari volunt ut infra dicetur. ¶Ac etiam quod ipse Dominus Benedictus jamdiu ex deuotione quam gerit ad prefatam ecclesiam et monasterium sancti fridianj' (etc. etc.) ¶ Statuit et decreuit suis sumptibus fundare unam capellam in prefata ecclesia sancti fridianj sub honore et uocabulo sancte Anne matris eiusdem Intemerate virginis marie ¶ Et iam fundauit locum dicti cappelle in calce dicte ecclesie versus miridiem ubi ad presens est dictus locus pro dicta capella de nouo fundatus erectus et edificatus' (f. 17r) 'In quo etiam intendit facere et quod ibi sit altare cum ancona et alijs suis debitis et competentibus ornamentis ac etiam fulcimentis que sunt ad manus magistrorum qui conducunt ea et quamprimum erunt perfecta ea poni facient in dicta Capella.' The document says later on that the Patronage of the Chapel was to be with Benedetto and Paolo Buonvisi and then to pass to their heirs. Part of this document, but without the piece at the end concerning the artists, was printed from the notary's draft by M. Ridolfi, *Scritti d'Arte e d'Antichità*, 1879, p. 355. What appear to be wills in connection with the founding of the chapel, of 3 November, 1503, and 16 August, 1510, are referred to in the *Inventario del R. Archivio di Stato in Lucca*, Vol V, 1946, p. 98; G. C. Williamson, *Francesco Raibolini called Francia*, 1901, pp. 111 ff., refers to the latter. These documents do not appear to be in the Archivio di Stato at Lucca, and are perhaps to be found in the Archivio Notarile there (ser Benedetto Franciotti notary). (3) Montgomery Carmichael (MS. in the Gallery archives) stated that the Buonvisi family held the Camaldolese abbacy of Cantignano *in commendam*; indeed Cardinal Francesco Buonvisi (1625–1700) was abbot of Cantignano (*Inventario* as in note 2, Vol. V, 1946, p. 114, No. 42). A Camaldolese association would certainly justify a white habit for S. Benedict; but it does not seem certain that Cantignano was still Camaldolese when the picture was painted. E. Repetti, *Dizionario Geografico Fisico Storico della Toscana*, I, 1833, p. 30, says that the abbey of Cantignano was given to the prior of Camaldoli to reform in 1277, but was in 1419 suppressed and 'aggregato con la sua chiesa e possessi ai canonici delle cattedrale di Lucca.' Nevertheless, G. B. Mittarelli and A. Costadoni, *Annales Camaldulenses*, in their 7th volume, 1762, seem to imply that the connection between Camaldoli and Cantignano was not broken. In any case, Benedetto Buonvisi is described in 1511 as a merchant and citizen of Lucca, and would seem to have had no connection with Cantignano. (4) So in the 1929 catalogue. Already so in the eighteenth century; see Oretti, MS. B 107 of the Biblioteca dell'Archiginnasio at Bologna. The Camaldolese association referred to in the previous note would justify the presence of S. Romuald on the picture just as well as S. Benedict in a white habit; but there would still be no convincing reasons for supposing that the saint really is S. Romuald. (5) Williamson, *loc. cit.* (6) Size, 0·95 × 1·81; from the Solly Collection. Berlin, 1931 Catalogue, p. 617, No. 121 (as copy); better in the 1883 Catalogue, p. 163, No. 121 (as copy); 1834 Catalogue (No. 253), as a repetition by Francia. Photograph in the Gallery archives, kindly sent by

Friedrich Winkler. Crowe and Cavalcaselle, *History of Painting in North Italy*, ed. Borenius, II, 1912, p. 277, call it a copy; Berenson in his 1932 Lists calls it an original. The Berlin picture has a Holy Woman between the Virgin and the right-hand angel; the X-Ray reveals no trace of an extra Holy Woman on No. 180. (7) Vasari, 1550, p. 535; Milanesi's edition, Vol. III, p. 543. Mentioned in the chapel, as by Francesco Francabio (*sic*), in a MS. by Pietro Paolini (1603–1681); see Montgomery Carmichael, *Francia's Masterpiece*, 1909, pp. 117/8. (8) Vincenzo Marchiò, *Il Forestiero Informato delle Cose di Lucca*, 1721, p. 286, as by Francesco Francabigio. Also mentioned as in the chapel by Oretti, MS. B 107 of the Biblioteca dell'Archiginnasio at Bologna. (9) Recorded in Room V in a MS. on the Buonvisi pictures, in the National Gallery Library. The MS. was presented by G. C. Williamson, who published a note on it in *The Connoisseur*, January–April, 1904, p. 189, dating it too early. It is possible that Nos. 179/180 were not removed from S. Frediano, until a substitute altarpiece was put up. This is by Stefano Tofanelli (1752–1812); its exact date has not been established, but it was sent by him to Lucca from Rome, where he went in 1768 and which he left *ca.* 1800. See Giacomo Sardini and Tommaso Trenta, *Memorie e Documenti per servire all'Istoria del Ducato di Lucca*, VIII, 1822, pp. 175, 184, 189. (10) *Inventario del R. Archivio di Stato in Lucca*, V, 1946, p. 100. (11) There are various letters concerning the sale of the Buonvisi pictures, including Nos. 179/180, in the Archivio di Stato at Lucca, *Intendenza della Lista Civile*, 10, No. 4 (*Inventario del R. Archivio di Stato in Lucca*, Vol. III, 1880, p. 80). On 14 October, 1823, Francesco Buonvisi (presumably Francesco Montecatini calling himself Buonvisi) pressed for a decision. The sale had certainly taken place by 1829; cf. Tommaso Trenta, *Guida del Forestiere per la Città e Contado di Lucca*, 1820, p. 101, where Nos. 179/180 are mentioned as still with the Buonvisi heirs, and the revised edition by A. Mazzarosa, 1829, pp. 85 and 87, where they are mentioned as in the Palazzo Ducale at Lucca. Williamson, *loc. cit.*, says that Nos. 179/180 were sold by the last of the Buonvisi heirs, Principessa Elisa Poniatowski née Montecatini; it is true that the Buonvisi property did eventually pass to her and thence to her husband Carlo, but this appears to have been considerably later. Some facts about the fate of the Buonvisi property are printed in the *Inventario del R. Archivio di Stato in Lucca*, Vol. V, 1946, p. 100. (12) The Queen of Etruria died in 1824. No. 180 has on the back CL under a crown; the compiler does not know if this means that it was purchased by Carlo Lodovico or (as would seem more likely) merely that it belonged to him. (13) Letters in the Gallery archives. (14) Letters of 1841 and 8 January, 1860, in the Gallery archives.

638   THE VIRGIN AND CHILD WITH TWO SAINTS

One of the saints is a martyr, the other holds a book.

Wood, painted surface, $30\frac{3}{4} \times 24\frac{1}{2}$ (0·78×0·625); including a black band, which runs along all four sides up to the edges of the panel, $32\frac{1}{2} \times 25\frac{1}{2}$ (0·825×0·65).

The picture has suffered from flaking, and has been considerably restored.

Generally accepted as an autograph Francia, and not by one of his imitators;[1] so far as the condition allows one to judge, this appears a reasonable view. Lipparini[2] dates No. 638 *ca.* 1495/99; but it would appear to be rather later.

COPY: Parts of the two central figures and the landscape were copied in a drawing by Degas.[3]

PROVENANCE: From the Collection of Col. Bourgeois at Paris;[4] purchased with the rest of the Edmond Beaucousin Collection, Paris, 1860.

REPRODUCTION: *Illustrations, Italian Schools*, 1937, p. 142. *Plates, Earlier Italian Schools*, 1953, Vol. I, p. 161.

REFERENCES: (1) E.g. by Crowe and Cavalcaselle, *Painting in North Italy*, I, 1871, p. 567 (Borenius edition, II, 1912, p. 279); and by G. C. Williamson, *Francesco Raibolini called Francia*, 1901, p. 144. Jacobsen in the *Repertorium für Kunstwissenschaft*, 1901, p. 365, calls it a studio piece. (2) G. Lipparini, *Francesco Francia*, 1913, p. 102. (3) Acquired in 1950 by A. S. F. Gow of Cambridge; photograph in the Gallery archives. On the same sheet is a copy of No. 1300 of the present catalogue, follower of Leonardo da Vinci. (4) National Gallery Report.

2487   BARTOLOMEO BIANCHINI

He holds a letter with the remains of an inscription, *Bar*(tolomeo?) *Blanchino | bono*(niae?).

Wood, painted surface, $22\frac{1}{4} \times 16$ (0.565×0.405).
Very good condition.

The sitter was a Bolognese humanist of noble family; he appears to have been esteemed by his contemporaries, but has left very little in the way of writings. He was alive in 1497 and dead before 1528.[1] There is evidence[2] that he was friendly with Francia; and a *Holy Family* by Francia at Berlin bears on the parapet the inscription, BARTHO-LOMEI SVMPTV BIANCHINI MAXIMA MATRVM | HIC VIVIT MANIBVS FRANCIA PICTA TVIS.[3]

No. 2487 is generally accepted as a work of Francia.[4] Both it and the Berlin *Holy Family* are early works and it has been suggested that they may once have formed a diptych;[5] this is however unlikely. No. 2487 would from the pose of the body necessarily have been on the left; the sitter would have had the eyes turned away from the Virgin and Child, and S. Joseph would have been very awkwardly placed in between. Besides, the inscription on the parapet at Berlin would seem awkward without any corresponding inscription here.

PROVENANCE: Duke of Buckingham's Collection at Stowe; Sale, 14 September, 1848 (lot 282), bought by J. M. and S. M. Smith.[6] Acquired from Smith by Lord Northwick in May, 1850.[7] Lent by Lord Northwick to the British Institution, 1850 (No. 58);[8] seen at Thirlestaine House, Cheltenham, by Waagen.[9] *Hours in Lord Northwick's Picture Galleries*, 1858 (No. 113).[10] Lord Northwick Sale, 19 August, 1859 (lot 1591), bought by Nieuwenhuys.[11] Stated to have belonged to the Princesse de Sagan.[12] Bought by George Salting, ca. 1889;[13] exhibited at the Burlington Fine Arts Club, 1894 (No. 23). Lent to the National Gallery from 1903; Salting Bequest, 1910.

REPRODUCTION: *Illustrations, Italian Schools*, 1937, p. 145. *Plates, Earlier Italian Schools*, 1953, Vol. I, p. 162.

REFERENCES: (1) See Carlo Malagola, *Della Vita e delle Opere di Antonio Urceo detto Codro*, 1878, pp. 296 ff. Bianchini has an entry in the *Biographie Universelle*. (2) Malagola, *op cit.*, p. 268, or C. C. Malvasia, *Felsina Pittrice*, I, 1678, p. 49. (3) Berlin, 1931 Catalogue, No. 125; size, 0.54×0.40; reproduced in the Illustrations. (4) E.g. by Crowe and Cavalcaselle, *History of Painting in North Italy*, I, 1871, p. 558 (ed. Borenius, II, 1912, p. 271). (5) See Thieme-Becker, and the Berlin Catalogue, 1931. (6) As Raphael; but in the printed priced catalogue, it is noted that the picture is probably by Francia. There is some confirmatory evidence of the early provenance on the back of the picture;

but in any case the descriptions suffice to make the identification sure. (7) As Francia; Smith's *Day-Book* (1848–1867) at the Victoria and Albert Museum, p. 104. (8) As Raphael. (9) Waagen, *Treasures*, III, 1854, p. 199, as Francia. (10) As Raphael. (11) As Raphael. (12) Burlington Fine Arts Exhibition Catalogue, 1894 (No. 23). (13) Salting MSS.

Ascribed to FRANCESCO FRANCIA

2671 MOURNING OVER THE DEAD CHRIST (FRAGMENT OF A PREDELLA?)

Present, Christ, the Virgin, the Magdalen, SS. Joseph of Arimathaea and Nicodemus; some drapery on the right belonged, perhaps, to another Holy Woman.

Wood, painted surface, $12 \times 13\frac{1}{2}$ (0.305×0.34); painted up to the edges all round, and obviously cut at the left and right.

A good deal worn and retouched, so that the style is somewhat affected.

The attribution to Francia as a late work is not unreasonable, but the condition makes it subject to caution. No. 2671 is a fragment of some obviously small panel, perhaps from a predella.

The standing figure of the Virgin, and to a less degree the figure of Christ, correspond fairly well with an engraving by Marcantonio.[1]

VARIANTS: Christ and the two figures at His head and feet correspond fairly with a picture at Leningrad.[2] Larger pictures, less closely connected, are at Turin,[3] at Parma,[4] No. 180 above (q.v.), and its variant at Berlin.

PROVENANCE: Label on the back, *Sig Principe di Cellammare*, so perhaps from the Cellamare Palace at Naples; also *Francesco Filiasi*, written twice, and (on the wood) ..*o xino*. Bought by George Salting *ca.* 1900;[5] lent by him to the Burlington Fine Arts Club, 1902 (No. 20). Salting Bequest, 1910.

REPRODUCTION: *Illustrations, Italian Schools*, 1937, p. 144. *Plates, Earlier Italian Schools*, 1953, Vol. I, p. 164.

REFERENCES: (1) There are two variants, Bartsch Nos. 34 and 35. B.34 is reproduced by B. Delessert, *Notice sur la Vie de Marc Antoine Raimondi*, 1853; the Virgin's right arm is bare. B. 35, where the Virgin's right arm is covered by a sleeve, is reproduced by Henri Delaborde, *Marc-Antoine Raimondi*, 1888, p. 107; Delaborde does not consider B. 34 to be by Marcantonio. P. Pouncey (letter of 19 January, 1948, in the Gallery archives) says that there is no evidence for dating either of these prints. Marcantonio was one of Francia's pupils. A picture in S. Pietro at Modena is a fairly exact derivation from the print (photograph Anderson, No. 10184, as Ortolano?). (2) Reproduced by Venturi, *Storia dell' Arte Italiana*, Vol. VII, Part III, Fig. 725, as Giacomo Francia; also reproduced in *L'Arte*, 1912, p. 214. Berenson, in his 1932 Lists, accepts it as by Francesco Francia. Hermitage Catalogue, 1958, Vol. I, p. 205, No. 145, size 0.24×0.335. (3) Turin, 1899 Catalogue, No. 155; size, 1.61×1.30; reproduced by G. Lipparini, *Francesco Francia*, 1913, p. 91. (4) Parma, Catalogue by Corrado Ricci, 1896, pp. 69/70, No. 123; size, 2.97×2.33; reproduced by Lipparini, *op. cit.*, p. 97. (5) Salting MSS. Cf. *L'Arte*, 1901, p. 293.

After Francesco FRANCIA

3927 THE VIRGIN AND CHILD WITH AN ANGEL

Inscribed on the parapet, in almost effaced letters: OPVS FRAN-CIAE AVR(EFIC)IS / (M)CCCCLXXXX*.

Wood, painted surface, 23 × 17½ (0·585 × 0·445); painted up to the edges all round, but the picture is very unlikely to have been cut.

It was established beyond reasonable doubt in 1955 that this picture is of fairly recent date, presumably the XIX Century.

The date inscribed on it is 1490, not 1492 as at one time read.

VERSIONS: A picture corresponding with No. 3927, but without the inscription and from which No. 3927 may have been copied, was in the T. G. Morgan Grenville Sale, 18 June, 1954 (lot 23), bought by L. Koetser[1]. A picture with a similar Virgin and Child, but with S. Catherine of Alexandria and the little S. John instead of the angel, and with a different landscape, was owned by G. Glück.[2]

PROVENANCE: Spitöver-Haas Collection, Rome; acquired by Ludwig Mond in 1893,[3] and lent by him to the R.A., 1894 (No. 152). Mond Bequest, 1924.

REPRODUCTION: *Illustrations, Italian Schools*, 1937, p. 144. *Plates, Earlier Italian Schools*, 1953, Vol. I, p. 163.

REFERENCES: (1) Reproduced in *The Illustrated London News*, 18 December, 1954, p. 1126. (2) 0·60×0·50; photograph in the Gallery archives. (3) J. P. Richter, *The Mond Collection*, 1910, II, p. viii.

Bernardino FUNGAI
1460–1516 or later

Sienese School. Baptized as Bernardino Cristofano di Nicholo d'Antonio di Pietro da Fonghaia; Fungaia being a place on the slopes of Monte Maggio, not far from Siena. He is mentioned as a pupil of Benvenuto di Giovanni's in 1482. Bacci records two authenticated works: a *Coronation of the Virgin* in the Servi at Siena is documented and dated between 1498 and 1501, and an altarpiece in the Gallery at Siena is signed and dated 1512. A picture in the Accademia at Venice (Catalogue, 1955, No. 192) has a doubtful signature.

Many pictures are currently ascribed to Fungai, who appears to have been eclectic.

Literature: Pèleo Bacci, *Bernardino Fungai*, 1947; especially, for the justification of some of the statements made above, pp. 12, 27/8, 41 ff. and 94.

1331 TONDO: THE VIRGIN AND CHILD WITH CHERUBIM

In the background, (left) the Nativity with S. Joseph and the Annunciation to the Shepherds, (right) the cavalcade of the Three Kings and their followers.

Wood, oval (meant for circular), painted surface, 47×46½ (1·195 × 1·18); painted up to the edges all round.

Cleaned in 1954; well preserved.

The Virgin and Child are on a design used several times with variations by Perugino.[1] The pattern of the Virgin's brocade recurs in other pictures accepted as Fungai's.[2]

It is generally agreed that No. 1331 is by Fungai.

PROVENANCE: Probably acquired in Siena in 1827.[3] Lent by J. W. Faulkner to the British Institution, 1865 (No. 70),[4] and to Leeds, 1868 (No. 33).[5] Lent by William Graham to the R.A., 1879 (No. 201). Graham Sale, 8 April, 1886 (lot 258), bought by Laurie for William Connal,[6] who presented it in 1891.

REPRODUCTION: *Illustrations, Italian Schools*, 1937, p. 146. *Plates, Earlier Italian Schools*, 1953, Vol. I, p. 165.

REFERENCES: (1) E.g. a picture at Vienna, 1938 Catalogue, No. 32 (Klassiker der Kunst *Perugino*, Plate 200). The pose (inverted) is used by Fungai on his signed altarpiece at Siena (Van Marle, *Development of the Italian Schools of Painting*, Vol. XVI, Fig. 278). (2) E.g. Van Marle, *op. cit.*, Vol. XVI, Figs. 273, 279. (3) See Ettore Romagnoli, *Biografia Cronologica de' Bellartisti Senesi*, MS. in the Biblioteca Comunale at Siena, Vol. V, p. 343: 'In Siena acquistò nel 1827. un tondo con M.V. e SS. il mio amico mons: faushnere che portò a Londra sua patria.' Bacci, *Bernardino Fungai*, 1947, p. 120, reads the name as Fauslinere. (4) As Domenico Fungai. Cf. Crowe and Cavalcaselle, *History of Painting in Italy*, III, 1866, p. 376. (5) As Bernardino Fungai. The label of the Leeds Exhibition was on the back. (6) Letter from W. Connal, 14 May, 1891, in the Gallery archives.

2764 THE VIRGIN AND CHILD WITH TWO SAINTS

Wood, painted surface, $24\frac{1}{4} \times 16\frac{1}{2}$ (0.62×0.42); painted up to the edges all round.

In indifferent condition.

In the 1929 catalogue, the saints were called SS. Peter and Paul.

It is generally agreed that No. 2764 is by Fungai.[1]

VERSION: A version with only slight differences was in an Anon. Sale at the Hôtel Drouot, Paris, 21 April, 1910 (lot 41).[2]

PROVENANCE: From the collection of Jules Soulages of Toulouse (largely formed *ca.* 1830–40). Brought to England with the rest of the collection by a syndicate. Soulages Catalogue by J. C. Robinson, 1856 (No. 581).[3] Exhibited at Manchester, 1857 (Provisional Catalogue, No. 1091; Definitive Catalogue, No. 125).[4] Bought by the South Kensington Museum in 1865 (Inv. No. 766–65).[5] Exhibited at Leeds, 1868 (No. 93a).[6] Lent to the National Gallery from 1895 until 1960, when it was returned to the Victoria and Albert Museum.[7].

REPRODUCTION: *Illustrations, Italian Schools*, 1937, p. 146. *Plates, Earlier Italian Schools*, 1953, Vol. I, p. 166.

REFERENCES: (1) Ascribed to Fungai by Crowe and Cavalcaselle, *History of Painting in Italy*, III, 1866, p. 376. (2) Size, 0.68×0.46; as Matteo di Giovanni; reproduced in the sale catalogue. (3) As *Holy Family*, attributed to Vivarini. (4) Exhibited as by Antonio Vivarini. (5) Cf. the South Kensington (Victoria and Albert Museum) Catalogue, *National Gallery of British Art*, Part I, Oil Paintings, 1893, p. 188, as attributed to Vivarini. (6) As Bartolomeo Vivarini. (7) It was given the inventory number 2764 at the National Gallery in 1915. From 1910 until 1915, No. 2764 had been the right-hand part of No. 1699 (in the 1929 catalogue as Sweertz; *The Dutch School*, catalogue by Neil MacLaren, 1960, as Michiel Nouts?).

Agnolo GADDI
active 1369, died 1396

A Florentine painter, a son of Taddeo Gaddi. According to Vasari, on his father's death (in 1366) he was put in the charge of Jacopo del Casentino (for morals) and Giovanni da Milano (for painting); no doubt he had previously been trained by his father. In any case, he was in 1369 working in the Vatican as an assistant, probably to his brother Giovanni. Frescoes in S. Croce, Florence, are attributed to him by a good tradition. A series of frescoes in the cathedral of Prato (1392/5) is a certain late work; some panels in S. Miniato, Florence, are also apparently documented as his and of 1393/6. It is probable that in all these works the execution is partly by assistants. Other pictures have at one time or another been ascribed to Agnolo Gaddi, but critical opinion about most of them has varied considerably.

Ascribed to Agnolo GADDI

568 PART(?) OF AN ALTARPIECE: THE CORONATION OF THE VIRGIN

Wood, arched top, $71\frac{3}{4} \times 37$ ($1\cdot82 \times 0\cdot94$); painted up to the edges all round.

The picture is in good condition for a work of the period, but is not free from retouches on some of the important parts. Nevertheless, except for a split down the middle, some damage at the bottom, and the renewal of the gold background, it may be held to be in satisfactory state.

No. 568 is rather closely derived from the central panel of the Baroncelli Coronation in S. Croce, Florence, which bears Giotto's signature but is not usually ascribed to Giotto's own hand.[1] The Baroncelli Coronation is flanked by four panels of adoring angels and saints; there is no evidence whether there were ever any side panels to No. 568.

There seems to be at present a good deal of agreement that the picture is by Agnolo Gaddi, perhaps an early work.[2]

PROVENANCE: Stated to be from the Convent of the Minori Osservanti of S. Miniato, near Florence;[3] possibly San Miniato al Tedesco is intended.[4] Purchased with the Lombardi-Baldi Collection, Florence, 1857.[5]

REPRODUCTION: *Illustrations, Italian Schools*, 1937, p. 12. *Plates, Earlier Italian Schools*, 1953, Vol. I, p. 167.

REFERENCES: (1) The fact was already noted in the N.G. Report, 1858. Cf. W. Gibson in *Apollo*, 1926, IV, p. 120. The Baroncelli picture is reproduced by Van Marle, *Development of the Italian Schools of Painting*, III, Fig. 184. (2) Roberto Salvini, *L'Arte di Agnolo Gaddi*, 1936, p. 29 (note 12), with bibliographical references. (3) N.G. MS. Catalogue. The picture is listed as a Giotto with no provenance in an undated Lombardi-Baldi Catalogue, No. 8; the copy of the catalogue in the Uffizi Library is claimed to be of 1845. (4) It should nevertheless be noted that according to Repetti, *Dizionario . . . della Toscana*,

Vol. V, 1843, p. 91, the church and convent of S. Francesco at San Miniato was 'abitato dai Minori Conventuali.' Alternatively, it may be noted that S. Francesco (or S. Salvatore) al Monte is a church of the Minori Osservanti, and is situated quite close to the S. Miniato on the outskirts of Florence; but that identification presents some difficulties, and is unlikely to be favourably considered without some supporting evidence. (5) For the history of the Lombardi-Baldi Collection, see Appendix I.

GARBO (Raffaellino del)
See RAFFAELLINO del Garbo

GEROLAMO dai Libri
ca. 1474–1555 (?)

School of Verona. His age was declared as 18 in 1492; the date of death is from Vasari. He was the son and pupil of a miniaturist Francesco I dai Libri. The dominant influence on his style was that of Mantegna, but he was affected also by others, especially the Veronese such as Francesco Morone. There are several authenticated works.

748 THE VIRGIN AND CHILD WITH S. ANNE (SYMBOL-
      IZING   THE   IMMACULATE   CONCEPTION:
      CENTRAL PICTURE FROM A TRIPTYCH)

The Child is blessing, and holds an olive-branch in His left hand; the Virgin's left foot is set upon a dead dragon. Three music-making angels below; the central one holds a singing-book, with traces of words and music, and some new notes, falsely headed *Nº 4 Solfegio*. A *cartellino* contains the illegible remains of two (?) lines of writing; the last word of the first line looks like *decepta* (conceivably *concepta* was written). A signature, mostly false, but almost certainly based on the remains of a true one, runs along its lower part: HIERONIMVS.A.LIBRIS.F.[1]

Canvas, $62\frac{1}{4} \times 37$ ($1 \cdot 58 \times 0 \cdot 94$); this includes an addition at the bottom of $1\frac{1}{2}$ in. (4 cm.). The original picture may indeed have been cut slightly along the bottom, but not very much, to judge by the present height of Morando's *S. Roch* (No. 735; $61\frac{3}{4}$ in.), which was the left wing.

No. 748 has suffered considerably from rubbing, flaking and repainting.

This picture was the centre of a triptych in S. Maria della Scala at Verona, of which one wing was Morando's *S. Roch*, dated 1518 (No. 735 of this Gallery), the other a *S. Sebastian* by Torbido (missing);[2] although it is rather strange, Vasari (in the edition of 1568)[3] already noted this arrangement. It would be possible to hold that No. 748 was painted independently of the two wings, presumably a little before; but this seems unlikely. The very early association of No. 748 with figures of SS. Sebastian and Roch seems, in any case, to be confirmed by an engraving by Gian Jacopo Caralio or Caraglio (active 1526, died 1565).[4]

There the main group of No. 748, with the dead dragon, and the lemon-tree and rose-hedge of the picture, is fairly accurately reproduced; SS. Roch and Sebastian stand on either side. It is true that the saints in the engraving are copied (with slight variations) from another altarpiece by Gerolamo dai Libri, formerly in S. Giacomo della Pigna at Verona and now in the museum there;[5] but their insertion on the engraving seems to confirm that No. 748 was at the time associated with pictures of those saints. Finally, the rose lying on the ground in No. 735 does not appear to be an attribute of S. Roch; it may be taken as recalling the rose-hedge of the present picture, thus confirming to some extent that Nos. 735 and 748 were painted as parts of a single altarpiece.

An inscription on the already mentioned engraving by Caraglio gives a clue to the subject:

.STELLA . CELI . EXTIRPAVIT . QVE . LACTAVIT . DOMI-
NVM.
MORTIS . PESTEM . QVAM . PLANTAVIT . PRIMVS .
PARENS.HOMINV̄.
IPSA . STELA . NVNC . DIGNETVR . SIDERA . CONPENSERE.
QVORVM . BELA . PREBENT . NOBIS . DIRE . MORTIS . VLC-
ERA. AMĒ.

These verses also occur on an engraving of the Virgin and Child, accepted by Hind as being by Giovanni Antonio da Brescia.[6] The text there has some variations of spelling; also, in the third line, *compescere* for *compensere* and in the fourth, *plebem scindunt* for *prebent nobis*. The text there is, further, introduced by the following explanatory sentence: 'Questa oratiōē esta denōtiata da vno sāto hō p̄dicatore / al populo d̄ bologna cōtra peste el dice c̄h Qualūque psona / c̄h vna uolta el giorno ī honore d̄ la īmaculata cōceptiōē dira / la dita oratiōē nō potrᵃ mai morir di morbo chi no sa lezere / la porti adosso e qsto e sperimētato a firēza siena / Cortona e uoltera.'

Although the inscriptions on No. 748 were apparently different, these two engravings suggest that No. 748 and its wings were probably connected both with the Plague and with the Immaculate Conception. The recorded history of Verona favours this. In 1511, when the city was assailed by Plague, tempest and earthquake, a vow was made that the Feast of the Immaculate Conception should be celebrated; and in 1575, at another outbreak of Plague, the city vowed to make a solemn yearly procession on 8 December in honour of the Conception.[7]

The history and subjects of the pictures themselves offer further confirmation. That the main subject of the pictures is the Immaculate Conception could be deduced from their provenance; they come from a chapel dedicated to the Conception.[8] The placing of the Virgin's foot on a dragon in No. 748 (it should properly be upon the head of a serpent) seems clearly a reference to the words of God to the serpent in Genesis iii, 15, *Inimicitias ponam inter te et mulierem, et semen tuum et semen illius; ipsa conteret caput tuum*, etc.; this passage, which implies the contrast between the Fall of Man through Eve (and Adam) and his Redemption through the Virgin Mary, is included in the Office of the Immaculate

Conception (8 December).[9] It may be added that the presence of S. Anne in No. 748 is by no means in disaccord with the subject of the Immaculate Conception.[10]

The connection of the pictures with the Plague may also be considered certain. S. Roch (No. 735 by Morando) and S. Sebastian (the lost picture by Torbido) were the principal saints invoked against the Plague.[11] The connection of the Immaculate Conception with the Plague has already been noted; or, if it is preferred to consider the figures in No. 748 individually, invocation of the Virgin Mary against the Plague is too frequent to need illustration, and S. Anne was also sometimes invoked.[12] Further, the church of S. Maria della Scala at Verona, from which the pictures come, was particularly associated with prayers against the Plague.[13]

If it is asked whether any particular outbreak of Plague is recorded in these pictures, the answer is probably the outbreak of 1510/2,[14] to which glancing reference has already been made. There does not appear to have been Plague at Verona between that date and 1518, the date of Morando's S. Roch. It is perhaps worth suggesting that the dead dragon in No. 748 may have a secondary meaning as a symbol of the end of war; the olive-branch held by the Child in the picture is indeed the normal emblem of peace. Verona underwent a terrible siege in 1516, but the Peace of Noyon became effective there in January, 1517;[15] and Morando's S. Roch, as has been noted, is dated in the following year.

There exists a Veronese picture iconographically somewhat similar to No. 748 and its wings, an altarpiece of 1528 by G. F. Caroto in S. Fermo at Verona;[16] it shows S. Anne with the Virgin and Child, SS. Sebastian and Roch and other saints. Caroto's picture seems also to be an Immaculate Conception against the Plague. The chapel in which it hangs seems to have been dedicated to the Immaculate Conception.[17] With regard to the Plague, the picture is dated 1528, and there was an outbreak of Plague at Verona in 1527.[18] Further, according to Persico,[19] it was in 1571 (1575?) that the city erected (re-erected?) this chapel on the occasion of the Plague; certainly, a picture in it by Antonio Giarola (Coppa) is connected with the Plague of 1630.[20]

The style of No. 748 is Mantegnesque. Two of Mantegna's pictures at Verona were the early S. Zeno altarpiece (where the Virgin's left hand and arm are similar), and the Trivulzio altarpiece of 1497 (where there is a lemon-tree; also three music-making angels).[21] The attitude of the Child in No. 748 is perhaps reminiscent of Mantegna, No. 274 of this catalogue; but there is no need to postulate a precise Mantegnesque original for the whole picture.

The two outer angels in No. 748 recur fairly exactly in a (probably earlier) picture once at Berlin, which has been variously ascribed.[22]

ENGRAVING: For Caraglio's engraving, partly based on No. 748, see above.

PROVENANCE: As stated above, No. 748 and its wings formed an altarpiece in S. Maria della Scala at Verona, which was a Servite church. The pictures are first recorded by Vasari in 1568.[23] Vasari writes of an altar 'della Santificazione' (whatever that may mean); but the chapel was in fact dedicated to the Conception,[24] and had been conceded in 1510 to the Compagnia Laicale della B.V. In 1586 the altar was transferred to Niccolò de Bonis and his heirs, but some rights were retained in it by the Compagnia until it ceased to exist in 1611. The chapel was then ceded to the Portatori del Vino (Torcoloti);[25] their Patron was S. Roch, to whom the dedication of the altar was transferred. In the early eighteenth century, the pictures appear no longer to have been in place,[26] but they were not finally removed from the church until 1742.[27] They passed into the hands of Gian Bettino Cignaroli.[28] The wings passed from him into the possession of the Carli family at Verona, but No. 748 does not appear to have entered the Carli Collection; the next mention of it is of 1822 in the Collection of Francesco Caldana at Verona,[29] who also owned the wings. Purchased from the heirs of Cav. Andrea Monga at Verona, 1864.[30]

REPRODUCTION: *Illustrations, Italian Schools*, 1937, p. 159. *Plates, Earlier Italian Schools*, 1953, Vol. I, p. 168.

REFERENCES: (1) Eastlake (note-book, 1864) noted the remains of a signature on the picture before its restoration. (2) Torbido's figure, being in bad condition, was reduced to a half-length, then to a head, which Eastlake looked for in Verona but could not find; information from Eastlake's MSS. (3) Vasari, ed. Milanesi, V, pp. 294 and 328; these passages do not occur in the text of 1550. (4) Bartsch, XV, p. 71, No. 7; photograph in the Gallery archives. From what is known of his life, it seems probable that this engraving is early work; see his biography by V. G. Salvaro in *Madonna Verona*, 1917, pp. 83 ff. (5) R. Wittkower in the *Jahrbuch für Kunstwissenschaft*, 1927, p. 205 (Fig. 13) and p. 209, No. 12; *Capolavori dei Musei Veneti*, Illustrated Catalogue, 1946 (No. 179), reproduced. The design of the Virgin and Child on this picture has some similarities (inverted) to that of No. 748; the Child also holds a branch of olive. (6) A. M. Hind, *Early Italian Engraving*, Part II, 1948, Vol. V, No. 32, and Vol. VI, Plate 548. (7) *Cronica di Pier Zagata*, etc. (*Supplementi*), Part II, Vol II, 1749, pp. 91 and 98. (8) See under Provenance. (9) The Protestants later disputed this text, preferring *ipse* for Christ to *ipsa* for the Virgin; see E. Mâle, *L'Art Religieux après le Concile de Trente*, 1932, pp. 38 ff. The iconography of No. 748 may be compared with that of an altarpiece, accepted as being by Gerolamo dai Libri, in S. Polo at Verona; Wittkower, *loc cit.*, p. 204 (Fig. 12) and p. 208, No. 10. For the very frequent presence of the serpent in pictures of the Immaculate Conception, cf. for instance Tiepolo's picture at Vicenza (reproduced by Karl Künstle, *Ikonographie der Christlichen Kunst*, I, 1928, Fig. 384); see also Francesco Podesti's fresco in the Sala dell'Immacolata in the Vatican (E. G. Massi, *Descrizione delle Gallerie di Pittura nel Pontificio Palazzo Vaticano*, 1887, p. 51). (10) Cf. K. Künstle, *op. cit.*, I, pp. 328 ff. and 646 ff.; E. Mâle, *L'Art Religieux de la Fin du Moyen Âge en France*, 1922, Fig. 117 and pp. 217 ff.; Beda Kleinschmidt, *Die heilige Anna*, 1930, pp. 205 ff.; Guy de Tervarent, *Les Enigmes de l'Art du Moyen Age*, II, *Art Flamand*, 1941, p. 39. Cf. also a picture in S. Anna at Capodistria; reproduced in the *Inventario degli Oggetti d'Arte d'Italia, Provincia di Pola*, 1935, p. 29. For the presence of the Infant Christ in an Immaculate Conception, it is sufficient to cite Francisco Pacheco, *Arte de la Pintura*, 1649, p. 481, and refer to a picture by Francesco Vanni at Montalcino (Venturi, *Storia dell'Arte Italiana*, Vol. IX, Part VII, Fig. 584). (11) S. Roch was officially recognized at Verona as a powerful interceder against the Plague in 1480; Girolamo Dalla Corte, *Dell'Istorie della Città di Verona*, III, 1744, p. 106. In 1512, prayers at Verona against the Plague to God, the Virgin and SS. Roch, Sebastian and Zeno (the Patron of the city) were partially successful; Dalla Corte, *op. cit.*, III, p. 187. (12) See P. Heitz and W. L. Schreiber, *Pestblätter des XV Jahrhunderts*, 1901, p. 9 and Plates 8 and 9; Campbell Dodgson, *Woodcuts of the XV Century in the . . . British Museum*, I, 1934, No. 154 and Plate LIII; Beda Kleinschmidt, *Die heilige Anna*, 1930, pp. 423 f. For the connection between the Immaculate Conception and the Plague at Milan, see the entry for Leonardo da Vinci, No. 1093, note 65. (13) In 1452, a procession against the Plague went from the Cathedral to S. Maria della Scala; Dalla Corte, *op. cit.*, III, p. 90. (**14**) *Cronica di Pier Zagata*, etc., Part II, Vol. I, 1747, pp. 134, 143, 144, 147. (**15**) Zagata, *op. cit.*, Part II, Vol. I, p. 191; Dalla Corte, *op. cit.*, III, p. 252. (**16**) Venturi, *Storia dell'Arte Italiana*, Vol. IX, Part III, Fig. 609. (**17**) The evidence available to the compiler is imprecise. But it is called the chapel of the Conception by Pozzo, *Vite de' Pittori etc. Veronesi*, 1718, p. 235, in Zagata (Supplementi), *op. cit.*, Part II, Vol. II, 1749, p. 196, and by Persico, *Descrizione di Verona*, I, 1820, p. 196. It is true that Vasari (ed. Milanesi, V. p. 284) refers merely to a chapel dedicated to the Virgin; he is followed by Pozzo, *op. cit.* in other places, e.g., p. 26, and by (Lanceni), *Ricreazione Pittorica*, 1720, p. 71. (**18**) Zagata (Supplementi), *op. cit.*, Part II, Vol. II, p. 93. (**19**) Persico, *op. cit.*, I, 1820, p. 196. (**20**) Pozzo, *op. cit.*, p. 171; Lanceni, *op. cit.*, p. 72. (**21**) Venturi, *Storia dell'Arte Italiana*, Vol. VII, Part III, Figs. 97–106 and 167–170. (**22**) Berlin, No. 40; in the 1931 Catalogue as Venetian, and reproduced in the Illustrations. Venturi, *Storia dell'Arte Italiana*, Vol. VII, Part IV, Fig. 398, as Basaiti. Noted as having been destroyed in *Arte Veneta*, 1949, p. 191 (with reproduction). (**23**) Cf. note 3. (**24**) This and several of the statements following are from Giambattista Biancolini, *Notizie Storiche delle Chiese di Verona*, VIII, 1771, p. 193. (**25**) This is mentioned not only by Biancolini, *loc. cit.*, but also by Pietro Sgulmero, *Il Trino-Trittico di S. Maria della Scala in Verona*, 1905 (Nozze Simeoni-Colpi), p. 11. Wittkower, in the *Jahrbuch für Kunstwissenschaft*, 1927, p. 208, No. 9 gives an entry for No. 748; cf. also Dirce Viana, *Torbido*, 1933, p. 77. (**26**) Pozzo, *Le Vite de' Pittori etc. Veronesi*, 1718; on pp. 29, 34 and 42 he follows Vasari's record about the pictures, adding that they were no longer visible. They are not mentioned in the Guide to Verona by Lanceni entitled *Ricreazione Pittorica*, 1720. (**27**) Biancolini, *op. cit.*, III, 1750 (privilege, 1748), p. 177. A picture of the Virgin and Child with SS. Anne, Sebastian and Roch by Bernardin Gissardi was put up instead of them; Biancolini, *op. cit.*, IV, p. 828. Zannandreis, *Le Vite dei Pittori etc. Veronesi*, 1891, p. 488, mentions the picture, as by Bernardino Ghizzardi. (**28**) Cf. the previous note. Also an annotation of 1743 by Gian Bettino Cignaroli to Pozzo's book; communicated by Bernasconi in 1863, and printed by G. Biadego, *Di Giambettino Cignaroli*, R. Dep. di Storia Patria per la Venezia, 1890, p. 22. (**29**) *Descrizione delle Opere di Pittura di Eccellenti Maestri raccolte dal Sig. Francesco Caldana*, 1822 (No. 108), with identifying description; cf. Sgulmero, *op. cit.*, pp. 23/4. This break in the provenance is no reason for feeling any doubt at all about the identification of the picture, the tradition for which had been preserved. (**30**) Francesco Caldana died in 1854; several of his pictures passed into the Collection of Andrea Monga, who died in 1861. No. 748 was framed in the Monga Collection with several irrelevant pictures. To judge from Eastlake's note-book of 1864, the two side-pieces were probably the *S. George* and *S. Paul* now in the Verona Museum; *Capolavori della Pittura Veronese*, 1947, Nos. 66, 67, as Giovanni Caroto. There were also predella pictures, *The Last Supper* in the centre, *The Flagellation* right, *The Agony in the Garden* left.

See also Ascribed to Niccolò GIOLFINO, No. 749

GEROLAMO da Santacroce
active 1516, died 1556 (?)

One of numerous Santacroces established at Venice; some of them are known to have had connections with Bergamo. Gerolamo may be identical with a *garzone* in Gentile Bellini's workshop, mentioned in 1503 and 1507; and/or an assistant of Giovanni Bellini, mentioned in

1507 at the Doge's Palace. Signed and dated works from 1516 (Chicago).

There are plenty of examples of Gerolamo's mature style; the only question (if it is worth answering) being the extent of his son's and his grandson's participation. These humble works conserve a vaguely Bellinesque tradition, only slightly affected by the new style of Titian, etc. Gerolamo's earliest authenticated work of 1516 is derived from Bellini's San Zaccaria altarpiece of 1505; see the Ryerson Catalogue, *ca.* 1925, pp. 53/4, No. 2025. The attribution of works earlier than this is somewhat doubtful.

The entry in Thieme-Becker is under *Santacroce*.

Ascribed to GEROLAMO DA SANTACROCE

632 A YOUTHFUL SAINT READING (PANEL FROM AN ALTARPIECE)

Poplar,[1] transferred from another panel, painted surface, $46\frac{3}{4} \times 18\frac{3}{4}$ ($1 \cdot 185 \times 0 \cdot 475$).

Not free from damage, but the condition in general is good.

For the commentary, etc. see No. 633 below.

633 A SAINT WITH A FORTRESS AND BANNER (PANEL FROM AN ALTARPIECE)

Spruce,[2] painted surface, $46\frac{3}{8} \times 18\frac{3}{4}$ ($1 \cdot 18 \times 0 \cdot 475$); painted up to the edges at the top and left.

In better condition than the pendant, but there is a large patch on the forehead. *Pentimento* in his right hand.

No. 632 was formerly called S. John the Evangelist, which is quite possible but not certain. No. 633 was in the 1929 catalogue as S. George; the banner with a red cross on a white ground would be correct, but the fortress, and the lack of armour and dragon make the identification doubtful. If the fortress is assumed to stand for a city, it might indicate that the saint is the local Patron, and not be a permanent attribute; in that case, the original destination of the picture would be connected with this patronage. A very similar saint occurs on Crivelli's triptych of 1482 in the Brera;[3] he is S. Venantius, Patron of Camerino near Ancona. A less similar example is on Bellini's altarpiece at Pesaro, where the saint is in Roman armour; this saint like No. 633 has been called S. George, but is pretty certainly S. Terentius, Patron of Pesaro.[4]

The pictures were acquired as by Gerolamo da Santacroce, and the attribution has usually been accepted.[5] It seems possible to accept them among the early works; but this problem has not been thoroughly disentangled. The style is derived ultimately from the late works of Giovanni Bellini. It seems fairly similar to that of Previtali's middle period; this might confirm the attribution to Gerolamo da Santacroce, if he was a Bergamask—but that is not always admitted (see Thieme-Becker).

Ludwig[6] published an unproved hypothesis about these pictures. In 1503, the Dominicans of S. Zanipolo, Venice, erected an oratory for a miraculous picture of the Virgin, known as the *Madonna della Pace*. In 1664 Boschini[7] described the paintings surrounding the miraculous image as a lunette (?) of God the Father and on each side S. John the Evangelist and *un Santo, in habito da Cavaliere, con un stendardo nella mano*, by Carpaccio. The pictures were removed from their place not long afterwards. Boschini's attribution was very likely wrong; an inventory of 1708 attributes the 'God the Father' to Paolo Veronese and the two saints to Palma, and later inventories give no painter's name at all.[8] Ludwig's identification of the two saints as Nos. 632/3 is in any case overbold; for No. 632 is not certainly S. John the Evangelist, and No. 633 is not obviously dressed as a knight.

Ludwig sought to buttress his hypothesis with others. Lorenzo Gabriel, Bishop of Bergamo, died in 1512 and his brother Zaccaria built him a tomb in this oratory at S. Zanipolo, in which he was himself buried in 1519. It is not proved that either of the Gabriel brothers was responsible for the altarpiece. If they were, Ludwig might suppose (as he does) that Lorenzo's connection with Bergamo might be recalled by a representation of S. Alexander, Patron of that town; but it would remain very doubtful if No. 633 does represent S. Alexander.[9]

Even if all this were conceded, the precise date of 1512 would not follow for the pictures.[10]

PROVENANCE: On the back of No. 633 is the seal of the Venetian Academy, etc. (for export from Venice). Owned by Woodburn.[11] Purchased with the rest of the Edmond Beaucousin Collection, Paris, 1860.

REPRODUCTIONS: *Illustrations, Italian Schools*, 1937, pp. 159/60. *Plates, Earlier Italian Schools*, 1953, Vol. I, p. 169.

REFERENCES: (1) and (2) Letter from B. J. Rendle, of the Forest Products Research Laboratory, in the Gallery archives. (3) Venturi, *Storia dell' Arte Italiana*, Vol. VII, Part III, Fig. 292. (4) Gronau, Klassiker der Kunst *Bellini*, 1930, Plate 53. (5) E.g. by Fiocco in *L'Arte*, 1916, pp. 12 and 25 of the offprint. Pallucchini in *Arte Veneta*, 1951, p. 196, inclines to doubt. (6) G. Ludwig in the Prussian *Jahrbuch*, 1903, *Beiheft*, pp. 18/9. (7) Boschini, *Le Minere della Pittura*, 1664, p. 229. Cf. Sansovino, *Venetia Città Nobilissima*, ed. Stringa, 1604, f. 124r. (8) The Scuola della Madonna della Pace ceased to exist in 1801. (9) S. Alexander should apparently have fleur-de-lys, and not a red cross on a white ground, as in No. 633. He is shown (in armour) in a picture by Foppa in the Brera (name inscribed); reproduced by Ffoulkes and Maiocchi, *Vincenzo Foppa*, 1909, p. 120. Also, without the name inscribed, in a picture of 1506 by Francesco di Simone da Santacroce at Bergamo; reproduced in the *Rassegna d'Arte*, 1909, p. 192. (10) The date is accepted by Berenson in his Lists of 1932, 1936 and 1957. (11) N.G. MS. Catalogue.

GEROLAMO DA VICENZA
active 1488

Three signed pictures are recorded in Thieme-Becker. The largest is a *Martyrdom of S. Sebastian* in the Musée André at Paris (reproduced in the catalogue, 6th edition, 1929, p. 106); it comes from Sant'Angelo in

Vado, a place between Arezzo and Urbino, and the style seems to show some Umbrian influence. No. 3077 below is a fourth signed picture. It alone bears a date; it was painted in Venice. Borenius in Thieme-Becker, s.v. Pironi, abandoned a former suggestion that the painter is identical with *Gerolamo Pironi* (better, *Pittoni*), and accepts that he may rather be *Gerolamo di Stefano d'Alemania*. This man is indeed stated to be the only suitable candidate. He is recorded at Vicenza several times between 1481 and 1510; until 1494 at least, he seems to have been closely associated with Bartolomeo Montagna. See G. G. Zorzi in *Miscellanea di Storia Veneta*, Series III, Vol. 10, 1916, Part III, pp. 122 ff.; for Pittoni, the same writer, *Miscellanea di Studi e Memorie*, 1937, pp. 87 ff. See further Lionello Puppi's articles in *Vita Vicentina*, 1958 (Nos. 6–7) and 1959 (No. 3).

3077 THE DEATH AND ASSUMPTION OF THE VIRGIN

In an enclosure, the Virgin is lying on a bier, with Christ kneeling by her; above, the same two figures rise in a glory to Heaven. Many little angels hold tapers or play musical instruments. In front, the twelve Apostles; S. John(?) in the centre seems to be waving a taper. In the extreme foreground, centre, the Donor (?); two sisters of Religion (?) kneel in the middle distance at the left. Signed on the balustrade: HIERONIMVS.VINCENTINVS. / PINCSIT. / VENETIIS (some letters run together). 1488.

Wood, painted surface, $13\frac{1}{4} \times 9$ (0·335 × 0·225).
The condition is fairly pure, but the surface has been rubbed.

The treatment of the subject is in some degree similar to the traditional κοίμησις, but the Virgin is here raised in the body into Heaven. The details of the iconography seem due to individual caprice, as would be the painting of a donor without showing his face.

Part of the signature, sufficient for attribution, was first read by E. K. Waterhouse.[1] The picture was in 1929 catalogued as by Carpaccio, and is often connected with him, but there seems to the compiler to be little or no connection.[2] The style derives ultimately from Mantegna; the scale and disposition of the figures among the buildings may be compared with Jacopo Bellini's drawings, which are a good deal earlier. The architecture on the right is no doubt meant to be Venetian.

PROVENANCE: Purchased from Conte di Thiene, Vicenza, by Sir Austen Henry Layard;[3] exhibited at South Kensington, 1869 (No. 49);[4] Layard Bequest, 1916.[5]

REPRODUCTION: *Illustrations, Italian Schools*, 1937, p. 84. *Plates, Earlier Italian Schools*, 1953, Vol. I, p. 170.

REFERENCES: (1) Infra-red photographs, with direct magnification × 2, have been taken; these show most of the letters of the signature quite clearly. (2) Longhi thinks that the André picture signed by Gerolamo da Vicenza is by a different hand from the two other signed works mentioned in Thieme-Becker. This distinction seems unnecessary, but in any case No. 3077 may reasonably be classed with the André picture; Longhi, however, classes it with the others. See R. Longhi, *Officina Ferrarese*, 1934, pp. 161/2 (note 56) and p. 197. Later,

Longhi, without rejecting the signature, seems to call No. 3077 a copy from Carpaccio; see *Viatico per Cinque Secoli di Pittura Veneziana*, 1946, pp. 15 and 80. Carpaccio's authentic pictures of this subject are reproduced by Van Marle, *Development of the Italian Schools of Painting*, Vol. XVIII, Figs. 165 and 172. On p. 570 of the same volume, Van Marle gives a confused note about No. 3077; it is true that Berenson (1936 Lists) thought that it may be a copy after Carpaccio. Berenson did not maintain this view in his 1957 Lists. (3) Layard MSS. in the National Gallery, as from Count Tieni; doubtfully as Gerolamo dai Libri, perhaps following Crowe and Cavalcaselle, *Painting in North Italy*, I, 1871, p. 498. No. 3077 seems to have been bought at the same time as Gerard David, No. 3067, which was lent by Layard to the British Institution, 1862, and may have been bought by him in 1860 (*Sir A. Henry Layard, Autobiography and Letters*, ed. W. N. Bruce, 1903, II, p. 228). (4) As Unknown. (5) For the history of the Layard Collection, see Appendix IV.

Domenico GHIRLANDAIO
ca. 1448–1494

Florentine School. Domenico Bigordi, called Ghirlandaio, or in the Florentine form Grillandaio. Stated to have been a pupil of Baldovinetti. He was in Rome several times, e.g. in 1475; and in 1481/2 he was painting frescoes in the Sistine Chapel there. He also worked in San Gimignano and Pisa. Many documented and even more dated works of his exist. The chief problem concerning him is the separation of his autograph works from the productions of his very active studio; his brother Davide indeed seems to have been his partner rather than merely his assistant.

2902 A LEGEND OF SS. JUSTUS AND CLEMENT OF VOLTERRA (PREDELLA PANEL FROM AN ALTARPIECE)

S. Justus, behind whom is seen S. Clement, stands at a gate in the walls of a town, and distributes bread to some soldiers.

Wood, painted surface, $5\frac{1}{2} \times 15\frac{1}{2}$ (0·14 × 0·39). A black band continues round the picture to the edges of the panel; the total size is $6\frac{3}{8} \times 16\frac{3}{8}$ (0·16 × 0·415).

Good condition; damage in the landscape right centre.

The subject was formerly identified as David receiving the shewbread from Ahimelech (I Samuel xxi, I sqq.); the true subject was identified by Gronau.[1] SS. Justus and Clement penetrated into Volterra at a time when the town was starving under siege from the Vandals; in answer to the saints' prayer, the granaries of the Volterrans were filled with grain, and the Vandal camp was entirely deprived of food. According to a version of the legend, the saints ordered loaves to be put on the ground outside the city (*sterni panibus viam, et per circuitum civitatis*), thus following the instruction in *Romans*, xii, 20, 'if thine enemy hunger, feed him'. The Vandals were astonished that a city thought to be starving should use bread as paving stones; *alienati sensu et pavore concussi*, they went off in confusion.[2]

Gronau[3] identified No. 2902 as one of the predella panels to Ghirlandaio's high-altarpiece in S. Giusto alle Mura just outside Florence, which was moved in 1529/31 to S. Giusto della Calza within the city. For the history of the two churches concerned, the student is referred to the provenance below. The main panel was nearly purchased for the National Gallery in 1855, but the Tuscan Government refused permission to export, and the picture is now in the Uffizi.[4] It represents the Virgin and Child with Angels and SS. Michael, Justus, Zenobius and Raphael. The predella is identified as having been made up of the following five panels, from left to right: (a) The Fall of the Rebel Angels, at Detroit;[5] (b) the subject of the present entry; (c) The Marriage of the Virgin, (d) A Miracle of S. Zenobius, (e) Tobias and the Angel, these three all at New York.[6] The association of the five predella panels and the altarpiece in the Uffizi is quite satisfactory.[7]

The contract for Ghirlandaio's high-altarpiece in S. Giusto alle Mura is not known to be preserved. The church is claimed to have been built in 1487,[8] but it is extremely probable that Ghirlandaio's picture was already in position by June, 1486.[9] A date in the earlier 1480's might seem reasonable; actually, there is a statement (perhaps not reliable) that the picture was painted in 1479.[10]

On stylistic grounds, it seems difficult to make a distinction between a predella by Ghirlandaio's own hand and a predella from his studio; but, since it is known that Ghirlandaio frequently depended on assistants in the execution of his pictures, it is not unlikely that No. 2902 and its companions were partly or wholly executed by assistants. It is customary to suppose that the Detroit panel may have been executed by Ghirlandaio himself, the others not.[11]

PROVENANCE: Ghirlandaio's picture, of which No. 2902 has been identified as one predella panel, was the high-altarpiece of S. Giusto alle Mura, outside the walls of Florence.[12] This church belonged to the Gesuati of S. Jerome,[13] and was destroyed in preparation for the siege of Florence in 1529. In 1531, these Gesuati were given another church in Florence, which had previously been named S. Niccolò or S. Giovannino,[14] but became more usually known as S. Giusto della Calza;[15] the Ghirlandaio was set up as its high-altarpiece.[16] The Order of the Gesuati of S. Jerome was suppressed in 1668. S. Giusto della Calza was raised to the status of an abbey, and in 1671 was given in commendam to Cardinal Camillo de' Massimi. He sold it in 1672 to the representatives of the Casa del Rifugio, who sold it in 1675 to the Reformed Franciscans of Fiesole, who sold it in 1680 to the Congregation of Priests of S. Salvadore all'Arcivescovado; the dedication of the church was then changed to S. Giovanni Battista. Ghirlandaio's high-altarpiece remained in position in spite of these incidents. It is recorded by Richa, with its predella, in 1761.[17] It is recorded, with the predella described in much the same terms, in some guides to Florence of the nineteenth century; but they continued to repeat information, even when it had become untrue.[18] By 1828, the predella had been detached from the picture, and belonged to Metzger at Florence.[19] The present whereabouts of the main panel and the other four pieces of the predella are indicated in the text above. No. 2902 is next known to be recorded in the Gentleman from Blackheath Sale, London, 20 June, 1874 (lot 26), with a companion, no description of subject, as by Pintoricchio, bought by Waters;[20] the owner was apparently W. Angerstein or W. J. Farrer, and the pictures are claimed to have been in the Rogers Collection. Lady Lindsay Bequest, 1912.

REPRODUCTION: *Illustrations, Italian Schools*, 1937, p. 152. *Plates, Earlier Italian Schools*, 1953, Vol. I, p. 171.

REFERENCES: (1) Gronau in *Apollo*, October, 1926, pp. 72 ff. (2) This is the version of the legend in a MS. in the Laurenziana, given by Luigi Consortini, *La Badia dei SS. Giusto e Clemente presso Volterra*, 1915, pp. 97 ff.; it seems to fit No. 2902 better than the version summarized by Gronau. Consortini's book contains further information about the stories of these saints. Ghirlandaio presumably had some slightly differing source. The picture from which No. 2902 comes was the high-altarpiece of a church dedicated to S. Justus, and there need be no doubt that S. Justus of Volterra was the saint intended on the picture; Vasari says so. In point of fact, the church was originally dedicated to S. Justus of Lyons. Richa, *Notizie Istoriche delle Chiese Fiorentine*, IX, 1761, p. 104, argues (apropos of a relic) against this; but Domenico Moreni, *Notizie Istoriche dei Contorni di Firenze*, VI, 1795, pp. 22 ff., proves conclusively that Richa is wrong. Possibly the change to S. Justus of Volterra came about because the Feasts of S. Justus of Lyons and S. Octavianus of Volterra are on the same day (September 2). (3) Gronau, *loc. cit.* in Note 1, and further in *Art in America*, December, 1927, pp. 16 ff. (4) Uffizi, 1926 Catalogue, No. 881. Reproduced by Van Marle, *Development of the Italian Schools of Painting*, Vol. XIII, Fig. 28; reproduced with the predella in *Art in America*, December, 1927, p. 20. Papers concerning the negotiations for the purchase of the main panel by the National Gallery are in the Gallery archives; there is a piece on the subject in *Journals and Correspondence of Lady Eastlake*, 1895, II, pp. 72/5. (5) Detroit, 1930 Catalogue, No. 86; size, $6\frac{1}{2} \times 14\frac{1}{2}$. According to the photograph in the Gallery files, the band round this picture is not black, but is otherwise similar to that surrounding No. 2902. Reproduced in *Apollo*, October, 1926, p. 73, and by Van Marle, *op. cit.*, Vol. XIII, Fig. 30. (6) Metropolitan Museum, 1940 Catalogue, *Italian, Spanish and Byzantine Paintings*, Nos. 13. 119, 1, 2, 3, reproduced; sizes, $6\frac{1}{4} \times 16\frac{1}{4}-16\frac{3}{8}$. Gronau in *Art in America*, December, 1927, p. 20, records that they have round them bands similar to that of No. 2902. (7) It must be admitted that what appears to be the only authentic reference to the predella when still attached to the Uffizi altarpiece is that by Richa, *op. cit.*, IX, 1761, p. 103; he says that it represented episodes from the lives of SS. Justus and Zenobius. But Richa must have been careless. The predella belonged in 1828 to Metzger at Florence, and is thus described by Rumohr: 'Fünf Stück gradino, von dem Gemälde des Dom. Ghirlandajo in la Calza. sehr fein ausgebildete Geschichte der Erzengel. wohl Bastiano Mainardi,' with a size given that corresponds well (Prussian *Jahrbuch*, 1925, *Beiheft*, p. 7). It may be noticed that Rumohr's description of the subjects is at least as incomplete as Richa's. (8) By Antonio di Giorgio Marchissi (Marchesi); see Milanesi's Vasari, Vol. IV, p. 476 (note), followed by Thieme-Becker. The Gesuati had previously had another church on the same site, since ca. 1439; see Richa, *op. cit.*, IX, 1761, p. 98, and Moreni, *op. cit.*, VI, 1795, pp. 31 ff. (9) See the documents concerning Ghirlandaio's Innocenti altarpiece, as printed by P. E. Küppers, *Die Tafelbilder des Domenico Ghirlandajo*, 1916, pp. 87/8, Doc. II. The high-altarpiece of the Gesuati, i.e. S. Giusto alle Mura (without the painter's name) is there referred to; its frame was to serve as a model for the frame of the Innocenti altarpiece, then being prepared. (10) The date of 1479 is stated in MS. No. 226 of the Moreniana Library (attached to the Riccardiana) at Florence, Vol. II, p. 239. The manuscript is entitled *Compendio di Notizie Istoriche delle chiese di Firenze, e di alcune suburbane divise nei suoi quartieri*, and is based, but with corrections, upon Richa's printed work. Richa, in fact, in a somewhat incorrect correction, Vol. IX, 1761, p. 343, mentions the date as ca. 1479. (11) E.g. Gronau, *loc. cit.* in notes 1 and 3; Berenson's 1932 Lists. A stylistic association with predellas at Lucca and Florence was claimed by Gronau; cf. P. E. Küppers, *Die Tafelbilder des Domenico Ghirlandajo*, 1916, pp. 68/9. Francovich in the *Bollettino d'Arte*, August, 1926, p. 82, ascribes No. 2902 to Bartolomeo di Giovanni. (12) Albertini, *Memoriale*, 1510, 1863 reprint, p. 17. See also Vasari, 1550, p. 466 (brief);

1568, p. 457; ed. Milanesi, III, p. 257 (and p. 570). (13) For this Order, see Hélyot, *Histoire des Ordres Monastiques*, III, 1715, pp. 407 ff. They were founded by the B. Giovanni Colombini, and were in some places known as the *padri dell'aqua vita*. (14) Henceforth, most of the facts are from Richa, *Notizie Istoriche delle Chiese Fiorentine*, Vol. IX, 1761, pp. 97 ff.; also his Vol. VIII, 1759, pp. 328 ff. The foundation was originally an Oratory attached to a Hospital, known as S. Niccolò de' Frieri (Frères) and belonging to the Order of S. John of Jerusalem. It had been transferred in 1392 to females belonging to the same Order, and had become known as S. Giovannino. (15) This was because the hood of these Gesuati, when not worn over the head, had the appearance of a stocking; pictorial indications are given by Hélyot, *op. cit.*, III, p. 407, and by Doyé, *Heilige und Selige*, 1929, II, Plate 51. (16) See Vasari. (17) Richa, as in note 7. (18) E.g. *Guida della Città di Firenze*, 1824, pp. 205/6; *Guida della Città di Firenze e suoi Contorni*, 1828, p. 206; reprint of the same, 1830. (19) See the Prussian *Jahrbuch*, 1914, *Beiheft*, p. 62, and 1925, *Beiheft*, pp. 7, 10. Cf. further a letter from Lord Normanby, our Minister to the Tuscan Government, to the Duke of Casigliano, 18 October, 1855; and the *Journals and Correspondence of Lady Eastlake*, 1895, II, p. 75. (20) Christie's stencil mark for this sale is on the back of No. 2902; lot 26 appears to be the only suitable lot in the sale.

Studio of DOMENICO GHIRLANDAIO

1230 PORTRAIT OF A GIRL

Wood, painted surface, $17\frac{3}{8} \times 11\frac{1}{2}$ ($0 \cdot 44 \times 0 \cdot 295$); including strips added, $\frac{1}{2}$ in. at the left, $\frac{3}{4}$ in. at the right.

In general in very good state. *Pentimenti* in nose, beads, etc.

No. 1230 has been ascribed to Ghirlandaio himself by some writers; Berenson, in his 1932 Lists, calls it Ghirlandaio in great part. The inferior quality of the drawing seems to exclude Ghirlandaio's own hand. The former attribution in the Gallery to Mainardi may be correct, but owing to the paucity of evidence it would be undesirable to maintain this.

To judge from the coiffure, the date of No. 1230 is not far from 1490.[1]

PROVENANCE: In the James Whatman Collection, Maidstone.[2] Exhibited at the British Institution, 1859 (No. 91), at Leeds, 1868 (No. 60A), and at Maidstone, 1884.[3] Purchased, Walker Fund, at the James Whatman Sale, 2 July, 1887 (lot 38).

REPRODUCTION: *Illustrations, Italian Schools*, 1937, p. 208. *Plates, Earlier Italian Schools*, 1953, Vol. I, p. 172.

REFERENCES: (1) Cf. Ghirlandaio's Portrait dated 1488, formerly in the Morgan Library (Van Marle, *Development of the Italian Schools of Painting*, XIII, Frontispiece); No. 48 of the Exhibition of *Pictures from the Thyssen-Bornemisza Collection*, at the National Gallery, 1961. (2) As Raffaellino del Garbo, perhaps because ' Raphael ' is inscribed on the back. (3) Label on the back.

3937 THE VIRGIN AND CHILD

Wood, painted surface, rounded top, $35 \times 22\frac{3}{4}$ ($0 \cdot 89 \times 0 \cdot 58$); excluding additions to the panel in the spandrels at the top, and of about $\frac{1}{2}$ in. all round. Incised circular marks about $1\frac{1}{2}$ in. within the line of the painted

arch at the top, and about $\frac{1}{2}$ in. outside this line, may indicate some uncertainty in the painter's mind as to the exact size his picture was to have.

Good condition, so far as can be seen through the varnish; much of
the gold is new.

No. 3937 is related in composition to the central part of an altarpiece
at Pisa by Domenico Ghirlandaio or his studio.[1] It is thus probable that
No. 3937 was painted from a cartoon by Domenico Ghirlandaio; it may
have been produced as his from his shop, and it is indeed doubtful if
there exists any small picture of the Virgin and Child nearer to Domenico Ghirlandaio than No. 3937. The quality, however, does not correspond with what we expect from Ghirlandaio's own hand.[2] It was
formerly catalogued as by Sebastiano Mainardi; but it does not
appear to be by the same hand as No. 2502 below, which would have a
better claim than No. 3937 to be associated with Mainardi.

No. 3937 and No. 2502 below are examples of the Virgin and Child
seen framed in a window. It is possible that this arrangement is derived
from Donatellesque bas-reliefs.

PROVENANCE: In the Collection of Sir Charles Eastlake by 1857.[3] Lady Eastlake Sale, 2 June, 1894 (lot 69), bought by (Ludwig) Mond. Mond Bequest,
1924.

REPRODUCTION: *Illustrations, Italian Schools*, 1937, p. 209. *Plates, Earlier
Italian Schools*, 1953, Vol. I, p. 173.

REFERENCES: (1) Reproduced by P. E. Küppers, *Die Tafelbilder des Domenico
Ghirlandajo*, 1916, Plate XXIIIa. (2) Cf. Crowe and Cavalcaselle, *History of
Painting in Italy*, II, 1864, p. 492. J. P. Richter, *The Mond Collection*, 1910, II,
pp. 424 ff., expresses some unconvincing views about the style of this picture.
(3) Waagen, *Treasures*, IV, 1857, p. 115 (as Ghirlandaio). It was probably acquired by Eastlake before 1855; pictures acquired by Eastlake after 1855 were
all (?) offered to the Gallery in 1867, but No. 3937 was not.

Follower of DOMENICO GHIRLANDAIO

2489 PORTRAIT OF A YOUNG MAN IN RED

Wood, painted surface, $15\frac{1}{4} \times 10\frac{7}{8}$ (0·39 × 0·275). This excludes some
new framing, which is fixed over the front of the panel round the edges.
The total size of the panel is $17\frac{3}{8} \times 12\frac{7}{8}$ (0·44 × 0·33); but it is uncertain
if the original field of the picture was ever much larger than it is at
present.[1]

Excellent condition.

From the following of Domenico Ghirlandaio; clearly not by Domenico's own hand. In the 1929 catalogue, it was ascribed to Sebastiano
Mainardi; so far as that name has a meaning,[2] it does not fit the style of
No. 2489. Küppers ascribed the picture to the Master of S. Sebastian,
an invention of his own.[3] Francovich called it Davide Ghirlandaio.[4]
Berenson (1932 Lists) ascribes No. 2489 to the young Granacci; but
hardly anything is known of Granacci's early style.

PROVENANCE: Col. 385 is written on the back; 6 and an I (?) under a crown appear at one time to have been on the front.[5] From the Barberini Collection, Rome.[6] Exported from Italy *ca.* 1903.[7] George Salting Bequest, 1910.

REPRODUCTION: *Illustrations, Italian Schools*, 1937, p. 208. *Plates, Earlier Italian Schools*, 1953, Vol. I, p. 174.

REFERENCES: (1) In Anderson's photograph No. 915 of this picture (as Masaccio), when it was still in the Barberini Collection at Rome, the field is indeed larger than it is now in the picture; but the extra strips, to judge from the photograph, appear to have been new, except probably at the top. (2) See his biography in this catalogue. (3) P. E. Küppers, *Die Tafelbilder des Domenico Ghirlandajo*, 1916, pp. 60/1. (4) Géza de Francovich in *Dedalo*, August, 1930, p. 139. Davide's most authentic picture, a *S. Lucy with Donor* in S. Maria Novella at Florence, is reproduced by Van Marle, *Development of the Italian Schools of Painting*, Vol. XIII, Fig. 87. Francovich in *Dedalo*, July, 1930, p. 86, does not admit the documentation for this picture, and uses other works for attributions to Davide. According to various documentary evidence, Davide was the most important assistant, or rather the partner, of Domenico Ghirlandaio; it is doubtful if the work of the two brothers will ever be disentangled. (5) Anderson photograph, No. 915 (as Masaccio). (6) As a self-portrait by Masaccio —see Anderson's photograph, No. 915. So recorded by X. Barbier de Montault, *Les Musées et Galeries de Rome*, 1870, p. 343, No. 67. Apparently it had previously been called Ghirlandaio; see Cavalcaselle e Crowe, *Storia della Pittura in Italia*, Vol. VII, 1896, pp. 461/2. Cavalcaselle's description of the background is inaccurate, but it cannot be doubted that he was writing of No. 2489. Presumably it is the picture called Mainardi in the index to Burckhardt's *Cicerone*, 6th edition by Bode, Part II, 1893, p. 86. (7) Dubious date-stamp on the back. It is recorded as still in the Barberini Collection in Lafenestre and Richtenberger, *Rome, Les Musées*, etc., 1905, p. 156.

2502   THE VIRGIN AND CHILD WITH S. JOHN

In the background on the right are various buildings of Rome, commented on below.

Wood, rounded top, painted surface, $31\frac{1}{4} \times 18\frac{1}{2}$ (0·79 × 0·47); painted up to the edges all round.

Considerably overcleaned, especially in the shadowed parts of the flesh; this is most marked in the lower part of the picture—for instance, much of S. John's face is seriously damaged. Some of the gold is new. There are various *pentimenti*, e.g. in the line of the Virgin's left arm and shoulder. The painter's first intention was to have the Virgin's right hand supporting Christ's right leg in the region of the knee; the underdrawing for this has come to show through partly.

On the right of the picture is a view of a town, which is not an exact record of Rome in the fifteenth century, but includes various buildings of Rome, tolerably well reproduced. The arched tower on the left is the Torre dei Conti, or possibly the Torre delle Milizie.[1] If one comes forward from it towards the right, one sees the Pantheon, the Column of Trajan or of Marcus Aurelius, the Arch of Constantine and the Colosseum. Behind the last is the Castel Sant' Angelo.[2] The group of buildings further back, between the Castel Sant' Angelo and the Pantheon, would be expected to be Old S. Peter's and the Vatican; although the buildings do not correspond very well with other records of them, this does appear to be true.[3]

It is not necessary to assume that the painter of No. 2502 had visited Rome; drawings of the buildings by somebody else would have served his purpose well enough.

No. 2502 was formerly ascribed to Sebastiano Mainardi.[4] It is explained in Mainardi's biography in this catalogue that the evidence concerning him is too slight to justify the use of his name; but No. 2502 is the picture in the National Gallery that seems the least unlikely to be by him.

VERSION: A version without the S. John was in the Ernst Rosenfeld Collection, New York; 1948, Coll. Mrs. Arthur Stein, New York.[5]

PROVENANCE: In the Collection of Conte Guido di Bisenzo at Rome by 1835.[6] The Bisenzo Collection was bought en bloc in 1847 by Lord Ward[7] (created Earl of Dudley in 1860). Exhibited at Manchester, 1857 (Provisional Catalogue, No. 59; Definitive Catalogue, No. 88).[8] In the George Salting Collection by ca. 1875;[9] Salting Bequest 1910.

REPRODUCTION: *Illustrations, Italian Schools*, 1937, p. 209. *Plates, Earlier Italian Schools*, 1953, Vol. I, p. 175.

REFERENCES: (1) Compare various views of the Torre dei Conti in H. Egger, C. Hülsen and A. Michaelis, *Codex Escurialensis, Ein Skizzenbuch aus der Werkstatt Domenico Ghirlandaios*, 1905/6, Vol. I, pp. 111/2 and 142, and Vol. II, Plates 40v, and 57v. The Torre delle Milizie seems less likely, but cf. for instance H. Egger, *Römische Veduten*, II, 1931, Plates 114, 115. (2) Cf. *Codex Escurialensis*, as in the previous note, Vol. I, pp. 63, 90 and 94, and Vol. II, Plates 7v, 26v and 30v. The constructions at the top have been a good deal modified since. (3) With help kindly supplied by Dr. Jacob Hess, the compiler after some doubts came to the conclusion that these buildings are meant for Old S. Peter's and the Vatican. The details are very inaccurate, as can be seen from numerous other records of these buildings; but the general arrangement corresponds quite well with the view shown in Hartmann Schedel's *Liber Chronicorum*, 1493, and the rather similar view in a map of Rome in the Museo Civico at Mantua. See G. B. de Rossi, *Piante Icnografiche e Prospettiche di Roma*, 1879, Plates V and XI; see also J. Tombu in *The Burlington Magazine*, Vol. L (1927), pp. 325 ff. What appears to be an accurate view of this region, with S. Peter's partly reconstructed, is in the background of a *Meeting of SS. Francis and Dominic*, Italian School ca. 1590, in the Mrs. E. M. Sargant Sale, 20 March, 1959, lot 45 (photo in the Gallery archives). (4) Crowe and Cavalcaselle, *History of Painting in Italy*, II, 1864, pp. 370 and 495, first ascribed it to Mainardi. (5) Van Marle, *Development of the Italian Schools of Painting*, Vol. XIII, p. 194; *Memorial Catalogue of Paintings by Old and Modern Masters collected by Edward R. Bacon*, New York, 1919, p. 214, No. 270 (reproduced). Reproduction after cleaning in the Gallery archives, kindly supplied by the Frick Library, New York. (6) Engraved in *L'Ape Italiana delle Belle Arti*, Vol. I, 1835, Plate XXVII (pp. 42/3, article by G. Melchiorri). (7) Cf. *Kunst-Blatt*, 1847, p. 152. (8) It was exhibited as by Pesello, an attribution authorized by Waagen, *Treasures*, II, 1854, p. 231. (9) Salting MSS.

Style of DOMENICO GHIRLANDAIO

2490 COSTANZA CAETANI

Inscribed. GHOS/TANZA | DEMED/ICIS IO/ANFRA/NCISC/ HVS D/OMINI | FRANC/ICI DE | GHAE/TANIS | VXOR.

Wood, painted surface, $22\frac{1}{2} \times 14\frac{3}{4}$ (0·57 × 0·375). Including the frame (which seems to be the original one; the bottom piece of it is missing), the size is $25\frac{1}{4} \times 17\frac{1}{4}$ (0·64×0·44).

Considerably damaged by wide cracks.

It has sometimes been doubted whether No. 2490 is an old picture; but the cleaning of it in 1935 offered no confirmation at all that it is a forgery.

The sitter was born *ca.* 1469,[1] and is recorded at Florence in 1489 and 1507.[2] A man obviously her husband is recorded on inscriptions at Castelfalfi (where the picture was in the nineteenth century) as alive in 1475 and dead by 1530.[3]

No. 2490 was lent to the Gallery in 1895 as by Domenico Ghirlandaio; it was catalogued as by him in 1929, but previously for a time had been catalogued as by Lorenzo di Credi.[4] Berenson (1932 Lists) maintains that it is by Domenico Ghirlandaio (early). Küppers[5] ascribes some other pictures to the same hand, as by the 'Maler der Constanza Medici.' Francovich[6] ascribes it to Davide Ghirlandaio. It seems near in style, or at least in character, to a female portrait at Berlin, No. 80.[7]

PROVENANCE: Formerly in the castle of Castelfalfi near Montajone (west of Florence), which had belonged to a man obviously the husband of the sitter.[8] In the nineteenth century, the castle belonged to the Biondi family, and No. 2490 was sold from there, it is stated about 1890, to Bardini.[9] Apparently owned by Sir George Donaldson in 1894.[10] Lent by George Salting to the National Gallery from 1895; Salting Bequest, 1910.

REPRODUCTION: *Illustrations, Italian Schools*, 1937, p. 152. *Plates, Earlier Italian Schools*, 1953, Vol. I, p. 176.

REFERENCES: (1) Florence, Archivio di Stato, Portate al Catasto by her father, Averardo de' Medici, Q. S. Giovanni, Gonfalone Leon d'Oro: 1470, *Gostāza* aged 4 (months, apparently), f. 111; and 1480, *Gostanza* aged 12 years, f. 155v. (2) Kindly communicated by Bernard Berenson, who sent the following passage, the result of research in the Florentine archives: 'Ghostanza era figlia di Averardo di Bernardo de' Medici, è ricordata nel 1489 e nel 1507 nei libri delle decime insieme con suo marito Giovan Francesco di M. Francesco di Benedetto Gaetano. Averardo fu magistrato nel 1464 e 1484, gonfaloniere nel 1485 e nel 1513. Dal Litta non risulta questa figlia.' (Averardo de' Medici is recorded on Tav. XVIII of Litta's *Famiglie Celebri d'Italia*.) (3) See *Miscellanea Storica della Valdelsa*, 1911, fasc. 1/2, p. 3 of offprint, *Cenni Storici su Castelfalfi* by G. P. Castelfalfi came politically into the Florentine sphere in 1370. (4) Ascribed to Lorenzo di Credi by Sir Claude Phillips in *The Burlington Magazine*, Vol. XVII (1910), p. 15. (5) P. E. Küppers, *Die Tafelbilder des Domenico Ghirlandajo*, 1916, pp. 66 ff. (6) Francovich in *Dedalo*, August, 1930, p. 134. (7) No. 80 of the 1931 Berlin Catalogue, attr. Lorenzo di Credi, with a note of other attributions for it; reproduced in the Berlin Illustrations. (8) Reference as in note 3; ascribed to Botticelli. (9) Some documents to this effect are in the Gallery archives. (10) Reference in a letter in the Gallery archives.

MICHELE GIAMBONO
active 1420–1462

Michele (di Taddeo) Bono, called *Giambono*. Venetian School. There are signed pictures at Venice and in Rome (Palazzo Venezia, Hertz Bequest). A product of International Gothic in a Venetian nuance, he may have been influenced by Jacobello del Fiore; it is pretty clear that he was affected by Gentile da Fabriano, who was working in Venice probably *ca.* 1409/14.

Literature: Evelyn Sandberg-Vavalà in the *Journal of the Warburg and Courtauld Institutes*, 1947, pp. 20 ff.

3917   A SAINT WITH A BOOK (PANEL FROM AN ALTAR-
        PIECE)

Poplar,[1] painted surface, $15\frac{1}{4} \times 11\frac{1}{4}$ (0·385 × 0·285); painted up to the edges all round.

Good condition. The black background may have been repainted (see below).

Formerly called *S. Mark.*

This would appear to be a panel from the upper tier of a polyptych. Suggestions for the reconstruction of the polyptych from which No. 3917 may have come have been made recently as follows.[2]

A *S. Michael*[3] in the Berenson Collection at Settignano is held to have been the central panel of the main tier. As side panels of the main tier, a *Bishop* and a *Pope* at Padua, a *S. Peter* at Washington and a *S. John the Baptist* in the Bardini Museum at Florence are suggested. This reconstruction appears convincing,[4] although it is not certain that the main tier consisted only of these five pictures.[5] The upper tier, it is suggested by Evelyn Sandberg-Vavalà, included No. 3917, a martyr bishop (Franciscan?) at Padua, a bishop in the Gardner Museum at Boston, and a S. Stephen in the Gibert (formerly Frizzoni) Collection at Bellagio.[6] These half-length figures seem to correspond quite well with the figures of the main tier, and the suggestion is very plausible. Sandberg-Vavalà notes that the black background of No. 3917 is an anomaly, since all (?) the other pictures have blue backgrounds; perhaps the background here has been repainted. She also notes that the Gibert *S. Stephen* must have been cut down.

The proposed reconstruction of this polyptych seems defensible, but it is not known what was its place of origin. Several of the panels were in the nineteenth century in Padua.[7]

The attribution of No. 3917 to Giambono seems to be due to Richter,[8] and is generally accepted[9].

PROVENANCE: Formerly with Guggenheim, Venice; bought by J. P. Richter, 1884. Acquired by Ludwig Mond, 1891.[10] Exhibited at the New Gallery, 1894/5 (No. 200). Mond Bequest, 1924.

REPRODUCTION: *Illustrations, Italian Schools*, 1937, p. 154. *Plates, Earlier Italian Schools*, 1953, Vol. I, p. 177.

REFERENCES: (1) Letter from B. J. Rendle, of the Forest Products Research Laboratory, in the Gallery archives. (2) R. Longhi, *Viatico per Cinque Secoli di Pittura Veneziana*, 1946, p. 50; independently, and more elaborately, E. Sandberg-Vavalà in the *Warburg and Courtauld Journal*, 1947, pp. 20 ff. (3) G. McN. Rushforth in *The Burlington Magazine*, Vol. XX (1911/2), pp. 106/7, argues unconvincingly that the subject is not S. Michael. (4) All these pictures are reproduced by Sandberg-Vavalà, *loc. cit.* (5) Crowe and Cavalcaselle, *Painting in North Italy*, 1871, I, p. 296, mention, as being from a single altarpiece, the two saints at Padua, and three pictures in the Collection of Galeazzo Dondi dall'Orologio at Padua, S. John Baptist, S. Peter and a bishop. It seems likely, although not proved, that the first two Dondi dall' Orologio pictures are the two now in the Bardini Museum and at Washington. Crowe and Cavalcaselle's text would then seem to imply that the bishop was also at full-length, like the others; but it is not known where such a picture may now be. (6) All these pictures are reproduced by Sandberg-Vavalà, *loc. cit.* (7) The full-lengths, *Bishop* and *Pope*, at Padua are from the Leonardo Emo Capodilista Collection at Padua, 1864. The half-length martyr bishop at Padua is from the Stefano Piombin Collection at Padua, 1887. (Cf. A. Moschetti in the *Bollettino d'Arte*, 1924/5, pp. 276 ff., and the same, *Il Museo Civico di Padova*, 1903, pp. 94 and 107.) The Bardini and Washington Saints, as noted in note 5, may be from the Dondi dall' Orologio Collection at Padua. The Berenson *S. Michael* may also be from the Dondi dall' Orologio Collection at Padua, to judge from the description of a picture there by Crowe and Cavalcaselle, *Painting in North Italy*, 1871, I, pp. 295/6. It is true that this is not proved; the first sure record of this *S. Michael* is at some auction in London as 'School of Germany', where it was bought by J. P. Richter who owned it in 1895. (See J. P. Richter, *The Mond Collection*, 1910, I, p. 62, and Berenson, *Study and Criticism*, Vol. I, p. 93.) (8) J. P. Richter, *The Mond Collection*, 1910, I, p. 59. (9) Testi, *Storia della Pittura Veneziana*, Vol. II, 1915, pp. 24 and 33/4, is perhaps the only writer to express doubt, and then not much. (10) J. P. Richter, *The Mond Collection*, 1910, Table of Contents for Vol. I.

GIAMPIETRINO
active first half of the sixteenth century

The name 'Giampietrino' has been written by Leonardo in the *Codice Atlantico*, f. 264; there is a not very ancient tradition that a *Giovanni Pedrino* was Leonardo's pupil. The name has been rather strangely telescoped with that of a *Pietro Rizzo* or *Riccio*, a Leonardo pupil recorded by Lomazzo (*Trattato*, 1584, pp. 679 and 695). Whatever these names may have meant, there is no sure means of connecting any of them with the group of paintings labelled by tradition 'Giampietrino'. One of the best traditions for 'Giampietrino's' name is attached to the Brivio *Egeria* (Suida, *Leonardo und sein Kreis*, 1929, Fig. 276); see Passavant in *Kunst-Blatt*, 1838, p. 291.

'Giampietrino's' works are (by definition) all attributions. An altarpiece at one time in the Cathedral of Pavia, and now in S. Marino there, is dated 1521. 'His' most characteristic pictures are half-lengths of the Virgin and Child, or nude biblical and classical women. The style is near to that of Marco d'Oggiono, reflecting the influence of Leonardo da Vinci and sometimes Cesare da Sesto. There is no standard of autograph quality, and it is uncertain if all the attributed pictures are really from one studio.

'GIAMPIETRINO'

3097   CHRIST CARRYING HIS CROSS

Poplar,[1] painted surface, $23\frac{1}{2} \times 18\frac{1}{2}$ ($0 \cdot 595 \times 0 \cdot 47$); painted up to the edges all round.

Rather rubbed; it has also suffered from flaking. But, so far as can be seen at present, in fair state.

It may go back ultimately to a design by Leonardo; a (not very similar) drawing of the *Head of Christ* by Leonardo is at Venice.[2]

VERSIONS: Several are known, in the Academy at Vienna,[3] at Turin,[4] in the collections of A. v. Reisinger (Vienna),[5] of Baron Herzog (Budapest),[6] of Lopez Cepero (Seville).[7]

PROVENANCE: Bought *ca.* 1865 from Baslini of Milan by Sir A. H. Layard;[8] exhibited at South Kensington, 1869 (No. 31); Layard Bequest, 1916.[9]

REPRODUCTION: *Illustrations, Italian Schools*, 1937, p. 270. *Plates, Earlier Italian Schools*, 1953, Vol. I, p. 178.

REFERENCES: (1) Letter from B. J. Rendle, of the Forest Products Research Laboratory, in the Gallery archives. (2) Reproduced by Suida, *Leonardo und sein Kreis*, 1929, Fig. 97. (3) Suida, *op. cit.*, Fig. 99. (4) Turin, 1899 Catalogue (No. 138). Photograph Alinari, No. 14842. (5) Frimmel, *Geschichte der Wiener Gemäldesammlungen, Die Galerie in der Akademie*, 1901, p. 136. (6) Suida, *op. cit.*, p. 214. (7) Noted by E. K. Waterhouse. (8) Letters, Morelli to Layard, 2(5?) October, 1865, and 3 January, 1866; Layard to Morelli, 1 January, 1866 (British Museum, Add. MSS. 38963 and 38966, Layard Papers, Vols. XXXIII and XXXVI). A. Venturi in *L'Arte*, 1912, p. 452, is not accurate. See also the Layard MSS. in the National Gallery. (9) For the history of the Layard Collection, see Appendix IV.

3930 SALOME

Poplar,[1] painted surface, $27 \times 22\frac{1}{2}$ ($0 \cdot 685 \times 0 \cdot 57$); painted up to the edges all round.

Very fair condition; rather rubbed.

VERSION: Somzée Sale, Brussels, 24 May, sqq., 1904 (lot 404), as Luini, reproduced in the catalogue.

PROVENANCE: Bought from M. Guggenheim, Venice, in 1895 by Ludwig Mond;[2] exhibited at the Burlington Fine Arts Club, 1898 (No. 57); Mond Bequest, 1924.

REPRODUCTION: *Illustrations, Italian Schools*, 1937, p. 269. *Plates, Earlier Italian Schools*, 1953, Vol. I, p. 179.

REFERENCES: (1) Letter from B. J. Rendle, of the Forest Products Research Laboratory, in the Gallery archives. (2) J. P. Richter, *The Mond Collection*, 1910, Table of Contents to Vol. II.

GIANNICOLA DI PAOLO
active 1484, died 1544

Giannicola di Paolo, a Perugian painter, called Smicca, and formerly erroneously called Manni. First mentioned in 1484, first mentioned as a painter in 1493. Vasari says that he was a pupil of Perugino, by whom he was certainly much influenced at the outset; later, he was influenced by diverse painters.

Ascribed to GIANNICOLA DI PAOLO

1104   THE ANNUNCIATION

The Virgin's prie-dieu is inscribed AVE GRATIA (apparently old); her prayer-book is marked with the letters D and H.

Wood, painted surface, $24 \times 41\frac{1}{2}$ (0·61 × 1·055); top corners cut. The size of the panel is $24\frac{3}{4} \times 42\frac{1}{4}$ (0·63 × 1·075); painted up to the edges all round, except in parts of the spandrels in the top corners. Part of the painting at the edges is only a lay-in; the true size of the picture, as given first, is indicated by contour lines.

Good condition.

Perhaps from the upper part of an altarpiece in compartments.

The attribution to Giannicola di Paolo does not appear to have been rejected; if the picture is by him, as seems likely enough, it would be a fairly early work, still strongly under Perugino's influence.

PROVENANCE: Perhaps in the Monaldi Collection, Perugia, by 1872.[1] Purchased from the Marchese Perolo Monaldi, 1881.

REPRODUCTION: *Illustrations, Italian Schools*, 1937, p. 210. *Plates, Earlier Italian Schools*, 1953, Vol. I, p. 180.

REFERENCE: (1) Mariano Guardabassi, *Indice-Guida dei Monumenti Pagani e Cristiani...nella Provincia dell' Umbria*, 1872, p. 201, No. 40, as Perugian School. That this reference is to No. 1104 is rendered doubtful by the *Elenco dei Quadri della Galleria del fu Marchese Giovanni Battista Monaldi di Perugia*, 1878, where the only corresponding picture seems to be No. 90, School of Perugino, size given as 1·31 × 0·89.

NICCOLÒ GIOLFINO

ca. 1476/7–1555

One of a large family of Veronese artists, and the second with the name of Niccolò. His age was declared as 13 in 1490, as 25 in 1501. He is generally said to have been a pupil of Liberale da Verona. There are many authenticated works.

Ascribed to NICCOLÒ GIOLFINO

749   PORTRAITS OF THE GIUSTI FAMILY OF VERONA(?)
(TWO FRAGMENTS FROM AN ALTARPIECE)

Canvas, each $22 \times 30\frac{3}{4}$ (0·56 × 0·78).

Good condition on the whole. There seems to be a *pentimento* in the *profil perdu* of the most prominent lady; another in the part of the man's sleeve visible in the women's section.

It is clear from its appearance that No. 749 is no predella, but the lower part of an undivided altarpiece: Mantegna had started the fashion for bust figures emerging above the bottom side of a frame, a motive the Veronese painters frequently repeated. The canvases are demonstrably cut at the tops and inner sides; so it would seem that the original altarpiece was on canvas. There is a very slight gap between the two fragments.

Eastlake in 1864[1] came across the two pictures forming No. 749 in the Monga Collection at Verona; they were surmounted by three other compartments, which he said were ruined, representing the Madonna with flanking saints. The central Madonna was shorter than the other two pieces, and had the following inscription under it: *Haec tabula a Nicolao Giolfino picta in Sacello S. Mariae a Stellis olim sita a familia nobilium Justorum juspatrona commissa et cum propriis imaginibus devotis expressa posteriori tempore distracta et in quinque partibus defracta nunc in unum restituta MDCCCLIII.*

The three upper compartments are identifiable from the inscription with a *Virgin and Child* (0·77 × 0·59) and *SS. Roch and Sebastian* (each, 1·24 × 0·49) among the pictures bequeathed in 1911 by Bortolo Monga to the Commune of Verona;[2] the attribution has been changed to Antonio da Vendri, they were exhibited for a time in the Convent of S. Girolamo and are now Nos. 2283–4–5 of the Verona Gallery.

It appears almost impossible on stylistic grounds to associate No. 749 and the three Verona pictures together, and it is more reasonable to suppose that the Monga family made a mistake.[3] But it is possible that the most striking parts of the Monga assemblage, the portraits, do really come from S. Maria in Stele or Stelle, where Lanceni[4] in 1720 noted a Giolfino altarpiece with SS. Bartholomew and Roch and 'alcuni ritratti,' and which was associated with the Giusti family.[5] The tradition that the present pictures are portraits of that family is therefore not entirely to be rejected, although there seems to be no means of identifying the sitters; indeed, some of the six men and nine women are only caps and napes.

The costumes seem to be in a fairly advanced sixteenth-century style, and may indicate a date of *ca.* 1520. No. 749 is usually accepted as a work by Giolfino,[6] but does not appear to be fully characteristic of him. A nineteenth-century association with Gerolamo dai Libri appears more satisfactory,[7] although an attribution to Gerolamo himself could not be accepted.

PROVENANCE: As stated above, perhaps from Santa Maria in Stelle, near Verona. By 1820 a *Virgin and Child with SS. Lucy and Catherine* had taken the place of the altarpiece called Giolfino there;[8] indeed, it is probable that the two fragments here numbered 749 had by then already entered the collection at Verona of Francesco Caldana, who was buying from *ca.* 1816.[9] Purchased from the heirs of Cav. Andrea Monga, Verona, 1864.[10]

REPRODUCTION: *Illustrations, Italian Schools*, 1937, p. 155. *Plates, Earlier Italian Schools*, 1953, Vol. I, p. 181.

REFERENCES: (1) Eastlake's note-book, 1864. (2) See the catalogue of the Monga Collection in *Madonna Verona*, 1914, VIII, p. 122 (No. 38), where the inscription is recorded. The S. Roch has since then been cut down to a half-length. There appear to be at present considerable gaps between the fields of the pictures. The S. Sebastian has been photographed by Alinari, No. 43657. (3) The Gerolamo dai Libri altarpiece, No. 748 of this Gallery, was framed up with several irrelevant pictures when in the Monga Collection. (4) (Lanceni), the part of his Guide of 1720 dealing with the Province of Verona, entitled *Divertimento Pittorico*, p. 138. (5) Persico, *Descrizione di Verona*, etc., II, 1821, p. 148. Dirce

Viana, *Francesco Torbido*, 1933, pp. 20/1. For the place, see Antonio Pighi, *S. Maria in Stele*, 1903. (6) Jacobsen in the *Repertorium für Kunstwissenschaft*, 1901, p. 351, suggests rather Michele da Verona. J. P. Richter, *Italian Art in the National Gallery*, 1883, p. 74, thinks it is not Giolfino, but more probably one of Morando's imitators. (7) See note 9. (8) Persico, *op. cit.*, II, 1821, p. 148. (9) Persico, *op. cit.*, I, 1820, pp. 130/1, with description that corresponds. The pictures there mentioned are ascribed to Gerolamo dai Libri or, if not, to a better hand. The Monga family, although they had framed up the two fragments as parts of a Giolfino altarpiece, also thought that these parts were by Gerolamo dai Libri (Eastlake's note-book), which is confirmation of the Caldana provenance. It may be mentioned that other Caldana pictures certainly passed into the Monga Collection. No additional information concerning the pictures is to be found in the *Descrizione delle Opere di Pittura di Eccellenti Maestri raccolte dal Sig. Francesco Caldana*, Verona, 1822 (No. 128), where Persico's description is merely quoted. (10) Andrea Monga died in 1861.

GIOTTO
1266 (?)–1337

Born probably at Colle near Vespignano in the Mugello. There is some evidence for a date of birth 1266 (or 1267), or else 1276; the matter is disputed (cf. C. Brandi in *Scritti in Onore di Lionello Venturi*, 1956, I, pp. 81 ff.). He is recorded at Florence from 1311; also active at Padua, Rome, Naples and probably Assisi.

The distinction between his own paintings and those of his studio has been, and is, the subject of lengthy dispute; it cannot here be fully discussed. His key works are admitted to be a cycle of frescoes in the Arena Chapel at Padua; these are ascribed to Giotto by a tradition worthy of all respect, but are not in the strictest sense documented.

Giotto's panel pictures are more doubtful than his frescoes. The one generally admitted, the altarpiece in the Uffizi, is not documented, being first mentioned in 1417 or 1418. A Crucifix in S. Maria Novella at Florence may be held to be documented, but the attribution has been often rejected. Two signed altarpieces in S. Croce, Florence, and in the Gallery at Bologna, are usually rejected. For Giotto's pictures, see Giulia Sinibaldi and Giulia Brunetti, *Pittura Italiana del '200 e '300, Catalogo della Mostra Giottesca di Firenze del 1937*, 1943, pp. 301 ff.

Giotto is often considered the founder of the modern school of painting.

Ascribed to GIOTTO

5360 PENTECOST (PANEL FROM A SERIES)

The twelve Apostles are shown gathered together in an enclosure; tongues of fire are on their heads, and the Holy Ghost descends in the form of a dove. Outside, the multitude of the different nations are marvelling, each man at hearing the Apostles speak his own language.

Wood, painted surface, $18 \times 17\frac{1}{4}$ (0·455 × 0·44); painted up to the edges all round.

In good condition for a picture of its date. The figures are by no means free from repaint, but the worn appearance of the flesh is partly an illusion due to the surface condition.

The subject is from *Acts* ii, 1–13. It is unusual to omit the Virgin Mary from the scene, but Giotto does this in his fresco of the subject at Padua.[1]

No. 5360 is one of a series of unknown extent and unknown provenance.[2] The other existing panels, reasonably presumed to be from the same series, are: *The Crucifixion with S. Francis*, *The Last Supper* and *Christ in Hell*, all three at Munich; *The Epiphany* at New York; *The Presentation in the Temple* in the Gardner Museum at Boston; and *The Entombment* in the Berenson Collection at Settignano.[3] *The Crucifixion* shows two donors. It is possible that these panels once ornamented the cupboard doors of some sacristy, but since the extent of the series is unknown, its original arrangement is also unknown.[4]

The series is usually not ascribed to Giotto's own hand; but some critics, and Philip Hendy in particular, maintain that it is by Giotto himself.[5] The date is usually supposed to be rather later than that of the frescoes at Padua; this does not seem to be provable, but the general appearance of the pictures would not accord very well with an earlier date. The compiler feels that the problems of attribution to Giotto himself are almost hopelessly confused, even for the frescoes; that the status of panel pictures of large size, which might be expected to conform a good deal to the frescoes, is even more dubious; and that it is impossible to obtain any sure evidence of what Giotto's style for small figures may have been. Some weaknesses of execution in the series from which No. 5360 comes seem, nevertheless, difficult to reconcile with any idea of Giotto's mature style; since critics in general incline not to consider the series as early work, it would seem likely that it is not by Giotto himself, but a production of the studio.[6]

PROVENANCE: With three others of the series, in the Prince (Stanislas) Poniatowski of Florence Sale, London, 9 February, 1839; No. 5360 was lot 104, bought by Hall. Bequeathed by William Coningham, a well-known collector, to his son, W. J. C. Coningham, who bequeathed it to his widow. She gave it in 1922 to Major Henry Coningham. Bequeathed to the National Gallery by his widow, Geraldine Emily Coningham, in memory of Mrs. Coningham of Brighton and of her husband, Major Henry Coningham, 1942.[7]

REPRODUCTION: *Plates, Earlier Italian Schools*, 1953, Vol. I, p. 182.

REFERENCES: (1) Venturi, *Storia dell'Arte Italiana*, Vol. V, Fig. 297. (2) Neither seem likely ever to be established. It is perhaps worth mentioning a passage in Vasari, ed. Milanesi, Vol. I, pp. 395/6, where a picture by Giotto with small figures is stated to have been brought from Sansepolcro to Arezzo by Piero Saccone, and to have been broken up; some pieces were retrieved by Baccio Gondi and taken to Florence. The subject or subjects of this work are not indicated by Vasari. *The Last Supper* at Munich was acquired in 1805, the other two pictures at Munich in 1813. The four other existing pictures of the series are first recorded in the Prince (Stanislas) Poniatowski of Florence Sale, London, 9 February, 1839, lots 101–104. Lot 101, bought by Hall, called *The Nativity*, is the New York panel. Lot 102, *The Presentation*, is the Boston panel; it was bought at the sale by Simes, and bought later in the century from the Simes

Collection by Henry Willett (P. Hendy, *Gardner Museum Catalogue*, 1931, p. 171). Lot 103, *The Entombment*, bought by Hall, is the Berenson panel; lot 104, *Pentecost*, is N.G. No. 5360. (3) Five of these are reproduced, with elaborate catalogue entries, by Giulia Sinibaldi and Giulia Brunetti, *Pittura Italiana del '200 e '300, Catalogo della Mostra Giottesca di Firenze del 1937*, 1943, pp. 337 ff. The sixth, *The Presentation in the Temple*, is reproduced and discussed at length by P. Hendy, *Gardner Museum Catalogue*, 1931. (4) A point in Hendy's catalogue, p. 171, needs correction; he says 'an inscription on the back of *The Entombment* states that till recently it was joined to *The Epiphany*.' The inscription, kindly communicated by Miss Nicky Mariano, reads: 'A picture divided in two parts; first part representing the *Birth* of our Saviour, and the second part showing his *Entombment*: Early Italian School. From the Collection of the late General C. R. Fox.' The two pictures were merely framed together; this is made quite clear by the entry in the General Fox Sale, 4 July, 1874, lot 37, 'Early Italian, The Nativity and the Entombment—in one frame,' bought by Daniell. The two pictures had *not* been framed together at the time of the Poniatowski Sale, 1839. (5) Philip Hendy in the Gardner catalogue, already cited, and in *The Burlington Magazine*, Vol. LIII (1928), pp. 17 ff. R. Longhi in *Proporzioni*, II, 1948, p. 51, also accepts this series as by Giotto himself. (6) For a bibliography of the critics, see Sinibaldi and Brunetti, *op. cit*. (7) Information concerning the Coningham provenance in the Gallery archives.

GIOVANNI d'Alemagna
active 1441 (?), died 1449/50
See under Antonio VIVARINI

GIOVANNI Battista of Faenza,
known as Bertucci
active 1495 (?), died 1516

Known as *Giovanni Battista Bertucci the Elder* (he had a grandson of the same names); other recorded names are *Utili, Braceschi, Dei Pittori*. Active at Faenza. Doubtfully recorded in 1495, surely from 1498. He is recorded to have collaborated sometimes with his brother Girolamo, whose works have not been identified. A Triptych, signed by Giovanni Battista and dated 1506, is at Faenza, and is the basis for attributions. A *Virgin and Child with the little S. John*, stated to be signed I.B.P, was in the D. C. E. Erskine Sale, 5 December, 1922 (lot 17), reproduced in the catalogue. No. 282 below may be documented, as is explained in the entry for it. His style appears to have been influenced by Costa and Perugino.

Giovanni Battista has been confused under his name of Utili with a painter now identified as Biagio di Antonio of Florence, who is recorded intermittently at Faenza between 1476 and 1504. (No works have survived that have so far been positively proved to be Biagio's: but something near proof is achieved by Ennio Golfieri and Antonio Corbara in the *Atti e Memorie dell'Accademia . . . La Colombaria*, 1947, pp. 435 ff.; summary in *Emporium*, January, 1948, pp. 30/1.)

Literature: Carlo Grigioni, *La Pittura Faentina*, 1935, pp. 194 ff., 276 ff.

282 THE VIRGIN AND CHILD IN GLORY (CENTRAL PANEL FROM AN ALTARPIECE)

The Virgin, supporting the Child, is seated upon clouds. She has a lily in her left hand.

Wood, painted surface, rounded top, $70\frac{1}{2} \times 32$ (1.79×0.815); painted up to the edges at the sides. The paint at the rounded top has probably been extended a little beyond the original, especially at the sides; the exact original measurements are not clear.

Good condition.

A picture formerly in Lord Aldenham's Collection[1] is fairly obviously from the same altarpiece as No. 282. It shows a saint at full length, turned towards the spectator's left; it is a youthful saint, in a dress suitable for an apostle, holding a book, a lily and a pen, and receiving inspiration from a cloud. He is reasonably supposed to be S. John the Evangelist.

Another picture, obviously the pendant to the Aldenham picture, appeared (as Pacchia) at Christie's, 9 July, 1948 (lot 99). It represents a Dominican Saint, turned towards the spectator's right, holding a lily, a book and a church, with a brooch with rays on his breast, and receiving inspiration from a cloud; clearly S. Thomas Aquinas.[2]

In these two pictures, the design of the parapet corresponds exactly with that on No. 282; the marble flooring also corresponds very closely, although the pattern seems to be of diamonds, not of circles within diamonds as in No. 282. It would seem very unreasonable to doubt that the three pictures come from the same ensemble.

No. 282 is stated to come from the Hercolani Collection at Bologna, and it would be difficult to doubt that this is true.[3] It would appear to have been the central part of an altarpiece in five compartments, in the Hercolani Collection by 1770, and ascribed there to Girolamo Marchesi da Cotignola.[4] The four other pieces were described in that collection as side pictures representing S. Dominic and S. John,[5] and two smaller pictures with half-figures of S. Jerome and S. Stephen.[6] These pictures are stated to have come from an altar somewhere in Romagna.[7]

No. 282, probably the picture called Girolamo Marchesi in the Hercolani Collection, was acquired by the National Gallery as by Lo Spagna; the attribution to Giovanni Battista (Bertucci) is due to Crowe and Cavalcaselle,[8] is generally accepted and seems very reasonable.

It is indeed possible that No. 282 is a documented work by this painter. The provenance, probably given as from somewhere in Romagna when in the Hercolani Collection, and more recently claimed to be probably from S. Maria degli Angeli at Faenza,[9] cannot be stated for sure; but the following evidence suggests that No. 282 may in fact come from S. Andrea at Faenza.

On 21 April, 1512,[10] Giovanni Battista contracted with sister Clarice

Manfredi of the Third Order of S. Dominic to paint the chapel of S. Thomas Aquinas, and an altarpiece for that chapel, in S. Andrea at Faenza. The altarpiece was to represent in the centre the Virgin holding the Child and at least two angels. A separate picture on the right of the Virgin was to show S. Thomas Aquinas and another unspecified figure; a picture on the left was to show S. John the Evangelist and another unspecified figure. Upper compartments above the side pictures were to contain (1) S. Jerome and (2) S. Stephen. A central upper compartment was to show Christ carrying the Cross. A predella was to show scenes of the lives of the various saints, and the Manfredi arms. On 19 March, 1516, the parties agreed that the complete work had been done and the complete payment for it made.

If the terms of this contract are compared with the description of the altarpiece in the Hercolani Collection (already suggested to have included No. 282, the Aldenham picture, and its pendant), one considerable difference may be noted. The side panels in the Hercolani Collection were claimed to be S. Dominic and S. John, not S. Thomas Aquinas with another saint, S. John the Evangelist with another saint.[11] The Hercolani assemblage further is not known to have had a picture of Christ carrying the Cross, or a predella. Nevertheless, the resemblances between the contract and the Hercolani pictures, and hence with No. 282 and the Aldenham picture and its pendant, are fairly close; and one may say that possibly No. 282 is the central part of the altarpiece, ordered in 1512, delivered in 1516, for the chapel of S. Thomas Aquinas in S. Andrea at Faenza.

The church shown in the background of No. 282 has been identified, apparently on very weak grounds, as perhaps S. Maria foris portam or S. Maria degli Angeli at Faenza.[12]

The design of the Virgin and Child on No. 282 has been stated to be not unlike a Pintoricchio of 1508 in S. Andrea at Spello;[13] but it is more likely to be derived from Perugino than from Pintoricchio.[14]

PROVENANCE: Possibly, as explained above, part of the altarpiece of the chapel of S. Thomas Aquinas in S. Andrea at Faenza. Apparently recorded with four other pieces in the Hercolani Collection at Bologna;[15] in any case, there is authority for saying that it came from the Hercolani Collection,[16] and it seems to have been there at least from 1770 until 1828.[17] First surely recorded in Lord Orford's Collection at Wolterton by Waagen;[18] purchased at the (Orford) sale, 28 June, 1856 (lot 267).[19]

REPRODUCTION: *Illustrations, Italian Schools*, 1937, p. 39. *Plates, Earlier Italian Schools*, 1953, Vol. I, p. 183.

REFERENCES: (1) Size, 51 × 21 in.; photograph in the Gallery archives. Lord Aldenham Sale, 24 February, 1937 (lot 123), as Lo Spagna, with the statement that it had been bought in 1846 from Count Cini at Rome. Exhibited at the R.A., 1886 (No. 200), as Roman School, and at the Burlington Fine Arts Club, 1906 (No. 16), as Giovanni Bertucci. What seems unquestionably the same picture was lent by Jacob M. Heimann to the Leonardo da Vinci Exhibition at Dallas, Texas, 1949 (No. 124), reproduced, as by Raphael; provenance given as Hercolani, Bologna and the Vatican, Rome; certificates (presumably as Raphael) from various authorities, including the Brera and the Vatican. (2) Called S. Dominic in the Sale Catalogue; size, 51 × 24 in.; photograph in the Gallery archives. While it may be admitted that the iconography of S. Dominic and of S. Thomas is sometimes a little confusing (cf. for instance the Lanino of the Cook Collection, No. 116, reproduced in the large Cook Catalogue), there can be no doubt that the saint in the 1948 Sale is S. Thomas; he has not S. Dominic's star, but a brooch with rays on his breast, which stands for S. Thomas's sun. This picture was in Mr. Earle's Collection at Leamington in 1856, as S. Dominic by Lorenzo da Costa (Scharf sketchbook, No. 43, p. 122, and General Notes, No. I, p. 39, in the National Portrait Gallery; photograph of the page of the sketchbook in the National Gallery archives). (3) At the Orford Sale of 1856, where the picture was bought, the catalogue gives no provenance; Waagen, *Treasures*, III, 1854, p. 434, records the picture in Lord Orford's Collection without provenance. But in the National Gallery MS. Catalogue, and thereafter in the printed catalogues, the provenance from the Hercolani Collection is stated; it is probable that Eastlake had reliable information on the point. (4) See the letter of 5 July, 1770, from Luigi Crespi to Innocenzo Ansaldi, printed in Bottari and Ticozzi, *Raccolta di Lettere*, VII, 1822, pp. 103/4. The central part is described as the Virgin and Child in a 'gloria d'angioli, e sotto alcuni altri che suonano diversi stromenti con bel paese in lontananza.' What is undoubtedly the same picture is described by Oretti (Bologna, Biblioteca dell'Archiginnasio, MS. B 384) as panel, 'La Madonna col Bambino Gesù con alcuni Puttini sotto, che suonano, fra i quali vi è un piccolo Paese con sopra Gloria d'Angeli.' Unlike No. 1051 below, No. 282 is not recorded in Oretti's MS. B 104, nor in Petronio Bassani's *Guida di Bologna*, 1816. See further in note 6. (5) It has already been noted that the Aldenham picture probably represents S. John the Evangelist, and that a Hercolani provenance has been claimed for it, and that its pendant has been called S. Dominic. (6) Bottari and Ticozzi, *loc. cit.* Crespi actually says that the five pieces were framed separately in the Hercolani Collection, and that the two half figures had originally been below the others; but it is fairly obvious that they had been above S. Dominic and S. John. On pp. 101/2, Crespi describes (with some mistakes) Costa, No. 629 of the National Gallery (reproduced in the *Illustrations, Italian Schools*, 1937, p. 109), and says that the half figures of that picture had been below, which appears to be impossible. In an effort to secure more exact knowledge concerning these pictures in the Hercolani Collection, the compiler obtained leave from the Avv. Ambrosini of Bologna to consult his Hercolani inventories. In the *Quadreria Ercolani dall'Inventario Legale del Notaio Angelo Felicori*, dated 22 April, 1828, the following entries occur: f. 2r., *S. Domenico del Pinturicchio, S. Giò: del Pinturichio*; f. 2v., *S. Girolamo del Cotignola, S. Lorenzo del Cotignola*; f. 6r., *B.V. col figlio, ed angeli del Cotignola*. In another inventory, *Nota dei Quadri esistenti nella Galleria Hercolani*, no entry possible for No. 282 could be found, but the following might refer to the side panels: f. 1v., *S. Girolamo, in tavola, attribuito a Muziano, ma più antico*; f. 1v., *Mezza figura di un S.º Diacono in tavola*; f. 3v., *Due laterali in tavola, nell'uno S. Giò: Envangelista nell'altro S Tommaso d'Acquino dello stesso Cottignola* (the word 'stesso' presumably refers back—a long way—to an altarpiece in no way connected with No. 282, etc., and ascribed to Ercole da Cottignola). This second inventory is not dated, but 183(illegible) has been added at the top, and 1830 on the cover, in later writing. It is also added at the end, in later writing, that the Hercolani Collection began to be dispersed from 1834 onwards. The compiler does not claim that these inventories throw much light on the problem, but they seem to make it probable that the altarpiece of five compartments, noted in the Hercolani Collection by Crespi in 1770, was, at least in part, still there in the early 1830's. (7) Bottari and Ticozzi, *loc. cit.* The words actually used are 'uno sportello d'un altare in Romagna'; Crespi also calls Costa No. 629 of the National Gallery a 'sportello' (cf. the previous note). (8) Crowe and Cavalcaselle, *History of Painting in Italy*, Vol III, 1866, pp. 354/5. (9) This statement appears first to have been made in the anonymous article on Bertucci in Thieme-Becker, III, p. 518. (10) Carlo Grigioni, *La Pittura Faentina*, 1935, pp. 315/7. (11) The absence of the second saints on the two side panels could be explained only by a modification of the contract. The identification of one figure in the Hercolani assemblage as S. Dominic instead of S. Thomas Aquinas can be explained on examination of the picture that indeed was called S. Dominic in the sale room, but certainly represents S. Thomas. In No. 282, the Virgin holds a lily; in the Aldenham picture, S. John (?) holds a lily; the Dominican on the pendant holds a lily; and indeed the probable Dominican origin of the pictures would justify these lilies. If the saint in the Hercolani Collection showed a Dominican with a lily, he would as likely as not have been identified as S. Dominic, even if another emblem suitable for S. Thomas Aquinas had been attached to him. In any case, this saint may have been called S. Thomas Aquinas in an inventory of 1830 (?) (see note 6). For S. Thomas with a lily, cf. what is reasonably thought to have been the high altarpiece of this very church of S. Andrea at Faenza, reproduced in the *Atti e Memorie dell' Accademia . . . La Colombaria*, 1947, p. 454. (12) R. Buscaroli, *La Pittura Romagnola del '400*, 1931, p. 288; Carlo Grigioni, *La Pittura Faentina*, 1935, p. 296. (13) Crowe and Cavalcaselle, *History of Painting in Italy*, III, 1866, pp. 354/5. The observation is exact; the picture is reproduced by Van Marle, *Development of the Italian Schools of Painting*, Vol. XIV, Fig. 183. (14) Cf. for instance (inverted) the altarpieces at Fano and Senigallia, Klassiker der Kunst *Perugino*, 1914, Plates 67 and 74. (15) See note 4. (16) See note 3. (17) See notes 4 and 6. (18) Waagen, *Treasures*, III, 1854, p. 434, as Lo Spagna. (19) As Lo Spagna, an attribution retained by the National Gallery until 1888. Then catalogued until 1898 as Umbrian School.

1051 THE INCREDULITY OF S. THOMAS

Left and centre, S. Thomas assures himself of the reality of Christ's Wounds; right, S. Anthony of Padua introduces a donor. Left background, S. Jerome (?) near a Crucifix, outside a cave.

Wood, painted surface, $40\frac{3}{4} \times 65\frac{1}{2}$ ($1 \cdot 035 \times 1 \cdot 66$); painted up to the edges all round.

Somewhat damaged from flaking and cracking.

The attribution to Giovanni Battista seems to have been made first in the National Gallery,[1] and is now generally accepted.

PROVENANCE: From the sacristy of the church of the PP. Minori Conventuali at Faenza.[2] In the Hercolani Collection at Bologna before 1777.[3] Recorded there in 1816 and *ca.* 1830.[4] E. Solly Sale, London, 8 May, 1847 (lot 21), bought by Domville; (Sir W. Domville) Sale, 25 May, 1850 (lot 31), bought by Smith.[5] Bought in 1850 from Smith by Lord Northwick;[6] in his Collection at Thirlestaine House, Cheltenham, where seen by Waagen.[7] Exhibited at Manchester, 1857 (Provisional Catalogue, No. 145; Definitive Catalogue, No. 211).[8] *Hours in Lord Northwick's Picture Galleries*, 1858 (No. 272); Northwick Sale, 3 August, 1859 (lot 568), bought by Colnaghi for Miss Solly.[9] Bequeathed by Miss Sarah Solly, 1879.[10]

REPRODUCTION: *Illustrations, Italian Schools*, 1937, p. 39. *Plates, Earlier Italian Schools*, 1953, Vol. I, p. 184.

REFERENCES: (1) In the 1898 Catalogue it was suggested that No. 1051 is by the same hand as No. 282 above. (2) This is stated by Oretti and (less assuredly) by Calvi; see the next note. Carlo Grigioni, *La Pittura Faentina*, 1935, p. 297, says that No. 1051 is probably from the high altar of S. Tomaso at Faenza. (3) See Oretti, MS. at the Biblioteca dell' Archiginnasio at Bologna, B 384. The reference occurs in a piece written for the marriage of Filippo Hercolani and Corona Cavriani, which had taken place by 1777; see P. Giuseppe Antonio Predieri, *Nel Primo Ingresso al Gonfalonierato di Giustizia del Marchese Filippo Hercolani*. Oretti in another MS. in the same Library (B 104, Part I) records

No. 1051 twice. On p. 61, Palazzo Hercolani in Strada maggiore dalla Chiesa di S.ª Catterina di Strada maggiore (a collection 'assai pregiata è raguardevole, è massime di Tauole d'altare raccolte dal Marchese Marco Antonio Ercolani'), he notes that No. 1051 had been *nella Sag.ª de Sud.ᵢ Frati*, i.e. of S. Francesco at Faenza; on p. 135 in 'Casa Ercolani Senatoria dalli Servi,' he notes No. 1051 as being on canvas (*sic*) and by Perugino. These references appear to apply to a single Hercolani Palace, in the street recently (but not still) named after Mazzini. No. 1051 is also recorded (with a long description) by J. A. Calvi, *Versi e Prose sopra una Serie di Eccellenti Pitture* in the Hercolani Collection, 1780, p. 20, as Perugino. (4) Petronio Bassani, *Guida agli amatori delle Belle Arti . . . per la città di Bologna*, I, i, 1816, p. 210, as Perugino. In an inventory kindly communicated by the Avv. Ambrosini of Bologna, *Nota dei Quadri esistenti nella Galleria Hercolani*, No. 1051 is recorded on f. 4*v.*, *Cristo, con S. Gio.ᵍ e S. Francesco, in tavola, del Perugino*. The inventory is not dated, but 183(illegible) has been added at the top and 1830 on the cover, in later writing. At the end, also in later writing, it is stated that the Hercolani Collection was being dispersed from 1834 onwards. (5) In both cases as Perugino. (6) Smith's Day Book, 1848–67, in the Victoria and Albert Museum, p. 120 (17 July, 1850); confirmatory note by Lord Northwick in the copy of the sale catalogue at Northwick Park (in 1948). (7) Waagen, *Treasures*, III, 1854, p. 201, as Girolamo Mocetto. (8) Exhibited as Raphael; Crowe and Cavalcaselle, *History of Painting in Italy*, II, 1864, p. 578, note this while making their own attribution of it to Palmezzano. (9) In both cases as Perugino. (10) Catalogued at the National Gallery from 1880 until 1898 as Umbrian School.

GIOVANNI Francesco da Rimini
active 1441, died 1470 or earlier

A picture signed and dated 1459 is in S. Domenico at Bologna; No. 2118 below is signed and dated 1461. There is no need to doubt that the painter of these pictures is identical with a painter of the same name, recorded at Padua, 1441/4. In any case, he is recorded several times at Bologna during the last ten years or so of his life.

Literature: Mostra di Melozzo, Forlì, Catalogue, 1938, pp. 66 ff.

2118   THE VIRGIN AND CHILD WITH TWO ANGELS

Signed: .IOVANES . FRANCISCVS . DE . RIMINO . FECIT . MCCCCLXI.

Wood, painted surface, 25½ × 18½ (0·645 × 0·475); painted up to the edges except at the top, and perhaps cut to a slight extent at the sides.

Considerably damaged. The signature is damaged and restored, but the reading is sure.

PROVENANCE: Doubtless the picture in the Hercolani Collection at Bologna by 1777,[1] and recorded as still there in 1816 and 1837.[2] In 1902, No. 2118 belonged to Cav. Achille Cantoni at Milan.[3] Lawrie and Co. Sale, London, 28 January, 1905 (lot 61), bought by Sulley; passed to George Salting soon after.[4] Lent to the Gallery by Salting in 1905, and presented by him in 1907.

REPRODUCTION: *Illustrations, Italian Schools*, 1937, p. 307. *Plates, Earlier Italian Schools*, 1953, Vol. I, p. 185.

REFERENCES: (1) See the Oretti MSS. in the Biblioteca dell'Archiginnasio at Bologna, B 384, Description of the Hercolani Collection for the marriage of

Filippo Hercolani and Corona Cavriani, f. 6*v.*, Small Virgin and Child with angels' heads, signed *Jovanes de Rimino fecit* MCCCCLXI. This marriage had taken place by 1777; see verses by P. Giuseppe Antonio Predieri, *Nel Primo Ingresso al Gonfalonierato di Giustizia del Marchese Filippo Hercolani.* The picture is referred to also in another passage of the Oretti MSS., noted by Corrado Ricci in the *Rassegna d'Arte*, II, 1902, pp. 134/5. It is no doubt the undescribed Gioanni da Rimino mentioned in the Hercolani Collection in *Pitture Scolture ed Architetture . . . di Bologna*, publ. Longhi, 1782, p. 286. (2) Petronio Bassani, *Guida agli amatori delle Belle Arti . . . per la città di Bologna*, I, i, 1816, p. 210, *Q. con la Maddona ed il Bambino m.f. di Gio. da Rimini.* (Gaetano Giordani), *Collezioni di Codici Manoscritte e di Quadri vendibili in Bologna* (Hercolani), 1837, 2nd part (pictures), p. 12: *Rimini* (da) *Francesco, B. Vergine, e due Angeli; mezze figure in tavola.* The picture is also listed in an inventory, kindly communicated by the Avv. Ambrosini of Bologna, *Nota dei Quadri esistenti nella Galleria Hercolani*, f. 3*v.*, *Tavolina antica, con la B.V. il Bamb? e due teste di Serafino, di Giovanni da Rimini del 1461 ben conservata.* This inventory is not dated, but has the date 183(illegible) added at the top and 1830 added on the cover, in later writing. See also the mention in E. Förster's *Handbuch für Reisende in Italien*, 2nd edition, 1842, p. 165, or 4th edition, 1848, p. 177; but it cannot be deduced from this with certainty that the picture was still in the Hercolani Collection. (3) Corrado Ricci in the *Rassegna d'Arte*, II, 1902, p. 135. (4) Cf. *L'Arte*, 1905, pp. 212 f.

GIOVANNI Martini da Udine

ca. 1453–1535

His name was really *Mioni*, and he was the son of Martino da Tolmezzo. There are several authenticated paintings, also retables in carved wood; he was influenced by Alvise Vivarini and other Venetians. See Bruno Molajoli's Catalogue of the Pordenone Exhibition, 1939, pp. 34 ff., where also there are several reproductions.

Ascribed to GIOVANNI Martini da Udine

778 ALTARPIECE: THE VIRGIN AND CHILD WITH S. GEORGE, S. JAMES THE GREATER AND A DONOR

Wood, painted surface, $97\frac{1}{2} \times 57$ ($2 \cdot 48 \times 1 \cdot 45$); painted up to the edges all round. It is framed to show a flat-arched top, but in fact only comparatively small pieces are missing from the two corners, and the original form was probably the usual square top.

The paint is fairly pure, but suffers much from the cracking of the panel.

It was acquired as by Martino da Udine (Pellegrino da San Daniele), to whom it is still ascribed by some critics;[1] but it is more likely to be by Giovanni Martini.[2] The style reflects to some extent that of Carpaccio, and a date in the early years of the sixteenth century is probable.

PROVENANCE: Once owned by Conte Ugo Valentinis at San Daniele;[3] purchased from V. Azzola, Venice, 1867.

REPRODUCTION: *Illustrations, Italian Schools*, 1937, p. 219. *Plates, Earlier Italian Schools*, 1953, Vol. I, p. 186.

REFERENCES: (1) E.g. by Borenius in Thieme-Becker, s.v. Pellegrino da San Daniele. (2) First ascribed to him by Frizzoni in the *Archivio Storico Italiano*, 1879, p. 417; cf. his *Arte Italiana del Rinascimento*, 1891, p. 327. This attribution was doubtfully accepted by Jacobsen in the *Repertorium für Kunstwissenschaft*, 1901, p. 357; positively by Bruno Molajoli in the Catalogue of the Pordenone Exhibition, 1939, p. 34 and by Pallucchini in *Arte Veneta*, 1951, p. 196. (3) Provenance stated in the Director's Report of Proceedings on the Continent, 17 February, 1868.

GIOVANNI DA MILANO
active *ca.* 1346–1369 (?)

Apparently from Caversaccio near Uggiate (region of Como); known from his signed pictures, etc., as Giovanni da Milano. First recorded at Florence in 1346 (Exhibition Catalogue, *Arte Lombarda*, Milan, 1958, p. 19). He joined the Physicians' Guild at Florence in 1363, and became a Florentine citizen in 1366. He seems to be identical with the Iohannes de Mediolano, working in the Vatican in 1369. There is a signed altarpiece of his at Prato; a *Pietà* in the Academy at Florence is signed and dated 1365. It was also in 1365 that he was working on his documented frescoes in the Rinuccini Chapel in S. Croce, Florence.

579A THREE PINNACLES FROM AN ALTARPIECE: THE ALMIGHTY, THE VIRGIN, AND ISAIAH

The Almighty holds two golden keys and a globe with seven stars. Isaiah holds a scroll inscribed: ECCE VIRGO CŌCIPIET (*Isaiah* vii, 14). Above each of the three figures is a seraph in a quatrefoil.

Wood. Compartment with *The Almighty*, pointed top, painted surface, $25\frac{1}{4} \times 10$ (0·64 × 0·255); the other two, pointed tops, painted surfaces, each, $22\frac{3}{4} \times 10$ (0·575 × 0·255); the three quatrefoils with seraphs, each, painted surface, diameter *ca.* $2\frac{1}{2}$ (0·065). Including the frames, the central panel is $37 \times 14\frac{3}{4}$ (0·94 × 0·375); the others $35\frac{1}{4} \times 14\frac{3}{4}$ (0·895 × 0·375). The frames are new at the sides and bottoms; but the decorative work at the tops round the seraphs may be old, and even parts of the outer mouldings at the tops.

Cleaning completed in 1956. The figures are in very fair state, Isaiah being the least well preserved. The gold backgrounds with their patterning now correspond with the original intention, but are considerably restored. Two horizontal lines, now mostly painted out, cross the mouth of the Almighty; there is no certainty that these are more than an indication of intention, not carried as far as the painting stage. By some mistake, the stamping of the pattern of the haloes continues across the neck and beards of Isaiah and the Almighty.

The three pictures seem obviously to have been pinnacles of an altarpiece. They go well together as three, but it cannot be excluded that they are the remains of a series of five or even more.

The iconography deserves some comment. The Almighty was clearly intended as the Apocalyptic Figure with a two-edged sword across His mouth; indeed, it seems clear that the intention was not changed, since the Figure as it is corresponds with most of the description in Revelation i, 13 sqq. It would seem that the representation of this Figure as the centre pinnacle of an altarpiece did not continue for long in Italian painting.[1] The subject of the two outer panels may be thought suggestive of the Annunciation, which was sometimes included in the pinnacles of an altarpiece, and with which Isaiah is sometimes prominently associated.[2] But the compiler is reluctant to believe that the Annunciation would have been represented without S. Gabriel,[3] so this subject would seem to be excluded for No. 579A unless some panels of similar size are missing; and while the figure on the left does seem clearly to be the Virgin, it may further be noted that in several *Annunciations* by Giovanni da Milano the pose of the Virgin is different. The intention would perhaps have been clear when the altarpiece was intact.[4]

No. 579A was ascribed to Giovanni da Milano by Crowe and Cavalcaselle,[5] and the attribution is generally accepted.[6]

PROVENANCE: Perhaps from the Camaldolese Abbey of S. Giovanni Decollato del Sasso near Arezzo.[7] In the Lombardi-Baldi Collection at Florence, 1845 (No. 11);[8] purchased with other pictures from Lombardi and Baldi, 1857.[9]

REPRODUCTION: *Illustrations, Italian Schools*, 1937, p. 157. *Plates, Earlier Italian Schools*, 1953, Vol. I, p. 187.

REFERENCES: (1) The compiler can cite examples associated with Giotto, in the altarpiece at Bologna and in the Stefaneschi Triptych, now in the Vatican Gallery (Klassiker der Kunst *Giotto*, reproductions on pp. 206 and 191). (2) E.g. the Annunciation with Isaiah and Jeremiah assigned to Raffaellino del Garbo, in S. Francesco at Fiesole; reproduced by O. H. Giglioli, *Fiesole* (Catalogo delle Cose d'Arte e di Antichità d'Italia), 1933, p. 173. (3) There is indeed a XV Century relief, suspiciously suggestive of the Annunciation without S. Gabriel, in the Castello Sforzesco at Milan; S. Vigezzi, *La Scultura in Milano*, 1934, Vol. I, p. 147, No. 448 and Vol. II, Plate XXIII. (4) On the two pictures recorded in note 1, the Bologna polyptych has no figures in the pinnacles at the sides; the Stefaneschi Triptych, on the face with the Apocalyptic Figure, has apparently Abraham and Isaac on one pinnacle, and a figure perhaps of the Old Testament on the other, and shows further figures in the spandrels and pilasters. (5) Crowe and Cavalcaselle, *History of Painting in Italy*, Vol. I, 1864, pp. 367 and 409. (6) E.g. by Toesca, *Il Trecento*, 1951, p. 763. (7) See the entry for No. 579, ascribed to Niccolò di Pietro Gerini. In the Lombardi-Baldi Collection, the pictures forming No. 579A were believed to be the pinnacles of No. 579; it is not credible that they were commissioned with No. 579 to form an altarpiece, but it may well be that Nos. 579 and 579A came to Lombardi and Baldi from the same church. No. 579, as is noted in the entry for it, may indeed come from the Abbey near Arezzo, but is highly likely to have been originally in the Angeli at Florence. No. 579A was first given a separate number in the 1888 Catalogue. (8) The catalogue is not dated, but the copy in the Uffizi Library is claimed to be of 1845. The attribution of No. 579A (and of No. 579, to which No. 579A was attached) was to Tadéus Gaddi. No. 579A was long catalogued at the National Gallery as of the School of Taddeo Gaddi; first as Giovanni da Milano in the 1912 Catalogue. (9) For details concerning the Lombardi-Baldi Collection, see Appendix I.

Style of GIOVANNI DA MILANO

1108 CHRIST AND THE VIRGIN WITH SAINTS

Above, Christ and the Virgin. Below, six saints, from left to right: S. John the Baptist, a Bishop with a book, S. Lawrence, S. Catherine of Alexandria, S. Clare (?) and S. Lucy.

Wood, painted surface, $15\frac{3}{4} \times 11$ (0·40 × 0·28). Including the framing, which is pretty clearly original, the size is $18 \times 13\frac{1}{2}$ (0·45 × 0·34).

Rather worn, but on the whole not badly preserved.

Previously catalogued as Sienese. P. Pouncey suggested a connection with Giovanni da Milano, with which Berenson (oral, 1936) agreed.[1] Pouncey classed it as from the studio of Giovanni da Milano, but this seems rather too precise for No. 1108, especially as the quality is low.

PROVENANCE: Purchased from Alessandro Castellani, Rome, 1881.

REPRODUCTION: *Illustrations, Italian Schools*, 1937, p. 330. *Plates, Earlier Italian Schools*, 1953, Vol. I, p. 188.

REFERENCE: (1) Notes by P. Pouncey in the Gallery archives.

GIOVANNI DA ORIOLO
active 1439, died 1480/8

Giovanni di Giuliano, from Oriolo close to Faenza; also named *Recordati, Savoretti* (?), *Marcio*. From 1439, active at Faenza; employed *ca.* 1447 by Lionello d'Este, Marquis of Ferrara. His only identified picture is No. 770 below.

Giovanni di Andrea (Calegari) da Riolo was a different painter.

Literature: Carlo Grigioni, *La Pittura Faentina*, 1935, pp. 53 ff.; Catalogue of the Melozzo Exhibition at Forlì, 1938, pp. 64/5 and Plate 37.

770 LIONELLO D'ESTE

Inscribed, LEONELLVS.MARCHIO.ESTĒSIS. Signed, OPVS IOHĀNIs ORIOLI.

Wood, painted surface, $21\frac{1}{2} \times 15\frac{1}{2}$ (0·545 × 0·395).

Good condition on the whole, but with some retouches on important parts, e.g. the eye, nostril and lips.

It is possible that this picture is of *ca.* 1447, and was the subject of a payment of 21 June, 1447.[1] Lionello d'Este was born in 1407 and died in 1450.

PROVENANCE: Purchased by Sir Charles Eastlake during the period of his Directorship (1855–1865).[2] Purchased from Lady Eastlake, at the price Sir Charles Eastlake had paid for it, 1867.

REPRODUCTION: *Illustrations, Italian Schools*, 1937, p. 261. *Plates, Earlier Italian Schools*, 1953, Vol. I, p. 189.

REFERENCES: (1) The text of the document is given by Gaetano Ballardini, *Giovanni da Oriolo*, 1911, p. 22, and by Carlo Grigioni, *La Pittura Faentina*, 1935, p. 63. Ballardini makes some comments on the document, which does seem to record payment for a portrait of someone, who may well be Lionello himself. (2) Ever since No. 770 entered the Gallery, it has been claimed to come from the Costabili Collection at Ferrara. But there appears to have been only one portrait of Lionello d'Este in that collection, Catalogue, Part IV, 1841 (No. 406), and that is certainly the Pisanello now at Bergamo.

GIOVANNI DI PAOLO
active 1420, died 1482

Sienese School. Also known as Giovanni dal Poggio, from the district of Siena where he lived. Sometimes assumed to be identical with a Giovanni di Paolo born in 1403; but he was already painting in 1420, and was therefore probably born several years before 1403. His first extant signed and dated work is of 1426; thereafter a considerable number of authenticated panels by him exist. He may have painted little in the last years of his long life. There have been several recent essays on him; one is by Pèleo Bacci, *Documenti e Commenti per la Storia dell'Arte*, 1944, pp. 65 ff.

3402   SS. FABIAN AND SEBASTIAN

At each of the bottom corners of the picture, a small figure of a Brother of the Misericordia kneels, in black with a white veil over his face, holding what may be a collecting spoon.

Wood: size of the picture, $33\frac{1}{4} \times 21\frac{1}{2}$ (0·845 × 0·545); size including the frame, $35\frac{1}{2} \times 24$ (0·905 × 0·605).

Good condition on the whole, in spite of a number of repairs. *Pentimenti* in several outlines. The frame appears to be the original one, except at the bottom, where it is new.

Apparently a votive picture, complete. Brethren of the Misericordia are still to be seen at Siena, attending funerals, etc. It need not be doubted that the sainted Pope is S. Fabian, whose feast falls on the same day as S. Sebastian's;[1] they are not infrequently represented together in pictures, especially in the early Spanish School.[2]

This picture was published as a Giovanni di Paolo by Borenius,[3] and Pope-Hennessy[4] accepts it as a late, autograph work. Van Marle[5] ascribed it to Giacomo del Pisano, a name that would be hard to justify; Hutton[6] doubted if it was by Giovanni di Paolo, and suggested some Pisan follower. Although the picture is inferior to the works of Giovanni di Paolo's best time, it seems reasonable to accept Pope-Hennessy's view.

PROVENANCE: Charles Butler Sale, 26 May, 1911 (lot 138),[7] bought by the Carfax Gallery, presumably for Robert Ross, a former director. Lent by Robert Ross to the Burlington Fine Arts Club, 1915/6 (No. 2). Presented through the National Art-Collections Fund, in memory of Robert Ross, 1919. Exhibited at the National Gallery, N.A.C.F. Exhibition, 1945/6 (No. 22).

REPRODUCTION: *Illustrations, Italian Schools*, 1937, p. 158. *Plates, Earlier Italian Schools*, 1953, Vol. I, p. 190.

REFERENCES: (1) At San Gimignano, the two saints were associated against the Plague; Pecori, *Storia di San Gimignano*, 1853, pp. 166 and 223. Relics of both saints are recorded in a 1482 inventory of the Cathedral at Siena; Borghesi and Banchi, *Nuovi Documenti*, 1898, p. 266. (2) Cf., for instance, Post, *History of Spanish Painting*, Vol. IV, Part I, p. 215. (3) Borenius in *The Burlington Magazine*, Vol. XXVIII (1915), p. 3. (4) John Pope-Hennessy, *Giovanni di Paolo*, 1937, pp. 126 and 143. (5) Van Marle, *Development of the Italian Schools of Painting*, Vol. IX, p. 458. (6) E. Hutton, *The Sienese School in the National Gallery*, 1925, p. 58. (7) As *SS. Gregory and Sebastian,* with identifying description, as by Giovanni del Poggio (Giovanni di Paolo lived in the contrada del Poggio Malavolti in Siena).

5451   THE BAPTISM OF CHRIST (PREDELLA PANEL FROM AN ALTARPIECE)

S. John the Baptist baptizes Christ in the Jordan; God the Father and the Holy Ghost are seen above. Seven angels.

Wood, painted surface, $12\frac{1}{8} \times 17\frac{1}{2}$ (0·31 × 0·445). The panel, being much bowed, has had some of the surface cut away at each side, in order to fit it into a frame; the amount of the original painted surface concerned is about $\frac{1}{2}$ in. wide in each case, over most of the height. There is no evidence if the picture did or did not once continue farther than the ends of the present panel, right and left.

For the commentary, etc., See No. 5454 below.

5452   THE HEAD OF S. JOHN THE BAPTIST BROUGHT TO HEROD (PREDELLA PANEL FROM AN ALTARPIECE)

Salome is seen dancing on the right.

Wood, painted surface, $12\frac{1}{4} \times 14\frac{5}{8}$ (0·31 × 0·37). This panel includes a band of grey paint on the left, which appears not to have been cut. On the right, the band of grey paint is certainly complete. These bands of grey paint are part of the structure of the picture, standing for walls at the sides, and are included in the measurements. At the right, outside the measurements given above, there is a narrow moulding forming a division, then a band of gold $\frac{5}{8}$ in. wide.

For the commentary, etc., see No. 5454 below.

5453   THE BIRTH OF S. JOHN THE BAPTIST (PREDELLA PANEL FROM AN ALTARPIECE)

S. Zacharias is seated on the right, writing the child's name.

Wood, painted surface, $12\frac{1}{8} \times 14\frac{3}{8}$ (0·305 × 0·365). The edges right and left are comparable with those left and right of the preceding panel. On the right were the remains of a band of grey paint about $\frac{1}{2}$ in. wide; most of the original painted surface has been shorn away, to fit the bowed panel into a frame. On the left, the band of grey paint is intact. These areas, which form part of the picture, as in No. 5452, are included in the measurements given above. Further on the left is a narrow moulding forming a division, then the remains of a band of gold $\frac{5}{8}$ in. wide.

For the commentary, etc., see No. 5454 below.

5454 S. JOHN THE BAPTIST RETIRING TO THE DESERT (PREDELLA PANEL FROM AN ALTARPIECE)

The youthful saint is shown at two stages of his ascetic journey.

Wood, painted surface, $12\frac{1}{4} \times 15\frac{1}{4}$ (0·31 × 0·385). At each side, there are narrow mouldings, forming divisions, not included in the above measurements. Then follow narrow panels painted with flowers; a little gold, forming a sort of mount round them, makes their height a little less than that of the principal picture. The flower picture on the left measures $11\frac{5}{8} \times 1\frac{3}{8}$ (0·295 × 0·035); that on the right, $11\frac{1}{2} \times 1\frac{5}{8}$ (0·295 × 0·04). The outer mouldings of these flower compartments, left for the left picture, right for the right picture, have been shaved away.

The measurements given above for Nos. 5451/4 are from what remained of the original pictures. Nos. 5451/4 have since been somewhat adapted to fit their new frames.

The condition is on the whole good. The panel worst preserved is No. 5452, where a good deal of the original paint has flaked away on a line approximately horizontal, going through the top of the head of the soldier kneeling, and Salome's neck; also on Herod's face. In No. 5451, there is a damage in the face of God the Father, and the blue sky along the horizon has mostly been worn away, leaving black. Other damages in the four panels are of less importance.

These four panels are clearly part of a predella. No. 5451 would seem to have formed the central panel. Nos. 5452 and 5453 are similar to each other in construction and size, perhaps the panels on the extreme right and left. No. 5454 seems to be an inner panel, the pendant to which is missing; the pendant would also presumably have had flowers at its sides, dividing it from its neighbours. The arrangement of the existing panels, from left to right, is thus likely to have been (1) No. 5453; (2) No. 5454; (3) No. 5451; (4) 5452. The original predella may have consisted of 5 panels, or 7, or even 9. It is not quite certain if the whole original predella represented scenes from the life of the Baptist; even if it did, the scenes were not necessarily all arranged in chronological order.[1]

The altarpiece from which the pictures come is not known.[2] Perhaps one that might be considered is the one at New York, signed and dated 1454; but the measurements appear not to fit.[3] There appears, therefore, to be no documentation for the attribution of Nos. 5451/4; but it would be perverse to doubt it.

No. 5451 is closely derived from Ghiberti's panel of *The Baptism* on the Font of the Baptistery at Siena.[4] No. 5452 is derived, though less closely, from Donatello's panel of *The Head of S. John Brought to Herod*, on the same Font.[5] Ghiberti's and Donatello's panels were delivered in Siena in October/November, 1427; it should be added that the Font as a whole was not completed until several years later.[6]

Nos. 5452, 5453 and 5454 are closely similar in composition to scenes of the same subjects by Giovanni di Paolo in the Münster and Chicago Museums.[7] Those panels are part of a large series of scenes of the *Life of S. John*, from which *The Baptism* is missing. The principal differences are due to the tall shape of the Münster-Chicago panels. It is not known how that series was originally arranged; it certainly did not form the predella of an altarpiece.[8] There is no evidence for deciding if that series or the National Gallery predella was painted first. The dates attributed to the Münster-Chicago series have varied greatly.[9]

A predella panel by Giovanni di Paolo of *The Baptism*, in the Ashmolean Museum at Oxford, corresponds fairly closely with No. 5451.[10]

VERSIONS: See the preceding two paragraphs.

PROVENANCE: Nos. 5451/4, framed in two frames, were lent by Charles Butler to the R.A., 1887 (Nos. 187, 188); to the New Gallery, 1893/4 (Nos. 17, 18); to the R.A., 1896 (Nos. 146, 153); and to the Burlington Fine Arts Club, 1904 (Nos. 27, 28). They had been acquired by J. Pierpont Morgan by 1909,[11] and appear to have remained in England. Listed for sale in the Morgan Sale at Christie's, 31 March, 1944 (lot 121), they were acquired before the sale, half the purchase money being given by the National Art-Collections Fund, 1944. Exhibited at the National Gallery, N.A.C.F. Exhibition, 1945/6 (No. 35). Cleaned Pictures Exhibition at the National Gallery, 1947/8 (Nos. 18–21).

REPRODUCTIONS: *Plates, Earlier Italian Schools*, 1953, Vol. I, pp. 191–194. All except No. 5453, in their condition before the cleaning in 1944, were reproduced in the large catalogue of the Burlington Fine Arts Club Sienese Exhibition, 1904; photographs of all of them before this cleaning were taken by the National Gallery.

REFERENCES: (1) Cf. the predella to Domenico di Bartolo's altarpiece at Perugia, reproduced in *L'Arte*, 1936, pp. 107, 111; better reproductions in F. Mason Perkins, *Pitture Senesi*, 1933, Plates 111–113. (2) A single figure of S. John the Baptist in the Henry Harris Sale, 25 October, 1950 (lot 196), is clearly irrelevant; the size of the painted surface is only *ca.* 23 × 7½ in. (3) 1940 Catalogue, *Italian, Spanish and Byzantine Paintings*, pp. 90/1, No. 32.100.76. In a letter of 12 March, 1947, Mrs. A. TenEyck Gardner of the Metropolitan Museum kindly gave further precisions about this altarpiece. She came to the same conclusion as the compiler, that Nos. 5451/4 do not fit well as the predella of that altarpiece. It may nevertheless be added that predellas of Sienese altarpieces often do fit badly. (4) Reproduced by J. von Schlosser, *Leben und Meinungen des ... Lorenzo Ghiberti*, 1941, Plate 49. (5) Klassiker der Kunst *Donatello*, 1907, Plate 28. (6) See P. Bacci, *Jacopo della Quercia*, 1929, pp. 178, 184/6; or Milanesi, *Documenti per la Storia dell'Arte Senese*, II, 1854, pp. 92, 134. (7) All reproduced in *The Burlington Magazine*, Vol. XXXIII (1918), p. 47. (8) P. Bacci, *Documenti e Commenti per la Storia dell'Arte*, 1944, pp. 87 ff., suggests that they may come from Giovanni di Paolo's own chapel dedicated to S. John the Baptist, in S. Egidio, Siena. (9) John Pope-Hennessy, *Giovanni di Paolo*, 1937, p. 89, as 1455/60; and his note on p. 111, No. 75, quoting former suggestions. R. Langton Douglas in *The Burlington Magazine*, Vol. LXXII (1938), pp. 44/7, as 1436/8; same volume, p. 95, Pope-Hennessy's reply. C. Brandi in *Le Arti*, 1941, pp. 325 f., as *ca.* 1450. (10) Ashmolean Catalogue, 1951 (No. 179). Reproduced in *The Burlington Magazine*, Vol. XXV (1914), p. 326. (11) Berenson, *Central Italian Painters*, 1909.

GIOVANNI del Ponte
ca. 1385–1437/42 (?)

Giovanni di Marco; he had a studio near S. Stefano a Ponte, Florence. Several mentions of his activity are recorded, but the only extant documented work is a series of frescoes of the early 1430's in S. Trinita, Florence. He seems to have collaborated in these with his partner, Smeraldo di Giovanni; but it would be possible to suppose that one or other of the partners rather than both executed these frescoes, if the terms of partnership made it necessary for both partners to acknowledge receipts of money. A considerable group of paintings with the same stylistic peculiarities exists; it is customary to call them Giovanni del Ponte.

'GIOVANNI del Ponte'

580 TRIPTYCH: THE ASCENSION OF S. JOHN THE EVANGELIST, WITH SAINTS

Centre panel: Christ or God, surrounded by haloed worthies (presumably of the Old Testament, David being identifiable), lifts S. John the Evangelist into heaven from a pit dug at the foot of an altar. Above, the scene is apparently the Descent into Hell. Christ with the banner of the Redemption is in a medallion in the centre; left, the broken gates of Hell, with Satan still foolishly clutching the key and two diabolic monsters. On the right, apparently Adam and Eve, followed by S. John the Baptist, who introduces an unhaloed soldier, possibly a man who had bequeathed money for the picture to be painted.

Left wing: From left to right, 1, S. Bernard, his book inscribed.$. BER. 2. S. Scholastica, with the name on the background above,.S. SCOLASTICA. 3, S. Benedict, his book inscribed B. 4, S. John the Baptist, his scroll inscribed.ECCE.AGNVS.DEI.QVITO.....A. Above, S. Michael in a medallion.

Right wing: From left to right, 1, S. Peter. 2, S. Romuald, his book inscribed.$.RVMV. 3, S. Catherine of Alexandria. 4, S. Jerome (?), his book inscribed PENITENCIA. / AGGERE.EST. / PERPETRAT/A. .MALA.PR/AGERE.ET. / PRAGENDO. / NON. PER/PETRARE. Above, in a medallion, S. Raphael with Tobias.

Left pilaster: At the top, in a medallion, a saint with a staff (?), holding a book inscribed AI. Next, S. Cosmas, name inscribed.COSMO. Lowest, S. Francis.

Right pilaster: At the top, in a medallion, S. Nicholas. Next, S. Damian, name inscribed $.DAMIAN. Lowest, S. Margaret.

Predella: Three scenes from the life of S. John the Evangelist. From left to right, 1, two haloed figures give money to the poor, while on the right S. John baptizes them (?) and others; 2, the Vision in Patmos; 3, S. John saved from a cauldron of boiling oil into which Domitian had put him. Extreme left, S. Apollonia, apparently with S. Agatha's breast as an emblem instead of her proper tooth, but with the name inscribed S.APO/LONIA. Extreme right, S. Viridiana with two snakes, and the name inscribed (S) VERDI/ANA.

580A PINNACLES TO THE ABOVE ALTARPIECE

Centre, the Trinity; left, S. Gabriel; right, the Virgin Annunciate.

Wood. The sizes of the painted surfaces are as follows: principal scene, cusped and rounded top, $48 \times 24\frac{1}{2}$ ($1 \cdot 22 \times 0 \cdot 62$); medallion above, diameter 8 ($0 \cdot 20$); total width of the *Descent into Hell*, $25\frac{3}{4}$ ($0 \cdot 655$). Groups of saints at the sides, cusped and rounded tops, $45\frac{1}{2} \times 24$ ($1 \cdot 155 \times 0 \cdot 61$); medallions above, diameter $5\frac{1}{2}$ ($0 \cdot 14$). Pilasters: medallions, each, diameter 4 ($0 \cdot 10$); middle figures, each, cusped top and bottom, $17 \times 4\frac{1}{2}$ ($0 \cdot 43 \times 0 \cdot 115$); lowest figures, each, cusped at the top, $17 \times 4\frac{1}{2}$ ($0 \cdot 43 \times 0 \cdot 115$). Including the frame, the total height of the altarpiece without the predella or pinnacles is $65\frac{1}{2}$ ($1 \cdot 66$), the total width including the pilasters $98\frac{1}{4}$ ($2 \cdot 50$). *Predella:* painted surfaces, centre scene, $12 \times 22\frac{1}{2}$ ($0 \cdot 305 \times 0 \cdot 57$); side scenes, each, $12 \times 21\frac{1}{2}$ ($0 \cdot 305 \times 0 \cdot 545$); side figures, each, 12×6 ($0 \cdot 305 \times 0 \cdot 15$). Including the frame, the total size of the predella is $15\frac{1}{2} \times 98\frac{1}{4}$ ($0 \cdot 395 \times 2 \cdot 50$). *Pinnacles:* centre, painted surface, $17 \times 10\frac{3}{4}$ ($0 \cdot 43 \times 0 \cdot 27$), or including its frame, $28\frac{1}{4} \times 14\frac{1}{4}$ ($0 \cdot 715 \times 0 \cdot 36$). Side pinnacles, each, painted surface, $16\frac{3}{4} \times 9\frac{1}{2}$ ($0 \cdot 425 \times 0 \cdot 24$); including the frame, $26\frac{3}{4} \times 13\frac{1}{4}$ ($0 \cdot 68 \times 0 \cdot 34$).

An altarpiece apparently complete, and in good condition on the whole. The frame is in essentials old, but regilt, a good deal restored, and possibly somewhat modified in form at the sides.

The altarpiece is dedicated to S. John the Evangelist. The central scene of his *Ascension* has strictly no known authority, but could be deduced from the legends of his death. According to the *Acts of John*, the Saint had a trench dug at the tomb of a Christian, laid his clothes in the trench, stood in it himself, uttered a prayer to God and then laid himself in the trench and died. Some versions add that on the next day his body was not found, since it had been translated by the power of Christ; others say that a light appeared over the Apostle, and then manna was seen issuing from the tomb. The *Golden Legend* places the spot before the altar of a church dedicated to S. John, and speaks of the light and the manna. In Italian, especially Florentine, painting for a time it was customary to represent S. John bodily ascending; the first example seems to be the fresco usually accepted as by Giotto, in the Peruzzi Chapel in S. Croce, Florence.[1]

As for the predella, the central scene of the *Vision in Patmos* is closely derived from the fresco of the subject in the already mentioned Peruzzi chapel in S. Croce.[2] The incidents of the vision are taken from various parts of *Revelation*; the Son of Man with a sickle in his hand being from Chapter xiv, v. 14, the Woman and Child and the Dragon from Chapter xii, and the four Angels in the four corners of the world holding the four winds from Chapter vii, v. 1. In accordance with Florentine tradition, the winds are symbolized as lions.[3]

The predella scene on the right calls for little comment; S. John is said to have been put into a cauldron of boiling oil by Domitian outside the Latin Gate at Rome, and when it did him no harm, he was exiled to Patmos.[4] The scene on the left actually shows two haloed young men giving money to the poor, and on the right S. John baptizing two unhaloed young men (the same ?), while two others prepare themselves. It is likely enough that the scene was meant to represent the story of the philosopher Craton, who persuaded two brothers to convert all their property into precious stones and then to destroy the stones. S. John rebuked Craton, and on being challenged recreated the jewels. All three men were converted; the stones were sold, and the money was given to the poor. The predella scene may well have been intended to represent all this, but does so very inadequately.

The scene of the *Descent into Hell* is obscure in the topography and the actors. The group on the right seems to be issuing from Hell; in that case, the two leading figures are almost certainly Adam and Eve, although he has a halo (but she is crushed up against the frame,) and although both are dressed in the height of respectability.[5] The former suggestion was that the haloed figure is S. John the Evangelist;[6] but his coiffure does not correspond with his other appearances in the picture. The soldier introduced by S. John the Baptist appears with so marked a gesture that he is probably the Donor of the altarpiece, or perhaps rather someone who had bequeathed money for it to be painted; admittedly, it is peculiar that such a man should be represented as being in Hell at the period of the Crucifixion.

The Saints in this picture also present some obscurities. The text on S. Jerome's (?) book is a grossly corrupt form of a patristic tag, *Poenitentiam agere est perpetrata mala plangere et plangenda non perpetrare.* These words appear to have been written in the first instance by S. Gregory the Great. From their appearance in the picture, it may be deduced that the painter was not at ease in reading and writing; it is more difficult to say for sure if the clerk who gave him the text intended S. Jerome, or someone else.[7] It seems fairly clear that S. Apollonia is shown with the emblem of S. Agatha; it is not surprising that painters should sometimes have been confused in these matters.[8] S. Verdiana or Viridiana is said to have been a nun; she lived for 34 years in a cell at Castelfiorentino with two snakes, and is mentioned in the fiftieth story of Boccaccio's *Decameron.*[9]

The altarpiece was formerly attributed to Jacopo del Casentino, apparently on the ground that Vasari says Jacopo painted at Pratovecchio, whence this picture comes. If, on the other hand, the attribution was based on good evidence, the Jacopo del Casentino in question would not be the same man as the Jacopo del Casentino with whom a number of pictures are associated in modern criticism. It is indeed probable that there were two; but in any event it is admitted that Nos. 580 and 580A are in the style of the pictures called by custom Giovanni del Ponte. This attribution for them was first made by Toesca;[10] Gamba says that the present altarpiece is the earliest work of the group.[11]

PROVENANCE: From the Camaldolese Nunnery of S. Giovanni Evangelista at Pratovecchio, not far from Camaldoli;[12] it could have been painted as its high-altarpiece. By 1845 in the Lombardi-Baldi Collection, Florence,[13] whence purchased with other pictures, 1857.[14]

REPRODUCTIONS: *Illustrations, Italian Schools*, 1937, p. 157. *Plates, Earlier Italian Schools*, 1953, Vol. I, pp. 195–203.

REFERENCES: (1) Van Marle, *Development of the Italian Schools of Painting*, Vol. III, Fig. 87. Representations of S. John's empty tomb without his ascension do also occur in Italian painting, e.g. in the predella of a picture of *S. John the Evangelist* assigned to Berto di Giovanni, in the Gallery at Perugia. See G. Cecchini, *La Galleria Nazionale dell'Umbria in Perugia*, 1932, p. 166, No. 307; there is a small reproduction in the exhibition catalogue, *Four Centuries of Painting in Umbria*, Perugia, 1945, No. 47. (2) Carlo Carrà, *Giotto*, 1924, Plate CXXX. (3) Scenes of S. John's story similar to the Florentine traditions, and in particular with the winds as beasts, occur also in Spain; cf. C. R. Post, *A History of Spanish Painting*, Vol. VII, Part II, p. 566 and Figs. 212 and 261. (4) The origin of this story seems to be obscure; cf. M. R. James, *The Apocryphal New Testament*, 1926, p. 229. (5) In a *Coronation* ascribed to Giovanni del Ponte in the Academy at Florence, there is a somewhat similar scene of the *Descent into Hell*, with figures obviously Adam and Eve fully dressed. Reproduced by Van Marle, *Development of the Italian Schools of Painting*, Vol. IX, Fig. 46. (6) In the Lombardi-Baldi catalogue, referred to in the provenance, this part was supposed to represent SS. John the Baptist and Evangelist presenting the family of the donor. (7) Migne, *Patrologia Latina*, Vol. 76, Col. 1256, Section 1609B, for S. Gregory. A reference is added by Kaftal, *Iconography of the Saints in Tuscan Painting*, 1952, Col. 524, to an Epistle of S. Jerome (Migne, *Patrologia Latina*, Vol. 30, Col. 243, Section III); but the connection is by no means precise. (8) What seems to be a case of a Jeremiah with a text from Isaiah is reproduced in *Dedalo*, 1932, p. 848 (comment on pp. 842 and 853). (9) A long life of S. Viridiana is given by Giuseppe Maria Brocchi, *Vite de' Santi e Beati Fiorentini*, I, 1741, pp. 169 ff. The religious order to which she belonged is varied, apparently, according to taste (cf. Richa, *Notizie Istoriche delle Chiese Fiorentine*, II, 1755, pp. 227 ff.; also III, 1755, pp. 361 f.). Remembering the case of S. Anthony the Great, she asked for temptations; two large snakes were granted to her, which beat her with their tails. A good representation of her is reproduced by Sirén, *Giotto and Some of His Followers*, II, 1917, Plate 188. (10) Toesca in *L'Arte*, 1904, p. 49. (11) Gamba in the *Rivista d'Arte*, 1906, p. 166. (12) N.G. MS. Catalogue, and printed catalogue, 1858; cf. Vasari, ed. Milanesi, I, p. 671. The house was a nunnery subject to the Angeli at Florence; see Gregorio Farulli, *Istoria Cronologica del nobile, ed antico Monastero degli Angioli di Firenze*, etc., 1710, pp. 254 and 260, or the same author (or Pietro Farulli, or Francesco Masetti), *Teatro Storico del Sacro Eremo di Camaldoli*, etc., 1723, p. 311. This nunnery was the subject of a series of articles (by D. Parisio Ciampelli?) in *Il Sacro Speco di S. Benedetto di Subiaco*, a periodical consulted in the Library of S. Paolo fuori le Mura, Rome. The author had access to various documents, which might be worth tracing and consulting for the history of No. 580. In Vol. XXIX of *Il Sacro Speco*, November, 1923, pp. 204/7, and in Vol. XXX, April, 1924, p. 44, it is stated that the nunnery was suppressed in 1808/10; that inventories were made in April, 1808 (by Pietro Maccioni, Luigi Fantoni and Geppino di Vito Ceccarelli), and in June, 1808; and that the pictures were auctioned on 26/7 November, 1810, being bought mostly by Frosini. The compiler searched several later numbers of the periodical without finding the continuation of this series of articles, which may not have been published. (13) No. 14, as Jacques de Casentino, of a Lombardi-Baldi Catalogue (*Collection de Tableaux Anciens*, etc.); the catalogue is not dated, but the copy in the Uffizi Library is claimed to be of 1845. (14) For the history of the Lombardi-Baldi Collection, see Appendix I.

Gerolamo GIOVENONE
active 1513, died 1555

Active at Vercelli. There are signed and dated works of 1513 and 1514 at Vercelli and Turin; of 1527 at Bergamo. A *S. Ambrose* in San Francesco, Vercelli, is held to be part of an altarpiece ordered in 1527 and paid for in 1535; it is unreasonable to contest this view. His early style is closely connected with that of Defendente Ferrari, of whom he may have been a pupil, or with whom he may have been a co-pupil of Giovanni Martino Spanzotti. His later work is strongly under the influence of Gaudenzio Ferrari; the *S. Ambrose*, even, being ascribed to Gaudenzio by Berenson.

1295 ALTARPIECE: THE VIRGIN AND CHILD, WITH SAINTS AND DONORS

The Saint to the left is S. Bonaventure, to the right S. Francis; each protects a male donor.

Poplar,[1] rounded top, original painted surface, $81 \times 48\frac{1}{2}$ ($2 \cdot 06 \times 1 \cdot 23$). The top 2 in. (5 cm.) of the panel is a new addition; the line of the original rounded top just passes beyond the original panel, which presumably has been shaved. The paint has been made up to the edges at the sides, and extended to form a slightly larger arch at the top; total painted area, $82 \times 52\frac{1}{2}$ ($2 \cdot 085 \times 1 \cdot 335$).

The picture is in fair, but not altogether reliable, state; to cite one example, the eye of the donor to the left has been considerably changed by restoration.

The identity of the Saint on the left used at one time to be questioned, but a Franciscan Saint who is also a Cardinal Bishop must be S. Bonaventure. It is true that the exact form of his emblem here, a thorny Crucifix with a pelican on top, is unusual.[2]

The attribution does not seem to have been doubted in print,[3] and is provisionally accepted here. The picture is near in style to Defendente Ferrari, but not under the influence of Gaudenzio; as it is more developed than Giovenone's authenticated works of 1513/4, it may be supposed to date from *ca.* 1520, on the assumption that Gaudenzio's dominance over Giovenone did not take place until *ca.* 1525/30. The costume of the donors does not seem to conflict with the date suggested.

PROVENANCE: Purchased from Antonio Carrer, Venice, 1889.[4]

REPRODUCTION: *Illustrations, Italian Schools*, 1937, p. 158. *Plates, Earlier Italian Schools*, 1953, Vol. I, p. 204.

REFERENCES: (1) Letter from B. J. Rendle, of the Forest Products Research Laboratory, in the Gallery archives. (2) No. 562 at Berlin, Schongauer School (reproduced in the Berlin Illustrations), contains S. Bonaventure (wrongly called S. Jerome on the plate) with a leafy Crucifix. A Crucifix, not leafy, but apparently with a pelican on top, is at Sainte-Lucie-de-Tallano (Plate I of G. Moracchini and D. Carrington, *Trésors Oubliés des Eglises de Corse*, 1959). In Vittorio Crivelli, e.g. at Cambridge, No. 1060 (small reproduction in *The Principal Pictures in the Fitzwilliam Museum*, 1929), a pelican is shown above the *lignum vitæ* held by S. Bonaventure. For the *lignum vitæ* with pelican, see especially the fresco ascribed to Taddeo Gaddi in the Refectory of S. Croce, Florence (reproduced by Sirèn, *Giotto and some of his Followers*, II, 1917, Plate 123). (3) Admitted by Berenson, 1932 Lists, and by A. M. Brizio, *La Pittura in Piemonte*, 1942, p. 220. (4) As ascribed to Defendente Ferrari. This attribution was due to or accepted by Morelli: letter to Layard, 5 February, 1890 (British Museum, Add. MS. 38965, Layard Papers, Vol. XXXV).

GIROLAMO *See* GEROLAMO

GIUSTO DE' MENABUOI
active 1363/4, died 1387/91

A Florentine painter, who worked much at Padua, and is often referred to as Giusto Padovano (Justus of Padua). The date 1363 (perhaps 1364 n.s.) is on a signed picture. From the early 1370's at least, he was at Padua, where his principal work is a series of frescoes (not strictly documented) in the Baptistery.

Literature: Sergio Bettini, *Giusto de' Menabuoi*, 1944.

701 TRIPTYCH: THE CORONATION OF THE VIRGIN, AND OTHER SCENES

Central panel: The Virgin is crowned by Christ. Foreground, from left to right, S. Margaret, an unidentified female saint, SS. Catherine, Peter, John the Baptist and Paul. At the sides are other saints, angels, etc., including SS. Ambrose (with his scourge), Francis, Dominic, Benedict (?), Anthony Abbot (?), Stephen (?), Lawrence (?).

Left wing: The Nativity (with two midwives) and the Announcement to the Shepherds. Above, in the spandrels, two unidentifiable figures of Prophets (?), done in gold under glass; at the top, the Angel of the Annunciation.

Right wing: Christ Crucified, with the Holy Women and S. John; the Cross being marked.Y.N.R.I. Above, in the spandrels, Daniel and David, the names being inscribed *daniel* and ( )*avit*, done in gold under glass; at the top, the Virgin Annunciate.

Reverse of the wings: the two wings when folded together show six scenes, which reading from left to right and from top to bottom are, S. Joachim's Offering Rejected, the Angel appearing to S. Joachim, the Meeting at the Golden Gate, the Birth of the Virgin, the Presentation of the Virgin, and the Marriage of the Virgin (with S. Joseph's rod in blossom, and an unsuccessful suitor breaking his own rod).

Reverse of the central panel: Red paint, with the signature towards the middle: (ju)*stus pinxit in mediol.*

At the base of the central panel, at the front, is the date pounced on a gold ground: *ano.dñi.m./.ccc.lxvii.*

Poplar, central panel, pointed top, $17\frac{1}{2} \times 8\frac{3}{8}$ (0·445 × 0·21); including the framing, none of which appears to be old, $19 \times 9\frac{3}{4}$ (0·48 × 0·25).

The gold ground on which is the date is $1\frac{1}{8} \times 12\frac{1}{8}$ (0·03 × 0·31), on a piece of wood with wedge-shaped restorations at the ends. The sizes of the scenes on the inside of the wings are: lower scene, pointed top, $11\frac{1}{8} \times 4\frac{1}{2}$ (0·28 × 0·115); spandrels, *ca.* $1\frac{1}{2} \times 1\frac{1}{4}$ (0·04 × 0·03); upper scene, $6\frac{5}{8} \times 4$ (0·17 × 0·10), irregular. The width of the two wings differs slightly. Total size, including the framing, $19 \times 5\frac{1}{4}$ (0·48 × 0·135).

Considerably restored. The triptych has been altered somewhat, presumably for the reframing; although there is no reason to suppose that the fields of the pictures have been reduced, unless perhaps by a very slight amount, the central panel itself has almost certainly been cut, and presumably the wood of the wings has been cut too. The parts cut away would presumably have been covered by an original framing more massive than the present framing. The wood forming the base may well not have been reduced in width, but there is no definite evidence concerning this.

The cutting of the central panel is indicated by the state of the signature, the authenticity of which is not doubted.[1] The last letter, read as an 'l', is here recorded for the first time; it had been almost completely covered over by a careless application of the gold paint used for the frame, and was uncovered in 1959. This letter is now on the extreme edge of the wood, and it seems incredible that this should have been so originally. The wood assumed to be missing here, with (for symmetry) much the same amount missing from the other side, could have made the original width of the central panel about the same as the width of the base at present.

As for the signature itself, the beginning of the first word is illegible, but the word was read as *Justus* already in 1827.[2] There is no evidence for saying that anything preceded it on a part of the wood cut away. The name of the place is certainly Milan; there might have been room, before a cutting of the panel, for the unabbreviated word *mediolano*.[3]

It was left doubtful before whether the gold with the date, at the base of the central panel, is authentic; but it appears undesirable to doubt it.[4] The date was recorded already in the Œttingen-Wallerstein Catalogue of 1827.

The *Presentation* and the *Angel of the Annunciation* in No. 701 correspond in some degree with Giusto de' Menabuoi's treatment of the same subjects in the Baptistery at Padua, probably not later than 1376.[5] The *Coronation of the Virgin* is somewhat similar to a fresco of the subject in the Santo at Padua, which Bettini attributes to Giusto and dates in the 1380's.[6] A Tyrolese *Coronation of the Virgin* at Stams seems to show some compositional connection with No. 701, and may possibly be derived from it.[7]

PROVENANCE: Stated to have been in the Collection of Count Joseph von Rechberg, Mindelheim, and bought in 1816 by Prince Ludwig von Œttingen-Wallerstein.[8] Alternatively, stated to have been acquired from the lithographer Stunz at Munich, i.e. J. B. Stuntz.[9] Œttingen-Wallerstein Catalogues, *ca.* 1826 and 1827 (No. 18). Exhibited at Kensington Palace (for sale), 1848 (Nos. 15–23), bought with the rest of the collection by the Prince Consort. At Kensington Palace.[10] Exhibited at Manchester, 1857 (Provisional Catalogue, No. 288; Definitive Catalogue, No. 38). Presented by Queen Victoria at the Prince Consort's wish, 1863.

REPRODUCTIONS: *Illustrations, Italian Schools*, 1937, p. 181. *Plates, Earlier Italian Schools*, 1953, Vol. I, pp. 205–206.

REFERENCES: (1) The comments on the condition of the triptych, corrected from the first edition of this catalogue, are based on a technical examination carried out by N. S. Brommelle and Joyce Plesters. It should be mentioned that, at the back, the gesso under the red paint on which is the signature differs in composition from the gesso under gold in various places; in point of fact, it is the composition of the latter that is unusual, the gesso under the red paint being of the type commonly found in Italian pictures. (2) Œttingen-Wallerstein Catalogue, 1827 (No. 18). (3) The compiler is much indebted to Professor Francis Wormald for comments on the lettering. The transcription was given with several faults in the first edition of this catalogue; Longhi in *Paragone*, March 1957, p. 7, and July 1957, p. 40, rightly claims that the place referred to must be Milan. At one time it was wrongly supposed to be Arquà. In comment on the transcription *mediol*, the form of the *d* with an upright stroke does, indeed, occur, as Longhi points out, at the time (see plates in Toesca's *La Pittura e la Miniatura nella Lombardia*, 1912); the letter here cannot be said to be well written, but doubt that it is a *d* may be abandoned. The mark after the *i* seems not to be an apostrophe, but a dot mixed up with an accidental blemish. The last letter, being as noted at the edge of the wood, could theoretically be, not an *l*, but the left-hand part of a different letter; *l* should not be doubted. A reproduction of the signature (with the *l* almost completely covered) is on Plate 13 of *Paintings and Drawings on the Backs of National Gallery Pictures*, 1946. (4) Longhi, *loc. cit.*, in previous note, protested against the doubt. The technical examination already referred to revealed nothing suspicious; the only point might seem the craquelure, which is markedly different at the base and in the rest of the triptych, but the expansions and contractions of the base are likely to have been different from those of the other parts. It is, perhaps, not common to have an inscription in such a place consisting only of a date; but compare some pictures associated more or less closely with Daddi (Memorial Catalogue of the *Mostra Giottesca* Exhibition held at Florence in 1937, 1943, Nos. 155, 156, 169, with reproductions and comments on the condition). It is patent that the date in No. 701 is carelessly and tastelessly executed; but this is not an argument against the authenticity of the inscription—indeed, it has been suggested above that the position of the signature, when the central panel was intact, may have been asymmetrical. (5) Sergio Bettini, *Giusto de' Menabuoi*, 1944, Plates 85 and 81, and p. 17. (6) Bettini, *op. cit.*, Plates 140 sqq. and p. 101. (7) Burger-Schmitz-Beth, *Deutsche Malerei vom Ausgehenden Mittelalter*, II, 1917, p. 240 (Fig. 288). (8) Letter from Dr. Noack, 20 November, 1909, noted by E. K. Waterhouse. See further *Kunst-Blatt*, 1824, pp. 318 and 353. (9) See G. Grupp in the *Jahrbuch des Historischen Vereins für Nördlingen und Umgebung*, Vol. VI, 1917, p. 97. (10) Waagen's Catalogue, 1854 (No. 13); see also Waagen, *Treasures*, IV, 1857, pp. 221/2.

GOZZOLI *See* BENOZZO DI LESE

GRECO-ROMAN

Various portraits of this class were recorded in the catalogue of 1929. All those there recorded, except Nos. 3931 and 3932 below, were lent to the British Museum in 1936; some of them, under the heading *Greco-Alexandrian Portraits*, were in the Exhibition of Greek Art at the Royal Academy, 1946 (Nos. 316–323). The three examples at present in the National Gallery are merely listed here; they are outside the tradition of the main schools of European painting as represented in the National Gallery Collection.

3931   A YOUNG WOMAN

Wood, $16\frac{1}{4} \times 8\frac{1}{2}$ (0·41 × 0·22).[1]

PROVENANCE: Found in the neighbourhood of the village of Er-Rubiyat, N.E. of Medînet-el-Faiyûm. Acquired from a Greek dealer by Th. Graf. of Vienna, and from him in 1893 by Ludwig Mond.[2] Exhibited at the Grafton Gallery, Fair Women, 1894 (No. 1 or No. 32). Mond Bequest, 1924.

REPRODUCTION: *Plates, Earlier Italian Schools*, 1953, Vol. I, p. 207.

REFERENCES: (1) Measurements from the 1929 Catalogue. (2) J. P. Richter, *The Mond Collection*, 1910, II, Table of Contents and pp. 597 ff. Richter gives a reference to George Ebers, *Die hellenistischen Portraits aus dem Fayum*, 1893, p. 11.

3932   A MAN WITH A WREATH

Wood, $16\frac{1}{2} \times 8\frac{3}{8}$ (0·42 × 0·22).[1]

PROVENANCE: From Er-Rubiyat and Th. Graf, as No. 3931 above. Ludwig Mond Collection, 1893; Mond Bequest, 1924.

REPRODUCTION: *Plates, Earlier Italian Schools*, 1953, Vol. I, p. 207.

REFERENCE: (1) Measurements from the 1929 Catalogue.

5399   A YOUNG WOMAN WITH A WREATH

Wood, $11\frac{1}{4} \times 7\frac{1}{2}$ (0·285 × 0·19); cut at the top corners.

PROVENANCE: Presented by Major R. G. Gayer-Anderson Pasha, and Col. T. G. Gayer-Anderson, C.M.G., D.S.O., 1943.

REPRODUCTION: *Plates, Earlier Italian Schools*, 1953, Vol. I, p. 207.

INGEGNO *See* ANDREA DI ALOIGI

ITALIAN SCHOOL

2084   PORTRAIT OF A YOUNG MAN

Reverse: marbling.

Wood, painted surface, $22 \times 17\frac{1}{4}$ (0·56 × 0·435); painted up to the edges all round.

There seems no doubt that this picture is a forgery. In Berenson's

Lists, 1932, as a copy after Botticelli; in the 1936 edition, Berenson adds r. (for ruined, repainted or restored). Ascribed by Van Marle to Sellaio.[1]

PROVENANCE: John Samuel Collection. Lent by his nieces, the Misses Cohen, to the New Gallery, 1893/4 (No. 99);[2] bequeathed with other pictures by the Misses Cohen, as the John Samuel Collection, 1906.[3]

REPRODUCTION: *Illustrations, Italian Schools*, 1937, p. 136. *Plates, Earlier Italian Schools*, 1953, Vol. I, p. 208.

REFERENCES: (1) Van Marle, *Development of the Italian Schools of Painting*, Vol. XII, pp. 390/2. (2) As Pietro Pollaiuolo. (3) In the 1929 Catalogue as Florentine.

2250 BUST OF ANDREA MANTEGNA IN RELIEF

Size: not measured.

Plaster cast of a bust of Andrea Mantegna in circular framing, with a rectangular framing added outside. The original bronze is on Mantegna's tomb in S. Andrea at Mantua.[1] It was traditionally ascribed to Sperandio, which is now rejected; Gian Marco Cavalli (living 1475–1508), Bartolomeo Melioli (*ca.* 1448–1514) or Mantegna himself have been suggested as possible authors.[2]

PROVENANCE: Presented by Henry Vaughan, 1883.

REPRODUCTION: *Plates, Earlier Italian Schools*, 1953, Vol. I, p. 208.

REFERENCES: (1) Reproduced by Carlo d'Arco, *Delle Arti e degli Artifici di Mantova*, I, 1857, Plate 52; by Bode in the Prussian *Jahrbuch*, 1889, p. 214; by Fiocco, *Mantegna*, 1937, Plate 296; and elsewhere. (2) For Cavalli and Melioli, see G. F. Hill, *A Corpus of Italian Medals*, 1930, I, pp. 47 and 61/2. For the attributions, see Bode in the Prussian *Jahrbuch*, 1889, pp. 211 ff., Fabriczy in *L'Arte*, 1888, pp. 428/9, and G. Fiocco, *Mantegna*, 1937, pp. 102/3. No effort has been made to write a complete entry for No. 2250.

3130 PORTRAIT OF AN OLD MAN

Canvas, 30 × 24¾ (0·765 × 0·625).

The picture has suffered a great deal from rubbing; two new patches.

It has been the subject of various attributions. Traditionally Giovanni Bellini, it was called Gentile Bellini by Frizzoni,[1] and catalogued in 1929 as of his school. In Layard's Collection it was variously given to Titian or Giorgione.[2] Berenson (1932 Lists) calls it Domenico Morone (?).

PROVENANCE: Sale (?) mark 329 C (not identified) on the back. Sir William Boxall, who died in 1879, bequeathed it to Sir A. H. Layard;[3] Layard Bequest, 1916.[4]

REPRODUCTION: *Illustrations, Italian Schools*, 1937, p. 30. *Plates, Earlier Italian Schools*, 1953, Vol. I, p. 209.

REFERENCES: (1) Frizzoni in the *Gazette des Beaux-Arts*, 1896, ii, p. 460. (2) Layard MSS. in the National Gallery. (3) Layard MSS. in the National Gallery. (4) For the history of the Layard Collection, see Appendix IV.

3831 PORTRAIT GROUP

Wood, 16 × 14¾ (0·406 × 0·365).[1]

This picture appears to be modern; there is some evidence, not altogether convincing, that it is by Icilio Federico Joni.[2]

PROVENANCE: Purchased from Hanson Walker, Florence Fund, 1923.

REPRODUCTION: *Plates, Earlier Italian Schools*, 1953, Vol. I, p. 210.

REFERENCES: (1) Measurements from the 1929 Catalogue. (2) Some discussion of No. 3831 (as an old picture) was published in *The Burlington Magazine*, Vol. XLIV (1924), pp. 195 f.; see also the 1929 Catalogue (School of Melozzo). On grounds of costume, Stella Mary Pearce suggests that it was painted soon after 1913; see her article in *The Bulletin of the Needle and Bobbin Club*, Vol. 44, 1960, pp. 23 ff.

4741 THE VIRGIN AND CHILD WITH TWO ANGELS

Inscribed on the background $\overline{\text{MP}}\ \overline{\Theta\text{V}}$.

Reverse: A painted Cross with triangles and circles at the ends of the four arms. Also, in a nineteenth-century hand, *Giunta Pisano / Secolo XII.*

Wood. The main part of the picture is, rounded top, 11¾ × 8½ (0·30 × 0·215). The size of the panel, which was entirely covered with gold or paint, is 14⅜ × 10½ (0·365 × 0·265). Hinge marks on the right, about 2¼ in. from the top and the bottom, are visible at the back (on the left when seen from the back).

Very good condition.

The motive of the Virgin and Child embracing, as on No. 4741, occurs frequently in Byzantine and early Italian painting.[1] The Cross on the reverse may be distantly derived from Crosses of two types, found on Byzantine ivories.[2]

There is a picture at Budapest representing *Christ on the Cross*, of the same size as No. 4741, with similar compartments on the front, and with the same Cross painted on the reverse.[3] Garrison thinks that the two panels formed a diptych, with No. 4741 at the left, the Budapest picture (hinge marks on the left) at the right.[4]

No. 4741 was traditionally ascribed to Giunta Pisano (active 1229–1254), and was considered in the 1939 Supplement to the Catalogue to be in his tradition.[5] Vavalà rather doubtfully associates No. 4741 with a picture at Pisa, the namepiece of the 'Master of S. Martino.'[6] Offner (verbal, 1947) associates it with a picture in S. Maria Maggiore at Florence, classed as by, or in the following of Coppo di Marcovaldo (active 1260–1274).[7] Garrison calls it Sienese under strong Pisan influenze.[8] It seems, at present at least, impossible to make satisfactory attributions for pictures such as No. 4741, or even to define for sure from what district of central Italy (Pisa, Florence, Siena, etc.) they come.

PROVENANCE: Purchased *ca.* 1890[9] at Assisi by W. B. Chamberlin, by whom presented, 1934.

REPRODUCTIONS: Front: *Illustrations, Italian Schools*, 1937, p. 283; *Plates, Earlier Italian Schools*, 1953, Vol. I, p. 211. The reverse is reproduced in *Paintings and Drawings on the Backs of National Gallery Pictures*, 1946, Plate 42.

REFERENCES: (1) See Curt H. Weigelt in *Art Studies*, VI, 1928, pp. 195 ff., and E. Sandberg-Vavalà, *L'Iconografia della Madonna col Bambino nella Pittura Italiana del Dugento*, 1934, pp. 57 ff. (p. 60, No. 173 is No. 4741). (2) One type seems sometimes to record Constantine's Vision of the Cross; the other type, less like the Cross on No. 4741, seems to record the Cross of Constantine in the Forum at Byzantium. See Adolph Goldschmidt and Kurt Weitzmann, *Die Byzantinischen Elfenbeinskulpturen*, II, *Reliefs*, 1934, pp. 22/3 and Plate LXIII. E. B. Garrison, *Italian Romanesque Panel Painting*, 1949, p. 107, refers to the circles at the ends of the cross as the heavenly *cibi*, or Foods of Grace; but this seems to be a mistake (letters from H. Buchtal in the Gallery archives). (3) Budapest, Catalogue by G. von Térey, I, *Byzantinische, Italienische, etc. Meister*, 1916, p. 7, No. 18c, with reproduction; 1937 Catalogue in Hungarian, p. 260, No. 31, with reproduction. (4) Garrison, *op. cit.*, Nos. 272, 273. (5) The catalogue entry in the 1939 Supplement, which contains many of the references given here, was written by P. Pouncey. (6) E. Sandberg-Vavalà, *op. cit.*, 1934, p. 60, No. 173. For the picture at Pisa, see Giulia Sinibaldi and Giulia Brunetti, *Pittura Italiana del Duecento e Trecento*, 1943, pp. 79 ff., with reproductions; Garrison, *op. cit.*, No. 392, as Raniero di Ugolino. (7) Sinibaldi and Brunetti, *op. cit.*, pp. 205 ff., with reproductions; Garrison, *op. cit.*, No. 219. (8) Garrison, *op. cit.*, No. 273. (9) The documents in the Gallery archives indicate that this is the probable date.

JACOMETTO VENEZIANO
active *ca.* 1472, died before 1498

In a letter of 10 September, 1497, it is mentioned that he was by then dead. There are several very early references to him by the Anonimo Morelliano (Marcantonio Michiel), who records works by him in various collections at Venice and Padua. From these his activity from *ca.* 1472 can be deduced. He was, it seems, chiefly a miniaturist. Attributions of pictures to him can be made on comparison with two little portraits in the Liechtenstein Gallery at Vaduz, which (in spite of difficulties of interpretation) do seem beyond reasonable doubt identifiable with a work described by the Anonimo (reproduced by Van Marle, *Development of the Italian Schools of Painting*, Vol. XVII, Fig. 229; a version of the man's portrait in the Collection of the Duke of Buccleuch is reproduced in *The Connoisseur*, Vol. XVIII, 1907, p. 141). The Anonimo also says that the figure or face of Antonello's *S. Jerome* (No. 1418 of this catalogue) was like Jacometto or even may have been repainted by Jacometto; there seems to be no justification for believing that Jacometto ever touched No. 1418, but what the Anonimo says furnishes at least a clue to what the Anonimo expected Jacometto's pictures to look like.

No full study of Jacometto in the light of recent researches is available at the time of writing; but it may be held that Nos. 2509 and 3121 below are reasonably ascribed to him. See further *The Burlington Magazine*, 1953, p. 208 (Giles Robertson) and 1955, p. 295 (E. K. Waterhouse).

There have been various wrong attempts to identify Jacometto with

Jacopo de' Barbari; e.g. by Luigi Servolini, *Jacopo de' Barbari*, 1944. Servolini's introductory chapter headed *Jacometto* is, nevertheless, a useful collection of references; these include some not given above.

Ascribed to JACOMETTO Veneziano

2509 PORTRAIT OF A BOY

Wood, painted surface, $9 \times 7\frac{3}{4}$ (0·23 × 0·195); painted up to the edges all round.

Excellent state.

J. Wilde (oral), on comparison with the Liechtenstein portraits mentioned in the biography above, ascribes No. 3121 below to Jacometto. Berenson in 1895[1] maintained that No. 2509 is by the same hand as No. 3121; this seems to the compiler undoubtedly true, and the recent cleaning of both pictures has done much to confirm the identity of hand.[2] Wilde accepts this, and ascribes No. 2509 as well as No. 3121 to Jacometto. It was desirable to explain the steps taken for the attribution, since No. 2509 is somewhat different in character from No. 3121, being more Antonellesque and indeed considerably better in quality.

Former attributions for No. 2509 were unsatisfactory. Traditionally Antonello, it was called Andrea Solari by Crowe and Cavalcaselle;[3] later it was often accepted as an Alvise Vivarini;[4] and more recently it has been called a Giovanni Bellini.[5]

VERSION: A damaged version with halo and palm, and a wreath in the hair, is in the Correr Museum at Venice; inscribed, .S.F.[6]

PROVENANCE: No. 2509 is very probably the Andrea Solari sold by Moreau to Comte Duchâtel, Paris, *ca.* 1856, and is certainly the picture seen in the Duchâtel Collection by Eastlake in 1860.[7] Presumably, Paris, Exhibition in 1866 (No. 4); Paris, Alsaciens-Lorrains Exhibition, 1874 (No. 3).[8] Bought by George Salting in 1889.[9] Exhibited at the New Gallery, 1894/5 (No. 142);[10] on loan to the National Gallery from 1895. Salting Bequest, 1910. Cleaned Pictures Exhibition at the National Gallery, 1947/8 (No. 29).

REPRODUCTION: *Illustrations, Italian Schools*, 1937, p. 388. *Plates, Earlier Italian Schools*, 1953, Vol. I, p. 213.

REFERENCES: (1) Berenson, *Lorenzo Lotto*, 1895, p. 110. (2) Pallucchini in *Arte Veneta*, 1951, p. 195, thinks that it is not by the same hand as No. 3121. (3) Crowe and Cavalcaselle, *Painting in North Italy*, 1871, II, pp. 59 and 98; ed. Borenius, II, 1912, pp. 382 and 433. (4) Cf. Berenson, *Venetian Painters*, 1894, 1895, 1897. See also especially Berenson, *Lorenzo Lotto*, 1895, pp. 110/1. Berenson says that the only alternative attribution would be to Jacopo de' Barbari; but this could not be accepted. (5) Gronau, Klassiker der Kunst *Bellini*, 1930, p. 122; Berenson, 1957 Lists (with a question mark). L. Dussler, *Giovanni Bellini*, 1935, pp. 99 f., inclines to accept the attribution to Giovanni Bellini. See also C. H. Collins Baker in *The Burlington Magazine*, Vol. L (1927), pp. 23 ff., who holds that Nos. 2509 and 3121 are not by the same hand. (6) Reproduced since cleaning in the *Bollettino d'Arte*, 1952, p. 261, with note; Correr Catalogue, 1957, pp. 51 f., where it is claimed to be by a different hand from No. 2509. Berenson, 1957 Lists, as Giovanni Bellini (?). (7) Eastlake's note-books, 1856 and 1860. See also the engraving in the *Gazette des Beaux-Arts*, 1862, I,

p. 9. (8) As Antonello. (9) Salting MSS. It seems to have come on to the market by 1887. In a letter from Layard to Morelli, 19 March, 1887 (British Museum, Add MS. 38968, Layard Papers, Vol. XXXVIII), Layard says that a little head had been offered to the National Gallery, ascribed to Antonello, but in Layard's opinion by the same hand as No. 3121 below; formerly belonging to 'un Duc Français', it had been sold when Layard wrote, to an unknown purchaser. The compiler has not found in the National Gallery papers anything concerning this incident; but it appears quite likely that No. 2509 is referred to. (10) As Antonello.

3121 PORTRAIT OF A MAN

Reverse: in gold on a black ground, two crossed sprays of myrtle, tied with a knot, and the inscription FELICES TER ET AMPLIVS / QVOS / IRRVPTA TENET COPVLA.

Wood, painted surface, $10\frac{1}{4} \times 7\frac{1}{2}$ (0·26 × 0·19); painted up to the edges at the sides. The reverse was originally of the same dimensions, but an inch or so is now covered round the edges, where the panel has been strengthened; the paint here was probably plain.

The flesh is not free from damage, especially to the left, but the original character is well preserved.

The inscription is from Horace, *Odes*, Book I, No. XIII, lines 17/8.

The attribution to Jacometto is due to J. Wilde (oral), on comparison with the Liechtenstein portraits mentioned in the biography above. It seems convincing. As some confirmation of his stylistic attribution, Wilde mentions that the technique of the reverse is very similar here and in the Liechtenstein pictures.

Former attributions were to Carpaccio or Antonello,[1] Alvise Vivarini,[2] and Giovanni Bellini (?)[3]; these are for the compiler all unsatisfactory. Berenson in 1895 claimed that No. 3121 is by the same hand as No. 2509 above; in the compiler's view, this is certainly right.[4]

PROVENANCE: Bought in 1871[5] from the Manfrin Collection, Venice, by Sir A. H. Layard.[6] Layard Bequest, 1916.[7]

REPRODUCTIONS: *Illustrations, Italian Schools*, 1937, p. 388 (front). *Plates, Earlier Italian Schools*, 1953, Vol. I, p. 214 (front). The reverse is reproduced in *Paintings and Drawings on the Backs of National Gallery Pictures*, 1946, Plate 35.

REFERENCES: (1) Layard MSS. in the National Gallery. (2) First by Morelli; letter to Layard, 25 December, 1871 (British Museum, Add. MS. 38963, Layard Papers, Vol. XXXIII). This attribution was accepted for a time by Berenson; *Venetian Painters*, 1894, 1895, 1897, and *Lorenzo Lotto*, 1895, pp. 108 ff. This is also the view of Pallucchini in *Arte Veneta*, 1951, p. 195 and of C. Gilbert in *Scritti in Onore di Lionello Venturi*, 1956, Vol. I, p. 282. (3) Berenson's Lists, 1957. (4) Berenson, *Lorenzo Lotto*, 1895, p. 110. (5) See the references in notes 2 and 6. (6) Layard MSS. in the National Gallery. The provenance is there stated; also in a letter from Layard to Lady Eastlake, 7 January, 1872 (British Museum, Add. MS. 38972, Layard Papers, Vol. XLII). Confirmation can be found in Crowe and Cavalcaselle, *Painting in North Italy*, 1871, I, p. 213, and ed. Borenius, I, 1912, p. 214 (picture in the Manfrin Collection, called Carpaccio, and ascribed by Crowe and Cavalcaselle to the school of Bernardino of Milan). It is true that Crowe and Cavalcaselle themselves give just the number, 139, of the Manfrin Collection; the identifying description (presumably from some Manfrin Catalogue) is added by Borenius. As a matter of fact, No. 3121 is listed in the Manfrin Catalogue of 1872 (although by then it had been sold); the catalogue gives the identifying description, but the number is 159, not 139. No. 3121 is probably No. 40 of the 1856 Manfrin Catalogue, *Testa*, Vettore Carpaccio, Tavola, 0·27 × 0·22 (same size as in the 1872 Catalogue); otherwise it may be thought to be No. 353, *Ritratto*, Incerta, Tavola, 0·24 × 0·16. The Manfrin Collection was formed, at least in part, by Conte Girolamo Manfrin, who died in 1801 according to *Il Forestiere Istruito...della Città di Venezia*, 1822, p. 295. According to the catalogue of the À. M. Plattis Sale, Paris, 13/4 May, 1870, the collection was formed *ca.* 1748 (perhaps meaning from that date onwards) and in 1848 was divided between the Marquise Bortolina Plattis veuve du Baron Sardagna and the Marquis Antonio Maria Plattis. According to the Manfrin Sale Catalogue of 1897, the collection was divided in 1849 between the Marchese Antonio Plattis and the Marchesa Bortolina Plattis nei Sardagna; her part, or some of it, remained in the Palazzo Manfrin until 1897. A. Venturi in *L'Arte*, 1912, p. 456, says that No. 3121 (the identity is quite clear) was bought in 1871 at the Monte de' pegni at Rome by Morelli, from whom Layard had it; but this is a mistake. No. 3121 (under the name of Vivarini) was indeed being looked after by Morelli during its restoration in Italy at this time. As for what Morelli bought, he wrote to Layard on 30 November, 1870 'per lei tengo un piccolo e grazioso busto di guerriero di marmo, di scuola lombarda.' The passage in its context rather implies that this had been acquired by Morelli at the Monte de' pegni. So Layard understood; and Morelli wrote on 5 March, 1871 (postscript dated the 7th), that it was a 'busto di marmo (non quadro),' not from the Monte de' pegni, but from the Pecennardi (*sic*) Collection at Cremona. See letters from Morelli to Layard, British Museum, Add. MS. 38963, Layard Papers, Vol. XXXIII. (7) For the history of the Layard Collection, see Appendix IV.

JACOPO DI CIONE
active 1365–1398

Also called *Robiccia*. Florentine School; a brother of Orcagna's. He is not very clearly documented as from 1368 completing an altarpiece dedicated to S. Matthew in the Uffizi (ordered of Orcagna in 1367), and as completing in 1373 a *Coronation of the Virgin* for the Florentine Mint, now in the Academy at Florence (ordered in 1372). He is documented also as collaborating in a several times restored fresco of *The Annunciation* at Volterra; but Offner rejects his participation in this work. In view of various difficulties concerning him, the pictures in the National Gallery often ascribed to him are classed in this catalogue as in the style of Orcagna.

Literature: The article in Thieme-Becker is under the name Orcagna. See also R. Offner in *The Burlington Magazine*, Vol. LXIII (1933), p. 84.

See Style of ANDREA DI CIONE, called ORCAGNA, Nos. 569–578, No. 1468

JUSTUS OF PADUA *See* GIUSTO DE' MENABUOI

LEONARDO da Vinci
1452–1519

At Florence from youth until *ca.* 1482; then at Milan until 1499 or possibly 1500. Thereafter chiefly at Florence until 1506; then chiefly at Milan again until 1513. 1513/6, at Rome and elsewhere in Italy; 1517, at le Clos-Lucé (Cloux), Amboise, where he died.

Leonardo had varied talents. He was a sculptor, although little if any of his work in sculpture survives. He paid some attention to architecture, and a great deal to engineering and the natural sciences. He is recorded to have been a good musician.

According to Vasari, Leonardo was a pupil of Verrocchio, in whose house he was certainly living in 1476. The pictorial work of Verrocchio is a subject by no means clear; stylistic judgment, nevertheless, confirms the tradition that Leonardo painted an angel in a *Baptism* ascribed to Verrocchio, in the Uffizi at Florence.

Pictures painted by Leonardo's own hand are few. There exist, on the other hand, many authentic drawings, mostly at Windsor.

1093 'THE VIRGIN OF THE ROCKS' (CENTRAL PICTURE FROM AN ALTARPIECE)

The Virgin stretches out her hand above the Infant Christ, Who, supported by an angel, is blessing S. John the Baptist. S. John, protected by the Virgin, is shown with a cross and holding a scroll inscribed, ECCE A/GNIVS.

Wood, rounded top, painted surface, $74\frac{5}{8} \times 47\frac{1}{4}$ (1·895 × 1·20). The paint continues to the edges top and bottom, but there is no reason to suppose that the picture has been cut there; on the contrary, indented lines in the painted surface at the bottom and round the arch at the top suggest that the height intended to be visible was only $73\frac{1}{2}$ (1·865). On each side, the spring of the arch is marked by a deep horizontal scratch, length about $\frac{3}{4}$ in. (2 cm.); for the whole straight part of the panel below these scratches, a strip about $\frac{3}{4}$ in. wide on each side is unprimed and unpainted, so that the width of the painted surface here is only $45\frac{3}{4}$ (1·16).[1]

No. 1093 was cleaned in 1948/9. A good deal of later paint was removed; and some of the forms are now different from what is seen in reproductions made before, e.g. the fingers of the Virgin's left hand and the line of her left shoulder,[2] the Child's left arm near the elbow, the hair of the Child.

The picture is in good condition for a work of its size and date. The chief damage is in the dark part of the angel's dress, where a considerable amount of paint has flaked away in the past. The Virgin's right hand (except for part of the thumb) is not authentic; but the evidence available concerning Leonardo's work underneath was too slight to justify cleaning away the overpainting. It is not certain if the haloes and the cross of S. John are contemporary. There is a damage above S. John's right eye. The picture is worn to a different extent in different places; thus, the patterning on the Virgin's left sleeve is much worn, the face of the Virgin a little, the flesh of S. John hardly at all. The paint on the Child's head is very thin, but the weak appearance there is due partly to *pentimenti*, described below. There are some sizeable cracks in the paint, e.g. in the Virgin's dress, in S. John's hands and in the foliage top left.

The picture is unfinished, notably in the Child's right hand; also, among other places, the Child's back, both hands of the angel, the right wing of the angel and a few places in the rocks.

It contains many *pentimenti*. The most important is in the head of the Child. Originally this was turned slightly upwards; also more towards the spectator, though less so than the head of the angel.[3] There are others in the lines of Christ's body; one is prominent in his right foot. Among further *pentimenti*, it may be mentioned that there were at least two previous attempts at S. John's head, and the ball of the thumb of the Virgin's outstretched left hand shows an obvious correction.

Finger-marks in the paint are visible, especially in much of the flesh.[4]

For the commentary, etc., see under No. 1662 below.

Associate of LEONARDO da Vinci (Ambrogio or Evangelista Preda)

1661   AN ANGEL IN GREEN WITH A VIELLE (LEFT WING TO NO. 1093 ABOVE)

Poplar,[5] painted surface, 46 × 24 (1·17 × 0·605). Painted up to the edges all round, and (to judge from the niche) cut at the top; the step at the bottom is somewhat less deep than in the case of No. 1662 below. Down the left-hand side, and included in the above measurements, there is an addition of 3 in. (7½ cm.), also of poplar.[5]

The general state is satisfactory; but the modelling of the face is slightly disturbed by cracks and some repaint. The background down both sides has been much repainted.

For the commentary, etc., see under No. 1662 below.

Associate of LEONARDO da Vinci (Ambrogio or Evangelista Preda)

1662   AN ANGEL IN RED WITH A LUTE (RIGHT WING TO NO. 1093 ABOVE)

Poplar,[5] painted surface, 46¾ × 24 (1·185 × 0·605). Painted up to the edges all round, and (like No. 1661 above) presumably cut at the top. A piece ¾ in. (2 cm.) wide at the top, 1¼ in. (3 cm.) at the bottom, included in the above measurements, has been added on the left-hand side.

In better condition than its pendant. Damages in the red dress are of little importance.

X-Ray photographs[3] seem to show that the chin was once about $\frac{1}{4}$ in. higher up, and that the nose was once shorter; but since it seems clear that the eye has not been moved, these were probably changes in the proportions but not in the pose of the face. The original space allowed for the hair left the shoulder visible where it was joined by the collar; when the hair was extended, it at one time covered more of the neck than at present—as indeed can be seen on the surface. There are also some alterations in the collar. The right arm once descended more steeply from the shoulder; this was because the lute was once some 3 in. to the right, and 1 in. lower down than at present. It is not clear how the right hand was shown.

These three pictures, Nos. 1093, 1661 and 1662, come from the altarpiece of the chapel of the Confraternity of the Immaculate Conception in S. Francesco Grande at Milan.

The documentary evidence concerning this altarpiece is long and complicated.[6] The order here followed is: the founding of the Confraternity's chapel; the commission for the altarpiece, given in 1480 to Giacomo del Maino; the commission to complete the altarpiece and paint three pictures for it, given in 1483 to Leonardo da Vinci, Evangelista Preda and Giovanni Ambrogio Preda; the settlement in 1506 of a dispute concerning the altarpiece; further information from appeals made by the artists in the interval 1483–1506; and discussion of an obscurity concerning the side pictures. After this summary of the documentary evidence, there will follow some comments on the hypothesis that No. 1093 is not the picture commissioned in 1483 by the Confraternity. Lastly, some remarks on style and iconography.

In 1475 Fra Stefano da Oleggio delivered some sermons in S. Francesco Grande at Milan, in the course of which he proposed that a Chapel dedicated to the Immaculate Conception should be built, and that a Confraternity of the Conception should be formed. The legal status of the Confraternity with respect to S. Francesco Grande was defined on 1 June, 1478; and on 8 May, 1479, they commissioned Francesco Zavattari and Giorgio della Chiesa to paint the vaulting of the Chapel.

On 8 April, 1480, the Confraternity commissioned Giacomo del Maino to make the ancona or altarpiece. This was to be according to designs to be given to him by the prior of the Confraternity and two others. Intaglio (meaning wood carving) is referred to in the contract. There is no mention of any gilding or colouring of the carvings; there is further no mention of any pictures to be done, and it seems to the compiler not certain that any were then intended.[7] The ancona was to be ready by the Feast of S. Michael (29 September), 1480. This, however, seems not to have been achieved; a dispute arose between Giacomo del Maino and the Confraternity, and the text of a decision on the matter, dated 7 August, 1482, has been preserved. The Confraternity were to pay a certain sum to Giacomo del Maino in final settlement for the work he had done; Giacomo del Maino was obliged to provide an 'absides' (shutter?) to be hinged (?) in front of the image of the Virgin on the ancona.[8]

Whatever Giacomo del Maino may have contracted to do in 1480, it is certain that the ancona as delivered by him was not in a finished state; for on 25 April, 1483, Leonardo da Vinci, Evangelista Preda and Giovanni Ambrogio Preda[9] were commissioned to do work on what was undoubtedly the same ancona. A list of the work these three were to do is included in the contract.

The image of the Virgin, mentioned in the document of 1482, seems certainly the same as *la nostra dona nel mezo*, etc., in the list of 1483; this was to be gilded and coloured by Leonardo and the Preda brothers. According to the text of 1483, it seems to have represented the Immaculate Conception, with God the Father, seraphim and angels. It seems to have been the centre of the main tier of the altarpiece. For it is the first item on the list; its presumed subject and position would suit both the title of the Confraternity and the heading of the list (*lancona dela conceptione*); and Giacomo del Maino's shutter (?) would most naturally have been for the principal compartment of the whole altarpiece.[10]

The list goes on to specify the execution of two groups of four angels, in one case singing, in the other making music, for which the spaces were still blank. Probably they were to be on each side of the central relief; or just possibly they were missing parts of the central relief itself. It seems in any case certain from the text that they were to be carvings. This is deduced partly from the position of the passage concerning them in the document; also because there is no reference to these angels being *dipinti in piano* (an expression used in this contract to specify pictures), or even specifically to their being coloured at all.[11]

Various other figures and ornaments already carved were to be gilt or coloured by Leonardo and the Preda brothers. It is not possible to understand the details, since the work is not known to exist.[12] In certain cases, the carvings were to be altered where they were not satisfactory.[13]

Among all this woodwork, three pictures were to be inserted. They are referred to in a single sentence, which has often wrongly been supposed to apply to the central picture alone. The part that does apply to the central picture (*la tauolla de mezo*) specifies the Virgin and Child with 'the' angels; it is not necessary here to quote the original text, since the words are clear, but what significance should be attached to them will receive some comment in note 17. The part referring to the side pictures is obscure, and will be the subject of comment later on in the text.

These pictures, if it is true that a relief of the *Immaculate Conception* was in the middle of the main tier of the altarpiece, must have been for an upper tier.[14] It is in any case probable that Giacomo del Maino had left certain spaces in his frame, which in 1483 would have been considered suitable for the insertion of pictures.

The payment for all the work on the altarpiece was to be 800 lire imperiali, and whatever more was recommended after completion by Agostino de' Ferrari (a friar of S. Francesco Grande) and two members of the Confraternity to be elected for this purpose. A special condition concerned the possibility of Leonardo's leaving Milan; the text appears incapable of precise interpretation as it stands,[15] but it is clear that the Confraternity attached the greatest importance to Leonardo's presence. Leonardo and the Preda brothers were made jointly responsible for all the work on the altarpiece.

All the work was to be finished by the Feast of the Conception (8 December), 1483. It was not. The date of delivery is not known, and at an unknown date the parties entered into a dispute. The settlement of this dispute is dated 27 April, 1506.

What is stated to have happened since 1483 is as follows. The artists had received 830 lire imperiali (30 more than the 800 definitely promised in 1483), as a complete payment for the work; there is a glancing reference to what is explicitly known from other sources, that the artists did not consider this sum enough. The work had not been finished to time, and was still unfinished in 1506. Leonardo had left Milan several years before (actually, in 1499 or 1500); Evangelista Preda had died (another source indicates that he may have died in 1490).

It is clear that in 1506 the Confraternity considered the original contract still valid. Even the umpires were as had been specified in 1483, Fra Agostino de' Ferrari and two members of the Confraternity;[16] and there are many references to the terms of the contract of 1483, without any suggestion at all that any of these terms had been changed. In particular, it is recorded in 1506 that the work on the altarpiece was to be 'per modum et formam prout latius in instrumento superinde confecto continetur,' i.e. according to the list of work of 1483.

It is clear that, apart from questions of money, the main matter of dispute was the central picture; clearly not on account of some change in its subject, which is described in 1506 as the Virgin and Child with S. John the Baptist,[17] but because it was still unfinished, indeed apparently the only part of the altarpiece still unfinished.

In dealing with the dispute, the umpires of 1506 diligently examined the altarpiece, and consulted with the parties and with art experts. They decided that the central picture must be finished within two years by the hand of Leonardo, provided that Leonardo came to Milan within that period and not otherwise. As a final settlement for all claims (mentioned as an excess beyond their obligations of 1483), the Confraternity were to pay an extra 100 lire imperiali in 1507, and again the same sum in 1508.

Leonardo did come to Milan in the period specified; the extra money was paid in 1507 and presumably in 1508.[18]

Various documents from the interval between 1483 and 1506 have been preserved. They are of interest chiefly for the history of the dispute. They also offer confirmation of various facts already recorded; but only in a few points do they give new information of value for the history of the altarpiece. In an appeal, which is not dated, and where the addressee is not recorded,[19] Leonardo and Ambrogio Preda state that the central picture of the Virgin and Child had been painted by Leonardo; there is also a reference to the side pictures, which will be mentioned presently. An appeal by Ambrogio Preda to the King of France (who was also

Duke of Milan), with a date 9 March, 1503, that it should be attended to, contains nothing that need be recorded here; but according to a connected Milanese document of 23 June, 1503, the altarpiece had been delivered several years before.

It remains to consider the documentary evidence concerning the side pictures. The passage concerning them in the contract of 1483 is so constructed that the whole must be quoted, although only the latter part refers to the side pictures. Abbreviated forms, where expanded, are printed in italics. 'Item.la tauolla de mezo facta.depenta in piano. la nra dona.*con*lo suo fiollo./ eli angolli.facta aolio in tucta.*per*fetione. *con*qlli doy.(*pro* ?)fecti vano./ depenti piani.coli colori.fini come edicto de sop.' In English, the latter part of this sentence is as follows: 'with these' (angels) 'two . . . are to be painted flat' (i.e. pictures, not painted reliefs) 'with fine colours as said above' (in earlier parts of the document). The word omitted from the translation is not clear, and must be the subject of a note.[20]

Fortunately, there is a way of deciding what it was agreed that the artists should do. In their undated appeal, Leonardo and Ambrogio Preda state that they had contracted[21] to paint two large angels in oil. It has already been remarked that no major change from the contract was admitted to have taken place. If it must be a change from what is written in the contract to Nos. 1661/2, one may suppose that such a change followed by agreement, and that in their dispute the parties were in accord in not mentioning the change, or rather in saying or implying that there had not been one; it would be pleasant, if indeed a change is insisted on, that some more reasonable account than this of what happened should be proposed.

The two angels were delivered to the Confraternity some years before 1503. There is no suggestion that they were unfinished in 1506. It is clear from the undated appeal that they were not painted by Leonardo.

It is the genesis of the Confraternity's altarpiece that has been the subject of comment hitherto. In the compiler's opinion, the three pictures ordered of Leonardo and the Preda brothers in 1483 are identical with Nos. 1093, 1661 and 1662 of the National Gallery. There exist, indeed, numerous records of pictures in the Confraternity's chapel, that are certainly the same as Nos. 1093, 1661 and 1662; these records (see below, under Provenance) go back to the sixteenth century.

In the case of No. 1093, nevertheless, an odd circumstance has caused various writers to question the identity. A variant of the composition, acceptable as by Leonardo, and earlier in style than No. 1093, is in the Louvre.[22] The origin of the Louvre picture is not known.[23] It has often been suggested that the Louvre picture is the one commissioned by the Confraternity in 1483, and that at some time No. 1093 was substituted for it in the Confraternity's altarpiece.

Three further points have been put to the compiler, in favour of the idea that somehow or other a substitution did take place. (1) If No. 1093 was ordered in 1483, the Louvre picture, which is earlier in style, already existed then. The Confraternity's frame also existed, independently.

How did it happen that Leonardo had a composition available, that fitted an independently existing frame? But coincidences do occur; this one may seem less striking, when it is remembered that the size and shape of the picture are fairly common;[24] and the compiler cannot exclude the possibility that the frame was modified.[25] (2) It is claimed that the inexact indication of the picture's subject in the contract of 1483 (see note 17) is more difficult to justify if the composition was already in existence. This seems correct. (3) 1483 has been claimed, on stylistic grounds, to be too early a date for No. 1093; the compiler feels forced to answer that, in his view, 1483 seems too late for the style of the picture in the Louvre.

The compiler cannot concede that these arguments, nor even the existence in the National Gallery and the Louvre of two similar pictures by Leonardo, make a substitution probable. It remains to see if such a thing is possible.

It is possible that in 1483 Leonardo began to paint the picture now in the Louvre for the Confraternity, but did not deliver it to them, and sold it to someone else; and then painted No. 1093 for the Confraternity. This hypothesis raises considerable difficulties.[26] It is not necessary here to assess how far it is likely to be true, since it hardly affects the status of No. 1093; all the documents would still apply to No. 1093, the only change being in the date at which it was begun.[27]

It is in the compiler's view impossible that substitution of a picture already delivered took place between 1483 and 1506. It is true that, in their appeals, the artists pleaded that Leonardo's Madonna should be returned to them; but Leonardo's Madonna, so far as he can see, could not possibly have been returned to them.

It is possible that a substitution took place after 1506 (or preferably 1508);[28] but the objections to this theory are very strong. (1) In 1506, not only Ambrogio Preda, but also several art experts examined the Confraternity's picture, which according to this theory was then the Louvre version; sometime later, the picture now in the National Gallery would have been put up in the Confraternity's altarpiece. How is it that no tradition concerning this exchange has survived?[29] (2) According to this theory, the picture now in the Louvre must contain some parts that were not finished in 1506. Maybe the present condition of that picture makes it impossible to see if this could be accepted as true; it is, on the other hand, easy to see that No. 1093 contains some parts not finished now. (3) The style of the green angel (No. 1661) seems to the compiler to be imitated in part from that of No. 1093,[30] certainly not from the version in the Louvre; how could this have happened, if the theory is true?

In the above discussion of hypotheses concerning substitution, it has been necessary to make some references to the style of the pictures. On stylistic grounds, the compiler accepts No. 1093 as being by Leonardo; many critics have denied this.[31] Nos. 1661 and 1662 are not by Leonardo. No. 1662 is not Leonardesque, parts of No. 1661 are Leonardesque; and the pictures are peculiar in being bad pendants, and in one being partly copied from the other.[32] Presumably they are by Evangelista and Ambrogio Preda, or one of them at different dates. The dates of these pictures are indeed not accurately established; nor is the date of No. 1093.[33]

The subject represented in No. 1093 has been reserved for discussion last. What seem certainly wrong deductions about this have been made by several writers, including the compiler.[34] If, as is claimed above, the central relief of the altarpiece represented *The Immaculate Conception*, that cannot be the subject of the central picture, whether it was in the main tier or an upper tier. The subject of No. 1093 is *The Virgin and Child with S. John and an Angel in a Landscape.* The peculiar setting has caused various attempts to link it with the Bible or with Christian legends;[35] but nothing clearly suitable to the picture has been found. It must not be forgotten that other pictures show sacred figures in landscapes with pierced rocks.[36] It seems most likely that Leonardo's curious mind led him to develop a theme already traditional in an unusual way.[37]

The instrument held by the green angel (No. 1661) is known as a vielle, viol or fiedel; it has four strings and a bourdon string.[38]

DRAWINGS: The genesis of Leonardo's design for *The Virgin of the Rocks* may perhaps be traced in a drawing at New York;[39] but a less indirect development from the various designs on this sheet is found in a composition known in several versions.[40]

A sheet of drawings, acceptable as by Leonardo, and certainly for the most part connected with the Louvre or National Gallery versions of *The Virgin of the Rocks*, was until recently bound as ff. 253 and 256 of the Arundel Codex, in the Department of MSS. at the British Museum. Many of these drawings are barely visible by ordinary light.[41]

A drawing in the Louvre has sometimes been thought to be by Leonardo, and may be thought to be for the head of S. John.[42]

A *Female Head* at Turin, clearly by Leonardo, is usually claimed to be for the head of the angel in the Louvre picture.[43] A drapery study at Windsor, clearly by Leonardo, has been claimed to be for the angel in No. 1093.[44] A bust of an infant at Windsor, acceptable as by Leonardo, has some similarity to the Christ, in the London version rather than in the Paris version; it probably has no connection.[45]

Various other drawings have been associated with one or other of the versions; many of them are indeed connected, but are not acceptable as by Leonardo, and are outside the scope of the present entry.[46]

VERSIONS AND COPIES, ETC.: A varying version, earlier in style than No. 1093, is in the Louvre; it has been referred to in the commentary above.

Many copies are known, both of the Louvre version and of No. 1093; some are Milanese work of the sixteenth century, some are later. It appears that nothing definite can be deduced from the existence or nature of these copies concerning the origin of No. 1093 and the Louvre picture. Lists of these copies, long but not complete, have been published by Malaguzzi Valeri;[47] one of the pictures to be added to these lists is No. 1861 below. The copy by Vespino at the Ambrosiana in Milan has been referred to in note 2. Perhaps a special mention should be made of an embroidery after the Louvre version in the Museo del Santuario di S. Maria sopra Varese.[48]

Partial derivations from Leonardo's design are also frequent. Since Leonardo tended to repeat his motives (thus, the Virgin's outstretched left hand in No. 1093 recurs rather similar in the *Madonna with the Yarn Winder*),[49] a derivation precisely from the *Virgin of the Rocks* is not always certain. The matter is too complicated for the present entry. It must suffice to list some pictures more or less connected: two versions of a *Virgin and Child with S. John* by Bernardino de' Conti (Virgin partly, and rocks);[50] Boltraffio's altarpiece from Lodi, now at Budapest (Christ and rocks);[51] a tondo reproduced by Suida (Christ and S. John);[52] a picture in the Seminario at Venice (Christ);[53] and the Elton Hall Cesare da Sesto (S. John).[54] The head of the Virgin in a picture at Zürich has a general similarity to the head of the Virgin in No. 1093.[55] A figure occurring twice in the border of Fra Antonio da Monza's miniature of *Pentecost* at Vienna seems to be derived from the S. John.[56] A picture at Nancy by Perugino is derived from the *Virgin of the Rocks*, or perhaps from some similar composition.[57] A picture even more curiously pillaged from Leonardo appeared as a Sodoma in the Somzée Sale, Brussels, 24 sqq. May, 1904 (lot 449).[58]

A special note may be made for Luini; is it possible that, when he came under Leonardo's influence, he was particularly affected by No. 1093? What seems to be only a copy of No. 1093 at Affori is ascribed to Luini's own hand by Suida.[59] In a *Holy Family* in the Prado, some elements seem to be derived from the *Virgin of the Rocks*.[60] A Luinesque design, known from versions in the Ambrosiana and elsewhere,[61] is partly derived from the *Virgin of the Rocks*; for a composition, inverted from these and considerably varied, see the entry for Luini, No. 3935 of this catalogue.

A bas-relief, derived with variations from No. 1093, is in the Castello Sforzesco at Milan.[62]

No derivations seem to be known of the *Angels*, Nos. 1661, 1662.[63]

PROVENANCE:[64] As explained above, No. 1093 (the compiler does not doubt its identity) and Nos. 1661 and 1662 were ordered in 1483, with a dispute lasting until 1508, as part of the altarpiece of the chapel of the Immaculate Conception in S. Francesco Grande, Milan. An inscription connected with the Plague, with a date of 1576 and mentioning incidentally a date of 1524, seems to refer to this altarpiece.[65] The location of the chapel in the church was changed in 1576;[66] but it is not known that any alteration was then made to the altarpiece.[67] No. 1093 is recorded three times by Lomazzo, who had gone blind in 1571, in books printed in 1584 and 1590; twice the picture is misleadingly called by Lomazzo the *Conception*, the third of Lomazzo's descriptions is so detailed that one can feel sure that he was describing No. 1093, not the variant now in the Louvre.[68] Besta (*ca.* 1598) mentions No. 1093.[69] Borsieri (1619) mentions No. 1093, with wrong provenance.[70] Mazenta (*ca.* 1635) mentions all three pictures, apparently.[71] The Sant' Agostini mention all three pictures.[72] Torre (1672/4) mentions all three pictures, with the words 'entro vaga tauola' for the frame, and with a wrong provenance different from Borsieri's.[73] Scaramuccia (1674) mentions No. 1093.[74] Much of S. Francesco fell down in 1688, but little reconstruction was necessary for this chapel, and it is not known that any change was made to the altarpiece.[75] Paraini (1716)[76] and Latuada (1738)[77] mention all three pictures, with Torre's wrong provenance. Sormani (1752) mentions No. 1093.[78] At some time No. 1093 was removed from the church, Nos. 1661 and 1662 remaining behind with the rest of the altarpiece. It seems probable that this happened in 1781; 1781 is the year in which the Confraternity of the Conception was annexed to the Hospitals of S. Caterina alla Ruota and La Senavra,[79] and No. 1093 is known to have been sold by the Hospital of S. Caterina alla Ruota in 1785. The evidence, nevertheless, is not conclusively in favour of the year 1781 for the removal of No. 1093. Gerli[80] says apparently that No. 1093 had gone from the church. The date printed in Gerli's book is 1784; but it has been claimed that some copies were issued in 1774. This date of 1774, according to the evidence so far produced, seems rather fantastic;[81] but if it is true that Gerli in 1774 said that No. 1093 had left the church, then presumably it had. Bartoli (1776, but he was possibly working on out-of-date information) apparently mentions all three pictures in S. Francesco Grande.[82] An inventory of 1781 mentions what seems undoubtedly to be the altarpiece, without specific reference to No. 1093 or to Nos. 1661 and 1662; since the valuation given for the altarpiece was 300 lire, and No. 1093 alone was sold four years later for more than 5 times that amount, it seems likely that No. 1093 had already been detached from the altarpiece.[83] Chiusole (1782, but he may have been working on out-of-date information) mentions No. 1093 in the church (wrongly as the *Conception*).[84] An anonymous guide to Milan of 1783 (maybe again with out-of-date information) mentions all three pictures in the church.[85] Bianconi[86] (1787) records the altarpiece and Nos. 1661 and 1662 in the church, noting that No. 1093 had previously been removed to a Luogo Pio; Bianconi is a fairly careful writer, and it may be accepted that, in 1787 or not very long before 1787, Nos. 1661 and 1662 were still there. An inventory of 1798 seems to mention the altarpiece and Nos. 1661 and 1662 as still in the church; 1798 is the year in which S. Francesco Grande was secularized.[87]

Provenance of No. 1093. Whatever may be the exact year in which No. 1093 was removed from S. Francesco Grande to the Hospital of S. Caterina alla Ruota, it was sold by the latter institution in 1785 to Gavin Hamilton.[88] 'Mr. Hamilton, of Rome' (undoubtedly the same) brought it immediately to England, where it was seen on 24 December, 1785, obviously in London, by C. J. Greville (description and provenance given). C. J. Greville recorded on 1 February, 1786, that 'Mr. Hamilton has sold his fine picture' (obviously the same) 'to Lord Lansdowne.'[89] Seen and described in Lord Lansdowne's Collection at Shelburne (Lansdowne) House in 1802/3 by Goede.[90] Although faultily described, it is presumed to be identical with a picture in the Lansdowne Sale, 20 March, 1806 (lot 47);[91] also to be identical with a picture stated to have been bought before 1817 at a Lansdowne Sale by Hill, and sold by him a month after his purchase to Lord Suffolk.[92] Perhaps the picture lent by Lord Suffolk to the British Institution, 1818 (No. 3);[93] recorded in Lord Suffolk's Collection by Buchanan (1824).[94] Perhaps the first statement in print identifying the picture from S. Francesco at Milan with Lord Suffolk's is of 1843.[95] No. 1093 was lent by Lord Suffolk to the British Institution, 1851 (No. 41) and 1858 (No. 7), and to the R.A., 1870 (No. 6). Purchased from the Earl of Suffolk, 1880.

Provenance of Nos. 1661 and 1662. It has been mentioned above that these pictures were still in S. Francesco at Milan *ca.* 1787, and may still have been there in 1798, in which year the church was secularized. At some time they entered the Melzi d'Eril Collection at Milan; they may have been acquired by Conte Giacomo Melzi, who died in 1802. Recorded (with a provenance from S. Francesco) in a Melzi Catalogue, not dated, but of the early nineteenth century.[96] At the death of Count Giacomo, the Melzi Collection was divided between his nephews, Francesco (Duca di Lodi) and Luigi, and was later reunited in the possession of the latter's son, Giovanni Francesco. He died in 1832; in 1835 a division of the pictures was effected between his three children, Duca Lodovico Melzi, Don Giovanni Melzi and Donna Barbara, who married Duca Tommaso Gallarati Scotti.[97] On the death of Lodovico in 1886, the ducal title passed to his brother Giovanni, and it was from him that Nos. 1661 and 1662 were purchased in 1898. Exhibited at the R.A., *Leonardo de Vinci*, 1952 (Nos. 246, 248).

REPRODUCTIONS: *Illustrations, Italian Schools*, 1937, p. 183 (No. 1093, before cleaning), p. 290 (Nos. 1661, 1662). *Plates, Earlier Italian Schools*, 1953, Vol. II, pp. 215–218.

REFERENCES: (1) Measurements by Cecil Gould. (2) These parts now correspond much more closely than they did before with the copy of No. 1093 in the Ambrosiana at Milan. This copy, which seems to be fairly careful, is by Vespino, and is mentioned as his in Cardinal Federico Borromeo's original list of pictures (1618), *La Madonna grande di Leonardo copiata*, etc., with a size that corresponds (see *Guida Sommaria...della Biblioteca Ambrosiana*, 1907, pp. 59 and 136). (3) Visible only under the X-Ray; X-Rays of this region and some others were reproduced in a pamphlet on the picture, written by the compiler and published by the National Gallery in 1947. It is presumably a chance that one of the copies of the design shows the Child not in profile; the pose does not correspond precisely with the original pose of the Child in No. 1093. The copy is reproduced by F. Malaguzzi Valeri, *La Corte di Lodovico il Moro*, II, 1915, Fig. 463. X-Rays of the heads of Nos. 1661/2 are reproduced by Ian Rawlins, *From the National Gallery Laboratory*, 1940, Plates 31, 33. (4) See Sir Charles Holmes in *The Burlington Magazine*, Vol. XXXIX (1921), p. 107, and Alan Burroughs in *Art Studies*, VIII, 2, 1931, p. 68, note 1. (5) Letter from B. J. Rendle, of the Forest Products Research Laboratory, in the Gallery archives. (6) The texts of the documents concerning *The Virgin of the Rocks* may be consulted as follows. G. Biscaro in the *Archivio Storico Lombardo*, 1910, pp. 125 ff., for the texts before the contract of 1483 and for this contract (with a photographic reproduction of the list of work to be done, in the copy signed by the parties). L. Beltrami, *Documenti e Memorie riguardanti la Vita e le Opere di Leonardo da Vinci*, 1919, for the contract of 1483 (without the photographic reproduction); also for all the later documents up to 1508 (two appeals by the artists and connected document, settlement of 1506 and connected document, supplementary payments of 1507 and 1508), except for one brief sentence, which is printed by F. Malaguzzi Valeri, *La Corte di Lodovico il Moro*, II, 1915, p. 391. All the texts from 1483 to 1508 are also printed by Aldo de Rinaldis, *Storia dell' Opera Pittorica di Leonardo da Vinci*, 1926, pp. 67 ff. By the kindness of Prof. Costantino Baroni, the compiler has seen photographs of many of these documents; various corrections to the printed texts need to be made, but for the most part the corrections do not affect the discussion in the present entry. Most of the documents preserved are not the copies signed by the parties, but are notary's drafts or copies. An account of the documentary evidence, written by the compiler, was published by the National Gallery in 1947; it deals with certain aspects of the problem more fully than the present entry. Several corrections to what is there said have been made here. The compiler has been fortunate enough to discuss *The Virgin of the Rocks* with Cecil Gould, A. E. Popham and Johannes Wilde, whose comments have been most valuable; these scholars, nevertheless, are not to be held responsible for the views here put forward. Since the first edition of the present catalogue, a good deal has been published about No. 1093 and its variant in the Louvre, partly in interpretation of the documents, and the compiler finds it convenient to record straightaway some of these publications. H. Beenken in the *Festschrift für Hans Jantzen*, 1951, pp. 132 ff., takes up again the idea that Leonardo's original picture was ceded by the Confraternity following on an undated appeal by Leonardo and Ambrogio Preda, which he dates in the 1490's. This idea is supposed to be supported by the wording of an appeal of *ca.* 1503 made by Preda alone, but Beenken's interpretation of this is for the compiler manifestly wrong; the compiler considers that the return of the picture following on the undated appeal is entirely excluded. One may, nevertheless, admire Beenken's efforts to cut free from the tangle in which he entangles himself. According to him, the Confraternity disgorged Leonardo's picture in the 1490's and received a substitute, which substitute Preda was asking them to disgorge in 1503. Beenken suggests that Preda passed off the substitute picture as his own work, in order that the Confraternity might be less disinclined to let it go; but it had been left unfinished, so that a buyer cognizant of Leonardo's habits would think it was by Leonardo. According to Heydenreich (*Leonardo da Vinci*, English edition, 1954, p. 188), Beenken's interpretation is convincing. Giorgio Castelfranco in *Leonardo, Saggi e Ricerche*, 1954, pp. 451 ff., and in the large *Storia di Milano*, Vol. VIII, 1957, pp. 491/2, has taken up again the idea that a substitution occurred between Preda's appeal of *ca.* 1503 and the settlement of the dispute in 1506; this also is excluded. The idea is based on the facts that Leonardo's picture was delivered, but is first referred to as unfinished in the settlement of 1506. Yet the deduction that the picture referred to in 1506 was a different one is untenable; it is sufficient here to cite a passage in the settlement, that Leonardo had left Milan 'jam pluribus annis prox. preteritis non finitis dictis laborerijs'. Mirella Lev

D'Ancona in *The Iconography of the Immaculate Conception* (Monographs on Archaeology and Fine Arts sponsored by the Archaeological Institute of America and the College Art Association of America, No. VII, 1957) wrote at length about *The Virgin of the Rocks*, partly from the point of view of the iconography; much the same in *Arte Lombarda*, Vol. I, 1955, pp. 98 ff. It seems wild. A statement that may be new (pp. 64 and 78 of the English text) is that in No. 1093 the flowers under the Virgin's mantle are violets, lilies and roses; this is incorrect. Her publication in English was followed by correspondence in *The Burlington Magazine*, June 1958, p. 218; April 1959, pp. 149/50; and June 1959, p. 245, when it was stopped; something of what she there wrote will be considered later on in the present entry. The compiler has not found these writings of much service for the understanding of the problem; but he has endeavoured to sift them and, partly in connection with what remained, has made several corrections to his entry. He takes this occasion to recall that a search in the Milanese archives might produce new documents. **(7)** The existing documents do not make clear the appearance of the Confraternity's altarpiece as it eventually turned out; yet it may be thought that it would have been classed as an altarpiece of mixed pictures and carvings, rather than as a group of pictures in an elaborate frame, or a carved altarpiece with some pictures thrown in. So far as the compiler is aware, such mixed altarpieces are unusual in the Renaissance in Lombardy; the nearest he can cite are an altarpiece at Sernio, and one at Morbegno that surrounds a fresco (reproduced in the *Inventario degli Oggetti d'Arte d'Italia, Provincia di Sondrio*, 1938, pp. 257 and 189). It may be supposed that these are not fully comparable; and the compiler thinks that the point should be borne in mind, although it is by no means proved, that originally the Confraternity did not intend to have pictures in their altarpiece. **(8)** Biscaro, *loc. cit.*, p. 161, gives the text as follows: 'ita quod dictus magister Jacopus teneatur in dicto oppere tradere et consignare absidem illam que vadit ante imaginem beatissime virginis marie ad modum incastri (?) suis propriis expensis et que asides computetur in dicto precio'. Biscaro on p. 129 translates *absides* or *asides* as *tavola*, perhaps meaning shutter; the Morbegno altarpiece mentioned in the previous note did have shutters. The compiler remains uncertain if this is the correct meaning; one alternative, it seems, might be a canopy, to be fixed over the image. **(9)** The two Predas were actually half-brothers; they will, for convenience here, sometimes be referred to as the Preda brothers. **(10)** The compiler records what seems implied by the text; it should not be forgotten that the scale of Giacomo del Maino's carvings has not been established. It may be thought preferable to suppose a relief of the Immaculate Conception in the middle of an upper tier, in which case presumably the 'absides' was not a shutter; in the Morbegno altarpiece mentioned in note 7 the Assumption is at the top, and one of the dedications of the church is (and presumably already was) to the Assumption. **(11)** Mirella Levi D'Ancona in *The Burlington Magazine*, April 1959, p. 150, argues against this interpretation; but the compiler has not been able to grasp her meaning. **(12)** It is stated in *L'Arte*, 1954, pp. 77/8, that the frame is in the Sormani Collection at Milan; but this is incorrect (letter from G. A. Dell'Acqua in the Gallery archives). **(13)** *Et de reconzare lintagli che non stiano bene*. In the copy of the list of work to be done, signed by the contracting parties, this phrase is seen to have been added. **(14)** The pictures would clearly not have been on shutters in front of the wood carvings, nor presumably on the back of the altarpiece. Perhaps some confirmation of the position in an upper tier may be found in an inventory of 1798; see note 87. **(15)** The compiler in his pamphlet of 1947 endeavoured to make sense of the passage, by suggesting that the word *ancona* was used for the central picture and not for the whole altarpiece; he felt that this interpretation was justified by a phrase used in the settlement of 1506, *tabulam seu anconam*, where the words seemed to him to be used as being equivalent. Even if the compiler still maintained that the picture was the centre of the main tier, and not of an upper tier as he now inclines to believe, he would withdraw this suggestion; *ancona* is used normally in these documents as meaning the whole altarpiece, not a part. The compiler remarked in his pamphlet that, with *ancona* meaning the whole altarpiece, the passage does not make sense; this seems to him still true. (16) It may be remarked that this had been arrived at in a roundabout way. Both parties had appealed to the King of France; thereupon an arbiter, Bernardino de' Busti, had been appointed. No details are known concerning Bernardino de' Busti's intervention; but clearly he referred the parties back to the procedure laid down in the contract of 1483. (This Bernardino de' Busti is presumably the man who seems to have died in 1529; V. Forcella, *Iscrizioni delle Chiese...di Milano*, VIII, 1891, pp. 195/6). (17) In view of the references in 1506 to the contract of 1483, it may seem impossible to believe that the subject had been changed; but in that contract, the central picture was specified as to represent the Virgin and Child with 'the' angels. It seems that, in this very brief passage, a specific mention of S. John the Baptist was considered unnecessary. As will be explained presently, the compiler does not doubt that the picture referred to is identical with No. 1093. No. 1093 shows S. John the Baptist and one angel, for which the descriptions in 1483 and 1506 would both be incorrect; but the passage of 1483 is the more difficult to excuse. (18) The receipts of 1508 are not actually known to have been signed; the documents preserved are notary's drafts. (19) In his pamphlet, the compiler argued for a date 1504/6; this has not been found convincing. He made some modifications to his views in the first edition of this catalogue, and is willing now to go further. He thinks his suggestion that the appeal was addressed to Bernardino de' Busti is wrong, since the letter begins *Ill.mo et Ex.mo Signore*; this form seems to have been reserved for ruling princes (such as Lodovico il Moro), their near relatives, and apparently other people of prominent position (see what appear to be examples in Rosmini, *Dell'Istoria di Milano*, Vol. IV, 1820, pp. 381 ff. and Giovio, *Opera, Lettere*, Vol. I, 1956, No. 180 (p. 334) and Vol. II, 1958, Nos. 223 (p. 34) and 276 (p. 104)). It is probable that the form could have been used to the French Governor of Milan; the compiler has come across hardly any letters addressed to him, but the one in Beltrami, *Documenti*, No. 179, is suggestive of the form. It seems nevertheless unlikely that the appeal was sent to the Governor about 1502, as has sometimes been claimed. The arguments for its dating are, so far as the compiler is aware, by no means conclusive, and it seems to him unnecessary to record them here in detail; it must suffice that, on balance of probability, he now inclines to think that this appeal was addressed to Lodovico il Moro. Motta, who published it, dates it '1484–1494, non dopo forse nè prima di certo'. It is most probable that it is later than the death of Evangelista Preda, which took place probably *ca.* 1490; but there would not seem to be good reasons for assigning a particular year in the 1490's to it. This appeal is, in the compiler's view, clearly related to Ambrogio Preda's appeal of *ca.* 1503, and the idea that it was followed by the return of the picture to the artists seems impossible to bring into accord with the documents. (20) The compiler is advised that the abbreviation would naturally be taken for *pro* (this according to the list of work to be done signed by the contracting parties). The word has been supposed to be 'prophcts' (undefined); but, as indicated in the next paragraph of the text, angels and not prophets are stated to have been ordered in 1483. It may be pointed out that the abbreviations for *pro* and *per*, without being interchangeable, are often very like each other; unfortunately, while there are several examples of *per* in this document, there is no *pro* for comparison. In his pamphlet of 1947, and in the first edition of this catalogue, the compiler included some remarks that should have been phrased differently or omitted. One thing to add is that photographs of one of the drafts of the contract are available to the compiler; the abbreviations there have a somewhat different form from those in the list of work signed by the parties, and there is there a distinction, noticeably clearer than in the signed list, between the abbreviation of the disputed word and the examples of *per*. If it is insisted that 'prophets' is the reading, the later conduct of the parties seems peculiar, as is indicated in the continuation of the text above; further on in the text, peculiarities in Nos. 1661/2 are referred to, and it may be thought that these may somehow link up with peculiarities in the contract for the two pictures and in the parties' references (or lack of references) to the matter. The compiler cannot think of anything better than this to make the 'prophets' acceptable; and thinks his suggestion of 'perfecti' instead has much in its favour, even if this is held definitely to be different from what is written. The most obvious meaning for this word would be 'well painted': 'with these (angels), two (others) are to be well painted on a flat surface', etc. A demand in the contract that the side pictures should be well painted, but less well than the central panel (*in tucta. perfetione*), seems to the compiler unobjectionable. Alternatively, J. Wilde suggested that *perfecti* may mean 'at whole length' (cf. N. Zingarelli, *Vocabulario della Lingua Italiana*, 1936/7, pp. 1123 and 782). A statement on this problem was made by Mirella Levi D'Ancona in *The Burlington Magazine*, April 1959, p. 150. She applies the phrase with the 'prophets' to the central panel, which the compiler cannot conceive is right; her comments do not extend beyond the contract itself. She would have, thus limited, a good case for the reading 'prophets', if it might not be thought that she threw it away by her in-accuracies; but her statement that *profeti* is a noun and *perfecti* an adjective is correct. (**21**) It is true that in their appeal Leonardo and Ambrogio Preda do not cite the date of their contract; the student should verify for himself that the contract of 1483 is certainly referred to. (**22**) Reproduced in the Klassiker der Kunst *Leonardo*, 1931, p. 20, and frequently elsewhere. There is a long entry for it in *Hommage à Léonard*, Paris, 1952, pp. 7 ff. There are several differences in the design; in particular, the angel in the Louvre is pointing with his right hand at S. John the Baptist. Cecil Gould, who measured the two pictures within a few days of each other, gave the size of the Louvre picture as $77\frac{1}{2} \times 47$ ($1 \cdot 97 \times 1 \cdot 195$), excluding about $\frac{1}{4}$ in. of binding at the sides and bottom. Cecil Gould's measurements for No. 1093 have already been given. (**23**) First recorded as existing at Fontainebleau in 1625. (**24**) In the National Gallery, for instance, altarpieces by Bergognone (No. 298) and Lanino (No. 700) are of similar shape, and near in size. (**25**) See note 13. The compiler cannot exclude that changes in the shape of the frame may there be referred to, although he feels that this inter-pretation of the text is somewhat strained. (**26**) Leonardo's conduct would seem dishonest; and why is there nothing in the settlement of 1506 concerning this incident? (**27**) The status of the picture in the Louvre would be changed. But the problems concerning the Louvre picture, except where they directly affect No. 1093, are outside the scope of the present entry. (**28**) Such a substitution was proposed to the compiler in a form that maybe reduces its improbability to a minimum. In their undated appeal, Leonardo and Ambrogio Preda say that one way of satisfying them would be for the Confraternity to give back Leonardo's picture to them, and keep the rest of the ancona for the money already paid; they mention that other offers had been made for Leonardo's picture. They did not get it back; assume therefore that Leonardo painted a replica for one of the people who had wanted to buy the original. This purchaser (assumed to be owning No. 1093) and the Confraternity (assumed to be owning the picture now in the Louvre) might after 1506 or 1508 have exchanged pictures. This suggestion was put forward coupled with a dating of the undated appeal in the 1490's. In the absence of confirmatory evidence, the compiler does not think that this theory is likely to be accepted as true; but it would certainly settle one major difficulty in believing that a substitution took place after 1506, which is how the Confraternity could have managed to get a substitute picture then. (**29**) It is true that artistic records for Milan are rather scanty. But Lomazzo mentions No. 1093 three times, with no hint of an exchange of pictures. He was a Milanese writer, who published his books in 1584 and 1590, having gone blind in 1571; he was acquainted with Francesco Melzi (*Trattato dell'Arte de la Pittura*, 1584, p. 106), who is presumed to have known something of Leonardo's work both at Milan and in France. Admittedly, Borsieri and Torre make curious statements about the provenance (q.v.), but the compiler has been unable to use these for a substitution theory. (**30**) What dirt there is on No. 1661 probably makes it look more Leonardesque than the painter intended. (**31**) As indicated previously, the picture was freed from a good deal of disfiguring repaint in 1948/9. On the whole, critics have tended to reject the authenticity of No. 1093, although recently there has been a movement in its favour. Much on the attribution can be found in the Leonardo bibliography by E. Verga, 1931 (analytical index for *The Virgin of the Rocks* by Heydenreich in the *Zeitschrift für Kunstwissenschaft*, 1932, p. 71). The question of how far Leonardo received studio assistance in the execution of No. 1093 is likely to have different answers from different writers. Sir Kenneth Clark (*Leonardo da Vinci*, 1958) well says on p. 51 that Leonardo's theories of painting led him away from our affections; on pp. 128/9 he more fully expresses his view on Leonardo's considerable share in the execution of No. 1093. The compiler, with the opinion constantly in his mind that Leonardo disliked the commission, goes further than Clark, and thinks that studio intervention was limited to minor parts, e.g. S. John's cross and the haloes (if these are contemporary), and possibly (but not certainly) some of the flowers and rocks. It is worth recording that some of the pentimenti would be surprisingly elaborate for a studio work, especially in a studio that was probably not one of the efficient factories of the time. (32) The compiler wrote at more length on this in his pamphlet of 1947. (33) With regard to the dating of No. 1093, the compiler will here make only the briefest comments. One is that the dating of Leonardo's works in general is far from fixed. Secondly, if it is admitted that No. 1093 is the picture ordered in 1483, it seems certain from the story of the dispute that not everything of what is now seen was painted in that year. With regard to the parts unfinished in 1506, these would naturally include the parts unfinished now. The compiler is unable to identify any further parts in No. 1093 as clearly painted between 1506 and 1508; it is possible that Leonardo may have done little work for the Confraternity at this time, although he (or at any rate his partner) accepted money from them. (34) In the compiler's pamphlet, 1947, pp. 7/8. (35) It seems useless to list the variations; but it may be noticed that Dr. R. Eisler in *The Burlington Magazine*, Vol. XC (1948), p. 239, produced a new interpretation, for which he cited no authority. D. W. Robertson in *Renaissance News*, Vol. VII, 1954, pp. 92 ff., refers to the *Song of Songs*, II, 3/4, but the compiler does not find this convincing. (36) E.g. Pintoricchio several times; for prominent rocks, Mantegna's *Madonna of the Quarries*. It seems clear to the compiler that there is nothing in the subject of No. 1093 that demands explanation by means of some Christian legend. (The association of the little S. John with the Virgin and Child was in 1483 a traditional theme; it is true that it seems then to have been quite a recent tradition, as the compiler explained in his pamphlet.) (37) Cf. Sir Charles Holmes, *The National Gallery, Italian Schools*, 1923, pp. 71 ff. (38) Letter from W. F. H. Blandford in the Gallery archives. (39) A. E. Popham, *The Drawings of Leonardo da Vinci*, 1946, pp. 69/70 and No. 159, reproduced. Cf. also Popham, No. 160. (40) Cf. Borenius in *The Burlington Magazine*, Vol. LVI (1930), pp. 142 ff. (41) Published by Popham in *The Burlington Magazine*, 1952, pp. 127 ff., with full discussion; he thinks that they were made for the Louvre picture. He further suggests that a hand in a sheet of various studies at Windsor, comparable in style, may be connected with the *Virgin of the Rocks*. (42) Berenson, *Drawings of the Florentine Painters*, 1938, No. 1067 and Fig. 487. Seidlitz in *L'Arte*, 1907, p. 325, calls the drawing Preda. Popham, in *The Burlington Magazine*, 1952, p. 128, thinks that it is not an original Leonardo. Suida, *Leonardo und sein Kreis*, 1929, p. 130, follows Calvi in connecting it with the Academy Cartoon (Popham, Nos. 176–180, reproduced). As Popham pointed out to the compiler, a copy of this drawing, with a female head above, is at Chatsworth, ascribed to Boltraffio; reproduced by E. Müntz, *Leonardo da Vinci*, 1898, Vol. I, Plate VI. (43) Popham, *op. cit.*, p. 69 and No. 157, reproduced. (It should be mentioned that Popham does not hold to the view expressed on p. 69, that the picture ordered of Leonardo in 1483 is *The Virgin of the Rocks* in the Louvre). (44) Popham, *op. cit.*, p. 69 and No. 158, reproduced. (Popham is now disinclined to believe that this drawing is in any way connected with *The Virgin of the Rocks*.) (45) Popham, *op. cit.*, pp. 71/2 and No. 171A, reproduced. (46) It is sufficient here to refer to Seymour de Ricci's Catalogue of the Louvre, *Ecoles Etrangères, Italie et Espagne*, 1913, pp.

169 f.; Malaguzzi Valeri, *La Corte di Lodovico il Moro*, II, 1915, pp. 414 ff.; E. Müntz, *Leonardo da Vinci*, 1898, esp. Ch. VI. (**47**) F. Malaguzzi Valeri in *Pagine d'Arte*, 30 January, 1914, p. 27, and his *La Corte di Lodovico il Moro*, II, 1915, pp. 416 ff. (**48**) See Costantino del-Frate, *S. Maria sopra Varese*, 1933, pp. 172 ff. and Plate CXXXIV. The date of the embroidery is disputed. (**49**) Three versions are reproduced in the Klassiker der Kunst *Leonardo*, 1931, Plates 65–67 (two with the right hand outstretched, one inverted with the left hand outstretched). (**50**) Both are reproduced in the large volume, *Leonardo da Vinci*, published in connection with the Leonardo Exhibition at Milan, 1939, p. 50. There is a clearer reproduction of the version in the Brera in the Klassiker der Kunst *Leonardo*, 1931, Plate 83. (**51**) Suida, *Leonardo und sein Kreis*, 1929, Fig. 203. (**52**) Suida, *op. cit.*, Fig. 65. (**53**) Reproduced by V. Moschini, *La Raccolta del Seminario di Venezia*, 1940, p. 33. Another version is reproduced in *The Burlington Magazine*, Vol. L (1927), p. 182. (**54**) Suida, *op. cit.*, Fig. 290. The connection with the *Virgin of the Rocks* was noted by Fumagalli, *Scuola di Leonardo*, 1811, apropos of a copy of this design in the Brera (*Catalogo*, 1908, No. 272). (**55**) Suida, *op. cit.*, Fig. 54; on pp. 251/2, Suida claims that the signature is that of Fernando de Llanos, not that of Francesco Napoletano. Sir Kenneth Clark, *Leonardo da Vinci*, 1958, p. 129, claims that there is a stylistic connection with No. 1093, but does not definitely couple the two pictures together. (**56**) Paolo d'Ancona, *La Miniature Italienne du Xe. au XVIe. Siècle*, 1925, Plate L. This miniature is datable between 1492 and 1503. (**57**) Klassiker der Kunst *Perugino*, 1914, Plate 153. (**58**) Reproduced in the sale catalogue. (**59**) Suida, *op. cit.*, p. 235. Reproduced in the *Rassegna d'Arte*, 1913, p. 31, and the large volume, *Leonardo da Vinci*, 1939, p. 48. For this picture, see also A. Annoni in *Atti del Convegno di Studi Vinciani* (Accademia Toscana di Scienze e Lettere 'La Colombaria'), 1953, pp. 26 ff. (**60**) Klassiker der Kunst, *Leonardo*, 1931, Plate 82. (**61**) A version in the Ambrosiana is reproduced by Fumagalli, *Scuola di Leonardo*, 1811; also, together with a version from the Dal Verme Collection, now also in the Ambrosiana, by Luca Beltrami, *Luini*, 1911, pp. 538/9. See also the *Rassegna d'Arte*, 1913, p. 30 (version belonging to Mrs. Clara Henfrey). (**62**) Dated at the beginning of the XVI Century in the *Guida al Castello Sforzesco*, 1957, p. 61; photo in the Gallery archives. (**63**) It has been claimed by G. Fogolari in the *Rassegna d'Arte*, 1914, p. 29, and by Suida in the *Monatshefte für Kunstwissenschaft*, 1920, p. 265, that two angels in an altarpiece in S. Lorenzo at Serravalle, ascribed to Francesco da Milano, are derivations; but the connection seems to be of the slightest. Reproduced in the *Rassegna d'Arte*, 1914, p. 27, wrongly lettered as in the Cook Collection. (**64**) It has been thought useful to give a good many references to old mentions of the pictures, especially in view of the variety of their errors. (**65**) See Serviliano Latuada, *Descrizione di Milano*, IV, 1738, p. 246; cf. also Vincenzo Forcella, *Iscrizioni delle Chiese . . . di Milano*, III, 1890, p. 145 (No. 202). There need be no doubt at all that the stone with this inscription has been preserved, and that it is the one now in the atrium of S. Ambrogio at Milan, near the right-hand door, as is claimed by Diego Sant'Ambrogio in the *Bollettino della Società Pavese di Storia Patria*, December, 1901, p. 479. (The text of the inscription now in S. Ambrogio, without reference to the one formerly in S. Francesco, is given by Forcella, *op. cit.*, III, 1890, p. 259, No. 328.) Apart from the similarity of the text itself, there is definite evidence that some monuments did go from S. Francesco to S. Ambrogio. Don Gabrio Maria Nava, abbot of S. Ambrogio, in a letter of 27 June, 1807, to the draft of which are attached two lists (one dated 15 June, 1807), asked that certain inscriptions and monuments in S. Francesco should be transferred to S. Ambrogio, where he would put them up 'nell'Area dell'anzidetta basilica'; S. Francesco was at that time in process of being pulled down. Partial agreement to Nava's request was given on 10 July, 1807; and some of the items mentioned are in fact now in S. Ambrogio. The inscription of 1576, it is true, is not mentioned. But Nava in his letter said that he was willing to receive further items from S. Francesco, if found; he also said that in S. Ambrogio 'sono già stati in occasione della profanazione degli Altari della

Chiesa di S. Fr., collocati altri monumenti antichi.' (See Aristide Calderini in *Aevum*, April/September, 1940, pp. 219 ff., and (for the drafts with comments) Luca Beltrami, *Cimeli Dispersi della Chiesa di S. Francesco Grande in Milano*, 1913, pp. 9 ff.) It should be added that there are a few differences between the existing inscription and the records of the one formerly in S. Francesco, including for the first word of the first line PICTA instead of VIRGO, which seems to imply that the inscription was connected with a picture. The inscription (existing form; there are verbal differences in the recorded form) ends up: ANNO MDLXXVI, V. CAL. SEP/HOC ALTARE IPSI VIRGINI/HONORIS ERGO DICAVIT; this date, which seems to refer precisely to the dedication of the altar, seems to fit in with the change of location of the Confraternity's Chapel, discussed in the next note. It might be thought that the inscription may not refer to the Confraternity's altarpiece, but to another near by; Placido Puccinelli, *Memorie Antiche di Milano* (attached to his *Zodiaco della Chiesa Milanese*), 1650, p. 72, calls it 'Altra Iscrittione presso la Cappella della Concettione,' and apparently the same thing is stated in an eighteenth-century MS. by Fusi (see Forcella, *op. cit.*, III, p. 145). But this view would be difficult to maintain in the face of what is said by Latuada, *loc. cit.*, and by Besta, MS. of *ca.* 1598 (A. Calderini in *Aevum*, April/September, 1940, p. 203); and it seems that doubt should cease altogether, if the inscription is read in connection with the following passage: 'Nel principio della quarentena' (i.e., soon after 29 October, 1576) 'il Castiglione uno de i Senatori, delegato di P.V., oltra l'ordinaria cura ch'egli haueua di detta sua porta, per ouuiar al progresso della peste, che in essa per la Dio gratia era minore che nelle altre porte . . . propose alli deputati della sua porta, che si facesse una uniuersale communione, che fu poi non solo compitamente essequita nella chiesa di S. Francesco che è in detta porta, all'altare dedicato ad honore e riuerenza della concettione della beata Vergine, cantata una messa solenne, et sporta larga elemosina ad ornato di detto altare, ma vnanimi si uotorno à far ogn'anno in tal giorno l'istessa congregatione, et communione nella detta chiesa, si come fu nell'anno del 1524. uotato di celebrar detta festa.' (Giacomo Filippo Besta, *Vera Narratione del Successo della Peste che afflisse l'inclita Città di Milano, l'anno 1576*, 1578, f. 30r, and f. 25v for the date of quarantine.) The compiler has placed the reference to this inscription first in the provenance, because of the mention of the date 1524; but the evidence of the inscription and of the passage just quoted from Besta, it may be admitted, does not provide proof that the altarpiece was in the Confraternity's chapel in 1524. (66). This change, which is referred to by Paolo Morigia, *Historia dell'Antichità di Milano*, 1592, p. 377, is described in some detail by Diego Sant'Ambrogio. The earlier chapel of the Conception was within the church and immediately to the left of the entrance, which was a single door in the centre of the façade. On 7 February, 1576, it was determined to construct a lateral door at this spot. On 4 April, 1576, S. Carlo Borromeo asked Conte Giano dal Verme to agree to the altar of the Conception's being moved to a chapel at that time dedicated to S. Bonaventure; and on 14 and 17 April, 1576, representatives of the dal Verme and Visconti families, who shared the patronage of this chapel, renounced their rights in it in favour of the Confraternity of the Conception. The Confraternity's new chapel was the one at the end of the right-hand aisle, where Leonardo's picture is recorded by various later writers. See Diego Sant'Ambrogio, *loc. cit.* in previous note, pp. 479 ff., and in the *Archivio Storico Lombardo*, 1902, 3rd series, Vol. XVII, pp. 147/8. Cf. also Aristide Calderini in *R. Istituto Lombardo, Rendiconti, Classe di Lettere e Scienze Morali e Storiche*, Vol. LXXIII, 1939/40, pp. 107/8 (pp. 11/2 of the offprint), and in *Aevum*, April/September, 1940, p. 203 (Besta's description of *ca.* 1598). It had already been decided to ask the members of the Confraternity to agree to the change on 28 January, 1576 (Ambrosiana, Archivio Spirituale, Sezione X, Visita Pastorale, Vol. 28, Q. 21). The change had already taken place by 11 August, 1576, as is seen from a letter of that date from S. Carlo Borromeo (Ambrosiana, Archivio Spirituale, Sezione XII, Ordini Religiosi e Congregazioni, Vol. 3, f. 181r): 'et quod cum capella dicte scole conceptionis, que alias erat in dicta ecclesia sancti francisci penes parietem frontispicii dicte ecclesiae constructa, ex ordine prelibati Reveren dissimi episcopi famaguste uisitatoris apostolici funditus fuerit ob maiorem ecclesie decorem demolita, scola uero ipsa et eius altare cum eius titulo honoribus et oneribus in aliam amplam capellam in capite ecclesie existentem fuerit translata, capellaque ipsa nunc maxima impensa per ipsos scolares instauretur et pulcherimis picturis et icona ornetur.' It should be noted that the Confraternity possessed not only a chapel in S. Francesco, but also a room for business (Luogo Pio). According to a document of 1 June, 1478, published by Biscaro in the *Archivio Storico Lombardo*, 1910, pp. 156 ff., this *Luogo Pio* was to be built in a spot described, which was at or near the west end of the church. It is known from later records to have been in the atrium of S. Francesco: see Torre, *Il Ritratto di Milano*, 1674, pp. 201 and 203, and (after reconstruction of the church with alterations, 1688) Latuada, *op. cit.*, IV., 1738, pp. 245 and 256; also Aristide Calderini in *Aevum*, April/September, 1940, p. 201 (Besta's description of ca. 1598), p. 215 (Paraini's description of 1716) and Plate 4 (plan of 1723). (67) The letter from S. Carlo Borromeo, 11 August, 1576, quoted in the previous note, refers to the altarpiece; but it does not seem necessarily to imply any change. Besta (*ca.* 1598) also seems to leave the matter open; see A. Calderini in *Aevum*, April/September, 1940, p. 203. (68) G. P. Lomazzo, *Trattato dell'Arte de la Pittura*, 1584, p. 171 (p. 175, which is not the reference, is also numbered 171 in error): (following on Leonardo's *S. Anne*) 'Et ancora nella tauola che si vede nella Capella della Conceptione in Santo Francesco di Milano, della quale occorrerà ragionare anco nel libro de i lumi, doue si vede in Santo Giouanni Battista mentre in ginocchio con le mani aggionte se'inchina à Christo, il moto dell'vbedienza, & riuerenza puerile, & nella Vergine il moto d'vna allegra speculatione, mentre rimira questi atti, & ne l'angelo il moto della Angelica beltà in atto di considerare la gioia che da quel misterio era per risultarne al mondo, in Christo fanciullo là diuinità, & sapienza, & però là Vergine stà in ginocchio tenendo con là destra S. Giouanni, stendendo la sinistra in fuori in scorto, & cosi l'Angelo tenendo Christo con la mano sinistra il quale stando assiso mira S. Giouanni & lo benedice.' Id., *id.*, p. 212: 'quella tauola di Leonardo Vinci . . . che è in Santo Francesco in Milano doue è dipinta la Concettione della Madonna.' Id, *Idea del Tempio della Pittura*, 1590, p. 132: '& in Milano in Santo Francesco la Concettione della Vergine' (among other works by Leonardo). Cf. Cecil Gould in *The Burlington Magazine*, Vol. XC (1948), pp. 328 f. Although the identity of No. 1093 appears certain from Lomazzo's description in the first reference, it may be added that E. Solmi deduces from the mention of the angel's left hand supporting Christ that the Louvre picture is referred to (*Archivio Storico Lombardo*, Series IV, Vol. VIII, 1907, p. 305). Vasari does not mention the altarpiece in S. Franceso Grande; this is curious because he was in Milan in 1566 at least (*Der literarische Nachlass*, II, ed. K. and H. W. Frey, 1930, p. 239; for an earlier visit, see W. Kallab, *Vasaristudien*, 1908, p. 254). Vasari does mention other works of art in S. Francesco (1550 edition, pp. 596 and 711; ed. Milanesi, IV, pp. 152 and 543). (69) 'Qui si vede una pittura di detta Vergine molto rara.' See A. Calderini in *Aevum*, April/September, 1940, p. 202; on p. 200, Calderini says that Besta's MS. seems to have been finished by 1598. (70) Girolamo Borsieri. *Supplimento della Nobiltà di Milano*, 1619, p. 71, as having been presented by S. Carlo Borromeo. This may be a confusion with the version of Leonardo's *S. Anne*, at one time in the sacristy of S. Maria presso S. Celso at Milan; this picture had apparently belonged to S. Carlo Borromeo (Ambrogio Mazenta, *Le Memorie su Leonardo da Vinci*, ed. Luigi Gramatica, 1919, p. 47; *The Burlington Magazine*, Vol. XX (1911/2), pp. 129 f.; Leonardo Exhibition at Los Angeles, 1949 (No. 35), lent by the University of California at Los Angeles, Willitts J. Hole Collection). (71) Ambrogio Mazenta, *Le Memorie su Leonardo da Vinci*, ed. Luigi Gramatica, 1919, p. 47; on p. 18, the editor claims that 1635 is the date of the *Memorie*. (72) Agostino Sant'Agostino, *L'Immortalità, e gloria del Pennello, Ouero Catalogo delle Pitture Insigni . . . di Milano*, 1671, p. 42: 'Nella Capella della Concettione vi è l'Ancona con la Beata Vergine, e S. Gio. Battista, & à lato due tauolette con due Angioli, che suonano, opere del Celebre *Leonardo*

da Vinci.' Agostino and Giacinto Sant'Agostini, *Catalogo delle Pitture Insigni,
che stanno esposte al publico nella Città di Milano*, seventeenth century (?), p. 87:
'l'ancona con la B. Vergine, & à lato due Angioli sopra tauola del celebre *Leonardo
da Vinci.'* (73) Carlo Torre, *Il Ritratto di Milano*, 1674 (passed for publication
1672), p. 203, with a confused attribution for the angels. Torre says that this
Tauola (presumably meaning the whole altarpiece) had been in S. Gottardo; cf.
the compiler's pamphlet of 1947, p. 9, also a sentence (not mentioning any
picture) in Paolo Morigia, *Historia dell'Antichità di Milano*, 1592, p. 117, and a
passage in Besta's description of *ca.* 1598, printed by A. Calderini in *Aevum,*
April/September, 1940, p. 202. (74) Luigi Scaramuccia, *Le Finezze de Pennelli
Italiani*, 1674, p. 138. (75) The only precise evidence, so far as the compiler is
aware, is in a letter from Annibale Cantoni, 22 August, 1696, concerning the reconstructions: 'le Capelle di S. Franᶜᵒ et Imacolata Conceṭᵉ non si sono totalᵉ
toccate, ma bensi in qualche parte polizzate et fatte più chiare' (printed by A.
Calderini in *Aevum*, April–September, 1940, p. 210). For the history of S. Francesco in general, see the same author in *R. Istituto Lombardo, Rendiconti,
Classe di Lettere e Scienze Morali e Storiche*, Vol. LXXIII, 1939/40, pp. 97 ff.
(76) Michele Paraini, printed by A. Calderini in *Aevum*, April/September, 1940,
pp. 213/4. (77) Latuada, *op. cit.*, IV, 1738, pp. 245/6. (78) Nicolò Sormani,
Giornata Terza de' Passeggi . . . nella città . . . di Milano, 1752, p. 38: 'l'effigie
dell' Immacolata è di Leonardo de' Vinci.' (79) Something about these institutions may be read in B. Borroni, *Il Forastiere in Milano*, 1808, pp. 47 and 220;
F. Pirovano, *Milano nuovamente descritta*, 1822, pp. 394/5; 1824 edition of the
latter, same pages. Cf. also Giovanni Angelo Marelli's note, 'S. Catterina alla
Rotta sopreso le monache 1782. Si è qui fatto il novo spedale delli esposti et
altri luogi pii qui unito' (published by V. Forcella, *Chiese e Luoghi Pii Soppressi
in Milano dal 1764 al 1808*, in the *Archivio Storico Lombardo*, 1889, p. 649). (80)
Disegni di Leonardo da Vinci incisi e publicati da Carlo Giuseppe Gerli, 1784, p. 4.
Cf. Cecil Gould in *The Burlington Magazine*, Vol. XC (1948), p. 329. (81) Dr. R.
Eisler in *The Burlington Magazine*, Vol. XC (1948), p. 329. (82) Francesco
Bartoli, *Notizie delle Pitture . . . d'Italia*, I, 1776, p. 162. (83) See G. Biscaro in
the *Archivio Storico Lombardo*, 1910, pp. 145/7 and F. Malaguzzi Valeri, *La
Corte di Lodovico il Moro*, II, 1915, p. 393. Item No. 1, where the description is
unclear and probably rough, seems accepted as being identical with the Con-
fraternity's altarpiece. Other furniture is then listed. No. 10 is 'un quadro del-
l'Immacolata con cornice e piccola cimasa dorata—L.15'; for reasons the compiler cannot understand, several writers have assumed that this item No. 10 was
No. 1093. It might have been anything; maybe the 'tavoletta che si tiene pen-
dente da un Pilastro,' according to Latuada, *op. cit.*, IV, 1738, p. 247. (84)
Adamo Chiusole, *Itinerario delle Pitture etc. d'Italia*, 1782, p. 110. (85) *Nuova
Guida della Città di Milano*, Milan, Sirtori, 1783, p. 72, all three as by Leonardo.
(86) (Carlo Bianconi), *Nuova Guida di Milano*, 1787, pp. 279/80; he records
Torre's wrong provenance as a rumour. (87) See F. Malaguzzi Valeri, *La Corte di
Lodovico il Moro*, II, 1915, p. 395. Malaguzzi Valeri doubts if the Confraternity's
altarpiece is referred to; but the altarpiece described in 1798, to judge from
Malaguzzi Valeri's quotation, perhaps corresponds sufficiently with the altarpiece described in the inventory of 1781 (see note 83). In 1798 there are mentioned 'nella sommità dell'ancona due pezzi di quadri rappresentanti due
angioli'; if these are identical with Nos. 1661/2, it is perhaps some confirmation
that Nos. 1093, 1661 and 1662 formed the upper tier of the Confraternity's
altarpiece. S. Francesco was secularized in 1798 (cf. V. Forcella in the *Archivio
Storico Lombardo*, 1889, p. 656). The church became a store-house; the conven-
tual buildings first a military hospital, then in 1799 or 1800 an orphanage. In
1805, both church and buildings were handed over to Napoleon's *vélites.* Destruction was proposed in 1806, and in 1807/13 a barracks was built on the site,
now known as the Caserma Garibaldi. See A. Calderini in *R. Istituto Lombardo,
Rendiconti, Classe di Lettere e Scienze Morali e Storiche*, Vol. LXXIII, 1939/40,
p. 114 (p. 18 of the offprint), and (for the documentation) the same author in
Aevum, April–September, 1940, pp. 216 ff. (88) See the *Raccolta Vinciana*, II,

pp. 81 ff. There is a reference to the sale in Della Valle's edition of Vasari, V, 1792, p. 69, a note probably based on a manuscript by Venanzio de Pagave; this seems to be the source of various references to the sale in an inexact form, which were current until the discovery of the documents published in the *Raccolta Vinciana*. (89) Historical Manuscripts Commission, 14th Report, Appendix, Part I, *The MSS. of the Duke of Rutland*, Vol. III, 1894, pp. 270, 280. F. W. Burton in *The Nineteenth Century*, 1894, p. 84, says that there is a reference to the picture in one letter in the Hamilton-Lansdowne correspondence; the compiler found nothing in the Lansdowne Marbles Sale Catalogue, 1930, pp. 77 ff. Cf. also Buchanan, *Memoirs*, 1824, II, p. 264: 'the large composition which formerly belonged to the Lansdowne collection, and afterwards passed into the collection of the Earl of Suffolk; a picture which appears to be the original of that now at the Louvre, and is very superior to it in every respect.' No. 1093 is also probably referred to by Buchanan, *op. cit.*, I, pp. 27/8, with a correction in Vol. II, p. 380. (90) C. A. G. Goede, *England, Wales, Irland und Schottland*, 4th part, Dresden, 1805, pp. 40/1. A picture that seems clearly distinct appeared in the John Edward Breen Sale, Fourth Day, 31 May, 1805, lot 172, thus described: '*L. D'Vinci* Virgin, Child, St. John, and Angel.—*A matchless performance, particularly described in the Life of this great Master, possessing all the excellencies to be found in his best works.*' The Breen pictures were on view on Monday, 27 May, which is the day on which Charles and Mary Lamb saw at a sale a picture on which she wrote some verses (letter of Charles Lamb to Dorothy Wordsworth, 14 June, 1805). These verses were printed in the 1818 edition of *The Works of Charles Lamb*, following on some by Charles Lamb himself; Charles' verses are entitled LINES ON THE CELEBRATED PICTURE BY LIONARDO DA VINCI, CALLED THE VIRGIN OF THE ROCKS, Mary's are entitled ON THE SAME. See *The Works of Charles and Mary Lamb*, ed. E. V. Lucas, Vol. V, 1903, pp. 39 and 301 (the annotation appears somewhat confused; titles checked from the 1818 edition). (91) 'An upright picture, representing the Virgin, the Infant Saviour, St. John and Elizabeth (sic).' (92) *The Farington Diary*, Vol. VIII, p. 104, 9 December, 1816; statement by Hill Jr. that his father bought a Leonardo for 389 gs. at a Lansdowne Sale, and sold it a month later (after removing some repaint) to Lord Suffolk for 2000 gs. The compiler has been unable to find the name of the purchaser of lot 47 of the Lansdowne Sale of 20 March, 1806; one priced copy at the Courtauld Institute gives the price as 155 gs., another at the same place gives £185, a third at the Victoria and Albert Museum gives 185 gs. It may be added that at a Lansdowne *et al.* Sale, 26 May, 1810 (lot 32), there was a Leonardo, *Holy Family with St. Elizabeth*; but this was sold for 30 gs., and not to Hill (information from Messrs. Christie's). Since there may be some mistake in Farington's note, it may be that No. 1093 did not pass directly from Lord Lansdowne to Hill. In the catalogue of a sale at Stanley's, of The Intended Ornaments to the Gallery of a late Distinguished Marshal of France, 2nd Day, 11 June, 1816, lot 52 was: 'LIONARDO DA VINCI, La Vierge aux rochers: this inestimable Picture from a Convent at Milan, and of which a duplicate is known to exist, has been long celebrated as the *chef d'œuvre* of the accomplished Lionardo . . .' (no price or buyer's name in the copy in the Victoria and Albert Museum). In the catalogue of a sale also at Stanley's, of A Gentleman Leaving England, 2nd Day, 3 July, 1816, lot 120 was: 'L. DA VINCI, LA VIERGE AUX ROCHERS. This Masterly production was painted expressly for the Monastery of the Dominicans at Milan, the same for which he also painted the celebrated Picture of the Last Supper. The latter occupied the Refectory, and this the Dormitory; from whence it was removed by the order of a late French Marshal, on the Conquest of Italy. . . .' (no price or buyer's name in the copy in the Victoria and Albert Museum). So far as the compiler is aware, it cannot be excluded that these entries refer to No. 1093; but cf. note 90. (93) Lord Suffolk owned another Virgin and Child attributed to Leonardo, and lent by him to the British Institution, 1851 (No. 2) and 1858 (No. 11). G. Scharf, *Artistic and Descriptive Notes . . . in the British Institution*, 1858, says that it is by a distant follower. This is identified as a ' Giampietrino ' in *The Burlington Magazine*, July 1955, *Notable Works of Art now on the Market*, Plate II; it is there stated that this is the picture exhibited at the British Institution in 1818. Possibly it is the *Holy Family* mentioned in Lord Suffolk's possession by J. W. Brown, *The Life of Leonardo da Vinci*, 1828, p. 254; there stated to have been in the Giustiniani Collection at Rome, so possibly identical with No. 48 of Part II of the 1638 Giustiniani inventory, published by L. Salerno (*The Burlington Magazine*, April 1960, p. 137). Presumably it is the undescribed Leonardo da Vinci mentioned in Lord Suffolk's Collection in *The Picture of London for* 1802, p. 215, and in later editions of this guide-book. (94) Cf. note 89 above. (95) Schorn and Förster's Vasari, III, i, 1843, p. 45. There is an account of Lord Suffolk's picture in Waagen, *Treasures*, III, 1854, pp. 168/9. (96) Nos. 133, 134. This catalogue is reprinted by Giulio Carotti, *Capi d'Arte app. a S.E. la Duchessa Joséphine Melzi d'Eril-Barbò*, 1901; these items on p. 180. It may be that Schorn and Förster's Vasari, as in the previous note, is the first dated record in print of these pictures as in the Melzi Collection. There are MS. accounts of them in Mündler's Diary, 1858, and Eastlake's note-book, 1858. (97) These details are from Carotti, as in the previous note.

After LEONARDO DA VINCI

1861 'THE VIRGIN OF THE ROCKS'

A copy of No. 1093 above, with a different landscape background; S. Joseph and the ass appear as small figures in the right distance.

Canvas, painted surface (sight), $18\frac{1}{4} \times 14\frac{1}{4}$ (0·465 × 0·36).
Damaged in parts, e.g. in the Virgin's left hand.
This poor copy seems to be of the seventeenth century.

PROVENANCE: J. M. Parsons Bequest to the South Kensington (Victoria and Albert) Museum, 1870;[1] on loan to Birmingham in 1882.[2] Lent to the National Gallery from 1895 until 1960, when it was returned to the Victoria and Albert Museum.

REPRODUCTION: *Plates, Earlier Italian Schools*, 1953, Vol. II, p. 219.

REFERENCES: (1) *Catalogue of the National Gallery of British Art at South Kensington*, Part I, 1893, p. 188, No. 529/70. (2) Birmingham, Museum and Art Gallery, *Catalogue*, 1888 (No. 183).

Follower of LEONARDO DA VINCI

1300 THE VIRGIN AND CHILD

Wood, painted surface, $23\frac{1}{2} \times 17\frac{1}{4}$ (0·60 × 0·44); painted up to the edges all round.

Good condition. There are *pentimenti* in the landscape by the Virgin's left shoulder, and in Christ's right leg.

The executant of this picture is unidentified, but the design is more or less directly Leonardo's. The Litta Madonna[1] shows the Child in a rather similar pose, inverted; an engraving based on that, with the Child the same way round as on No. 1300, is reproduced by Suida.[2] The Virgin's head in No. 1300 is almost exactly taken from *The Madonna with the Yarn-winder.*[3] Leonardo's later style is reflected in the draperies and even the semi-Netherlandish colour of No. 1300. Its date may be presumed to be from his second Milanese period or soon after. Jacobsen[4] ascribes the picture to the following of Cesare da Sesto.

VERSIONS, ETC.: A variant or copy, with the Virgin's eyes turned towards the spectator, and a different background, is in private possession at Pavia.[5] A drawing by Degas after No. 1300 appeared in the 4th Degas Sale, Paris, 2/4 July, 1919 (lot 114b);[6] another was acquired by A. S. F. Gow of Cambridge in 1950.[7]

PROVENANCE: Purchased with rest of Edmond Beaucousin Collection, Paris, 1860.[8] On loan at the South Kensington Museum, 1862–1889.

REPRODUCTION: *Illustrations, Italian Schools*, 1937, p. 234. *Plates, Earlier Italian Schools*, 1953, Vol. II, p. 220.

REFERENCES: (1) Suida, *Leonardo und sein Kreis*, 1929, Fig. 50. (2) Suida, *op. cit.*, Fig. 59; for variants, see Suida, Figs. 61, 62, and Boltraffio, No. 728 of this catalogue. (3) One version is reproduced by Suida, *op. cit.*, Fig. 133. (4) Jacobsen in the *Repertorium für Kunstwissenschaft*, 1901, p. 358. (5) Photograph in the Gallery archives, supplied by Prof. Wart Arslan, April, 1948. (6) Reproduced in the album and by J. Rewald, *The History of Impressionism*, 1946, p. 48. (7) Photograph in the Gallery archives; on the same sheet is a drawing after Francia, No. 638 of the present catalogue. (8) As Melzi.

1438　THE HEAD OF S. JOHN THE BAPTIST

Inscribed, MDXI / II.KL.FEB.

Walnut,[1] original painted surface, $18 \times 15\frac{1}{4}$ (0.455×0.385); painted up to the original edges all round (there are small additions to the panel except at the top).

Good condition in general, except for undercleaning. There is a *pentimento* on the lip and chin.

The date is presumably 31 January, 1511.

There is some evidence that Leonardo painted a Head of S. John in a Charger;[2] this tradition is confirmed by the existence of many Milanese versions of the subject in the early sixteenth century.[3] As the hand of No. 1438 has not been determined, it seems best to associate it with Leonardo's following; Jacobsen[4] thinks the painter is Martino 'Piazza,' which seems not justifiable (see his biography in this catalogue).

PROVENANCE: Stated to be from the Collection of Cardinal Stoppani, Rome.[5] Doubtless the picture seen by Mündler in 1858 in the possession of Prof. Geromini, Cremona.[6] Acquired from a dealer in Modena[7] by James C. Watt, from whom purchased, Walker Fund, 1895.

REPRODUCTION: *Illustrations, Italian Schools*, 1937, p. 235. *Plates, Earlier Italian Schools*, 1953, Vol. II, p. 221.

REFERENCES: (1) Letter from B. J. Rendle, of the Forest Products Research Laboratory, in the Gallery archives. (2) See Suida, *Leonardo und sein Kreis*, 1929, p. 156. It is possible that the popularity of the subject is due in the first place to Gentile Bellini; see the story, of which the details are suspicious, related by Ridolfi, *Le Maraviglie dell'Arte*, 1648, I, pp. 40/1. (3) The earliest date is 1507 on the Andrea Solari in the Louvre. For the varying designs of this subject, see Suida in the *Repertorium für Kunstwissenschaft*, 1902, p. 338; *The Burlington Magazine*, Vol. VII (1905), pp. 75/6; the *Rassegna d'Arte*, 1907, p. 17; and Kurt

Badt, *Andrea Solario*, 1914, pp. 210/2. (**4**) Jacobsen in the *Repertorium für Kunstwissenschaft*, 1901, p. 358. (**5**) N.G. MS. Catalogue. Giovanni Francesco Stoppani (1695–1774) became a cardinal in 1753; see Migne's *Dictionnaire des Cardinaux* and G. Moroni, *Dizionario di Erudizione Storico-Ecclesiastica*. (**6**) Mündler's Diary; he says that there exists a pamphlet proving it to be by Leonardo or Raphael. Mündler's description is not enough for identification; but the Geromini provenance is stated in the N.G. MS. Catalogue, presumably on information from the vendor. (**7**) N.G. Report, 1895.

LIBERALE DA VERONA
ca. 1445–*ca.* 1526

School of Verona. His age was declared as 10 in 1455. He was active as a miniaturist at Monte Oliveto near Siena, and at Siena, from 1467 until 1476. He seems to have spent the next years wandering; but by 1492 at latest he seems to have settled at Verona. There are two signed pictures, one of which is dated 1489. There is evidence that he was alive in 1525 and dead in 1527 (letter from Raffaello Brenzoni in the Gallery archives). Of the various influences that have been discerned in his works, the chief would seem that of Mantegna.

Literature: Raffaello Brenzoni, *Liberale da Verona*, 1930 and in *L'Arte*, 1954, pp. 9 ff.

1134 THE VIRGIN AND CHILD WITH TWO ANGELS

Wood, painted surface, 24 × 17¾ (0·61 × 0·45); painted up to the edges all round.

Very fair condition.

The attribution to Liberale is generally accepted.

PROVENANCE: Purchased from Paolo Fabris, Venice, 1883.

REPRODUCTION: *Illustrations, Italian Schools*, 1937, p. 184. *Plates, Earlier Italian Schools*, 1953, Vol. II, p. 222.

1336 DIDO'S SUICIDE (FROM A CASSONE?)

Poplar,[1] painted surface, 16¾ × 48½ (0·425 × 1·23); painted up to the edges left and right.

Very fair state.

The subject is from the *Æneid*, IV, 504 sqq.; Dido, abandoned by Æneas, committed suicide on a pyre in her palace at Carthage. The details of the picture do not follow Virgil very exactly.

The two soldiers on the extreme right are copied from the two outside figures in a print by Dürer, '*Five Lansquenets and an Oriental on Horseback.*'[2] The two small figures, left centre behind the pyre, are (inverted) from two of the central figures of the same engraving, the arms of the man on the left being changed. It is possible that the pose of the negro's legs in the foreground towards the right is taken from the same print.

Dürer's print is an early one; dated *ca.* 1494 by Tietze and Tietze-Conrat, and 1495/6 by Panofsky.[3] The poses of several of the other figures on the picture are markedly Mantegnesque.

The attribution to Liberale is usually accepted; it is due to Morelli, who saw the picture at Colnaghi's soon after the Dunn-Gardner Sale.[4]

PROVENANCE: Anon. Sale, Phillips, 30 April, 1851 (lot 92).[5] In the Collection of Lord Northwick at Thirlestaine House, Cheltenham; Catalogue, 1858 (No. 245);[6] Sale, 3 August, 1859 (lot 538),[7] bought by Rhodes for Cecil Dunn-Gardner of Brighton. Dunn-Gardner Sale, London, 27 June, 1881 (lot 78),[8] bought by Colnaghi, from whom bought by Edward Habich,[9] and from then on loan at the Cassel Gallery.[10] Purchased with other pictures from Edward Habich, Cassel, 1891; lent by the National Gallery to the R.A., 1892 (No. 159).[11]

REPRODUCTION: *Illustrations, Italian Schools*, 1937, p. 184. *Plates, Earlier Italian Schools*, 1953, Vol. II, pp. 223–224.

REFERENCES: (1) Letter from B. J. Rendle, of the Forest Products Research Laboratory, in the Gallery archives. (2) Noted by P. Pouncey. (3) Tietze and Tietze-Conrat, *Dürer-Katalog*, I, 1928, No. 43, reproduced on p. 152. E. Panofsky, *Albrecht Dürer*, II, 1945, No. 195. (4) J. P. Richter was present; he reported this, many years later, to E. K. Waterhouse. The authorship of the attribution is confirmed in letters from Layard to Morelli, 24 August, 1883 and Morelli to Layard, 8 September, 1883 (British Museum, Add. MSS. 38964 and 38967, Layard Papers, Vols. XXXIV and XXXVII). (5) As Ippolito Scarsella. Lord Northwick's own copy of the sale catalogue, kindly lent by Capt. E. G. Spencer-Churchill, proves the identity; Lord Northwick noted that the picture had become his, and suggested an attribution to Beccafumi. (6) As Beccafumi. (7) As Ippolito Scarsella. (8) As Ippolito Scarsella. (9) J. P. Richter, as in note 4. (10) See the Prussian *Jahrbuch*, 1882, *Amtliche Berichte*, p. LXXXIII. (11) As Liberale.

LIBRI *See* GEROLAMO DAI LIBRI

FILIPPINO LIPPI
1457(?)–1504

Son of Fra Filippo Lippi. The year of his birth is doubtful; 1457 is usually considered the most probable, although Gronau in Thieme-Becker does not exclude a date *ca.* 1452. He was brought up at Prato. He was in Spoleto with his father from 1467; he left soon after his father's death, at the end of 1469 or the beginning of 1470. He may at once have been placed in Botticelli's studio in Florence; he was certainly living with him *ca.* 1472 (Horne, *Sandro Botticelli*, 1908, pp. 31/2). The date 1480 is doubtfully associated with a *S. Jerome* once in the Florentine Academy (later Uffizi; recorded as Filippino's by Vasari), and with the important *Vision of S. Bernard* in the Badia at Florence (documented as Filippino's). Thereafter several documented and dated pictures and frescoes exist. He was in Rome from 1488 for a few years.

293 ALTARPIECE: THE VIRGIN AND CHILD WITH
SS. JEROME AND DOMINIC

S. Jerome is on the left; in the distance behind is another, small figure
of S. Jerome in penitence, and his lion preparing to fight with a bear.
S. Dominic is on the right; the building behind him may seem to be a
hospital, and is perhaps surmounted by a statue of the Virgin and Child.
In the distance towards the middle S. Joseph with the ass is seen.

Predella: divided by painted framing into five compartments. Centre,
the dead Christ is supported in the tomb by S. Joseph of Arimathaea (?);
various instruments of the Passion lie on the tomb. Right, S. Mary
Magdalene; left, S. Francis. The two end compartments contain the
arms of the Rucellai family.

Wood. Main panel, painted surface, $80 \times 73\frac{1}{4}$ ($2 \cdot 03 \times 1 \cdot 86$), approx.;
the preparation, and here and there beginnings of paint, continue be-
yond these measurements to the edges of the panel. The total painted
surface of the predella is 8×93 ($0 \cdot 205 \times 2 \cdot 36$); painted up to the edges
at the ends. The sizes of the three central compartments are: Dead
Christ, $6 \times 19\frac{1}{4}$ ($0 \cdot 15 \times 0 \cdot 49$); the Magdalen, $6 \times 19\frac{3}{4}$ ($0 \cdot 15 \times 0 \cdot 505$);
S. Francis, $6 \times 20\frac{1}{4}$ ($0 \cdot 15 \times 0 \cdot 515$).

Cleaned in 1959. Very good condition. Some wearing; the areas most
affected are parts of the Virgin's mantle and parts of the gold decoration.
Several *pentimenti* in the main panel, e.g. on the Virgin's left shoulder
and left hand, in the Child's left hand, and in S. Dominic's head.

It comes from a chapel belonging to the Rucellai family in the Vallombrosan church of S. Pancrazio, Florence. This does not mean the celebrated Rucellai Chapel attached to that church, and containing the
so-called 'S. Sepolcro.' In the seventeenth and eighteenth centuries,
the picture was shown in another, but apparently contiguous, Rucellai
chapel, dedicated to S. Jerome,[1] and there is no reason to suppose that
it had ever been anywhere else.

The dedication of the chapel would explain the presence of S. Jerome
on this picture. Perhaps S. Dominic was chosen, because S. Dominic
was particularly associated with the Hospital attached to S. Pancrazio;
he gave Fra Guido the habit there in 1216.[2]

The chapel has on the floor in front of the altar DE ORICEL—
LARIIS.ET EORVM DESCENDENTIBVS / MCCCCLXXXV.
FILIORVM.PHILIPPI.VANNIS.[3] The picture may, therefore, be
associated with the branch of the Rucellai family descending from
Filippo di Vanni (1391–1462). It may date from about 1485, which is,
further, the date when the church of S. Pancrazio was consecrated.[4]

VERSIONS, ETC.: A copy (?) of the figure of S. Jerome was in the Stefano
Bardini Sale, London, 30 May, 1902 (lot 629); Plate 112, No. 708, of the album.
The design of the Child recurs with some variations in a *tondo* referred to in the
entry for No. 927 below. In an altarpiece at Todiano di Preci,[5] the Child again
corresponds quite closely, and here the Virgin also shows considerable similarities. A composition exists both in a drawing and a painting, showing the
dead Christ, S. Joseph of Arimathaea (?), and two angels; the two main figures
are in some respects like the two figures in the central part of the predella here.[6]

PROVENANCE: From the chapel of S. Jerome, belonging to the Rucellai family, in S. Pancrazio, Florence. Probably referred to by Albertini (1510),[7] and certainly by Vasari (1550).[8] The church of S. Pancrazio was suppressed in 1808 or 1809;[9] the picture remained the property of the Rucellai family,[10] and was purchased from Cav. Giuseppe Rucellai in 1857.

REPRODUCTION: *Illustrations, Italian Schools*, 1937, p. 186. *Plates, Earlier Italian Schools*, 1953, Vol. II, pp. 225–226.

REFERENCES: (1) Bocchi-Cinelli, *Le Bellezze della Città di Firenze*, 1677, p. 205; Richa, *Notizie Istoriche delle Chiese Fiorentine*, III, 1755, p. 320 (as Filippo Lippi). For the chapels, see G. Guasti, *Le Cappelle Rucellai in San Pancrazio*, 1916. (2) Richa, *op. cit.*, III, pp. 6 and 325. It is perhaps confirmation that the building in the landscape behind S. Dominic may seem to be a hospital. (3) G. Guasti, *op. cit.*, p. 6. The branch of the Rucellai family descending from Filippo di Vanni failed in 1604; see Luigi Passerini, *Genealogia e Storia della Famiglia Rucellai*, 1861, Tavola VII. (4) Richa, *op. cit.*, III, p. 310. A Scharf, *Filippino Lippi*, 1935, No. 40, dates No. 293 *ca.* 1485; Katharine B. Neilson, *Filippino Lippi*, 1938, p. 120, dates it between 1485 and 1496. (5) Ascribed to Filippino; published by A. Fabbi in the *Rivista d'Arte*, Vol. XXXIV (Annuario 1959), 1961, pp. 121/2 and Figs. 5, 6. (6) Scharf, *op. cit.*, Nos. 29 and 184, Figs. 62 and 63. (7) Albertini, *Memoriale*, ed. Horne, p. 14; the reference is not precise. (8) Vasari, 1550, p. 515; Vasari, ed. Milanesi, III, p. 464. (9) Vasari, ed. Milanesi, III, p. 371; G. Guasti, *op. cit.*, p. 4. (10) In the late 1820's it was in the Rucellai Palace, in the part then occupied by the Layard family, over the bed where the youthful Sir A. H. Layard slept; see *Sir Henry Layard, Autobiography and Letters*, 1903, Vol. I, p. 27.

927 AN ANGEL ADORING (FRAGMENT)

At the bottom is the top of a head, presumably that of the Infant Christ or the little S. John. On the right are the remains of drapery or limbs, possibly unfinished.

Wood, 22 × 10 (0·56 × 0·255); painted up to the edges all round.

The paint has been a good deal abraded in parts. A strip down the left side is considerably cleaner than the rest.

No. 927 is a fragment of a picture, which perhaps represented the Virgin and Child (with S. John?), with angels in adoration. Another fragment of an angel at Strasbourg may be a part of the same work;[1] but Scharf (formerly) and Neilson have claimed that No. 927 is several years later in date than the Strasbourg fragment.[2] In favour of the claim that the two fragments may have belonged together, it should be mentioned that a *tondo* of *The Virgin and Child with Two Angels* appeared at Christie's in 1939, in which the left-hand angel is derived from No. 927, and the right-hand angel from the figure at Strasbourg.[3]

PROVENANCE: Sir Augustus Wall Callcott Sale, 10 May, 1845 (lot 404), bought by Wynn Ellis.[4] Exhibited at the R.A., 1871 (No. 281).[5] Wynn Ellis Bequest, 1876.

REPRODUCTION: *Illustrations, Italian Schools*, 1937, p. 187. *Plates, Earlier Italian Schools*, 1953, Vol. II, p. 227.

REFERENCES: (1) A. Scharf, *Filippino Lippi*, 1935, Fig. 17. (2) Scharf, *op. cit.*, Nos. 53/4; Strasbourg, *ca.* 1485, N.G. No. 927, *ca.* 1495. Katherine B. Neilson, *Filippino Lippi*, 1938, pp. 73/4, seems to follow Scharf's dating approximately. In his *Filippino Lippi* (Schroll, 1950), No. 91, Scharf accepts that No. 927 and the Strasbourg fragment belong together, and dates them *ca.* 1495/8. **(3)** Hon. Mrs. Post Sale, 24 February, 1939 (lot 83), as Verrocchio; photograph in the Gallery archives. In this derivation, nothing appears that corresponds with the head of Christ or S. John (?) or the forms on the right side of No. 927. The attitude of the Child in this *tondo* is very nearly that of No. 293 above, but the Virgin is mostly different. **(4)** In the sale as by Filippino Lippi; for the purchaser, see the *Report from the Select Committee on the National Gallery*, 1853, question No. 9954. **(5)** As by Filippo Lippi.

1124   THE ADORATION OF THE KINGS

In the background are various small figures, Tobias and the Angel, S. Francis receiving the Stigmata, S. Jerome before a Crucifix, S. Benedict (?), the Magdalen or S. Mary of Egypt, and two other scenes with unidentified figures.

Wood, $22\frac{3}{8} \times 33\frac{3}{4}$ (0·57 × 0·86). Painted up to the edges all round; but various incised lines indicate that the picture has not been cut, at any rate not more than a negligible amount.

Very good state.

The picture is now usually accepted as an early work by Filippino.[1] It used, like No. 1412 below, to be ascribed to 'Amico di Sandro;' but most of the pictures formerly called 'Amico di Sandro' are now usually held to be early works of Filippino.[2] No. 1124 is apparently under Botticelli's influence. Gamba even thinks that the design is Botticelli's. He claims that the composition, especially in the figures of the Virgin and Child, is more or less repeated by Botticelli in a later work, the unfinished *Adoration of the Kings* in the Uffizi,[3] but the connection is not close; No. 1124 would appear, for some figures at least, to be closer to the *Adoration of the Kings*, No. 592 of this Gallery, catalogued as by Botticelli.

PROVENANCE: Apparently from the Palazzo Capponi, Florence.[4] First recorded in the Beckford Collection, Bath, by Passavant and Waagen.[5] It passed by inheritance to Beckford's son-in-law, the 10th Duke of Hamilton; seen at Hamilton Palace by Waagen.[6] Exhibited at the R.A., 1873 (No. 193). Purchased at the Hamilton Sale, 24 June, 1882 (lot 397).[7]

REPRODUCTION: *Illustrations, Italian Schools*, 1937, p. 63. *Plates, Earlier Italian Schools*, 1953, Vol. II, pp. 228–229.

REFERENCES: **(1)** Berenson's Lists, 1932. C. Gamba in *Miscellanea di Storia dell'Arte in Onore di I. B. Supino*, 1933, p. 473. A. Scharf, *Filippino Lippi*, 1935, No. 23. It had already been noted as a Filippino by Crowe and Cavalcaselle, *History of Painting in Italy*, ed. Douglas, IV, 1911, p. 274. **(2)** Amico di Sandro (referring to Sandro Botticelli) was invented by Berenson in the *Gazette des Beaux-Arts*, 1899, I, pp. 459 ff., and II, pp. 21 ff., as the author of a group of pictures. Most of these Berenson himself, in his Lists of 1932, ascribes to the young Filippino. Katharine B. Neilson, *Filippino Lippi*, 1938, pp. 23, 27, thinks that some of the pictures are by a painter distinct from Botticelli and from Filippino; she continues to call No. 1124 Amico di Sandro, but classes No. 1412 below, which she says is not by the same hand, as a Filippino. **(3)** Gamba, *loc. cit.*, in note 1; the picture is reproduced in the Klassiker der Kunst *Botticelli*, 1926, Plate 102. **(4)** *Mae Franc. Capponi* is written on the back, also Botticelli's name. The picture seems to have retained an attribution to Botticelli when in the Beckford Collection in England; cf. Waagen, *Treasures*, III, 1854, p. 304.

The Capponi referred to is probably Marchese Franceso Pier Maria Capponi (1688–1753); see Tav. XV of Litta, *Celebri Famiglie in Italia*, Capponi family. **(5)** Passavant, *Kunstreise*, 1833, p. 151; Waagen, *Kunstwerke*, 1837, II, pp. 333/4 (with identifying descriptions). In both cases as by Filippo Lippi. **(6)** Waagen, *Treasures*, III, 1854, p. 304. **(7)** As Botticelli. In the 1929 Catalogue as School of Botticelli.

1412 THE VIRGIN AND CHILD WITH S. JOHN

The book on the parapet is inscribed with imitations of letters, which do not form an inscription.

Poplar,[1] $23\frac{1}{4} \times 17\frac{1}{4}$ (0.59×0.435); painted up to the edges all round.

Fair condition. The picture has suffered from cracking, whence a number of damages, e.g. on the Virgin's neck and the left hand of S. John. Although parts are reasonably pure, the condition in general is not altogether reliable.

In the same group as No. 1124 above, q.v.[2]

PROVENANCE: Bought in Florence by Sir Charles Eastlake.[3] Lady Eastlake Sale, 2 June, 1894 (lot 65),[4] bought by Agnew for the National Gallery.

REPRODUCTION: *Illustrations, Italian Schools*, 1937, p. 62. *Plates, Earlier Italian Schools*, 1953, Vol. II, p. 230.

REFERENCES: **(1)** Letter from B. J. Rendle, of the Forest Products Research Laboratory, of 12 October, 1935, in the Gallery archives. From 1917 to 1925 the picture was withdrawn from exhibition as a forgery, on a false identification of the wood of the panel as American basswood or butternut. **(2)** A. Scharf, *Filippino Lippi*, 1935, No. 36. Katharine B. Neilson, *Filippino Lippi*, 1938, p. 27, calls it Filippino, but thinks it is by a different hand from No. 1124 above. **(3)** Stated in the 1894 Sale catalogue. It appears to be one of the pictures offered to the National Gallery by Lady Eastlake in 1867, in which case it was bought by Sir Charles Eastlake between 1855 and 1865. **(4)** As Botticelli.

4904 MOSES BRINGS FORTH WATER OUT OF THE ROCK

The figure behind Moses is perhaps Aaron.

Canvas, transferred from panel, $30\frac{3}{4} \times 54\frac{1}{4}$ (0.78×1.375).

The upper part of this picture is much damaged. The main figures are in fair state for a transferred picture, although by no means free from damage.

The story of Moses smiting the rock in the desert and causing water to flow from it occurs with slight variations in Exodus xvii, 1–7, and in Numbers xx, 7–13.

This picture is in Filippino's late style.[1] No. 4905 below is obviously a pendant. It is possible that other pictures now missing continued the series; on the reverse of the Habich drawing, mentioned in the section *Drawings*, is the sketch of a composition which Kurz thinks may illustrate how Pharaoh adopted the young Moses, and how the High Priest of Heliopolis, aware of the impending doom of the Egyptians, wanted to kill the child.[2] Perhaps the pictures ornamented the wainscoting of some room.

It is possible that some figures in Bacchiacca's picture of this subject in the Giovanelli Collection at Venice may be freely derived from No. 4904.[3]

DRAWINGS: Two connected drawings exist. One was in the Habich Collection at Cassel;[4] the other is at Christ Church, Oxford.[5]

PROVENANCE: Once owned by Cav. William Spence at Florence.[6] Owned in 1873 by Sir Bernhard Samuelson, 1st Bart.[7] (created 1884). He died in 1905, and the picture passed to his son, Sir Henry Bernhard Samuelson, who lent it to the Grafton Galleries, 1911 (No. 26). Bequeathed by Sir Henry Bernhard Samuelson, Bart., in memory of his father, 1937. Cleaned Pictures Exhibition at the National Gallery, 1947/8 (No. 32).

REPRODUCTION: *Plates, Earlier Italian Schools*, 1953, Vol. II, p. 231.

REFERENCES: (1) A. Scharf, *Filippino Lippi*, 1935, No. 8, dates it *ca.* 1500; Katharine B. Neilson, *Filippino Lippi*, 1938, p. 152, agrees. Sir Claude Phillips published Nos. 4904 and 4905 in *The Art Journal*, 1906, pp. 1 ff., suggesting that they are to be identified with two pictures, subject not given, recorded by Vasari (ed. Milanesi, III, p. 467) as painted for Matthias Corvinus. Certainly they are not identical with two pictures painted by Filippino for Matthias Corvinus before 1488, which represented the Virgin and Child and other saints; see the passage in Filippino's will in Scharf, *op. cit.*, p. 90. In any case, Matthias Corvinus died in 1490, and Nos. 4904/5 would seem on stylistic grounds to be rather later. (2) O. Kurz in *The Burlington Magazine*, Vol LXXXIX (1947), p. 147. The reverse of the drawing is reproduced in the *Rassegna d'Arte*, 1906, p. 42, and by Scharf, *op. cit.*, Fig. 187. (3) Reproduced in the *Gazette des Beaux-Arts*, November/December, 1947, p. 155. The possible connection was pointed out by P. Pouncey. (4) Berenson, *Drawings of the Florentine Painters*, 1938, No. 1272A, as Filippino; reproduced in the *Rassegna d'Arte*, 1906, p. 41. (5) Berenson, *op. cit.*, 1938, No. 1382A, as School of Filippino; reproduced by Berenson in his Vol. III, Fig. 258. (6) This is from the catalogue of the Grafton Galleries Exhibition, 1911, No. 26. The picture is there recorded to be on panel, so presumably the transference to canvas took place since; the catalogue of 1911 says that there was then a label on the back, to the effect that the picture had belonged to Spence, and that it had at one time or another been attributed to Piero di Cosimo. (7) Label on the frame.

4905   THE WORSHIP OF THE EGYPTIAN BULL-GOD, APIS

Wood, painted surface, 30¾×54 (0·78×1·37); painted up to the edges all round.

The picture is, on the whole, in very good condition, except for the red dresses of three of the principal figures.[1] It appears at one time to have been intended to be about ½ in. shorter at each end; the painting of strips at each side is in fact not fully completed.

This is obviously a pendant to No. 4904 above, q.v.[2]

The subject is somewhat obscure. The bull in the sky is indeed undoubtedly the Egyptian Apis, with a crescent moon on his shoulder.[3] He is shown in the sky, as O. Kurz pointed out, in accordance with a story told by Petrus Comestor and others;[4] Apis used to rise suddenly out of a river, and when the Egyptians gathered round him with music and chanting, he rose into the air and moved above their heads as if he were playing the cithara.

Kurz argues that No. 4905 shows the Egyptians worshipping Apis;

but he does not give convincing reasons why so recondite a subject should have been chosen.[5]

It is a tradition that the Golden Calf of the Israelites (Exodus xxxii) was an image of the Egyptian Apis; and it seems probable that Filippino in No. 4905 is illustrating in a learned way the subject of the *Worship of the Golden Calf*. This would fit well with the subject of the pendant (No. 4904 above); and it may be held that the tents in the background of the two pictures symbolize in each case the journeyings of the Israelites in the desert.[6] There are, nevertheless, various difficulties in accepting this explanation of the subject. It is usual in the *Worship of the Golden Calf* to find both Moses and Aaron; yet their absence here is not fatal to the identification.[7] It is more serious that Apis himself is shown in No. 4905, and not a golden image of Apis, as it should be.[8] One may, perhaps, imagine that Filippino's patron wanted a very learned representation of the subject, and in his enthusiasm failed to see that he was bungling the story.

An attempt has been made to attach an astrological meaning to No. 4905.[9] This idea may have been introduced to explain why the Bull is shown in the sky; but Kurz has given a different and satisfactory explanation of that. There is indeed a tradition identifying Apis with the zodiacal sign of Taurus;[10] but there is no reason to suppose that Filippino's patron had this tradition present in his mind when he commissioned the picture.

DRAWINGS: The main figures with the hind feet of the Bull occur distributed over two drawings at Berlin. They seem to be moderately exact copies. An extra figure is shown on one drawing, to the right of the tambourine girl (last but one from the left on the picture); no trace of any such figure is to be found on the picture, either by normal light or under the X-Ray. One figure in the picture is omitted from the drawings.[11]

PROVENANCE: Possibly, like No. 4904 above, once owned by Cav. William Spence at Florence.[12] Owned by 1873 by Sir Bernhard Samuelson, 1st Bart.[13] (created 1884). He died in 1905, and the picture passed to his son, Sir Henry Bernhard Samuelson, who lent it to the Grafton Galleries, 1911 (No. 28). Bequeathed by Sir Henry Bernhard Samuelson, Bart., in memory of his father, 1937. Cleaned Pictures Exhibition at the National Gallery, 1947/8 (No. 31).

REPRODUCTION: *Plates, Earlier Italian Schools*, 1953, Vol. II, p. 232.

REFERENCES: (1) For a further account of the condition, see the catalogue of the Cleaned Pictures Exhibition at the National Gallery, 1947/8 (No. 31). (2) No. 4905 is recorded by A. Scharf, *Filippino Lippi*, 1935, No. 9, and by Katharine B. Neilson, *Filippino Lippi*, 1938, pp. 152/4. (3) See F. J. Mather in *The Burlington Magazine*, Vol. XX (1911/2), pp. 362/3. (4) O. Kurz in *The Burlington Magazine*, Vol. LXXXIX (1947), pp. 145 ff. (5) Kurz, *loc. cit.* and (in answer to criticism by Giles Robertson) p. 228. (6) Kurz, p. 228, makes another suggestion for the tents in No. 4905; it seems unlikely in itself, but is of some value for the defence of Kurz' view of the subject. (7) For the absence of Moses, see what Kurz says on p. 145. There is also some justification for the omission of Aaron; see R. Eisler in *The Burlington Magazine*, Vol. XC (1948), pp. 58/9. (8) Eisler, *loc. cit.*, thinks that one of the domestic animals shown in the background of No. 4905, on the right, is the image of the Golden Calf; this suggestion does not appear to be sensible. (9) Vaguely suggested by Sir Claude Phillips in *The Art Journal*, 1906, pp. 1 ff., this was taken up by Sir George Hill in *The Burlington Magazine*,

Vol. XX (1911/2), pp. 171/2; it is maintained by Eisler in *The Burlington Maga-zine*, Vol. XC (1948), pp. 58/9, although by that time Kurz' explanation of why the Bull is in the sky had already been made. **(10)** Eisler, *loc. cit.* **(11)** See C. Hülsen, *Das Skizzenbuch des Giovannantonio Dosio*, 1933, Plates XX and XXIII. On p. 11 it is noted that these drawings are connected with No. 4905, and it is stated that they, like some others in the assemblage, are not by Dosio. The refer-ence was supplied by E. Gombrich and O. Kurz. **(12)** The catalogue of the Grafton Galleries Exhibition, 1911, which notes a label to this effect on the back of No. 4904, makes no note of any such thing for No. 4905; there is no such label on the back of No. 4905 now. **(13)** Label on the frame.

See also SANDRO BOTTICELLI, Nos. 592, 1033

FRA FILIPPO LIPPI
ca. 1406 (?)–1469

He took his vows, after at least a year's novitiate, as a Carmelite in Florence, 1421. He remained for about 11 years in the Carmine at Florence, being first mentioned as a painter there at the beginning of 1431. In 1434 he is mentioned at Padua; 1437, again in Florence. He was much patronized by the Medici family. From 1452 for many years he was working intermittently at Prato; in 1467/9, he was working at Spoleto, where he died.

Several documented and dated pictures are known. The chronology of his works, nevertheless, was confused before the publication of various articles in the *Rivista d'Arte*, 1936. There can be no doubt that Filippo Lippi's style was formed in imitation of Masaccio, who was painting in the Carmine at Florence, *ca.* 1427(?). Lippi was slow in abandoning a Masaccesque uncouthness, but eventually evolved a more delicate style, usually said to be imitated from Fra Angelico. Many of his later works took years to complete, and were executed partly or wholly by pupils.

248   S. BERNARD'S VISION OF THE VIRGIN

Wood, top corners cut to form an irregular hexagon; size, $38\frac{1}{2} \times 41\frac{3}{4}$ (0·98 × 1·06). Painted up to the edges all round, but the paint along the three top edges is new.

Gravely damaged; but (among important parts) the Virgin's face and the face of the angel on the right are very fairly preserved.

The subject of *The Vision of S. Bernard*, which occurs in several celebrated Florentine pictures, is variable and imprecise. No. 248 does not illustrate the so-called *Lactatio*, when the Virgin comforted S. Ber-nard with her milk,[1] nor the appearance of the Virgin with SS. Benedict and Lawrence to S. Bernard,[2] nor presumably the story of S. Bernard's hearing the *Salve Regina* from the Virgin surrounded by angels.[3] Two earlier pictures of *The Vision of S. Bernard* are accompanied by texts. One, a picture in the Accademia at Florence ascribed to Orcagna, etc.,[4] contains inscriptions which are partial and slightly varied quotations from the *Liber de Passione Christi et doloribus et planctibus matris ejus*, ascribed to S. Bernard.[5] This text, which is fragmentary, is a dialogue between the Virgin and apparently S. Bernard, in which the Virgin explains her sufferings at the Passion. The quotation used for the picture at Florence is as follows: 'Dic mihi si in Jerusalem eras quando fuit captus filius tuus, et vinctus, et ductus, ad Annam tractus? At illa: in Jerusalem eram, quando hoc audivi, et gressu quo potui ad Dominum meum flens perveni.'[6] It is probable that an introductory part of the text, now missing, would have explained how the Virgin with angels appeared to the Saint. Another picture, by Giovanni da Milano at Prato, is entitled *Doctrina Sancti Bernardi Confessoris*.[7]

No. 248 has no texts, and it is impossible to be sure what incident is intended. The two pictures just referred to may provide a clue; but it must be pointed out that Filippino Lippi's picture in the Badia at Florence has different inscriptions, and that the iconography of the subject appears to have been by no means fixed. It should not, however, be doubted that S. Bernard is the saint here represented.

The shape would be suitable for a position over a door; and there is some evidence that No. 248 may have been an overdoor in the Palazzo Vecchio at Florence. Baldinucci cites a payment of 16 May, 1447, for a Virgin and S. Bernard to be placed before the door of the Cancelleria there.[8] Vasari lists two overdoors in the Palazzo Vecchio, representing the Annunciation and S. Bernard.[9] The Anonimo Magliabechiano, however, records only the Annunciation.[10] Although the evidence is confused, it is quite possible that No. 248 is referred to by Baldinucci and Vasari. An *Annunciation* at Washington (Kress Loan) is similar in shape to No. 248, except that the proportion of width to height is greater;[11] it is thought that it may be the picture of that subject referred to by Vasari and the Anonimo Magliabechiano.

No. 248 is usually accepted as being by Fra Filippo Lippi. Berenson, however, in his 1936 Lists, says that Lippi was assisted, possibly by Don Diamante. Berenson accepts the date of 1447 for the picture, and the supposed date of 1430 for Don Diamante's birth; since attributions even to Don Diamante's mature period are extremely uncertain, and since No. 248 is much damaged, the attribution of No. 248 to him would present considerable difficulties. Œrtel ascribes the execution of No. 248 probably to Neri di Bicci, which is not satisfactory.[12]

PROVENANCE: First surely mentioned in the E. Joly de Bammeville Collection, Paris, in 1850;[13] purchased at the Bammeville Sale, London, 12 June, 1854 (lot 53).[14]

REPRODUCTION *Illustrations, Italian Schools*, 1937, p. 189. *Plates, Earlier Italian Schools*, 1953, Vol. II, p. 233.

REFERENCES: (1) The *Lactatio* was illustrated often at a later date, e.g. by Murillo in the Prado (*Klassiker der Kunst*, 1923, pp. 63/4); an Italian example occurs on the choir-stalls of Chiaravalle Milanese by Carlo Garavaglia, 1645. For an earlier example, see M. Meiss in *The Art Bulletin*, 1936, p. 461 and Fig. 26. (2) Bollandists, 20 August, p. 272. This subject does appear in art occasionally, e.g. on the Chiaravalle choir-stalls mentioned in the previous note, and in a picture in S. Ambrogio at Milan (T. Hümpfner, *Ikonographie des Hl. Bernard*, 1927, Plates 78 and 47). (3) Bollandists, 20 August, p. 248. (4) Van Marle, *Development of the Italian Schools of Painting*, Vol. III, Fig. 261. (5) Migne, *Patrologia Latina*, Vol. 182 (1854), Col. 1133 sqq. (6) This text is used also for the figure of S. Bernard in No. 1468 of this Gallery, Style of Orcagna. (7) *Catalogo della Galleria Comunale di Prato*, 1912, p. 14, with reproduction; also reproduced by Van Marle, *Development of the Italian Schools of Painting*, Vol. IV, p. 229. (8) Baldinucci, *Notizie*, I, 1845, p. 508. The position appears to have been near to the chapel, which was—and is—dedicated to S. Bernard; see A. Lensi, *Palazzo Vecchio*, 1929, p. 16. That chapel was possibly dedicated to S. Bernard because of the important functions in the State of the Cistercians of the Badia at Settimo; Richa, *Notizie Istoriche delle Chiese Fiorentine*, I, 1754, p. 305. The popular tradition that the original dedication was to the Vallombrosan B. Bernardo Uberti and became transferred by a confusion to S. Bernard of Clairvaux is rejected by Giulianelli in Richa, *op. cit.*, X, 1762, pp. 219 ff. and by (Follini and Rastrelli), *Firenze Antica e Moderna*, V, 1794, pp. 366/7; also by Richa, *op. cit.*, II, 1755, p. 233, who claims that the foundation stone of the Palazzo Vecchio was laid on the feast of S. Bernard, 20 August, 1298 (but contrast Frey, *Die Loggia dei Lanzi*, 1885, pp. 183/5). (9) Vasari, ed. Milanesi, II, p. 617; 1550 edition, p. 396. (10) Anonimo Magliabechiano, ed. Frey, 1892, p. 97. On the same page a small picture of S. Bernard is recorded in the Murate at Florence; that picture appears to be otherwise unknown. (11) Washington, Catalogue, 1941, No. 536; Illustrations, 1941, p. 130; size, 40½×64. (12) R. Œrtel, *Fra Filippo Lippi*, 1942, pp. 67/8. (13) Mrs. Jameson, *Legends of the Monastic Orders*, 1850, p. 153, as Gozzoli. (14) As Masaccio.

666   THE ANNUNCIATION

On the parapet centre is a device in grisaille, three feathers or plumes, and a ring (discussed below).

Wood, rounded top, 27×60 (0·685×1·52); painted up to the edges all round.

Considerably damaged, but less in the figures than elsewhere, and still preserving much of its original quality.

For the commentary, etc., see No. 667 below.

667   SEVEN SAINTS

From left to right, SS. Francis, Lawrence, Cosmas (or Damian), John the Baptist, Damian (or Cosmas), Anthony Abbot and Peter Martyr.

Wood, rounded top, 26¾×59¾ (0·68×1·515); painted up to the edges all round.

More damaged than its pendant, No. 666 above; the quality of most of the heads and hands is to a varying degree disturbed by repaint.

Nos. 666 and 667 were sold in the nineteenth century from the Palazzo Riccardi (formerly Medici) at Florence. A Medicean origin for the two pictures is indeed fairly sure, although there do not appear to be any old records of them, and their purpose, presumably as overdoors to judge by their shape, is not very clear.

The three feathers in a diamond ring form a well-known Medicean device. It is true that the Rucellai family also used the device of two, even in one case three, feathers in a diamond ring.[1] The Medici also sometimes used only two feathers,[2] so the matter is confusing. But in the case of Nos. 666/7, the device may reasonably be associated with the Medici, since the pictures come from Palazzo Riccardi, and further, Fra Filippo is known to have been employed a good deal by the Medici family.

The device was, according to Giovio, first used in the Medici family by Lorenzo the Magnificent;[3] Lorenzo certainly used it,[4] but it was certainly also used by his father, Piero the Gouty,[5] and perhaps by his grandfather, Cosimo *Pater Patriæ*.[6]

The saints in No. 667 also seem to have been connected with the Medici. They recur (with the addition of S. Julian) in an altarpiece by Baldovinetti in the Uffizi,[7] where also S. Peter Martyr, instead of the more usual S. Dominic, balances S. Francis. Baldovinetti's altarpiece came in 1796 from the chapel of the Medicean Villa at Cafaggiolo,[8] for which it may be assumed to have been painted; and Cafaggiolo at that period seems to have been associated with Cosimo *Pater Patriæ*, his son Piero the Gouty and his grandsons, Lorenzo the Magnificent and Giuliano.[9]

The saints on No. 667 and on Baldovinetti's picture, therefore, probably had a connection with the branch of the Medici family descending from Cosimo *Pater Patriæ*. The following tentative explanation of them is proposed. Giovanni Bicci de' Medici is considered to be the man who first firmly established the fortunes of the Medici family; S. John the Baptist is in the centre of No. 667. According to Litta, Giovanni Bicci had four sons, Antonio, Damiano, Cosimo *Pater Patriæ* and Lorenzo; these are the names of the four saints nearest to the Baptist.[10] Cosimo's son was named Piero; and S. Peter Martyr is one of the remaining saints. The last saint is S. Francis; and Piero's father-in-law was named Francesco.

In Baldovinetti's picture, the eighth saint, the one missing from No. 667, is S. Julian; Giuliano was the name of the younger brother of Lorenzo the Magnificent. Baldovinetti's picture has been thought to have been painted to celebrate the birth of Giuliano in 1453.[11] This may be true; in any case the absence of S. Julian from No. 667, if the proposed explanation is on the right lines, perhaps implies that Giuliano was not yet in existence.

Lorenzo the Magnificent was born in 1449. The subject of No. 666, *The Annunciation*, would seem hardly suitable for a birth; perhaps rather for an heir not born, but expected. If Nos. 666/7 were painted in his honour, it is suggested that they might date from 1448. Alternatively it could be suggested that the expected birth is that of Giuliano or a sister; but this seems less probable.[12]

On stylistic grounds, a date of *ca.* 1457/8 has been suggested;[13] but the arguments for precisely these years do not seem to be entirely convincing.

PROVENANCE: Both pictures were acquired shortly before 1848 from Palazzo Riccardi by the Metzger brothers of Florence.[14] No. 666 was seen at their shop by Eastlake in 1855, at which time No. 667 had already been sold to Alexander Barker.[15] No. 667 is mentioned in Waagen's Supplement as in the Barker Collection,[16] and was exhibited at the British Institution in 1858 (No. 21);[17] purchased from Alexander Barker, 1861. No. 666 was acquired by Sir Charles Eastlake in or after 1855, and was presented by him at the time that No. 667 was purchased.

REPRODUCTIONS: *Illustrations, Italian Schools*, 1937, pp. 188/9. *Plates, Earlier Italian Schools*, 1953, Vol. II, pp. 234–236.

REFERENCES: (1) The use of the device by the Medici and the Rucellai is discussed, apropos of Nos. 666/7, in an article by the compiler in *Critica d'Arte*, January, 1950, pp. 356 ff. For the use by the Rucellai of three feathers in a diamond ring, see the original frame of No. 227 of this catalogue, an altarpiece classed as by Botticini, which has the Rucellai arms in the predella. It has been suggested that the use of this device by the Rucellai is dependent upon its use by the Medici; Stegmann and Geymüller, *Die Architektur der Renaissance in Toscana*, 1885 sqq., III, p. 10, point out that Bernardo, the son of the builder of Palazzo Rucellai, was betrothed in 1461 and was married in 1466 to Nannina, a sister of Lorenzo the Magnificent. But this argument does not seem valid for the Botticini, No. 227. That altarpiece may not unreasonably be associated with Gerolamo di Piero di Cardinale Rucellai, whose tomb is close to where the picture hung; and Gerolamo was only a fourth cousin of Bernardo. (2) Two feathers in a diamond ring may be seen on supports for the capitals in at least four rooms on the ground floor at Palazzo Riccardi; on supports for the capitals in the cloister of the Badia at Fiesole, a Medicean building; and on the tomb of Piero and Giovanni di Cosimo in S. Lorenzo at Florence (L. Planiscig, *Andrea del Verrocchio*, 1941, Plate 24). (3) Giovio, *Dialogo dell'Imprese Militari et Amorose*, Lyons, 1559, pp. 40 ff. Giovio specifies the colours of the feathers as red, white and green. There is an example with these colours, associated with Pope Leo X, in the Museo Artistico Industriale at Rome; *Catalogo della Mostra Medicea*, Florence, 1939, No. 49. It may nevertheless be doubted if the colours were considered important, since the device is frequently shown in stone or bronze. (4) The evidence of miniatures is decisive; cf. E. Barfucci, *Lorenzo de' Medici e la Società Artistica del suo Tempo*, 1945, Fig. 106 and pp. 297 f. See further in the article in *Critica d'Arte* mentioned in note 1. (5) It appears on the Cappella del Crocefisso in S. Miniato at Florence, which cannot be dissociated from Piero. See Venturi, *Storia dell'Arte Italiana*, Vol. VIII, Part I, Figs. 187 and 194; Stegmann and Geymüller, *op. cit.*, II, Plate XI; Berti, *San Miniato*, 1850, pp. 65 f. and 151. It has been mentioned in note 2 that it appears on the tomb of Piero and his brother Giovanni in S. Lorenzo at Florence; L. Planiscig, *Andrea del Verrocchio*, 1941, Plate 24. (6) It apparently does not appear on Cosimo's tomb. The already mentioned Badia at Fiesole is in great part due to the munificence of Cosimo: see Vespasiano da Bisticci, *Vite di Uomini Illustri*, ed. Ludovico Frati, III, 1893, p. 49; A. J. Rusconi, *Fiesole*, 1931, p. 70; *Catalogo delle Cose d'Arte e di Antichità d'Italia, Fiesole*, by O. H. Giglioli, 1933, p. 70 (inscription of 1462). The cloister of the Badia was certainly built in Cosimo's life-time, in 1459; see C. von Fabriczy, *Filippo Brunelleschi*, 1892, pp. 588/9, 606. Some further arguments in favour of Cosimo could perhaps be drawn from Palazzo Riccardi, where the device occurs very frequently; but it seems uncertain which parts of the construction were seen to by Cosimo himself. Perhaps Benozzo's frescoes of *ca*. 1459 in the chapel offer the best evidence. Apparently only three figures in these frescoes can be distinguished as connected with the Medici family; Cosimo is possibly symbolized by the old man, whose horse's trappings are ornamented with groups of peacock's feathers, also interlaced diamond rings with the motto *semper*, also the Medici *palle* in a diamond ring and the three feathers alternately. The device is found on the doorway of the Medici Bank at Milan, now in the Castello Sforzesco there; the compiler is not convinced that this should be dissociated from Cosimo. (7) Reproduced by Van Marle, *Development of the Italian Schools of Painting*, Vol. XI, Fig. 157.

(8) See Ferdinando Ranalli, *Storia della Pittura dal suo Risorgimento*, etc., I, 1841, No. 19. A Chapel at this Villa was already in existence in 1464; see E. Müntz, *Les Collections des Médicis*, 1888, p. 51. A chapel dedicated to SS. Cosmas and Damian is mentioned by G. M. Brocchi, *Descrizione della Provincia del Mugello*, 1748, p. 50. (9) See further in the article in *Critica d'Arte*, mentioned in note 1. (10) Litta, *Famiglie Celebri d'Italia*, Tav. VIII of the Medici family; he says that Antonio and Damiano died very young in 1398 and 1390. G. Pieraccini, *La Stirpe de' Medici di Cafaggiolo*, I, 1924, p. 13, says that he has found no confirmation of the existence of Antonio and Damiano; but Litta could hardly have invented them. (11) Ruth Wedgwood Kennedy, *Alesso Baldovinetti*, 1938, p. 55. (12) Giles Robertson in *The Burlington Magazine*, 1953, p. 28. objects to part of this commentary; but the compiler thinks that some of his criticisms misinterpret the text above. He fully agrees that the suggestion concerning the choice of *The Annunciation* for one of the pictures is doubtful; but he does not think that what is printed above (without alteration from the first edition of this catalogue) is impossible or too confidently phrased. (13) Pudelko in the *Rivista d'Arte*, 1936, pp. 52/4; R. Œrtel, *Fra Filippo Lippi*, 1942, pp. 41 f.; Mary Pittaluga, *Filippo Lippi*, 1949, pp. 202/3. (14) Vasari, Le Monnier edition, IV, 1848, p. 118. Some search in old Medici inventories for these pictures revealed nothing. (15) Eastlake's note-book, 1855. (16) Waagen, *Treasures*, IV, 1857, pp. 71/2. (17) Cf., besides the catalogue, George Scharf, *Artistic and Descriptive Notes* on this exhibition, 1858, pp. 42/3. The picture was then supposed to contain portraits of Cosimo and Lorenzo de' Medici, Savonarola, etc.

Ascribed to FRA FILIPPO LIPPI

3424 THE VIRGIN AND CHILD

In the spandrels at the top, under the frame, are two coats of arms, referred to below.

Wood. The size of the panel is 30×24 ($0 \cdot 765 \times 0 \cdot 61$). The size of the original painted surface was probably a little less; the paint at the edges is damaged and made up, except at the bottom—where the picture may have been cut a little.

On the whole, the condition is satisfactory.

The main part of the picture has a rounded top. Originally the spandrels right and left at the top were painted somewhat in the manner of the *Virgin and Child* at Washington (formerly Berlin);[1] some remnant of the original work is to be found on the right. For the most part these spandrels are now covered with more recent and very coarse paint, itself a good deal damaged, including two coats of arms; there may have been coats of arms on the original, but it is not certain.

The coat on the left is that of the Strozzi family. On the right are the arms of two families impaled. Those on the left belong to the Ruggieri family of Padua, and to some non-Italian families also; those on the right could belong to Tergola da Villa Rappa of Padua, Turretini of Lucca, da Vinci of Tuscany, and others. It is not possible to make any deduction from these arms, except that the picture was owned at some time by some member of the Strozzi family, of which there were innumerable branches. Even if it were sure that the arms are copied from arms originally on the picture, it would not be sure that they were copied correctly. In point of fact, the present arms may indicate the owner at the time they were put on, and not the person who had originally commissioned the picture.

The picture was formerly catalogued as by Filippo Lippi. Although very near to the works of his mature style, it is rather weak and lifeless for him, and is probably in part at least of studio execution. Mendelsohn ascribes it to a painter influenced by Lippi and perhaps Pesellino;[2] but it seems unnecessary to go outside the immediate orbit of Lippi. Pudelko gives it a wrong inventory number, confuses it with another picture, and ascribes it to an assistant.[3] Berenson (1932 and 1936 Lists) accepts it as Lippi, Œrtel[4] does not; Mary Pittaluga[5] thinks the head of the Virgin is probably by Lippi, the rest by Don Diamante.

PROVENANCE: Bought by Lord Brownlow in Florence in 1874.[6] Exhibited at the Burlington Fine Arts Club, 1906 (No. 28) and 1919 (No. 7); presented by Lord Brownlow, 1919.

REPRODUCTION: *Illustrations, Italian Schools*, 1937, p. 187. *Plates, Earlier Italian Schools*, 1953, Vol. II, p. 237.

REFERENCES: (1) Washington, 1941 Catalogue, No. 401, and Illustrations, 1941, p. 129. (2) Henriette Mendelsohn, *Fra Filippo Lippi*, 1909, pp. 195 ff. (3) Pudelko in the *Rivista d'Arte*, 1936, p. 56. (4) R. Œrtel, *Fra Filippo Lippi*, 1942, p. 69. (5) Mary Pittaluga, *Filippo Lippi*, 1949, p. 204. (6) N.G. Catalogue, 1920.

See also PESELLINO, Nos. 727, etc.

LIPPO DI DALMASIO
ca. 1352 (?)–1410 or later

Of a Bolognese family named *Scannabecchi*. He is supposed to have been born *ca.* 1352 (Antonio Bolognini Amorini, *Vite de' Pittori ed Artefici Bolognesi*, I, 1841, p. 16); he is first surely recorded as existing in 1373. His father Dalmasio was also a painter. Between 1377 and 1389 he was living, perhaps constantly, at Pistoia; thereafter at Bologna. He made his will in 1410, and was dead by 1421. Several signed works have survived. In addition to the bibliography in Thieme-Becker (s.v. Scannabecchi), see Francesco Filippini and Guido Zucchini, *Miniatori e Pittori a Bologna*, 1947, s.v. *Dalmasio* and *Lippo*.

752 'THE MADONNA OF HUMILITY'

The Virgin, holding the Child, is seated in a meadow, with a glory behind her; she has a crown of twelve stars, and the moon is at her feet. Signed: *.lippus dalmasii pinxit.*

Canvas, perhaps transferred from panel, $43\frac{1}{4} \times 34\frac{1}{4}$ ($1 \cdot 10 \times 0 \cdot 87$).

Much damaged and repainted,[1] so that the style is considerably affected.

The moon and the stars refer, as is quite common with the 'Madonna of Humility,' to Revelation xii, 1. It seems clear that the glory behind the Virgin represents the words in the same verse, 'clothed with the sun.'[2]

PROVENANCE: In the Malvezzi Collection at Bologna in 1773,[3] and therefore presumably the same as the undescribed picture owned by Lucio Malvezzi in 1678.[4] Recorded in 1816 in the Hercolani Collection, Bologna,[5] where it still was in 1861.[6] Purchased from Michelangelo Gualandi, 1866.

REPRODUCTION: *Illustrations, Italian Schools*, 1937, p. 190. *Plates, Earlier Italian Schools*, 1953, Vol. II, p. 238.

REFERENCES: (1) It was retouched by Domenico Pedrini in 1773; Francesco Filippini and Guido Zucchini, *Miniatori e Pittori a Bologna*, 1947, p. 160, referring to Oretti, MS. B 123 at Bologna, p. 72. The passage concerning the condition is: 'ma tutta volta in quattro pezzi rimessa in una nuova tela, il Betusti (?) la fece ritoccare al Sr Domenico Pedrini l'anno 1773.' (X-Rays of some parts of No. 752 do reveal various tears.) (2) For a picture by or after Paolo da Modena at Modena, which is iconographically similar and has 'LA NOSTRA DONNA D UMILTA' inscribed on it, see M. Meiss in *The Art Bulletin*, 1936, p. 438 and Fig. 7, and R. Pallucchini, *I Dipinti della Galleria Estense di Modena*, 1945, No. 3 and Fig. 3. For a picture, also iconographically similar, on which the text from *Revelation* is quoted, see the Ranuccio d'Arvari at Legnago; reproduced by Trecca in *Madonna Verona*, 1909, pp. 149 f., and by Fiocco, *ib.*, 1912, pp. 229 ff. (3) Oretti, MS. B 123 in the Biblioteca dell'Archiginnasio at Bologna. Oretti appears to record No. 752 twice; on p. 71 'Casa Maluezi del Sig^r Luzio, un altra Imag^e della Madonna,' and p. 72 (an addition to the first form of the MS.), 'Casa del Senatore Maluezzi,' with identifying description and the record of the condition quoted in note 1. Oretti, in another MS. also in the Biblioteca dell'Archiginnasio at Bologna (B 104, Part I), also appears to record No. 752 twice. On p. 54, in the Palazzo Malvezzi, Palazzo del Sig^re Luzio, è incontro alla Chiesa de PP. di S. Giacomo, he mentions *Una Madonna di Lippo Dalmasio*; on p. 100, Palazzo Malvezzi del Sr Senatore da S. Sigismondo, Aggiunta di altre pitture, he notes *Una Madonna col Bambino di Lippo Dalmasio*. (4) Carlo Cesare Malvasia, *Felsina Pittrice*, I, 1678, p. 30. (5) Petronio Bassani, *Guida agli amatori delle Belle Arti . . . per la città di Bologna*, I, i, 1816, p. 211, *Q. La B.V. col Bambino ec., m.f.* On p. 206, the author records that Conte Astorre Hercolani married Marchesa Maria Malvezzi da S. Sigismondo, through whom some Malvezzi property passed into the Hercolani possession. (6) The picture was seen by Eastlake in the Hercolani Collection in 1861; it was No. 9 of an inventory of January, 1861, *Collezione della principessa donna Maria Hercolani in Bologna* (inventory kindly communicated by the Avv. Ambrosini of Bologna). No. 752 is also recorded by Crowe and Cavalcaselle, *History of Painting in Italy*, II, 1864, p. 209.

AMBROGIO LORENZETTI
active 1319–1347

A Sienese painter, occasionally active at Florence; younger (?) brother of Pietro Lorenzetti. A *Virgin and Child* at Vico l'Abate, not signed or documented but acceptable as his, is dated 1319. Several authenticated works exist; e.g. some frescoes in the Palazzo Pubblico at Siena, and *The Presentation* in the Uffizi at Florence.

1147   FRESCO: A GROUP OF POOR CLARES (FRAGMENT)

Fresco, irregular shape; greatest height, 23 in. (0·585); greatest width, 20½ in. (0·52).

Considerably damaged; but the face of the principal figure is not badly preserved.

This fragment comes from the Chapter House of S. Francesco, Siena, apparently from a large wall-painting, the subject of which was perhaps *The Body of S. Francis halted at S. Damiano, Assisi, and wept over by S. Clare and her Companions.*[1]

The frescoes discovered in the Chapter House of S. Francesco, Siena, in the middle of the last century include (besides No. 1147) two large Franciscan scenes and a *Crucifixion,* now in the church; a *Resurrected Christ* and a head from a decorative border, still in the Chapter House (now Refectory); probably Nos. 3071 and 3072 below;[2] and a few other small fragments.[3]

All these frescoes were associated with the Lorenzetti, perhaps because Ambrogio is recorded by Ghiberti and other writers to have painted frescoes in the cloister of the convent. The Chapter House frescoes seem to be distinct from those.[4] There is general agreement that some of the existing works are by Ambrogio Lorenzetti, and some probably by Pietro. There is enough original work left on No. 1147 for us to be confident that it is by Ambrogio.

PROVENANCE: The Chapter House frescoes in S. Francesco, Siena, were discovered under whitewash shortly before 1855.[5] It was apparently at once that No. 1147 was removed by the *maestro di casa* to his own room, where it remained apparently unrecorded. Purchased from him through Charles Fairfax Murray and Cav. P. Lombardi of Siena, 1878.[6]

REPRODUCTION: *Illustrations, Italian Schools,* 1937, p. 194. *Plates, Earlier Italian Schools,* 1953, Vol. II, p. 239.

REFERENCES: (1) The habit is correct for Poor Clares; but it chances that the parts of the figures shown make them look rather like Dominicans. The subject suggested occurs in S. Francesco, Assisi; reproduced by Van Marle, *Development of the Italian Schools of Painting,* Vol. III, Fig. 103. (2) Ascribed to Pietro Lorenzetti. (3) The two Franciscan scenes are Van Marle, *op. cit.,* Vol. II, Figs. 254/7; the *Crucifixion* is Van Marle, Vol. II, Fig. 239, Cecchi, *Pietro Lorenzetti,* 1930, Plates XCV–XCVIII, or G. Sinibaldi, *I Lorenzetti,* 1933, Plate XV; the *Resurrected Christ* is Cecchi, Plate XCIX, or Sinibaldi, Plate XVI; the head is Cecchi, Plate C. (4) E. von Meyenburg, *Ambrogio Lorenzetti,* 1903, pp. 14 and 23 ff.; Sinibaldi, *op. cit.,* pp. 172 ff., 197 f., 212 ff. Nevertheless, Toesca, *Il Trecento,* 1951, p. 588, claims identity. (5) The original positions of the four subject pieces are described by Milanesi in the *Monitore Toscano,* 27 January, 1855; reprinted in his *Sulla Storia dell'Arte Toscana, Scritti Varj,* 1873, pp. 357 ff. He notes that other fragments come from a second room, formerly part of the same Chapter House; No. 1147 may be one of these other fragments. The two Franciscan scenes were transferred to the church in 1857; see V. Lusini, *Storia della Basilica di S. Francesco in Siena,* 1894, p. 214. (6) Letter from C. Fairfax Murray, 2 August, 1877, in the Gallery archives; N.G. MS. Catalogue, and Report for 1878.

PIETRO LORENZETTI

A Sienese painter, brother of Ambrogio Lorenzetti. He may be identical with a Petruccio Lorenzo who did some slight painting in the

Palazzo Comunale at Siena in 1306; but his first authenticated work is an altarpiece of 1320 in the Pieve at Arezzo. Several other authenticated works exist, e.g. *The Birth of the Virgin* in the Cathedral Museum at Siena, referred to in the entry for No. 1113 below.

Ascribed to PIETRO LORENZETTI

1113   S. SABINUS BEFORE THE GOVERNOR(?) (PREDELLA PANEL FROM AN ALTARPIECE)

The scene is probably that where the Governor of Tuscany, Venustianus (later canonized), summoned the Bishop S. Sabinus and his two deacons, SS. Marcellus and Exuperantius, before him, and tried to make them worship an image of Jupiter.

Wood, painted surface, $12 \times 10\frac{3}{4}$ (0.305×0.27). Including the original frame, the total size is $14\frac{3}{4} \times 13$ (0.375×0.33). The frame is original, but not in one piece with the picture; the top 1 in. of the panel (below the frame along the top) is further an (original) addition.

Very good condition, in spite of some prominent scratches.

In November, 1335, Pietro Lorenzetti received the first payment for an altarpiece for the chapel of S. Savino in Siena Cathedral. The central part of this altarpiece, representing *The Nativity of the Virgin*, and signed and dated 1342, is now in the Cathedral Museum. Flanking panels, representing S. Sabinus and S. Bartholomew, are missing. No description of a predella for this altarpiece is known, but it is certain that there was a predella; in December, 1335, master Ciecho was paid for translating the legend of S. Sabinus into the vernacular for the purposes of the picture.[1]

That Pietro Lorenzetti should require help over the story of the Sienese S. Sabinus is not surprising; the Bollandists themselves have confessed that they know practically nothing of him.[2] He was certainly a Patron of Siena, and he appears in Duccio's *Maestà*, which was the high-altarpiece of the Cathedral.[3] He is traditionally identified with S. Sabinus of Assisi. This Bishop, with his deacons Marcellus and Exuperantius, was imprisoned at Assisi by Venustianus, the Governor of Tuscany. He summoned them before him, and tried to make them worship a small statue of Jupiter of coral, covered with gold mesh. Sabinus threw it on the ground; Venustianus cut off his hands and tortured the deacons.[4] Venustianus was later converted; still later, Sabinus was martyred in the year 303, at Spoleto.

The above story corresponds quite well with the scene in No. 1113; so it is likely that Fairfax Murray[5] was right in supposing it to be from the predella of Pietro Lorenzetti's S. Savino altarpiece. The question then arises whether the execution is by Pietro himself (predella quality), or from his studio, or by a follower. The attribution to Pietro is sometimes accepted; but DeWald and Sinibaldi incline to attribute the picture to a follower known as the Master of the Dijon Triptych.[6]

A predella panel in the Vatican, where the subject is apparently *Christ before Pilate*, is very close indeed in style to No. 1113, and it is possible that it comes from the same altarpiece.[7]

PROVENANCE: Presented by Charles Fairfax Murray, 1882. Cleaned Pictures Exhibition at the National Gallery, 1947/8 (No. 13).

REPRODUCTION: *Illustrations, Italian Schools*, 1937, p. 195. *Plates, Earlier Italian Schools*, 1953, Vol. II, p. 240.

REFERENCES: (1) For the whole of this paragraph, see Pèleo Bacci, *Dipinti Inediti e Sconosciuti di Pietro Lorenzetti*, etc., 1939, pp. 90 ff. (2) *Acta Sanctorum*, 30 October, Vol. 62 (1883), p. 235. (3) Shown in Van Marle, *Development of the Italian Schools of Painting*, II, Fig. 11; the name is inscribed, but Van Marle has it wrong. Some more about S. Sabinus can be found in Enzo Carli, *Vetrata Duccesca*, 1946, pp. 46/7. (4) Cf. L. Iacobilli, *Vite de Santi e Beati dell'Umbria*, Vol. III, 1666, pp. 249/50. The story, with some variation, is illustrated in two scenes of the Arca di San Savino at Faenza; see L. Dussler, *Benedetto da Majano*, 1924. Plates 1 and 2. (5) Fairfax Murray *ap.* Crowe and Cavalcaselle, Italian edition, III, 1885, p. 201. (6) E. T. DeWald in *Art Studies*, 1929, p. 158; Giulia Sinibaldi, *I Lorenzetti*, 1933, p. 177. (7) Van Marle, *op. cit.*, II, fig. 226. Sinibaldi, *op. cit.*, pp. 177/8 and Plate XXVII, says that a predella panel in the Mason Perkins Collection may be connected, at least in style; it does not appear to be from the same series.

3071   FRESCO: A CROWNED FEMALE FIGURE (FRAGMENT)

Perhaps an allegorical figure of one of the Virtues.

Fresco, irregular shape; greatest height, 15 in. (0·38); greatest width, 13 in. (0·33).
Much damaged and repainted.
Incised lines forming a gable top, and apparently the remains of similar lines at the left and left bottom, indicate pretty clearly that this figure was once in a hexagon. It is no doubt from the decorative border framing a large fresco. See further in the entry for No. 3072 below.

3072   FRESCO: A FEMALE SAINT IN YELLOW (FRAGMENT)

Fresco, irregular shape; greatest height 15½ in. (0·39); greatest width, 11 in. (0·28).
A good deal damaged.
In a cusped medallion; sufficient parts of the border exist for the shape to be quite clear. The fragment is tipped slightly as framed at present.

Nos. 3071 and 3072 are stated in 1864 and 1869 to be from S. Francesco at Siena.[1] In his MS. Catalogue, Layard dubiously inserted S. Agostino as the name of the church, but it is fairly certain that this was due merely to a lapse of memory.[2] There can, indeed, be little doubt that Nos. 3071 and 3072 are from the Chapter House of S. Francesco, just like No. 1147 above (Ambrogio Lorenzetti). It may be added that a head in a hexagon, apparently of similar size to No. 3071, still exists in the Chapter House (now Refectory) of S. Francesco;[3] and that the framing of two Franciscan scenes, now removed to the church, contains cusped medallions with armorial decoration, similar in shape to the medallion of No. 3072.[4] Both No. 3071 and 3072 are clearly fragments from the borders of large frescoes, which are not necessarily identical with any of those that have survived.

Nos. 3071 and 3072 were formerly ascribed in the Gallery to Ambrogio Lorenzetti. No. 3072 appears to be in the style of Pietro, who appears to have painted other frescoes also in the Chapter House.[5] No. 3071 may seem too much damaged for attribution, but it is reasonable to class it with No. 3072.

PROVENANCE: Purchased by Sir Austen Henry Layard 'from a man who had cut them out of the wall.'[6] As explained above, Layard dubiously says that the wall was in S. Agostino, Siena; but they are mentioned in 1864 by Crowe and Cavalcaselle as being from S. Francesco, presumably the Chapter House. Exhibited at the South Kensington Museum, 1869 (Nos. 41, 42). Layard Bequest, 1916.[7]

REPRODUCTIONS: *Illustrations, Italian Schools*, 1937, p. 194; *Plates, Earlier Italian Schools*, 1953, Vol. II, pp. 241–242 (framed as octagons).

REFERENCES: (1) Crowe and Cavalcaselle, *History of Painting in Italy*, II, 1864, p. 136; South Kensington Museum Exhibition, 1869 (Nos. 41, 42). For the S. Francesco frescoes, see the entry for Ambrogio Lorenzetti, No. 1147, above. (2) The text is 'fragments of a fresco painted in the church of S. Agostino (?) at Siena—described by Ghiberti & Vasari.' The lighter colour of the ink for 'S. Agostino (?)' shows that the space was left blank at first; then the name was inserted and blotted at once. Ghiberti and Vasari record frescoes by Ambrogio Lorenzetti both in S. Francesco and in S. Agostino at Siena: Ghiberti, *I Commentarii*, ed. Schlosser, 1912, i, pp. 40/1, and ii, pp. 142/4, and Vasari, ed. Milanesi, Vol. I, pp. 521/2. What appear to be fragments of the S. Agostino series are reproduced by G. Sinibaldi, *I Lorenzetti*, 1933, Plate XXXIII. (3) E. Cecchi, *Pietro Lorenzetti*, 1930, Plate C. Sinibaldi, *op. cit.*, pp. 216/7, gives the size as 0·42 × 0·35; possibly 0·35 × 0·42 was meant. (4) One of these borders appears partially in the reproduction by L. Gielly, *Les Primitifs Siennois*, 1926, Plate XLVII. (5) Sinibaldi, *op. cit.*, pp. 197/8, calls Nos. 3071/2 Ambrogio, which indeed appears to be the generally accepted view. But on pp. 216/7 she cites the variations of criticism concerning the head in a hexagon at S. Francesco, which appears to be closely related; and in any case a comparison with No. 1147 above, which appears to be clearly by Ambrogio, makes another name for Nos. 3071/2 desirable. (6) Layard MS. Catalogue in the National Gallery; cf. note 2. (7) For the history of the Layard Collection, see Appendix IV.

LORENZO DI CREDI
ca. 1458–1537

Florentine School. In his mother Lisa's tax declaration of 1470 (unpublished; Florence, Archivio di Stato, Quartiere Santo Spirito, Gonfalone Ferza, p. 99 of 2nd volume), Lorenzo's age was given as 12; in her, published, declaration of 1480/1, his age was given as 21. There is alternative, but greatly inferior, evidence that he was born in 1456 (inscription on the back of a portrait at Washington, 1942 Catalogue, *Works of Art from the Widener Collection*, No. 634; photographs of the inscription are in the Gallery files). Lorenzo was the son of Andrea, a goldsmith. He had some training as a sculptor, but was chiefly active as a painter. He is recorded as a painter in Verrocchio's studio in 1480/1, and was apparently there constantly until Verrocchio's death in 1488.

Not many documented or dated works by Lorenzo exist. An altarpiece in the Louvre (Seymour de Ricci's Catalogue, *Ecoles d'Italie et d'Espagne*, 1913, No. 1263; Mlle. Blumer in the *Bulletin de la Société de l'Histoire de l'Art Français*, 1936, p. 278, No. 173) is documented. The date of 20 February, 1493 (1494 n.s.), records apparently its completion; see Prof. Medici in the *Rivista Europea*, Vol. XXI (1880), p. 237 (evidence quoted in *L'Arte*, 1906, p. 258, is imprecise with regard to the date; the date of 1503 given in Colnaghi's *Dictionary of Florentine Painters*, 1928, p. 79, is a mistake). A *S. Bartholomew* in Orsanmichele certainly, and a *Nativity* in the Uffizi possibly, may be considered documented, and of before 1510 (see Albertini's *Memoriale* of 1510). An altarpiece in S. Maria delle Grazie at Pistoia is documented as of *ca.* 1510 (Vasari, ed. Milanesi, Vol. IV, p. 566; the provenance is vouched for by F. Tolomei, *Guida di Pistoia*, 1821, p. 81). A *S. Michael* in the Cathedral of Florence is implied to be documented as of *ca.* 1523 (Vasari, ed. Milanesi, Vol. IV, pp. 200 and 568). All these pictures, except the *S. Bartholomew* in Orsanmichele, are reproduced by Van Marle, *Development of the Italian Schools of Painting*, Vol. XIII; the *S. Bartholomew* is reproduced in the *Rivista d'Arte*, 1932, p. 435.

There is enough fact to form a good idea of Lorenzo di Credi's style, but his chronology is not very sure. He would seem to have been a painter who developed little; this can be stated positively as regards his mature works, but the evidence concerning his earliest style is weak. This matter of dating is relevant to Lorenzo's possible or probable participation in an altarpiece in the Cathedral of Pistoia, which is commented on in the biography of Verrocchio. In any event, it need not be doubted that Lorenzo's style was strongly influenced by that of the young Leonardo da Vinci.

Lorenzo di Credi does not appear to have painted in fresco. He had several pupils, and inferior repetitions of his designs were no doubt sometimes executed by these.

593 THE VIRGIN AND CHILD

Tobias and the Angel are seen in the background.

Wood, painted surface, $28 \times 19\frac{1}{2}$ (0·71 × 0·495); painted up to the edges all round.

Very good condition.

This appears to be an early work.[1]

VERSIONS: Figures on the same design as the Virgin and Child here occur in the Vatican;[2] in the Esmond Harmsworth Collection;[3] and (a tondo, with S. Joseph and the little S. John added) now or formerly in Russia.[4] Free variants of the design are not uncommon.

PROVENANCE: From the Collection of the Cav. Mancini, Florence.[5] In the Lombardi-Baldi Collection, Florence, by 1852;[6] purchased thence with other pictures, 1857.[7]

REPRODUCTION: *Illustrations, Italian Schools*, 1937, p. 113. *Plates, Earlier Italian Schools*, 1953, Vol. II, p. 243.

REFERENCES: (1) Cf. Thieme-Becker, s.v. Credi. Degenhart dates it *ca.* 1485 in the *Rivista d'Arte*, 1932, p. 444, or *ca.* 1485/90 in the *Münchner Jahrbuch*, 1932, p. 159. (2) Reproduced by Degenhart in the *Münchner Jahrbuch*, 1932, p. 112, as Gianjacopo di Castrocaro (Mattoncini). It used to be numbered 147 at the Vatican, and is No. 340 of the 1933 *Guida*, p. 150; size, 0·75 × 0·57. (3) Reproduced in *The Burlington Magazine*, Vol. XLII (1923), p. 49, size 0·883 × 0·654, and lent by the Hon. Esmond Harmsworth to the Daily Telegraph Exhition at Olympia, 1928 (X 7), with reproduction; in each case as Piero di Cosimo. (4) *Les Anciennes Ecoles de Peinture dans les Palais et Collections Privées Russes*, 1910, p. 23, with reproduction (Coll. Prince Kotchoubey). (5) N.G. Report; this name is also written on the back of the panel. (6) Vasari, Le Monnier edition, Vol. VIII, 1852, p. 206. (7) For the history of the Lombardi-Baldi Collection, see Appendix I.

648 THE VIRGIN ADORING THE CHILD

In the background, the Announcement to the Shepherds.

Wood, painted surface, 34 × 23¾ (0·865 × 0·605); painted up to the edges all round.

Good condition, but less good than No. 593 above.

This appears to be an early work.[1]

VARIANTS: No exact version of the design appears to be known. A picture at Dresden is fairly closely related,[2] and another design not very dissimilar is repeated frequently.[3]

PROVENANCE: In the Collection of Karl Aders, a German merchant living in London; exhibited for sale at 10 Warwick Street, 1835 (?), No. 44; Sale, Foster's, 1 August, 1835 (lot 101), bought by Longdile; Anon (H. C. Robinson or rather Aders Trust) Sale, Christie's, 26 April, 1839 (lot 30), bought by Rodd.[4] In Lord Northwick's Collection, Thirlestaine House, Cheltenham by 1846, and seen there by Waagen;[5] *Hours in Lord Northwick's Picture Galleries*, 1858 (No. 287); Northwick Sale, 3 August, 1859 (lot 579), bought by Chr. J. Nieuwenhuys.[6] Purchased with the rest of the Edmond Beaucousin Collection, Paris, 1860.

REPRODUCTION: *Illustrations, Italian Schools*, 1937, p. 113. *Plates, Earlier Italian Schools*, 1953, Vol. II, p. 244.

REFERENCES: (1) Degenhart in the *Rivista d'Arte*, 1932, p. 443, and in the *Münchner Jahrbuch*, 1932, p. 158, dates it *ca.* 1477/8; but this appears to be too early. (2) Dresden Catalogue, *Die Romanischen Länder*, 1929, No. 14, with reproduction. (3) Cf. for instance, Van Marle, *Development of the Italian Schools of Painting*, Vol. XIII, Figs. 201–3. (4) At the 1835 (?) Exhibition and 1835 Sale, the size is given as 2 ft. 10 in. × 1 ft. 11 in., and there is no description; in the 1839 Sale, the size is not given, but the description (including the Announcement to the Shepherds in the background) corresponds well. In Lord Northwick's own copy of the 1835 Sale, consulted by kind permission of Capt. E. G. Spencer-Churchill, there is a note presumably in Lord Northwick's writing 'Mine very fine.' There is no note in Lord Northwick's copy of the 1839 Sale, but the picture is certainly the same. (5) See *The Art-Union*, 1846, p. 256, 'Virgin Worshipping the Saviour,' and the 1846 Northwick Catalogue, No. CCCCXLVIII. Waagen, *Treasures*, Vol. III, 1854, p. 196, No. 2. (6) The Northwick provenance is given in the N.G. Report.

Don LORENZO Monaco
before 1372–1422 or later

He was Piero di Giovanni, of Siena, apparently. In 1390 he was a novice, and in 1391 took his vows and the name of Lorenzo at the Camaldolese monastery of S. Maria degli Angeli, Florence. Vasari says that he was 55 years old at his death, which took place not earlier than 1422 and apparently not later than 1424 (Mirella Levi D'Ancona in *The Art Bulletin*, 1958, p. 175). His activity as a painter is first surely recorded in 1399. At least two documented works still exist, and some frescoes in S. Trinita at Florence are, further, partly authenticated. He also painted miniatures.

215   ADORING SAINTS (LEFT PORTION OF AN ALTARPIECE)

From left to right: first row, 1, S. Benedict, his book inscribed PASSI/ONIB' / XP̄I P / PATI/ĒTIÁ/ PĀTIC¹/PEMUR / U/T / R/E/G/NI EI/ MERE (amur esse consortes—from the Prologue of his Rule); 2, S. John the Baptist; 3, S. Matthew, his book with an inscription from his *Gospel*, II, 1, CUM N/ATUS / ESSET / Y̅H̅S̅ Ī BE/ THLEM / IUDE IN / DIEBUS / H/ER/ODI/S RE/GIS. Second row: 1, S. Catherine or S. Reparata (?); 2, S. Stephen; 3, S. Paul, his book inscribed, *ad galathas*. Third row: 1, S. Francis; 2, S. Augustine or S. Ambrose (?). Fragments of two angels are visible on the right.

Wood, painted surface, pointed top, $71\frac{1}{2}\times41\frac{1}{4}$ ($1\cdot815\times1\cdot05$); the measurements given are those of the original part of the painted surface. The arch forming the top starts a little way in from the sides of the panel, and is not quite symmetrical with the picture as it exists now; its spring starts $2\frac{1}{2}$ in. in on the left, 1 in. in on the right. Some additions to the panel on the left have been made, to make the effect more symmetrical. The panel has been cut at the top a little, so that the arch is now round, but it was originally slightly pointed; it is also cut about 6 in. at the bottom (new addition here, with reconstruction of the step, etc.). The right side originally joined on to the left side of No. 1897 below, but there is now a gap between the two edges, as will be explained presently. Cut also at the left, but probably to a negligible extent.[1]

Considerably worn in the heads and the shadows; the two heads best preserved are those of S. Matthew and S. Catherine (?).

For the commentary, etc., on No. 215, see No. 1897 below.

216   ADORING SAINTS (RIGHT PORTION OF AN ALTARPIECE)

From left to right: first row, 1, S. John Evangelist, his book inscribed from his *Gospel*, I, 1, IN PRIN/CIPIO ER/AT VĒB/UM.ET / VERB/UM E/RAT / APUD / DEUM. / ET DE/US ER/AT VER/ BUM. HO/C ERAT; 2, S. Peter; 3, S. Romuald. Second row: 1, S.

Philip (?); 2, S. Lawrence; 3, an unidentified saint. Third row: 1, S. Gregory; 2, S. Dominic. Fragments of two angels are visible on the left.

Wood, painted surface, pointed top, $70\frac{1}{2} \times 40$ (1.79×1.015); the measurements given are those of the original part of the painted surface. As with No. 215 above, the arch forming the top is not quite symmetrical with the picture as it exists now; its spring starts $\frac{1}{2}$ in. in on the left, $1\frac{1}{2}$ in. in on the right. The picture is very slightly cut at the top; there is also a small modern addition at the top to make the arch a little taller. Cut about 1 in. more than No. 215 is at the bottom (new addition here, with reconstruction of the step, etc.). The left side originally joined on to the right side of No. 1897 below, but there is now a gap between the two edges, as will be explained presently. Cut a little (perhaps about 1 in.) at the right.

In good condition in general; much better than No. 215 above.

For the commentary, etc., on No. 216, see No. 1897 below.

1897　THE CORONATION OF THE VIRGIN (CENTRE PORTION OF AN ALTARPIECE)

Christ crowns the Virgin. Seven angels below; the two on the left and the two on the right are fragmentary, and continue in Nos. 215/6 above. At the bottom, the remains of an inscription: ...S. FLORENT... (letter) (PE ?)R... ME. SUE. ET. SU (other parts of this inscription must have been on Nos. 215/6 above, but have been cut away).

Wood, painted surface, pointed top, $85\frac{1}{2} \times 45\frac{1}{2}$ (2.17×1.15). The arch starts some way in, and at its spring the width of the picture is only 39 in. (0.99). The vertical measurements are taken at the bottom to where the original canvas covering the panel stops; this edge of the canvas has not been cut. The original paint may have continued a little lower, the edge of the panel being at present about $\frac{1}{4}$ in. below the edge of the canvas; but for a height of about 1 in. along the bottom there are no remains at all of the original paint. Cut left and right, as will be explained presently.

The main part of No. 1897 is well preserved. The two angels on the left are largely modern reconstructions. At the bottom a large hole in the centre has been covered by restoration, the lower part of the central angel's drapery being mostly new. The lowest parts of the draperies of the angels on either side are also mostly new.

Nos. 215, 216 and 1897, in spite of what is sometimes said,[2] are certainly parts of the same picture. This seemed highly probable even before the recent cleaning. The gap between No. 1897 and No. 215 is $2\frac{3}{4}$ in. (0.07); No. 215 stops $5\frac{1}{2}$ in. (0.14) above the bottom of the panel of No. 1897. This can be calculated accurately, because parts of the haloes of the two angels on the left of No. 1897 continue on No. 215; there are also remains of keys at the back, which give confirmation of the measurements. The gap between No. 1897 and No. 216 is almost exactly the same as the other; the difference at the bottom is about $6\frac{1}{2}$ in. (0.615), with a margin of error of less than $\frac{1}{2}$ in. These measurements are not quite so accurate as the others, because haloes and keys do not help; but there is good evidence from the angels' wings and the floor pattern in No. 216. The sight size of the three pictures arranged together is $85\frac{1}{2} \times 131\frac{1}{2}$ ($2 \cdot 17 \times 3 \cdot 34$).

The altarpiece in its original form was clearly not divided as a triptych, but presented a single painted surface with a three-arched top. The arrangement corresponds with that of Lorenzo Monaco's *Coronation of the Virgin* in the Uffizi, which is signed and dated 1414 (1413 o.s.). Although in the Uffizi picture the scene takes place on a rainbow in heaven instead of the flooring here, and although that picture is a good deal more elaborate, there are many close correspondences between the two. Indeed, the two altarpieces could fairly be called free variants of the same design.

There can be no doubt at all that the Uffizi picture was the high-altarpiece of the Camaldolese church of S. Maria degli Angeli, Florence.[3] Nos. 215, 216 and 1897 are also Camaldolese pictures, as is indeed natural in works held to be by a painter of that Order, and is confirmed by the presence of S. Romuald and the white habit for S. Benedict.[4] It seems difficult to doubt that the National Gallery pictures are the principal surviving pieces of a *Coronation* stated to have existed in the Camaldolese monastery of S. Benedetto fuori della Porta a Pinti, just outside Florence.[5]

The relative dates of the Uffizi and National Gallery altarpieces cannot be settled with absolute certainty. According to the inscription on it, the Uffizi altarpiece was given (?) by the painter and his relatives in replacement of another picture;[6] there is nothing to show that this earlier picture was by Lorenzo Monaco, but if it was, it might have been moved to S. Benedetto when the more elaborate work was completed. Alternatively, and considerably better, since S. Benedetto was built in imitation of the Angeli,[7] it could be argued that its altarpiece was painted in imitation of the altarpiece at the Angeli.

Although the attribution of Nos. 215/6 to Lorenzo Monaco is now usually accepted, No. 1897 (wrongly supposed to be distinct) is sometimes called a school-piece;[8] this seems to be an aberration. Indeed, the quality of Nos. 215/6 is clearly less fine than that of No. 1897.

The Uffizi altarpiece retains its pilasters, pinnacles and predella. The National Gallery picture would have had a predella; its similarity to the Uffizi picture is so great that, by analogy, some probable identifications of what its predella was can be made. This matter is discussed in the entry for No. 2862 below.

DRAWING: A drawing in the Uffizi seems to be for No. 215.[9] Six figures in two rows are shown. The front row corresponds very well with the picture. In the second row of the drawing, the first figure agrees pretty well with the S. Catherine or Reparata (?) of the picture; S. Stephen is in the place occupied in the picture by S. Paul; but the middle figure in the drawing is not S. Paul. A curved line in the right bottom of the drawing suggests that the figures were intended to be on a rainbow (as in the Uffizi picture), and not on the ground as in No. 215. A figure of S. Benedict enthroned on the reverse of the drawing seems irrelevant.

PROVENANCE: Probably, as explained above, an altarpiece of S. Benedetto fuori della Porta a Pinti, Florence, which was founded in 1395–1401. This monastery was destroyed for strategic reasons during the siege of Florence in 1529/30; the altarpiece was brought to S. Maria degli Angeli, Florence, where Vasari saw it in the Alberti Chapel in the cloister.[10] It is still mentioned there by Bocchi-Cinelli (1677), del Migliore (1684), Richa (1759) and Follini-Rastrelli (1792).[11] No record of when it was removed has been discovered.

Provenance of No. 215: Cardinal Fesch Collection, Rome; 1841 Catalogue (No. 2283); Sale, designed for 22/5 March, 1844, and taking place in March–April, 1845 (lot 990), bought by Satzbeuh.[12] It passed to William Coningham, who presented it together with No. 216 in 1848.[13]

Provenance of No. 216: Taken from Florence to Rome on speculation; purchased there from J. Freeborn by William Coningham,[14] who presented it together with No. 215 in 1848.

Provenance of No. 1897: Discovered in 1830 or 1840 in a chapel of a former Camaldolese abbey, at that time a house for Camaldolese novices (?), at Elmo or Adelmo, near Cerreto.[15] This house is stated to have been secularized under the French dominion at the beginning of the nineteenth century, when the building with the picture in it was purchased by the Landi family of the neighbouring Certaldo. Seen in the Landi Collection by Crowe and Cavalcaselle.[16] Purchased shortly before 1900 from 11 members of the Landi family by M. Galli-Dunn of Florence, from whom purchased, Clarke Fund, 1902. The three panels were in the Cleaned Pictures Exhibition at the National Gallery, 1947/8 (Nos. 14–16).

REPRODUCTIONS: *Illustrations, Italian Schools,* 1937, p. 196 (Nos. 215/6 before cleaning), p. 197 (No. 1897 before cleaning). *Plates, Earlier Italian Schools,* 1953, Vol. II, pp. 245–248.

REFERENCES: **(1)** It should be stressed that Nos. 215, 216 and 1897 have all been cleaned recently, and differ considerably from the reproductions of them made before cleaning. Reproductions of them after cleaning are in *Critica d'Arte,* September, 1949, Figs. 151, 152 and 148 (in the last case, before restoration); see also Figs. 153/5 for the three pictures together, with fragments of what was probably the predella. **(2)** E.g. by Osvald Sirèn, *Lorenzo Monaco,* 1905, pp. 65 ff. Crowe and Cavalcaselle, *History of Painting in Italy,* I, 1864, p. 554, rightly associated the pictures together; see also an article by the writer of the present catalogue in *Critica d'Arte,* September, 1949, pp. 202 ff. **(3)** Vasari, ed. Milanesi, II, pp. 18/9; Gaye, *Carteggio,* II, 1840, p. 433. Confirmation of the identity is afforded by the mention of Prior Matteo in the inscription on the picture, which is dated 1413 (1414 n.s.); Don Matteo di Guido Cardinali was elected Prior of the Angeli in 1399 and died in 1421, as can be found in Farulli's books mentioned in note 10 (cf. the quotation in O. Sirèn, *Don Lorenzo Monaco,* 1905, pp. 180/1). The Uffizi picture yielded its place on the high altar to an Alessandro Allori, which was painted in 1593 (Venturi, *Storia dell'Arte Italiana,* Vol. IX, Part VI, p. 82). **(4)** Various reformed Benedictines, including the Camaldolese, regarded S. Benedict as their original founder; but in their pictures they showed him dressed, not in his own black, but in the white habit they themselves had adopted. **(5)** Mentioned by Vasari, *loc. cit.* The church was for a brief time dedicated to S. Matthew, then to S. Benedict (Domenico Moreni, *Notizie Istoriche dei Contorni di Firenze,* VI, 1795, pp. 61/2). If its altarpiece was painted for the church and not transferred from the Angeli (see the next paragraph in the text above), the prominent position accorded to S. Matthew on No. 215 would be an argument in favour of the provenance. The altarpiece of the *cappella maggiore* of this church had two holes made in it by lightning on 13 June, 1511 (Luca Landucci, *Diario Fiorentino,* ed. del Badia, 1883, p. 310); there is no confirmatory evidence on the pictures themselves that Nos. 215/6 and 1897 have been struck by lightning. **(6)** See the (fragmentary) inscription in Gaye, *Carteggio,* II, 1840, pp. 433/4. **(7)** By a disposition of 1395, which took effect in 1400/1; cf. G. Richa, *Notizie Istoriche delle Chiese Fiorentine,* VIII, 1759, p. 271, and the corrections by Domenico Moreni, *Notizie Istoriche dei Contorni di Firenze,* VI,

1795, pp. 60/1. See also note 10. (8) E.g. Sirèn, *op. cit.*, p. 189; partly school. Mirella Levi D'Ancona, in *The Art Bulletin*, 1958, pp. 180 and 184 and in *Commentari*, 1958, pp. 257/8, claims that the execution of Nos. 215/6 as well as of No. 1897 is not by Lorenzo Monaco, and that they are possibly by the follower who painted a *Virgin and Child* at Bologna; there does not seem to be a very close connection with that picture, which has at various times been called autograph. Studio participation in some work of Lorenzo Monaco may fairly be claimed, and most people would consider Nos. 215/6 and 1897 a lesser work than the Uffizi *Coronation* (as indeed might be expected from what is known of the original destinations); but there does not seem to be justification for classing Nos. 215/6 and 1897 under any name except that of Lorenzo Monaco. (9) Sirèn, *op. cit.*, Plates XXII, XXIII; Berenson, *Drawings of the Florentine Painters*, 1938, No. 1391A (not accepting that it is for No. 215). (10) Not in Vasari's 1550 edition; Milanesi's edition, II, p. 19. It is true that Vasari and other writers refer to a *Coronation of the Virgin*, without mention of the flanking saints; but there is no need to suppose that the S. Benedetto altarpiece had been broken up at an early date. For the foundation of S. Benedetto and the removal of its contents to the Angeli at the time of the Siege of Florence, see also Gregorio Farulli, *Istoria Cronologica del nobile, ed antico Monastero degli Angioli di Firenze*, etc., 1710, pp. 272 and 280; or the same author or Pietro Farulli or Francesco Masetti, *Teatro Storico del Sacro Eremo di Camaldoli*, etc., 1723, pp. 65 and 68. (11) Bocchi-Cinelli, *Le Bellezze della Città di Firenze*, 1677, p. 492 (not in the original edition of 1591 by Bocchi alone). Ferdinando Leopoldo del Migliore, *Firenze Città Nobilissima*, 1684, p. 332. Richa, *op. cit.*, VIII, p. 163. (Follini and Rastrelli), *Firenze Antica e Moderna*, IV, 1792, pp. 83/4. (12) As Gaddo Gaddi in both catalogues; identifying description in the second one. (13) Both as Taddeo Gaddi. (14) Letter from William Coningham in the Gallery archives. This letter refers to Freeborn as the consul at Rome, so his initial could be supplied from *The Royal Calendar*. J. Freeborn was in Rome by 1839 and during the 1840's; these dates should perhaps be extended. (15) Vasari, ed. Milanesi, II, pp. 19/20, as 1830; in the Le Monnier edition of Vasari, II, 1846, p. 211, the date is given as 1840. It is stated at one time to have belonged to the Camaldolese of Florence (cf. also Pecori, *Storia di San Gimignano*, 1853, p. 408); it is close to the monastery of S. Pietro at Cerreto (where the Uffizi picture was discovered in the nineteenth century), which was itself attached to the Angeli at Florence by a Bull of 1414. Repetti (*Dizionario . . . della Toscana*, Vol I, 1833), says that in his time it belonged to the Camaldolese of S. Giusto at Volterra. Some further information about the provenance of the picture is in a letter from C. A. de Cosson, 1901, in the Gallery archives, who says that the house at Elmo had been for novices. It may be mentioned that No. 1897 has on the back a scribble with 1762 and various illegible words; this has been photographed, although it appears useless for the history of the picture. (16) Crowe and Cavalcaselle, *op. cit.*, I, 1864, p. 554.

2862   S. BENEDICT ADMITTING SS. MAURUS AND
       PLACIDUS INTO THE BENEDICTINE ORDER
       (FRAGMENT OF A PREDELLA PANEL)

Wood, painted surface, $11\frac{1}{8} \times 15\frac{1}{8}$ (0·285 × 0·385); excluding a false edging of green. The painted surface was originally cut at the left-hand corners top and bottom; the triangles, which have been made up with new paint, have a height and width of $2\frac{3}{4}$ in. (0·07). The panel has been reduced in thickness.

Somewhat damaged.

It need not be doubted that the subject (which does not occur in the Golden Legend) is correctly identified; it was fairly popular in old pictures. No. 2862 is clearly the fragment of a predella; a scene or scenes must have continued on the right, which would have had the corners cut on the right. The whole panel would then have had the form of a much flattened octagon.

Under Nos. 215, 216 and 1897 above, there is a discussion of that altarpiece and the nearly related picture at the Uffizi. The Uffizi picture retains its predella, representing the Nativity, the Adoration of the Kings and four panels of legends of S. Benedict. Nos. 215, etc., are so like the main part of the Uffizi picture that it is probable that they had a predella with similar subjects.[1]

The predella panels that may be considered for this purpose are No. 2862; No. 4062 below; *The Death of S. Benedict*, on loan to the Gallery from Sir Richard Barrett Lennard;[2] and a panel of *Miracles of S. Benedict* in the Vatican.[3] The halo patterns in the four pictures correspond.

No. 2862 has the corners of the panels cut at the left; No. 4062 also has the corners cut at the left. Sir Richard Barrett Lennard's picture has the corners cut at the right; the Vatican panel has the corners cut at the right. The cuts seem to be all of the same size.

Further, No. 4062 and Sir Richard Barrett Lennard's picture are certainly parts of one panel; No. 4062 being the left part, the other the right. The rocky landscape joins on, except for a probable loss of a couple of millimetres; this is not clear at the bottom, but is clear at the top.[4] This part of the predella, then, was a flattened octagon, width about $40\frac{3}{4}$ in. ($1\cdot04$).

It is also highly probable that No. 2862 joined on to the Vatican picture. That also represents early incidents in S. Benedict's life, and the total width would correspond very exactly with that of the other two. To judge from the photographs, the landscapes at the two edges fit together quite well.[5]

The subject of No. 2862 does not occur in the predella of the Uffizi picture; but the two scenes shown at the Vatican do occur there, on separate panels. The two scenes in No. 4062 below are repeated very exactly on a single panel in the Uffizi. Sir Richard Barrett Lennard's *Death of S. Benedict* is also repeated at the Uffizi, where also the revelation of the event to S. Maurus is included.

These pictures, therefore, seem to be in sufficient agreement with the predella at the Uffizi to make it probable, by analogy, that they formed part of the predella of Nos. 215, 216 and 1897 above. The matter is, however, not quite certain; No. 5224 below, ascribed to Lorenzo Monaco, may be thought evidence that Lorenzo Monaco may have painted other predellas with scenes of S. Benedict's life.

It is possible that Lorenzo Monaco in his treatment of the incidents concerning S. Benedict here and at the Uffizi was slightly influenced by Spinello Aretino's series of frescoes in S. Miniato al Monte, Florence, datable soon after 1387.[6]

The execution of No. 2862 and the connected works is rather weak; it is uncertain if they are by Lorenzo Monaco (of predella quality) or by an assistant in his studio.[7]

PROVENANCE: Owned by 1854 by Captain James Stirling of Glentyan, Ren-
frewshire, who died in 1872 without issue.[8] It passed to his great-nephew,
Graham Charles Somervell, who lent it to the Old Masters and Scottish National
Portraits Exhibition at Edinburgh, 1883 (No. 509);[9] Sale, 23 April, 1887 (lot
153), always as by Masaccio. Bought by Henry Wagner at the Sale, and lent by
him to the New Gallery, 1893/4 (No. 67), and to the Grafton Gallery, 1911 (No.
17). Presented by Henry Wagner, 1912.

REPRODUCTION: *Illustrations, Italian Schools*, 1937, p. 198. *Plates, Earlier
Italian Schools*, 1953, Vol. II, p. 249.

REFERENCES: (1) The Uffizi predella is reproduced by R. Salvini and L.
Traverso, *Predelle*, 1959, pp. 61/2. Pudelko in *The Burlington Magazine*, Vol.
LXXIII (1938), pp. 247/8, attempts to supply also some of the pinnacles and
pilasters of the National Gallery altarpiece; but there is not sufficient evidence
at present for discussing anything but the predella. (2) Photo in the Gallery
archives. Size, $11\frac{1}{4} \times 20\frac{3}{8}$ (0·285 × 0·52). Reproduced (as at the National Gallery)
in *Critica d'Arte*, September, 1949, Fig. 159. (3) Vatican, 1933 Guide, No. 193;
0·30 × 65; photograph Anderson, No. 23966. Reproduced by P. d'Achiardi,
I Quadri Primitivi della Pinacoteca Vaticana, 1929, Plate XXXa, and in *Critica
d'Arte*, September, 1949, Fig. 157. The subjects are: a monk of Subiaco being
drawn from his prayers by the Devil; and S. Benedict resuscitating a young
monk killed by a fall of masonry during the building of Monte Cassino. (4) Even
the worm-holes of the two panels correspond well. And on the back is confirmation; No. 4062 is marked 469 in pigment, and the other picture has 468, apparently in the same writing. (5) The predella of Orcagna's altarpiece in S. Maria
Novella has panels fairly similar in shape to what is claimed here (Venturi, *Storia
dell'Arte Italiana*, Vol. V, Fig. 619). Dr. Redig de Campos, in a letter of 11
July, 1947, kindly confirmed that the Vatican picture has been cut at the left,
and has its corners cut at the right. (6) Six are reproduced by Georg Gombosi,
Spinello Aretino, 1926, Plates 14–16; fourteen by Venturi, *Storia dell'Arte
Italiana*, V, Figs. 687–700. (7) Mirella Levi D'Ancona in *The Art Bulletin*, 1958,
p. 180, and in *Commentari*, 1958, pp. 257/8, says that the execution is not Lorenzo
Monaco's; she does not ascribe them certainly to Torelli (to whom she ascribes
many works). (8) The existence of the picture is reported by Waagen, *Treasures*,
III, 1854, p. 314, as Masaccio: for its identity with No. 2862 and its attribution
to Lorenzo Monaco, see Crowe and Cavalcaselle, *A New History of Painting in
Italy*, ed. Douglas II, 1903, p. 302, and IV, 1911, p. 63. The information does
not appear in the 1864 edition of Crowe and Cavalcaselle, but is to be found in
the Italian edition, II, 1883, p. 346. For the identity of the owners, see Burke's
Landed Gentry, 1921 edition, s.v. Stirling of Kippendavie and Somervell of
Sorn. (9) Exhibition label on the back; cf. Graves, *Century of Loan Exhibitions*,
1st Addenda.

4062 INCIDENTS   IN   THE   LIFE   OF   S.   BENEDICT
      (FRAGMENT OF A PREDELLA PANEL)

Left, S. Benedict instructs S. Maurus to go to the help of S. Placidus,
whose imminent death by drowning had been revealed to S. Benedict.
Centre, S. Maurus walks over the water as if it had been land, and seizes
S. Placidus by the hair. Right, S. Benedict visits his sister S. Scholastica
at her nunnery, and is detained there overnight by a storm, the effect of
her prayers.

Wood, painted surface, $11\frac{1}{4} \times 20\frac{3}{8}$ (0·285 × 0·52); painted up to the
edge at the right. On the left, the corners of the paint were originally cut
off top and bottom; the triangles, which have been made up with new
paint, have a height and width of $2\frac{3}{4}$ in. (0·07).

The picture is in good condition, although there are some obtrusive retouches.

The stamping of the halo of S. Maurus in the centre has been forgotten.

As explained in the entry for No. 2862, No. 4062 and a *Death of S. Benedict* on loan to the Gallery from Sir Richard Barrett Lennard were originally in one piece, and probably part of the predella of Nos. 215, 216 and 1897 above. The composition of No. 4062 corresponds quite closely with a panel of the same two scenes in the predella of Lorenzo Monaco's *Coronation of the Virgin* in the Uffizi.

PROVENANCE: Purchased, Florence Fund, from Canon A. F. Sutton, 1925.

REPRODUCTION: *Illustrations, Italian Schools*, 1937, p. 198. *Plates, Earlier Italian Schools*, 1953, Vol. II, p. 250.

Ascribed to DON LORENZO MONACO

3089 ILLUMINATED LETTER B, CUT FROM A CHORAL BOOK

The miniature shows Abraham and the Angels (see below); the back contains music and fragments of words, but no illumination.

Vellum, $14\frac{1}{2} \times 13\frac{1}{8}$ (0·37 × 0·33), approx.[1]

The identification of the subject of the miniature as *Abraham and the three Angels* (Genesis xviii, 1 sqq.) seems certainly to be correct.[2] Mirella Levi D'Ancona[3] accepts it, adding that it symbolizes the Trinity. This symbolism has indeed a long tradition, and was fairly often illustrated;[4] it may be that the idea here is the differing tradition, that two of the angels were indeed angels, but the third (the dominant one in the account given in the Bible) was God.[5] This seems suggested by the fact that in No. 3089 the central angel, rather more richly clothed than the other two, has a short beard, as if Christ; if it had been desired to emphasize that Abraham's three visitors were or symbolized the three Persons of the Trinity, they could have been shown exactly alike—and all with beards.[6] The intention in No. 3089 seems, nevertheless, somewhat confused; the bearded figure does seem to be shown winged, i.e. as an angel,[7] and the halo of this figure does not differ from the haloes of the other two.

The scene is shown in a letter that is certainly a B, and this may confirm the association with the Trinity, since the first word in the introit of the mass of the Trinity is 'Benedicta';[8] the compiler does not think that this would exclude the interpretation of the single beard, suggested above.

No. 3089 is traditionally ascribed to Lorenzo Monaco; this was doubted by Berenson (1932 Lists), and strongly doubted in the first edition of the present catalogue. Mirella Levi D'Ancona[9] ascribes it to 'Don Silvestro De' Gherarducci', which is better. The traditional classification, although clearly wrong, is nevertheless retained at present;

attributions to Don Silvestro would seem to be in need of sifting, and there is some doubt if his name should be used at all.[10]

PROVENANCE: Purchased by Sir Austen Henry Layard at the J. G. von Quandt Sale, Dresden, 1 sqq. October, 1860 (lot 365[11]); further recorded as Layard's in 1861.[12] Exhibited at the South Kensington Museum, 1869 (No. 33).[13] Layard Bequest, 1916.[14]

REPRODUCTION: *Illustrations, Italian Schools*, 1937, p. 199. *Plates, Earlier Italian Schools*, 1953, Vol. II, p. 251.

REFERENCES: (1) The size is that given by the 1929 Catalogue. (2) The compiler is much indebted to Professor Francis Wormald for his kind help. (3) Mirella Levi D'Ancona in the *Rivista d'Arte*, 1957, p. 22. (4) See the illuminations, more or less contemporary with No. 3089, reproduced by W. Braunfels, *Die Heilige Dreifaltigkeit*, 1954, Fig. 12 (leaf from an Antiphonary in the Morgan Library, New York, attributed to Spinello Aretino) and by Offner, *Corpus*, Section III, Vol. II, Part II, Add. Plate VIII (attributed to the Pacino workshop). See further Offner, *Corpus*, Section III, Vol. VI, pp. 145 ff., in an account of the iconography of the Trinity, and (for Russian traditions) V. Lasareff in the *Gazette des Beaux-Arts*, December, 1959, pp. 289 ff. (5) For both traditions, see A. Calmet, *Commentaire Littéral sur tous les Livres de l'Ancien et du Nouveau Testament*, Vol. I, 1724, p. 156, and remarks by Pope Benedict XIV in J. Molanus, *De Historia SS. Imaginum et Picturarum*, 1771, pp. 487 ff. Abraham's visitors all have haloes, but one also a mandorla, in a mosaic in S. Maria Maggiore at Rome; reproduced by Toesca, *Storia*, I, *Il Medioevo*, 1927, Fig. 102. (6) For the scene so treated, cf. the panel ascribed to Bonifacio Bembo at Cremona; reproduced by A. Puerari, *La Pinacoteca di Cremona*, 1951, Fig. 42. See further in the *Petites Heures du Duc de Berry* (Paris, Bibliothèque Nationale, MS. Latin 18014, f. 188), where the illustration is accepted as representing Abraham and the Angels; reproduced in the *Monuments et Mémoires Piot*, Vol. III, 1896, Plate XI. Also a tapestry at Brussels, reproduced by Baldass, *Die Wiener Gobelinssammlung*, 1920, No. 25 and by T. Ehrenstein, *Das Alte Testament im Bilde*, 1923, p. 147, Fig. 32. Baldass says that this tapestry is Brussels work of the 2nd quarter of the XVI Century; the symbolical intention here is confirmed by the presence of an allegory of the Trinity among allegories of moral qualities in the framing of the tapestry. It is true that in all these cases the visitors do not appear to be winged. (7) A very strange illustration by Rembrandt shows three bearded figures, two of them winged; reproduced by L. Münz, *A Critical Catalogue of Rembrandt's Etchings*, 1952, Vol. I, Plate 206. (8) Compare the miniatures in the Morgan Library, mentioned in note 4. (9) Mirella Levi D'Ancona, *loc. cit.* in note 3. (10) It may be that the best justification for using the name was in a collection of cut-out miniatures, once belonging to W. Y. Ottley. As Mirella Levi D'Ancona, *loc. cit.*, p. 8, points out, one of these (representing SS. Peter and Paul) was in the catalogue of the Ottley Sale, 12 May, 1838, lot 185, claimed to be signed; confirmation of the claim is desired. (11) The acquisition is recorded in the Layard MSS. in the National Gallery; attribution, Memmi (?). Miss T. Lans of the Rijksbureau voor Kunsthistorische Documentatie at The Hague kindly consulted the sale catalogue of 1860, where No. 3089 is clearly identifiable as lot 365 (as Abraham and the Angels, School of the Gaddi). (12) Framemaker's date; there is also a label of some loan exhibition, 1 May, 1862, and a number 108 that may be connected. (13) Italian School, fourteenth century. (14) For the history of the Layard Collection, see Appendix IV.

5224 S. BENEDICT IN THE SACRO SPECO AT SUBIACO (FRAGMENT)

The young S. Benedict in his cave is receiving his food from S. Romanus; the food is being let down in a basket at the end of a rope, to which is attached a bell to call S. Benedict's attention. A small devil is about to break the rope. Right, an angel, a fragment of another legend once illustrated farther to the right. In a false framing of gold, with a false coat of arms at the top, and the new words ME DUCE at the bottom.

Wood. The size within the framing is $11\frac{1}{2} \times 10\frac{1}{4}$ (0·29 × 0·26); the size of the panel is $14\frac{1}{4} \times 11$ (0·36 × 0·28).

Much rubbed; also undercleaned.

So far as examination has been carried at present, this seems to be a fragment of an old picture, possibly of a predella. It is clearly not connected with No. 2862 etc., above, if only because S. Benedict's halo does not correspond with the haloes of that series.[1] Top and bottom there is gilding, under some or all of the new decorative work, also under the present field of the picture for about $\frac{1}{2}$ in.[2]

The main part of the story is told in the Golden Legend. The angel in No. 5224 probably belongs to what is almost a continuation of the same story. A priest was preparing his own Easter repast, but on hearing from Christ or an angel that S. Benedict was in danger of starving, went and found the saint in his cave and shared his meal with him. The angel on the picture is clearly enough pointing with one hand to S. Benedict, and with the other to the interior of a building mostly outside the field of the picture at present, in which it may be assumed that the priest was shown.[3]

What remains of the original picture here is much in the style of Lorenzo Monaco, but not certainly or even probably by his own hand.[4]

PROVENANCE: With Bottenwieser, Berlin. Purchased from Agnew in 1927 by Lord Rothermere, who lent it to the Italian Exhibitions at the R.A., 1930, No. 68 (Memorial Catalogue, No. 47),[5] and at Paris, 1935 (No. 316). Presented by Viscount Rothermere, 1940.

REPRODUCTION: Plates, Earlier Italian Schools, 1953, Vol. II, p. 251.

REFERENCES: (1) Nevertheless, Mirella Levi D'Ancona in Commentari, 1958, p. 258, inclines to associate it with the others. (2) It is difficult to guess why the gilding was put on, unless it was meant to show as a surround to the picture itself; no such arrangement was made for No. 4062 above, and if this was the arrangement for No. 5224, the exposed surface would have been taller than those of Nos. 4062, 2862, etc. (3) An example of this subject is reproduced by Van Marle, Italian Schools, Vol. III, Fig. 198. (4) Mirella Levi D'Ancona, loc. cit. in note 1, thinks it is not by Lorenzo Monaco; she does not ascribe it certainly to Torelli (to whom she ascribes many works). (5) With the provenance as stated above.

LORENZO D'ALESSANDRO DA SANSEVERINO
active 1468, died 1503

Active in the Marches. He was influenced by Niccolò di Liberatore, Crivelli and others. Several authenticated works by him exist. He is not to be confused with an earlier painter, Lorenzo Salimbeni da Sanseverino. See Luigi Serra, L'Arte nelle Marche, II, 1934, pp. 269 ff.

249 ALTARPIECE: THE MARRIAGE OF S. CATHERINE OF
     SIENA

The Virgin is seated centre, her halo inscribed.AVE.GRATIA.
PLENA.DO. She holds the Child, His halo inscribed SVM LVX.; He
is offering a ring to S. Catherine, her halo inscribed SANTA.KTER-
INA.DE SEN. Behind S. Catherine stands S. Dominic, his halo
inscribed .SANCTVS.DOMINICVS. On the other side stands S.
Augustine, his halo inscribed S.AVGVSTINVS. Before him kneels a
Dominican beatus, probably the Blessed Costanzo da Fabriano. Signed:
LAVR / ENTIVS.I.I. / SEVERᴵNAS / PISꞮT.

Wood, painted surface, $57 \times 57\frac{1}{4}$ ($1 \cdot 445 \times 1 \cdot 455$).
Good condition on the whole; most of the gold on the Virgin's robe is
new.

This picture comes from Fabriano (see the provenance), so the tradition that the unnamed Dominican beatus is the Blessed Costanzo da
Fabriano is probably correct.[1] For a long time, National Gallery catalogues have called him S. Demetrius of Spoleto; but no Dominican is
recorded who would have been called that.[2] The Bammeville sale catalogue (see the provenance) identified him with the B. Raymond of
Capua; but this appears unlikely.[3] The B. Costanzo of Fabriano died at
Ascoli in 1481 (1482 n.s.?). His head was transferred to the Benedictine
nuns of S. Sebastiano, Fabriano in 1502 (1503 n.s.?), and is now in the
Cathedral there.[4] If the identification is correct, No. 249 was certainly
painted after the B. Costanzo's death; but it is not necessary to believe
that it was painted on the transfer of his head from Ascoli to Fabriano.

PROVENANCE: First recorded in the sacristy of the Dominican church of S.
Lucia, Fabriano.[5] Purchased at the E. Joly de Bammeville Sale, London, 12
June, 1854 (lot 55).

REPRODUCTION: *Illustrations, Italian Schools*, 1937, p. 199. *Plates, Earlier
Italian Schools*, 1953, Vol. II, p. 252.

REFERENCES: (1) A. Ricci, *Memorie storiche delle arti . . . della Marca di Ancona*,
1934, I, p. 194 (with identifying description), and J. D. Passavant, *Rafael von
Urbin*, 1839, I, p. 428. (2) There appear to have been two B. Demetrius of
Spoleto; one a Franciscan who died in 1459, the other a Franciscan tertiary
who died in 1491. See Jacobilli, *Vite de' Santi, e Beati dell'Umbria*, I, 1647,
pp. 418 f. and II, 1656, pp. 329 f. (3) His connection with S. Catherine of Siena,
nevertheless, did sometimes cause him to be painted in association with her. See
Milanesi, *Documenti per la Storia dell'Arte Senese*, III, 1856, pp. 267 f., and
Venturi, *Storia dell'Arte Italiana*, Vol. IX, Part VII, Figs. 587/9. (4) Venanzo
Benigni, *Compendioso Ragguaglio delle Cose . . . di Fabriano* (ca. 1730), 1924,
p. 41. (5) References as in note 1.

LORENZO Veneziano

active 1356 (?)–1372

The dates given are from his signatures; cf. L. Testi, *Storia della
Pittura Veneziana*, I, 1909, pp. 209/10.

Ascribed to LORENZO Veneziano

3897 THE 'MADONNA OF HUMILITY' WITH SS. MARK AND JOHN THE BAPTIST (PART OF AN ALTARPIECE)

On the central picture, SC̃A / MARIA D'LAUMI / LITADE. .S. / MAR / CHVS:—(the M has been slightly altered by restoration) on the background of S. Mark's picture. The Baptist holds a scroll, ECCE / A(G ?)N' / DEI / ECCE / QVI / TOLIS / PECA / TA / MVN / DI. / MIS / ERE / RE; his name is on the background, S. / .IOHĒS / .BT̃I.

The three pictures with their framework are on one panel; total size (excluding the outermost moulding of the frame all round, which is new), $12\frac{1}{4} \times 22\frac{1}{2}$ (0·31 × 0·575). The three pictures each have cusped tops; sizes of the picture surfaces (centre) $9\frac{1}{8} \times 7\frac{1}{8}$ (0·23 × 0·18), (sides) $9\frac{1}{8} \times 4\frac{3}{4}$ (0·23 × 0·12).

Good condition; the chief damage is in the left-hand bottom corner of S. Mark's compartment. The gilding of the framework is new, and the panel is considerably warped.

Perhaps the central part of a predella.

The 'Madonna of Humility' in the centre has the crescent moon at her feet, and there are stars on the background; cf. Venetian School, No. 4250.

Acquired as by Tommaso da Modena, an attribution generally rejected. Evelyn Sandberg-Vavalà ascribed it to Lorenzo Veneziano, with which Toesca and Berenson agree.[1] Luigi Coletti[2] called it Giovanni da Bologna. Hans Gronau (oral, 1936) put it between Paolo Veneziano and Lorenzo Veneziano. F. Bologna ascribed it to a painter he names the Master of Arquà.[3]

PROVENANCE: In the collection of the Rev. J. Fuller Russell, where probably seen by Waagen;[4] exhibited at Manchester, 1857(?);[5] at the R.A., 1878 (No. 200); Sale, 18 April, 1885 (lot 99), bought by (Henry) Wagner. Exhibited at the New Gallery, 1893/4 (No. 25); presented by Henry Wagner, 1924.

REPRODUCTION: Illustrations, Italian Schools, 1937, p. 358. Plates, Earlier Italian Schools, 1953, Vol. II, p. 253.

REFERENCES: (1) E. Sandberg-Vavalà in Art in America, February, 1930, pp. 54 ff. Toesca, Il Trecento, 1951, p. 711 and Berenson, 1957 Lists. (2) Luigi Coletti in L'Arte, 1931, p. 135. (3) F. Bologna, in Arte Veneta, 1951, pp. 24 ff. In Arte Veneta, 1952, pp. 17 f., he does not agree that this painter is identical with the Master of S. Elsino, i.e. the author of Venetian School, No. 4250 of this Gallery; the style of Nos. 3897 and 4250 does indeed seem to be different. (4) Waagen, Treasures, 1854, II, p. 462, as Berna or Barna da Siena; the description does not fit too well, but it is probably the picture. Waagen may well be responsible for the attribution to Barna, which was still current at the 1893/4 exhibition. (5) It does not seem to be either in the provisional or in the definitive catalogue of the exhibition; but there are genuine Manchester labels on the back.

Bernardino LUINI
active 1512, died 1532

Active at Milan, Lugano, etc. Although his works have made him the most popular of Milanese painters, very little is known of him; thus, his date of birth has been put at *ca.* 1460 and also at *ca.* 1490. The date of 1512 is that of a fresco at Chiaravalle (Milan).

An altarpiece in the Musée André, Paris, No. 663, is signed by Bernardino of Milan and dated 1507, but the painter is often supposed not to be Luini; Frizzoni's views are given in the *Rassegna d'Arte*, 1914, pp. 201 ff., Suida's in *Leonardo und sein Kreis*, 1929, p. 233. It is, in fact, almost as difficult to reject as to accept this picture. Frizzoni rightly points out that the general style is not Lombard at all, being if anything Veronese; on the other hand, some parts are distinctly Luinesque, and the rejection of Luini's authorship would suggest that he was exercising an influence on a painter of different training as early as 1507. It is accepted by Ottino, *Luini*, 1956, No. 209.

It is clear that some reserve is necessary in defining Luini's formation. Undoubtedly, he was very strongly influenced by Leonardo, some of whose designs he copied; but he seems before this to have been affected by non-Leonardesque traditions current at Milan (Bramantino, Solari and even Bergognone).

There are plenty of authenticated works of Luini; also innumerable copies and schoolpieces.

Literature: Angela Ottino della Chiesa, *Bernardino Luini*, 1956.

18 CHRIST AMONG THE DOCTORS

Poplar,[1] painted surface, $28\frac{1}{2} \times 33\frac{3}{4}$ (0·725 × 0·855); painted up to the edges all round.

So far as can be seen, this appears to be a seriously damaged picture; in particular, an X-radiograph suggests that little of the original face of Christ is preserved. A few small *pentimenti*, e.g. in the ear of the man left.

The subject of No. 18 is traditionally *Christ among the Doctors* (Luke ii, 41 sqq.); but it has sometimes been thought to be rather *Christ disputing with the Pharisees*, on the ground that He was only twelve on the other occasion, but seems to be older on the picture.[2] It is uncertain what age Luini intended his Christ to be; He seems here to be standing, and the other figures seem to be sitting, which might explain why He appears as tall.[3] *Christ disputing with the Pharisees* is not a well defined theme; but *Christ among the Doctors* occurs frequently. In a fresco of the latter subject by Luini at Saronno,[4] there is a head of a man rather like that of the man on the left in No. 18.

What can be seen of the style of No. 18, especially the two heads on the left, justifies the opinion that it is an original Luini, although some details of the hands are weak. It was traditionally ascribed to Leonardo de Vinci, whose name has been written three times on the back.[5]

VERSIONS: Numerous; they may be all copies. A few to be mentioned are: Milan, at one time in the Casati Collection;[6] Milan, Arcivescovado;[7] Spada Gallery, Rome;[8] Perugia (No. 355; ex-S. Domenico there); Earl of Yarborough Sale, 12 July, 1929 (lot 50);[9] and No. 2088 below (part).

PROVENANCE: No. 18 was in Rome by the seventeenth century; it is an Aldo-brandini picture, that belonged to Donna Olimpia Aldobrandini, Principessa di Rossano, who married secondly Camillo Pamphilj in 1647, and died in 1681.[10] Later owned by their son, Cardinal Benedetto Pamphilj (Cardinal 1681, died 1730),[11] and recorded in Palazzo Pamphilj al Corso in 1759 and 1763.[12] Much Aldobrandini property had passed by entail from Cardinal Ippolito Aldo-brandini (died 1638) to the already mentioned Olimpia. At her death, the Rossano title passed to the Borghese, but the Aldobrandini fortune passed to certain members of the Pamphilj family, who assumed the name of Aldo-brandini. In the first instance, much of the Aldobrandini property went to one of Olimpia's sons, Giovanni Battista; what clearly appears to be No. 18 went to another son, Cardinal Benedetto, but he at his death bequeathed his fortune to the family. Olimpia's last direct heir was Donna Maria Livia Aldobrandini (Pamphilj), wife of Prince Altieri. She died in 1760; the Pamphilj title passed to the Doria-Landi, but a lawsuit over the Aldobrandini inheritance between the Borghese and the Colonna was won by the Borghese in 1769. The arrangement arrived at was that the Aldobrandini fortune and title should be held by the second son of the head of the Borghese family.[13] It is therefore no difficulty that the Aldobrandini-Pamphilj version of No. 18 should pass to the Borghese;[14] and what is certainly No. 18 is recorded in Palazzo Borghese in 1776,[15] and in 1787 in the part of Palazzo Borghese occupied by Prince Aldobrandini.[16] No. 18 was imported into England by Day in 1800/1.[17] Buchanan seems to have been entrusted with its sale in May, 1808;[18] at about that time, if not already by 1807, it was acquired by Lord Northwick.[19] Exhibited at the British Institution, 1816 (No. 31); acquired from Lord Northwick by the Rev. W. Holwell Carr in 1824;[20] Holwell Carr Bequest, 1831.

REPRODUCTION: *Illustrations, Italian Schools*, 1937, p. 203. *Plates, Earlier Italian Schools*, 1953, Vol. II, p. 254.

REFERENCES: (1) Letter from B. J. Rendle, of the Forest Products Research Laboratory, in the Gallery archives. (2) The subject is thus identified in the entry of the 1626 inventory, given in note 10; but the compiler still thinks that No. 18 shows Christ among the Doctors. (3) Or He may be on a high seat; cf. a Cima at Warsaw (reproduced in Berenson, 1957 Lists, Plate 461). (4) Repro-duced by Ottino, *Luini*, 1956, Plate 146. (5) For the attribution to Luini, see Carlo Amoretti, *Memorie Storiche . . . di Lionardo da Vinci* (attached to the *Trattato della Pittura*), 1804, p. 168; Ignazio Fumagalli, *Scuola di Leonardo da Vinci in Lombardia*, 1811 (no page number); Waagen, *Kunstwerke*, I, 1837, pp. 184/5. Accepted as an original Luini by Ottino, *Luini*, 1956, No. 84. Sir Kenneth Clark (*Catalogue of the Drawings of Leonardo da Vinci at Windsor Castle*, 1935, Vol. I, Nos. 12524/5 and *Leonardo da Vinci*, 1939, p. 129 or 1958, pp. 118/9) points out that two drapery studies by Leonardo at Windsor correspond with details of a globe-bearing Christ, bought in at the Yarborough Sale in 1929 (photograph in the Witt Library). He goes on to say that Leonardo may also have made a cartoon corresponding more or less with No. 18, from which No. 18 would be derived. But the Yarborough *Christ* does not correspond closely with the Christ in No. 18; and further objections to the claim are stated by E. Panofsky, *Dürer*, 1945, Vol. I, p. 115. See also J. Bialostocki in the *Journal of the Warburg and Courtauld Institutes*, 1959, pp. 17 ff. (6) Engraved (as Luini) in Fumagalli, *op. cit.* in previous note. (7) Monti Bequest, 1650; mentioned in Fumagalli, *op. cit.* (8) Reproduced by E. Lavagnino, *La Galleria Spada in Roma*, 1933, p. 18, and by Zeri, *La Galleria Spada*, 1954, Fig. 122. Presumably it is the Spada picture referred to in note 11 (cf. Zeri's entry for the picture, No. 130). (9) Later in the Brigadier R. J. Cooper Sale, 12 December, 1947 (lot 9);

photograph in the Gallery archives. **(10)** Dr. Paola Della Pergola kindly sent an
extract from the inventory of Olimpia Aldobrandini, 1626 (No. 85): ' Un quadro
con Christo che disputa con li farisei di mani di Leonardo da Vinci del N⁰ 177'.
No. 18 has written on the back ' N⁰ 177. DI LEONARDO DAVINCI', so
there seems no doubt at all about the identification. **(11)** Further evidence for the
provenance is in a drawing of a closely corresponding composition on f. 4r. of
Padre Sebastiano Resta (1635–1714), *Correggio in Roma*, MS. probably ca.
1710/4 in the British Museum Print Room (Malcolm, Add. 180). Under the
drawing is the following inscription, noted by P. Pouncey: ' Il Quadro di mano
di Leonardo da Vinci di questa Disputa di Cristo con i Dottori/Stà in Galleria
Pamfilia trà quadri della qᵐ Sigʳᵃ Principessa di Rosano' (i.e. Olimpia Aldobrandini) ' peruenuti/nel figlio Cardˡᵉ' (i.e. Benedetto, Cardinal 1681–1730). ' In
Napoli io n'hebbi un fatto dal Louino, che donai al Sig Cardˡᵉ Spada prima/che
andasse Nunzio in Francia' (presumably Fabrizio Spada, 1643–1717, Nuncio ca.
1672/5). ' Si osserui l'idea della faccia del Cristo benche giouine: non il resto.'
Other evidence from Resta concerning the existence of a version in the Pamphilj
Collection is in the Department of MSS., British Museum, Lansdowne 802,
Book F, No. 17, where Resta refers to a ' tela' (*sic*) ' di quattro palmi per traverso,
Sta in Galeria del Sig Card. Panfilio.' (For this MS., see A. E. Popham in *Old
Master Drawings*, Vol XI, June, 1936, pp. 1 ff. On p. 17, No. VI, Popham
gives the full text of the inscription, and reproduces on Plate 6 the drawing
Resta says is connected with No. 18; the fact that Resta is wrong about the status
of the drawing in no way impugns his statement concerning the picture in the
Pamphilj Collection). **(12)** Still as Leonardo. Vasari, ed. Bottari, II, 1759,
p. 22. Filippo Titi, *Descrizione delle Pitture, etc. esposte al Pubblico in Roma*,
1763, p. 320 (not in the editions of Titi dated 1674, *Studio di Pittura*, 1686,
Ammaestramento Vtile, e curioso . . ., and 1721, *Nuovo Studio di Pittura . . .*).
Titi, 1763, p. 281 (not in Titi of 1674, 1686 and 1721) refers to a copy of the
Pamphilj picture by P. Biagio Betti in S. Silvestro al Quirinale. On p. 282 of the
1763 edition (1686 edition, p. 258; 1721 edition, p. 302), Titi mentions in the
Libreria of the same church a picture of the same subject by Biagio Botti, presumably the same man. F. Baumgart (*Zeitschrift für Kunstgeschichte*, 1934, pp.
231/2) reproduces a picture of this subject in this church, which he states is by
Biagio Betti; Baumgart's picture is not a copy of No. 18, but a copy of a Dürer
print. Baumgart is, nevertheless, not justified in deducing that it was a picture
similar to the one he reproduces that was in the Pamphilj Collection. **(13)** Much
of this is from the *Enciclopedia Italiana* and from Moroni's *Dizionario di Erudizione Storico-Ecclesiastica*; cf. also Teodoro Amayden, *La Storia delle Famiglie
Romane*, ed. C. A. Bertini, 1910/5. Further discussion of these family arrangements would appear excessive here. In an inventory of one of Olimpia Aldobrandini's sons, Giovanni Battista, referred to in the entry for Mantegna, No.
1417, note 17, the compiler did not identify any picture corresponding with No.
18; the record may be there, or the property of his brother, Cardinal Benedetto,
may have been considered as separate. **(14)** In the catalogue of the Leonardo
Exhibition at Los Angeles, 1949 (No. 28), a version of No. 18 lent by Stuart
Borchard (as ' Leonardo Composition') is claimed to be the Pamphilj version; no
justification of this statement is made. **(15)** *Viaggiana*, 1776, p. 135. **(16)** Ramdohr, *Ueber Mahlerei etc.*, 1787, I. p. 307. For two later references, see F.
Noack in the *Repertorium für Kunstwissenschaft*, 1929, p. 224. **(17)** Buchanan,
Memoirs, 1824, II, p. 5 (No. 9), as from the Aldobrandini Cabinet, with the later
ownership of Lord Northwick and Holwell Carr stated. **(18)** *Catalogue of a
Select Collection etc. from the Aldobrandini Villa etc.* (agent, Buchanan), at 18
Oxendon Street, Haymarket, 24 May, 1808, No. 1, as from the Villa Aldobrandini; in this catalogue this phrase seems to cover both the Villa Aldobrandini and the Aldobrandini Cabinet, which are distinct headings in the
Day catalogue (previous note). The 1808 catalogue seems to be careless in its
headings; thus No. 2, Raphael, *S. Catherine*, which is presumably No. 168 of
the National Gallery, is stated to be from the Villa Aldobrandini, but it
appears to be a Borghese, not an Aldobrandini picture. **(19)** Mentioned in Lord

Northwick's Collection in *The Picture of London for* 1807, p. 299. (20) *Somerset House Gazette*, 31 July, 1824.

3935   THE VIRGIN AND CHILD WITH S. JOHN

Poplar,[1] painted surface, $34\frac{3}{4} \times 26$ (0·885 × 0·66); painted up to the edges all round.

Very good state. Many *pentimenti*. S. John's head was at one time as in the Fogg version, listed below, being a little more frontal and tipped somewhat; his original right eye being to the left of his present one, his original ear being higher up and more in perspective. There are a good many other, smaller variations in this figure, the most noticeable being in the hands. Christ's ear was once lower; and there is a second outline to His cheek and forehead to the right.

An early work. The influence of Bergognone and Bramantino, which has been claimed,[2] is perhaps discernible; but Richter is wrong in saying that there is no trace of Leonardo's. Not only is S. John's hair Leonardesque; the whole right part of the composition seems clearly to be derived, although inverted and with variations, from the *Virgin of the Rocks*. Luini seems to have been strongly affected by that picture, as was pointed out in the entry for it, in the section *Versions and Copies*; it was in Leonardo's studio for completion about 1506/8, but it is not to be accepted that No. 3935 is so early.[3]

VERSIONS: A version is in the Fogg Art Museum (Naumburg Bequest, 1930), ex-Pepys Collection, and ex-the George C. Thomas Sale, New York, 12 November, 1924 (lot 64);[4] some of the variations are the subject of comment above. Several other designs by Luini show in parts loose connections with the design of No. 3935.

PROVENANCE: Unidentified seal on the back. Acquired by Ludwig Mond, 1893;[5] exhibited at the Burlington Fine Arts Club, 1898 (No. 27); Mond Bequest, 1924.

REPRODUCTION: *Illustrations, Italian Schools*, 1937, p. 202. *Plates, Earlier Italian Schools*, 1953, Vol. II, p. 255.

REFERENCES: (1) Letter from B. J. Rendle, of the Forest Products Research Laboratory, in the Gallery archives. (2) B.F.A.C. Catalogue, 1898 (No. 27); J. P. Richter, *The Mond Collection*, Vol. II, 1910, pp. 339/40. (3) So early a dating was mentioned, though with restrictions, in the first edition of this catalogue. Ottino, *Luini*, 1956, No. 83, who thinks No. 3935 only rather early, objects; and even if the André picture is excluded from Luini's works, it does seem most unlikely that Luini was painting in the style of No. 3935 so early. (4) Photograph in the Gallery archives. Reproduced by Reinach, *Répertoire*, I, p. 220, and in the Thomas Sale Catalogue; also, together with a reproduction of No. 3935, by Luca Beltrami, *Luini*, 1911, pp. 540/1, and by Ottino, *Luini*, 1956, Figs. 98, 99. (5) Richter, *op. cit.*, Table of Contents to Vol. II. Richter (oral) says that it was bought from a German dealer, who said he had got it from a sale in Berlin.

Studio of BERNARDINO LUINI

3090   THE VIRGIN AND CHILD

Poplar,[1] painted surface, $19\frac{1}{4} \times 17\frac{1}{4}$ (0·49 × 0·44); painted up to the edges at the sides.

A good deal retouched.

It has been called an original;[2] the style is now hardly recognizable, but it seems at best a studio-piece. Berenson (1932 Lists) marks it with an s.

VERSIONS: An original, with some variations and S. Joseph added, is in the Louvre.[3] Another variant, of poor quality, is at Bâle (Bachofen-Burckhardt Stiftung, photograph in the Gallery archives).

PROVENANCE: From Count Borromeo passed to Baslini, Milan, from whom Sir A. H. Layard bought it *ca.* 1863.[4] Exhibited at South Kensington, 1869 (No. 10), and at the R.A., 1870 (No. 62); Layard Bequest, 1916.[5]

REPRODUCTION: *Illustrations, Italian Schools*, 1937, p. 204. *Plates, Earlier Italian Schools*, 1953, Vol. II, p. 256.

REFERENCES: (1) Letter from B. J. Rendle, of the Forest Products Research Laboratory, in the Gallery archives. (2) Cf. for instance Frizzoni in the *Gazette des Beaux-Arts*, 1896, II, p. 469. Ottino, *Luini*, 1956, No. 82, inclines to think it an original. (3) Cf. Malaguzzi Valeri in the *Rassegna d'Arte*, 1913, p. 32 (reproduced, p. 30). (4) Layard MSS. in the National Gallery. No. 3090 seems to be identical with a picture noted in the Conte Giberto Borromeo Collection at Genoa by Eastlake in his note-book, 1857. This Borromeo Collection had been brought from Milan (Mündler's *Diary*, 1 May, 1857), and did not remain long in Genoa. (The Casa dei Borromei at Milan seems to have been occupied by Austrian troops from *ca.* 1855, the family not returning to it until after 1860; see *Journals and Correspondence of Lady Eastlake*, II, 1895, p. 172). When Eastlake in 1863 visited the Giberto Borromeo Collection at Milan, he did not note any picture that could be identical with No. 3090, so it may already have been sold. According to the Layard MSS. in the National Gallery, No. 3090 seems to have been bought at the same time as Bonsignori, No. 3091; see the entry for that picture, where the date of acquisition is given as *ca.* 1863. A. Venturi in *L'Arte*, 1912, p. 451, says 1864. No. 3090 is mentioned in letters from Morelli to Layard, 26 October, 1864, and Layard to Morelli, 5 December, 1864 (British Museum, Add. MSS. 38963 and 38966, Layard Papers, Vols. XXXIII and XXXVI). (5) For the history of the Layard Collection, see Appendix IV.

After BERNARDINO LUINI

2088 CHRIST

Poplar,[1] painted surface, $29 \times 22\frac{3}{4}$ (0·735 × 0·58); painted up to the edges all round.

Much damaged.

A copy of the central figure of No. 18 above; it does not seem to be contemporary.

PROVENANCE: Stated to come from the Strozzi Collection, Ferrara.[2] Passed into the John Samuel Collection; exhibited at the R.A., 1871 (No. 290). Exhibited at the New Gallery, 1893/4 (No. 170), lent by the Misses Cohen, nieces of John Samuel. Bequeathed with other pictures by the Misses Cohen, as the John Samuel Collection, 1906.

REPRODUCTION: *Plates, Earlier Italian Schools*, 1953, Vol. II, p. 257.

REFERENCES: (1) Letter from B. J. Rendle, of the Forest Products Research Laboratory, in the Gallery archives. (2) John Samuel *Catalogue*, 1895 (No. 13); cf. G. C. Williamson, *Luini*, 1907, p. 105.

3936 S. CATHERINE

Poplar,[1] painted surface, $28 \times 23\frac{1}{2}$ (0.715×0.60); painted up to the edges all round.

In fairly good state, apparently.

J. P. Richter, who was consulted about Ludwig Mond's purchase of No. 3936 only at the last moment, thought that it was probably an original, but with the proviso that certainty could only be reached if the picture were cleaned;[2] there seems, nevertheless, little justification for calling it anything but a copy.[3] Among the various versions known, that in the Hermitage has been called an original;[4] but Richter satisfied himself that that picture is inferior to No. 3936.

VERSIONS: One is at Leningrad, said to be from the French Royal Collection; bought in 1815 from the Collection of the Empress Josephine at Malmaison.[5] Another, of inferior quality, but apparently from the French Royal Collection, is in the Louvre (until recently at Compiègne).[6] There are numerous others.

PROVENANCE: From the Corsi Collection, Florence, and in the Howard Collection at Corby Castle by 1825.[7] Lent by P. H. Howard to the British Institution, 1849 (No. 74);[8] to Manchester, 1857 (not in the Provisional Catalogue; Definitive Catalogue, No. 209); to the British Institution, 1866 (No. 57); and to Leeds, 1868 (No. 234).[9] Anon. Sale at Christie's, 29 June, 1889 (lot 83), bought by Lesser Lesser, by whom exhibited at the R.A., 1892 (No. 164).[10] Bought from Lesser by Ludwig Mond in 1892;[11] exhibited at the Burlington Fine Arts Club, 1898 (No. 29); Mond Bequest, 1924.

REPRODUCTION: *Illustrations, Italian Schools*, 1937, p. 203. *Plates, Earlier Italian Schools*, 1953, Vol. II, p. 258.

REFERENCES: (1) Letter from B. J. Rendle, of the Forest Products Research Laboratory, in the Gallery archives. (2) Letters from J. P. Richter in the Gallery archives. (3) Berenson, 1932 Lists, calls No. 3936 Luini in great part. Ottino, *Luini*, 1956, No. 85, does not express a definite opinion on the authenticity, but is reluctant to consider it merely a copy; she records several other versions. (4) Cf. A. Venturi in *L'Arte*, 1898, p. 316. (5) Somof's Hermitage Catalogue, *Ecoles d'Italie et d'Espagne*, 3rd edition, 1891, No. 72, reproduced p. 90; 1958 Catalogue, Vol. I (Italian, etc. Schools), pp. 68/9, No. 109, reproduced. (6) *Inventaire des Tableaux du Roy rédigé en 1709 et 1710 par Nicolas Bailly*, ed. F. Engerand, 1899, pp. 2/3; already in Le Brun's Inventory of 1683. Jacques Dupont (letter of 27 January, 1949) gave some confirmation of Engerand's identification, and Michel Florisoone sent a photograph. (7) Provenance stated in Neale's *Views of Seats*, Second Series, Vol. II, 1825; there is a seal with the Corsi arms on the back of the picture. (8) Here and at the two next exhibitions as Luini. (9) As Leonardo, ex-Corsi. (10) There are on the back of No. 3936 labels of the Manchester, Leeds and R.A. Exhibitions. (11) Richter, *The Mond Collection*, 1910, Table of Contents to Volume II.

ZANOBI MACHIAVELLI
ca. 1418–1479

Florentine School. For the dates of birth and death (beyond reasonable doubt the right man), see the *Rivista d'Arte*, 1916, pp. 67 ff. Recorded as active for the Badia at Fiesole in 1464 (1465 ?). Later, at least in 1475/6, active in Pisa. Several signed works exist. Vasari says that he was a pupil of Benozzo (Gozzoli).

586 TRIPTYCH: THE VIRGIN AND CHILD WITH SAINTS

Centre, the Virgin and Child with angels. Left wing, a Bishop Saint and S. Nicholas of Tolentino. Right wing, SS. Bartholomew and Monica.

Wood. The size of the central panel is $64\frac{3}{4} \times 28\frac{1}{2}$ ($1\cdot645 \times 0\cdot725$); painted surface, pointed top, $64\frac{1}{2} \times 27\frac{3}{4}$ ($1\cdot64 \times 0\cdot71$). Left wing, panel, $57 \times 23\frac{1}{2}$ ($1\cdot45 \times 0\cdot595$); painted surface, pointed top, $56\frac{1}{4} \times 23\frac{1}{2}$ ($1\cdot43 \times 0\cdot595$); the measurements include a new addition to the panel down the right side, 1 in. wide. Right wing, panel, $56 \times 24\frac{1}{4}$ ($1\cdot425 \times 0\cdot62$); painted surface, pointed top, $56 \times 23\frac{1}{4}$ ($1\cdot425 \times 0\cdot595$); the measurements include a new addition to the panel down the right side, $1\frac{1}{4}$ in. wide.

The backgrounds have been regilt, and it is undecided if the original fields of the pictures corresponded exactly with the present ones, or if originally the pictures had pointed tops. The condition of the figures is fair.

It is possible that No. 586 comes from the same ensemble as Nos. 587/8 below; the matter is discussed in the entry for those pictures.

No. 586 is stated to come from S. Spirito at Florence, and was identified with Fra Filippo Lippi's Barbadori altarpiece there.[1] The identification is wrong,[2] but No. 586 may all the same come from S. Spirito; S. Spirito is an Augustinian church, and No. 586 contains Augustinian saints.

The attribution to Fra Filippo Lippi was accepted with some reserves by the National Gallery when the pictures were acquired.[3] Crowe and Cavalcaselle[4] were the first to make the attribution to Machiavelli.

From this altarpiece may perhaps come a predella panel ($0\cdot225 \times 0\cdot48$), which was in the Spiridon Sale, Amsterdam, 19 June, 1928 (lot 16), and is now in the Rijksmuseum at Amsterdam (vom Rath Bequest).[5] This is ascribed to Machiavelli by Berenson,[6] and the subject is S. Nicholas of Tolentino saving a man from hanging.[7]

The pose of the Child in No. 586 is perhaps derived from Domenico Veneziano's altarpiece in the Uffizi,[8] and is repeated more or less in other pictures by Machiavelli.[9]

PROVENANCE: Stated to be from S. Spirito at Florence, as explained above; stated to have been in the sacristy, and to have been removed to the convent at the end of the eighteenth century.[10] Stated to have been later in the Primicerio Crociani's Collection at Montepulciano.[11] By 1845 in the Lombardi-Baldi Collection at Florence, No. 43 of the Catalogue.[12] Purchased with other pictures from Lombardi and Baldi, 1857.[13]

REPRODUCTION: *Illustrations, Italian Schools*, 1937, p. 204. *Plates, Earlier Italian Schools*, 1953, Vol. II, p. 259.

REFERENCES: (1) See Vasari, Le Monnier edition, IV, 1848, p. 119. (2) Fra Filippo Lippi's Barbadori altarpiece is in the Louvre; Van Marle, *Development of the Italian Schools of Painting*, Vol. X, Fig. 253. Cf. I. B. Supino, *Fra Filippo Lippi*, 1902, pp. 55 ff., and Mlle. Blumer in the *Bulletin de la Société de l'Histoire de l'Art Français*, 1936, p. 286. (3) Compare the National Gallery Report for 1858, p. 62. In the National Gallery Catalogue, 1862, it was suggested that the

Virgin and Child is partly by Fra Filippo Lippi, the angels and side figures by Alesso Baldovinetti. (4) Crowe and Cavalcaselle, *History of Painting in Italy*, II, 1864, pp. 518/9. (5) As School of Uccello; reproduced in the Spiridon sale catalogue, and in the *Verslag van den Hoofddirecteur*, Rijkmuseum, Amsterdam, for 1941. This picture was in the Toscanelli Sale, 9/23 April, 1883 (lot 67), and Plate XV of the Album, as Benozzo. Toscanelli acquired some pictures that had previously belonged to Lombardi and Baldi; the compiler has no proof that this was so in this case. (6) Berenson in *Dedalo*, 1932, pp. 692 (reproduction) and 698. (7) P. Baudouin de Gaiffier, S.J., *Le Pendu Miraculeusement Sauvé*, in the *Revue Belge d'Archéologie et d'Histoire de l'Art*, 1943, pp. 141 ff, esp. p. 143, No. 4. (8) Van Marle, *Development of the Italian Schools of Painting*, Vol. X, Fig. 192. (9) E.g. in the signed example at Dublin; Van Marle, *op. cit.*, Vol. XI, Fig. 377. (10) See the National Gallery Report for 1858, p. 62. If these statements of location in S. Spirito are considered to be merely confusions with Fra Filippo Lippi's Barbadori altarpiece, it may be that No. 586 was in a chapel belonging to the Capponi da S. Frediano family, the first in the right hand transept of S. Spirito, as is claimed by W. and E. Paatz, *Die Kirchen von Florenz*, Vol. V., 1953, pp. 153 and 156. The picture of that chapel is recorded by Richa, *Notizie Istoriche delle Chiese Fiorentine*, Vol. IX, 1761, pp. 22/3, as by Fra Filippo Lippi, *Maria, il Bambino Gesù, e Santi*; it is recorded, apparently, as still there by Follini and Rastrelli, *Firenze Antica e Moderna*, Vol. VII, 1797, p. 366. The picture of a different subject, now in this place in the church, was already there in 1819; see L.F.M.G. Gargiolli, *Description de la Ville de Florence*, 1819, II, p. 150. So far as the compiler is aware, Richa's picture could be the right one; but further details on the matter would be welcome. If this location is right for No. 586, it is not probable that Nos. 587/8 below were associated. The chapel in question is of the normal form for S. Spirito, that is with its wall on a curve; although later on large altarpieces were squeezed into these chapels, it can be claimed that usually in the XV and early XVI Centuries the width of the altarpiece and its frame did not greatly exceed 85 in. (11) See the National Gallery Report for 1858, p. 62. (12) The catalogue is not dated; but the copy in the Uffizi Library is claimed to be of 1845. (13) For the history of the Lombardi-Baldi Collection, see Appendix I.

587 LEFT WING OF AN ALTARPIECE: SS. JOHN THE BAPTIST AND EVANGELIST

The Baptist's scroll is inscribed ECCE AGN / PE.

Wood. Size of the panel, rounded top, $52\frac{1}{8} \times 22\frac{7}{8}$ ($1 \cdot 325 \times 0 \cdot 58$); original (?) painted surface, rounded top, $50\frac{3}{4} \times 20\frac{1}{2}$ ($1 \cdot 29 \times 0 \cdot 52$).

Figures in fair state. Regilt, so that it is not certain if the present field of the picture corresponds exactly with the original one.

For the commentary, etc., see No. 588 below.

588 RIGHT WING OF AN ALTARPIECE: SS. MARK AND AUGUSTINE

On S. Augustine's mitre is the Resurrected Christ, and Christ in the Tomb with the Virgin, S. John and the Magdalen (?).

Reverse: a drawing of a female in profile, on the unprimed wood.

Wood. Size of the panel, rounded top, $52\frac{1}{8} \times 22\frac{3}{4}$ ($1 \cdot 325 \times 0 \cdot 58$); original (?) painted surface, rounded top, $51 \times 20\frac{1}{2}$ ($1 \cdot 295 \times 0 \cdot 52$).

Figures in fair state. Regilt; it is not certain if the present field of the picture corresponds exactly with the original one.

Nos. 587 and 588 are obviously fragments of one altarpiece. In the National Gallery Report for 1858, the suggestion was made that they may have been from the same ensemble as No. 586 above. Against this, it may be remarked that the pictures forming No. 586 have at present pointed tops, whereas Nos. 587/8 have, and perhaps always had, round tops; that the scale of the figures, and indeed the sizes of the panels, are slightly smaller in Nos. 587/8 than in No. 586; and that a pentaptych, with a pair of saints on each of the four wings, would be unusual and unwieldy.[1] A further point that may be against the association is made at the end of note 10 to the entry for No. 586. In favour, it may be noted that Nos. 587/8 are parts of an Augustinian altarpiece, that No. 586 is also Augustinian, and that the saints represented here are not repeated in No. 586. The style of the pictures is also close, and the step on which the saints stand corresponds in the various pictures.

No. 587 was already attributed to Machiavelli by 1919.[2] Both pictures were catalogued as his in the National Gallery catalogue of 1929; the attribution is accepted by Berenson in his Lists of 1932.

PROVENANCE: If Nos. 587/8 are from the same altarpiece as No. 586 above, the earlier part of the provenance for No. 586, as given in the entry for it, would be valid for Nos. 587/8 also. Nos. 587/8 are stated to have been in a collection at Montepulciano, but not certainly the same as that in which No. 586 was.[3] By 1845 they were, like No. 586, in the Lombardi-Baldi Collection at Florence.[4] Purchased with other pictures from Lombardi and Baldi, 1857.[5] No. 587 was lent to Edinburgh, 1862–1927;[6] No. 588 was lent to Dublin, 1862–1926.[7]

REPRODUCTIONS: *Illustrations, Italian Schools*, 1937, pp. 206/7. *Plates, Earlier Italian Schools*, 1953, Vol. II, p. 260. The drawing on the reverse of No. 588 is reproduced in *Paintings and Drawings on the Backs of National Gallery Pictures*, 1946, Plate 7.

REFERENCES: (1) Such things seem to be rather of an earlier time; cf. the Giovanni da Milano in the Uffizi, reproduced in part by Van Marle, *Development of the Italian Schools of Painting*, Vol. IV, Fig. 115. Cf. also the altarpiece reproduced by Van Marle, *op. cit.*, Vol. III, Fig. 336. (2) It was on loan to Edinburgh, and appears as Machiavelli in the Edinburgh Catalogue, 45th edition, 1919. It was ascribed to Fra Filippo Lippi in the 43rd edition, 1912; the 44th edition has not been consulted. (3) In the National Gallery Report for 1858, p. 63, it is stated: 'it appears that they came from the same collection at Montepulciano, where that altarpiece (i.e., No. 586) was found.' This implies that Eastlake had tried without success to obtain a positive assurance on the point. In the National Gallery Catalogue, 1858, it is stated that Nos. 587/8 were obtained by Lombardi and Baldi at Montepulciano 'with' No. 586, but the Primicerio Crociani Collection is not explicitly mentioned. (4) Lombardi-Baldi Catalogue, Nos. 37, 38, as Masolino. The catalogue is not dated, but the copy in the Uffizi Library is claimed to be of 1845. (5) In the National Gallery Catalogue, 1858, as School of Fra Filippo Lippi. For the history of the Lombardi-Baldi Collection, see Appendix I. (6) Lent as Alesso Baldovinetti (N.G. Report for 1863, p. 123); in Edinburgh Catalogues, 1900 (No. 103), 1908 (No. 104), 1912 (No. 104), as ascribed to Fra Filippo Lippi; Edinburgh Catalogues, 1919 (No. 456) and 1924 (No. 456) as Machiavelli. Both No. 587 and No. 588 were wrongly ascribed to Zoppo by A. Venturi in *L'Arte*, 1927, pp. 62/3. (7) Lent as Alesso Baldovinetti (N.G. Report for 1863, p. 123); in Dublin Catalogues, 1871 (No. 2), as School of Fra Filippo Lippi, and 1914 (No. 412), as Giusto d'Andrea or Andrea di Giusto.

Sebastiano MAINARDI
active 1493, died 1513

From San Gimignano. He is often stated to be recorded as active there in 1474 or 1475, although this cannot really be deduced from what is said by Luigi Pecori, *Storia della Terra di San Gimignano*, 1853, p. 512. Mainardi was certainly active in Pisa in 1493/4. He married a sister of Domenico Ghirlandaio; she was born *ca.* 1475, so it is probable that the marriage did not take place very long before Ghirlandaio's death in 1494.

There is no doubt that Mainardi was a pupil and/or assistant of Ghirlandaio's; but his importance in Ghirlandaio's studio is not well defined. Among the works of collaboration between the two that Vasari (in the edition of 1568) mentions, is a fresco of *The Assumption of the Virgin* in S. Croce, Florence. This is sometimes considered the basis for identifying Mainardi's style; but Albertini, writing 58 years before Vasari, ascribed the fresco to Ghirlandaio without mentioning Mainardi, and in any case a work by Mainardi on Ghirlandaio's cartoon (as Vasari calls it) would give but a partial indication of Mainardi's characteristics.

In point of fact, there is only one existing work that can be called a documented example of Mainardi; a series of frescoes in the chapel of S. Bartolo in S. Agostino at San Gimignano is stated to have borne Mainardi's initials and the date 1500. The more important part of these frescoes is reproduced (very small) in *Cronache d'Arte*, 1927, p. 171. It is generally admitted that these frescoes show the decadence of Mainardi's art; in other words, they do not correspond very well with the numberless Ghirlandaiesque pictures that have been ascribed to him. His name has indeed been used as a peg on which to hang many of Ghirlandaio's schoolpieces, some of which are closely related in style to each other.

In view of the difficulty of reasonable attribution to Mainardi, the pictures in the National Gallery formerly catalogued as his are now classified in the following of Ghirlandaio.

See Studio of Domenico GHIRLANDAIO, Nos. 1230, 3937:

Follower of Domenico GHIRLANDAIO, Nos. 2489, 2502

MANNI (Giannicola) *See* GIANNICOLA di Paolo

Giovanni MANSUETI
active 1485, died 1527(?)

Venetian School. He was a pupil of Bellini (perhaps both Gentile and Giovanni Bellini). The date of death does not seem to have been clearly established; compare Ludwig in the Prussian *Jahrbuch*, 1905, Supplement, p. 62, with Paoletti, *La Scuola Grande di S. Marco*, 1929, p. 159. There exist several signed works.

1478 SYMBOLIC REPRESENTATION OF THE CRUCIFIXION

In the centre, the Trinity; the Virgin and S. James the Greater, S. John and S. Peter stand at the foot of the Cross, and the Magdalen with SS. Joseph of Arimathaea and Nicodemus kneel in front. Two *putti* behind hold the spear and sponge. Signed (?), *J de mansuet(is?)*. 1492 (much retouched, and possibly false).

Canvas, 51 × 48¾ (1·295 × 1·24).
Considerably rubbed and restored.

The signature is much damaged and not beyond suspicion; but if it is false, it may be copied from the genuine signature of Mansueti. On stylistic grounds, the picture is acceptable as his.

Since its acquisition, the picture has been said probably to have been used as a banner, but this supposition is unnecessary. The kneeling figure holding pincers was in the 1929 catalogue doubtfully called S. Peter Martyr, but the pincers obviously refer to the Descent from the Cross; this saint and the other saint kneeling opposite must be S. Joseph of Arimathaea and S. Nicodemus.

VERSION: The Trinity alone, in very similar but not identical figures, reappears in a picture in S. Simeone Grande, Venice.[1] The figure of God the Father is fairly similar to one in an *Assumption* at Padua.[2]

PROVENANCE: Possibly a picture mentioned by Sansovino in S. Maria de' Crocicchieri (now, Gesuiti), Venice.[3] Probably in the Manfrin Collection, Venice.[4] Said to have been owned by the Hon. Julian Fane and Lady Desborough.[5] Purchased through Agnew at a Diplomatist's Sale, Christie's, 18 July, 1896 (lot 106).

REPRODUCTION: *Illustrations, Italian Schools*, 1937, p. 210. *Plates, Earlier Italian Schools*, 1953, Vol. II, p. 261.

REFERENCES: (1) *Cinque Secoli di Pittura Veneta, Catalogo della Mostra*, 1945 (No. 41), and Fig. 21. (2) Padua Gallery, Catalogue, 1957, reproduced on p. 100. (3) Sansovino, *Venetia Città Nobilissima*, 1581, f. 61r; Stringa's edition, 1604, f. 147v; Martinioni's edition, 1663, pp. 168/9. (4) *Catalogo dei quadri esistenti nella Galleria Manfrin in Venezia*, 1856 (No. 372): *Cristo in Croce con Santi*, Mansueti Giovanni, Tela, 1·32 × 1·26. Cf. F. Zanotto, *Nuovissima Guida di Venezia*, 1856, p. 346: 'Cristo in Croce, con la Vergine e S. Giovanni'; and Crowe and Cavalcaselle, *Painting in North Italy*, I, 1871, p. 223, or ed. Borenius, I, 1912, p. 226. In a MS. list of the Manfrin pictures (1851) in the National Gallery Library, Stanza H, No. 40 is 'Giovanni Mansueti, Cristo in Croce con varj Santi.' Eastlake in his note-book for 1855 mentions in the 7th room of the Manfrin Collection a 'Crucifixion or Italian Trinity—Mansueti.' In his note-book, 1857, No. 312 is 'Italian Trinity & other figs. Mansueti—not desirable.' In his note-book, 1862, No. 181 is 'Mansueti—Ital. Trinity—Sts—architect.' The Manfrin Collection was formed, at least in part, by Conte Girolamo Manfrin, who died in 1801 according to *Il Forestiere Istruito . . . della Città di Venezia*, 1822, p. 295. According to the catalogue of the A. M. Plattis Sale, Paris, 13/4 May, 1870, the collection was formed *ca.* 1748 (perhaps meaning from that date onwards) and in 1848 was divided between the Marquise Bortolina Plattis veuve du Baron Sardagna and the Marquis Antonio Maria Plattis. According to the Manfrin Sale Catalogue of 1897, the collection was divided in 1849 between the Marchese Antonio Plattis and the Marchesa Bortolina Plattis nei Sardagna; her part or some of it remained in the Palazzo Manfrin until 1897. (5) Statement in the 1913 Catalogue. Presumably the reference is to the Hon. Julian Henry Charles Fane, d. 1870, whose daughter's husband was created Lord Desborough in 1905.

Andrea MANTEGNA
ca. 1430/1–1506

Painter and engraver. Born probably at Isola di Carturo, between Vicenza and Padua (near Piazzola). The date of his birth is from the inscription recorded on a lost picture, and is not likely to be wrong. He moved to Padua at an early age, where he was adopted by Francesco Squarcione. He joined the Guild there between 1441 and 1445 (M. Urzì in the *Archivio Veneto*, 5th Series, Vol. XII, 1932, p. 219). He lived with Squarcione for 6 years, but Squarcione may be thought too feeble a painter to have influenced him much, except perhaps in a taste for Roman antiquities. Mantegna (who was precocious) was no doubt affected by the Bellini (he married the daughter of Jacopo Bellini in 1453), and by Pizolo. Perhaps more important for his development were the Florentine artists whose works were to be seen at Padua; principally Donatello, probably also Uccello and Fra Filippo Lippi. After painting much of the Ovetari Chapel in the Eremitani at Padua (see note), and other works at Padua and probably Venice, Mantegna moved to Mantua in 1459/60, where he remained in the service of the Gonzagas for the rest of his life. He was at Rome in 1488/90; but his work in the Vatican has been destroyed. He was a formative influence on Correggio.

Note. In view of the importance of dating Mantegna's work in the Eremitani Chapel, to which reference is made in several parts of the present catalogue, some account of Mantegna's chief frescoes in the Chapel (which was terribly damaged during the last war) appears to be desirable.

On 16 May, 1448, frescoes to decorate the Chapel were commissioned, half to be by Antonio Vivarini and Giovanni d'Alemagna, half by Niccolò Pizolo and Andrea Mantegna. By 27 September, 1449, Mantegna had partly painted figures of SS. Peter, Paul and Christopher in the apse of the Chapel, and it was agreed that Mantegna should finish these. It was also agreed that Mantegna should paint five of the stories of S. James in the main part of the Chapel, Pizolo doing the sixth.

Pizolo died in 1453. He had been responsible for painting the apse of the Chapel (apart from Mantegna's three figures); he had done about three-quarters of his work, but in particular seems not to have touched the space at the end, destined for *The Assumption of the Virgin* (blank, except conceivably for accessory figures, in February, 1454). Pizolo had presumably not touched the single scene from the story of S. James, allocated to him in the main part of the Chapel.

By January, 1457, *The Assumption of the Virgin* and 'the story' (it seems clearly all six stories) of S. James had been completed; on 14

February, the painter Pietro da Milano certified that they were by Mantegna.

The frescoes of S. Christopher on the other wall of the main part of the Chapel had been allocated originally to Antonio Vivarini and Giovanni d'Alemagna, who had not touched them at all at the time of Giovanni's death in 1449/50. It is clear that Antonio did nothing to this wall after Giovanni's death either; a payment he received in November, 1451, being presumably for work on the vaulting. Presumably the commission was transferred to other painters. There is reason to believe that the two uppermost frescoes, which are anonymous, were painted in 1450 or 1451, for the two immediately below have signatures (or at least very old inscriptions with the names) of Ansuino da Forlì and Bono da Ferrara; and Ansuino received a payment (at the same time as Mantegna) in October, 1451, while Bono received two payments in July, 1451, and seems to have left Padua very soon after.

On stylistic grounds, the two lowest frescoes on this (the S. Christopher) wall are by Mantegna. E. Tietze-Conrat (*Mantegna*, 1955) is one of the writers who puts them before several of the S. James frescoes on the opposite wall; the compiler thinks (as he thought before) that the arguments for putting them late, and perhaps latest of all, are stronger. It is not clear that a date for them can be deduced from the known documents concerning the Chapel.

The documents concerning the painting of this chapel are the Lazzarini (Moschetti) documents and the Rigoni documents, to which reference is given in Thieme-Becker; also further documents published by E. Rigoni in *Arte Veneta*, 1948, pp. 141 ff., where some deductions concerning dates, etc., seem to be unsure.

274 ALTARPIECE: THE VIRGIN AND CHILD WITH THE MAGDALEN AND S. JOHN THE BAPTIST

S. John holds a scroll with the words (ec)CE AGNV(s Dei ec)CE Q(ui tollit pec)CATA M(un)DI, and the signature, *Andreas Mantinia C.P.F.*

Canvas, present picture surface, $53\frac{3}{4} \times 45$ ($1 \cdot 36 \times 1 \cdot 14$); the picture is edged with a red-spotted black band, and the total painted area is $54\frac{3}{4} \times 46$ ($1 \cdot 39 \times 1 \cdot 165$).

Cleaned in 1957. Exceptionally good condition; some losses on the Virgin's cheeks and neck; a little rubbing, e.g. on the Magdalen's hair, right side. A *pentimento* in the Baptist's left shoulder.

The speckled band is not simply a band, but the remains of a marble window, as can be seen clearly in the right-hand bottom corner. This painted framework is partly overpainted, partly overcleaned; in particular, the parts in perspective at the left and top are almost all missing. At the top, the paint of the framework came down to touch what now appears as the top of the canopy, this canopy being imagined as behind it and cut off by it; what is seen of the front valance is indeed noticeably less tall than the back. The outermost edges of the canvas have probably all been cut, except possibly the one on the left.

The C.P. of the signature is often interpreted as *Civis Patavinus*; Mantegna did sign himself *Patavus* in 1474 in the Sala degli Sposi,[1] but in several documents from his later years (including his will) he is described as a citizen of Mantua. An old suggestion of *Comes Palatinus* would therefore seem equally good; the signature on his frescoes of 1489/90 in the Vatican was *Andreas Mantinia Comes Palatinus eques auratae militiae pinxit*.[2] He seems to have acquired the title from the Emperor in 1469,[3] which would then be a *terminus a quo* for No. 274. The spelling *Mantinia* can also be used as an argument against an earlier date.[4] The style would suggest an even later date (towards 1500 ?).

At the time of its acquisition, the execution was sometimes held to be in part by G. F. Caroto,[5] which seems very unlikely.

PROVENANCE: Said to have been owned by Cardinal Cesare Monti, Archbishop of Milan, who died in 1650; the original statement to this effect seems due to a misconception,[6] but there is also a tradition, first recorded in 1859,[7] that it was placed in the private chapel of Palazzo Monti in 1610. However that may be, the Palazzo Monti at Milan became in due course the Palazzo Andreani, where the picture came to light between 1787 and 1796.[8] Engraved in the Mario Andreani Collection in 1813.[9] It passed (by inheritance ?) to the Mellerio family, then to Conte Somaglia at Palazzo Mellerio, Milan.[10] The last named sold it to Baslini in 1855, who sold it to Roverselli, from whom purchased, 1855.

REPRODUCTION: *Illustrations, Italian Schools*, 1937, p. 211. *Plates, Earlier Italian Schools*, 1953, Vol. II, p. 262.

REFERENCES: (1) Knapp, Klassiker der Kunst *Mantegna*, 1910, Plate 42. (2) Cf. Kristeller, *Mantegna*, 1901, p. 300. (3) Kristeller, *op. cit.*, p. 202/3. (4) Cf. note 4 to the entry to No. 1417 below. (5) E.g. by Crowe and Cavalcaselle, *Painting in North Italy*, I, 1871, p. 482, or ed. Borenius, 1912, II, p. 189. The suggestion is due to a statement concerning Caroto by Vasari (not in the 1550 edition; ed. Milanesi, Vol. V, p. 280). (6) In Borroni's *Forastiere in Milano*, 1808, I. p. 49; the text is apparently taken—and mistaken—from (Bianconi), *Nuova Guida di Milano* (Stamperia Sirtori), 2nd edition, 1796, p. 119. (7) N.G. Catalogue, 1859; not in the edition of 1858. (8) (Bianconi), *Nuova Guida di Milano* (Stamperia Sirtori), 2nd edition, 1796, p. 119; not in the description of the Palazzo Andreani in the first edition, 1787, p. 103. (9) Zanconi and Carpani, *Raccolta delle migliori dipinture* etc., 1813, No. 8. (10) N.G. MS. Catalogue, and Eastlake's note-book and travelling report.

902   THE INTRODUCTION OF THE CULT OF CYBELE AT ROME ('THE TRIUMPH OF SCIPIO')

On a litter at the left is a stone (considered to be the goddess herself), her statue and a figure of Victory. The woman half kneeling in the centre is presumably Claudia Quinta (see below). On a banner and on the drummer-boy's collar are inscribed SPQR. Two tombs bear the inscriptions: SPQR / GN SCYPIO / NI CORNELI / VS F.P. ('filius posuit'), and P SCYPIONIS / EX HYSPANIENSI / BELLO / RELIQVIAE. Along the lower edge of the picture in the centre is S HOSPES NVMINIS IDAEI C. (These inscriptions have been retouched.)

Canvas (?) in monochrome: the area exposed is $29 \times 105\frac{1}{2}$ ($0.735 \times$

2·68). The bottom and left side are true edges. At the top in places nearly ½ in. of the painted surface is folded over the edge of the stretcher; but the limit of the stuff is very ragged, and in places there is no fold at all, so the reduction of the picture here (if any) would seem very slight. The right side is folded back over the whole depth of the stretcher (a little over 1 in. or 3 cm.), and ends in a clean cut; the part folded over is painted, but the moulding of the doorway immediately above the top step is the only detail distinguishable. A triangle at the right bottom corner, of which the exposed height is 8 in. (0·205), width 6 in. (0·15), has been inserted; this fragment also continues painted over the right edge of the stretcher. It seems not to be of contemporary execution. It may be noted that the threads of the original support, where it joins on to this insertion, are much distorted; since the original paint is not distorted, it seems that the strain on the stuff took place before the paint was put on. It is a likely deduction that the painted triangle now inserted was not intended in the original picture, and that a transverse part of the original stretcher caused the strain.

In general, a good deal of Mantegna's quality is preserved; but there is much damage. The parts most affected are the priest at the extreme left (much damaged), the shoulder, etc., of the man walking in front of the litter, the drapery and hands of Claudia Quinta, and the legs and right arm of the drummer-boy; other parts also are damaged. A few *pentimenti*; in particular, the priest on the left seems not to have had at first a mitre.

Cybele[1] was a goddess with many names, such as the Great Mother of the Gods or (as in the inscription here) the Idæan Deity; a principal seat of her worship was at Pessinus, the capital city of the Tolistobogi in Asia Minor, where she was called Agdistis. In the course of the Punic War, in 204 B.C., the Sibylline Books were found to declare that Hannibal might be driven out of Italy if she were brought from Pessinus (or perhaps rather in fact from Pergamum) to Rome. This was done. On their way the envoys stopped at Delphi, to consult the oracle there; good hope of success was promised, provided that the goddess was received by the worthiest man in Rome. The Senate designated Publius Cornelius Scipio Nasica, who is therefore referred to on the picture as her host,[2] S.C., by decree of the Senate. The vessel bringing the goddess, or more exactly the sacred stone identified with her, to Rome ran on to a shoal at or near Ostia; Claudia Quinta, a Roman matron whose chastity had been doubted, pulled the vessel free by means of a rope or, according to some, her girdle or scarf, and thus convinced the people of her innocence.

Mantegna has chosen, it seems, the moment of the goddess' arrival at Rome; the Oriental character of her worship, which persisted for a long time, is stressed. The woman half kneeling in the centre would be Claudia Quinta, whom Mantegna perhaps imagines as publicly thanking the goddess for favour received. Invented tombs of Scipio's father and uncle, who had fallen fighting in Spain about 211 B.C., are flattering references to that family; this is natural, for the Francesco Cornaro, who commissioned what is presumably this picture, claimed to be a descendant.[3] But Scipio himself is not apparent.[4] According to Livy, indeed, he merely received the goddess on the ship at Ostia, and carrying her to land, entrusted her to various Roman matrons to take to Rome; Ovid's account of his actions is just 'Nasica accepit'. He is sometimes supposed to be the figure in No. 902 standing behind Claudia Quinta; but that man is talking about her to another, and would be playing very ill the part of 'host to the Idæan Deity.' Besides, this particular Scipio was distinguished as Nasica on account of his nose, and Mantegna might seem to have tried to avoid the point.

Material evidence has been noted above that the picture has been cut at the right. It is possible that a considerable area is missing, in which Scipio might have been flatteringly presented; but it seems more likely that Scipio was reserved for another picture, since it appears certain, as will be explained presently, that No. 902 was intended to be part of a series. It is true that the drummer-boy in No. 902 seems to be calling the attention of someone outside the field of the picture, and that the trumpet emerging from the doorway top right is peculiar; but the inscription HOSPES NUMINIS IDAEI is fairly in the centre. Further, the probabilities concerning the right-hand bottom corner, as noted above, seem to exclude sufficient room for Scipio in any part cut away, at least if the line where original and insertion now join is imagined as continuing straight.

The circumstances of the commission for what is assumed to be No. 902 were as follows. On 1 January, 1506 (1505 o.s.),[5] Bembo wrote to Isabella d'Este that his friend Francesco Cornaro many months before had commissioned Mantegna to paint several pictures; the sizes and price had been agreed, and an advance payment had been made. Now (presumably in the autumn of 1505) Mantegna had written that he could not continue the work without an increase in payment; would Isabella straighten the matter out? On 31 January, 1506,[6] Isabella replied that she would do her best, as soon as Mantegna's health permitted his attending to such things.

Mantegna was at this time engaged (among other work) on a picture for Isabella herself,[7] and it is therefore doubtful if he did any more for Francesco Cornaro before his own death on 13 September, 1506. This is confirmed by the fact that his sons Lodovico and Francesco, who quarrelled about the estate in general, and about the Cornaro picture, agreed at least that the Cornaro family had no claim on it;[8] so presumably no conditions satisfactory to Mantegna had been reached.

At whatever moment Mantegna left off his works for Francesco Cornaro, what is assumed to be No. 902 (which alone had been begun)[9] must have been at his death in a more or less presentable state; for almost at once Cardinal Gonzaga expressed a desire to have it,[10] and it had in fact passed into his hands at some time before 26 November, 1506.[11]

The execution of No. 902 is sometimes in part attributed to an assistant, but the style (where the picture is not damaged) offers no confirmation of this.

A bust of Cybele reappears in Mantegna's *Triumph of Cæsar*, also with a crown of towers,[12]. A youth playing a drum and a pipe at the same time appears in a project for part of the *Triumph of Cæsar*.[13]

DRAWING: A drawing with a few variations of the priest on the left, etc., is at Bremen.[14]

ENGRAVING: By F. Novelli.[15]

PROVENANCE: As stated above, No. 902 is presumably a picture ordered by Franceso Cornaro of Venice, *ca.* 1504/5. Mantegna died on 13 September, 1506; on 2 October, 1506, one of his sons (Lodovico) was taking steps to sell it to Cardinal Sigismondo Gonzaga, who in fact had it shortly after. The other son (Francesco) tried to get it back on 26 November, but Lodovico was being paid for it in instalments by the Cardinal in 1507.[16] It is very probable that No. 902 is the picture concerned; in any case, No. 902 did eventually reach the Palazzo Cornaro, later Mocenigo a S. Polo, Venice. It was noted there in 1815 by Moschini;[17] bought thence by (Antonio) Sanquirico.[18] In the collection of George Vivian, who lent it to the British Institution, 1835 (No. 157) and 1844 (No. 77), to the Manchester Exhibition, 1857 (Provisional Catalogue, No. 289; Definitive Catalogue, No. 102), and to the R.A., 1871 (No. 274). Purchased from Captain Ralph Vivian, 1873.

REPRODUCTION: *Illustrations, Italian Schools*, 1937, p. 213. *Plates, Earlier Italian Schools*, 1953, Vol. II, pp. 263–264.

REFERENCES: (1) For the subject, see especially Ovid's *Fasti*, ed. Sir J. G. Frazer, III, 1929, pp. 217, 227 ff., 236 ff., 248 f. The other principal source for the story is Livy. (2) The reference to Scipio as host of the Idaean Deity is from Juvenal, *Satires*, III, 138. (3) It is assumed that No. 902 is identical with the picture ordered from Mantegna by Francesco Cornaro. The only description of that is 'quella opera di Scipion Cornelio' (D'Arco, *Delle Arti e Degli Artefici di Mantova*, Vol. II, 1857, No. 86). While it cannot be said that the identity is proved, it would appear unreasonable to feel much doubt about it. (4) Giles Robertson in *The Burlington Magazine*, January, 1953, p. 28, suggested that the figure here identified as Claudia Quinta is Scipio; to his regret, the compiler cannot think that this is right. The costume of the figure, although apparently not at all correct as Roman costume, seems decidedly female. The figure is not wearing a toga, and the compiler knows of no reason why Mantegna should show Scipio without a toga. It is further doubtful if the attitude is one of hospitality, even hospitality of whatever peculiar form is suitable for a goddess. Ovid more-over says that Claudia Quinta, before freeing the ship, thrice lifted her palms to heaven and, bending the knee and with dishevelled hair, prayed for the miracle that in fact followed; the moment cannot be the same as in Mantegna's picture, but it may seem that Ovid's words influenced him if (as seems most difficult to deny) the figure in the centre is Claudia Quinta. One may even wonder if the band of stuff curling in front of the figure's right leg is not meant for the girdle or scarf by which according to some accounts (not Ovid's) the miracle was effected; but this point is more doubtful. (5) D'Arco, *op. cit.*, No. 68. (6) *Gazette des Beaux-Arts*, 1896, I, p. 226. (7) D'Arco, *op. cit.*, No. 75. (8) D'Arco, *op. cit.*, Nos. 86 and 89. (9) The others were only prepared canvases; D'Arco, *op. cit.*, No. 89. It has been claimed that a picture formerly in the Cook Collection, and in 1951 in the Kress Loan to Washington, formed part of the same series as No. 902; see the large Cook catalogue, I, 1913, No. 133 (School of Giovanni Bellini, reproduced), and *Paintings and Sculpture from the Kress Collection Acquired by the Samuel H. Kress Foundation 1945–1951*, Washington, 1951, No. 30 (Giovanni Bellini, reproduced). Nos. 1125 A and B below (Follower of Mantegna) are also suggested as part of the same decoration; see the entry for them, and cf. E. Tietze-Conrat, *Mantegna*, 1955, p. 186. One could not feel much confidence in these suggestions, in the absence of any records in support. (10) D'Arco, *op. cit.*, No. 86. (11) D'Arco, *op. cit.*, No. 89. (12) Knapp, *Klassiker der Kunst*

Mantegna, 1910, Plate 51. For the attribute, see Lomazzo, *Arte della Pittura*, 1584, pp. 605/6. Further indications in H. A. J. Munro's Lucretius, Commentary to Book II, vv. 606/10, where passages from Virgil, Ovid and Spenser are quoted; also Frazer as in note 1, p. 217. (13) Drawing at Chantilly; reproduced by Kristeller, *Mantegna*, 1901, p. 285. The motive occurs also elsewhere. (14) Reproduced in *The Burlington Magazine*, Vol. LXIX (1936), p. 134. (15) There is an impression in the Correr Library at Venice (Stampe, C 2). (16) See D'Arco, *op. cit.*, Nos. 68, 86, 89, 92. (17) Giannantonio Moschini, *Guida di Venezia*, 1815, II, p. 237 (cf. the next note). (18) Vasari, ed. Milanesi, III, p. 424.

1145 SAMSON AND DELILAH

Inscribed on the tree-trunk: FOEMINA / DIABOLO TRIBVS / ASSIBVS EST / MALA PEIOR.

Linen, in monochrome, $18\frac{1}{2} \times 14\frac{1}{2}$ (0·47 × 0·37). These measurements do not include a black band about $\frac{1}{2}$ in. wide all round, some parts of which have been trimmed.

Good condition on the whole, though rubbed in parts. There are many very small losses, some apparently under old retouches (which may be fairly numerous over parts of the picture).

Late work. The execution is occasionally ascribed to the studio,[1] but it seems unreasonable not to class it as by Mantegna himself.

Other Old Testament subjects in a similar technique and of approximately of the same size are *Judith* in Dublin;[2] *The Judgment of Solomon* in Paris;[3] and *The Sacrifice of Abraham* and *David and Goliath* at Vienna.[4] The quality of the execution varies considerably, but it is possible that they are from one series. There is some rather doubtful evidence that the two at Vienna at least come from the Ducal Collection at Mantua.[5]

The inscription is a proverb, which seems to have become current long ago.[6]

PROVENANCE: No. 1145 was sold in 1883 as belonging to the Collection known as the Sunderland drawings. Some or all of these drawings were bought before 1728 from Bartolomeo Buonfiglioli at Bologna by Procurator Zaccaria Sagredo of Venice;[7] they (?) belonged in 1761 to Consul Joseph Smith at Venice and are said to have been purchased in 1763 by Consul (John) Udny and imported into England. They thereafter formed part of the Duke of Marlborough's library at Blenheim.[8] No. 1145 was purchased at the Sunderland Sale, 15 June, 1883 (lot 82).

REPRODUCTION: *Illustrations, Italian Schools*, 1937, p. 214. *Plates, Earlier Italian Schools*, 1953, Vol. II, p. 265.

REFERENCES: (1) E.g. by Knapp, Klassiker der Kunst *Mantegna*, 1910, Plate 126. (2) E. Tietze-Conrat, *Mantegna*, 1955, Plate 123. 1956 Catalogue (No. 442); size, 0·46 × 0·36. (3) Tietze-Conrat, *op. cit.*, Plate 129. Seymour de Ricci's Catalogue, *Ecoles Etrangères, Italie et Espagne*, 1913, p. 89; size, 0·465 × 0·37. (4) Tietze-Conrat, *op. cit.*, Supplementary Figs. 29 and 30; 1938 Catalogue, Nos. 81A and 81B; sizes, 0·485 × 0·36/365. (5) A. Luzio, *La Galleria dei Gonzaga*, 1913. On p. 119, No. 381 of the 1627 Gonzaga Inventory, there is listed a small grisaille of David with the head of Goliath; on p. 124, No. 509 of the 1627 Inventory, four grisailles of Tobias, Esther, Abraham and Moses are listed. On p. 318 (1709 Inventory) four grisailles, size apparently 18 × 36 in. each, Judith and other subjects, are listed. (6) Tietze-Conrat, *op. cit.*, p. 184, gives a reference to the XIV

Century Adolphus, conveniently printed in *P. Leyseri Historia Poetarum et Poematum Medii Aevi*, 1741, p. 2028 and in T. Wright, *A Selection of Latin Stories*, 1842, p. 186. A nearer form of the proverb was current in English, the earliest reference known to the compiler being in T. T(wyne?), *The Schoolemaster*, 1583 (1576 edition not consulted), Book IV, Ch. 19; cf. also John Clarke, *Paroemiologia Anglo-Latina*, 1639, p. 118. (7) See the *Raccolta di Lettere*, Bottari's edition, II, 1757, p. 151 or Bottari-Ticozzi's edition, II, 1822, p. 186. Giuseppe Campori, *Raccolta di Cataloghi*, 1870, p. 616, gives the date of sale as 1727. The rest of the provenance for the Buonfiglioli Collection is from the 1883 sale catalogue, corrected by the statements in Joseph Smith's will (K. T. Parker, *Canaletto Drawings at Windsor Castle*, 1948, p. 60). There are further comments on the Buonfiglioli (Bonfiglioli) and Sagredo Collections in other volumes on the drawings at Windsor; see particularly *Venetian Drawings* (XVII–XVIII centuries) by A. F. Blunt and E. Croft-Murray, 1957, p. 24, list of pictures and drawings acquired in 1752 from Sagredo by Consul Smith. The compiler considers that the early provenance for No. 1145 is far from established. (8) The Earldom of Sunderland is one of the Duke of Marlborough's titles; but it is not recorded when the collection was acquired for Blenheim.

1417 THE AGONY IN THE GARDEN

Five *putti* appear to the kneeling Christ, bearing Instruments of the Passion (Column, Cross, Sponge and Spear). The three Apostles are asleep in the foreground; behind, Judas and a crowd of soldiers approach along the road from Jerusalem. Signed OPVS / ANDREAE / MANTEGNA.

Wood, painted surface, $24\frac{3}{4} \times 31\frac{1}{2}$ (0·63 × 0·80).

Excellent state; the chief damages are on Christ's dress. A few small *pentimenti*, e.g. on the sole of Christ's right foot.

The picture has been sometimes identified with a small work (undescribed), painted by Mantegna for Giacomo Antonio Marcello in 1459.[1] Critics who have rejected this suggestion as unproved have varied considerably in the dating, Tietze-Conrat giving *ca.* 1450,[2] Knapp after 1464;[3] nor is this variation surprising, since Mantegna's style was fairly stable and not many dated works are known. The case may be put as follows.

Towards 1470–5, it seems, Mantegna changed his signature to the form *Mantinia*;[4] which therefore suggests that No. 1417 is probably of earlier date. On the other hand Mantegna, although brilliantly precocious, seems not to have found his style quite so soon as has been supposed. Thus, the figures of SS. Peter, Paul and Christopher on the vaulting of the Eremitani Chapel are Mantegna's work of *ca.* 1449, but were not classed as his until the documentary proof was discovered;[5] even the polyptych of 1453/4 in the Brera conserves primitive traces; and some at least of the most mature and striking of the Eremitani frescoes are not earlier than 1454.[6]

A further argument against a very early date is found in Mantegna's *Agony in the Garden* at Tours, part of an altarpiece of 1457/9 from S. Zeno, Verona.[7] This picture and No. 1417 have a general similarity; but in No. 1417 the design appears clearer and the realism more ably carried through, which seems to indicate a later date. At Tours, an angel brings Christ a cup, according to tradition; in No. 1417, the *putti* with the Instruments of the Passion seem to be iconographically unusual,[8] and it may be thought that this is more likely to follow than to precede the normal rendering. There seems, therefore, some reason for putting No. 1417 between 1460 and 1470; and, as it is after all rather like the picture at Tours, preferably towards the beginning of that period.

The design is often said to be derived from a drawing by Jacopo Bellini, which Goloubew dates from the 1440's; it has at least a general similarity[9]. There is, indeed, in No. 1417 one other possibie, though very small, point of contact with Jacopo. The town of Jerusalem in No. 1417 contains many fanciful structures, among which is a column with reliefs in spiral (perhaps for Trajan's Column), surmounted by an equestrian statue that is probably a reminiscence of Donatello's Gattamelata;[10] a monument almost exactly similar (except that the reliefs are not in spiral) occurs in the background of one of Jacopo's drawings.[11] In this point Mantegna may have imitated Jacopo, or Jacopo Mantegna, or both may have followed some Squarcionesque invention, or the parallel may be a chance.

Another design, in which some details (such as the pose of the Christ) do seem directly connected, is Giovanni Bellini's No. 726 of this Gallery. As is stated in the entry for that, the little that is known of Bellini's origins makes it likely that he imitated Mantegna rather than *vice versa*.

Other compositions in a general way similar were produced by Crivelli;[12] by Ercole de' Roberti[13] (who in his turn was copied by Zaganelli);[14] and by Carpaccio.[15] It is uncertain if any of these are derived directly from any of the existing versions by Mantegna or the Bellini.

COPIES: The miniature No. 1417A below (reproduction in the *Illustrations, Italian Schools*, 1937, p. 177) is a copy with variations; there, an angel brings Christ a cup and the *putti*, increased in number and with a more complete set of the Instruments of the Passion, have been moved to the decorative border. An old drawing after Judas and his followers is in the British Museum.[16]

PROVENANCE: Clearly identifiable as an Aldobrandini picture, in the Collection by 1626, perhaps already by 1611.[17] In the Collection of Cardinal Fesch in France, then (from 1815) at Rome; 1841 Catalogue (No. 1372); Sale, 1845 (lot 687), bought by Artaria.[18] Owned by Farrer.[19] W. Coningham Collection, 1845/6;[20] Sales, London, 9 June, 1849 (lot 58), bought in, and 12 April, 1851 (lot 57), bought by Chaplin. In the Thomas Baring Collection by 1853;[21] exhibited at Manchester, 1857 (Provisional Catalogue, No. 290; Definitive Catalogue, No. 98), and at the R.A., 1870 (No. 58). Mr. Baring bequeathed his pictures to his nephew, Lord Northbrook; Catalogue, 1889 (No. 192); purchased from the Earl of Northbrook, 1894. Cleaned Pictures Exhibition at the National Gallery, 1947/8 (No. 25).

REPRODUCTION: *Illustrations, Italian Schools*, 1937, p. 212. *Plates, Earlier Italian Schools*, 1953, Vol. II, p. 266.

REFERENCES: (1) E.g. by Crowe and Cavalcaselle, *Painting in North Italy*, I, 1871, p. 382, or ed. Borenius, 1912, II, p. 85; texts concerning the Marcello picture are Docs. 6 and 7 of Kristeller's *Mantegna*, London, 1901, pp. 468/9 (German edition, Docs. 17, 18, 19). (2) E. Tietze-Conrat, *Mantegna*, 1955, p. 185; she suggests that the Marcello picture may be the *S. Sebastian* at Vienna.

(3) Knapp, Klassiker der Kunst *Mantegna*, 1910, Plate 100. G. Fiocco, *Mantegna*, 1937, p. 202, seems even to date it in the Roman period (1488/90). (4) *Mantegna* and *Mantinia* each appear in different spellings, *Mantinia* and its variants being the proper Latin form; they are two distinct groups. It need not be doubted that the statement in the text concerning the change of form is substantially true. One or two exceptions could be produced; but it remains very unlikely that a picture signed *Mantegna*, as No. 1417 is, would be later than *ca.* 1475. (5) Knapp, Klassiker der Kunst *Mantegna*, 1910, pp. 148/9, as Pizolo; the *Eternal*, the other figure on p. 148, really is by Pizolo. (6) See the note to Mantegna's biography above. (7) Knapp, Klassiker der Kunst *Mantegna*, 1910, Plate 86. (8) What might be a *putto* offers Instruments of the Passion in Altobello Meloni's *Agony in the Garden* in Cremona Cathedral; reproduced in *Proporzioni*, III, 1950, Plate CLXXI. An angel is associated with Instruments of the Passion in an *Agony* ascribed to the studio of Lazzaro Bastiani; Venice, Accademia, Catalogue (XIV and XV Centuries), 1955, No. 59, reproduced. An angel offers Instruments of the Passion in the Cup in Bergognone, No. 1077A and Niccolò di Liberatore, No. 1107 of the present catalogue. In a relief in Rodez Cathedral there are several angels, and one offers the Crown of Thorns and the Nails as well as the Cross (which by itself is not unusual); reproduced by Marguérite de Bévotte, *La Sculpture à la Fin de la Période Gothique dans la Région de Toulouse, d'Albi et de Rodez*, 1936, Plate XXVIII. More or less comparable examples in *The Agony in the Garden* may be found occasionally in later pictures too. Cf. further the note (for angels), col. 306, in the edition of Molanus' *De Historia SS. Imaginum*, in Vol. XXVII of Migne's *Theologiae Cursus Completus*, 1843. (Wingless) *putti* with the Instruments of the Passion are seen in Antonio Vivarini and Giovanni d'Alemagna's *Coronation of the Virgin* (reproduced by Van Marle, *Development of the Italian Schools of Painting*, Vol. XVII, Fig. 6); cf. also the figures framing a *Virgin and Child* ascribed to Mantegna at Berlin, No. 27 (winged), and Crivelli's *Virgin and Child* at Verona (wingless; reproduced by Crowe and Cavalcaselle, *Painting in North Italy*, ed. Borenius, 1912, I, p. 82). (9) In the London sketch-book; Goloubew, *Les Dessins de Jacopo Bellini*, 1908/12, I, Plate L. Goloubew (no doubt rightly) rejects the date of 1430 on the first page of this sketch-book; he may be correct in putting it at 1440/50, but *prima facie* it would not seem necessary to date it so early. Marcel Röthlisberger in *The Burlington Magazine*, 1956, p. 363, or in *Saggi e Memorie di Storia dell'Arte*, II, 1959, pp. 62/3, comments on novelties in the iconography of the drawing (town and approaching figures in the background). These do indeed seem to be foreign to the preceding Italian tradition for this subject; although Jacopo Bellini may not have been the first to introduce them (see the Giovanni di Paolo in the Vatican, reproduced by Van Marle, *Italian Schools*, Vol. IX, Fig. 274), it may be thought that there is for this reason a connection between Jacopo Bellini's drawing and No. 1417. (10) Donatello's Gattamelata was unveiled perhaps in 1453. (11) A *Crucifixion* in the sketch-book at Paris, which Goloubew dates rather after than before 1450; see his *Dessins de Jacopo Bellini*, 1908/12, II, Plate XXXVI. An equestrian statue on top of a column appears also in the *Triumph of Caesar*; a poor reproduction in Knapp, Klassiker der Kunst *Mantegna*, 1910, Plate 55. (12) Drey, *Carlo Crivelli*, 1927, Plate III. (13) Venturi, *Storia dell'Arte Italiana*, Vol. VII, Part III, Fig. 509. (14) Venturi, *Storia dell' Arte Italiana*, Vol. VII, Part III, Fig. 774. (15) Venturi, *Storia dell'Arte Italiana*, Vol. VII, Part IV, Fig. 459. (16) British Museum, *Italian Drawings, The Fourteenth and Fifteenth Centuries*, catalogue by A. E. Popham and Philip Pouncey, 1950, I, No. 167, and II, Plate CLV. (17) D.ssa Paola Della Pergola kindly gave a reference to an Aldobrandini inventory of 1611 (No. 18), but the identification of the picture is there doubtful. She also cited the inventory of Olimpia Aldobrandini, 1626 (No. 178): 'Un quadro con Christo orante nell'horto con cinque angeli che tengono li misterij della passione con tre discepoli et la turba di mano di Andrea mantegna del N° 339.' This seems clearly identical with No. 1417. See also the *Inventarium bonorum repertorum post obitum clar:mem: Pripīs D. Joīs Baptē Pamphilij Aldni*, Die 18 Nouembris, 1709 (Rome, Archivio di

Stato, not. Paolo Fazio, No. 2661): 'Vn quadro in tauola con Nr̄o Sigr̄e che ora nell'Orto con cinque Angeli, che tengono li misteri della Passione con li trè Apostoli, e la turba alto palmi trè di mano d'Andrea Mantenga con cornę dorata.' The pages of this inventory are not numbered; this entry occurs in a section dated 15 March, 1710. Aldobrandini property passed from Donna Olimpia Aldobrandini, Principessa di Rossano (died 1681) to her sons, the already mentioned Giovanni Battista Pamphilj and Cardinal Benedetto Pamphilj. The last direct heir of Donna Olimpia died in 1760, and in 1769 a lawsuit over the Aldobrandini inheritance between the Borghese and the Colonna was won by the Borghese. The arrangement arrived at was that the Aldobrandini fortune and title should be held by the second son of the head of the Borghese family. See further in the entries for Luini, No. 18, and Botticelli, No. 1034, note 24. (18) With identifying description. (19) *Report from the Select Committee on the National Gallery*, 1853, question 7026. (20) *Le Cabinet de l'Amateur*, Vol. IV, 1845/6, p. 142. (21) Reference as in note 19.

5641 THE HOLY FAMILY WITH S. JOHN

There are the remains of an inscription...DEI on the scroll held by S. John. For the treatment of the subject, see the commentary below.

Canvas, 28 × 20 (0·71 × 0·505).

This picture is seriously damaged, having suffered much from rubbing and flaking; considerably restored.[1]

The most prominent figure in the picture is the Infant Christ, Who stands holding a branch of olive and a globe; it has indeed been customary to entitle No. 5641 *Imperator Mundi*,[2] but there is no doubt, peculiar as the treatment is, that No. 5641 is a *Holy Family with S. John*. The Virgin appears to be within a stone parapet, on the edge of which Christ and S. John are standing.[3] It has been suggested that this construction is the mystic well (*fons signatus*) often associated with the Virgin;[4] but Mantegna might have thought twice about suspending the Virgin in a well. The picture is so much damaged that it is impossible to say what the Virgin is doing. In Canella's engraving and in Cavenaghi's reconstruction, she was holding a branch of olive in her right hand; there is no trace of this in what remains of Mantegna's paint. In Canella's engraving she held her right forearm in her left hand; in Cavenaghi's reconstruction she held a book; it seems to be rather a fold of her mantle, and has now been so reconstructed. The possibility that she was holding a needle in her right hand and was represented sewing cannot be excluded.[5]

In spite of its condition, there appears to be no doubt that No. 5641 is an original Mantegna.

VERSION : A variant ascribed to Mantegna, size 0·71 × 0·44, with S. Elizabeth (?) instead of S. Joseph, and other variations, was reproduced in an Anon. Sale, Hôtel Drouot, Paris, 23 November, 1927 (lot 30): ex-Couvreur and Dollfus Collections; now in the Petit Palais, Paris.[6]

ENGRAVING: Engraved by C.(?) Canella.[7]

PROVENANCE: Recorded in 1856 in the Collection at Verona of Cav. Andrea Monga (1794–1861).[8] Acquired from the Monga Collection in 1885 by J. P. Richter, and in his collection at Florence until 1891.[9] Purchased from him by Ludwig Mond; exhibited at the R.A., 1893 (No. 151). Mond Bequest, 1924; but with life-interests reserved for Lord and Lady Melchett. Exhibited at the R.A., 1930 (No. 241; Memorial Catalogue, No. 183). Entered the National Gallery in 1946.

REPRODUCTIONS: For the engraving of *ca.* 1830/40, see note 7. Reproductions of No. 5641 as restored by Cavenaghi are frequent, e.g. in the *Souvenir* of the Italian Exhibition at the R.A. 1930, p. 45. In its present state, in *Plates, Earlier Italian Schools,* 1953, Vol. II, p. 267.

REFERENCES: (1) The picture is recorded (rather roughly) in one state in an engraving by Canella (see the Section *Engraving*). Richter (letter of 9 January, 1931, in the Gallery archives) took it to Cavenaghi when he acquired it; Cavenaghi stripped it, and the picture has become known with Cavenaghi's re-constructions on it. The picture was cleaned again in 1946/8, and now differs in various respects from the previous reproductions of it. (2) See J. P. Richter, *The Mond Collection,* I, 1910, pp. 255 ff. (3) An arrangement not altogether dissimilar occurs in Lord Northampton's Bellini (Klassiker der Kunst *Bellini,* 1930, Plate 107), and in a Montagna at Vicenza (Venturi, *Storia dell'Arte Italiana,* Vol. VII, Part IV, Fig. 263). (4) Richter, *loc. cit.* (5) O. Kurz was kind enough to consider this problem. He inclined to think that the Virgin originally held in her right hand a plant somewhat in the shape of a Cross, and cited as probably similar a picture at Dresden (Klassiker der Kunst *Mantegna,* 1910, Plate 112). In a derivative (?) from No. 5641, mentioned under *Version* in text, the Virgin is re-presented sewing; Kurz admitted that this might indicate the original form in No. 5641, and cited another case in the *Madonna Cucitrice* by Giovanni Fran-cesco Caroto at Modena (R. Pallucchini, *I Dipinti della Galleria Estense,* 1945, Fig. 126; Venturi, *Storia dell'Arte Italiana,* Vol. VII, Part IV, Fig. 531). (6) Mündler (Diary, August, 1856) saw what may have been the same picture in the Palazzo Marescalchi at Bologna. (7) The engraving is reproduced by Richter, *The Mond Collection,* I, 1910, Plate L. P. Pouncey (letter of 8 October, 1948) dated it roughly 1830/40; it is presumably the same as an engraving of which Richter in a letter of 9 January, 1931, stated that he owned an impression, and which he dated *ca.* 1730. The initial of the engraver appears in Richter's repro-duction to be C.; he is possibly the painter Carlo Canella, born at Verona in 1800, whose existence is recorded by Roberto Bassi-Rathgeb, *Il Pittore Giuseppe Canella,* 1945, pp. 27/8. (8) Mündler's Diary, 1 November, 1856; see also 1/2 October, 1857, and Eastlake's note-book, 9 September, 1864. For Cav. Andrea Monga's dates, see Serafino Ricci in *Miscellanea di Storia Veneta,* Series II, Vol. III, 1895, pp. 10, 21. (9) J. P. Richter, *The Mond Collection,* Table of Contents to Vol. I, and letter of 9 January, 1931, in the Gallery archives.

After ANDREA MANTEGNA

1417A ILLUMINATED INITIAL D

Within it, the Agony in the Garden, derived from Mantegna No. 1417 above. On the letter itself are five winged *putti* with the Instruments of the Passion; on the left two with column and scourge, on the right three with spear, sponge, hammer and pincers.

Vellum, $7\frac{1}{2}$ (0·19) square.

Evidently cut from some choral book or other manuscript of the fifteenth or at latest, early sixteenth century. The composition is derived from Mantegna's picture, No. 1417 above, but the iconography is more normal. Here, as often, an angel appears before Christ with a cup, and Mantegna's *putti* with the Instruments of the Passion have been placed (with great differences) in the framing, which forms the letter itself.

PROVENANCE: In the collection of the Earl of Northbrook by 1889;[1] presented by him at the time the Mantegna was purchased from him, 1894.

REPRODUCTION: *Illustrations, Italian Schools*, 1937, p. 177. *Plates, Earlier Italian Schools*, 1953, Vol. II, 268.

REFERENCE: (1) Catalogue of the Northbrook Collection by J. P. Richter, 1889, p. 142.

Follower of ANDREA MANTEGNA

1125A THE VESTAL VIRGIN TUCCIA WITH SIEVE

Poplar,[1] painted surface, $28\frac{1}{2} \times 9$ (0·725 × 0·23); painted up to the edges all round, and probably cut a little at the sides and top.
Apparently well preserved.
For the commentary, etc., see under No. 1125B.

1125B SOPHONISBA DRINKING POISON(?)

Wood, painted surface, $28\frac{1}{2} \times 9$ (0·725 × 0·23). These measurements include an addition of $1\frac{1}{8}$ in. (3 cm.) on the right, and of $\frac{1}{2}$ in. (1 cm.) at the top; the paint continues up to all the original edges. The original size would clearly have been the same as that of No. 1125A.
Less well preserved than No. 1125A.

Tuccia was a Vestal Virgin accused of unchastity; to prove her innocence she carried a sieve full of water from the Tiber to the temple. Sophonisba was a Carthaginian; her second husband, Masinissa, to avoid handing her over as a captive to Scipio, sent her a bowl of poison. These identifications (of which the first seems certain, the second very probable) were made by Kristeller;[2] the pictures had before been called *Summer* and *Autumn*.

Morelli and Frizzoni[3] thought the two pictures were fakes. In a technical examination, nothing was found inconsistent with their being of Mantegna's time; and it seems undesirable to doubt it, even though stylistically some details might seem suggestive of a more recent date. The quality of the pictures seems clearly to be unworthy of Mantegna himself, so that one may think that they are the work of some competent follower or even studio assistant of Mantegna's later time. Many critics do not accept the execution as by Mantegna himself.[4]

PROVENANCE: On the backs, *Antonio Mantegna* with the numbers 109 and 110. In the Duke of Hamilton's Collection at Hamilton Palace; seen there by Waagen.[5] Purchased at the Hamilton Sale, 24 June, 1882 (lot 398).

REPRODUCTIONS: *Illustrations, Italian Schools*, 1937, p. 214. *Plates, Earlier Italian Schools*, 1953, Vol. II, p. 269.

REFERENCES: (1) Letter from B. J. Rendle, of the Forest Products Research Laboratory, in the Gallery archives. (2) P. Kristeller, *Andrea Mantegna*, 1901,

p. 372. (3) See Frizzoni, *Arte Italiana del Rinascimento*, 1891, p. 299. But Morelli himself, *The Galleries of Munich and Dresden*, tr. Ffoulkes, 1893, p. 175, says merely 'able imitator.' (4) E.g. Kristeller, *loc. cit.* (school); Knapp, Klassiker der Kunst *Mantegna*, 1910, Plate 125 (studio); Berenson, 1932 Lists, marked with a p. In the catalogue of *Paintings and Sculpture from the Kress Collection Acquired by the Samuel H. Kress Foundation 1945–1951*, Washington, 1951, p. 82, it is claimed that Nos. 1125A and B formed part of the same decoration as Mantegna, No. 902 above; the height does correspond, but without further evidence the association would appear very uncertain. (5) Waagen, *Treasures*, 1854, III, pp. 304/5.

Imitator of ANDREA MANTEGNA

639 "NOLI ME TANGERE" (PANEL FROM A SERIES)

Wood, painted surface, 16¾ × 12¼ (0·425 × 0·31).
Good condition.

Clearly from the same series as Nos. 1106 and 1381 below. At one time ascribed to Francesco Mantegna, a son of Andrea, of whom no authenticated works are known. They are generally held to be by a follower (pupil) of Mantegna,[1] but it seems possible that they are later imitations. There is a good deal of crackle, but the technique of the painting seems unlikely.

The style may be derived largely from Mantegna's upright engravings of *The Deposition* and *The Entombment*.[2] It is possible that the vine growing on a withered tree and the bee-hive are derived from Mantegna's *Agony in the Garden* at Tours, a panel once in San Zeno at Verona.[3]

PROVENANCE: Francis Duroveray Sale, London, 2 March, 1850 (lot 238), bought by Nieuwenhuys.[4] Purchased with the rest of the Edmond Beaucousin Collection, Paris, 1860.

REPRODUCTION: *Illustrations, Italian Schools*, 1937, p. 215. *Plates, Earlier Italian Schools*, 1953, Vol. II, p. 270.

REFERENCES: (1) G. Fiocco, *Mantegna*, 1937, pp. 207/8, seems to think that they are by Crivelli. (2) Knapp, Klassiker der Kunst *Mantegna*, 1910, Plates 143/4. (3) Knapp, *op. cit.*, Plate 86. (4) The provenance is indicated in the N.G. Report for 1860, and there is some confirmatory description in the sale catalogue.

1106 THE RESURRECTION (PANEL FROM A SERIES)

Wood, painted surface, 16¾ × 12¼ (0·425 × 0·31).
Good state, except that some of the faces are rubbed.
See the note to No. 639 above.

PROVENANCE: From the Capponi Palace, Florence.[1] Acquired with No. 1381 by the Rev. John Sanford in 1832;[2] Catalogue (for sale), 1838 (No. 21); not in Sanford Sale, 1839. W. Coningham Sale, 9 June, 1849 (lot 39), bought by Webb.[3] Perhaps G. H. Morland Sale, 9 May, 1863 (lot 117), bought by Herrman. Coll. His de la Salle, Paris; Sale, London, 27 November, 1880 (lot 93), bought by Danlos. Purchased from A. W. Thibaudeau, 1881.

REPRODUCTION: *Illustrations, Italian Schools*, 1937, p. 215. *Plates, Earlier Italian Schools*, 1953, Vol. II, p. 270.

REFERENCES: (1) Inscription on the back. (2) See *The Burlington Magazine*, 1955, p. 213, Nos. 26, 27; the exact date of acquisition can be deduced from a Sanford note-book belonging to the Barber Institute at Birmingham (references on pp. 13, 15, 16, 30). (3) With identifying description, as ex-Sanford.

1381   THE MARIES AT THE SEPULCHRE (PANEL FROM A SERIES)

Wood, painted surface, 16¾ × 12¼ (0·425 × 0·31).
Good condition.
The scene is according to Mark xvi, 1 sqq.
See the note to No. 639 above.

PROVENANCE: From the Capponi Palace, Florence.[1] Acquired with No. 1106 by the Rev. John Sanford in 1832;[2] Catalogue (for sale), 1838 (No. 22); not in Sanford Sale, 1839. W. Coningham Sale, 9 June, 1849 (lot 40), bought by Farrer.[3] Lent by Lord Taunton to the British Institution, 1860 (No. 40), and by Lady Taunton to the R.A., 1870 (No. 143). Bequeathed by Lady Taunton, 1892.

REPRODUCTION: *Illustrations, Italian Schools*, 1937, p. 216. *Plates, Earlier Italian Schools*, 1953, Vol. II, p. 271.

REFERENCES: (1) Inscribed on the back. (2) See note 2 to No. 1106 above. (3) With description; cf. No. 1106 above.

MARCO DEL BUONO
1402 (?)–1489 (?)

Florentine School. The date of birth and death are from Milanesi's Vasari, II, p. 682. Member of the Physicians' Guild at Florence, 1426. By 1446 he was a partner with Apollonio di Giovanni, almost entirely for the production of *cassoni*; his partner died in 1465. For the records of this activity, see Schubring, *Cassoni*, 1923, pp. 443 ff. (also Gualandi, *Memorie*, IV, 1843, p. 140).

See FLORENTINE SCHOOL, No. 4906

MARCO D'OGGIONO
apprenticed *ca.* 1490 (?), died after 1524

Milanese School. Supposed to be the *Marco* in Leonardo da Vinci's studio, 1490; in 1521, mentioned as well known. He was alive in 1524; perhaps as late as 1529 (Suida, *Bramante Pittore e il Bramantino*, 1953, p. 206). Lanzi says that he died in 1530, but cf. E. Motta in the *Archivio Storico Lombardo*, 1891, p. 259. For his activity at Savona in 1501/2, see

W. Suida in the *Raccolta Vinciana*, XV–XVI, 1935/9, pp. 127 ff. An altarpiece of *The Three Archangels* in the Brera, and an altarpiece formerly in the Crespi Collection are signed; an altarpiece at Besate (Abbiategrasso) is semi-documented and datable 1524. (The two last are reproduced by Frizzoni in *L'Arte*, 1905, pp. 416, 419.) Some frescoes in the Brera from Santa Maria della Pace, Milan, are also authenticated works (Vasari, Lomazzo, etc.). His style is strongly under the influence of Leonardo's, and is rather like 'Giampietrino's.'

1149 THE VIRGIN AND CHILD

Wood, painted surface, $26\frac{1}{4} \times 21$ (0·665 × 0·535); painted up to the edges all round.

Much damaged and repainted.

An example of the *Madonna of Humility*, the Virgin being seated on the ground.

The attribution appears to be generally accepted.[1]

DRAWING: A pricked drawing, apparently for the head of the Virgin here, is in the Victoria and Albert Museum.[2]

PROVENANCE: Manfrin Collection, Venice; presumably 1856 Catalogue (No. 214)[3] and 1872 Catalogue (No. 46);[4] purchased thence, 1883.

REPRODUCTION: *Illustrations, Italian Schools*, 1937, p. 217. *Plates, Earlier Italian Schools*, 1953, Vol. II, p. 271.

REFERENCES: (1) Accepted by Frizzoni, *Arte Italiana del Rinascimento*, 1891, pp. 348/9; Suida, *Leonardo und sein Kreis*, 1929, p. 294; Berenson, 1932 Lists. It may be due to Morelli (letter to Layard, 17 May, 1883; British Museum, Add. MS. 38964, Layard Papers, Vol. XXXIV). (2) See W. G. Constable in *Old Master Drawings*, September, 1927, pp. 20/1, Plate 25. (3) *Madonna con Bambino*, Cesare da Sesto, Tavola, 0·69 × 0·53. The Manfrin Collection was formed, at least in part, by Conte Girolamo Manfrin, who died in 1801 according to *Il Forestiere Istruito . . . della Città di Venezia*, 1822, p. 295. According to the catalogue of the A.M. Plattis Sale, Paris, 13/4 May, 1870, the collection was formed *ca.* 1748 (perhaps meaning from that date onwards) and in 1848 was divided between the Marquise Bortolina Plattis veuve du Baron Sardagna and the Marquis Antonio Maria Plattis. According to the Manfrin Sale catalogue of 1897 the collection was divided in 1849 between the Marchese Antonio Plattis and the Marchesa Bortolina Plattis nei Sardagna; her part or some of it remained in the Palazzo Manfrin until 1897. (4) As Cesare da Sesto.

MARGARITO OF AREZZO
active 1262 (?)

Called Margaritone by Vasari, who devotes a good deal of space to him as an early painter of his home town. There is uncertainty about his dates, although several signed pictures have survived. A documentary mention of 1262 apparently refers to him. His pictures are most probably of the second half of the thirteenth century; the evidence is insufficient for a more exact statement.

564 THE VIRGIN AND CHILD ENTHRONED, WITH SCENES OF THE NATIVITY AND THE LIVES OF THE SAINTS

A Retable or Altar Frontal. Centre, the Virgin and Child within a mandorla; in the corners, the four Evangelists represented by their symbols. Scenes on each side, from left to right and top to bottom: 1, The Nativity, with the Announcement to the Shepherds; inscribed, DE PARTV VIRGINIS MARIE & ADNVTIATIŌE PASTORVM. 2, S. John the Evangelist in a cauldron of boiling oil; he was put into one by Domitian outside the Latin Gate at Rome, and when it did him no harm, he was exiled to Patmos. Inscribed, HIC BEAT' JOĦES EV̄G. A FERVORE OLEI LIBERATVR. 3, S. John the Evangelist resuscitating Drusiana; inscribed, HI SC̄S JOĦES EV̄G SVSCITAT DELVSIANAM. 4, S. Benedict tempted in the Sacro Speco at Subiaco. The temptation was the thought of a beautiful woman he had seen at Rome; S. Benedict conquered it by rolling in the brambles outside his cave. Inscribed, HI .S̄. BN̄EDICT' PIECIT SE Ī SPINAS FVGIĒS DIABOLI T̄ETATIŌE. 5, The Decapitation of S. Catherine. After the torture of the wheel (which is her proper attribute), S. Catherine was beheaded and angels carried her body to the summit of Mount Sinai. Inscribed, HI SC̄A CATTARINA SVSCEPIT MA(R)TIRIV̄ & Ī MŌTE SINJ AB ĀGLIS Ē DLATA. 6, Miracle of S. Nicholas. The devil in disguise had given some pilgrims about to visit S. Nicholas a deadly oil, with the request that they would anoint the walls of his house with it. S. Nicholas appeared and warned them of the danger; they threw the oil into the sea, which burst into flame. Inscribed, HI SC̄S NICOLAVS PRECEPIT NAVTIS VT VAS COL/TVM A DIABVLO Ī MARI PICERĒT. 7, S. Nicholas by miracle saves three innocent men from decapitation. Inscribed, HI SC̄S NICOLAVS LIBERAT CŌDĒNATOS. 8, S. Margaret in prison is swallowed by a dragon, and escapes unhurt; the cross by means of which the miracle was performed is seen floating in the air, top left. Inscribed, HI SC̄A MARGARITA..........ORE ERVPTIS / VISCERIBVS........ The picture is signed, centre bottom, MARGARIT' DE ARITIO ME FECIT.

Wood, $30 \times 66\frac{1}{2}$ (0.76×1.69), excluding the framing and the top of the Virgin's mandorla which extends over part of the framing. Total size, $36\frac{1}{2} \times 72$ (0.925×1.83). The individual scenes are approximately within rectangles formed by painted lines, the inside measurements of which are $10\frac{1}{8} \times 9\frac{7}{8}$ (0.26×0.25), each.

The picture is obviously damaged, but is not badly preserved for a work of the time, except towards the right. The paint and gold on the framing are new.

No. 564 was probably rather a retable than an altar frontal.[1]

The picture, a signed specimen of a not altogether obscure painter, was included in the purchase of part of the Lombardi-Baldi Collection 'to show the barbarous state into which art had sunk even in Italy previously to its revival.'[2] Anatole France at greater length says much the same thing.[3]

PROVENANCE: Wrongly supposed to come from S. Margherita, Arezzo.[4] Acquired before 1845 in the neighbourhood of Arezzo by Lombardi and Baldi of Florence;[5] purchased with other pictures from their collection, 1857.[6]

REPRODUCTION: *Illustrations, Italian Schools*, 1937, p. 217. *Plates, Earlier Italian Schools*, 1953, Vol. II, pp. 272–274.

REFERENCES: (1) Giacomo de Nicola in *Vita d'Arte*, July, 1912, p. 3, protests against the view that such things formed altar frontals, which (at least later on) were very inferior works. (2) N.G. Report, 1858. Cf. also Appendix I. (3) Anatole France, *L'Ile des Pingouins*, Livre III, Ch. V. (4) Vasari, Le Monnier edition, I, 1846, p. 303, or ed. Milanesi, I, p. 360. Vasari's description of the S. Margherita picture does not fit. (5) For the provenance, see the N.G. Report, 1858. For the date, see the Lombardi-Baldi Catalogue (*Collection de Tableaux Anciens*, etc.), n.d., but the copy in the Uffizi Library is claimed to be of 1845, (No. 5); also the 1846 Vasari, as in previous note. (6) For the history of the Lombardi-Baldi Collection, see Appendix I.

MARCO MARZIALE
active 1493–1507

He described himself as a Venetian, and a pupil of Gentile Bellini. From January, 1493, he was working for the Venetian State at a modest wage, but he seems to have moved about 1500 from Venice to Cremona. There are several signed pictures.

Literature: B. Geiger in the Prussian *Jahrbuch*, 1912, pp. 1 ff. and 122 ff.

803 ALTARPIECE: THE CIRCUMCISION

The Infant Christ, the Virgin and the priest are in the centre; an old woman (Anna the prophetess?) and S. Joseph with two pigeons stand behind the Virgin. Of the other figures, the man in profile on the right is Tommaso Raimondi, and opposite him is his wife Doralice Cambiago, on whose garments the letter D is repeatedly embroidered; the kneeling boy is presumably their son, perhaps the Marco who died in 1568. The arches of the vaulting are inscribed with the verses from Luke ii, 29 sqq.: NVNC DIMITTIS SERVVM TVVM DOMINE SECVNDVM VERBVM TVVM / IN PACE QVIA VIDERVNT OCVLI MEI SALVTARE TVVM QVOD / PARASTI ANTE FATIEM OMNIVM POPVLORVM / LVMEN AD REVELATIONEM GE(nti)VM ET GLORIAM PLEBIS TVE ISRAEL (the variations of lettering are not here reproduced). Signed on a *cartellino*: MARCVS MARTIALIS VENE/TVS IVSSV M^{CI} EQVITIS / ET IVR̃CON. D. THOME / .R. OPVS HOC.P.AN. / M^O CCCCC^O, followed by a monogram consisting of an M with a horizontal bar through it and a form of cross above.

Canvas, $87\frac{1}{2} \times 59\frac{1}{2}$ (2·22 × 1·51).

In very good condition; remarkably so for a canvas picture of the date.

The Donor, Tommaso Raimondi, was a jurist and poet who died in 1510. The man with a book next to him has been supposed to be his brother Eliseo, in which case the woman behind S. Joseph would be Eliseo's wife, Lorenza degli Osi.[1]

VARIANT: The picture is partly repeated from a half-length composition of 1499 by Marziale, once in the Conservatorio delle Penitenti, Venice, and now in the Correr Museum.[2]

PROVENANCE: Described by Panni in 1762 as the high-altarpiece of S. Silvestro, Cremona, for which it was no doubt painted.[3] Apparently still there in 1794,[4] but (according to Sacchi) hidden during the Revolutionary period.[5] By ca. 1827 it had entered the collection of the Marchese Sommi-Picenardi, Torri de' Picenardi, near Cremona.[6] This collection passed by inheritance to the Marchese Araldi Erizzo, whose creditors sold this and other pictures to Baslini in 1869; purchased from Baslini, Milan, 1869.

REPRODUCTION: *Illustrations, Italian Schools*, 1937, p. 220. *Plates, Earlier Italian Schools*, 1953, Vol. II, p. 275.

REFERENCES: (1) Cf. Gussalli in the *Rassegna d'Arte*, 1912, pp. 181 f. (2) Correr Catalogue, 1957, pp. 110 f., with reproduction after cleaning. Also reproduced by Geiger in the Prussian *Jahrbuch*, 1912, p. 9; Geiger thinks that it is derived from a Gentile Bellini of this subject, which is recorded to have existed. (3) A. M. Panni, *Distinto Rapporto*, 1762, pp. 145/6; the church adjoined the Palazzo Raimondi. (4) Giuseppe Aglio, *Le Pitture e le Sculture della città di Cremona*, 1794, p. 92. (5) F. Sacchi, *Notizie Pittoriche Cremonesi*, 1872, p. 169. (6) Catalogue of ca. 1827, No. 71, referred to by Geiger, *loc. cit.*, p. 16. Most of the Picenardi pictures were collected by Conte Giovanni Battista Biffi of Cremona, a cousin of the Picenardi, who died in 1807. The Picenardi property was in 1816 made over to the grandsons of a sister, Gerolamo and Antonio Sommi-Picenardi. It was their father, Serafino Sommi (who died in 1857, aged 90), who from 1817 was building the Bibliopinacoteca at the Torri de' Picenardi, where the pictures were transferred ca. 1827. See Guido Sommi-Picenardi, *Le Torri de' Picenardi*, 1909, pp. 61/2, 71/2, 138/9, 141 and 147.

804 ALTARPIECE: THE VIRGIN AND CHILD WITH SAINTS

To the left S. Gall, with the Baptism of Christ and S. Paul on his crozier; and S. John the Baptist with a scroll inscribed, ECCE AGNVS DEI: to the right, SS. Bartholomew and James the Greater. On the vaulting of the apse behind: (Regi) NA.CELI.LET(a)RE.ALELVIA. O(?). Signed on a *cartellino*: MARCVS MARCI / ALIS VENETVS. P / .M.D. VII.

Wood, rounded top, painted surface, 87 × 56 (2·205 × 1·42); painted up to the edges except at the top.

Very good condition.

S. Gall is identified on account of the picture's provenance; the prominence accorded to S. Bartholomew may indicate the Donor's Christian name. S. James' hat is ornamented not only with the usual cockle shell, but also with a stamped design surmounted by a crown, a pair of crossed keys, and a black head of Christ over crossed keys on a white ground; these badges may have been common badges of pilgrims, though the head of Christ (perhaps from the *Vera Icon*, preserved at S.

Peter's) and the crossed keys suggest Rome rather than Compostella.[1] The sentence on the vaulting is an Easter antiphon in the Roman Catholic church.[2]

The style of No. 804 is predominantly Venetian, and the angel is reminiscent of one in Bellini's S. Giobbe altarpiece;[3] but there seem also to be traces of Perugino's influence.[4]

PROVENANCE: Described by Panni in 1762 as the high-altarpiece of S. Gallo (also called the SS. Trinità) at Cremona, for which it was doubtless painted.[5] Bought from the church by Conte Giovanni Battista Biffi in 1791.[6] He was a cousin of the Picenardi, and died in 1807. No. 804 is mentioned in 1818 in the collection of the Marchese Sommi-Picenardi at Cremona;[7] ca. 1827 transferred to the Torri de' Picenardi. The collection passed by inheritance to the Marchese Araldi Erizzo, whose creditors sold this and other pictures to Baslini of Milan in 1869;[8] purchased from Baslini, 1869.

REPRODUCTION: *Illustrations, Italian Schools*, 1937, p. 219. *Plates, Earlier Italian Schools*, 1953, Vol. II, p. 276.

REFERENCES: (1) A badge with crossed keys appears also on S. Roch's pilgrim's hat in Morando, No. 735, and in other Italian pictures of pilgrims. Badges of the black face of Christ and (separately) the crossed keys are on a S. Roch by Francesco Morone at Venice (photograph Alinari, No. 32299). (2) J. J. M. Timmers, *Symboliek en Iconographie der Christelijke Kunst*, 1947, p. 459. (3) Klassiker der Kunst *Bellini*, 1930, Plate 85. (4) There is an altarpiece by Perugino in S. Agostino, Cremona; Klassiker der Kunst *Perugino*, 1914, Plate 36. (5) A. M. Panni, *Distinto Rapporto*, 1762, p. 124. (6) See Geiger in the Prussian *Jahrbuch*, 1912, p. 123. Giuseppe Aglio, *Le Pitture e le Sculture della città di Cremona*, 1794, p. 141, confirms that it had been removed from the church at the time he wrote. (7) Grasselli, *Guida . . . di Cremona*, 1818, p. 191. (8) See Guido Sommi-Picenardi, *Le Torri de' Picenardi*, 1909, pp. 71, 138/9, 141 and 153 (No. 143); see also the entry for No. 803 above, for a summary of the Biffi, Sommi and Picenardi relationships.

MASACCIO
1401–1427/9

Tommaso di Giovanni, called from early times Masaccio; Vasari says that the nickname was given him because of his carelessness in practical affairs. Born at San Giovanni Valdarno, some 30 miles from Florence. Living in Florence by 1422. Pisa, 1426. Died at Rome; of the three possible years, 1428 is more likely than 1427 or 1429. His teacher is unknown; possibly it was Mariotto di Cristofano, a painter of his home town; probably it was not Masolino, as various post-Vasarian writers have claimed.

The only work documented as by Masaccio is a polyptych painted for the Carmine at Pisa. It can hardly be doubted that several fragments of this picture survive, No. 3046 being the central part; but since there is not in the strictest sense proof of identity, a better basis for the study of Masaccio is provided by some frescoes in the Brancacci Chapel in the Carmine at Florence. These are recorded already by 'Manetti' as being partly by Masaccio (see Vasari, *Vita di Filippo Brunelleschi*, ed. Carl Frey, 1887, pp. 205/6). Not all the frescoes painted in this chapel have survived. Concerning those that have, and excluding a part painted later by Filippino Lippi, two views are held. According to some critics, everything is by Masaccio, but at different dates; according to others, only the more forceful and original frescoes are by Masaccio, and the rest is claimed to be by Masolino, who, according to Albertini's *Memoriale* of 1510 and Vasari, did paint frescoes in this chapel.

Masaccio, and Giotto a century earlier, are the two founders of Italian Renaissance painting.

There was active at Florence, and elsewhere in the fifteenth century, a sculptor called Masaccio (Maso di Bartolommeo).

3046   THE VIRGIN AND CHILD (CENTRAL PART OF AN ALTARPIECE)

Wood, painted surface, $53\frac{1}{4} \times 28\frac{3}{4}$ (1·355 × 0·73); painted up to the edges all round. These measurements exclude additions to the panel of $\frac{5}{8}$ in. all round. The picture itself has a pointed top; the two spandrels with gold patterning above the arch are in essentials old. The bottom is at present covered with new, plain paint, and the panel has certainly been cut here; marks on the back of the panel, which suggest that originally there were two horizontal battens, imply in that case that the cut at the bottom may be of about 8 in. or more. It is further likely that the panel has been cut at the top and sides, but the field of this picture, the central part of an altarpiece, is probably not greatly reduced at the top and sides.

This is obviously a damaged picture, but there are considerable remains of the original work. Of the flesh parts, the Virgin's face is almost entirely free from repaint, although rubbed; the Child's head is in similar condition, but a little less good. The Virgin's hands and the Child's feet are much damaged. The condition of the other flesh parts is between these two extremes. There are considerable remains of the original draperies, and of the gold, especially at the top.

In the church of the Carmine at Pisa,[1] Giuliano di Colino degli Scarsi da S. Giusto had a chapel constructed by Pippo di Giovanni di Gante of Pisa; it was begun in 1425, and seems to have been dedicated to S. Julian. The carpentry of the altarpiece for the chapel was carried out by Antonio di Biagio of Siena. The painting of the altarpiece was by Mazo di Giovanni of Florence, pop. S. Michele Visdomini, i.e. Masaccio.[2] The *paliotto* of the altar was painted with a figure of S. Julian and decorative work by Cola d'Antonio of Florence; the *cortina* was painted by Mariano di Piero della Valenzana of Pisa.

Masaccio's work of painting the altarpiece was begun on 19 February, 1426, and he received his first payment on the following day. His final payment was on 26 December, 1426, before the delivery of the altarpiece was made.[3] Andrea di Giusto is recorded to have been a garzone of Masaccio's at the time. His painter brother Giovanni (real name Vittorio, apparently) seems also to have been in Pisa in that year.

Masaccio's picture is recorded *in situ* by Vasari, in general terms in the edition of 1550, and with a detailed description in the edition of 1568;[4] it is to be deduced that between 1550 and 1568 Vasari had carefully examined the picture, or that a correspondent had carefully examined it for Vasari.[5] The picture is described in 1568 as a polyptych. The central part represented the Virgin and Child, '& a' piedi sono alcuni Angioletti, che suonano, uno de' quali sonando un liuto, porge con attenzione l'orecchio all'armonia di quel suono.' At the sides were SS. Peter, John the Baptist, Julian and Nicholas. In the predella, stories of these four saints, and in the centre the Adoration of the Kings with followers and their horses. Above, many saints, and a Crucifixion in the centre. So far Vasari; according to the documents concerning the chapel, the combined height of the altar and the altarpiece was about $8\frac{2}{3}$ braccia (roughly 15 ft.).[6]

Vasari's appears to be the only book that certifies the presence of the altarpiece in the chapel (of S. Julian) at the Carmine, Pisa.[7] It is true that both Borghini and Baldinucci mention this altarpiece;[8] but there seems nothing to prove that they did more than rearrange Vasari's words, and Tronci, describing the Carmine at Pisa towards the year 1635, says nothing at all about Masaccio's picture.[9] The Church was largely reconstructed in the later sixteenth century,[10] and it is probable that Masaccio's polyptych was removed from its place at some time during this period. There are said to be grounds for believing that it, or parts of it, remained in the monastery buildings.[11]

The identification of an altarpiece removed to an unknown place at so early a date, maybe in the sixteenth century, is difficult to prove; but a very high probability can be claimed for panels that on the one hand accord with Vasari's description, and on the other can on stylistic grounds be ascribed to Masaccio or his studio. It should be remarked, apropos of the second condition, that Masaccio died when still very young, and it is not possible that he painted very many altarpieces.

No. 3046 is on stylistic grounds acceptable as a Masaccio, and it accords pretty well with Vasari's description of the central part of the Pisan altarpiece.[12] The predella is reasonably identified with pictures at Berlin representing the *Adoration of the Kings* and stories of SS. Peter, John the Baptist, Julian and Nicholas.[13] A *Crucifixion* at Naples is reasonably thought to be from the upper tier.[14] Four saints at Berlin are held to be from the pilasters; two of the saints are Carmelites, and the identification is not unreasonable.[15] Two larger saints, obviously pendants, have been identified as from the upper tier; this is very possible, and it is indeed likely that the two pictures do come from Pisa.[16] Finally, No. 3627 of the present catalogue (Florentine School) has been supposed to be from the frame of the Pisan polyptych; unlike the fragments listed hitherto, this seems to have no claim to belong.

There exists in the Museo Gregoriano in the Vatican a bronze figure (Etruscan, probably 2nd century B.C.), in many ways so similar to the Child in No. 3046 that it seems likely that Masaccio saw some version of it.[17]

A relief of Donatello's, of which varying versions have survived, has been said to be influenced in its arrangement by the angels of No. 3046.[18]

PROVENANCE: For the history of the altarpiece of which No. 3046 is reasonably supposed to have been the central part, see above; that altarpiece is recorded in the Carmine at Pisa by Vasari (1550 and 1568), and is not recorded by Tronci *ca.* 1635. No. 3046 belonged to Miss Woodburn in 1855;[19] Samuel Woodburn Sale, 9 June, 1860 (lot 21), bought by Clarke.[20] Stated to have belonged to the Rev. F. H. Sutton by 1864.[21] In the collection of the Rev. A. F. Sutton, Brant Broughton, 1907.[22] Exhibited at the Grafton Galleries, 1911 (No. 7). Purchased, Temple-West Fund, from Canon Sutton, with the aid of a contribution from the N.A.C.F., 1916. Exhibited at the National Gallery, N.A.C.F. Exhibition, 1945/6 (No. 28).

REPRODUCTION: *Illustrations, Italian Schools*, 1937, Frontispiece. *Plates, Earlier Italian Schools*, 1953, Vol. II, p. 277 (after removal of a band marking the arch).

REFERENCES: (1) See both L. Tanfani Centofanti, *Notizie di Artisti tratte dai Documenti Pisani*, 1897, pp. 176/81, and E. Somaré, *Masaccio*, 1924, pp. 162/3. (2) There is no other record that Masaccio lived in the district of S. Michele Visdomini at Florence; but it would appear unnecessary to labour the point that the Mazo here referred to is identical with Masaccio. Cf. the evidence of Masaccio's work at Pisa, referred to in notes 4 and 7. (3) The document of 26 December, 1426, seems to demand delivery of the completed picture on that day. (4) Vasari's two texts are conveniently printed side by side by E. Somaré, *Masaccio*, 1924, pp. 172/3. (5) Vasari did visit Pisa during the period in question. (6) Document printed by Tanfani Centofanti, *op. cit.*, p. 180. (7) That Masaccio worked in Pisa is already recorded by 'Manetti'; cf. Somaré, *op. cit.*, p. 167. (8) Raffaello Borghini, *Il Riposo*, 1584, p. 314. Filippo Baldinucci, *Notizie dei Professori del Disegno*, I, 1845, p. 475 (the first edition of this part of Baldinucci's work was published in 1728). (9) Information kindly supplied by Prof. G. Isnardi, letter of 21 January, 1948, in the Gallery archives, from the copy of Tronci's MS. in the Soprintendenza ai Monumenti at Pisa. Can. Paolo Tronci was born in 1585 and died in 1648. In the part of his MS., *Il Duomo di Pisa*, published by Pèleo Bacci, 1922, p. viii, the editor says that Tronci finished his MS. soon after 1635. It may be added that Mario Salmi, *Masaccio* (*ca.* 1933, p. 111; 1948, pp. 177/8), is somewhat confused about what since Tronci's time has been said about Masaccio's altarpiece at Pisa. Alessandro da Morrona, *Pisa Illustrata* (1st edition, III, 1793, pp. 290/1; 2nd edition, III, 1912, pp. 278/9), mentions in the sacristy of the Carmine at Pisa an altarpiece without attribution, which is clearly identical with one recorded by Pandolfo Titi, *Guida per il Passeggiere . . . di Pisa*, 1751, pp. 229/30, as by Antonio Sogliani. Morrona also mentions, separately, that Borghini and Baldinucci wrote of a Masaccio altarpiece in the Carmine, of which Morrona could find no trace at the time he wrote. Giovanni Poggi in *Miscellanea d'Arte*, 1903, p. 183, gives a correct account of this, and says that the Sogliani picture is now in the church of the Carmine at Pisa. (10) Prof. Isnardi's letter, referred to in the previous note, gives the date of reconstruction as between 1560 and 1590. A. da Morrona, *Pisa Illustrata*, III, 1812, pp. 273/4, says the construction was well forward in 1568, and finished except for the façade in 1574, and that the church was consecrated in 1612. (11) Langton Douglas and G. de Nicola, edition of Crowe and Cavalcaselle, *History of Painting in Italy*, IV. 1911, p. 61. U. Procacci, *Tutta la Pittura di Masaccio*, 1951, p. 26, says that the altarpiece 'andò smembrata e dispersa' in the XVIII Century. (12) The picture was published, as being by Masaccio and the central part of the Pisan altarpiece, by Berenson in the *Rassegna d'Arte*, 1907, p. 139, and 1908, pp. 81 ff. Both these claims have sometimes been doubted, e.g. somewhat by Langton Douglas and G. de Nicola, *op. cit.*, in the previous note, IV, 1911, pp. 60/1; but doubt appears unreasonable. (13) Berlin, 1931 Catalogue,

Nos. 58 A, B, E. Nos. 58 A and B were acquired from the Palazzo Capponi at Florence in 1880. No. 58 E was acquired in 1908 on the Florentine market (cf. Douglas and de Nicola, *op. cit.* in note 11, IV., 1911, p. 60); the execution is inferior and is ascribed to Andrea di Giusto. For reproductions of these and other fragments about to be mentioned, see for instance Mario Salmi, *Masaccio*, *ca.* 1933. (14) Naples, Catalogo by Aldo de Rinaldis, 1928, No. 36; acquired in 1901 from L. de Simone, Naples. (15) Berlin, 1931 Catalogue, No. 58 D; first recorded in the New Gallery Exhibition, London, 1893/4 (No. 27), as Masaccio, lent by Charles Butler. (16) One, *S. Paul*, is at Pisa, Museo Civico, 1906 Catalogue, pp. 158/9, No. 27; from the Zucchetti Collection at Pisa, 1796. For a fragmentary inscription on the back, stated to be of the late seventeenth century, see A. Schmarsow, *Masaccio-Studien*, II, 1896, p. 78, and the catalogue of the *Quattro Maestri* Exhibition at Florence, 1954 (No. 3). The other, apparently *S. Andrew*, is in the Lanckoronski Collection. A *S. Paul*, formerly in the A. Bayersdorfer Collection, is said by Fabriczy in the *Gazette des Beaux-Arts*, 1892, II, p. 329, to be perhaps from the Pisan altarpiece; this picture appears to be identical with the Lanckoronski *S. Andrew*, which was given to Prince Lanckoronski by Bayersdorfer (information kindly supplied by J. Wilde). A sketch reconstruction of the altarpiece is given by Mario Salmi, *Masaccio*, 1948, Plate 35. (17) See R. Offner, supplementary note (on loose page) to his contribution to *Studies in the History of Art dedicated to William E. Suida*, 1959. (18) These reliefs are the subject of comment by W. L. Hildburgh in *The Art Bulletin*, March, 1948, pp. 11 ff.; H. W. Janson, *ib.*, June, 1948, pp. 143 ff.; and W. L. Hildburgh, *ib.*, September, 1948, pp. 244 ff. The connection with No. 3046 is not close. (19) On the back is a label with MISS WOODBURN / MARCH 13, 1855, and the number 70 added. (20) A cutting from the sale catalogue is on the back, which makes the identification certain; the picture was then ascribed to Gentile da Fabriano. (21) This is stated in the catalogue of the Grafton Galleries Exhibition, 1911. (22) *Rassegna d'Arte*, 1907, p. 139. The Rev. A. F. Sutton succeeded his uncle, the Rev. F. H. Sutton, as Rector of Brant Broughton in 1889 (information from Burke's *Peerage*).

Follower of MASACCIO

3648   THE NATIVITY (PREDELLA PANEL FROM AN ALTARPIECE)

The Virgin and Child, S. Joseph, the ox, the ass and one midwife; in the background, the Announcement to the Shepherds.

Wood, painted surface, $8\frac{1}{2} \times 25\frac{7}{8}$ (0·215 × 0·655). This includes about $\frac{1}{2}$ in. of plain gold at each end; the corners of the picture itself are slightly cut, to form an octagon. A black line runs round the whole picture, at the edges of the panel top and bottom, but inside the gold at the ends.

Condition good in general.

This picture appears to be by a rather remote follower of Masaccio, showing some influence of Fra Filippo Lippi.[1] It was ascribed by Langton Douglas and G. de Nicola to Andrea di Giusto.[2] W. Stechow[3] calls it workshop of Masaccio, and does not exclude the possibility that it was the central panel (which was a *Nativity*) of the predella of an altarpiece once in S. Maria Maggiore at Florence.[4] A. Schmarsow[5] rejects this, claiming that No. 3648 was never the middle of a predella, and that workshop of Masaccio is too precise a relation; he sees in it Umbrian influence, and suggests early Boccati. Berenson in his 1932 Lists dubiously suggests the Master of the Castello Nativity,[6] which seems more reasonable. Parronchi inclines to consider favourably an attribution to Uccello.[7]

PROVENANCE: Lent by Sir Henry Howorth to the Burlington Fine Arts Club, 1907 (No. 2),[8] and 1920 (No. 8).[9] Presented by Sir Henry Howorth through the N.A.C.F., in memory of Lady Howorth, 1922. Exhibited at the National Gallery, N.A.C.F. Exhibition, 1945/6 (No. 30).

REPRODUCTION: *Illustrations, Italian Schools*, 1937, p. 221. *Plates, Earlier Italian Schools*, 1953, Vol. II, p. 278.

REFERENCES: (1) This was the opinion of Mario Salmi, *Masaccio, ca.* 1933, pp. 82 and 130/1. In the edition of 1948, p. 165, Salmi calls it Master of the Castello Nativity; cf. note 6. (2) In their edition of Crowe and Cavalcaselle, *History of Painting in Italy*, IV, 1911, p. 64. (3) W. Stechow in *Kunstchronik* (supplement to the *Zeitschrift für Bildende Kunst*), February, 1930, p. 127. (4) For the different things Vasari in 1550 and 1568 says about this altarpiece, which he calls Masaccio, see E. Somaré, *Masaccio*, 1924, p. 171, col. 1, and p. 172, col. 2. For what are thought to be some of its principal parts, see Mario Salmi, *Masaccio, ca.* 1933, pp. 128/9; Salmi accepts these fragments as being by Masolino. (5) A. Schmarsow in *Kunstchronik*, April, 1930, pp. 2/3. (6) This name was given for a grouping of several pictures by Berenson in the J. G. Johnson Catalogue, I, 1913, pp. 17 ff. Among more recent articles on him, see especially Berenson in *Dedalo*, 1932, pp. 831 ff., and two articles by U. Procacci and M. Salmi in the *Rivista d'Arte*, 1935, pp. 405/21; also M. Salmi, *Masaccio*, 1948, p. 165, as noted in note 1, for the attribution of No. 3648. (7) Parronchi in *Paragone*, No. 89, 1957, p. 27. (8) As Florentine, ascribed to Fra Filippo Lippi or Pesellino. (9) As Florentine *ca.* 1450, close to Pesellino.

See also Ascribed to MASOLINO, No. 5962

MASOLINO
ca. 1383–after 1432 (?)

Florentine School, though born at or connected with Panicale (in the Valdelsa?). Perhaps an assistant of Ghiberti's, 1403/7. 1423, Physicians' Guild at Florence. 1425/7, Hungary. Documented works at Castiglione d'Olona, Empoli (1424) and Todi (1432, apparently). A picture at Bremen, not signed, is dated 1423. There does not seem to be any clear evidence concerning how long he lived (see Procacci in the *Rivista d'Arte*, 1953, pp. 42/3, on former claims that he died in 1440 or 1447).

The question of Masolino's relation to Masaccio has at different times received different answers, and is too complicated for discussion here.

Ascribed to MASOLINO

5962   SS. JOHN THE BAPTIST AND JEROME (PART OF AN ALTARPIECE)

S. John's scroll is inscribed ECCE....VS.DEI. S. Jerome's book is marked with various letters, and with the inscription INPRIN-

CIPIO.C/REAVIT.DEVM / CELVM.ETTERRA' / TERRA. AVTEM / EIAT.INNANIS / ET VACVA.ET / SPIRITVS. DOM/MINI . FEREBA / TVR . SVPER / AQVAS . ECETE / RA (derived from the first two verses of Genesis i).

Poplar,[1] pointed top, painted surface, $45 \times 21\frac{1}{2}$ ($1 \cdot 14 \times 0 \cdot 55$).

The arch has been cut about 3 cm. at the top; at the time of acquisition the spandrels were made up with new gold. Perhaps trimmed slightly at the sides and bottom.

The figures are in very good condition, and most of the original gold background is preserved. There appear to be changes in the outlines of S. John the Baptist's foot, which the compiler cannot interpret precisely.

For the commentary, etc., see under No. 5963.

5963 A POPE AND S. MATTHIAS (PART OF AN ALTAR-PIECE)

The Pope holds a book; he is perhaps S. Liberius (see below). S. Matthias holds a book and an axe stained with blood.

Poplar,[2] (now transferred to hardboard), pointed top, painted surface, $45\frac{1}{4} \times 21\frac{1}{2}$ ($1 \cdot 145 \times 0 \cdot 55$).

The arch has been cut about 3 cm. at the top; at the time of acquisition the spandrels were made up with new gold. Perhaps trimmed slightly at the bottom, but an incised line $1\frac{1}{2}$ cm. up seems to mark the intended edge of the picture; the paint, however, continues below it, and the measurements given above are to the edge of the paint. Perhaps slightly trimmed at the sides.

Less well preserved than No. 5962, but the heads are in good condition.

Nos. 5962 and 5963[3] once formed a single panel painted on both sides. The conservation of the pictures has necessitated some recent modifications to the backs, but at the time of acquisition various knots in the wood corresponded precisely;[4] it is, therefore, certain that the two pictures have been at some time sawn apart.[5]

Nos. 5962 and 5963 are to be associated with *The Miracle of the Snow* and *The Assumption* at Naples;[6] these two pictures also have been sawn apart, since there also various knots in the wood correspond precisely. Early association may reasonably be deduced from seventeenth-century Farnese inventory stamps on the backs of all four pictures (preserved separately for Nos. 5962/3 since the recent treatment).[7] Proof of a still earlier association follows from a detail in the panels themselves. The two pictures at Naples have at the backs both on the left and on the right the marks of a tie, certainly from before the time when the panels were sawn apart. Each mark is a hollow roughly square, with the marks of nails extending horizontally further in;[8] the sawing apart of the panels was done very exactly in the centre, and the marks are close reflections of each other. These Naples pictures are taller than Nos. 5962/3, where, at the time of acquisition, the corresponding tie-marks were at the extreme tops of the panels; these marks, the significance of which is quite clear when taken in conjunction with the marks at Naples, were to the right for No. 5962, to the left for No. 5963, seen in each case from the side of the painted surface.[9]

These four pictures were clearly the central part (Naples) and one wing (National Gallery) of a triptych painted on both faces. A triptych, not a polyptych; since the tie-marks of Nos. 5962/3 were in one corner only, in each case.

The other wing of this double-faced triptych is clearly the *SS. John Evangelist* (apparently) *and Martin*, and the *SS. Peter and Paul* (size, $1·073 \times 0·525$, each) in the J. G. Johnson Collection at Philadelphia.[10] There the backs have been cradled, so the association cannot be proved from the panels themselves. It is useful to record that the two Johnson pictures and Nos. 5962/3 were all together in the Cardinal Fesch Sale of 1845;[11] it is more important, and also certain, that the two Johnson pictures, just like Nos. 5962/3 and the two at Naples, were in the Farnese Collection at Rome in the seventeenth century.[12]

On one face of this triptych were No. 5962 and *SS. John the Evangelist* (?) *and Martin*; both these pictures show one saint turning slightly backwards and one in three-quarter profile. No. 5963 and *SS. Peter and Paul* were on the other face; both show one saint almost frontal and one in pure profile. The two pictures mentioned first are painted in strong relief, the other two more softly; it is therefore probable that the central picture for the first two was *The Miracle of the Snow*, which has much more depth than *The Assumption*.

This triptych was originally associated with the Roman family of the Colonna. S. Martin at Philadelphia has the Colonna arms on the orphrey of his cope;[13] it is even probable that this bishop symbolizes Pope Martin V (d. 1431), who was a Colonna. In No. 5962 S. John the Baptist holds, not the usual cross, but a cross supported on a column, which seems clearly to allude to the Colonna arms.[14] The references to the Colonna on these two side pictures, and not on the other two, may suggest that these pictures were at the front rather than the back of the altarpiece.

There are strong iconographical arguments that this triptych comes from S. Maria Maggiore at Rome. The subject of *The Miracle of the Snow* (at Naples) is the foundation of S. Maria Maggiore itself;[15] such a subject (in a central position) could have been represented in any picture in that church, or else in some church, oratory or chapel dedicated to the Virgin of the Snow. The subject as represented at Naples includes Christ and the Virgin in a circular glory, and this is a strong argument for the first alternative; for this form is followed in a mosaic on the façade of S. Maria Maggiore, earlier than the picture,[16] and in Mino's later relief for the ciborium,[17] but (so far as the compiler knows) it was not customary to follow this form in representations of the subject elsewhere.[18]

Another strong argument for the provenance from S. Maria Maggiore is the presence of S. Matthias, a saint rather rarely represented, in No. 5963; the body of S. Matthias is one of the principal relics in S. Maria Maggiore.[19] Further, the Assumption of the Virgin (represented at Naples), admittedly a great feast throughout the Church, is particularly associated with S. Maria Maggiore,[20] and was also represented on Mino's already mentioned ciborium;[21] S. Jerome (in No. 5962), admittedly one of the most frequently represented of saints, is also particularly associated with that church.[22] If S. Liberius, the founder of the church, is the Pope shown in No. 5963, this, too, would be an argument for the provenance; his identity has, indeed, been proposed because of the provenance, but the argument is not reduced merely to a vicious circle, since it can be said that the features of the Pope in No. 5963 accord pretty well with those of S. Liberius in *The Miracle of the Snow* at Naples, and that there is thus some support for the identification. So far as the compiler is aware, the connection of the other saints shown in the pictures with S. Maria Maggiore is not sufficiently precise to be worth mentioning.

These arguments for a provenance from S. Maria Maggiore fit in with a record by Vasari, who was clearly describing one side of the triptych under discussion. His text is as follows:[23] 'Una nella chiesa di Santa Maria Maggiore, in una cappelletta vicina alla sagrestia; nella quale sono quattro Santi tanto ben condotti, che paiono di rilievo; e nel mezzo Santa Maria della Neve; ed il ritratto di papa Martino di naturale, il quale con una zappa disegna i fondamenti di quella chiesa; ed appresso a lui è Sigismondo II imperatore. . . .'

In Vasari's time, the sacristy was approximately on the site of the present Cappella Paolina,[24] and from the archives of S. Maria Maggiore, Dr. Ugo Procacci has been able to identify the *cappelletta* as one near this and near the East end of the church, described as between columns and situated between the choir and the North aisle. The picture of *The Miracle of the Snow* could be expected to be on the side facing the altar, and that this was the arrangement receives confirmation from the picture itself; the choir was six steps higher than the aisle, and the design of *The Miracle of the Snow* does suggest that the spectator should be placed higher with regard to it than for *The Assumption*, which would have faced the aisle. The *cappelletta* was dedicated to S. John the Baptist, which (according to the reconstruction already proposed) accords with the position of that saint on No. 5962. It was a chapel of the Colonna family.[25]

It is possible that this triptych included some further, minor parts, although the compiler knows of no evidence that that was so. A predella panel in the Vatican, representing *The Death of the Virgin*, has by some critics been associated;[26] so has another predella panel, representing *The Marriage of the Virgin*, which was destroyed during the last war.[27] *Christ Crucified with the Virgin and S. John* in the Vatican has been proposed for a position above the main panels.[28] Two pictures at Washington representing *The Annunciation* have also been associated;[29] but there was clearly no room for them on this altarpiece.

With regard to the attribution, Vasari considered *The Miracle of the*

Snow, and presumably No. 5962 and the *SS. John the Evangelist* (?) *and Martin*, to be by Masaccio. Some modern critics have followed Vasari in their attribution of the altarpiece; but most prefer an attribution to Masolino, except for No. 5962. No. 5962 has been ascribed by several writers to Masaccio, but the compiler inclines to think it impossible that they are right.[30] The considerable difference of style between Nos. 5962 and 5963 is perhaps in part explained by their being from different faces of an altarpiece; but this seems hardly to suffice and, if Masaccio is not involved, it seems probable that the painting of the altarpiece was shared by Masolino and assistants, or was in part by some different painter.[31] S. John the Baptist is the most Masaccesque figure of the four at the National Gallery; this figure may be imitated from the lost S. John the Baptist on Masaccio's polyptych at Pisa, which occupied the same position on the altarpiece.[32]

There is no definite evidence for the date.[33]

PROVENANCE: The reasons have been given above for believing that No. 5962 was the front, and No. 5963 the back of the left wing of a double-faced triptych, which was associated with the Colonna family and was in S. Maria Maggiore at Rome. It is beyond reasonable doubt identical with a triptych mentioned in the church by Vasari (text of 1568; not in the edition of 1550). It is not known when the triptych left the church, nor how it passed into the Farnese Collection;[34] but it certainly was in Palazzo Farnese at Rome, with the three panels sawn apart to form six pictures, in 1653 and 1697.[35] The two central pictures were sent from the Farnese Palace to Naples in 1760;[36] it is not known what happened to the four side pictures.[37] It may, nevertheless, be presumed that they remained together, since all four were in the collection of Cardinal Fesch in Paris, then (from 1815) in Rome. Nos. 5962 and 5963 are Nos. 1315 and 1340 of the Fesch Catalogue, 1841;[38] Fesch Sale, Rome, 1845 (lots 864 and 865),[39] bought (with the two other side pictures, now at Philadelphia) by Baseggio. They were in the Adair Collection at Flixton Hall, being acquired probably by Sir R. Shafto Adair, 1st Bart., who was buying pictures *ca.* 1850.[40] Purchased, Colnaghi Fund, with a contribution from the National Art-Collections Fund, from Major-General Sir Allan Adair, through Messrs. Christie, Manson and Woods, 1950.

REPRODUCTIONS: *Plates, Earlier Italian Schools*, 1953, Vol. II, pp. 279–280.

REFERENCES: (1) As is about to be explained, the wood of No. 5962 is the same as that for No. 5963, for which see the next note. (2) The Forest Products Research Laboratory kindly examined specimens of wood from No. 5963. (3) The compiler has discussed the pictures with Johannes Wilde, who made several valuable suggestions. (4) Photographs of the untouched backs have been taken at the Gallery. (5) It might be suggested that the panel was sawn in two before the pictures were painted; but this is rendered unlikely by the thinness of the resulting panels, and seems to be excluded altogether by what is said in the next paragraph concerning the backs of the two pictures at Naples. (6) Reproduced by Salmi, *Masaccio*, 1948, Plates 175/6. Sizes, 1·44 × 0·76 and 1·42 × 0·76, according to the Naples Catalogue by Aldo de Rinaldis, 1928. They once had pointed tops, and have probably been cut about 2–3 cm. at the tops. The compiler is much indebted to Dott. Bruno Molajoli, who granted him special facilities for studying these pictures. (7) For comment on these Farnese stamps, see note 12. (8) On the left side (seen from the front) of *The Miracle of the Snow*, the lower edge of the tiemark is 1·12 m. from the bottom of the picture, the upper edge 1·165 m. In *The Assumption* the corresponding mark is 4 cm. lower, that picture having been cut at the bottom by that amount more than *The Miracle of the Snow.* (**9**) These tie-marks show on the photographs of the backs of Nos. 5962/3 taken before treatment; there is also a detail photograph of the mark for No. 5963. For No. 5963, the lower edge of the tie-mark was 1·11 m. from the bottom of the panel; its height, which clearly had been reduced when the top of the panel was cut, was *ca.* 3 cm. No trace of nails was visible. Measurements for the mark of No. 5962 were not taken, but it is seen from the photograph to correspond. The amount of wood cut away from the tops of the panels in these corners cannot be stated; it is uncertain whether the tie-mark was originally open at the top as well as on one side (as was the case when the pictures were acquired), or whether it was like the tie-marks at Naples (but with very much less of the panel above it). John Pope-Hennessy in *The Burlington Magazine,* January 1952, p. 31, claimed that the two pictures at Naples are from an upper storey of the altarpiece; the compiler cannot accept this. (**10**) Published by L. Venturi in *L'Arte*, 1930, pp. 165 ff. (also in his *Pitture Italiane in America*, 1931, Plate CLVII); Salmi, *op. cit.*, Plates 177/8; Johnson Collection, *Reproductions,* 1953, Plates 22/3. Acquired from Kleinberger in 1916; previously in the Earl of Northesk Sale, Sotheby's, 30 June, 1915 (lot 111), as Tuscan School. Mr. Henri Marceau (letter of 16 November, 1950, in the Gallery archives) kindly gave a number of facts concerning the pictures, including the unfortunate news that the backs have been cradled. (**11**) All as Gentile da Fabriano, with identical measurements given, all bought by Baseggio. No. 5962 was No. 864–1315 of the Fesch Sale, No. 5963 was No. 865–1340; the Fesch labels were still on the backs when the pictures were acquired by the National Gallery. The two Philadelphia pictures are identifiable from the descriptions as No. 866–1339 (*SS. Peter and Paul*), and No. 867–1317 (*SS. John the Evangelist*(?) *and Martin*). (**12**) The statement that all six pictures were in the Farnese Collection is certainly correct, but needs some explanation. In an inventory of Palazzo Farnese at Rome, of goods received into the charge of Innocenzo Sacchi, 31 December, 1653 (Parma, Archivio di Stato, Miscellanea Storica—Raccolta di Manoscritti—No. 86, in the volume dealing with the furnishings), the six pictures are thus described. P. 309: ' Un quadro bislongo cō ū Pontefice cō la Zappa in mano che da principio alla Chiesa di S. Maria Mag͞re in tauola cornice di noce.' ' Un'altro dell'istessa grandezza, è cornice simile cō la madonna in mezzo circondata da cherubini.' (Two consecutive entries, for the pictures at Naples). P. 333: ' Un quadro in tauola cornice di noce fondo dorato con S. Pietro, è S. Pauolo in piedi mano di Pierino del Vago' (Johnson). P. 334: ' Un quadro, cornice di noce fondo dorato con ū Papa in piedi, et ū religioso con un accetta in mano pure in piedi' (No. 5963). P. 337: ' Un quadro in tauola fondo dorato, cornice di noce cō S. Giro- lamo, è S. Gio: Batt͞a in piedi' (No. 5962). P. 339: ' Un quadro fondo dorato con Papa con ū pieuale mitria è pastorale, et ū altro Santo in piedi con un libro alla sinistra cornice di noce' (Johnson; these four pictures all in the same room). From these descriptions alone, the student might be prepared to accept the identifications, in spite of the attribution of one of the Johnson pictures to Pierino del Vaga, and of the claim that the S. Martin on the other Johnson picture is a Pope. The proof depends on an inventory of Farnese property, still at Rome, of 1697, which with some variations repeats the descriptions of 1653. For the 1697 inventory includes numbers; a Farnese stamp (with a lily, as reproduced in *Le Gallerie Nazionali Italiane*, Vol. V, 1902, p. 209) also includes numbers; this stamp has been preserved on the backs of the two Naples pictures, and for Nos. 5962/3; and in all four cases the numbers correspond. *The Miracle of the Snow* at Naples is No. 479, ' Un quadro bislungo con un Pontefice con la zappa in mano che dà un prencipio alla Chiesa di S. Maria Maggiore in tavola, con fondo dorato cornice di noce.' *The Assumption* is No. 453, ' Un quadro bislongo fondo dorato con la Madonna in mezzo circondata da cherubini in tavola cornice di noce.' One Johnson picture was No. 290 (no record of this number on the back), ' Un quadro in tavola cornice di noce fondo dorato con S. Pietro e S. Paolo.' N.G. 5963 is No. 282, ' Un quadro cornice di fondo dorato con un Papa in piedi.' N.G. 5962 is No. 296, ' Un quadro in tavola fondo dorato cornice di noce con S. Girolamo e S. Gio Batta in piedi.' The second Johnson picture was No. 277 (no record of this number on the back), 'Un quadro fondo dorato con un Papa, Piviale, mitria e Pastorale con un altro Santo in piedi con un libro alla sinistra cornice di noce.' (The four wings all in one room.) The manuscript of the 1697 inventory, which was in the Archivio di Stato at Naples, was destroyed during the last war; the above texts are from a copy kindly pointed out by Prof. de Franciscis; a less complete transcription was printed in *Le Gallerie Nazionali Italiane*, Vol. V, 1902, pp. 271 ff. It should be added that the 1653 inventory was the subject of an article by Pierre Bourdon and Robert Laurent-Vibert in the *Mélanges d'Archéologie et d'Histoire*, Ecole Française de Rome, Vol. XXIX, 1909, pp. 145 ff. (13) Mr. Henri Marceau (letter of 16 November, 1950) gave the information that this part of the picture is a bit rubbed, but that the colours appear to be correct (white column on a red ground). (14) It may be mentioned that the Easter candelabrum in S. Maria Maggiore at Rome, which is stated to have been the gift of a Colonna, has the form of a column; cf. Pasquale Adinolfi, *Roma nell'Età di Mezzo*, II, 1881, p. 181. It should on the other hand be noted that something similar to the cross and column in No. 5962 may be seen in the left hand section of No. 569 of the National Gallery, Style of Orcagna. (15) For the story, see the Naples Catalogue by Aldo de Rinaldis, 1928, p. 189. (16) By Filippo Rusuti or assistants; reproduced by Emilio Lavagnino and Vittorio Moschini, *Santa Maria Maggiore*, *ca.* 1923, Fig. 9; the connection was pointed out by R. Longhi in *Critica d'Arte*, 1940, p. 168. (17) Reproduced in *L'Arte*, 1890, p. 94. (18) As examples, it may be noted that Christ and the Virgin in a circular glory are absent from the story of the Foundation of S. Maria Maggiore as represented in the predella of Stefano di Giovanni's Chiusdino altarpiece (so far as the condition allows one to judge; reproduced by Enzo Carli, *Sassetta e il Maestro dell'Osservanza*, 1957, Plates 20–26); and from the predella of Matteo di Giovanni's altarpiece in S. Maria delle Nevi at Siena (reproduced in *La Diana*, 1934, p. 170). The form is not followed in the predella of *The Annunciation* at Brescia, assigned to Jacopo Bellini (Berenson, 1957 Lists, Plate 64), nor in a window in Orsanmichele, Florence (see Werner Cohn in the *Mitteilungen des Kunsthistorischen Institutes in Florenz*, 1959, pp. 8/9). Christ and the Virgin do appear fairly closely imitated in an engraving in Heinrich Reitzmann, *Hystoria de festo nivis gloriosissime dei genetricis et virginis Marie in ea forma qua Roma in Basilica ejusdem ad Mariam majorem nuncupata, ubi mirabile sumpsit exordium, observatur*, 1515; reproduced by H. A. Schmid, *Die Gemälde und Zeichnungen von Matthias Grünewald*, Textband, 1911, p. 210. It may be added apropos of the picture at Naples that Valentino Leonardi, *La Tavola della Madonna della Neve nel Museo Nazionale di Napoli*, 1906, claims that the background corresponds with a view to be seen from S. Maria Maggiore itself. (19) Cf. Paulus de Angelis, *Basilicae S. Mariae Maioris de Urbe . . . Descriptio et Delineatio*, 1621, p. 110. The compiler will not labour the point that the relic was already there at the time of Masolino's pictures; cf. for instance Adinolfi, *op. cit.*, p. 176. In some reference books, it is claimed that sometimes S. Matthew is represented with the same emblem (an axe); but the compiler doubts if the axe was an accepted emblem for S. Matthew. Cf. for instance S. Matthew and S. Matthias side by side, names inscribed, in an altarpiece by Pietro di Miniato at Prato; reproduced by Van Marle, *Development of the Italian Schools of Painting*, Vol. III, Fig. 311. Cf. also B. van Orley's S. Matthias, reproduced by Friedländer, *Die Altniederländische Malerei*, Vol. VIII, Plate LXVI. If in spite of this it were claimed that the saint on No. 5963 could possibly be S. Matthew, this argument for the provenance from S. Maria Maggiore would not stand; although in point of fact there is in that church a relic of S. Matthew as well as the body of S. Matthias (Angelis, *loc. cit.*). (20) The three great feasts of the year at S. Maria Maggiore are Christmas, the Miracle of the Snow and the Assumption; cf. for instance Lavagnino and Moschini, *op. cit.*, p. 102. (21) Reproduced in *L'Arte*, 1890, p. 100. Although the iconography does not correspond, the general effect is not dissimilar. It is possible that the relief is imitated from the picture at Naples; but the picture includes the nine angelic orders, and corresponds rather with the mosaic in the apse at S. Maria

Maggiore, where it seems that the nine angelic orders are present at the Coronation of the Virgin. (22) Cf. for instance Adinolfi, *op. cit.*, pp. 188 ff. (23) Vasari, ed. Milanesi, II, pp. 293/4 (text of 1568); not in Vasari, 1550. (24) See the notes by Onofrio Panvinio (1530–1568), published by G. Biasiotti, in the *Mélanges d'Archéologie et d'Histoire*, École Française de Rome, Vol. XXXV, 1915, on p. 35; it is remarked that these notes are probably from before 1566. (25) The compiler is greatly indebted for this information to Dr. Ugo Procacci, who hopes to publish it himself with more detail. In the first edition of this catalogue, the compiler discussed at some length several Colonna chapels in the church, without satisfying himself that any could be identified with the one referred to by Vasari. The various records used by the compiler are most confusing and, while it may well be that some of the references do apply to what is clearly the right chapel, it seemed undesirable to reprint them in the present edition. In *Paragone*, January 1952, p. 12, Longhi suggested that originally the pictures formed the high-altarpiece of the church. Changes of arrangement in S. Maria Maggiore were indeed frequent, and the compiler knows of no proof that the original location of the pictures had not already been abandoned by the time of Vasari. The Colonna connections of the pictures could be thought to refer to Pope Martin V (d. 1431). Yet, pending some confirmatory record, Longhi's proposal seems unlikely; the triptych would seem small to be the high-altarpiece of that church, and the details concerning the *cappelletta*, given in the text above, would seem to suit the pictures curiously well if that had not been their original location. (26) Reproduced by Van Marle, *Development of the Italian Schools of Painting*, Vol IX, Fig. 173; Salmi, *op. cit.*, p. 222, rejects the association. The compiler is indebted to Dr. Redig de Campos for the information that there is no Farnese stamp on the back, and that nothing is known of its early provenance. (27) Published by John Pope-Hennessy in *The Burlington Magazine*, Vol. LXXXII (1943), pp. 30/1; from the Artaud de Montor Collection, and later in the Fuller Russell Sale, 18 April, 1885 (lot 104). (28) Salmi, *op. cit.*, Plate 211; he discusses it on p. 222, and rejects the association. As with the other picture in the Vatican (information from Dr. Redig de Campos), no Farnese stamp on the back, and nothing known of its early provenance. (29) Salmi, *op. cit.*, Plates 180/1; discussion on pp. 209/10. John Walker (letter of 20 December, 1950, in the Gallery archives) kindly gave the information that there are no traces of Farnese stamps on the backs. (30) The comment now printed in the text has been modified in some degree from the first edition of the catalogue; Nos. 5962/3 were unpublished at that time, and the compiler could only (privately) suppose that claims of Masaccio's authorship would be printed, since No. 5962 is in some ways (but only in some) strongly suggestive of Masaccio. Note 46 of the first edition read: 'The problem of Masaccio and Masolino seems likely to go on receiving contradictory solutions from the critics, unless new and important documentary evidence is discovered. In spite of the uncertainty of the subject, the compiler feels strongly that no part of the S. Maria Maggiore triptych could be accepted as by Masaccio, without transferring at the same time to Masaccio various other works now usually assigned to Masolino. From these works, the developed style of Masaccio is absent; if proof of Masaccio's authorship were produced, they would be early works.' The compiler inclines now to think an early dating excluded. This is not only on account of the historical considerations so far published by Procacci (in the *Rivista d'Arte*, 1953, pp. 3 ff.), but also for stylistic reasons; he cannot at present conceive a stylistic development for Masaccio from No. 5962 to the picture in the Uffizi, No. 3046, etc. Here is a selection of what has been written recently about this S. Maria Maggiore altarpiece. Sir Kenneth Clark in *The Burlington Magazine*, November 1951, pp. 339 ff., gives consideration to the difficulties of the problem; he claims that Masaccio received the commission in 1425/6, completed No. 5962, began *SS. John the Evangelist and Martin* and perhaps *The Miracle of the Snow*, then left Rome, and that the other side of the altarpiece is by Masolino *ca.* 1428 or soon after. The claims with regard to Masaccio seem to the compiler incredible on stylistic grounds, if it is agreed that No. 3046 is part of Masaccio's Pisan altarpiece of 1426; for the claim that Masaccio visited Rome in 1425, see Procacci's strong denial in the *Rivista d'Arte*, 1953, pp. 40 ff. Longhi in *Paragone*, January 1952, pp. 8 ff., says that No. 5962 (and only this part) is by Masaccio; he and Masolino received the commission together early in 1425, and No. 5963 is Masolino's work of that year. The altarpiece, left unfinished, was taken up again by Masolino and an assistant in 1428/31. Salmi in *Commentari*, 1952, pp. 14 ff., says that the commission was given in 1428 to Masolino and Masaccio together, and that No. 5962 is by Masaccio. Millard Meiss in *The Art News*, April 1952, pp. 24 ff., says that No. 5962 (and only this part) is by Masaccio, the date being 1422/3; he comments on certain weaknesses of realization. Procacci, in the 2nd edition of his *Tutta la Pittura di Masaccio*, 1952, pp. 36/7, says that the triptych is very unlikely to be earlier than 1425 and conjectures that in 1428 Masolino and Masaccio began it together. He proposes that Masaccio laid in the arrangement of the figures and the faces in No. 5962, and that he completed some details such as S. John the Baptist's foot; then he died, and Masolino weakened this picture in completing it. Cesare Brandi in *Studi in Onore di Matteo Marangoni*, 1957, pp. 169/70, while stressing how curious the relation between Masolino and Masaccio seems to have been, associates No. 5962 with Masaccio; but he thinks that the flowers there are uncharacteristic of him, and suggests that the picture was begun by Masaccio and finished after his death by someone else. F. Hartt in *The Art Bulletin*, 1959, p. 163, says that No. 5962 is an early work by Masaccio. If the conditions of life at Rome exclude work in S. Maria Maggiore at this time, Hartt suggests three alternative ways by which the date could still stand: that the work was carried out in the Lateran in 1423 and later moved to S. Maria Maggiore; or that it was ordered from Rome in 1423, but executed in Florence and sent to Rome later; or that it was ordered from Rome in 1423 but suspended, Masaccio later bringing No. 5962 to Rome but dying before he could undertake the rest (which is by Masolino). These suggestions do not seem exactly to fit the claims of anarchy at Rome made by Procacci in the *Rivista d'Arte*, 1953, esp. pp. 47 f., 51 ff.; Procacci clearly thinks that a Roman commission of any kind in 1423 is most unlikely. Hartt seems to favour his second alternative, but his arguments in support do not convince, and this explanation would not accord very well with the view (which indeed does seem likely) that *The Miracle of the Snow* at Naples is imitated from a mosaic at S. Maria Maggiore. In 1960 the compiler was so fortunate as to have conversations on the subject with Dr. Ugo Procacci and with Dr. Ulrich Middeldorf. Procacci maintained his view that a date before 1424 is extremely unlikely, although he cannot actually disprove it (provided that the picture is assumed to have been then painted *at Florence*); if not so early, the pictures are demonstrably not from before 1428. He can prove that, in the Spring of 1428, Masolino travelled to Rome; Masaccio followed some months later, and died probably within a few weeks of his arrival. Procacci considers that what one sees of No. 5962 cannot be Masaccio's work of 1428, which indeed seems most clear. He would still be ready to admit that Masaccio began to lay in No. 5962, but the paint one sees would be by someone else, execution by whom would noticeably have weakened Masaccio's conception. This view might indeed be thought to correspond with the character of No. 5962; but then X-radiographs should perhaps look more Masaccesque than does the picture by normal light, and the compiler has been unable to satisfy himself that they do. Procacci now thinks that some work by a painter distinct from Masaccio and from Masolino should be postulated. Dr. Middeldorf said that he thinks that No. 5962 probably dates from *ca.* 1435; he sees in it certain characteristics of Fra Angelico's style at that time, while finding S. John's leg and the flowers suggestive of Domenico Veneziano. The compiler does not see a markedly close connection with the latter, but does think that in some respects No. 5962 is close to Fra Angelico's *Deposition* from S. Trinita; execution of any part by Fra Angelico, nevertheless, seems most difficult to conceive. (31) Procacci, as has been recorded in the previous note, thinks that some painter distinct from Masaccio and from Masolino is involved. (32) This can be deduced from Vasari's description of the Pisan altarpiece (ed.

Milanesi, II, p. 292); and from the arrangement of the predella at Berlin, reasonably held to be the predella of the Pisan altarpiece (see reproductions in Salmi, *op. cit.*, Plates 32, 35). One may further wonder if there is not in this figure some reflection of Donatello. It should be added that the church held by S. Jerome may reasonably be thought suggestive of Masaccio, as Millard Meiss stressed to the compiler; the preceding comments apply for the Masaccesque quality only of the S. John. (33) Since dating and attribution are in this case inseparable, some records of ideas for the date have already been given in note 30. The compiler wishes to add that, if a break in the execution is postulated, execution of the parts by Masolino at different dates would seem to him worthy of consideration. (34) The compiler has not come across a record of a Farnese chapel in S. Maria Maggiore. Many of the Farnese pictures in the Palace at Rome came from the collection of Fulvio Orsini (d. 1600), but this triptych is not traceable in the inventory published by P. de Nolhac in the *Gazette des Beaux-Arts*, 1884, I, pp. 427 ff. It was recorded in note 31 of the first edition that a Colonna chapel in S. Maria Maggiore that has sometimes been identified as the right one belonged in 1610 to Giulia, wife of Marzio Duca di Zagarolo. Her grandson Pompeo (d. 1661) was the last of this Colonna branch, and on his death his possessions passed to a cousin Stefano, Duca di Bassanello, whose father's first wife had been Isabella, natural daughter of Ranuccio Farnese. She had died in 1645. (See Litta, *Famiglie Celebri d'Italia*, Colonna, Tav. VI and X.) It seems improbable that the pictures passed via this Colonna-Farnese connection; there are some further connections between the families, which seem even more unpromising. (35) See note 12. (36) Naples Catalogue, 1928, p. 192. (37) Not in Sale, Lugt 1630. (38) As period of Fra Angelico. (39) As Gentile da Fabriano. Labels with the Fesch numbers of 1841 and 1845 from the backs of Nos. 5962/3 are preserved. No. 5962 also had in pigment on the wood ' N? 759 . d . C.,' No. 5963 'N? 754 . d . C.' These are probably Fesch marks (earlier than the labels of 1841); Foppa, No. 729 of the present catalogue, which is a Fesch picture, has fairly similar on the back ' N? 758 d(u?)) Cat.' The numbers do not correspond with those of the Fesch inventory of 1839 (Rome, Archivio di Stato, Archivio dei Notari Capitolini, Ufficio 11, Not. Augusto Appollonj). The reference in the Fesch catalogue of 1845 to a rumour of four pendants by Fra Angelico in a church at Perugia is clearly a confusion with the Fra Angelico still at Perugia (Klassiker der Kunst *Fra Angelico*, 1924, Plates 81 sqq.). (40) Information from Major-General Sir Allan Adair. There had been a fire in 1846, and pictures were being purchased for Flixton at the Blayds Sale, 1849, etc.; see the catalogue of the Adair Sale, 8 December, 1950.

MASTER OF THE BAMBINO VISPO
active early fifteenth century

'The Master of the Lively Child,' a name invented by Sirèn in *L'Arte*, 1904, pp. 349 ff. It is applied to a number of works, in some of which the Infant Jesus is in a twisted attitude; they are somewhat related to Lorenzo Monaco in style, and are even more markedly in the 'International Gothic' current. Attempts to attach to this group the names of various Tuscan artists are rejected by Berenson in *Dedalo*, 1932, pp. 177 ff.

It is supposed that the Master of the Bambino Vispo had an early period at Valencia in Spain; see G. Pudelko in *Art in America*, 1938, pp. 47 ff., and R. Longhi in *Critica d'Arte*, Nos. XXV/VI, 1940, pp. 183/5. Longhi ascribes to the Master of the Bambino Vispo some of the works ascribed by C. R. Post (*History of Spanish Painting*, see especially

Vol. VII, Part II, pp. 790 ff.; Vol. VIII, Part II, pp. 647 ff.; Vol. IX, Part II, pp. 765 ff.) to 'The Gil Master.' One of the items ascribed to the 'Gil Master' by C. R. Post (albeit with some reserves) is the 'Spanish' primitive, No. 4190 of the National Gallery (Catalogue of the German School, 1959, as Tyrolese).

Among the works ascribed to the Master of the Bambino Vispo, a *Last Judgment* at Munich (1938 Catalogue in English, No. 10201) is dated by Pudelko 1415. Various fragments, including two wings, once at Bonn (on loan from Berlin), and at Stockholm, are supposed to be parts of an altarpiece ordered for the Cathedral of Florence in 1422.

The grouping called the Master of the Bambino Vispo has undergone a considerable extension recently; there is disagreement whether certain items belong or not.

Ascribed to the MASTER OF THE BAMBINO VISPO

3926   THE BEHEADING OF A FEMALE SAINT (PREDELLA PANEL FROM AN ALTARPIECE?)

Wood, original painted surface, $16 \times 24\frac{3}{4}$ (0·405 × 0·63); painted up to the edges all round, but it is new paint along the edges.

Good condition; Cleaned in 1961. Largish damages in the gold.

Several female saints were decapitated; there does not appear to be any clue to indicate which one is represented here.[1]

No. 3926 was ascribed by Richter[2] and Van Marle[3] to Giovanni del Ponte, which is not satisfactory, although not very far out. It was ascribed to the Master of the Bambino Vispo by Berenson.[4]

A *Death of the Virgin* at Chicago, also ascribed by Berenson to the Master of the Bambino Vispo, corresponds in size and halo patterns with No. 3926.[5] The two pictures are possibly parts of one predella, the Chicago picture being obviously a centre piece.

PROVENANCE: By 1838, in the collection of Conte Guido di Bisenzo, Rome.[6] The Bisenzo Collection was bought *en bloc* in 1847 by Lord Ward[7] (created Earl of Dudley in 1860). Apparently mentioned in his collection by Waagen.[8] Exhibited at the R.A., 1871 (No. 322).[9] Dudley Sale, 25 June, 1892 (lot 68),[10] bought by Richter for Ludwig Mond. Exhibited at the R.A., 1893 (No. 148).[11] Mond Bequest, 1924.[12]

REPRODUCTION: *Illustrations, Italian Schools*, 1937, p. 137. *Plates, Earlier Italian Schools*, 1953, Vol. II, p. 281.

REFERENCES: (1) In a rather similar *Martyrdom of S. Catherine* at Berlin (1931 Catalogue, No. 1063, ascribed to Niccolò di Pietro Gerini), angels in the background carry the saint's body to the summit of Mount Sinai, which identifies the subject there beyond any doubt. It may be thought that two damages in the gold background of No. 3926, on each side of the mountain, might be spaces where angels were, and that the top of the picture including the body of S. Catherine may have been cut away. This is possible, but cannot be proved. (2) J. P. Richter, *The Mond Collection*, 1910, ii. pp. 395 ff. (3) Van Marle, *Development of the Italian Schools of Painting*, Vol. IX, p. 72, as *The Decapitation of S. Elizabeth* (wrong). (4) Berenson in the J. G. Johnson Catalogue, I, 1913, p. 10, and in his Lists, 1932. This attribution is accepted by Pudelko in *Art in America*, 1938, p. 57, and by Longhi in *Critica d'Arte*, Nos. XXV/VI, 1940, pp. 183/5. (5) Chicago, Ryerson Bequest, Typescript *ca.* 1926, pp. 13 ff., No. 2052. The attribution is accepted by Pudelko, *loc. cit.*, p. 54, who apparently considers it earlier than No. 3926, and by Longhi, *loc. cit.* First recorded in the D. P. Sellar Sale, Paris, 6 June, 1889 (lot 18). Reproduced in the catalogue of the Jean Dollfus Sale, Paris, 1 April, 1912 (lot 51), and by Pudelko, *loc. cit.*, Fig. 4. Size, $16\frac{3}{8} \times 25\frac{7}{8}$. (6) Engraved in *L'Ape Italiana delle Belle Arti*, IV, 1838, Plate XXXIV (pp. 57/9, article by G. Melchiorri). (7) *Kunst-Blatt*, 1847, p. 152. (8) Waagen, *Treasures*, II, 1854, p. 233, as *The Martyrdom of S. Catherine of Siena*; Waagen ascribes the picture to Ambrogio Lorenzetti, noting that it had been called Lorenzo di Bicci. It is clearly Waagen's picture for which an attribution to the Bicci seems to be approved by Crowe and Cavalcaselle, *History of Painting in Italy*, II, 1864, p. 147. (9) Painter unknown. (10) As Giotto. (11) As School of Giotto, *Martyrdom of S. Catherine*. (12) Formerly catalogued at the National Gallery as Florentine School.

MASTER OF THE CASSONI
fifteenth century

A few furniture pieces, some traditionally ascribed to Dello, were grouped together by Venturi, *Storia dell'Arte Italiana*, Vol. VII, Part I, p. 431; this list was considerably extended, under the name of the Master of the Cassoni, by Schubring, *Cassoni*, 1923, Nos. 186 sqq. The works are Florentine of about the middle of the fifteenth century (two items are of 1448 and 1468); they may have been produced from a single workshop, but this is denied by R. Carità in the *Bollettino d'Arte*, 1949, p. 273. Schubring (p. 110) takes as his basis for the group a *desco* at Turin, which is a variant of No. 3898 below. Schubring's suggestion (p. 111) that his Master of the Cassoni may be identical with Apollonio di Giovanni or Marco del Buono is claimed to be unjustifiable by W. Stechow in the *Bulletin of the Allen Memorial Art Museum*, Oberlin College, June, 1944, pp. 13 ff.

Ascribed to the MASTER OF THE CASSONI

3898 BIRTH PLATE: THE TRIUMPH OF LOVE

On a richly decorated car, from which flames emerge, the naked, winged Love stands with his bow and arrows. Many people accompany the car. In the foreground, Aristotle ridden by Phyllis, and Samson and Delilah.

Reverse: Two coats of arms (mentioned below) are suspended from a lemon-tree and an orange-tree; an egret (?) in the foreground, the sun above.

Wood, twelve-sided, diameter $24\frac{1}{4}$ (0·615); including the frame, which is in all probability the original one, 27 (0·685).

Good condition.

The *desco da parto*, or birth plate, was used in Florence for bringing food to women in labour.[1]

The subject of the obverse of No. 3898 is loosely derived from Petrarch's *Triumph of Love*. The verses by Petrarch worth quoting in this connection are:

> Sovr'un carro di foco un garzon crudo
> con arco in man e con saette a' fianchi;
>   nulla temea, però non maglia o scudo,
> ma su gli omeri avea sol due grand'ali
> di color mille, tutto l'altro ignudo:
>   d'intorno innumerabili mortali. . . .
> Poco dinanzi a lei vedi Sansone,
> vie più forte che saggio, che per ciance
> in grembo a la nemica il capo pone.[2]

The incident of Aristotle and Phyllis does not occur in Petrarch's *Triumphs*; according to a widely diffused story, Aristotle fell in love with Phyllis, who demanded that he should be bridled and carry her on his back.[3] The incident clearly illustrates the power of love, and is sometimes added to the *Triumph of Love* in Italian art.[4]

The coats of arms on the reverse of No. 3898 have not been identified. The arms on the right, consisting principally of three red crescents on a gold ground, have wrongly been supposed to be those of the Strozzi. The arms on the left are supposed by Schubring to be those of the Wiesel family; but this would appear improbable.[5]

No. 3898 is accepted by Schubring as being by his Master of the Cassoni.[6] The classification is convenient, but the identification of individual hands for pictures such as this seems to be somewhat subjective.

VERSION: There is a very similar *desco* at Turin.[7]

PROVENANCE: Presumably Anon. Sale, 1859, bought by Bohn.[8] Henry G. Bohn Catalogue, 1884, p. 146; Sale, 19 March, 1885 (lot 137), bought by Wagner.[9] Lent by Henry Wagner to the New Gallery, 1893/4 (No. 81).[10] Presented by Henry Wagner, 1924.[11]

REPRODUCTIONS: *Illustrations, Italian Schools*, 1937, p. 221 (front). *Plates, Earlier Italian Schools*, 1953, Vol. II, p. 282 (front). The reverse is reproduced in *Paintings and Drawings on the Backs of National Gallery Pictures*, 1946, Plate 38.

REFERENCES: (1) For the use, see especially Baldinucci, *Notizie*, I, 1845, p. 502; for the word, E. Müntz, *Les Collections des Médicis*, 1888, p. 63. Cf. E. Müntz in the *Chronique des Arts*, 1889, p. 260, and in *Monuments Piot*, 1894, pp. 218 ff. See also Masaccio's *Desco* at Berlin, the subject painted on which shows a desco being used; Berlin, 1931 Catalogue, No. 58c, reproduced in the Berlin Illustrations. (2) Petrarch, *Le Rime Sparse e i Trionfi*, ed. E. Chiòrboli, 1930: p. 304, *Trionfo d'Amore*, I, lines 23–28, and p. 315, *Trionfo d'Amore*, III, lines 49–51. See also *Die Triumphe Francesco Petrarcas*, ed. C. Appel, 1901, pp. 180/1 and 197. (3) See for instance A. Borgeld, *Aristoteles en Phyllis*, 1902, or E. Mâle, *L'Art Religieux du XIIIe Siècle en France*, 5th edition, 1923, pp. 337 ff. (Campaspe instead of Phyllis). (4) See Schubring, *Cassoni*, 1923, No. 198 (a variant of No. 3898, mentioned under the heading *Version* in the text), and Nos. 201, 202. Cf. also A. M. Hind, *Early Italian Engraving*, Vol. I, 1938, A.I. 18, and Vol.

II, 1938, Plate 18. (5) Schubring, *Cassoni*, 1923, Nos. 199, 200. The arms of the Wiesel family are not given in the plates of Rietstap's *Armorial Général*. In any case, it is doubtful if the animal depicted on No. 3898 is meant to be a weasel; an infra-red photograph of it is reproduced by Ian Rawlins, *From the National Gallery Laboratory*, 1940, Plate 43. (6) Schubring, *op. cit.*, Nos. 199, 200. (7) Schubring, *op. cit.*, No. 198 and Plate XLIII; Turin, 1899 Catalogue, No. 107, attr. Dello. (8) As Uccello; see Redford, *Art Sales*, 1888, II, p. 258. The identity of the sale has not been established. (9) As Orcagna. Christie's stencil mark for the Bohn Sale is on the side of No. 3898. Sometimes, e.g. in the 1929 National Gallery catalogue, No. 3898 is wrongly said to come from the Charles Butler Collection. (10) As Dello Delli. (11) As by the Master of the Cassoni.

MASTER of the Story of GRISELDA
active *ca.* 1500

Named from the three pictures, Nos. 912/4 below. A series of famous persons of antiquity is in part ascribed to the same hand; that series seems to have been done for the most part under the direction of Signorelli. The influence of Signorelli is indeed marked in Nos. 912/4; also, to a less extent, that of Pintoricchio. Some parallels with the Sienese School suggest that the painter was active at Siena; indeed, part of the series of famous persons is ascribed to Neroccio, Francesco di Giorgio and Pacchiarotto. The date of the works is *ca.* 1500. Berenson's doubtful identification of the painter as Fungai (*Central Italian Painters of the Renaissance*, 1909) was later abandoned by him; a suggestion of Bernardino di Mariotto, in the National Gallery catalogue of 1913, is also untenable.

Literature: Giacomo di Nicola in *The Burlington Magazine*, Vol. XXXI (1917), pp. 224 ff. See also A. Venturi in *L'Arte*, 1900, pp. 235/8; Berenson in *Dedalo*, 1931, pp. 750 ff.; A. S. Weller, *Francesco di Giorgio*, 1943, pp. 222 ff.

912 THE STORY OF PATIENT GRISELDA, PART I

Left background, the Marquis Gualtieri di Saluzzo hunts the stag. Left foreground, the Marquis and his followers come upon his chosen bride Griselda, a poor girl carrying water. Right background, the Marquis goes to announce his marriage, on the condition of absolute obedience on the part of his wife, at the house of his bride's father; a little further forward, he leads Griselda away. Right foreground, Griselda at the Marquis' invitation takes off her poor clothes, which lie on the ground; an attendant holds rich clothes for her to put on. Centre, before a triumphal arch adorned with horses and unidentified sculptures, the Marquis marries Griselda.

Wood, painted surface, $24\frac{1}{4} \times 60\frac{3}{4}$ (0.615×1.545); painted up to the edges top and bottom.

A good deal repainted; Griselda's drapery, in the scene where she has taken off her poor clothes, seems new.

For the commentary, etc., see under No. 914 below.

913   THE STORY OF PATIENT GRISELDA, PART II

The Marquis puts his wife's obedience to the test. Left background, (1) a servant receives his instructions from the Marquis; (2) Griselda gives her baby to the servant; (3) the servant takes it away (to kill it on orders from the Marquis, Griselda falsely thinks). Centre foreground, under a loggia, the Marquis pretends to have received Papal permission to dissolve his marriage; Griselda hands him back her ring. Right centre foreground, in the presence of the Marquis, Griselda strips off her rich clothes. Right foreground, Griselda goes away, dressed only in a shift. Right background, Griselda returns to her father's house; a woman at the foot of some steps holds the poor clothes Griselda had discarded when she left it.

Wood, painted surface, $24\frac{1}{4} \times 60\frac{3}{4}$ (0·615 × 1·545); painted up to the edges top and bottom.

Much repainted.

For the commentary, etc., see No. 914 below.

914   THE STORY OF PATIENT GRISELDA, PART III

Extreme right background, the Marquis summons Griselda from her father's house and instructs her in what he wants her to do in view of his pretended second marriage. Left background, Griselda goes off and sweeps the Marquis' house in preparation for the supposed new bride. Centre background, Griselda's two children arrive in a splendid cortège; the elder, who is a girl, is the alleged new bride for the Marquis. Right background, Griselda welcomes the supposed bride and her brother, not knowing who they are. Right foreground, the two children are seated at table with the Marquis; Griselda, standing, praises them, still not knowing who they are. Left foreground, the Marquis reveals that Griselda's trials were invented to test her obedience to him; she is, as she always has been, his wife, and the alleged bride and her brother are Griselda's children, not killed as she had thought. The two last scenes are at the ends of a long table, the centre of which is occupied by the guests for the Marquis' pretended second wedding. The table is set under a loggia ornamented with unidentified reliefs.

Wood, painted surface, $24\frac{1}{4} \times 60\frac{3}{4}$ (0·615 × 1·545); painted up to the edges top and bottom.

Damaged and repainted, but probably less so than Nos. 912/3 above.

The three pictures form a fairly careful illustration to the last story of Boccaccio's *Decameron*. The theme of wifely obedience made the story very popular; Chaucer's Clerk's Tale in *The Canterbury Tales* is taken from Petrarch's Latin version of it.

The three pictures clearly form a complete series. It would seem that they may have been let into the wainscoting of a room, rather than into three cassoni.[1]

The costumes make a date of *ca.* 1500 likely.

PROVENANCE: Nos. 912/4 were apparently bought by Alexander Barker in Italy.[2] In his Collection by *ca.* 1854.[3] Exhibited at Leeds, 1868 (Nos. 18–20), and at the Burlington Fine Arts Club, 1871 (Nos. 57, 61, 64).[4] Purchased at the Barker Sale, 6 June, 1874 (lots 85, 86, 87).[5]

REPRODUCTIONS: *Illustrations, Italian Schools*, 1937, p. 368. *Plates, Earlier Italian Schools*, 1953, Vol. II, pp. 283–284.

REFERENCES: (1) P. Schubring, *Cassoni*, 1923, Nos. 536/8. (2) This is stated in the N.G. MS. Catalogue. The writer of the entry certainly consulted the restorer who had repaired the pictures for Barker about their condition, and may have had the information about the provenance from him. (3) They are clearly the pictures referred to by Waagen, *Treasures*, IV, 1857, p. 75, as Pintoricchio; this passage in conjunction with Waagen's remarks on p. 71 suggests that 1854 is the date on which Waagen saw the pictures. (4) In both cases as by Pintoricchio. (5) As by Pintoricchio; catalogued at the Gallery, 1894–1929, as Umbrian School.

MASTER OF THE OSSERVANZA
active *ca.* 1436

The name is applied to a group of pictures, the frontiers of which are not yet fixed, formerly ascribed to Stefano di Giovanni (Sassetta), but separated from him by Alberto Graziani (following a suggestion of Longhi's) in *Proporzioni*, II, 1948, pp. 75 ff.; see also Enzo Carli, *Capolavori dell'Arte Senese*, 1946, pp. 58 ff., and John Pope-Hennessy in *The Burlington Magazine*, Vol. XC (1948), p. 360. His triptych in the Osservanza near Siena, from which he has been given his name, is dated 1436. Berenson, *Sassetta*, 1946, p. 52, Cesare Brandi, *Quattrocentisti Senesi*, 1949, Chapter III, and John Pope-Hennessy in *The Burlington Magazine*, 1956, p. 370, think that this group is by the young Sano di Pietro. But this does not seem satisfactory; and the claim is rejected by Enzo Carli, *Sassetta e il Maestro dell'Osservanza*, 1957, pp. 89 ff. (with many illustrations).

5114 TRIPTYCH: THE BIRTH OF THE VIRGIN

Wood, painted surfaces, central panel, $10\frac{5}{8} \times 7\frac{3}{4}$ (0·27 × 0·195); left panel, $11\frac{1}{4} \times 3\frac{3}{8}$ (0·285 × 0·085); right panel $11\frac{1}{4} \times 3\frac{5}{8}$ (0·285 × 0·09). The frames, which are fixed round the panels, are probably altogether new.

Good condition; but somewhat more damaged than might appear at first sight. It is doubtful if the three panels have been framed up quite correctly; the cornice mouldings in the pictures should be on a line, but are not. Several *pentimenti* in the outlines.

This triptych was ascribed by Morelli to Sano di Pietro,[1] but since then has more usually been called Stefano di Giovanni (Sassetta).[2] The compiler, in consultation with Enzo Carli and John Pope-Hennessy, found the attribution to the Osservanza Master quite satisfactory.[3] It shows some connections with a large picture of the same subject at Asciano, also acceptable as by the Osservanza Master.[4]

PROVENANCE: In the Trivulzio Collection at Milan; first known to be recorded by Mündler in 1858.[5] Acquired by Lord Rothermere before 1932;[6] bequeathed by Viscount Rothermere, 1940.

REPRODUCTION: *Plates, Earlier Italian Schools*, 1953, Vol. II, pp. 285–286.

REFERENCES: (1) Label on the back. Recorded(?) under this name in Berenson's *Central Italian Painters*, 1897 and 1909. (2) See Cagnola's notes in the *Rassegna d'Arte*, 1904, p. 142, and 1906, p. 63; Berenson's *Central Italian Painters*, 1909 (as well as under Sano?); J. Pope-Hennessy, *Sassetta*, 1939, p. 117. (3) This sentence is repeated from the first edition of this catalogue—Pope-Hennessy in *The Burlington Magazine* 1956, p. 369, still holds this view; Carli, *Sassetta e il Maestro dell'Osservanza*, 1957, p. (123), after further consideration suspends judgment (picture wrongly located at Washington). (4) Enzo Carli, *Capolavori dell'Arte Senese*, 1946, Plates C sqq. (5) Mündler's Diary, 6 March, 1858; he thought it might be late fourteenth-century Florentine. Its provenance has been confused apropos of a picture exhibited at Matthiesen's, London, 1946 (No. 4), which may be from an Anon. Sale, 22 April, 1942 (lot 97). (6) P. G. Konody, *Works of Art in the Collection of Viscount Rothermere*, 1932, Plate 20.

MASTER OF THE PALA SFORZESCA
active ca. 1495

The *Pala Sforzesca* is an altarpiece of 1494/5 in the Brera, with portraits of Lodovico il Moro and his family as donors; its style shows a combination of the old Lombard manner (Foppa, etc.), and Leonardo's. Several other pictures have been ascribed to the same hand; the scale is different, but there can be little doubt that they are nearly related. The painter has been named Zenale, Bernardino de' Conti, Ambrogio Preda, Antonio da Monza and Jacopo de Mottis; the *Pala Sforzesca* seems to differ considerably from the authenticated works of all these.

Literature: Malaguzzi Valeri in the *Rassegna d'Arte*, 1905, pp. 44 ff.; the same, Brera Catalogue, 1908, pp. 186/8; Mario Salmi in *Cronache d'Arte*, November-December, 1927, pp. 388 ff.; Suida, *Leonardo und sein Kreis*, 1929, pp. 179 ff.

Ascribed to the MASTER OF THE PALA SFORZESCA

3899 S. PAUL (FROM AN ALTARPIECE?)

Walnut,[1] painted surface, $9\frac{3}{8} \times 5\frac{1}{4}$ (0·24 × 0·135); perhaps very slightly cut at the bottom.

Very good condition.

The picture entered the Gallery as School of Verrocchio; in the 1929 Catalogue as Milanese School. Ascribed by Salmi[2] and Suida[3] to the Master of the Pala Sforzesca; there seems no reason to doubt that it is from the same group as No. 4444 below. Ascribed by Berenson (1932 Lists) to Butinone; the book does seem in Butinone's style.[4]

Five small Apostles in the Castello Sforzesco at Milan are reproduced by Salmi;[5] these are very similar in style, but variations in the architectural setting make it clear that they are from another series. A *S. Andrew* reproduced by Suida[6] is less like in style and is also from a different series.

PROVENANCE: There is an unidentified seal on the back. Presented by Henry Wagner, 1924.

REPRODUCTION: *Illustrations, Italian Schools*, 1937, p. 236. *Plates, Earlier Italian Schools*, 1953, Vol. II, p. 287.

REFERENCES: (1) Letter from B. J. Rendle, of the Forest Products Research Laboratory, in the Gallery archives. (2) Salmi, *loc. cit.* in the biography above. (3) Suida, *op. cit.*, in the biography above, p. 181. (4) Berenson does not admit the separate existence of a *Master of the Pala Sforzesca*; he ascribes the Pala Sforzesca to Bernardino de' Conti (?), No. 3899 and the five Apostles to be mentioned at Milan to Butinone. (5) Salmi, *loc. cit.* (6) Suida, *op. cit.*, Fig. 186.

4444   THE VIRGIN AND CHILD WITH SAINTS AND DONORS

The Saints (from left to right) are S. James the Great, a deacon (S. Lawrence or Stephen?), S. Bernardino (?) and a young male saint.

Wood, painted surface, $22 \times 19\frac{1}{4}$ (0.555×0.49); painted up to the edges all round.

Good condition in general, though parts of the flesh have rather numerous retouches. There is a *pentimento* in the hand of the taller male donor in the front row.

Ascribed to the Master of the Pala Sforzesca by A. Venturi.[1] It is very near in style to the Cora Madonna;[2] both of these pictures seem to be a little earlier than the Pala Sforzesca itself, perhaps *ca.* 1490.

PROVENANCE: Prince Jérome Napoleon Sale, Christie's, 11 May, 1872 (lot 324), with identifying description,[3] bought in. Coll. John Bell, Glasgow; Sale, Christie's, 25 June, 1881 (lot 781),[4] with identifying description, as from Prince Napoleon's Collection, bought by Patrichio. Exhibited at the Burlington Fine Arts Club, 1898 (No. 6), lent by Sir George Donaldson, from whom purchased in 1898 by Vernon J. Watney.[5] Presented by Lady Margaret Watney in memory of her husband, Vernon J. Watney, 1929.

REPRODUCTION: *Plates, Earlier Italian Schools*, 1953, Vol. II, p. 288.

REFERENCES: (1) Venturi in *L'Arte*, 1898, p. 315. (2) Suida, *Leonardo und sein Kreis*, 1929, Fig. 183. Berenson (1932 Lists) ascribes both No. 4444 and the Cora Madonna to Bernardino de' Conti (?). (3) As Zenale. (4) As Zenale. (5) Letter in the Gallery archives.

MASTER OF PRATOVECCHIO
See TUSCAN SCHOOL, No. 584

MATTEO DI GIOVANNI
active 1452, died 1495

His family came from Sansepolcro, and he himself may have been born there; but he is classed in the Sienese School. He was in Siena in partnership with Giovanni di Pietro in 1452 and still in 1457, apparently working as a beginner on comparatively humble tasks. A number of authenticated pictures by him exist.

1155   THE ASSUMPTION OF THE VIRGIN (CENTRAL PANEL
        FROM AN ALTARPIECE)

The Virgin's halo is inscribed REGINA.CELI.LETARE (from an
Easter antiphon). In the foreground, S. Thomas is receiving the Virgin's
girdle. Christ is seen at the top of the picture; also two haloed groups,
including David and S. John the Baptist.

Wood, irregular top, $130\frac{1}{2} \times 68\frac{1}{2}$ ($3 \cdot 31 \times 1 \cdot 73$).[1]
Excellent state.

This picture is stated to have been the central panel of an altarpiece
in S. Agostino, Asciano,[2] and is stated to have borne a date 1474.[3] Side
panels are stated to have existed, and it is reasonably supposed that two
of them survive, SS. Michael and Augustine, in the Collegiata of S.
Agata at Asciano.[4]

PROVENANCE: From S. Agostino at Asciano, as explained above. Found by
Romagnoli in 1800 in the woodstore of the monastery, No. 1155 was taken charge
of by the Gonfaloniere D. Francesco Bambagini of Asciano. Later, but apparently before 1835, it was hung in the choir of S. Agostino, Asciano.[5] At some
time, probably after 1838 and certainly before 1863, it was acquired by the
Griccioli family, and was placed by them on the high altar of the chapel in their
villa near Siena, the former abbey of S. Eugenio or Monastero.[6] Purchased from
Girolamo Griccioli through Charles Fairfax Murray, 1884.

REPRODUCTION: *Illustrations, Italian Schools*, 1937, p. 222. *Plates, Earlier
Italian Schools*, 1953, Vol. II, p. 289.

REFERENCES: (1) Measurements from the 1929 Catalogue; this picture has not
been examined out of its frame with reference to the present catalogue entry. (2)
Romagnoli, *Biografia Cronologica de' Bell'Artisti Senesi*, MS. in the Communal
Library at Siena, Vol. IV, p. 673; cf. John Pope-Hennessy, *Matteo di Giovanni's
'Assumption' Altarpiece*, in *Proporzioni*, III, 1950, p. 81. (3) E. Micheli, *Guida
Artistica della Città e Contorni di Siena*, 1863, p. 138. (4) G. F. Hartlaub, *Matteo
da Siena*, 1910, p. 72 and Plate VI. John Pope-Hennessy, *loc. cit.*, pp. 81 ff.,
accepts the association and reproduces the pictures after cleaning on Plates
LXXVII–LXXVIII. He further suggests that two panels of the *Virgin Annunciate* (Plate LXXX) and the *Annunciatory Angel* most probably formed two of
the upper panels of this altarpiece. Also that a saint in the Berenson Collection
(Plate LXXIX) may originate from the superstructure or pilasters. (5) All this is
from Romagnoli, as in note 2; he gave his MS. to the library in 1835. (6)
Romagnoli's *Cenni Storici-Artistici di Siena*, 3rd edition, 1852, p. 105, does not
record it in S. Eugenio; Romagnoli had died in 1838 (cf. p. 7). E. Micheli, *op.
cit.*, p. 138. In the Romagnoli MSS. in the Library at Siena, the statement that
the picture had been moved to S. Eugenio is an addition, apparently in Milanesi's
handwriting.

1461   S. SEBASTIAN

Wood, rounded top, painted surface, $49\frac{3}{4} \times 23\frac{1}{2}$ ($1 \cdot 265 \times 0 \cdot 60$).
Excellent state. Frame partly original, but renewed round the arch.
Presumably a complete picture as it stands.

Berenson, in his 1932 Lists, ascribed the angels to Cozzarelli; in his
1936 Lists, the landscape and the angels are so ascribed.

Hartlaub[1] calls No. 1461 a late work; Maria Luisa Gengaro[2] less
reasonably calls it an early work.

DERIVATION: A *S. Sebastian* of 1495 at Siena, reasonably ascribed to Cozzarelli, is similar in character to No. 1461, and is perhaps freely derived from it.[3]

PROVENANCE: Purchased from Stefano Bardini, Florence, 1895.

REPRODUCTION: *Illustrations, Italian Schools*, 1937, p. 220. *Plates, Earlier Italian Schools*, 1953, Vol. II, p. 290.

REFERENCES: (1) G. F. Hartlaub, *Matteo da Siena*, 1910, p. 128. (2) Maria Luisa Gengaro in *La Diana*, 1934, pp. 152 ff. and 164. (3) Siena, Catalogo by C. Brandi, 1933, p. 56, No. 296; photograph in the Gallery archives.

Imitator of MATTEO DI GIOVANNI

247   CHRIST CROWNED WITH THORNS

The halo is inscribed .YH̄S. / XPS. / .NAZA. Round the edge is the inscription, .IN NOMINE.IH̄V.OMNE.GEN / V.FLECT CELES/TIVM.TERESTIVM. & INFENO.

Wood, painted surface, $8\frac{1}{2} \times 8\frac{1}{2}$ (0·21 × 0·21); including the framing, $9\frac{1}{2} \times 9\frac{1}{2}$ (0·24 × 0·24).

The inscription is derived from *Philippians*, II, 10. Its use here may be supposed connected in some way with its occasional appearance on S. Bernardino's plaque with IHS on it;[1] but cf. also some prints chiefly consisting of the Monogram and text.[2]

This picture appears to be of comparatively recent manufacture.[3]

The style is imitated from Matteo di Giovanni,[4] but no exact original by Matteo appears to be known.

PROVENANCE: Purchased at the E. Joly de Bammeville Sale, 12 June, 1854 (lot 50).[5]

REPRODUCTION: *Illustrations, Italian Schools*, 1937, p. 223. *Plates, Earlier Italian Schools*, 1953, Vol. II, p. 291.

REFERENCES: (1) See Kaftal, *Iconography of the Saints in Tuscan Painting*, 1952, col. 197. (2) Schreiber, *Handbuch der Holz- und Metallschnitte des XV. Jahrhunderts*, IV, 1927, Nos. 1808 sqq. and V, 1928, Nos. 2754–2754 f.; a reproduction in Timmers, *Symboliek en Iconographie der Christelijke Kunst*, 1947, Plate 28; another in Campbell Dodgson, *Woodcuts of the XV Century in the British Museum*, II, 1935, Plate XCVI. (3) Verbal confirmation from H. Ruhemann and others. (4) Ascribed to Matteo di Giovanni by Crowe and Cavalcaselle, *History of Painting in Italy*, III, 1866, p. 134. The picture has been mentioned often in subsequent literature; e.g. by G. F. Hartlaub, *Matteo da Siena*, 1910, pp. 129/30, and by Maria Luisa Gengaro in *La Diana*, 1934, p. 172. (5) As Niccolo Alluno.

MATTEO DI PACINO
See Style of ORCAGNA, Nos. 569–578

Filippo MAZZOLA
active 1490, died 1505

Active at Parma. There are several signed works; dated from 1491. Perhaps a pupil of Francesco Tacconi, but an imitator especially of Giovanni Bellini. Indeed, he may on one picture at Padua have called himself a disciple of the latter; the signature there has been claimed to run *Filipus Maz*(olus) *d*(is.) *Joanis* / (Bel)*li*?(ni p.)—see A. Moschetti in the *Bollettino del Museo Civico di Padova*, Vol. X, 1907, p. 151, and L. Grossato's Padua Catalogue, 1957, p. 102. He was the father of Parmigianino.

1416   THE VIRGIN AND CHILD WITH S. JEROME(?) AND THE B. BERNARDINO DA FELTRE (?)

The B. Bernardino (?) holds a staff, a book and a model of the Holy Sepulchre with Christ in the tomb against a cross marked INRI. Signed, .PHILIPPVS.MAZOL(L ?)A. P. P.

Wood, painted surface, $22 \times 29\frac{1}{4}$ (0.56×0.745); painted up to the edges all round.

Considerably damaged by flaking, and somewhat repainted.

One need not feel much doubt that the Franciscan *beatus* is Bernardino, born at Feltre in 1439, died at Pavia in 1494, although he was not formally beatified until 1653.[1] The B. Bernardino was active particularly in North Italy, and was responsible for the establishment or development of the *Monte di Pietà* in many Italian towns. It was customary, therefore, to show him with the *Pietà*; cf. for instance the record of the image on his tomb.[2]

It may be deduced that No. 1416 was probably painted between 1494, the date of the B. Bernardino's death, and 1505, the date of Filippo Mazzola's death.

PROVENANCE: Some time before 1837 in the collection at Rome of the landscape painter Giovanni Maldura (*ca.* 1772–1849).[3] Presumably Anon. Sale, Christie's, 17 March, 1890 (lot 111), bought by Murray.[4] Purchased from C. Fairfax Murray, Lewis Fund, 1894.

REPRODUCTION: *Illustrations, Italian Schools*, 1937, p. 224 (with the parapet and signature cut off). *Plates, Earlier Italian Schools*, 1953, Vol. II, p. 291.

REFERENCES: (1) Father Exupère of the Museo Francescano at Assisi kindly suggested the identification. (2) Bollandists, 28 September, p. 889. There is a picture of him with the *Pietà*, and with the name inscribed, in the Oratorio di S. Maria delle Grazie at Parma; recorded in the *Inventario degli Oggetti d'Arte d'Italia, Provincia di Parma*, 1934, p. 64. In the Congregazione di Carità at Mantua there is a picture ascribed to F. Scutellari, with the name inscribed, the emblem being apparently the *Monte di Pietà*; reproduced in the *Inventario, cit., Provincia di Mantova*, 1935, p. 57. The B. Bernardino is further presumably the figure occurring in a picture in S. Bartolomeo at Parma, ascribed to Francesco Maria Rondani; recorded in the *Inventario, cit., Provincia di Parma*, 1934, p. 18, as the B. Bernardino da Siena. *Mostra Parmense di Dipinti Noti ed Ignoti*, Parma, 1948 (No. 116), as S. Bernardino da Siena; reproduced on Plate XXVIII. The figure in that picture has not the name inscribed, but was already called the

B. Bernardino by Ireneo Affò, *Vita del Graziosissimo Pittore Francesco Mazzola detto il Parmigianino*, 1784, p. 8. Another example, without the name inscribed, is at Faenza, ascribed to Scaletti; recorded by R. Buscaroli, *La Pittura Romagnola del Quattrocento*, 1931, pp. 259 ff. A figure with a *Pietà*, without the name inscribed, is in the Monastero di S. Cecilia at Città di Castello. G. Magherini and E. Giovagnoli, *La Prima Giovinezza di Raffaello*, 1927, p. 14 (Plates VII, VIII), say that it is either the B. Bernardino da Feltre or the B. Barnaba da Terni; the latter, whose life and connection with the *Monte di Pietà* at Perugia, etc., are recorded by Jacobilli, *Vite de' Santi, e Beati dell'Umbria*, I, 1647, pp. 261 ff., and by Wadding, *Annales Minorum*, Vol. XIV (1735), seems unlikely except (perhaps) in Umbrian pictures. The B. Marco da Monte Santa Maria in Gallo seems also unlikely; but cf. the print recorded by A. M. Hind, *Early Italian Engraving*, Vol. I, 1938, B. III. 8 and Vol. III, 1938, Plate 205. (3) An engraving of the picture with the name of the then owner was pointed out by Father Exupère of Assisi, who was kind enough to send a photograph of it. The engraving is signed by G(iuseppe) Craffonara (1790–1837), and appears to be unrecorded. The engraving, so far as its rather rough quality allows one to judge, shows no variations from No. 1416 in its present state. (4) As P. Mazzuolo.

MICHELE DA VERONA
ca. 1470–1536/44

His age was declared as 12 in 1482. There are several signed works, of which the chief is a large *Crucifixion* of 1501 in the Brera.

1214 CORIOLANUS PERSUADED BY HIS FAMILY TO SPARE ROME

Canvas, $36\frac{3}{4} \times 47\frac{1}{4}$ (0·93 × 1·20). Apparently not cut; what seems to be the original canvas continues beyond the edges of the paint.

Very fair condition.

The subject is described in Plutarch, *Life of Coriolanus*. Coriolanus, after being banished from Rome, prepared to attack the city; he was persuaded to desist by his mother Volumnia, his wife Virgilia, his children, and Valeria. Shakespeare follows Plutarch, and further agrees with Michele da Verona in introducing only one child. There is said to be better authority for calling his mother Veturia, and his wife Volumnia. See also Signorelli, No. 3929.

The attribution appears to be acceptable.[1]

PROVENANCE: Apparently in 1820 in the collection at Verona of Francesco Caldana, who was buying from *ca.* 1816.[2] Purchased out of the Walker Fund from J. P. Richter, Milan, 1886.

REPRODUCTION: *Illustrations, Italian Schools*, 1937, p. 232. *Plates, Earlier Italian Schools*, 1953, Vol. II, p. 292.

REFERENCES: (1) As Michele da Verona in Crowe and Cavalcaselle, *Painting in North Italy*, ed. Borenius, II, 1912, p. 215; also in Berenson's Lists, 1932. (2) Persico, *Descrizione di Verona*, etc., 1820/1, I, pp. 130/1, as Francesco Mantegna; II (Appendice), p. 320, as Michel Veronese. The rather rare subject makes the identification likely. Cf. also the *Descrizione delle Opere di Eccellenti Maestri raccolte dal Sig. Francesco Caldana*, 1822 (No. 6): 'Di Michel Facci Veronese. L'incontro di Vettuvia e di Coriolano, di Francesco Mantegna, citato nella Descrizione di Verona Parte prima, e corretto nell' Appendice alla pag. 320.' It should be added that Michele de' Fachai (Facci) was at one time confused with Michele da Verona; see Zannandreis, *Le Vite dei Pittori . . . Veronesi*, 1891, p. 103. J. P. Richter (oral communication) thought he bought it from a Veronese collection or (if not) the Canella Collection, Venice; in *The Mond Collection*, 1910, I, p. 48, he says he bought it from a private collection at Venice, where it was called Carpaccio.

MILANESE SCHOOL

2089   THE VIRGIN AND CHILD (FRAGMENT?)

Fresco, rounded top, painted surface, $29 \times 17\frac{3}{4}$ (0.735×0.45). Very seriously damaged.

Formerly catalogued as from the School of Boltraffio; possibly rather nearer the picture in the Cora Collection assigned to the Master of the Pala Sforzesca,[1] but the style is no longer recognizable.

PROVENANCE: Lent by William Graham to the R.A., 1885 (No. 222); Graham Sale, 9 April, 1886 (lot 365), bought by Samuel. John Samuel Collection; bequeathed his nieces, by the Misses Cohen, 1906.

REPRODUCTION: *Illustrations, Italian Schools*, 1937, p. 44. *Plates, Earlier Italian Schools*, 1953, Vol. II, p. 293.

REFERENCE: (1) Reproduced by Suida, *Leonardo und sein Kreis*, 1929, Fig. 183.

2251   BONA OF SAVOY (?)

Full length, in profile; the flowers she holds are columbines.

Canvas, $55 \times 23\frac{3}{4}$ (1.395×0.605), approx.; the edges are very ragged. Much damaged.

The sitter, at one time wrongly called Beatrice d'Este, has been called Bona of Savoy, born 1449, the wife of Galeazzo Maria Sforza, and Regent after his death, 1476–80. The costume suggests a rather later date. It is true that she did not die until 1503; but her circumstances after 1480 were perhaps too difficult for portrait-making. Still, the profile resembles that on a medal of her.[1]

Ascribed by Cook[2] to Zenale, but no attribution seems possible.

PROVENANCE: Acquired from the Ravaisson Collection, Paris, in 1889 by Sir George Donaldson;[3] exhibited at the Burlington Fine Arts Club, 1898 (No. 7); lent by Sir George Donaldson to the National Gallery, 1907, and presented by him, 1908.

REPRODUCTION: *Illustrations, Italian Schools*, 1937, p. 233. *Plates, Earlier Italian Schools*, 1953, Vol. II, 294.

REFERENCES: (1) Hill, *Corpus*, 1930, No. 669, Plate 116. (2) Herbert Cook in *The Burlington Magazine*, Vol. V (1904), p. 200; formerly called Ambrogio Preda. (3) Document in the Gallery archives.

Gerolamo MOCETTO
living 1458–1531

Painter and engraver; he was born probably not long before 1458, and he made his will in 1531. He was from a family established at Murano, and he was active in Venice, also (probably *ca.* 1517) in Verona. He was influenced by Mantegna and Giovanni Bellini.

1239 THE MASSACRE OF THE INNOCENTS (FRAGMENT?)

Herod is seated right. Signed, HEROL / EMO / MOCETO / P. For the commentary, etc., see No. 1240 below.

1240 THE MASSACRE OF THE INNOCENTS (FRAGMENT?)

Each canvas (presumably transferred from wood), $26\frac{3}{4} \times 17\frac{1}{2}$ (0.675×0.445).
Very fair state.

No. 1239 seems intended to continue the scene of No. 1240 on the right, but the architecture is confused. The treatment of the theme as it stands in two scenes is most peculiar. There were already two pieces with almost exactly the same fields at the time of Strange's ownership;[1] but it seems possible that Nos. 1239/40 are fragments of a single, rather large work, if a considerable gap is postulated between the two. No. 1239 seems in any case to have been cut somewhat at the left, and No. 1240 at the right.

The mother throwing up her arms on No. 1240 is copied from the Magdalen in Mantegna's engraving of *The Entombment* (horizontal); the head of the mother with a turban in the same picture is taken from the Holy Woman supporting Christ in the same engraving. The two infants lying together in No. 1240 are from Mantegna's engraving, *Bacchanalian with a Wine-Press*.[2]

In Mocetto's engraving of *The Killing of the Sow* recur: (1) the soldier standing on the right of No. 1239; (2) the kneeling soldier and his companion in the centre of No. 1239 (both naked in the engraving); (3) the two women left centre in No. 1239, one with her hand on the other's shoulder; (4) (with considerable variations) the mother (who holds a child), in the centre of No. 1239; (5) the helmeted figure by her side (nearest to Herod) in No. 1239; (6) the kneeling soldier in the centre of No. 1240 (naked in the engraving). The soldier on the extreme right of No. 1240 seems to recur (with variations) in Mocetto's engraving, *The Altar of Sacrifice* (holding a torch). The female figure in No. 1240, with face hidden by a mother's upraised arm, recurs with variations in the same engraving (next figure).[3] The soldier mentioned first in the above list, with considerable variations, and reversed, recurs in the fragment of a fresco ascribed to Mocetto, *Scipio and the Celtiberian Maid*, No. 476 of the Verona Gallery.[4]

ENGRAVINGS: See under Provenance. For related engravings, see above.

PROVENANCE: Nos. 1239 and 1240 were engraved when in the collection at Venice of John Strange (1732–1799).[5] Strange left Italy at the end of 1786;[6] Nos. 1239/40 remained at Venice in the possession of Giovanni Maria Sasso,[7] who still owned them at the time of his death in 1803.[8] Coll. Marquis de Sivry, Venice; Sale, Paris, 18/9 April, 1853 (lots 57, 58).[9] In 1859, owned by the Vicomte de Janzé, Paris;[10] Sale, Paris, 24/5 April, 1866 (lots 29, 30).[11] Purchased from J. P. Richter, Florence, 1888.[12]

REPRODUCTIONS: *Illustrations, Italian Schools*, 1937, pp. 236/7. *Plates, Earlier Italian Schools*, 1954, Vol. II, pp. 295–296.

REFERENCES: (1) See under Provenance. (2) Klassiker der Kunst *Mantegna*, 1910, Plates 131 and 139. (3) A. M. Hind, *Early Italian Engraving*, Vol. V, 1948, p. 163, Nos. 6 and 7, and Vol. VII, 1948, Plate 721. (4) See Barclay Baron in *Madonna Verona*, January–June, 1909, pp. 84/5, No. 5. Photograph Alinari, No. 43642. (5) Engraved for Giovanni Maria Sasso's *Venezia Pittrice*, which never appeared. Impressions are in the Correr Library at Venice (Stampe, B 11 and C 2). In the engraving of No. 1239, the signature has an I above the first E of *Herolemo*, which appears not to be there now. Both the engravings are lettered: *Dal Quadro di Girolamo Moceto / nella Raccolta di S.E. il Sigr. Cavr Giovanni Strange Residente di S.M. Britanica appresso la Serenisma Repubca di Venezia*. No engraver's name is given; it may have been Sasso himself (see Note 7). The National Gallery MS. Catalogue gives this information wrongly, confusing John Strange with Sir Robert Strange (1721–1792). (6) This is deduced from the Strange letters, Epistolario Moschini, in the Correr Library at Venice. The *Dictionary of National Biography* says that Strange was British Resident at Venice until 1788. (7) Strange Letters in the Correr Library, Venice, letter 55, Strange to Sasso, 8 November, 1792: 'Mi rincresce però che Ella se ne sia riservati si pochi e fra questi giusto alcuni che ero già per chiedergli qui, per la mia raccolta e sono li due compagni Girolamo Mocetto, giacche Ella li ha incisi a nome mio, nel suo libro.' (8) Hume correspondence, 10 November, 1803. (9) With identifying description. According to Giulio Lecomte, *Venezia*, 1844, p. 264, a de Sivry, who lived for thirty years at Palazzo Martinengo in Venice, died in 1842, bequeathing his pictures to de Bon. (10) See E. Galichon in the *Gazette des Beaux-Arts*, 15 June, 1859, pp. 322 and 334/5. (11) The reference kindly checked by Charles Sterling. (12) Richter seems to have bought them in London in 1886; letter from Morelli to Layard, 12 September, 1886 (British Museum, Add. MS. 38965, Layard Papers, Vol. XXXV).

BARTOLOMEO MONTAGNA
living 1459, died 1523

Bartolomeo Cincani, called Montagna. Active chiefly at Vicenza. He seems to have been trained at Venice, where he was living in 1469; his teacher is unknown, and his early style is to some extent a matter of guesswork, but there are several authenticated and dated examples of his mature and late periods. See especially G. G. Zorzi in *Miscellanea di Storia Veneta*, Series III, Vol. 10, 1916, Part III, pp. 85 ff.

802   THE VIRGIN AND CHILD

Wood, painted surface, $25\frac{1}{2} \times 21\frac{1}{2}$ (0.645×0.545); painted up to the edges all round.

In unsatisfactory condition, except for parts of the landscapes. None of the features of the two faces are in pure condition, and the modelling of both figures has been affected. The Child's fingers are entirely over-painted; the fingers of the Virgin's right hand are the best preserved prominent parts.

The attribution used sometimes to be doubted,[1] but the bad condition explains the somewhat odd effect, and the picture is now generally held to be an authentic early work.

PROVENANCE: Seen in 1862 in the Collection of Conte Carlo Castelbarco at Milan.[2] Purchased from Baslini, Milan, 1869.

REPRODUCTION: *Illustrations, Italian Schools*, 1937, p. 239. *Plates, Earlier Italian Schools*, 1953, Vol. II, p. 297.

REFERENCES: (1) E.g. by Borenius, *The Painters of Vicenza*, 1909, p. 93. (2) Eastlake's note-book, 1862, as Liberale, with identifying description.

3074 THREE SAINTS (FRAGMENT)

Left, S. Zeno; centre, S. John the Baptist, whose scroll is inscribed ECCE AGNVS (much retouched); right, a female saint with book and palm. Signed on a *cartellino*: *Bart(b?)olomeus mō | tanea pinxit* (much retouched, but doubtless following more or less a genuine signature).

Canvas, transferred from wood, 40½ × 55½ (1·03 × 1·41). The transference has left the edges ragged and unclear; there seems no material reason why it should not have been cut on all four sides. Frizzoni[1] positively says that the saints were once at full length, which seems very likely. Crowe and Cavalcaselle[2] wrongly call it a fresco; it seems obviously a transferred panel picture.

No. 3074 has been seriously damaged. The *cartellino* with signature may be an insertion; the X-Ray indicates that it is completely surrounded by a gap in the original paint, and it is not impossible that it was originally in a different place, presumably at the foot of the picture. The spelling *Montanea* is perhaps imitated from the Latin form of Mantegna's name; the form appears on Montagna's S. Bartolomeo altarpiece at Vicenza,[3] but as it is rare, it may here be a false reconstruction. On the other hand, the first three letters of the signature, *Bar*, are to all appearances authentic; and these may be held to suffice for documenting the attribution.

The female martyr has been called S. Catherine of Alexandria.

Probably from Montagna's middle period.

DRAWING: Borenius[4] thinks a head in the British Museum may be for the S. John; as he admits, the lighting and expression differ.

PROVENANCE: Stated to be from a chapel belonging to the Tanara family in the village of San Giovanni Ilarione between Verona and Vicenza.[5] Bought at Verona from the Tanara family by Sir A. H. Layard in 1856;[6] exhibited at South Kensington, 1869 (No. 12); Layard Bequest, 1916.[7]

REPRODUCTION: *Illustrations, Italian Schools*, 1937, p. 238. *Plates, Earlier Italian Schools*, 1953, Vol. II, p. 298.

REFERENCES: (1) Frizzoni in the *Gazette des Beaux-Arts*, 1896, II, p. 462. (2) Crowe and Cavalcaselle, *Painting in North Italy*, I, 1871, p. 433, or ed. Borenius, 1912, II. p. 134. (3) Crowe and Cavalcaselle, *op. cit,* I, 1871, p. 433, or II, 1912,

p. 134; Borenius, *The Painters of Vicenza*, 1909, p. 27. (4) Borenius, *op. cit.*, pp. 104/5, with reproduction. British Museum, *Italian Drawings, The Fourteenth and Fifteenth Centuries*, catalogue by A. E. Popham and Philip Pouncey, 1950, No. 176 and Plate CLXI. (5) Layard MSS. in the National Gallery. (6) Layard MSS. in the National Gallery, and *L'Arte*, 1912, p. 449. Presumably, No. 3074 is one of the 'tavole' by Montagna and others, seen in Casa 'Tanáro' (for sale) in January, 1856, by Mündler (*Diary*). (7) For the history of the Layard Collection, see Appendix IV.

Ascribed to BARTOLOMEO MONTAGNA

1098   THE VIRGIN AND CHILD

Canvas, transferred from panel, $23\frac{1}{4} \times 20$ (0.59×0.51).
Severely damaged.

The attribution appears usually to have been accepted, but is doubted by J. P. Richter (oral) and by Jacobsen;[1] the picture may well have been a genuine Montagna, but is too much damaged to see clearly.

PROVENANCE: Purchased from Baslini, Milan, 1881.

REPRODUCTION: *Illustrations, Italian Schools*, 1937, p. 239. *Plates, Earlier Italian Schools*, 1953, Vol. II, p. 299.

REFERENCE: (1) Jacobsen in the *Repertorium für Kunstwissenschaft*, 1901, pp. 358/9, seems to incline to Speranza.

1696   FRESCO: THE VIRGIN AND CHILD (FRAGMENT)

Fresco (sight), $33 \times 22\frac{3}{4}$ (0.84×0.58).
Considerably damaged.

Formerly catalogued as by Giovanni Bellini, or of his school. There is general agreement now in favour of Montagna; but it is too much damaged for the compiler to express a definite opinion if it is by Montagna himself, or by a follower.[1]

PROVENANCE: On the (modern) frame are two shields, one with the arms, on a white (?) ground three black (?) fleur-de-lys surmounted by a red label of three points; the other with an inscription, DIPINTO 1481. NEL CORO / DELLA CHIESA DI MAGRÈ / VICINO A SCHIO. VICENZA.[2] It was in the Layard Collection, but not in the main part of it at Venice;[3] Lady Layard ceded her life-interest in it to the National Gallery in 1900.[4]

REPRODUCTION: *Illustrations, Italian Schools*, 1937, p. 37. *Plates, Earlier Italian Schools*, 1953, Vol. II, p. 300.

REFERENCES: (1) Pallucchini in *Arte Veneta*, 1951, p. 195, does not doubt that it is by Montagna. L. Coletti, *Cima da Conegliano*, 1959, Plate 154, hesitates between Cima and Montagna; but the compiler does not think that Cima is involved. (2) Borenius went to Magrè, but could not verify the provenance or date; see *The Painters of Vicenza*, 1909, p. 10. It is perhaps legitimate to record in connection with No. 1696 the following reference to a document of 11/2 December, 1486: 'Pacta inter M. Bartholomeum Montagna pictorem et Iohannem de Magrade.' The document itself has not been discovered: see G. G.

Zorzi in *Miscellanea di Storia Veneta*, Series III, Vol. 10, 1916, Part III., p. 93.
(3) It is recorded in a list of pictures in the London house, brought before the
National Gallery Trustees on 28 January, 1913. (4) For the history of the Layard
Collection, see Appendix IV.

Paolo MORANDO
ca. 1486–1522

School of Verona. His age was declared as 28 in 1514, when he was
stated to be the son of Thadeus Cavazzola q.m. Jacobi de Morando.
Since Vasari's time it has been customary to refer to him under the name
of Cavazzola, but there is no doubt that Morando is more correct.
According to Vasari (edition of 1568), he was a pupil of Bonsignori and
Francesco Morone. His earliest dated work is of 1508; there are several
other authenticated works, some of them dated.

735   S. ROCH (LEFT WING OF A TRIPTYCH)

Signed: PAVLVS / MORĀDVS / .V (with abbreviation signifying
ver).P.and dated M.D.(XVIII).

Canvas, $61\frac{3}{4} \times 21\frac{3}{4}$ ($1·57 \times 0·55$). The bottom foot or so is only $17\frac{1}{4}$ in.
($0·435$ m.) wide; presumably the picture has been cut at the sides, al-
though in its present state of repaint at the edges this cannot be stated
for sure.

Considerably worn and repainted.

S. Roch, with an ulcer in the thigh due to the plague, was turned out
of Piacenza; but his dog brought him every day a loaf, and an angel
tended his wound.[1] In the more accurate representations of him, the
dog has the loaf in his mouth. Morando has further not indicated the
proper role of the angel, who seems here to be promising a heavenly
reward. S. Roch is here correctly shown as a pilgrim; the crossed keys
on his hat may have been a common badge of pilgrims to Rome, and
reappear (with other badges) in Marziale, No. 804 of this catalogue, and
elsewhere.

No. 735 was the left wing of a triptych, of which the other wing was a
S. Sebastian by Torbido (missing); the centrepiece was Gerolamo dai
Libri, No. 748, in the entry for which the whole matter is more fully discussed. The date of No. 735 is still legible as MDXVIII, although only
the MD is prominent; it was clear and correctly read by Cignaroli in
1743.[2] In the middle of the nineteenth century, the date was wrongly
supposed to be MDXX.[3]

PROVENANCE: Mentioned by Vasari (text of 1568) as part of a triptych in S.
Maria della Scala, Verona.[4] In the early eighteenth century it seems no longer to
have been in place,[5] but it was not removed from the church until 1742.[6] No.
735 and the other wing by Torbido were taken (through the hands of Cignaroli)
to Casa Carli, Verona.[7] They both passed between *ca.* 1816 and 1820 into the
collection of Francesco Caldana, Verona.[8] Acquired *ca.* 1838 from the Caldana
Collection by Cesare Bernasconi, Verona,[9] from whom purchased, 1864.

REPRODUCTION: *Illustrations, Italian Schools*, 1937, p. 240. *Plates, Earlier Italian Schools*, 1953, Vol. II, p. 301.

REFERENCES: (1) The story is given according to Mrs. Jameson, *Sacred and Legendary Art*, 1883, Vol. II, pp. 425 ff. (2) Annotation by Cignaroli to Pozzo's *Le Vite de' Pittori etc. Veronesi*, of 1718; communicated by Bernasconi in 1863. Also printed by G. Biadego, *Di Giambettino Cignaroli*, R. Deputazione di Storia Patria per la Venezia, 1890, p. 22. (3) So in the reproductions in the Bernasconi Catalogue, 1851, No. 82, and in (Aleardi), *Di Paolo Morando*, etc., 1853, Plate 20. (4) Vasari, ed. Milanesi, Vol. V, p. 294; not in the text of 1550. For further details of the provenance, see the entry for Gerolamo dai Libri, No. 748. (5) Cf. Gerolamo dai Libri, No. 748, note 26. (6) This and the following information is taken from Cignaroli, as in note 2, and from Bernasconi's comments in the Gallery archives. Cf. also Gerolamo dai Libri, No. 748, note 27. (7) The statement in earlier editions of the National Gallery catalogue that the altar in S. Maria della Scala belonged to the Cagnoli family is due to a communication from Bernasconi. It seems certainly wrong (cf. the entry for Gerolamo dai Libri, No. 748); but the Carli property may have passed by descent to the Cagnoli. (8) G. B. da Persico, *Descrizione di Verona*, etc., 1820/1, I, pp. 130/1, ascribing both pictures to Morando, and transferring the signature and date from No. 735 to the Torbido; errors corrected in Vol. II (Appendice), p. 320. Persico does not record from whom Caldana bought the two pictures; but Cignaroli's annotation concerning the date makes it clear that they are indeed the same as the Carli ones. This receives further confirmation in the *Descrizione delle Opere di Eccellenti Maestri raccolte dal Sig. Francesco Caldana*, 1822 (cf. Pietro Sgulmero, *Il Trino-Trittico di S. Maria della Scala in Verona*, 1905, Nozze Simeoni-Colpi). No. 124 of this 1822 Catalogue is 'Di Franc. Morando detto Cavazzola Veronese. S. Rocco, figura al naturale all'ombra d'un Albero con sovrastante Angelo,' with references to Vasari and Persico. The Torbido must be No. 120 of the catalogue, 'Di Paolo Morando detto Cavazzola. S. Sebastiano legato ad un albero,' with references to Persico, I, p. 131, and II, Appendix, p. 120 (wrongly for p. 320). (9) Recorded in the Bernasconi Collection by G. B. da Persico, *Verona e la sua Provincia*, 1838, p. 213; the date is confirmed in Bernasconi's communication in the Gallery archives.

777 THE VIRGIN AND CHILD, S. JOHN THE BAPTIST AND AN ANGEL

Signed: PAVLVS. / V (with abbreviation signifying *ver*).P̄.

Canvas, $29\frac{3}{4} \times 25\frac{1}{2}$ (0·755 × 0·645).

The picture has been somewhat rubbed and restored, but the faces of the Virgin, the Child and S. John are in good condition. The last two letters of *Paulus* in the signature have been retouched.

COPY: A copy by Lorenzo Muttoni is recorded.[1]

PROVENANCE: In the Portalupi Collection at Verona before 1836;[2] purchased from Conte Lodovico Portalupi, 1867.[3]

REPRODUCTION: *Illustrations, Italian Schools*, 1937, p. 240. *Plates, Earlier Italian Schools*, 1953, Vol. II, p. 302.

REFERENCES: (1) Diego Zannandreis, *Le Vite dei Pittori etc. Veronesi*, ed. Biadego, 1891, p. 98; it is not clear from what the author says who this Lorenzo Muttoni was. (2) Zannandreis, *loc. cit.*, with identifying description. The author was born in 1768 and died in 1836; Biadego in his introduction, p. xxii, says that the book was written *ca.* 1831/4. No. 777 was engraved when in the Portalupi Collection in (Aleardi), *Di Paolo Morando*, etc., 1853, Plate 21. (3) In the first edition of Crowe and Cavalcaselle, *Painting in North Italy*, I, 1871, p. 502,

No. 777 is confused with a picture now in the Verona Museum (ex-Bernasconi Collection); this confusion is corrected in the edition by Borenius, II, 1912, p. 210.

Domenico MORONE
ca. 1442(?)–after 1517

School of Verona. His age was declared as 13 in 1455/6, as 25 in 1465. R. Brenzoni, *Domenico Morone*, 1956, p. 3, thinks that he may have been born *ca.* 1438/9. Not very many of his works survive. The most important is the *Fight between the Gonzagas and the Buonaccolsi*, signed and dated 1494, formerly in the Crespi Collection and now at Mantua.

1211 SCENE AT A TOURNAMENT

The letters SPQ(R) on the banneret hanging from a trumpet. A banner with an eagle above the grand stand.

1212 SCENE AT A TOURNAMENT

Each, spruce,[1] painted surface, $17\frac{7}{8} \times 19\frac{3}{8}$ (0.455×0.49); painted up to the edges all round.

No. 1211 is in fairly pure state, but is a good deal worn and cracked; No. 1212 is less well preserved.

The setting of the two pictures is the same; the subjects are probably merely fanciful. The pictures may have come from a *cassone*.

The authorship seems clearly the same as that of the Gonzaga-Buonaccolsi Fight, signed and dated 1494, at Mantua.[2] The difference in style and quality between these three pictures and all others assigned to Domenico Morone is somewhat mysterious; Berenson[3] suggests a temporary influence of Gentile Bellini.

From the costume, Nos. 1211/2 may be dated fairly precisely *ca.* 1490.[4]

PROVENANCE: Purchased without attribution from Guggenheim, Venice, by J. P. Richter,[5] from whom purchased, Walker Fund, 1886.

REPRODUCTIONS: *Illustrations, Italian Schools*, 1937, p. 246. *Plates, Earlier Italian Schools*, 1953, Vol. II, pp. 303–304.

REFERENCES: **(1)** Letter from B. J. Rendle, of the Forest Products Research Laboratory, in the Gallery archives. **(2)** R. Longhi in *Arte Veneta*, 1947, pp. 188 ff., ascribes Nos. 1211/2 to Carpaccio. But comparison with the picture at Mantua seems to show that the attribution of Nos. 1211/2 to Domenico Morone is right, unless indeed the authorship of that picture is put in question; and the compiler fails to see any close connection with the sure works of Carpaccio. The attribution to Carpaccio is, nevertheless, accepted as very plausible by T. Pignatti, *Carpaccio*, 1958, p. 17, who goes on to say that the banner in the two pictures shows the black eagle of the arms of the House of Este. What is shown is a single-headed black eagle on a red banner; this does not suit Este. Pallucchini in *Arte Veneta*, 1951, p. 195, also inclines to accept the attribution to Carpaccio. Fiocco, *Carpaccio*, 1958, pp. 8 and 36, rejects this attribution, and thinks rather of the style of Ercole de' Roberti. **(3)** Berenson, *Three Essays in*

Method, 1927, pp. 1 ff. (*Nine Pictures in Search of an Attribution*). (4) Note by
Stella M. Pearce in the Gallery archives. (5) J. P. Richter, oral communication;
cf. also *The Mond Collection*, 1910, I, p. 48.

Francesco MORONE
ca. 1471–1529

School of Verona. His age was given as 1 in 1472. He was the son and
pupil of Domenico Morone, and a friend of Gerolamo dai Libri. There
are many sure works.

285 THE VIRGIN AND CHILD

Wood, painted surface, $24\frac{1}{2} \times 17$ (0·625 × 0·435); painted up to the
edges all round.

Excellent state.

Acquired as by Pellegrino da San Daniele,[1] and ascribed by Mündler[2]
to Gerolamo dai Libri, by whom a replica at Verona was then supposed
to be. There is now agreement about the attribution to Francesco
Morone;[3] Wittkower[4] calls it very late work; Moschini associates it with
the S. Maria in Organo picture of 1503[5].

VERSION: The same group inverted is at Verona.[6] A *Virgin and Child* at Venice
corresponds closely in some details.[7]

PROVENANCE: Baron Francesco Galvagna Collection, Venice, by 1844;[8] purchased with the rest of the collection, 1855.

REPRODUCTION: *Illustrations, Italian Schools*, 1937, p. 247. *Plates, Earlier
Italian Schools*, 1953, Vol. II, p. 305.

REFERENCES: (1) Already so ascribed by Gianjacopo Fontana, *Manuale ad Uso
del Forestiere in Venezia*, 1847, p. 238 and *Venezia Monumentale Pittoresca*,
1850 (?), p. 168 of text volume. (2) Mündler's Diary, 31 January and 10 March,
1856. (3) This attribution did not appear in the National Gallery catalogue until
the edition of 1864; but already in his note-book of 1857, Eastlake remarked on
the stylistic similarity of No. 285 to Francesco Morone's signed picture in S.
Maria in Organo at Verona. (4) R. Wittkower in the *Jahrbuch für Kunstwissenschaft*, 1927, p. 204, Nos. 26 and 27. (5) Moschini in the *Bollettino d'Arte*,
1932/3, pp. 241 ff. (6) Venturi, *Storia*, Vol. VII, Part IV, Fig. 501. (7) Sandra
Moschini Marconi, *Gallerie dell'Accademia di Venezia*, Catalogue, XIV and XV
Centuries, 1955, No. 158, with reproduction. (8) Giulio Lecomte, *Venezia*, 1844,
p. 276, as Bernardino di S. Daniele. See also the references in note 1.

NARDO DI CIONE
active ca. 1343, died ca. 1365

Florentine School; a brother of Orcagna's. It is not sure if *Nardo* is an
abbreviation for *Bernardo* or *Lionardo*. He joined the Physicians' Guild
at Florence at a date not far from 1343. All attributions to him are based
on Ghiberti's statement that he painted some still extant frescoes in the
Strozzi Chapel in S. Maria Novella at Florence; later sources tend to

attribute these frescoes to Orcagna, but Ghiberti's statement appears to be quite reliable.

Literature: Thieme-Becker, s.v. Orcagna.

581 ALTARPIECE: THREE SAINTS

Left, a saint with a book. Centre, S. John the Baptist, with a scroll inscribed EGO.VOS.CLAMANTE / .IN.DEXERTO.PARATE. VIA. (Matthew iii, 3, etc.). Right, S. James Major.

Wood. A picture with triple arched top. Formerly framed with dividing colonnettes, so as to appear as three pictures; but the original gold background and painted floor are continuous. Sight size, $53\frac{3}{4} \times 57$ ($1\cdot365 \times 1\cdot45$) approx. The total size of the original wood, measured from the back, is $62\frac{3}{4} \times 58$ ($1\cdot595 \times 1\cdot475$), the top edge being in the shape of three triangles with their topmost points cut off.

Good condition. A little worn; the outlines of the heads are rather damaged, especially that of S. James. Framing new.

The left-hand saint was formerly called S. John the Evangelist; but he is not certainly characterized.

No. 581 is either a complete altarpiece, or the central part of an altarpiece, presumably dedicated to S. John the Baptist. It is indeed not unlikely that some predella scenes, and perhaps some small panels on the pilasters at the sides, or pinnacles at the top, are missing; it is less likely that large saints, similar to the three preserved, are missing from the left and right sides. A triptych mainly consisting of three figures of saints is admittedly rather unusual in early Italian painting, except in the Venetian School; but a triptych with S. Julian in the centre at San Gimignano is to some extent comparable.[1] It is in any case wrong to suppose, as has sometimes been done, that the three saints of No. 581 were three of the side panels of some large polyptych, perhaps with the Virgin and Child in the centre; as has been noted above, No. 581 has a continuous pictorial surface, and S. John the Baptist clearly forms a centre between the other two saints. A *S. Peter* in SS. Stefano e Cecilia at Florence has by several writers wrongly been supposed to be part of the same altarpiece as No. 581.[2]

The attribution of No. 581 to Nardo was made by Offner.[3] But see also his entry in *Corpus*, Section IV, Vol. II, 1960, pp. 37 ff.

PROVENANCE: Stated to be from the Hospital Church of SS. Giovanni e Niccolò, near Florence.[4] Purchased with other pictures from Lombardi and Baldi, Florence, 1857.[5]

REPRODUCTION: *Illustrations, Italian Schools*, 1937, p. 259. *Plates, Earlier Italian Schools*, 1953, Vol. II, p. 306 (colonnettes removed).

REFERENCES: (1) Van Marle, *Development of the Italian Schools of Painting*, Vol. IX, Fig. 39. (2) See Offner's rejection of this view in *The Burlington Magazine*, Vol. LXIII (1933), p. 83, with reproduction on p. 82, Plate IIIc. (3) R. Offner in *Art in America*, April, 1924, pp. 101/2; the same, *Studies in Florentine Painting*, 1927, pp. 97 ff. The attribution is accepted by H. D. Gronau, *Andrea Orcagna und Nardo di Cione*, 1937, p. 57. It seems so convincing that it is unnecessary to list here other, unsatisfactory attributions for No. 581. (4) National

Gallery Catalogue, 1858, presumably on information supplied to Eastlake. The place intended has not been identified. W. and E. Paatz, *Die Kirchen von Florenz*, II, 1941, p. 279, think that S. Giusto or Giovanni Battista della Calza at Florence may have been meant. This seems just possible, but not likely; for the church concerned, see Richa, *Notizie Istoriche delle Chiese Fiorentine*, Vol. IX, 1761, pp. 97 ff. (5) As Spinello, as which catalogued until 1906; thenceforward as Orcagna. (Crowe and Cavalcaselle, *History of Painting in Italy*, 1864, I, p. 440, and II, p. 18, had suggested School of Orcagna for it.) For details concerning the Lombardi-Baldi Collection, see Appendix I.

NICCOLAIO *See* Style of ORCAGNA, Nos. 569–578

NICCOLÒ di Buonaccorso
active 1372, died 1388

Sienese School. He joined the guild of painters at Siena at an undefined date (there is no authority for the year 1356, which has been claimed). A work signed and dated 1387 is referred to by Milanesi as in a bad state. No. 1109 below is the only other signed work.

1109 THE MARRIAGE OF THE VIRGIN: PANEL FROM A TRIPTYCH (?)

S. Joseph holds a leafy rod, from which a dove emerges. SS. Joachim and Anna behind, among the spectators. Signed: NICHOLAVS: BONACHVRSI : DE SENIS : ME PÑXT.

Reverse: a patterned design, without figures.

Wood. The size of the picture, cusped and rounded top, is $17 \times 10\frac{1}{2}$ (0.43×0.265); the total size including the framing is 20×13 (0.51×0.33). On the reverse, the size of the pattern, excluding the mouldings forming the framing, is $18\frac{3}{4} \times 11\frac{3}{4}$ (0.475×0.295).

The front is in good condition, except for the framework, which has been regilt. The reverse has been considerably damaged.

Two other panels clearly from the same series are known. One, *The Presentation of the Virgin*, was in the Hospital of S. Maria Nuova at Florence, and is now in the Uffizi;[1] the other, *The Coronation of the Virgin*, is in the Lehman Collection, New York.[2]

It is possible that No. 1109 was at one time in S. Maria Nuova, with the *Presentation*.[3] The fact that the painter adds *from Siena* to his name in the signature suggests that in any case it was probably painted for some destination other than Siena.

PROVENANCE: Doubtless identical with a picture (subject undescribed) seen by Fairfax Murray for sale in Florence in 1877;[4] purchased from C. Fairfax Murray, 1881.

REPRODUCTIONS: The front is reproduced in the *Illustrations, Italian Schools*, 1937, p. 253 and in the *Plates, Earlier Italian Schools*, 1953, Vol. II, p. 307; the back in *Paintings and Drawings on the Backs of National Gallery Pictures*, 1947, Plate 24.

REFERENCES: (1) English Catalogue of the Uffizi by E. Pieracini, 1910, p. 110, No. 14; size, 0·51 × 0·34. Photograph, Sopraintendenza, No. 25916. It is described (while still in S. Maria Nuova) by Cavalcaselle e Crowe, *Storia della Pittura in Italia*, III, 1885, p. 255. Its transference to the Uffizi is referred to by E. Ridolfi in *Le Gallerie Nazionali Italiane*, IV, 1899, pp. 169/70. It is certainly from the same series as No. 1109, and its back has a decoration exactly corresponding to that of No. 1109. (2) Lehman Catalogue, 1928, No. XXXVI, reproduced; size, $17\frac{5}{8} \times 10\frac{7}{16}$ (0·448 × 0·266), presumably excluding the frame. 2nd edition of the Catalogue of the Lehman Exhibition, Paris, 1957 (No. 298). It is also described and reproduced in the *Rassegna d'Arte*, 1914, pp. 98/9. It is presumed to be identical with an *Assumption*, stated by Langton Douglas to have been in the Sciarra Collection; see Crowe and Cavalcaselle, *History of Painting in Italy*, III, 1908, p. 133, note. (3) Ridolfi, *loc. cit.*, seems to imply this, but he may not have had positive information. (4) Letter of 6 December, 1877, in the Gallery archives.

NICCOLÒ DI LIBERATORE
active *ca.* 1456, died 1502

Niccolò di Liberatore of Foligno; called *Alunno* by a confusion of Vasari's. Active much at Foligno; also elsewhere in Umbria and in the Marches. Many signed and dated works exist. He may have been a pupil of his father-in-law, Pietro di Giovanni Mazzaforte. His earliest surviving work is a picture of 1457 or 1458 at Deruta; it seems to be copied from a Benozzo at Vienna (see the entry in this catalogue for Fiorenzo di Lorenzo, No. 1103). Later, Niccolò appears to have undergone some Venetian influence (Antonio Vivarini, Crivelli).

1107   TRIPTYCH: CHRIST ON THE CROSS, AND OTHER SCENES

Centre panel, Christ on the Cross; below, on one side, the Virgin supported by two Holy Women, on the other side S. John. S. Francis embraces the foot of the Cross, where the blood from Christ's feet has run down; the blood from His other wounds is caught in cups by angels. On the framing, just above the top of the Cross, are the letters, .I.N.R.I. Signed on a *cartellino*: .*NicolAi fulginatis*. | .*Mº.ccccº Lxxxvij*.

Left wing, in two divisions. In the upper, *The Agony in the Garden*; the cup offered by the angel contains the Cross, Spear and Sponge. SS. Peter, James and John are asleep in the foreground; behind, Judas and the soldiers approach. In the lower division, *The Way to Calvary*. The Virgin, accompanied by two Holy Women, is helping Christ to support the Cross. The two Thieves are in front.

Right wing, in two divisions. In the upper, *The Resurrection*. In the lower, *Mourning over the Dead Christ*; the body of Christ is mourned over by the Virgin and S. John, at the foot of the Cross marked .I.N.R.I.

The frame, which is original, has a pediment. The base of the pediment is painted on the front with two swags, and at the sides with a simple circular design (the one on the right mostly destroyed). In the triangular space above, in relief, is *yhs* within a sun, under a crown.

Reverses of the Wings. Simple painted framework, and painted marbling (red and green), in areas corresponding closely with the divisions on the fronts of the wings.

Wood. Central panel, painted surface, $36\frac{1}{4} \times 22\frac{3}{4}$ ($0 \cdot 92 \times 0 \cdot 575$); including the frame-mouldings surrounding this panel, $39\frac{1}{4} \times 25\frac{3}{4}$ ($1 \cdot 00 \times 0 \cdot 655$). Scenes on the wings, each, painted surface, $17 \times 9\frac{3}{4}$ ($0 \cdot 43 \times 0 \cdot 25$). Sizes of the wings including framing, (left) $39\frac{1}{4} \times 13$ ($1 \cdot 00 \times 0 \cdot 33$); (right) $39\frac{1}{4} \times 12\frac{3}{4}$ ($1 \cdot 00 \times 0 \cdot 325$). The height of the pediment over the central panel is ca. 18 in. ($0 \cdot 46$ m.); the top finial has been broken away, so the original height was about 2 in. more. The backs of the wings are completely covered with paint, and need no separate measurements.

Excellent state. Even much of the gilding on the frame, even the hinges of the wings appear to be original. The base on which the central panel stands at present is new; but some such base must have been made originally, since the central panel can be seen at the back to continue down to within $\frac{1}{2}$ in. of the bottom of the present base.

VARIANT: A *Resurrection* in the pinnacle of a polyptych in S. Niccolò at Foligno, apparently of 1492, is rather similar to the *Resurrection* here.[1]

PROVENANCE: From the convent of S. Chiara at Aquila; presumably painted for it, since it is obviously a Franciscan picture, and recorded there in 1848.[2] It disappeared from there during the Unification of Italy, in 1870.[3] Purchased from Signora Maria Gianzana, through Alessandro Castellani of Rome,[4] 1881.

REPRODUCTIONS: *Illustrations, Italian Schools*, 1937, p. 254 (all the scenes). *Plates, Earlier Italian Schools*, 1543, Vol. II, p. 308 (also including the pediment). Photographs exist of the pediment alone and of the backs of the wings.

REFERENCES: (1) Van Marle, *Development of the Italian Schools of Painting*, Vol. XIV, Fig. 33. For the date, see Adamo Rossi, *I Pittori di Foligno*, 1872, pp. 35/6. (2) A. Signorini, *L' Archeologo nell'Abruzzo*, 1848, p. 190. Crowe and Cavalcaselle, *History of Painting in Italy*, III, 1866, p. 132, also note it as there. (3) Rossi, *op. cit.*, p. 35. (4) Rather than from Alessandro Castellani; see Burton's letter of 1887, in the Gallery archives.

NICCOLÒ DI PIETRO GERINI
active 1368, died 1415

A painter active at Florence, Prato and Pisa. The records of his pictures and frescoes, some of which still exist, indicate a career of collaboration with other painters. It is possible to be sure that Niccolò's work was not of high quality, and that his style was without very marked peculiarities. For the theory that he was partly concerned in the S. Pier Maggiore Altarpiece, see the entry, Style of Orcagna, Nos. 569 sqq.; for an essay on what his style is believed to be, see R. Offner, *Studies in Florentine Painting*, 1927, pp. 83 ff.

Ascribed to NICCOLÒ DI PIETRO GERINI

579 TRIPTYCH: THE BAPTISM OF CHRIST, WITH SS. PETER AND PAUL

Centre, S. John baptizes Christ; the Almighty and the Holy Spirit above. At the top, an angel in a medallion. Left wing, S. Peter, with the (apparently old) inscription S.PETRUS.APL. Right wing, S. Paul, with the (apparently old) inscription SCS.PAULUS.APS. Predella in two divisions: left, the angel (S. Gabriel) appearing to S. Zacharias, and the birth of S. John the Baptist; right, S. John the Baptist decapitated, the Feast before Herod and Salome bringing the Baptist's head to Herodias. At the extreme ends of the predella, S. Benedict (left) and S. Romuald (right).

Wood. The size of the painted surface of the central scene is 63×30 ($1 \cdot 60 \times 0 \cdot 76$), cusped and pointed top; of the medallion, 5 ($0 \cdot 125$) in diameter; of the saints at the sides, each, $48\frac{1}{2} \times 14\frac{1}{2}$ ($1 \cdot 23 \times 0 \cdot 37$), cusped and pointed tops. Including the frame, but excluding the predella, the total size is $75 \times 67\frac{1}{2}$ ($1 \cdot 90 \times 1 \cdot 71$). The scenes of the predella are each $13\frac{1}{4} \times 26\frac{3}{4}$ ($0 \cdot 335 \times 0 \cdot 68$); the saints of the predella each $13\frac{1}{4} \times 4\frac{1}{2}$ ($0 \cdot 335 \times 0 \cdot 115$); all the corners being cut. The total size of the predella with its framing is $18\frac{3}{4} \times 78\frac{3}{4}$ ($0 \cdot 475 \times 2 \cdot 00$).

In good condition in general; obvious damages on Christ's body, etc., and along the bottom of the predella. The frame is in essentials old, but has been a good deal restored, and entirely regilt.

The predella panel with the Feast before Herod, etc., seems to be derived from a fresco by Giotto in the Peruzzi Chapel in S. Croce at Florence.[1]

No. 579 is a Camaldolese altarpiece, dedicated to S. John the Baptist, from which are missing pinnacles and probably pilasters with single saints down the sides. When it entered the Gallery, and previously when it was in the Lombardi-Baldi Collection at Florence, three pinnacles by Giovanni da Milano, No. 579A, were attached to it; nothing is known of when they were first added to it.[2]

When No. 579 entered the Gallery, there was recorded below the central compartment a half-obliterated inscription, to the effect that the picture was painted by order of Filippo Neroni in 1337 (?).[3] The only possible place for the inscription is the strip of the frame running along the bottom. This is now covered with new gold. Removal of some pieces of the gold revealed a sheet of iron. As the removal of the iron might have disrupted the whole altarpiece, it was thought best not to try, and the gold was fixed back again on top.

The Gallery catalogue maintained the date 1337 (with which was associated an attribution to Taddeo Gaddi) until 1863; thereafter, the date was changed to 1387.[4] The change may have been made to meet the wishes of Crowe and Cavalcaselle, who in 1864 published their preference on stylistic grounds for the year 1387 rather than 1337.[5] There is evidence that 1387 is right; see note 9.

There is a tendency nowadays to ascribe No. 579 to Niccolò di Pietro Gerini, whose œuvre is not too well defined. Uncertainty has also been expressed. Sirèn in 1904 called it Niccolò di Pietro Gerini with the collaboration of Lorenzo di Niccolò in the predella; in 1908 he called it Jacopo di Cione, while seeing in it much of Gerini too; in 1920 he called it Niccolò di Pietro Gerini or his studio, feeling then that no distinction between his autograph and studio productions was possible.[6] Khvoshinsky and Salmi call it Jacopo di Cione.[7] Jacopo di Cione is at present a name with little meaning;[8] so far as it has a meaning, the name seems misapplied to No. 579.

PROVENANCE: Apparently originally in the Angeli at Florence, and removed thence at an unknown date.[9] Stated to be from the Abbey del Sasso di Camaldoli.[10] Possibly what was meant is the Camaldolese Abbey of S. Giovanni Decollato del Sasso near Arezzo, for which No. 579 could have served as the high-altarpiece.[11] By 1845, in the Lombardi-Baldi Collection at Florence;[12] purchased thence with other pictures, 1857.[13]

REPRODUCTION: Illustrations, Italian Schools, 1937, p. 254 (without the predella). Plates, Earlier Italian Schools, 1953, Vol. II, pp. 309–310.

REFERENCES: (1) Van Marle, Development of the Italian Schools of Painting, Vol. III, Fig. 84. (2) Already noted as attached in a Lombardi-Baldi Catalogue (Collection de Tableaux Anciens, etc.), No. 11; the catalogue is not dated, but the copy in the Uffizi Library is claimed to be of 1845. (3) N.G. Catalogue, 1858, as Taddeo Gaddi (text not given); for the location, see the N.G. Report for 1858. Scharf in April/May, 1858, thus copied the inscription: CCCXXII. DOMN . PHILIPP' NERONIS . FECIT . FIERI . HANC . . . . (C?)E AGEELE . MA . . . . SVE . & SUORUM MON. (Scharf sketchbooks, No. 51, f. 52r, in the National Portrait Gallery; photograph in the National Gallery archives). (4) Some confusion about the time at which the date 1337 was changed to 1387 is caused by the N.G. MS. Catalogue and the N.G. Report for 1858, both of which give 1387. The entry in the MS. Catalogue is perhaps of 1858. The N.G. Report for 1858 was not printed until 1867. No record has been found at the Gallery of completing the obliteration of the inscription. (5) Crowe and Cavalcaselle, History of Painting in Italy, 1864, I, p. 367. (6) Sirèn in L'Arte, 1904, p. 338; Sirèn, Giottino, 1908, pp. 79 and 90; Sirèn in Thieme-Becker, s.v. Gerini. (7) Basile Khvoshinsky and Mario Salmi, I Pittori Toscani, II, I Fiorentini del Trecento, 1914, p. 32. The authors' reference to this picture on p. 56 was by mistake; see their Errata-Corrige. (8) See the entry, Style of Orcagna, Nos. 569 sqq. (9) The evidence for the original location is given by W. Cohn in the Rivista d'Arte, 1956, pp. 66/7. Don Filippo di Nerone Stoldi was a monk at the Angeli from 1357 to 1409. His mother Angiola and his stepbrother Federigo left property to the Angeli, to be sold, and the money to be used for the construction of a chapel dedicated to S. John the Baptist; this chapel was built and furnished after the death of Federigo in 1383, with a dedication to S. Giovanni Decollato, and the first mass was said in it in 1387. These facts, so far as one can judge from the doubtful records of the inscription on the picture, make it highly probable that No. 579 was the altarpiece of the Stoldi Chapel in the Angeli. It may be added (a) that Farulli (Istoria Cronologica . . . degli Angioli di Firenze, 1710, p. 22) mentions also Filippo di Nerone Alberti as a monk at the Angeli, but this may be a mistake for Filippo di Nerozzo (L. Passerini, Gli Alberti, 1869, Vol. I, Tav. III); and (b) that the Stoldi Chapel appears clearly to have been distinct from one of 1387/8, dedicated to S. Jacopo e S. Giovanni Decollato, founded by Bernardo di Cino de' Nobili (Richa, Notizie Istoriche delle Chiese Fiorentine, Vol. VIII, 1759, pp. 148/9, 166). (10) N.G. 1858 Catalogue, s.v. Taddeo Gaddi. (11) A mention of this Abbey is made by Farulli, op. cit., 1710, p. 196; also by Richa, op. cit., Vol. VIII, 1759, p. 159. This Abbey, however, appears to have contained black Benedictines, and although connected with the Camaldolese not to have become itself Camaldolese until 1413/4. See G. B. Mittarelli and A. Costadoni, Annales Camaldulenses, V, 1760, pp. 308/9 and VI, 1760, p. 264. Further, E. Repetti, Dizionario Geografico Fisico Storico della Toscana, V, 1843, p. 202, says that it was by then a ruin; a ruin is an unlikely place for No. 579 to come from, and it is not known at what date the Abbey was still intact. (12) No. 11 of a Lombardi-Baldi Catalogue, not dated, but the copy in the Uffizi Library is claimed to be of 1845. (13) For the history of the Lombardi-Baldi Collection, see Appendix I.

See also Style of ORCAGNA, Nos. 569–578

ANDREA DI CIONE, called ORCAGNA
active ca. 1343, died 1368/9

Florentine painter, sculptor and architect; the name *Orcagna* appears to be a corruption of *Arcangelo*. He matriculated with the Physicians *ca.* 1343; cf. Carl Frey, *Die Loggia dei Lanzi*, 1885, pp. 101 ff. and 332/3, and Rufus Graves Mather in *L'Arte*, 1936, p. 54 and Fig. 4. A date of birth *ca.* 1308 is sometimes accepted on the authority of Vasari, who says that he lived for sixty years; but as Vasari wrongly gives his date of death as 1389, the matter may be considered uncertain. For the true date of death, see *L'Arte*, 1938, p. 352, where it is given as 1368; in the plate of the document opposite p. 351, the year appears rather to be 1369, and Baldinucci (*Notizie*, 1845 edition, i, p. 259) also read 1369 in this passage, without indeed understanding what the date signified.

For Orcagna's work in fresco, the student may consult the catalogue of the *II Mostra di Affreschi Staccati*, Florence, 1958, Nos. 16–21 and 101–135. The key to his style in pictures is an altarpiece in S. Maria Novella at Florence, which he contracted to paint in 20 months some time in 1354; there was however, a little delay in the execution, the picture being signed and dated 1357. Less important is a *S. Matthew* in the Uffizi; Orcagna contracted to paint it in September, 1367, but as he was sick, his brother Jacopo di Cione promised in August, 1368, to finish it, so that the extent of Orcagna's participation is uncertain.

Orcagna was the first painter of his time at Florence. The Orcagnesques, that is other painters working in a similar style whether consciously imitated from Orcagna or not, are hard to differentiate; they sometimes collaborated, their stylistic peculiarities are often weakly marked, and the documents concerning their works are confusing and insufficient. A general heading *Style of Orcagna* is therefore in many cases more justifiable than attributions to individual names.

Style of ORCAGNA

569 ALTARPIECE: THE CORONATION OF THE VIRGIN, WITH ADORING SAINTS

Centre panel, Christ crowns the Virgin Mary; music-making angels below.

Left panel, five rows of saints, A–E, numbered from right to left: A. 1. S. Peter; on his knee is the model of a church, which stands for the Church, and also for S. Pier Maggiore at Florence, where No. 569 formed part of the high-altarpiece. In the tympanum over the main entrance of the model-church are a Cross and crossed keys. 2. S. Bartholomew. 3. S. Stephen. B. 1. S. John the Evangelist, holding a book with a quotation reduced from *Revelation* vii, 9; *Vjdi tur/bam ma/gnā quaz / dinumeā/re nemo / poterat. / ex omībus / gentibus / stantes an/te thronū / &in conspectu* (con abbr.)/*agni amicti.* 3. S. Miniato(?). 4. S. Zenobius (?). 5. S. Francis. 6. The Magdalen, her robe embroidered with X̄P̄S and ĪH̄S. C. 1. S. Philip. 3. S. Blaise. 4. S. Gregory. 5. S. Benedict. 6. S. Lucy. D. 2. S. Luke (?). 4. S. Ambrose (?). 5. One of the Magi (?). E. 1 and 2. The two remaining Magi (?). 3. S. Reparata (?).

Right panel, five rows of saints, A–E, numbered from left to right: A. 1. S. Paul, holding a book with a quotation from II *Corinthians* iii, 18: *Nos ōs / reuelata / facie glo/riam do/mini spe/culantes / in eadem / ymagi/nē trans/formam' / a clarita/te in cla/ritatem / tanquā.* 2. S. Matthew, holding a book with a fragment from his gospel, i, 1: *Libē / intio / ihu x / filij d / filij a/braaz.* 3. S. Lawrence. B. 1. S. John the Baptist. 3. S. Julian (?). 4. S. Nicholas. 5. S. Dominic. 6. S. Catherine of Alexandria. C. 1. S. James the Greater. 3. S. Ivo of Brittany (?). 4. S. Bernard (?). 5. S. Anthony Abbot. 6. S. Agnes. D. 2. S. Mark (?). 4. S. Augustine (?). 5. S. Jerome. 6. S. Scholastica. E. 3. S. Ursula (?).

Wood. Central panel, pointed top, painted surface, $81\frac{1}{2} \times 44\frac{3}{4}$ ($2 \cdot 065 \times 1 \cdot 135$); side panels, with twin pointed tops, each, painted surface, $66\frac{1}{2} \times 44\frac{1}{2}$ ($1 \cdot 69 \times 1 \cdot 13$). The painted parts extend to the edges of the panels, except along the bottom.

See the commentary to No. 578 below.

570   THE TRINITY (PANEL FROM AN ALTARPIECE)

Wood, irregular top, painted surface, $34\frac{1}{4} \times 15\frac{3}{4}$ ($0 \cdot 87 \times 0 \cdot 40$); the painted parts of this picture and of all the subsequent pictures up to No. 578 continue to the edges of the panels.

See the commentary to No. 578 below.

571   SERAPHIM, CHERUBIM AND ANGELS ADORING (PANEL FROM AN ALTARPIECE)

Wood, irregular top, painted surface, $34\frac{1}{4} \times 14\frac{3}{4}$ ($0 \cdot 87 \times 0 \cdot 375$).

See the commentary to No. 578 below.

572   SERAPHIM, CHERUBIM AND ANGELS ADORING (PANEL FROM AN ALTARPIECE)

Wood, irregular top, painted surface, $34\frac{1}{4} \times 14\frac{3}{4}$ ($0 \cdot 87 \times 0 \cdot 375$).

See the commentary to No. 578 below.

573   THE ADORATION OF THE SHEPHERDS (PANEL FROM
      AN ALTARPIECE)

The announcement to the shepherds is in the background.
For the size and commentary, see No. 578 below.

574   THE ADORATION OF THE KINGS (PANEL FROM AN
      ALTARPIECE)

For the size and commentary, see No. 578 below.

575   THE RESURRECTION (PANEL FROM AN ALTARPIECE)

The letters S P Q R occur on two of the soldiers' shields.
For the size and commentary, see No. 578 below.

576   THE MARIES AT THE SEPULCHRE (PANEL FROM AN
      ALTARPIECE)

For the size and commentary, see No. 578 below.

577   THE ASCENSION (PANEL FROM AN ALTARPIECE)

For the size and commentary, see No. 578 below.

578   PENTECOST (PANEL FROM AN ALTARPIECE)

Above, the Holy Ghost descends upon the Virgin and the assembled
apostles; below, the people marvel that each man hears his own language
spoken.

Nos. 573/578, wood, irregular tops, each, painted surface, $37\frac{1}{2} \times 19\frac{1}{2}$
(0.95×0.49).

Nos. 569/578 are in good condition for pictures of the fourteenth
century, despite some obvious blemishes. In the side panels of No. 569,
many of the faces are to a varying degree worn and restored; of the
smaller panels, No. 570 is perhaps the most damaged. The surface of
the paint suffers somewhat in effect from uneven cleaning. Most of the
gold is old, except in Nos. 570 and 576; in those two pictures, the whole
backgrounds, including God the Father's crown in No. 570, are new.
In Nos. 571 and 572, about 4 or $4\frac{1}{2}$ in. at the tops (10 or 11 cm.) are new
additions; and the triangular pieces of gold right and left near the
bottom of the two pictures are also new. In Nos. 573, 574, 575, 577 and
578, a couple of inches at the tops are new.

In a good many cases, the outlines of the painted figures do not precisely correspond with the incised outlines for them. The most prominent *pentimento* is in the angel's wing or drapery on the right of No. 572,
which was intended to come further down.

These pictures come from S. Pier Maggiore at Florence, as will be
explained presently.

It is an iconographical oddity in No. 569 that the Magi are apparently
among the groups of adoring saints. As for the dubious identifications of

saints, the patrons of Florence are likely to appear in a picture such as this, which may justify the suggestions for SS. Zenobius, Miniato and Reparata. S. Reparata ought properly to appear as a martyr; the figure here identified as her has no palm, but a figure apparently accepted as S. Reparata in Daddi's polyptych in the Uffizi has no palm either.[1] SS. Mark and Luke may be expected, since the two other Evangelists are present; the figures identified hold pens and correspond well enough with the types traditional for these saints. SS. Ambrose and Augustine are suggested since SS. Gregory and Jerome are certainly present, and the four figures often appear together as the four Doctors of the Church. S. Blaise is certainly identifiable, and later on at least the church of S. Pier Maggiore possessed an important relic of this saint; S. Ursula is dubiously identified, since (later on, at least) the head of one of her companions was another prized relic.[2] S. Julian was a very popular saint at Florence at the time of this picture, and is likely to be Right Panel, B 3, as suggested; otherwise, he might be Right Panel, E 2. S. Ivo is suggested on comparison with a figure with the name inscribed in a *Coronation of the Virgin* by 'Giovanni del Ponte' in the Florentine Academy (No. 458).[3]

In No. 574, it is an iconographical caprice that the Child should be handing the first King's gift to S. Joseph; but in a Giotto studio piece in New York, for instance, S. Joseph is already holding the gift. The scene in No. 576 is according to Luke xxiv, 1 sqq. Meiss[4] claims that the composition of No. 578 is derived from Andrea da Firenze's fresco of the subject in the Spanish Chapel at S. Maria Novella, Florence; he also compares the Christ hovering above the tomb in No. 575 with Andrea da Firenze's treatment of the subject.

In spite of a break in the provenance, it cannot be doubted that Nos. 569/578 are the principal remains of the high altarpiece of S. Pier Maggiore at Florence, a church belonging to Benedictine nuns. They were ascribed by Vasari[5] to Orcagna himself, and they are indeed fairly closely in his style; but one cannot suppose that they contain anything whatever of Orcagna's own work.

The documents[6] concerning the altarpiece are very incomplete, but show that it was begun apparently in November, 1370 (after Orcagna's death), and finished at the end of 1371 or soon after. The painter Niccolaio is mentioned in connection with it, also Matteo di Pacino; the documents preserved do not prove that no other painter took part in it.

In November, 1370, Niccolaio was employed to design the picture (*disegnare la tavola*); he was paid a sum that is substantial, but probably less than one-tenth of the total cost of an altarpiece such as this. His work continued for 14 working days over a period of three weeks; the document does not certainly imply that the designing was then finished. It has been suggested[7] that Niccolaio merely designed some elaborate framework for the altarpiece, and that the painter of the pictures had begun his own part of the work independently several months before; but Niccolaio is described as a painter, and is mentioned as the designer of the picture, not the frame. It would seem therefore most unlikely that his work was confined to the frame, or even to the mere gilding of the pictures; he would appear also to have drawn in the outlines of the compositions, either on cartoons or on the panels themselves, and this would possibly have fixed some of the morphological details now visible[8] It is not recorded if it was Niccolaio or someone else who thereafter executed the paintings.

Niccolaio seems to have had an important, and possibly the principal, part in producing the pictures. He may well be identical with the Niccholaio who, in partnership with a certain Simone, contracted to paint a picture for the Florentine Mint, now in the Accademia at Florence.[9] In October, 1372, Simone and Niccholaio were paid for part of this work, but they did not finish it, and in October, 1373, Jacobo Cini was paid for completing it. These two payments cover the whole work of painting that picture; the money that Simone and Niccholaio received is practically equal to what Jacobo Cini received. The style of that picture, which is also a *Coronation of the Virgin*, is very close indeed to that of No. 569; it is not unreasonable to suppose that the two pictures each contain a substantial amount of work by the same Niccolaio. The picture at Florence is on a larger scale than No. 569, so there is no question of the same cartoons having been used for the figures in the two pictures that correspond.

Niccolaio is often assumed to be Niccolò di Pietro Gerini. It is not known with certainty what Gerini's style was like in 1370; the characteristics, such as they are, of his later style are not apparent in Nos. 569/78. Another possible, but even more doubtful, candidate would be Niccolò di Tommaso. His name, unlike Gerini's, does indeed appear in the form Niccolaio in the list of the Florentine Company of S. Luke;[10] his only authenticated work, on the other hand, is a triptych in S. Antonio Abate at Naples, signed and dated 1371 (recently cleaned), which offers little resemblance to Nos. 569/78.[11] It is very doubtful if the National Gallery pictures can be ascribed, even in part, to the same hand as the Naples triptych; it is certain that some other pictures, which have on comparison with it been attributed to Niccolò di Tommaso, differ considerably.[12]

The other painter mentioned in the extant documents concerning Nos. 569/78 is Matteo di Pacino.[13] It is recorded that a *colmo* was removed from his house some time during 1370; it is not stated, but it appears likely, that he had been painting this *colmo*. One picture is known, signed and dated 1360, by Matteo di Pacino;[14] it is in an Orcagnesque style, and a good deal weaker than any part of Nos. 569/78, but it is possible that, working ten years later on another man's design, he might have produced some parts of the present altarpiece.[15]

It is usual in modern criticism to ascribe Nos. 569/78 in great part or entirely to Orcagna's brother, Jacopo di Cione.[16] It is very difficult to be sure what characteristics of style Jacopo di Cione had. On the one hand, he promised in August, 1368, to finish a *S. Matthew* (now in the Uffizi), which Orcagna had contracted to paint in September, 1367;[17] it is not known how much Orcagna had done, nor (since he was a sick man) if he had done it himself, nor indeed what Orcagna's style was like in 1367/8, nor even if Jacopo di Cione did finish the picture, nor at what date. It would nevertheless seem probable that the scenes of S. Matthew's legend in this picture, which appear very unlike Orcagna's work, are due to Jacopo di Cione; the style of these scenes appears very similar to that of *The Crucifixion*, No. 1468 below. Secondly, the already mentioned picture for the Florentine Mint was finished in 1373 by Jacobo Cini, often identified as Jacopo di Cione.[18] It has already been suggested that this picture and Nos. 569/78 have some work by Niccolaio in common; it is generally assumed, since they are so like, that they were also both executed in part by Jacopo di Cione. So far as the National Gallery is concerned, there would thus seem some reason for ascribing No. 1468 below to Jacopo di Cione, and Nos. 569/78 to Jacopo di Cione in part; unfortunately a comparison of the originals, while confirming that they are quite closely alike, does not confirm that they are in part certainly by the same hand. It seems therefore prudent not to associate Jacopo di Cione's name either with No. 1468 or with Nos. 569/78; but it should be repeated that the existing documents concerning Nos. 569/78 do not exclude that he executed part or even all of them. It is nevertheless probable that the design at least is due to one Niccolaio, who cannot be certainly identified; and it is possible that some of the painting was done by Matteo di Pacino.

There are no ancient records of how Nos. 569/78 were arranged, and the original frame is missing. The three panels of the Coronation and adoring saints are obviously the main part; H. D. Gronau and R. Offner[19] have given strong reasons for believing that the six pictures Nos. 573/8 formed the upper tier, with Nos. 570/2 as pinnacles above. The documents mention that there was a predella ; the identification of most of this by Gronau and then by Offner has recently been completed by Klara Steinweg.[20] The pictures are in the Rhode Island School of Design at Providence, in the J. G. Johnson Collection at Philadelphia, three in the Vatican (one substantially cut), and a fragment until recently in the von Quast Collection at Radensleben and now in the Thyssen-Bornemisza Collection at Lugano.[21] These six panels contain stories of S. Peter, as they should for the predella of the high-altarpiece of a church dedicated to that saint,[22] and the tooling of the gold on them is quite closely similar to that of Nos. 569/78; the identification therefore seems beyond reasonable doubt. Offner more dubiously also suggested that six small figures of saints in the van Gelder and Hutton Collections came from the pilasters of the altarpiece;[23] but this is not convincing.

PROVENANCE: Painted to be the high-altarpiece of S. Pier Maggiore at Florence, it was after a time removed to the chapel belonging to the della Rena family.[24] The church was destroyed following an accident in 1783.[25] Although there is no known reason to suppose that the della Rena family had commissioned the picture, they appear to have taken it away with them when their chapel ceased to exist, and it is stated that the pictures thereafter passed by inheritance into the possession of the Marchese Roberto Pucci.[26] Acquired from him in 1846 by Francesco Lombardi and Ugo Baldi;[27] purchased with most of the rest of the Lombardi-Baldi Collection, Florence, 1857.[28]

REPRODUCTIONS: *Illustrations, Italian Schools*, 1937, pp. 255–258. *Plates, Earlier Italian Schools*, 1953, Vol. II, pp. 311–322.

REFERENCES: (1) R. Offner, *Corpus of Florentine Painting*, Section III, Vol. III, 1930, Plate XIV[15]. (2) G. Richa, *Notizie Istoriche delle Chiese Fiorentine*, I, 1754, p. 138. (3) Van Marle, *Development of the Italian Schools of Painting*, Vol. IX, 1927, Fig. 46. A figure on Rossello di Jacopo Franchi's altarpiece, No. 8460 of the Academy of Florence, probably also represents S. Ivo. (4) M. Meiss, *Painting in Florence and Siena after the Black Death*, 1951, pp. 33, 39. (5) Vasari, ed. Milanesi, I, p. 595. (6) The texts are printed by O. Sirèn, *Giottino*, 1908, pp. 100/1, and by H. D. Gronau in *The Burlington Magazine*, Vol. LXXXVI (1945), p. 144. (7) H. D. Gronau, *loc. cit.*, p. 140. (8) R. Offner in *Studies, Museum of Art*, Rhode Island School of Design, 1947, pp. 59/61, interprets the meaning of the documents much as is suggested in the text here, but thinks that Niccolaio's drawings did not do more than fix the compositions; the picture, according to Offner (*loc. cit.*, p. 53), is, as we see it, essentially a Jacopo di Cione, although it 'cannot conceal an admixture of hands.' (9) The documents are printed by Sirèn, *op. cit.*, pp. 101/2. (10) Gualandi, *Memorie . . . risguardanti le Belle Arti*, VI, 1845, p. 186: *Niccolaio masi dipintore* (died?) 1405, and *Niccholo di piero dipintore* (died?) 1414. (11) R. Offner, *Studies in Florentine Painting*, 1927, Fig. 10 (before cleaning), between pp. 126 and 127. (12) Offner, *op. cit.*, pp. 109 ff. For Berenson's mention of Niccolò di Tommaso in connection with Nos. 569, etc., see note 16. (13) Died 1374; see *L'Arte*, 1938, Fig. 2 opp. p. 352. (14) Reproduced by A. Muñoz, *Pièces de Choix de la Collection du Comte Grégoire Stroganoff*, II, 1911, Fig. VI, and by Berenson in *Dedalo*, 1931, p. 985. (15) There are indeed slight divergencies of style between various parts of Nos. 569/78; and it is a curious fact that the saints who appear both in the large panels and in the small scenes differ rather markedly in feature. H. D. Gronau (*loc. cit.*) has stated that *colmo* means one of the top parts of Nos. 569/78. This may be so; but it could also mean one of the main parts, if one may judge from the use of the word *colmus* in a document of 1372 concerning the Abbey of Passignano (Milanesi, *Documenti per la Storia dell'Arte Senese*, I, 1854, pp. 269/71). (16) E.g. Sirèn, *op. cit.*, p. 80, as probably mostly by Jacopo di Cione; Berenson, 1932 Lists, as probably planned by Andrea (Orcagna) and executed by Jacopo di Cione with the aid of Niccolò di Tommaso and Niccolò di Pietro (Gerini); H. D. Gronau, *loc. cit.*, p. 140, as Jacopo di Cione assisted; Gronau's views as previously expressed were approved by Offner in *The Burlington Magazine*, Vol. LXIII (1933), p. 84. R. Offner in *Studies, Museum of Art*, Rhode Island School of Design, 1947, pp. 43 ff. Klara Steinweg in *Rendiconti della Pontificia Accademia Romana di Archeologia*, Vols. XXX–XXXI, 1957/9, pp. 231 ff., makes further comments on the style. (17) The documents are printed by Sirèn, *op. cit.*, pp. 99/100. For an analysis of this picture, see H. D. Gronau, *Andrea Orcagna und Nardo di Cione*, 1937, pp. 23 ff. (18) A Sienese painter Jacopo di Cino was in existence at the right time; he seems most unlikely. (19) H. D. Gronau, *loc cit.*, p. 143; one could also compare the structure of the Rinuccini altarpiece (Van Marle, *op. cit.*, III, 1924, Fig. 294). Van Marle, *ib.*, pp. 497 and 618, obscurely suggests that a *Death and Assumption of the Virgin*, which he attributes to Niccolò di Pietro Gerini, is from the same ensemble. Although the provenance of Nos. 569/78 is not in the strictest sense proved, it would be reckless to dispute it, and accepting it means that Nos. 569/78 belong to one and the same ensemble, which indeed has not been doubted. It would nevertheless have been difficult to associate all the panels together, if they had been scattered and the provenance forgotten; thus, even in Nos. 573/8, which manifestly form a series, there are some variations in the halo patterns, and the differences in the tooling between the large and the small panels are considerable. But the reconstruction by H. D. Gronau and R. Offner appears reasonable, and it seems undesirable to suppose either that Nos. 569/78 come from more than one altarpiece, or that other small scenes of the lives of the Virgin or of Christ are missing. (20) H. D. Gronau, *loc. cit.*, pp. 140 ff., with reproductions of four panels. R. Offner, *loc. cit.*, Figs. 1

and 3–6. Steinweg, *loc. cit.* in note 16, with reproductions of all six. (21) Schloss Rohoncz Collection, Catalogue, 1958, No. 311a. (22) Steinweg, *loc. cit.*, comments on the iconographical programme. (23) R. Offner, *loc. cit.*, Figs. 13A, 13B. (24) Mentioned in Vasari's 2nd edition; ed. Milanesi, I, p. 595. F. Bocchi, enlarged by G. Cinelli, *Le Bellezze della Città di Firenze*, 1677, pp. 353/4; Richa, as in note 2, p. 145. Both these writers state that the picture had been the high-altarpiece, which indeed the character of the picture and of the documents confirms. The date of its removal from the high altar has not been established, but it may have been taken away when Desiderio da Settignano's ciborium was set up. It was pretty clearly no longer on the high altar in the middle of the sixteenth century; apart from Vasari's not very clear references, see a letter of 1566 quoted by F. Moisè, *Santa Croce di Firenze*, 1845, p. 124. (25) (Follini and Rastrelli), *Firenze Antica e Moderna*, III, 1791, p. 375, and VIII, 1802, p. 335. (26) National Gallery Catalogue, 1859, presumably on information supplied to Eastlake. It is the break in the provenance at this point that justifies the statement in note 19 that the provenance is not in the strictest sense proved; but there seems to be no justification for disputing it. Follini and Rastrelli, *Firenze Antica e Moderna*, V, 1794, p. 99, say that at the time of the ruin of S. Piero Maggiore the pictures were taken away by the owners of the chapels, or sold. (27) Vasari, ed. Milanesi, I, p. 595; and N.G. MS. Catalogue. (28) For the history of the Lombardi-Baldi Collection, see Appendix I.

1468 SMALL ALTARPIECE: THE CRUCIFIXION

In the centre, Christ hangs on the Cross, marked .$\overline{\text{I}}.\overline{\text{N}}.\overline{\text{R}}.\overline{\text{Y}}$. Angels receive in basins the blood from the Wounds in His hands and side. Left, the good thief (S. Dismas); he is haloed, and two angels carry up his soul to heaven. Right, the bad thief (Gestas); two devils hold a brazier (?) above his head. In the foreground, centre, the Virgin is supported by the Magdalen and three other Maries; S. John stands near. Left, the soldiers casting lots, apparently. Right, various figures, including a soldier with a shield marked S.P.Q.R. A little behind is a man with the Sponge at the end of a pole, and various groups of soldiers on horseback, some with S.P.Q.R. on their jerkins or the banners attached to their spears. The rider with a spear near the Cross, with his right hand to his mouth, may be meant for S. Longinus. A man towards the right is breaking the legs of the bad thief.

Left and right of this scene are compartments one above the other, with saints. Left, SS. John the Baptist and Paul; right, SS. James the Greater and Bartholomew.

The predella contains five roundels, set in decorative raised work. From left to right: (1) A female saint with a red cross and a book. (2) S. Bernard, holding a book inscribed: *Dic mat' | domini si | in ierusalē | eras quā|do captus | fuit filiuˢ | tuus & uī|tus. Cui | illa R'it. | In ierusa|lem erā | quādo | hoc aud*(i)*|ui. & gres*(su). (3) The Virgin and Child. (4) S. Anthony Abbot (?), in white, with book, crutch and black hog (?). (5) S. Catherine of Alexandria, with wheel, crown and palm.

At the top are seven canopied cusps, the insides painted blue with stars. Two pilasters at the sides are ornamented with decorative raised work and with shields (indecipherable remains of blue and red).

Wood. Picture of the Crucifixion, painted surface, cusped top, $42\frac{1}{2} \times 33$ ($1\cdot08 \times 0\cdot84$); measured to the top of the painted surface in the central cusp, which is higher than the others. S. John the Baptist, painted surface, pointed top, $19\frac{1}{2} \times 5\frac{1}{8}$ (0.495×0.13); S. Paul, painted surface, pointed top, $20\frac{1}{4} \times 5\frac{1}{8}$ (0.515×0.13); S. James, painted surface, pointed top, $20 \times 4\frac{7}{8}$ (0.505×0.125); S. Bartholomew, painted surface, pointed top, $20 \times 4\frac{7}{8}$ (0.505×0.125). There are simple mouldings, not included in the above measurements, separating these five compartments. The diameter of the roundels in the predella is in each case $5\frac{7}{8}$ (0.15). For the whole altarpiece, including the framing, the greatest height is $60\frac{1}{2}$ (1.54), the greatest width $54\frac{1}{2}$ (1.385).

Cleaned in 1955/6. There are various damages, e.g. in the head of the white horse next the Cross; but in general the altarpiece is very well preserved. Most of the gold is original; the part most restored is on the canopies. The predella is on a separate piece of wood, attached to the main panel, which continues behind. The pilasters are on separate pieces of wood from the main panel. They appear to be not only original, but in their correct position. One change carried out during the cleaning was the removal of a strip of wood about 3 cm. high, that ran along the bottom of the central panel and of the compartments with S. Paul and S. Bartholomew; the rocky edge to the ground in *The Crucifixion* is now clearly visible.

The inscription on the book held by S. Bernard is from the *Liber de Passione Christi et doloribus et planctibus matris ejus*, ascribed to S. Bernard. The full text runs: 'Dic mihi si in Jerusalem eras quando fuit captus filius tuus, et vinctus, et ductus, ad Annam tractus? At illa: in Jerusalem eram, quando hoc audivi, et gressu quo potui ad Dominum meum flens perveni.'[1] The same text is quoted on *The Vision of S. Bernard* ascribed to Orcagna and others, in the Academy at Florence.[2]

From the rather prominent position of S. Bernard, No. 1468 may perhaps have had a Cistercian destination. It is rather small to have been over the altar of a chapel; it could have been in some sacristy, or in a private oratory.

It is usual in modern criticism to ascribe No. 1468 to Jacopo di Cione,[3] a brother of Orcagna's. That attribution may be correct; but it is explained in the entry for Nos. 569/78 above why it is undesirable, in the present state of knowledge, to make use of Jacopo's name. It is noted in that entry that No. 1468 is very close in style to the scenes in the S. Matthew altarpiece in the Uffizi.

PROVENANCE: Stated in the 1823 Fonthill Sale Catalogue to have come from the Camposanto at Pisa. Not in the Beckford Sale Catalogue, Fonthill, 1822 (sale not held); but in the Beckford and additions Sale, Fonthill, 10 October, 1823 (lot 34), bought by Bentley.[4] Coll. Rev. J. Fuller Russell, where seen by Waagen;[5] exhibited at the R.A., 1877 (No. 151); Fuller Russell Sale, 18 April, 1885 (lot 123), bought by Ash.[6] Bequeathed by the Rev. Jarvis Holland Ash, 1896.[7]

REPRODUCTION: *Illustrations, Italian Schools*, 1937, p. 180. *Plates, Earlier Italian Schools*, 1953, Vol. II, pp. 323–326. The picture has been photographed since the cleaning.

REFERENCES: (1) Migne, *Patrologia Latina*, Vol. 182, Col. 1133 sqq. (2) Reproduced by Van Marle, *Development of the Italian Schools of Painting*, Vol. III, Fig. 261. (3) E.g., by H. D. Gronau in Thieme-Becker (article under Orcagna);

approved by Offner in *The Burlington Magazine*, Vol. LXIII (1933), p. 84. Cf. also Sirèn, *Giotto and Some of His Followers*, 1917, I, pp. 258/9. (**4**) As Andrea Orcagna. The provenance from Fonthill is stated in the Fuller Russell Sale Catalogue. It is genuinely a Beckford picture, being mentioned (with provenance from the Campo Santo di Pisa) in John Rutter, *A Description of Fonthill Abbey*, 2nd edition, 1822, p. 52. (**5**) Waagen, *Treasures*, Vol II, 1854, p. 463, as Spinello. (**6**) As Spinello. The chalk marks of the Fuller Russell Sale are still on the back of the picture. No. 1468 has been confused with another picture by Langton Douglas and S. Arthur Strong in their edition of Crowe and Cavalcaselle, *History of Painting in Italy*, Vol. II, 1903, p. 179, as Daddi (original edition, Vol. I, 1864, pp. 453/4, as Bernardo of Florence). This other picture was in the Ottley Collection; Waagen, *Kunstwerke*, 1837, I, p. 396; probably Warner Ottley Sale, 30 June, 1847 (lot 20), as Taddeo Gaddi. Seen by Waagen, *Treasures*, Vol II, 1854, p. 264, as Spinello, in the Eastlake Collection; Eastlake Sale, 2 June, 1894 (lot 54), bought by H. Quilter. Quilter Sale, 7 April, 1906 (lot 75), as Early Florentine. To judge from the description and the size, this picture is identical with the Orcagnesque *Crucifixion* in the Lehman Collection, New York, reproduced by Sirèn, *Giotto and Some of His Followers*, 1917, II, Plate 218. (**7**) As Spinello, and so catalogued until 1906; then catalogued as by Jacopo di Cione.

3894 'NOLI ME TANGERE' (PANEL FROM A SERIES?)

The Magdalen kneels before Christ.

Wood, painted surface, $21\frac{3}{4} \times 14\frac{7}{8}$ (0·555×0·38). The measurements exclude $\frac{1}{4}$ in. of black paint along the bottom, which may correspond with an original edging. The width given is that for the lowest 6 in., where on each side the picture goes up to the edges of the panel, but has apparently not been cut; higher up, the width of the picture is only $14\frac{1}{8}$ (0·36). No. 3894 has been cut at the top, the patterning at the edge of the gold showing clearly that the picture originally had a lobed top; at present the top $\frac{1}{2}$ in. of gold is covered with black paint, but this has been included in the measurements given.

Very good condition. Several *pentimenti* in the outlines.

Catalogued in 1929 as by Jacopo di Cione. Roger Fry doubtfully suggested Agnolo Gaddi,[1] which Salvini does not admit.[2] In Berenson's Lists of 1932 as Giottesque after 1350, close to Giovanni da Milano. It is near in style to the predella of Orcagna's Strozzi altarpiece in S. Maria Novella at Florence,[3] and perhaps even closer to a *Crucifixion* in the Lehman Collection, New York,[4]

PROVENANCE: Stated to be from the Abate Casali's Collection at Florence.[5] Lent by Edward Granville Harcourt Vernon to Manchester, 1857 (Provisional Catalogue, No. 26; Definitive Catalogue, No. 21);[6] Sale, 18 June, 1864 (lot 275), bought by Bale.[7] Charles Sackville Bale Sale, 14 May, 1881 (lot 294), bought by Wagner.[8] Exhibited at the New Gallery, 1893/4 (No. 28), and at the Grafton Galleries, 1911 (No. 18). Presented by Henry Wagner, 1924.[9]

REPRODUCTION: *Illustrations, Italian Schools*, 1937, p. 180. *Plates, Earlier Italian Schools*, 1953, Vol. II, p. 327.

REFERENCES: (**1**) Fry in *The Burlington Magazine*, Vol. XX (1911/2), p. 72. This attribution is accepted by E. Sandberg-Vavalà in *The Art Bulletin*, 1936, p. 423. (**2**) R. Salvini, *L'Arte di Agnolo Gaddi*, 1936, p. 185, as Gerinesque under Gaddesque influence. (**3**) Good reproductions of two parts in *L'Arte*, 1937, p. 39. (**4**) Lehman Catalogue, 1928, No. VI, with reproduction; Sirèn, *Giotto and*

Some of his Followers, 1917, II, Plate 218. For a suggested provenance for this picture, see note 6 to the entry for No. 1468 above. (5) In the Manchester Exhibition Catalogue. He may be identical with the Abate (?) Giulio Cesare Casali, Florence, who in 1857 owned four saints, which in 1857/8 were acquired by Jarves and are now at Yale (Catalogue by O. Sirèn, 1916, Nos. 27/8, as Lorenzo di Niccolò, reproduced); information from Eastlake's note-book, 1857, and Mündler's Diary, 1857 and 1858. (6) As Orcagna; there is a Manchester Exhibition label on the back of No. 3894. (7) As Taddeo Gaddi; cutting from the sale catalogue on the back of No. 3894. The buyer is recorded in Scharf's sketchbook, No. 69, ff. 7*v* and 8*r*, in the National Portrait Gallery. (8) Here, and in the two subsequent exhibitions, as Taddeo Gaddi. (9) As Jacopo di Cione.

ORIOLO (GIOVANNI) *See* GIOVANNI DA ORIOLO

GIACOMO PACCHIAROTTO
1474–1540 or later

Sienese School. A certain amount is known about his life; he spent his time partly in fighting. It seems, on the other hand, very difficult to justify attaching his name to pictures. Apparently an authenticated work, and the only one, is a fresco of *ca.* 1520 in the Palazzo Ex-Pretorio at Casole d'Elsa (Borghesi e Banchi, *Nuovi Documenti*, 1898, p. 442; photograph in the Gallery files, sent by Enzo Carli). It is doubtful if this fresco is by the same hand as the works usually now ascribed to Pacchiarotto; a coherent stylistic group, nevertheless, is indicated by the modern use of the name Pacchiarotto, and No. 1849 below belongs to this group. It may be mentioned that, in the older books on Sienese painting, he was confused with Gerolamo del Pacchia; a traditional attribution to Pacchiarotto has therefore little value, and in many cases can be proved to have none.

Ascribed to GIACOMO PACCHIAROTTO

1849 ALTARPIECE: THE NATIVITY WITH SAINTS

An altarpiece complete in its original frame. Centre, the Virgin adoring the Child, with S. Joseph, the ox and the ass; above, God the Father between two angels. Left, S. John the Baptist holding a scroll inscribed ECCE / ИƆ / DEI, S. Stephen and a shepherd (?). Right, SS. Jerome and Nicholas. In the predella, from left to right, (1) the Agony in the Garden, with SS. Peter, James and John; (2) the Betrayal of Christ, with S. Peter cutting off the ear of Malchus; (3) Christ on the Cross, marked .I.N.R.I., with the Virgin, S. John and S. Mary Magdalene; (4) the Deposition, with the Virgin, S. John, S. Mary Magdalene and S. Joseph of Arimathaea (?); (5) the Resurrection. At each end of the predella is a coat of arms; left, in the top left-hand corner a white castle on a red ground, the rest gold (Cerretani); right, per pale, (1) a lion rampant, apparently silver (the red underpainting shows in large patches), on a ground now dark, and (2) Piccolomini. On the pilasters of the frame, from top to bottom, are: left, SS. Gabriel, Peter and Francis; right, the Virgin Annunciate, SS. Paul and Lucy.

Wood. Main picture, painted surface, rounded top, $73\frac{3}{4} \times 61$ ($1 \cdot 875 \times 1 \cdot 55$). The height of the predella scenes is $8\frac{1}{2}$ ($0 \cdot 215$); the widths, from left to right, are $9\frac{1}{2}$ ($0 \cdot 245$), $10\frac{1}{2}$ ($0 \cdot 265$), $9\frac{1}{4}$ ($0 \cdot 24$), 11 (0.28) and $9\frac{1}{2}$ (0.24). The size of the figures on the pilasters is, rounded tops, $9 \times 2\frac{1}{2}$ ($0 \cdot 23 \times 0 \cdot 065$), or in a few cases slightly larger. The total size including the frame is, rounded top, $92\frac{1}{2} \times 76\frac{3}{4}$ ($2 \cdot 35 \times 1 \cdot 95$).

This altarpiece has been considerably damaged, but the style remains sufficiently visible. The frame is the original one, but partly restored, and mostly regilt.

The scene of the Nativity takes place in a shed before a cave; a similar arrangement occurs in Botticelli's picture, No. 1034 of this catalogue. In various representations of the Nativity, other Persons of the Trinity as well as the Christ Child are shown;[1] here there is God the Father, but not the Holy Ghost. The figure without a halo in the main scene, on the left behind S. Stephen, is probably a shepherd;[2] alternatively, he might be the donor of the picture, but this seems unlikely. In the predella of No. 1849, the dark halo of Judas at the Betrayal is to be noted.

The arms at the left end of the predella are those of the Cerretani family at Siena.[3] The other coat shows per pale, unidentified at the spectator's left, Piccolomini at the right.[4]

No. 1849 is in the style called Pacchiarotto's, and is accepted by Berenson in his Lists of 1932; it is explained in the biography above that attributions to Pacchiarotto are uncertain.

VARIANTS: A predella of five scenes in S. Girolamo at Siena includes the Crucifixion with figures corresponding to those in the Crucifixion here; and a Deposition closely similar to the one here, but inverted.[5]

PROVENANCE: From the Cerretani Collection at Siena. Noted, with this provenance, and with identifying description, by Mündler at a dealer's in Rome in May, 1858.[6] Acquired by Agnew's through Fairfax Murray in Rome.[7] Purchased from Agnew's, 1901.

REPRODUCTION: *Illustrations, Italian Schools*, 1937, p. 259. *Plates, Earlier Italian Schools*, 1953, Vol. II, pp. 328–330.

REFERENCES: (1) Cf. Van Marle, *Development of the Italian Schools of Painting*, Vol. VII, Fig. 122, for God the Father without the Holy Ghost at the Nativity. (2) Compare the figure in a composition not altogether unrelated to No. 1849 in S. Agostino at Massa Marittima (Van Marle, *op. cit.*, Vol. XVI, Fig. 283). (3) This coat of arms occurs several times in the *tavolette di biccherna* at Siena. (4) Some search in the Archivio at Siena gave no certain result; but it is suggested that the unidentified coat may be meant for Docci. Docci should be a golden lion rampant holding a club, on a blue ground, which is not what is shown here; but Docci may nevertheless be meant. Tommaso di Girolamo di Lodovico Docci married Faustina di Pietro d'Aldobrando Cerretani in 1530; nothing about Girolamo could be found, but Lodovico di Tommaso Docci, possibly the grandfather, married Margarita di Giovanni Piccolomini in 1460. The compiler claims no certainty for this identification; but has been able to find nothing else that

could fit the arms on the picture, among families at Siena, involving both Piccolomini and Cerretani. It is true that Marcantonio Piccolomini, son of Calidonia
di Bindo Bindi, married in 1525 Laura Cerretani, and that Spinello Piccolomini,
son of Caterina Tolomei, married Virginia Cerretani (see A. Lisini and A.
Liberati, *Genealogia dei Piccolomini di Siena*, 1900, Plate III); but neither of
these cases would seem to offer any justification for the lion on No. 1849 associated with the Piccolomini arms. (5) F. Mason Perkins, *Pitture Senesi*, 1933, p.
163 and Fig. 170, as by a painter related to Andrea di Niccolò and Giacomo
Pacchiarotto. (6) Mündler's Diary, as style of Fungai. The dealer's name is given
as Menchetti or Menghetti. (7) Letters in the Gallery archives of 4 December,
1901 and 7 February, 1948.

PEDRINI (Giovanni) *See* 'GIAMPIETRINO'

Pietro PERUGINO
living 1469, died 1523

Pietro Vannucci, known as Perugino from the principal scene of his
activity, Perugia. There is good evidence that he was born at Castel
(now Città) della Pieve, near Chiusi. He is said by Giovanni Santi to
have been of the same age as Leonardo da Vinci (born in 1452); this is
probably roughly true, although Vasari says that he was born *ca.* 1445/6.
It is probable that he remained in Città della Pieve until 1470; but this
is often denied. Vasari says that he was trained by some inferior painter
at Perugia, and this may be true; but his style seems to have been formed
chiefly at Florence, where he is listed as a member of the Company of
S. Luke in 1472. The tradition that he was in Florence the pupil, or
perhaps rather the assistant, of Verrocchio is probable. Other statements about his early period are very uncertain, though some recent
critics lay stress on a tradition that he was a pupil of Piero della Francesca. His first surviving sure work is a fragmentary fresco at Cerqueto
(about 12 miles south of Perugia), which was signed and dated 1478.

Perugino's first important sure works are some frescoes in the Sistine
Chapel in Rome, part of a series carried out by several painters in 1481/2.
Thereafter Perugino divided his time for the most part between Florence
and Perugia or its district. He painted many frescoes and pictures,
and ran an active studio; one of his pupils was (it seems) Raphael.

Literature: Fiorenzo Canuti, *Il Perugino*, 1931.

181 THE VIRGIN AND CHILD WITH S. JOHN
Inscribed on the Virgin's mantle PETRUS.PERUGINUS.

Wood, painted surface, $27 \times 17\frac{1}{2}$ (0.685×0.445). Painted up to the
edges all round; but the edges of the picture (except for the modifications about to be noted) consist of a painted framing, so that the present
surface of the picture cannot have been reduced to any notable extent
at the sides and bottom.

Very good condition in general, although not free from retouches,
including some on prominent parts. Beneath the right-hand side of the

parapet, the Virgin's drapery and the outlines of S. John's body once continued as far as the painted framing. The paint on this part of the parapet appears to be entirely new; but the alteration appears to have been made by Perugino in the course of his work, since on the one hand the position of the Child's feet has not been changed, and on the other X-Rays reveal no clear step in the parapet towards the middle of the picture. The picture once had a rounded top; spandrels right and left in the sky are in new paint, in the outer parts on insertions in the panel. X-Rays reveal the original arrangement clearly; it may be calculated that about 3 in. is missing from the top of the picture at the centre. Most of the gold is new. The inscription in gold appears to be entirely new; possibly it follows old indications, but the spelling *Peruginus* instead of *Perusinus* does not allay suspicion that it is invented.

No. 181 was accepted as being an early work in the first edition of this Catalogue; but there is some reason to date it soon after 1500.[1]

A S. John with somewhat similar outlines occurs in a tondo, of which three versions are known.[2]

PROVENANCE: On the back is an unidentified seal, water (?), two columns (?), a star and a motto NON POTVI (?). No. 181 is said to have been brought from Perugia by Pizzetta, a picture-cleaner; but it is almost certainly the picture in the Ph. Panné Sale, London, 26 March, 1819 (lot 110), *Virgin, Infant Christ and St. John, the latter in prayer: on thick panel*, 27 × 17½, stated to have been bought by Piazzetta. Pizzetta sold it, apparently *ca.* 1820, to William Beckford of Font-hill.[3] Included by mistake in the Beckford Sale, Fonthill, 16 (for 15) Oct., 1822 (lot 78), and bought back by Beckford.[4] Seen in the Beckford Collection at Bath by Waagen.[5] Purchased from Beckford, 1841.

REPRODUCTION: *Illustrations, Italian Schools*, 1937, p. 268. *Plates, Earlier Italian Schools*, 1953, Vol. II, p. 331.

REFERENCES: (1) Perugino's datable early works are very few, and the execution of some of those clearly dragged. Degenhart in the *Rivista d'Arte*, 1932, p. 442, dates No. 181 before 1472; W. Bombe, Klassiker der Kunst *Perugino*, 1914, pp. XIV/XV, dates it *ca.* 1480; O. Fischel in the Prussian *Jahrbuch*, 1917, p. 71, dates it shortly after 1491; Umberto Gnoli, *Pietro Perugino*, 1923, p. 54, says perhaps 1485/90. Other writers also have suggested times in the 1480's or early 1490's. Against a date in the 1480's or early 1490's, it is thought that the hair-dressing of the Virgin is most characteristic of the years soon after 1500. On stylistic grounds, Zeri in the *Bollettino d'Arte*, 1953, p. 131, says 1500/10, and E. Camesasca, *Tutta la Pittura del Perugino*, 1959, pp. 175/6, *ca.* 1500/5. The compiler does not agree with Zeri's judgment of the picture's quality, the execution of which seems refined; but if the picture is really of *ca.* 1505, the possibility that it was executed by a hand other than Perugino's should be borne in mind. Crowe and Cavalcaselle, *History of Painting in Italy*, III, 1866, p. 250, suggest the participation of Lo Spagna for it. (2) One at Verona is Klassiker der Kunst *Perugino*, 1914, Plate 197, as Studio (Verona 1913 Catalogue, No. 34); another is at Berlin, No. 138, as School of Perugia, reproduced in the Berlin Illustrations; the third is at Stuttgart, 1957 Catalogue, p. 196 (reproduced in Reinach, *Répertoire*, I, p. 233). (3) Cyrus Redding, *Memoirs of William Beckford*, 1859, II, p. 375, quoting a letter from Beckford of 6 July, 1840; Beckford says that he had bought the picture 20 or 30 years before from Pizzetta, who told him that he had had it from Perugia. (4) The 1822 sale did not, in fact, take place. The Font-hill property, including the items listed for sale in 1822, had been acquired by Farquhar; Beckford bought back No. 181 from him. See Cyrus Redding, *op. cit.*, pp. 239 and 257. (5) Waagen, *Kunstwerke*, 1837, II, p. 327.

288   THREE PANELS OF AN ALTARPIECE: THE VIRGIN
AND CHILD WITH SS. RAPHAEL AND MICHAEL

Centre, the Virgin and Child with an angel; left, S. Michael; right, S. Raphael and the young Tobias. Signed on S. Michael's panel, PETRVS PĒRVSINV(S) / PINXIT, the first P being new. On the other side panel, there are some miscellaneous letters on the dresses of the angel and of Tobias, mostly new.

Wood. The painted surfaces of the pictures are at present, rounded tops: centre panel, $50 \times 25\frac{1}{4}$ (1.27×0.64); side panels, $49\frac{3}{4} \times 22\frac{3}{4}$ (1.265×0.58). These measurements exclude black edging all round all the pictures. This edging, most of the parts of the pictures forming the rounded tops, a wide strip at the bottom of the central panel and other smaller strips elsewhere are on additions to what remains of the original panels. The sizes of the original painted surfaces, so far as they have been preserved, are: centre panel, $44\frac{1}{2} \times 25\frac{1}{4}$ (1.13×0.64); S. Michael's panel, 45×22 (1.14×0.56); S. Raphael's panel, $44\frac{1}{2} \times 22$ (1.13×0.56). These original panels have been cut down somewhat from what Perugino produced. Copies suggest that about 1 in. is missing from the tops, and several inches from the bottoms.[1] In the central panel, probably the whole of the cushion on which the Child is seated was shown. On S. Michael's panel, there was a recumbent figure of Satan; part of his wing, beginning near S. Michael's right heel and crossing the shield, and part of the outline of his head, just under S. Michael's right foot, are still detectable under the repaint, but most of Satan's body has been cut away. On S. Raphael's panel, the dog of Tobias was shown; its head near the angel's right foot is still detectable, but the body has been cut away.

The pictures are in general in good condition, except for the over-paintings just mentioned, and a good deal of repaint along the edges where the original panels join on to the additions. There are some rather prominent damages in some of the dresses; but the most damaged of the important parts is Tobias' left hand. Among the *pentimenti*, it may be mentioned that the mountain behind Tobias' head was once some 4 in. higher, and that his fish is painted on top of his dress, etc.

No. 288 is part of an altarpiece painted for the Certosa near Pavia. Only two documents concerning its commission are now known.[2] One is a letter of 10 October, 1496, from Jacopo d'Antonio, a woodworker of Florence, to Fra Gerolamo of the Certosa. He says that both Perugino and Filippino Lippi would have been nearly finished with the altarpiece each had contracted to paint for the Certosa, and that he himself would have gone ahead with the frames, if any money had come through. It is likely enough that neither Perugino nor Filippino Lippi had even begun his picture at that time. The second document is a letter from Lodovico il Moro to his representative at Florence, of 1 May, 1499; he there threatens the painters with the withdrawal of the money advanced to them, if their altarpieces for the Certosa were not produced in a reasonable time.

It is usually assumed that Perugino made haste to complete his work after this threat. There is no evidence that he did; there is some evidence that he did not. In the first place, Filippino Lippi had delivered nothing at the time of his death in 1504;[3] since Filippino was not frightened by a threat, there is no need to suppose that Perugino was. Secondly, it does not appear certain that Perugino ever completed his altarpiece for the Certosa. The associated pieces are the three panels here catalogued, and a panel of *God the Father*, still *in situ*.[4] These do not form a complete altarpiece by themselves, and they were in fact framed at the Certosa in an altarpiece of six compartments; but the remaining two panels in this frame, representing *The Annunciation*, do not appear to have been by Perugino.[5] What evidence there is indicates rather that they were by Albertinelli;[6] it is even reasonable to believe that they were documented works by Albertinelli,[7] and further that they are the pictures of 1511 now at Geneva.[8]

If it were conceded that Perugino never completed his altarpiece for the Certosa, the date of No. 288 would be left somewhat vague.[9] This vagueness of dating would be of some importance for the attribution. Several critics have thought they saw the hand of the youthful Raphael in No. 288.[10] If the execution of the pictures were accepted as of *ca.* 1499, this would be unlikely;[11] but it appears legitimate, if desired, to choose for this or that part of them any year at the beginning of the sixteenth century that might seem suitable for Raphael's participation. Nevertheless, the attribution of anything in No. 288 to Raphael is only a guess.

VERSIONS AND COPIES: Copies of all the three panels of No. 288 are, as already mentioned in note 1, in the Certosa near Pavia.[12] A picture, apparently only a copy, and corresponding closely with the central panel of No. 288 before it was cut down, is in the Diocesan Museum at Trent.[13] A good version of the main figures of the central panel, with the infant S. John added, is in the Pitti Gallery at Florence.[14] A tondo with the main figures of the central panel, apparently not by Perugino's hand, is recorded in the Liechtenstein Gallery.[15] Other copies and variants of the central panel are known; an important one is a derivation in an altarpiece at Arona by Gaudenzio Ferrari, commissioned in January, 1510, and delivered in 1511.[16] A copy of S. Michael showing the figure of Satan (as in the copy at the Certosa, mentioned above) was owned by the Rev. Mr. Sutton.[17] A copy of the top part of S. Michael is recorded at Darmstadt.[18] Figures somewhat similar to this S. Michael occur in an altarpiece at Florence, and in the Cambio at Perugia.[19] What may be a copy of the *Tobias and the Angel* before it was cut down was in Lady Galway's Sale, 24 October, 1947 (lot 140).

DRAWINGS: Several connected drawings are known. Fischel accepts as genuine a head and hands of the Virgin at Venice, a boy (for the angel of the central panel) at Stockholm, a man in armour for S. Michael at Windsor, and the figures of S. Raphael and Tobias in contemporary Renaissance costume at Oxford.[20]

PROVENANCE: As explained above, the three panels of No. 288 were the principal parts of an altarpiece in six compartments in the Certosa near Pavia; the chapel where the pictures hung was dedicated to S. Michael. The Carthusians of Pavia were suppressed by Joseph II in 1782, and the three pictures included in No. 288 were taken to the Accademia at Milan in 1784;[21] they seem to have been intended for the Gallery at Vienna,[22] but, not proving acceptable, were sold in January, 1786,[23] to Count Giacomo Melzi d'Eril of Milan, who died in 1802.[24] No. 151 of an early nineteenth-century Melzi catalogue. At the death of Count Giacomo, the Melzi collection was divided between his nephews Francesco (Duca di Lodi) and Luigi, and was later reunited in the possession of the latter's son, Giovanni Francesco. He died in 1832; in 1835 a division of the pictures was effected between his three children, Duca Lodovico Melzi, Don Giovanni Melzi and Donna Barbara, who married Duca Tommaso Gallarati Scotti. The three panels forming No. 288 were among the pictures that passed to Duke Lodovico Melzi, from whom they were purchased in 1856.[25]

REPRODUCTIONS: *Illustrations, Italian Schools*, 1937, p. 272. *Plates, Earlier Italian Schools*, 1953, Vol. II, pp. 332–334.

REFERENCES: (1) The copies are in the chapel in the Certosa near Pavia, from which No. 288 came. They are square-topped; Satan, Tobias' dog and the whole of the cushion on which the Infant Christ is seated are there shown. The copies presumably record the original fields of No. 288; they are reproduced in the Prussian *Jahrbuch*, 1917, *Beiheft*, Fig. 125. See further under *Versions*. According to the N.G. MS. catalogue, S. Michael in No. 288 is shown without the arched top, but cut at the bottom as now, in the background of a portrait (stated to be of 1802) of Count Giacomo Melzi (who died in 1802) in the Hospital at Milan. This portrait is no doubt the one by Antonio Schieppati. Part of it, not showing the Perugino, is reproduced as the frontispiece to Giulio Carotti's *Capi d'Arte appartenenti a S.E. la Duchessa Joséphine Melzi d' Eril-Barbò*, 1901; photograph of the whole of it in the Gallery archives, kindly supplied by Gian Alberto Dell'Acqua. The reproduction of the Perugino appears to be too fanciful for a precise deduction concerning its condition at the time to be made. (2) The texts of the documents have been several times printed, e.g. by F. Canuti, *Il Perugino*, 1931, II, Docs. 253/4, and by A. Scharf, *Filippino Lippi*, 1935, Docs. XVIII and XXI. (3) For some drawings by Filippino in view of his altarpiece (a *Pietà*), see A. Scharf, *Filippino Lippi*, 1935, pp. 47 ff. Milanesi in his edition of Vasari, III, p. 475, says that Filippino's contract was of 7 March, 1494 (1495 n.s.); but this matter appears irrelevant to the history of No. 288, since Perugino need not have had his contract on the same date as Filippino had his, and in any case it is likely enough that no work had been begun by 10 October, 1496. The lay-in of Filippino's *Pietà* remained in the possession of his widow until 1511, in which year she came to a settlement about it with the representatives of the Certosa. The document in question does not appear to have been published, but it is summarized by Milanesi in his edition of Vasari, IV, p. 227 (see also III, p. 475). According to this, Filippino's widow agreed to pay back 40 of the 45 ducats her husband had received as an advance. She was to pay 20 of these ducats to the Certosa; she was to hand over the remaining 20 ducats and Filippino's unfinished picture to Mariotto Albertinelli (then in partnership with Fra Bartolommeo), who on 25 June, 1511, contracted with the Certosa to paint for them for this price a picture instead of, and similar to, Filippino's. When Fra Bartolommeo and Albertinelli dissolved their partnership on 5 January, 1513 (1512 o.s.), both Filippino's unfinished *Pietà* and the beginning of Albertinelli's substitute *Pietà* were agreed to be Albertinelli's property; see P. Vincenzo Marchese, *Memorie dei più insigni Pittori*, etc., *Domenicani*, II, 1854, p. 366. (4) Reproduced in the Klassiker der Kunst *Perugino*, 1914, Plate 80. Reproduced in its position in the altarpiece in the Certosa in the Prussian *Jahrbuch*, 1917, *Beiheft*, Fig. 125. This panel has clearly had a piece added at the top. (5) The two pictures now occupying these positions, and reproduced in the Prussian *Jahrbuch*, 1917, *Beiheft*, Fig. 125, are by Ambrogio Bergognone, and are part of what was once a different altarpiece, in the Certosa. The stone framing of the Perugino altarpiece dates from *ca.* 1650 (letter from Wart Arslan, 19 February, 1948, in the Gallery archives); the pictures in this frame before the breaking up of the altarpiece in 1784 may, therefore, not be the same as the ones in the chapel at the beginning of the sixteenth century. Several panels by Perugino could, if desired, be assumed to have been lost at an early date. But this does not seem very likely, and in any case there is no evidence for discussing anything except the pictures that were in the frame of *ca.* 1650. (Prior Matteo Valerio, who was at the Certosa from 1604 until 1645, in his notes says only ' San Michele di Pietro Perugini'; see the *Archivio Storico Lombardo*, 1879, p. 141). Old descriptions of the Certosa are unfortunately meagre, and some writers who do mention Perugino's altarpiece mention only Perugino's name; thus, F. Bartoli, *Notizia delle Pitture, Sculture ed Architetture* . . . *d'Italia*, II, 1777, pp. 68/9, in a fairly detailed account ascribes the whole altarpiece to Perugino, and Oretti, who visited the Certosa di Pavia on 31 August, 1772, mentions the six pieces as Perugino's (Bologna, Biblioteca dell'Archiginnasio, MS. B 96 *bis*, pp. 4/5). The evidence is, nevertheless, strong that the 5th and 6th panels in the frame were not by Perugino; (Lalande), *Voyage d'un François en Italie*. new edition, VIII, 1770, p. 310, J. J. Volkmann, *Historisch-Kritische Nachrichten von Italien*, III, 1771, p. 757, and the *Nuova Guida della Città di Milano*, etc., publ. Sirtori, 1783, p. 105, are explicit in this sense. See further in the next note. (6) See Carlo Magenta, *La Certosa di Pavia*, 1897, p. 294. Magenta quotes an old MS. inventory, 'L'annunziata aggiunta al quadro di lui (Perugino) è opera di Biagio di Bindo Fiotentino'; the name is interpreted as that of Mariotto (di Biagio di Bindo) Albertinelli, though it is difficult to imagine why such a form should have been recorded. Magenta goes on to quote, with reserves about its accuracy, from the list by Fenini of pictures sent to France in 1796: 'Arcangelo di Biagio Bindi,' 'Vergine Annunziata' (apparently without attribution). (7) By 3 July, 1511, Mariotto Albertinelli (in partnership with Fra Bartolommeo) had received 12 ducats for the paintings that had been done for the Certosa; see P. Vincenzo Marchese, *Memorie dei più insigni Pittori*, etc., *Domenicani*, II, 1854, p. 68. This can hardly be applied to the *Pietà* that Mariotto contracted to paint in substitution for Filippino's altarpiece, if Milanesi's summary of the document referred to in note 3 is correct. In the first place, Mariotto had contracted to paint the *Pietà* on 25 June, 1511, so the 'paintings' could hardly have been 'done' by July 3rd; secondly, Mariotto was to receive his payment for the *Pietà* from Filippino's widow, not directly from the representatives of the Certosa. It is therefore probable that the payment of 3 July, 1511, was for pictures other than the *Pietà*; it seems reasonable to suppose that the two panels of *The Annunciation* are referred to. (8) Signed by Fra Bartolommeo and Albertinelli together, and dated 1511; reproduced by Venturi, *Storia dell'Arte Italiana*, Vol. IX, Part I, Fig. 275. The size of each panel is, according to the Geneva Catalogue of 1928, p. 51, 1·09 × 0·55; so far as can be calculated from the plate in the Prussian *Jahrbuch*, 1917, *Beiheft*, Fig. 125, they would have fitted well into the spaces allowed by the frame. It seems not to be a strong objection that the signature on the Geneva pictures seems not recorded in any account of the Certosa di Pavia; visitors to the Certosa could hardly have seen it, and the inventories are presumably careless. Mme. Adhémar (letter of 26 November, 1947) has kindly furnished confirmation of the provenance of the Geneva pictures: (*a*) in the *Inventaire de Napoléon 1er.* is recorded 'La Vierge de l'Annonciation,' size 1·18 × 0·59, premier envoi d'Italie (Musée de Genève); (*b*) in the *Livre des envois aux Départements*, Département du Léman-Genève, 'La Vierge et l'Ange de l'Annonciation de Fra Bartolomeo tableaux formant pendant,' 3 ft. 5 in. × 1 ft. 9 in., 1 er. envoi d'Italie, 27 floréal an XII. Mlle. Blumer, in her study of pictures captured by Napoleon in Italy, gives the provenance of the Geneva pictures as Milan 1796, Paris 8 November, 1796, Geneva 1801; see the *Bulletin de la Société de l'Histoire de l'Art Français*, 1936, p. 263, Nos. 86, 87. The pictures were deposited in S. Germain at Geneva on 23 March, 1805 (Edouard Chapuisat, *La Municipalité de Genève*, II, 1910, p. 308); the church, where they remained for some time, is wrongly called Sainte Madeleine by Crowe and Cavalcaselle, *History of Painting in Italy*, ed. Borenius, VI, 1914, p. 74. (9) Various considerations suggest that a date of delivery later than *ca.* 1510 is unlikely, and some confirmation of this is afforded by Gaudenzio Ferrari's altarpiece at Arona, commissioned in January, 1510, and delivered in 1511; but see further under *Versions*. (10) E.g. E. Müntz, *Raphaël, Sa Vie, Son Œuvre et*

Son Temps, 1881, p. 54. (**11**) There are some sensible remarks on this subject by Crowe and Cavalcaselle, *Raphael: His Life and Works*, 1882, I, pp. 34 ff. (**12**) They are traditionally ascribed to Galeazzo Pasterelli, 1586; cf. Canuti, *op. cit.*, I, p. 129 (date given as 1585), and Magenta, *op. cit.*, p. 293. In Prior Matteo Valerio's list of items in the Certosa, several works are mentioned as being by Galeazo Posbonelli (*sic*), and paid for in 1586, but not these copies: see the *Archivio Storico Lombardo*, 1879, p. 141. The error (if error it is) is perhaps due to G. L. Calvi, *Notizie sulla vita . . . dei . . . pittori . . . in Milano*, II, 1865, p. 253 (Galeazzo Posterelli). The copies are reproduced in the Prussian *Jahrbuch*, 1917, *Beiheft*, Fig. 125. (**13**) For the Trent picture, see G. B. Emert, *Fonti Manoscritte Inedite per la Storia dell'Arte nel Trentino*, 1939, pp. 125 and 174, giving a bibliography of references; see also Vincenzo Casagrande, *Catalogo del Museo Diocesano di Trento*, 1908, No. 17, size given as 1·32 × 0·74. There is a reproduction of this picture in the Gallery archives. (**14**) Klassiker der Kunst *Perugino*, 1914, Plates 81/3; A Iahn-Rusconi, *La R. Galleria Pitti in Firenze*, 1937, No. 219. (**15**) Klassiker der Kunst, Plate 84. (**16**) Reproduced by E. Halsey, *Gaudenzio Ferrari*, 1908, p. 38. This picture has been mentioned in note 9 as an argument for believing that Perugino's Pavia picture had been delivered by *ca.* 1510. The argument is of some weight, but is not quite cogent. Gaudenzio Ferrari could have made his derivation from some other version by Perugino, especially as his relations with Perugino may have been fairly close. See, for this last point, the derivation from Perugino's *Pietà* in the Pitti Gallery (Klassiker der Kunst *Perugino*, 1914, Plate 40) at Vercelli, reproduced by Vittorio Viale, *Gotico e Rinascimento in Piemonte*, 1939, Plate 125; on pp. 166/7, it is true, Viale expresses some doubt about the attribution of the Vercelli picture to Gaudenzio, and Anna Maria Brizio, *La Pittura in Piemonte*, 1942, p. 103, rejects the attribution. (**17**) Photograph at Windsor; see C. Ruland, *The Raphael Collection in the Royal Library at Windsor Castle*, 1876, p. 115, B.I.9, and letter from Sir Owen Morshead, 29 July, 1947, in the Gallery archives. This picture was lent (as by Raphael) to the R.A., 1878 (No. 204) by the Rev. F. H. Sutton, and was presumably lot 33 of the Canon Sutton Sale, 12 February, 1926. (**18**) Ruland, *op. cit.*, p. 115, B.I.7.; *Die Gemälde Sammlung des Grossherzöglichen Museum zu Darmstadt*, 1885, No. 514. (**19**) Klassiker der Kunst *Perugino*, 1914, Plates 87 and 107. What appears to be a derivation from the former, with a dragon under his feet, occurs in a picture in S. Francesco at Fiesole; reproduced by O. H. Giglioli, *Catalogo delle Cose d'Arte e di Antichità d'Italia, Fiesole*, 1933, p. 172. The latter does not represent S. Michael. It is likely enough that Perugino derived his figures from Donatello's *S. George* (Klassiker der Kunst *Donatello*, 1907, Plates 7–9). (**20**) O. Fischel in the Prussian *Jahrbuch*, 1917, *Beiheft*, pp. 47/50, Nos. 52, 53, 54, 56; all reproduced. *The Italian Drawings of the XV and XVI Centuries . . . at Windsor Castle*, by A. E. Popham and Johannes Wilde, 1949, p. 175, No. 21; Oxford, *Catalogue of Drawings*, by K. T. Parker, Vol. II, *Italian Schools*, 1956, No. 27. For a copy of Tobias and the Angel, see *British Museum, Italian Drawings, the Fourteenth and Fifteenth Centuries*, catalogue by A. E. Popham and Philip Pouncey, 1950, I, No. 200. (**21**) Silvola's inventory of 21 January, 1784, according to Luca Beltrami, *Ambrogio Fossano*, 1895, pp. 67 f. See also Canuti, *op. cit.*, I, p. 129. (**22**) See Giovanna del Convito in the *Archivio Storico Lombardo*, 1933, p. 510 .(**23**) Mündler was shown the documents concerning the purchase; diary, 18 March, 1856. Cf. also Giulio Carotti, *Capi d'Arte appartenenti a S.E. la Duchessa Joséphine Melzi d' Eril-Barbò*, 1901, p. 10. (**24**) The history of the divisions of the Melzi property is to be found in Carotti, *op. cit.*, pp. 9 ff. and 140 ff. Carotti also reprints the undated Melzi catalogue. (**25**) For the circumstances of the export from Italy, see F. Malaguzzi-Valeri in the *Repertorium für Kunstwissenschaft*, 1903, pp. 372 ff.

1075 ALTARPIECE: THE VIRGIN AND CHILD WITH SS. FRANCIS AND JEROME

Wood, painted surface, 73 × 60 (1·855 × 1·525). The edges of the paint are rather irregular; outside the measurements given, the panel has been gessoed up to its edges.

Good condition.

On 7 April, 1507, Giovanni di Matteo Schiavone, a woodworker at Perugia, made a nuncupative will, by which he directed that a chapel in S. Maria de' Servi at Perugia should be built, and a picture painted for it; the subject of the picture was to be the Virgin of Loreto with SS. Jerome and Francis. Giovanni died almost at once. On 7 June, 1507, his executors, including Prior Niccolò of the Servi at Perugia, contracted with Perugino for the painting of the picture. Perugino was to get the woodwork made and then to paint with his hand the Virgin standing with the Child 'ad similtudinem illius de Loreto,' and SS. Jerome and Francis. Everything was to be complete by September, 1507; it is not known if Perugino delivered the picture, which is No. 1075, to time.[1]

The references to the 'Virgin of Loreto' were perhaps intended to specify a Virgin standing with the Child under a canopy, with angels holding the supporting pillars, which symbolizes the transport of the Holy House of Loreto. Perugino can hardly be said to have followed this iconographical form in No. 1075, but perhaps the pedestal on which the Virgin here stands and the wall surrounding the figures may be attempts to refer to the subject.[2]

The contract for No. 1075 specified a *pledula*, which has been interpreted to mean a predella; but no suitable predella pictures have been identified.[3] The original frame of No. 1075 is now in the Gallery at Perugia; it has been adapted to fit another picture, certainly now contains no spaces for predella pictures, and cannot reasonably be supposed ever to have done so.[4]

It may be doubted if the execution of No. 1075 is, as was demanded in the contract, entirely by Perugino's hand.[5]

VERSIONS AND COPIES: A copy of 1822 by Giuseppe Carattoli is in S. Maria Nuova (over the side door) at Perugia; the original had been removed from this church the year before (see the provenance).[6] A bust length of the Virgin and Child at Spoleto reproduces fairly exactly the upper part of the central figures of No. 1075.[7] A similar group recurs in a picture in the Louvre, No. 1540;[8] No. 1573A of the same Gallery is stated to repeat this design.[9] The figure of S. Francis recurs with variations in a gonfalone of 1499 at Perugia,[10] and in several pictures by or ascribed to Tiberio d'Assisi.[11] The angels in No. 1075 are on a design frequently used by Perugino.[12]

DRAWING: A drawing claimed to be for the S. Jerome is recorded.[13]

PROVENANCE: As explained above, commissioned in 1507 for S. Maria de' Servi at Perugia. This church was one of the buildings pulled down to make space for the fortress known as the *Rocca Paolina*; the fortress was built in 1540/3, and it was in 1542 that the Servites moved to another church, known as S. Maria Nuova.[14] No. 1075 was moved to the new church, and was hung over an altar dedicated to S. Francis, belonging to the Cecconi family; it is not certain if the Cecconi had acquired rights in the picture before the move or not.[15] In any case, the picture remained in the church, the ownership or patronage passing by bequest from the Cecconi to the Crispolti and then to Baron Fabrizio della Penna Senior.[16] He paid money for removing the picture to his house in 1821.[17] Penna Catalogue, 1875 (No. 38). Purchased from Baron Fabrizio della Penna, grandson of the first named, Perugia, 1879.

REPRODUCTION: *Illustrations, Italian Schools*, 1937, p. 271. *Plates, Earlier Italian Schools*, 1953, Vol. II, p. 335.

REFERENCES: (1) See F. Canuti, *Il Perugino*, 1931, II, Docs. 418 and 419; they are notaries' copies of the documents. A slightly different text of the second document is given by W. Bombe, *Geschichte der Peruginer Malerei*, 1912, pp. 378/9. (2) An inscribed example of a 'Virgin of Loreto' of the type referred to is at Spelonga, by Panfilo da Spoleto, 1482; reproduced by L. Serra, *L'Arte nelle Marche, Periodo del Rinascimento*, 1934, Fig. 456. For the whole subject, see Corrado Ricci, *Per l'Iconografia Lauretana*, in the *Rassegna d'Arte*, 1916, pp. 265 ff. (3) The text of the contract for No. 1075, which is Canuti, *op. cit.*, Doc. 419, has been printed with several errors; with the kind help of Dr. Ignazio Baldelli of the Biblioteca Comunale at Perugia, the original document in the Archivio Notarile at Perugia has been consulted. The relevant words are 'cum pledula et paramentis brocatorum'; and, though the writing of the document is very bad, 'pledula' must be taken as sure. The word may mean merely a pedestal or base; a reason against its meaning predella in the modern sense is that no subjects to be painted on it are specified. In view of the construction of the frame, referred to in the next sentence in the text, the interpretation of the word as predella would almost necessarily mean that Perugino failed to carry out this part of the contract. (4) Cf. U. Gnoli, *Pietro Perugino*, 1923, p. 55. Prof. Achille Bertini Calosso was kind enough to send a photograph of the frame, which is round the picture Plate 117 of the Klassiker der Kunst *Perugino*, 1914. (5) Longhi in *Paragone*, May 1955, p. 23, claims the intervention of Raphael, especially for the Child. A. Venturi, *Storia*, Vol. VII, Part II, p. 694, had thought the picture executed by Andrea d'Aloigi under Perugino's direction. (6) Serafino Siepi, *Descrizione Topologico-Istorica della Città di Perugia*, I, 1822, p. 282. (7) Reproduced by Venturi, *Storia dell'Arte Italiana*, Vol. VII, Part II, Fig. 538, as Andrea d'Assisi (L'Ingegno). (8) Reproduced in the *Gazette des Beaux-Arts*, 1896, I, p. 285, as Lo Spagna. (9) Seymour de Ricci's Louvre Catalogue, *Ecoles Etrangères, Italie et Espagne*, 1913, pp. 146 and 156. (10) U. Gnoli, *Pietro Perugino*, 1923, Plate XXXIV; Perugia Catalogue, 1932, p. 151, No. 349. (11) Van Marle, *Development of the Italian Schools of Painting*, Vol. XIV, pp. 412 ff. (12) In No. 1441 below, and in other cases corresponding even more closely. (13) Antonio Mezzanotte, *Della Vita e delle Opere di Pietro Vannucci . . . il Perugino*, 1836, p. 198 (Coll. Francesco Conestabile della Staffa, Perugia). The record seems doubtful, since the drawing appears not to be identifiable in the *Catalogue Descriptif des Anciens Tableaux et des Dessins appartenant à M. le Comte Scipion Conestabile della Staffa*, 1871 (2nd edition, 1872). (14) See William Heywood, *A History of Perugia*, 1910, p. 331. It is Cesare Crispolti, *Perugia Augusta*, 1648, p. 125, who says that it was in September, 1542, that the Servites moved from S. Maria de Servi. (15) Canuti, *Il Perugino*, 1931, II, Doc. 420, gives a text with many errors, corrected with the kind help of Dr. Ignazio Baldelli. The date is 19 May, 1663; it is stated that 'Dominorum Cecconium perusina familia' had in the past built in S. Maria Nuova an altar dedicated to S. Francis, over which was No. 1075, 'etsi e (*sic*) eadem Tabula quae in altari eiusdem Familiae existebat in eorundem fratrum antiquiori Ecclesia, tunc temporis sita in portae Heburneae Regione occasione constructionis Perusinae Arcis demolita.' On the other hand, it was recorded by P. Giuseppe Bruni, mid-eighteenth century, that the Servites ceded the altar of S. Francis in 1557 to Pietro Antonio Cecconi; see G. B. Vermiglioli, *Di Bernardino Pinturicchio . . . Memorie*, 1837, pp. 211 ff., and Canuti, *op. cit.*, II, Doc. 423. For yet different information, see Antonio Mezzanotte, *Della Vita e delle Opere di Pietro Vannucci . . . il Perugino*, 1836, pp. 51 ff. (16) Perhaps the first mention of it in print is by Giovanni Francesco Morelli, *Brevi Notizie delle Pitture . . . di Perugia*, 1683, pp. 80/1. For the ownerships, see Mezzanotte, *op. cit.*, p. 53. (17) Canuti, *op. cit.*, II, Docs. 421 and 422. See also Serafino Siepi, *Descrizione Topologico-Istorica della Città di Perugia*, 1822, I, p. 282, and II, p. 478. It would appear that the ownership of the picture may have lapsed and passed to the

Servites, who certainly claimed to have sold the picture to Baron Fabrizio della Penna Senior; see Fabrizio della Penna, *Il Quadro del Perugino nella Galleria Penna in Perugia*, 1878.

1441 FRESCO: THE NATIVITY

The Virgin, S. Joseph and several shepherds adore the Infant Christ.

Fresco, transferred to canvas: pediment shaped. In three pieces: central piece, pointed top, $100\frac{1}{4} \times 51\frac{1}{2}$ ($2 \cdot 545 \times 1 \cdot 31$); right hand piece, trapezoid, $87\frac{3}{4} \times 92\frac{1}{4}$ ($2 \cdot 23 \times 2 \cdot 34$); left hand piece, trapezoid, $88\frac{1}{4} \times 91\frac{3}{4}$ ($2 \cdot 24 \times 2 \cdot 33$).

Much damaged and repainted. Transferred in 1843.[1]

This fresco comes from the Oratory of the Confraternity of the Annunziata, also called S. Maria Assunta, at Fontignano. Fontignano, about 15 miles from Perugia, is close to the road from that place to Città della Pieve. Perugino died there in 1523.

It is supposed that No. 1441 is Perugino's last work.[2] The fresco was over the arch separating the nave and chancel of the Oratory at Fontignano; at the sides of the arch were painted SS. Roch and Sebastian,[3] the saints invoked against the Plague, and it was of the plague that Perugino died at Fontignano in 1523. If all the three frescoes were done at the same time, 1523 is therefore likely enough.[4]

There is no documentation to confirm the attribution of these works to Perugino.

VERSIONS: The design is one that was frequently repeated by Perugino with variations.[5] The Virgin also connects with No. 288 above and its variants; the angels recur in No. 1075 above, etc., with variations.

DRAWING: A drawing formerly in the A. G. B. Russell Collection is supposed to be for the head of S. Joseph, but this appears doubtful.[6]

PROVENANCE: A stated above, from the Oratory of the Confraternity of the Annunziata at Fortignano;[7] removed from the wall in 1843 on the instructions of its purchaser, P. Nazzareno Bonomi, Vicario Generale de' RR. PP. Paolotti di S. Spirito in Perugia.[8] It remained for some time in a private house in Perugia.[9] Purchased in 1862 from W. B. Spence of Florence by the Victoria and Albert Museum.[10] Lent since 1895.

REPRODUCTION: *Illustrations, Italian Schools*, 1937, p. 273. *Plates, Earlier Italian Schools*, 1953, Vol. II, p. 336.

REFERENCES: (1) See S. Massari, *Del Presepe di Fontignano, Ultimo Dipinto di Pietro Vannucci detto il Perugino*, etc., 1844, p. 3; it is noted that No. 1441 and other frescoes, among various damages, had been whitewashed at the beginning of the nineteenth century. At the end of the book, there is an etching of No. 1441 by Massari, giving a slightly larger field all round than now. (2) It has been occasionally alleged that No. 1441 is unfinished; but there seems to be no evidence for saying this, so far as the condition of the fresco enables one to see. (3) Baldassare Orsini, *Vita, etc., di Pietro Perugino*, 1804, p. 214. These saints, over life-size, were detached from the wall, apparently at the same time as No. 1441, and were in very bad state in 1844; Massari, *op. cit.*, p. 4. They are now missing. Mündler, in his Diary, 16 September, 1856, says that they had been sold. Eastlake on the same visit to Perugia, calling them SS. Silvester (*sic*) and Roch, says that one had been sold in Florence, one in Gubbio. Crowe and Cavalcaselle, *History of Painting in Italy*, III, 1866, p. 243, say they had been sold to Count della Porta. They are, however, not in the list of pictures belonging to Count Carlo della Porta at Gubbio, given by O. Lucarelli, *Guida Storica di Gubbio*, 1886, pp. 59/61. (**4**) A fresco ascribed to Perugino, still on the wall in another part of the church, is actually dated 1522. See Orsini, *op. cit.*, pp. 214/5 (date given as 1522, then 1521); F. Canuti, *Il Perugino*, 1931, I, p. 228. A reproduction of the whole, including the date, is given by E. Camesasca, *Tutta la Pittura del Perugino*, 1959, Plate 218a. (**5**) Perhaps the nearest are Klassiker der Kunst *Perugino*, 1914, Plates 112, 125, 158. (**6**) Reproduced in *The Connoisseur*, May, 1923, p. 3. (**7**) Mentioned *in situ* by Orsini, *op. cit.*, 1804, p. 214. (**8**) Massari, *op. cit.*, p. 3. (**9**) Mündler, Diary, 16 September, 1856, says it was the Casa Martotelli. Eastlake in his notebook, same visit, says the house or the picture belonged to Don Nazzareno Bonomi, who certainly had been the owner earlier (see the provenance above). Crowe and Cavalcaselle, *History of Painting in Italy*, III, 1866, p. 243, say that the picture remained until 1862 for sale with Angelo Morrettini, Perugia. (**10**) Catalogue, Part II, *Water Colour Paintings, etc.*, 1893, p. 225; inv. no. 7856/62. See also the National Gallery *Descriptive and Historical Catalogue*, Foreign Schools, 1898.

After Pietro PERUGINO

1431 THE BAPTISM OF CHRIST

Wood, painted surface, $12\frac{3}{4} \times 23\frac{1}{4}$ (0.325×0.59); excluding a black band round the edges, which to a slight extent covers the edges of the picture itself. Size of the panel, $13\frac{3}{4} \times 24\frac{3}{4}$ (0.35×0.63).

The picture appears to be on canvas stuck on to panel; the panel has been gessoed round the edges, to raise them to the level of the picture. The panel may be quite old; the picture is not, but is a modern copy of a Perugino at Rouen.[1]

PROVENANCE: Purchased from Godfrey Kopp, Rome, 1894.

REPRODUCTION: *Plates, Earlier Italian Schools*, 1953, Vol. II, p. 337.

REFERENCE: (**1**) The picture by Perugino at Rouen, which differs slightly from No. 1431 in the trees and the landscape, is reproduced in the Klassiker der Kunst *Perugino*, 1914, Plate 54. From time to time, some writing has accrued around No. 1431; since the painting is not old, it is sufficient to cite *L'Arte*, 1907, p. 159.

Follower of Pietro PERUGINO

702 THE VIRGIN AND CHILD IN A MANDORLA WITH CHERUBIM

Wood, painted surface, $18 \times 12\frac{3}{4}$ (0.46×0.32); painted up to the edges all round. To judge from the stamped pattern round the edges at the top, the picture has been very slightly cut left and right.

In general a well preserved picture, so far as can be seen. The gold work, although of poor quality, appears to be largely original.

No. 702 is a version of a very popular design, of which numerous variants have survived. The execution of No. 702 appears to be more in the style of Perugino than of anyone else. It is possible that the original of the numerous versions was by Perugino himself;[1] this is however not certain, some of the existing versions being in the style of Pintoricchio or other painters. Some versions have been ascribed to Antonio da Viterbo (Pastura), an imitator of Perugino and Pintoricchio;[2] it is nevertheless very improbable that he invented the design and, on stylistic grounds, unlikely that he executed No. 702.

VERSIONS: No attempt is made here to list all the existing versions, some of which have a landscape background instead of the mandorla with cherubim. A version with the mandorla and cherubim, formerly belonging to Major-General John Sterling and later to J. Pierpont Morgan, is said by Crowe and Cavalcaselle to be the finest known, and to be by Pintoricchio.[3] Other versions with the mandorla and cherubim are at Budapest,[4] Paris,[5] Tuscania (Municipio),[6] in the Cook Collection,[7] in the Brera at Milan[8] and at Darmstadt.[9] A variant where the design of the Virgin and Child is changed was in the Henri Rouart Sale, Paris, 11 December, 1912 (lot 49).[10] Versions without the mandorla and cherubim are in the Fogg Art Museum at Cambridge, Mass.;[11] the Bufalini Collection at Città di Castello;[12] and the former Benson Collection.[13]

PROVENANCE: No. 702 was bought by Count Joseph von Rechberg in Paris in August, 1815, and sold by him in September, 1815, to Prince Ludwig Kraft Ernst von Œttingen-Wallerstein, Schloss Wallerstein.[14] Catalogues of ca. 1826 and 1827 (No. 17); exhibited with other Œttingen-Wallerstein pictures at Kensington Palace (for sale), 1848 (No. 25),[15] bought with the rest of the collection by the Prince Consort. Waagen's Catalogue, 1854 (No. 17).[16] Exhibited at Manchester, 1857 (Provisional Catalogue, No. 42; Definitive Catalogue, No. 115).[17] Presented by Queen Victoria at the Prince Consort's wish, 1863.[18]

REPRODUCTION: *Illustrations, Italian Schools*, 1937, p. 367. *Plates, Earlier Italian Schools*, 1953, Vol. II, p. 337.

REFERENCES: (1) Oskar Fischel in the Prussian *Jahrbuch*, 1917, p. 57, ascribes the composition to Perugino at an early period. (2) For him, see E. Steinmann, *Antonio da Viterbo*, 1901. (3) Crowe and Cavalcaselle, *History of Painting in Italy*, III, 1866, pp. 164/5 (as in the collection or Sir Anthony Stirling), or ed. Borenius, V, 1914, pp. 274/5. The picture was exhibited at the R.A., 1910 (No. 5). (4) Budapest, 1937 Catalogue (in Hungarian), No. 62, as Pintoricchio; reproduced in G. von Térey's Budapest Catalogue, *Romanische Meister*, 1916, p. 63. (5) Paris, Louvre, Seymour de Ricci's Catalogue, *Ecoles Etrangères, Italie et Espagne*, 1913, p. 155, No. 1573, as School of Perugino; reproduced by Van Marle, *Development of the Italian Schools of Painting*, Vol. XV, Fig. 202, as Antonio da Viterbo. (6) Reproduced in the Catalogue, *La Pittura Viterbese*, Viterbo, 1954, Plate 51; partly reproduced by Van Marle, *op. cit.*, Vol. XV, Fig. 201, and by Venturi, *Storia dell'Arte Italiana*, Vol. VII, Part II, Fig. 551. It has some landscape and angels outside the mandorla at the sides and top. (7) Cook Catalogue, Vol. I, No. 56, reproduced, as School of Pintoricchio. (8) Brera, No. 474, as Umbrian School; 1908 Catalogue, p. 270; more recent catalogue (n.d.), No. 129. (9) Darmstadt, 1885 Katalog, No. 513, as Umbrian School. (10) As Ingegno (Andrea di Aloigi); reproduced in the catalogue. (11) Catalogue, 1919, No. 34, reproduced, as Umbrian School. The evidence concerning a traditional attribution of Raphael is summarized in the catalogue, from the book by David Farabulini, *Sopra una Madonna di Raffaello d'Urbino*, 1875. (12) Reproduced by Venturi, *Storia dell'Arte Italiana*, Vol. VII, Part II, Fig. 449, as Pintoricchio. (13) Reproduced by Venturi, *Storia*, Vol. VII, Part II, Fig. 554, as Antonio da Viterbo. (14) Letter from Werner Noack, 20 November, 1909, noted by E. K. Waterhouse. (15) As Raphael. (16) As Niccolò Alunno, with a note that M. Hartzen inclined to Pintoricchio. Cf. also Waagen, *Treasures*, IV, 1857, pp. 222/3. (17) As Niccolò Alunno. (18) Ascribed to Ingegno (Andrea di Aloigi) when it entered the Gallery; changed in 1888 to Umbrian School.

2484 THE VIRGIN AND CHILD, WITH SS. DOMINIC AND CATHERINE OF SIENA, AND TWO DONORS

Wood, painted surface, $14 \times 12\frac{1}{2}$ ($0 \cdot 355 \times 0 \cdot 315$); painted up to the edges all round. The bottom $\frac{7}{8}$ in. is on a different piece of wood from the main part; but the join is covered at the back, and the front is much repainted, so that it has not been possible to say if this is an original addition or not. The top 1 in. also appears to be wholly new paint, but this is on the main panel, and not on an addition.

Considerably repainted.

Formerly ascribed without grounds to Andrea di Aloigi, L'Ingegno. The condition does not prevent one from seeing that the picture is in the unattributable class; it is by some feeble follower of Perugino.

PROVENANCE: In the Conte Guido di Bisenzo Collection, Rome, by 1836.[1] This collection was bought *en bloc* in 1847 by Lord Ward[2] (created Earl of Dudley in 1860). Among the Ward pictures on view for some years at the Egyptian Hall.[3] Exhibited at the R.A., 1871 (No. 317) and 1892 (No. 179). Dudley Sale, 25 June, 1892 (lot 40), bought by G. Salting. By November, 1892, it had passed to Wickham Flower,[4] who lent it to the New Gallery, 1893 (No. 138). Flower Sale, 17 December, 1904 (lot 42), bought by Agnew. George Salting Bequest, 1910.

REPRODUCTION: *Illustrations, Italian Schools*, 1937, p. 173. *Plates, Earlier Italian Schools*, 1953, Vol. II, p. 338.

REFERENCES: (1) Engraved (as Ingegno) while in this collection for *L'Ape Italiana delle Belle Arti*, II, 1836, Plate XXVIII; pp. 46/7, article by G. Melchiorri. (2) *Kunst-Blatt*, 1847, p. 152. (3) *The Athenaeum*, 1851, p. 722. (4) Label on the back. The Salting MSS. are not clear about Salting's purchase, sale and repurchase of the picture.

See also Follower of ANDREA DEL VERROCCHIO, No. 781

PESELLINO
ca. 1422–1457

Florentine School. Francesco di Stefano, known as *Pesellino*. Confused in old source-books with his maternal grandfather Giuliano (Pesello), who may have given Francesco his earliest training in painting. His age was declared as 5 in 1427. In 1453 he entered into partnership with Piero di Lorenzo and Zanobi di Migliore for three years; his partnership with the former continued until his death. His only documented work is the part he painted of the altarpiece catalogued below. There is, however, a pre-Vasarian tradition that he painted the predella to Fra Filippo Lippi's altarpiece in S. Croce, Florence (now divided between the Uffizi and the Louvre), probably about 1440; it is indeed probable that Lippi was his chief instructor in painting. A number of pictures, mostly with figures on a small scale, are reasonably ascribed to him.

A different Francesco di Stefano, painter at Florence, has sometimes been confused with Pesellino; e.g. by R. G. Mather in *The Art Bulletin*, March, 1948, pp. 53 ff.

PESELLINO
(finished in the studio of FRA FILIPPO LIPPI)

ALTARPIECE: THE TRINITY WITH SAINTS

This altarpiece was broken into several pieces, which entered the Gallery at different dates, and have different inventory numbers, viz. 727, 3162, 3230, 4428, 4868 a, b, c, d. One further piece is lent by H.M. The Queen, and has no inventory number.

727 THE TRINITY

For all details, see under No. 4868 below.

3162 ANGEL ON THE RIGHT

For all details, see under No. 4868 below.

3230 ANGEL ON THE LEFT

For all details, see under No. 4868 below.

4428 SS. ZENO AND JEROME

For all details, see under No. 4868 below.

LENT SS. JAMES THE GREAT AND MAMAS (WITH THREE LIONS)

For all details, see under No. 4868 below.

4868A S. MAMAS IN PRISON THROWN TO THE LIONS

4868B THE BEHEADING OF S. JAMES THE GREAT

4868C S. ZENO EXORCISING THE DAUGHTER OF THE EMPEROR GALLIENUS

4868D S. JEROME AND THE LION

Wood. The sight size of the main panel, painted surface, is $72\frac{1}{2} \times 71\frac{1}{2}$ ($1·84 \times 1·815$).[1] The sizes of the pictures forming the predella, in each case with the corners cut, are: a, $10\frac{5}{8} \times 15\frac{1}{2}$ ($0·27 \times 0·395$); b, $10\frac{3}{4} \times 15$ ($0·275 \times 0·38$); c, $10\frac{3}{4} \times 15\frac{3}{8}$ ($0·275 \times 0·39$); d, $10\frac{3}{8} \times 15\frac{3}{4}$ ($0·265 \times 0·40$).

In the case of each of these predella panels, grey paint continues beyond the area of the pictures to the edges of the panels; the sizes of the panels are roughly 1 in. more each way than the pictures.

The condition is good; but on the main panel, a piece in the right bottom corner, size $22\frac{1}{2} \times 22$ ($0\cdot57 \times 0\cdot56$), is of recent manufacture.[2] The fragments into which this panel had been broken, when fitted together again, left a few gaps along some of the joins, but the necessary reconstructions do not cover any of the important parts of the picture. There are some *pentimenti* in the predella, in part visible only by means of the X-Ray; in the scene with S. James, the executioner's dress and right leg were once different; in the scene with S. Zeno, the emperor's left eye was originally shown as open, the woman standing on the left was once apparently facing three-quarters to the front, and there are other changes; in the scene with S. Jerome, his hands were once somewhat different. X-Rays of the main panel show practically nothing at all, partly owing to the heavy cradling of this part.

S. Mamas was so called because as an infant he referred to his foster-mother Ammia as *mama*. He was martyred; he appears to have suffered both prison and the onset of wild beasts, but not concurrently, as indicated on the predella.[3] His identification, like those of the other saints, is nevertheless certain, as can be seen from the documents about to be summarized.

Although there is a break in the provenance, there can be no doubt at all that Nos. 727, etc., form the picture concerning which the documents have been published and commented upon by Pèleo Bacci.[4]

On 10 September, 1455, the Company of Priests of the Trinity at Pistoia decided to commission an altarpiece for their church.[5] The priest Pero ser Landi, treasurer of the Company, had a few days before obtained from Lorenzo, a painter in Florence, a drawing, which was shown to the Company; this drawing may well have corresponded in subject, but by no means necessarily in arrangement, with the picture thereupon commissioned. The Company decided that their picture should represent the Trinity, in honour of which they existed; that it should include figures of S. James the Great, Patron of Pistoia, of S. Zeno, Patron of the clergy of Pistoia, and of S. Jerome; and, at the particular request of Pero ser Landi, that the fourth saint should be S. Mamas. The predella is not referred to.[6] The negotiations for commissioning the picture were put into the hands of Pero ser Landi and Filippo di ser Giovanni.

Within a few days, Pero ser Landi went to Florence and arranged that Pesellino should paint the picture; he stayed on this occasion six days in Florence, and settled the design with the painter. Various payments to Pesellino followed during the succeeding months. On 29 July, 1457, Pesellino died.[7] It is possible that his health had been poor for some time; certainly, on 10 July, Pero ser Landi had endeavoured to settle accounts with him, and had had the picture valued by Fra Filippo Lippi and Domenico Veneziano.

The valuers are stated to have considered the picture half finished at Pesellino's death, and this seems to be approximately correct.[8] The design had been settled in September, 1455; it is certain that since that time Pesellino had done a good deal to the picture.[9]

At the end of September, 1458, the unfinished picture was brought from Florence to Pistoia; about a month later it was sent to Prato, where Fra Filippo Lippi was commissioned to finish it. Several payments to Fra Filippo Lippi were made, partly via Don Diamante and Domenico, a pupil of Fra Filippo's; and in June, 1460, the picture was delivered at Pistoia.

It may be added that Lippi as part of his contract painted a dossale or paliotto for the altar, which was delivered at Pistoia in 1467; Bacci has been able to identify this dossale with the *Madonna della Misericordia* once at Berlin.[10] The dossale appears to have been delivered not quite complete and was put in order on its arrival by a local painter, Giovanni di Piero di Tommeo.

The documents indicate precisely that the picture was begun by Pesellino and finished by Fra Filippo Lippi; they do not indicate which parts were painted by whom. It is reasonable to assume that, for the main panel at least, the whole design was laid in by Pesellino; so that whatever part of this was finished by Lippi would have been done following more or less precisely Pesellino's forms. Indeed, the only at all prominent parts of this main panel that might pass as purely Lippi's are the hands of God the Father, and the Dove. Nevertheless, Gronau[11] seems to be right in seeing a difference of style between the saints on the right and those on the left; if the execution of SS. James and Mamas is indeed not Pesellino's, the comparatively good quality would seem to indicate the workmanship of Lippi himself, not of one of his assistants. The landscape of the main panel is in a loose technique that seems Lippesque, and is comparable with the landscapes of the predelle, which are usually ascribed throughout to Lippi's studio. The compiler would not be willing to exclude Pesellino's participation entirely from these predelle, but admits that most of what is now seen appears Lippesque. Their rough quality, and Lippi's methods of getting work done at the period in question, indicate an execution wholly or at least in part by studio assistants.[12]

DRAWINGS: Drawings connected with the saints on the main panel are at Florence[13] and Frankfort.[14] A drawing in the British Museum is vaguely connected with the female figure standing on the left of the scene with S. Zeno and the daughter of the Emperor Gallienus.[15]

DERIVATIVE: The two angels recur in a *Nativity* in the Louvre.[16]

PROVENANCE: As explained above, the altarpiece was painted for the Compagnia della SS. Trinità at Pistoia. Mentioned in an inventory of 1492.[17] The Confraternity was suppressed *ca.* 1783, and the altarpiece is said to have been then sold to an unknown foreigner.[18] It is probable that there was not very much delay in dividing it into several pieces, some of which may have left Italy fairly soon.

Provenance of No. 727. This central piece entered the collection of William Young Ottley, who was living in Italy, *ca.* 1791/9; it was later seen in his collection by Waagen.[19] Warner Ottley Sale, 30 June, 1847 (lot 19), bought by the

Rev. Walter Davenport Bromley. Seen in the Davenport Bromley Collection by Waagen;[20] purchased at the Davenport Bromley Sale, 13 June, 1863 (lot 172).

Provenance of No. 3162 (the Angel on the right). This and its companion appear to have been owned by Lombardi at Florence.[21] In any case, bought by the Countess Brownlow from Pinti, *ca.* 1867.[22] Lent by the Countess Brownlow to the New Gallery, 1893/4 (No. 109),[23] and by Lord Brownlow to the Burlington Fine Arts Club, 1906 (No. 19). Bequeathed by the Countess Brownlow, 1917.

Provenance of No. 3230 (the Angel on the left). Apparently, like No. 3162 above, with Lombardi in Florence. Lent[24] by Lord Somers to the British Institution, 1866 (No. 37), and to the R.A., 1873 (No. 182); lent to the R.A., 1896 (No. 159), by Lady Henry Somerset (daughter of the 3rd Earl Somers). Purchased from Lord Somers, Temple-West Fund, 1917.

Provenance of No. 4428 (SS. Zeno and Jerome). Waagen[25] saw in the Ottley Collection not only No. 727 above, as already recorded, but also 'on two other panels, SS. James and Zeno.' It is probable that the accuracy of Waagen's notes was affected by the description of the altarpiece in the 2nd edition of Vasari,[26] and that Waagen actually saw No. 4428 and the Queen's panel, to be discussed presently. No. 4428 is first definitely recorded in 1906 in the Collection of the German Emperor William (II).[27] After the 1914–18 war it was shown for a time at the Schloss Museum at Berlin;[28] presented by the National Art-Collections Fund, in association with and by the generosity of Sir Joseph Duveen, Bart., 1929.

Provenance of The Queen's panel (SS. James and Mamas). Like No. 4428 above, pretty clearly seen by Waagen in the Ottley Collection. Bought in 1846 from Warner Ottley through Gruner, and presented by Queen Victoria to the Prince Consort on 26 August, 1846.[29] It hung for many years at Osborne, but was transferred in 1902 to Buckingham Palace.[30] Lent from the Royal Collection since 1919.

Provenance of No. 4868. Found in some buildings attached to S. Desiderio at Pistoia, which had belonged to a nunnery suppressed in 1786; the Gelli family obtained these buildings for use as a factory.[31] Some writing on the back of the scene with S. Zeno suggests that this panel at least was in the hands of Antonio Gherardin between 7 April and 1 May, 1879; perhaps for repair. In any case, the four predella panels were lent by Cav. Antonio Gelli to an Exhibition at Pistoia, 1899, Sala XVI, No. 2. After his death, they passed to his daughter, Signora Michelozzi-Roti, in Florence. Later in the Felix M. Warburg Collection, New York; presented by Mr. and Mrs. Felix M. Warburg, through the National Art-Collections Fund, 1937.

The reconstructed altarpiece was included in the N.A.C.F. Exhibition at the National Gallery, 1945/6 (No. 31).

REPRODUCTIONS: *Illustrations, Italian Schools,* 1937, p. 275 (without the predella). *Plates, Earlier Italian Schools,* 1953, Vol. II, pp. 339–344.

REFERENCES: (1) The sizes of the individual pieces into which the main panel had been broken are, according to the 1929 catalogue: No. 727, cruciform, 72×39 (1.82×0.99); No. 3162, 17×24 (0.43×0.61); No. 3230, $18\frac{3}{4} \times 24$ (0.47×0.61); No. 4428, $32\frac{1}{2} \times 22\frac{3}{8}$ (0.82×0.57); The Queen's fragment, $55\frac{1}{2} \times 25\frac{1}{2}$ (1.41×0.65). The shapes of the individual fragments are indicated in the Book of Illustrations, *Italian Schools,* 1923, p. 134. (2) It was painted to the order of the National Gallery by Prof. E. W. Tristram in 1929/30. (3) Some indications about S. Mamas can be found in *The Burlington Magazine,* Vol. XVI (1909/10), p. 233, and Vol. XX (1911/2), pp. 351 ff. (4) Pèleo Bacci, *Documenti e Commenti per la Storia dell'Arte,* 1944, pp. 113 ff. Partial publication of the documents had taken place at various times previously, but Bacci's latest work supersedes these approximations. The summary of the events as given in the text is rather short; the student is referred to Bacci for further details. (5) Old sources, such as Vasari, call the church S. Jacopo, but it was dedicated to the Trinity. See, for instance, Giuseppe Dondori, *Della Pietà di Pistoia,* 1666, p. 166 (misprinted 162). Similarly, in the eighteenth-century Oretti MSS. in the Biblioteca dell'Archiginnasio at Bologna (B 5), the picture (as scuola di Masaccio) is mentioned as the high-altarpiece of the 'Chiesa della SS^ma Trinità, Congrega di Preti.' (6) For a predella in intarsia, which was probably something quite different, see Bacci, *op. cit.*, pp. 121/2. The existing predella is first surely referred to in 1465; Bacci, *op. cit.*, pp. 146/7. (7) On 2 August, 1457, the Company were warned not to make any further payments for the work that had been done by Pesellino, pending settlement of a dispute between Pesellino's widow and his partner in business, Piero di Lorenzo di Pratese; for this reason, the final payment to Pesellino's widow was not made until 14 June, 1458. The matter would have been hardly worth mentioning here, if it had not in the past been supposed that Piero di Lorenzo assisted Pesellino in painting the picture. There is not the slightest evidence in favour of such a view, and very strong evidence against. (8) Pesellino's widow, on the other hand, claimed that it was 'quasi fornita.' The view taken by the valuers that it was half finished is, nevertheless, fairly well confirmed by the amounts of money paid for Pesellino's work, and then for Fra Filippo Lippi's work. (9) Bacci, *op. cit.*, p. 131, gives an argument to show that the figure of S. Mamas at least was far advanced at the time of Pesellino's death; the argument is good as far as it goes, but does not prove that the surface of that figure as now seen is Pesellino's work. (10) Berlin, 1931 Catalogue, No. 95, reproduced in the Illustrations; recorded in *Arte Veneta*, 1949, p. 192, to have been destroyed in the last war. Bacci's identification is quite sure; but it may be added that some confirmation that Berlin No. 95 comes from Pistoia can perhaps be found in Vasari, ed. Milanesi, Vol. II, p. 625, note 3. The note is excessively confused. But the picture recognized by the inhabitant of Pistoia is identified as No. 170 of the Berlin 1841 Catalogue, which is the later No. 95. Previously to Bacci's discovery, the dossale had been wrongly identified with a series of 18 small single figures, lent by Sir John Leslie to the R.A., 1885 (Nos. 252 and 256), as Filippino, and sold in an Anon. Sale at Christie's, 9 July, 1926 (lot 129), as Filippino, as coming from the Carmine at Florence. Some of these figures are now in the Courtauld Institute Galleries (*Catalogue of the Lee Collection*, 1958, No. 73), at Washington, and at Worcester, Mass.; others are in private collections. They are all reproduced by Mary Pittaluga, *Filippo Lippi*, 1949, Figs. 170/1. (11) Gronau in the *Rivista d'Arte*, 1938, p. 130. P. Toesca in the *Enciclopedia Italiana*, s.v. Pesellino, see traces of participation by Fra Filippo in the figure of God the Father. (12) Mary Pittaluga (*Rivista d'Arte*, 1950, pp. 235, 239) claims that on documentary grounds Pesellino's participation is excluded from the predella; this, however, does not appear to be so (Bacci, *op. cit.*, pp. 121/2). Berenson in his latest Lists thinks that Nos. 4868B and D show the participation of Don Diamante, and No. 4868C that of the Master of S. Miniato. M. Pittaluga in *L'Arte*, 1941, pp. 22 ff., and her *Filippo Lippi*, 1949, p. 204, agrees with Berenson about Nos. 4868B and D, ascribes No. 4868C to Fra Filippo Lippi (?) and a helper, and No. 4868A to a different helper of Fra Filippo. P. Toesca in the *Enciclopedia Italiana*, s.v. Pesellino, calls No. 4868B Pesellino, No. 4868C Fra Filippo, No. 4868D near Fra Filippo, and No. 4868A perhaps Piero di Lorenzo. (13) Two drawings: Berenson, *Drawings of the Florentine Painters*, 1938, Fig. 180, and No. 1838A, Fig. 182. (14) Berenson, *op. cit.*, No. 1846B, Fig. 185. (15) Berenson, *op. cit.*, No. 1387, Fig. 169. British Museum, *Italian Drawings, the Fourteenth and Fifteenth Centuries*, catalogue by A. E. Popham and Philip Pouncey, 1950, I, No. 150, and II, Plate CXXXVIII. (16) Louvre, Seymour de Ricci's Catalogue, *Ecoles Etrangères, Italie et Espagne*, 1913, No. 1343, as Filippo Lippi. Ascribed by Gronau to Don Diamante, and reproduced by him in the *Rivista d'Arte*, 1938, p. 132. (17) Bacci, as in note 4, p. 117. (18) Tolomei, *Guida di Pistoia*, 1821, p. 97. For a mention of the altarpiece still *in situ* in the eighteenth century, see note 5. (19) Waagen, *Kunstwerke*, 1837, I, p. 397. (20) Waagen, *Treasures*, III, 1854, p. 375. (21) Recorded, as by Fra Filippo Lippi, by Crowe and Cavalcaselle, *History of Painting in Italy*, II, 1864, p. 336. In a Lombardi-Baldi Catalogue, No. 42, one angel only is listed, as by Masaccio; the catalogue is not dated, but the copy in the Uffizi Library is claimed to be of 1845. (22) MS. note by Collins Baker in his copy of the 1915 Catalogue.

(23) As Masaccio. (24) As Masaccio. (25) Waagen, *Kunstwerke*, 1837, I, p. 397. (26) Vasari, ed. Milanesi, III, p. 38. (27) Paul Seidel, etc., *Gemälde alter Meister im Besitze des deutschen Kaisers*, 1906/7, pp. 81/2, as Ligurian School. It may be that No. 4428 was bought, like the Queen's panel, by Queen Victoria. Her eldest daughter, the Princess Royal, married the Emperor Frederick (III) in 1858; a gift to her might explain how the picture turned up in the German Imperial Collection, that is, in the possession of their son, the Emperor William (II); but no evidence has been found that this actually happened. (28) Where identified in 1922 as Pesellino by Hans Kauffmann; see *The Burlington Magazine*, Vol LIV (1929), pp. 223 and 145. (29) From the Osborne Catalogue, 1876, p. 88, No. 119, kindly communicated by Benedict Nicolson; no earlier reference to the picture as being in the Royal Collection has been discovered. Queen Victoria's diary refers to several pictures on 26 August, 1846, but not to this Pesellino (kindly communicated by Sir Owen Morshead). (30) See L. Cust, *The Royal Collection*, I, *Buckingham Palace*, 100 Photogravures, 1905. (31) Bacci, as in note 4, p. 117.

MARTINO 'PIAZZA'
active *ca.* 1513–1522

Properly *de' Toccagni*; assumed to have been known as *Piazza*. In conjunction with his brother Albertino, active at Lodi. Passavant says that he died in 1527. Only one documented picture survives, and that is documented as being by both brothers; see Angiola Maria Romanini in the *Bollettino d'Arte*, 1950, pp. 123 ff.

Three pictures with monograms are also recorded; Mündler seems to have been the first to say that the monograms may stand for Martino 'Piazza.' The three pictures are: (1) No. 1152 below; the monogram is described in the text. (2) A *Nativity* in the Ambrosiana at Milan; only the letters M P P are present. (3) A *Virgin and Child with S. John*, in 1857 in the Bortolan (Mantovani-Orsetti) Collection at Treviso. Mündler copied the monogram, which is similar to that on No. 1152 below, except that a single P takes the place of M P P, and the wings are shown lower down. This picture appeared as Penni in the Conte della Torre di Rezzonico Giovio and Mantovani-Orsetti (eredità Bortolan di Treviso) Sale at Milan, 31 May and following days, 1898 (lot 18); reproduced in the sale catalogue, and by Reinach, *Répertoire*, I, p. 219.

Whether or not these three pictures are by the same hand, it appears doubtful if any of them are really by Martino 'Piazza.' One difficulty about accepting the monogram as his is that, while Martino's sons were certainly called Piazza in 1529, there is no proof that Martino himself used this name.

Ascribed to MARTINO 'PIAZZA'

1152 S. JOHN THE BAPTIST IN THE DESERT

Signed with a monogram: the letters M P P are surmounted by a T; a small drop hangs from each end of the cross-bar of the T, and its stem passes between a pair of wings.

Poplar,[1] painted surface, $27\frac{1}{4} \times 20\frac{1}{2}$ (0·69×0·52); painted up to the edges all round.

Good condition; many *pentimenti* in the outlines.

For the doubtful attribution, see the biography above.[2]

PROVENANCE: Seen by Mündler in 1856 in the possession of Sr. Bozzi, Milan;[3] purchased from Pietro Vergani, Milan, 1883.[4]

REPRODUCTION: *Plates, Earlier Italian Schools*, 1953, Vol. II, p. 345.

REFERENCES: (1) Letter from B. J. Rendle, of the Forest Products Research Laboratory, in the Gallery archives. (2) Angiola Romanini of Pavia kindly wrote to the compiler on this subject; letter of 1 March, 1948, in the Gallery archives. (3) Mündler's Diary, with identifying description. (4) As Martino Piazza.

PIER FRANCESCO FIORENTINO
active 1474–1497

A priest, active for the most part at San Gimignano. There are two signed works: one of 1494 in S. Agostino at San Gimignano is reproduced in *Dedalo*, July, 1926, p. 87; the other of 1497 in the Gallery at Montefortino is reproduced in the *Inventario delle Cose d'Arte e di Antichità d'Italia, Provincie di Ancona e di Ascoli Piceno*, 1936, p. 296. For further evidence concerning him, see G. Poggi in the *Rivista d'Arte*, 1909, pp. 65 ff. He appears to have been a follower of Benozzo (Gozzoli).

He has in the past been credited with a large number of pictures deriving from Fra Filippo Lippi and apparently Pesellino. These pictures differ considerably from Pier Francesco's sure works. They have sometimes been ascribed to a pseudo-Pier Francesco Fiorentino; but this is unjustifiably precise. The existing works do not form a group; they are copies of varying style and quality from certain designs. It is clear that there was a demand among the Florentine public of the time for religious pictures of certain types; one or more factories were formed to meet the demand, the resulting works being now unattributable.

See FLORENTINE SCHOOL, No. 1199

PIERO DI COSIMO
ca. 1462, after 1515

Florentine School. Son of Lorenzo di Piero. By 1480, pupil of Cosimo Rosselli, whose christian name he attached to his own. According to Vasari (edition of 1550) he assisted Cosimo Rosselli in the Sixtine Chapel at Rome (frescoes of 1481/2), and he appears to have stayed with Rosselli for a long time. Vasari (edition of 1550) says that he died in 1521; he was certainly still alive in 1515 (see Vasari, ed. Milanesi, Vol. V, p. 25).

There are no documented works by Piero di Cosimo. Vasari, in his edition of 1550, mentions a number of identifiable pictures, and all attributions are based on these.

698   A MYTHOLOGICAL SUBJECT

A nymph partly naked is lying on the ground, with a wound in her neck. A satyr seems to be grieving over her; a dog looks on. In the background, an estuary with various birds and animals.

Reverse: A drawing on the unprimed wood, perhaps for the decorative pilaster of some frame.

Wood, painted surface, $25\frac{3}{4} \times 72\frac{1}{4}$ (0·65 × 1·83). Painted up to the edges all round, but the paint is not quite finished on the edges at the sides. The drawing on the reverse is about 22 in. long.

Cleaned in 1952/3. Fairly well preserved. There are many *pentimenti* in the outlines; the dog once had its tongue out, apparently.

The subject of No. 698 was doubtfully accepted by Eastlake as being *The Death of Procris*,[1] and this has often been admitted. It appears unlikely. According to the classical story, which is told with some variations, Cephalus killed Procris by mistake with a magic spear, and a dog sometimes called Laelaps was also associated with Cephalus and Procris. The correspondence with No. 698 is slight. To account for the satyr here Schubring[2] refers to the 'Fabula di Caephalo' by Nicolò da Correggio, a play produced in Ferrara in 1487. Nicolò da Corregio does speak of a faun who stimulated the jealousy of Procris against Cephalus; but this seems to be a poor justification for the presence here of a faun or satyr, and for the absence here of Cephalus. It may therefore rather be that No. 698 represents a different, hitherto unidentified subject; conceivably a subject from some Renaissance poem rather than from classical legend[3]

It appears probable that No. 698 is not a cassone front, as it has often been called; it may rather have ornamented some wainscoting.[4]

PROVENANCE: From the Collection at Florence of Conte Ferdinando Guicciardini (1782–1833).[5] Probably passed to his son, Conte Carlo.[6] With Lombardi and Baldi at Florence, probably by 1856[7] and certainly by 1858.[8] Purchased from Francesco Lombardi, Florence, 1862.

REPRODUCTIONS: *Illustrations, Italian Schools,* 1937, p. 278 (front); *Plates, Earlier Italian Schools,* 1953, Vol. II, p. 346 (front); both before cleaning. The reverse is reproduced in *Paintings and Drawings on the Backs of National Gallery Pictures,* 1946, Plate 12.

REFERENCES: (1) Eastlake's note-book, 1858. (2) P. Schubring, *Cassoni,* 1923, pp. 52/3 and No. 404. Schubring refers back to A. d'Ancona, *Origini del Teatro Italiano,* 1891, II, pp. 5 ff. (3) Irving Lavin, in the *Warburg Journal,* 1954, pp. 260 ff., nevertheless accepts the identification of the subject as the Death of Procris; he has the weighty support of Erwin Panofsky for this view. The picture no doubt would be so identifiable if a literary source much closer to it than Nicolò da Correggio's play were found, or if other pictures of the same series and showing Cephalus were found; but in the present state of knowledge the compiler does not feel justified in accepting the identification, even though he has no alternative subject to propose. C. A. Holborow, in the *Bulletin of the History of Medicine,* March–April 1959, pp. 168 ff., suggested that the female

figure may be shown as having undergone a tracheostomy, possibly after drowning; it seems difficult to bring this into accord with the action shown in the
picture, but it is a fair point that the water in the background may not be irrelevant to the subject. (4) See what is said in the entry for Botticelli, No. 915. (5)
The Guicciardini arms are on a label and a seal on the back, and they are of the
form used by Conte Ferdinando di Lorenzo Guicciardini. No. 698 is not recorded
in the Guicciardini inventory of 1807, referred to in the entry for No. 1033,
Botticelli. Letter in the Gallery archives from Conte Paolo Guicciardini, 11
September, 1948. (6) The label and seal referred to in the previous note are of
the same form as those on the back of Florentine School, No. 585, which is
stated to have belonged to Conte Carlo. No. 585 and No. 698 were both later
with Lombardi and Baldi at Florence, and it seems probable that they were sold
together from the Guicciardini Collection. (7) Eastlake's note-book, 1856 (not
explicit). In a letter from Eastlake to Wornum, 1 October, 1862, Eastlake says
that No. 698 was originally selected with other pictures from Lombardi-Baldi
for purchase in 1857, but in the difficulty of arranging the price, it was omitted.
(8) Eastlake's note-book, 1858; also mentioned in Eastlake's note-book, 1861.

4890 THE FIGHT BETWEEN THE LAPITHS AND THE
      CENTAURS

The scene is before a cave, at the marriage-feast of Pirithous, King of
the Lapiths, with Hippodame. The centaurs were invited, as being near
relatives of Pirithous. The fight began when the drunken centaur
Eurytus or Eurytion tried to rape Hippodame, seizing her by the hair;
the two figures are seen in the foreground, towards the right. The man
about to hurl a wine-bowl at Eurytus is Theseus. The centaur using a
candelabrum as a weapon is Amycus; the centaur preparing to hurl a
smoking altar, Gryneus. Further to the right, Theseus (a second time)
has leapt on the back of the centaur Bienor; Theseus holds the centaur's
hair with his left hand, and prepares to beat his face in with an oak-
trunk. In the right middle-distance, the centaur struggling to uproot a
tree is most probably Petreus; in that case, the man about to hurl a
lance at him is Pirithous. In the middle-distance towards the left, the
centaur Dictys, fleeing from Pirithous, is impaled on an ash; the man
above him with a stone is apparently a confusion for the centaur
Aphareus, who tried to avenge Dictys. At the extreme left, in the foreground, the figure felling a centaur is doubtless Hercules. In the foreground in the middle is a group of two centaurs. Cyllarus, with golden
hair and a black body, is dying near the javelin that killed him; his lover
Hylonome, with hair combed and wreathed with flowers, and with a
wild beast's skin over her flank, lays her hand upon Cyllarus' wound and
kisses him.

Wood, painted surface, $28 \times 102\frac{1}{2}$ (0·71 × 2·60); painted up to the
edges all round.
Cleaned in 1954/5. Good condition.
The subject is taken from the *Metamorphoses* of Ovid, Book XII,
vv. 210 sqq. Piero di Cosimo has in parts followed Ovid very closely;
almost everything recorded above in the description of the picture
corresponds with Ovid. There are various other figures in the picture,
not described above; these seem to be due to the painter's fancy, or

perhaps in a few cases to a misunderstanding of Ovid. Ovid further mentions several incidents in the fight, that Piero di Cosimo does not illustrate.[1]

No. 4890 is likely to have formed part of the decoration of a room. There exist three other pictures by Piero di Cosimo, of the same height but not of the same width as No. 4890;[2] Panofsky, chiefly because of the subject-matter of the pictures, thinks that these three belong to one series, but that No. 4890 does not belong.[3] No old records are known, certainly referring to No. 4890.[4]

The execution of No. 4890 is in parts coarse; but there is no good reason to suppose that it is not by Piero di Cosimo himself.

PROVENANCE: With Gagliardi, Florence, at least by 1885; brought to England, ca. 1892.[5] Coll. John Burke, London.[6] With a London dealer ca. 1902;[7] presumably the Carfax Gallery was meant.[8] In the Collection of Charles Ricketts and Charles Shannon by 1905.[9] Exhibited at the Burlington Fine Arts Club, 1919 (No. 31); at the Italian Exhibition at the R.A., 1930 (No. 234; Memorial Catalogue, No. 298). Charles Ricketts died in 1931. No. 4890 was deposited on loan at the National Gallery from 1933. Paris, *Exposition de l'Art Italien*, 1935 (No. 496; but not in the catalogue). Bequeathed by Charles Haslewood Shannon, 1937.

REPRODUCTION: *Plates, Earlier Italian Schools*, 1953, Vol. II, pp. 347–348.

REFERENCES: (1) For the interpretation of the subject, see H. P. Horne in *The Architectural Review*, 1902, ii, pp. 61 ff. Comments on the medical interest of the picture were made by S. Squire Sprigge in *The Lancet*, 19 July, 1902, p. 167, and in *The Burlington Magazine*, Vol. XXVIII, 1915/6, pp. 195/6. (2) (*a*) Oxford, Ashmolean Museum; 1951 Catalogue (No. 328); stated to be from Palazzo Rucellai, Florence; size, 0·71 × 1·96. Exhibited at the R.A., 1930 (No. 225; Memorial Catalogue, No. 299). Reproduced in *The Burlington Magazine*, Vol. XXXVIII (1921), p. 133; in the *Souvenir* of the R.A. Exhibition of 1930, p. 50; by R. Langton Douglas, *Piero di Cosimo*, 1946, Plates XV–XVI. (*b*) and (*c*) New York, Metropolitan Museum; Catalogue, *Italian, Spanish and Byzantine Schools*, 1940, pp. 58 ff.; sizes 27¾ × 66½/¾. Reproduced in the catalogue, and by R. Langton Douglas, *Piero di Cosimo*, 1946, Plates XI–XIV. (3) E. Panofsky, *Studies in Iconology*, 1939, pp. 33 ff., esp. pp. 51/2. Panofsky further discusses two pictures at Hartford and Ottawa (R. Langton Douglas, *Piero di Cosimo*, 1946, Plates IV–VIII). The ex-Benson (Hartford) picture is the subject of correspondence between Panofsky and Langton Douglas in *The Art Bulletin*, 1946, pp. 286 ff.; 1947, pp. 143 ff.; 1947, p. 284. (4) Vasari mentions a Vespucci room and a Pugliese room decorated by Piero di Cosimo, but there is no good reason for believing that No. 4890 came from either of them; see Vasari, 1550, pp. 590/1, and Milanesi's edition, Vol. IV, pp. 139 and 141/2. The Vespucci series is likely to have included two pictures formerly in the Sebright Collection, and now at the Fogg Art Museum, Cambridge, Mass., and at Worcester, U.S.A.; see E. Panofsky in the *Worcester Art Museum Annual*, II, 1936/7, pp. 33 ff., and R. Langton Douglas, *Piero di Cosimo*, 1946, Plates XL–XLV. Panofsky, *Studies in Iconology*, 1939, pp. 57 ff., thinks that the Pugliese series probably included the Oxford and New York pictures. (5) Burlington Fine Arts Club, Catalogue of the Signorelli Exhibition, 1893, p. xvi. Possibly it had remained with Gagliardi for some time; Mündler in his Diary, 10 September, 1857, records at Gagliardi's 'a singular composition by *L. Signorelli*, a profane subject,' which might conceivably be No. 4890. It was certainly at Gagliardi's, as Piero di Cosimo, but with an attribution to Signorelli recorded, in 1885-7; see letters from J. P. Richter to Layard, 5 November, 1885, 9 December, 1886, and 16 October, 1887 (British Museum, Add. MSS. 39039, 39041, 39042, Layard

Papers, Vols. CIX, CXI, CXII). (6) Berenson, *Florentine Painters*, 1896.
F. Knapp, *Piero di Cosimo*, 1899, p. 39. (7) H. P. Horne in *The Architectural
Review*, 1902, ii, p. 61. (8) Cf. *The Athenaeum*, 7 June, 1902, p. 728. (9) Reinach,
Répertoire, Vol. I, 1905, p. 688.

Ascribed to PIERO di Cosimo

895 PORTRAIT OF A MAN IN ARMOUR

In the background is a view of Piazza della Signoria at Florence, discussed below.

Wood, $27\frac{3}{4} \times 20\frac{1}{4}$ (0·705 × 0·515); painted up to the edges at the sides.

In good condition on the whole, though somewhat repainted in the
face and right hand.

The view of the Palazzo Vecchio and the Loggia dei Lanzi in the
background, although sketchy, is in general very accurate.[1] A rather
earlier view, taken from a similar place, occurs in a fresco by Domenico
Ghirlandaio of *ca.* 1485 in S. Trinita, Florence, and may be compared.[2]
The parapet or *ringhiera* at the base of the Palazzo Vecchio is there
shown in a similar form, and is indeed recorded to have existed.[3] The
marzocco or lion at the corner of it has been destroyed,[4] but its base
shown on the picture is still in use for a different *marzocco*.[5] The lions
at the corners of the cornice of the Palace are also recorded to have
existed.[6] Lensi reproduces a drawing showing one such lion in a position
a few feet higher; he does not say what authority he has for the drawing,
and the picture is perhaps more accurate.[7] The decoration over the main
door of the Palace, rather summarily indicated, still exists; it is a space
with a pointed top, the ground decorated with fleur-de-lys, with two
lions below. It now has other ornamentation too, including a cross at
the bottom;[8] the mark on the picture below the lions is perhaps a shield,[9]
that does seem to be ornamented with a cross.

The Loggia dei Lanzi is seen on the picture very much as it is now.
The street between the Loggia and the Palazzo Vecchio is now quite
different, with the buildings housing the Uffizi Gallery, etc. The church
shown on the picture at the left of it, immediately behind the Palazzo
Vecchio, is S. Piero Scheraggio.[10]

For the date of the picture it is important that Michelangelo's *David*
is shown at the door of the Palazzo Vecchio. This statue was unveiled in
position on 8 September, 1504.[11] It is apparently shown on the far side
of the door; but this is merely an appearance due to imperfectly realized
perspective. Baccio Bandinelli's group of *Hercules and Cacus* is not
shown on the picture; this was set up as a pendant to the *David* in
1534.[12] The picture therefore dates from between 1504 and 1534.

The picture was bequeathed as a portrait of Francesco Ferrucci,
which there seems to be no reason to believe; Ferrucci, born 1489, died
1530, was active as a soldier during the last two years of his life. As an
alternative name for the sitter, Malatesta Baglioni was suggested in a
letter of 1907 in the Gallery archives; there are no arguments in favour

of this. In the 1929 catalogue, the ornamentation over the door of the Palazzo Vecchio was misunderstood, and the sitter was therefore wrongly supposed to be a member of the Vitelleschi family, and related to the Orsini.

The attribution of No. 895 to Piero di Cosimo is due to J. P. Richter, and is usually accepted;[13] it seems to be more likely than not, but not quite certain. Gamba's attribution to Ridolfo Ghirlandaio seems less satisfactory.[14]

PROVENANCE: Presented in accordance with the wishes of the late Sir Anthony Coningham Stirling, K.C.B., 1871.[15]

REPRODUCTION: *Illustrations, Italian Schools*, 1937, p. 277. *Plates, Earlier Italian Schools*, 1953, Vol. II, p. 349.

REFERENCES: (1) Cf. A. Lensi, *Palazzo Vecchio*, 1929, p. 268, for a modern photograph from much the same view-point. (2) Reproduced in part by Lensi, *op. cit.*, p. 31; cf. also Van Marle, *Development of the Italian Schools of Painting*, Vol. XIII, fig. 15. (3) Lensi, *op. cit.*, p. 24. (4) Lensi, *op. cit.*, p. 296. Its position was changed in 1564; *Diario Fiorentino di Agostino Lapini*, ed. Corazzini, 1900, p. 140. (5) Reproductions in Lensi, *op. cit.*, pp. 316 and 325. (6) Lensi, *op. cit.*, p. 24. They were removed in 1762; Lensi, *op. cit.*, p. 287. (7) Lensi, *op. cit.*, p. 297. Lensi, p. 94, reproduces one of the versions of *Savonarola's Martyrdom*, which shows these lions higher still. In a Bellotto at Budapest, presumably accurate, the lions are shown very much as in No. 895; H. A. Fritzsche, *Bernardo Belotto*, 1936, Plate 53. (8) Reproduction in Lensi, *op. cit.*, p. 321; cf. Lensi, pp. 106, 110, 116, 315. A red cross on a white ground is the arms of the Florentine people; Lensi, *op. cit.*, p. 3. (9) Cf. the views reproduced by Lensi, *op. cit.*, pp. 223 and 277. (10) A list of views of S. Piero Scheraggio is given by P. Sanpaolesi in the *Rivista d'Arte*, 1934, p. 7. For the building of the Uffizi, see U. Dorini in the *Rivista Storica degli Archivi Toscani*, 1933, pp. 1 ff.; but the buildings sketched in this picture, between S. Piero Scheraggio and the Loggia, do not appear to be identifiable. (11) Lensi, *op. cit.*, p. 104. (12) Lensi, *op. cit.*, p. 119. (13) Cf. Frizzoni in the *Archivio Storico Italiano*, 1879, pp. 258/9, and his *Arte Italiana del Rinascimento*, 1891, p. 252; J. P. Richter, *Italian Art in the National Gallery*, 1883, pp. 35/6. (14) Gamba in *Dedalo*, January, 1929, p. 488 (15) As by Costa.

PIERO DELLA FRANCESCA
active 1439, died 1492

Also called *Piero dei Franceschi* and *Piero del Borgo*; the latter name refers to the town of Sansepolcro (or Borgo San Sepolcro), of which Piero was a native, and in which he lived for much of his life.

The first mention of Piero is of September, 1439. He was than apparently an assistant of Domenico Veneziano's, who was at that time painting frescoes in S. Egidio (S. Maria Nuova) at Florence. This is the only record of Piero's presence in Florence; it is not known how long he remained with Domenico Veneziano, either before or after September, 1439, in Florence or elsewhere.

Piero was in Sansepolcro in 1442. In 1445 he contracted to paint a polyptych there, which is now in the museum of the town; it was to be executed by his own hand within three years, but the execution appears to have dragged. Thereafter, Piero painted many pictures and frescoes, in Sansepolcro; at Urbino, where he was much employed at the Court; and at Rimini, Ferrara, Arezzo and elsewhere. Various works have survived, documented, and dated or approximately datable. He appears to have gone blind during the last few years of his life.

Piero attained some distinction as a mathematician, writing books on geometry and perspective. His pictorial work exercised a considerable influence in many places of central and northern Italy.

665   PART(?) OF AN ALTARPIECE: THE BAPTISM OF CHRIST

S. John baptizes Christ; the Holy Ghost descends as a Dove; three angels stand on the left.

Wood, rounded top, painted surface, $66 \times 45\frac{3}{4}$ ($1 \cdot 67 \times 1 \cdot 16$). The arch at the top starts a little way in on each side; but the paint has been made up, about $2\frac{1}{2}$ in. on each side at the spring, to form a wider arch.

Certain statements concerning the amount of overcleaning suffered by No. 665 appear to be very much exaggerated; but it is true that some overcleaning has taken place, e.g. on the face of the angel right, to a less extent on that of the central angel, on the beard of S. John, in the gold work. The picture has a very heavy craquelure, and there is a vertical split down the middle, badly restored. *Pentimenti* in the feet of the angel on the left. Much of the drapery of the angel on the right to the right of the tree-trunk, and his wing, are painted over the landscape; but part of his arm in this area, not extending so far as the present outline, is in solider paint, possibly or probably without landscape underneath. It may therefore seem likely that the outlines of this angel have been extended to the right, in a correction by the artist; yet it should be noted that landscape is painted under the headdress and raised hand in two of the background figures, and that some branches of the tree on the left seem to have been painted beneath the trunk of the principal tree.

No. 665 is recorded in the early nineteenth century as the central panel of a triptych, then in the Cathedral of Sansepolcro.[1] The remaining part of the triptych is now in the Museum at Sansepolcro,[2] except indeed for part of the frame, including a tondo of *God the Father*, which was above No. 665 and is now missing.[3] The only existing part of this assemblage that is attributable to Piero della Francesca is No. 665. The rest is reasonably attributed to Matteo di Giovanni.[4]

There is some reason to believe that Matteo's pictures were painted to fit round No. 665. All the pictures were together in the nineteenth century; no picture by Matteo di Giovanni that could once have been the central panel of the triptych has been identified; and all the pictures are stated to come from the high-altar of S. Giovanni Battista at Sansepolcro,[5] where a central scene of *The Baptism* would clearly have been suitable. These are quite strong arguments for believing that Matteo's pictures were painted to fit round No. 665. Nevertheless, an element of doubt remains, since Matteo's pictures are grossly discordant with No.

665 in style and in scale.⁶ It is therefore just possible that Matteo's pictures are the remains of an altarpiece entirely by him, that his central panel was later removed or destroyed, and that No. 665 was substituted for it.

Matteo di Giovanni's predella contains at one end the arms of the Graziani family.⁷

No. 665 is generally admitted to be a very early work by Piero della Francesca.⁸

The figure of the catechumen taking off his clothes in the right middle-distance of No. 665 appears to be imitated by Signorelli in his *Baptism of Christ* of 1508 in S. Medardo at Arcevia; that figure is by a pupil of Signorelli's, but apparently following a drawing by Signorelli himself.⁹ A relief of *The Baptism* in Arezzo Cathedral, ascribed by Pope-Hennessy to the very early time of Donatello, seems to show some connections with No. 665.¹⁰

PROVENANCE: Stated to have been the centre piece of a triptych, of which the rest is by Matteo di Giovanni, on the high-altar of the Priory of S. Giovanni Battista at Sansepolcro.¹¹ This priory was suppressed in 1808.¹² No. 665 and the surrounding pieces of the altarpiece were hung in the Sacristy of the Cathedral (S. Giovanni Evangelista) at Sansepolcro.¹³ No. 665 was bought from the Bishop and Chapter in 1859 by Sir J. C. Robinson on behalf of Matthew Uzielli.¹⁴ On loan at the South Kensington Museum, 1860/1. Purchased at the Uzielli Sale, London, 13 April, 1861 (lot 184).¹⁵

REPRODUCTION: *Illustrations, Italian Schools*, 1937, p. 140. *Plates, Earlier Italian Schools*, 1953, Vol. II, p. 350 (here including the additions that change the shape of the top).

REFERENCES: (1) See the provenance. (2) *Mostra di Opere d'Arte Trasportate a Firenze durante la Guerra*, 1947, No. 55; reproduced in the *Rassegna d'Arte*, 1905, pp. 49–51, and better by G. F. Hartlaub, *Matteo da Siena*, 1910, Plates III, IV. (3) Margherita Pichi, *Vita di Pietro della Francesca . . . scritta da Giorgio Vasari*, with notes by Francesco Gherardi Dragomanni, 1835, p. 22. (4) M. Logan in the *Rassegna d'Arte*, 1905, as in note 2. (5) See the provenance. (6) See the reproduction of all the pictures together in G. F. Hartlaub, *op. cit.*, Plate III. (7) This was pointed out by G. Magherini-Graziani, *L'Arte a Città di Castello*, 1897, p. 205. Although the detail of the arms on the predella is somewhat imprecise, there need be no doubt about the identification, especially as one branch of the Graziani family was prominent at Sansepolcro at about the right time. A connection between a Graziani and the Priory of S. Giovanni Battista at Sansepolcro, whence No. 665 is stated to come, has indeed not been found. Simeone Graziani, abbot of S. Giovanni *Evangelista* (later the Cathedral), restored that church in 1480 and his tomb is dated 1509; he was succeeded by his brother Galeotto, who became the first Bishop of Sansepolcro in 1520 and died in 1522. See Pietro or Gregorio Angelo Farulli, *Annali e Memorie . . . di S. Sepolcro*, 1713, p. 41; Lorenzo Coleschi, *Storia della Città di Sansepolcro*, 1886, pp. 144/5, 166, 195; T. C. I. Guide to Italy. Galeotto Graziani has indeed been called abbot of S. Giovanni *Battista* at Sansepolcro by Ughelli, as quoted by A. M. Gratianus, *De Scriptis Invita Minerva*, I, 1745, p. 80; but this appears to be a mistake. (8) E.g. by R. Longhi, *Piero della Francesca*, 1946, p. 175. (9) *Inventario degli Oggetti d'Arte d'Italia*, VIII, *Provincie di Ancona e Ascoli Piceno*, 1936, pp. 51 and 53 (reproduction); for the documents concerning the picture, see A. Anselmi in *L'Arte*, 1892, pp. 196/7. (10) *Studies in the History of Art, dedicated to William E. Suida*, 1959, pp. 47 ff., with reproduction. (11) In point of fact, what appears to be the only reference to it when still in S. Giovanni Battista is the mid-XVIII century mention of a *fresco* of the Baptism and other saints by Piero (Coleschi, *op. cit.*, p. 184); G. F. Pichi, *La Vita e le Opere di Piero della Francesca*, 1892, p. 107, claims that this cannot be something different and otherwise unknown, but must be a faulty description of No. 665, etc. M. Pichi, 1835 (as in note 3), p. 22, states the provenance from S. Giovanni Battista. **(12)** This is the date given by G. F. Pichi, *op. cit.*, 1892, p. 106. **(13)** See M. Pichi, *op. cit.*, 1835, p. 22. The altarpiece is also mentioned by Giacomo Mancini, *Istruzione Storico-Pittorica . . . di Città di Castello*, 1832, I, p. 340 (reprint of a letter of 1828), and II, p. 268. **(14)** J. C. Robinson, *Catalogue of the various works of Art forming the Collection of Matthew Uzielli*, 1860, No. 819. **(15)** The following curious passage is quoted from a letter from Eastlake to Layard, 15 April, 1861 (British Museum, Add. MS. 38987, Layard Papers, Vol. LVII): 'It is a most undoubted & characteristic specimen, fortunately almost unrestored, & so it will remain—but the great objection to it is its very ruined state. This weighs with me so much that I am at this moment undecided whether to place it in the N. Gallery (where it cannot have a good place) or to take it myself.'

769 S. MICHAEL (PANEL FROM A POLYPTYCH)

He holds a dead dragon's head, and tramples on the dragon's body. Inscribed on his armour, * ANGELVS * POTENTIA DEI * LVCHA.

Wood, painted surface, pointed top, $52\frac{3}{8} \times 23\frac{3}{8}$ ($1 \cdot 33 \times 0 \cdot 595$). Painted up to the edges at the sides and bottom. It is probable that the painted area has not been reduced at the sides; it is possible that a little has been cut away along the bottom. By analogy with other pictures of the same series as No. 769, mentioned later on in the commentary, it would appear that the top of the painting in No. 769 was originally rounded; this is confirmed roughly by the shape of the gesso preparation on No. 769, which continues a little outside the painted surface of the arch.

No. 769 has suffered a good deal from overcleaning and flaking. There are numerous retouches; the floor has been repainted with a false, centralized perspective, and the dragon has had its neck extended.

No. 769 contains various *pentimenti*. Some of these are confusing, since Piero appears to have been in the habit of completing his forms, even when they were due to be covered by other forms; thus, the dragon's head is painted under the sword, and the parapet is painted under the dragon's head. There are in any case corrections in some of the outlines of the legs, in the lower line of the wing at the left under S. Michael's arm, and in the line of the body at the left. The corrections to the body have caused some confusion where the inscription is. It appears superficially that the first * of the inscription as recorded above is preceded by traces of a B.[1] An infra-red photograph of this part gives no support at all, and suggests a mark merely decorative. X-Rays confirm what is indeed apparent on the surface, that there are numerous attempts at the outline in this part.

The part of the picture most interesting in its condition is the right-hand bottom corner. It has already been noted that the perspective of the floor, as seen at present, is modern. It will be explained presently that the pendant to No. 769 is *A Saint* in the Frick Collection, New York.[2] That picture has in the left-hand bottom corner a marble step, above which are traces of a second step; they clearly were connected with a throne on a missing panel placed between the Frick *Saint* and No. 769. Meiss deduces that under the repaint two similar steps should exist on No. 769, in the right-hand bottom corner.[3] The X-Ray photographs of No. 769 confirm this deduction, but with some additional detail. The lower step is clearly marked under X-Rays in No. 769.[4] Faint traces of the upper step are also visible under X-Rays.[5] The lower step is very much more distinct than the upper step, both in the X-Ray photographs of No. 769 and on the surface of the Frick *Saint*.

Nor is this all. Over the upper surface of the lower step on No. 769, and considerably beyond it to the left, X-Rays reveal folds of drapery (?) and patterns of flowers, perhaps brocade of the same drapery. Some of these flowers are detectable in ordinary light; some of them show red, which may have been their colour. The X-Ray images are not very clear; but one may say that perhaps at one time the richly decorated dress of a figure on the central panel, presumably the Virgin, spread into No. 769 and enveloped the lower step; the upper step could not have been included at that moment. It appears impossible at present to decide whether Piero first intended the two steps, or the single step covered with drapery (?). The lines marking the upper step would seem to indicate that it as well as the lower step was intended from the first. The back part of the lower step was intended to be hidden, because its outline continues only to the floor-line level of the parapet; and since the drapery (?) does not appear to have covered this back part very much, one could argue that it was intended to be covered by the upper step. These arguments go far to show that Piero first intended two steps; but against that view is the obvious fact that the Frick picture now shows two steps, and not one step covered with drapery. The faint condition of the upper step, on the surface in the Frick picture and in the X-Ray photograph for No. 769, adds to the puzzle. Removal of the repaint from the floor of No. 769 might make a solution to the problem possible.

Possibly connected with the problem of the steps on No. 769 is the condition of the right edge. Most of the bit of panelling of the parapet at the edge, and a wedge shaped area above (at the height of the sword and hand) appear to be almost bare of original paint. But the exact meaning of this condition appears too difficult to attempt to explain until the picture is cleaned.

The inscription on No. 769 is an unsolved puzzle. From its position, it must refer to S. Michael. The words are ANGELUS POTENTIA DEI LUCHA. *Angelus* applies to S. Michael.[6] It was suggested in the first edition of this catalogue that *potentia* is presumably in the ablative: 'by the Power of God.' The great act that S. Michael by the Power of God performed was his victory over Satan or Lucifer. This is indeed shown in symbol on picture No. 769, but the compiler cannot produce a reasonable expansion of the letters LUCHA to signify 'conquered Lucifer.' Alternatively, *potentia* could be a nominative, and would be so according to an interpretation of the inscription suggested by Professor D. S. Robertson.[7] He proposed that the last word read originally MICHA

(for Michael); this may be thought desirable, and it is not excluded that
the LV may be found a falsification of MI, but the compiler cannot find
any trace at present of MI. If this last word is Michael, *Potentia Dei*
would presumably be in apposition, indicating some characteristic of S.
Michael. Professor Robertson comments upon this matter, but does not
cite anything convincingly in support.[8] It may be that cleaning of the
inscription would lead to a sure interpretation of it, but it must at present
be recorded as unexplained; a secondary meaning attached to it is mentioned in note 18 and the corresponding part of the commentary.[9]

On 4 October, 1454, Piero della Francesca contracted to paint the
high-altarpiece of S. Agostino at Sansepolcro.[10] The subject was not
specified in the contract,[11] but it is there stated that the altarpiece was
to be a polyptych, the woodwork for which had already been carpentered. A good deal of the money was provided by Angelo di Giovanni di
Simone d'Angelo, partly at his own wish, and partly to carry out the
wishes of his deceased brother Simone and of Simone's wife Johanna,[12]
and for the souls of his forbears. Piero della Francesca promised to
finish the altarpiece within eight years, with paintings on the front only
and not on the back. By 14 November, 1469, the altarpiece had apparently been completed;[13] Piero on that date received a payment of part of
the money still due to him.

The last sure record of this high altarpiece *in situ* is of 1550.[14] In
spite of this, there are good reasons for believing that No. 769 formed
part of it.

No. 769 is on pictorial grounds (identity of the parapet, etc.) certainly
from the same series as *A Saint* (already mentioned) in the Frick Collection, New York; *S. Nicholas of Tolentino* in the Poldi-Pezzoli Museum
at Milan; and *S. Augustine* at Lisbon.[15] The order from left to right is,
on pictorial grounds, clearly *S. Augustine*; No. 769; a missing central
panel; the Frick *Saint*; and *S. Nicholas of Tolentino*.[16]

The presence of two Augustinian Saints in this polyptych indicates
an Augustinian provenance. Since the four pictures are clearly by Piero
or at least from his studio,[17] this affords a presumption that they are the
remains of Piero's polyptych in S. Agostino at Sansepolcro. Some confirmation can be found from the two inner saints of the polyptych, No.
769, and the Frick *Saint*. It is rather to be expected that these prominently placed saints may recall the donors. On No. 769, which was in a
more important place than the Frick *Saint*, the inscription begins with
the word *Angelus*, the name of the principal donor of the S. Agostino
altarpiece.[18] An identification for the Frick *Saint* can also be suggested
in connection with the donors of the S. Agostino altarpiece.[19] It is indeed not proved that the existing panels come from this high-altarpiece
in S. Agostino at Sansepolcro; but it would be unreasonable to feel
much doubt about it.[20]

Two small figures, which do seem to be Augustinian saints, and a
clearly similar *S. Apollonia* are sometimes thought to have formed minor
parts of the S. Agostino altarpiece.[21] Longhi adds that in his opinion a
Crucifixion may have been the central panel of the predella.[22]

PROVENANCE: It is explained above why No. 769 is reasonably considered to be part of the high-altarpiece of S. Agostino at Sansepolcro, which Piero della Francesca contracted to paint in 1454 and had apparently completed by 1469. This high-altarpiece is mentioned by Vasari in 1550.[23] The Augustinians of Sansepolcro were turned out of their church in 1555; the church passed to the Clarissans, who reconstructed it and reconsecrated it in 1557.[24] The Augustinians removed to the Pieve di S. Maria at Sansepolcro, which became commonly known as S. Agostino. The new church of S. Agostino was demolished in 1771 and reconstructed by Venanzio Righi in 1773; this Augustinian community was suppressed in 1808.[25] It is not known if Piero's high-altarpiece for the old S. Agostino (S. Chiara) remained somewhere in that church after 1555, nor if it was removed to the new S. Agostino (Pieve di S. Maria).[26] No. 769 is first surely recorded as a single panel, with a false Mantegna signature, at Fidanza's, Milan, in 1861.[27] Bought, most probably at that time, by Sir Charles Eastlake. Purchased from Lady Eastlake, at the price Sir Charles Eastlake had paid for it, 1867.

REPRODUCTION: *Illustrations, Italian Schools*, 1937, p. 138. *Plates, Earlier Italian Schools*, 1953, Vol. II, p. 351.

REFERENCES: (1) Millard Meiss in *The Art Bulletin*, March, 1941, p. 58, accepts this B. He deduces that the inscription may among other things refer to the Blessed Angelo Scarpetti, the object of a local cult in the church at Sansepolcro from which No. 769 is reasonably considered to come; but this suggestion cannot be accepted—it would indeed be difficult to accept, even if the B were there. (2) Reproduced by Meiss, *loc. cit.*, p. 53, next to a reproduction of No. 769; Mirella Levi D'Ancona in the large Frick Catalogue, Vol. XII, 1955, pp. 61 ff. (3) On the reproductions mentioned in the previous note, these steps have been marked. (4) It shows under X-Rays only as far as the floor-level line of the parapet, just as the corresponding line on the surface of the Frick *Saint* does. Assuming that both were intended from the beginning to indicate steps, and not simply variations in the floor, this proves that the back parts of the steps were intended to be hidden. (5) The lines marking the horizontal base of the top step, and the horizontal edge of the lower step, continue on No. 769 a good deal farther than is necessary, just as they do on the Frick picture. (6) A possible reason why *Angelus* rather than *Arcangelus* was chosen is recorded in note 18; even without that, the word does not present great difficulty. (7) D. S. Robertson in *The Burlington Magazine*, May 1953, p. 170. (8) Francis Wormald and other scholars were good enough to search for texts using similar words in reference to S. Michael, but nothing closely comparable was found. The compiler can cite one pictorial case that may be from the tradition followed by Piero. In the Gallery at Arezzo (P 23) is a fresco, classed as Aretine, end of the XIV Century, and coming from the near-by Puliciano. It shows Christ and four Saints, one of whom must be S. Michael; and the shield held by this figure is inscribed POTENTIA DEI. The compiler does not know if these two words are referred to S. Michael himself or to his protective shield; scholars may be able to find support from them for the case (nominative or ablative) of *potentia* in Piero's inscription. There is a poor reproduction of the fresco in A. del Vita, *La Pinacoteca di Arezzo*, 1921, Plate 12. (9) Another secondary meaning suggested for it is rejected in note 1. Two other principal meanings proposed for it, and commented on by Meiss, *loc. cit.*, p. 58, are clearly wrong. One is that the inscription is a signature of Luca Signorelli. The other is that the first three words are a quotation from S. Luke; but they are not. (10) The two known documents concerning this picture are printed from Milanesi's transcriptions by Millard Meiss in *The Art Bulletin*, March, 1941, pp. 67/8. They appear to be notary's copies, without the signatures of the contracting parties; there is no reason to question their authority. (11) The subject is recorded to have been specified in a separate document, which has not been discovered. (12) Meiss, *loc. cit.*, pp. 59 and 68, claims that Johanna, after being the wife of Simone, became the wife of Angelo himself; but this appears to be a mistake. (13) Mirella Levi D'Ancona, *loc. cit.*, p. 70, thinks that it was not finished by

1469. (**14**) Vasari, 1550, p. 362 (no description of the subject). The passage is repeated exactly in the 1568 edition of Vasari, I, p. 355 (Milanesi's edition, Vol. II, p. 493); Vasari does not record that the church had changed hands in the interval, and it is clear that the mention of 1568 is no proof that Piero's picture was still on the high altar in 1568. (**15**) See Millard Meiss in *The Art Bulletin*, March, 1941, pp. 53 ff.; Sir Kenneth Clark in *The Burlington Magazine*, Vol. LXXXIX (1947), pp. 205 ff., with reproductions of all four pictures; letters from Sir Kenneth Clark, Millard Meiss and Roberto Longhi in *The Burlington Magazine*, Vol. LXXXIX (1947), pp. 285 ff. Earlier references to some of the pictures can be found from these references. (**16**) He used to be called S. Thomas Aquinas, and was first correctly identified by Borenius in *The Burlington Magazine*, Vol. XXIX (1916), p. 162. (**17**) The attribution of No. 769 and the Poldi-Pezzoli picture to the more or less mythical Fra Carnevale was accepted by Venturi, *Storia dell'Arte Italiana*, Vol. VII, Part II, pp. 103 ff.; but it need not be taken seriously. It can be admitted without discussion that the pictures are by Piero della Francesca, perhaps with the intervention of the studio in their weaker parts. (**18**) It is reasonable to believe that the inscription could have a secondary meaning in connection with the donor; S. Michael may be assumed to have been Angelo's patron saint. (**19**) The Frick *Saint* is a saint of apostolic character, reading a book. According to the documents, the person most concerned with the S. Agostino altarpiece after Angelo di Giovanni was his brother Simone. There seems to be no reason why the Frick *Saint* should not be S. Simon—not Simon Peter, who would probably have been characterized unmistakably, but Simon Zelotes. Millard Meiss in *The Art Bulletin*, March, 1941, p. 59, does not consider this identification, and proposes S. John the Evangelist, to recall Angelo's father Giovanni and his sister-in-law Giovanna. This seems possible, but less likely. (**20**) Some impediment to the identification of the S. Agostino altarpiece has been caused by the following circumstances. The Augustinians were in 1555 turned out of their church, which was transferred to Poor Clares, who reconstructed it and reconsecrated it in 1557 (L. Coleschi, *Storia della Città di Sansepolcro*, 1886, p. 179; Vasari, *Vita di Pietro della Francesca*, publ. Margherita Pichi with notes by F. G. Dragomanni, 1835, p. 20). The Augustinians removed to another church. In their former church (S. Chiara), the high-altarpiece representing an *Assumption* became identified with Piero's polyptych. But that picture (reproduced by Meiss, *loc. cit.*, p. 56) is manifestly a Franciscan, and not an Augustinian altarpiece, and further is not a polyptych; nor indeed is it reasonable to attribute it to Piero della Francesca. It is presumed that the Clarissans brought the picture with them when they moved into S. Agostino. (**21**) The matter is discussed by Millard Meiss in *The Art Bulletin*, March, 1941, pp. 66/7; he reproduces the two Augustinian saints formerly in the Liechtenstein Collection, Vienna (now Frick Collection, New York). See further Mirella Levi D'Ancona in the large Frick Catalogue, Vol. XII, 1955, pp. 68 ff. The *S. Apollonia*, formerly in the Lehman Collection at New York, and now at Washington, is reproduced by R. Longhi, *Piero della Francesca*, 2nd edition, 1946, Plate CCIII, and in *Paintings and Sculpture from the Kress Collection*, National Gallery of Art, Washington, 1945, p. 49. (**22**) Longhi, *op. cit.*, pp. 186/7 and Plate CCIV. The association of this picture is more doubtful than for the three saints above mentioned. (**23**) Vasari, 1550, p. 362. The passage is repeated in the edition of 1568; it has already been noted that this is no proof that Piero's polyptych was then still over the high altar of that church. (**24**) L. Coleschi, *Storia della Città di Sansepolcro*, 1886, p. 179; cf. also Vasari's *Vita di Pietro della Francesca*, publ. Margherita Pichi with notes by F. G. Dragomanni, 1835, p. 20. (**25**) Coleschi, *op. cit.*, pp. 181/2; Giacomo Mancini, *Istruzione Storico-Pittorica . . . di Città di Castello*, 1832, II (*Memorie di Alcuni Artefici del Disegno*), pp. 222, 270; MS. Index in the Archivio di Stato at Florence. (**26**) Giacomo Mancini, *op. cit.*, Vol. II, p. 272, mentions in S. Chiara at Sansepolcro that 'Nel parapetto del coretto delle monache vi sono alcuni quadretti in tavola, alcuni de' quali sembrano di mano di *Pietro della Francesca*, ed altri di alcun *quattrocentista* della scuola fiorentina.' But these need not be thought connected with Piero's S. Agostino altarpiece, and might seem rather to be the pictures referred to by Lorenzo Coleschi, *Storia della Città di Sansepolcro*, 1886, p. 180, as still in S. Chiara there: 'E di più nel Coretto delle Monache, o cantoria, si ammirano otto belle vignette a tempera, in cui sono effigiati diversi Santi, reputate della Scuola senese, e più particolarmente di Girolamo della Genga per vedervisi dipinti dei cavalli, che il Genga ebbe gran vaghezza di rappresentare, ed è pure stimata della stessa scuola una bella tavola a tempera, in Sagrestia, che rappresenta un Cristo risorto con alcuni Santi da ambo i lati.' For some other pictures, in Mancini's own collection, apparently not connected either, see Mancini, *op. cit.*, Vol. I, pp. 270, 272. (27) Eastlake's note-book, 1861.

908   THE NATIVITY

The Virgin kneels before the Child; S. Joseph is seated on a saddle. Behind, five angels, the ox and the ass, and two shepherds, one apparently pointing to the star.

Wood, painted surface, $49 \times 48\frac{1}{4}$ ($1 \cdot 245 \times 1 \cdot 23$);[1] painted up to the edges left and right.

This picture has been called unfinished, and this may be true. Thus, the lutes appear now not to have any strings, which Piero della Francesca might or might not have intended to put in; but even if he did put the strings in, they may have been removed by overcleaning, which has clearly removed, for instance, yellow patterning from the Virgin's bodice. The extremely unfinished appearance of some parts of the picture, especially of the two shepherds and of S. Joseph, is probably to be attributed to overcleaning rather than to anything the painter left undone.[2] The outlines showing in these parts are the painter's original underdrawing. The overcleaning has taken place intermittently over much of the picture, e.g. the angels' dresses. The picture has also been damaged by flaking along vertical cracks; a large damage through the Child's legs is due to a burn. It is also damaged by cracks in the paint, e.g. on the Virgin's dress. In spite of these extensive blemishes, No. 908 is not to be considered as in bad condition for a picture of the fifteenth century.

Pentimenti in the position of the Child's legs (best seen under the X-Ray), in the shepherd's upraised arm, in the position of the ox, in the line of S. Joseph's forehead, in the rock separating the middle distance from the distant landscape left, etc.

It is suggested that one of the shepherds in No. 908 is pointing to the Star; the Star strictly should be for the Magi, but there appears to have been no rigid distinction for this matter in pictures. The braying ass in No. 908 is rather unusual, but should not be supposed to be satirical in intention.[3]

No. 908 appears to show some Netherlandish influence; in particular, the motive of the Child resting on the ground on a corner of the Virgin's mantle, although it could be derived for instance from Fra Filippo Lippi, was very frequently used by Memlinc and other Netherlandish painters.[4]

No. 908 is considered by Longhi to be a late work.[5]

PROVENANCE: This picture appears to have remained with the descendants of the painter's brother Marco, at Sansepolcro.[6] Giambattista, the last of the Franceschi, by will of 1698 made his sister Margherita or her husband his heir; she was the wife of Ranieri Benedetto Marini.[7] No. 908 is first recorded in 1825 in the possession of Giuseppe Marini-Franceschi of Sansepolcro; he sent it for storage at the Uffizi in Florence.[8] Noted as still in Florence (for sale) in 1836.[9] The picture appears to have been returned for a time to Sansepolcro, and to have been hung in the private chapel of the Marini-Franceschi.[10] It was nevertheless about 1848 in Florence, in the keeping of Cav. Frescobaldi, apparently a relative of the owner.[11] Giuseppe Marini-Franceschi died in March or April, 1858; a month after his death Mündler noted that No. 908 was not at Sansepolcro, but with Cav. Frescobaldi at Florence.[12] Seen by Eastlake in Florence in 1861;[13] it appears that he would have bought the picture for himself,[14] if he had not been forestalled by Alexander Barker of London.[15] Purchased at the Barker Sale, 6 June, 1874 (lot 70).

REPRODUCTION: *Illustrations, Italian Schools*, 1937, p. 141. *Plates, Earlier Italian Schools*, 1953, Vol. II, p. 352.

REFERENCES: (1) This picture is not quite rectangular, being a little higher at the right than at the left; the measurements given for the height are an average. (2) In 1826, Giuseppe Marini-Franceschi admitted that No. 908 was in a damaged state; see the *Repertorium für Kunstwissenschaft*, 1900, p. 389. Giles Robertson in *The Burlington Magazine*, 1953, p. 28, thinks the picture unfinished. (3) For the star, see for instance Van Marle, *Development of the Italian Schools of Painting*, Vol. III, Figs. 124 and 125; Fig. 124 shows the Nativity with shepherds and the star, Fig. 125 shows the Adoration of the Kings without the star. An example of a braying ass is in *The Adoration of the Kings* at Padua, reproduced in Crowe and Cavalcaselle, *Painting in North Italy*, ed Borenius, I, 1912, p. 223; another is in the Butinone in the Castello Sforzesco at Milan, Plate XLVII of the 1957 *Guida*. (4) Friedländer, *Die Altniederländische Malerei*, Vol. VI, Fig. 28, is one case; there are many others. For Fra Filippo Lippi, see Van Marle, *Development of the Italian Schools of Painting*, Vol. X, Fig. 246. (5) R. Longhi, *Piero della Francesca*, 1946, p. 124. The attribution by A. Venturi, *Storia dell'Arte Italiana*, Vol. VII, Part II, p. 98, to the more or less mythical Fra Carnevale has no justification; cf. what Longhi, *op. cit.*, 1946, p. 183, says apropos of the altarpiece in the Brera. (6) See the genealogical tree given by Evelyn (Marini-Franceschi), *Piero della Francesca*, 1912, p. 18. (7) *Repertorium für Kunstwissenschaft*, 1900, p. 389; Evelyn, *op. cit.*, p. 17. This will, now in the Archivio di Stato at Florence (rog. Ottavio Pippi), contains no mention of No. 908. (8) *Repertorium für Kunstwissenschaft*, 1900, p. 389. (9) *Kunstblatt*, 1836, p. 349. Margherita Pichi, *Vita di Pietro della Francesca . . . scritta da Giorgio Vasari*, with notes by Francesco Gherardi Dragomanni, Nozze Franceschi Marini-Frescobaldi, 1835, p. 23, notes the picture as being ' presso il nobile sig. Giuseppe Franceschi Marini,' but this perhaps indicates the ownership rather than the location. (10) Evelyn, *op. cit.*, p. 135. (11) Vasari, Le Monnier edition, IV, 1848, pp. 14/5. Giuseppe Marini-Franceschi married Caterina Frescobaldi *ca.* 1835; see Pichi, *op. cit.* (12) Mündler's Diary. (13) Eastlake's note-book, 1861. (14) National Gallery, MS. Catalogue. There seems little reason to doubt that this is true. But it seems desirable to quote what seems to be a less reliable account, in a letter from Layard to Morelli. 18 June, 1874. ' Il m'a été offert il y a quelques années pour 80 napoleons—et Eastlake et moi après l'avoir examiné nous l'avons rejeté même à ce prix.' (British Museum, Add. MS. 38966, Layard Papers, Vol. XXXVI.) (15) According to W. Weisbach in the *Repertorium für Kunstwissenschaft*, 1900, p. 390, the agent for the sale was Ugo Baldi; this may be merely a corruption of Cav. Frescobaldi.

After PIERO DELLA FRANCESCA (?)

1062   A BATTLE

Wood, painted surface, $28 \times 37\frac{1}{4}$ (0·71 × 0·945); the picture is in a fixed framing, but the paint probably continues up to the edges all round.

Fair state.

There seems to be no sufficient clue on the picture to indicate what particular battle is represented.

The costume of certain figures, for instance the man in armour on the left, indicates a date of *ca.* 1530/40.[1] Various details, nevertheless, seem to reflect an earlier style. J. Lauts[2] suggests that No. 1062 is a copy (with considerable variations) from some lost work by Piero della Francesca; to judge from the central figure on a white horse, or the group of warriors in the middle distance on the left, Lauts would seem to be right. The actual execution of No. 1062 appears to be Ferrarese,[3] and Lauts suggests that the picture may be derived from one of the frescoes by Piero della Francesca, mentioned by Vasari as having been in the Palace at Ferrara.[4] This is possible; even if it were not accepted, No. 1062 could still be derived from a lost Piero della Francesca.[5]

PROVENANCE: In the possession of W. Benoni White, by 1863 at latest;[6] purchased at his sale, 23 May, 1879 (lot 81).[7]

REPRODUCTION: *Illustrations, Italian Schools*, 1937, p. 132. *Plates, Earlier Italian Schools*, 1953, Vol. II, p. 353.

REFERENCES: (1) Letter from Sir James Mann, 20 August, 1931, in the Gallery archives. (2) J. Lauts (letter of 19 August, 1949) agrees with this dating. J. Lauts in the *Zeitschrift für Kunstgeschichte*, Vol. X, 1941, pp. 67 ff. (3) Lauts, *loc. cit.*, associates it loosely with the style of Dosso Dossi. (4) Vasari, 1550 edition, p. 361; ed. Milanesi, Vol. II, p. 491 (with a note wrongly identifying the Palace as Schifanoia). Nothing is known of the subjects painted. Vasari says that the work was done for Borso d'Este (d. 1471), and that it was destroyed by Ercole vecchio (who succeeded Borso) 'per ridurre il palazzo alla moderna.' The reconstruction to which Vasari refers seems clearly to be that of 1479; 'cusì fu messa tuta la parte nova a terra e anche de la vechia' (Zambotti, *Diario Ferrarese*, in Muratori, *Rerum Italicarum Scriptores*, Vol. XXIV, Part VII, 1937, p. 68). There was further a fire in the Palace in 1509 (L. N. Cittadella, *Notizie Relative a Ferrara*, 1864, p. 322). It would remain unexplained how the composition of one of these frescoes could have been known to a painter of *ca.* 1530/40; perhaps some copies were made at the time of the demolition. See further J. Lauts in *The Burlington Magazine*, May 1953, p. 166, where a picture at Baltimore with characteristics similar to those of Nos. 1062 is reproduced. The picture at Florence there referred to seems to be further away. (5) Some other suggestions concerning No. 1062 have been printed. Jacobsen in the *Repertorium für Kunstwissenschaft*, 1901, p. 347, says that No. 1062 is between Ercole de' Roberti and Dosso Dossi. A. Morassi in *The Burlington Magazine*, Vol. LVIII (1931), p. 129, attributes the picture to Fogolino. Pudelko in *The Art Bulletin*, 1934, p. 257, thinks that it may be derived from Pisanello. (6) See the title page of the sale catalogue. (7) As Mantegna; there is an old label with this name on the back of the picture.

PINTORICCHIO
active 1481, died 1513

Bernardino di Betto of Perugia, called *Pintoricchio* or *Sordicchio*. According to Vasari's evidence, he may have been born *ca.* 1454; he joined the painters' guild at Perugia in 1481. His chief works are frescoes in the Borgia Apartments in the Vatican, and in the Piccolomini Library in Siena Cathedral; he was also active at Perugia and Spello. Many authenticated works exist.

693   S.   CATHERINE   OF   ALEXANDRIA   WITH   AN ECCLESIASTICAL DONOR

Wood, painted surface, $22\frac{1}{4} \times 15$ (0.565×0.38); painted up to the edge at the bottom.

So far as can be seen, not in bad condition; most of the gold is new.

PROVENANCE: Bequeathed by Lieut.-General Sir William George Moore, of Petersham,[1] 1862.

REPRODUCTION: *Illustrations, Italian Schools*, 1937, p. 279. *Plates, Earlier Italian Schools*, 1953, Vol. II, p. 354.

REFERENCE: (1) As by Pintoricchio.

703   THE VIRGIN AND CHILD

A coat of arms centre bottom, not identified.

Wood. The size of the painted surface, which is the same as that of the panel, is $22\frac{5}{8} \times 15\frac{3}{4}$ (0.575×0.40); the paint, in part at least, has been made up to the edges. These measurements include a painted framing. The size of the picture itself is, rounded top, 21×14 (0.535×0.355); probably cut at the top, where a little of the arch is missing.

The picture is perhaps not in bad condition *au fond*; but it has been much repainted, and its character is somewhat altered.

VERSION: An unfinished version is at Trevi.[1]

PROVENANCE: Bought in Paris, August, 1815, by Count Joseph von Rechberg, who sold it in September of the same year to Prince Ludwig von Œttingen-Wallerstein.[2] Catalogues of *ca.* 1826 and 1827 (No. 20). Exhibited with other Œttingen-Wallerstein pictures (for sale) at Kensington Palace, 1848 (No. 24); the collection was bought *en bloc* by the Prince Consort. Waagen's Catalogue, 1854 (No. 18).[3] Exhibited at Manchester, 1857 (Provisional Catalogue, No. 79; Definitive Catalogue, No. 130).[4] Presented by Queen Victoria, at the Prince Consort's wish, 1863.

REPRODUCTION: *Illustrations, Italian Schools*, p. 279. *Plates, Earlier Italian Schools*, 1953, Vol. II, p. 355.

REFERENCES: (1) Reproduced by Venturi, *Storia dell'Arte Italiana*, Vol. VII, Part II, Fig. 447. (2) Information recorded by E. K. Waterhouse, from a letter from Werner Noack, 20 November, 1909. Cf. G. Grupp in the *Jahrbuch des Historischen Vereins für Nördlingen und Umgebung*, Vol. VI, 1917, p. 100. (3) The information in this entry is repeated in Waagen, *Treasures*, IV, 1857, p. 223. (4) For the identification, see W. Burger, *Trésors d'Art exposés à Manchester en 1857*, 1857, p. 39.

911   FRESCO: SCENES FROM THE ODYSSEY

Penelope is seated at her loom; behind her hang the bow and quiver of her husband Odysseus. A maid (Eurycleia?) is on the ground by her.

The young man approaching Penelope is presumably her son Telemachus, just returned from a journey in search of his father. The man
with a hawk is presumably one of Penelope's suitors. Behind him are a
man with a turban (perhaps the soothsayer Theoclymenus), and a man
apparently lamenting the condition of affairs (conceivably the swineherd
Eumæus). Still further behind, Odysseus enters the room, disguised as a
beggar.

In the background, two earlier scenes from the *Odyssey* are shown.
The Sirens form the nearer incident; to protect themselves against their
alluring song, Odysseus' crew have their ears stopped (it should be with
wax), and Odysseus himself is tied near the mast of his ship. The ship
is ornamented with many coats of arms, alternately those of the Petrucci
family of Siena, and a red cross on a white ground (Genoa?). The ship's
flag shows a golden cross on a red ground. The second scene, further
back, shows Circe, who transforms men into swine, and Odysseus, who
was not changed by her enchantments. A castle carries the Petrucci arms
on the tower.

Fresco, transferred to canvas, $49\frac{1}{2} \times 59\frac{3}{4}$ ($1\cdot255 \times 1\cdot52$), including
narrow bands forming the edging. The right side has been left some-
what irregular by the painter; the measurement of width is given along
the bottom, where the paint continues a little further than at the top, and
beyond the edging as marked at the top.

Much damaged.

Odysseus was prevented for ten years after the fall of Troy from
returning to his home in Ithaca. His wife Penelope was pestered by
many suitors. She put them off for a time, saying she could consider
none until she had finished weaving a shroud for her father-in-law
Laertes; she wove it during the day, and unwove it each night. Eventually, Telemachus set out on a journey, to obtain news whether his father
was alive or dead. He learnt nothing useful on his journey, but on getting
back to Ithaca, he discovered Odysseus disguised as a beggar in the hut
of the swineherd Eumæus. Father and son returned to their house a
little apart; Odysseus thereupon destroyed the suitors.

The story is that of the Odyssey, but the painter of No. 911 appears
to have been badly advised about what is described as happening in that
poem. Penelope is here shown as weaving, but the ruse of the web had
been discovered some time before Odysseus' return (*Odyssey*, II,
93 sqq.). The maid here shown may be the nurse Eurycleia, who recognized Odysseus soon after his return on seeing a peculiar scar (*Odyssey*,
XVII, 31 sqq., and XIX, 349 sqq.). The bow hanging behind Penelope
is clearly that of Odysseus, which none of the suitors were presently to be
proved capable of drawing (*Odyssey*, XXI). The young man in the centre
of the picture is presumably Telemachus, just returned from his journey
in search of news of his father; but the scene takes place in a different
setting in the *Odyssey* (XVII, 31 sqq.). Presumably the man with a hawk
in the picture is the sole representative of Penelope's numerous suitors,
unless indeed he is one of the followers of Telemachus. The man in a
turban could be the soothsayer Theoclymenus, whom Telemachus had

picked up (*Odyssey*, XV, 222 sqq.). The sentimental man could be the swineherd Eumaeus; he did burst into tears on seeing the bow belonging to his absent master (*Odyssey*, XXI, 80 sqq.). The beggar entering at the door is undoubtedly Odysseus in disguise.

The scene with the Sirens in the background is also somewhat confused in this picture; the figures diving off a rowing boat into the sea appear to be a fanciful addition to the story (*Odyssey*, XII, 165 sqq.). The story of Circe is in the *Odyssey*, X, 198 sqq.

No. 911 comes from the Palazzo del Magnifico (Pandolfo Petrucci) at Siena; Signorelli, Nos. 910 and 3929 of this Gallery, are from the same series, which is datable approximately 1509. What is known about the original scheme of decoration is discussed in the entry for No. 910 in this catalogue. The Petrucci arms, occurring many times in No. 911, have no eagle impaled, quartered or in chief, such as occurs in other fragments from this ensemble.[1] The red cross on a white ground may stand for Genoa, which was of great importance to the Sienese for its maritime trade.[2] The significance of the golden cross on a red ground has not been explained.

It is generally accepted that No. 911 is by Pintoricchio. Although the fresco is much damaged, it seems likely that it is Pintoricchio's own work, and not merely a studio piece. Pintoricchio was apparently recalled to Siena on or about 24 April, 1508, to work or resume work for Pandolfo Petrucci;[3] it is possible that the execution of No. 911 may be part of the work referred to.

The Petrucci arms occur on No. 911, but not those of the Piccolomini family. It could from this be argued that No. 911 is not later than September, 1509; a marriage of some importance to Pandolfo Petrucci took place then, between his son Borghese and Vittoria Piccolomini.[4] It is probable, but not certain, that the Piccolomini arms would have been added to the picture, if the marriage had already taken place before its completion.

PROVENANCE: From the Palace of Pandolfo Petrucci at Siena, as stated above. With Nos. 910 and 3929 (Signorelli), it was transferred from the wall in 1842 or 1844, to the order of E. Joly de Bammeville of Paris.[5] Not in the Bammeville Sale, London, 1854. All three frescoes passed into the Collection of Alexander Barker, where seen by Waagen.[6] Just possibly exhibited at Leeds, 1868 (No. 11).[7] Purchased at the Barker Sale, 6 June, 1874 (lot 84).

REPRODUCTION: *Illustrations, Italian Schools*, 1937, p. 280. *Plates, Earlier Italian Schools*, 1953, Vol. II, p. 356.

REFERENCES: (1) See the entry for Signorelli, No. 910, Note 31. (2) This was suggested by Dr. Giovanni Cecchini of the Archivio di Stato at Siena. (3) This is deducible from the inscription on Pintoricchio's altarpiece in S. Andrea, Spello; see Corrado Ricci, *Pintoricchio*, English edition, 1902, pp. 216/7. (4) G. A. Pecci, *Memorie Storico-Critiche della Città di Siena*, I, 1755, pp. 77, 241. The Petrucci and Piccolomini arms are associated in other parts of the decoration from which No. 911 comes; see the entry for Signorelli, No. 910, Note 31. (5) Waagen, *Mantegna und Signorelli* (from Raumer's *Historisches Taschenbuch*, 1850), p. 569; Vasari, Le Monnier edition, VI, p. 153. (6) Waagen, *Treasures*, IV, 1857, pp. 73/5. Waagen wrongly maintains that the subject is *Collatinus and Lucretia*. Della Valle, *Lettere Sanesi*, III, 1786, p. 320, had wrongly thought that it was

Paris and Helen. The scenes from *The Odyssey* in the background of No. 911 are sufficient to disprove these views. **(7)** *Scene from the History of the Family of the Piccolomini of Sienna.* This would appear rather to be lot 82 of the 1874 Sale; in the sale catalogue, nevertheless, it is lot 84 and not lot 82 that is said to have been exhibited at Leeds.

See also Ascribed to FIORENZO DI LORENZO, No. 2483

PISANELLO
living 1395, died 1455 (?)

Medallist and painter; properly *Pisano*. From the time of Vasari (1550) his christian name was supposed to be *Vittore*; no christian name occurs on any authentic picture or medal, and Vasari's form may be merely a corruption from his frequent signature 'Pisanus *Pictor*.' Early in this century Biadego discovered some documents, referring not simply to *Pisano* or *Pisanello*, but giving also a christian name *Antonio*; there seems to be no doubt that this Antonio Pisano is the identical man, although the matter has been disputed, and some of the points made against the identification do not seem to have been fully met. From the extensive literature on the subject, in addition to the references given by Hill in Thieme-Becker, may be cited Testi, *Storia della Pittura Veneziana*, II, 1915, p. 138; A. Venturi in *L'Arte*, 1908, pp. 467 ff.; and especially Zippel in *L'Arte*, 1902, pp. 405 ff.

Pisanello, according to the Biadego and other documents, was born not long before the end of 1395, perhaps at Pisa, but if so, he would have moved at an early age to Verona; he kept up an association with Verona for most of his life, but was often absent. He painted in the Sala del Gran Consiglio at Venice in conjunction with or following after Gentile da Fabriano; the work has perished. Mentioned at Mantua in 1422 and 1425; in Rome, 1431/2. At least from 1438 (indeed, no doubt earlier) his most regular employment was for the Este and Gonzaga courts at Ferrara and Mantua; but he was also in Milan and Venice. 1449, Naples.

He is now famous chiefly as a medallist, and for his drawings. Much of his painted work has perished, and few of his existing paintings can be surely dated.

Pisanello's style is an outcome of International Gothic, which flourished at Verona as well as elsewhere in Europe; Stefano da Verona may have influenced him; so probably did Gentile da Fabriano.

776 THE VIRGIN AND CHILD WITH SS. GEORGE AND
    ANTHONY ABBOT

Signed: *pisanus | pi̅*.

Poplar,[1] painted surface, $18\frac{1}{2} \times 11\frac{1}{2}$ (0·47 × 0·29).

Eastlake[2] noted in 1858, 'Blue sky almost rubbed to ground. The armour and dress of S. George once beautifully finished but now almost obliterated,' etc. The restorer who soon after gave the picture its present appearance was pleased with his work, and considered changing his name from *Giuseppe* to *Vittore* (then supposed to be Pisanello's).[3] So far as the flesh parts are concerned, the face of S. George is the best preserved and is in very fair state; there is repaint under the eye and on his cheek and chin. S. Anthony's flesh is in bad condition. The repaint on the flesh parts of the Virgin and Child includes most of the accents, so that the general effect is false.

The fantastic signature is conceived as part of the flora of the soil. The two horses' heads to the right recur in a rather similar way on Pisanello's fresco in S. Anastasia, Verona;[4] they are natural enough in the scene there, but it is surprising that here should be two. It has been claimed that the composition with the Virgin and Child in the sky is a derivation from miniatures.[5] The Virgin and Child here may be thought to be clothed with the sun, presumably in reference to the Apocalyptic Woman and Child (Revelation xii, 1); or it may be thought that there is some connection with the Vision of Augustus and the Sibyl.[6]

There is no means of establishing a date for the picture, but there is general agreement that it is a fairly mature work.[7]

DRAWINGS: Hill[8] thinks that a compositional sketch showing five figures in a row, of which the central three are apparently S. Anthony, the Virgin (with the Child) and S. George, may represent the first idea for the picture; this view is sometimes disputed, but seems defensible. Less uncertainly, two drawings after Pisanello indicate an early idea for the picture;[9] on one sheet are two figures who might well be SS. Anthony and George, on the other the Virgin and Child not very different from the picture. Some drawings of horses' heads may be connected (though not very closely) with this picture or the S. Anastasia fresco.[10]

PROVENANCE: In the Costabili Collection at Ferrara; catalogue, IV, 1841 (No. 405); still there in 1858.[11] Bought by Sir Charles Eastlake, and sent to England in 1862.[12] Presented by Lady Eastlake in memory of Sir Charles Eastlake, P.R.A., First Director of the National Gallery, 1867.

REPRODUCTION: *Illustrations, Italian Schools*, 1937, p. 284. *Plates, Earlier Italian Schools*, 1953, Vol. II, p. 357.

REFERENCES: (1) Letter from B. J. Rendle, of the Forest Products Research Laboratory, in the Gallery archives. (2) Eastlake's note-book, 1858. (3) Cf. Frizzoni, *Arte Italiana del Rinascimento*, 1891, p. 303. (4) Hill, *Pisanello*, 1905, Plate 15. (5) G. M. Richter in *The Burlington Magazine*, Vol. LV (1929), p. 128. (6) Mirella Levi D'Ancona, *The Iconography of the Immaculate Conception*, 1957, pp. 27/8, appears to think that No. 776 is an Immaculate Conception; the compiler cannot distinguish the crescent moon which she seems to claim under the Virgin, and the painter's signature does not consist of small snakes. For Augustus and the Sibyl (mentioned by her), see a picture at Stuttgart assigned to the early Venetian School; Plate 31 of the catalogue of the Italian Exhibition at Stuttgart, 1950. (7) Hill, *Pisanello*, 1905, p. 236, as *ca.* 1443/8. (8) Hill, *Pisanello*, 1905, p. 157, and *Drawings by Pisanello*, 1929, No. 3 and Plate III. (9) Hill, *Pisanello*, 1905, Plates 43 and 44. (10) The two nearest seem to be Hill, *Drawings by Pisanello*, 1929, Nos. 33 and 36, Plates XXIX and XXXII. (11) Eastlake's note-book, and Mündler's Diary for 1858. (12) Letter in the Gallery archives.

1436   THE VISION OF S. EUSTACE (?)

The Crucifix is inscribed INRI.

Wood, painted surface, $21\frac{1}{2} \times 25\frac{3}{4}$ (0.545×0.655); painted up to the edges all round.

The picture is much worn, and has been extensively made up with many small retouches. The face of the saint has been repainted on the forehead, nose, etc.

The scene represents a huntsman who sees a stag with a crucifix between its horns. This story, with the subsequent conversion of the huntsman, is told both of S. Eustace and of S. Hubert. Although the soldier S. Eustace should properly be shown in armour, it is most likely that the saint here is S. Eustace rather than S. Hubert.[1] S. Hubert may indeed not have been represented in early Italian art;[2] and it would appear that the story of S. Hubert is an adaptation of the story of S. Eustace, and that it was introduced at a date not precisely defined, but maybe later than the date (also undefined) of No. 1436.[3] In any case, it is rather unusual for the saint to remain horsed before his Vision; but he does so in Jacopo Bellini's drawings.[4]

The attribution of No. 1436 to Pisanello was made by Bode and Tschudi,[5] and has usually been accepted; but G. M. Richter[6] follows Manteuffel in rejecting it. So far as the condition of the picture permits a judgment, there seems no reason to disagree with Hill[7] in classing it as an authentic work, earlier than No. 776. There is no trace of letters on the scroll.

COPY: Hill[8] mentions a sixteenth century copy, then in private hands at Marseilles, and now owned by Conte Vittorio Cini at Venice; the lake in No. 1436 with some of the birds has been moved with changes to the foreground, and distant hills and buildings form the background of that picture, and there are several other variations.

DRAWINGS: Among Pisanello's drawings of animals, etc., there are many that correspond more or less with details of the picture; but it is not certain that any of them were actually made for it.[9]

PROVENANCE: On the back a label, *Albrecht Dürer / A. fincke / (Berlin)*.[10] In the Ashburnham Collection, London, by 1878;[11] exhibited at the New Gallery, 1893/4 (No. 163); purchased from the Earl of Ashburnham, 1895.

REPRODUCTION: *Illustrations, Italian Schools*, 1937, p. 284. *Plates, Earlier Italian Schools*, 1953, Vol. II, p. 358.

REFERENCES: (1) Bode and Tschudi in the Prussian *Jahrbuch*, 1885, p. 16, as S· Eustace; it has since then been called S. Hubert sometimes, e.g. in the exhibition of 1893/4, and by Müntz in the *Gazette des Beaux-Arts*, 1901, II, pp. 226/7. (2) Mrs. Jameson, *Sacred and Legendary Art*, II, 1883, p. 735, says that she knows of no examples. S. Eustace, on the other hand, certainly does occur; cf. the work of 1462, with the name inscribed, and no armour, at Florence, reproduced by Van Marle, *Development of the Italian Schools of Painting*, Vol. X, Fig. 235. (3) Letter from J. Maquet-Tombu, 2 March, 1948, in the Gallery archives. She kindly called the compiler's attention to the scene on the Font of 1446 at Hal (reproduced in *Belgische Kunstdenkmäler*, I, 1923, Fig. 263). A S. Hubert holding a stag with crucifix is on a Lochner at Munich, No. H.G. 502 (Plate 3 of recent editions of the Catalogue). The exact date at which S. Hubert's Vision was first introduced has not been established; but it was probably not much before 1450 in Northern Europe, and perhaps after that in Italy. There are some comments on this problem in L. Huyghebaert, *Sint Hubertus*, 1949. (4) V. Goloubew, *Les Dessins de Jacopo Bellini*, I, 1912, Plates XXX and LXXXVIII, and II, 1908,

Plate XXXVII. See also a fresco (certainly of S. Eustace) reproduced by Mario Salmi, *L'Abbazia di Pomposa*, 1936, Vol. I, Fig. 319. (5) Bode and Tschudi as in note 1. (6) G. M. Richter in *The Burlington Magazine*, Vol. LV (1929), pp. 134 ff. (7) Hill, *Pisanello*, 1905, pp. 62 ff. and 236, as *ca.* 1435/8. (8) Hill, *Pisanello*, 1905, p. 65. Photograph in the Gallery archives, kindly sent by B. Berenson. (9) Alfred Hentzen, *Die Vision des Heiligen Eustachius von Antonio Pisanello* (*Der Kunstbrief*, No. 48), 1948, claims that a few drawings are definitely studies for No. 1436: (*a*) horse and rider in the Louvre (Hentzen, Fig. 13; B. Degenhart, *Pisanello*, Turin, 1945, Plate 83); (*b*) back part of horse in the Louvre (Hentzen, Fig. 14); (*c*) hound before the horse (perhaps Degenhart, Plate 82, in the Louvre); (*d*) head of dog by horse's foreleg; (*e*) studies of a crucified man in the Louvre (Hentzen, Fig. 2). The last is on the reverse of (*a*); see A. Venturi, *Giorgio Vasari: Gentile da Fabriano e il Pisanello*, 1896, p. 104, No. 2368 (with Guiffrey's note) and the Verona Exhibition Catalogue, *Da Altichiero a Pisanello*, 1958, No. 104 and Plates CXIV and CXIX. Other drawings may be connected with No. 1436 (see Hentzen's other reproductions) without being made for it. On this subject, Hill, *Pisanello*, 1905, pp. 68 ff. makes some prudent remarks. See also Hill, *Drawings by Pisanello*, 1929, Nos. 32, 41, 42, 63, 64, 65, with reproductions. (10) A letter in the Victoria and Albert Museum from John Sheepshanks to William Smith, 11 October, 1851, refers without details to Mr. Fincke (apparently of Vienna), who was sending an Albert Durer for sale to England. (11) MS. Catalogue in the N.G. Library. See also Bode and Tschudi as in note 1; Bode saw it in 1882 or earlier (letter from Burton to Layard, 14 June, 1885, British Museum, Add. MS. 39038, Layard Papers, Vol. CVIII). The picture had been called Dürer, with a casual suggestion of Foucquet.

See also BONO DA FERRARA, No. 771

Antonio del POLLAIUOLO

ca. 1432–1498

Piero del POLLAIUOLO

ca. 1441, not later than 1496

Florentine School. They were brothers. For the dates of birth, see R. G. Mather in *The Art Bulletin*, March, 1948, p. 32, and Maud Cruttwell, *Antonio Pollaiuolo*, 1907, pp. 3/4. For Piero's date of death, see Cruttwell, *op. cit.*, pp. 252/3. Antonio, and probably Piero also, died in Rome.

Both brothers were sculptors and painters, Antonio (apparently) being primarily a goldsmith and worker in bronze, Piero being primarily a painter.

Several documented pictures by Piero exist. (A) of a series of *The Seven Virtues* in the Uffizi, three are documented as Piero's of 1469/70. (B) an altarpiece at San Gimignano is signed and dated 1483. (C) a portrait of Galeazzo Maria Sforza in the Uffizi is presumably the one mentioned as Piero's in a Medici inventory of 1492.

Documented pictures by Antonio do not exist, but he is known to have been a painter. According to a letter dated 1494, *The Labours of Hercules*, lost, but known to have been three pictures, were done in 1460 by both brothers. Antonio is further listed as 'goldsmith and painter' in 1473 in the books of the Compagnia di San Luca at Florence (Horne, *Sandro Botticelli*, 1908, p. 20).* Antonio, in his signature on the bronze tomb of Pope Sixtus IV, describes himself as famous in silver, gold, painting and bronze. And, in the epitaph on Antonio's own tomb, he is described as 'pictor insign.'

These references to Antonio's painting seem rather meagre; and there is little evidence that he *was* famous among his contemporaries as a painter. It is true that Luca Landucci (*Diario Fiorentino*, ed. Iodoco del Badia, 1883, p. 3) refers to the Pollaiuolo brothers as goldsmiths, painters and sculptors; Giovanni Santi also, in his chronicle, couples the brothers together among painters. But most early mentions, if they refer to the particular class of Antonio's work, do not refer to his painting. Albertini, in his *Memoriale* of 1510, lists several pictures as by Piero del Pollaiuolo, none as by Antonio. The *Anonimo Magliabechiano* and the *Libro di Antonio Billi* record one picture as being by Piero on Antonio's design; all the other pictures they mention are ascribed to Piero.

It is Vasari (1550) who first stressed Antonio's activity as a painter, partly in collaboration with Piero. But even at this late period, it appears doubtful if Benvenuto Cellini agreed with Vasari's views (*I Trattati dell'Oreficeria e della Scultura*, ed. Carlo Milanesi, 1857, pp. 7 and 13).

More recent critics have tended to accept Vasari's authority concerning Antonio's prominence as a painter. They may claim some justification from the existing works; for some Pollaiuolesque pictures are clearly superior to others, and superior to Piero's documented pictures. Since certain works that are not painting are demonstrably by Antonio and clearly of high merit, there has been a tendency to ascribe the best pictures to Antonio. Collaboration between the two brothers is often postulated.

While there is general agreement among modern critics concerning Antonio's importance as a painter, there is little agreement concerning which parts of which pictures are by Antonio, which by Piero. In the present state of knowledge, it is prudent to catalogue Nos. 292 and 928 below under the names of both brothers. It seems indeed unlikely that their work in painting will ever be convincingly disentangled; a careful study of the value of the evidence concerning Piero would, nevertheless, be welcome.

Ascribed to ANTONIO and PIERO DEL POLLAIUOLO

292 ALTARPIECE: THE MARTYRDOM OF S. SEBASTIAN

The Saint, tied to a tree, is being shot at by six archers. In the middle distance on the left is a ruined piece of architecture, ornamented with two bas-reliefs of unidentified subject, and with two moors' heads in

* Another document of the Compagnia di San Luca is often referred to; first, it seems, by Berenson, *Drawings of the Florentine Painters*, 1903, I, p. 18. It is printed by Horne, *op. cit.*, Doc. XI, and affords no evidence concerning Antonio del Pollaiuolo's activity as a painter.

profile. Groups of soldiers, mostly on horseback, one holding a banner marked SPQR, are distributed over the landscape in the middle distance; a moorish figure is, in two cases, included among these groups.

Wood, $114\frac{3}{4} \times 79\frac{3}{4}$ (2·915 × 2·025); painted up to the edges all round. The picture has the appearance of having been trimmed slightly all round.

Cleaning completed in 1954. Good condition. A false halo for S. Sebastian was removed during the cleaning; the picture has suffered somewhat from bitumen, and some areas, e.g. the archer left centre, have numerous small losses. *Pentimenti* in the legs of the archer right, and elsewhere.

S. Sebastian was not actually killed by his ordeal with the arrows, but this episode is properly referred to as a part of his martyrdom. Although the distant landscape in No. 292 is reminiscent of the scenery in the Arno valley, and although the little town in the distance on the left vaguely suggests fifteenth-century Florence, it is probably meant to symbolize Rome, in or near which S. Sebastian was shot at. Indeed, the two columns with spiral decoration in this little town fairly clearly stand for the Columns of Marcus Aurelius and Trajan at Rome. The company of archers who shot arrows at the Saint is said to have been from Maure-tania;[1] but the two moors in the background of the picture are not well explained for this reason. They probably, and the two moors' heads on the building to the left certainly, refer to the arms of the Pucci family, who commissioned the picture.[2]

No. 292 was the principal altarpiece in the Oratory of S. Sebastiano, attached to the church of the SS. Annunziata at Florence.[3] This oratory belonged to the Pucci family,[4] who, as already stated, commissioned the picture. According to Vasari,[5] it was done to the order of Antonio Pucci; he died in 1484, and was buried in the oratory.[6] According to Vasari's second edition, the date of the picture is 1475.[7] There is a pre-Vasarian tradition that the model for the Saint was Gino di Lodovico Capponi. He was born on 21 December, 1453, and died in April, 1498. The fact that his son Lodovico was interested in art, being a picture-collector of some eminence, makes more probable the accuracy of the tradition about Gino in the picture; his birth in 1453, and his apparent age on the picture, offer some confirmation of Vasari's date of 1475.[8]

As could be deduced from the biography given above, the earliest sources cite this picture as the work of Piero del Pollaiuolo.[9] Vasari says that it was painted by Antonio.[10] More recent critics have variously divided the picture up between the brothers.[11] It can reasonably be said that the bodies of the two archers in the near middle distance are inferior in execution to the faces and to the five principal figures.

The legs of Pollaiuolo's *David* at Berlin are similar in pose to those of the archer on the left.

A *S. Sebastian* supposedly by Pollaiuolo is recorded in the eighteenth century to have been in S. Jacopo sopr'Arno at Florence,[12] but is not now known to exist.

COPIES AND DERIVATIONS: Eastlake noted a copy of No. 292 in the Hercolani Collection at Bologna in 1861.[13] In a Neri di Bicci at Volterra the figure of S. Sebastian seems fairly clearly to be derived; this picture is dated 1478.[14] It is often alleged that Botticelli's *S. Sebastian* at Berlin (apparently of 1474) is in some way connected with No. 292; but there seems to be little, if any, connection.[15] Signorelli, on the other hand, seems to have been inspired in a general way by No. 292 in his picture of the *Martyrdom of S. Sebastian* (1498) at Città di Castello.[16] A figure in a predella at Empoli, ascribed to Botticini, seems to be derived from No. 292.[17] A picture at Modena, supposed to be more or less a copy of No. 292, is not at all closely connected.[18] A picture by the Master of Santa Inés would seem to be partially derived from No. 292.[19] A picture by Fabrizio Boschi (died 1642) in S. Felicita, Florence, is supposed to be derived from No. 292; another by Francesco Morosini (XVII century) in S. Remigio, Florence, is also apparently derived.[20]

DRAWINGS: Drawings in Berlin,[21] Cambridge (Fogg),[22] Dublin,[23] Florence (Uffizi)[24], Paris (Louvre)[25] and the Janos Scholz Collection[26] may perhaps show some connection with the picture.

ENGRAVINGS: Two figures lying on the ground in the battle scene on the lower bas-relief on the picture recur with some variations in a Pollaiuolo School engraving.[27] An anonymous Florentine engraving of *The Martyrdom of S. Sebastian* appears to be partly inspired by No. 292.[28]

PROVENANCE: The picture is first recorded in 1510,[29] in an oratory attached to the SS. Annunziata at Florence; it remained there until the nineteenth century.[30] It was probably in the 1830's that it was removed to the Palazzo Pucci at Florence.[31] Purchased from Marchese Roberto Pucci, 1857.

REPRODUCTION: *Illustrations, Italian Schools*, 1937, p. 285. *Plates, Earlier Italian Schools*, 1953, Vol. II, p. 359.

REFERENCES: (1) *Les Petits Bollandistes*, I, p. 494. (2) The commission by the Pucci is first stated by Vasari (cf. note 5); but it is implicit in Albertini's *Memoriale* of 1510 (1863 reprint, p. 13). Nor can the matter be considered in any degree doubtful; cf. the reference to Richa in note 3. For the Pucci arms, see Litta, *Famiglie Celebri d'Italia*, s.v. Pucci. They are only suggested on No. 292; they occur correctly on two of the Nastagio degli Onesti panels ascribed to Botticelli (Schubring, *Cassoni*, 1923, Nos. 399, 400, Plate XCV). (3) See especially Richa, *Notizie Istoriche delle Chiese Fiorentine*, VIII, 1759, pp. 52 f. (4) Richa, *op. cit.*, VIII, p. 53, says that the oratory was made over to the Pucci family in 1452. (5) Vasari, 1550 edition, p. 500; ed. Milanesi, III, pp. 292 f. (6) See Litta, *op. cit.*, in note 2. (7) The date is not given in the 1550 edition of Vasari. See the reference to what seems to be a derivation of 1478 in note 14 and the corresponding text. (8) For the Gino tradition, see *Il Libro di Antonio Billi*, ed. Frey, 1892, p. 27; *Il Codice Magliabechiano*, ed. Frey, 1892, p. 103. This tradition was accepted by Vasari. For Gino, see Litta's *Famiglie Celebri d'Italia*, Vol. X, s.v. Capponi, Tavola XVII. Some careless critics have imagined the sources meant Gino di Neri Capponi, a politician who died in 1420. According to Baldinucci (*Classici Italiani* edition, VIII, 1811, p. 282), Jacopo Chimenti da Empoli in his *Martyrdom of S. Sebastian* in S. Lorenzo at Florence also made the saint's head an excuse for a portrait. (9) Albertini, *Memoriale*, 1510, 1863 reprint, p. 13; Billi and the Anonimo Magliabechiano as in the previous note. (10) Vasari, as in note 5. (11) Cf., for instance, Sergio Ortolani, *Il Pollaiuolo*, 1948, pp. 212/3. (12) Richa, *Notizie Istoriche delle Chiese Fiorentine*, X, 1762, pp. 355 f. (13) Eastlake's note-book. (14) Reproduced by Corrado Ricci, *Volterra*, 1905, p. 90. (15) Horne, *Sandro Botticelli*, 1908, pp. 32 f. (16) Klassiker der Kunst *Signorelli*, 1927, p. 60. (17) Bacci in the *Bollettino d'Arte*, 1924/5, Anno IV, Vol. 2, pp. 345 and 350. (18) Cavalcaselle e Crowe, *Storia della Pittura Italiana*, Vol. VI, pp. 138/9. But see R. Pallucchini, *I Dipinti della Galleria Estense di Modena*,

1945, No. 502, Fig. 196. (19) See C. R. Post in the *Gazette des Beaux-Arts*, November 1953, pp. 222/3 and Fig. 4. (20) For the Boschi, see Venturi, *Storia dell'Arte Italiana*, Vol. IX, Part VII, Fig. 402 and p. 720. The other was pointed out by A. E. Popham; photograph, Cipriani No. 6248. (21) Berenson, *Drawings of the Florentine Painters*, 1938, No. 1911; S. Ortolani, *Il Pollaiuolo*, 1948, Plate 113, and note on p. 214. (22) Berenson, *op. cit.*, No. 1898D. Agnes Mongan and Paul J. Sachs, *Drawings in the Fogg Museum of Art*, 1940, Vol. I, No. 38, and Vol. II, Fig. 34. (23) Berenson, *op. cit.*, No. 1951C and Fig. 92; the connection is very doubtful. (24) Gernsheim photograph, No. 2197. The drawing shows two horsemen and four foot soldiers similar in character to the groups in the background of the picture, but not corresponding precisely with any of them. (25) This is a sheet from the 'Verrocchio Sketch-book,' and is referred to by Maud Cruttwell, *Antonio Pollaiuolo*, 1907, p. 158. Reproduction in the Gallery archives. (26) Exhibited at Oakland and Berkeley, 1961, *Drawings from Tuscany and Umbria*, No. 66, with comment and reproduction in the catalogue. (27) Van Marle, *Development of the Italian Schools of Painting*, Vol. XI, Fig. 225. A. M. Hind, *Early Italian Engraving*, Vol. I, 1938, D. I. 2., and Vol. III, 1938, Plate 265. One of these recumbent figures occurs also in a drawing at Windsor, No. 059 (photograph in the Gallery archives). (28) A. M. Hind, *Early Italian Engraving*, Vol. I, 1938, B. III. 14, and Vol. III, 1938, Plate 211. (29) Albertini, *Memoriale* of 1510 (1863 reprint, p. 13). (30) The oratory itself was reconstructed at the beginning of the seventeenth century, but the picture remained in it. (31) It is recorded in the Palazzo Pucci by Federico Fantozzi, *Nuova Guida di Firenze*, 1849, p. 382. W. and E. Paatz, *Die Kirchen von Florenz*, I, 1940, p. 184, quote the reference as of 1842, which is the date of an earlier edition of Fantozzi. Various guides to Florence of the nineteenth century record the picture as still in the chapel (e.g. *Guida della Città di Firenze*, publ. Antonio Campani, 1830, pp. 84/5); but these guides sometimes go on repeating information that has become out of date. Rosini, *Storia della Pittura Italiana*, Plates, Vol. I, 1839, Plate LIII, says the picture is 'presso gli eredi Pucci di Firenze,' which may indicate that it had already left the chapel. It is indeed probable that the picture was removed to Palazzo Pucci in or soon after 1830, the year of some repairs to the chapel (F. Bigazzi, *Iscrizioni e Memorie della Città di Firenze*, 1886, p. 379); this is stated to be so by Morris Moore, *Purchase of a Pollaiolo*, 1857, p. 4.

928   APOLLO AND DAPHNE

Wood, painted surface, $11\frac{5}{8} \times 7\frac{7}{8}$ (0·295 × 0·20); painted up to the edges all round.

Good condition. The foliage (which has apparently darkened) seems to be painted on top of the sky; at least, it does not show up under X-rays.

The story of Apollo and Daphne is told with some variations. Briefly, Apollo pursued her; she prayed for protection against the ravisher, and was transformed into a laurel-tree ($\delta\acute{\alpha}\varphi\nu\eta$).

This picture is usually accepted as an early work by Antonio del Pollaiuolo. The attribution to Antonio, claimed to be a better man than Piero, is little more than a recognition of its high quality; the early dating may be correct, but is not based on factual evidence.

Schubring suggests that No. 928 once formed part of a *cassone*.[1]

PROVENANCE: Acquired by William Coningham in Rome, 4 January, 1845;[2] Sale, 9 June, 1849 (lot 28), bought by White. Wynn Ellis Bequest, 1876.

REPRODUCTION: *Illustrations, Italian Schools*, 1937, p. 286. *Plates, Earlier Italian Schools*, 1953, Vol. II, p. 360.

REFERENCES: (1) Schubring, *Cassoni*, 1923, No. 334. W. Stechow, *Apollo und Daphne*, 1932, p. 20, says a drawing dated 1525, identified as by Erhard Schön, in the Ecole des Beaux-Arts at Paris, is a free copy; a direct connection appears unlikely (photograph in the Gallery archives). (2) There is an inscription to this effect on the back.

EVANGELISTA PREDA
active 1483, died 1490 or later

Elder half-brother of Giovanni Ambrogio Preda; his date of birth is unknown, but it was probably *ca.* 1450 or a few years before (cf. Malaguzzi Valeri, *La Corte di Lodovico il Moro*, III, 1917, p. 5). He was associated at Milan in 1483 with Ambrogio and with Leonardo da Vinci in the contract for the altarpiece containing the *Virgin of the Rocks*. He made his will in 1490, and may have died soon after; in any case, he was dead by 1503. His style is unknown.

See under LEONARDO DA VINCI, Nos. 1093, 1661, 1662

GIOVANNI AMBROGIO PREDA
ca. 1455–after 1508

Milanese School. His name is often given in Latin forms *de Predis*, etc. He is recorded as a minor in 1467, and there seems to be good reason for placing his date of birth within a year or so of 1455; see G. Biscaro in the *Archivio Storico Lombardo*, 1910, pp. 132 and 225, and Malaguzzi Valeri, *La Corte di Lodovico il Moro*, III, 1917, pp. 5 ff. He is referred to as a miniature painter in 1472. In 1482, employed by Lodovico il Moro; in 1491 in Rome (*Warburg and Courtauld Journal*, 1958, p. 297); in 1493 at Innsbruck, employed by the Emperor Maximilian I, for whom he worked intermittently on pictures and on designs for medals and tapestries. He might be a man referred to as still alive in 1522.

In 1483, he, his elder half-brother Evangelista and Leonardo da Vinci contracted for an altarpiece, of which the pictures (as eventually completed) are the *Virgin of the Rocks* and its wings in the National Gallery; see under Leonardo da Vinci, Nos. 1093, 1661, 1662.

Preda's indisputable picture is the portrait of the Emperor Maximilian I at Vienna, signed and dated 1502. Morelli, first in his *Berlin Gallery*, then in his *Borghese Gallery*, attributed therefrom several works to Preda, most of which are still accepted as his; but the only other picture assignable to him alone on objective evidence is No. 1665 below.

Too little is known of him for his style to be convincingly defined. He may have begun in an old Lombard way; the principal exponent of this style was Foppa. He was at one time in partnership with Leonardo; if No. 1665 below is accepted, he came strongly under Leonardo's influence.

1665 FRANCESCO DI BARTOLOMEO ARCHINTO (?)

He holds a scroll inscribed. 1494. ; then ET(ATI? in monogram)S. AÑO. 20. ; then a monogram. AMPRF. (apparently).

Wood, painted surface, 21 × 15 (0·535 × 0·38).

The picture suffers from a heavy crackle, the marks of which have been in places reduced by repaint.

The identification of the sitter appears uncertain, but was traditional in the Archinto Collection.[1] According to the Burlington Club Catalogue of 1898,[2] Francesco was born in 1474; this would be confirmation if proved. Litta gives no date of birth, but records that he was alive in 1507, and died in 1551.[3]

The monogram on the picture has been given as correctly as possible above.[4] A plausible interpretation is Am(brosius) Pr(eda) F(ecit). It would seem capricious to doubt the attribution for No. 1665, unless an interpretation of the inscription excluding Preda is made. According to Suida,[5] it is almost impossible that No. 1665 should be by the same hand as the *Maximilian* at Vienna; but an interval of eight years with unknown circumstances might explain the difference of style. The Vienna picture is the only clear standard for stylistic comparison; Preda's part in the altarpiece of the *Virgin of the Rocks* is too ill defined to be relevant,[6] and attributed works could hardly have a claim for retention against a picture in all probability signed. It is, however, by no means clear that acceptance of No. 1665 involves rejection of the main body of ascriptions to Preda.

Probably the nearest picture to No. 1665 in style is the *Portrait of a Man* in the Brera, No. 790; some participation by Leonardo is often assumed for that.[7] The influence of Leonardo is apparent in No. 1665; it is also apparent that Leonardo had no part in the execution. It would be possible to imagine some indications by Leonardo for the design; but the few facts known about Preda's partnership with Leonardo seem to exclude collaboration in that case,[8] and there is no proof that Preda had close contact with Leonardo in other cases.

PROVENANCE: In Palazzo Archinto, Milan, apparently at least by 1842/3.[9] Comte Joseph Archinto Sale, Paris, 18 May, 1863 (lot 27).[10] Bought in 1863 from Farrer (?) by W. Fuller Maitland of Stansted Hall.[11] Exhibited at the British Institution, 1864 (No. 10); at Leeds, 1868 (No. 122); at the R.A., 1872 (No. 215);[12] at the New Gallery, 1893/4 (No. 185); at the Burlington Fine Arts Club, 1898 (No. 49). Purchased from W. Fuller Maitland, 1898.

REPRODUCTION: *Illustrations, Italian Schools*, 1937, p. 289. *Plates, Earlier Italian Schools*, 1953, Vol. II, p. 361.

REFERENCES: (1) Engraved as Francesco in Litta, *Famiglie Celebri d'Italia*; the text concerning the Archinto family is dated 1842/3. It is true that Litta says nothing about the location of the portrait. Cf. also Mündler's Diary, 1856. (2) Burlington Fine Arts Club, Milanese Exhibition, 1898 (No. 49). (3) Litta, *op. cit.* (4) There is available at the National Gallery a photograph, taken with direct magnification × 4. A recent critic to treat of this monogram is E. Möller in the Prussian *Jahrbuch*, 1939, p. 92; Möller reproduces a drawing of it, which is not quite accurate, and suggests AM PREDA, which appears impossible. (5) Suida, *Leonardo und sein Kreis*, 1929, pp. 174/5. No. 1665 is admitted as Preda by

Berenson, 1932 Lists, and by others. (6) See the entry under Leonardo da Vinci. (7) Cf. for instance what Suida says, *op. cit.*, p. 175 (with reproduction). (8) See the entry under Leonardo da Vinci. (9) Litta, as in note 1 (not explicit). For Morelli's evidence of 1847, see *L'Arte*, 1894, p. 250; for Frizzoni's of *ca.* 1848, see the *Gazette des Beaux-Arts*, 1898, II, pp. 390/1. See also Mündler's Diary, 1856. The picture was traditionally called Leonardo. (10) Léonard de Vinci, Portrait de M. Archinto. (11) Stansted Hall Catalogue, and MSS. in the Gallery archives; 'Farrer' is not given there, but his name appears in the N.G. 1929 Catalogue. (12) In these three exhibitions as Leonardo.

5752 PROFILE PORTRAIT OF A LADY

The buckle of her belt is ornamented with a moor's head between the letters L at the left and O at the right.

Walnut,[1] painted surface, $20\frac{1}{2} \times 14\frac{1}{2}$ (0.52×0.37).

The picture is a good deal worn on the hair and neck; the features on the whole are well preserved. *Pentimenti* in the outline of her forehead and nose, and in the back of her neck.

The moor's head and letters on the buckle have been associated with Lodovico il Moro, Duke of Milan, and the sitter has therefore rashly been identified with one of his mistresses, Lucrezia Crivelli[2] or Cecilia Gallerani.[3] Malaguzzi Valeri rejects both these names.[4] It is doubtful if even an association with Lodovico il Moro is correct; a moor's head was not one of his usual emblems, although there is evidence that he occasionally used it.[5]

No. 5752 is generally accepted as being a work of Ambrogio Preda; it has been seen in his biography above that the evidence concerning his style is not entirely satisfactory, but the attribution to him of No. 5752 is nevertheless reasonable.

PROVENANCE: For many years before 1907 in the Collection of the Earl of Roden, Tullymore Park, near Newcastle, Co. Down.[6] Lent by the Earl of Roden to the R.A., 1907 (No. 20). Sold in 1919 (?) to Colnaghi's,[7] it remained in the private collection of Otto Gutekunst, a partner in the firm. Probably exhibited at Agnew's, November–December 1922 (No. 8); lent by Otto Gutekunst to the R.A. 1930 (No. 323; Manorial Catalogue, No. 272).[8] Presented by Mrs. Gutekunst in memory of her husband, 1947.

REPRODUCTION: *Plates, Earlier Italian Schools*, 1953, Vol. II, p. 362.

REFERENCES: (1) Letter from B. J. Rendle, of the Forest Products Research Laboratory, 17 September, 1948, in the Gallery archives. (2) Doubtfully by A. Edith Hewett in *The Burlington Magazine*, Vol X (1906/7), pp. 309 ff. (3) H. Cook in *L'Arte*, 1907, pp. 151 f. (4) F. Malaguzzi Valeri, *La Corte di Lodovico il Moro*, Vol. I, 1913, p. 512. (5) See Malaguzzi Valeri, *op. cit.*, Vol. I, pp. 7, 8, 42, 398. A figure of Italy brushed by a moorish boy is given as an emblem of Lodovico by P. Giovio, *Dialogo dell' Imprese Militari et Amorose*, 1574, pp. 43/4; but this may be a mistake by Giovio, since a miniature derivation of the emblem with Lodovico not symbolized as a moor is reproduced by Malaguzzi Valeri, *op. cit.*, Vol. I, p. 357. For Lodovico il Moro's customary emblems, see Malaguzzi Valeri, *op. cit.*, Vol. I, pp. 320 ff.; Luca Beltrami, *Il Castello di Milano*, 1894, pp. 715 ff.; his portrait from the Trivulzio Collection in the Castello Sforzesco (reproduced in *Pantheon*, 1930, p. 446); and the cushion of his tomb in the Certosa di Pavia (reproduced in Litta, *Famiglie Celebri d'Italia*, last plate of the Sforza family). In spite of what is said in *The Burlington Magazine*, Vol. X

(1906/7), p. 309, the moor's head and letters on the buckle appear to be the only emblems on No. 5752. (6) *The Burlington Magazine*, Vol. X (1906/7), p. 309. (7) Suida, *Leonardo und sein Kreis*, 1929, p. 280. Reinach, *Répertoire*, IV, 1918, p. 16, says that it was on the market in 1913. (8) As a Portrait of Lucrezia Crivelli.

See also LEONARDO DA VINCI, Nos. 1093, 1661, 1662

Andrea PREVITALI
active 1502, died 1508

From 1502 to 1510, the signatures are some spellings of *Andreas Bergomensis* or *Andreas Cordelle Agi*; then (with one exception) some form of *Previtali*. Morelli's theory that two different painters were involved is convincingly disposed of by Irene Kunze in *The Burlington Magazine*, Vol. LXXI (1937), pp. 261 ff. He was from Bergamo. On several of his earlier pictures he describes himself as a pupil of Giovanni Bellini, from whom indeed he borrowed various motives. On his return to Bergamo towards 1511 he came under the influence of Lotto.

695   THE VIRGIN AND CHILD WITH A DONOR

S. Catherine is in the middle distance to the right.

Wood, painted surface, 21 × 27 (0·535 × 0·69); painted up to the edges all round.

Good condition, except for the Virgin's right hand, which is much damaged. Most of the small local damages are obvious, but also include parts of the donor's eye and S. Catherine's face. Most of the gold is new.

Early work, perhaps *ca.* 1505. The motive of the Virgin touching the donor's head was probably invented by Giovanni Bellini.[1]

VERSIONS: A signed variant, with a different donor, was in the Porto Collection, Vicenza, then in the Yerkes Collection, New York, and is now at the Wadsworth Atheneum, Hartford.[2] There is also a signed variant of the Virgin and Child alone.[3]

PROVENANCE: Manfrin Collection, Venice;[4] purchased thence, 1862.

REPRODUCTION: *Illustrations, Italian Schools*, 1937, p. 292. *Plates, Earlier Italian Schools*, 1953, Vol. II, p. 363.

REFERENCES: (1) Cf. Gronau, Klassiker der Kunst *Bellini*, 1930, Plates 116 and 151. (2) Reproduced in *The Burlington Magazine*, Vol. LXXI (1937), p. 263, Plate Ic. Wadsworth Atheneum, Exhibition, *Twenty-one Years of Museum Collecting*, April/May, 1949 (No. 32); confirmatory letter from C. C. Cunningham, 13 May, 1949, in the Gallery archives. (3) Reproduced in *The Burlington Magazine, loc. cit.*, p. 266, Plate IIa. (4) Where it was called Cima. Presumably 1856 Catalogue (No. 299). It was ascribed to Previtali by Mündler, in whose diary it is several times mentioned; e.g. on 17 October, 1857, apropos of a picture in the Frizzoni Collection, which however is not on the same design (photograph, Marcozzi, Milan, No. 457). The Manfrin Collection was formed, at least in part, by Conte Girolamo Manfrin, who died in 1801, according to *Il Forestiere Istruito . . . della Città di Venezia*, 1822, p. 295. According to the catalogue of the A. M. Plattis Sale, Paris, 13/4 May, 1870, the collection was formed *ca.* 1748 (perhaps meaning from that date onwards), and in 1848 was divided between the Marquise Bortolina Plattis veuve du Baron Sardagna and the Marquis Antonio Maria Plattis. According to the Manfrin Sale Catalogue of 1897, the collection was divided in 1849 between the Marchese Antonio Plattis and the Marchesa Bortolina Plattis nei Sardagna; her part or some of it remained in the Palazzo Manfrin until 1897.

1409 THE VIRGIN AND CHILD WITH SS. JOHN THE BAPTIST AND CATHERINE

The child wears a piece of coral. Signed: + 1504 / *Andreas.cordelle. agij.dissipulus. / iouānis.bellini.pinxit,* followed by a mark of which the first portion is like a 2 or a z.

Wood, painted surface, $25\frac{3}{4} \times 33\frac{3}{4}$ (0·655 × 0·855); painted up to the edge at the top.

A good deal damaged, though most of the flesh is pure.

The figure of S. John is derived from a picture ascribed to Giovanni Bellini in the Academy at Venice (ex-Giovanelli).[1] The mark at the end of the signature seems hard to explain; the second member has a long tail to it, and can hardly be a 4 as Ludwig maintains.[2]

VERSION: A fairly exact repetition, not signed, is in S. Giobbe, Venice.[3]

PROVENANCE: Duke of Buckingham Collection, Stowe, by 1817;[4] Sale, 24th Day, 15 September 1848 (lot 389), bought by Sir Charles Eastlake; purchased at Lady Eastlake's Sale, 2 June, 1894 (lot 53).

REPRODUCTION: *Illustrations, Italian Schools,* 1937, p. 291. *Plates, Earlier Italian Schools,* 1953, Vol. II, p. 364.

REFERENCES: (1) Gronau, Klassiker der Kunst *Bellini,* 1930, Plate 152; cf. Gronau, *Spätwerke,* 1928, pp. 18/9. (2) Ludwig in the Prussian *Jahrbuch, Beiheft,* 1903, pp. 58/9; his drawing of the mark is incorrect. (3) Reproduced on the same page as No. 1409 in Crowe and Cavalcaselle, *Painting in North Italy,* ed. Borenius, 1912, Vol. I, p. 280. (4) 1817 *Description,* p. 48, as Andrea Covelli.

2500 THE VIRGIN AND CHILD

Wood, painted surface, $19\frac{3}{4} \times 26$ (0·50 × 0·66); painted up to the edges all round.

A good deal damaged by the cracking of the panel; the paint is also rather heavily cracked, but the shadows seem not worn. Small *pentimenti* in the outlines of the Child.

No. 2500 seems to be rather similar in style to a picture of 1510, once at Dresden.[1] It was perhaps painted by Previtali at Bergamo, before the influence of Lotto set in.

PROVENANCE: In the hands of Antonio Grandi, Milan, *ca.* 1908;[2] George Salting Bequest, 1910.

REPRODUCTION: *Illustrations, Italian Schools,* 1937, p. 292. *Plates, Earlier Italian Schools,* 1953, Vol. II, p. 365.

REFERENCES: (1) Reproduced in *The Burlington Magazine,* Vol. LXXI (1937), p. 262, Plate Id. (2) Cf. the reproduction in *L'Arte,* 1908, p. 52.

2501 SALVATOR MUNDI

Signed: ANDREAS.PRIVITALVS.P.M.D.XVIIII.

Poplar,[1] painted surface, $24\frac{1}{4} \times 20\frac{3}{4}$ (0·615 × 0·53); painted up to the edges all round.

Excellent state.

PROVENANCE: Possibly the picture offered to the Gallery by Lord Ronald Sutherland Gower in 1902; he had bought it many years previously.[2] Lent by George Salting to the Gallery from 1903; Salting Bequest, 1910.

REPRODUCTION: *Illustrations, Italian Schools,* 1937, p. 293. *Plates, Earlier Italian Schools,* 1953, Vol. II, p. 366.

REFERENCES: (1) Letter from B. J. Rendle, of the Forest Products Research Laboratory, in the Gallery archives. (2) Letter in the Gallery archives.

3087 SALVATOR MUNDI

Poplar,[1] painted surface, $18\frac{3}{4} \times 15$ (0·475 × 0·38); painted up to the edges all round.

Excellent state.

Compare with No. 2501 above; perhaps a little earlier, but also from Previtali's Bergamask period.

VARIANT: A rather closely similar picture is at Seattle; exhibited, *2500 Years of Italian Art,* November–December 1957 (No. 113); photograph in the Gallery archives.

PROVENANCE: Bought by Mündler in 1863 from a chemist in Bergamo, and sold by him in that year to Sir A. H. Layard;[2] exhibited at South Kensington, 1869 (No. 19); Layard Bequest, 1916.[3]

REPRODUCTION: *Illustrations, Italian Schools,* 1937, p. 293. *Plates, Earlier Italian Schools,* 1953, Vol. II, p. 367.

REFERENCES: (1) Letter from B. J. Rendle, of the Forest Products Research Laboratory, in the Gallery archives. (2) Letter from Layard to Morelli, 30 November, 1863, British Museum, Add. MS. 38966 (Layard Papers, Vol. XXXVI); summarized by A. Venturi in *L'Arte,* 1912, p. 452. Cf. also the Layard MSS. in the National Gallery. The chemist may have been Prospero Arrigoni; Eastlake visited this collection in 1854, and noted a head of Christ by Palmezzano, which sounds unlikely for No. 3087. (3) For the history of the Layard Collection, see Appendix IV.

Ascribed to ANDREA PREVITALI

3111 THE VIRGIN AND CHILD WITH TWO ANGELS

Wood, transferred to canvas, $26\frac{1}{2} \times 36\frac{1}{2}$ (0·67 × 0·925).

There is a good deal of the damage frequent on transferred pictures; it also suffers badly from cracks.

The attribution to Previtali is due probably to Eastlake.[1] Mündler[2] in 1857 judiciously remarked that it was like a Boccaccino, but that the landscape was very like that of Previtali, and that it might be the work of the latter painter. Since then, a variant recognizably in the style of Boccaccino has turned up; the execution clearly differs. No. 3111, therefore, seems likely to be a work of Previtali on a Boccaccino design;[3] but some critics have thought it a Boccaccino—e.g. Berenson (1932 Lists).[4]

VARIANT: The version by Boccaccino, or at least in his style, was in the Liphardt Collection.[5]

PROVENANCE: Seen in 1856/7 in the collection of Count Castellani (previously of Count Bertolazone d'Arache) at Turin.[6] Bought from Mündler by Sir Ivor Guest, who exchanged it for another picture with his brother-in-law Sir A. H. Layard;[7] exhibited at South Kensington, 1869 (No. 38);[8] Layard Bequest, 1916.[9]

REPRODUCTION: *Illustrations, Italian Schools*, 1937, p. 294. *Plates, Earlier Italian Schools*, 1953, Vol. II, p. 368.

REFERENCES: (1) Eastlake's note-book, 1856; see note 6. (2) Mündler's Diary, 1857. (3) This is Gronau's view in *Apollo*, IV, 1926, pp. 75 f.; he refers again to the subject in *Belvedere*, 1929, II, p. 253. (4) But in the 1957 Lists it is recorded as a Previtali. A. Puerari, *Boccaccino*, 1957, pp. 185/6, seems to accept No. 3111 as Previtali's, and suggests a date of 1515/20. (5) Reproduced in Gronau's articles; see note 3. (6) Eastlake's note-book, 1856; it was called Lotto, but Eastlake suggested Previtali. Mündler's diary, 1856 and 1857. In the Le Monnier Vasari, V, 1849, p. 188, a catalogue of the collection of the 'Marchese d'Harache' is referred to; the compiler has not seen this. Dr. Vittorio Viale kindly sent a copy of the undated *Inventario di quadri, stampe e statue dell'ill.mo Sig. Conte Bertolazone d'Arache e di Banna, Collaterale nella R.a Camera* (Turin, Biblioteca del Re, MSS., Misc. Patria, Vol. 156), but No. 3111 does not appear to be recorded there. Mündler, in his Diary, 11 April, 1856, says that 'Conte Castillane' was nephew and heir to 'Conte Harrach.' To judge from the catalogue of the Arache Sale at Paris, 1859, *Castellani* is the right spelling. (7) Layard MSS. in the National Gallery. (8) As Boccaccino. (9) For the history of the Layard Collection, see Appendix IV.

4884 SCENES FROM AN ECLOGUE OF TEBALDEO*

1. Damon broods on his unrequited love.
2. Thyrsis asks Damon the cause of his sorrow.
3. Damon takes his life.
4. Thyrsis finds the body of Damon.

Painted area of each of the four $7\frac{3}{4} \times 7\frac{1}{4}$ (0·2 × 0·185). On two strips of wood, each *c.* $17\frac{3}{4} \times c. 7\frac{3}{4}$ (0·453 × 0·2).

Good condition in general. A little worn in places.

Perhaps intended as part of a piece of furniture.

The attribution to Previtali, suggested by Pouncey, was first published by G. M. Richter,[1] who demonstrated that many features in No. 4884 were almost identical with comparable elements in authentic works by Previtali.[2] These resemblances are indeed so striking as to leave little doubt that Previtali was the author of No. 4884. Nevertheless, some caution must be observed in view of the fact that no works of humanist subject definitely by Previtali are known, nor any in which he approaches

*This entry is by Mr. Cecil Gould and is reprinted from his catalogue of *The Sixteenth-Century Venetian School*, 1959.

quite so close to Giorgione, Richter's analogies being drawn, with one exception, from the backgrounds of Previtali's religious pictures. The identification of the subject is due to Dr. Ernst Gombrich.[3] The Arcadian story of the suicide of Damon the shepherd on account of his unrequited love for Amaryllis occurs in the second eclogue of the Ferrarese poet, Antonio Tebaldeo, printed in the Venetian edition of his works (1502).

PROVENANCE: Until 1936 in the collection of Count da Porto, at Schio, near Vicenza, who alleged that it had been in the Manfrin collection, Venice. Subsequently with Podio at Venice.[4] Purchased, 1937 (Grant-in-Aid and Temple-West Fund, with a contribution from the N.A.-C.F.).

REPRODUCTION: *Burlington Magazine*, Vol. LXXI (1937), p. 201.

REFERENCES: (1) Letter to the *Burlington Magazine*, Vol. LXXII (1938), p. 33. This had followed an article by Kenneth Clark (*Burlington Magazine*, Vol. LXXI (1937), p. 199) attributing the scenes, with reserve, to Giorgione himself, and a letter from Tancred Borenius (*Burlington Magazine*, Vol. LXXI (1937), p. 286) favouring an attribution to Palma Vecchio which the same writer also suggested in a letter to *The Times* newspaper of 21st October, 1937. Immediately Richter suggested Previtali, however, Borenius veered and supported it (same issue of the *Burlington Magazine*). In the course of the lengthy correspondence conducted chiefly in *The Times* and *Daily Telegraph* Georg Gronau supported the attribution to Giorgione (*The Times*, 23rd November, 1937) as did Ludwig Justi (in a statement in the Gallery archives). The attribution to Previtali was supported by A. Morassi (*Giorgione*, 1942, pl. 180) and by R. Longhi (*Viatico per Cinque Secoli* . . ., 1946, p. 64). Berenson (*Lists*, 1957) calls No. 4884 a 'Giorgionesque furniture painting'. (2) There would be no point in recapitulating Richter's analysis here, but one element which he himself did not stress may be indicated. The curious and naive form of the sheep in No. 4884 recurs in an almost identical form in the background of the *Madonna and Child* at Detroit, which is a signed work of Previtali. (3) Gombrich's results were published by Clark (*loc. cit.*). There can be no reasonable doubt that the identification is correct—cf., in particular, Tebaldeo's mention of Damon's breaking his lyre before killing himself (*E tu, mia cetra, sopra questo sasso / spezata rimarai, poi chel tuo sono / mai non mosse colei per cui sol lasso*). In the third scene of No. 4884 the broken instrument is shown on the ground. See also the entry in the Supplement (1939) to the National Gallery catalogue of 1929. (4) Letter from G. M. Richter to the *Daily Telegraph*, 26th January, 1938. This provenance renders dubious a rumour current at the time of purchase that No. 4884 had come from Malta. There is, however, no confirmation of the Manfrin provenance.

RAFFAELLINO DEL GARBO
living 1479 (?), died *ca.* 1527 (?)

Florentine School.

Vasari wrote a life of Raffaellino del Garbo, but there is some doubt about what one should understand by that. The problem revolves around three names, Raffaellino del Garbo, Raffaelle Carli and Raffaelle dei Capponi.

To mention first the pictures, (A) there are no documented Garbos. His basic works are a *Resurrection* in the Uffizi and a *Pietà* at Munich; these are mentioned (it must be admitted, rather obscurely) by the

Anonimo Magliabechiano and by Vasari. (B) signed Carlis of 1501 and 1502 exist in the Ringling Museum at Sarasota (ex-Benson) and at San Francisco (Kress Collection, ex-Corsini). A fresco of 1503, in a building attached to S. Maria Maddalena dei Pazzi at Florence, is documented as by Raffaello di Bart? Carli. (C) there is one signed Capponi, an altarpiece of 1500 in the Uffizi. It may be added that a few other works, signed or documented as by Raffaelle *tout court*, can be associated with (A), (B) or (C).

On the documentary side, (*a*) Raffaellino del Garbo must be identified with Raphael Bartolomei Nicolai Capponi, pictor nel Garbo; see especially the records concerning his son Bartolommeo, as given by C. Frey, *Die Loggia dei Lanzi*, 1885, p. 358, and by Colnaghi in his *Dictionary of Florentine Painters*, 1928, p. 226. (*b*) Raffaelle Carli is presumably the Raffaelle di Bartolommeo di Giovanni di Carlo, who is recorded as orphaned in 1479. It might appear that the name of Carli's grandfather is different from that of Garbo's grandfather, but this is not necessarily so. Carli, after being orphaned in 1479, was taken up by the Capponi family; if his benefactor was Niccolò Capponi (there were several Niccolò Capponis alive at the right time), he might out of gratitude have referred to himself as Raffaelle di Bartolommeo di Niccolò Capponi. Unfortunately, the documents concerning him have not been published, but merely summarized by Milanesi in his edition of Vasari, IV, pp. 250/1. (*c*) Raffaelle dei Capponi could obviously be identical with (*a*) or (*b*) or both; indeed, it would be difficult to reject his identity with (*a*), in view of the passage already referred to in Colnaghi's *Dictionary*.

Some further records, less important for the documentary side of the problem, can be found by the student without difficulty; e.g. on consulting Katherine B. Neilson, *Filippino Lippi*, 1938, pp. 186 ff. It is enough here to say that it is a pity that the texts of all the documents are not published, but that, on the documentary information available, (*a*) Garbo, (*b*) Carli and (*c*) Capponi appear to be identical.

It is satisfactory that (*a*), (*b*) and (*c*) appear to be identical; unfortunately, on the stylistic side, it is not always admitted that (A), (B) and (C) are. Berenson, in his *Drawings of the Florentine Painters*, 1938, I, pp. 107 ff., claims that the works of (B), Carli and (C), Capponi are identical, but distinct from the works of (A), Garbo. The theory according to Berenson's development of it does great violence to probability. It would be slightly better, if the pictures in group (A) cannot be accepted as by the same hand as the others, to say that Vasari was mistaken in ascribing them to Raffaellino del Garbo; this would indeed leave us free to consider Garbo, Carli and Capponi as one, but such a mistake by Vasari, and before him by the *Anonimo Magliabechiano*, is difficult to believe. In point of fact, various critics now tend to accept the unity of the groups on stylistic as well as on documentary grounds; cf. for instance Gronau in Thieme-Becker s.v. Garbo; A. Scharf in the Prussian *Jahrbuch*, 1933, pp. 151 ff.; C. H. Smyth in *The Art Bulletin*, 1949, pp. 209 f.

Until general agreement on this problem is reached, attributions are bound to be uncertain. It does not even appear desirable to record here indications concerning the style of the authenticated pictures; but it may be stated that, in any case, the painter or painters were eclectic and second-rate. It may be added that, according to Vasari, Raffaellino del Garbo died in 1524, aged 58; but the date should probably be *ca.* 1527 (cf. Colnaghi, *Dictionary of Florentine Painters*, 1928, p. 225, col. 2, top).

Ascribed to RAFFAELLINO DEL GARBO

3101   PORTRAIT OF A MAN

Wood, painted surface, $20\frac{3}{8} \times 13\frac{7}{8}$ (0·515 × 0·35); spandrels left and right at the top, so that the picture has roughly the shape of a flattened arch. Painted up to the edges all round, but certainly not cut to any appreciable extent.

In indifferent condition. Most of the important parts have been retouched to a greater or less extent; but it is probable that the character of the picture has not been greatly altered.

There are many *pentimenti*. The X-Ray reveals at least three other attempts at the right hand; his right shoulder once stood out further. At the top, the yellow curtains are painted over the central hanging; some incised lines at the top (not covered by the existing X-Rays) may indicate some attempt at a different arrangement, but seem irrelevant.

This picture was catalogued in 1929 as by Botticelli, and Berenson in his Lists of 1932 accepted the attribution. But the picture is painted in a more nearly cinquecento style than ever Botticelli achieved; the semi-Umbrian landscape is foreign to Botticelli; and in any case, the execution appears to be that of a fumbler. Further, the picture reflects the style of Filippino Lippi nearly as much as Botticelli's. It was Morelli[1] who suggested for it the name of Raffaellino del Garbo; this attribution is clearly not wide of the mark, and would indeed be hardly doubtful, if the name Raffaellino del Garbo had in itself a clear meaning.

PROVENANCE: 'Alberto Duro' on the back. Bought by Sir Austen Henry Layard not later than 1865 from Arrigoni of Bergamo.[2] Exhibited at Leeds, 1868 (No. 38),[3] and at South Kensington, 1869 (No. 46). Layard Bequest, 1916.[4]

REPRODUCTION: *Illustrations, Italian Schools*, 1937, p. 60. *Plates, Earlier Italian Schools*, 1953, Vol. II, p. 369.

REFERENCES: (1) Noted in the Layard MSS. in the National Gallery. Morelli, in a letter to Layard, 2(5 ?) October, 1865, actually said School of Filippino, and 'très probablement' Raffaellino del Garbo (British Museum, Add. MS. 38963, Layard Papers, Vol. XXXIII). No. 3101 is accepted as Raffaellino's by A. Scharf in the Prussian *Jahrbuch*, 1933, p. 159; also by Frizzoni in the *Gazette des Beaux-Arts*, 1896, II, pp. 473 ff. (2) Presumably this was Prospero Arrigoni, a chemist; Eastlake visited his collection in 1854, but did not record in his note-book any picture that could be identical with No. 3101. It is not known under what attribution Layard acquired the picture; Layard notes that Molteni (who restored it) thought it a Foppa, and Bertini a Signorelli. Most of this is from the Layard MSS. in the National Gallery; the date of acquisition from a letter from Layard to Morelli, 13 October, 1865 (British Museum, Add. MS. 38966, Layard Papers, Vol. XXXVI). (3) As 'A Portrait, said to be Lorenzo de' Medici' by Filippino Lippi; Thode had suggested Filippino—see Ulmann in the *Repertorium für Kunstwissenschaft*, 1894, p. 106. (4) For the history of the Layard Collection, see Appendix IV.

4902 TONDO: THE VIRGIN AND CHILD WITH TWO ANGELS

Canvas, transferred from panel; circular, diameter $33\frac{1}{4}$ (0·845).

Considerably damaged and restored.

Ulmann[1] thought that this is only a copy of a picture in Berlin, mentioned in the next section; but it appears oversubtle to postulate a separate hand for No. 4902, especially when its damaged state is remembered.

VERSION: A tondo at Berlin corresponds with the design of No. 4902, except for some differences in the draperies and landscape.[2]

PROVENANCE: Exhibited at the New Gallery, 1893/4 (No. 118),[3] lent by Sir Bernhard Samuelson. He died in 1905, and the picture passed to his son, Sir Henry Bernhard Samuelson, who bequeathed it in memory of his father, 1937.

REPRODUCTION: *Plates, Earlier Italian Schools*, 1953, Vol. II, p. 370.

REFERENCES: (1) H. Ulmann in the *Repertorium für Kunstwissenschaft*, 1894, p. 103. (2) Berlin, 1931, Catalogue, No. 90; reproduced in the Illustrations; size, 0·84 in diameter. The Berlin picture is generally accepted as a Raffaellino del Garbo; cf. for instance Berenson, *Drawings of the Florentine Painters*, 1938, I, p. 109. For the somewhat dubious meaning attached to this name, the student is referred to the biography above. According to the Berlin Catalogue, there is a free variant of the same design in the Musée André, Paris. (3) As by Garbo.

4903 TONDO: THE VIRGIN AND CHILD WITH THE MAGDALEN AND S. CATHERINE OF ALEXANDRIA

Canvas, transferred from panel; circular, diameter $50\frac{1}{2}$ (1·28).

Considerably damaged and restored.

This picture, formerly called Botticelli or Filippino Lippi, was ascribed to Raffaellino del Garbo by Crowe or Cavalcaselle.[1]

DRAWINGS: A drawing at Christ Church, Oxford, has been called a study for No. 4903.[2] A drawing of two hands in the British Museum seems to be a study for the Virgin's hands in No. 4903.[3]

PROVENANCE: In the Pucci Collection at Florence by 1849,[4] and seen there by Eastlake in 1855.[5] By 1907[6] in the collection of Sir Henry Bernhard Samuelson, who bequeathed it in memory of his father, 1937.

REPRODUCTION: *Plates, Earlier Italian Schools*, 1953, Vol. II, p. 371.

REFERENCES: (1) Mentioned as not seen in the first edition of Crowe and Cavalcaselle, II, 1864, p. 429. With the attribution to Raffaellino del Garbo in Cavalcaselle e Crowe, *Storia della Pittura in Italia*, VII, 1896, p. 152; Crowe and Cavalcaselle, *History of Painting in Italy*, IV, ed. Douglas and de Nicola, 1911, p. 304. Eastlake, who saw the picture in the Pucci Collection in 1855, had already noted in his note-book that it is possibly by Raffaellino del Garbo. No.

4903 is admitted as Garbo by Berenson in his 1932 Lists. A. Scharf in the Prussian *Jahrbuch*, 1933, p. 163, says that the style of No. 4903 can be used as an argument that Garbo and Carli were the same man. See also the biography above. (2) Berenson, *Drawings of the Florentine Painters*, 1938, II, No. 768, and III, Fig. 259; Scharf, *loc. cit.* (3) British Museum, *Italian Drawings, The Fourteenth and Fifteenth Centuries*, catalogue by A. E. Popham and Philip Pouncey, 1950, I, No. 61, and II, Plate LXIV. (4) Vasari, Le Monnier edition, V, 1849, p. 114 (as Botticelli). (5) Eastlake's note-book; see also Crowe and Cavalcaselle, as in note 1. (6) In which year it was reproduced for the Arundel Portfolio.

See also FLORENTINE SCHOOL, No. 2492

RIMINI (Giovanni Francesco da)
See GIOVANNI Francesco da Rimini

Ercole de' ROBERTI
active 1479, died 1496

Ercole d'Antonio de' Roberti, also referred to as Ercole de' Grandi, was a Ferrarese painter; he is first mentioned at Ferrara in 1479. From 1486 onwards he was working for the Este court there. There are some grounds for believing that he was born in the early 1450's.

Much confusion has been caused by the alleged activity of an Ercole di Giulio Cesare de' Grandi, who is said to have died in 1531. This man may possibly have existed. At least one Ercole of repute, distinct from Ercole de' Roberti, seems to have been known of in Bologna (Giovanni Filoteo Achillini, *Viridario*, written in 1504; printed in 1513 and in Giuseppe Guidicini, *Cose Notabili della Città di Bologna*, I, 1868, p. 405; apparently faulty French translation in the *Revue Universelle des Arts*, X, 1859, pp. 463 ff.); but there are no good grounds for attributing any existing picture to any such person.

In view of other possible Ercoles, the evidence concerning Ercole de' Roberti's works is not sufficient for complete certainty of attribution. Nothing produced by him for the Ferrarese court has been identified. The key work is an altarpiece of 1480 from Ravenna, now in the Brera at Milan; the documents concerning this picture refer to Ercole, without giving the family name. Other works associated with Bologna are identified with good traditions as by Ercole da Ferrara: frescoes in the Garganelli chapel in the Cathedral, of which there is good reason to hold that one head, now at Bologna, survives (Guido Zucchini in *Proporzioni*, 1943, pp. 81 ff.; *Bollettino d'Arte*, 1958, p. 375), and *Scenes from the Passion* now in Dresden and Liverpool, indubitably the ones formerly in S. Giovanni in Monte. The author of these works is assumed to be the Ercole de' Roberti active at the Ferrarese court, and this is unlikely to be wrong. A few other pictures can be ascribed with confidence to the same hand.

There is a confused but good tradition that Ercole was a pupil of

Francesco del Cossa, whom he appears to have assisted for some years.

The best account of the evidence concerning Ercole de' Roberti, impugning the existence of Ercole di Giulio Cesare de' Grandi, is by Giacomo Bargellesi in the *Rivista di Ferrara*, 1934, No. 9. See also F. Filippini in the *Bollettino d'Arte*, 1917, pp. 49 ff.

1217 THE ISRAELITES GATHERING MANNA

Moses and Aaron stand on the left; Moses (?) appears again in a group in the background.

Wood transferred to canvas, painted surface, $11\frac{3}{8} \times 25$ (0.29×0.635).

Very fair condition. The transference was carried out in 1829.[1] The receptacle for manna on the right probably had its base shown resting on the ground, as in the copy at Dresden mentioned presently; in this area of No. 1217 the original paint is missing, and the base is concealed in the reconstruction by manna.

The subject is from Exodus xvi, 1 sqq.

A composition known from a copy,[2] and identified as representing *Melchizedek blessing Abraham* (Genesis xiv, 18), seems to have been a pendant to No. 1217. Possibly, if not parts of a predella, the two pictures decorated some piece of furniture; see further the comment to No. 1127 below, note 4.

COPY: A copy of No. 1217 is at Dresden.[3] The composition appears to have been imitated, though only loosely, in No. 3103 of this Gallery, in the *Summary Catalogue* of 1958 as by a follower of Costa.

PROVENANCE: Probably an Aldobrandini picture (with the presumed pendant), coming from Lucrezia d'Este, Duchess of Urbino, who lived much at Ferrara, and bequeathed most of her property to Cardinal Pietro Aldobrandini in 1598.[4] No. 1217 is indubitably the picture once owned by Dr. Niccola Martelli; by 1829 it had passed to his grandsons and heirs, Luigi Martelli and his brothers, who sold it to Cardinal Fesch.[5] Fesch Catalogue, 1841 (No. 2118); Sale, Rome, 1845 (lot 863), bought by Del Re.[6] No. 1217 was in Lord Ward's Collection by 1859;[7] Lord Ward became Earl of Dudley in 1860, and lent the picture to the R.A., 1871 (No. 306).[8] Purchased from Lord Dudley's heirs, Clarke Fund, 1886. Cleaned Pictures Exhibition at the National Gallery, 1947/8 (No. 30).

REPRODUCTION: *Illustrations, Italian Schools*, 1937, p. 309. *Plates, Earlier Italian Schools*, 1953, Vol. II, p. 372 (after cleaning in 1940).

REFERENCES: (1) See the *Notizie ed Osservazioni sopra un quadro di Masaccio rappresentante gli ebrei che raccolgono la manna nel deserto*, p. IV. (2) Mentioned in the Chigi Collection by A. Venturi in *L'Arte*, 1889, pp. 359/60; it was later in the (Fairfax ?) Murray Sale, Berlin, 6/7 November, 1929 (lot 291), Plate XLI; size, 0.293×0.658. See also R. Longhi, *Officina Ferrarese*, 1934, note 88 and Plate 99. (3) Dresden Catalogue, *Die Romanischen Länder*, 1929, p. 21, No. 47, reproduced; size, 0.295×0.66. Longhi, *loc. cit.*, implies that this copy is the pendant copy to the Murray picture mentioned in the previous note. The chief difference between No. 1217 and the Dresden picture is that the latter shows some extra mountains in the background; the field of the Dresden picture is also very slightly different. (4) See Paola Della Pergola's publication of the Inventory of Lucrezia d'Este, 1592, in *Arte Antica e Moderna*, July–September, 1959, pp. 342 ff., Nos. 118/9. D.ssa Della Pergola kindly wrote that she traces the two pictures in Aldobrandini Inventories of 1626 and 1682, which she is preparing to publish. See also the *Inventarium bonorum repertorum post obitum clar: mem: Prīpīs D. Joīs Baptē Pamphilij Aldni*, Die 18 Nouembris, 1709 (Rome, Archivio di Stato, not. Paolo Fazio, No. 2661): 'Vn quadro di Elia in tauola con la pioggia della manna di Moisè bislongo, alto palmo uno, et un quarto di mano del Grande —Vn quadro simile con Melchisadech in abito bianco con due figure auanti (?) inginocchioni, e molte altre atorno di mano del Grande, alto palmo uno, et un quarto in tauola guasto, e scrostato.' The pages of this inventory are not numbered; the entries occur in a section dated 20 March, 1710. The compiler does not understand the words 'di Elia,' which seems to be the correct reading; but the two entries seem to refer to No. 1217 and the presumed pendant, for (in view of the provenance) they are likely to have been the originals, not the copies. Much Aldobrandini property passed from Donna Olimpia Aldobrandini, Principessa di Rossano (died 1681) to her sons, the already mentioned Giovanni Battista Pamphilj and Cardinal Benedetto Pamphilj. The last direct heir of Donna Olimpia died in 1760, and in 1769 a lawsuit over the Aldobrandini inheritance between the Borghese and the Colonna was won by the Borghese. The arrangement arrived at was that the Aldobrandini fortune and title should be held by the second son of the head of the Borghese family. See further in the entries for Luini, No. 18; Botticelli, No. 1034, note 24; and ascribed to Roberti, No. 1127, note 5. No. 1217 might be *Il Popolo Ebreo nel deserto, Giovanni Bellini*, in the Borghese Inventory (actually of *ca.* 1790), published in *Archivi*, 1937, p. 222, 2nd Room, No. 49. (5) See the pamphlet referred to in note 1. It was called Masaccio, an alleged signature *T. Guidi* being in the left bottom corner; there appear to be some remains of this on No. 1217 now. (6) In both cases as Masaccio. (7) Eastlake's note in his note-book, when he was in Dresden and saw the copy there. Cf. also Crowe and Cavalcaselle, *History of Painting in Italy*, II, 1864, p. 380. (8) As Unknown.

Ascribed to ERCOLE DE' ROBERTI

1127 THE LAST SUPPER

Christ is seated, holding the Host, between S. Peter and S. John. Of the other apostles, Judas is prominent on the right. The scene is set in architecture ornamented with bas-reliefs; an antique sacrifice is seen in the centre, and right and left the Adoration of the Kings or Shepherds, and the Flight into Egypt can be identified with some probability.

Wood, painted surface, $11\frac{3}{4} \times 8\frac{1}{4}$ (0·30 × 0·21).
Considerably damaged, e.g. in most of the front of the tablecloth; the heads on the whole are well preserved.
Said to have been the door of a tabernacle.[1]
Longhi[2] admits the attribution to Ercole, which seems more likely than not. It has, nevertheless, often been rejected.[3] It may be demonstrable that it comes from the same series as No. 1217 above and its presumed pendant.[4]

PROVENANCE: Apparently the picture acquired by W. Y. Ottley in December, 1798, from the Villa Aldobrandini at Rome and brought to England by March, 1799; exhibited for sale by private contract at 31 Margaret Street, Cavendish Square (No. 26); later in the W. Y. Ottley Sale, 25 May, 1811 (lot 31).[5] Lent by the Duke of Hamilton to the R.A., 1873 (No. 164); purchased, Hamilton Sale, 1 July, 1882 (lot 759).[6]

REPRODUCTION: *Illustrations, Italian Schools*, 1937, p. 308. *Plates, Earlier Italian Schools*, 1953, Vol. II, p. 373.

REFERENCES: (1) According to the Ottley Sale catalogue, and assuming that the provenance is correct. (2) R. Longhi, *Officina Ferrarese*, 1934, p. 71. (3) Berenson, 1936 Lists, as Ferrarese close to Roberti. Frizzoni, *Arte Italiana del Rinascimento*, 1891, p. 283, rejects it on grounds of quality. Venturi, *Storia dell'Arte Italiana*, Vol. VII, Part III, p. 751, as by a miniaturist follower of Roberti. Filippini in *Il Comune di Bologna*, 1933, No. 9, ascribes it to Guido Aspertini; he is known to have been Roberti's pupil, but no certain works by him exist. (4) Paola Della Pergola in her publication of the Inventory of Lucrezia d'Este, 1592, in *Arte Antica e Moderna*, July–September 1959, records on pp. 350/1 that F. Zeri has found XVI Century copies of No. 1217, the Melchizedek picture (its presumed pendant) and No. 1127, and thinks that the originals came from one predella. The compiler has not seen Zeri's article and can offer only provisional comments. No. 1217 and the Melchizedek do seem to have been in the same collections from 1592. No. 1127 may have the same provenance (No. 117 of the 1592 Inventory, 'una Cena'); at the time of writing, it is not established if later (Aldobrandini) Inventories confirm precisely the identification, yet No. 1127 does seem to have been acquired in 1798 from the Villa Aldobrandini (with an attribution to Masaccio, which was the name for No. 1217 too). The heights of Nos. 1217 and 1127 correspond closely; and while No. 1127 is more ornate and thus makes a somewhat different impression from No. 1217, it may be thought that the style of the two pictures corresponds well enough. A strong argument for the association is that the Gathering of the Manna and the scene of Abraham and Melchizedek are the two typologies of the Eucharist in the *Biblia Pauperum*. The *Speculum Humanae Salvationis* adds a third, the Paschal Lamb (Exodus, xxii, 1 sqq.); and it should be remarked that a picture apparently of this subject ('il sacrificio dell'Agnello figura del Testamento Nuovo'), ascribed like the others to Grandi, is included in No. 11 of the 1592 Inventory of Lucrezia d'Este. For these typologies, see Timmers, *Symboliek en Iconographie der Christelijke Kunst*, 1947, p. 247; J. Lutz and P. Perdrizet, *Speculum Humanae Salvationis*, 1907, Vol. I, p. 208; and H. Cornell, *Biblia Pauperum*, 1925, pp. 272/3. Zeri's claim that No. 1127, etc. are from a predella is supported by the shape and size of the known pictures, and there may be strong evidence in favour; the compiler cannot cite any Eucharistic predella strictly comparable. Pictures that do seem comparable are those by Livio Agresti at Forlì, each 0·24 × 0·42, showing Christ giving the Communion to the Apostles, a Miracle of the Host, the Paschal Lamb, and Abraham and Melchizedek; these Eucharistic pictures seem never to have formed a predella or part of one (see Filippo Guarini, Catalogue of the Forlì Gallery, 1874, Nos. 67, 69, 71, 73, or better Angelo Zoli, *Cenni Storici sulla Cattedrale di Forlì*, 1882, pp. 26 ff., and the *Guida per la Città di Forlì*, 1838, p. 11). If these Agresti pictures are indeed considered analogous, No. 1127, etc., may be thought to have ornamented some piece of church furniture. It may finally be remarked that the monastery of the Corpus Domini at Ferrara was rather closely connected with the Court (cf. Marc'Antonio Guarini, *Compendio Historico ... delle Chiese ... di Ferrara*, 1621, pp. 283 ff.); so the Robertis may have been made for there, passing thence to Lucrezia d'Este. (5) As by Masaccio, which was the attribution in the Hamilton Collection; the identification is probable, but cannot be proved. The title of the exhibition catalogue begins *Private View of Twenty-Six Capital Pictures, purchased at Rome, in Dec.* 1798; Ottley's name is not printed, but there is no doubt that he was the owner. For further details of the Aldobrandini inheritance, see the entries for Luini, No. 18 and Botticelli, No. 1034, note 24. The compiler did not identify any picture corresponding with No. 1127 in an inventory of Giovanni Battista Pamphilj Aldobrandini, referred to in the entries for Roberti, No. 1217 above, and Mantegna, No. 1417, note 17; the record may be there, but cf. Luini, No. 18, note 13. (6) In both cases as by Masaccio.

1411   THE ADORATION OF THE SHEPHERDS, AND THE
        DEAD CHRIST (TWO PICTURES)

Left, the Adoration of the Shepherds, with the Annunciation to the
Shepherds in the background. Right, Christ in the Tomb, with S.
Jerome in penitence; in the middle distance, the Stigmatization of S.
Francis; in the background, the Deposition. The cover of the tomb has
the mark I̅( ).

Wood, each panel, painted surface, $7 \times 5\frac{3}{8}$ (0.178×0.135); painted up
to the edges top and bottom.
Good condition.

The two pictures clearly belong together; it is not known if there were
any further parts of the series.[1] A picture in S. Maria Calchera at Brescia,
assigned to Moretto, also shows Christ in the Tomb and the penitent
S. Jerome, a third equally prominent figure there being identified as
S. Dorothy.[2]

No. 1411 is often ascribed to Roberti,[3] but that does not appear quite
satisfactory. Pouncey[4] thinks that, if not by Roberti, it may be by a
painter with a style allied to the miniaturist Marmitta. No. 1411 is sometimes classed together with No. 1127 above;[5] but there appears to be
some difference of style.

PROVENANCE: In the Costabili Collection at Ferrara in 1838.[6] Still there in
1858,[7] but bought then or soon after by Sir Charles Eastlake, who died in 1865.
Lent by Charles Eastlake Smith to the Burlington Fine Arts Club, 1894 (No.
11).[8] Purchased at the Lady Eastlake Sale, 2 June, 1894 (lot 71).[9]

REPRODUCTIONS: Illustrations, Italian Schools, 1937, p. 308. Plates, Earlier
Italian Schools, 1953, Vol. II, p. 374.

REFERENCES: (1) In an Este inventory of 1493, two folding anconette are recorded, painted (?) with The Nativity and Christ in the Tomb; Campori, Raccolta
di Cataloghi, 1870, p. 2. (2) Reproduced by A. Morassi, Brescia (Catalogo delle
Cose d'Arte e di Antichità d'Italia), 1939, p. 381. (3) E.g. by R. Longhi, Officina
Ferrarese, 1934, p. 71. Crowe and Cavalcaselle, Painting in North Italy, 1871, I,
p. 548, ascribe it to Costa. (4) Pouncey, ms. For some Marmitta reproductions,
see Paolo d'Ancona, La Miniature Italienne, 1925, Plates LVI, LVII, and Toesca
in L'Arte, January–June, 1948, pp. 33 ff. (5) E.g. by Venturi, Storia dell'Arte
Italiana, Vol. VII, Part III, p. 751; and by F. Filippini in Il Comune di Bologna,
1933, No. 9, who ascribes it to Guido Aspertini (but see the entry for No. 1127
above). (6) C. Laderchi, Catalogo della Quadreria Costabili, I, 1838, Nos. 59, 60,
as Costa. (7) Eastlake's note-book and Mündler's Diary. (8) As Roberti. (9) As
Grandi.

ROMAN SCHOOL (?) FIRST TO SECOND CENTURY (?)

2980   MOSAIC: CRANE, PYTHON AND LIZARD (FRAGMENT)

Mosaic, (sight) $9\frac{1}{4} \times 11\frac{1}{2}$ (0.235×0.29).

The attribution is preserved from the 1929 Catalogue.[1] No comment is
made here concerning No. 2980; it is outside the tradition of the main
schools of European painting as represented in the National Gallery
Collection.

PROVENANCE: Lt.-Col. J. H. Ollney Bequest, 1836/7.[2] Exhibition of Greek Art at the Royal Academy, 1946 (No. 315).[3] On loan to the British Museum since 1954.

REPRODUCTION: *Plates, Earlier Italian Schools*, 1953, Vol. II, p. 375.

REFERENCES: (1) Page 414. (2) Mentioned in the National Gallery Minutes as Antique, A Fragment of a Tessellated Pavement. (3) As probably Greek-Alexandrian work, first century.

ROMAN SCHOOL (?) TWELFTH CENTURY (?)

3403 MOSAIC: 'THE WATER OF LIFE' (FRAGMENT)

Mosaic, $19\frac{5}{8} \times 20$ (0·50 × 0·51).[1]

PROVENANCE: Apparently in a sale at Sotheby's, 18 June, 1890 (lot 52).[2] Presented by Henry Wagner, through the National Art-Collections Fund, 1919. On loan to the Victoria and Albert Museum since 1953.

REPRODUCTION: *Plates, Earlier Italian Schools*, 1953, Vol. II, p. 375.

REFERENCES: (1) Measurements from the 1929 Catalogue. The attribution and title are preserved from the 1929 Catalogue; no comment is here made concerning this mosaic, which is outside the tradition of the main schools of European painting as represented in the National Gallery Collection. No. 3403 was published in *The Burlington Magazine*, Vol. XXXV (1919), p. 75. (2) According to the 1920 Catalogue. In 1929 the lot number is given as 12, but 52 should be right, to judge from a cutting in the National Gallery archives.

SANTACROCE *See* GEROLAMO DA SANTACROCE

GIOVANNI SANTI
active 1469, died 1494

More properly *Giovanni di Sante*. His family moved from Colbordolo to Urbino in 1450; presumably he did too, if (as is probable) he was already alive. He was active at Urbino, partly for the Court. There are several signed works; dated from 1484. He is thought to have been influenced by Melozzo, whose friend he certainly was; he himself expressed great admiration for Mantegna. He was the father of Raphael.

751 THE VIRGIN AND CHILD

Wood, painted surface, $26\frac{3}{4} \times 19\frac{1}{4}$ (0·68 × 0·49); painted up to the edges all round.

Good condition on the whole. Certain outlines have been retouched, e.g. the Virgin's chin; more extensive, but still local, damages in the landscape and sky.

The attribution to Giovanni Santi was made by Crowe and Cavalcaselle,[1] and is generally accepted.

PROVENANCE: Coll. Conte Mazza, Ferrara, by 1864.[2] Purchased from him in 1865 by Michelangelo Gualandi, Bologna, from whom purchased, 1865.[3]

REPRODUCTION: *Illustrations, Italian Schools*, 1937, p. 318. *Plates, Earlier Italian Schools*, 1953, Vol. II, p. 376.

REFERENCES: (1) Crowe and Cavalcaselle, *History of Painting in Italy*, Vol II, 1864, pp. 588/9. (2) See the previous note. (3) According to a letter from Lady Eastlake to Wornum, 27 November, 1865, Eastlake (who was dying) had not seen the picture, but determined to buy it on learning that it was accepted as a Giovanni Santi by Cavalcaselle. Count Mazza demanded a quick sale, so Eastlake authorized Gualandi to buy it, on the understanding that the National Gallery should have it if the Trustees approved; otherwise, Eastlake would have taken it for himself.

SASSETTA *See* STEFANO DI GIOVANNI

GIORGIO SCHIAVONE
1436/7-1504

His name was *Ćulinović*. *Schiavone* means Slavonian; he was actually a Dalmatian. Both epithets occur inscribed on some pictures. By error his christian name, which he is not known to have used for signatures, was long supposed to be Gregorio. He was apprenticed in Squarcione's shop in Padua from 1456 to *ca.* 1459. In 1462 he was in Zara, in 1463 in Sebenico where he spent most of the rest of his life, though he did occasionally revisit Padua. He seems not to have done much painting except during his first Paduan period; none of his signed works are dated, but the signatures stress his dependence on Squarcione and these pictures are perhaps most reasonably ascribed to the period 1456/62. As is the case with other Squarcionesques, his works show a distinct influence of Fra Filippo Lippi, who had been active at Padua in the 1430's; but the style is mainly a caricature of that adopted by Mantegna, who was Squarcione's most distinguished pupil.

630 POLYPTYCH OF TEN PANELS

Lower Row (from left to right):

(*a*) *S. Anthony of Padua*

   Wood, painted surface, 26 × 9 (0·66 × 0·23); painted up to the edges all round.

(*b*) *S. Bernardino*, with the monogram $\overline{\text{IHS}}$.

   Wood, painted surface, 28½ × 10 (0·72 × 0·255); painted up to the edges all round.

(*c*) *The Virgin and Child Enthroned*

   The Child wears a piece of coral. Signed on a *cartellino*, .OPVS. SCLAVONI.DISIPVLI. / SQVARCIONI.S. (for the *pentimento*, see below).

Wood, painted surface, $36 \times 13\frac{3}{4}$ (0·915 × 0·35); painted up to the edges all round.

(*d*) *S. John the Baptist*, with a scroll inscribed, EC(ce) AG / N(us) / DEI.

Wood, painted surface, $28\frac{1}{2} \times 10$ (0·72 × 0·255); painted up to the edges all round.

(*e*) *S. Peter Martyr*

Wood, painted surface, 26×9 (0·66 × 0·23); painted up to the edges all round.

Upper Row (from left to right):

(*f*) *S. Jerome*

Wood, painted surface, $12\frac{3}{4} \times 9\frac{3}{4}$ (0·325 × 0·25); painted up to the edges all round.

(*g*) *S. Catherine*

Wood, painted surface, 12×9 (0·305 × 0·23); painted up to the edges all round.

(*h*) *Pietà*

Wood, painted surface, $14\frac{3}{4} \times 10\frac{1}{4}$ (0·375 × 0·26); painted up to the edges all round.

(*i*) *S. Sebastian*

Wood, painted surface, 12×9 (0·305 × 0·23); painted up to the edges all round.

(*j*) *A Female Saint*, with book and palm

Wood, painted surface, $12\frac{3}{4} \times 9\frac{3}{4}$ (0·325 × 0·25); painted up to the edges all round.

Good condition, except for the gold backgrounds, which are new. The third word of the signature originally read DISIPVLVS; the two last letters (with the tail of the preceding L) are partly blotted out by repaint, but the final I seems to be genuine. It is most probable that this is a *pentimento*; in the course of time, and by the effect of some over-cleaning (compare the seals attaching the *cartellino*), the first reading presumably came to show through and had to be painted out. Waagen[1] in an inaccurate transcription made a point of reading the nominative; but the I might have been difficult to distinguish if the VS had been at that time more prominent, and Waagen's statement cannot be accepted as proof that the I has been added since.

When in the Dennistoun Collection,[2] the panels were in a different, and wrong, arrangement. The present form is obviously correct in the main, though there may be some inversions between the outer and inner figures of the two rows. Presumably some at least of the panels have been reduced in size. Since all the gold is new, there is little evidence for saying if the exposed surfaces were meant to end in square tops or with some arch-work. The larger scale of the central figures has plenty of precedent, e.g. in Squarcione's polyptych of 1449/52,[3] and in Mantegna's *Altarpiece of S. Luke* of 1453/4[4]; indeed, the general disposition of the latter is rather closely similar to that of No. 630.

It has been remarked in the biography above that the works certainly by Schiavone seem to be most probably from within a year or two of 1460. It may be noted in passing that S. Bernardino was canonized in 1450.[5] A comparatively early date for No. 630 is partly confirmed by the representation of S. Sebastian; clothed S. Sebastians seem to have been particularly in a Vivarinesque tradition,[6] and in general aspect also this figure recalls Antonio Vivarini. The *Dead Christ Supported by Putti*, which is obviously of Donatellesque derivation, is an early example of this form in a picture; see the comment to Crivelli No. 602, which is in all probability later. The female saint top right was formerly called S. Cecilia, the reason not being given. The figure in grey with a cardinal's hat was formerly called S. Anthony Abbot, but is certainly S. Jerome.[7]

VARIANTS: A version of the *Pietà* by a different hand, with a swag and candelabra added and some other variations, is at Berlin.[8] The lower limbs of the Child recur fairly exactly in a *Virgin and Child* signed by Schiavone, at Berlin.[9] SS. Anthony of Padua and Peter Martyr and some details of the Virgin and Child are repeated in a small altarpiece by Schiavone in the Musée André, Paris.[10]

PROVENANCE: No. 630 is presumably the picture from an altar in S. Niccolò at Padua, belonging to the Frigimelica family, and removed to Palazzo Frigimelica apparently in the eighteenth century.[11] This house passed in time to the Salvadego family, but the picture does not seem to be mentioned again at Padua. No. 630 was in the Collection of James Johnston of Straiton at Edinburgh, formed from 1829 onwards; Catalogue, 2nd edition, 1835 (No. 17); Sale, bought by James Dennistoun of Dennistoun, Edinburgh.[12] Seen by Waagen;[13] Dennistoun Sale, London, 14 June, 1855 (lot 20), bought by Nieuwenhuys. Purchased with the rest of the Edmond Beaucousin Collection, Paris, 1860.

REPRODUCTION: *Illustrations, Italian Schools*, 1937, p. 327 (wrongly numbered 530). *Plates, Earlier Italian Schools*, 1953, Vol. II, p. 377.

REFERENCES: (1) Waagen, *Treasures*, 1854, III, pp. 280/1. (2) See the description in Waagen, *loc. cit.* (3) Venturi, *Storia dell'Arte Italiana*, Vol, VII, Part III, Fig. 1. (4) Venturi, *op. cit.*, Fig. 91. (5) The features are perhaps a little more authentic than might be imagined, since S. Bernardino is stated to have visited Squarcione at Padua (Scardeone, *De Urbis Patavii Antiquitate*, reprint by P.v.d.Aa, Leyden, n.d., Col. 422); but the point must not be pressed. (6) Cf. the entry for Crivelli, No. 724. (7) Cf. the figure in Benozzo, No. 283 of this catalogue, or the figure in the polyptych by Antonio and Bartolomeo Vivarini at Bologna, where a lion and church are also included; reproduced (not very clearly) by Testi, *Storia della Pittura Veneziana*, Vol. II, 1915, p. 381. (8) Photograph in the Gallery archives. The picture had been in the depot, but was to be exhibited in 1939. (9) Reproduced in the Berlin Illustrations, and in Venturi, *op. cit.*, Fig. 18. (10) Venturi, *op. cit.*, Fig. 25. (11) No. 630 seems clearly identical with the ten pictures on gold grounds, of which the Virgin and Child was signed OPVS.SCLAVONI.DISCIPVLI.SQVARCIONI, or (in another reference) *Opus.Sclavoni.Discipuli.Squarcioni.S.* See Giovambatista Rossetti, *Descrizione ... di Padova*, 1765, p. 239 and pp. 330/1, or 3rd edition, 1780, p. 248 and pp. 344/5. Bonifazio Frigimelica, who became doctor of law at Padua before 1444 (Portenari, *Della Felicità di Padova*, 1623, p. 283), is said to appear as a portrait in one of Mantegna's Eremitani frescoes; see Vasari, ed. Milanesi, III, p. 391. He was actually the legal representative of Imperatrice Ovetari in 1452;

cf. L. Testi, *Storia della Pittura Veneziana*, II, 1915, p. 741, and *Arte Veneta*, 1948, p. 147. **(12)** The Earl of Crawford and Balcarres kindly communicated a catalogue of the Dennistoun Sale of 1855 annotated by Dennistoun's widow; No. 630 is stated to have been bought at Johnston of Straiton's Sale in Edinburgh at Tait's Room for £8 8s. There were several sales of this Collection; there is some reason to believe that the one in question was in 1841, but the compiler has not seen the catalogue. Mr. David Baxendall kindly sent an extract from the catalogue of the Johnston Collection of 1835. **(13)** Waagen, *loc. cit.*, in note 1, with identifying description.

Ascribed to GIORGIO SCHIAVONE

904 THE VIRGIN AND CHILD

The Child wears a piece of coral. On the pilaster, left, is an . A . , and lower down the right-hand half of an E (?) followed by a stop; on the right-hand pilaster, . P . , and lower down a stop followed by the left part of an Ω (?).

Wood, painted surface, $22 \times 16\frac{1}{4}$ ($0 \cdot 56 \times 0 \cdot 415$); perhaps slightly trimmed at the lower edge, but this is not likely.

So far as can be seen at present, this picture is considerably worn and extensively retouched.

The picture has not been cut at the sides, and the two lower letters (if they are letters) were therefore always incomplete. A reading downwards on the left and then up on the right would give A E Ω P (?), which at least suggests an abbreviation sometimes used, A E O P E F, or *Alpha et Omega Principium et Finis* (from the Apocalypse).[1] It is probable that some phase of this class was intended. On two pictures,[2] and in a rather similar place, Schiavone puts S P Q R; fanciful as this is, it may be held to give some local colour. On a *Virgin and Child* in the Correr Museum, ascribed to Schiavone,[3] a *cartellino* on the parapet carries the letters R C; which, *faute de mieux*, might be held to stand for *Regina Coeli*.

Crowe and Cavalcaselle,[4] however, who read only A P on No. 904, thought it was a signature, and suggested Antonio da Pavia, a late Mantegnesque, whom further they identified with Antonio della Corna;[5] but the style demands an early Mantegnesque, or rather a Squarcionesque. Besides, if the letters are a signature, P might stand for *pinxit*; but it is unlikely that a signature was intended.

The picture is usually admitted to be by Giorgio Schiavone; its condition renders a certain doubt prudent. The style seems slightly different from that of No. 630. Criticism is perhaps incapable of disentangling the Squarcionesques; for instance, at one time or another, a *Virgin and Child* signed by Squarcione at Berlin and another signed by Zoppo at Lord Wimborne's have been ascribed to Schiavone on grounds of style.[6] No. 904 is certainly near to Schiavone; but not necessarily by his hand.

PROVENANCE: In the Collection of Alexander Barker, London, by 1871;[7] purchased at the Sale, 6 June, 1874 (lot 49).[8]

REPRODUCTION: *Illustrations, Italian Schools*, 1937, p. 328. *Plates, Earlier Italian Schools*, 1953, Vol. II, p. 378.

REFERENCES: (1) A variant of this inscription is on the hem of the dress of S. Mary Cleophae in a Strigel at Nuremberg (1937 Illustrations, Plate 192). (2) At Berlin and Turin; reproduced by Venturi, *Storia dell'Arte Italiana*, Vol. VII, Part III, Figs. 18 and 24. (3) Correr Catalogue, 1957, pp. 73/4, reproduced; there is comment on the difficulty of interpreting the letters R.C., but the suggestion given in the text above is not referred to. (4) Crowe and Cavalcaselle, *Painting in North Italy*, I, 1871, p. 345, or ed. Borenius, 1912, II, p. 48; cf. also p. 419 of the first edition (p. 120 of the 2nd edition). (5) Crowe and Cavalcaselle, *op. cit.*, II, 1871, p. 73, or II, 1912, pp. 402/3. (6) Reproduced by Venturi, *Storia dell'Arte Italiana*, Vol. VII, Part III, Figs. 2 and 5. (7) See Crowe and Cavalcaselle, as in note 4. (8) As Vivanni, i.e. Vivarini.

SEGNA di Bonaventura
active 1298, died 1326/31

Sienese School. Apparently a nephew of Duccio's. Recorded at Arezzo in 1319. Four signed works exist. See Pèleo Bacci, *Fonti e Commenti per la Storia dell'Arte Senese*, 1944, pp. 3 ff. (Review by Enzo Carli in *Emporium*, April–June, 1944, pp. 58/9.)

Style of SEGNA di Bonaventura

567 CRUCIFIX

The Virgin and S. John are shown at the ends of the cross, left and right. Inscribed (new): IHS NAZARENUS / R.E.X / IUDEORUM.

Wood. Total size, including the framing, $84 \times 72\frac{1}{2}$ ($2 \cdot 135 \times 1 \cdot 84$). The outer $\frac{3}{8}$ in. of this framing all round is new wood; the inner part may be original. Size of the panels of the Virgin and S. John, excluding the framing, each, $14 \times 8\frac{1}{2}$ ($0 \cdot 355 \times 0 \cdot 22$).

Much damaged. Over a part of Christ's left arm and hand, length $12\frac{1}{4}$ in. ($0 \cdot 31$), the paint is wholly new; over about 4 in. ($0 \cdot 10$) of His right arm, the paint is wholly new. The figure of Christ in general is in poor preservation. S. John is well preserved, the Virgin less well than S. John. The stamped background behind the Virgin and S. John, and on part of Christ's halo, preserves the original pattern with some remains of the original gold over it. The patterning on the picture not stamped, but merely painted and gilt, is new, perhaps following old indications. The framing has been regilt.

By analogy with other Crucifixes of the time, a roundel of God the Father should once have surmounted No. 567.

No. 567 was ascribed to Segna at the National Gallery since the catalogue of 1858. This attribution has not always been accepted; Berenson, in his Lists of 1932, includes No. 567 under Segna's name with a question-mark, and F. Mason Perkins in Thieme-Becker s.v. Segna rejects the attribution. It is certainly wrong.

It is neverthless convenient to maintain a loose connection with Segna in the form of the ascription for No. 567, since a rather similar Crucifix at Moscow is a signed work of Segna's.[1] Other Crucifixes, in varying degrees nearer to No. 567 than the Moscow picture, are at (1) S. Polo in Rosso near Gaiole;[2] (2) the Siena Gallery, No. 21;[3] (3) Pienza, S. Francesco;[4] (4) Arezzo, Badia (SS. Flora e Lucilla);[5] (5) Massa Marittima Cathedral;[6] (6) Chianciano, Museo d'Arte Sacra;[7] (7) the Siena Gallery, No. 36.[8] The relations between these pictures and No. 567 and Segna are at least difficult to define;[9] it should further be remembered that No. 567 is in unreliable condition.

PROVENANCE: From the Vanni Collection at Siena.[10] Purchased with other pictures from the Lombardi-Baldi Collection, Florence, 1857.[11]

REPRODUCTION: *Illustrations, Italian Schools*, 1937, p. 328. *Plates, Earlier Italian Schools*, 1953, Vol. II, pp. 379–380.

REFERENCES: (1) Reproduced in *The Burlington Magazine*, Vol. XLVII (1925), p. 153. (2) F. Mason Perkins, *Pitture Senesi*, 1933, Plate 67. (3) Siena, Catalogo by Cesare Brandi, 1933, p. 280, No. 21, as Follower of Segna; photograph in the Gallery archives. (4) Photograph, Ministero della Pubblica Istruzione, No. 5724, in the Gallery archives; reproduced in *Vita d'Arte*, July, 1912, p. 5. It is often stated to be connected, e.g. by Brandi, *op. cit.*, p. 280. (5) Usually admitted to be by Segna; reproduced in *L'Arte*, 1912, p. 34, and by Van Marle, *Development of the Italian Schools of Painting*, II, Fig. 84. (6) Reproduced in *L'Arte*, 1912, p. 31, and by Van Marle, *op. cit.*, II, Fig. 86. (7) Exhibition, *Dipinti Senesi del Contado e della Maremma*, Siena, 1955, catalogue by Enzo Carli, pp. 52 ff., with reproductions. (8) Siena, Catalogo by Cesare Brandi, 1933, p. 71, No. 36, as Follower of Duccio (formerly called Massarello di Gilio). Reproduced by Van Marle, *op. cit.*, II, Fig. 58. (9) Carli, *loc. cit.* in note 7, makes a careful analysis. (10) National Gallery Catalogue, 1858, no doubt on information supplied to Eastlake. (11) For details concerning the Lombardi-Baldi Collection, see Appendix I.

JACOPO DEL SELLAIO

ca. 1441–1493

A Florentine, son of Arcangelo, a saddler. Vasari says that he was a pupil of Fra Filippo Lippi. In 1472 he was a member of the Compagnia di San Luca at Florence. He was in partnership with Filippo di Giuliano, at least in 1473 and in 1480/1.

There are three works in varying degrees authenticated. (1) An *Annunciation* in S. Lucia dei Magnoli at Florence is of *ca.* 1473, and may be by either Jacopo del Sellaio or Filippo di Giuliano, although the existing document does not actually say this. (2) A *Pietà* at Berlin, from S. Frediano at Florence, is documented as Sellaio's and as of *ca.* 1483 (1484 n.s.); the documents are in the Archivio di Stato at Florence (especially Compagnia di S. Frediano, Registro nọ 112, especially f. 58). (3) A *Crucifixion*, also from S. Frediano at Florence, and now in another church now dedicated to S. Frediano there, is traditionally assigned to Sellaio, but is apparently not documented as his; it appears to be not earlier than 1490.

The basis for the identification of Sellaio's work would perhaps be made more clear by the full publication of the documents. Many pictures have indeed been ascribed to him; some of these form a coherent group, so far as the very moderate quality allows one to judge. The two pictures in the National Gallery formerly ascribed to Sellaio do not appear to belong to this group; and it is best in this catalogue to do without Sellaio's name.

See Follower of SANDRO BOTTICELLI, No. 916

FLORENTINE SCHOOL, No. 2492

SIENESE SCHOOL

1317   THE MARRIAGE OF THE VIRGIN (PANEL FROM A SERIES)

Before the High Priest the Virgin is being married to S. Joseph, whose blossoming rod is surmounted by a dove. Right, S. Anne and two other women. Left, disappointed suitors are breaking their rods.

Wood, painted surface, 16 × 13 (0·41 × 0·33); painted up to the edges all round.

The condition is reliable in general, though the picture is somewhat worn and in some places restored. Only a part of the gold is original.

Berenson and Hans Gronau identified as from the same series a panel in the Vatican representing *The Birth of the Virgin*, size 0·41 × 0·335.[1] This appears convincing. A panel of *The Crucifixion* in the Museo dell' Opera del Duomo at Siena, size 0·40 × 0·70, is among the pictures noted by Berenson as probably by the same hand;[2] this indeed seems very possible, but is not to be admitted as sure. Cesare Brandi thinks that the picture at Siena is from the same series as the other two;[3] he thinks that it would have formed the central part of a predella, with the National Gallery and Vatican pictures at its sides. He also thinks that this predella might have belonged to an altarpiece now in the Siena Gallery.[4] Brandi's suggestions appear very difficult to accept; it is more prudent to say that the National Gallery and Vatican panels are almost certainly from one ensemble, which may have been a predella.

The date of No. 1317 is probably the beginning of the fifteenth century.

The names associated with No. 1317 and other pictures and frescoes ascribed to the same hand (Gualtieri di Giovanni, Master of the Life of Mary, Gregorio di Cecco) are somewhat speculative.[5]

PROVENANCE: Purchased from A. Borgen, London, Clarke Fund, 1890.

REPRODUCTION: *Illustrations, Italian Schools*, 1937, p. 330. *Plates, Earlier Italian Schools*, 1953, Vol. II, p. 381.

REFERENCES: (1) Berenson in *Dedalo*, November, 1930, pp. 329 ff., esp. p. 340, and Hans Gronau in *The Burlington Magazine*, Vol LVII (1930), p. 299, each with reproductions of both pictures. The Vatican panel is No. 187 of the 1933 Catalogue. (2) Berenson, *loc. cit.*, p. 340. There is an entry for this picture on pp. 56/7 of Enzo Carli's *Il Museo dell'Opera*, etc., Siena, 1946. John Pope-Hennessy, *Giovanni di Paolo*, 1937, pp. 23 and 50, inclined then to consider it an early Giovanni di Paolo, but this is unacceptable. (3) Cesare Brandi in *Le Arti*, 1941, p. 233 and Fig. 5, or *Giovanni di Paolo*, 1947, pp. 5/6 and 68 and Fig. 11. (4) Siena, Catalogo by Cesare Brandi, 1933, No. 140, pp. 184/5, reproduced; also reproduced by Berenson, *loc. cit.*, p. 330. (5) Berenson, *loc. cit.*, pp. 329 ff.; Carli, *op. cit.*, pp. 56/7 and 58.

4491   S. MARY MAGDALENE (PANEL FROM A POLYPTYCH)

Wood, cusped and pointed top, painted surface, $23\frac{1}{2} \times 13\frac{1}{4}$ ($0·595 \times 0·335$). Possibly shaved at the bottom. The measurements are taken to the extreme point of the present panel; actually, the piece at the top, $2\frac{1}{4}$ in. ($0·055$) high, is a modern addition, the original having presumably been broken away.

Fair state. The decorative framework towards the top is in part old, and the patterning of it is to be considered authentically what the painter intended; it was once gilt, but is now painted over.

For the commentary, etc., see No. 4492 below.

4492   S. PETER (PANEL FROM A POLYPTYCH)

Wood, cusped and pointed top, painted surface, $23\frac{1}{2} \times 13\frac{1}{4}$ ($0·595 \times 0·335$). Possibly shaved at the bottom. A piece $2\frac{1}{4}$ in. ($0·055$) high at the top is new, as with No. 4491 above.

Fair state. As with No. 4491 above, the pattern of the framework is authentically what the painter intended.

Nos. 4491 and 4492 are obviously two panels from the right side of a polyptych. Evelyn Sandberg-Vavalà claimed a *Virgin and Child* once in Palazzo Venezia and now in Palazzo Barberini at Rome as the central panel.[1] The style does seem very close. The framework on that picture is similar to the framework of Nos. 4491/2; but perhaps not enough to make the identification sure.

Evelyn Sandberg-Vavalà discusses the relationship of the pictures with Lippo Memmi. Berenson (1909 Lists) ascribed Nos. 4491/2 to Andrea Vanni, and in his 1932 Lists doubtfully to Barna. It seems best to class them as anonymous.[2]

PROVENANCE: Belonged to the Cumming family since the middle of the nineteenth century.[3] In the early twentieth century, they belonged to Charles D. Cumming of 'Hayling,' Epsom,[4] who deposited them with Sir Charles Holroyd (d. 1917). Presented through Mr. Holroyd by the Misses Cumming, in memory of their father, Charles D. Cumming, 1930.

REPRODUCTIONS: *Illustrations, Italian Schools*, 1937, p. 370. *Plates, Earlier Italian Schools*, 1953, Vol. II, p. 382.

REFERENCES: (1) E. Sandberg-Vavalà in *The Burlington Magazine*, Vol. LXXI (1937), p. 177. The picture at Rome is reproduced by Vavalà; it was exhibited at the R.A., 1930 (No. 56; Memorial Catalogue, No. 14 and Plate VIII), as by Simone Martini. Museo di Palazzo Venezia, *Catalogo* by A. Santangelo, I, *Dipinti*, 1947, p. 26; *Catalogo della Galleria Nazionale, Palazzo Barberini, Roma*, by Nolfo di Carpegna, 1955, p. 42. It comes from a private collection at Chieti; see *L'Arte*, 1904, p. 309. (2) This was the view of P. Pouncey in the National Gallery *Supplement to the Catalogue*, 1939, where the pictures are dated *ca.* 1350. (3) A note of the history of the pictures by E. K. Waterhouse is in the Gallery archives. (4) In Berenson's *Central Italian Painters*, 1909, p. 261, the pictures are listed with a misprint of this address.

Luca SIGNORELLI
1441(?)–1523

The date of birth is from Vasari, and may be too early. Signorelli was from Cortona, and there is a good tradition that he was a pupil of Piero della Francesca. Active at Cortona, Arezzo, Florence, Rome, Orvieto and other Italian towns. His chief work is a series of frescoes in the Cathedral of Orvieto; there are many other authenticated works. He ran an active studio.

910 FRESCO: THE TRIUMPH OF CHASTITY: LOVE DISARMED AND BOUND

The God of Love is being bound by Petrarch's Laura, the embodiment of Chastity. Lucretia and Penelope are among those who pull out the feathers of his wings and break his bow and arrows; other ladies not identified assist in the victory over him. Of the three Roman soldiers on the right, the two most prominent are probably (Julius?) Caesar and Scipio (the great Africanus). A banner shows a white ermine on a green ground. Left background, an earlier moment of the Triumph, the Capture of Love. Right background, a later incident; Chastity in her triumphal car displays Love as her prisoner. The costumes of the figures and the banner in these two scenes are fairly accurately repeated from the main scene. Signed on a *cartellino:* LVCAS CORITIVS (i.e. of Cortona; damaged, but legible).

Fresco, transferred to canvas, $49\frac{1}{2} \times 52\frac{1}{2}$ ($1 \cdot 255 \times 1 \cdot 335$), including narrow bands forming the edging.

Much damaged.

The subject is taken, in part accurately, from Petrarch's *Triumphs*. The relevant parts of Petrarch's text are as follows:

The disarming and binding of Love:

> *Ivi ben mille gloriose salme*
> *Torre gli vidi, la faretra e l'arco,*
> *E legarli per força ambe le palme*
> *Dietro dal dosso, e lui impedito e carco,*
> *Non de l'usate spoglie, ançi di ferro,*
> *E d'ogni sua baldança ignudo e scarco.*

Laura binds Love:

> Ell'avea in dosso, il dì, candida gonna,
>   Lo scudo in man che mal vide Medusa.
>   D'un bel diaspro er'ivi una colonna,
> A la qual d'una in meçço Lethe infusa
>   Catena di diamante e di topatio,
>   Che s'usò fra le donne, oggi non s'usa,
> Legarlo vidi, etc.

Lucretia and Penelope:

>   infra le quali
> Lucretia da man destra era la prima;
> L'altra Penelope. Queste gli strali
>   Avean speçato, e la pharetra a lato
>   A quel protervo, e spennachiato l'ali.

Caesar and Scipio (from a later passage):

> Scolpito per le fronti era il valore
>   De l'onorata gente, dov'io scorsı
>   Molti di quei che legar vidi Amore.
> Da man destra, ove gli occhi in prima porsi,
>   La bella donna avea Cesare e Scipio.

The banner:

> Era la lor victoriosa insegna
>   In campo verde un candido ermellino,
>   Ch'oro fino e topaçi al collo tegna.[1]

It is thus seen that Signorelli has in part followed Petrarch fairly well; but No. 910 differs a good deal from the customary representations of the *Triumph of Chastity* on *cassoni*, etc.[2] The scene in the background of No. 910 on the right is most often chosen alone for this subject. The armed men on the right-hand side of No. 910 (Caesar? Scipio? and another) do not normally appear on other pictures; it may indeed be doubted if Signorelli has followed Petrarch's intention in putting them where he has.

No. 910, No. 3929 below and No. 911 (Pintoricchio) are frescoes detached from a room in the Palazzo del Magnifico (Pandolfo Petrucci) at Siena.

This room is now almost entirely deprived of its decorations; but there exist two detailed descriptions of it when it was still intact, by della Valle and by the Abate Giovanni Girolamo Carli.[3] It is situated high up in the Palace, overlooking the Via dei Pellegrini.[4] The size of the room is 6·74 × 5·14 or 6·29 metres (about 22 ft. by 17 ft. or 20½ ft.).[5] The centre of each wall appears to have been occupied by a door or a window, on each side of which was a fresco, making 8 in all. Della Valle and G. G. Carli listed the frescoes on the walls in the same order, which it is convenient to follow for the present description.

1. *The Calumny of Apelles*, signed by Signorelli.[6] This fresco is stated to be still on the wall, but covered with whitewash.[7]

2. *The Festival of Pan*, signed by Signorelli. This fresco is stated to be still on the wall, but covered with whitewash.[8] It is reasonably supposed that the composition is preserved in a drawing in the British Museum (ex-Fenwick).[9]

3. No. 910 of the National Gallery, the subject of the present entry. Signed by Signorelli.[10]

4. No. 3929 below; signed by Signorelli.[11]

5. A subject called by della Valle *Scipio and the Celtiberian Maid*, but perhaps wrongly. To judge from G. G. Carli's description, printed in Appendix III, this fresco would seem to be identical with a fresco called Pintoricchio, once apparently in the E. Joly de Bammeville Collection at Paris.[12] It is known that the three frescoes from the Palazzo Petrucci now in the National Gallery were removed from the wall to the order of Joly de Bammeville; it is possible that he owned also this *Scipio* (?), but there appears to be no record of its present whereabouts.[13]

6. No. 911 of the National Gallery, Pintoricchio.[14]

7. *The Ransoming of Prisoners*, No. 333 of the Gallery at Siena.[15]

8. *Æneas' Flight from Troy*, No. 334 of the Gallery at Siena.[16]

These eight frescoes on the walls of this room in the Palazzo del Magnifico at Siena were only part of the decoration. Carved woodwork formed the seating round the walls, and carved wooden pilasters served as framing on the walls between the frescoes; some of this woodwork is now in the Gallery at Siena.[17] The floor was covered with maiolica tiles;[18] many of these have been preserved, chiefly in the Victoria and Albert Museum,[19] but also at Berlin[20] and probably in the Louvre.[21] The ceiling was an elaborate construction of stucco. The central part was set with 20 small frescoes, and with a fresco of four putti supporting the Petrucci arms in the middle;[22] all but two of these frescoes are now in the Metropolitan Museum at New York.[23] A few fragments of the ceiling are still *in situ*; but nothing can be said about them.[24]

While it need not be doubted that the subjects illustrated in this room were chosen by some humanist for Pandolfo Petrucci, the general scheme does not appear to be comprehensible.

This room was decorated to the order of Pandolfo Petrucci, known as il Magnifico. He was born in 1451 (apparently 1452 n.s.) and gradually acquired more and more power in Siena, especially after the death of his brother Jacopo in 1497; it was not, however, until after his return in 1503 from a brief exile that he became master of the city. He died in 1512, having retired somewhat from public life during the preceding few months.[25]

The date of No. 910, of the two other frescoes in the National Gallery and of the whole decoration can be established as *ca.* 1509. This date of 1509 actually occurs on at least one of the already mentioned tiles.[26] There are various reasons for believing that this is the approximate date of the whole decoration.

The Palace itself was bought by Pandolfo Petrucci from the Accarigi family.[27] The date of the purchase is not known, but it may have been at the time of Pandolfo's return from exile in 1503; for in 1504 he was cutting trees on Monte Amiata in connection with extensions to it.[28] Some new walls in the Palace were built by Domenico di Bartolomeo da Piacenza; by 14 December, 1508, this man had completed his work.[29]

A domestic incident is relevant to the date of the decoration. On 22 September, 1509, Pandolfo Petrucci's eldest son Borghese (b. 1490) married Vittoria Piccolomini. The marriage was strongly opposed by the Piccolomini, and it is said that the bride's mother died of grief when it happened.[30] The tiles many times, and the woodwork three times, contain the Petrucci and Piccolomini arms associated, impaled or quartered.[31] It is difficult to believe that this could have been done before the marriage was settled. It should be added that the Petrucci arms without Piccolomini are shown in the centre of the ceiling, and on Pintoricchio's fresco, No. 911 of the National Gallery.

The biographies of the painters concerned in the decoration offer some further confirmation of a date of ca. 1509. The painters are: Signorelli, who signed four of the frescoes; Pintoricchio, to whom No. 911 of the National Gallery is reasonably attributed; and possibly Gerolamo Genga, who is said to have worked much in Pandolfo Petrucci's Palace.[32] The only years after 1500 in which Signorelli is actually known to have been in Siena are 1506 and 1509.[33] Pintoricchio was in Siena a good deal off and on during the early years of the sixteenth century; but in particular on 24 April, 1508, Pandolfo Petrucci was urging him to return to Siena, apparently to work or rather to resume work for him.[34] Genga is known to have been in Siena in 1510, 1511 and perhaps 1512.[35]

No. 910, which carries Signorelli's signature, is certainly by that painter or from his studio; the bad condition makes it impossible to say how far the execution was by Signorelli's own hand.

PROVENANCE: From the Palazzo del Magnifico at Siena, as explained above.[36] With No. 3929 below, and No. 911 (Pintoricchio), transferred from the wall in 1842 or 1844, to the order of E. Joly de Bammeville of Paris.[37] Not in the Bammeville Sale, London, 1854. All three frescoes passed into the Collection of Alexander Barker, where seen by Waagen.[38] Purchased at the Barker Sale, 6 June, 1874 (lot 72).

REPRODUCTION: *Illustrations, Italian Schools*, 1937, p. 331. *Plates, Earlier Italian Schools*, 1953, Vol. II, p. 383.

REFERENCES: (1) The quotations are from the critical text, *Die Triumphe Francesco Petrarcas*, edited by Carl Appel, 1901; IV, 94 sqq. (from the earlier, but less usual text); IV, 118 sqq.; IV, 131 sqq.; VI, 19 sqq.; V, 19 sqq. Other passages (IV, 76 sqq. and 169 sqq.) are to a minor extent relevant to what is seen on No. 910. Since the divisions of Petrarch's *Triumphs* vary considerably in different editions, it is desirable to cite also *Le Rime Sparse e i Trionfi*, ed. Ezio Chiòrboli, Laterza, 1930. The text of the first quotation above is not admitted in this edition; the other four are to be found on pp. 328/9, vv. 118 sqq. and 131 sqq. (both in the *Trionfo della Pudicizia*), p. 343, vv. 19 sqq. (*Trionfo della Fama*) and p. 331, vv. 19 sqq. (*Trionfo della Morte*). (2) For Petrarch's *Triumphs* in art, see P. Schubring, *Cassoni*, 1923, where many plates and further bibliographical references may be found. (3) P. Guglielmo della Valle, *Lettere Sanesi*, III, 1786, pp. 319 ff. and 331, with corrections in his edition of Vasari, IV, 1791, pp. 332 ff. The account by the Abate Carli is here printed in Appendix III. There is also a brief reference in Bottari's edition of Vasari, II, 1759, p. 681. It may be mentioned that G. G. Carli records a second room with decorations in the Palazzo del Magnifico. So far as the compiler is aware, the only existing fragment that could come from this room is a fresco of *Minerva* in the Platt Collection, U.S.A., ascribed to Genga and claimed to be from the Palace of Pandolfo Petrucci; see G. H. Edgell, *A History of Sienese Painting*, 1932, p. 288 and Fig. 441. A *Venus* in the Petrucci Palace is the subject of two contemporary poems (printed in the *Repertorium für Kunstwissenschaft*, 1880, p. 59); there is no reason to suppose that it was part of the decoration of either of these rooms. (4) With the kind assistance of Prof. Raffaello Niccoli, the compiler was enabled to examine what remains of the room. (5) See A. Franchi in *L'Art*, Vol. XXIX, 1882, p. 148; the alternative measurement is from *Arte Italiana Decorativa e Industriale*, Anno X, 1901, p. 63. (6) The subject is indeed not thus identified by della Valle or G. G. Carli. But their descriptions, and the inscriptions they record, make the identification certain; see R. Förster in the Prussian *Jahrbuch*, 1887, pp. 29 ff., 89 ff. and especially p. 109; or R. Vischer, *Luca Signorelli*, 1879, pp. 312 ff. (7) Vasari, Le Monnier edition, VI, p. 153; ed. Milanesi, III, p. 702. (8) As in the previous note. (9) Berenson, *Drawings of the Florentine Painters*, 1938, No. 2509^{k-3} and Fig. 121. British Museum, *Italian Drawings, The Fourteenth and Fifteenth Centuries*, catalogue by A. E. Popham and Philip Pouncey, 1950, No. 236 and Plate CCVIII. (10) The signature here, and on No. 3929 below, and (in Greek letters) on fresco No. 1, has the word *Coritius* instead of Signorelli's usual *Cortonensis*. Corythus was the legendary founder of Cortona; Signorelli or his adviser knew this probably from Vergil (e.g. *Æneid*, III, 170). (11) The references to this fresco by della Valle and G. G. Carli are meagre, but there can be no doubt of its identity. (12) Vasari, Le Monnier edition, V, p. 274 (name as Bonneville); Milanesi's edition, III, pp. 504/5. Waagen, *Mantegna und Signorelli* (from Raumer's *Historisches Taschenbuch*, 1850), pp. 569/70, mentions the three National Gallery frescoes in the Joly de Bammeville Collection, Paris, but not this *Scipio* (?). Indeed, on p. 559 and p. 593, note 87, Waagen implies that in 1841 he had looked for this and frescoes Nos. 1 and 2 in vain in the Palazzo del Magnifico. Nor is any such work identifiable in the Bammeville Sales, 1854 (London) or 22 June, 1893 (Paris). (13) It may be mentioned that it is certainly not identical with a picture at Strasbourg, 1912 *Verzeichnis*, No. 264, as Genga; 1938 *Catalogue*, No. 242, as Genga. This was already noted by Giacomo de Nicola in *The Burlington Magazine*, Vol. XXXI (1917), p. 228. The work at Strasbourg is (as Hans Haug kindly pointed out) not a fresco; it is some 30 cm. higher than Nos. 910, etc. (size, 1·53 × 1·83); and it contains the Piccolomini arms without Petrucci. The subject, which appears to be *The Rape of the Sabines*, is in disaccord with della Valle's description of fresco No. 5, and in hopeless disaccord with G. G. Carli's description. Photograph in the Gallery archives. (14) Della Valle in his *Lettere Sanesi* numbers the frescoes in two series of four; No. 6, which is No. 2 of the second series, is referred to by mistake as No. 3, which is the number also, and correctly, given to No. 7. (15) Siena, *Catalogo* by Cesare Brandi, 1933, p. 333, No. 333, as by Genga; Venturi, *Storia dell'Arte Italiana*, Vol. IX, Part V, Fig. 340. The subject has not been identified. There is a free variant of it in the sketchbook at Lille that has been identified as by Jacopo Ripanda; it was apparently Ripanda's variant that was used for a dish in the British Museum. There the subject is supposed to be *Ariovistus, Cæsar's Ambassadors, and the Æduan Hostages*; but it does not appear to correspond with what is recorded by Caesar in his *Gallic War*. See J. Byam Shaw in *The Burlington Magazine*, Vol. LXI (1932), pp. 18 ff.; he there reproduces Ripanda's drawing, the dish in the British Museum, and a dish dated 1524 in the Louvre, which shows a variant of the design. (16) Siena, *Catalogo* by Cesare Brandi, 1933, p. 333, No. 334, as by Genga. Venturi, *Storia dell'Arte Italiana*, Vol. IX, Part V, Fig. 339. (17) This woodwork, ascribed to Barili, is recorded in the Siena Catalogue, 1903, pp. 180 ff. (Sculture), Nos. 3–16, with measurements; more elaborate records of measurement, kindly supplied by Enzo Carli, are in the Gallery archives. Three of the pilasters are reproduced by Venturi, *Storia dell'Arte Italiana*, Vol. VIII, Part I, Fig. 691; drawings of another pilaster and of one of the bases are reproduced by A. Franchi in *L'Art*, Vol. XXIX, 1882, pp. 148,150.

Photographs of most of the woodwork, supplied by Enzo Carli, are in the Gallery
archives. The provenance of this woodwork can be established with precision.
Della Valle's and G. G. Carli's descriptions include various identifying details.
According to (Ettore Romagnoli), *Nuova Guida della Città di Siena*, publ. Guido
Mucci, 1822, p. 48, the woodwork removed from the Palazzo del Magnifico
passed to the Cardinal Archbishop of Siena, i.e. Antonio Felice Zondadari,
who died in 1823. The following passages from Romagnoli's manuscript *Biografia Cronologica de' Bellartisti Senesi*, pre-1835, Vol. V, in the Biblioteca
Comunale at Siena, indicate what happened. (P. 469): 'La residenza intagliata
da Antonio (Barili) per una Camera del Palazzo del magnifico Pandolfo nel 1511.
è pure un famigerato squisitissimo lavoro, tolto da quel locale non ha gran
tempo, e posseduto poscia da S.E. il cardinal Arcivescovo Antonfelice Zondadari di buona memoria.' (P. 478): 'La sopra notata Residenza del Palazzo Petrucci
dopo la morte dell'Eminentissimo Card: Zondadari cioè circa il 1833. la vidi
situata in una stanza della canonica del Duomo. Essa contiene undici pilastri
lavoratissimi di castagno filettati d'Oro. Sono ornati di figure rappresentanti
virtù. Vi sono ancora le tre Grazie, le armi Petrucciane varie sfingi, uccelli, e
putti bellissimi. Le cornici che cingevano la sala nell'impostatura della volta
sono lavorate dallo stesso Barili, bellissime ancor esse, e degne d'esser situate in
qualche pubblico locale a meraviglia dell'osservatore.' (Note added, apparently
in Milanesi's writing: 'È ora nell'Accademia di Belle Arti di Siena.') (18) The
evidence that the maiolica tiles were in this room of the Palazzo del Magnifico
is in G. G. Carli's description; see Appendix III. (19) Victoria and Albert
Museum: Fortnum's *Catalogue, Maiolica*, 1873, p. 132, Nos. 4915–5386/'57 and
1659–1661/'56. See also Bernard Rackham, *Catalogue of Italian Maiolica*, 1940,
No. 386. Many of these tiles show the Petrucci arms, which will be the subject
of comment presently. Rackham reproduces some on Plate 62, and photographs
of many others are in the Gallery archives. Under No. 955 (reproduced Plate
154), Rackham refers to some more recent tiles as being also from the Petrucci
Palace; however that may be, they are certainly not part of a recorded restoration of 1600 in the workshops of Pantaneto, which was carried out on a different
set of tiles in the Santuario di S. Caterina at Siena (see the text of the reference
given by Rackham). (20) O. von Falke, *Majolika*, 1907, Fig. 55; one of the tiles
reproduced includes the Petrucci arms. (21) Louvre: Alfred Darcel, *Notice des
Fayences Peintes Italiennes*, etc., 1864, pp. 103 ff., Nos. G 111–140. See also G.
Ballardini, *Corpus della Maiolica Italiana*, I, 1933, Figs. 44, 47. Some of these
tiles in the Louvre are from the Campana Collection at Rome, Nos. 285–96
according to Darcel; indeed, in the Campana Catalogue, undated but apparently of 1859, Class X (*Dipinture in Majolica*), Sala A, Nos. 285–97 are claimed
to be 12 (*sic*) tiles or sets of tiles, called Urbino ware, no provenance given.
Although there are no Petrucci arms on the tiles in the Louvre, it appears probable that a few of them do come from the Petrucci Palace, as claimed; one of the
tiles reproduced by Ballardini is on a design that occurs in the Victoria and
Albert Museum collection. (22) Portions of this ceiling when still intact have
been reproduced from drawings by A. Franchi in *L'Art*, Vol. XXIX, 1882, p.
185, and by Corrado Ricci in *Arte Italiana Decorativa e Industriale*, Anno X,
1901, pp. 61 ff. and Plate 43. Owing to various partitions erected inside the
room, the drawings were done under great difficulty, and the Petrucci arms,
which form the centre of the vault, are shown facing different ways in the two
reproductions; but there is no doubt that these drawings are substantially
correct. The one reproduced by Franchi is of superior authority; it is possible
that Ricci's is derived from it. Apart from the central frescoes, the decoration of
this ceiling included eight (?) moral texts, of which della Valle gives the text of
seven (some are visible on the drawing in *L'Art*, Vol. XXIX, 1882, p. 185); the
nine Muses (drawings of Terpsichore, Eratho and Calliope are reproduced by
Ricci, *loc. cit.*, Figs. 126, 127 and 129); and apparently three other subjects.
Ricci's Fig. 124, *Brennus*, is stated to have been in one of the lunettes, on the
wall under the vaulting. (23) As Pintoricchio; Catalogue, *Italian, Spanish and
Byzantine Paintings*, 1940, pp. 110/2, Nos. 14.114, 1–22, with reproductions of

three of them. All are reproduced in the Metropolitan Museum *Bulletin*, January, 1921, Part II. (24) The proprietor made difficulties; Prof. Raffaello Niccoli and Prof. Enzo Carli of the Soprintendenza at Siena spared no effort in the compiler's favour, but in vain. (25) For Pandolfo Petrucci, see especially G. A. Pecci, *Memorie Storico-Critiche della Città di Siena*, I, 1755. (26) Reproduced by Rackham, *op. cit.*, Plate 62; Victoria and Albert Museum photograph, No. 71058. A doubtful reading of the same date is also claimed for one of the tiles in the Louvre; see A. Darcel, *Notice des Fayences Peintes Italiennes*, etc., 1864, p. 103, No. G 111. The compiler thinks that here also 1509 is intended, but 1502 is a possible reading. (27) G. A. Pecci, *Memorie Storico-Critiche della Città di Siena*, I, 1755, p. 206. (28) Pecci, *loc. cit.* In the already mentioned Guide to Siena by Romagnoli, 1822, p. 48, this date of 1504 is cited, and the frescoes in the room are also attributed to the year 1499, which is inadmissible. Patzak in Thieme-Becker, XIII, p. 386, s.v. Genga, wrongly suggests a date of *ca.* 1498 for three of the frescoes. (29) Borghesi e Banchi, *Nuovi Documenti per la Storia dell'Arte Senese*, 1898, pp. 382/3. (30) Pecci, *op. cit.*, pp. 77, 241. (31) Associated on the pilaster to the left on Fig. 691 of Venturi, *Storia dell'Arte Italiana*, Vol. VIII, Part I (Alinari photograph, 8927). Impaled on the wooden base of a pilaster reproduced by A. Franchi in *L'Art*, Vol. XXIX, 1882, p. 150. Quartered on the other wooden base (photograph in the Gallery archives), and frequently on the tiles. Apropos of the Petrucci arms themselves, it may be mentioned that they occur sometimes plain (as in Pintoricchio, No. 911 of the National Gallery), but often with an eagle in chief, and (in the tiles) quartered with an eagle. Dr. Giovanni Cecchini of the Archivio di Stato at Siena pointed out that many Sienese families were in the habit of adding the Imperial eagle in chief to their own arms; the Petrucci among many others certainly did so (cf. A. Lisini, *Le Tavolette Dipinte di Biccherna e di Gabella del R. Archivio di Stato in Siena*, 1901, Plates LXXXVII and LXXXX). The quartering with the Imperial eagle is a different matter; perhaps Pandolfo Petrucci, as tyrant of the city, thought he could permit himself this. It may be considered in some way comparable that two of the pilasters in the Gallery at Siena have three little coats of arms towards the bottom, Petrucci, Petrucci and apparently the Balzana (Siena). Presumably Pandolfo Petrucci identified himself with the city of Siena, and may therefore have considered an alliance with the Emperor to be a reasonable way of indicating his status. (32) This is Vasari's statement; not in the 1550 edition; ed. Milanesi, VI, p. 316. Although Vasari explicitly says that Genga worked in Pandolfo Petrucci's Palace, his vagueness about Genga's subjects would allow us perhaps to doubt his accuracy, if we wish. Conceivably, Genga may have worked in another Palace, begun by Pandolfo's brother Jacopo Petrucci, in 1489, and now rebuilt as the Palazzo del Governo; cf. Pecci, *op. cit.*, II, 1755, pp. 27, 46/7. However that may be, it is customary to associate Genga's name with some of the frescoes from Pandolfo Petrucci's Palace. There is only one authenticated picture by Genga of about the right time, *The Transfiguration* in the Mueso dell'Opera del Duomo at Siena (Vasari, ed. Milanesi, VI, p. 316, as of 1510; Enzo Carli, *Il Museo dell'Opera*, etc., 1946, p. 34, as of 1512). Photograph in the Gallery archives, kindly sent by Enzo Carli; reproduced in the *Rassegna Marchigiana*, Anno VI, 1927/8, p. 233. The style of this picture differs somewhat from that of the two frescoes from Palazzo Petrucci now in the Gallery at Siena. The next documented picture by Genga is one of 1513/8 in the Brera; reproduced by Venturi, *Storia dell'Arte Italiana*, Vol. IX, Part V, Fig. 338. (33) R. Vischer, *Luca Signorelli*, 1879, pp. 356, 358. (34) This is from an inscription in the form of a letter, serving as a signature to Pintoricchio and Eusebio da S. Giorgio's altarpiece in S. Andrea at Spello; see Corrado Ricci, *Pintoricchio*, English edition, 1902, pp. 215/7. (35) Milanesi, *Documenti per la Storia dell'Arte Senese*, III, 1856, pp. 47/8 (September, 1510); R. H. H. Cust, *Giovanni Antonio Bazzi*, 1906, p. 116 (August, 1511). For 1512, see note 32 above. (36) The earliest sure references to the series from which No. 910 comes are those by Mancini (as quoted by della Valle, *loc. cit.*), and by Fabio Chigi, 1625/6, 'al Palazzo del Magnifico sono stanze dipente da Luca Signorelli da Cortona' (*Bullettino Senese di Storia Patria*, 1939, p. 333; p. 53 of the offprint). The Palazzo del Magnifico passed away from the Petrucci family at an undefined, but certainly fairly early, date. On the main floor landing, the arms of the Silvestri family have been added in the vaulting; G. G. Carli (see Appendix III) and della Valle in his edition of Vasari (1791) say that the Palace belonged in their time to the Savini. The rooms were adapted to the use of the occupiers; but the decorations of which No. 910 formed a part do not appear to have been disturbed until the early nineteenth century. (37) Waagen, *Mantegna und Signorelli* (from Raumer's *Historisches Taschenbuch*, 1850), p. 569; Vasari, Le Monnier edition, VI, p. 153. (38) Waagen, *Treasures*, IV, 1857, pp. 73/5.

1128 ALTARPIECE: THE CIRCUMCISION

The Virgin, the Child, S. Joseph and S. Simeon are distinguished by haloes. Signed: LVCAS / CORTONENSIS / PINXIT.

Wood, painted surface, $101\frac{3}{4} \times 71$ ($2 \cdot 585 \times 1 \cdot 80$). The edges of the paint are rather ragged at the sides.

The condition of No. 1128 is somewhat complicated.

It will be stated presently that No. 1128 is, beyond all reasonable doubt, identical with a picture (Vasari wrongly says a fresco) once at Volterra; Vasari says that the Child in the Volterra *Circumcision* had suffered from damp, and had been repainted by Sodoma.[1] There is also a record that No. 1128 was restored in 1732 by Ippolito Cigna.[2] Various restorations have occurred since.

To deal first with the principal *pentimenti* by Signorelli himself, many of which are revealed only by X-Rays. The Christ Child was originally very different, with His head almost in profile looking downwards, His right arm at His side, His right leg turned back and His left leg a little further back than now. It is nevertheless certain that Signorelli, and not any later restorer, altered the pose to approximately what it is now. The Virgin's right hand was originally rather lower, and probably supported the Child from below. There are various *pentimenti* in the right hand of the priest, and in the left hand of S. Joseph. Of the heads, that of the woman on the right was once further to the left, and tipped a little downwards. The man next her has *pentimenti* in the turban, and his eyes seem originally to have been turned towards the Child. The woman behind the Virgin was originally a bearded old man (?) facing towards the spectator's right, with long heavy hair falling on the shoulders; there are various alterations in this part, which are extremely confused. S. Joseph next her has a change in the line of his head. The two heads to the left are additions by Signorelli; originally there was architecture, and one male head (perhaps a tonsured priest) looking downwards over S. Joseph's shoulder. The four principal feet show many changes in the outlines.

As for Sodoma, it is very probable that he repainted the head, hands and feet of the Child, and part of the Virgin's right hand. His work was, no doubt, chiefly in this area, but may not have been confined to it; for instance, the ends of the largest toes of S. Joseph's right foot may have been retouched by him.

Modern repaints are chiefly to cover places where the horizontal battens have parted. Although some of these are disturbing, the picture does not contain an exceptional amount of modern work for an altarpiece of the fifteenth century.

There can be no reasonable doubt that No. 1128 is the picture formerly in the Chapel of the Circumcision, belonging to the Compagnia del Santissimo Nome di Gesù in S. Francesco at Volterra.[3] It is true that Vasari, who is the first to mention this Volterra picture, calls it a frecso;[4] but there are at least two records of it *in situ*, that on the one hand refer back explicitly or implicitly to Vasari, and on the other clearly indicate that it was a picture.[5] There is thus no impossibility that the Volterra *Circumcision* and No. 1128 are identical. There is a strong argument that they are in the condition of the Christ Child on No. 1128; Vasari, as has already been mentioned, says that this part of the Volterra *Circumcision* was repainted by Sodoma,[6] and most critics agree that this part of No. 1128 shows evidence of Sodoma's style.[7]

If, as seems highly probable, No. 1128 is the picture from Volterra, it is probably of *ca.* 1491. Two altarpieces by Signorelli at Volterra are dated in that year;[8] it is indeed probable that Signorelli was living in the town at the time.[9]

DRAWING: A drawing of a man in approximately the same pose as the woman on the right of No. 1128 is recorded in the Marignane Collection, Paris.[10]

PROVENANCE: As explained above, in all probability from the Chapel of the Circumcision, belonging to the Compagnia del Santissimo Nome di Gesù in S. Francesco at Volterra. The Volterra picture is recorded *in situ* in 1756 and in 1782,[11] but it seems to have been removed not very long afterwards.[12] No. 1128 was probably in the Lansdowne Sale, London, 19 March, 1806 (lot 67).[13] No. 1128 was certainly in the Duke of Hamilton's Collection at Hamilton Palace.[14] Exhibited at the R.A., 1873 (No. 162). Purchased at the Hamilton Sale, 1 July, 1882 (lot 769).

REPRODUCTION: *Illustrations, Italian Schools*, 1937, p. 334. *Plates, Earlier Italian Schools*, 1953, Vol. II, p. 384.

REFERENCES: (1) Vasari, not in 1550 edition; ed. Milanesi, Vol. III, p. 685. (2) Frizzoni, *Arte Italiana del Rinascimento*, 1891, p. 246, says that there was information to this effect on the back of the picture; the information is not there now, but it is difficult to believe that Frizzoni is unreliable. (The picture entered the Gallery in 1882, and was cradled in 1886.) It may be considered some confirmation that Cigna appears to have restored Signorelli's *Annunciation* at Volterra in 1731 (R. Vischer, *Luca Signorelli*, 1879, p. 317). Cigna's association with No. 1128 could be used to confirm that No. 1128 does come from Volterra; but the argument for this, which is set out lower down in the commentary, is sufficient by itself. (3) There is a record of another picture of *The Presentation in the Temple*, ordered of Signorelli at Cortona in 1521. But that picture, now often ascribed to Papacello, has not left Cortona, being until recently in the Spedale there and now in the Picture Gallery of the town. See R. Vischer, *Luca Signorelli*, 1879, pp. 260, 377, 381; Girolamo Mancini, *Vita di Luca Signorelli*, 1903, p. 222 (reproduction); Mario Salmi in the *Bollettino d'Arte*, 1923/4, p. 181; Van Marle, *Development of the Italian Schools of Painting*, Vol. XVI, p. 132. (4) Vasari; not in 1550 edition; ed. Milanesi, Vol. III, p. 685. Some further confusion has been added to Vasari by his editor (Le Monnier edition, Vol. VI, p. 138), who refers to a MS. by Ormanni and apparently another MS. as indicating two different

Circumcisions by Signorelli at Volterra. But this is corrected by Girolamo Mancini, *Luca Signorelli*, 1903, p. 73, who cites Ormanni's MS. thus, 'la Circoncisione a s. Francesco nella Cappella del SS̅m̅o̅ Nome di Gesù.' (5) See the Oretti MSS. in the Biblioteca dell'Archiginnasio at Bologna, B 5, a collection of various items. In the *Nota delle Pitture, Sculture che si vedono nelle Chiese di Volterra fatta l'anno 1756*, the following passage occurs on f. 5r.: 'S. Francesco, Compagnia del SS̅m̅o̅ Nome. A mano dritta si vede La Capl̅a̅ della Circoncisione con una Tav̅a̅ di Luca da Cortona della q̅l̅e̅ dice il Vasari Par: 11. a ⁵²⁷' (a reference to the 1568 edition) 'che *Gio: Ant?* Razzi da Vercelli d? il Soddoma vi rifece il Bambi? Gesù poco feliceme, avendo questa Tav̲a̲ assai patito, e specialme il d? Bamb?' In the *Nota delle migliori Pitture Sculture, che si vedono nelle Chiese di Volterra fatta da Ippolito Cigna, S. Francesco, Compagnia del Sm̅o̅ Nome*, there is the following passage: '2. A destra nella Capl̅a̅ della Circoncisione la Tav̲a̲ è dipinta da Luca da Cortona, e il Sodoma vi rifece il Bamb? Gesù.' (6) For Sodoma's visit to Volterra, see Vasari; not in 1550 edition; ed. Milanesi, Vol. VI, p. 397. Sodoma is thought to have been in Volterra in 1539; cf. R. H. H. Cust, *Giovanni Antonio Bazzi*, 1906, pp. 225/7. The date is deduced from Vasari. Vasari says that he worked there for Lorenzo di Galeotto de' Medici. This man is recorded in Litta's *Celebri Famiglie d'Italia*, Tavola XVIII of the Medici family; Litta makes no mention of Volterra, nor does he give his date of birth, but says his father died in 1528. (7) Frizzoni, however, disagrees; *Arte Italiana del Rinascimento*, 1891, pp. 245/6. (8) Klassiker der Kunst *Signorelli*, 1927, Plates 43/4. (9) Cf. R. Vischer, *Luca Signorelli*, 1879, pp. 90/1. Mario Salmi, *Luca Signorelli*, 1953, p. 49, suggests that it is a few years earlier than 1491. (10) Berenson, *Drawings of the Florentine Painters*, 1938, No. 2509^H-11, and Fig. 118. Berenson is inclined to disbelieve that this drawing was actually done for No. 1128. (11) See Oretti's MS., quoted in note 5, and Adamo Chiusole, *Itinerario . . . d'Italia*, 1782, p. 198. (12) It is not mentioned in A. F. Giachi, *Saggio di Ricerche su . . . Volterra*, II, 1786, pp. 194 ff. (*Delle Tavole delle Chiese*). G. Leoncini, *Illustrazione sulla Cattedrale di Volterra*, 1869, p. 93, says that the Confraternity was suppressed at the end of the eighteenth century, and that a relic of the Holy Name from it, after being for a short time in the Bishop's Palace, was placed in the Cathedral, in a chapel dedicated to the Virgin, in 1791. Pietro Torrini, *Guida per la Città di Volterra*, 1832, pp. 165/6, says that the building attached to S. Francesco at Volterra that had belonged to the Compagnia del SS. Nome was in his time a 'magazzino'. (13) The description in the sale catalogue is meagre, but it is clearly implied that the form of the signature on that picture corresponded with the form on No. 1128. (14) Waagen, *Treasures*, III, 1854, p. 299.

1133   ALTARPIECE: THE ADORATION OF THE SHEPHERDS

In the left background is the Announcement to the Shepherds. Centre background, under a portico, a scene apparently illustrating the decree of taxation by Augustus. Signed on the portico, . LVCE . DECOR-TONA . P . O . beneath a monogram perhaps standing for L S.

Wood, painted surface, 85 × 67 (2·15 × 1·70), approximately; the edges of the paint are rather ragged.

Good condition.

There need be little doubt that No. 1133 is the *Nativity* formerly in S. Francesco at Città di Castello,[1] and recorded there by Vasari in 1550.[2] According to three old sources, the S. Francesco picture was painted in 1496.[3]

It is sometimes stated that No. 1133 reveals the influence of van der Goes' altarpiece, now in the Uffizi; some Netherlandish influence is indeed most probable, but the similarities between No. 1133 and the van der Goes are not very close.

No. 1133 is clearly not one of Signorelli's better pictures; but the evidence is insufficient for saying how far he was helped by assistants in its execution.

VARIANTS: Some figures in No. 1133 recur fairly exactly in a picture of the same subject now in the Museo Diocesano at Cortona.[4] Cf. also a predella in the Uffizi,[5] where however the correspondence is less.

DRAWING: There is a drawing in the British Museum, squared, showing three of the shepherds and one of the angels.[6]

PROVENANCE: Probably from S. Francesco at Città di Castello; this has been stated above, and the evidence will be given presently. The S. Francesco altar-piece may have been ordered by a member of the Tiberti family,[7] but by 1541 the altar where it hung seems to have belonged to the Biccheri;[8] the chapel may have been the one formerly containing the relics of the B. Giacomo (which were later transferred to another chapel).[9] The church of S. Francesco was re-modelled between 1707 and 1727,[10] and Signorelli's picture was apparently re-moved to a position over the main door of the church and then to the refectory, where it apparently remained until the Napoleonic suppression of the convent.[11] No. 1133 is first certainly recorded in 1826 at Città di Castello in the collection of Giacomo Mancini,[12] who in 1832 himself said that it is the S. Francesco picture.[13] There is secondhand verbal evidence that, on the suppression of S. Francesco, the picture from there was sold to a priest Manfucci, that Can. Giulio Mancini persuaded Manfucci that the sale had been illegitimate, and when the picture had been handed back acquired it for himself, after which it is assumed that the picture passed from Can. Giulio Mancini to Giacomo Mancini;[14] there may in any case have been some peculiar circumstances attending the acquisition by Giacomo Mancini, since among his frequent references to the picture only one apparently gives a clue to the provenance.[15] No. 1133 remained for some decades in the Mancini Collection at Città di Castello;[16] acquired thence by Bardini, from whom purchased, Lewis Fund, 1882.

REPRODUCTION: *Illustrations, Italian Schools*, 1937, p. 332. *Plates, Earlier Italian Schools*, 1953, Vol. II, p. 385.

REFERENCES: (1) See the provenance. Since No. 1133 certainly comes from a collection at Città di Castello, it may be considered more likely than not that it was painted for a church there; and, apart from the positive evidence in the provenance that it came from S. Francesco, the other *Nativities* recorded in other churches at Città di Castello do not appear to fit. The one formerly in S. Agostino does not appear to be now certainly traceable, but it seems wrong to suggest, as has sometimes been done, that it is identical with No. 1133; Giacomo Mancini, *Memorie di alcuni artefici del disegno . . . in Città di Castello*, 1832, I, p. 60, and II, p. 69, says that the S. Agostino picture included a 'capanna' (the second volume of Mancini's work is sometimes referred to under the title *Memorie di alcuni Pittori, Scultori ed Architetti Tifernati*). Mario Salmi, *Luca Signorelli*, 1953, p. 52, suggests that it may be the picture now at Naples (Cata-logue of the Signorelli Exhibition, 1953, No. 15, reproduced), but this is doubt-ful. A lunette in fresco formerly in S. Maria Nuova obviously does not compete, and in any case was destroyed in 1789; see Giacomo Mancini, *op. cit.*, I, p. 201, and II, pp. 69/70; *Genuina e Distinta Relazione dell'Oribilissimo Terremoto scoppiato in Città di Castello la mattina del 30. Settembre 1789*, p. 3; Girolamo Mancini, *Luca Signorelli*, 1903, p. 29. Another picture of *The Nativity* is alleged to have existed in S. Domenico at Città di Castello (see G. Magherini-Graziani, *L'Arte a Città di Castello*, 1897, p. 340), but this does not appear to be recorded elsewhere. (2) Vasari, 1550 edition, pp. 521/2, says that it was 'cosa con disegno,

& amore da lui lauorata'; these words are omitted from the 1568 edition, I, p.
527. (3) Angelo Conti, *Fiori Vaghi delle Vite de' Santi, e Beati Delle Chiese, e
Reliquie della Città di Castello*, 1627, p. 157, 'La Natiuità del Saluatore di Luca
Signorelli nel 1496.' For the other two records, see G. Magherini-Graziani,
L'Arte a Città di Castello, 1897, pp. 198 and 340. The former is a MS. by
Certini of the early eighteenth century; the latter is an anon. MS. of *ca.* 1650
(letter from C. Fasola, 13 April, 1939, in the Gallery archives). In spite of this
evidence, Magherini-Graziani rejects the date of 1496 for No. 1133. (4) Repro-
duced in the catalogue of the Signorelli Exhibition, 1953 (No. 62). In a note to
the Klassiker der Kunst *Signorelli*, 1927, p. 212, Dussler wrongly says that his
Plate 180 is a replica (except for some angels) of this picture. (5) Klassiker der
Kunst *Signorelli*, 1927, Plate 42. (6) British Museum, *Italian Drawings, The
Fourteenth and Fifteenth Centuries*, catalogue by A. E. Popham and Philip
Pouncey, 1950, Vol. I, No. 235, and Vol. II, Plate CC. (7) Magherini-Graziani,
op. cit., p. 198. The text cited seems to imply that a Tiberti and his wife a Caval-
canti were buried near the altar in 1348, but not necessarily to imply that the
Tiberti still owned the altar when Signorelli painted his picture. Manni (as
quoted by R. Vischer, *Luca Signorelli*, 1879, p. 378) seems to say that the S.
Francesco picture was painted for the Bourbon del Monte family. Giacomo
Mancini was related to this family (*Istruzione Storico-Pittorica*, I, 1832, p. 279),
which might furnish a clue as to how the picture became his. (8) Magherini-
Graziani, *op. cit.*, p. 198. The ownership of the altar in 1541 by the Biccheri
family is clearly a correct record; the doubt is whether Signorelli's picture was
over that altar. (9) For the position in the church, see Giacomo Mancini,
Memorie di alcuni artefici del disegno, 1832, I, p. 142, and II, p. 72; Magherini-
Graziani, *op. cit.*, p. 340, quotes a text giving a different position. (10) Giacomo
Mancini, *op. cit.*, 1832, I. pp. 137 f. (11) Magherini-Graziani, *op. cit.*, p. 198.
(12) Giacomo Mancini, *op. cit.*, 1832, I, p. 315 (a reprint from an article of 1826).
(13) Giacomo Mancini, *op. cit.*, 1832, II, p. 67. (14) Magherini-Graziani, *op. cit.*,
pp. 198/9. (15) See note 13. (16) Seen there by Bode in 1875; Bode, *Mein Leben*,
1930, I, p. 117.

1776 THE ADORATION OF THE SHEPHERDS (PREDELLA
      PANEL FROM AN ALTARPIECE)

Wood, painted surface, $6\frac{3}{4} \times 25\frac{1}{2}$ (0·17×0·65); painted up to the edges
all round, but the condition of the painted framing shows that the pic-
ture itself (which has rounded ends) has not been cut.

Fairly good condition.

PROVENANCE: It is not known from what altarpiece this panel comes. It is
first recorded in 1856 in the Collection of Agostino Castellani at Cortona.[1] Later
owned by Conte Colonna Ferretti at Cortona.[2] Purchased from P. and D.
Colnaghi, who had had it from E. Volpi,[3] 1900.

REPRODUCTION: *Illustrations, Italian Schools*, 1937, p. 333. *Plates, Earlier
Italian Schools*, 1953, Vol. II, p. 386.

REFERENCES: (1) Mentioned by Mündler in his Diary, 20 September, 1856.
The identification is from Eastlake's note-book, 1857, where the picture is described without any possibility of doubt. Crowe and Cavalcaselle, *History of
Painting in Italy*, III, 1866, p. 28, also mention it as belonging to the heirs of
Agostino Castellani; Borenius in the 1914 edition, V, p. 111, wrongly connects
this mention with another picture, once in the Baldelli-Tommasi Collection,
and now in the Museo dell'Accademia Etrusca at Cortona, reproduced by
Girolamo Mancini, *Vita di Luca Signorelli*, 1903, p. 225. (2) N.G. Catalogue,
1901. (3) Verbal information from J. Byam Shaw, 1947.

1847   ALTARPIECE: THE VIRGIN AND CHILD WITH SAINTS

Centre, the Virgin stands on cherubs' heads, holding the Child; she is crowned by two angels. Left, SS. Sebastian and Jerome. Right, SS. Christina and Nicholas; on his cope are embroidered figures of SS. Peter, Bartholomew, James the Greater and others. Inscribed on a *cartellino*: . EGREGIVM . QVOD . CERNIS . OPVS . MAGISTER. / ALOYSIVS . PHYSICVS . EXGALLIA . ET . TOMA/SINA . EIVS . VXOR . EXDEVOTIONE . SVIS . / SVMPTIBVS . PONI . CVRAVERVNT . LVCA . SI/GNORELLO . DECORTONA . PICTORE . INSI / GNI . FORMAS . INDVCENTE . AÑO . D . M . D . XV.

Wood, rounded top, painted surface, 104½×76 (2·65×1·93), excluding an edging in black paint all round.

A good deal damaged, especially in the upper part, especially in the dresses.

The inscription gives some facts about the origin of this picture, which are elaborated in a document of 10 September, 1515.[1] Signorelli is there stated to have painted the picture 'omni suo labore et magisterio,' *ca.* July–August, 1515. It was painted for a physician, Lodovicus de Rutenis (Rodez), in return for past and future professional services to Signorelli and his family. The physician is recorded in other sources as inhabiting Perugia and Montone (between Umbertide and Città di Castello);[2] No. 1847 was painted for S. Francesco at Montone, where the physician had built a chapel dedicated to S. Christina.

The predella of No. 1847 is now in the Brera at Milan.[3]

In spite of the documentary evidence, it is somewhat difficult to accept No. 1847 as being entirely from Signorelli's own hand.

PROVENANCE: For the early part of the provenance, see above. No. 1847, from which the predella had already been separated, was still visible at Montone in the late eighteenth century.[4] Later, it was put aside and lost; it was searched for, and acquired not long before 1826, by Giacomo Mancini of Città di Castello.[5] It remained in the Mancini Collection until towards the end of the nineteenth century,[6] and was probably purchased direct from there by E. Volpi of Florence, from whom purchased, 1901.

REPRODUCTION: *Illustrations, Italian Schools*, 1937, p. 332. *Plates, Earlier Italian Schools*, 1953, Vol. II, p. 387.

REFERENCES: (1) Apparently the notary's copy; first printed by A. Rossi, and reprinted by R. Vischer, *Luca Signorelli*, 1879, pp. 360 f. (2) Vischer, *op. cit.*, pp. 360 f. (3) Brera, Catalogo by F. Malaguzzi Valeri, 1908, No. 506; size, 0·15 × 2·03; photographs in the Gallery archives. It represents incidents in the life of S. Christina. (4) Annibale Mariotti, *Lettere Pittoriche Perugine*, 1788, p. 274. (5) Giacomo Mancini, *Istruzione Storico-Pittorica . . . di Città di Castello*, 1832, I, pp. 312 ff., reprinted from the *Giornale Arcadico di Roma*, 1826. (6) Recorded as still there in Berenson's *Central Italian Painters*, 1897, and by Magherini-Graziani, *L'Arte a Città di Castello*, 1897, pp. 207 ff.

2488   THE HOLY FAMILY

Wood, painted surface, 31¾×25½ (0·81×0·65); painted up to the edges all round. There is a small insertion in the top right corner.

Much restored. The features of the Virgin and Child and the Child's hands are among the parts reasonably pure. X-Rays do not reveal any detail under the black background, top left.

A work of Signorelli's middle period; Dussler suggests a date of *ca.* 1490/5.[1]

PROVENANCE: Bought by George Salting in 1904.[2] Exhibited at the Burlington Fine Arts Club, Umbrian Exhibition, 1909 (No. 28). Salting Bequest, 1910.

REPRODUCTION: *Illustrations, Italian Schools*, 1937, p. 331. *Plates, Earlier Italian Schools*, 1953, Vol. II, p. 388.

REFERENCES: (1) Klassiker der Kunst *Signorelli*, 1927, Plate 55. (2) Salting MSS.

3929 FRESCO: CORIOLANUS PERSUADED BY HIS FAMILY TO SPARE ROME

The scene is the camp of the Volscians, who are besieging Rome (presumably the city shown in the background). The Volscian general is the exiled Roman Coriolanus, who is seen on the right, his head encircled with a wreath. Coriolanus' mother Volumnia is the aged figure, with her raised hand persuading her son to have pity on Rome. Next her is Coriolanus' wife Virgilia, holding one of his children; another is running forward to clasp his knees. The other prominent woman is presumably Valeria, who had had first the idea of going with Coriolanus' family and other women to beg him to spare Rome. In the middle distance on the left, four figures presumably stand for the priests and soothsayers, who a short while before had unsuccessfully tried to soften Coriolanus. Signed on a *cartellino*, LVCAS CORITIV(S).

Fresco, transferred to canvas, 49½ × 49½ (1·255 × 1·255). These measurements include narrow bands forming the edging left and top; the bands are not apparent on the other two sides in the present condition of the picture, but it may be excluded that any considerable part of the picture itself has been cut away.

Much damaged.

The subject is described at length in Plutarch's *Life of Coriolanus*; see also Shakespeare's play, Act V, Scene III. According to other accounts, held to be of better authority than Plutarch, Coriolanus' mother was named Veturia, and Volumnia was his wife. See also Michele da Verona, No. 1214.

This fresco, like No. 910 above and No. 911 (Pintoricchio), comes from the Palazzo del Magnifico (Pandolfo Petrucci) at Siena. The decoration of the room from which it comes is fully discussed in the entry for No. 910 above; also the reasons for accepting a date of *ca.* 1509.

Although the picture is signed by Signorelli,[1] it was formerly in the Gallery wrongly ascribed to Gerolamo Genga.[2] How far the execution is by Signorelli's own hand is, on account of the condition, impossible to say.

The group of horsemen in the middle distance on the right is repeated with variations from a group in Signorelli's fresco of *S. Benedict and*

Totila at Monte Oliveto near Siena, apparently of *ca.* 1497–1501.[3] A pricked drawing in the British Museum shows the same group, but does not correspond very precisely either with the figures at Monte Oliveto, or with those here. The size of the drawing is, however, the same as here; since the group at Monte Oliveto is slightly larger, the drawing might rather be for No. 3929.[4]

DRAWING: In the British Museum, see the preceding paragraph.

DERIVATION: There is a free derivation from No. 3929 in a maiolica plaque in the Victoria and Albert Museum, No. 4277–'57.[5]

PROVENANCE: From the Palazzo del Magnifico at Siena, as stated above. With No. 910 above and No. 911 (Pintoricchio), transferred from the wall in 1842 or 1844 to the order of E. Joly de Bammeville of Paris.[6] Not in the Bammeville Sale, London, 1854. All three frescoes passed to the Alexander Barker Collection, where seen by Waagen.[7] Barker Sale, 6 June, 1874 (lot 71), bought by Leyland.[8] Lent by F. R. Leyland to the R.A., 1876 (No. 194). Leyland Sale, 28 May, 1892 (lot 98), bought by Frickenhaus. Lent by Ludwig Mond to the Burlington Fine Arts Club, 1893 (No. 17). Mond Bequest, 1924.

REPRODUCTION: *Illustrations, Italian Schools*, 1937, p. 151. *Plates, Earlier Italian Schools*, 1953, Vol. II, p. 389.

REFERENCES: (1) The unusual form *Coritius* instead of *Cortonensis* occurs also on No. 910 above, and is commented on in Note 10 of the entry for that picture. (2) This is due to the influence of J. P. Richter, *The Mond Collection*, 1910, II, pp. 535 ff. Vasari, ed. Milanesi, VI, p. 316 (text of 1568; not in the 1550 edition), says that Genga did much work in Pandolfo Petrucci's Palace. It is hardly worth bothering to discuss the attribution to Genga of a picture signed by Signorelli; but it may be mentioned that Genga's only authenticated work of this time is *The Transfiguration* of 1510 or 1512 in the Cathedral Museum at Siena (Vasari, *loc. cit.*; Enzo Carli, *Il Museo dell'Opera*, etc., Siena, 1946, p. 34). Reproduced in the *Rassegna Marchigiana*, Anno VI, 1927/8, p. 233. Photograph in the Gallery archives, supplied by Enzo Carli. An authenticated Genga of 1513/8 is in the Brera at Milan; reproduced by Venturi, *Storia dell'Arte Italiana*, Vol. IX, Part V, Fig. 338. (3) *Klassiker der Kunst Signorelli*, 1927, Plate 67. (4) The drawing is Berenson, *Drawings of the Florentine Painters*, 1938, No. 2509^{E-1}, and it is reproduced the exact size of the original by W. Y. Ottley, *The Italian School of Design*, 1823, p. 17. British Museum, *Italian Drawings, The Fourteenth and Fifteenth Centuries*, catalogue by A. E. Popham and Philip Pouncey, 1950, No. 237 and Plate CCIII. The size of the figures in the Monte Oliveto fresco is slightly larger than for the figures in No. 3929; letter from Enzo Carli, 3 December, 1947, in the Gallery archives. (5) See Pierre Verlet in *The Burlington Magazine*, Vol. LXXI (1937), p. 183, with reproductions. The plaque is in Rackham's *Catalogue of Italian Maiolica* at the Victoria and Albert Museum, 1940, No. 259. See further Rackham in *The Burlington Magazine*, Vol. XCIII (1951), p. 110. (6) Waagen, *Mantegna und Signorelli* (from Raumer's *Historisches Taschenbuch*, 1850), p. 569; Vasari, Le Monnier edition, VI, p. 153. (7) Waagen, *Treasures*, IV, 1857, pp. 73/5. (8) The buyer's name is taken from Redford's *Art Sales*.

3946 PREDELLA: ESTHER BEFORE AHASUERUS, AND
         THREE VISIONS OF THE TRIUMPH OF S. JEROME

From left to right: (i) the apparition of SS. John the Baptist and Jerome to S. Augustine; S. Jerome has two crowns above his head, S. John the Baptist has three: (ii) the apparition of Christ and S. Jerome to Sulpicius Severus and two monks: (iii) Esther's intercession with

Ahasuerus on behalf of the Jews: (iv) the apparition of Christ and S. Jerome to Cyril.

Wood, painted surface, $11\frac{5}{8} \times 83\frac{5}{8}$ (0·295 × 2·125). Painted up to the edge at the right; the picture has possibly been cut there, but it is unlikely that a whole scene has been cut away, although there is only one scene with S. Jerome on this side of the central compartment, and two on the other side. The left side of the central scene is $29\frac{1}{2}$ in. from the left edge of the picture, and its right side is $60\frac{1}{2}$ in. from this edge; its centre is therefore 45 in. from the left instead of $41\frac{3}{4}$ in., which would be the centre of the whole picture as it stands. It is therefore just possible that a scene some $6\frac{1}{2}$ in. wide is missing from the right, but this space appears inadequate.[1] Further, Signorelli was clearly confused about the disposition of this predella; for instance, the division on the left side of the central scene is pitifully inadequate.

Fair state; the scene on the extreme left is the most damaged. Some marks on the landscape of the scene at the right may be *pentimenti*, or some peculiarity in the lay-in of the picture; they are less clear by X-Rays than by normal light, and they appear not to indicate any changes of significance.[2]

The subject of the central panel is from the apocryphal *Rest of the Chapters of the Book of Esther*, Chapter xv.[3] The three scenes with S. Jerome illustrate visions said to have been had by various people at the time of S. Jerome's death, all indicating his peculiar sanctity. Signorelli's illustrations correspond well with the stories as given in the *Divoto Transito del Glorioso Sancto Hieronymo*, Florence, Bonacorsi, 1490 (1491), Chapters XXVII, XXVI and XXII;[4] the fairly slight variations may be due to negligence or convenience, or some slightly different forms of the legends may have been used for the pictures. The scene on the left is when S. Augustine was preparing to write an epistle in honour of S. Jerome, who had just died; SS. John the Baptist and Jerome appeared to him, the former with three crowns on his head, the latter with only two. It was explained that the two crowns were those worn by Virgins and Doctors; the third, that of Martyrs, could not be worn by S. Jerome, who did not perish by the knife, although what he had suffered for the faith made him in a more general sense a true Christian martyr. The picture differs from the text of 1491 in a few points; e.g. the text says that the two saints were in white garments ornamented with gems, and that they were accompanied by a multitude of angels. The second scene is of the vision granted to (Sulpicius) Severus and his companions at Tours at the time of the death of S. Jerome; the vision was of the soul of S. Jerome being received into heaven by Jesus Christ. Here again the text of 1491 differs somewhat from the picture; according to the text, Severus had three companions, of whom two were monks, and the vision showed not only angels but the whole court of heaven. The third scene, on the right, is the vision at the time of S. Jerome's death vouchsafed to Cyril; there appeared Christ, S. Jerome and many angels, each with a lighted taper. The text of 1491 mentions a mystic road from Cyril's monastery leading up to heaven;[5]

it also says that Christ was on S. Jerome's right hand, whereas in the picture He is on S. Jerome's left. Cyril is also claimed to be a Bishop, apparently of Jerusalem.[6]

J. P. Richter[7] plausibly suggested that No. 3946 formed the predella to an altarpiece commissioned for the Compagnia di S. Gerolamo at Arezzo and now in the Gallery of that town.[8] This altarpiece, size 3·415 × 2·33,[9] represents the Virgin and Child with various other figures, including (as is natural) S. Jerome. The scene with Esther in No. 3946 also suits the Arezzo altarpiece. Esther's mediation is considered a type of the Virgin Mary; the altarpiece at Arezzo shows the Virgin and Child, and includes various mystic references to the Virgin.[10]

The Arezzo picture was commissioned on 19 September, 1519, to be finished by July, 1520; it was to have a *gradino* one braccio (58 cm.) high.[11] Vasari[12] says that he remembered the altarpiece being delivered at Arezzo when he was 8, i.e. *ca.* 1519; but the date of delivery may have been slightly later. On 16 September, 1522, Signorelli and the Confraternity came to a compromise about the picture, which (it is implied) had by then been delivered. If six months later the blue of the Virgin's mantle was considered unsatisfactory, it was to be redone in ultramarine by the hand of Guglielmo de Marcillat.[13] On 20 December, 1522, this same Guglielmo de Marcillat made a drawing for the decoration in stone of the altar where Signorelli's altarpiece was to be put; it is quite clear that it was not then in position.[14]

Whether or not No. 3946 was the predella of the Arezzo picture, it appears clearly to be a late work of Signorelli's; although the execution is rather coarse, it may be largely by Signorelli's own hand, but Salmi claims a good deal of intervention by Papacello.[15]

PROVENANCE: Probably, as explained above, the predella of an altarpiece of 1519–1522 at Arezzo; the contract for that specifies a predella, but no later mention of that predella is known. No. 3946 was probably in the E. Joly de Bammeville Sale, London, 12 June, 1854 (lot 49), bought by Grüner. It passed through the hands of Sir J. C. Robinson, and was purchased in 1886 by J. P. Richter, who sold it to Ludwig Mond in the following year.[16] Signorelli Exhibition at the Burlington Fine Arts Club, 1893 (No. 14); New Gallery, 1897/8 (No. 144). Mond Bequest, 1924.

REPRODUCTION: *Illustrations, Italian Schools*, 1937, p. 333. *Plates, Earlier Italian Schools*, 1953, Vol. II, p. 390.

REFERENCES: (1) See further in note 9. (2) See further in note 5. (3) See also *The Book of Esther*, v, 1, 2. The allegorical significance of this scene in the predella is the subject of comment presently. (4) Extracts from the relevant passages are translated by J. P. Richter, *The Mond Collection*, 1910, II, pp. 501 ff.; cf. also Louise Pillion in the *Gazette des Beaux-Arts*, 1908, I, pp. 303 ff. (5) It does not appear likely that the *pentimenti* or marks already mentioned in this part of the picture are the painted out remains of the mystic road. (6) Probably S. Cyril, the Bishop of Jerusalem who died in 386, is intended; but S. Jerome did not die until 420. It appears that these stories of S. Jerome were invented long after S. Jerome's death; see, for instance, the Bollandists (30 September, p. 420), E. Panofsky (in *Studies in Art and Literature for Belle da Costa Greene*, 1954, p. 106) and especially Helen I. Roberts in *The Art Bulletin*, 1959, pp. 283 ff. (7) J. P. Richter, *op. cit.*, II, pp. 510 f. (8) Klassiker der Kunst *Signorelli*,

1927, Plate 145; Arezzo, Catalogo by Mario Salmi, 1921, pp. 47/8, No. 46. Mirella Levi D'Ancona, *The Iconography of the Immaculate Conception*, 1957, p. 36, says that No. 3946 (or part of it) was probably the predella of Signorelli's *Immaculate Conception* at Cortona; that picture does not appear to be connected with S. Jerome, and there is a record (R. Vischer, *Luca Signorelli*, 1879, p. 377) that its predella showed scenes of the life of the Virgin. (9) The fact that the altarpiece at Arezzo is wider than No. 3946 could be used as an argument that No. 3946 has been cut; but see the remarks at the beginning of the commentary. (10) For the significance of Esther, see J. P. Richter, *op. cit.*, II, pp. 492 ff. See also (with regard to *Immaculate Conceptions*) Montgomery Carmichael, *Francia's Masterpiece*, 1909, Chapter II. (11) See R. Vischer, *Luca Signorelli*, 1879, p. 363, and Girolamo Mancini, *Vita di Luca Signorelli*, 1903, p. 218. The full text of the contract does not appear to have been published. The contract appears to be the only place where the predella is mentioned; the history of the picture can be followed clearly, but mentions of it before it reached the Arezzo Gallery (e.g. G.A. Angelucci, *Memorie Istoriche per ... Arezzo*, 1819, p. 120) do not include anything about the predella. (12) Vasari, ed. Milanesi, III, pp. 692/3. In the edition of 1550, p. 524, the picture is mentioned, but Vasari's indication of date is not given in that text. (13) Girolamo Mancini, *Guglielmo de Marcillat*, 1909, p. 83; the passage is quoted by Salmi in his Arezzo *Catalogo*, 1921, p. 48. (14) Girolamo Mancini, *Guglielmo de Marcillat*, *loc. cit.* in previous note; Vasari, ed. Milanesi, IV, p. 429 (1550 edition, p. 681), indicates that Marcillat's work was a stone framing to the picture itself. (15) Mario Salmi, *Luca Signorelli*, 1953, p. 68. (16) J. P. Richter, *The Mond Collection*, 1910, II, p. vii. Richter seems to have bought it in London; letter from Morelli to Layard, 12 September, 1886 (British Museum, Add. MS. 38965, Layard Papers, Vol. XXXV).

Don SILVESTRO De' Gherarducci
See Ascribed to Don LORENZO Monaco, No. 3089

Andrea SOLARI
active 1495 or before, died 1524

A Milanese, brother of the sculptor Cristoforo Solari (il Gobbo). There are several signed and dated works, from 1495 to 1515; the signatures are in Latin, and are some form of *Andreas de Solario* or *Andreas Mediolanensis*. For the date of death, see W. Suida in *The Art Quarterly*, Winter, 1945, p. 16.

Solari's earliest signed work, *The Virgin and Child with SS. Joseph and Jerome* of 1495 in the Brera, is from Murano. It is very probable that Solari visited Venice, and that he there underwent the influence of the Venetian followers of Antonello; No. 923 below, probably of before 1495, is important in this connection. At Milan, Solari was influenced by Leonardo da Vinci, but was not one of Leonardo's closest followers. From 1507 to 1509 or later, he was working in Normandy for Cardinal d'Amboise.

734 GIOVANNI CRISTOFORO LONGONI

He holds a letter addressed, *Nobili Joanni Christophoro | Longono Amico*. On the parapet in front is inscribed: IGNORANS QVALIS

FVERIS . QVALISQVE FVTVRVS . SIS QVALIS . STVDEAS POSSE VIDERE DIV. Signed: .ANDREAS. D / .SOLARIO. / . F . / . 1505.

Poplar,[1] $31\frac{1}{4} \times 23\frac{3}{4}$ (0.79×0.605). Painted up to the edges all round. A modern addition of about 2 in. at the top was removed after the picture was purchased (Eastlake's note-book, 1863).

Much repainted in the flesh. The landscapes are in good condition, except that the foliage is rubbed. Small *pentimenti* in the cap, the line of his left shoulder, the landscape to the left.

The sitter is presumably the man (a) appointed a *notarius Provixionum Mediolani* in 1494; (b) mentioned in an inscription of 1498.[2]

PROVENANCE: On the back, A R, and several unidentified seals. Said to be from the Casa Lampognana (Milan ?),[3] or from Dr. Faccioli, Verona.[4] Purchased from Baslini, Milan, 1863.

REPRODUCTION: *Illustrations, Italian Schools*, 1937, p. 338. *Plates, Earlier Italian Schools*, 1953, Vol. II, p. 391.

REFERENCES: (1) Letter from B. J. Rendle, of the Forest Products Research Laboratory, in the Gallery archives. (2) For (a) see C. Santoro, *Gli Uffici del Dominio Sforzesco*, 1948, p. 165, ' Io. Christophorus de Longono'. For (b) see V. Forcella, *Iscrizioni delle Chiese, etc. di Milano*, I, 1889, p. 70. In neither case is he described as Noble; this description might be expected to be used in the first document. (3) Eastlake's letter to Wornum, 5 September, 1863. (4) N.G. MS. Catalogue.

923   A MAN WITH A PINK

Poplar,[1] original panel, $20\frac{3}{8} \times 16\frac{1}{8}$ (0.515×0.41). The original painted surface seems to be only $19\frac{1}{2} \times 15\frac{1}{4}$ (0.495×0.385).

Good state; the hair damaged by cracking and overcleaning. There are *pentimenti* in the hair and the lines of the cap.

Formerly called *A Venetian Senator*.[2]

Attributed to Andrea Solari by Mündler.[3] It should be assigned to his Venetian period, and probably dated even earlier than the picture of 1495 (from Murano) in the Brera at Milan.[4] It seems somewhat reminiscent of Netherlandish painting.

PROVENANCE: By 1842 in the Palazzo Grillo-Cattaneo or Palazzo Gavotto, near the Piazza del Portello, Genoa.[5] In the Villa (Frederico) Mylius at Genoa in 1872, whence acquired by Baslini in 1873.[6] Purchased from Baslini, Milan, 1875.

REPRODUCTION: *Illustrations, Italian Schools*, 1937, p. 338. *Plates, Earlier Italian Schools*, 1953, Vol. II, p. 392.

REFERENCES: (1) Letter from B. J. Rendle, of the Forest Products Research Laboratory, in the Gallery archives. (2) The costume does not appear to indicate a Senator, but (assuming that the sitter is a Venetian) one of several classes of Magistrate; see Cesare Vecellio, *Degli Habiti Antichi et Moderni*, 1590, p. 105 (1598 edition, p. 81). (3) Mündler's Diary, 1 May, 1857. (It had been called a Bellini.) (4) Kurt Badt, *Andrea Solario*, 1914, p. 192, says *ca.* 1492/3. (5) Recorded in the Palazzo Grillo-Cattaneo by E. Förster, *Handbuch für Reisende in Italien*, 2nd edition consulted, 1842, p. 242. Recorded by Alizeri, *Guida di*

Genova, Vol. II, Part I, 1847, p. 486; for the identity with No. 923, cf. *L'Arte*,
1891, p. 285. According to the N.G. MS. Catalogue, it had belonged to the
Marchesa Grillo-Cattaneo, who married the Marchese Girolamo Gavotti; but
Alizeri implies that the collection had been formed recently by the Gavottos.
(6) Bode, *Mein Leben*, I, 1930, pp. 74 and 93/4. It was already with Baslini in
1873; Morelli, in a letter to Layard, 11 December, 1873, says that he had recommended that the Director of the National Gallery should buy it (British
Museum, Add. MS. 38963, Layard Papers, Vol. XXXIII).

Studio of ANDREA SOLARI

2504   THE VIRGIN AND CHILD

Wood, painted surface, $24 \times 18\frac{1}{4}$ (0.61×0.465). The picture appears
to be painted all round up to the edge of the original panel, which seems
to have been let into another, which is of poplar.[1]

Excellent state, though it suffers here and there slightly from undercleaning.

Formerly passing as a Salai or a Cesare da Sesto, it is usually classed
as an old copy of a lost Solari,[2] though Frizzoni and Berenson think it
an original.[3] The design seems to have some relationship to that of
Raphael's *Madonna of the Tower*, No. 2069 of this Gallery, which might
be earlier.[4] A design somewhat similar in part appears in the Cesare da
Sesto sketchbook in the Morgan Library, New York.[5]

VERSION: A version, closely corresponding in the forms except that the Child
has a drapery, and probably of inferior quality, is at Budapest (Pállfy Bequest).[6]

PROVENANCE: Presumably the picture in the Pourtalès-Gorgier Collection,
Paris; Catalogue by J.-J. Dubois, 1841 (No. 62); Sale, 27 May, etc., 1865 (lot
107).[7] Certainly exhibited at the R.A., 1894 (No. 118), lent by Andrew McKay.[8]
Bought by George Salting in 1894;[9] exhibited at the Burlington Fine Arts Club,
1898 (No. 20); lent to the National Gallery from 1902; Salting Bequest, 1910.
Exhibited at Birmingham, *Italian Art*, 1955 (No. 101).

REPRODUCTION: *Illustrations, Italian Schools*, 1937, p. 337 (wrongly numbered
2054). *Plates, Earlier Italian Schools*, 1953, Vol. II, p. 393.

REFERENCES: (1) Letter from B. J. Rendle, of the Forest Products Research
Laboratory, in the Gallery archives. (2) E.g. by Suida, *Leonardo und sein Kreis*,
1929, p. 290 (copy); the same in Thieme-Becker (workshop replica); K. Badt,
Andrea Solario, 1914, p. 193 (copy); Venturi in *L'Arte*, 1898, p. 316 (probably a
copy). The attribution to Solari may be due to Mündler; cf. Badt, *op. cit.*, p. 6.
(3) Frizzoni in the *Gazette des Beaux-Arts*, 1898, ii, p. 397; Berenson, 1932
Lists. (4) Some other derivations from Raphael's design are known. A pricked
drawing of the design is in the British Museum (ascribed by Berenson to Bres-
cianino; cf. *Study and Criticism*, Vol. II, pp. 39 ff.) (5) Reproduced in Fairfax
Murray's *Two Lombard Sketchbooks*, 1910, Plate 61. (6) Catalogue in German of
the Pállfy Bequest, 1913, No. 104. The Pállfy version is probably the one
from the Aguado Sale, Paris, 1843, where it was noted to be on the same design
as the Pourtalès version (presumably No. 2504); cf. *Le Cabinet de l'Amateur*,
1843, p. 146. It was certainly bought from Moreau in Paris in 1861. (7) As
Salaino. But cf. Crowe and Cavalcaselle, *Painting in North Italy*, II, 1871, p. 59,
or ed. Borenius, Vol. II, 1912, p. 382. (8) Label on the back. (9) Salting MSS.

Antonio de SOLARIO
active 1502–1518 (?)

Known (since 1623 at least) as *lo Zingaro*; his existence was for a time wrongly doubted. In his signatures he calls himself a Venetian, but he is first certainly recorded in 1502 at Fermo; he seems to have been active for several years in the Marches. Since 1623, he is said to have painted some frescoes of the life of S. Benedict at Naples, with the approximate date of 1495; some of these indeed seem to be by the same hand as the signed pictures (two of which are dated 1508 and 1514), but the date may be wrong. There is a very uncertain record (of 1636) that he was working at Montecassino in 1518. The Withypoll triptych (of which the wings are Nos. 646/7 below), and a record by John Leland of two paintings by him apparently in England, in the sixteenth century, have been considered indications that he may have visited England; see L. Bradner in *Publications of the Modern Language Association*, Vol. LXXI, 1956, pp. 834/5. It may be thought that further evidence in favour of this is provided by the picture lent by the Marquess of Salisbury to the R.A., 1960 (No. 26).

There can be little doubt that he was trained in Venice, his style reflecting mixed influences of several of the leading painters there. It is often said that his landscapes are like Pintoricchio's; but it is by no means certain that they could not be derived from Carpaccio or other Venetians. There is no good reason for supposing any connection with Andrea Solari, who was, however, most probably in Venice about 1495.

Literature: Gronau in Thieme-Becker.

646 S. CATHERINE OF ALEXANDRIA (LEFT WING OF A TRIPTYCH)

Reverse: Amid decorative scroll-work, two *putti* support a medallion, in which is a half-length figure of S. John the Baptist with a lamb and the inscription: ECCE AGNVS DEI :. Above is a tablet with AVE GRACIA PLENA/DOMINVS TECUM. Below are the arms of Withypoll, *per pale or and gules three lions passant guardant within a bordure all counterchanged.*

For the commentary, etc., see No. 647 below.

647 S. URSULA (RIGHT WING OF A TRIPTYCH)

Reverse: Similar to the other, except that the saint is S. Paul. The tablet has BENEDICTA TV INTER / MVLIERES ET . B(enedictus). F(ructus). V(entris). T(ui) (*Luke* i, 42). Below are the arms of Withypoll, quartered with Gant or Gaunt, *barry azure and or, on a bend engrailed gules three spearheads argent.*

Wood, each, $33\frac{1}{4} \times 16$ (0·84 × 0·40).[1]

Various old attributions need not be recorded since the discovery of the central panel now at Bristol (ex-Duke of St. Albans),[2] which

includes a portrait of Paul Withypoll (name inscribed), and is signed by
Antonio de Solario and dated 1514. It should, however, be mentioned
that Venturi[3] and Berenson[4] had stated the correct attribution for Nos.
646 and 647 long before. The paintings on the reverses are clearly contemporary and, contrary to what is sometimes stated, are rather closely
connected in style with the pictures on the front (compare the faces of
the *putti* with that of the angel accompanying S. Catherine, etc.); compare also the cornucopias at the top with those above the throne on
Antonio de Solario's Osimo altarpiece.[5] It is, however, possible that the
painting of the reverses is not by Antonio's own hand.

Paul Withypoll[6] (there are various spellings) was a son of John
Withypoll of Bristol; his mother (whose arms he quarters) was Alison,
daughter of John a Gaunt or Gant of Cardiff. He was a prosperous
merchant taylor, who lived chiefly in London; there is a record that he
married in 1510, and he died in 1547. The presence of S. John the Baptist on the reverse of No. 646 may well be due to the fact that that saint
is the Patron of the Guilds of Merchant Taylors both in Bristol and in
London; it has been claimed that Paul Withypoll was a member of the
Bristol Guild,[7] certainly he was a member of the London Guild.[8] The
compiler does not know if he visited Italy.[9] The central panel is apparently on oak, which might be thought to support the idea mentioned
in the biography above, that Antonio de Solario came to England.[10]
Paul Withypoll's portrait on the central panel is accompanied by a
cartellino with the inscription, ORATE. PRO. ANIMA / PAVLI
WITHIPOL; this formula is often used of dead people, but there is no
reason to suppose that the *cartellino* is later than the painting.[11]

PROVENANCE: The triptych may be presumed to have remained in the Withypoll family, descending to Elizabeth, great-great-great-grand-daughter of Paul,
who married in 1642 the 6th Viscount Hereford. This claim can be made, since
the central panel seems clearly identifiable, from a note by Tom Martin the
antiquary (1697–1771), in Sudbourne Hall, Suffolk ('where the late Lord Hereford dyed');[12] this note may be from soon after 1748.[13] Sudbourne was sold in
1753 to the then Earl of Hertford, and the compiler does not know what happened to the picture. Nos. 646/7 were probably in the James Wadmore Sale, 5
May, 1854 (lots 23, 24).[14] Purchased[15] with the rest of the Edmond Beaucousin
Collection, Paris, 1860. Lent to the South Kensington Museum, 1862–1889.
Lent to Bristol since 1937. The whole triptych was exhibited at the R.A., 1956/7
(No. 8).

REPRODUCTIONS: (obverses), *Illustrations, Italian Schools*, 1937, p. 174.
Plates, Earlier Italian Schools, 1953, Vol. II, p. 394. The reverses are reproduced
in *Paintings and Drawings on the Backs of National Gallery Pictures*, 1946, Plates
9 and 10 (with the inventory numbers inverted).

REFERENCES: (1) Measurements from the 1929 Catalogue; the pictures have
not been examined with a view to the present entry. (2) Reproduced in *The
Burlington Magazine*, Vol. LXIX (1936), p. 229, and in the Bristol Catalogue,
1957, Plate 45 (entry for it on p. 109). (3) Venturi, *Storia dell'Arte Italiana*,
Vol. VII, Part IV, 1915, p. 667. (4) Berenson in *Art in America*, Vol. 3, June
1915, p. 165; reprinted in his *Venetian Painting in America*, 1916, p. 48. (5)
Van Marle, *Italian Schools*, Vol. XVIII, Fig. 272. (6) Much information about
him and his family is given by G. C. Moore Smith, *The Family of Withypoll*,
1936. Withypoll pedigrees may also be found in *The East Anglian*, N.S. Vol. X,

1903/4, pp. 302/4, and in J. S. Corder, *Christchurch or Withepole House*, 1893, p. 28. **(7)** Information in the Gallery archives from Everard Green, 1890, from an unspecified Bristol book; the compiler did not find any mention of Paul Withypoll in Francis F. Fox, *Some Account of the Ancient Fraternity of Merchant Taylors of Bristol*, 1880. **(8)** Cf. Moore Smith, *op. cit.* **(9)** Moore Smith, *op. cit.*, p. 14, admits the possibility. The Withypoll family had dealings with the Bank of S. George at Genoa, but the compiler has not found a mention of any Withypoll in the printed works on this bank that he has consulted. **(10)** Actually fabric on oak; but H. Schubart kindly wrote that in many instances the edge of the painting extends over the edge of the canvas, so it seems not doubtful that the oak support is the original one. **(11)** Information from H. Schubart. **(12)** Moore Smith, *op. cit.*, p. 96. It is quite likely that the picture is the one noted by Evelyn in 1677 at Lord Hereford's house Christchurch at Ipswich (*Diary*, ed. de Beer, 1955, Vol. IV, p. 115). The land at Ipswich had been bought by Paul Withypoll and his son Edmund in 1545; the existing house was probably not begun by Paul, but rather by Edmund soon after his father's death. It is further possible that the picture is referred to in passing in connection with Paul Withypoll's will ('the Table'; Moore Smith, *op. cit.*, p. 22, checked). **(13)** From information given in G.E.C., the note seems to be from after the death of the 10th Viscount. **(14)** As Ghirlandaio; the description in the sale catalogue tallies very well. **(15)** As Ridolfo Ghirlandaio. From 1892 catalogued as Umbrian School; 1913, School of the Marches; 1920, Italian School.

2503   THE VIRGIN AND CHILD WITH S. JOHN

On S. John's scroll, ECE A. Signed *Antonius desolario / uenetus f.*

Canvas transferred from panel, $14\frac{3}{8} \times 11\frac{3}{4}$ (0.365×0.295). An inscription dated 1865 on the back of the canvas refers to the transference.

In exceptionally good state for a transferred picture. Rosini's[1] remarks might be construed as criticism of the condition, but as he reproduces the picture enlarged into a tondo, he seems obviously irresponsible. Moschini,[2] on the other hand, can no doubt be trusted when he says that some dealer, probably towards 1825, painted out the signature in order to pass the picture as a Leonardo or a Raphael.

PROVENANCE: Obviously not (as sometimes suggested) the Andrea Solari catalogued in the Carignan Collection and sold in 1742, which is presumably No. 1530 of the Louvre. No. 2503 was acquired by the Abate Luigi Celotti, Venice, a little before 1828;[3] in his collection in Florence *ca.* 1832.[4] In the Leuchtenberg Collection, Munich (later Leningrad), apparently by 1840;[5] 1845 Catalogue, 2nd room (No. 52); 1851 Catalogue (plates), 2nd edition (No. 2). Acquired by Asher Wertheimer, London, *ca.* 1903,[6] it passed to Salting *ca.* 1907.[7] George Salting Bequest, 1910.

REPRODUCTION: *Illustrations, Italian Schools*, 1937, p. 339. *Plates, Earlier Italian Schools*, 1953, Vol. II, p. 395.

REFERENCES: **(1)** Rosini, *Storia della Pittura Italiana*, Vol. III, 1841, p. 28, and Plates, 1840, No. XXXVII ('in Monaco'). **(2)** Moschini, *Memorie della Vita di Antonio de Solario*, etc., 1828, p. 24, with engraving by Francesco Novelli. **(3)** Moschini as in note 2. **(4)** See *Kunst-Blatt*, 1832, pp. 151 f. **(5)** Rosini, as in note 1. With regard to the Leuchtenberg family, the Beauharnais known as Prince Eugène died in 1824. The heads of the family during the ownership of No. 2503 appear to have been his son Maximilian (d. 1852), Maximilian's son Nicholas (d. 1890), Nicholas' son Nicholas (d. 1928). **(6)** See Fry in *The Burlington Magazine*, Vol. I (1903), p. 353; Berenson's comments appeared in the June number, Vol. II, p. 114. **(7)** *The Burlington Magazine*, Vol. XI (1907), p. 376, note 3, and *L'Arte*, 1908, p. 79.

Lo SPAGNA
active 1504, died 1528

Giovanni di Pietro, a Spaniard, known as *Lo Spagna*; he was active at Perugia, Todi, Macerata, Trevi, Spoleto, etc. Possibly recorded at Perugia in 1470; first certainly recorded at Perugia, in 1504. He imitated Perugino, and to a less extent Raphael. Several authenticated works exist; but his style is marked with little originality.

Ascribed to Lo SPAGNA

691 CHRIST CROWNED WITH THORNS

Wood, painted surface, $15\frac{7}{8} \times 12\frac{3}{4}$ (0·405 × 0·325); including a narrow band of red paint, forming a framing.

Good condition; some retouches, mostly to cover old flaking.

This picture does not appear to be by Lo Spagna;[1] but the old attribution is left, in the absence of any better one.

PROVENANCE: Bequeathed by Lieut.-General Sir William George Moore, 1862.

REPRODUCTION: *Illustrations, Italian Schools*, 1937, p. 341. *Plates, Earlier Italian Schools*, 1953, Vol. II, p. 396.

REFERENCE: (1) The attribution has been doubted by several critics, e.g. by Crowe and Cavalcaselle, *History of Painting in Italy*, III, 1866, p. 327.

1032 THE AGONY IN THE GARDEN

Christ kneels centre; in the foreground, SS. Peter, James and John. In the right middle distance, Judas leads forward the soldiers, one of whom carries a banner with SPQR (new?).

Wood, painted surface, $23\frac{3}{4} \times 26\frac{1}{2}$ (0·60 × 0·67), excluding narrow strips added left and right; painted up to the edges all round.

Good condition on the whole.

This picture was published by Passavant as a Raphael; the letters R V that Passavant claimed to see on S. Peter's robe are now not there, and Passavant's provenance for the picture, which would support his attribution, seems wrong.[1] No. 1032 is based in the main on Perugino's picture of the same subject in the Uffizi;[2] the apostle on the right is near in pose to a figure in Perugino's *Transfiguration* in the Vatican,[3] and the soldier with legs astride in the right middle distance may be derived from Perugino's figure of Lucius Sicinius in the Cambio at Perugia.[4] The execution of No. 1032 is by some quite competent Peruginesque; it is usually admitted to be by Lo Spagna,[5] but his authorship cannot be considered certain.

VERSIONS: A version of Christ without the apostles, and with the angel somewhat varied, is No. 1812 below. A picture in 1935 in a private collection at

Chicago[6] is perhaps identical with a copy recorded in Rome in the nineteenth century.[7] A copy by John Linnell[8] appeared in the Mrs. T. H. Riches Sale, 18 October, 1950 (lot 150); photograph in the Gallery archives. For Perugino's version of this subject, see above.

DRAWINGS: Fragments of a pricked cartoon, the four principal figures, are in the Uffizi;[9] they correspond in size with the figures on No. 1032. Other drawings are apparently not connected.[10]

PROVENANCE: By 1829 in the Collection of Prince Gabrielli at Rome.[11] Bought by Woodburn; lent by W. Coningham to the British Institution, 1844 (No. 5).[12] Coningham Sale, 9 June, 1849 (lot 60), bought by J. Coningham. Coll. W. Fuller Maitland, Stansted Hall;[13] lent by him to Manchester, 1857 (Provisional Catalogue, No. 147; Definitive Catalogue, No. 134), and to the R.A., 1873 (No. 176). Purchased from W. Fuller Maitland, 1878.

REPRODUCTION: *Illustrations, Italian Schools*, 1937, p. 340. *Plates, Earlier Italian Schools*, 1953, Vol. II, p. 397.

REFERENCES: (1) J. D. Passavant, *Rafael von Urbin*, II, 1839, pp. 31 ff. Passavant says that No. 1032 is the same as a picture called Raphael by Vasari (ed. Milanesi, IV, pp. 322/3); but Vasari's description does not correspond with No. 1032, and there is a large break in the provenance. (2) Klassiker der Kunst *Perugino*, 1914, Plate 25. (3) Klassiker der Kunst *Perugino*, 1914, Plate 119. (4) Klassiker der Kunst *Perugino*, 1914, Plate 107. (5) E.g. by Crowe and Cavalcaselle, *History of Painting in Italy*, III, 1866, pp. 308/9. Berenson's Lists of 1932 and 1936, owing to an unfortunate confusion, do not express his views; he accepts both No. 1032 and No. 1812 below as being by Lo Spagna—letter from Miss Nicky Mariano, 12 February, 1939, in the Gallery archives. (6) Photograph in the Gallery archives. (7) Passavant, *Rafael von Urbin*, III, 1858, p. 88; Crowe and Cavalcaselle, *Raphael: His Life and Times*, 1882, I, p. 238. (8) Mentioned by Alfred T. Story, *The Life of John Linnell*, 1892, Vol. I, p. 3. (9) Fischel in the Prussian *Jahrbuch*, 1917, *Beiheft*, p. 147, No. 138; photographs in the Gallery archives. (10) The drawing of two apostles, mentioned by Passavant, *Rafael von Urbin*, II, 1839, p. 557, No. 340, as in the Lawrence Collection, and III, 1858, p. 303, No. 22, as in the King of Holland's Sale, 1850, is apparently the one now at Weimar; Fischel in the Prussian *Jahrbuch*, 1917, Fig. 42, and *Beiheft*, No. 22. Fischel's Figs 43 and 44 (at Windsor) are not connected with the design of No. 1032. (11) Passavant, *Rafael von Urbin*, II, 1839, pp. 31 ff. Passavant also says that the picture had belonged to the Gabrielli family since the time of the B. Forte de' Gabrielli, Prior of the Camaldolese Monastery at Urbino in the seventeenth century; but there seems to be some confusion here, since the B. Forte died in 1040, and Dom Cottineau, *Répertoire . . . des Abbayes et Prieurés*, II, 1939, Col. 3243, records no Camaldolese house at Urbino. (12) For Woodburn, see Passavant, *Rafael von Urbin*, III, 1858, p. 88. Henceforward, the picture appeared as a Raphael until its acquisition by the National Gallery. (13) *Report from the Select Committee on the National Gallery*, 1853, question 9837; Waagen, *Treasures*, III, 1854, pp. 4/5.

1812   CHRIST AT GETHSEMANE

At each side (hidden by the frame) is a painted decoration, including the Nails with the Crown of Thorns, and two Scourges.

Reverse: remains of dark paint and a very simple pattern (a circle, etc.).

Wood, painted surface, $13\frac{3}{8} \times 10\frac{1}{8}$ (0·34×0·26), painted up to the edges all round. The size of the picture alone, without the decoration at the sides, is $13\frac{3}{8} \times 5\frac{1}{4}$ (0·34×0·13). What remains of the reverse is perhaps confined to the area of this central part.

The front is in good condition. The execution of the decorative work at the sides is very coarse, and may be on pieces of wood separate from the picture itself. This decorative work may be of later date, and the same may be true of the decoration on the reverse.

A companion panel represents *Christ Carrying the Cross:* there is similar painted decoration at the sides, including the Spear and Sponge, and a Hammer and Pincers (?). This companion piece is in the collection of the Duke of Sutherland,[1] and is said to have been over the altar of the chapel of the Riccardi Palace, Florence.[2]

The figure of Christ in No. 1812 corresponds closely with the figure in No. 1032 above; but No. 1812 does not appear to be by the same hand as No. 1032. Berenson, however, attributes both pictures to Lo Spagna, as is explained in the entry for No. 1032 above.

PROVENANCE: As noted above, a companion panel is said to have been in Palazzo Medici (Riccardi) at Florence. On the back of No. 1812 is a label, perhaps of the eighteenth century, *All'Ill*mo *et Ecc*mo *Sig*re *Giovanni Hiccolini Imbascatore di Toscana In Roma.*[3] Also on the back is the monogram GDH under a crown, which there is good reason for interpreting as that of D. Gaspar de Haro y Guzmán, Marqués de Carpio, Marqués de Heliche, Conde Duque de Olivares, Spanish Ambassador in Rome in 1682, and Viceroy of Naples from 1682 until his death in 1687.[4] On the back of No. 1812 are also two impressions of an unidentified seal. No. 1812 was owned by Henry Farrer in 1850, who is said to have had it from Russia.[5] Lent by Farrer to Manchester, 1857 (Provisional Catalogue, No. 146; Definitive Catalogue, No. 128).[6] Henry Vaughan Bequest, 1900.

REPRODUCTION: *Illustrations, Italian Schools,* 1937, p. 340 (central part only). *Plates, Earlier Italian Schools,* 1953, Vol. II, p. 398. The reverse has been photographed.

REFERENCES: (1) Exhibited at the British Institution, 1835 (No. 79). (2) Information from William Martin; cf. Lord R. S. Gower, *Stafford House,* 1910, no pagination, with reproduction; cf. Lord R. S. Gower, *Stafford House,* 1910, no pagination, with reproduction. The picture is also reproduced in the *Rassegna d'Arte,* 1914, p. 58. (3) Giovanni Niccolini, 1544–1611, was Tuscan Ambassador at Rome for some 24 years from 1587; see Richa, *Notizie Istoriche delle Chiese Fiorentine,* I, 1754, p. 121; Luigi Passerini, *Genealogia e Storia della Famiglia Niccolini,* 1870, pp. 58 ff.; *Diario Fiorentino di Agostino Lapini,* ed. Corazzini, 1900, p. 261. Probably this is the man meant; the inscription on the picture is not contemporary with him, and may have been copied from an earlier one, with Niccolini misread as Hiccolini. (4) See Angel M. de Barcia, *Catálogo de la Colección de Pinturas del . . . Duque de Berwick y de Alba,* 1911, pp. 260/1. It is recorded there that D. Gaspar de Haro's pictures bore an identifying mark; further, several pictures with marks similar to that on No. 1812 correspond with pictures mentioned in the published parts of his inventory. (5) Passavant, *Rafael von Urbino,* III, 1858, p. 164, with identifying description. (6) As Raphael. Manchester Exhibition labels are on the frame.

GIOVANNI MARTINO SPANZOTTI
active 1480, died 1525/8

From Casale; active chiefly at Vercelli, Chivasso and Turin. He has long been known as the painter to whom Sodoma was apprenticed; his own work is somewhat mysterious. A triptych at Turin is signed; it is

in a rather primitive, Gothic style, and dates perhaps from the 1480's.
A *Baptism* in the Cathedral of Turin is in a much more developed style.
Spanzotti received a commission in 1508, and was paid in 1510, for
what has been admitted to be this picture, but can with some difficulty
be assumed to have been something different. A *Jesus among the Doctors*
in the Civic Museum of Turin is stylistically rather like the *Baptism*,
and carries a monogram, which has been interpreted without very much
forcing as Spanzotti's signature. A trouble with these two pictures is
that they differ considerably from the earlier, signed triptych, and are
close in style to Defendente Ferrari. Anna Maria Brizio argues that the
available evidence is not proof of Spanzotti's authorship of the *Baptism*
and the *Jesus among the Doctors*; she maintains that these and a few
other connected works are by Defendente. It is possible and perhaps
easier to admit that Spanzotti developed from a primitive style to a style
also adopted by Defendente. It is further certain that other Piedmontese
painters also painted in a very similar way. It follows that the attribution
of pictures in this manner that are not signed or documented is doubtful.
   Literature: Vittorio Viale, *Gotico e Rinascimento in Piemonte*, 1939,
pp. 57 ff.; the three key works are reproduced on Plates 40, 51 and 54.
Anna Maria Brizio, *La Pittura in Piemonte*, 1942, pp. 45 ff. and 252 ff.;
L. Mallé in the *Bollettino della Società Piemontese di Archeologia e di
Belle Arti*, 1952/3, pp. 76 ff.

See Style of DEFENDENTE FERRARI, Nos. 1200, 1201

SPINELLO ARETINO
active 1373, died 1410/1

From Arezzo. On some confused indications by Vasari, he has been
said to have been born *ca.* 1333; but he may have been born after 1345.
Vasari (edition of 1568) claims to have read a date 1361 on one of his
pictures. First surely recorded in 1373. 1386 or later, member of the
Physicians' Guild at Florence. He settled indeed in Florence for some
time, but without breaking his connection with Arezzo; active also at
Pisa and Siena. The date of death seems to be 1411 rather than 1410
(*Rivista d'Arte*, 1917/8, pp. 63/4). Several authenticated works exist.

276 FRESCO: TWO HALOED MOURNERS (FRAGMENT FROM
      THE BURIAL OF S. JOHN THE BAPTIST)
Fresco, $19\frac{3}{4}$ (0·50) square (sight).
   The figures are in fair state for a fresco of the date; part of the back-
ground at the top is new.
   In 1348, Vanni Manetti wrote instructions in his will that his chapel
in the Carmine at Florence should be painted; he was still alive in 1357.[1]
The decoration, as carried out, consisted principally of six scenes of the

life of S. John the Baptist. The Carmine was largely destroyed by fire on 28/9 January, 1771. These frescoes, in point of fact, suffered comparatively little from the fire itself; and Thomas Patch in 1772 published engravings of the six scenes.[2] Patch's engravings are a very rough rendering of the style of the originals; but there is no doubt at all that he copied the compositions with considerable exactness, marking apparently with some care on his engravings the parts where the intonaco had peeled off (leaving the underdrawings visible), and the parts that had been renewed.

Patch further sawed off from the walls some fragments of the original frescoes; the rest or most of the rest was presumably destroyed in the reconstruction of the church. No. 276 is from the *Burial of S. John Baptist*; a haloed figure from the same fresco is in the Ammanati Chapel in the Camposanto at Pisa.[3] There are five other fragments from the series in the same chapel at Pisa; the head of Christ from the *Baptism*, two angels from the same, the head of S. Zacharias from the *Naming of S. John*, the harpist from the Herod scene, and the head of S. Elizabeth from the *Visitation*.[4] Part of the serving maid behind S. Elizabeth in the last scene appeared in the Lord O'Hagan Sale, 19 May, 1939 (lot 73), and is now in the Boymans–van Beuningen Museum at Rotterdam.[5] Salome from the Herod scene, and a group of three women with the Infant Baptist from the *Naming of S. John* are at Liverpool.[6] There is also a fragment at Pavia claimed to be from the same series.[7]

The subject of the *Burial of the Baptist* is rather uncommon. In the present fresco several of the figures taking part in the burial, including the two in No. 276, have haloes; according to the Bible the Baptist was buried by his own disciples. Some of the Apostles had been disciples of the Baptist, but the compiler has not found a text indicating that Apostles (or some other saints) took part in the burial; haloed figures do, nevertheless, sometimes occur in pictures.[8] The two figures in No. 276 were on the right of the composition, at the top end of the headless body being put into the tomb.

The frescoes in the Manetti Chapel in the Carmine were ascribed by Vasari to Giotto.[9] Doubt about this attribution had already been expressed, before the date of Manetti's will (1348) was known. The fragments were ascribed to Spinello Aretino by Vitzthum,[10] and this attribution has been generally accepted. Procacci dates them soon after 1387.[11]

PROVENANCE: Sawn from the wall of the Manetti Chapel, known as the Chapel of St. John the Baptist or S. Lucy, in the Carmine at Florence after the fire of 1771 by T. Patch, as explained above. Imported into England by the Hon. C. F. Greville;[12] Sale, 31 March, 1810 (lot 76).[13] Coll. Samuel Rogers by 1818;[14] exhibited at the British Institution, 1848 (No. 87); purchased at the Rogers Sale, 3 May, 1856 (lot 721).

REPRODUCTION: *Illustrations, Italian Schools*, 1937, p. 341. *Plates, Earlier Italian Schools*, 1953, Vol. II, p. 399.

REFERENCES: (1) See Vasari, ed. Milanesi, Vol. I, p. 376. An elaborate account of these frescoes is given by Ugo Procacci, *L'Incendio della Chiesa del Carmine*

del 1771, in the *Rivista d'Arte*, 1932, pp. 141 ff.; esp. pp. 212 ff. (2) Small reproductions of Patch's engravings are given by Procacci, *loc. cit.*, Figs. 6–11. (3)
Reproduced by Procacci, *loc. cit.*, Fig. 15. All the pieces in the Camposanto
at Pisa were given by Carlo Lasinio; see R. Grassi, *Descrizione . . . di Pisa*, II,
1837, p. 174. (4) For two of them, see Van Marle, *Development of the Italian
Schools of Painting*, Vol. III, Figs. 331 and 332; all the other pieces at Pisa are
reproduced by Procacci, *loc. cit.* (5) In the sale as Sienese School; photograph
in the Gallery archives. In the van Beuningen Exhibition at Rotterdam, 1949
(No. 78); Catalogue of the van Beuningen Collection by D. Hannema, 1949
(No. 78) and Plate 116, wrongly as The Virgin. (6) Liverpool (Roscoe Collec-
tion); Brockwell's Catalogue, 1928, No. 55 as Florentine and No. 79 as A.
Lorenzetti; reproduced by Procacci, *loc. cit.*, Figs. 16, 17. Ralph Fastnedge in
the Liverpool *Bulletin*, October 1954, p. 42, Nos. 30/1 and *Cleaned Pictures*,
Liverpool, 1955, Nos. 2/3. They were both bought in at the William Roscoe
Sale, 27 September, 1816 (lots 6, 7), as Giotto. (7) Procacci, *loc. cit.*, p. 223 and
Fig. 18, as from the *Decollation*. It does not correspond with the figure of S.
John as indicated in Patch's engraving of this scene; indeed, according to Patch,
the intonaco had fallen away in this region, and nothing but the underdrawing
on the wall had been left. Procacci believes that the fragment now at Pavia
must have been loose after the fire, and that it was removed before Patch made
his engraving. (8) For the Biblical texts, see Matthew xiv, 12 and Mark vi, 29.
The scene occurs in the background of the fresco of *The Banquet of Herod* in the
Baptistery at Castiglione d'Olona, and one of the figures there does seem to have
a halo; see the reproduction given by R. Longhi, *Fatti di Masolino e di Masaccio*,
in *Critica d'Arte*, July–December 1940, Plate 127, Fig. 30. In the burial scene
in a series at Albizzate, two of the figures have haloes; reproduced in the
Rivista d'Arte, 1941, p. 157. Haloed figures carry the headless body in a fragmentary fresco in the Oratorio di S. Giovanni at Urbino; Zampetti, *Gli Affreschi
di Lorenzo e Jacopo Salimbeni*, etc., 1956, p. 26 and Plate XXXIV, considers
this one of the frescoes in the Oratory later than those of the Salimbeni.
(9) Vasari, *loc. cit.* in note 1 (1550 edition, p. 141). (10) Vitzthum in *L'Arte*,
1906, pp. 199 ff. (11) Procacci, *loc. cit.*, pp. 226 ff. (12) See Tresham and Ottley's
British Gallery, 1818, Plate 1. The statement in the Rogers Sale catalogue of
1856 that No. 276 had belonged to Towneley before belonging to Greville may
be a confusion from what Tresham and Ottley say. A Towneley provenance,
on the other hand, is acceptable for the Rotterdam fragment; see the introductory note to the Lord O'Hagan Sale of 1939 and the catalogue of the British
Institution Exhibition, 1848 (No. 95). (13) As Masaccio. (14) Tresham and
Ottley, as in note 12.

1216   FRESCO: S. MICHAEL AND OTHER ANGELS (FRAG-
       MENT FROM THE FALL OF LUCIFER)

Fresco transferred to canvas, $45\frac{3}{4} \times 67$ ($1\cdot16 \times 1\cdot70$).[1]
Much damaged. For the commentary, etc., see No. 1216 B below.

1216 A   FRESCO: DECORATIVE BORDER (FRAGMENT FROM
         THE FALL OF LUCIFER)

The donor in a white religious habit kneels between medallions of a
saint and angel. Inscribed: +HOC.OPUS.FECIT.FIERI.XPO-
FANUS.HU.

Fresco transferred to canvas, $22 \times 60\frac{1}{2}$ ($0\cdot56 \times 1\cdot54$), approx.
Much damaged. For the commentary, etc., see No. 1216 B below.

1216 B FRESCO: DECORATIVE BORDER (FRAGMENT FROM
THE FALL OF LUCIFER)

Medallions of a saint and angel. Inscribed: .UCII.CA.....
ANNO (?) DNI......, followed at some distance by III, possibly part
of the day of the month.

Fresco transferred to canvas, 22 × 50 (0·56 × 1·27), approx.
Much damaged.

The left-hand side of No. 1216 B seems to join on to the right-hand
side of No. 1216 A. All three pieces are from a large fresco of the Fall of
Lucifer; another fragment is in the Gallery at Arezzo.[2] The whole composition (without the decorative border) was engraved[3] before it was
broken up and mostly destroyed. No. 1216 was not cut horizontally
from the fresco; the right-hand end was considerably higher than the
left-hand end, the angle of the bottom edge being at about 20° to the
horizontal.

The fresco was painted for the Compagnia di Sant'Angelo or S.
Michele Arcangelo at Arezzo.[4] Vasari tells the story that Spinello made
his Lucifer so horrible that it gave him bad dreams, so that he soon
died;[5] Gombosi, however, doubts a late date,[6] and Berenson[7] thinks the
execution is from Spinello's studio.

Spinello's fresco of the same subject in San Francesco at Arezzo contains a S. Michael not very dissimilar to No. 1216.[8]

PROVENANCE: From the Compagnia di Sant'Angelo or S. Michele Arcangelo,
Arezzo, as explained above; this Confraternity was suppressed in 1785,[9] and the
three fragments were removed from the wall in 1855 on the instructions of Sir
Austen Henry Layard, who had acquired them.[10] Exhibited at Manchester, 1857
(Provisional Catalogue, Nos. 184 and 195; Definitive Catalogue, No. 39); and
at South Kensington, 1869 (Nos. 2–4). Presented by Sir Henry Layard, 1886.[11]

REPRODUCTIONS: Illustrations, Italian Schools, 1937, p. 342. Plates, Earlier
Italian Schools, 1953, Vol. II, p. 400.

REFERENCES: (1) Size from the 1929 Catalogue; No. 1216 has not been
examined out of its frame with reference to the present entry. (2) Arezzo, 1921
Catalogue, No. 8; photograph in the Gallery archives. From the right-hand side,
about halfway up. (3) Carlo Lasinio, Affreschi Celebri del XIV e XV Secolo, 1841,
Plate XXXII (bound as Plate XXVII in the National Gallery copy); the engrav-
ing is actually dated 1821, and was executed by Paolo Lasinio. A copy by
Ermini, also without the border, is reproduced by U. Pasqui and U. Viviani,
Guida illustrata . . . di Arezzo e dintorni, 1925, Fig. 110. (4) Cf. note 9. (5)
Vasari, ed. Milanesi, I, p. 692 (1550 edition, p. 208). According to the Arezzo
Catalogue, 1921, the district where the fresco was situated is still known as the
borgo dei diavoli. (6) G. Gombosi, Spinello Aretino, 1926, p. 91. (7) Berenson,
1932 lists. (8) Photograph Soprintendenza, No. 128. (9) Numerous papers con-
cerning this confraternity are in the Archivio di Stato at Florence (Compagnie
Soppresse, indexed under S. Michele Arcangelo). According to the index, it
would appear most unlikely that any of these papers would throw any light on
the date or origin of Spinello's fresco. (10) See L'Arte, 1912, p. 449, and the
Layard MSS. in the National Gallery. For an account of the fresco not long
before its removal from the wall, see Lord Lindsay, Sketches of the History of
Christian Art, II, 1847, pp. 319/20. (11) For the history of the Layard Collection,
see Appendix IV.

See also FLORENTINE SCHOOL, No. 3120

STEFANO DI GIOVANNI, called SASSETTA
1392(?)–1450

Sienese School; usually known as *Sassetta*, an appellation for which there appears to be no contemporary evidence. His father was from Cortona, but he may have been born at Siena in 1392. There is what could hardly be doubted as evidence of his activity in 1423; certainly from 1426. A documented altarpiece of 1430/2 is in the Contini Collection; other authenticated works exist.

4757   THE WHIM OF THE YOUNG S. FRANCIS TO BECOME A SOLDIER (PANEL FROM AN ALTARPIECE)

On the left, the young S. Francis, about to set out for the wars, gives away to a knight poorer than himself the clothes he had prepared for his expedition. On the right, S. Francis is asleep; an angel indicates to him a castle in the sky, bedecked with flags and coats of arms, each one with a red cross on a white ground.

Wood, painted surface, trefoiled top, $34\frac{1}{4} \times 20\frac{5}{8}$ (0·87 × 0·525). The painted surfaces of this and the following pictures are not quite precisely measurable, since the edges have been newly painted over.

The frames of this and the following pictures, although much cut about, restored and regilt, preserve some old parts. The grouping in two twos and a three dates from 1935. The patterning and shapes of the spandrels at the tops may be said certainly to correspond with the original forms; but the four square tops and the three shaped tops are not necessarily round the right pictures, a point commented on below. In No. 4757, as in the others of the series, marks where were the capitals of the colonnettes at the sides are visible on the pictures.

The condition of No. 4757 is in general good; but some of the restorations have changed colour and become obtrusive. There is a *pentimento* in what may be the horse's tail, and the landscape in the centre seems once to have had a higher hill.

The two incidents represented in No. 4757 were closely connected; the date was probably *ca.* 1205, in any case before S. Francis of Assisi (1182–1226) had founded the Franciscan Order. Intending to go to the wars in Apulia, S. Francis had prepared for himself rich clothes to be knighted in, but he gave them away in an access of generosity to a knight poorer than himself. Following upon this, one from God showed him while he slept a fair palace with arms marked with the cross of Christ hanging on the walls, and told him that these all belonged to him and to his soldiers. S. Francis at first understood the dream literally, but soon realized his mistake and renounced his military expedition. The dream indeed symbolizes the army of Franciscan friars in the Church Militant. It was a step in S. Francis' conversion from the world, and was thought to have been granted to him because of his generosity to the poor knight the day before.

This story, like many stories of S. Francis, is told with differences by different writers.[1] The summary above corresponds sufficiently with what Stefano would have been instructed to paint.

For the further commentary, etc., see under No. 4763 below.

4758 S. FRANCIS RENOUNCES HIS EARTHLY FATHER (PANEL FROM AN ALTARPIECE)

Bishop Guido of Assisi covers S. Francis with his pallium. The saint is otherwise naked; he has given back, or thrown back, his clothes to Pietro di Bernardone, the man he no longer recognizes as his father. The father is hardly restrained from attacking his perverse son.

Wood, painted surface, trefoiled top, $34\frac{1}{2} \times 20\frac{3}{4}$ (0·875 × 0·525), approx. (edges restored).

Not free from damage, but in good condition in the important parts.

The incident occurred not very long after those illustrated in No. 4757, and was a further step in S. Francis' conversion from the world. S. Francis had been inspired to give to the church some money belonging to his father. His father appealed to the civil courts, and, when they proved unhelpful, to the Bishop of Assisi; S. Francis tore off his clothes, exclaiming that all that stuff was his father's, and that he no longer recognized any father but God. The Bishop covered the saint with his pallium. The father's violence, stressed in No. 4758, belongs properly to an earlier phase of his struggle with his son.[2]

For the further commentary, etc., see under No. 4763 below.

4759 THE POPE ACCORDS RECOGNITION TO THE FRANCISCAN ORDER (PANEL FROM AN ALTARPIECE)

The Pope, probably Innocent III, blesses S. Francis. A crowned figure is seated among the Cardinals present at the ceremony. Over a door is a coat of arms with crossed keys, and crossed keys form the decoration of the hanging behind the Pope.

Wood, painted surface, trefoiled top, $34\frac{1}{2} \times 20\frac{1}{2}$ (0·875 × 0·52).

The condition is in general good; some of the reds of the cardinals' robes have been restored.

S. Francis, with the eleven disciples he then had, went to Rome ca. 1210; they received Pope Innocent III's blessing, and his authorization to preach. A more formal recognition of the Franciscan Rule was received from Pope Honorius III in 1223.[3] The earlier incident is probably here intended; the later should strictly show a document being handed by the Pope to S. Francis, the earlier can reasonably be illustrated without such a document.

The crowned figure in No. 4759 is mysterious. Stefano may perhaps have been influenced by Ambrogio Lorenzetti's fresco in S. Francesco, Siena, where a crowned figure also occurs. That fresco is often called *S. Louis of Toulouse Receiving the Franciscan Habit from Pope Boniface VIII*; but No. 4759 represents S. Francis and not S. Louis of Toulouse.[4] There may have been some tradition that a king was present at

S. Francis' interviews with Innocent III or Honorius III; but no such tradition appears to be recorded. A possible explanation is as follows. To persuade Innocent III to grant his request, S. Francis recounted to him an allegory of a king, whose children by a poor wife asked for his protection and were willingly granted it, because they were indeed his children.[5] Franciscan legends often changed and expanded as time went on (cf. for instance No. 4761 below); it is not impossible that the allegorical king should have come to have a corporeal existence.

One of the cardinals in No. 4759 is wearing a blue robe instead of the normal scarlet. A blue cardinal's hat occurs in Catena No. 694 of the National Gallery.[6]

For the further commentary, etc., see under No. 4763 below.

4760   THE STIGMATIZATION OF S. FRANCIS (PANEL FROM AN ALTARPIECE)

In the sky is a visionary figure of Christ, with arms extended as if on the Cross, and with six seraph's wings. S. Francis kneels in ecstasy, and the Wounds of Christ are miraculously impressed upon his body. In a recess is a cross, with the letters .I.N.R.I., the Nails and the Crown of Thorns. Brother Leo wonderingly observes the event. The door of a chapel in the background is ornamented with an image of the Virgin and Child.

Wood, painted surface, trefoiled top, $34\frac{1}{2} \times 20\frac{3}{4}$ (0·875 × 0·525).

Good condition. *Pentimenti* in the saint's habit, and in the rock behind him.

The Stigmatization, or Impression on S. Francis' body of the Five Wounds of Christ, occurred in 1224; the scene was Mount Alvernia, or La Verna, not far from Bibbiena, and between the upper valleys of the Arno and the Tiber. It would have been correct, but is often not the case in pictures, for the vision of Christ to be shown nailed to the Cross; here the Cross has been transferred to a makeshift oratory in the foreground. S. Francis was alone at the time of the event, but it became customary in pictures to show Brother Leo as a witness.[7]

For the further commentary, etc., see under No. 4763 below.

4761   S. FRANCIS BEARS WITNESS TO THE CHRISTIAN FAITH BEFORE THE SULTAN (PANEL FROM AN ALTARPIECE)

S. Francis, shown stigmatized, and making the sign of the cross, prepares to walk through the fire. Brother Illuminato and the Sultan's magicians look on with different feelings. The Sultan himself is seated on the left.

Wood, painted surface, trefoiled top, 34 × 21 (0·865 × 0·535), approx. (edges restored).

Considerably damaged. S. Francis' head is well preserved except at the top, and the group of heads on the right is in good condition; those on the left much less good.

The date of this incident is *ca.* 1219, at the time of the siege of Damietta during the 5th Crusade. S. Francis, accompanied by Brother Illuminato, went forward from the crusaders' camp and reached the presence of the Sultan. He was apparently al-Malik al-Kamil, Sultan of Egypt, who reigned from 1218 until 1238. He listened to S. Francis patiently, and sent him and his companion back with a safe-conduct. S. Francis expressed his readiness to go through the fire for his faith, but was not called upon to undergo this test.[8]

For the further commentary, etc., see under No. 4763 below.

4762   THE LEGEND OF THE WOLF OF GUBBIO (PANEL FROM AN ALTARPIECE)

The scene is before the town-gate of Gubbio. The wolf, the remains of whose former victims are shown in the background, stretches out its right paw, which S. Francis takes; they are agreeing that the wolf should give up its habits of rapine, and be fed at the public expense in return. A notary writes down the pact. S. Francis is shown with the Stigmata.

Wood, painted surface, trefoiled top, $34 \times 20\frac{1}{2}$ (0.865×0.52).

Probably the most damaged picture of the seven in the National Gallery.

The notary here shown is not mentioned in the traditional story.[9]

For the further commentary, etc., see under No. 4763 below.

4763   THE FUNERAL OF S. FRANCIS (PANEL FROM AN ALTARPIECE)

The saint is stretched out on the bier; the lady Jacopa kisses his hands, and the doubting knight Jeronimo assures himself of the wound in his side. A bishop, presumably meant for Guido of Assisi, reads the funeral service. The church where the scene is laid is shown with an altarpiece representing the Virgin and Child, SS. Peter and Paul, and in the pinnacles God and the Annunciation.

Wood, painted surface, trefoiled top, $34\frac{3}{4} \times 20\frac{7}{8}$ (0.88×0.53).

The right side of the picture (bishop, acolyte, etc.) is much damaged; the central Franciscan mourner has a damaged face, and another damage crosses his breast and that of the Franciscan on his right. The rest of the picture, although by no means free from damage, is better preserved.

S. Francis died in 1226, in a hut close by the Porziuncula, near Assisi; he was buried in Assisi, in the church of S. Giorgio (now attached to S. Chiara), but his remains were soon after transferred to the church of S. Francesco, built in his honour. The scene in No. 4763 is a combination of the death and the funeral. The bishop is presumably Guido (cf. No. 4758), although he was apparently absent from Assisi at the time. The lady Jacopa was a Roman matron and a supporter of S. Francis, who called her 'Brother Jane'; she was the only woman admitted at the saint's death. Her name is given as *de Septemsoliis*, and she appears to have married a Frangipani; she appears to have been a Franciscan tertiary, and to have died at Assisi. S. Francis had begun a letter to her, summoning her to his death-bed, but she came of her own accord before the letter was completed. The story of the doubting knight is parallel to that of S. Thomas in the Gospels; many stories of S. Francis came to correspond more and more closely with the stories concerning Christ.[10]

Possibly SS. Peter and Paul are shown on the altarpiece of the church in No. 4763 because of S. Francis' particular devotion to those saints.[11]

There can be no reasonable doubt that Nos. 4757/63 are part of the high-altarpiece of S. Francesco, Sansepolcro, which Stefano di Giovanni contracted to paint in 1437, and delivered in 1444. A central portion of that altarpiece (in the Berenson Collection) is indeed identified with certainty.[12] The structure and patterning of the frame there correspond closely with the frames here, which are in essentials old. The provenance of the National Gallery series would be for that reason alone very probable; the style and the subject fit perfectly.

On 5 September, 1437,[13] Stefano signed a contract in Sansepolcro for the high-altarpiece of San Francesco there. It was to be made in height, breadth and form similar to a construction previously intended for the high-altarpiece, and already carpentered and gessoed (but not painted).[14] Stefano was to paint the altarpiece on both sides, the figures and scenes to be settled by the friars. Stress was laid on the painter putting his best work into it. It was to be handed over finished in Siena within 4 years; whereupon Stefano was to go to Sansepolcro, set up the altarpiece there, and make good any damage that might have happened during the journey.[15] The payments were to be in three equal parts, at the beginning, middle and end of the work.

On 5 June, 1444,[16] in Sansepolcro, Stefano and the friars solemnly agreed that the painter had set in place the high-altarpiece complete, and that he had received the full payment, apparently in three lots as laid down in the contract of 1437.

No description of this high-altarpiece in situ is known, and its subject and construction are therefore in some degree uncertain; but the following panels were clearly main parts of it. (1) S. Francis Triumphant[17] in the Berenson Collection, already mentioned as certainly from this altarpiece. (2) Full-length figures of S. John the Baptist and The Blessed Ranieri with a pater noster, also in the Berenson Collection, and framed as wings to No. 1 in the form of a triptych.[18] (3) The seven scenes in the National Gallery. (4) An eighth scene, now at Chantilly.[19] (5) Three large pictures, published by Enzo Carli, and recently acquired by the Louvre; these consist of The Virgin and Child, similar in size and shape to the S. Francis Triumphant, and two full-length saints, similar in size and shape to the two in the Berenson Collection. The form of the frame and the halo patterns leave no doubt that the association of No. 5 is correct; the three pictures and the three in the Berenson Collection are clearly identical with the six recorded by Romagnoli as being from the Sansepolcro altarpiece.[20]

It is reasonable to assume that no more large pictures from this altarpiece remain to be found; if that is so, it clearly was a pentaptych. Carli's proposed reconstruction appears in the main convincing. The front would have had *The Virgin and Child* in the centre, flanked on each side by two full-length saints. *S. Francis Triumphant* would have formed the centre of the back; the eight scenes would have been arranged at the sides. This scheme for the back seems convincing, but the detailed arrangement of the various scenes cannot be fixed with certainty. In Nos. 4758, 4759, 4761 and 4763 the sky at the top is symbolized by gold; in the other four panels the sky is blue. This is one obvious distinction; the other was in the frames (now changed). The frames of Nos. 4757, 4758, 4761 and 4762 had their corners cut at the top; the others were square.[21] Obviously the square frames would have been placed below the others. It seems impossible to arrive at an acceptable arrangement if one admits these two conditions as valid; presumably therefore the conditions have been changed. The frames of the National Gallery panels, but not the one at Chantilly, were detachable; it is legitimate to suppose that the seven National Gallery frames have have been taken off at some time, and put back wrong. In that case, Carli proposes to arrange the scenes as follows: top row, left to right, Nos. 4758, 4759, 4761, 4763; bottom row, left to right, Nos. 4757, Chantilly, 4762 and 4760.[22] It is to be noted that in this arrangement all the blue skies are in the lower row, and all the gold skies in the upper row; the chronological arrangement of the scenes is, further, not as clear as one would wish, but the order seems to be as good as the conditions allow.

The altarpiece certainly included a predella; Pope-Hennessy identified one of the predella panels with a picture at Berlin, and other scenes from the legend of the B. Ranieri are recorded to have existed, clearly also predella panels.[23] The altarpiece may also have included pinnacles.[24]

PROVENANCE: The reasons for accepting Nos. 4757/63 as parts of the high-altarpiece of S. Francesco, Sansepolcro, are given above. A reconstruction of the church was undertaken in 1752, and it was re-opened for the cult in 1760; the altarpiece is stated to have remained until 1810 in the friary (which was suppressed in point of fact in the year 1808), and then to have been bought by Cavalier Sergiuliani of Arezzo.[25] The Sigg. Sergiuliani presented what may have been the whole altarpiece to the Canonico (Giulio Anastasio?) Angelucci of Arezzo, who in turn gave some parts at least to his brother, Priore Pietro Antonio Angelucci of Montecontieri, near Asciano, who still owned them *ca.* 1823.[26]. It is probable that the Canonico Angelucci's gift to his brother did not include Nos. 4757/63 or the Chantilly panel: what were obviously these eight pictures are stated to have been sold in 1819 or later by the Abate Angelucci of Arezzo to the Florentine dealer, Carlo del Chiaro.[27] A few years before 1839, they are stated to have passed into the collection of Count Anatole Demidoff at Florence.[28] Presumably he did not keep them long, since in 1840 Frédéric Reiset bought the panel now at Chantilly.[29] Six of the National Gallery panels (i.e., not No. 4762) are stated to have been acquired from a church in Corsica by Emmanuel Chalandon of Lyons, who lent them to the Exposition Rétrospective at Lyons in 1877.[30] Nos. 4758 and 4761 were lent by Chalandon to the Exhibition at Siena in 1904, Catalogue p. 335, Nos. 10108 and 10107. The six Chalandon pictures were purchased by Duveen from Georges Chalandon in 1925.[31] No. 4762 passed by inheritance from the Comte de Martel at Cour-Cheverny to the Comtesse de Féligonde,[32] from whom Duveen bought it in

1926. All seven were bought in 1927 by Clarence Mackay of Long Island (New York). Purchased from him through Duveen, Grant-in-Aid and Temple-West Funds, with contributions from the National Art-Collections Fund, Benjamin Guinness and Lord Bearsted, 1934. Exhibited at the National Gallery, N.A.C.F. Exhibition, 1945/6 (No. 34).

REPRODUCTIONS: *Illustrations, Italian Schools*, 1937, pp. 320–322; *Plates, Earlier Italian Schools*, 1953, Vol. II, pp. 401–407 (without the frames). Reproduced as previously framed, and in an earlier state, in *The Burlington Magazine*, Vol. III (1903/4), pp. 9, 12, 15, 18, 20, 24, 27.

REFERENCES: (1) The modern biography of S. Francis that has been consulted as a check is that by Johannes Joergensen, French edition, 1909. The exact sources used for Stefano's pictures, Nos. 4757/63, would be difficult to trace; nor is it worth while going into the matter very deeply—that would be interesting in a study of Franciscan legends in art, but is perhaps not of prime importance for these isolated examples. It may nevertheless be noted that the story of No. 4757 as painted by Stefano corresponds closely with S. Bonaventure's *Life of S. Francis*, Italian edition by Mons. Leopoldo Amoni, 1888, pp. 18/9, and with the *Legenda Trium Sociorum*, ed. PP. Marcellino da Civezza and Teofilo Domenichelli, 1899, Chapter II; less well with the *Legenda Secunda* of Thomas de Celano, Part I, Chapter II, and still less well with that writer's *Legenda Prima*, Part I, Chapter II, edition of P. Eduardus Alenconiensis, 1906. These sourcebooks are of considerably earlier date than Stefano's picture. Benozzo's fresco of 1452 in S. Francesco, Montefalco, is nearer in time, and although not quite identical, is clearly based on similar Franciscan traditions; reproduced by Van Marle, *Development of the Italian Schools of Painting*, Vol. XI, Fig. 85. The inscription at the base of Benozzo's fresco is: QVAL.B.F. DEDIT . VESTIMENTVM . SV̄V . CVIDĀ . PAVPI . N(sic)ILITI . NOCTE . VERO . SEQVĒTI . OSTĒDIT . SIBI . X̄PS . MĀGNV̄ . PALATIV̄. ARMIS . MILITARIBVS . CVMCRVCIBVS . INSIGNITVM. (2) The story occurs with variants in Thomas de Celano, *Legenda Prima*, Part I, Chapter VI; *Legenda Secunda*, Part I, Chapter VII; S. Bonaventure's *Life*, pp. pp. 27/8; *Legenda Trium Sociorum*, Chapter VI. For the editions referred to, see note 1. (3) Cf. Thomas de Celano's *Legenda Prima*, Part I, Chapter XIII, etc. (4) Ambrogio Lorenzetti's fresco is reproduced by Van Marle, *op. cit.*, Vol. II, Fig. 256. The reason for the customary identification of the subject seems to be the presence of the king, supposed to be Charles II of Anjou, the father of S. Louis of Toulouse; the argument would apply equally to No. 4759, and would here clearly be false. It may be that Stefano was influenced in No. 4759 by Ambrogio Lorenzetti's fresco; but according to the customary view, Stefano, in order to establish the design for his *Recognition of the Franciscan Order*, would have looked at a fresco of another subject, and then not realized that it was another subject. Yet even without dragging Stefano into the matter, one can see that Ambrogio Lorenzetti's fresco is unlikely to represent *S. Louis of Toulouse Receiving the Franciscan Habit from Boniface VIII*; S. Louis of Toulouse, for instance, did not receive the Franciscan habit from the Pope. For pictures undoubtedly representing S. Louis' retirement from the world, see the predella of Simone Martini's picture at Naples, reproduced by W. Rolfs, *Geschichte der Malerei Neapels*, 1910, Plate 19, and by E. Cecchi, *Trecentisti Senesi*, 1948, Plate 84. (5) *Legenda Trium Sociorum*, Chapter XIII, pp. 84/5 of the edition cited in note 1; the story can also be read in the Bollandists, 4 October, p. 590. (6) This may be based on the fact that cardinals wear violet for mourning or penitence; see X. Barbier de Montault, *Le Costume et Les Usages Ecclésiastiques*, Vol. I, n.d., p. 58. A cardinal in blue with a red hat is seen to the left in one of the S. Silvester frescoes in S. Croce, Florence (Sirèn, *Giotto and some of his Followers*, 1917, II, Plate 175). For further information about the apparently difficult subject of cardinals not in scarlet, see Cecil Gould's catalogue, *The Sixteenth-Century Venetian School*, 1959, entry for Catena No. 694, and notes by Stella M. Pearce in the Gallery archives. (7) A detailed account of the Stigmatization may be found in the *Fioretti di San Francesco*; there are many others. (8) There are accounts of this incident in S. Bonaventure's *Life* (pp. 110/1 of the edition cited in note 1), and in No. XXIII of the *Fioretti*. The details of S. Francis' journey to the Holy Land are meagre and unsure; according to François Van Ortroy (*Analecta Bollandiana*, 1912, pp. 451 ff.), S. Francis would have set out in 1219, in June or soon after, and would have been back in Italy by the end of 1220 or the beginning of 1221. (9) The story is No. XX of the *Fioretti*. (10) Much of this is from the *Fioretti* (*Fourth Consideration of the Holy Stigmas*); cf. also S. Bonaventure's *Life*, ed. cit. in note 1, p. 163, etc. A good deal about the Lady Jacopa can be found in Sabatier's edition of the *Speculum Perfectionis*, 1898, pp. 273 ff. (11) Cf. S. Bonaventure's *Life*, ed. cit. in note 1, p. 105. It may be repeated from note 1 that notes 1–11 do not claim to give the detailed justification for every statement made concerning the Franciscan legend. (12) The reference is to the *S. Francis Triumphant*, which with two flanking saints is reproduced by John Pope-Hennessy, *Sassetta*, 1939, Plate XXII. The frame of this *S. Francis* used, according to Rosini, *Storia della Pittura Italiana*, Vol. I of the Plates, 1839, Plate L, to carry the following inscription: CRISTOFORVS FRANCISCI FEI E ANDREAS IOHANNIS TANIS OPERARIVS A MCCCCXXXXIIII. The date is correct for the Sansepolcro high-altarpiece, and the names of the clerks of works correspond with those mentioned in the documents for that picture (cf. Appendix II and Borghesi e Banchi, *Nuovi Documenti per la Storia dell'Arte Senese*, 1898, pp. 119 and 142). It is true that in 1444 Paltonus Iohannis Tani is stated to be acting in lieu of Andreas; but that is no objection. In a document of 1430, what are presumably the same names have been transcribed as Christoforo Francisci Tofani and Sandro Johannis Tani or Tucci; Milanesi in *Il Buonarroti*, Series III, Vol. II, No. III, 1885, p. 83 (reprinted in his *Nuovi Documenti per la Storia dell'Arte Toscana*, 1901, pp. 81/2). (13) This contract is here printed as Appendix II, by kind permission of Monsignor Angelo Mercati; it need not be doubted that this is the document seen in S. Francesco at Siena by Della Valle, *Lettere Sanesi*, III, 1786, p. 44. An inferior text is printed by Borghesi e Banchi, *Nuovi Documenti per la Storia dell'Arte Senese*, 1898, pp. 119 f.; also by Pope-Hennessy, *Sassetta*, 1939, p. 127. Neither of these two documents, nor the document of 1444 about to be referred to, contain Stefano's signature; but it would be most unreasonable to doubt that Stefano did in fact sign other copies of the 1437 and 1444 documents, on the dates mentioned. (14) This was clearly the work of carpentry ordered from Bartolommeo di Giovannino d'Angelo of Sansepolcro on 2 August, 1426. Bartolommeo contracted to make the structure of the high-altarpiece for S. Francesco, Sansepolcro, suitably for painting on both sides, with flowers and ornaments similar to the high-altarpiece of the Badia at Sansepolcro. See Milanesi in *Il Buonarroti*, Series III, Vol. II, No. III, 1885, p. 82 (No. 96); reprinted in his *Nuovi Documenti per la Storia dell'Arte Toscana*, 1901, p. 80. On p. 83 (No. 99) (pp. 81/2 of the reprint), Milanesi gives a document of 9 October, 1430, according to which Antonio di Giovanni d'Anghiari, a painter living at Sansepolcro, agreed to paint the front side of this high-altarpiece, which was then in position; the figures and scenes were to be chosen by the friars, and the work was to be done in $3\frac{1}{2}$ years. It is not known why Antonio did not execute the painting. A reason why Bartolommeo's woodwork was not used by Stefano is suggested in the next note. (15) It is clear that Stefano was going to do the work in Siena; presumably it was not worth while transporting the woodwork already existing from Sansepolcro to Siena, so Stefano started afresh. (16) Borghesi e Banchi, *op. cit.*, pp. 142 ff.; also printed by Pope-Hennessy, *op. cit.*, pp. 127/9. (17) The attitude of S. Francis is perhaps derived from some such source as S. Bonaventure's *Life, ed. cit.* in note 1, pp. 54 or 116. (18) Reproduced by Pope-Hennessy, *op. cit.*, Plate XXII, flanking the *S. Francis*. The three pictures fit together reasonably as a triptych, but it will be noted presently that this seems clearly to be a wrong reconstruction. The framing is in essentials old, but it is presumed that the base of the frame, binding the three pictures together, is not old; indeed, the central part of the base, under the *S. Francis*, is recorded to have borne an inscription (cf. note 12), but apparently has none now. Berenson in *The Burlington Magazine*, Vol. III (1903/4), p. 172, first suggested the Blessed Ranieri's name; apart from any other arguments, the subjects of the predella of the altarpiece, referred to in note 23, may be said to make the identification certain. The B. Ranieri was buried beneath the high altar of S. Francesco at Sansepolcro, and was the object of a local cult. See the Bollandists, Nov. 1, pp. 390 ff., or Lodovico Jacobilli, *Vite de' Santi e Beati dell'Umbria*, III, 1661, pp. 3/4. He joined the Franciscan community as a lay-brother and died in 1304; he was formally beatified by Pius VII in 1802. According to the writers quoted, his mother was a Rasini of Sansepolcro, and his father was a Mariani of Arezzo. Lorenzo Coleschi, however, *Storia della Città di Sansepolcro*, 1886, p. 191, says that according to his authorities, whom he cites, his father was a Rasini or Bambini, his mother a Strofilati, or *vice versa*. Léon Kern in his scholarly essay in the *Revue d'Histoire Franciscaine*, 1930, pp. 233 ff., rejects much of this, and various other stories, as legend. (19) Associated by Langton Douglas in *The Burlington Magazine*, Vol. I (1903), p. 314 (all eight scenes associated by Berenson, *ib.*, Vol. III (1903/4), pp. 3 ff. and 171 ff.). Pope-Hennessy, *op. cit.*, Plate XXI. The subject is *The Meeting of S. Francis with Three Girls*, one of whom said to him: *Welcome, Lady Poverty*. The story is told in Thomas de Celano, *Legenda Secunda*, Part II, Chapter LX, and in S. Bonaventure's *Life*, p. 86 (*edd. cit.* in note 1), but the subject is considerably developed in the Chantilly picture. (20) The compiler is greatly indebted to Enzo Carli for discussing with him the arrangement of the altarpiece. Carli published the pictures in *The Burlington Magazine*, Vol. XCIII (1951), pp. 145 ff., and the student is referred to his article for further details. For the reference to Romagnoli, see note 26. (21) See the reproductions in *The Burlington Magazine*, Vol. III (1903/4), pp. 9, 12, 15, 18, 20, 24, 27, 30. (22) Pope-Hennessy, *op. cit.*, pp. 107 ff., inverts the positions of the picture at Chantilly and No. 4760. M. Henri Malo, Keeper of the Musee Conde at Chantilly, kindly confirmed that the frame there is fixed and cannot have been changed. (23) Pope-Hennessy, *op. cit.*, p. 106. Reproduced in the Berlin Illustrations, *Die Italienischen Meister 13. bis. 15. Jhrht.*, 1930, p. 114. Obviously the same picture was, with a pendant (?), in Cardinal Fesch's Collection in France, then (from 1815) at Rome, as School of Angelico. In the inventory of Cardinal Fesch's effects, begun on 5 September, 1839 (Rome, Archivio di Stato, Archivo dei Notari Capitolini, Ufficio 11, Notaio Augusto Appollonj, Vol. 611; copy in Rome, Archivio Storico Capitolino, Notaio Augusto Appollonj, 1839, No. 141), the following entries for the pictures were made on 7 November, 1839:'12853. Quadro in tavola alto piede uno, e un terzo, largo piede uno, e undici dodicesimi rappresentante un S. Francescano che apparisce in Visione ad un Cardinale della maniera del Beato Angelico Scudi Quaranta.' '12858. Quadro in tavola alto piede uno, e un terzo, largo piede uno, e cinque sesti rappresentante un Coro di Francescani della maniera del Beato Gio: Angelico molto guasto dal restauro Scudi Quaranta.' The Berlin picture, with the Franciscan Saint become S. Francis, was in the Fesch Sale Catalogue of 1841, No. 1329, with wrong size; in George's Catalogue, Part IV, 1845, No. 868, with full description. What was called the pendant was No. 1334 of the 1841 Catalogue, and No. 869 of the 1845 Catalogue, where the description is as follows: 'Suite du sujet précédent. Saint François, ayant rassemblé sa communauté dans l'église de son couvent, ordonne des prières pour le repos de l'âme du cardinal,' wood, same size to a fraction as the other. Both these pictures were bought by the 'Principe di Canino,' i.e. the son of Lucien Bonaparte, Charles-Lucien-Jules-Laurent; they appeared in his sale at Christie's, 12 March, 1853 (lots 36, 37). The identity of the Berlin picture with one of the predella panels of Stefano's altarpiece is established by Léon Kern, *Le Bienheureux Rainier de Borgo San Sepolcro*, in the *Revue d'Histoire Franciscaine*, 1930, p. 282, quoting Giovanni Antonio Castiglione, *Gli Honori de gli antichi Disciplinati*, 1622, pp. 44 ff.; the reference kindly supplied by Dr. Kaftal and John Pope-Hennessy. See Kaftal, *Iconography of the Saints in Tuscan Painting*, 1952, col. 885. The story, which is not findable in the normal sources concerning the B. Ranieri, was that the people of Sansepolcro decided to embalm the body of the saint when he died in 1304; four of the citizens went to Rome to ask for a special balm from a cardinal, who was ill but received them willingly, having the night before had a vision concerning their arrival. The cardinal gave the balm, and later went to Sansepolcro to pay homage to the B. Ranieri. It is not clear how the story of the missing pendant (?) fitted in. For two other scenes, clearly once part of this predella, see Kern, *loc. cit.*, pp. 281/2; the two scenes described are, (*a*) the miser of Citerna, whose death and damnation (with demons in animal shape) the B. Ranieri prophesied; (*b*) the delivery of 90 paupers from the prisons of Florence by the intervention of the B. Ranieri. (**24**) It has been suggested that a picture of *Christ on the Cross with S. Francis*, size 0·808 × 0·405, belonging to Freiherr von Preuschen, Stuttgart, and exhibited at Stuttgart, 1950 (No. 94), may have been a pinnacle of the present altarpiece. See further Kurt Bauch in the *Festschrift zum 60. Geburtstag von C. G. Heise*, 1950, pp. 103 ff., with reproduction. H. D. Gronau (*The Burlington Magazine*, Vol. XCII, 1950, p. 322, with reproduction in a different frame) objects that the tooling of the haloes in the Stuttgart picture is too unlike those of the National Gallery and Chantilly panels. The difference is certainly very great for the halo of Christ, but apparently much less for that of S. Francis. The haloes of the Berenson triptych should perhaps also be considered in this connection, and the compiler feels that the association of the Stuttgart panel is neither proved nor disproved. It is accepted by Carli, *Sassetta e il Maestro dell'Osservanza*, 1957, p. 56. (**25**) The first part of this is from Lorenzo Coleschi, *Storia della Città di Sansepolcro*, 1886, p. 169; he says nothing about the altarpiece. The second point is from Romagnoli's MS. in the Biblioteca Comunale at Siena, *Biografia Cronologica de' Bellartisti Senesi*, Vol. IV, p. 428, as follows: ' questa tavola esprime la natività di G.C. e fu situata sino al 1810 nel coretto interno del convento: a quell'epoca il P. Sereni (?) l'ebbe e unitamente agli altri religiosi decisero di venderla al Cav.ʳ Sergiuliani di Arezzo.' Romagnoli on later information corrected what he here says about the subject; see the next note. (**26**) This is based on a passage in Romagnoli's MSS., Vol. IV, p. 432; cf. the quotation in Pope-Hennessy, *op. cit.*, pp. 129/30, note 4. No christian names are given for the Canonico Angelucci of Arezzo; but an Abate Giulio Anastasio Angelucci published books on Arezzo in 1816 and 1819, and seems to be the right man. What Romagnoli in this passage stated about the subjects of the pictures is in correction of what he had previously written (see the previous note) and is from a letter of 1823 from the Canonico Angelucci. It is clear that the parts described in the present passage are the *S. Francis Triumphant* and two full-length saints in the Berenson Collection, and the *Virgin and Child* and two full-length saints published by Enzo Carli. (**27**) Rosini, *Storia della Pittura Italiana*, II, 1840, pp. 165 and 193/4, and Vol. I of the Plates, 1839, Plate XXV (the Chantilly picture); the other seven pictures are mentioned as representing scenes of S. Francis, but are not illustrated or described. The central panel of the Berenson portion is mentioned by Romagnoli as by Stefano di Giovanni; it is still under this attribution that it appears in Rosini, *op. cit.*, III, 1841, p. 20, and Vol. I of the Plates, 1839, Plate L. The 8 scenes, however, are not identifiable in Romagnoli's description, and are not called Stefano by Rosini; he says that the Abate Angelucci considered them Piero della Francescas, and he himself suggested Agnolo Gaddi. It seems therefore unlikely that the 8 scenes were with the Berenson portion at Montecontieri; it is more likely that the Abate Angelucci, perhaps not realizing that they were connected, kept them for himself. (**28**) Rosini, as in the previous note, Vol. II, p. 194. In 1840 Anatole Demidoff was made Principe di San Donato by the Grand Duke of Tuscany (Cesare da Prato, *Firenze ai Demidoff*, 1886, p. 67). No other record of the pictures in the Demidoff Collection has yet been found; but it is true that some del Chiaro pictures were bought by Prince Demidoff (Vasari, ed. Milanesi, Vol. II, p. 625, note 5). (**29**) From the catalogue of the Frédéric Reiset Sale, Paris, 28 April, 1879 (lot 35); the sale in point of fact did not take place by auction, because the Duc d'Aumale bought the Reiset Collection *en bloc*. (30) Apparently as Fra Angelico; the pictures are mentioned in the *Gazette des Beaux-Arts*, 1877, ii, p. 265. One of the frames still retains a fragmentary label of the Exposition Rétrospective at Lyons (date missing). For the christian name of the owner, and the provenance, see J.-B. Giraud's Memorial Volume on the Lyons Exhibition of 1877, 1878, p. 5. The provenance from Corsica, if true, is curious. One cannot help remembering that the Berlin picture, part of the predella, had belonged to Cardinal Fesch; and that a large number of Cardinal Fesch's pictures passed by bequest to the town of Ajaccio and to other places in Corsica. But no record of the Chalandon pictures was found in the inventory of the effects of Cardinal Fesch at Rome, begun on 5 September, 1839 (Rome, Archivio di Stato, Archivio dei Notari Capitolini, Ufficio 11, Notaio Augusto Apollonj, Vol. 611; copy in Rome, Archivio Storico Capitolino, Notaio Augusto Appollonj, 1839, No. 141). (31) Henceforward, much of the provenance is from a letter from Duveen's, 12 December, 1934, in the Gallery archives. (32) Presumably Odette de Martel, the wife of Comte Charles de Féligonde (*Bottin Mondain* for 1928).

Francesco TACCONI
active 1458–1500

A Cremonese; he was in Venice *ca.* 1489/91. A. Puerari, *Boccaccino*, 1957, reproduces on Fig. 5 one of his organ shutters for S. Mark's, Venice, and on pp. 29 ff. suggests some attributions to him.

286   THE VIRGIN AND CHILD

Signed: .OP.FRANCISI. / .TACHONI.1489. / .OCTV.

Lime,[1] painted surface, $39\frac{1}{4} \times 20\frac{3}{4}$ ($1\cdot00 \times 0\cdot53$); painted up to the edge at the top.
Good condition.

The design reappears in several versions at half-length, some with signatures of Giovanni Bellini, and is nearly related to the latter painter's No. 280 in this Gallery; in the entry for that picture the matter is more fully discussed.

PROVENANCE: Stated to be from the Savorgnan Collection, Venice;[2] by 1824 it belonged to Baron Francesco Galvagna, Venice;[3] purchased with the rest of the Galvagna Collection, 1855.

REPRODUCTION: *Illustrations, Italian Schools*, 1937, p. 344. *Plates, Earlier Italian Schools*, 1953, Vol. II, p. 408.

REFERENCES: (1) Letter from B. J. Rendle, of the Forest Products Research Laboratory, in the Gallery archives. (2) The Savorgnan provenance is recorded in the National Gallery Catalogue, 1856, presumably on information supplied to Eastlake. It should be noted that the Galvagna Collection was housed in the Palazzo Savorgnan; according to Gianjacopo Fontana, *Cento Palazzi . . . di Venezia*, 1865, p. 316, Galvagna bought the Palace in 1826. (3) See Vidoni, *La Pittura Cremonese*, 1824, p. 124. Mentioned in the Galvagna Collection by Giulio Lecomte, *Venezia*, 1844, p. 276 and by Gianjacopo Fontana, *Manuale ad Uso del Forestiere in Venezia*, 1847, p. 238.

Cosimo TURA
not long before 1431–1495

Cosimo Tura, also known as Cosmè, was the first important Ferrarese painter. He is described as an infant in a document of 1431, so he was presumably born not long before. He is recorded as active at Ferrara from 1451. Much of his work was for the Este court, but almost all of this has been lost. Of his surviving pictures, two organ shutters in the Cathedral Museum at Ferrara are documented and dated 1469; a picture of 1484 at Modena is also documented.

Tura appears to have been influenced chiefly by the Squarcionesques, in particular by the young Mantegna. He could also have seen works by Piero della Francesca and Rogier van der Weyden, and appears to have been somewhat affected by their styles.

772 THE VIRGIN AND CHILD ENTHRONED (CENTRAL PANEL FROM AN ALTARPIECE)

The Virgin is holding the sleeping Child, perhaps about to wake him. Six angels. The throne is ornamented with two tablets containing some of the words of the Ten Commandments in Hebrew, and (above) with the symbols of the Four Evangelists. On the organ case is the remnant of an inscription...ER / ..LLA / ...GENS(?) / ...T.A.. / ..R(?) TVM.. / ...DDE..DI.. / ...M...SA / ...T.. / ...(S?)... (See below).

Wood, painted surface, rounded top, $94\frac{1}{4} \times 40$ ($2 \cdot 39 \times 1 \cdot 02$). Cleaned in 1951/2. In general, in very good condition, though there are some losses, especially in the lower part. Painted up to the edges at the sides and bottom, but apparently not cut. Small *pentimenti* in the outlines.

The association of the Old and New Testaments on the throne has an obvious symbolic meaning.

No. 772 formed part of an altarpiece, recorded to have been on an altar near the chapel of S. Maurelio in S. Giorgio fuori, Ferrara, which was a monastery belonging to the Congregation of Monte Oliveto.[1]

Baruffaldi gives an account of the S. Giorgio altarpiece in its original form; he says there were eight compartments, but describes only six[2] and some scenes in the predella. Various parts, identifiable as being from this altarpiece, have survived. They are No. 772; the right-hand panel, in the Colonna Gallery, Rome;[3] the head of S. George at San Diego, California, a fragment from the left-hand panel, which according to Baruffaldi represented SS. Peter and George with a kneeling monk;[4] and a *Pietà* in the Louvre, which was the uppermost compartment.[5] Figures apparently representing SS. Benedict and Bernard were most probably fitted in above the side-panels (the Colonna picture is considerably less tall than No. 772), and below the *Pietà*; these are now missing.[6] The predella is stated by Baruffaldi to have shown scenes from the lives of SS. Benedict and Bernard. Longhi[7] thinks that the central panels of the predella were three *tondi* now in America (Metropolitan, Gardner and Fogg Art Museums) representing the *Flight into Egypt*, the

Circumcision, and the *Adoration of the Kings*; there is no record that it was actually so, and such *tondi* would be of peculiar form for predella panels. Longhi's chief argument is that one of the *tondi* contains a tablet showing Moses, similar to the tablets with the Ten Commandments in No. 772; the similarity may indicate that the two panels are from the same altarpiece, but may merely symbolize that the tablets are in each case Mosaic.

The altar where No. 772, etc., can be accepted as having hung is stated to have belonged to the Roverella family,[8] and it is not to be doubted that the altarpiece was connected with that family. Baruffaldi records that he saw on the case or the base of the organ in No. 772 an inscription, of which the following words were legible: *Surge Puer Roverella*, and of which various letters are now visible since the cleaning of 1951/2. He later found that this is a quotation from *Lodouici Bigi Pictorii Ferrariensis poetae Tu/multuariorū carminū* Lib. III, 1492, where the text is as follows:

Imago uirginis excitātis filiū.
Surge puer. rouorella fores gens pultat. apertum
Redde aditum. pulsa lex ait: intus eris.[9]

The (missing) monk on the left wing of the altarpiece is indeed described by Baruffaldi as knocking at something; which may be assumed to indicate that some member of the Roverella family had died, and was demanding entrance into Paradise, though it may be added that the inscription does not seem certainly to limit itself to one member of the family. The problem is to guess which Roverella he was, and whether the kneeling monk on the extant right panel was also certainly a Roverella. Baruffaldi thought that the figure now missing was Lorenzo Roverella, Bishop of Ferrara from 1460, died 1474; Baruffaldi admitted that he was not represented as a Bishop, but said that he closely resembled Lorenzo as shown on his tomb of 1476, still in S. Giorgio at Ferrara.[10] A strong claimant to be one of the two kneeling figures is Lorenzo's brother, Niccolò, died 1480, general of the Olivetan congregation; he was already prior of S. Giorgio in 1479, when the church after restoration was re-dedicated to SS. George, Maurelius and Lawrence.[11] Another brother, Bartolomeo, died 1476, had been a cardinal since 1461, and seems even less likely than Bishop Lorenzo.[12] Niccolò is thus highly probable for one of the donors; the other, according to the inscription, should also be a Roverella, but it is not possible to identify him with much probability.

These historical facts suggest for No. 772, etc., a date either before Niccolò's death in 1480, or (if it is he who is demanding entrance into Paradise) not very long after.

PROVENANCE: The altarpiece, of which, as explained above, No. 772 must be a part, was in S. Giorgio, Ferrara. It suffered damage, apparently chiefly in the left wing, during the siege of Ferrara in 1709;[13] it was then dismembered, and various parts were distributed in various places in the monastery. No. 772 is stated to have been in the Filippo Zafferini Collection, which was at one time in Ferrara, but in 1819 apparently in Brescia.[14] No. 772 was later in the Federico Frizzoni Collection at Bergamo; Eastlake saw it there in 1855,[15] and then or soon after obtained it in exchange for a Cariani.[16] Purchased from Lady Eastlake, at the price Sir Charles Eastlake was calculated to have paid for it, 1867.

REPRODUCTION: *Illustrations, Italian Schools*, 1937, p. 360. After cleaning in *Plates, Earlier Italian Schools*, 1953, Vol. II, p. 409.

REFERENCES: (1) Girolamo Baruffaldi, *Vita di Cosimo Tura* (of *ca.* 1706), publ. with notes by Giuseppe Petrucci, 1836, pp. 17 f. The same, *Vite de' Pittori e Scultori Ferraresi* (written after the dismemberment of the altarpiece in 1709), publ. with notes by Giuseppe Boschini, I, 1844, pp. 77 ff. The same, additions to Carlo Brisighella, *Descrizione delle Pitture etc. di Ferrara*, Bologna, Biblioteca dell'Archiginnasio, MS. B 175. The identity of No. 772 is established by the inscription, which is commented on presently. Further, the three figures on a side panel in the Colonna Gallery, about to be mentioned in the text, correspond with Baruffaldi's description, and details of the architecture in the Colonna picture correspond very closely indeed with those on No. 772. It is true that, in one redaction, Baruffaldi refers to eight angels instead of the six that are on No. 772, but the rest of Baruffaldi's description of the central panel corresponds well with No. 772. The location of the altarpiece is also indicated by Marc' antonio Guarini, *Compendio Historico dell'Origine* etc. *di Ferrara*, 1621, p. 394. Agostino Superbi, *Apparato de gli Hvomini Illustri della Città di Ferrara*, 1620, p. 122, speaks of a Tura, obviously this one, near a chapel later dedicated to S. Francesca Romana, which was indeed near the chapel of S. Maurelio. The altarpiece of the chapel of S. Maurelio itself was also by Tura, but was a different picture. (For the dates of Baruffaldi's MSS., see *Lettera di Giampietro Cavazzoni Zanotti da premettersi alle Vite Inedite .. di Girolamo Baruffaldi Seniore*, 1834, pp. 20 ff., C. Laderchi, *La Pittura Ferrarese*, 1856, pp. 4 ff. and C. Padovani, *La Critica d'Arte e la Pittura Ferrarese*, 1954 (1955), pp. 104 ff. See further Roberto Longhi, *Officina Ferrarese*, 1934, pp. 36 ff. (2) As already noted, Baruffaldi in one redaction mentions eight angels in No. 772, instead of the six that are there. (3) Venturi, *Storia dell'Arte Italiana*, Vol. VII, Part III, Fig. 402. (4) The identification appears to be perfectly satisfactory; cf. Longhi, *Ampliamenti nell'Officina Ferrarese*, 1940, pp. 3 f. and Plate I; San Diego, *Catalogue of European Paintings*, 1947, p. 39 (reproduced). This fragment is oval, but has been enlarged to form a rectangle. (5) Venturi, *Storia dell'Arte Italiana*, Vol. VII, Part III, Fig. 405. Baruffaldi does not give enough description to prove the identity of the Louvre picture, but it would seem very unreasonable to doubt it. There is, nevertheless, some confusion about its provenance. C. Cittadella, *Catalogo Istorico de' Pittori e Scultori Ferraresi*, I, 1782, p. 51, says that such a picture had been in S. Giorgio; in Vol. IV, 1783, p. 308, he mentions a *Pietà* in the Zafferini Collection. Since what is presumably the Louvre *Pietà* is stated to have been later in the Zafferini collection (reference as in note 14), both mentions by Cittadella presumably refer to the Louvre picture. Antonio Frizzi, however, *Guida del Forestiere per la Città di Ferrara*, 1787, p. 135, mentions what is presumably the Louvre picture as still in S. Giorgio; presumably Frizzi was working on out-of-date information. The Louvre picture was at Baslini's, Milan, in April and August, 1857, and by May, 1858, in the Campana Collection, Rome (Mündler's Diary: Eastlake's note-book). (6) Petrucci, in his notes to Baruffaldi, 1836, pp. 36/7, says all that is known of their fate. (7) Longhi, *Officina Ferrarese*, 1934, pp. 37 ff. and Plates 44/5. Sergio Ortolani, *Cosmè Tura Francesco del Cossa Ercole de' Roberti*, 1941, p. 56, does not accept Longhi's suggestion, and E. Ruhmer, *Tura*, 1958, p. 177, doubts it. Salmi, *Cosmè Tura*, 1957, pp. 31 ff., argues in favour of it, and gives a reconstruction of the altarpiece only slightly different from Longhi's. (8) See Baruffaldi; it is also stated rather confusedly by G. A. Scalabrini, *Memorie Istoriche delle Chiese di Ferrara*, 1773, *Borghi*, pp. 25 and 29. (9) It is on the sheet marked f iiii, r; the author was born in 1454. In the British Museum copy of the book, there is a note in old writing: *Questi duoi versi sono in una Tauola d'Altare in S. Giorgio dipinta da Cosmo Tura detto Cosmè Pittore Ferrarese*. The second line refers to *Matthew* vii, 7, or *Luke* xi, 9, *pulsate, et aperietur vobis*. The remnant of this inscription, uncovered by cleaning in 1952, has been given above; published with reproduction by the compiler in *The Burlington Magazine*, June 1952, p. 168. On a Tura at Venice of the Virgin and sleeping Child (in an attitude not dissimilar to No. 772), there is the following inscription: .SVIGLIA EL TVO FIGLIO DOLCE MADRE PIA / PER FAR IN FIN FELIC(E L'ALM)A MIA. (10) He does in fact wear a mitre on his tomb; see L. Planiscig, *Bernardo und Antonio Rossellino*, 1942, Plate 86. (11) Scalabrini, *op. cit.*, 1773, *Borghi*, p. 20. Scalabrini prints the date as 1476, but it was apparently 1479; see Guarini, *op. cit.*, p. 390, and especially Andrea Borsetti, *Svpplemento al Compendio Historico del Signor D. Marc' Antonio Guarini*, etc., 1670, p. 236. Niccolò Roverella was still prior of S. Giorgio at his death in 1480; see B. Zambotti, *Diario Ferrarese*, ed. Pardi (Muratori, *Rerum Italicarum Scriptores*, new ed., Vol. XXIV, Part VII, 1937), p. 77. (12) Information about the Roverella family is to be found in Litta's *Famiglie Celebri d'Italia*, and in Zambotti, as in previous note, p. 7. According to a copy of Caleffini's chronicle in the British Museum, Add. MS. 22324, f. 19r., Cardinal Bartolomeo was the heir of Bishop Lorenzo. It may be mentioned that the kneeling figure in the Colonna panel is under the protection of S. Paul; S. Maurelius, who is also present, was one of the patrons of Ferrara. On the left panel, S. George is the other principal patron of Ferrara; and it seems likely that the missing donor was under the protection of the other saint there, S. Peter. Ruhmer, *op. cit.*, p. 176, says that No. 772 includes the Estensian emblem of fire, seen in his Plates 53/5. It would be by no means strange for this picture to include some Estensian emblems, but the compiler certainly cannot prove that what is shown in No. 772 is one. It is true that A. Venturi in the *Rivista Storica Italiana*, Vol. II, 1885, p. 734, mentions 'el fogo' as one, 'una fiamma con lingue serpentine di fuoco'; this may refer to what can be seen in the Sala delle Imprese and/or the Sala degli Sposi in Palazzo Schifanoia, Ferrara, but what is seen in No. 772 is different. In the *Bibbia di Borso*, so rich in such emblems, there seems to be nothing nearer than a basin with four flames (example reproduced by H. J. Hermann, *Zur Geschichte der Miniaturalmalerei am Hofe der Este in Ferrara*, offprint of 1900, p. 30); Tammaro De Marinis in the *Enciclopedia Italiana*, Vol. VI, pp. 924/5, says that this was an emblem of Ercole d'Este. It is worth noting that something rather similar to what is seen on No. 772 is found at the tops of the four outside pilasters of the tomb of Bishop Roverella (1476) in S. Giorgio at Ferrara (L. Planiscig, *Bernardo and Antonio Rossellino*, 1942, Plate 86); but the compiler is reluctant to believe that these details in No. 772 are meant as a special emblem. (13) Baruffaldi, *op. cit.*, I, 1844, p. 80; Scalabrini, *op. cit.*, *Borghi*, pp. 23/5. (14) Baruffaldi, *op. cit.*, 1836, note by Petrucci, p. 36, referring to the *Indice e Descrizione di una partita di quadri esistenti in Brescia*, 1819. By the kindness of Gian Alberto Dell'Acqua and Cesare Gnudi, a typescript of this catalogue was made for the National Gallery Library, from a copy in the Biblioteca Comunale at Ferrara. There is no mention in it of Zafferini; this is supplied, doubtless on good authority, by Petrucci, *loc. cit.*. No. 1 of the catalogue is doubtless the *Pietà* in the Louvre. No. 2 (the only other Tura) is thus described: 'Rappresenta la Madonna in Seggio Reale col Bambino in braccio, circondata da una architettura greca, e da una Gloria d'Angeli filarmonici.' This seems certainly to be No. 772, although the size is given as: 'Alto piedi 6; largo piedo 9, pollici 6.' It would seem from what Petrucci, *loc. cit.*, says that at the time he wrote (1836) the Zafferini pictures were deposited with the firm of Rosini e Fiorani at Brescia, perhaps for sale. (15) Eastlake's note-book. (16) It is mentioned in the Eastlake Collection by Waagen, *Treasures*, IV, 1857, p. 116. For the Cariani exchange, see Gustavo Frizzoni in the *Archivio Storico Italiano*, 1879, p. 276, or his *Arte Italiana del Rinascimento*, 1891, p. 281; the Cariani picture is reproduced in *L'Arte*, 1910, p. 181.

773 S. JEROME (FRAGMENT)

In the background is seen a kneeling layman (perhaps the donor), accompanied by a monk.

Wood, painted surface, $39\frac{3}{4} \times 22\frac{1}{2}$ ($1 \cdot 01 \times 0 \cdot 57$). Painted up to the edges all round, but apparently not cut at the sides, nor probably very much at the bottom.

The picture is damaged in some places, e.g. in the saint's right foot; but the condition on the whole is good.

Another fragment of this picture, which was clearly once attached (with a small gap) along the top of No. 773 towards the left, is in the Brera at Milan; it shows the figure of Christ in the sky, and this is the object of S. Jerome's gaze in No. 773.[1] The whole would have formed a devotional picture of S. Jerome, probably complete in itself rather than one panel of a polyptych. There is a tradition, for which there appears to be no ancient authority, that it came from the Certosa (S. Cristoforo) at Ferrara.[2] The Order to which the monk in the background of No. 773 belongs has not been identified, but in any case he is not a Carthusian. The layman is said to represent Borso d'Este, which is obviously wrong.[3]

PROVENANCE: Coll. Rizzoni, Ferrara, *ca.* 1783.[4] In 1836 in the Costabili Collection, Ferrara.[5] Bought thence by Sir Charles Eastlake not earlier than 1858.[6] Purchased from Lady Eastlake, at the price Sir Charles Eastlake had paid for it, 1867.

REPRODUCTION: *Illustrations, Italian Schools*, 1937, p. 359. *Plates, Earlier Italian Schools*, 1953, Vol. II, p. 410.

REFERENCES: (1) See G. Bargellesi in the *Cenobio degli Artisti*, 15 May, 1928, pp. 11/2, and his *Notizie di Opere d'Arte Ferrarese*, 1955, pp. 17 ff. In the latter, he reproduces the Brera fragment in connection with the top part of No. 773; this is also done (more exactly) by Salmi, *Cosmè Tura*, 1957, Plate XXVI. E. Ruhmer, *Tura*, 1958, p. 42, deduces from the arrangement of the Brera and National Gallery fragments that the original picture was one and a half times as high and twice as wide as No. 773; the compiler does not follow this. It may be added that, in the Brera fragment, Christ is shown against a ray in the sky; traces of the continuation of this ray are visible in the top left-hand corner of No. 773 (increased in Bargellesi's and Salmi's reproductions). The Brera piece has often wrongly been called a fragment from the *Stigmatization of S. Francis;* Sergio Ortolani, *Cosmè Tura Francesco del Cossa Ercole de' Roberti*, 1941, pp. 60/1, wrongly supposes that it does not join on to No. 773. (2) Baruffaldi, *Vita di Cosimo Tura*, 1836, note by G. Petrucci, p. 37. (3) C. Cittadella, *Catalogo Istorico de' Pittori e Scultori Ferraresi*, IV, 1783, p. 308 (among other wild statements). (4) Cittadella, as in previous note. (5) Petrucci, as in note 2; see also C. Laderchi, *Descrizione della Quadreria Costabili*, I, 1838, No. 13. (6) Eastlake's and Mündler's note-books; in 1858 in both, the picture is still recorded in the Costabili Collection at Ferrara.

905   THE VIRGIN: FRAGMENT OF AN ANNUNCIATION

What appear to be the rays preceding the Dove are visible on the left.

Wood, painted surface, $17\frac{3}{4} \times 13\frac{3}{8}$ ($0 \cdot 45 \times 0 \cdot 34$). Painted up to the edges all round, and clearly cut all round.

Considerably restored in parts, e.g. in the Virgin's features; but the style of Tura, although weakened, is still clearly discernible in the picture.[1]

PROVENANCE: Possibly identical with a picture in the Costabili Collection at Ferrara.[2] Lent by Alexander Barker to the British Institution, 1863 (No. 40), and 1865 (No. 73); possibly to Leeds, 1868;[3] and to the Burlington Fine Arts Club, 1871 (No. 50). Purchased at the Barker Sale, 6 June, 1874 (lot 54).

REPRODUCTION: *Illustrations, Italian Schools*, 1937, p. 361. *Plates, Earlier Italian Schools*, 1953, Vol. II, p. 411.

REFERENCES: **(1)** E. Ruhmer, *Tura*, 1958, pp. 47/8, 84 and 171 (end of note on his Plates 9–12) calls No. 905 a studio piece; but it seems to the compiler clearly a damaged autograph work. (2) C. Laderchi, *Descrizione della Quadreria Costabili*, I, 1838, No. 20. (3) A Leeds, 1868, label is on the back of the frame, but the picture is not listed in the catalogue; perhaps it was asked for, but not exhibited.

3070   AN ALLEGORICAL FIGURE

A female figure is seated, holding a branch of cherries; her dress is unlaced below the waist. Her feet rest on a stone, which crushes some flowers or weeds. The throne on which she is seated is ornamented with six figures of dolphins, a shell and a string of red and white beads. There are two small figures in the background: on the right, a man hammering (?) in a cave; on the left, a rider among rocks.

Wood, painted surface, $45\frac{3}{4} \times 28$ ($1 \cdot 16 \times 0 \cdot 71$). Painted up to the edges all round; obviously somewhat cut at the top, the bottom and the left, and possibly also on the right.

Considerably damaged by flaking.

This picture is stated to be identical with one of *Summer* from a series of the *Four Seasons*, first recorded at the beginning of the eighteenth century in the offices of the Inquisition, attached to S. Domenico at Ferrara.[1] No. 3070 does not obviously represent one of the Seasons; a picture at Berlin, stated on equal authority to be from the same series,[2] could easily represent *Autumn*;[3] the Berlin picture would form a not particularly good pendant to No. 3070. In spite of this uncertainty, it need not be denied that No. 3070 was one of the four pictures, as claimed; the identification of the two that appear to be missing (cf. note 15) might settle the matter.

The series is recorded without provenance in the eighteenth century; but the pictures are unlikely to have been painted for the Inquisition, or for the friary of S. Domenico. A secular provenance seems, indeed, indicated; in the absence of evidence, one of the Este Palaces would appear likely. This matter will be discussed further presently.

The question of what No. 3070 does represent has exercised some critics. The dolphins and the shell ornamenting the throne give the figure a marine appearance; but this may have nothing to do with the subject. Dolphins appear in some of the decorative work carried out for Borso d'Este, e.g. in the Palazzo di Schifanoia at Ferrara; possibly the dolphin was one of Borso's emblems, though it was not one of the usual ones, and if No. 3070 was painted for Borso, the dolphins might thus receive their explanation.[4] A shell is frequently used to ornament a niche, and may be thought in itself not to be significant. It is therefore not necessary that No. 3070 should represent a marine goddess, such as Amphitrite.[5] The unlacing of the dress in the picture might seem to have a lascivious meaning, but appears rather to be merely the fashion of the time.[6] There remain the branch of cherries and the figures in the background. The fruit would be available in late spring or early summer, and if No. 3070 represents one of the Seasons, *Spring* would be less unlikely than *Summer*; the month of *May* would perhaps be more suitable than either. As for the background figures, the figure on the right is so much damaged that it is not clear what he is doing; on the left, some additional figure may have been cut away. The compiler, therefore, can make no use of these for the interpretation.

It has already been suggested that No. 3070 may be part of some decoration carried out for one of the Este Palaces. It is often assumed that it comes from the room at Belfiore known as the Studio of Borso; neither the room nor Belfiore have survived.[7] Cosimo Tura is known to have been working for this room from 1458 until 1463;[8] No. 3070 is acceptable as a work by Tura, and (so far as we know) an early work. The provenance from Belfiore, is however, very uncertain, the evidence concerning what Tura did paint there being apparently very slight.[9] Further, Tura painted pictures for the Studio of Ercole d'Este.[10]

There exists the following group of Ferrarese pictures of comparable character; to judge from the perspective, all of them were intended to be hung rather high. (1) No. 3070, the only one of the group clearly by Tura. (2) Its presumed pendant, the *Autumn* (?) at Berlin, there wrongly ascribed to Cossa, size $1 \cdot 15 \times 0 \cdot 71$.[11] (3) Pannonio's *Ceres* (as *Summer*?), at Budapest, size $1 \cdot 365 \times 0 \cdot 82$.[12] This picture contains the *paraduro*, one of the emblems of Borso d'Este; it was presumably painted for him, but not necessarily for Belfiore. It would accord much better than No. 2 as a pendant to the National Gallery picture; but it is highly probable that the two have been separated at least since the beginning of the eighteenth century.[13] (4) and (5) Two allegorical figures in the Strozzi Collection, sizes $1 \cdot 22 \times 0 \cdot 72$ each.[14] Both of them contain emblems of Borso d'Este (the unicorn under a palm-tree, and the watering-place for doves); their status is therefore similar to No. 3. Although there appears to be no reason why they should have been called *Winter* and *Spring*, it is just conceivable that they were hung with Nos. 1 and 2 in the eighteenth century in the offices of the Inquisition at Ferrara.[15] They would not form bad pendants to No. 3070. Nos. 4 and 5 seem to the compiler to be by the same hand. (6) and (7) Two female figures, at Budapest, sizes $1 \cdot 05 \times 0 \cdot 387/383$ respectively.[16] No Este emblems. Nos. 6 and 7 are apparently by the same hand as No. 2. (8) *Charity*, in the Poldi Museum at Milan, size $1 \cdot 17 \times 0 \cdot 80$. No Este emblems. Apparently by a follower of Tura influenced by Rogier van der Weyden.[17]

It may be said that these pictures, whether or not any of them were originally associated with No. 3070, offer little help in elucidating its subject. In case it is supposed that some of them may come from Belfiore, it may be recalled that a painter Angelo del Macagnino, none of whose works have been identified, was active from 1447 at Ferrara, and in particular at Belfiore.[18] Bono da Ferrara may also have been active there *ca.* 1450/2; [19] but it seems not to have been suggested that any of the pictures are by Bono.

PROVENANCE: Apparently first recorded at the beginning of the eighteenth century, as one of a series of the *Four Seasons*, in the offices of the Inquisition attached to S. Domenico at Ferrara; the series is still recorded in the same place in 1770 and 1782.[20] It may be accepted that No. 3070 was really one of this set; the claim is made in the catalogue of the Costabili Collection at Ferrara, where No. 3070 was by 1836.[21] Noted by Eastlake and Mündler as still in the Costabili Collection at Ferrara in 1858.[22] Acquired by Sir Austen Henry Layard, probably in 1866.[23] He lent it to Leeds, 1868 (No. 35), and to the South Kensington Museum, 1869 (No. 18). Layard Bequest, 1916.[24]

REPRODUCTION: *Illustrations, Italian Schools*, 1937, p. 361. *Plates, Earlier Italian Schools*, 1953, Vol. II, p. 412.

REFERENCES: (1) G. Baruffaldi, *Vita di Cosimo Tura* (ca. 1706), ed. G. Petrucci, 1836, pp. 19 and 37. C. Laderchi, *Catalogo della Quadreria Costabili*, I, 1838, No. 15. (2) Costabili Catalogue, as in note 1, No. 16; there is no description. Mündler in his *Diary*, 1858, p. 59r, says that both the Costabili figures were seated on thrones; but this must be one of Mündler's rare slips, and No. 16 must be the Berlin picture. See Crowe and Cavalcaselle, *History of Painting in North Italy*, I, 1871, p. 518; Costabili Catalogue, 1871 (No. 7); Costabili Sale Catalogue, Milan, 27/9 April, 1885 (lot 30). See also the Berlin Catalogue, 1931, No. 115A (Cossa); Illustrations, Italian 13–15 Cents., p. 36. (3) If not *Autumn*, it should be one of the autumnal months. See further E. Ruhmer, *Francesco del Cossa*, 1959, pp. 68 ff. (4) Dolphins forming the arms of the Virgin's throne appear in a drawing in the British Museum, with apparently no marine signification. See British Museum, *Italian Drawings, The Fourteenth and Fifteenth Centuries*, catalogue by A. E. Popham and Philip Pouncey, 1950, I, No. 256, and II, Plate CCXVII. (5) This is suggested by Gombosi in *The Burlington Magazine*, Vol. LXII (1933), p. 71. The article is a detailed account of the group of Ferrarese pictures mentioned later on in the text; but the writer's statements are to be considered with caution. This identification for No. 3070 is followed by E. Ruhmer, *Tura*, 1958, p. 172, who thinks that the figures in the background are Vulcan and Mars. (6) Cf. the Poldi and Strozzi pictures, mentioned later on in the text. (7) According to Caleffini's chronicle, Belfiore was burnt in 1483 and was being rebuilt in 1494; this information is noted by C. Padovani, *La Critica d'Arte e la Pittura Ferrarese*, 1954 (1955), pp. 536, 538. Belfiore appears to have been still in existence in 1632 (see A. Frizzi, *Memorie per la Storia di Ferrara*, 2nd edition, ed. Laderchi, III, 1850, p. 388). Ruhmer, *Tura*, 1958, p. 172, objects to the provenance from Belfiore for No. 3070. (8) The documents are printed by A. Venturi in the Prussian *Jahrbuch*, 1888, pp. 7/8. In his text, Venturi gives the date of his first document as 1458; in his transcription of the document, it is 1459. The context suggests that 1458 is correct; this is confirmed by Campori in the *Atti e Memorie delle RR. Dep. di Storia Patria, Provincie Modenesi e Parmensi*, Series III, Vol. III, 1885, p. 548. (9) Evidence concerning a series of Muses in the Studio is given in a MS. by Lodovico Carbone, stated to be of 1475/6; see A. Lazzari, *Il 'Barco' di Lodovico Carbone*, in *Atti e Memorie della Deputazione Ferrarese di Storia Patria*, Vol. XXIV, 1919, pp. 5 ff. C. Padovani, *op. cit.*, p. 546, quotes a passage. According to Carbone, there were two Muses by Angelo del Macagnino; the others were painted (or completed?) by Tura. The first two seem clearly the same as the two recorded by Ciriaco d'Ancona, apparently in 1449 (text in the Prussian *Jahrbuch*, 1940, p. 162); Ciriaco's text may suggest that some of the others may have been, wholly or partly, also by Angelo, which indeed may seem to be confirmed by Campori, *loc. cit.* in note 8, p. 536. (10) Venturi in the Prussian *Jahrbuch*, 1888, pp. 26/7. In the period 1477/81, for the studio of Ercole, Tura painted three figures of nude women and repaired four others of women, not stated to be nude, original authorship not given. The room is sometimes said to have been at Belfiore, but the compiler does not know if this is established. (11) See notes 2 and 3. Venturi, *Storia dell'Arte Italiana*, Vol. VII, Part III, Fig. 388. (12) Venturi, *Storia dell'Arte Italiana*, Vol. VII, Part III, Fig. 430. No doubt it is the same as the

Michele Pannonio, *Donna seduta rappresentante l'abbondanza*, wood, 1.38 × 0.81, No. 1047 of the *Catalogo de' Quadri* etc. . . . *esistenti nella Galleria del Sagro Monte di Pietà di Roma*, December, 1857; no earlier record of its provenance is known. (13) It is very doubtful if the Budapest picture could have been one of the series of four in the offices of the Inquisition at Ferrara. They were all called Tura; but the Budapest picture is signed by Pannonio. Further, the missing pictures are supposed to have been *Winter* and *Spring*; the Budapest *Ceres* could only be *Summer*. See further in note 15. (14) Venturi, *Storia dell'Arte Italiana*, Vol. VII, Part III, Figs. 431/2. H. Beenken in the Prussian *Jahrbuch*, 1940, pp. 153/4, thinks that they represent *Hope and Prudence*. See also Ruhmer, *Cossa*, 1959, pp. 67 f. (15) The Strozzi pictures appear to be first recorded by Crowe and Cavalcaselle, *History of Painting in North Italy*, I, 1871, p. 518. Their identity with the *Winter* and *Spring* from the series of the Inquisition, doubtful as it may seem, does not appear capable of disproof. The two Inquisition pictures are said to have passed to the sacristy of the Carmelite church of S. Girolamo at Ferrara, and thence to Filippo Pasini; see Baruffaldi, *Vita di Cosimo Tura*, 1836, p. 37 (note by Petrucci). What happened to them after 1836 is not recorded. (16) Venturi, *Storia dell'Arte Italiana*, Vol. VII, Part III, Figs. 386/7; see also Ruhmer, *Cossa*, 1959, pp. 66 f. They are generally called *Angels*, and according to the Budapest Catalogue, 1937, pp. 94/5, one panel has an inscription ΣΩΣΙ ΚΡ, which is interpreted as Σώσει Κύριος. Gombosi, *loc. cit.*, called them *Muses*, and therefore thinks they are from a series of *Muses* recorded as being possibly the work of Angelo del Macagnino; see notes 9 and 18. (17) Venturi, *Storia dell'Arte Italiana*, Vol. VII, Part III, Fig. 440. Ruhmer, *Tura*, 1958, pp. 18/9, thinks it partly by Tura; see further his *Cossa*, 1959, pp. 67 f. (18) Campori, *loc. cit.* in note 8, p. 536; Giuseppe Colucci, *Delle Antichità Picene*, Vol. XV, 1792, pp. CXLIV/V; Prussian *Jahrbuch*, 1940, pp. 161/2. Angelo's nuncupative will was read before witnesses on 5 August, 1456, and was registered in 1458; it appears doubtful whether he died in 1456 or 1457 or 1458. See Milanesi, *Documenti Senesi*, II, 1854, pp. 293/5. (19) Campori, *loc. cit.*, p. 544, doubtfully. (20) Baruffaldi, *Vita di Cosimo Tura*, ed. Petrucci, 1836, p. 19. C. Barotti, *Pitture e Sculture . . . di Ferrara*, 1770, p. 66. C. Cittadella, *Catalogo Istorico de' Pittori e Scultori Ferraresi*, I, 1782, p. 54. It is possible, but not certain, that the two later authors are repeating information that had become untrue. In the Oretti MSS. in the Biblioteca dell'Archiginnasio at Bologna, B 175 is a *Descrizione delle Pitture, e Sculture, che adornano le Chiese, et Oratorj della Città di Ferrara*, Opera Postuma di Carlo Brisighella (who died in 1710), apparently written out and added to by Baruffaldi with notes added later by Barotti. On. p. 389 is a passage about the four pictures in the Inquisition, that adds nothing to the passage in Baruffaldi referred to at the beginning of this note; indeed this part of the manuscript (pp. 351 ff.) is not by Brisighella, but by Baruffaldi himself. But there is an addition (by Barotti?), 'J Quadri del Tura mancano da molto tempo.' (21) C. Laderchi, *Catalogo della Quadreria Costabili*, I, 1838, No. 15; Petrucci's note to Baruffaldi, *op. cit.*, 1836, p. 37. (22) Eastlake's note-book; Mündler's Diary. (23) A letter from Layard to Morelli, 20 October, 1866 (British Museum, Add. MS. 38966, Layard Papers, Vol. XXXVI), refers to acquisitions just made from the Costabili Collection, but without listing the pictures. (24) For the history of the Layard Collection, see Appendix IV.

TUSCAN SCHOOL

584 SIDE PARTS OF AN ALTARPIECE

There are two panels with two large saints each: left SS. Michael and John the Baptist; right, a Bishop and a Female Martyr, each with a book.

Above, S. Gabriel and the Annunciate Virgin in circular medallions. Still higher, pinnacles with the Virgin and S. John the Evangelist. The pilasters left and right each contain three saints on the front, and three on the outer side. From top to bottom: I, Left, front, (a) S. Benedict in a white habit; (b) a Pope with a book; (c) a bearded monk in white with a book. II, Left, side, (a) a young man holding a heart and a book (S. Ansanus?); (b) a Bishop with a book; (c) S. Peter. III, Right, front, (a) S. Romuald (?; clean-shaven); (b) S. Catherine of Alexandria; (c) a young man with three arrows and a book (S. Sebastian?). IV, Right, side, (a) S. Jerome; (b) S. Paul; (c) a female martyr holding a cup with lid (S. Mary Magdalene?).

Wood. Painted surfaces of the large panels, pointed tops, $37 \times 19\frac{1}{2}$ (0.94×0.495), approximately. Diameter of the medallions, painted surface, $5\frac{1}{4}$ (0.135). Painted surfaces of the pinnacles, pointed tops, $12\frac{3}{4} \times 7$ (0.325×0.18). Painted surfaces of the saints on the pilasters: the four top ones, $11\frac{3}{4} \times 4\frac{1}{4}$ (0.30×0.11), approximately; the eight others, $10\frac{1}{4} \times 4\frac{1}{4}$ (0.26×0.11), approximately. So far as can be seen the frame is to a considerable extent old, although so much cut about that it is not worth while giving measurements, and wholly regilt. The four sets of saints one above another on the fronts and sides of the pilasters are each upon a single piece of wood.

Good condition.

Fragments of an altarpiece in compartments. The two pinnacles clearly flanked a central pinnacle of Christ on the Cross; the Virgin, as sometimes occurs, must have been turning away from the Cross, towards the spectator's left.[1] Several of the saints on the picture are not identifiable; this may be due to confusions by the painter. On the left-hand pilaster, II (a) should be the same as a saint appearing in other Florentine works, identifiable as S. Ansanus.[2] On the right-hand pilaster, III (a) with a crutch and a book, seems to be meant for S. Romuald, although it is extraordinary to show him clean shaven. III (b) is from the wheel obviously S. Catherine; but it is extraordinary that she should wear a wreath of red and white roses.[3] III (c) may be meant for S. Sebastian, although he is not marked as a martyr. IV (c) is marked as a martyr, but may all the same be meant for the Magdalen.

The altarpiece, from the presence apparently of S. Romuald, and of S. Benedict in white, may be considered Camaldolese. It comes indeed from the Camaldolese nunnery of S. Giovanni Evangelista at Pratovecchio, for which it could have been painted.

In the church at Pratovecchio is a picture apparently representing the Virgin of the Assumption, size given as 0.88×0.58; Longhi[4] claims that this is the (somewhat reduced) central picture for No. 584. To judge from the reproductions, he is right in ascribing it to the same hand, but it seems rather awkward as the centre of the present altarpiece. The awkwardness might seem less if the picture has been considerably cut down; and the strangeness of the painter may be thought to make the association less doubtful than it would otherwise be.[5] Longhi further thinks that the predella of the altarpiece is a *Death of the Virgin* in the

Gardner Museum at Boston;[6] this in his reconstruction-plate has an appearance perhaps too strange. It should be remarked that a female figure at the extreme left of the Boston picture is not a saint and is presumably the donatrix; her dress is black and white, and it would be difficult to look on her as a Camaldolese nun.

Longhi[7] classes No. 584 as by the Master of Pratovecchio, claiming that it is by the same hand as several pictures, including a triptych known as the 'Poggibonsi altarpiece,' which is sometimes ascribed to Castagno.[8] To judge from the reproductions, an association with the 'Poggibonsi altarpiece' appears reasonable. No. 584 was in the 1929 Catalogue ascribed to Castagno; it may be under the influence of some such painter as Giovanni di Francesco, and may not be purely Florentine.[9] From the provenance, it seems likely to be by a Tuscan painter, although this has sometimes been denied.[10] Longhi, who has a high opinion of its quality, considers that it is Florentine.

The date may be not long after 1450; though for a work of so provincial a quality the date may be rather later.

PROVENANCE: From the Camaldolese nunnery of S. Giovanni Evangelista at Pratovecchio.[11] In the Lombardi-Baldi Collection at Florence by 1845;[12] purchased with other pictures from Lombardi and Baldi, 1857.[13] Lent to Edinburgh, 1862–1934.[14]

REPRODUCTIONS: *Illustrations, Italian Schools*, 1937, p. 92 (front only). *Plates, Earlier Italian Schools*, 1953, Vol. II, pp. 413–416 (all the parts).

REFERENCES: (1) Cf. for instance Giovanni Bellini's picture in the Correr Museum at Venice; Klassiker der Kunst *Bellini*, 1930, Plate 24. (2) It should be accepted as certain that in Florentine art S. Ansanus may be shown with a heart (sometimes marked with a sacred Monogram); the compiler does not know the source for this. The identity of a frescoed figure, although no name is visible, in the SS. Annunziata at Florence can indeed hardly be doubted; it is in a chapel firmly stated to have been founded (in 1453) with a dedication to S. Ansanus, and its position suggests that it was over the altar. See Pellegrino Tonini, *Il Santuario della Santissima Annunziata*, 1876, pp. 121 ff. and 300/1 (Doc. LXIII); reproduced by Salmi, *Il Beato Angelico*, 1958, Plate 117a. Further, a picture with the name inscribed shows the Saint holding what must indeed be a heart, being red, although unfortunately the emblem is damaged (Luciano Berti, *Il Museo della Basilica a S. Giovanni Valdarno*, 1959, No. 7, Paolo Schiavo; supplementary information and photograph kindly sent by Dr. Berti). A picture of a saint holding a heart, in 1928 in the Acton Collection at Florence, is also inscribed (SCS. SANUS. MARTIR); but the compiler knows this only from a photograph (in the Witt Library, as Lorenzo di Niccolò Gerini). What is visible of saints with a heart in S. Felice and in S. Niccolò at Florence, and at Peretola, shows no identifying inscriptions, and the compiler knows of no documentation; the same is to be said of an example in the Gallery at Empoli (No. 82 of the *Itinerario*, 1956/7), and one in a predella once in S. Bartolomeo at Quarata (Salmi, *Paolo Uccello*, etc., 1938, Plate 112). A comparable figure, doubtfully accepted as S. Ansanus, is in the Oratorio della Madonna del Buon Consiglio at Prato; A. Marquand, *Andrea della Robbia*, 1922, Vol. II, pp. 130/1 and Fig. 213. The compiler does not know if this emblem was used for S. Ansanus outside the orbit of Florence, in particular at Siena, where S. Ansanus is often represented. All he can say is that a wood statue in SS. Simone e Giuda at Lucca holds a heart, and it may be thought that there is support for the identification of S. Ansanus in this case, although the compiler does not know how reliable the support is; Pèleo Bacci, *Francesco di Valdambrino*, 1936, Plate 9. (3) S.

Catherine is indeed shown with a wreath of roses (and her usual crown) in
Pietro di Giovanni d'Ambrogio's banner in the Musée Jacquemart-André at
Paris; detail reproduced by J. Pope-Hennessy, *Sienese Quattrocento Painting*,
1947, Plate 21. But it may be questioned if this wreath is considered an emblem
particular to her. The banner shows 'S. Catherine in Glory', and the six virtues
present have wreaths of roses too; they do not have the wheel, crown and palm
that S. Catherine has, and one of them has a sword of her own, whereas in this
particular picture S. Catherine has no sword. It would seem that the crowns of
roses, common to S. Catherine and to her virtues, indicate something suitable to
them all in this scene of S. Catherine in Glory. (4) Longhi in *Paragone*, November 1952, pp. 10 ff. (referred to also in *Paragone*, March 1951, p. 58). The
picture was No. 279 of the Arezzo Exhibition of 1950. (5) Salmi in *Commentari*,
1951, p. 195, accepts the attribution of the Pratovecchio picture, but seems
reserved about the association with No. 584. Hartt in *The Art Bulletin*, 1959,
p. 234, accepts both claims. (6) Catalogue, 1931, as Caporali, reproduced; letter
from George L. Stout, 28 September, 1959, in the Gallery archives. (7) Longhi
in *Paragone*, November 1952, pp. 10 ff.; cf. Longhi in *Critica d'Arte*, V (1940),
p. 100. (8) See G. M. Richter, *Andrea del Castagno*, 1943, Plates 11–15. On p.
11, Richter makes some statements about the former repaintings on the picture.
It was in fact reproduced in a different condition in the catalogue of the A.
Sambon Sale, Paris, 25/8 May, 1914 (lot 221), as Verrocchio School. The central
panel was reproduced in yet another state in an advertisement in *The Burlington
Magazine*, Vol. XXXVII (1920), No. 209, as Domenico Veneziano. (9) Crowe
and Cavalcaselle, *History of Painting in Italy*, III, 1866, pp. 57/8, give it to the
following of Domenico di Bartolo and Vecchietta. (10) A. Venturi, *Storia dell' Arte
Italiana*, Vol. VII, Part III, p. 656, suggested Girolamo di Giovanni da Camerino;
the same in *L'Arte*, 1925, p. 100, as Antonio Cicognara. (11) National Gallery
Catalogue, 1859, presumably on information supplied to Eastlake. Cf. the entry
for 'Giovanni del Ponte,' No. 580, note 12. (12) Catalogue, No. 54; the catalogue
is not dated, but the copy in the Uffizi Library is claimed to be of 1845. (13) For
the history of the Lombardi-Baldi Collection, see Appendix I. (14) It is recorded
in some editions of the Edinburgh Catalogue, e.g. 1900, No. 117; 1908, No. 120;
1924, No. 453.

TUSCAN (?) SCHOOL

1842   HEADS OF ANGELS: FRAGMENT OF A FRESCO

Fresco, irregular (ovoid) shape: 11×15 (0.28×0.38), approx.

Apparently in reasonably pure state, though with many obvious
lacunæ. The gold work seems to have been much renewed, but the halo
patterns are certainly authentic.

What is now the horizontal position for the fragment would pretty
clearly have been incorrect for the whole composition; the present fragment would probably have been tipped considerably to the left.

From a fresco of unknown subject.

No. 1842 was attributed on entering the Gallery to the Tuscan School;
it was ascribed by Berenson[1] to Stefano di Giovanni, called Sassetta, and
supposed by him to be from Stefano's fresco on the Porta Romana at
Siena. Pope-Hennessy[2] noted that the halo pattern of No. 1842 differs
from that of Stefano's work on the Porta Romana; he called No. 1842 a
restored work by Sano di Pietro, who did indeed finish Stefano's fresco
on the Porta Romana after Stefano's death.[3] The compiler doubts if
No. 1842 is Sienese.

The fresco in point of fact may have come from Florence. Tito Gagliardi,[4] writing from London but apparently an inhabitant of Florence, says that it had been bought in the *Convento delle Poverine*, Via della Scala, at Florence, and that he possessed another fragment in Italy. One is indeed not forced to believe that No. 1842 was part of the structure of this Florentine convent; it may have been brought in from elsewhere as a fragment. The identity of the convent is unfortunately obscure; the Convent of S. Gerolamo delle Poverine at Florence, which might seem to be the one indicated, was in the street now called the Via Tripoli,[5] but the Via della Scala is at the other end of the town.

PROVENANCE: See above. Henry Vaughan Bequest, 1900.

REPRODUCTION: *Illustrations, Italian Schools*, 1937, p. 319. *Plates, Earlier Italian Schools*, 1953, Vol. II, p. 417.

REFERENCES: (1) Berenson in the *Rassegna d'Arte*, 1904, p. 142. (2) John Pope-Hennessy, *Sassetta*, 1939, p. 147. (3) John Pope-Hennessy, *Sassetta*, 1939, pp. 121, 146; Emile Gaillard, *Sano di Pietro*, 1923, pp. 75/81. The halo pattern of Sano's work there does not correspond with No. 1842 any more than Stefano's does (see Enzo Carli, *Sassetta*, 1957, Plates 74 sqq.). (4) Letter stuck on the back, 23 July, no year. (5) An account of the convent is given in Richa, *Notizie Istoriche delle Chiese Fiorentine*, II, 1755, pp. 296 ff.; for the location, cf. Federigo Fantozzi, *Nuova Guida ... della Città ... di Firenze*, 1849, p. 168.

Paolo UCCELLO

ca. 1397–1475

Florentine School. Paolo di Dono, called Uccello. The date of birth is deduced from tax declarations of 1427, etc., and is no doubt fairly exact. He was assisting Lorenzo Ghiberti on the doors of the Florentine Baptistery in or after 1407, apparently for four or five years (Vasari, ed. K. Frey, I, 1911, p. 356). In 1415 he entered the Physicians' Guild at Florence as a painter. He was active chiefly at Florence; but he carried out a mosaic in 1425 at Venice, and was still there in 1427. Several authenticated works exist. His interest in perspective has been the subject of much critical comment.

583 NICCOLÒ MAURUZI DA TOLENTINO AT THE BATTLE OF SAN ROMANO (FROM A SERIES)

Niccolò is on horseback in the centre; above him is a standard showing several times a device of knotted cords ('Solomon's knot'), black on a white ground, and at the top the fragment of another, unidentified device. A rider in front of him wears a surcoat, partly decorated barry undy, black and silver; the helmet of a rider towards the left is ornamented with a red cross on a silver ground. Two shields lie about, one being quartered silver and red; the other being quartered green, and silver and red divided in zigzag. The bannerets hanging from the trumpets on the left bear in chief a red cross on a white ground; the rest may be a cross saltire of several colours on a red ground.

Wood, painted surface, $71\frac{1}{2} \times 126$ ($1\cdot82 \times 3\cdot20$); to a very slight degree, not rectangular. Painted up to the edges all round; for cuts, see later on, in the commentary.

The picture is, at the time of writing, under treatment, which has involved modifications to the support; the cleaning is not yet finished. Its condition is very good for a work of its size and date; worn in places; some losses, especially along joins. Almost all the armour had been overpainted; the original armour is well preserved in general. The cleaning of this has revealed a striking increase in refinement, but very little change in the forms; a few changes in the colours of the plumes. There is a *pentimento* in the profile of the young bare-headed rider.

The condition of the top part of the picture is peculiar. The two top corners, though old, are not original. These pieces are of trapezoid shape. The lines forming their bases where they join on to the original seem to be pretty well horizontal and straight. The oblique lines of junction from the inner ends of these horizontals to the top of the picture are curved, as if forming part of an arch on each side; the complete arch would, it seems, rise at its middle point some two to three feet, or even more, above the present upper edge of the picture.[1] The approximate measurements of the piece at the left are: height, $17\frac{3}{4}$ in. ($0\cdot45$); width at the top, $9\frac{3}{4}$ in. ($0\cdot245$); width at the bottom, 2 in. ($0\cdot05$). The approximate measurements of the piece at the right are: height, $17\frac{1}{4}$ in. ($0\cdot44$); width at the top, 20 in. ($0\cdot505$); width at the bottom, 12 in. ($0\cdot305$). The paint on these pieces is quite old; as will be explained presently, there is some reason to believe that it is of the XVI Century (though hardly early in that century). It may be in association with this that extensive overpainting along the top of the picture was carried out. At the time of writing, the cleaning here has not proceeded very far, and the forms of the original cannot be described with any precision; but it can be said that most if not all of the parts hitherto seen as sky will turn out to be landscape, which thus may uninterruptedly rise to the present top of the picture. The original paint in this area is well preserved in parts, but there is a good deal of damage, especially towards the left.

Two other pictures, easily acceptable as from the same series as No. 583, are in the Uffizi (signed)[2] and in the Louvre.[3] It is beyond reasonable doubt that these three pictures are identical with three, listed as representing the *rotta di san Romano*, in Palazzo Medici (now Palazzo Riccardi) at Florence in 1492; the three existing pictures can confidently be claimed to have been in the Grandducal Collection at Florence at the end of the XVIII Century (seen under Provenance), and it would seem highly improbable that they had not all been in the Medici Collection during several centuries.[4] It is deducible that the pictures in the inventory of 1492 were on panel, as the existing pictures are;[5] the sizes given in 1492, so far as they can be understood, correspond quite well.[6] A further argument for the identification is found in the subject claimed in 1492, that is, the Battle of San Romano. There, the chief captain on the Florentine side was Niccolò Mauruzi da Tolentino; as already recorded, a standard in No. 583 shows a device of knotted cords ('Solomon's knot'), and this device was used by Niccolò da Tolentino, though it appears uncertain if the colours here, black on a white ground, are correct for him.[7]

Acceptance of the identification should involve acceptance of the subject; the record in the inventory of 1492 could hardly, indeed, be totally wrong, yet there might be some error in it, and one or two of the pictures might show something other than the Battle of San Romano. The nature of the battle might seem to justify doubt; fought near Montopoli between the Florentines and the Sienese on 1 June, 1432, it appears to have been of dubious importance, even of dubious result.[8] Why should these pictures have been painted, recording it? In partial answer to this, one can say that Cosimo de' Medici (Pater Patriae) was friendly with Niccolò da Tolentino,[9] who died indeed in 1435, but whose memory appears to have remained green in Florence for some time.[10]. Further, the existing pictures, without joining on to each other pictorially, seem to go quite well together as three, which is support of a kind for the view that they show the same battle; the picture in the Louvre may be thought to be of a force coming up to help, and Micheletto Attendolo, the second commander of the Florentines, did come up with reinforcements for Niccolò da Tolentino at the Battle of San Romano.

The three pictures were together, as already mentioned; there were also three others (lost), the subjects of which can hardly have referred to the Battle of San Romano;[11] all six were in a room known in 1492 as the *camera di Lorenzo* (the Magnificent, b. 1449). It seems likely that they had all been commissioned by the Medici; but their original location need not have been the same in the Palace. This problem must be considered in connection with the already mentioned newer top corners of No. 583; similar top corners are found in the pictures in Florence and Paris.[12] In an inventory of 1598, pictures that must be these three Battle-pieces are recorded as framed together, in Palazzo Medici, but not in the *camera di Lorenzo*;[13] it is reasonable to suppose that the six top corners were added and painted to make the pictures presentable as one unit, and that before 1598 (though not necessarily originally) such top corners had been missing. Baldini[14] suggests that the pictures could have been at one time of this unusual form, in order to fit at each side of bracket capitals supporting the vault of a room. One is, indeed, at a loss to suggest any other explanation; yet the matter has, unfortunately, not ceased to be obscure. The top corners are at present cut asymmetrically; the cuts on No. 583 and the Louvre picture being wide on the right and narrow on the left, those on the Uffizi picture being narrow on the right and wide on the left. It is true that bracket-capitals supporting the vault of a XV Century room in Florence may be expected themselves to vary —that is, those in the corners of the room are likely to be of much less spread than any others; and this is actually the case in the room rightly or wrongly identified as the *camera di Lorenzo* in Palazzo Medici.[15] But to link the existing variations in the top corners of the pictures with such variations in the capitals necessarily involves placing the pictures on more than one wall. Baldini thus puts two pictures side by side and the third on a wall at right angles, and this reconstruction does seem the most reasonable, under the conditions. Conceivably Lorenzo the Magnificent, furnishing his room with material to hand, might have made do with such an arrangement; yet, given a room in the Palace large enough for the three pictures to be in a line,[16] it would seem surprising if the original commission had been for any such thing. It should be added that the lighting of the three Battle-pieces, perhaps not greatly stressed, does in each case come from the left.

The room that is (rightly or wrongly) identified as the *camera di Lorenzo* adds to the difficulty of understanding this matter. On a short wall, where Baldini puts two of the pictures, the distance from one bracket-capital to the next is approximately 3·70 m.;[17] on a long wall, where he puts the third Battle-piece, the distance is approximately 3·30 m. The present widths of the three pictures are almost exactly the same; so, given the conditions, the variation in the spaces seems most awkward. Further, the two spaces available on the short wall are each considerably more than the width of the pictures, so much so that one wonders how any elaboration of framing could have made it necessary for the top corners of the pictures to be cut. Again, the vaulting in this room rises very steeply for some way above the capitals, which themselves do not spread widely, and this hardly suits the angle of the curves formed by the newer corners where they join on to the original part of the pictures. The compiler cannot solve the problem. Baldini's explanation would seem to be on the right lines; but possibly the cutting of the pictures, whether or not this was done when they were painted, was for a room other than the one rightly or wrongly identified as the *camera di Lorenzo*.

It seems undesirable in this place to elaborate hypotheses that might (or perhaps would not) help in understanding the arrangement of the pictures; but it should be recorded that the cuts in the top corners may be no longer in their first form. Paint continues to the edges of the wooden support in the Uffizi and National Gallery pictures, so it is natural to suppose that the edges, and in particular the vertical sides, may have been cut; indeed, the paint at the sides of No. 583 has the appearance of having been at least trimmed. Yet substantial cutting here remains doubtful[18]—and might not be useful for understanding the problem!

On the other hand, there may have been large cuts at the tops of the pictures. There is material evidence that the top edge of the Uffizi picture has been at least trimmed; at the top edge of No. 583, what seemed to be some clean cuts in the canvas lying between the wood and the paint have been observed. On pictorial grounds, the truncated standard in No. 583 seems most strange; cutting might be considerable. It is not at present excluded that parts cut away at the tops formed arches or the larger parts of arches; in that case, the pictures could have covered, more or less completely, the top parts of sections of wall under vaulting. It should be mentioned that this does not seem to have been so in the *camera di Lorenzo* in 1492; the height of the pictures, perhaps or probably including the frame, is given as $3\frac{1}{2}$ braccia, or just over 2 m.[19] An attempt was made at the National Gallery to decide if the beginnings of arches right and left at the top are part of the original form of the picture or not, but without success; it does seem that there are strips of unpainted wood here, but these seem to be on both sides of the joins, that is, both on the original picture and on the inner edges of the newer corners, as if these areas had been tinkered with at some time.

No. 583 may have been trimmed along the bottom, but it is unnecessary, indeed undesirable, to suppose substantial cutting of the pictures along the lower edges.

The perspective might be expected to show how high the pictures were intended to be hung. The compiler experimented with No. 583, and thinks that this matter cannot be definitely decided, but that the bottom edge may well have been about six or seven feet from the ground. In 1492 the six pictures recorded were above some wainscoting, broken by two doors the height of which is given as about 2 m. The room now identified as the *camera di Lorenzo* has, and presumably originally had, a door in the short wall where Baldini places two of the Battle-pieces; the height of this door, from the ground to the underside of the lintel, is about 2·60 m. If it is indeed thought that the pictures were originally hung high, their being shaped to fit under vaulting should, perhaps, be thought to have been the original arrangement too.

As already recorded in note 11, one of the six pictures in the *camera di Lorenzo* was by Pesellino. If the Battle-pieces were painted for the Medici, and to go with this Pesellino, this provides a clue for their date; Pesellino was born *ca.* 1422 and died in 1457. A date in the 1450's would accord with what is known of the construction of the Palace.[20] Andrea dal Castagno's painting of Niccolò da Tolentino may also be thought to offer some support to this dating for the Uccellos; as already noted, it was ordered about October 1455.

PROVENANCE: As explained above, No. 583 is beyond reasonable doubt one of three Battle-pieces by Uccello, in Palazzo Medici (now Palazzo Riccardi) at Florence. These Medici pictures are recorded in an inventory of 1492,[21] by the Anonimo Magliabechiano,[22] by Vasari (editions of 1550 and 1568),[23] and in an inventory of 1598.[24] It seems clear that the three pictures remained in the Grandducal Collection until 1787, when what were obviously No. 583 and the Louvre picture were removed from the Gallery at Florence, presumably for sale.[25] No. 583 is stated to have been acquired in 1844 from the Giraldi Collection in Florence by Lombardi and Baldi in Florence,[26] who certainly had it in 1848.[27] Purchased with other pictures from Lombardi and Baldi, 1857.[28]

REPRODUCTION: *Illustrations, Italian Schools*, 1937, p. 362. *Plates, Earlier Italian Schools*, 1953, Vol. II, pp. 418/20. As has been noted, the picture is under treatment at the time of writing; important changes in the appearance are involved.

REFERENCES: (1) As is about to be explained, the Uccello in the Uffizi is similar in this respect, except that the wide corner is at the left and the narrow one at the right; a plate showing the forms there is given by Umberto Baldini in the *Bollettino d'Arte*, 1954, p. 232. (2) Uffizi, Florence; size, 1·82 × 3·23. The compiler is much indebted to Luisa Becherucci, Umberto Baldini and Gaetano Lo Vullo for help about this picture, which was examined and discussed under most favourable conditions. (3) Paris, Louvre; size, 1·80 × 3·16. (4) The claim for the provenance was made by E. Müntz, *Les Collections des Médicis*, 1888, p. 60, and was elaborated by H. P. Horne in *The Monthly Review*, 1901, pp. 114 ff. Horne's arguments (about to be summarized) are cumulatively strong; they are noticeably strengthened by the provenance of No. 583 and the Louvre picture at the end of the XVIII Century from the Grandducal Collection at Florence, which Horne had been unable to establish. The three pictures used to be identified as three out of four Battles by Uccello, recorded by Vasari in a garden at Florence at one time belonging to the Bartolini family (see Vasari, Le Monnier edition, Vol. III, 1848, p. 96). Vasari's description includes the name of Carlo Malatesta, and No. 583 was supposed to represent the battle of Sant'Egidio near Perugia in 1416, where Carlo Malatesta and his nephew Galeazzo were taken prisoner. Arguments against this (followed by a misguided attempt to date the picture after Uccello's death from the costume) were given by J. R. Planché in *The Journal of the British Archaeological Association*, Vol. XXXIV, 1878, pp. 171 ff.; for the battle itself, see William Heywood, *A History of Perugia*, 1910, p. 286, where further references are given. The identification was strongly attacked by Horne, *loc. cit.*; and since the three pictures clearly have a Medici provenance, an alternative Bartolini provenance would seem unnecessary to discuss. Decio Gioseffi in *Critica d'Arte*, 1958, pp. 146/8, thinks that the two provenances are most probably not alternatives; the Bartolini pictures would be identical with the Medici ones, which would have been placed in the Bartolini garden for a time in the XVI Century, and seen there by Vasari. It should be noted that Gioseffi's claim little affects the status of the three existing Battle-pieces; the chief result of accepting it would be to cancel three of the Bartolini pictures from the list of Uccello's recorded but lost works. Gioseffi goes to great pains to justify his view, but his attempt involves so many improbabilities (at least) that the compiler would be reluctant to linger over it. (5) Horne, *loc. cit.*, p. 124. Vasari (1550 edition, p. 254; text of 1568, ed. Milanesi, Vol. II, p. 208) says that they were on canvas; but Horne's demonstration seems quite satisfactory. (6) Cf. Horne, *loc. cit.*, pp. 125, 134; he seems in his deductions to pursue the matter too far. The height is given as $3\frac{1}{2}$ braccia (2,044 m.), possibly or probably including the frame. The widths of the three Battle-pieces are not given individually; all that is stated is the total width of these three and of three lost pictures, apparently distinct in subject but of the same height. This total width, 42 braccia or about $24\frac{1}{2}$ m., would with reasonable allowance for framing correspond well with the width not of 6 but of 7 pictures, if all were just over 3 m. wide, as the existing Uccellos now are. Gioseffi, *loc. cit.*, supposes that one of the lost pictures was twice as wide as the others; this might be correct, but Gioseffi maybe would not have made his proposal as he did, if the needs of the Bartolini garden had not lured him on. Students may care to imagine other explanations of the 42 braccia, not all mutually exclusive. (7) See Horne, *loc. cit.*, p. 129, quoting Sansovino. Niccolò da Tolentino's knot is shown on the painted monument to him by Andrea dal Castagno in the Cathedral of Florence (reproduced by Van Marle, *Italian Schools*, Vol. X, Fig. 210); there the knot is red on a white ground, as is pointed out by Richa, *Notizie Istoriche delle Chiese Fiorentine*, Vol. VI, 1757, p. 131, and by Salmi, *Paolo Uccello, Andrea del Castagno, Domenico Veneziano*, 1938, p. 165. It is a pity that Niccolò's coat of arms is not to be found on No. 583. Horne, *loc. cit.*, pp. 131 f., tries without much success to link a standard in the picture in the Louvre with Micheletto Attendolo da Cotignola, the second commander of the Florentines at the Battle of San Romano. He points out (pp. 133/4) that a red cross on a white ground, which appears in chief on the bannerets hanging from the trumpets in all three pictures, is the arms of the Florentine people. He says that other arms or devices shown on shields, etc., cannot be identified and appear to be fanciful. (8) Horne, *loc. cit.*, pp. 126 ff., gives some account of it; one cannot, it seems, even be certain that the Florentines won (cf. for instance Muratori, *Annali d'Italia*, Vol. XIII, 1820, p. 268). There is, nevertheless, some evidence that the battle was hailed as a victory, and an occasion of rejoicing, at Florence (D. Buoninsegni, *Storia della Città di Firenze*, 1637, p. 44). (9) Cf. W. Roscoe, *The Life of Lorenzo de' Medici*, 9th edition, 1847, p. 409. (10) He was honourably buried in the Cathedral of Florence (Horne, *loc. cit.*, p. 130); Andrea dal Castagno's painted monument to him (already mentioned) was ordered about October 1455. Some victory by him was celebrated at Florence in an annual procession; see Richa, *op. cit.*, Vol. IV, 1756, p. 257, or Roberto Razzòli, *La Chiesa d'Ognissanti in Firenze*, 1898, pp. 59/60. Richa says that the victory in question was in 1432; both say that it was on 21 August, which is not the day and month stated for the battle of San Romano. The compiler has not identified this victory. There is an entry for Niccolò in Litta. (11) Horne, *loc. cit.*, p. 137: 'uno dj battaglie & (?di) draghj et lionj et vno della storia diparis dimano di pagholo vcello & vno dimano difranc° dipesello entrovj vna chaccia'. Gioseffi, *loc. cit.* in note 4, needing a fourth Battle-piece for the Bartolini garden, tries hard to find one here. (12) See the careful article by Umberto Baldini in the *Bollettino d'Arte*, 1954, pp. 226 ff. (13) Baldini, as in previous note. The text of 1598 is: '3. quadri grandi, di giostre, antichi, tutti, in un' pezzo / con lor corniciette dorate, apicchati, almuro, alti / sopra alla porta del primo salone, nellandito, della / capella' (Horne, *loc. cit.*, p. 138, checked with the original ms.). No attribution is there stated. (14) Baldini, *loc. cit.* in note 12. (15) For the identification, see Baldini, *loc. cit.*; the compiler does not know if it can be proved. Stegmann and Geymüller, *Die Architektur der Renaissance in Toscana*, Vol. II, p. 19, locate it differently, apparently where the main staircase of the Palace now is; they say they make their deductions about the internal arrangements of the Palace from indications in the 1492 inventory and from Filarete. Horne, *loc. cit.*, p. 125, did not seek to locate the room, but deduced that its size was 24 × 18 braccia, or 45 ft. 9 in. × 34 ft. 3½ in. (about 14 × 10½ m.). The room now identified as the *camera di Lorenzo* measures 7·42 × 9·87 m., and Horne's estimated measurements may seem rather large for any room on the ground floor (as this was) of Palazzo Medici; he did not know of the cuts at the top corners of the pictures, and his reasoning can hardly stand if it was in the *camera di Lorenzo* that they served a purpose. (16) As mentioned in the previous note, the long wall of the room now identified as the *camera di Lorenzo* measures 9·87 m., sufficient for the three Battle-pieces as they now are. (17) Baldini reproduces only a rough sketch of the arrangement; an exact drawing is given by A. Parronchi in *Paragone*, May 1957, Plate 14. (18) On the right-hand side of the Uffizi picture, there is a part where the gesso projects slightly beyond the supporting wood; the paint above the gesso at this place seems to be original, in which case the gesso is too. Could the wood have been cut here when gesso and paint were already in place, so as to leave a slightly projecting area of gesso and paint? (19) A. Parronchi in *Paragone*, May 1957, p. 26 (note 15) suggests that there were detached lunettes on canvas above the pictures. This supposition seems designed as a sop to Vasari, who says that the pictures themselves were on canvas; but pictures partly on wood and partly on canvas seem most unlikely. Gioseffi, *loc. cit.* in note 4, does not think that the pictures ever had lunettes, detached or otherwise. (20) This matter is discussed by Horne, *loc. cit.*, pp. 119 ff. John Pope-Hennessy in his essay on No. 583 (The Gallery Books, No. 4, n.d.), pp. 4/5, says that the structure was completed in 1454. Benozzo was working on the frescoes in the chapel of the Palace in 1459. (21) Horne, *loc. cit.*, p. 137; E. Müntz, *Les Collections des Médicis*, 1888, p. 60. (22) Ed. Frey, 1892, p. 100: 'e quadrj delle giostre'. (23) Vasari, 1550, p. 254; text of 1568, ed. Milanesi, Vol. II, p. 208. (24) Horne, *loc. cit.*, p. 138; it should be remembered that no attribution is recorded. (25) Information most kindly sent by Dr. Ugo Procacci. (26) The evidence for this is apparently only what is stated in the National Gallery Catalogue of 1858 (or the N.G. MS. Catalogue, or the N.G. Report); presumably Eastlake had the information from Lombardi and Baldi. (27) Vasari, Le Monnier edition, Vol. III, 1848, p. 96. (28) For details concerning the Lombardi-Baldi Collection, see Appendix I.

6294 S. GEORGE AND THE DRAGON

Canvas,[1] $22\frac{1}{4}$ × $29\frac{1}{4}$ (0·565 × 0·74). Cut at the left and probably at the bottom, but to judge from the composition, not by very much.

Good condition, although worn in places. Many *pentimenti*. In particular, the level of the soil has been raised, the cave at one time descending much lower at the left; the arrangement of the grass has also been changed somewhat. The Princess' hands were once in a different position, and larger, with the girdle in her left hand instead of her right; her crown was intended to be at a steeper angle. A curved mark across the lower part of her dress has not been explained. The massed clouds on the right partly cover a continuation of the trees.

The story is told with variations; the standard version is in *The Golden Legend*, and this is the form followed in the picture. A dragon would stay at a distance from a certain city if regularly given food; in time the turn came for the King's daughter to be eaten, but S. George arrived in time to save her. He wounded the dragon with his lance, whereupon the Princess put her girdle round its neck and it followed her like a dog. The three went into the city; the King and all the people were baptized; then S. George killed the dragon with his sword. The picture shows the attack by S. George with his lance. The next incident is also adumbrated; the Princess has put her girdle round the dragon's neck, although (by some whim or carelessness) she continues to wear another girdle. The spiral of cloud in the sky must be to suggest celestial aid for S. George; the Figure of God is not shown, the miracle being expressed merely as a disturbance of nature.[2]

The picture was probably not much studied in the original before its acquisition by the National Gallery; some doubts about the attribution had from time to time been expressed, but these (especially since the recent cleaning) seem by no means justified.[3] From the costume, the date is *ca.* 1460.[4] A picture ascribed to Uccello, showing the same subject as No. 6294, but differing considerably in composition, is in the Musée Jacquemart-André at Paris.[5]

PROVENANCE: In the Lanckoronski Collection at Vienna, the first known record of it there being of 1898.[6] Purchased through Mr. Farago from Count Lanckoronski by special grant, with contributions from the Phillott and Temple-West Funds, 1959.

REPRODUCTION: In *The Burlington Magazine*, September–October 1959, p. 311 (after cleaning at the National Gallery).

REFERENCES: (1) There is no reason to suppose that it has been transferred from panel; see N. S. Brommelle in *The Museums Journal*, July 1959, pp. 87 ff., for this and other technical points. (2) In an article by the compiler in *The Burlington Magazine*, September–October 1959, pp. 309 ff., there are comments on various details of the iconography. (3) No. 6294 has been associated (in the compiler's view, wrongly) with an *Adoration* at Karlsruhe. The attribution to Uccello may now be more easily accepted by critics; some (unlike the compiler) class almost all Uccellesque pictures as by Uccello himself. For the opinions of various writers, see John Pope-Hennessy, *Paolo Uccello*, 1950, p. 152 and Enio Sindona, *Paolo Uccello*, 1957, p. 62; for Pope-Hennessy's opinion in favour of Uccello, see *The Manchester Guardian*, 28 January, 1959. An appreciation of the picture by Sir Philip Hendy was published in *The Listener*, 4 February, 1960, pp. 228/9. **(4)** Note by Stella Mary Pearce in the Gallery archives. **(5)** John Pope-Hennessy, *Paolo Uccello*, 1950, Plate 69. **(6)** Loeser in the *Repertorium für Kunstwissenschaft*, 1898, pp. 88/9.

UGOLINO DI NERIO
active 1317–1327

A painter recorded at Siena. It need not be doubted that Ugolino di Nerio is identical with the Ugolino of Siena who signed the high altarpiece of Santa Croce, Florence. All the pictures here catalogued as Ugolino's are fragments of that work; other fragments of it exist, and are referred to in the commentary to No. 1188; the piece of wood bearing the signature did still exist in the nineteenth century (Waagen, *Kunstwerke*, I, 1837, p. 395), but is now missing. Vasari says that Ugolino died at Siena; in the first edition of his *Vite* he gives the date as 1339, in the second edition 1349, but it is uncertain if he had good authority for stating either date.

The Santa Croce altarpiece is Ugolino's only authenticated work, but other pictures have been attributed to him. It is clear from the style of the Santa Croce altarpiece that Ugolino was a close follower of Duccio, the compositions of some of the scenes being derived with simplifications from Duccio's *Maestà* (1308/11).

1188   THE BETRAYAL (PREDELLA PANEL FROM AN ALTAR-PIECE)

Centre, Judas kisses Christ; left, S. Peter cuts off the ear of Malchus.

Wood. The size of the picture is $13\frac{1}{2} \times 21$ (0·345 × 0·53). The size of the panel is 16×23 (0·405 × 0·585), including $\frac{1}{2}$ in. along the bottom, which has been added as restoration.

The condition is good on the whole. The framing, although regilt, may be original, except for the strip along the bottom already indicated.

The composition corresponds fairly closely with the panel of the same subject in Duccio's *Maestà*.[1]

No. 1188, and all the other Ugolinos catalogued below, are fragments from a polyptych, which formed the high altarpiece of Santa Croce, Florence. The date of the altarpiece could be inferred with some probability, if the date at which the church was first used for the cult were known; but this appears not to have been fixed. The altarpiece was apparently commissioned by the Alamanni family.[2]

Vasari first surely recorded the existence of Ugolino's altarpiece, in the first edition of his *Vite*, 1550.[3] In July, 1566, the authorities of Santa Croce demanded, and were granted, leave to move the high altar forward into the church, to remove the altarpiece and to substitute a ciborium or a Crucifix; a ciborium on Vasari's designs, and executed by Dionigi Nigetti, was placed on the high altar on 7 April, 1569.[4] Ugolino's altarpiece was lost sight of, until identified in the Upper Dormitory of Santa Croce at the end of the eighteenth century by Della Valle.[5]

Della Valle saw the altarpiece apparently intact, and left some description of it; it was composed of various panels in several tiers. It can be deduced from Della Valle's statements and from the existing fragments that the predella consisted of seven panels; this gives the necessary information about the width. From the existing fragments it can be deduced that the height was of four tiers, leaving aside some small painted heads decorating the intervening framework. The altarpiece therefore consisted of: (1) the predella of seven panels; (2) the main tier, of the Virgin and Child and six single figures; (3) an upper tier of coupled figures, not more than 14 in all; (4) pinnacles, not more than seven in all.[6]

In Della Valle's time some parts of the altarpiece were already in bad condition, and at the beginning of the nineteenth century all (?) the parts considered worth preserving are stated to have been bought by an Englishman and imported into England.[7] In 1835 Waagen[8] visited the W. Young Ottley Collection and noted the following fragments: all seven predella panels; from the main tier, a fragment of the Virgin and Child, and 'five' of the side panels; from the upper tier, 'three' sets of coupled figures; of the pinnacles, four panels. Waagen also saw the signature, which was at that time attached to the picture now No. 1189 of the National Gallery.

The fragment of the Virgin and Child seems not to have been identified since Waagen. Waagen's account of the remaining fragments is often accepted as correct, but there was probably an error in his notes. The fragments catalogued for the Warner Ottley Sale on 30 June, 1847, were as follows:[9] all seven predella panels; from the main tier, *three* (SS. John Baptist, Peter and Paul); from the upper tier, *five* couple (two couple named as Philip and James, and Andrew and Bartholomew); and four other panels, which seem clearly to have been pinnacles, named Moses, Aaron, S. John and Daniel. It seems probable that Waagen recorded five items from the main tier and three from the upper tier, but should have written three from the main tier and five from the upper tier; then his account, except for the missing fragment of the Virgin and Child, would correspond with what was catalogued in the Ottley Collection in 1847.

The history of the altarpiece since the Ottley Sale in 1847 is best arranged according to the individual items.

Predella. All seven panels, (1) *The Last Supper*, (2) *The Betrayal*, (3) *The Flagellation*, (4) *The Way to Calvary*, (5) *The Deposition* (wrongly called *The Crucifixion* at the 1847 Sale), (6) *The Entombment* and (7) *The Resurrection*, which were lots 10, 11 and 81 of the 1947 Ottley Sale (bought in), reappeared as lot 55 of the Ottley Sale on 24 June, 1850, bought by (the Rev. J. Fuller) Russell. As their subsequent history is not complex, it is sufficient here to state that (1) is in the Robert Lehman Collection in America;[10] (2) is National Gallery, No. 1188; (3) is Berlin, No. 1635A; (4) is National Gallery, No. 1189; (5) is National Gallery, No. 3375; (6) is Berlin, No. 1635B; (7) is National Gallery, No. 4191.

Main Tier. *The Virgin and Child*, as already remarked, did not appear
in the 1847 Ottley Sale, nor in the sale of 1850; its present whereabouts
are unknown. Mrs. Coor, nevertheless, has identified what seems highly
likely to be the spandrels from above it, showing angels, in the Los
Angeles County Museum.[11] The three saints, lot 1 of the 1847 Sale,
bought in, and lot 56 of the 1850 Sale, apparently again bought in, are
now at Berlin. These three panels have arched tops, in the spandrels
above which are small panels of angels. Two further fragments of angels
alone, without the main figures, have survived; one is National Gallery,
No. 3378, the other is of No. 3 of the catalogue of the Cook Collection.
These made no individual appearance in the 1847 or 1850 Sales, but it
seems possible that N.G. No. 3378 at least was sold attached to the lower
side of one of the sets of coupled saints forming the upper tier.[12]

Upper Tier. The five pieces in the 1847 Sale were as follows:

Lot 2, Two Saints with books, in Gothic panel compartments, bt.
    Anthony.

Lot 3, Philip and James, bt. Anthony.

Lot 4, Andrew and Bartholomew, bt. Bromley Davenport.

Lot 5, Two Saints, bt. Edward.

Lot 6, Two Saints, bt. Anthony.

Lot 2 is identifiable as Berlin, No. 1635C; lot 3 as Berlin, No. 1635D;
lot 4 as National Gallery, No. 3473. Lots 5 and 6 should be Berlin, No.
1635E, and National Gallery, No. 3377, the National Gallery picture
being probably lot 6 rather than lot 5.[13]

Pinnacles. In the 1847 Sale appeared:

Lot 7, Moses and Aaron, bt. Edward.

Lot 8, St. John ⎫
Lot 9, Daniel   ⎬ bt. Anthony.

These fetched even smaller prices than the pieces of the upper tier, and
are clearly only the pinnacles. Lot 7 was bought in, and reappeared as
lot 57 of the 1850 Sale, again apparently bought in; it is clearly identical
with the two pictures, Nos. 1 and 2 of the Cook Collection.[14] Lots 8 and
9, being bought by Anthony, presumably passed into the Fuller Russell
Collection (cf. note 13). They are presumably identical with the pictures
from the upper part of the altarpiece, obscurely described by Waagen in
his *Treasures* of 1854:[15] 'the youthfully conceived St. John alone, and
the head of the (other) only seen.' All the Fuller Russell Ugolinos were
in an exhibition at the R.A. in 1878; the two pictures described by
Waagen must be No. 175, A Saint, small half figure, $18\frac{3}{4} \times 10\frac{1}{2}$; 190, A
Saint, small half figure, 15×10. These appeared in the Russell Sale,
18 April, 1885, lot 113, A Saint, and lot 114, A Saint, both bought by
Butler. They reappeared in the Charles Butler Sale, 25 May, 1911: lot
84, Daniel, The Prophet, in a loose red robe over a green dress, holding
in his left hand a scroll, on which is an inscription, $18\frac{1}{2} \times 10\frac{1}{4}$, bt. Carfax;
and lot 85, A Prophet, in red and green robes, holding a scroll, $13\frac{1}{2} \times 10$,
bt. Smith (for Wagner). The former is No. 89 of the 1913 Catalogue of
the J. G. Johnson Collection at Philadelphia; the other is National
Gallery, No. 3376. The only difficulty about these identifications is that

Waagen seems to have recorded the Johnson Daniel (which has the name inscribed) as a St. John. The 1847 Sale catalogue records both Daniel and St. John; it seems reasonable to suppose that the Daniel was then correctly identified, and that the figure then supposed to be St. John is National Gallery, No. 3376 (who is in point of fact Isaiah). It seems therefore that once again Waagen made a muddle of his notes; on seeing the two pictures, he was presumably told that one was St. John, never took in the name of Daniel at all, applied the name of St. John to the wrong picture and left the other anonymous.

If the above remarks are admitted to be sound, every part of Ugolino's altarpiece catalogued in the Ottley Sale of 1847 can be identified with a subsequently recorded picture. The parts seen by Waagen in 1835 in the Ottley Collection, but not in the 1847 Sale, are: the fragment of the central panel, representing the Virgin and Child; the signature, which was then attached to National Gallery, No. 1189, but is now missing; and possibly, but not probably, two single figures of saints from the main tier.

An *Isaiah* not recorded to have been in Ottley's possession, but sometimes claimed to be part of the Santa Croce altarpiece, is at Dublin, No. 2012.[16] The identification is impossible, since Isaiah already appears in National Gallery, No. 3376.

PROVENANCE: For the provenance until the Ottley Sale of 1847, see the commentary above. Warner Ottley Sale, 30 June, 1847, lot 11 with four other predella panels, bought by Browne, i.e. bought in. Ottley Sale, 24 June, 1850 (lot 55), with all the rest of the predella, bought by Russell. Coll. Rev. J. Fuller Russell, where seen by Waagen in 1851.[17] Exhibited at Manchester, 1857; Provisional Catalogue, No. 12 with the rest of the predella; Definitive Catalogue, No. 25a. Exhibited at the R.A., 1878 (No. 178). Fuller Russell Sale, 18 April, 1885 (lot 117), purchased out of the Clarke Fund for the National Gallery.

REPRODUCTION: *Illustrations, Italian Schools*, 1937, p. 364. *Plates, Earlier Italian Schools*, 1953, Vol. II, p. 421.

REFERENCES: (1) Van Marle, *Development of the Italian Schools of Painting*, Vol. II, Fig. 24. (2) G. Richa, *Notizie Istoriche delle Chiese Fiorentine*, I, 1754, p. 56, and F. Moisè, *Santa Croce di Firenze*, 1845, pp. 69/70, without precise evidence say that the church was being used by about 1320. The date is no doubt not far wrong; cf. W. and E. Paatz, *Die Kirchen von Florenz*, Vol. I, 1940, pp. 497 ff. The absidal chapel behind the altar is stated to have been constructed later, but this is irrelevant to the date of Ugolino's altarpiece; cf. Moisè, *op. cit.*, pp. 172/4. For the family of the donor, see the *Carteggio Inedito di D. Vinc. Borghini*, ed. A. Lorenzoni, I, 1912, pp. 102 ff.; for other connections of the Alamanni family with the high altar of S. Croce, and for what seems to be the family tomb, see Moisè, *op. cit.*, pp. 125 and 208, and Richa, *op. cit.*, I, p. 97. A very elaborate account of Ugolino's altarpiece, including a number of points not discussed in this catalogue, was published by Gertrude Coor-Achenbach in *The Art Bulletin*, September 1955, pp. 153 ff. (3) Vasari, 1550 edition, p. 154; 1568 edition, p. 143; Milanesi's edition, Vol. I, p. 454. It is perhaps recorded earlier as a Giotto in the *Anonimo Magliabechiano*, ed. Frey, 1892, p. 52. (4) See F. Moisè, *Santa Croce di Firenze*, 1845, pp. 122/4, and Agostino Lapini, *Diario Fiorentino*, ed. G. O. Corazzini, 1900, p. 163. See also *Der Literarische Nachlass Giorgio Vasaris*, ed. K. and H. W. Frey, II, 1930, p. 549, and F. Moisè, *op. cit.*, pp. 173/4. A storm in 1512 caused damage near the high altar, but presumably not to Ugolino's altarpiece; see *Diario Fiorentino di Luca Landucci*, ed. Iodoco del Badia, 1883, p. 320, and Richa, *op. cit.*, I, p. 60 (date given as 1514). **(5)** Della Valle, *Lettere Sanesi*, II, 1785, p. 202. **(6)** The Virgin and Child of the main tier was almost certainly on an extra wide panel, and it might be supposed therefore that it may not have left room for as many as six flanking figures; but five of these figures, in whole or in part, have survived, as will be explained below. Possibly the central section of the upper tier, and the central pinnacle on the topmost tier, may have been of different form from the parts at the sides; a *Crucifixion* in this space would be rather to be expected, for the high-altarpiece of Santa Croce, which had a predella of Passion Scenes without the Crucifixion. It seems probable that, whatever the exact form, the *Crucifixion* or other representation was surmounted by a separate pinnacle. **(7)** Vasari, ed. Milanesi, I, p. 454. It may be that the English purchaser there mentioned was Young Ottley himself, who was living in Italy *ca.* 1791/9. If the date of sale is really after 1799, the purchaser could still have been Ottley, unless it were proved that he never returned to Italy. The friary was suppressed in 1810; cf. F. Moisè, *Santa Croce di Firenze*, 1845, pp. 410 ff. **(8)** Waagen, *Kunstwerke und Künstler in England*, I, 1837, pp. 393/5. **(9)** Mr. Martin Asscher courteously allowed the compiler access to the auctioneer's copies of the sale catalogues of 1847 and 1850, which he possessed; the Frick Library of New York also kindly sent a typescript of part of the sale catalogue of 1847. **(10)** Reproduced in *Apollo*, February, 1935, p. 65; by Mrs. Coor, *loc. cit.*, Fig. 6; and on Plate III of the catalogue of the Lehman Exhibition, Paris, 1957 (2nd edition). **(11)** Mrs. Coor, *loc. cit.*, pp. 156 and 158 and Fig. 7. If, as seems very likely, this fragment is correctly identified, the width of the missing Virgin and Child would have been 75 cm., i.e. greater than the width of the surrounding saints; this is to be expected, by analogy with other polyptychs of the time. **(12)** In point of fact, there does not seem to be proof that No. 3378 was ever in the Ottley Collection, but it seems most unlikely that it was not. The fragment in the Cook Collection was bought in 1910 at Cheltenham, together with two pinnacles of Moses and Aaron. It may be that these three fragments had been sold from the Ottley Collection only shortly before, and that they are the same as the undescribed fragments of the upper tier, stated by Langton Douglas to have been *ca.* 1908 owned by Col. Warner Ottley (Crowe and Cavalcaselle, ed. Douglas, III, 1908, p. 24). It should be added that according to Mr. Martin Asscher's copy of the Ottley Sale Catalogue of 1847 there were two uncatalogued lots, 100 bought for ten guineas by E. O(ttley) and 101 bought for eight guineas by Hickman; but there is no indication at all of what pictures were included in these lots. **(13)** Anthony seems to have seen acting as agent for the Rev. J. Fuller Russell, whereas Edward was buying in for the Ottley family; and one set of coupled saints at Berlin could (so far as is known) have remained in the Ottley Collection until the beginning of the present century whereas National Gallery No. 3377 could not. The question of what Ugolinos did remain in the Ottley Collection is complicated by a list of pictures supplied to the Gallery in 1899 by Col. Warner Ottley. The only Ugolinos in the list are, (*a*) Two Saints with Books in Gothic panel Compartments, (*b*) Philip and James (2), and (*c*) Two Saints (2). The compiler finds it difficult to believe that pictures exactly corresponding with the above could have been in the Ottley Collection in 1899; it may be noted that Col. Ottley's descriptions tally with lots 2, 3 and 5 of the 1847 Sale, but lots 2 and 3 seem to have passed directly from Fuller Russell (sold 1885) to Charles Butler (sold 1911). **(14)** Reproduced by Mrs. Coor, *loc. cit.*, Figs. 4 and 5. **(15)** Waagen, *Treasures*, 1854, II, p. 462. **(16)** 1956 Catalogue, No. 1112; reproduced by Mrs. Coor, *loc. cit.*, Fig. 14. **(17)** Waagen, *Treasures*, 1854, II, p. 462.

1189 THE WAY TO CALVARY (PREDELLA PANEL FROM AN ALTARPIECE)

Christ carrying the Cross is in the centre; the Maries are on the left.

Wood. The size of the picture is $13\frac{1}{2} \times 21$ (0·345 × 0·53). The size of the panel is 16×23 (0·405 × 0·585).

The condition is very fair, but rather less good than for No. 1188 above. The framing, although regilt, may be original.[1]

For the altarpiece from which this panel comes, see the commentary to No. 1188 above.

PROVENANCE: For the provenance until the Ottley Sale of 1847, see the commentary to No. 1188 above. Warner Ottley Sale, 30 June, 1847, lot 11 with four other predella panels, bought by Browne, i.e. bought in. Ottley Sale, 24 June, 1850 (lot 55), with all the other predella panels, bought by Russell. Coll. Rev. J. Fuller Russell, where seen by Waagen in 1851.[2] Exhibited at Manchester, 1857; Provisional Catalogue, No. 12 with the rest of the predella; Definitive Catalogue, No. 25c. Exhibited at the R.A., 1878 (No. 184). Fuller Russell Sale, 18 April, 1885 (lot 119), purchased out of the Clarke Fund for the National Gallery. Exhibited at Birmingham, *Italian Art*, 1955 (No. 108).

REPRODUCTION: *Illustrations, Italian Schools*, 1937, p. 365. *Plates, Earlier Italian Schools*, 1953, Vol. II, p. 422.

REFERENCES: (1) As Mrs. Coor in *The Art Bulletin*, September, 1955, pp. 155/6, points out, No. 1189 would have been the central section of the predella. It has been remarked in note 11 to the entry for No. 1188 that the Virgin and Child above it was almost certainly wider than the flanking saints of the main tier. No. 1189 is not wider than other predella panels; if it is assumed that No. 1189 has not been cut, it may well be, as Mrs. Coor suggests, that it was flanked by decorative strips, perhaps with the coats of arms of the donors. (2) Waagen, *Treasures*, 1854, II, p. 462.

3375 THE DEPOSITION (PREDELLA PANEL FROM AN ALTARPIECE)

The Maries, SS. John, Nicodemus and Joseph of Arimathaea are present. On the Cross is the inscription (I)C.XC, for Jesus Christ, instead of the usual I.N.R.I.

Wood. The size of the picture is $13\frac{1}{2} \times 20\frac{3}{4}$ (0·345 × 0·525). The size of the panel is 16×23 (0·405 × 0·585).

The condition is good on the whole. The framing, although regilt, may be original.

The composition corresponds fairly closely with the panel of the same subject in Duccio's *Maestà*.[1]

For the altarpiece from which this panel comes, see the commentary to No. 1188 above.

PROVENANCE: For the provenance until the Ottley Sale of 1847, see the commentary to No. 1188 above. Warner Ottley Sale, 30 June, 1847, lot 11 with four other predella panels, wrongly called *The Crucifixion*, bought by Browne, i.e. bought in. Ottley Sale, 24 June, 1850 (lot 55), with all the other predella panels, bought by Russell. Coll. Rev. J. Fuller Russell, where seen by Waagen in 1851.[2] Exhibited at Manchester, 1857; Provisional Catalogue, No. 12 with the rest of the predella; Definitive Catalogue, No. 25d. Exhibited at the R.A., 1878 (No. 186). Fuller Russell Sale, 18 April, 1885 (lot 120), bought by Wagner. Lent by Henry Wagner to the New Gallery, 1893/4 (No. 26), and to the Burlington Fine Arts Club, 1904 (No. 10); presented by Henry Wagner, 1918.

REPRODUCTION: *Illustrations, Italian Schools*, 1937, p. 366. *Plates, Earlier Italian Schools*, 1953, Vol. II, p. 423.

REFERENCES: (1) Van Marle, *Development of the Italian Schools of Painting*, Vol. II, Fig. 30. (2) Waagen, *Treasures*, 1854, II, p. 462.

3376 ISAIAH (PINNACLE FROM AN ALTARPIECE)

Inscribed across the background, the letters being much effaced: YSA / .AS. He holds a scroll, on which remain the letters (A)RI and NOMEN; these are the remains of an inscription from Isaiah vii, 14, *Ecce virgo concipiet, et pariet filium, et vocabitur nomen ejus Emmanuel.*

Wood, pointed top. The size of the picture is $13\frac{1}{2} \times 10$ ($0 \cdot 34 \times 0 \cdot 25$). The size of the panel is $18 \times 12\frac{1}{2}$ ($0 \cdot 46 \times 0 \cdot 32$). A strip $1\frac{5}{8}$ in. ($0 \cdot 04$) along the bottom is joined on, but is apparently old. Several inches have been cut away from the bottom, as can be seen from the position of the scroll and from the analogy of the other pinnacles of Ugolino's altarpiece; the pointed top appears to be of the original shape.

Considerably damaged, especially in the lower part.

For the altarpiece from which this pinnacle comes, see the commentary to No. 1188 above.

PROVENANCE: For the provenance until the Ottley Sale of 1847, see the commentary to No. 1188 above. Apparently Warner Ottley Sale, 30 June, 1847 (lot 8), wrongly as S. John, bought by Anthony. Coll. Rev. J. Fuller Russell, where seen (but not described) by Waagen in 1851.[1] Exhibited at the R.A., 1878 (No. 190), size given as 15×10. Fuller Russell Sale, 18 April, 1885 (lot 113 or 114), bought by Butler. Charles Butler Sale, 25 May, 1911 (lot 85), bought by Smith for Henry Wagner.[2] Presented by Henry Wagner, 1918.

REPRODUCTION: *Illustrations, Italian Schools*, 1937, p. 363. *Plates, Earlier Italian Schools*, 1953, Vol. II, p. 424.

REFERENCES: (1) Waagen, *Treasures*, 1854, II, p. 462. Some comment on the various errors of reference to this picture is made in the commentary to No. 1188 above, towards the end. (2) A letter from Henry Wagner of 20 December, 1911 (apropos of the gift of pictures Nos. 2862/3 to the Gallery), confirms this.

3377 SS. SIMON AND THADDEUS (JUDE) (FRAGMENT OF AN ALTARPIECE)

The names are inscribed on the background; for the figure on the left only...ON is now legible, for the figure on the right S.THA. In framing with a trefoil design at the top, and a strip of quatrefoil designs including three heads below.

Wood, top corners cut. The size of the compartments containing the large figures, trefoil tops, is $17 \times 8\frac{7}{8}$ ($0 \cdot 43 \times 0 \cdot 225$) each. The size of the strip along the bottom is $3\frac{1}{2} \times 20\frac{7}{8}$ ($0 \cdot 09 \times 0 \cdot 53$). The size of the panel is $26 \times 22\frac{1}{2}$ ($0 \cdot 66 \times 0 \cdot 57$), top corners cut; the panel is apparently the original panel, and is in one piece as seen from the back. The total size of the front, including all the framing, is $27\frac{3}{4} \times 24\frac{1}{2}$ ($0 \cdot 705 \times 0 \cdot 625$); the total of the front measured inside the frame is 24×21 ($0 \cdot 61 \times 0 \cdot 53$).

Much damaged. In general, the central parts of the frame, although regilt, seem to be original.

The reading of what remains of the letters for the saint on the left is difficult. In the first edition of this catalogue, it was given as C(O?), for S. James; but... ON for S. Simon is to be accepted as certain, since, as Mrs. Coor points out[1], the types of the Apostles in Ugolino's altarpiece correspond closely with those in Duccio's *Maestà*, where the names are clear.

For the altarpiece from which No. 3377 comes, see the commentary to No. 1188 above.

PROVENANCE: For the provenance until the Ottley Sale of 1847, see the commentary to No. 1188 above. Warner Ottley Sale, 30 June, 1847 (lot 6, probably, which was bought by Anthony). Coll. Rev. J. Fuller Russell, where seen by Waagen in 1851.[2] Exhibited at Manchester, 1857; not in the Provisional Catalogue; Definitive Catalogue, No. 27.[3] Exhibited at the R.A., 1878 (No. 189). Fuller Russell Sale, 18 April, 1885 (lot 110), bought by Wagner. Lent by Henry Wagner to the New Gallery, 1893/4 (No. 76),[4] and to the Burlington Fine Arts Club, 1904 (No. 2). Presented by Henry Wagner, 1919. Exhibited at the National Gallery, N.A.C.F. Exhibition, 1945/6 (No. 27).

REPRODUCTION: *Illustrations, Italian Schools*, 1937, p. 364. *Plates, Earlier Italian Schools*, 1953, Vol. II, p. 425.

REFERENCES: (1) Gertrude Coor-Achenbach in *The Art Bulletin*, September, 1955, p. 158. (2) Waagen gives no description, but it can be deduced with fair certainty that he saw No. 3377. (3) The label of the Manchester Exhibition is still on the back of the picture. (4) Wrongly called SS. Mark and Thomas. The two apostles on No. 3377 have usually been left anonymous; at the B.F.A.C. in 1904, one of the figures is called probably S. James the Less.

3378   TWO ANGELS (FRAGMENT FROM AN ALTARPIECE)

Wood. The size of the painted surface is $10 \times 20\frac{3}{4}$ ($0 \cdot 25 \times 0 \cdot 53$); of this, the two angels in the spandrels are the original part, the arched space separating them having been entirely regilt. The size of the original part of the panel is apparently $11 \times 22\frac{1}{4}$ ($0 \cdot 28 \times 0 \cdot 565$); the total size of the panel at present is $13 \times 23\frac{1}{2}$ ($0 \cdot 33 \times 0 \cdot 60$).

The angels are in quite good condition, but their gilt backgrounds suffer from an apparently bituminous crackle. The gilding of the arch, as already remarked, is new; the framework is new.

For the altarpiece from which this fragment comes, see the commentary to No. 1188 above. No. 3378 is the top part of one of the principal panels of the polyptych; originally, the figure of a saint was shown below the arch.

PROVENANCE: Possibly Warner Ottley Sale, 30 June, 1847, attached to lots 2, 3 or 6, bought by Anthony.[1] Coll. Rev. J. Fuller Russell, where seen by Waagen.[2] Exhibited at the R.A., 1878 (No. 183). Fuller Russell Sale, 18 April, 1885 (lot 115), bought by Wagner. Lent by Henry Wagner to the Burlington Fine Arts Club, 1904 (No. 3); presented by Henry Wagner, 1919.

REPRODUCTION: *Illustrations, Italian Schools*, 1937, p. 367. *Plates, Earlier Italian Schools*, 1953, Vol. II, p. 426.

REFERENCES: (1) Cf. the commentary to No. 1188 above; all these lots passed into the Fuller Russell Collection. (2) Waagen, *Treasures*, IV, 1857, p. 285. Waagen (cf. p. 284) records No. 3378 and No. 4191 below as having been acquired by the Rev. J. Fuller Russell after 1854; but No. 4191 appeared with all the other predella panels in the Ottley Sale of 1850, and the lot is marked in the auctioneer's copy of the catalogue as being bought by Russell.

3473   SS. BARTHOLOMEW AND ANDREW (FRAGMENT OF AN ALTARPIECE)

The names are inscribed on the background, (   )THOLO/MEU and S AN/DREAS.

Wood, top corners cut. The size of the compartments containing the figures, trefoil tops, is $17 \times 8\frac{7}{8}$ (0·43 × 0·225), each. The size of the panel is $21\frac{7}{8} \times 22$ (0·555 × 0·56), top corners cut; the total size of the front, including all the framing, is $24\frac{1}{4} \times 27\frac{1}{2}$ (0·62 × 0·70).

Damaged, and with considerable areas of repaint. In general, the inner parts of the frame are apparently original, but regilt.

For the altarpiece from which No. 3473 comes, see the commentary to No. 1188 above.

The two figures, especially S. Bartholomew, are derived from the representations of the same saints on Duccio's *Maestà*.[1]

PROVENANCE: For the provenance until the Ottley Sale of 1847, see the commentary to No. 1188 above. Warner Ottley Sale, 30 June, 1847 (lot 4), bought by Bromley Davenport. Seen in the Davenport Bromley Collection by Waagen;[2] Sale, 12 June, 1863 (lot 5), bought by Anthony. Exhibited at the R.A., 1878 (No. 182), lent by Lord Crawford; again at the Burlington Fine Arts Club, 1904 (No. 6); presented by the Earl of Crawford and Balcarres, through the National Art-Collections Fund, 1919.

REPRODUCTION: *Illustrations, Italian Schools*, 1937, p. 365. *Plates, Earlier Italian Schools*, 1953, Vol. II, p. 426.

REFERENCES: (1) Weigelt, *Sienese Painting of the Trecento*, n.d., Plates 18 and 19. (2) Waagen, *Treasures*, 1854, III, p. 374.

4191   THE RESURRECTION (PREDELLA PANEL FROM AN ALTARPIECE)

Wood. The size of the picture is $13\frac{1}{2} \times 20\frac{1}{2}$ (0·345 × 0·52). The size of the panel is $16 \times 22\frac{1}{4}$ (0·405 × 0·565); this excludes a narrow strip added down the right-hand side, but includes an insertion in the right-hand bottom corner, size $6 \times 2\frac{1}{4}$ (0·15 × 0·055), with a slanting top.

Much damaged, especially in the flesh of Christ; the background regilt.

For the altarpiece from which this panel comes, see the commentary to No. 1188 above.

PROVENANCE: For the provenance until the Ottley Sale of 1847, see the commentary to No. 1188 above. Warner Ottley Sale, 30 June, 1847, lot 11 with four other predella panels, bought by Browne, i.e. bought in. Ottley Sale, 24 June, 1850 (lot 55), with all the other predella panels, bought by Russell. Coll. Rev. J. Fuller Russell, where seen by Waagen.[1] Exhibited at Manchester, 1857; Provisional Catalogue, No. 12 with the rest of the predella; Definitive Catalogue, No. 25f. Exhibited at the R.A., 1878 (No. 188). Fuller Russell Sale, 18 April,

1885 (lot 122), bought by White. C. Holden-White Sale, 16 January, 1925 (lot 105), bought by Martin. Presented by Viscount Rothermere, 1926.

REPRODUCTION: *Illustrations, Italian Schools,* 1937, p. 366. *Plates, Earlier Italian Schools,* 1953, Vol. II, p. 427.

REFERENCE: (1) Waagen, *Treasures,* IV, 1857, p. 285. Cf. note 2 to No. 3378 above.

UMBRIAN (?) SCHOOL

4143   FRESCO: A SAINT (FRAGMENT)

He seems to be turning over the pages of a book with his right hand.

Fresco, transferred to canvas, $31\frac{1}{2} \times 25\frac{1}{2}$ (0·80 × 0·65). Much damaged.

For the commentary, etc., see No. 4145 below.

4144   FRESCO: A SAINT (FRAGMENT)

Seated at a desk, a pen in his left hand, gazing upwards as if to receive inspiration.

Fresco, transferred to canvas, $30\frac{1}{2} \times 24\frac{1}{2}$ (0·775 × 0·615). Much damaged.

For the commentary, etc., see No. 4145 below.

4145   FRESCO: A BISHOP SAINT (FRAGMENT)

Holding a book.

Fresco, transferred to canvas, $30\frac{3}{4} \times 25\frac{1}{2}$ (0·78 × 0·65). Much damaged.

The three fragments, Nos. 4143/5, are each within a medallion, and perhaps formed part of the framing of some large composition. Some modern inscriptions scratched into No. 4145 (1488 / .D.VLISSES *de...*, etc.) suggest that No. 4145 was, when on the wall, within convenient reach.

A fourth fragment, obviously of the same series, is in the Museum of Historic Art at Princeton, N.J.[1] A fifth (*Christ?*) was in 1933 owned by Torquato Malagola, Rome.[2]

Nos. 4143/5 are stated to come from the Palazzo del Podestà, Piazza Vittorio Emmanuele (now Piazza del Comune), Assisi;[3] the fifth fragment is stated to come from the Palazzo del Capitano del Popolo at Assisi, which is a more correct name. The building is also known as the Palazzo del Comune, apparently. Several other frescoes from this building, including one of several riders, are now on deposit in the Pinacoteca at Assisi;[4] none of them seems connected with Nos. 4143/5.

Nos. 4143/5 were ascribed by Sir Charles Holmes[5] to the following of Pietro Cavallini (b. *ca.* 1250?—still living 1308); but they appear to be works of the middle or even late fourteenth century. Since they come from Assisi, the hand may be Umbrian.

PROVENANCE: Stated, as explained above, to be from the Palazzo del Capitano del Popolo at Assisi; removed from the wall in 1923. Purchased from G. Dudley Wallis, 1926.

REPRODUCTIONS: *Illustrations, Italian Schools*, 1937, pp. 93/4. *Plates, Earlier Italian Schools*, 1953, Vol. II, p. 428.

REFERENCES: (1) Photograph in the Gallery archives; size, 0·80 × 0·65; subject, a bearded saint, called S. John. (2) Photograph and information in the Gallery archives; size, 0·56 × 0·66. (3) Document in the Gallery archives. It is possible that they had been uncovered not very long before being removed from the wall in 1923; Mariano Guardabassi, *Indice-Guida dei Monumenti Pagani e Cristiani . . . nella Provincia dell' Umbria*, 1872, p. 27, mentions only frescoed coats of arms in the Palazzo del Capitano del Popolo at Assisi. (4) They are the property of the Cassa di Risparmio di Perugia. For a list of the frescoes, see Emma Zocca, *Catalogo delle Cose d'Arte e di Antichità d'Italia, Assisi*, 1936, pp. 256/7; the one with riders is referred to by Van Marle, *Development of the Italian Schools of Painting*, V, p. 436 (Italian edition, I, p. 419). (5) Sir Charles Holmes in the *Festschrift für Max J. Friedländer*, 1927, pp. 209 ff.; and National Gallery Catalogue, 1929.

UTILI *See* GIOVANNI BATTISTA OF FAENZA

VENETIAN SCHOOL

631 PORTRAIT OF A LADY

Wood, painted surface, $14\frac{1}{2} \times 11\frac{3}{4}$ (0·37 × 0·30).

Good state, except for the left half of the background, which is almost entirely new. Painted spandrels form a rounded top; these had been hidden before the recent cleaning of the picture.

No satisfactory attribution has been made. Traditionally Gentile Bellini, it for long passed as a Bissolo,[1] but was in the 1929 edition of the catalogue called Bartolomeo Veneto.[2] Gronau[3] suggested Francesco Rizzo da Santacroce, Jacobsen[4] a pupil of Palma Vecchio, Berenson (1957 Lists) Pietro degli Ingannati (?). The painted framing at the top of the picture seems to be in a Northern tradition, in which case it might be by some German or Netherlander established at Venice. The costume is perhaps of 1510/20.

PROVENANCE: From the collection of Col. Bourgeois, Paris.[5] Purchased with the rest of the Edmond Beaucousin Collection, Paris, 1860.

REPRODUCTION: *Illustrations, Italian Schools*, 1937, p. 378 (before cleaning). *Plates, Earlier Italian Schools*, 1953, Vol. II, p. 429.

REFERENCES: (1) Cf. Crowe and Cavalcaselle, *Painting in North Italy*, I, 1871, p. 287, or ed. Borenius, 1912, Vol. I, p. 293. (2) This attribution seems to have been made by Morelli, and to be approved by Frizzoni, *Arte Italiana del Rinascimento*, 1891, p. 324. (3) Gronau in the *Gazette des Beaux-Arts*, 1895, I, p. 263. (4) Jacobsen in the *Repertorium für Kunstwissenschaft*, 1901, p. 342. (5) N.G. MS. Catalogue.

750 THE VIRGIN AND CHILD WITH SS. CHRISTOPHER
AND JOHN THE BAPTIST, AND DOGE GIOVANNI
MOCENIGO

The Christ Child is shown twice, once held by the Virgin, once by S. Christopher. S. John's scroll is inscribed ECCE AG(nus). The Doge holds a banner with the Lion of S. Mark, an inscription PAX / TIBI / MAR/CE / EVA/NGEL/ISTA / MEVS, and the Mocenigo arms; he kneels before an altar, on which are the Mocenigo arms and an inscription, VRBEM REM VE/NETAM SERVA / VENETVMQᴱ / SENA-TVM / ET MIHI SI ME/REOR VIRGO / SVPERNA (f)AVE.

Canvas, $72\frac{1}{2} \times 116\frac{1}{2}$ ($1\cdot84 \times 2\cdot96$). Beyond these measurements, a little of the painting is turned over the edges of the stretcher all round; e.g. the remaining part of the G of *Agnus*.

Condition very untrustworthy. Thus, many of the numberless light touches on the brocades and on the patterning on the banner seem to be false; these restorations may be fairly recent. It is possible that there are other, earlier restorations as well; yet it seems probable that the faces of the Virgin, the Child and S. John, and even S. Christopher's head and hand with the Child he carries, although considerably damaged and re-touched, are not seriously changed in character. The Doge's flesh seems to have suffered more. The high-lights in the landscape, painted in a loose technique, seem for the most part original. The inscription seems much retouched, but presumably follows old indications; the F needed for the last word is missing also on an engraving of the picture, which Ludwig said is of the seventeenth century.[1] A few comparatively slight *pentimenti*, e.g. in the Doge's head, and in the fingers of the Child blessing.

The coats of arms on No. 750 make it certain that the Doge is a Mocenigo, either Pietro (Doge, 1474–1476) or Giovanni (Doge, 1478–1485). The traditional identification of Giovanni is seen to be correct, because his Patron is here S. John; Giovanni's features on a medal correspond well enough.[2]

According to the Mocenigo archives (of an unspecified date) 'era costume della Repubblica Veneta che ogni Doge regnante regalasse un dipinto storico di Sua famiglia al Palazzo Ducale. Il Doge Giovanni Mocenigo ne commise l'esecuzione al Carpaccio. Ma essendo il Doge sudetto morto di peste nel 1485—poco prima che l'artista portasse il quadro a compimento—i suoi eredi lo acquistarono per la somma di duemila ducati.'[3]

These statements are applied to No. 750, but appear to be not entirely convincing. They have been accompanied by others, apparently not taken from the Mocenigo archives, but attributable rather to Giulio Cornoldi, *procuratore* of Count Mocenigo in 1866.[4] The picture, it is said, was painted on the occasion of the Plague in 1478/9. Cornoldi doubtless had seen a (false) date of 1479 on the picture;[5] as for the Plague, Cornoldi says that S. Christopher was invoked against the Plague (which was sometimes so), and that the vase on the altar in No.

750 is votive, 'acciò la Vergine si degni benedire ai farmachi pegli appestati.'

Admittedly, No. 750 may have been connected with some outbreak of the Plague; though the inscription (such as it is) seems to have rather a political tinge.

There was an outbreak of Plague in Venice in 1478/9; another in 1485 has already been mentioned. The earlier occasion would suit the false signature once on the picture; the other would suit better the statements in the Mocenigo archives, although even so these would make little sense.

It was necessary to record at some length this unsatisfactory documentation concerning the picture, in order that the student may understand that neither a connection with the Plague nor a date of 1479 are proved.

To pass on to the attribution, one must first consider if No. 750 is a fifteenth-century picture. The condition is not good, and the point is very hard to decide; indeed, most Venetian canvases of the fifteenth century are so much damaged that it is difficult to arrive at a reasonable standard for such things. It may, nevertheless, be noted that in some parts of No. 750, such as the impasto of S. Christopher's nose, where the paint is not new repaint, and perhaps is not old repaint, the technique would appear unlikely on a picture of 1478/85. It is certainly tempting to attribute the picture's poor quality to its being a copy; but it cannot be excluded that it may be a poor (and damaged) original.

Copy or not, No. 750 is traditionally ascribed to Carpaccio. The false signatures of Carpaccio, on the later state of the engraving and once on the picture, have been recorded in note 5. On stylistic grounds, no certainty can be reached, since the earliest authenticated Carpaccio is of 1490. There are, nevertheless, some grounds for thinking that No. 3098 of this catalogue may be a work by Carpaccio earlier than 1490; that picture, like No. 750, is much damaged. The most obvious point of comparison is the landscape; but it is only in photographs that the loosely painted landscapes in Nos. 3098 and 750 may be said to appear alike. So far as critical opinion is concerned, Berenson formerly listed No. 750 as by Carpaccio.[6] The compiler would be reluctant to accept No. 750 as Carpaccio's; but, if the picture were admitted to be only an old copy, would feel less difficulty in believing it to be a copy of Carpaccio.

It is inevitable that a Carpaccio as dubious as No. 750 should have been attributed to Lazzaro Bastiani.[7] It is more surprising that it should have been attributed to Gentile Bellini,[8] Giovanni Bellini,[9] or both Gentile and Giovanni Bellini.[10]

A rather similar portrait, identified as being Giovanni Mocenigo, is in the Correr Museum at Venice.[11] Another, also similar to the portrait in No. 750, is in the Frick Collection at New York;[12] this is traditionally identified as Andrea Vendramin (Doge, 1476–1478), but has also been called Giovanni Mocenigo.[13] Andrea Vendramin's features are authentically recorded in a miniature,[14] and are not unlike; so there is no necessity to reject the tradition for the Frick picture. Mayer,[15] on the other hand, marking the resemblance, supposed that the Doge in No. 750 was originally Andrea Vendramin, on whose death he was turned into Giovanni Mocenigo; this view seems rash, and it was perhaps put forward in favour of yet another portrait of a Doge, whom Mayer says is Giovanni Mocenigo.

ENGRAVING: See above.

PROVENANCE: Recorded *ca.* 1840 in the Collection of the Mocenigo di S. Polo at Venice.[16] Purchased from Conte Alvise Mocenigo di S. Eustachio, Venice, 1865.[17]

REPRODUCTION: *Illustrations, Italian Schools*, 1937, p. 29. *Plates, Earlier Italian Schools*, 1953, Vol. II, p. 430.

REFERENCES: (1) G. Ludwig, letter in the Gallery archives, apropos of an impression in the Albertina, of which Ludwig sent a photograph. This engraving, as A. E. Popham kindly confirmed, is from the same plate as a later impression in the Gallery archives, in which the only noticeable differences are some cross-hatching in the landscape centre, and the addition of a signature (referred to in note 5). The impression in the Albertina has been trimmed at the margins, and it is impossible to say if it ever had any lettering. The impression in the National Gallery is lettered as follows: *Il Doge Giovanni Mocenigo genuflesso supplicante la B.V. con li S.S. Giō Baīta. e Cristoforo./ Opera di Vittore Carpaccio Veneto dipinta l'anno 1479. esiste dal Sigʳ Giō. Maria Sasso.* In pencil, the first *e* of *esiste* has been given a capital letter, and (*il rame*)? has been added at the end; see further in note 16. On stylistic grounds, Popham inclined to date the engraving in the eighteenth century, but not so late as the activity of Sasso, who died in 1803. It is possible that Sasso took over a plate already made; certainly, the engraving was intended for use in Sasso's projected *Venezia Pittrice*, and there are other impressions of it in the Correr Library at Venice (Stampe, B11 and C2). It should also perhaps be mentioned that No. 750 is stated to have been 'fatto intagliare dal Sasso' in *Giovanni Bellini e Pittori Contemporanei*, publ. Giuseppe Orlandelli, 1840(?), p. 93 (from a reference on p. 95, the date might appear to be rather 1834). In *L'Arte*, 1897, p. 416, Ludwig says that the engraver's name was Jacobi. The engraving is not a good reproduction of the character of the picture, as seen now, and it contains certain mistakes in proportion (the Virgin's niche for instance is too low); but it is in many, quite minute details in accord with No. 750. It is therefore worth noting that on the engraving: (*a*) the lion on the banner has his head turned backwards; (*b*) there is no conical hill above S. John the Baptist's hand; (*c*) the cloud above the banner stretches a good deal further to the left, well beyond the staff of the banner; (*d*) the fruit in the sky has fewer leaves; (*e*) the decoration on the mouldings of the altar is omitted. In some or all of these cases, the engraving may have exactly reproduced the picture as it was at the time; but the X-Ray does not confirm this. (2) Hill, *Corpus*, 1930, No. 436, and Plate 82. The head from Giovanni Mocenigo's tomb is reproduced by Venturi, *Storia dell'Arte Italiana*, Vol. X, Part I, Fig. 273. It may be added that no medal of Pietro Mocenigo is recorded; the statue on his tomb in S. Zanipolo, which may be a fair likeness, is reproduced by Planiscig, *Venezianische Bildhauer der Renaissance*, 1921, p. 49. (3) Letter from Count Alvise Mocenigo, 1931, in the Gallery archives. (4) Document from Giulio Cornoldi, January, 1866, in the Gallery archives; he gives the text copied in 1931 (see the previous note), and adds statements apparently of his own. (5) This date is recorded in the lettering of the engraving (later state), mentioned in note 1; a signature is there shown (later state) on the top of the altar as VICTOR CARPATIO. Signature and date are mentioned on p. 93 of Orlandelli, as in note 1. In 1855/6, Mündler in his Diary records that the inscription on the picture was illegible. In 1865, when the picture was acquired for the National Gallery, it bore a signature MCCCLXXIX. VICTORE CARPATIO F. (N.G. Report, 1865, position not recorded); this was removed as false soon after. (6) Berenson, *Venetian Painters*, 1894, 1895, 1897. (7) Ludwig in *L'Arte*, 1897, pp. 415/6; Paoletti and Ludwig in the *Repertorium für Kunstwissenschaft*, 1900, p. 278; Ludwig and Molmenti, *Vittore Carpaccio*, 1906, pp. 19 ff. Pallucchini in *Arte Veneta*, 1951, p. 196, does not exclude Bastiani. (8) M. L(ogan) in *The Burlington Magazine*, Vol. III (1903), pp. 319/20. (9) Berenson, Lists of 1957. It is but fair to add that Giovanni Bellini's use of impasto is in a very advanced technique; but it seems unlike the paint of No. 750. (10) Gronau, Klassiker der Kunst *Bellini*, 1930, Plate 68; Gamba, *Giovanni Bellini*, 1937, pp. 89/90. (11) Ascribed to Gentile Bellini since its cleaning; see T. Pignatti in *The Burlington Magazine*, March 1953, p. 93 and the Correr Catalogue, 1957, pp. 43/4, with reproduction. (12) See Gronau in *Unknown Masterpieces*, Vol. I, 1930, Plate 16, and the large Frick Catalogue, I, 1949, p. 237; also reproduced by Van Marle, *Development of the Italian Schools of Painting*, Vol. XVII, Fig. 84. (13) By Gamba, *Giovanni Bellini*, 1937, p. 90. (14) Reproduced by Venturi, *Storia dell'Arte Italiana*, Vol. VII, Part IV, Fig. 343, and in the Burlington Arts Club, Early Venetian Exhibition, Catalogue, 1912, Plate L. Cf. F. Mason Perkins in *Apollo*, March, 1927, pp. 102 ff. (15) A. L. Mayer in *Pantheon*, 1930, pp. 17 ff. (16) *Giovanni Bellini e Pittori Contemporanei*, publ. Giuseppe Orlandelli, 1840 (?), p. 93. See also O. Mündler, *Essai d'une Analyse Critique . . . du Louvre*, 1850, p. 53. It is usually assumed that No. 750 had been in the Mocenigo possession since it was painted, and that is indeed likely enough. Yet the lettering on Sasso's engraving, recorded in note 1, could be held to be against this. Sasso actually says that he owned the picture, and this statement seems to have been corrected in the National Gallery impression to ownership of the plate. It would be possible to argue that Sasso sold the picture after the lettering was made on the engraving; yet it is not to be excluded that Sasso's lettering was badly expressed, and that Sasso never meant to claim ownership of the picture. (17) In National Gallery catalogues as Carpaccio from the time of acquisition. Changed in 1906 to Bastiani, then in 1913 to the School of Gentile Bellini.

3086 AUGUSTUS AND THE SIBYL

The Virgin and Child appear in the sky.

Poplar;[1] $7 \times 15\frac{1}{4}$ (0·175 × 0·385) is the size of the painted surface shown. The panel extends to $9\frac{3}{4} \times 18$ (0·245 × 0·455), and the four edges are ornamented with a painted border in leaf decoration, $\frac{5}{8}$ in. wide. The space between the two painted areas is now blank; no doubt it once had a moulding to serve as a framing, and the panel may be supposed to come from a piece of furniture.

Cleaned in 1957; the picture is a good deal damaged.

According to a widespread tradition, the Virgin and Child appeared to Augustus and one of the Sibyls, and pointed out the site of S. Maria d'Aracœli at Rome.[2]

The landscape is taken (it seems) from a *Resurrection* at Berlin, ascribed to Giovanni Bellini; the town and bridge (but not the castle on a hill) recur also in Andrea Busati, No. 3084 of this catalogue, in the entry for which the matter is more fully discussed.

In the 1929 Catalogue as School of Cima, but it is doubtful if an attribution could be made, even if the picture were in reliable condition. In Berenson's lists, *Venetian Painters*, 1894, 1895, 1897 as Carpaccio; 1932 as Giovanni Bellini (?); 1936 as Lazzaro Bastiani (?); 1957 as Diana (?). Fiocco half suggests Lattanzio da Rimini.[3] Pallucchini[4] inclines to Busati.

PROVENANCE: Bought from Richetti by Sir A. H. Layard;[5] Layard Bequest, 1916.[6]

REPRODUCTION: *Illustrations, Italian Schools*, 1937, p. 100. Including the border in the *Plates, Earlier Italian Schools*, 1953, Vol. II, p. 431.

REFERENCES: (1) Letter from B. J. Rendle, of the Forest Products Research Laboratory, in the Gallery archives. (2) Karl Künstle, *Ikonographie der Christlichen Kunst*, 1928, I, p. 309. (3) G. Fiocco, *Carpaccio* ('Valori Plastici'), p. 96. (4) Pallucchini in *Arte Veneta*, 1951, p. 196. (5) Layard MSS., in the National Gallery as Carpaccio. (6) As Gerolamo da Santacroce. For the history of the Layard Collection, see Appendix IV.

3543   S. JEROME IN A LANDSCAPE

His book is inscribed, IRAM / VINCE / PATIĒ / CIA. AM̄ / SIĒCIAz / SCRIPT / RARVM / CARNIS / VINSIA. / NŌ AMAĒ.

Cypress (?),[1] painted surface, $13\frac{1}{2} \times 10\frac{1}{2}$ (0.345×0.27); excluding an edging partly gilded of about $\frac{1}{4}$ in. all round except at the top, where the new gold presumably covers it.

Good condition except for a circular patch by the lion's head, and the new gold background.

The text is derived from a sentence by S. Jerome, *Iram vince patientia: AMA SCIENTIAM Scripturarum, et carnis vitia non amabis.*[2]

According to Van Marle[3], it is of the Veneto-Byzantine School, probably of the 2nd quarter of the fourteenth century; according to Minns,[4] it is Venetian of the late fourteenth century.

PROVENANCE: Given by Ruskin to William Ward; purchased from him by Alfred A. de Pass,[5] by whom exhibited at the Burlington Fine Arts Club, 1905 (No. 8),[6] and presented, 1920.[7]

REPRODUCTION: *Illustrations, Italian Schools*, 1937, p. 371. *Plates, Earlier Italian Schools*, 1953, Vol. II, p. 431.

REFERENCES: (1) Letter from B. J. Rendle, of the Forest Products Research Laboratory, in the Gallery archives. (2) S. Jerome's works in Migne, *Patrologia Latina*, Vol. 22, Col. 1078. (3) Van Marle, *Development of the Italian Schools of Painting*, Vol. IV, p. 39. (4) Kondakov, *The Russian Ikon*, 1927, p. 74, note by Minns. (5) Label on the back. William Ward (1829–1908), copyist of Turner, was closely associated with Ruskin; a volume of Ruskin's letters to him was published in 1922, but the compiler did not find any reference to No. 3543. (6) As Niccolò di Buonaccorso. (7) As Sienese School.

3893   PIETÀ

Christ is against the Cross and in the Tomb; two angels with censers. Inscribed, .I.N.R.I.

Poplar,[1] original painted surface, cusped top, $17\frac{1}{8} \times 10\frac{3}{4}$ (0.435×0.275). The rest of the panel has been covered with new gold, etc.; its rounded top has been slightly shaved. Total size, $20\frac{3}{4} \times 12$ (0.525×0.30).

The original part of the picture is on the whole in good condition.
This is derived from the 'Cristo di San Gregorio'; Christ is said to
have appeared to S. Gregory the Great at mass in Rome, at S. Croce in
Gerusalemme or elsewhere. The original image in S. Croce was engraved by Israel von Meckenem, and corresponds for the most part
with the present picture.[2]

The attribution to the Venetian School is retained from the 1929
Catalogue. Ascribed by Berenson (oral, 1927) to Niccolò da Guardia-
grele.[3]

PROVENANCE: Charles Butler Sale, London, 25 May, 1911 (lot 15),[4] bought by
(Henry) Wagner, by whom presented, 1924.[5]

REPRODUCTION: *Illustrations, Italian Schools*, 1937, p. 371. *Plates, Earlier
Italian Schools*, 1953, Vol. II, p. 432.

REFERENCES: (1) Letter from B. J. Rendle, of the Forest Products Research
Laboratory, in the Gallery archives. (2) Cf. E. Mâle, *L'Art Religieux de la Fin
du Moyen Age en France*, 2nd edition, 1922, pp. 98 ff. Mâle reproduces the
engraving (Bartsch, Vol. VI, No. 135), which is inscribed: *Hec ymago contrefacta
est ad instar et similitudinem illius prime ymaginis pietatis custodite in ecclesia sancte
crucis in urbe romana quam fecerat depingi sanctissimus gregorius pontifex magnus
propter habitam ac sibi ostensam desuper visionem.* For further references, see
Campbell Dodgson, *Woodcuts of the XV Century in the British Museum*, I, 1934,
No. 112, and E. Panofsky, '*Imago Pietatis*' in the Festschrift Friedländer, 1927,
pp. 261 ff. (3) His signed picture is reproduced by Van Marle, *Development of
the Italian Schools of Painting*, Vol. VIII, p. 453. (4) As School of Cimabue. (5)
As Venetian School.

4250 ALTARPIECE OF THE VIRGIN MARY

Centre, The Virgin and Child; there remains a fragment of the inscription, MARIA. / (Mate)R. HVM / (ili)S (or perhaps better, (ilitati)S).
For the iconography, see the commentary below.

Wood, painted surface (cusped top), 29 × 18 (0·735 × 0·455); measurements here and elsewhere to the edges of the painted area or the incised
lines marking the limits of the gold.

Left Side, Story of the Birth of the Virgin
    (a) (Outer Top) *S. Joachim's Offering Rejected;* with the name,
.S̃. / IVACHI / NVS.
    (b) (Inner Top) *The Angel appearing to S. Joachim;* with the name,
.S̃.IV / ACHI / NVS.
    (c) (Outer Bottom) *The Meeting at the Golden Gate;* with the
names, .S̃. ANA., and S̃ / IVACH / INV'.
    (d) (Inner Bottom) *The Birth of the Virgin;* with the names, .S̃.
ANA., and M̅P̅.Θ̅V̅.(Mother of God).

*Right Side, Miracles of the Virgin Connected with the Feast of the Con-
ception*
    (e) (Outer Top) *Helsinus Saved from Shipwreck.*
    The visionary prelate holds a scroll inscribed, *Vis. mo/rtem.
e/uader/e . conc/pciōe/z . Virg/inis . ce/lebra/bis . / vi . i/dus / dec*
(December 8th).

Reverse: on the back is a rough drawing of a head in profile.

(*f*) (Inner Top) *Helsinus Preaching in favour of the Celebration of the Conception.*

In the right-hand top corner (under the frame) is the obscure scribble, *quando chō/prasemo | le pare/dane (Per I?)*; the writing seems to be quite old.

(*g*) (Outer Bottom) *A French Canon Drowned by Devils.*

The Virgin appears in the sky, with the inscription $\overline{\text{MP}}.\overline{\ominus\text{V}}$.

(*h*) (Inner Bottom) *The Canon Restored to Life by the Virgin.*

The Virgin again appears, with the inscription $\text{MP}.\overline{\ominus\text{V}}$.

(*a*) and (*c*), (*b*) and (*d*), (*e*) and (*g*), (*f*) and (*h*) are on single pieces of wood; the four panels have each been covered with gesso over the whole front surface. The painted areas of the scenes vary slightly, the upper row being approximately $12 \times 10\frac{1}{2}$ (0·305 × 0·265), the lower row approximately $11\frac{1}{2} \times 10\frac{1}{2}$ (0·29 × 0·265), all with cusped tops.

Predella, Christ and the Twelve Apostles

Christ's book is inscribed: E(g)O S/ON LV/X. MO/NDI. | VIA./ VER/ITA/S. ET / VIT. The Apostles are each inscribed with their names: from left to right, S̄. / FELI/PV'., S̄. /MATEV', (S.Jac) HOBV'. / MINOR.,.S. / .MATIA.,.S̄. / .IACHOBV'.,.S. / . PETRV'.,.S. / .IOVANE / V̄A.,.S̄. / .BARTO/LOME/V'.,S̄. / .ANDRE/AS,.S̄. / TADEV'., S. / SIMON, S̄ / T(homas).

Wood,[1] in three pieces. From Philip to Bartholomew, the painted surface is $5\frac{1}{8} \times 49$ (0·13 × 1·245); painted up to the edges except at the bottom. Andrew and Thaddeus, painted surface, $5\frac{1}{4} \times 9\frac{3}{4}$ (0·135 × 0·25), exclusive of $\frac{1}{2}$ in. added to the panel on the left; painted up to the edges all round. Simon and Thomas, $5\frac{1}{4} \times 10\frac{3}{4}$ (0·135 × 0·275), exclusive of $\frac{1}{2}$ in. added to the panel on the right; painted up to the edges all round.

The condition in parts is fair, though there are considerable areas of new paint. The most important part affected on the central panel is about half of the Virgin's left hand. The scenes are on the whole the parts least injured.

This altarpiece may be intended as a representation of the Immaculate Conception. The two miracles of the Virgin are two of the three stories given in additions to the *Golden Legend* as alternative origins of the Feast of the Conception on 8 December.[2] (1) William the Conqueror, alarmed at the naval and military preparations in Denmark, sent Helsinus (Æthelsige), Abbot of Ramsey in Huntingdonshire, to enquire into the matter, which he did. On his way back, his vessel was menaced by a violent storm; but an angel dressed as a bishop appeared standing on the water, and said that they would all be saved from shipwreck if Helsinus vowed to celebrate and persuade others to celebrate the Conception of the Virgin on 8 December. (2)[3] A French canon, returning from fornication with a married woman, took a boat to cross the Seine, and at the same time began to recite the Office of the Virgin. A crowd of devils sent him and the boat to the bottom, and began to torment his soul; but three days later the Virgin among angels appeared, proved to the devils that the canon's soul was rightly hers, reinstated it in his body and, parting the waters, brought him safely to the bank. The Virgin made the canon promise that he would refrain from adultery, and that he would celebrate the Feast of her Conception on 8 December.

The pictures vary slightly from the stories as given above; but it seems likely that the painter was working from a literary source such as the *Golden Legend*, because these subjects are in pictures rare.[4] On the pictures of story No. 2, in one scene the devils are represented forcing the man's soul out of his mouth, and in the other angels are putting it back again.

The subjects on the left side of No. 4250 are also connected with the Conception and Birth of the Virgin, from what may be called the historical point of view.

The central panel is specifically described as representing a Madonna of Humility, though her attitude and the Child's differ somewhat from the traditional Venetian form; she has the moon at her feet, the sun as a brooch at her breast, and the background is ornamented with stars.[5]

It may be noted that it is here S. Paul who has been omitted from the company of the twelve Apostles. The emblem of S. James the Great is at present a whip, but it is clear that it has been changed by repaint from the usual pilgrim's staff.

Fiocco[6] ascribed the central panel to a follower of Lorenzo Veneziano, the rest to Stefano Veneziano (*plebanus* di Sant'Agnese). Coletti[7] ascribed the whole to Jacobello di Bonomo. These suggestions are not satisfactory; in particular, it seems very clear that the 'Virgin and Child' is not by a different hand from the rest. The picture is essentially Venetian, probably from towards the end of the fourteenth century, but Coletti seems justified in noting the 'Bolognese vivacity' of some details, and Longhi thinks it may come from the region of Rimini.[8]

PROVENANCE: On the back (twice) P. Laurati (i.e. Lorenzetti). William Graham Sale, 8 April, 1886 (lot 224), bought by Clifford.[9] Bequeathed by H. E. Luxmoore, 1927. Cleaned Pictures Exhibition at the National Gallery, 1947/8 (No. 17).

REPRODUCTIONS: *Illustrations, Italian Schools*, 1937, p. 370 (small). *Plates, Earlier Italian Schools*, 1953, Vol. II, pp. 433–436. The drawing on the reverse is reproduced in *Paintings and Drawings on the Backs of National Gallery Pictures*, 1946, Plate 39.

REFERENCES: (1) A piece of the predella was tested and found to be lime by B. J. Rendle, of the Forest Products Research Laboratory. (2) *The Golden Legend*, tr. W. Caxton, Temple Classics, II, 1928, pp. 126 ff. There are some variations in *La Légende Dorée*, Garnier edition, II, pp. 334 ff. It should be noted that similar miracles are recorded of the Virgin without reference to the Feast of the Immaculate Conception, although in the present case the association should not be doubted. A window in Orsanmichele, Florence, shows a scene that is comparable, but that (no doubt rightly) is not associated with the Conception by Werner Cohn in the *Mitteilungen des Kunsthistorischen Institutes in Florenz*, 1959, p. 9 (No. 9). Students desiring information about the legends may consult E. F. Wilson, *The Stella Maris of John of Garland*, 1946 or Sister Mary Vincentine Gripkey in *Mediaeval Studies*, Vols. XIV, 1952, pp. 9 ff. and XV, 1953, pp. 14 ff. (3) This story is in the Garnier edition of the Golden

Legend, but not in Caxton's translation. For these stories (the text was believed to be by S. Anselm), see further E. D. O'Connor, *The Dogma of the Immaculate Conception*, 1958, pp. 522 f. (4) The story of Helsinus does, however, appear in the predella of Francia's *Immaculate Conception* in S. Frediano at Lucca; see Montgomery Carmichael, *Francia's Masterpiece*, 1909, pp. 58 ff. (For further comment on this picture, see R. Ligtenberg in the *Mededeelingen van het Neder-landsch Historisch Instituut te Rome*, 1931, pp. 65 ff.) The same story was also on a window in S. Jean at Rouen; E. Mâle, *L'Art Religieux de la Fin du Moyen Age en France*, 2nd edition, 1922, p. 208. The miracle of the canon and that of Helsinus probably appear in a series in Winchester Lady Chapel; see M. R. James in *The Walpole Society*, Vol. XVII, 1928/9, p. 33, and Plate XXI. (5) The emblems are derived from the Apocalyptic Woman and Child (Revelation xii, 1); they often accompany representation of 'The Madonna of Humility.' They were used often in later pictures of or connected with the *Immaculate Conception* (cf. for instance Francesco Podesti's fresco in the Sala dell'Immacolata in the Vatican); even the presence of a Child in pictures of this subject was some-times considered defensible (see Francisco Pacheco, *Arte de la Pintura*, 1649, pp. 481 ff.). It may be added that M. Meiss (*The Art Bulletin*, 1936, p. 463) claims that there is no evidence of a reference to the Immaculate Conception in 'The Madonna of Humility'; but here clearly there is. (6) Fiocco, oral communica-tion. (7) Luigi Coletti in *L'Arte*, 1931, pp. 131 ff. (8) R. Longhi, *Viatico per Cinque Secoli di Pittura Veneziana*, 1946, p. 48. Works he thinks by the same hand are reproduced in the Catalogue of the Rimini Exhibition, 1935, Nos. 60/1, and by L. Serra, *L'Arte nelle Marche*, II, 1934, Figs. 474/5. For further dis-cussion of the attribution, see R. Pallucchini in *Arte Veneta*, 1950, p. 10, and F. Bologna, *ib.*, 1952, pp. 17/8. (9) As Sienese School; the stencil mark of the Graham Sale is on the back of the picture.

VERONESE SCHOOL

1135   TRAJAN AND THE WIDOW (1)

Spruce,[1] painted surface, $13\frac{3}{8} \times 12\frac{3}{8}$ (0·34×0·315); including the framing, which seems to be in one piece with the rest, $19 \times 18\frac{1}{4}$ (0·485 ×0·46).

For the commentary, etc., see No. 1136 below.

1136   TRAJAN AND THE WIDOW (2)

Spruce,[1] painted surface, $13\frac{1}{8} \times 12\frac{7}{8}$ (0·335×0·33); including the framing, which seems to be in one piece with the rest, $18\frac{7}{8} \times 18\frac{1}{2}$ (0·48×0·47).

Good condition; the gold of the framework is new.

Presumably from a cassone.

According to the story, the Emperor Trajan was persuaded to post-pone his affairs, and render justice to a widow for her dead child. The subject was very popular, and is described by Dante, *Purgatorio*, X, 76 sqq.[2]

Nos. 1135/6 might pass as modern imitations, if clearly authentic inscriptions on the backs did not prove that they existed already in 1756. They are probably genuine works of the late fifteenth century. They are not attributable, but seem to be of the School of Verona.[3]

PROVENANCE: On the back of No. 1135 is the inscription: *Vittor Carpaccio Autore | Sig°naroli⁴ Ass(i)curò essere l'Autore di qu(e)sti due quadri | donati in Venezia al Co. Teodoro Albani dalla Sigᵃ Conˢᵃ Catterina | Locatelli Terzi | Vittor Carpaccio | Autore Veneto 1756 | Signaroli assicura l'Autore antico | dal Mille e Cinquecento.* An inscription to exactly the same effect is on the back of No. 1136. Both purchased from Paolo Fabris, Venice, 1883.

REPRODUCTIONS: *Plates, Earlier Italian Schools*, 1953, Vol. II, pp. 437–438.

REFERENCES: (1) Letter from B. J. Rendle, of the Forest Products Research Laboratory, in the Gallery archives. (2) For the story and various illustrations, see Giacomo Boni in the *Nuova Antologia*, 1 November, 1906, pp. 3 ff. (3) P. Schubring ascribes them (or more exactly one of them) to Domenico Morone in his *Illustrationen zu Dantes Göttlicher Komödie*, 1931, Plate 217. The claim in the 1929 catalogue that the front part of the cassone, of which Nos. 1135/6 would have formed the sides, as in the Accademia at Venice presumably refers to No. 170 (Fig. 169) of the Venice Catalogue (XIV and XV Centuries), 1955; this, as is noted there, is not connected with Nos. 1135/6. (4) Presumably the painter Cignaroli.

Andrea del VERROCCHIO
ca. 1435–1488

Florentine School. *Andrea di Michele di Francesco Cioni.* In his father's tax declaration of 1446, his age was given as 12 (R. G. Mather in *The Art Bulletin*, 1948, p. 29; the date on the back, presumably when this tax return was attended to, is 28 February, 1446, 1447 n.s.). He studied as a goldsmith, apparently under Giuliano Verrocchi; he was apparently also a pupil of Donatello. Famous as a sculptor, especially in metalwork, and much employed by the Medici family.

His studio was important in the history of painting; Leonardo da Vinci, Lorenzo di Credi and probably Perugino being his pupils and/or assistants. Verrocchio was himself active as a painter as well as a sculptor; but the identification of his pictures is troublesome. Three works may be considered as in varying degrees authenticated.

(1) An altarpiece in the Cathedral of Pistoia is the subject of a document of November, 1485. The commission had been given to Verrocchio between 1474 and 1479. In the document it is stated on hearsay that Verrocchio would have finished the picture by 1479 if he had received all the money due to him, and that it was nearly, if not quite, finished in November, 1485. The ecclesiastical authorities at Pistoia, therefore, decided to take over the responsibility for the commission, which had been given originally by the executors of Bishop Donato dei Medici. They decided to ascertain if the picture was according to the specification and drawing agreed to in the original contract; to cause it to be finished, if it was not finished; and to pay Verrocchio the money still due, not later than October, 1486.

It is quite certain that Verrocchio received the original commission, and only one degree less certain that the existing picture follows Verrocchio's design. The amount of work already done on the picture by 1485 is uncertain; what happened after 1485 is uncertain. Stylistically, the picture resembles the work of Lorenzo di Credi, to whom indeed Vasari (edition of 1568) attributes it. Lorenzo di Credi may well have been the specialist for painting in Verrocchio's studio, though hardly at the time of the original contract (see the note on his date of birth in his biography in the present catalogue). If Lorenzo executed the picture on Verrocchio's design, it would give no clue to Verrocchio's style of painting; if Verrocchio painted some and Lorenzo the rest, X-Rays might help in isolating Verrocchio's style; if Verrocchio painted the whole picture (which seems indeed unlikely), his style would hardly be distinguishable from Lorenzo's.

(2) *The Baptism of Christ* in the Uffizi is ascribed to Verrocchio by the Anonimo Magliabechiano, Billi and Vasari (editions of 1550 and 1568). One of the angels is traditionally the work of Leonardo da Vinci; this attribution for the angel and a few other parts is acceptable. As for the rest of the picture, it is unfinished and damaged. For an attribution to Botticelli, see Ragghianti in *Critica d'Arte*, 1954, pp. 102 ff., 302 ff.

(3) A picture now at Budapest is apparently identical with one that Vasari (edition of 1568) mentions as Verrocchio's, adding that the painter himself was particularly pleased with it. Many modern critics believe that the picture is of inferior quality, unworthy of Verrocchio; Budapest Catalogue, 1954, No. 1386, as Verrocchio Studio.

It may be admitted that attributions of pictures to Verrocchio are to be treated with reserve.

Ascribed to ANDREA DEL VERROCCHIO

296 THE VIRGIN AND CHILD WITH TWO ANGELS

Wood, painted sufrace, $38 \times 27\frac{3}{4}$ (0·965 × 0·705). Painted up to the edges all round; it is indeed probable that the picture has been considerably cut down.

Cleaned in 1951. Good condition; but rubbed in some of the shadows of the flesh, e.g. on the Virgin's right temple. Some of the gold is new.

There has been a tendency recently among some critics to ascribe No. 296 to Verrocchio's own hand.[1] This is not accepted by everyone.[2] It has been indicated in the biography above that Verrocchio's pictorial style is very difficult to define. If the key-piece is assumed to be the *Baptism* in the Uffizi (in the parts not executed by Leonardo da Vinci), it is reasonable to maintain that No. 296 is not very far from Verrocchio, as was done first by Crowe and Cavalcaselle.[3] No. 296 has been grouped with a *Virgin with the Standing Child* at Berlin[4] and with another, inferior, picture at Frankfort;[5] it would indeed seem to be by the same hand as the former.[6] Any more precise statement about the authorship or dating would appear to be, in the present state of knowledge, undesirable;[7] but it may be added that the draughtsmanship in No. 296 is more mechanical than might be expected of Verrocchio.

DRAWINGS: There exist, it seems, no drawings certainly connected with No. 296. There are dubious connections with a compositional study in the Uffizi,[8] with a head in the Uffizi,[9] with a lily at Windsor[10] and with a *putto* in the Louvre.[11]

PROVENANCE: From the Contugi Collection at Volterra.[12] Purchased thence through L. Hombert of Florence,[13] 1857.

REPRODUCTION: *Illustrations, Italian Schools*, 1937, p. 386. *Plates, Earlier Italian Schools*, 1953, Vol. II, p. 439.

REFERENCES: (1) See especially Berenson, *Drawings of the Florentine Painters*, 1938, p. 52. No. 296 is also ascribed to Verrocchio by Degenhart in the *Rivista d'Arte*, 1932, p. 405. (2) Thus, Aldo Bertini in *L'Arte*, 1935, pp. 467/8, says it is not by Verrocchio himself. Cf. also *Critica d'Arte*, May, 1949, pp. 81/2. Günter Passavant, *Andrea del Verrocchio als Maler*, 1959, pp. 151/2, calls it a studio piece. (3) Crowe and Cavalcaselle, *History of Painting in Italy*, II, 1864, pp. 411/3, discussing the picture at some length, claim that it is more in Verrocchio's style than in that of other painters, and that the execution may have been by Lorenzo di Credi in Verrocchio's studio. In their Vol. III, 1866, p. 405, they say that it may have been executed in the shop of Verrocchio when Leonardo and Credi were employed there. (4) Berlin, 1931 Catalogue, No. 108; reproduced by Van Marle, *Development of the Italian Schools of Painting*, Vol. XI, Fig. 323. (5) Frankfort, 1924 Catalogue, No. 702; reproduced by Van Marle, *op. cit.*, Vol. XI, Fig. 324. (6) This claim is made in the Berlin catalogue of 1931, in the entry for No. 108. It is, like most of what has ever been said about No. 296, sometimes denied; e.g. by Aldo Bertini in *L'Arte*, 1935, pp. 467/8. (7) As a selection of various views concerning No. 296, it may be noted that: Mündler in the *Zeitschrift für bildende Kunst*, 1867, pp. 301/2, calls it one of the Pollaiuoli; Bode, in the *Repertorium für Kunstwissenschaft*, 1899, p. 391, calls it near Verrocchio; Maud Cruttwell, *Verrocchio*, 1904, p. 118, calls it not Verrocchio; Jens Thiis, *Leonardo da Vinci*, London, n.d., p. 67, calls it 'Alunno di Andrea' (a thing of his own invention); Sir Charles Holmes, *The National Gallery*, I, *Italian Schools*, 1923, p. 61, calls it studio of Verrocchio, perhaps helped by Leonardo da Vinci. Zeri in the *Bollettino d'Arte*, 1953, pp. 134 ff. and E. Camesasca, *Tutta la Pittura del Perugino*, 1959, pp. 41/2, calls No 296 early Perugino, to whom they ascribe No. 781 below also (see note 11 to the entry for that). (8) Berenson, *Drawings of the Florentine Painters*, 1938, No. 2796. Reproduced by Jens Thiis, *Leonardo da Vinci*, London, n.d., p. 66, and by O. Sirèn, *Léonard de Vinci*, 1928, II, Plate 16A. (9) Berenson, *op. cit.*, 1938, No. 2780E and Fig. 126. (10) This is mentioned with reserves by Sir Kenneth Clark, *Catalogue of Drawings by Leonardo da Vinci at Windsor*, 1935, I, No. 12418 (reproduced in Vol. II). (11) Berenson, *op. cit.*, 1938, No. 2783 and Figs. 122/3; the connection is claimed by Berenson in his text volume (Vol. I), p. 46. (12) Where it was called Piero della Francesca. (13) Hombert was merely the agent for the National Gallery (Board Minutes, 16 November, 1857). No. 296 appeared in the National Gallery Catalogue, 1858, as Domenico Ghirlandaio. In the edition of 1862, a note was added dubiously suggesting Antonio del Pollaiuolo. Later, the picture was catalogued as by that painter, then as Tuscan School, and latterly as School of Verrocchio.

Follower of ANDREA DEL VERROCCHIO

781   TOBIAS AND THE ANGEL

Tobias holds a roll of paper, marked *Ricord*.

Wood, painted surface, 33 × 26 (0·84 × 0·66); these measurements include a narrow black band along each edge.

Good condition; the restorations include a good deal of new gold.

The subject is to be found in the Book of *Tobit*, in the Apocrypha.[1] The roll of paper held by Tobias is no doubt the statement of money due to his father, Tobit; it was to collect this debt that Tobias and S. Raphael set out on their journey. Presumably the word *Ricord* on the picture is an attempt to indicate the character of the document.[2] S. Raphael holds what seems to be a box, half of the top being a flap that lifts up. This may reasonably be thought to contain the heart, liver and gall of the fish, which the angel told Tobias to take and put up safely (*Tobit*, vi, 4); these are important for later incidents in the story.[3]

The most famous of the Florentine versions of this subject is in a picture with the two other Archangels, in the Uffizi;[4] that picture is claimed by Mesnil to be from shortly before 1467,[5] and if it really is earlier, it may to some extent have influenced the composition of No. 781. S. Gabriel there rather than S. Raphael resembles S. Raphael here. It may be that Pollaiuolo's already mentioned picture at Turin established the manner of treating the theme for its period of great popularity at Florence. Parts of the landscape in No. 781 recur with variations in a picture of the subject at Bergamo and in the Rossi altarpiece (which includes the subject) at Berlin, dated 1475, assigned to Botticini; but in these cases the influence may be rather from than on No. 781.[6]

It seems impossible to say definitely who painted No. 781. The picture would appear to be Verrocchiesque, if No. 296 above is admitted to be Verrocchiesque; but it is apparently further than No. 296 from the *Baptism* at Florence. Bode, however, and others think that No. 781 is by Verrocchio himself.[7] Maud Cruttwell[8] thought that it is not Verrocchio. A. Venturi[9] thought it is by Antonio del Pollaiuolo, which is pretty clearly wrong. Berenson, in his Lists of 1932, called it near Verrocchio, perhaps executed by Botticini; the use of Botticini's name for No. 781 appears very strange. Ragghianti[10] ascribed it to the young Perugino; this at least brings in the name of a major painter, which seems desirable. The attribution to Perugino has had some success among Italian writers.[11] Suida[12] called the picture Verrocchio and Leonardo da Vinci, thinking that the fish and dog are Leonardo's work.

PROVENANCE: Formerly owned by Conte Angiolo Galli Tassi at Florence; he bequeathed it in 1863 with other property to the Arcispedale di S. Maria Nuova and other hospitals in Tuscany, for whose benefit it was sold.[13] Purchased from G. Baslini, Milan, 1867.[14]

REPRODUCTION: *Illustrations, Italian Schools*, 1937, p. 387. *Plates, Earlier Italian Schools*, 1953, Vol. II, p. 440.

REFERENCES: (1) A summary of the story is given in *A Few Saints from Pictures in the National Gallery*, 1946, under S. Raphael; the illustration there is a detail from Lorenzo di Credi's picture, No. 593 of the present catalogue, a group roughly similar to the group in No. 781. For the treatment of the theme in art, see Gertrude M. Achenbach in *Marsyas*, Vol. III (1943/5), 1946, pp. 71 ff. The great popularity of this theme in Florentine painting from about the middle of the XV Century, sudden and rather brief, has not been fully explained. S. Raphael has constantly been considered primarily a healer (and hence the Guardian Angel); an example that may be added to what is said in the article in *Marsyas* is the print reproduced by A. M. Hind, *Early Italian Engraving*, Vol. II, Plate 107. S. Raphael is also a protector for journeys; cf. for instance the inscription on the sculptured group on the Doge's Palace at Venice, 'Effice quaeso fretum Raphael reverende quietum' (Zanotto, *Il Palazzo Ducale di Venezia*, Vol. I, 1846, pp. 204 ff.). (2) This inscription appears also in Pollaiuolo's picture of the subject at Turin, which seems probably earlier than No. 781; see Colacicchi, *Antonio del Pollaiuolo*, 1943, Plate 52. (3) It may be compared with what the angel holds in various other versions of the subject. Nevertheless, E. Morpurgo, *L'Orologio Tascabile*, 1951, p. 29, denies this for No. 781 and claims that the object here is a watch. (4) Reproduced by Van Marle, *Italian Schools*, Vol. XI, Fig. 336. (5) J. Mesnil, *Botticelli*, 1938, p. 26. (6) See Günter Passavant, *Andrea del Verrocchio als Maler*, 1959, pp. 112/3 and Plates 105 and 109. (7) Bode in the *Repertorium für Kunstwissenschaft*, 1899, p. 391. Sergio Ortolani, *Pollaiuolo*, 1948, p. 192, also calls No. 781 Verrocchio himself, an early work. For Günter Passavant, *Andrea del Verrocchio als Maler*, 1959, No. 781 is one of the few autograph pictures by Verrocchio, and he devotes a whole chapter to it. (8) Maud Cruttwell, *Verrocchio*, 1904, p. 118. (9) A. Venturi in *L'Arte*, 1926, p. 56. (10) C. L. Ragghianti in *L'Arte*, 1935, p. 196. (11) It is accepted by Zeri in the *Bollettino d'Arte*, 1935, pp. 134 ff.; he also ascribes No. 296 above to Perugino, although it seems most doubtful if the two pictures can be by the same hand. Zeri is followed in both attributions by E. Camesasca, *Tutta la Pittura del Perugino*, 1959, pp. 40 ff. Since No. 781 may be thought to show some connections with established Peruginos, a cross-reference is given for it under Perugino's name. There is very little evidence concerning Perugino's early works; so far as the compiler can guess, his authorship of No. 781 is unlikely. (12) Suida in *Leonardo, Saggi e Ricerche*, 1954, p. 317 and plates. The compiler is not sure that a special category should be made for the dog and the fish; but thinks that the claim of Leonardo's intervention deserves careful discussion. (13) The Director's MS. Report of Proceedings on the Continent, January, 1868, gives an indication of the provenance. C. Morelli, *Gli Spedali di Parigi e di Londra–L'Arcispedale di Santa Maria Nuova*, etc., 1863, p. 3, and O. Andreucci, *Della Biblioteca e Pinacoteca dell'Arcispedale di S. Maria Nuova*, 1871, p. 21, say that the Galli Tassi bequest was for the benefit of S. Maria Nuova and of the other hospitals in Tuscany, and that the testator directed that the pictures, etc., included in the bequest should be sold. For the date of the bequest and spelling of the name, see (Isidoro del Lungo), *Il R. Arcispedale di S. Maria Nuova: I Suoi Benefattori: Sue Antiche Memorie*, 1888, p. 36. (14) As by A. Pollaiuolo.

ALVISE VIVARINI
living 1457, died 1503/5

The christian name is often given in the form *Luigi*; the date of birth on unsure evidence is often said to be *ca.* 1446. He was a son of Antonio, and nephew of Bartolomeo Vivarini; he was probably trained by the latter, and was influenced by Antonello and to some extent by Giovanni Bellini. An altarpiece at Montefiorentino is signed and dated 1475; there are many other authenticated works. Employed by the Venetian State from 1488. An altarpiece in the Frari at Venice was finished after his death by Basaiti. There is a recent article on him by C. Gilbert in *Scritti in Onore di Lionello Venturi*, 1956, I, pp. 277 ff.

Another painter at Venice, *Alvise Bavarin*, dead by 1502, used to be confused with Alvise Vivarini.

1872   THE VIRGIN AND CHILD

Signed: ALVVIXI VIVARIN.P (partly damaged).

Wood, painted surface, $27\frac{1}{4} \times 21$ (0·69 × 0·535); painted up to the edges all round.

The flesh and the landscape are in reasonably pure but somewhat cracked condition; the draperies conserve much old repainting, which at one time covered the landscape also.

A characteristic work, presented to the Gallery as evidence against some of Berenson's (later abandoned) attributions to Alvise.[1]

ENGRAVING: For Giovanni Maria Sasso's *Venezia Pittrice* (the landscape at that time repainted in a different form).[2]

PROVENANCE: Passed from the Correr Collection at San Giovanni Decollato, Venice, not later than 1803 into the Manfrin Collection, Venice;[3] Manfrin Catalogues, 1856 (No. 357)[4] and 1872 (No. 40); Manfrin Catalogue (for sale), 1892 (No. 17). Bought in 1893 from the Sangiorgi Gallery, Rome, by Charles Loeser of Florence,[5] who presented it in 1898.

REPRODUCTION: *Illustrations, Italian Schools*, 1937, p. 387. *Plates, Earlier Italian Schools*, 1953, Vol. II, p. 441.

REFERENCES: (1) Letters from the donor in the Gallery archives. (2) The work never appeared; impressions of the engraving in the Correr Library at Venice (Stampe B11 and C2). (3) Ownership stated on the engraving for Sasso, who died in 1803. The Manfrin Collection was formed, at least in part, by Conte Girolamo Manfrin, who died in 1801, according to *Il Forestiere Istruito . . . della Città di Venezia*, 1822, p. 295. According to the catalogue of the A. M. Plattis Sale, Paris, 13/4 May, 1870, the collection was formed *ca.* 1748 (perhaps meaning from that date onwards) and in 1848 was divided between the Marquise Bortolina Plattis veuve du Baron Sardagna and the Marquis Antonio Maria Plattis. According to the Manfrin Sale Catalogue of 1897, the collection was divided in 1849 between the Marchese Antonio Plattis and the Marchesa Bortolina Plattis nei Sardagna; her part or some of it remained in the Palazzo Manfrin until 1897. See also, for the picture, Moschini's *Isola di Murano*, 2nd edition, 1808, p. 16 (the first edition is of 1807), and I. Neümann-Rizzi's *Elogio dei Vivarini*, 1816/7, pp. 81/2 (the pagination appears to vary in different editions). The identity of the Manfrin picture with No. 1872 is further stated by the donor (letter of 24 January, 1898, in the Gallery archives). (4) Presumably; as Bartolomeo Vivarini. (5) Letter in the Gallery archives.

2672   PORTRAIT OF A MAN

Signed: .ALOVISIV(s).VIVARINVS / DE.MVRIANO.F / .1497. (worn here and there).

Wood, painted surface, $24\frac{1}{2} \times 18\frac{1}{2}$ (0·625 × 0·47); painted up to the edges all round.

The condition is good in general, but the shadows of the flesh have been worn and made up somewhat; the character of the features, however, is only very slightly affected. Small *pentimenti* in the left eyeball, right temple, etc.

PROVENANCE: In May, 1857, with Brison at Milan.[1] Bonomi Collection, Milan, by 1871.[2] Bonomi-Cereda Sale, Milan, 14/6 December, 1896 (lot 31 and Plate VI). Lent by George Salting to the Burlington Fine Arts Club, Winter, 1902 (No. 24); Salting Bequest, 1910.

REPRODUCTION: *Illustrations, Italian Schools*, 1937, p. 389. *Plates, Earlier Italian Schools*, 1953, Vol. II, p. 442.

REFERENCES: (1) Mündler's Diary: 'a portrait of an old man, by "Aloysius Vivarinus 1497." (2) Crowe and Cavalcaselle, *Painting in North Italy*, 1871, I, p. 65.

ANTONIO VIVARINI
active 1440 (?), died 1476 (?)/84

In the signatures of his pictures, *Antonio da Murano*. He collaborated with his brother-in-law, Giovanni d'Alemagna (who died in 1449/50), first at Venice, then from 1447 at Padua. Of the works of this early time, one (at Parenzo) is signed by Antonio alone,* none by Giovanni alone, several by both. The style of the two painters cannot be distinguished. Its Gothic character is said to have been influenced by Gentile da Fabriano, Pisanello or (through Giovanni d'Alemagna) German sources, and was very slightly affected by the 'Squarcionesques' at Padua.

In 1450, the probable year of Giovanni's death, Antonio collaborated with his brother Bartolomeo in an altarpiece at Bologna; the style is hardly altered, and this new collaboration went on for several years. There is an altarpiece signed by Antonio alone, not much more evolved, in the Vatican (1464).

Another Antonio da Murano, painter, was alive in Venice in 1496.

It is customary to give Antonio the chief place in the early works; but it is possible that Giovanni was the principal partner.

ANTONIO VIVARINI AND GIOVANNI D'ALEMAGNA

768 PANEL FROM AN ALTARPIECE: SS. PETER AND JEROME

Inscribed on the pedestal,.SANTVS PETRVS.SĀTVs.GERO-NIMVS.

Poplar,[1] painted surface, $55\frac{1}{4} \times 18$ ($1\cdot40 \times 0\cdot455$); painted up to the edges except at the bottom. The top $2\frac{3}{4}$ in. is an addition to the panel. Good condition, so far as it can be observed, but much of the gold is new; *pentimento* in S. Jerome's hat.

For the commentary, etc., see No. 1284 below.

1284 PANEL FROM AN ALTARPIECE: SS. FRANCIS AND MARK

S. Francis holds a Crucifix. Inscribed on the pedestal, .SĀCTS. FRANSISCVs.SANCTVS.MARCVS.

* In the *Inventario degli Oggetti d'Arte d'Italia, Provincia di Pola*, 1935, p. 126, it is stated that the date of 1440 for this picture is quite certain. It has often been disputed.

Wood, painted surface, $53\frac{1}{4} \times 17\frac{3}{4}$ ($1 \cdot 355 \times 0 \cdot 45$); painted up to the edges all round. Less well preserved than No. 768; the panel has cracked and the paint is worn. S. Mark's head and hands are considerably repainted, but the gold of the haloes is mostly original.

The lettering of the inscriptions is not free from caprice.

According to a mis-statement of Crowe and Cavalcaselle[2] (often made worse by misquotation), No. 768 is from the same altarpiece as a *Virgin and Child* then in Molteni's studio, and now in the Poldi-Pezzoli Museum, Milan;[3] this is palpably untrue. Crowe and Cavalcaselle, in a manner of self-correction, note that No. 768 is similar to a *Virgin and Child* in the Church of the Filippini (S. Tomaso Cantauriense) at Padua; and Pudelko[4] has convincingly stated that it is this picture that was the central panel for Nos. 768 and 1284. This *Virgin and Child* was not painted for its present position, but was given to the Church at Padua, it seems, in the eighteenth century;[5] it is not signed.

Pudelko thinks that the pictures are slightly earlier than a large work of 1446 at Venice; in any case, there seems little doubt that they are from the period of collaboration between Antonio Vivarini and Giovanni d'Alemagna. There is thus no need to ascribe Nos. 768 and 1284, as was done formerly in the Gallery, to Antonio alone.

PROVENANCE: Probably parts of a triptych, the wings of which contained the same saints as Nos. 768 and 1284, once in S. Moisè, Venice.[6] No. 768 is from the Zambeccari Collection, Bologna; it was seen there in 1857 by Mündler,[7] and was purchased thence by Sir Charles Eastlake, who died in 1865. Purchased from Lady Eastlake, at the price Sir Charles Eastlake had paid for it, 1867. No. 1284 was purchased from J. P. Richter, Clarke Fund, 1889.[8]

REPRODUCTIONS: *Illustrations, Italian Schools*, 1937, p. 390. *Plates, Earlier Italian Schools*, 1953, Vol. II, p. 443.

REFERENCES: (1) Letter from B. J. Rendle, of the Forest Products Research Laboratory, in the Gallery archives. (2) Crowe and Cavalcaselle, *Painting in North Italy*, I, 1871, p. 29, or ed. Borenius, I, 1912, p. 29. (3) Crowe and Cavalcaselle refer to a picture in Molteni's studio, and it is Borenius who identifies this with the Poldi-Pezzoli *Madonna*. Reproduced by Van Marle, *Development of the Italian Schools of Painting*, Vol. XVII, p. 25. Reproduced since its cleaning, and showing the original form of the top, in *Le Arti*, III, 1941, p. 299. (4) Pudelko in *The Burlington Magazine*, Vol. LXXI (1937), pp. 130 ff., where the three pictures are reproduced. The inscription on the pedestal of the Padua picture is *Dignare me laudare te Virgo sacrata da michi*; cf. the *Inventario degli Oggetti d'Arte d'Italia, Provincia di Padova*, 1936, p. 162. The size is $1 \cdot 48 \times 0 \cdot 665/67$; information kindly supplied by Rodolfo Pallucchini, in the Gallery archives. (5) Cf. Giovambatista Rossetti, *Descrizione delle Pitture etc. di Padova*, 3rd edition, 1780, p. 276; given by 'fu Signor Giuseppe Picchi, Assessore della nostra Serenissima Repubblica.' This passage is not in Rossetti's first edition, 1765. Giuseppe Picchi may be a man who died in 1755; see Cigogna, *Iscrizioni Veneziane*, IV, 1834, p. 203. (6) Boschini, *Le Minere della Pittura*, 1664, p. 104; 1674 ed., p. 80 (Sestier di S. Marco); he calls it Antonio da Murano. Not in Zanetti's revised edition of 1733. (7) Mündler's Diary; he ascribed the picture to Giovanni d'Alemagna. Recorded as Antonio Vivarini in the *Catalogo della Galleria del N.U. Sig.r Mse. Commendatore Don Camillo Zambeccari*, n.d., p. 28. (8) Richter (*The Mond Collection*, 1910, I, p. 48) says that he acquired it from a palace in Northern Italy, where it was without attribution.

Bartolomeo VIVARINI
ca. 1432 (?) — after 1499 (?)

Brother of Antonio Vivarini, who was clearly the elder. The dates of birth and death are according to information from two pictures discussed by Borenius in *The Burlington Magazine*, Vol. XIX (1911), pp. 192 ff. For the latter, see also Elizabeth E. Gardner in the Metropolitan Museum *Bulletin*, June, 1952, p. 287. He was certainly active from 1450 to 1491. He collaborated at first with his brother, though but for the signatures it is doubtful if his hand would be recognized in such early works of collaboration. In 1459, he signed alone a *S. John Capistran* in the Louvre; some other pictures are attributed to him at this period. His developed style is first clear in altarpieces of 1464 and 1465 at Venice and Naples; it obviously depends largely on Mantegna's San Zeno Altarpiece and similar works, and continues henceforward with little change, except for a varying participation by assistants. Some influence of his nephew Alvise is sometimes discernible in his later works.

284   THE VIRGIN AND CHILD WITH SS. PAUL AND
        JEROME

Signed: . OPVS . BARTOLMEI . VIVARINI . DEMVRANO . (retouched slightly; some letters fancifully placed).

Wood, painted surface, $37\frac{1}{2} \times 25$ (0.95×0.635); painted up to the edges all round, and perhaps cut somewhat.

Most of the picture is in very good condition: the gold haloes and background are new.

A fairly early work, probably.

PROVENANCE: From the Contarini Collection, Venice, it had passed into that of Conte Bernardino Cornian degli Algarotti, Venice, by 1816;[1] 1840 Catalogue (No. 1); purchased thence, 1855.

REPRODUCTION: *Illustrations, Italian Schools*, 1937, p. 389. *Plates, Earlier Italian Schools*, 1953, Vol. II, p. 444.

REFERENCE: (1) Cf. I. Neümann-Rizzi, *Elogio dei Vivarini*, 1816/7, pp. 63, 82, who does not give the provenance from the Contarini Collection. (The pagination of Neümann-Rizzi's work appears to vary in different editions.) The Contarini provenance is stated in the N.G. MS. Catalogue, presumably on information supplied by the former owner.

Marco ZOPPO
ca. 1432–*ca.* 1478

Marco (di Antonio) di Ruggero, lo Zoppo. He was born at Cento, but called himself a Bolognese. Apprenticed to Squarcione of Padua *ca.* 1453; but he left him in 1455, and went to Venice. He was in Bologna 1461/2, but is several times recorded again in Venice, where he died. There are several authenticated works. See V. Lazzarini, *Documenti relativi alla Pittura Padovana*, 1909, and I. B. Supino, *Nuovi Documenti su Marco Zoppo Pittore*, Nozze Morpurgo-Castelnuovo, 1925.

590 PIETÀ

The dead Christ is supported by S. John the Baptist and another saint.

Wood, painted surface, $10\frac{3}{8} \times 8\frac{1}{4}$ (0·265 × 0·21).
Very good condition.

The back is coloured to imitate marble; this seems to be contemporary. This may suggest that No. 590 is a complete picture, perhaps painted for private devotion; but it may be one panel from a small altarpiece, such as Giorgio Schiavone, No. 630.

The attribution seems to be due to Crowe and Cavalcaselle.[1]

VERSION: In the Stefano Bardini of Florence Sale at Christie's, 30 May, 1902 (lot 624).[2]

PROVENANCE: On the back (in Italian) an attribution to Dürer, attested by many famous painters including Sig. Benvenuti; presumably the painter born 1769, died 1844. The writing may be that of Prof. Rosini of Pisa, in whose collection the picture was.[3] Later at Florence, owned by Francesco Lombardi and Ugo Baldi;[4] purchased from them with other pictures, 1857.[5]

REPRODUCTION: *Illustrations, Italian Schools*, 1937, p. 393. *Plates, Earlier Italian Schools*, 1953, Vol. II, p. 445.

REFERENCES: (1) Crowe and Cavalcaselle, *Painting in North Italy*, 1871, I, pp. 349 and 521; ed. Borenius, 1912, II, pp. 52 and 229. Cf. also Frizzoni in the *Archivio Storico Italiano*, 1879, p. 277. (2) In the Portfolio published by Bardini in connection with the sale, it is Plate 111, No. 703. (3) N.G. Report, 1857. (4) As Mantegna, according to the National Gallery Report for 1857, where reference is given to the printed catalogue of the Lombardi-Baldi Collection. No. 590 is, however, not mentioned in the catalogue (claimed to be of 1845); perhaps it was included in the printed supplement, referred to in Appendix I. (5) As Tura. For the history of the Lombardi-Baldi Collection, see Appendix I.

3541 A BISHOP SAINT (PANEL FROM AN ALTARPIECE)

Wood, rounded top, painted surface, $19\frac{1}{2} \times 11\frac{1}{4}$ (0·495 × 0·285); painted up to the edges all round.

The picture has been somewhat overcleaned, and part of the surface is uneven from cracking; but the painted area is fairly pure, and part of the gold background is genuine.

Clearly from the upper tier of a polyptych. Borenius[1] published as from the same altarpiece two other pictures of approximately the same size; a *S. Paul* at Oxford,[2] and a *S. Peter* then in the Henry Harris Collection (later Kress, now Washington). A *S. Jerome* to all appearances from the same series is in the Walters Art Gallery at Baltimore.[3] In all four pictures, the halo pattern is closely similar. The shape of the pictures at the top cannot be determined precisely; rather indistinct marks on No. 3541 and on the Washington *S. Peter* suggest that the tops may have been in the form of a cusped arch. The panels themselves at Oxford and Washington have square tops; for No. 3541 and the Baltimore picture, the panels have rounded tops, but perhaps they have been cut down to this form.

No. 3541 and the Washington *S. Peter* face to the right; the saints at Oxford and Baltimore face to the left.

PROVENANCE: In the Collection of Alfred A. de Pass, by whom exhibited at the R.A., 1895 (No. 138); presented by him, 1920.

REPRODUCTION: *Illustrations, Italian Schools*, 1937, p. 393. *Plates, Earlier Italian Schools*, 1953, Vol. II, p. 446.

REFERENCES: (1) Borenius in *The Burlington Magazine*, Vol. XXXVIII (1921), pp. 9 ff., with reproductions (but see note 2). The two pictures are recorded in the Ashmolean Catalogue, 1951 (No. 483) and the Washington Catalogue, 1941 (No. 382). (2) The picture at Oxford was cleaned in 1946, and Borenius' reproduction of it is no longer true; photograph of it in its present state in the Gallery archives. There is practically speaking none of the original gold background left. Fortunately, just enough of the original halo has been preserved to prove that its form was closely similar to those of No. 3541 and the other two pictures mentioned in the text. The gold in the Oxford picture has been reconstructed to form a semicircle at the top, but there is nothing to prove that it was so originally. (Letter from John Woodward in the Gallery archives). (3) Photograph in the Gallery archives. Walters Catalogue, 1929 (No. 542); size, $19\frac{1}{2} \times 10\frac{3}{4}$.

APPENDIX I

THE LOMBARDI - BALDI COLLECTION

The Lombardi-Baldi pictures were acquired in 1857, and the following account was given in the *Report of the Director of the National Gallery* for 1857/8 (printed in 1867):

'NEGOTIATION respecting a Portion of the LOMBARDI-BALDI COLLECTION of WORKS by early Italian Masters.

'A collection of pictures, consisting of specimens of early Italian, and more particularly of Tuscan Masters, had been gradually formed in Florence, from the year 1838, chiefly by Signor Francesco Lombardi and Signor Ugo Baldi.

'The first printed catalogue was dated 1844. From time to time, after that date, the collection received important additions, and, in some instances, inferior works were exchanged for better examples of the masters.

'A second enlarged catalogue was printed in 1845; after which time the descriptions of additional pictures were furnished in a printed supplement and in manuscript.

'The number of specimens finally amounted to about 100; but as many were of small dimensions, or of inferior interest, the importance of the series was at no time commensurate with its extent. The most valuable works contained in it, forming about a fourth part of the entire Gallery, conferred on it, however, a merited reputation.

'The existence and character of the Lombardi-Baldi Collection were known to the Trustees of the National Gallery as early as 1847.

'It does not appear that any person connected with the National Gallery had an opportunity of seeing and reporting on the collection till I inspected it in 1855. But during the Session of 1853, Lord John Russell being then the organ of the Government in the House of Commons, a correspondence on the subject took place between the Treasury (through the Foreign Office), the Hon. P. Campbell Scarlett, then acting for Her Majesty's Minister at Florence, and the Trustees of the National Gallery.

'In a letter, dated Florence, 20th March 1853, addressed by Mr. D. Lewis Franklin to Lord John Russell, and which was referred to the Trustees (Minutes, 2nd May 1853), the collection was estimated at 15,000*l.*, including the expense of its transfer to England. On inquiry, it appeared, from a letter from the Hon. P. Campbell Scarlett, dated Florence, 19th May 1853, that the price demanded for the collection by the proprietors was 12,000*l.*, and that probably the offer of a lower sum would not be refused.

'On the 18th July 1853 (minutes of that date), Mr. Spence, an English artist residing chiefly in Florence, being for a time in London, attended at a meeting of the Trustees by their request, and furnished information respecting the pictures referred to, at the same time expressing his opinion of their importance.

'On the 1st of August following (Minutes of that date), the Trustees, aware that the proprietors refused to separate the collection, came to the conclusion that, with the information before them, it was not expedient to proceed with the question.

'The above particulars represent the extent of the inquiries that were made respecting the Lombardi-Baldi Gallery previously to 1855.

'Without reference to that collection, attention was particularly directed, in 1853, to the expediency of forming, by means of a chronological series of works by early masters, an historical foundation for a complete gallery of pictures. That view was taken by the Select Committee on the National Gallery in 1853, and a passage in the Report itself of that Committee, in which such opinion is expressed, thus concludes: "Your Committee think that the funds appropriated to the enlargement of the collection should be expended with a view not merely of exhibiting to the public beautiful works of art, but of instructing the public in the history of that art, and of the age in which, and the men by whom, those works were produced." (Report, &c., 1853, p. xvi.)

'This opinion was embodied, leaving a due latitude to the Trustees and Director, in the Treasury Minute, dated 27 March 1855, re-constituting the establishment of the National Gallery.

'The same opinion had been before expressed, in a debate on the National Gallery on the 8th of March 1853, by Lord John Russell, at that time the organ of the Government in the House of Commons, as follows: "There is one object which I have more than once stated in this House as worth striving for, an object which ought not to be attended with much difficulty; I mean the obtaining of a collection of works by the early Italian masters, many of which are indeed very beautiful in themselves, but which have a further value as showing the progress which led afterwards to the beautiful creations of Raphael and Da Vinci." (Hansard's Parl. Debates, vol. cxxiv., p. 1314.)

'Meanwhile the proprietors of the collection in Florence before referred to, while they declined to dispose of separate specimens, continued to ask so high a price for the entire gallery as to prevent the most willing bidders from coming to terms with them.

'In the autumn of 1855, when I first saw the Lombardi-Baldi pictures, I found the proprietors still unwilling to separate the collection. It appeared, therefore, that the only mode of obtaining possession of the best specimens would be to buy the whole gallery, and afterwards to sell the less important part of it.

'In 1856 an Act of Parliament was passed "to extend the powers of the Trustees and Director of the National Gallery, and to authorise the sale of Works of Art belonging to the Public."

'This seemed to remove the chief impediment to the acquisition of the Florentine Gallery in question. About the same time I received several letters from Members of the House of Commons of 1856, recommending the purchase. Further experience was, however, considered desirable, and the 'unsuccessful result of a sale of part of the Krüger pictures in February 1857 showed the difficulty of so disposing of works "unfit for or not required as part of the National Collection."

'Under these circumstances, being duly authorised, I made another attempt in the autumn of 1857 to induce the proprietors to dispose of a portion of their gallery, and finally succeeded.

'The number of works selected is strictly 22; but one of those works, originally a vast altarpiece by Orcagna, now consists of the chief portion in three compartments, and nine pictures in separate frames. The number of distinct pictures is therefore 31. Other altarpieces include many pictures, large and small, in one frame-work; the entire number, reckoning these as separate works, amounts to more than 60. The price paid for this portion of the collection was 7,000*l.*, with banker's commission, 7,035*l.*

'In the selection thus made, considerable difficulty was experienced, on the one hand, in confining such selection to the specimens which I considered the most eligible, and, on the other, in meeting the expectations of the proprietors by a proposal which, by including a sufficient number of works at a sufficient price, should reconcile them to the separation of their gallery. All the justly celebrated and all the most historically valuable pictures in the collection were comprehended; and notwithstanding the difficulty adverted to of stopping at that point, scarcely any others were admitted. The unsightly specimens of Margaritone and the earliest Tuscan painters were selected solely for their historical importance, and as showing the rude beginnings from which, through nearly two centuries and a half, Italian art slowly advanced to the period of Raphael and his contemporaries. In some few cases different names are, on good grounds, substituted for those given by the late proprietors.'

THE CONTRACT FOR STEFANO DI GIOVANNI'S ALTARPIECE IN S. FRANCESCO AT SANSEPOLCRO

A text of this contract was published by Borghesi e Banchi, *Nuovi Documenti per la Storia dell'Arte Senese*, 1898, pp. 119 f.; reprinted by John Pope-Hennessy, *Sassetta*, 1939, p. 127. A superior text, transcribed by Monsignor Angelo Mercati, Prefetto dell'Archivio Segreto Vaticano, is here printed, together with notes by him, by his kind permission. This document comes from S. Francesco at Siena, where it bore the number 339; there can be little doubt that it is the document referred to by Della Valle, *Lettere Sanesi*, III, 1786, p. 44. Its present collocation is Archivio Segreto Vaticano, Cancelleria della Nunziatura Veneta, No. 16201.

'In nomine Domini Amen. Anno a nativitate eiusdem millesimo quadringentesimo trigesimoseptimo indictione quintadecima, presidente sanctissimo in Christo patre et domino nostro domino Eugenio divina providentia papa quarto, mensis septembris die quinto, magister Stefanus Johannis pictor de civitate Senarum sponte et ex certa scientia deliberate et premeditate[1] promisit et convenit sollempniter Christoforo Francisci ser Fei et Andree Johannis Tani de terra Burgi sancti Sepulcri[2] operariis et superstitibus operum ecclesie sancti Francisci de dicto Burgo presentibus et pro dictis operibus recipientibus et legiptime stipulantibus facere[3] et construere unam tabulam ligneam ad altare maius dicte ecclesie sancti Francisci cum suis debitis proportionibus, cyboriis, ornamentis[4] et partibus ad latitudinem, altitudinem, mensuram[5] et similitudinem illius[5] tabule lignee iam constructe et inglissate[6] pro dicto altari, et ipsam tabulam sic construendam, ut supra, ornate pingere ab utroque ipsius tabule latere[7] et per totum ad illas ystorias et figuras prout declaratum extiterit[8] per guardianum et fratres dicti loci sancti Francisci de Burgo, ad aurum finum, açurrum finum et colores alios similiter cum[9] ornamentis et aliis secundum subtile ingenium et sue artis pictorie peritiam et quanto[10] plus venustius sciet[11] et poterit, omnique suo conatu omnibus et singulis ipsius magistri Stefani

---

(1) B. (Borghesi e Banchi) om. 'sponte—premeditate'. (2) B.: Tani de Burgo supradicto. (3) B.: presentibus et stipulantibus et recipientibus pro dictis operibus facere. (4) B.: proportionibus et bonis ornamentis. (5) B. om. (6) B.: ingesate. (7) B.: ab utroque latere eiusdem tabule. (8) B.add. 'sibi'. (9) B.: ad aurum finum et azurum et colores alios finos cum. (10) B.: ingenium sue artis pictorie, et quanto. (11) B.: sciret.

sumptibus et expensis ac[5] rebus[5] expedientibus,[5] et eamdem ad per-
fectum de predictis omnibus ductam[12] et ad finem usque completam
consignare et tradere promisit dictus magister in dicta civitate Senarum
hinc ad quatuor annos continuos proxime secuturos operariis predictis
et seu eorum numptio. Et hoc facere promisit dictus magister pictor pro
eo et ex eo quod dicti operarii per se et successores eorum promiserunt
et convenerunt[13] sollempniter dicto magistro presenti et pro se et suis
heredibus et iura sua habituris legiptime stipulanti et recipienti dare,[14]
tradere, solvere et numerare pro pretio, salario et mercede omnium predictorum eidem magistro Stefano, ut supra, stipulanti[15] florenos quin-
gentos decem ad rationem librarum quinque denariorum cortonensium
pro quolibet floreno in dicta civitate Senarum his terminis, videlicet
tertiam partem dicte quantitatis a principio ad voluntatem ipsius
magistri Stefani, et aliam tertiam partem quandocunque dictum labore-
rium fuerit ad medium sue perfectionis redactum,[16] et residuam tertiam
medietatem [sic] facto et expleto toto dicto laborerio[17] et deinde ad
omnem ipsius magistri petitionem et voluntatem ex pacto in dicta civitate Senarum, ubi se constituerunt dicti operarii soluturos quantitatem
predictam in terminis antedictis. Et pro cautela et observatione omnium
predictorum promiserunt et convenerunt sollempniter contrahentes
predicti offerre et dare sibi invicem et vicissim sufficientes et ydoneos
fideiussores, qui se et sua sollempniter et legiptime obligabunt et pro-
mictent quod partes et contrahentes suprascripti sibi invicem facient,
adtendent et observabunt omnia et singula supra et infrascripta hinc
inde promissa fideiussionis nomine et se principales in huiusmodi con-
stituendo, ita quod ex iure bene valeat et obligati sint quatenus hec
omnia et infrascripta non fierent et observarentur inter se plenissime,
et dictas fideiussiones prestare promiserunt hinc inde etiam ante ali-
quam solutionem prime rate quantitatis predicte in dicta civitate Senarum. Et demum perfecta dicta tabula promisit sollempniter dictus
magister Stefanus personaliter se transferre in dictam terram Burgi et
ipsam eamdem tabulam ad dictum altare maius ecclesie sancti Francisci
componere et aptare prout expedierit, que tamen conduci debeat de
dicta civitate ad dictam terram Burgi et ubi locari debet vecturis et expensis omnibus dictorum operariorum et rischo. Sed si eadem tabula in
conductione predicta modo aliquo in aliquibus figuris, picturis et
laborerio vastaretur, promisit idem magister ea reparare et ornatam
modo predicto apponere et statuere suo loco predicto, quia sic sollempniter ut supra in omnibus suis partibus actum et sollempni stipulatione
firmatum extitit inter eos. Et ea omnia et singula supra et infrascripta
promiserunt et convenerunt sollempniter dicti contrahentes sibi invicem
et vicissim sollempnibus stipulationibus intervenientibus inter eos firma
et rata habere, tenere, facere et observare et contra non facere vel venire
aliqua ratione vel causa de iure vel de facto, sub pena dupli dicte quan-

---

(12) B.add. 'ornatissime'. (13) B.: iuraverunt. (14) B. om. 'presenti—
recipienti'. (15) B. om. 'eidem—stipulanti'. (16) B.: fuerit ad medium seu perfec-
tioni reductum. (17) B.: et residuam tertiam partem; facto toto dicto laborerio.
Con quest'ultima parola termina il testo di B.

titatis his semper ratis manentibus premissis et sollempniter stipulatis, cum dampnis et expensis ac interesse litis et extra reficiendis in totum, prout faciens et seu substinens sine aliis probationibus suo tantum dixerit iuramento, pro quibus omnibus et singulis firmiter observandis et adimplendis obligaverunt sibi invicem dicti operarii bona dictorum operum et dictus magister Stephanus se et eius heredes personaliter et omnia sua bona realiter presentia et futura, renunptiantes in his beneficio, exceptioni et auxilio dictarum promissionum, conventionum et obligationum non factarum, dicte pene non apposite, non stipulate, non promisse, omniumque supra et infra scriptorum non sic se habentium et gestorum, presentis instrumenti non sic rite celebrati, doli mali, condictionis, indebiti, sine causa et ex iniusta causa quam metus causa, prescriptis verbis, privilegio fori et omnibus aliis legum iuris et statutorum auxiliis, beneficiis, exceptionibus, deffensionibus, iuribus et renunptiationibus quibuscunque, quibus contrahentibus et utrique ipsorum presentibus, volentibus et sponte confitentibus ego notarius infrascriptus precise percepi guarentigiam secundum formam statuti dicti Burgi.

'Actum in Burgo sancti Sepulcri in apoteca domus mee presentibus domino Malatesta Pieri de Captaneis Anibale domini Mastini Henrici ser Francisci ser Ferrantis de dicto Burgo testibus ad suprascripta vocatis et adhibitis et rogatis.

'Ego Franciscus Christofori Cisti de Burgo sancti Sepulcri imperiali auctoritate iudex ordinarius et notarius publicus predictis omnibus et singulis presens interfui et ea omnia rogatus scripsi et publicavi et signum meum apposui consuetum.'

APPENDIX III

THE PALAZZO DEL MAGNIFICO AT SIENA

(See the entry for Signorelli, No. 910)

There is in the Biblioteca Comunale at Siena (pressmark C VII 20) a volume made up of miscellaneous notes by the Abate Giovanni Girolamo Carli, some of which are dated in the 1770's. The passages of interest for the Palazzo del Magnifico are as follows. On f. 74 the author begins an account headed *Pitture di due Stanze del Palazzo già di Pandolfo Petrucci, ora de' Nobb. Sigg. Savini*. After giving a summary of the little that Vasari and other earlier writers had said, he goes on: 'Io ho fatto minute osservazioni nelle Stanze di quel Palazzo insieme col Sig.ʳ Francesco Corinti Pittore. Le Stanze dipinte sono 2. sole, e non *molte*. La prima ha il pavimento tutto di piccole lastre quadre di terra cotta vetrinate, e dipinte di gusto con fiorami, putti, Armi, &.ᶜ, non so, se lavorate in Siena, o in Urbino. Tutta esta Stanza è circondata da una residenza di legno intagliata con putti, uccelli, fogliami, &.ᶜ, probabilmente lavoro del Barili.

'Le 4. pareti di d.ᵃ Stanza sono ornate con grandi Pitture a fresco, cioè vi sono due Storie per ogni parte, in tutte 8. Sono tutte di una stessa mano indubitamente; nella maggior parte le figure sono ignude, e in diverse attitudini; il colorito è alquanto crudo, ma il disegno è corretto. Nel 1° Quadro è un Principe sul tribunale in atto di giudicare, con guardie intorno, e d'avanti molte donne, che in varie maniere strapazzazzano (*sic*) un giovane ignudo, e alcune implorano giustizia dal Principe. Nel 2.° è una specie di Baccanale con belli ignudi &.ᶜ Nel 3° sono molte donne, che legano un giovane, a cui hanno strappato l'ale; in lontananza sono bellissime figure piccole, che da una parte danno la caccia al d.° giovane, in altra lo conducono prigioniere in trionfo; sì in questo Quadro, che in altri, (f. 75) più figure hanno ornamenti d'oro, come nelle opere del Pinturicchio. Nel 4.° sono altre donne &.ᶜ Nel 5.° è una donna simbolica in trono con più altre femmine, e putti &.ᶜ Nel 6.° è Penelope al telajo con avanti i Proci, e in lontananza la Nave di Ulisse; a' piedi Penelope è un Gatto. Nel 7.° (che è conservatissimo) è un Giudice con avanti molti schiavi ignudi &.ᶜ Nel 8.° (ben conservato) si vede Enea con indosso anchise, e appresso Ascanio, e Creusa (bellissima fig.), e in lontananza l'incendio di Troja. Le composizioni di questi Quadri sono buone. Nel 1.° Quadro in un piedistallo è scritto:

HAΓNIA   Ma doveva scriversi:
               Η ΑΓΝΟΙΑ

KAKωNAITIA   KAKωN AITIA,

Cioè *Ignorantia maloru' causa.* E poco più sotto:

MHTE ΔIKHNΔIKAΣEIΣ ΠPIN   che doveva
AMΦOINMYOON AKOYΣEIΣ   scriver—

si così:

MHTE ΔIKHN ΔIKAΣEIΣ ΠPIN
AMΦOIN MYΘON AKOYΣEIΣ,   cioè

Neque jus decernas, priusqua' amboru' orationem auscultaveris.
Sotto al d° verso Greco è il seg. Latino:

INDICTAM AMBOBVS NOLI
DECERNERE CAVSSAM.   E più sotto:
ΛOYKAΣ O KOPITIOΣ EΠOIEI,   cioè

Lucas Cortonensis fecit.   Nel 2° Quadro poi leggesi:
LVCAS Ð CORTÕA.   Nel 3°
LVCAS CORITIVS.   E così nel 4°.

La volta di questa Stanza è tutta ornata di lavori di stucco, e di Pitture in varj piccoli spartimenti. Le Pitture parte sono a guazzo, parte a fresco, e rappresentano varie Istorie, e Favole, le Muse &ᶜ In mezzo è l'Arme di Casa Petrucci, che si figura sostenuta da 4. bei putti dipinti di grandezza al naturale. La maniera è diversa da quella del Signorelli, e vi è tradizione che sì questa volta, sì il fregio della Stanza contigua siano opera di Girolamo Genga: onde hanno sbagliato sì il Vasari, che il Bottari, attribuendo il primo tutte queste Pitture al Genga, e il secondo tutte al Signorelli. Il gusto di esta volta si accosta più al moderno, gli alberi (?) sono meno secchi, e più naturali, lo stile e più grandioso, il pennello più sciolto; ma il disegno, la composizione, e l'espressione sono assai inferiori al fare del Signorelli.

'(f. 76) La Stanza seconda ha intorno un largo fregio, in cui in 12. spartimenti (3. per facciata) sono in mezze figure al naturale varie Deità, Virtù, &ᶜ Gli ornati intorno sono a guazzo, e i dᵗ dipartimenti a fresco. Sono indubitamente della stessa mano della volta della Stanza precedente. Il colorito è sufficiente, qualche figura è ragionevole; ma l'invenzione è meschina, il disegno non correttissimo, le pieghe sono ordinarie, il fare tutto insieme ha del manierato, e del troppo uniforme; bensì la maniera esce dal secco, e grandeggia alquanto. Io non avea veduti più Pitture del Genga. Ma se tutte le sue cose son come queste (ch'ei fece nell'età d'an. 36.), egli fu Pittore assai mediocre, e non meritava, che il Vasari ne scrivesse la Vita, o almeno dovea farla con meno elogj. Io per me non credo, che queste Pitture fossero allora così applaudite in Siena, come dice il Vasari perchè la Città avea Pittori molto superiori al Genga: se pure non furono allora lodate per soggezione del Tiranno Petrucci, che le avea ordinate, ed a cui piacevano.'

On f. 16 of the Abate Carli's manuscript, there are some rough notes concerning the Palazzo del Magnifico; most of the rough notes concerning the principal room in the Palace must have been on other sheets, now missing. The following piece from f. 16 is here reproduced: 'Nella St.

contigua è un largo fregio con 12. spartimenti, cioè 3. per parte, ove in mezze figure al naturale sono varie Deità, Virtù &ᶜ Gli ornati intorno sono a guazzo, i dipartimenti a fresco. È la stessa mano del Genga. Qualche fig. è ragionevole, ma per lo più sono deboli è di disegno, e d'invenzione, il colorito è sufficiente. E un far un poco manierato, e troppo uniforme, pieghe meschine; ma nel tutto insieme la maniera ha qualche cosa di grande. Si vede, che fu Pittore mediocre, che non meritava, che ne fosse scritta la Vita dal Vasari, e allora in Siena n'era de' migliori, cioè verso il 1512. quando morì Pandolfo Petrucci.

'Il pavimento della prima St. sopradᵃ e di lastre quadre di terra cotta vetrinate e dipinte con putti, Armi Petrucci &ᶜ di buon gusto.

'In essa i sedili sono di legno forse lavoro del Barili, con putti, uccelli, fogliami, &ᶜ.'

Note. The letters *per* are in the manuscript written in an abbreviation, but are printed expanded.

APPENDIX IV

THE LAYARD COLLECTION

Many of the pictures formerly belonging to Sir Austen Henry Layard (1817–1894) are recorded in the present catalogue, and it seems desirable to give here a brief account of the collection.

Most of the pictures were acquired by Layard in Italy, and had already been brought by him to London by 1869. Layard was appointed in that year our Minister at Madrid. He thereupon lent most of his pictures and a few objects of art to the South Kensington Museum; after a short time, most or all of the collection was transferred to Dublin, where it remained for some years. In October, 1874, Layard bought Palazzo Cappello at Venice. He continued to be our Minister at Madrid until 1877, and then was stationed until 1880 at Constantinople; but many of the pictures were sent to Venice in 1875 and 1876, most of them from Dublin, a few from Madrid. A few were kept in London.

Layard died in 1894. He had already in 1886 presented to the National Gallery three fragments of a fresco by Spinello Aretino (Nos. 1216, 1216 A and 1216 B). In his will, he bequeathed to the National Gallery his pictures other than portraits, with a life-interest to Lady Layard. In 1900, she handed over to the National Gallery (from the part of the collection in London) a fresco now ascribed to Montagna (No. 1696). She died in 1912. A selection of pictures from the London house was accepted by the Trustees in 1913. The pictures from Venice were not incorporated in the National Gallery until 1916, partly because of export difficulties from Italy, partly because of a dispute concerning the meaning of the word 'portraits' in Layard's will.

The Layard pictures belonging to the Nation are now divided between the National and Tate Galleries. The inventory numbers of all the pictures are: 1216, 1216 A and B; 1696; 2946–2956 inclusive; 3066–3132 inclusive.

A bust of Layard, made by J. W. Wood in 1881, was presented to the National Gallery in 1943 by Vice-Admiral Arthur John Layard Murray; inventory number, 5449.

REFERENCES: Layard MSS. in the National Gallery; British Museum, Department of MSS., Add. MS. 38966, letters from Layard to Morelli (e.g. 21 May, 1874; 8 October, 1874; 16 March, 1875; 3 June, 1876); A. Venturi in L'Arte, 1912, pp. 449 ff. Among general accounts of the collection may be cited G. Frizzoni in the Gazette des Beaux-Arts, 1896, II, pp. 455 ff., and G. Lafenestre and E. Richtenberger, Venise, pp. 303 ff.

THE CORRESPONDENCE OF JEAN PAUL RICHTER AND GIOVANNI MORELLI

The printing of the present edition of the Catalogue was far advanced when I saw the publication of these letters: *Italienische Malerei der Renaissance im Briefwechsel von Giovanni Morelli und Jean Paul Richter 1876–1891*, edited by Irma and Gisela Richter, 1960. The letters make many references to pictures now in the National Gallery. Some are comments on the attribution, sometimes tentative; there are references also to condition and restorations; also sometimes there is information about provenance. So far as the present catalogue is concerned, a rather rapid search through the letters did not reveal much needing to be added. It was too late to incorporate anything in the entries for the pictures, but a few items are printed here as an Appendix; the *Index of Collections* has been adapted to refer to anything relevant among these items.

Ascribed to Gentile BELLINI, No. 1213.
The picture, already Richter's in 1885, seems then to have been in London. There is confirmation of Morelli's proposal of Malatini for the sitter. Letters from Richter, 6 June, 1885 and from Morelli, 13 July, 1885, pp. 411, 419.

Giovanni BELLINI, No. 3912.
Richter saw this picture at Menghini's, Mantua, about 1883; letter from Richter, 24 October, 1885, p. 441.

BOTTICELLI and his studio or following.
Morelli's views on the attribution of some National Gallery pictures, e.g. Nos. 592, 1033, 275 and 598, are given in his letter of 14 July, 1883, pp. 272/3.

Andrea BUSATI, No. 3084.
The record of Morelli's claims concerning the reading of the signature is mostly confirmed in his letter of 20 March, 1878, p. 36.

Michele GIAMBONO, No. 3917.
Richter's statement in the Mond Catalogue that he acquired this picture from Guggenheim, Venice, in 1884 seems to be wrong; for No. 3917 can hardly be different from the 'Brustbild des hl. Marcus von Michele Giambono', referred to in his letter of 21 April, 1887, pp. 505/6. The letter gives an account of various acquisitions, some just made, the rest apparently about to be made; it seems clear that they were all from two collections, one certainly at Verona, the other implied to be at Verona. From information recorded elsewhere about some of

the pictures listed, it seems clear that the two collections were Balladoro and Portalupi.

LIBERALE da Verona, No. 1336.

The authorship of the attribution to Liberale here receives confirmation; but it may be that Morelli saw the picture at Cavenaghi's rather than at Colnaghi's. Morelli's letters of 20 August and 10 November, 1882, pp. 229, 240.

MICHELE da Verona, No. 1214.

This picture, bought by Richter in 1885, is here recorded to have been in the Albrizzi Collection, which passed some years before 1885 to Genovesi, one of the proprietors of Danieli's Hotel at Venice. Letters from Richter of 8 March and 29 March, 1885, pp. 385/6, 388/9.

Gerolamo MOCETTO, Nos. 1239/40.

There is confirmation of Richter's acquisition, apparently in London, in 1886; letters from Richter, 1 July and 1 August, 1886, pp. 475, 480.

Domenico MORONE, Nos. 1211/2.

Richter bought these pictures from Guggenheim in 1885; Guggenheim had had them from Pietro 'Monza', Verona. There seems no doubt that this was Pietro, one of the sons of Andrea Monga. Letters from Richter of 7 February and 29 March, 1885, pp. 371/2, 389.

Antonio VIVARINI and Giovanni d'Alemagna, No. 1284.

This picture is among those recorded in Richter's letter of 21 April, 1887, pp. 505/6, commented on in this Appendix under *Giambono*; it seems clear, therefore, that it was bought in 1887 from the Balladoro or the Portalupi Collection at Verona.

LIST OF ATTRIBUTIONS CHANGED FROM THE CATALOGUE OF 1929 AND THE SUPPLEMENT OF 1939

Note: Changes in the qualification of a name (*ascribed to, studio of,* etc.) are not here listed. Nor are changes in the position of a catalogue entry, if they are not changes of attribution; for all such changes of position, where it seemed desirable, a cross-reference is given in the text.

Old Attribution	Inventory Number	New Attribution
BASAITI, Marco	281	BELLINI, Follower of Giovanni
BASAITI, Marco	599	BELLINI, Giovanni
BELLINI, Gentile	1440	BELLINI, Giovanni
BELLINI, Gentile	3098	CARPACCIO, Ascribed to Vittore
BELLINI, School of Gentile	750	VENETIAN SCHOOL
BELLINI, School of Gentile	3130	ITALIAN SCHOOL
BELLINI, School of Giovanni	1696	MONTAGNA, Ascribed to Bartolomeo
BOLTRAFFIO, School of	2089	MILANESE SCHOOL
BOTTICELLI, Alessandro	3101	RAFFAELLINO del Garbo, Ascribed to
BOTTICELLI, School of	1124	LIPPI, Filippino
BOTTICELLI, School of	1412	LIPPI, Filippino
CARPACCIO, Vittore	3077	GEROLAMO da Vicenza
CASTAGNO, Ascribed to	584	TUSCAN SCHOOL
CAVALLI, After Gian Marco	2250	ITALIAN SCHOOL
CAVALLINI, School of Pietro	4143 4144 4145	UMBRIAN (?) SCHOOL
CIMA, School of	3086	VENETIAN SCHOOL
FERRARESE SCHOOL, Early Sixteenth Century	1062	PIERO della Francesca, After (?)
FLORENTINE SCHOOL, Fifteenth Century	2084	ITALIAN SCHOOL
FLORENTINE SCHOOL, Fifteenth Century	3926	MASTER of the BAMBINO Vispo, Ascribed to
GENGA, Girolamo (?)	3929	SIGNORELLI, Luca
GHIRLANDAIO, School of	1299	FLORENTINE (?) SCHOOL
GOZZOLI, Benozzo	591	ANGELICO, Follower of Fra
GRYEF, Adriaen	3088	BARBARI, Jacopo de'
INGEGNO, Andrea di Luigi	2484	PERUGINO, Follower of Pietro
ITALIAN SCHOOL, Fifteenth Century	646 647	SOLARIO, Antonio de
ITALIAN SCHOOL, Fifteenth Century	1456	FRANCESCO di Antonio, Ascribed to
ITALIAN SCHOOL, Sixteenth Century	1417A	MANTEGNA, After Andrea
JACOPO DI CIONE	1468	ORCAGNA, Style of

Old Attribution	Inventory Number	New Attribution
JACOPO DI CIONE	3894	ORCAGNA, Style of
LIPPI, Filippino	598	BOTTICELLI, Follower of Sandro
LIPPI, School of Fra Filippo	589	BOTTICELLI, Follower of Sandro
LORENZETTI, Ambrogio	{ 3071 3072 }	LORENZETTI, Ascribed to Pietro
LORENZETTI, Ambrogio	3895	FLORENTINE SCHOOL
MACRINO d'Alba	{ 1200 1201 }	FERRARI, Style of Defendente
MAINARDI, Bastiano	1230	GHIRLANDAIO, Studio of Domenico
MAINARDI, Bastiano	2489	GHIRLANDAIO, Follower of Domenico
MAINARDI, Bastiano	2502	GHIRLANDAIO, Follower of Domenico
MAINARDI, Bastiano	3937	GHIRLANDAIO, Studio of Domenico
MARTINO da Udine, Ascribed to	778	GIOVANNI Martini da Udine, Ascribed to
MASACCIO	3627	FLORENTINE SCHOOL
MELOZZO, School of	3831	ITALIAN SCHOOL
MESSINA, School of	2618	ANTONELLO da Messina, Follower of
MILANESE SCHOOL, Fifteenth to Sixteenth Centuries	{ 779 780 }	BERGOGNONE, Ascribed to Ambrogio
MILANESE SCHOOL, Fifteenth to Sixteenth Centuries	1300	LEONARDO da Vinci, Follower of
MILANESE SCHOOL, Fifteenth to Sixteenth Centuries	1438	LEONARDO da Vinci, Follower of
MILANESE SCHOOL, Fifteenth to Sixteenth Centuries	{ 3080 3081 }	BERGOGNONE, Style of Ambrogio
MILANESE SCHOOL, Fifteenth to Sixteenth Centuries	3899	MASTER of the PALA Sforzesca, Ascribed to
MILANESE SCHOOL, late Fifteenth Century	4444	MASTER of the PALA Sforzesca, Ascribed to
ORCAGNA, Andrea	581	NARDO di Cione
PARENZO, Bernardo da	3336	BUTINONE, Ascribed to Bernardino
PIER Francesco Fiorentino	1199	FLORENTINE SCHOOL
PISAN (?) SCHOOL, Thirteenth Century	4741	ITALIAN SCHOOL
ROSSELLI, Ascribed to Cosimo	1196	FLORENTINE SCHOOL
SASSETTA, Stefano di Giovanni	1842	TUSCAN (?) SCHOOL
SELLAIO, Jacopo del	916	BOTTICELLI, Follower of Sandro
SELLAIO, Jacopo del	2492	FLORENTINE SCHOOL
SIENESE SCHOOL (?), Fourteenth or early Fifteenth Century	1108	GIOVANNI da Milano, Style of
TOMMASO da Modena	3897	LORENZO Veneziano, Ascribed to
UCCELLO, Ascribed to	585	FLORENTINE SCHOOL
UMBRIAN SCHOOL	702	PERUGINO, Follower of Pietro
UMBRIAN SCHOOL	{ 912 913 914 }	MASTER of the Story of GRISELDA

Old Attribution	Inventory Number	New Attribution
VENETIAN SCHOOL, Fifteenth to Sixteenth Century	2095	BELLINI, Follower of Giovanni
VENETIAN SCHOOL, Fifteenth to Sixteenth Century	3084	BUSATI, Andrea
VENEZIANO, Bartolommeo	631	VENETIAN SCHOOL
VIVARINI, Alvise	2509	JACOMETTO Veneziano, Ascribed to
VIVARINI, Alvise	3121	JACOMETTO Veneziano, Ascribed to

Picture No. 5115, in the first edition of the present catalogue as Italian School, is now classed as Ascribed to Andrea da Firenze.

INDEX TO RELIGIOUS SUBJECTS

The figures of the Trinity are not indexed; nor is the Virgin Mary, except for scenes of her life (section 3).

1. ARCHANGELS

2. FIGURES OF THE OLD TESTAMENT AND THE APOCRYPHA

* An asterisk denotes that the figure or scene is a minor part of the picture.

ELIJAH
  Duccio . . . No. 1330

ESTHER
  Signorelli, Luca . No. 3946

EVE
  (?) Angelico, Fra . No. 663
  (?) 'Giovanni del
    Ponte' . . No. 580

EZEKIEL
  Angelico, Fra . . No. 663

GOLIATH
  Cima da Conegliano,
    Giovanni Battista . No. 2505

HABBAKKUK
  Angelico, Fra . . No. 663

ISAAC
  *Francia, Francesco . No. 179

ISAIAH
  Angelico, Fra . . No. 663
  Duccio . . . No. 566
  Giovanni da Milano . No. 579A
  Ugolino di Nerio . No. 3376

JACOB
  Duccio . . . No. 566

JEREMIAH
  Angelico, Fra . . No. 663
  Duccio . . . No. 566

JOEL
  Angelico, Fra . . No. 663

JONAH
  Angelico, Fra . . No. 663

JONATHAN
  Cima da Conegliano,
    Giovanni Battista . No. 2505

JOSHUA
  Angelico, Fra . . No. 663

MOSES
  Angelico, Fra . . No. 663
  Botticini, Ascribed to
    Francesco . . No. 1126
  Duccio . . . No. 566
  Duccio . . . No. 1330
  Lippi, Filippino . . No. 4904
  Roberti, Ercole de' . No. 1217

NOAH
  Angelico, Fra . . No. 663

SAMSON
  Mantegna, Andrea . No. 1145
  Master of the Cassoni,
    Ascribed to . . No. 3898

TOBIAS
  'Giovanni del Ponte' . No. 580
  *Lippi, Filippino . . No. 1124
  *Lorenzo di Credi . No. 593
  Perugino, Pietro . No. 288
  Verrocchio, Follower
    of Andrea del . . No. 781

ZECHARIAH
  Angelico, Fra . . No. 663

3. SCENES OF THE LIFE OF CHRIST AND THE LIFE OF THE VIRGIN MARY

ADORATION OF THE KINGS,
  SHEPHERDS
  See under NATIVITY

AGONY IN THE GARDEN: BE-
  TRAYAL AND CAPTURE OF
  CHRIST

  Bellini, Giovanni . No. 726
  Bergognone, Ambrogio No. 1077A
  Mantegna, Andrea . No. 1417
  Mantegna, After
    Andrea . . . No. 1417A

  Niccolò di Liberatore No. 1107
  Pacchiarotto, Ascribed
    to Giacomo . . No. 1849
  Spagna, Ascribed to Lo No. 1032
  Spagna, Ascribed to Lo No. 1812
  Ugolino di Nerio . No. 1188

ANGEL APPEARING TO S.
  JOACHIM
  *Benozzo di Lese . No. 283
  Giusto de' Menabuoi . No. 701
  Venetian School . No. 4250

* An asterisk denotes that the figure or scene is a minor part of the picture.

* An asterisk denotes that the figure or scene is a minor part of the picture.

† The figure of the crucified Christ occurs also in certain miracles, such as those of SS. Eustace, Francis and Hubert; also in Crucifixes, and in representations of the Trinity.

* An asterisk denotes that the figure or scene is a minor part of the picture.

4. SAINTS OF THE NEW TESTAMENT PERIOD AND LATER

The figures are noted as beatified or canonized; this may not in every case be recognized by the Church.

Some saints of the New Testament period appear normally in certain scenes; in many such cases, the scenes are indexed in the previous section, but the individual saints are not indexed in this section.

* An asterisk denotes that the figure or scene is a minor part of the picture.

S. ALEXANDER
(?) GEROLAMO da Santa-
croce, Ascribed to . No. 633

B. AMANDUS (unidentified
Dominican)
ANGELICO, Fra . . No. 663

B. AMBROGIO SANSEDONIO
ANGELICO, Fra . . No. 663

S. AMBROSE
(?) BERGOGNONE, Style
of Ambrogio . . No. 3081
GIUSTO de' Menabuoi . No. 701
(?) LORENZO Monaco, Don No. 215
(?) ORCAGNA, Style of . No. 569

S. ANDREW
*BENOZZO di Lese . No. 283
BOTTICINI, Ascribed to
Francesco . . No. 1126
CRIVELLI, Carlo . . No. 788
UGOLINO di Nerio . No. 3473
See also APOSTLES

S. ANNE
ANGELICO, Fra . . No. 663
*BENOZZO di Lese . No. 283
FRANCIA, Francesco . No. 179
GEROLAMO dai Libri . No. 748
GIUSTO de' Menabuoi . No. 701
MASTER of the OSSER-
VANZA . . . No. 5114
NICCOLÒ di Buonaccorso No. 1109
SIENESE SCHOOL . . No. 1317
VENETIAN SCHOOL . No. 4250

S. ANSANUS
(?) TUSCAN SCHOOL . No. 584

S. ANTHONY ABBOT
ANGELICO, Fra . . No. 663
BARTOLO di Fredi, As-
cribed to . . No. 3896
(?) GIUSTO de' Menabuoi No. 701
LIPPI, Fra Filippo . No. 667
ORCAGNA, Style of . No. 569
(?) ORCAGNA, Style of . No. 1468
PISANELLO . . . No. 776

S. ANTHONY OF PADUA
ANGELICO, Fra . . No. 663
GIOVANNI Battista of
Faenza . . . No. 1051
SCHIAVONE, Giorgio . No. 630

S. APOLLONIA
(?) 'GIOVANNI del Ponte' No. 580

APOSTLES† (grouped together)
ANGELICO, Fra . . No. 663
BARNABA da Modena . No. 2927
VENETIAN SCHOOL . No. 4250

S. AUGUSTINE
ANGELICO, Fra . . No. 663
BOTTICINI, Francesco . No. 227
BOTTICINI, Ascribed to
Francesco . . No. 1126
(?) LORENZO Monaco,
Don . . . No. 215
LORENZO d'Alessandro
da Sanseverino . No. 249
MACHIAVELLI, Zanobi . No. 588
(?) ORCAGNA, Style of . No. 569
SIGNORELLI, Luca . No. 3946

S. AUREA
(?) DUCCIO . . No. 566

S. BALTHAZAR
See under KINGS; see also ADOR-
ATION OF THE KINGS under
NATIVITY in Section 3

S. BARNABAS
(?) ANGELICO, Fra . No. 663

S. BARTHOLOMEW
BOTTICINI, Ascribed to
Francesco . . No. 1126
*CRIVELLI, Carlo . . No. 788
FIORENZO di Lorenzo . No. 1103
FLORENTINE SCHOOL . No. 5930
MACHIAVELLI, Zanobi . No. 586
MARZIALE, Marco . No. 804
ORCAGNA, Style of . No. 569
ORCAGNA, Style of . No. 1468
*SIGNORELLI, Luca . No. 1847
UGOLINO di Nerio . No. 3473
See also APOSTLES

S. BENEDICT
ANGELICO, Fra . . No. 663
(?) BOTTICINI, Ascribed
to Francesco . . No. 1126
(?) FRANCIA, Francesco No. 179
'GIOVANNI del Ponte' . No. 580
(?) GIUSTO de' Menabuoi No. 701
*(?) LIPPI, Filippino . No. 1124
LORENZO Monaco, Don No. 215

* An asterisk denotes that the figure or scene is a minor part of the picture.
† Some or all of the Apostles appear normally in certain scenes, such as *The Agony in the Garden* or *Pentecost.*

* An asterisk denotes that the figure or scene is a minor part of the picture.

S. FRANCIS—*continued*
LIPPI, Fra Filippo . No. 667
LORENZO Monaco, Don No. 215
NICCOLÒ di Liberatore No. 1107
ORCAGNA, Style of . No. 569
PACCHIAROTTO, Ascribed
to Giacomo . . No. 1849
PERUGINO, Pietro . No. 1075
ROBERTI, Ascribed to
Ercole de' . . No. 1411
STEFANO di Giovanni
Nos. 4757–4763
VIVARINI, Antonio, and
Giovanni d'Alemagna No. 1284

B. GABRIELE
CRIVELLI, Carlo . . No. 668

S. GALL
MARZIALE, Marco . No. 804

S. GASPAR
See under KINGS; see also ADOR-
ATION OF THE KINGS un-
der NATIVITY in Section 3

S. GEORGE
(?) ANGELICO, Fra . No. 663
CRIVELLI, Carlo . . No. 724
(?) GEROLAMO da Santa-
croce, Ascribed to . No. 633
GIOVANNI Martini da
Udine, Ascribed to . No. 778
PISANELLO . . . No. 776
UCCELLO, Paolo . . No. 6294

S. GREGORY
ANDREA da Firenze, As-
cribed to . . No. 5115
ANGELICO, Fra . . No. 663
LORENZO Monaco, Don No. 216
ORCAGNA, Style of . No. 569

S. HELEN
ANGELICO, Fra . . No. 663

B. HENRY (unidentified Dominican)
ANGELICO, Fra . . No. 663

B. HENRY AMANDUS SUSO
(?) ANGELICO, Fra . No. 663

B. HENRY OF COLOGNE
(?) ANGELICO, Fra . No. 663

S. HILARY
ANGELICO, Fra . . No. 663

HOLY WOMEN (THE MARIES)
Often present in scenes of the
Passion such as THE CRUCI-
FIXION. In Section 3, there is
an index reference for MARIES
AT THE SEPULCHRE

S. HUBERT
(?) PISANELLO . . No. 1436

B. HUMBERT OF ROMANS
ANGELICO, Fra . . No. 663

S. IGNATIUS OF ANTIOCH
ANGELICO, Fra . . No. 663

S. IVO
(?) ORCAGNA, Style of . No. 569

B. JAMES (unidentified Dominican)
ANGELICO, Fra . . No. 663

B. JAMES OF BEVAGNA
(?) ANGELICO, Fra . No. 663

S. JAMES THE GREATER
BOTTICINI, Ascribed to
Francesco . . No. 1126
GIOVANNI Martini da
Udine, Ascribed to . No. 778
MANSUETI, Giovanni . No. 1478
MARZIALE, Marco . No. 804
MASTER of the PALA
Sforzesca, Ascribed
to . . . . No. 4444
NARDO di Cione . . No. 581
ORCAGNA, Style of . No. 569
ORCAGNA, Style of . No. 1468
PESELLINO   Lent; No. 4868B
*SIGNORELLI, Luca . No. 1847
See also APOSTLES

S. JAMES THE LESS
See APOSTLES

B. JAMES OF SALOMONIO
(?) ANGELICO, Fra . No. 663

B. JANE OF FLORENCE
ANGELICO, Fra . . No. 663

S. JEROME
ANGELICO, Fra . . No. 663
ANTONELLO da Messina No. 1418
BELLINI, Follower of
Giovanni . . No. 281
BENOZZO di Lese . No. 283

* An asterisk denotes that the figure or scene is a minor part of the picture.

* An asterisk denotes that the figure or scene is a minor part of the picture.

* An asterisk denotes that the figure or scene is a minor part of the picture.

* An asterisk denotes that the figure or scene is a minor part of the picture.

CLASSICAL HISTORY AND MYTH: ROMANCE

Very doubtful or impossible identifications are not here indexed

AMYCUS ⎱ See LAPITHS and
APHAREUS (?) ⎰ Centaurs

APOLLO

POLLAIUOLO, Ascribed to Antonio and
Piero del, No. 928
MASTER of the CASSONI, Ascribed to
the, No. 3898
VENETIAN SCHOOL, No. 3086

ARISTOTLE

AUGUSTUS
BIENOR. See LAPITHS and Centaurs
CAESAR, Julius (?)
CAMILLUS
CAMPASPE. See PHYLLIS
CENTAURS. See LAPITHS and Centaurs
CLAUDIA Quinta (?)
CORIOLANUS

SIGNORELLI, Luca, No. 910
FLORENTINE SCHOOL, No. 3826

MANTEGNA, Andrea, No. 902
MICHELE da Verona, No. 1214
SIGNORELLI, Luca, No. 3929
MANTEGNA, Andrea, No. 902

CYBELE
CYLLARUS. See LAPITHS and Centaurs
DAMON

PREVITALI, Ascribed to Andrea, No.
4884
POLLAIUOLO, Ascribed to Antonio and
Piero del, No. 928

DAPHNE

DICTYS. See LAPITHS and Centaurs
DIDO
EUMAEUS (?) ⎱
EURYCLEIA (?) ⎰
EURYTUS. See LAPITHS and Centaurs
FALERII. See SCHOOLMASTER of Falerii
GRISELDA

LIBERALE da Verona, No. 1336
PINTORICCHIO, No. 911

MASTER of the Story of GRISELDA,
Nos. 912/4

GRYNEUS ⎱ See LAPITHS and Centaurs
HERCULES ⎰
HELEN
HIPPODAME ⎱ See LAPITHS and Cen-
HYLONOME ⎰ taurs
LAPITHS and Centaurs
LUCRETIA
MARS
NARCISSUS

ANGELICO, Follower of Fra, No. 591

PIERO di Cosimo, No. 4890
SIGNORELLI, Luca, No. 910
BOTTICELLI, Sandro, No. 915
BOLTRAFFIO, Follower of Giovanni
Antonio, No. 2673
PINTORICCHIO, No. 911
ANGELICO, Follower of Fra, No. 591
PINTORICCHIO, No. 911
SIGNORELLI, Luca, No. 910

ODYSSEUS
PARIS
PENELOPE

PETRARCH. See TRIUMPHS of Petrarch
PETREUS (?). See LAPITHS and Cen-
taurs
PHYLLIS

MASTER of the CASSONI, Ascribed to
the, No. 3898

PIRITHOUS (?). See LAPITHS and Centaurs

INDEX OF PORTRAITS

Very doubtful or impossible identifications are not here indexed

INDEX OF COLLECTIONS

NUMERICAL INDEX

* Included in the entry for LEONARDO da Vinci, No. 1093.

LIST OF PAINTINGS ACQUIRED
SINCE 1961 REVISION

LEONARDO DA VINCI
1452–1519

6337 CARTOON: THE VIRGIN AND CHILD WITH
      SAINT ANNE AND SAINT JOHN THE BAPTIST

Black chalk, heightened with white, on paper, 141·5 × 104·6 (55$\frac{3}{4}$ × 41); not pricked for transfer to panel.
Purchased with a special grant, and contributions from the N.A.C.F., the Pilgrim Trust and through a public appeal organized by the N.A.C.F.; presented by the N.A.C.F., 1962.

MASTER OF SAN FRANCESCO
active late 13th century

Ascribed to the MASTER OF SAN FRANCESCO

6361 CRUCIFIX

Wood, 92·1 × 75 (36$\frac{1}{4}$ × 27$\frac{3}{4}$)
Purchased, with contributions from the N.A.C.F. and an anonymous donor, 1965.

UGOLINO DI NERIO
active 1317 to 1327

6484 MOSES (PINNACLE FROM AN ALTARPIECE)

Wood (poplar), pointed top, 55 × 31·5 (21$\frac{5}{8}$ × 12$\frac{3}{8}$)
Purchased by private treaty from the Trustees of the Doughty House Trust, 1983.

6485 DAVID (PINNACLE FROM AN ALTARPIECE)

Wood (poplar), pointed top, 55·5 × 31·5 (21$\frac{3}{4}$ × 12$\frac{3}{8}$)
Purchased by private treaty from the Trustees of the Doughty House Trust, 1983.

6486 TWO ANGELS (SPANDRELS FROM THE MAIN
      TIER OF AN ALTARPIECE)

Wood (poplar), 27 × 56 (10$\frac{1}{2}$ × 22)
Purchased by private treaty from the Trustees of the Doughty House Trust, 1983.